THE FILMGOER'S COMPANION

LESLIE HALLIWELL

The Filmgoer's Companion

THIRD EDITION, AGAIN REVISED AND ENLARGED

With a Foreword by
ALFRED HITCHCOCK

MacGibbon & Kee   London

Granada Publishing Limited
First published in Great Britain 1965
by MacGibbon & Kee Ltd
3 Upper James Street London W1R 4BP
Second edition (revised and enlarged) 1967
Reprinted 1968
Third edition (further revised and enlarged) 1970
Reprinted 1971

ISBN 0 261 63180 2

Printed in Great Britain by
Ebenezer Baylis and Son Ltd
The Trinity Press, Worcester, and London

This book is dedicated with affection to

C. K. DEXTER HAVEN

JAMES BLANDINGS

ELWOOD P. DOWD

FLOYD THURSBY

WALTER PARKS THATCHER

WOLF J. FLYWHEEL

CARL DENHAM

SHERIDAN WHITESIDE

SAUL FEMM

JOSEPH TURA

LONGFELLOW DEEDS

LAURA JESSON

AHMED BEN HASSAN

RUDOLF RASSENDYLL

LAWRENCE TALBOT

JAKIE RABINOWITZ

EDYTHE VAN HOPPER

WALDO LYDECKER

PHILIP MARLOWE

THEO KRETSCHMAR-SCHULDORFF

MAX CORKLE

DR LUDOVIC PRAETORIUS

LOLA FROHLICH

EMILY KOCKENLOCKER

MR LAUREL AND MR HARDY

. . . wherever they may be

FOREWORD

THIRTY OR FORTY years ago, when the idea of the cinema as an art was new, people started to write highbrow treatises about it. Unfortunately, few of the books seemed to have much connection with what one saw at the local picture house. Even earlier began the still-continuing deluge of fan magazines and annuals, full of exotic photographs but short on solid information. We film-makers had our own reference books, but these were often incomprehensible to the layman and gave him more undigested facts than he needed. Nobody wrote for the sensible middlebrow picturegoer who was keenly interested in the craft of cinema without wanting to make a religion of it.

The volume you hold in your hand aims to be the first comprehensive reference book in English for that numerous but neglected audience. I feel sure it will be welcome, for audiences are taking an increasingly serious interest in their films these days—even in the flippant ones.

A concise guide to film matters past and present is obviously a good thing to have on a handy shelf, especially when the best of the old films are constantly cropping up on TV. I hope it will prove possible to bring out revised and corrected editions on a regular basis. Not that many glaring errors will be discovered: the author has done his homework rather better than the villains in my films, who always seem to get found out sooner or later.

Speaking personally, I don't know whether it is more flattering or disturbing to find oneself pinned down like a butterfly in a book which recounts all the macabre details of one's career. But being a stickler for detail myself, I must, and do, submit; and I wish the enterprise well.

Alfred Hitchcock

INTRODUCTION

THIS BOOK IS for people who like the movies. Especially it's for those who enjoyed the golden ages of the 30s and 40s, now revisiting us on television, when the big studios of Hollywood turned out highly efficient and varied entertainment without being too pretentious about it. Nowadays, independent producers aim higher, which sometimes only means that they have further to fall; and most films are half as long again as they should be. But the good ones keep on turning up, and Jeanne Moreau and Elvis Presley and Peter O'Toole have fans just as enthusiastic as those of Bette Davis and George Formby and Rudolph Valentino.

Everyone who watches films, whether on TV or the big screens, frequently thinks of something he'd like to check: a star's age, a director's name, what else that funny little fellow with the moustache has been in. To find out the answer to this sort of question it's sometimes been necessary to consult upwards of a dozen fairly inaccessible volumes. This book aims to bring all the available sources together while at the same time excluding inessential or dated information. A fully comprehensive work on these lines would be almost the size of the *Encyclopaedia Britannica*; but this 'potted' one should satisfy most requirements.

The arrangement is completely alphabetical, and you won't find an index at the end because the whole book is one vast index. Most of the entries refer to actors, including not only stars but several hundred familiar names from the supporting cast, people whose valiant service has seldom been recorded. Then there are directors, producers, musicians, writers and photographers—the principal ones at least. The more important the person, the longer the entry, that's a rough general rule: routine contributors get a couple of lines, Edward G. Robinson spreads over half a page. All told, however, you'll find very few of your favourites missing: if they've stuck in your memory, they're probably here. As to the list of credits, the aim has been to give the first important picture, the most recent, and a sampling of the more significant titles in between: the peak period is usually when the dates are most closely crowded. Stage work has not normally been detailed nor has TV.

There are also notes on well-known film series, on films which have been frequently remade, on films with similar titles; on technical terms, on organisations, on general subjects like censorship and screen ratios. Finally you will find several hundred entries on individual films which seem in one way or another important, influential, or simply excellent of their kind. Unavoidably, many readers will disagree with the selection and/or the assessments: that must remain their privilege until a second edition, if called for, comes out, amended and improved according to comment received. (Bouquets, suggestions, corrections and threatening letters should be addressed c/o the publisher.)

The emphasis is firmly on Britain and Hollywood: the book is aimed at the general filmgoer, not at the egghead student of film culture who shuns commercial entertainments in favour of middle-European or Oriental masterpieces which never get further than the National Film Theatre or a very few art houses. However, references to important foreign films and personalities are fairly numerous, and even admitting its selectiveness in this field the book still ranges more widely than anything else published in English.

No one has been omitted simply because he is dead: the entries have been selected from the whole history of the cinema. But the silent period is covered in less detail than the talkies, and probably few readers will quarrel with that.

This is a collection of facts rather than opinions; if a few of the latter *have* crept in, they are usually the ones most generally held.

L.H.

London, July 1965

INTRODUCTION TO THE THIRD EDITION

THE MODEST PRINCIPLES expounded in the original introduction to this book still stand. The second edition, however, proved to be nearly twice as long, and this third edition is longer still. Almost nothing has been deleted; it remains to explain the additions.

To begin with, the existing entries have all been brought up to date (that is to say, to October 1969). Countless revisions and corrections have been made, and many entries have been considerably augmented by additional titles. Within one volume it is plainly not possible to do what many people have requested, namely to list every film with which every actor or director has been concerned: apart from the immensity of the task and the fact that the least important people would have the longest list of credits, records in many cases are such that absolute accuracy and completeness could not be guaranteed. However, it has seemed to me that in the cases of leading or typical figures a complete file is desirable, not only to document their own careers but to indicate the steps by which such careers are built. Several hundred entries, therefore, now aim to be complete and are noted by the symbol (†); for some others the list of sound films only is complete. Please do not interpret the symbol as necessarily meaning importance: typicality accounts for quite a number, and some other people simply made very few films! 'Incomplete' entries still try to indicate the beginning and end dates of a career, with the dates coming closest together over the most prolific period.

TV film series in which actors have regularly appeared are now dated, for the most part; I have continued to avoid listing live or taped series, which are less likely to be available to the student of the future.

The new entries are partly accounted for by the fact that new careers are starting all the time. I have also sought and found information about lesser character actors, cinematographers, art directors, composers, and about more leading figures of the silent era, a period which was previously somewhat thinly covered. There are more paragraphs on general topics and definitions, and very many more on themes and subjects which movies have particularly explored, from abortion to zombies and from Ancient Egypt to Devil's Island: these light-hearted mini-essays have proved very popular, though I stress again that they can never aspire to completeness. (So numerous are they in this edition that an alphabetical list is offered at the end of the book.) There are also entries on literary figures whose work has been adapted for films, and historical figures, including western heroes, who have been frequently impersonated; on national cinematic trends; on famous production companies; and on technical processes. On the whole most creative aspects of the industry are covered; trade matters are virtually ignored.

More films have been listed and described under their own titles, and in particular I have added many which may have little intrinsic merit but which have been popular enough to suffer several remakes; others are included because their titles are well-known but I suspect that comparatively few people could say what they are about. Otherwise, as before, I have tried to include all films which have had significance, either as masterworks in their own right, as influencing subsequent production, or simply as being very good of their kind. The information given is intended to be just sufficient for a student to 'place' a film, and to give him a key for further research.

Cross-referencing is kept to an absolute minimum: if it were done properly, the book would double its size again. Whatever the information you need, once you are used to the book there must be several ways of finding it.

A number of people have complained that the year of production appended to certain films tends to vary in different entries. I am grateful for any corrections under this heading, and can only plead the impossibility of cross-checking every possible date in so long a book. I aim to give the year when a film was completed and first publicly shown, but sometimes when release is held up for months over a year-end it is difficult to be sure what year to quote, and the decision is likely to vary according to the source consulted. Films first shown in January or February are usually assigned to the previous year. In the case of American TV series, the date '67', for instance, means that the series was booked for the 1967 season, which of course runs into 1968. In the fifties such series ran for 39 episodes, but this has been gradually dwindling to 26, and in recent years quite a lot are cut off at 17 or even 13.

The Companion has continued to find a kindly reception, and although basically cheerful rather than scholarly it does now, I hope, provide an 'enquire within upon the cinema' adequate to satisfy general and even much specialized curiosity on factual points. If it still seems nostalgic rather than forward-looking that is probably because I personally, working every day among films as buyer for a television station and as adviser to a weekly programme about the movies, find that I still get more genuine pleasure from the old ones than I do from the new. Despite the immense technical advances shown by the latter, they have lost a few essential ingredients: simplicity, innocence, and optimism being among them.

L.H.

London, October 1969

CORRECTIONS AND SUGGESTIONS will continue to be welcome and should be sent to me care of the publisher.

EXPLANATORY NOTES

PERSONAL DATES The birth year of a leading actor or actress is very often a matter for speculation: the older he gets, the later the official date sometimes becomes. I have normally chosen the earliest published date as being most likely to be accurate. Doubtful dates are prefaced by '*c.*' (*circa*). An asterisk in place of a date means that not even an informed guess can be made; this device is also used when someone has probably died but no confirmation can be found.

FILM DATES See penultimate paragraph of introduction to this edition.

REAL NAMES When known, and when different from professional names, these are given in brackets immediately after the subject's main dates.

FILM TITLES These frequently vary from country to country: I have normally given the title by which the film is known in its country of origin. Alternative titles have been thinned down in this edition, as they tend to be forgotten when the film is revived for TV: but see the article on *title changes*, which lists many of them.

Foreign language titles are translated only in cases where the original is not generally known: e.g. *Les Enfants du Paradis* and *Wild Strawberries* are used rather than *Children of Paradise* or *Smultronstallet*.

ABBREVIATIONS Lower-case *a*, *w*, *p*, *d* or *ph* bracketed behind a film title indicate actor, writer, producer, director, cinematographer. AA or BFA signify the winning of an Academy Award or British Film Academy Award, and where these letters appear immediately after the title of a film individually listed, it was considered best of its year.

NATIONALITIES I have tried to indicate hereditary origin

13

rather than place of birth or adopted citizenship. The fact that Joan Fontaine was born in Tokyo does not make her Japanese.

COMPLETE ENTRIES The symbol (†) prefixing an item means that an attempt has been made to supply all film credits rather than a selection. Partial completeness, e.g. talkies but not silents, is indicated in some cases at the end of the paragraph. See introduction.

ALPHABETICAL ORDER This is adhered to on normal dictionary lines. 'Mc' and 'Mac' are now treated as one, under 'Mac', as is the practice in telephone directories, though the spelling is of course kept distinct. Dino de Laurentiis comes under D, Erich Von Stroheim under V, Laura La Plante under L.

Fictional characters, who are separately listed at the end of the book, occur under their complete names, e.g. Sherlock Holmes under S and the Crime Doctor under C.

ACKNOWLEDGEMENTS

AS THIS BOOK has been compiled by a methodical gleaning of information from sources as diverse as old fan magazines, trade year books, publicity hand-outs, magazine articles and current reviews, it would be impossible to list each publication which has helped me. I would, however, like to pay due tribute to the ever-courteous staff of the British Film Institute's Information Department, and to the Institute's files and publications; without these the book would have lost much fullness and accuracy.

Hundreds of people have been interested enough to write to me personally with suggestions and corrections. I have tried to thank them all personally and wish to place on particular record the contributions of the following, most of whom sent me page upon page of notes: Malcolm Arthur, Roy Atkinson, Robert Bloch, Henry R. Davis, David Gilbey, Clyde Gilmour, Philip O. Greenhalgh, Gerald S. Gregory, C. E. Hearn, Philip Jenkinson, Philip Megrah, Howard R. Milton, Graham Murray, Robert Nagler, Bryan Niland, Alex Roberts, David Rode, John Stabler, Homero Thevenet, Roi A. Uselton.

I recall with gratitude the contributions made to the first edition by John Cutts, now working where the inspiration is (or used to be), in Hollywood. My chief thanks are still reserved for my wife Ruth, who during the years of writing, rewriting and proof-reading gave what help I asked, suffered the domestic accumulation of mountains of paper and publications, and allowed me to live a hermit-like nocturnal existence.

A

ABBOTT, BUD (1895–   ). American comedian, the 'straight man' half of Abbott and Costello, cross-talking vaudevillians of long experience whose film debut as supporting comics in *One Night in the Tropics* (39) led to a long series of starring comedies. *Rookies (Buck Privates)* (40), *Hold That Ghost* (41), *Ride 'Em Cowboy* (41), *Rio Rita* (42), *Who Done It* (42), *Pardon My Sarong* (43), *Lost in a Harem* (44), *The Naughty Nineties* (45), *The Time of Their Lives* (46), *On the Carpet* (an attempt at characterization rather than cross talk) (46), *The Wistful Widow of Wagon Gap* (48), *Abbott and Costello Meet Frankenstein* (49), *Abbott and Costello Meet the Killer* (50), *Abbott and Costello Meet the Invisible Man* (51), *Abbott and Costello Meet Dr Jekyll and Mr Hyde* (53), *Abbott and Costello Meet the Mummy* (54), *Dance with Me, Henry* (55), others. After a short-lived TV series, the team split in 1955. Bud Abbott (real Christian name: William) retired, and Lou Costello (qv) tried to mount solo projects but died in 1959.

ABBOTT, GEORGE (1889–   ). American writer-producer-director (or collaborator) of lively commercial plays, many of which were filmed: *Broadway, Three Men on a Horse, Room Service, On the Town, Where's Charley, The Pajama Game* (co-d film version), *A Funny Thing Happened on the Way to the Forum*, etc.

ABBOTT, JOHN (1905–   ). British-born character actor with staring eyes, specializing in eccentric parts; in Hollywood from 1941. *Mademoiselle Docteur* (debut) (38), *The Return of the Scarlet Pimpernel* (38), *The Saint in London* (40), *The Shanghai Gesture* (41), *They Got Me Covered* (42), *Jane Eyre* (43), *Secret Motive* (lead) (43), *The Vampire's Ghose* (45), *Deception* (46), *The Woman in White* (48) (a memorable performance, as the grotesque invalid Frederick Fairlie), *The Merry Widow* (52), *Public Pigeon Number One* (57), *Who's Minding the Store* (63), *Gambit* (66), others.

ABEL, ALFRED (1880–1939). German character actor of weighty personality. Best-known performances include *Dr Mabuse* (21), *The Phantom* (22), *Metropolis* (26), *Gold* (28), *Congress Dances* (31).

ABEL, WALTER (1898–   ). American actor with stage experience. Made Hollywood debut as d'Artagnan in *The Three Musketeers* (35); later specialized in harassed fathers and professional men. *The Green Light* (37), *Miracle on Main Street* (38), *Arise My Love* (40), *Hearts in Springtime* (41), *Holiday Inn* (42), *Star Spangled Rhythm* (43),

An American Romance (44), *Kiss and Tell* (45), *The Kid from Brooklyn* (46), *Dream Girl* (48), *Island in the Sky* (53), *The Indian Fighter* (55), *Bernardine* (57), *Raintree County* (57), *Handle with Care* (58), *Mirage* (65), etc. Much on stage in recent years.

ABIE'S IRISH ROSE. Anne Nichols' long-running Broadway comedy of the twenties, about a Catholic girl marrying into a Jewish family, has twice been filmed: by Victor Fleming in 1928, with Jean Hersholt, and by Eddie Sutherland in 1945, with Michael Chekov.

abortion, unmentionable on the screen for many years save in conti-nental dramas like *Carnet De Bal* (37), and officially ostracized exploitation pictures like *Amok* (38), was first permitted as a Hollywood plot point in *Detective Story* (51). Six years later, *Blue Denim* concerned an abortion that was prevented; and the later abortion scenes in *Sweet Bird of Youth* (62), *The Interns* (62) and *Love with the Proper Stranger* (64) scarcely displayed an obsession with the subject. Meanwhile however the British gave it full rein in *Saturday Night and Sunday Morning* (60), *The L-Shaped Room* (62), *Alfie* (65) and *Up the Junction* (68); by which time it had certainly lost its shock value. By 1969 Hollywood felt confident enough to use it as the plot point of a commercial thriller, *Daddy's Gone-a-Hunting*.

abstract film. One in which the images are not representational but fall into visually interesting or significant patterns: e.g. Disney's *Fantasia*, Norman McLaren's hand-drawn sound films, etc.

Academy Awards. Merit prizes given annually since 1927 by the Ameri-can Academy of Motion Picture Arts and Sciences. The award is in the form of a statuette known in the trade—for reasons variously explained—as Oscar. In this volume an Academy Award is noted by the letters AA after the film title.

accelerated motion. An effect obtained by running the camera more slowly than usual: when the resulting film is projected at normal speed, the movements seem faster because they occupy fewer frames than would normally be the case. The opposite of *slow motion* (qv).

ACCENT ON YOUTH, a successful Broadway play by Samson Raphael-son, about a lazy playwright spurred to new success by his young secretary, has been filmed three times. In 1935 Herbert Marshall and Sylvia Sidney were directed by Wesley Ruggles. In 1950 it turned up as *Mr Music*, with Bing Crosby and Nancy Olson directed by Richard Haydn; and in 1958 it emerged again as *But Not For Me*, with Clark Gable and Carroll Baker, directed by George Seaton. .

ACE IN THE HOLE (THE BIG CARNIVAL) (US 1951). Biting satire on the

American pursuit of the buck, with Kirk Douglas as a hard-boiled reporter who deliberately delays rescue operations on a man trapped in a cave so that his story will make national headlines. Brilliantly directed by Billy Wilder, from a script by himself and producer Charles Brackett.

ACHARD, MARCEL (1899–   ). French writer whose film scripts include *The Merry Widow* (34), *Mayerling* (36), *Alibi* (37), *The Strange Monsieur Victor* (38), *Untel Pére et Fils* (40), *Monsieur la Souris* (43), *Madame De* (52), *La Garconne* (57), *A Woman like Satan* (59). Directed *Jean de la Lune* (49), *The Paris Waltz* (50).

ACKLAND, RODNEY (1908–   ). British writer, sporadically in films from 1930. *Bank Holiday* (38), *49th Parallel* (41), *Thursday's Child* (also directed) (43), *Queen of Spades* (48), etc. Also successful playwright. Published autobiography, 'The Celluloid Mistress' (54).

ACORD, ART (1891–1931). American star of silent westerns: *A Man Afraid of his Wardrobe* (15), *In the Days of Buffalo Bill* (21), *The Oregon Trail* (23), etc. Sound ended his career.

ACOSTA, RODOLFO (1920–   ). Cold-eyed Mexican-American character actor, a frequent western villain or henchman. *The Fugitive* (48), *One Way Street* (50), *Yankee Buccaneer* (52), *Hondo* (54), *Bandido* (56), *The Tijuana Story* (leading role) (57), *Flaming Star* (60), *How the West Was Won* (62), *Rio Conchos* (64), *Return of the Seven* (66), *Nobody Loves Flapping Eagle* (70), many others. TV series: *High Chaparral* (67).

ACRES, BIRT (1854–1918). British cinematograph pioneer, later projector manufacturer.

action still. A photograph of a scene as it actually appears in the film, as opposed to one specially posed for publicity purposes. Sometimes called a frame blow-up. In TV, an 'action stills' programme has come to mean one consisting of still photographs given a semblance of life by camera movement.

actors have seldom been the subject of biopics. Anna Neagle appeared as Peg Woffington, with Cedric Hardwicke as David Garrick, in *Peg of Old Drury* (35), and Garrick was played by Brian Aherne in *The Great Garrick* (37). Miriam Hopkins was Mrs Leslie Carter in *Lady with Red Hair* (41), Charlie Ruggles (of all people) played Otis Skinner in *Our Hearts Were Young and Gay* (44), and Richard Burton was Edwin Booth in *Prince of Players* (54). Recently we have had Julie Andrews and Daniel Massey as Gertie Lawrence and Noel Coward in *Star*. Of the idols of its own creation, Hollywood has so far given us biographies of Valentino, Jean Harlow, Lon Chaney, Diana and John Barrymore, and Lilian Roth.

19

actor-directors

actor-directors are still a comparatively rare breed. Those who have directed themselves have not always been wise; but they include Charles Chaplin (always), Jacques Tati (always), Buster Keaton, Stan Laurel, Erich Von Stroheim, Jules Dassin, Tom Walls, Ray Milland, Richard Carlson, John Wayne (*The Alamo*), Burgess Meredith (*The Man on the Eiffel Tower*), Robert Montgomery (*The Lady in the Lake*), Gene Kelly, Laurence Olivier, Paul Henried (*For Men Only*), Marlon Brando (*One-Eyed Jacks*), Jean Cocteau, Frank Sinatra (*None But The Brave*), Ralph Richardson (*Home at Seven*), Peter Sellers (*Mr Topaze*), Nigel Patrick (*Johnny Nobody*), Peter Lorre (*Die Verlorene*), Jose Ferrer (*The Shrike*), Anthony Newley (*Heironymus Merkin*), and Peter Ustinov. Actors who have directed others include Lionel Barrymore, Dick Powell, Charles Laughton, Richard Haydn, John Cassavetes, James Cagney, Karl Malden, John Mills, Richard Attenborough, Ricardo Cortez, and Paul Newman.

The Actors' Studio. Lee Strasberg's drama school in New York was well publicized during the 50s as the source of 'method' acting, which was practised by Marlon Brando among others. It corresponded closely with the Stanislavsky system: actors underwent curious mental exercises to assimilate themselves into their characters. Now seems to have been more fashionable than influential.

ACUFF, EDDIE (1902–1956). American supporting comedian. *The Petrified Forest* (36), *The Boys from Syracuse* (40), *Hellzapoppin* (41), *The Flying Serpent* (56), *Blondie's Big Moment* (47), scores of others.

ADAIR, JEAN (1873–1953). American stage actress best remembered by film fans as one of the sweetly murderous aunts in *Arsenic and Old Lace* (44). Very occasional other movies include *Advice to the Lovelorn* (34), *Something in the Wind* (46).

ADAM, ALFRED (1909–). French character actor, usually of weak or villainous roles. *La Kermesse Héroique* (35), *Carnet de Bal* (37), *Boule de Suif* (45), *La Ferme du Pendu* (48), *The Witches of Salem* (56), *Maigret Sets a Trap* (61), etc.

ADAM, KEN (1921–). British art director, in films from 1947. *Queen of Spades* (48), *Around the World in Eighty Days* (56), *The Trials of Oscar Wilde* (60), *Dr Strangelove* (63), *Goldfinger* (64), *The Ipcress File* (65), *Thunderball* (65), *Funeral in Berlin* (66), *You Only Live Twice* (67), *Chitty Chitty Bang Bang* (68), etc.

ADAM, RONALD (1896–). British character actor specializing in well-bred but stuffy professional men. In hundreds of films and TV plays, including *The Drum* (38), *Escape to Danger* (43), *Green for Danger* (46), *Bonnie Prince Charlie* (48), *Angels One Five* (51), *Private's*

Progress (55), *Reach for the Sky* (56), *Cleopatra* (62), *The Tomb of Ligeia* (64), *Who Killed the Cat?* (66). Also on stage as actor, author and producer.

ADAMS, BEVERLY (1945–   ). Canadian born leading lady in Hollywood films; plays Lovey Kravezit in the Matt Helm films. *The New Interns* (64), *The Silencers* (66), *Birds Do It* (66), *Murderers' Row* (66), *The Torture Garden* (GB) (67), *The Ambushers* (67), etc.

ADAMS, CASEY (1917–   ). See under MAX SHOWALTER (his real name, which he has recently used).

ADAMS, DOROTHY (c. 1915–   ). American character actress, usually of timorous or sullen ladies. *The Flame of New Orleans* (41), *Laura* (44), *The Best Years of Our Lives* (46), *The Foxes of Harrow* (48), *Carrie* (52), *Three for Jamie Dawn* (56), *From the Terrace* (60), etc.

ADAMS, EDIE (1931–   ). American singer-comedienne, widow of Ernie Kovacs. *The Apartment* (60), *Call Me Bwana* (63), *It's a Mad Mad Mad Mad World* (63), *Love with the Proper Stranger* (64), *The Best Man* (64), *Made in Paris* (65), *The Oscar* (66), *The Honey Pot* (67).

ADAMS, GERALD DRAYSON (c. 1904–   ). Canadian screenwriter, former literary agent. *The Big Steal* (co-w) (51), *The Golden Horde* (51), *Flaming Feather* (54), *The Black Sleep* (56), *Kissing Cousins* (64), many other action films and much TV.

ADAMS, JILL (1931–   ). British leading lady, former model, who made a number of films in the 50s but has more recently concentrated on her private life as wife of a BBC commentator. *The Young Lovers* (54), *Doctor at Sea* (55), *Private's Progress* (55), *The Green Man* (56), *Brothers in Law* (57), *Carry On Constable* (60), etc.

ADAMS, JULIE (formerly JULIA) (1926–   ). American leading lady, in Hollywood from 1947. *Hollywood Story* (51), *Bright Victory* (51), *Where the River Bends* (52), *Mississippi Gambler* (53), *The Creature from the Black Lagoon* (54), *One Desire* (55), *Away All Boats* (56), *Slaughter on Tenth Avenue* (57), *Raymie* (60), *Tickle Me* (65), etc. Married Ray Danton.

ADAMS, NICK (1932–68) (Nicholas Adamschock). American leading man who usually played neurotic or aggressive types; never quite made the big time. *Somebody Loves Me* (debut) (52), *Mister Roberts* (55), *No Time for Sergeants* (58), *Pillow Talk* (59), *Hell is for Heroes* (62), *The Hook* (63), *Twilight of Honour* (63), *Monster of Terror* (*Die Monster Die*) (GB) (66), *Young Dillinger* (66), *Frankenstein Conquers the World* (Jap.) (66), *Fever Heat* (67), etc. TV series: *The Rebel*, *Johnny Yuma*.

ADAM'S RIB. 1. US 1923: Cecil B. De Mille marital drama with flashbacks to Genesis. 2. US 1949: brittle sex comedy with Spencer Tracy and Katharine Hepburn as married lawyers on opposite sides of a case. Written by Ruth Gordon and Garson Kanin, with neat direction by George Cukor, it introduced in supporting roles four striking newcomers: David Wayne, Jean Hagen, Tom Ewell and Judy Holliday.

ADAMS, ROBERT (1906–   ). West Indian Negro actor, former teacher, prominent in British films of the 40s. *Sanders of the River* (debut) (35), *King Solomon's Mines* (37), *Caesar and Cleopatra* (45), *Men of Two Worlds* (leading role) (47), etc.

ADAMS, TOM (1938–   ). Burly British leading man who played secret agent Charles Vine in *Licensed to Kill* (65), *Where the Bullets Fly* (66); also in *The Fighting Prince of Donegal* (66), *Fathom* (67), *Subterfuge* (69)

ADDAMS, DAWN (1930–   ). British leading lady, in Hollywood from 1950. Films mainly unremarkable, but was chosen by Chaplin to play opposite him in *A King in New York* (57). Other films include *Night into Morning* (US) (51), *Plymouth Adventure* (US) (52), *The Robe* (US) (53), *The Moon Is Blue* (US) (53), *Khyber Patrol* (54), *The Silent Enemy* (58), *The Two Faces of Dr Jekyll* (60), *The Black Tulip* (64), *Ballad in Blue* (65), *Where the Bullets Fly* (66), etc.

ADDINSELL, RICHARD (1904–   ). British composer whose greatest film success was his 'Warsaw Concerto' for *Dangerous Moonlight* (40). Also scored *The Amateur Gentleman* (36), *Fire over England* (37), *Goodbye Mr Chips* (39), *Gaslight* (40), *Love on the Dole* (40), *Blithe Spirit* (45), *Scrooge* (51), *Beau Brummell* (54), *The Prince and the Showgirl* (57), *The Admirable Crichton* (57), *The Waltz of the Toreadors* (62), etc.

ADDISON, JOHN (1920–   ). British composer, in films from 1948. *The Guinea Pig* (49), *Seven Days to Noon* (50), *The Man Between* (53), *Private's Progress* (55), *Reach for the Sky* (56), *Lucky Jim* (57), *I Was Monty's Double* (58), *Look Back in Anger* (59), *The Entertainer* (60), *A Taste of Honey* (61), *The Loneliness of the Long Distance Runner* (62), *Tom Jones* (AA) (63), *Guns at Batasi* (64), *Moll Flanders* (65), *Torn Curtain* (66), *A Fine Madness* (66), *The Honey Pot* (67), *Smashing Time* (67).

ADDY, WESLEY (1912–   ). American character actor, usually of humourless or sinister appearance. *The First Legion* (51), *My Six Convicts* (52), *Kiss Me Deadly* (55), *The Big Knife* (55), *Timetable* (57), *The Garment Jungle* (58), *Ten Seconds to Hell* (59), *Whatever Happened to Baby Jane* (62), *Seconds* (66), many others.

ADLER, BUDDY (1909–1960). American production executive. With Columbia 1947–54: produced *From Here to Eternity* (AA) (53). To Fox 1954: head of studio from 1956: produced *Anastasia* (57), *Inn of the Sixth Happiness* (58), *South Pacific* (58), etc. Real Christian name: Maurice.

ADLER, JAY (c. 1907–   ). American character actor, brother of Luther Adler; usually plays hoboes, small-time gangsters, etc. *No Time to Marry* (38), *My Six Convicts* (52), *99 River Street* (54), *The Big Combo* (55), *The Sweet Smell of Success* (57), *The Brothers Karamazov* (58), *Seven Guns to Mesa* (60), many others.

ADLER, LARRY (1914–   ). American harmonica virtuoso whose chief contribution to films is the score of *Genevieve* (53); also composed for *King and Country* (63), *High Wind in Jamaica* (64).

ADLER, LUTHER (1903–   ). American character actor, heavy-featured member of well-known theatrical family (brother Jay, sister Stella, etc.). Films include *Saigon* (47), *Wake of the Red Witch* (48), *House of Strangers* (49), *M* (51), *Rommel, Desert Fox* (51), *The Magic Face* (as Hitler) (51), *Hoodlum Empire* (52), *The Tall Texan* (53), *The Miami Story* (54), *The Girl in the Red Velvet Swing* (55), *The Last Angry Man* (59), *Cast a Giant Shadow* (66), *The Brotherhood* (68). A frequent TV guest star.

ADLER, STELLA (1895–   ). American stage actress, sister of Luther and Jay Adler. Rare films include *Love on Toast* (38), *My Girl Tisa* (48).

THE ADMIRABLE CRICHTON. Barrie's comedy, about master and man reversing roles after being shipwrecked on a desert island, has long fascinated film-makers. (Goldwyn is said to have lost interest after discovering that it was not what it sounded, a naval drama.) De Mille filmed it in 1919 as *Male and Female*, with Thomas Meighan and Gloria Swanson; a musical version, *We're Not Dressing*, turned up in 1934 with Bing Crosby and Carole Lombard; a further variation, *Our Girl Friday*, was filmed by Noel Langley in 1953 starring Kenneth More and Joan Collins; and in 1957 Kenneth More and Diane Cilento appeared in a more or less straight version of the play, under its original title, directed by Lewis Gilbert. More has since appeared on the stage in a musical adaptation, *Our Man Crichton*.

ADOREE, RENEE (1898–1933) (Jeanne de la Fonte). French star of American silent films; early circus experience. *Monte Cristo* (22); *Man and Maid* (22), *The Big Parade* (25), *Tin Gods* (26), *Flaming Forest* (27), *On Ze Boulevard* (27), *Mr Wu* (27), *The Cossacks* (28), *The Pagan* (29), *Call of the Flesh* (30), etc. Sound ended her career.

Adrian

ADRIAN (1903–1959). American costume designer, with MGM for many years; married Janet Gaynor. Christian name: Gilbert.

ADRIAN, IRIS (1913–   ) (I. A. Hostetter). American actress, former Ziegfeld Follies dancer, familiar from early 30s as wisecracking blonde, usually in second features. *Rumba* (35), *Our Relations* (37), *Professional Bride* (41), *The G-String Murders* (42), *Spotlight Scandals* (44), *I'm from Arkansas* (45), *Road to Alcatraz* (46), *The Paleface* (48), *G.I. Jane* (51), *Highway Dragnet* (54), *The Buccaneer* (59), *That Darn Cat* (65), *The Odd Couple* (68), many others.

ADRIAN, MAX (1903–   ). British character actor, on stage (including revue) from 1926; films very occasional. *The Primrose Path* (30), *Why Pick on Me?* (38), *Kipps* (41), *The Young Mr Pitt* (42), *Penn of Pennsylvania* (42), *Henry V* (44), *Pool of London* (50), *Pickwick Papers* (52), *Dr Terror's House of Horrors* (65), *The Deadly Affair* (67), *Julius Caesar* (70), etc.

advertising appears seldom as a background to movies, but when it does, satire is usually in the air, as in *Christmas in July*, *The Hucksters*, *Mr Blandings Builds His Dream House*, *It Should Happen To You*, *Good Neighbour Sam*, and *How to Succeed in Business without Really Trying*. It was played fairly straight in *Madison Avenue* and *The Narrowing Circle*.

AEROGRAD (USSR 1935). An influential propaganda piece, written and directed by Dovzhenko in the guise of a melodrama about interference by Japanese spies in the building of a Siberian airport.

aeroplanes: see *airplanes*.

THE AFFAIRS OF ANATOL (US 1921). A famous comedy of manners from Cecil B. de Mille's early period. Starring Wallace Reid and Gloria Swanson, it was adapted from a Schnitzler play about a newly married man who spends too much time sorting out other people's affairs instead of his own.

THE AFRICAN QUEEN (GB 1951). Immensely popular film version of C. S. Forester's yarn about a hard-bitten skipper and a prim spinster who become heroes—and lovers—during a perilous escape down an African river in 1915. Directed by John Huston from James Agee's script, with rich performances from Humphrey Bogart (AA) and Katharine Hepburn. Sam Spiegel was one of the first producers to submit Hollywood stars to the rigours of real African locations; and under the circumstances Jack Cardiff's photography is a remarkable achievement.

AGAR, JOHN (1921–   ). American leading man, once married to Shirley Temple; mainly in low-budgeters. *Fort Apache* (48), *Sands of Iwo Jima* (49), *The Magic Carpet* (52), *The Golden Mistress* (53), *Bait* (54), *Joe Butterfly* (56), *Daughter of Dr Jekyll* (57), *Journey to the Seventh Planet* (61), *Of Love and Desire* (63), *Cavalry Command* (65), *Waco* (66), *The St Valentine's Day Massacre* (67), etc.

L'AGE D'OR (France 1930). A surrealist film by Luis Bunuel and Salvador Dali, denigrating mankind and modern society in a succession of more or less unrelated sequences. Widely banned for alleged sacrilege and indecency, it now seems obscurely dull rather than sensational.

AGEE, JAMES (1909–1955). One of America's most respected film critics, he also wrote novels and screenplays (e.g. *The African Queen* [51]). A posthumous collection of his reviews was published under the title 'Agee on Film', and the screenplays followed. His play *A Death in the Family* was filmed in 1963 as *All the Way Home*.

AGOSTINI, PHILIPPE (1910–   ). French cinematographer. *Carnet de Bal* (co-ph) (37), *Les Anges du Pêche* (43), *Les Dames du Bois de Boulogne* (44), *Les Portes de la Nuit* (46), *Pattes Blanches* (48), *Le Plaisir* (co-ph) (51), *Rififi* (55), etc. Directed *Le Dialogue des Carmelites* (59), *La Soupe aux Poulets* (60), etc.

AH WILDERNESS. Eugene O'Neill's gentle small-town play was filmed in 1935 by Clarence Brown, with Lionel Barrymore, Wallace Beery and Eric Linden. In 1947 Rouben Mamoulian remade it as a semi-musical called *Summer Holiday*, with Walter Huston, Frank Morgan and Mickey Rooney.

AHERNE, BRIAN (1902–   ). Gentle-mannered British leading man of stage and screen. In British silent and early sound films: *Safety First* (26), *The Squire of Long Hadley* (27), *Shooting Stars* (28), *Underground* (29), *The W Plan* (32), *I Was a Spy* (33), *The Constant Nymph* (33), etc.; went to Hollywood and became the American ideal of the charming Englishman. *What Every Woman Knows* (34), *Sylvia Scarlett* (35), *Beloved Enemy* (36), *Merrily We Live* (38), *Juarez* (his best role, as Emperor Maximilian) (39), *Vigil in the Night* (40), *The Lady in Question* (40), *Smiling Through* (41), *The Man Who Lost Himself* (41), *My Sister Eileen* (43), *Forever and a Day* (43), *The Locket* (46), *Drums along the Amazon* (48), *I Confess* (53), *Prince Valiant* (54), *A Bullet Is Waiting* (54), *The Swan* (56), *The Best of Everything* (59), *Susan Slade* (61), *Lancelot and Guinevere* (as King Arthur) (63), *Rosie* (67), etc.

AHN, PHILIP (1911–   ). American actor of Korean parentage, seen in Hollywood films as an assortment of Asiatic types. *The General Died at Dawn* (36), *They Got Me Covered* (42), *I Was an American Spy* (51), *Love Is a Many Splendoured Thing* (55), *Never So Few* (59), many others.

AIMEE, ANOUK (1932–　　) (Françoise Sorya). French leading lady, originally known simply as 'Anouk'. *Les Amants de Verone* (48), *The Golden Salamander* (49), *Pot Bouille* (56), *La Tête Contre les Murs* (58), *La Dolce Vita* (59), *Lola* (62), *Eight and a Half* (63), *A Man and a Woman* (66), *The Appointment* (69), *The Model Shop* (US) (69), *Justine* (69), many others.

AINLEY, HENRY (1879–1945). British stage actor who was popular in occasional silent films such as *Sweet Lavender*, *The Prisoner of Zenda*, *Quinneys*, *She Stoops to Conquer* and *The Manxman*. Sound films: *The Good Companions* (32), *The First Mrs Fraser* (33), *As You Like It* (36).

AINLEY, RICHARD (1910–1967). British-born actor son of Henry Ainley. Appeared in *As You Like It* (36), *The Frog* (37), *A Stolen Life* (39), then went to Hollywood for *Lady with Red Hair* (41) and subsequently made occasional appearances: *The Smiling Ghost* (42), *White Cargo* (42), *Above Suspicion* (43), *Passage to Hong Kong* (49), etc. Retired as result of injuries received in World War II.

air balloons, of the spherical type with a hanging basket, have provided picturesque climaxes in films as diverse as *Trottie True*, *The Wizard of Oz* and *Charlie Bubbles*, while the initial part of the journey in *Around the World in Eighty Days* was accomplished in a splendidly ornate example of the species, and a dramatically-styled version was used in *Five Weeks in a Balloon*. Balloons were popular for comic gags in silent films, notably Buster Keaton's *Balloonatic*. The most charming adaptation of the idea was in *The Red Balloon*, at the end of which a group of toy balloons carried the boy hero off into the sky; and the director of that film next made *Stowaway in the Sky*, which was about an air balloon over France. Balloons also featured in *Those Magnificent Men in Their Flying Machines* and *The Great Race*.

Barrage balloons, a familiar sight in the Britain of World War II, seldom featured in films apart from the Crazy Gang's *Gasbags*; but zeppelins or dirigibles were featured in *Dirigible* itself, *Hell's Angels*, *Madame Satan* and recently *The Assassination Bureau*.

airplanes, one of the most exciting inventions of the twentieth century, have naturally been a popular source of cinematic thrills. Films about aviation itself began with the newsreel shots of attempts by early birdmen, some of them with tragic results: these have been well preserved in a Robert Youngson one-reeler of the early 50s, *This Mechanical Age*. In the 20s began the long series of spectacular aerial dramas: *Wings*, *Hell's Angels*, *Dawn Patrol*, *Lucky Devils*, *Devil Dogs of the Air*, *F.P.1*, *Wings of the Navy*, *Men with Wings*, *Test Pilot*, *Only Angels Have Wings*. British films on aviation were rare, exceptions being the exciting *Q Planes* and Korda's ill-fated documentary *Conquest of the Air*; but 1939 brought a need to show the nation's strength, and this was done superbly in such films as *The Lion Has*

Wings, Squadron Leader X, Target for Tonight, Coastal Command, Flying Fortress, Journey Together and *The Way to the Stars*. When America entered the war we were deluged with aerial melodramas, mostly with high-sounding titles and high propaganda content: *Eagle Squadron, International Squadron, I Wanted Wings, Winged Victory, A Wing and a Prayer, The Wild Blue Yonder, Bombardier, God Is My Co-Pilot, Flying Tigers, Captains of the Clouds, Dive Bomber, Air Force, Flight Command, Thirty Seconds over Tokyo,* and many others. Even Disney weighed in with the instructional *Victory Through Air Power*.

During the 40s began the still-continuing stream of biographies of aviation pioneers and air aces: *They Flew Alone* (Amy Johnson), *Flight for Freedom* (Amelia Earhart), *Captain Eddie* (Eddie Rickenbacker), *The McConnell Story, Reach for the Sky* (Douglas Bader), *The Dam Busters* (Dr Barnes Wallis and Guy Gibson), *The Spirit of St Louis* (Lindbergh), *The One That Got Away* (Franz von Werra), etc.

Post-war air dramas from Hollywood showed a considerable increase in thoughtfulness. The responsibility of power was examined in *Command Decision, Twelve O'clock High, The Beginning or the End, Strategic Air Command* and others, while the future of aviation was the subject of such films as *On the Threshold of Space, Towards the Unknown* and *X-15*. But there has also been room for spectaculars like *Lafayette Escadrille, Bombers B-52, The Longest Day* and *The Blue Max*, for such romantic dramas as *Blaze of Noon, Chain Lightning, Tarnished Angels* and *The Bridges at Toko-Ri*, and even for the more routine melodramatics of *Sky Commando, Battle Taxi, 633 Squadron, Sky Tiger, Jet Pilot, Flight from Ashiya* and *The Flight of the Phoenix*. Britain too has turned out routine recruiting thrillers like *The Red Beret* and *High Flight*, with a nod to civil aviation in *Out of the Clouds*; against these can be set the earnest probing of *The Sound Barrier* and *The Man in the Sky*, the affectionate nostalgia of *Angels One Five* and *Conflict of Wings*.

In films where aviation itself is not the main subject, planes can be used for a wide variety of dramatic purposes. In *Triumph of the Will* Hitler's arrival at Nuremberg was made to seem godlike by clever photography of his plane descending through the clouds. A very different effect was given in *The Best Years of Our Lives* which began with three war veterans being given a lift home in the nose of a bomber; and the same film, in the scene when Dana Andrews walks through a scrap yard full of the planes he has so recently been flying in the war, produced a ruefully moving sense of waste and futility. Godlike again was Raymond Massey's fleet of futuristic planes in *Things to Come*; and impeccable trick photography gave memorable punch to a musical, *Flying Down to Rio*, in which chorus girls apparently performed on the wings of planes in mid-air.

Any list of the most spectacular plane sequences should include

Aked, Muriel

Cary Grant being chased through the cornfield in *North by Northwest*; Claudette Colbert and Ray Milland escaping from Spain in *Arise My Love*; *King Kong* being cornered on the Empire State Building; the plane crashing into the sea in *Foreign Correspondent*; and, of course, the climactic sequences of films already mentioned such as *Hell's Angels*, *The Blue Max*, *The Sound Barrier* and *Dawn Patrol*. Comedy flying sequences can be equally thrilling, as shown by George Formby in *It's in the Air*, Abbott and Costello in *Keep 'Em Flying*, the Marx Brothers in *A Night in Casablanca*, Laurel and Hardy in *The Flying Deuces*, Duggie Wakefield in *Spy for a Day*, Ben Blue and Mickey Rooney in *It's a Mad Mad Mad Mad World*, Jimmy Edwards in *Nearly a Nasty Accident*, Pat Boone in *Never Put It In Writing*, W. C. Fields in *Never Give a Sucker an Even Break*, Spencer Tracy in *State of the Union*, Jack Lemmon in *The Great Race*, Fred MacMurray (flying a Model T) in *The Absent-minded Professor*, James Stewart in *You Gotta Stay Happy*, and practically the whole cast of *Those Magnificent Men in Their Flying Machines*. Air hostesses were featured largely in *Come Fly With Me* and *Boeing-Boeing*.

Plane crashes have been the dramatic starting point of many films including *Lost Horizon*, *Five Came Back*, *Back from Eternity*, *Fate Is the Hunter*, *The Night My Number Came Up*, *Broken Journey*, *The Flight of the Phoenix* and *Sands of the Kalahari*. The *fear* that a plane will crash has also been a potent source of screen melodrama, especially in such films as *No Highway*, *The High and the Mighty*, *Julie*, *Zero Hour*, *Jetstorm* and *Jet over the Atlantic*, which focus on the emotional reactions of passengers. The proximity of planes to heaven has been useful in fantasies like *Here Comes Mr Jordan*, *A Guy Named Joe*, *A Matter of Life and Death* and *The Flight That Disappeared*. Finally, plane-building was used as a symbol of power in *The Carpetbaggers*; and symbols of a more fearsome kind are the atomic bombers which figured so largely in *Dr Strangelove* and *Fail Safe*.

See also: *documentaries; helicopters.*

AKED, MURIEL (1887–1955). British character actress usually seen as comedy spinster or gossip. *A Sister to Assist 'Er* (31 and 38), *The Mayor's Nest* (32), *Rome Express* (32), *Friday the Thirteenth* (33), *Cottage to Let* (41), *Two Thousand Women* (44), *The Wicked Lady* (45), *The Happiest Days of Your Life* (50), *The Story of Gilbert and Sullivan* (53), many others.

AKINS, CLAUDE (1918–   ). American character actor often seen as surly western villain. *From Here to Eternity* (53), *The Caine Mutiny* (54), *The Sea Chase* (55), *Johnny Concho* (56), *The Defiant Ones* (58), *Porgy and Bess* (59), *Inherit the Wind* (60), *How the West Was Won* (62), *The Killers* (64), *Ride Beyond Vengeance* (66), *Return of the Seven*

(66), *Waterhole 3* (67), *The Devil's Brigade* (68), *Nobody Loves Flapping Eagle* (70), etc. Much on TV.

AKINS, ZOE (1886–1958). American playwright whose *The Greeks Had a Word for It* was filmed as *Gold Diggers* (qv); *The Old Maid* was later filmed with Bette Davis.

The Alamo, originally a cottonwood tree, gave its name to a Franciscan mission in San Antonio, where in 1836 180 Americans were overpowered and slaughtered by 4,000 Mexicans. As those who died included such legendary figures as Jim Bowie and Davy Crockett, the siege of the Alamo has figured in many a film, notably *The Last Command* (55) and *The Alamo* (60); while in *San Antonio* (45) Errol Flynn and Paul Kelly had a non-historic fight in the mission ruins.

ALBEE, EDWARD (1928–   ). American playwright whose only but significant contribution to cinema is *Who's Afraid of Virginia Woolf?* (66).

ALBERGHETTI, ANNA MARIA (1936–   ). Italian-American operatic singer who came to films as a teenager and has made occasional appearances: *Here Comes the Groom* (51), *The Stars Are Singing* (53), *The Medium* (54), *The Last Command* (55), *Ten Thousand Bedrooms* (57), *Cinderfella* (60), etc.

ALBERNI, LUIS (1887–1962). Spanish-American character actor who played countless small film roles: *Santa Fe Trail* (30), *Svengali* (31), *The Kid from Spain* (32), *Anthony Adverse* (36), *Captain Carey USA* (49), *What Price Glory* (52), etc.

ALBERS, HANS (1892–1960). German actor with stage experience. *The Blue Angel* (30), *Gold* (34), *Baron Munchausen* (43), *Der Letzte Mann* (remake) (55), many others.

ALBERT, EDDIE (1908–   ) (Eddie Albert Heimberger). American actor with radio and stage experience, who for thirty years has projected an 'honest Joe' personality. *Brother Rat* (39), *Four Wives* (39), *This Man Reuter* (40), *The Wagons Roll at Night* (41), *Bombardier* (43), *The Perfect Marriage* (46), *You Gotta Stay Happy* (48), *Carrie* (51), *Roman Holiday* (53), *I'll Cry Tomorrow* (55), *The Teahouse of the August Moon* (56), *The Sun Also Rises* (57), *Orders to Kill* (GB) (58), *Roots of Heaven* (59), *The Young Doctors* (61), *The Party's Over* (GB) (63), *Seven Women* (66), many others. Frequent TV guest star; has also starred in series *Green Acres* (65–69).

ALBERTSON, FRANK (1909–64). American light leading man, later character actor, in films since 1922 when he began as extra and prop boy. Innumerable appearances include *Just Imagine* (31), *A Connecticut Yankee* (31), *Room Service* (38), *Bachelor Mother* (39), *The Man from Headquarters* (40), *Mystery Broadcast* (43), *Arson Squad* (45), *The Hucksters* (47), etc.

29

ALBERTSON, JACK (c. 1910–   ). American character actor who started as a straight man in burlesque. Occasional films include *Man of a Thousand Faces* (57), *Period of Adjustment* (62), *A Tiger Walks* (64), *How to Murder Your Wife* (65), *The Subject was Roses* (AA) (68), *Justine* (69), *Rabbit, Run* (70).

ALBRIGHT, HARDIE (1903–   ) (Hardy Albrecht). American leading man of the early thirties. *Young Sinners* (31), *So Big* (32), *Song of Songs* (33), *The Scarlet Letter* (34), *Ladies Love Danger* (35), *Granny Get Your Gun* (40), *Pride of the Yankees* (42), *Angel on My Shoulder* (46), *Ski Patrol* (51) (last to date), etc.

ALBRIGHT, LOLA (1925–   ). American leading lady with varied experience before screen debut in 1948. A hit in *Champion* (49), but subsequent roles for her Stanwyck-like personality were hard to find. *The Good Humour Man* (50), *Arctic Flight* (52), *The Tender Trap* (56), *The Monolith Monsters* (57), *Seven Guns to Mesa* (60), *A Cold Wind in August* (61), *Kid Galahad* (62), *The Love Cage* (65), *Lord Love a Duck* (66), *The Way West* (67), *Where Were You when the Lights Went Out* (68), *The Impossible Years* (68), etc. Much on TV, including series *Peter Gunn* (58–61).

alcoholics have been familiar screen figures since the movies began: JACK NORTON and ARTHUR HOUSMAN (qv) made a living playing little else, and almost every top star, male or female, has had a big drunk scene. More serious studies of alcoholism have been given by Lars Hanson in *The Atonement of Gosta Berling*, Fredric March in *A Star Is Born* (James Mason in the later version), Ray Milland in *The Lost Weekend*, Susan Hayward in *Smash-Up* and *I'll Cry Tomorrow*, Gig Young in *Come Fill the Cup*, David Farrar in *The Small Back Room*, Burt Lancaster in *Come Back Little Sheba*, Henry Fonda in *The Fugitive*, Bette Davis in *Dangerous*, Van Johnson in *The Bottom of the Bottle*, Thomas Mitchell in *Stagecoach*, Charles Laughton in *Vessel of Wrath* (and Robert Newton in the remake, *The Beachcomber*), Jason Robards in *Long Day's Journey into Night*, Gregory Peck in *Beloved Infidel*, George Murphy in *Show Business*, David Farrar in *The Small Back Room*, James Dunn in *A Tree Grows in Brooklyn*, Joan Fontaine in *Something to Live For*, Myrna Loy in *From the Terrace*, Maurice Ronet in *Le Feu Follet*, Kenneth More in *Dark of the Sun*, and Jack Lemmon and Lee Remick in *Days of Wine and Roses*. Inebriation for comic effect was displayed by Jackie Gleason in *Papa's Delicate Condition*, Wallace Beery in *Ah Wilderness*, William Powell in *The Thin Man*, and James Stewart in *Harvey*.
See: Drunk Scenes.

ALCOTT, LOUISA M. (1832–88). American novelist whose cosy family tales *Little Women* (qv) and *Little Men* have been frequently plundered by movie-makers.

ALDA, ALAN (1936–   ). American leading man, son of Robert Alda. *Gone Are the Days* (63), *The Extraordinary Seaman* (68), *Paper Lion* (68), *The Moonshine War* (70).

ALDA, ROBERT (1914–   ) (Alphonso d'Abruzzo). American actor with radio and stage experience before film debut 1943. Played George Gershwin in *Rhapsody in Blue* (45); but after *Cloak and Dagger* (46) and *The Beast with Five Fingers* (47) his parts dwindled and he returned to Broadway with only occasional films: *Tarzan and the Slave Girl* (50), *Two Gals and a Guy* (51), *Beautiful But Dangerous* (Italian) (55), *Imitation of Life* (59), *Cleopatra's Daughter* (60), etc.

ALDO, G. R. (1902–1953) (Aldo Graziati). Italian cinematographer. *Miracle in Milan* (50), *Othello* (52), *Umberto D* (52), *Senso* (53), etc.

ALDON, MARI (1930–   ). American leading lady of the 50s; former ballet dancer. *Distant Drums* (51), *This Woman Is Dangerous* (52), *The Barefoot Contessa* (54), *Summertime* (55), etc. Recently inactive.

†ALDRICH, ROBERT (1918–   ). American director whose films tend toward an unsympathetic view of mankind: happy endings are rare. *Big Leaguer* (53), *World for Ransom* (53), *Apache* (54), *Vera Cruz* (54), *Kiss Me Deadly* (also produced) (55), *The Big Knife* (also produced) (55), *Autumn Leaves* (56), *Attack!* (also produced) (57), *Ten Seconds to Hell* (59), *The Angry Hills* (59), *The Last Sunset* (60), *Whatever Happened to Baby Jane* (also produced) (62), *Four for Texas* (also produced) (63), *Hush Hush Sweet Charlotte* (also produced) (64), *The Flight of the Phoenix* (also produced) (65), *The Dirty Dozen* (also produced) (66), *The Killing of Sister George* (also produced) (68), *The Legend of Lylah Clare* (also produced) (69), *Too Late the Hero* (also produced) (69). Since 1960 his films have been overlong for their content.

ALEKAN, HENRI (1909–   ). French cinematographer. *Mademoiselle Docteur* (37), *Bataille du Rail* (44), *La Belle et la Bête* (46), *Les Maudits* (47), *Une Si Jolie Petite Plage* (48), *Anna Karenina* (48), *Juliette ou la Clef des Songes* (50), *Austerlitz* (60), *Topkapi* (64), *Lady L* (65), *Triple Cross* (66), *Mayerling* (68), etc.

ALEXANDER, BEN (1911–1969). American boy actor of silent days: *Each Pearl a Tear* (16), *Hearts of the World* (18), *Penrod and Sam* (23), etc. Later in *All Quiet on the Western Front* (30), *Stage Mother* (34), *Born to Gamble* (36), *Convicts' Code* (39), *Pay the Devil* (57), others; famous on TV as police sergeant in *Dragnet* (52-59) and later in *The Felony Squad* (66-69).

ALEXANDER, JOHN (1897–   ). American stage actor with amiable personality, best remembered on screen as mad Uncle Teddy in

Arsenic and Old Lace (44). Also in *The Petrified Forest* (36), *Flowing Gold* (41), *A Tree Grows in Brooklyn* (44), *Mr Skeffington* (45), *The Jolson Story* (46), *Summer Holiday* (48), *Fancy Pants* (as Theodore Roosevelt) (50), *The Marrying Kind* (52), *One Foot in Hell* (60), etc.

ALEXANDER, KATHERINE (1901–). American actress specializing in sympathetic second leads. *The Barretts of Wimpole Street* (34), *The Painted Veil* (34), *The Dark Angel* (36), *The Great Man Votes* (39), *The Hunchback of Notre Dame* (39). *The Vanishing Virginian* (42), *The Human Comedy* (42), *John Loves Mary* (49), etc.

ALEXANDER NEVSKY (USSR 1938). Eisenstein's exciting historical spectacle has Cherkassov as the medieval warrior who conquered barbarian hordes in a battle on the ice at Nijni-Novgorod. The action sequences use music by Prokoviev in place of natural sound.

ALEXANDER THE GREAT (356–323 B.C.). A mighty warrior who became king of Macedonia at the age of twenty and quickly overran most of the Mediterranean before he died of a fever at the age of 33. He was played by Richard Burton in Robert Rossen's rather stolid 1956 biopic.

ALEXANDROV, GRIGORI (1903–) (G. Mormonenko). Russian director, former assistant to Eisenstein. *Jazz Comedy* (35), *Volga Volga* (38), *Spring* (47), *Glinka* (52), etc. Acted in *Battleship Potemkin* (26).

ALEXANDER, ROSS (1907–37). Budding American leading man of the early 30s. *The Wiser Sex* (32), *Flirtation Walk* (34), *A Midsummer Night's Dream* (35), *Captain Blood* (35), *Boulder Dam* (36), *China Clipper* (36), etc.

ALEXANDER, TERENCE (1923–). British light leading man, often in ineffectual roles. *The Woman with No Name* (51), *The Gentle Gunman* (52), *The Runaway Bus* (54), *Portrait of Alison* (55), *The One That Got Away* (57), *Danger Within* (59), *The League of Gentlemen* (60), *The Fast Lady* (62), *The Long Duel* (67), *Waterloo* (69), many others.

ALEXIEFF, ALEXANDRE (1901–). Franco-Russian animator who devised a method of illuminating pins stuck through a screen at various levels to produce a picture. Chief examples are *A Night on a Bare Mountain* (34) and the titles for *The Trial* (64).

ALFIE (GB 1966). Bill Naughton's amusing play about a cockney Lothario, while filmed rather flatly by Lewis Gilbert, with muddy colour and no subtlety, will presumably be remembered as another stage in the cinema's progress towards complete freedom in choice of subject matter: its crude attitude to sex, expressed in raw dialogue, kept box-offices busy and gave the world a new view of the British at play. Michael Caine played the long title role with relish, and even made it sympathetic.

ALGAR, JAMES (1914–   ). American writer-director of Disney True-Life Adventures and associated productions: *The Living Desert*, *The Vanishing Prairie*, *The African Lion*, *White Wilderness*, *Jungle Cat*, *The Legend of Lobo*, *The Incredible Journey*, *The Gnome-Mobile*, etc.

ALGIERS (US 1938). The film in which Charles Boyer did *not* say 'Come with me to the Casbah'. (The line was a Hollywood legend.) The film itself, though highly successful, was a spineless remake of Julien Duvivier's *Pepe Le Moko* (36), which had Jean Gabin, in a script by Ashelbé and Henri Jeanson, as a doom-laden but romantic criminal exile who finally sacrifices himself for a woman. Tony Martin later starred in *Casbah* (48), a further Hollywood remake in semi-musical form.

ALGREN, NELSON (1909–   ). American novelist who writes of life's seamy side. Books filmed include *The Man with the Golden Arm* and *A Walk on the Wild Side*.

ALIAS NICK BEAL (THE CONTACT MAN) (US 1948). A pleasingly successful modern version of 'Faust', with Thomas Mitchell as an honest politician almost corrupted by smooth, suave, diabolic Ray Milland. Effectively studio-set, with the magical moments understated and a general feeling of shape and style. Directed by John Farrow, photographed by Lionel Lindon, from Jonathan Latimer's script.

ALI BABA. The *Arabian Nights* story, of a poor camel-driver who outwits forty thieves by trailing them to their magic cave which opens to a password, has been a favourite with film-makers. Edison made a version in 1902, William Fox in 1919. In 1943 Jon Hall starred in *Ali Baba and the Forty Thieves*, while in 1952 Tony Curtis was *Son of Ali Baba*. (This film was remade, with much use of footage from the original, in 1964 as *Sword of Ali Baba*, starring Peter Mann). Meanwhile in 1954 Fernandel appeared in a French comedy version under Jacques Becker's direction. Eddie Cantor dreamed he was Ali Baba in *Ali Baba Goes to Town* (38), and the character has appeared in many other *Arabian Nights* films. A superior spelling was adopted for *The Adventures of Hajji Baba* (56) in which John Derek played the role.

ALICE IN WONDERLAND. This Victorian nonsense classic was written by Lewis Carroll (C. L. Dodgson) and published in 1865. Most film versions—and there were several silent ones—have included

B   33

material from *Through the Looking Glass*, published in 1871. Since sound there have been two American productions using actors (in 1931 with little-known players and in 1933 with Charlotte Henry and an all-star Paramount cast); a 1950 French version with Carol Marsh and Bunin's puppets; and a rather stiff and unimaginative Disney cartoon of 1951.

ALISON, DOROTHY (1925–   ). Australian actress resident in Britain. *Mandy* (52), *Turn the Key Softly* (53), *The Maggie* (54), *Reach for the Sky* (56), *The Long Arm* (56), *The Scamp* (57), *Life in Emergency Ward Ten* (59), *Georgy Girl* (66), etc.

ALL ABOUT EVE (US 1950). Writer-director Joseph L. Mankiewicz dipped his pen in venom when he wrote this story of the rise to fame of an unscrupulous actress, and won an Academy Award on both counts. Bette Davis blazed as the displaced idol, George Sanders as a waspish critic also won an Academy Award as best supporting actor, and Marilyn Monroe had a brief bit as a dumb blonde. Anne Baxter was Eve.

ALLAN, ELIZABETH (1908–   ). British leading lady with stage experience; adept at delicate or aristocratic heroines. *Alibi* (31), *Black Coffee* (31), *Michael and Mary* (32), *Nine Till Six* (32), *The Lodger* (33), *Java Head* (34), *David Copperfield* (US) (34), *Mark of the Vampire* (US) (35), *A Tale of Two Cities* (US) (36), *Camille* (US) (36), *Michael Strogoff* (US) (37), *Inquest* (38), *Saloon Bar* (40), *The Great Mr Handel* (42), *Went the Day Well* (42), *He Snoops to Conquer* (44), *No Highway* (51), *The Heart of the Matter* (54), *The Brain Machine* (55), etc. A popular TV personality 1955–60.

ALLAND, WILLIAM (1916–   ). American actor, originally with Orson Welles' Mercury Theatre: played the enquiring reporter in *Citizen Kane* (41). Later became staff producer for Universal-International: *It Came from Outer Space* (53), *This Island Earth* (56), *The Lady Takes a Flyer* (58), *The Rare Breed* (65), etc. Independently produced and directed *Look in Any Window* (61).

ALLBRITTON, LOUISE (1920–   ). American leading lady of the 40s, mainly in light comedy. *Not a Ladies Man* (debut) (42), *Who Done It* (42), *A Date with an Angel* (42), *Son of Dracula* (43), *Her Primitive Man* (44), *Men in Her Diary* (45), *San Diego I Love You* (45), *Tangier* (46), *The Egg and I* (47), *Walk a Crooked Mile* (48), *Sitting Pretty* (48), *The Great Manhunt* (50), etc. Recently inactive.

ALLEGRET, MARC (1900–   ). French director of superior commercial films. *Mam'zelle Nitouche* (31), *Fanny* (32), *Lac aux Dames* (34), *Les Beaux Yeux* (35), *Gribouille* (37), *Orage* (38), *Entrée de Artistes* (38), *L'Arlesienne* (42), *Petrus* (46), *Blanche Fury* (GB) (47).

Maria Chapdelaine (50), *Blackmailed* (GB) (51), *Futures Vedettes* (55), *Lady Chatterley's Lover* (55), *En Effeuillant La Marguerite* (56), *Un Drole de Dimanche* (58), *L'Abominable Homme des Douanes* (63), etc.

ALLEGRET, YVES (1907–   ). French director, brother of Marc Allegret. *Les Deux Timides* (41), *Dédée* (47), *Une Si Jolie Petite Plage* (48), *Manèges* (49), *Les Orgueilleux* (53), *Oasis* (54), *Germinal* (63), etc.

ALLEN, ADRIENNE (1907–   ). British light actress, mostly on stage. Mother of Daniel Massey, ex-wife of Raymond. *Loose Ends* (31), *Black Coffee* (31), *The Morals of Marcus* (35), *The October Man* (47), *Vote for Huggett* (49), *The Final Test* (53), *Meet Mr Malcolm* (54), etc.

ALLEN, BARBARA JO (c. 1904–   ) (also known as VERA VAGUE). American comedy actress, well known on radio with Bob Hope. *Village Barn Dance* (40), *Ice Capades* (41), *Mrs Wiggs of the Cabbage Patch* (42), *In Rosie's Room* (44), *Snafu* (46), *Square Dance Katy* (50), *The Opposite Sex* (56), etc.

ALLEN, CHESNEY (1894–   ). British light comedian, for many years teamed with Bud Flanagan and the Crazy Gang, from whose more violent antics he stood somewhat aloof. *A Fire Has Been Arranged* (34), *Underneath the Arches* (37), *Alf's Button Afloat* (38), *Gasbags* (40), *We'll Smile Again* (42), *Dreaming* (44), *Here Comes the Sun* (45), etc. Retired from show business.

ALLEN, COREY (1934–   ). American supporting actor specializing in depraved adolescents. *The Mad Magician* (54), *Night of the Hunter* (55), *Rebel without a Cause* (55), *The Shadow on the Window* (57), *Party Girl* (58), *Private Property* (lead) (60), *Sweet Bird of Youth* (62), etc.

ALLEN, ELIZABETH (1934–   ) (E. Gillease). American leading lady with stage experience. Films: *From the Terrace* (60), *Diamond Head* (63), *Donovan's Reef* (63). TV series: *Bracken's World* (69).

ALLEN, FRED (1894–1956) (John F. Sullivan). Baggy-eyed American radio comedian whose very occasional films included *Thanks a Million* (35), *Love Thy Neighbour* (41), *It's in the Bag* (*The Fifth Chair*) (45), *We're Not Married* (52), *Full House* (53). Published autobiography 1954: *Treadmill to Oblivion*.

ALLEN, GRACIE (1906-1964). American comedienne who projected a scatterbrained image for thirty years on radio, TV and films, usually with her husband George Burns. Occasional film appearances include *College Humour* (33), *We're Not Dressing* (34), *College Holiday* (36), *A Damsel in Distress* (38), *The Gracie Allen Murder Case* (39), *Mr and Mrs North* (42), *Two Girls and a Sailor* (44), etc.

35

ALLEN, IRVING (1905–   ). Polish-American producer. Hollywood experience from 1929; films include *Avalanche* (d) (47), *16 Fathoms Deep* (d) (50), *New Mexico* (p) (51), *Slaughter Trail* (p, d) (51). In Britain from early 50s as co-founder of Warwick Films (*Cockleshell Heroes, Zarak*, etc.). More recently: *The Trials of Oscar Wilde* (60), *The Hellions* (61), *The Long Ships* (64), *Genghis Khan* (65), *The Silencers* (66), *The Ambushers* (67), *Hammerhead* (68), *Cromwell* (69), etc.

ALLEN, IRWIN (1916–   ). American writer-producer who began with semi-instructional entertainments and then switched to fantasy. *The Sea Around Us* (50), *The Animal World* (56), *The Story of Mankind* (57), *The Big Circus* (59), *The Lost World* (also directed) (61), *A Voyage to the Bottom of the Sea* (also directed) (62), *Five Weeks in a Balloon* (also directed) (63), etc. Recently turning out TV series in similar vein: *Voyage to the Bottom of the Sea, Lost in Space, Time Tunnel, Land of the Giants*, etc.

ALLEN, LEWIS (1905–   ). British-born director with stage experience; busy in Hollywood from the mid-forties. *Our Hearts Were Young and Gay* (44), *The Uninvited* (44), *The Unseen* (45), *Those Endearing Young Charms* (46), *Mrs Loring's Secret* (46), *The Perfect Marriage* (46), *Desert Fury* (47), *Chicago Deadline* (48), *Valentino* (51), *Sons of the Musketeers* (52), *Suddenly* (54), *Illegal* (55), *Another Time Another Place* (58), *Whirlpool* (59), *Decision at Midnight* (MRA film) (63), etc.

ALLEN, LEWIS M. (1922–   ). American producer with theatrical experience. *The Connection* (60), *The Balcony* (63), *Lord of the Flies* (64), *Fahrenheit 451* (66).

ALLEN, PATRICK (1927–   ). Lantern-jawed British leading man who after playing assorted villains and heroes in routine films established himself as TV's *Crane*. *1984* (55), *The Long Haul* (57), *High Tide at Noon* (57), *Dunkirk* (58), *Tread Softly Stranger* (58), *I Was Monty's Double* (58), *Never Take Sweets from a Stranger* (60), *The Traitors* (62), *Captain Clegg* (62), *The Night of the Generals* (66), *Night of the Big Heat* (67), *When Dinosaurs Ruled the Earth* (69), etc.

ALLEN, REX (1922–   ). American singing cowboy, popular on radio and in vaudeville. Made many second features from the late 40s: *Arizona Cowboy, Under Mexicali Stars, The Old Overland Trail, The Phantom Stallion*, etc.

ALLEN, STEVE (1921–   ). American radio and TV personality who played the title role in *The Benny Goodman Story* (55), and was also in *I'll Get By* (51), *College Confidential* (59), *Warning Shot* (66).

ALLEN, WOODY (1935–   ) (Allen Stewart Konigsberg). American night club comedian and playwright who has made some chaotic film appearances: *What's New Pussycat* (66), *Casino Royale* (67), *What's Up Tiger Lily* (67), *Take the Money and Run* (69), etc.

ALLGEIER, SEPP (1890–1968). German cinematographer. Best-known films include *Diary of a Lost Girl* (29), *The White Hell of Pitz Palu* (29), *William Tell* (33).

ALLGOOD, SARA (1883–1950). Irish character actress, long with the Abbey Theatre and from 1940 in Hollywood. *Blackmail* (30), *Juno and the Paycock* (30), *The Passing of the Third Floor Back* (35), *Storm in a Teacup* (37), *Lady Hamilton* (41), *How Green Was My Valley* (42), *Jane Eyre* (43), *The Lodger* (44), *Between Two Worlds* (44), *The Spiral Staircase* (45), *Kitty* (46), *Ivy* (47), *Mother Wore Tights* (48), *Cheaper by the Dozen* (50), etc.

Allied Artists Corporation. An American production company, more recently involved in TV, which flourished throughout the 30s and 40s as a purveyor of routine crime and comedy second features. Its policy was to put out the poorer product under the banner of its subsidiary, MONOGRAM PICTURES CORPORATION; the 'quality' AA product was little in evidence until the 50s, when films like *Love in the Afternoon*, *The Friendly Persuasion* and *Al Capone* came from this stable. Meanwhile the Monogram films, boasting, such attractions as Frankie Darro, the East Side Kids, the Bowery Boys, Bela Lugosi and Charlie Chan, had their faithful following, and in France attracted highbrow cineastes to such an extent that Jean-Luc Godard dedicated his film *À Bout de Souffle* to Monogram.

ALLISTER, CLAUDE (1891–   ) (Claud Palmer). British character actor associated with monocled silly-ass roles. Algy in *Bulldog Drummond* (29); later in *The Private Life of Henry VIII* (32), *The Private Life of Don Juan* (34), *Dracula's Daughter* (US) (36), *Captain Fury* (US) (39), *Charley's American Aunt* (US) (41), *Kiss the Bride Goodbye* (44), *Gaiety George* (46), *Quartet* (48), *Kiss Me, Kate* (53), etc.

ALL QUIET ON THE WESTERN FRONT (US 1930). Erich Maria Remarque's book, showing World War I from the point of view of the German soldier, was turned into a milestone of cinema history by director Lewis Milestone, cinematographer Arthur Edeson and composer David Brockman. Lew Ayres, Louis Wolheim, Slim Summerville headed the cast. AA best picture.

ALL THAT MONEY CAN BUY (US 1941). From Stephen Vincent Benet's story 'The Devil and Daniel Webster', this delightfully American film put the Faust legend into a nineteenth-century farming setting peopled by real historical characters. Edward

37

Arnold as lawyer Webster and James Craig as the young farmer were both outshone by Walter Huston as Mr Scratch, the amiable devil. Bernard Herrman's vibrant music (AA) perfectly counterpointed William Dieterle's zestful direction and production. The film has also, at various times, been known as *The Devil and Daniel Webster* and *Daniel and the Devil*.

ALL THE KING'S MEN (US 1949). A notable film version, written and directed by Robert Rossen, of Robert Penn Warren's exposé of American state politics, paralleling the career of the corrupt Huey Long of Louisiana. AA best picture; Broderick Crawford best actor; Mercedes Cambridge best supporting actress. John Ireland also was excellent as the jaundiced narrator.

ALLWYN, ASTRID (1909–). Swedish-American leading lady of minor movies in the thirties. *Reputation* (32), *Only Yesterday* (33), *Follow the Fleet* (36), *Dimples* (37), *Love Affair* (39), *Mr Smith Goes to Washington* (39), *Unexpected Uncle* (41), *No Hands on the Clock* (last to date) (42), etc.

ALLYSON, JUNE (1917–) (Ella Geisman). Husky-voiced American leading lady, trained as a dancer. Appeared in Hollywood shorts from 1937, then danced and sang on Broadway. After repeating her stage role in *Best Foot Forward* (43), she was contracted by MGM as teenage lead in big wartime musical *Two Girls and a Sailor* (44). Was subsequently cute in many comedies and musicals, with occasional dramatic ventures. *Music for Millions* (45), *Two Sisters from Boston* (46), *The Secret Heart* (46), *Till the Clouds Roll By* (46), *Good News* (47), *Little Women* (as Jo) (49), *So Bright the Flame* (52), *The Glenn Miller Story* (53), *Executive Suite* (54), *Woman's World* (54), *The Shrike* (55), *You Can't Run Away from It* (56), *The Opposite Sex* (56), *My Man Godfrey* (57), *Stranger in My Arms* (59), etc. TV series: *The June Allyson Show* (59–61). Widow of Dick Powell.

ALOMA OF THE SOUTH SEAS. This sentimental romance was a silent success in 1927, with Gilda Grey and Percy Marmont. In 1941 Paramount remade it in colour, with Dorothy Lamour, Jon Hall, and lots of crocodiles and volcanoes.

ALPERSON, EDWARD L. (1896–1969). American independent producer, mainly of hokum pictures; former film salesman. *Black Beauty* (47), *Dakota Lil* (50), *Invaders from Mars* (53), *New Faces* (54), *The Magnificent Matador* (56), *I Mobster* (59), many others.

ALTON, JOHN (1901–). Hungarian-born cinematographer, in Hollywood from 1924. Won Academy Award for *An American in Paris* (51). Others: *Atlantic City* (44), *Father of the Bride* (50), *The People Against O'Hara* (51), *The Big Combo* (55), *The Teahouse of the August Moon* (56), *The Brothers Karamazov* (58), *Elmer Gantry* (60).

ALTON, ROBERT (1906–1957) (Robert Alton Hart). American director, mainly of musical sequences: *Strike Me Pink* (36), *Showboat* (51), *There's No Business Like Show Business* (55), many others. Directed features: *Merton of the Movies* (47), *Pagan Love Song* (50).

ALVARADO, DON (1900–1967) (José Paige). American 'latin lover' of the 20s: later appeared in character roles. *The Loves of Carmen* (26), *Drums of Love* (27), *The Battle of the Sexes* (28), *The Bridge of San Luis Rey* (29), *Rio Rita* (29), *Morning Glory* (33), *The Devil is a Woman* (35), *The Big Steal* (50), etc.

ALWYN, WILLIAM (1905–   ). British composer. Has worked for films since 1936: *Odd Man Out* (47), *The Fallen Idol* (48), *The Card* (52), *Manuela* (57), *The Running Man* (63), many others.

AMATEAU, ROD (1923–   ). American radio writer who briefly became a film director (*The Rebel* [51], *Monsoon* [52]) and then turned his attention to half-hour comedy TV films, of which he has since made many hundreds.

THE AMATEUR GENTLEMAN. Jeffrey Farnol's Regency novel, of an innkeeper's son who becomes involved with highwaymen and London society, was a popular subject for British movies. In 1920 Maurice Elvey directed Langhorne Burton; 1926 saw Sidney Olcott directing Richard Barthelmess in a Hollywood version; and in 1936 Douglas Fairbanks Jnr was the star of a sound version directed by Thornton Freeland.

AMATO, GIUSEPPE (1899–1964) (G. Vasaturo). Italian producer. *Four Steps in the Clouds* (42), *Open City* (45), *Shoe Shine* (46), *Bicycle Thieves* (49), *Umberto D* (52), *Don Camillo* (52), *La Dolce Vita* (59), many others.

AMBLER, ERIC (1909–   ). Popular British novelist (works filmed include *The Mask of Dimitrios, Journey Into Fear, Hotel Reserve*). Also screenwriter: *The Way Ahead* (44), *The October Man* (47), *The Magic Box* (51), *The Card* (52), *The Cruel Sea* (54), *A Night to Remember* (57), *The Wreck of the Mary Deare* (59), etc.

AMBLER, JOSS (1900–1959). British character actor, often seen as heavy father or police inspector. *The Citadel* (38), *The Black Sheep of Whitehall* (41), *The Agitator* (44), *The Long Arm* (56), many others.

AMECHE, DON (1908–   ) (Dominic Amici). American leading man with stage and radio experience; an adequate light hero of mainly trivial films. *Sins of Man* (debut) (36), *Ramona* (first star role) (36), *You Can't Have Everything* (37), *Alexander's Ragtime Band* (38), *In Old Chicago* (38), *The Three Musketeers* (musical version; as D'Artagnan) (39), *The Story of Alexander Graham Bell* (39), *Swanee River* (as Stephen

Foster) (40), *Lilian Russell* (40), *Down Argentine Way* (40), *That Night in Rio* (41), *Confirm or Deny* (42), *Something to Shout About* (42), *Heaven Can Wait* (under Lubitsch, his best performance) (43), *Happy Land* (43), *A Wing and a Prayer* (44), *A Genius in the Family* (46), *Will Tomorrow Ever Come* (47), *Sleep My Love* (48), *Phantom Caravan* (54), *Fire One* (55), *A Fever in the Blood* (60), *Picture Mommy Dead* (66), etc. Since 1950 has been mainly on Broadway stage and in TV (especially as circus ringmaster).

AMERICA, AMERICA (US 1964). A long and painstaking account, directed by Elia Kazan from his own autobiographical book, of the struggles of a poor Turk to emigrate to America. Splendidly photographed by Haskell Wexler, with a stalwart central performance from Stathis Giallelis; but needlessly uncommercial.

AN AMERICAN IN PARIS (US 1951). One of Hollywood's most pleasing musicals, a five-time Academy Award winner. Splendid MGM production values, sympathetic direction by Vincente Minnelli, Gershwin tunes and careful colour photography helped to give the excitement to which the performances of Gene Kelly, Oscar Levant and Nina Foch contributed. The final musical sequence remains unexcelled as a film ballet. AA best picture, best cinematography (Alfred Gilks, John Alton), best costume design, best scoring, best screenplay (Alan Jay Lerner).

AMERICAN MADNESS (US 1932). One of the most notable early sound dramas on a social theme, in this case the American pursuit of the dollar, with Walter Huston as an honest banker driven to desperation by the corruption around him. Written by Robert Rossen and directed by Frank Capra; after its box-office failure they subsequently expressed their social comment and popular sentimental feeling in comedy vein.

AN AMERICAN TRAGEDY. Theodore Dreiser (qv) published his downbeat novel in 1925, about an ambitious but callow youth who is forced by the social system and his own weakness into murdering his sweetheart. Josef Von Sternberg's 1931 film version, though not entirely to his own liking, was a more vigorous and cinematic treatment than George Stevens' portentous 1951 remake, *A Place in the Sun*. The stars of the first version were Phillips Holmes, Sylvia Sydney and Frances Dee; of the second, Montgomery Clift, Shelley Winters and Elizabeth Taylor.

AMES, LEON (1903–) (Leon Wycoff). American stage actor, a specialist in harassed or kindly fathers and professional men, e.g. *Meet Me in St. Louis* (44), *Little Women* (49). Other films include *The Murders in the Rue Morgue* (debut) (32), *East Side Kids* (39), *Crime Doctor* (43), *Son of Lassie* (44), *The Lady in the Lake* (46),

Merton of the Movies (47), *The Violent Hour* (50), *On Moonlight Bay* (52), *Sabre Jet* (53), *Peyton Place* (57), *From the Terrace* (60), *The Monkey's Uncle* (65), *On a Clear Day You Can See Forever* (69). On TV has played the lead in series *Life with Father* (54) and *Father of the Bride* (61), and a supporting role in *Mister Ed* (63–66).

AMFITHEATROF, DANIELE (1901–   ). Russian composer, in Hollywood from 1938. Scores include *I'll Be Seeing You* (43), *Letter from An Unknown Woman* (48), *The Lost Moment* (48), *Rommel, Desert Fox* (51), *The Naked Jungle* (54), *Trial* (55), *Heller in Pink Tights* (60), many others.

AMES, RAMSAY (1924–   ). American leading lady of the early 40s. *Ali Baba and the 40 Thieves* (42), *The Mummy's Tomb* (42), *Calling Dr Death* (43), etc.

AMIS, KINGSLEY (1922–   ). British novelist. Books filmed include *Lucky Jim*, *That Uncertain Feeling* (as *Only Two Can Play*), *The Egyptologists* (project).

amnesia has been a favourite theme of the movies, and the line 'Who am I?' long since became immortal. Heroes and heroines who have suffered memorably from the affliction include Ronald Colman in *Random Harvest*, John Hodiak in *Somewhere in the Night*, Joan Crawford in *Possessed*, and Gregory Peck in *Mirage*. In *Portrait of Jennie* Jennifer Jones was a ghost who forgot she was dead, and the same might be said of the passengers in *Outward Bound*, its remake *Between Two Worlds*, and *Thunder Rock*. In *While I Live* (*Dream of Olwen*) Carol Raye was the characteristic film amnesiac, emerging out of the mist complete with theme tune; but the scriptwriters of *The Mummy's Curse* win the prize for audacity, with their heroine who manages to forget that she's a 3,000-year-old mummy – and look the part of a modern maiden! Perhaps the cutest twist of all was in the film *Black Angel*, in which Dan Duryea, having spent an hour of running time trying to find out who killed his wife, discovers that he did it himself while suffering from amnesia. The same thing happened to Boris Karloff in *Grip of the Strangler*. Latest sufferers: George Peppard in *The Third Day*, Joan Fontaine in *The Witches*, James Garner in *Mister Buddwing*. The matter was put to comic use by William Powell in *I Love You Again*.
  See also: *psychology*.

AMYES, JULIAN (1917–   ). British director: *A Hill in Korea* (56), *Miracle in Soho* (57); also TV director and executive.

anamorphic lens. One which, in a camera, 'squeezes' a wide picture on to standard film; in a projector, 'unsqueezes' the image to fill wide screen; e.g. CinemaScope, Panavision, other similar processes.

B*   41

ANASTASIA (GB 1956). An interesting Hollywood investigation into a puzzle of recent history, namely the fate of the Czar's daughter alleged to have been executed during the Russian revolution. Written by Arthur Laurents from a TV play by Marcelle Maurette, and directed by Anatole Litvak, it marked Ingrid Bergman's (AA) return to the Hollywood screen after her European 'exile'. In a somewhat less fictionalized version of the story, *Is Anna Anderson Anastasia?* (Germany 1957), Lilli Palmer played the enigmatic claimant.

ANCHORS AWEIGH (US 1945). Musical with Gene Kelly and Frank Sinatra as sailors on leave. Remarkable only as a forerunner of *On the Town* and for Kelly's delightful dance with a cartoon mouse.

Ancient Egypt has not been a popular stopping place for movie-makers. Several films based on the Bible (qv), notably *The Ten Commandments*, have stayed awhile, and there were detailed reconstructions in *The Egyptian* and *Land of the Pharaohs*. Otherwise it has been most frequently seen in flashbacks in *The Mummy* (qv) and its sequels.

ANDERS, GLENN (1889–). American stage actor who has made occasional film appearances, usually sinister: *Laughter* (31), *By Your Leave* (35), *Nothing but the Truth* (41), *The Lady from Shanghai* (48), *M* (51), *Behave Yourself* (52), etc.

ANDERS, LUANA (c. 1940–). American leading lady of minor movies. *Life Begins at Seventeen* (58), *The Pit and the Pendulum* (61), *The Young Racers* (63), *Dementia 13* (*The Haunted and the Hunted*) (63), etc.

ANDERS, MERRY (c. 1932–). American light leading lady. *Les Misérables* (52), *Phffft* (54), *The Dalton Girls* (57), *Violent Road* (58), *The Hypnotic Eye* (60), *20,000 Eyes* (61), *House of the Damned* (63), *Tickle Me* (65), etc. TV series: *How to Marry a Millionaire* (58).

ANDERSEN, HANS CHRISTIAN (1805–75). Danish writer of fairy tales, impersonated by Danny Kaye in Goldwyn's 1952 biopic. Many of his tales were filmed by Disney as Silly Symphonies, and one of them was the basis of *The Red Shoes* (48).

ANDERSON, DAPHNE (1922–) (Daphne Scrutton). British light actress chiefly associated with the stage. *Trottie True* (49), *The Beggar's Opera* (52), *Hobson's Choice* (54), *A Kid for Two Farthings* (55), *The Prince and the Showgirl* (57), *Snowball* (60), *Captain Clegg* (62), etc.

ANDERSON, EDDIE 'ROCHESTER' (1905–). Negro comedian long associated with Jack Benny on radio and TV. His gravel voice and rolling eyes were familiar in many films of the 30s and 40s, including

Three Men on a Horse (35), *Green Pastures* (36), *Jezebel* (38), *You Can't Take It with You* (38), *Gone with the Wind* (39), *Topper Returns* (41), *Tales of Manhattan* (42), *The Meanest Man in the World* (42), *Cabin in the Sky* (leading role) (43), *Broadway Rhythm* (44), *The Show-off* (46). More recently in TV: Jack Benny Show (53–65). Made guest appearance in *It's a Mad Mad Mad Mad World* (63).

ANDERSON, G. M. ('BRONCHO BILLY') (1882–   ). American silent actor, an unsuccessful vaudeville performer who drifted into films in *The Great Train Robbery* (03). Later co-founded the Essanay company and made nearly four hundred one-reel Westerns starring himself. Retired in the 20s and became Max Aronson (his real name) again. Special Academy Award 1957 'for his contribution to the development of motion pictures'.

ANDERSON, JEAN (1908–   ). British stage and screen actress often cast as sympathetic nurse, tired mother, or spinster aunt. *The Mark of Cain* (debut) (47), *Elizabeth of Ladymead* (49), *White Corridors* (51), *The Franchise Affair* (51), *A Town Like Alice* (56), *Heart of a Child* (57), *Robbery under Arms* (57), *Solomon and Sheba* (59), *Half a Sixpence* (67), many others.

ANDERSON, DAME JUDITH (1898–   ). Distinguished Australian-born stage actress, long in US. Her occasional films include *Blood Money* (34), *Rebecca* (as Mrs Danvers) (40), *Free and Easy* (41), *Lady Scarface* (41), *King's Row* (42), *Laura* (44), *Ten Little Niggers (And Then There Were None)* (45), *The Spectre of the Rose* (46), *The Furies* (50), *Salome* (53), *The Ten Commandments* (56), *Macbeth* (59), *Cinderfella* (60), *Don't Bother to Knock* (GB) (61), *A Man Called Horse* (69).

ANDERSON, LINDSAY (1923–   ). British documentarist and critic. *O Dreamland* (53), *Thursday's Children* (54), *Every Day Except Christmas* (57), etc. Directed features: *This Sporting Life* (63), *The White Bus* (67), *If* (68).

ANDERSON, MAX (1914–59). British documentary director, with the GPO Film Unit from 1936, later Crown Film Unit. Best known for *The Harvest Shall Come* (41), *Daybreak in Udi* (48).

ANDERSON, MAXWELL (1888–1959). American playwright, many of whose plays were filmed: *What Price Glory, Mary of Scotland, Winterset, Joan of Lorraine* (as *Joan of Arc*), *Elizabeth the Queen* (as *Elizabeth and Essex*), *Key Largo, The Bad Seed*. Also wrote screenplay of *All Quiet on the Western Front* (30), *The Wrong Man* (56), etc.

ANDERSON, MICHAEL (1920–   ). British director. *Waterfront* (50), *Hell Is Sold Out* (51), *Night Was Our Friend* (52), *Will Any Gentleman* (53), *The Dam Busters* (55), *1984* (55), *Around the World in Eighty Days* (US) (56), *Yangtse Incident* (56), *Chase a Crooked Shadow* (57),

Anderson, Michael Jnr

Shake Hands with the Devil (59), *The Wreck of the Mary Deare* (50),
All the Fine Young Cannibals (US) (60), *The Naked Edge* (61), *Flight
from Ashiya* (62), *Wild and Wonderful* (63), *Operation Crossbow* (65),
The Quiller Memorandum (66), *The Shoes of the Fisherman* (68), *Tai-
Pan* (70), etc.

ANDERSON, MICHAEL JNR (1943–   ). British juvenile lead, former
child actor, son of director Michael Anderson. *The Moonraker* (57),
The Sundowners (60), *In Search of the Castaways* (61), *Play it Cool* (62),
The Greatest Story Ever Told (65), *Major Dundee* (65), *The Sons of
Katie Elder* (65), *The Glory Guys* (65), *Hall of Mirrors* (69), etc. TV
series: *The Monroes* (66).

ANDERSON, RICHARD (1926–   ). American leading man, mainly in
routine or secondary roles. *Forbidden Planet* (56), *Paths of Glory* (57),
The Long Hot Summer (58), *Seven Days in May* (64), *Seconds* (66), etc.
TV series: *Perry Mason.*

ANDERSON, RONA (1926–   ). Scottish actress who made film debut
in *Sleeping Car to Trieste* (48). Subsequent films, mainly routine,
include *Poets' Pub* (49), *Home to Danger* (51), *Black Thirteen* (54),
The Flaw (55), *Stock Car* (55), *Man with a Gun* (58), *Devils of Darkness*
(65), *The Prime of Miss Jean Brodie* (69).

ANDERSON, WARNER (1911–   ). American stage and screen actor:
many solid supporting performances. *Destination Tokyo* (44),
Command Decision (48), *Destination Moon* (50), *The Caine Mutiny* (54),
The Blackboard Jungle (55), *Rio Conchos* (64), etc. TV series: *The
Doctor* (52), *San Francisco Beat* (54–55), *Peyton Place* (64–69).

ANDERSSON, BIBI (1935–   ). Swedish actress. *Smiles of a Summer Night*
(55), *The Seventh Seal* (56), *Wild Strawberries* (57), *The Face* (58), *So
Close to Life* (60), *The Devil's Eye* (61), *Persona* (66), *Duel at Diablo*
(US) (66), *A Question of Rape* (67), etc.

ANDERSSON, HARRIET (1932–   ). Swedish actress, a member of
Ingmar Bergman's company. *Summer with Monika* (52), *Sawdust and
Tinsel* (53), *A Lesson in Love* (54), *Smiles of a Summer Night* (55),
Through a Glass Darkly (62), *To Love* (64), *Now About These Women*
(65), *The Deadly Affair* (GB) (66), etc.

ANDES, KEITH (1920–   ). American light actor, usually in secondary
roles. *The Farmer's Daughter* (47), *Clash by Night* (52), *Blackbeard the
Pirate* (52), *Back from Eternity* (56), *The Girl Most Likely* (57), etc.
TV series: *Glynis* (63).

ANDRESS, URSULA (1936–   ). Swiss-born glamour star, in international films. *The Loves of Casanova* (It.) (54), *Dr No* (62), *Four
for Texas* (63), *Fun in Acapulco* (64), *She* (64), *What's New Pussycat*
(65), *The Tenth Victim* (65), *Once Before I Die* (66), *The Blue Max*
(66), *Casino Royale* (67), *The Southern Star* (69), etc.

ANDREWS, DANA (1909–   ). American leading man who in recent years has declined into routine character roles. *Lucky Cisco Kid* (38), *Tobacco Road* (41), *Belle Starr* (41), *Berlin Correspondent* (42), *The Purple Heart* (43), *Laura* (44), *Fallen Angel* (45), *The Best Years of Our Lives* (46), *A Walk in the Sun* (46), *Boomerang* (47), *Britannia Mews* (48), *My Foolish Heart* (50), *I Want You* (51), *Elephant Walk* (53), *Duel in the Jungle* (54), *Comanche* (56), *Night of the Demon* (GB) (57), *Madison Avenue* (60), *Crack in the World* (65), *The Satan Bug* (65), *In Harm's Way* (65), *Town Tamer* (65), *The Loved One* (65), *Spy in Your Eye* (66), etc.

ANDREWS, EDWARD (c. 1914–   ). Beaming, bespectacled American character actor equally at home in sinister, hearty or henpecked roles. Long stage experience before screen debut as villain of *The Phenix City Story* (56); now in many films and TV appearances every year. *The Tattered Dress* (57), *Tea and Sympathy* (57), *The Fiend Who Walked the West* (58), *Elmer Gantry* (60), *Kisses for My President* (64), *Send Me No Flowers* (64), *The Glass Bottom Boat* (66), *Birds Do It* (66), etc. Many TV guest star appearances.

ANDREWS, HARRY (1911–   ). Tough-looking British stage and screen actor. Often plays sergeant-majors or other no-nonsense characters. *The Red Beret* (debut) (52), *A Hill in Korea* (56), *Moby Dick* (56), *Ice Cold in Alex* (58), *The Devil's Disciple* (59), *Solomon and Sheba* (59), *Circle of Deception* (60), *The Best of Enemies* (62), *Lisa* (*The Inspector*) (62), *55 Days at Peking* (62), *The Informers* (63), *The System* (64), *The Hill* (65), *Sands of the Kalahari* (65), *Modesty Blaise* (66), *The Deadly Affair* (66), *The Jokers* (67), *Danger Route* (67), *The Charge of the Light Brigade* (68), *The Night They Raided Minsky's* (US) (68), *A Nice Girl Like Me* (69), *The Battle of Britain* (69), *Country Dance* (70), *The Gaunt Woman* (70), etc.

†ANDREWS, JULIE (1935–   ) (Julia Vernon or Wells). British-born super-star of international films; performed in music halls from childhood. The original stage Eliza of *My Fair Lady*. *Mary Poppins* (AA) (64), *The Americanisation of Emily* (64), *The Sound of Music* (65), *Torn Curtain* (66), *Hawaii* (66), *Thoroughly Modern Millie* (67), *Star!* (as Gertrude Lawrence) (68), *Darling Lili* (69), *She Loves Me* (70).

THE ANDREWS SISTERS: PATTY (1918–   ), MAXINE (1916–   ) and LAVERNE (1913–67). American close harmony singing group popular in light musicals of the forties. *Argentine Nights* (40), *Hold That Ghost* (41), *Moonlight and Cactus* (43), *Road to Rio* (47), etc.

ANDRIOT, LUCIEN (1897–   ). French-American cinematographer, long in Hollywood. *Gigolo* (26), *White Gold* (27), *The Valiant* (28), *Hallelujah I'm a Bum* (33), *Anne of Green Gables* (34), *The Gay Desperado* (36), *The Lady in Question* (40), *The Hairy Ape* (44), *The*

Southerner (45), *Ten Little Niggers* (45), *Dishonoured Lady* (47), many others; recently working in TV.

ANGEL, DANNY (DANIEL M.) (1911–   ). British producer, in films from 1945. *Mr Drake's Duck* (50), *Albert R.N.* (53), *The Sea Shall Not Have Them* (54), *Reach for the Sky* (56), *Carve Her Name With Pride* (57), *The Sheriff of Fractured Jaw* (58), *West Eleven* (63), etc.

ANGEL, HEATHER (1909–   ). British-born leading lady of the 30s; in Hollywood from 1933; still seen in supporting roles and on TV. *City of Song* (30), *Berkeley Square* (33), *The Informer* (35), *Pride and Prejudice* (40), *Time to Kill* (42), *In the Meantime, Darling* (44), *The Saxon Charm* (48), *The Premature Burial* (62), etc.

ANGELI, PIER (1932–   ) (Anna Maria Pierangeli). Italian leading lady who after some stage and film experience at home, applied for and got the leading role in MGM's *Teresa* (51). Subsequent roles less notable: *The Devil Makes Three* (52), *The Flame and the Flesh* (53), *The Silver Chalice* (55), *Port Afrique* (GB) (56), *Somebody Up There Likes Me* (57), *The Vintage* (57), *Merry Andrew* (58), *The Angry Silence* (GB) (59), *Sodom and Gomorrah* (62), *The Battle of the Bulge* (65), etc.

angels made appearances in many silent films: *Intolerance, The Four Horsemen of the Apocalypse, The Sorrows of Satan*, and the many versions of *Uncle Tom's Cabin* and *Faust* were among them. Since sound they have remained a favourite Hollywood device, but have naturally tended to lose their wings and become more whimsical, less awesome and often of somewhat ambiguous reality, to be explained away in the last reel as a result of the hero's bump on the head. The last completely serious angels were probably those in the all-Negro *Green Pastures* (36); since then they have been played by Claude Rains in *Here Comes Mr Jordan*, Jeanette Macdonald in *I Married an Angel*, Kenneth Spencer (and others) in *Cabin in the Sky*, Jack Benny (and others) in *The Horn Blows at Midnight*, Henry Travers in *It's a Wonderful Life*, Leon Ames in *Yolanda and the Thief*, Kathleen Byron and a great many extras in *A Matter of Life and Death*, Robert Cummings in *Heaven Only Knows*, Cary Grant in *The Bishop's Wife*, several actors in *Angels in the Outfield*, James Mason in *Forever Darling*, Diane Cilento in *The Angel Who Pawned Her Harp*, and John Philip Law in *Barbarella*.

Used in a figurative sense, the word 'angel' has continued to be a favourite title component: *I'm No Angel, Angel, The Dark Angel, Angels with Dirty Faces, Angels Wash Their Faces, Angel and the Badman, Angel Face, Angel Baby, Angels in Disguise, The Angel Wore Red, Angels One Five, Angels in Exile*, etc.

See also: *fantasy.*

ANGELS WITH DIRTY FACES (US 1938). A typical example of the period when Hollywood's gangster melodramas had to point a moral: the character played by James Cagney pretended to be a coward on his way to the electric chair so that he would not become an object of hero-worship for the Dead End Kids. As so often, Pat O'Brien was an Irish priest. Despite good direction by Michael Curtiz, there was precious little fun to be had from this type of social melodrama: the genre quickly declined and the Dead End Kids turned into comedians (in a so-called sequel, *The Angels Wash Their Faces*).

ANGELUS, MURIEL (1909–) (M. A. Findlay). British leading lady of the 30s who had a brief Hollywood career before retiring in 1940. *The Ringer* (30), *Hindle Wakes* (31), *The Light that Failed* (39), *Down Went McGinty* (40), *The Way of All Flesh* (40), etc.

ANGERS, AVRIL (1922–). British character comedienne whose film appearances have been infrequent. *Skimpy in the Navy* (50), *Lucky Mascot* (51), *The Green Man* (56), *Devils of Darkness* (65), *The Family Way* (66), *Two a Penny* (68), etc.

ANHALT, EDWARD (1914–). American screenwriter who once worked with his wife EDNA (1914–): *Bulldog Drummond Strikes Back* (48), *Panic in the Streets* (50), *The Sniper* (52), *Not as a Stranger* (54), *The Pride and the Passion* (56), *The Young Lions* (58), etc. Now works alone: *A Girl Named Tamiko* (63), *Becket* (64), *Hour of the Gun* (67), *The Boston Strangler* (68), etc.

ANIMAL FARM (GB 1954). Britain's only full-length cartoon, a major achievement of the Halas and Batchelor studios, but on the whole too conventionally animated to bring out the full satiric flavour of George Orwell's fable.

animals, as Walt Disney knew, are a sure way to success at the box office, with dogs well established as number one providers. Dog stars of the movies have included Rin Tin Tin, Strongheart (his closest rival), Ben (Mack Sennett's comedy dog), Pete (of 'Our Gang'), Asta (of the 'Thin Man' series), Daisy (so popular in the 'Blondie' films that he starred in his own movies), and of course the immortal Lassie. Less publicized canines have successfully taken on dramatic roles in such films as *The Voice of Bugle Ann*, *Oliver Twist*, *Umberto D*, *Greyfriars Bobby*, *Owd Bob*, *Old Yeller*, *Savage Sam*, *The Ugly Dachshund* and *The Spy with a Cold Nose*; while Dick Powell was reincarnated as a very handsome Alsatian in *You Never Know*. Rhubarb has been the only 'starred' cat, though felines have played important roles in *The Cat and the Canary*, *The Cat Creeps*, *Cat Girl*, *Shadow of the Cat*, *Breakfast at Tiffany's*, *The Incredible Journey*, *A Walk on the Wild Side*, *The Three Lives of*

47

Thomasina, That Darn Cat, The Torture Garden (with its diabolical pussy), *The Wrong Box, The Goldwyn Follies* (in which the Ritz Brothers were memorably assisted by hundreds of cats to sing 'Hey Pussy Pussy'), *The Bluebird* (in which a sleek black feline was humanized very satisfyingly into Gale Sondergaard), *The Tomb of Ligeia, Eye of the Cat*, and several versions of *The Black Cat*. Other animals to achieve something like stardom have included Balthasar the donkey, Flipper the dolphin, Gentle Ben the bear, Cheta the chimp (in the Tarzan films), Clarence the Cross-eyed Lion (not to mention Fluffy), the Zebra in the Kitchen, Lucy the elephant (in *Hannibal Brooks*), and her cousin Zenobia, and a great many horses including Rex ('King of the Wild Horses'), Tarzan (with Ken Maynard), Champion (with Gene Autry) and Trigger (with Roy Rogers). *Doctor Dolittle* recently starred a host of animals from pigs to giraffes; but perhaps one shouldn't count the anthropoids in *Planet of the Apes*.

animation. The filming of static drawings, puppets or other objects in sequence so that they give an illusion of movement. Sometimes called 'stop-frame animation' because only one frame of film is exposed at a time.

ANKA, PAUL (1941–   ). American pop singer, subject of the documentary *Lonely Boy* (62). Acted in *The Longest Day* (62) and composed the score.

ANKERS, EVELYN (1918–   ). British leading lady who appeared during the 40s in a number of Hollywood films, mostly of the exploitation type; then retired. *The Villiers Diamond* (GB) (33), *The Wolf Man* (41), *The Great Impersonation* (42), *The Mad Ghoul* (44), *Pillow of Death* (45), *Queen of Burlesque* (46), *Spoilers of the North* (47), *Tarzan's Magic Fountain* (49), *The Texan Meets Calamity Jane* (50), etc.

ANKRUM, MORRIS (1896–1964). American stage actor seen in many films as lawyer, judge or Western villain. *Light of the Western Stars* (40), *Tales of Manhattan* (42), *The Harvey Girls* (45), *Joan of Arc* (48), *Rocketship XM* (50), *My Favourite Spy* (51), *Son of Ali Baba* (52), *Apache* (54), *Earth Versus the Flying Saucers* (56), *Badman's Country* (59), many others.

ANNA AND THE KING OF SIAM. Anna Leonowens' autobiography of her experiences as governess at an eastern court seemed in 1946 a strange choice for a Hollywood film, especially when Rex Harrison was cast as the King and Linda Darnell as his leading mistress. But Irene Dunne kept the strange mixture palatable, and John Cromwell's direction was smooth. The plot was immediately adapted by Rodgers and Hammerstein as a musical, filmed with great success in 1956 as *The King and I*. Walter Lang directed Deborah Kerr and Yul Brynner in the leading roles.

ANNABELLA (1909–   ) (Suzanne Charpentier). French leading lady, a René Clair discovery, once married to Tyrone Power. *Napoleon* (26), *Le Million* (32), *Le Quatorze Juillet* (33), *Under the Red Robe* (GB) (36), *Dinner at the Ritz* (GB) (37), *Wings of the Morning* (GB) (37), *Suez* (US) (38), *Hôtel du Nord* (38), *Bomber's Moon* (US) (42), *Tonight We Raid Calais* (US) (43), *13 Rue Madeleine* (US) (46), *Don Juan* (Sp.) (50), etc. Retired.

ANNA CHRISTIE (US 1930). Early talkie version of Eugene O'Neill's waterfront play, advertised by the famous slogan, 'Garbo Talks!' Previously filmed in 1923 with Blanche Sweet.

ANNA KARENINA. Tolstoy's novel has been filmed many times, twice with Garbo (as *Love* in 1927, and again in 1935). The latter version, directed by Clarence Brown with Basil Rathbone as Karenin, was not eclipsed by Korda's 1948 British remake with Vivien Leigh and Ralph Richardson, though Julien Duvivier's direction achieved some pretty effects.

ANNAKIN, KEN (1914–   ). British director, a former journalist whose first film was *Holiday Camp* (46). Variable output since then includes *Miranda* (48), *Hotel Sahara* (51), *The Planter's Wife* (52), *Three Men in a Boat* (56), *Across the Bridge* (57), *The Swiss Family Robinson* (60), *Very Important Person* (61), *The Longest Day* (63), *The Fast Lady* (63), *Those Magnificent Men in Their Flying Machines* (65), *The Battle of the Bulge* (65), *The Biggest Bundle of Them All* (66), *The Long Duel* (67), *Monte Carlo or Bust* (69).

ANNA LUCASTA. Philip Yordan's melodramatic play was originally (1944) set among Negroes, but on Broadway they became Polish immigrants, and it was this version which was first screened, in 1949, with Paulette Goddard as the bad girl of the family who comes back to help in a domestic crisis. In 1959 the Negro version was finally filmed with Eartha Kitt and Sammy Davis Jnr. Yordan wrote both screenplays.

ANNE OF GREEN GABLES. L. M. Montgomery's popular novel for girls about an orphan teenager who comes to live with crusty relations and finally charms them into her way of thinking, was a great screen success for Mary Miles Minter in 1926. In 1934 Anne Shirley appeared in a sound remake, and followed it up in 1941 with a sequel, *Anne of Windy Willows*.

ANN-MARGRET (1941–   ) (Ann-Margaret Olson). Swedish-born leading lady, in America from 1946, latterly groomed as Hollywood sex symbol. *State Fair* (61), *Bye Bye Birdie* (62), *Viva Las Vegas* (63), *The Pleasure Seekers* (64), *Kitten with a Whip* (64), *Bus Riley's*

Back in Town (64), *Once a Thief* (65), *Stagecoach* (66), *The Swinger* (66), *Murderers' Row* (67), *The Tiger and the Pussycat* (Italian) (67).

ANNIS, FRANCESCA (1944–   ). British leading lady, former juvenile player. *The Cat Gang* (58), *Cleopatra* (62), *The Eyes of Annie Jones* (63), *Flipper's New Adventure* (*Flipper and the Pirates*) (US) (64), *The Pleasure Girls* (65), *Run with the Wind* (66), *The Walking Stick* (69), etc.

ANOUILH, JEAN (1910–   ). Noted French playwright who has written screenplays since 1936: *Monsieur Vincent* (47), *Caroline Chérie* (50), *A Night with Caroline* (52), *Le Chevalier de la Nuit* (53), etc. Several of his plays have been filmed: *The Waltz of the Toreadors*, *Becket*, etc.

'ANOUK'; see AIMEE, ANOUK.

À NOUS LA LIBERTÉ (France 1931). René Clair's classic social satire about mass production, a forerunner of 'Modern Times'. Photographed by Georges Perinal, with music by Georges Auric; leading players Raymond Cordy, Henri Marchand.

ANSARA, MICHAEL (1922–   ). American actor with stage experience, specializing in Indian roles. *Only the Valiant* (51), *The Robe* (53), *Sign of the Pagan* (54), *Diane* (55), *The Lone Ranger* (58), *The Comancheros* (62), *Guns of the Magnificent Seven* (69), etc. TV series: *Broken Arrow* (56–58), *Law of the Plainsman* (59).

ANSTEY, EDGAR (1907–   ). British documentary producer (*Housing Problems* [35], *Enough to Eat* [36], etc.) who has for many years been chief films officer for British Transport.

ANTHONY, JOSEPH (1912–   ) (J. A. Deuster). American director from stage and TV; former small part actor and dancer. *The Rainmaker* (56), *The Matchmaker* (58), *Career* (59), *All in a Night's Work* (61), *The Captive City* (63), etc.

ANTHONY, TONY (1937–   ). American leading man having some success in tough Italian westerns. *A Stranger in Town* (67), *The Stranger Returns* (68), etc.

Anti-Semitism was understandably not a popular subject with film-makers when the function of movies was simply to entertain. Amiable comic Jews were permitted, in *Abie's Irish Rose*, *Potash and Perlmutter*, and the Cohen and Kelly series; and it was readily acknowledged that Jewry provided a flow of star talent without which show business could not continue. But thoughtful movies on the Jewish plight were almost non-existent, unless one counts such epics as *The Wandering Jew* (33) and *Jew Suss* (34). Occasionally came a cry from Europe, as in *Professor Mamlock* (36), but it was not really until *The Great Dictator* (40) that the film-going public was made aware of what was happening to the Jews in Germany. For propaganda purposes the Nazis put out a number of anti-semitic films such as *Ohm Kruger* and another version of *Jew Suss*; the only real reply during the second world war was a gentle British movie called *Mr Emmanuel*. In *Tomorrow the World* (44), from the play about an ex-Nazi youth in America, the subject was touched on; but not till the reconstruction days of 1947 could a spade really be called a spade. In a taut murder thriller called *Crossfire*, the victim was changed from a homosexual to a Jew; then came *Gentleman's Agreement*, in which a gentile reporter posed as a Jew to expose anti-Semitism in America. Perhaps this interest was stimulated by the immense popularity of *The Jolson Story*, with its sympathetic portrait of a Jewish home; but the confusion in American minds is demonstrated by the fact that David Lean's *Oliver Twist* was banned in 1948 because of Alec Guinness' 'caricature' of Fagin! During the last decade or so there seems to have been sporadic interest in the subject. The birth of Israel generated such movies as *Sword in the Desert, Exodus, Judith* and *Cast a Long Shadow*, and Christopher Isherwood's Berlin stories of the early thirties became first a play and film called *I Am a Camera* and later a musical and film called *Cabaret*. Poignant recollections of World War Two by a girl who died in Auschwitz produced a book, play and film called *The Diary of Anne Frank*, and a little British film called *Reach for Glory* took a swipe at the consequences of intolerance. Currently the world's most successful stage musical is *Fiddler on the Roof*, soon to be filmed; dealing with the Russian pogroms, the story has been filmed many times before in Yiddish, usually under the title *Tevye the Milkman*.

ANTONIONI, MICHELANGELO (1912–   ). Italian director whose reputation was boosted in the 50s by the ardent support of high-brow film magazines. Co-scripts all his own films, which largely jettison narrative in favour of vague incident and relentless character study. *Cronaca di un Amore* (50), *Le Amiche* (55), *Il Grido* (57), *L'Avventura* (59), *La Notte* (60), *L'Eclisse* (62), *The Red Desert* (64), *Blow-Up* (GB) (66), *Zabriskie Point* (US) (69), etc.

THE APARTMENT (US 1960) (AA/BFA). A typically mordant comedy from director Billy Wilder, scripted by himself and I. A. L. Diamond. This one lifts the lid off New York office life, only to discover something not far removed from a Capra soft centre. Jack Lemmon finds some sympathy in the part of a clerk who avenges his status by letting out his apartment to house the amorous affairs of his bosses.

APPLAUSE (US 1929). One of the most professionally fluent of early talkies, with director Rouben Mamoulian trying, and usually bringing off, every cinematic trick in the book as well as some of his own. On its own level the story works too: a hokey but powerful melodrama of mother love against the tawdry background of burlesque. Written by Garrett Fort from a novel by Beth Brown; photographed by George Folsey. With Helen Morgan, Joan Peers, Henry Wadsworth.

The Arabian Nights. This collection of ancient eastern tales, more properly called *The Arabian Nights Entertainment*, was first collected around 1450, but Sir Richard Burton's unexpurgated Victorian translation is the one generally used. The tales, presented as told by the heroine Scheherezade, have been plundered innumerable times by film-makers. See the entries under *The Thief of Bagdad* and *Ali Baba*; note also films based on Aladdin, Sindbad the Sailor and various genies in bottles.

ARBEID, BEN (1924–). British producer: *The Barber of Stamford Hill* (62), *Private Potter* (63), *Children of the Damned* (64), etc.

ARBUCKLE, ROSCOE 'FATTY' (1887–1933). Grown-up fat boy of American silent cinema whose career was ruined after his involvement in a 1921 scandal in which a girl died. Though he never again appeared before the camera, he directed a few films under the name 'Will B. Good'. The few of his two-reel slapstick comedies which survive are still funny.

arc. A high-powered lamp used in projectors and studio lighting, its illumination consisting of an electrical discharge between two carbon rods.

ARCHARD, BERNARD (1922–). Lean, incisive British actor with repertory experience; became famous on TV as *Spycatcher*. *Village of the Damned* (60), *The List of Adrian Messenger* (63), *Face of a Stranger* (66), etc.

ARCHAINBAUD, GEORGE (1890–1959). American director, mainly of routine Westerns. *The Lone Ranger* (19), *Men of Steel* (25), *College Coquette* (29), *The Lost Squadron* (32), *The Return of Sophie Lang* (36), *Thanks for the Memory* (38), *Untamed* (40), *The Kansan* (43), *Woman of the Town* (44), *King of the Wild Horses* (47), *Hunt the Man Down* (51), many others.

ARCHER, JOHN (1915–) (Ralph Bowman). American leading man of routine second features. *Flaming Frontier* (38), *White Heat* (49), *Destination Moon* (50), *A Yank in Indo-China* (52), *Rodeo* (53), *The Stars Are Singing* (53), *No Man's Woman* (55), *Emergency Hospital* (59), etc.

ARDEN, EVE (1912–) (Eunice Quedons). Lanky American comedienne: Broadway experience, including the Ziegfeld Follies, preceded long Hollywood career as wisecracking friend of the heroine. Her astringent personality saved many a 40s comedy from total boredom. *Stage Door* (37), *Comrade X* (40), *Whistling in the Dark* (41), *The Doughgirls* (44), *Night and Day* (45), *Mildred Pierce* (45), *The Voice of the Turtle* (47), *The Unfaithful* (47), *Curtain Call at Cactus Crick* (50), *Three Husbands* (50), *We're Not Married* (52), *Our Miss Brooks* (55), *Anatomy of a Murder* (59), *The Dark at the Top of the Stairs* (62), *Sergeant Deadhead* (66), etc. TV series: *Our Miss Brooks* (52–55), *The Eve Arden Show* (59), *The Mothers-in-Law* (67).

ARDEN, ROBERT (1921–   ). Anglo-American actor resident in Britain; former vocalist. *Two Thousand Women* (44), *No Orchids for Miss Blandish* (48), *Confidential Report* (56), many second features and TV series *Saber of London*. Now TV journalist.

ARISE MY LOVE (US 1940). This amiable mock-heroic romantic comedy-drama is notable as Hollywood's most prompt response to the outbreak of World War Two in Europe. Claudette Colbert and Ray Milland make an agreeable team as a newspaperwoman and an aviator involved in world events from the Spanish Civil War to the sinking of the *Athenia*, and Billy Wilder's slightly cynical script ends with an implicit command for America to wake up. In the circumstances, Mitchell Leisen's direction is perhaps just a little too impeccable. AA best original story: Benjamin Glazer, John Toldy.

†ARKIN, ALAN (1934–   ). American character actor; stage experience. *The Russians are Coming, The Russians are Coming* (66), *Woman Times Seven* (67), *Wait Until Dark* (67), *Inspector Clouseau* (68), *The Heart Is a Lonely Hunter* (68), *Popi* (69), *Catch 22* (69).

ARKOFF, SAMUEL Z. (1918–   ). American executive producer, co-founder with James H. Nicholson of American-International Pictures.

ARLEN, HAROLD (1905–   ). American song composer ('Happiness Is Just a Thing Called Joe', 'That Old Black Magic', 'Blues in the Night', 'Stormy Weather', 'Accentuate the Positive', many others). Film scores include *Strike Me Pink* (36), *The Wizard of Oz* (AA for 'Over the Rainbow') (39), *Cabin in the Sky* (43), *A Star Is Born* (54), *I Could Go On Singing* (63), etc.

ARLEN, RICHARD (1899–   ) (Richard Van Mattimore). American leading man who rose from extra to star in the 20s, later became the durable hero of scores of 'B' pictures, and still plays bits. *Wings* (27), *The Four Feathers* (29), *Island of Lost Souls* (32), *Tiger Shark* (32), *Alice in Wonderland* (as the Cheshire Cat) (33), *Three-Cornered Moon* (33), *Helldorado* (34), *The Devil's Pipeline* (41), *Aerial Gunner* (43), *Minesweeper* (43), *Buffalo Bill Rides Again* (46), *The Blazing*

Forest (52), *Devil's Point* (GB) (54), *Law of the Lawless* (63), *The Best Man* (64), *Apache Uprising* (65), many others.

ARLETTY (1898–   ) (Leonie Bathiat). Celebrated French actress of stage and screen adept at the portrayal of world-weary, sophisticated women. *Un Chien Qui Rapporte* (31), *La Guerre des Valses* (33), *Aloha* (37), *Hotel du Nord* (38), *Le Jour Se Leve* (39), *Les Visiteurs du Soir* (42), *Les Enfants du Paradis* (44), *L'Amour Madame* (52), *L'Air de Paris* (54), *Huis Clos* (54), *Les Petits Matins* (*Girl on the Road*) (61), *La Gamberge* (62), etc.

ARLING, ARTHUR E. (1906–   ). American cinematographer. *Gone with the Wind* (co-ph) (39), *The Yearling* (AA) (46), *The Homestretch* (47), *You're My Everything* (49), *Wabash Avenue* (50), *Red Garters* (54), *I'll Cry Tomorrow* (55), *Pay the Devil* (57), *The Story of Ruth* (60), *Notorious Landlady* (62), *My Six Loves* (63), *Straitjacket* (63), *The Secret Invasion* (64), many others.

ARLISS, GEORGE (1868–1946) (George Augustus Andrews). Distinguished British stage actor who in middle age was persuaded to face the cameras for *The Devil* (21) and *Disraeli* (21), and stayed in films to present a gallery of classic if highly theatrical characterizations, both in Britain and in Hollywood. *The Green Goddess* (23 and 30), *The Ruling Passion* (23), *Disraeli* (sound: AA) (30), *Old English* (31), *The Man Who Played God* (31), *Alexander Hamilton* (31), *The Working Man* (33), *Voltaire* (33), *Cardinal Richelieu* (34), *The House of Rothschild* (34), *The Iron Duke* (35), *Dr Syn* (38), etc.

ARLISS, LESLIE (1901–   ). British writer who worked on *Orders Is Orders* (32), *Jack Ahoy* (34), *Rhodes of Africa* (36), *Pastor Hall* (39), *The Foreman Went to France* (42). Then turned director and made some of the popular Gainsborough costume melodramas of the 40s. *The Night Has Eyes* (42), *The Man in Grey* (43), *Love Story* (44), *The Wicked Lady* (45), *A Man about the House* (47), *Idol of Paris* (48), *The Woman's Angle* (52), *Miss Tulip Stays the Night* (55), *See How They Run* (55), etc.; recently directing TV films.

ARMENDARIZ, PEDRO (1912–1963). Massive Mexican actor with expansive personality; became a star in his own country, then moved on to Hollywood and Europe. *Isle of Passion* (41), *Maria Candelaria* (43), *The Pearl* (46), *The Fugitive* (47), *Maclovia* (48), *Fort Apache* (48), *Three Godfathers* (48), *Tulsa* (48), *We Were Strangers* (49), *The Torch* (50), *El Bruto* (52), *Lucretia Borgia* (53), *Border River* (54), *The Conqueror* (56), *Manuela* (57), *The Wonderful Country* (59), *Francis of Assisi* (61), *From Russia with Love* (63), etc.

ARMETTA, HENRY (1888–1945). Italian-born character actor, long in US, where he was on stage before coming to Hollywood 1929.

Typecast as excitable, gesticulating foreigner. *Strangers May Kiss* (30), *The Unholy Garden* (31), *The Man Who Reclaimed His Head* (34), *The Big Store* (40), *Anchors Aweigh* (45), many others.

ARMS AND THE MAN. Bernard Shaw's military comedy has only once been filmed straight: this was in 1931 (GB) with Barry Jones as Bluntschli. The stage musical comedy *The Chocolate Soldier* was based on it, but when this was filmed in 1941 Shaw's libretto was abandoned. *The Guardsman*, made in 1932 with Alfred Lunt and Lynn Fontanne, bears some resemblance to it.

ARMSTRONG, LOUIS (1900–   ). Famous, gravel-voiced Negro jazz trumpeter, affectionately known as 'Satchmo' (satchel-mouth). Sporadic screen appearances, chiefly in guest spots, include *Pennies from Heaven* (36), *Cabin in the Sky* (43), *New Orleans* (47), *Glory Alley* (51), *High Society* (56), *The Five Pennies* (59), *Paris Blues* (61), *A Man Called Adam* (66), *Hello Dolly* (69); also a semi-biopic, *Satchmo the Great* (57).

ARMSTRONG, ROBERT (1896–   ). American character actor usually seen as cop, gangster or sheriff. *The Main Event* (27), *Big Money* (30), *The Tip-Off* (31), *King Kong* (leading role as the foolhardy film producer Carl Denham) (32), *Son of Kong* (34), *G-Men* (35), *Mystery Man* (37), *Sky Riders* (41), *Outside the Law* (41), *Gangs of the Waterfront* (45), *Mighty Joe Young* (50), *Las Vegas Shakedown* (55), many others.

army comedies have always been popular, and most well-known comedians have at least one to their credit: Laurel and Hardy in *Pack Up Your Troubles*, *Blockheads* and *Great Guns*; Abbott and Costello in *Buck Privates*; Jimmy Durante and Phil Silvers in *You're in the Army Now*; the Ritz Brothers in *We're in the Army Now*; Bob Hope in *Caught in the Draft*; Norman Wisdom in *The Square Peg*; Martin and Lewis in *At War With the Army*; Wheeler and Wolsey in *Half Shot at Sunrise*; Arthur Lucan in *Old Mother Riley Joins Up*; Jerry Lewis in *The Sad Sack*; Frank Randle in *Somewhere in England*.

Other British successes in the genre include *Carry on Sergeant*; *Private's Progress*; *I Only Arsked*; *Idol on Parade*; *Reluctant Heroes*; *On the Fiddle*. Hollywood has contributed *Operation Mad Ball*; *No Time for Sergeants*; *The Teahouse of the August Moon*; *What Did You Do in the War Daddy?*

Outstanding TV series on the subject: Britain's *The Army Game*, America's Bilko series (*You'll Never Get Rich*) with Phil Silvers.

ARNALL, JULIA (1931–   ). Austrian-born actress resident in Britain. *Man of the Moment* (54), *I Am a Camera* (55), *Lost* (56), *House of Secrets* (56), *Man without a Body* (57), *Mark of the Phoenix* (59); later played small roles in *The Quiller Memorandum* (66), *The Double Man* (67), etc.

ARNAUD, YVONNE (1892–1958). French actress and pianist, long popular on the British stage. Films include *On Approval* (31), *A Cuckoo in the Nest* (33), *The Improper Duchess* (36), *Stormy Weather* (36), *Neutral Port* (40), *Tomorrow We Live* (42), *Woman to Woman* (46), *The Ghosts of Berkeley Square* (47).

ARNAZ, DESI (1915–) (Desiderio Alberto Arnaz y de Acha). Diminutive but explosive Cuban who began his career as a singer and later formed his own Latin-American band. Performed in minor film musicals during 40s, then married Lucille Ball, founded Desilu Studios, and appeared in the long-running TV series *I Love Lucy* (50–61). Later films include *The Long Long Trailer* (54), *Forever Darling* (56). Inactive as performer since their divorce but produced TV series *The Mothers-in-Law* (67–69).

ARNE, PETER (1922–). Anglo-American actor in British films from 1955, usually as dastardly villain. *Time Slip* (55), *The Purple Plain* (55), *The Moonraker* (57), *Ice Cold in Alex* (58), *Danger Within* (58), *The Hellfire Club* (61), *The Black Torment* (64), *Khartoum* (66), etc.

ARNESS, JAMES (1923–). Giant (6' 6") American actor who drifted into films from advertising. Played minor parts including the title role in *The Thing* (52); then routine leads in such films as *Them* (54), *The First Travelling Saleslady* (56). Created role of Marshal Dillon in long-running TV series *Gunsmoke* (55–69), which he now produces and owns.

ARNO, SIG (1895–) (Siegfried Aron). German comedy actor in US from early 30s; latterly typecast as funny foreigner. *Manon Lescaut* (26), *Pandora's Box* (28), *The Loves of Jeanne Ney* (28), *Diary of a Lost Girl* (29), *The Star Maker* (38), *The Great Dictator* (40), *The Palm Beach Story* (42), *Up In Arms* (44), *The Great Lover* (48), *On Moonlight Bay* (51), *The Great Diamond Robbery* (53), many others. More recently acting in Germany.

ARNOLD, EDWARD (1890–1956) (Guenther Schneider). Plump but dynamic American actor who in the 30s played leads in such films as *Rasputin and the Empress* (32), *Roman Scandals* (33), *Diamond Jim* (25), *The Glass Key* (35), *Come and Get It* (36), *Crime and Punishment* (36), *Easy Living* (37), *The Toast of New York* (37), *You Can't Take It with You* (38), *Mr Smith Goes to Washington* (39). During the 40s and 50s the roles became smaller and more conventional, but he never lost his popularity. *All That Money Can Buy* (41), *The War Against Mrs Hadley* (42), *Eyes in the Night* (42), *Mrs Parkington* (44), *Weekend at the Waldorf* (45), *The Hucksters* (47), *Dear Ruth* (47),

Annie Get Your Gun (50), *Belles on Their Toes* (52), *City That Never Sleeps* (53), *Living It Up* (55), *The Ambassador's Daughter* (56), many others.

ARNOLD, JACK (1916–). American director, with Universal since 1952. *It Came from Outer Space* (53), *The Glass Web* (53), *The Creature from the Black Lagoon* (54), *Tarantula* (55), *Red Sundown* (56), *The Tattered Dress* (57), *The Incredible Shrinking Man* (57), *Pay the Devil* (57), *High School Confidential* (58), *The Mouse That Roared* (GB) (59), *No Name on the Bullet* (59), *A Global Affair* (63), *Hello Down There* (68), etc. Now producer.

ARNOLD, MALCOLM (1921–). British composer: *The Sound Barrier* (52), *Island in the Sun* (56), *The Bridge on the River Kwai* (AA) (57), *Inn of the Sixth Happiness* (58), *Tunes of Glory* (60), *The Chalk Garden* (63), many others.

ARNOUL, FRANÇOISE (1931–) (Françoise Gautsch). Sultry French leading lady of sex melodramas in the 50s. *Quai de Grenelle* (50), *Forbidden Fruit* (52), *Companions of the Night* (53), *La Rage au Corps* (53), *The Sheep Has Five Legs* (54), *French Can-Can* (55), *The Face of the Cat* (57), *The Devil and the Ten Commandments* (61), *Le Dimanche de la Vie* (66), etc.

ARNT, CHARLES (1908–). American character actor often seen as snoop, suspicious character, or just plain ordinary fellow. *Ladies Should Listen* (35), *Remember the Night* (40), *Blossoms in the Dust* (41), *Cinderella Jones* (46), *Dangerous Intruder* (leading role) (46), *That Brennan Girl* (47), *Wabash Avenue* (50), *Veils of Bagdad* (53), *Miracle of the Hills* (59), many others.

AROUND THE WORLD IN EIGHTY DAYS. Jules Verne's globe-trotting Victorian lark was first filmed by Richard Oswald in Germany in 1919. In 1956 Michael Todd made it the subject of the first of the giant-screen extravaganzas in 70mm, and the impact of location photography, much expense, and 44 stars in cameo roles was enough to gain it the year's best picture Academy Award, despite its many glaring faults. Michael Anderson directed rather uncertainly from a screenplay by S. J. Perelman, James Poe and John Farrow; David Niven as the imperturbable Phileas Fogg led the revels.

ARSENAL (USSR 1929). A notable propaganda piece, written and directed by Dovzhenko, contrasting trench warfare in 1918 with a workers' revolt at home.

ARSENE LUPIN. The gallant French jewel thief and part-time detective created at the beginning of the century by Maurice Leblanc, has been the subject of many films, the first being a Vitagraph 1917 version starring Earle Williams. In 1932 the Barrymore brothers were in *Arsène Lupin*, John taking the title role; in 1938 Melvyn Douglas was in *Arsène Lupin Returns*; Charles Korvin took over in 1944 for *Enter Arsène Lupin*; in 1957 there was Robert Lamoureux in *The Adventures of Arsène Lupin*; and in 1962 Jean-Claude Brialy starred in *Arsène Lupin Contre Arsène Lupin*.

ARSENIC AND OLD LACE (US 1944). Frank Capra's no-holds-barred film version of the macabre farce by Joseph Kesselring, with Cary Grant registering nineteen double takes to the minute as the astonished nephew, Josephine Hull and Jean Adair as the murderous aunts, and John Alexander as Uncle Teddy. The Boris Karloff stage role ('Jonathan') was taken over by Raymond Massey, with Peter Lorre as the cringing Dr. Einstein.

art director. Technician responsible for designing sets, sometimes also costumes and graphics.

art house. American term (now displacing 'specialized hall' in GB) for cinema showing classic revivals and highbrow or off-beat new films of limited commercial appeal.

ARTHUR. The legendary British king of the 5th or 6th century, central figure of the courtly love tradition and alleged creator not only of the democratic Round Table but of the idyllic city and palace of Camelot, has figured in several movies, especially in recent years when we seem to have had need to cherish our legends. There have been three sound versions, to begin with, of *A Connecticut Yankee at King Arthur's Court* (qv); in the 1949 version Cedric Hardwicke played the King as having a perpetual cold. In 1945, Arthur Askey dreamed he was a member of the Round Table in *King Arthur Was a Gentleman*; in 1964 Disney presented in cartoon form the childhood of Arthur in *The Sword in the Stone*. In slightly more serious vein, Mel Ferrer was Arthur in *Knights of the Round Table* (54), with Robert Taylor as Lancelot and Ava Gardner as Guinevere: Anthony Bushell had the role in *The Black Knight* (54) and Mark Dignam took over in *Siege of the Saxons* (64). In the 1963 *Lancelot and Guinevere*, the three roles were taken respectively by Brian Aherne, Cornel Wilde and Jean Wallace; in the 1967 musical *Camelot* (qv) by Richard Harris, Franco Nero, and Vanessa Redgrave. TV series on the subject have included *Sir Lancelot* and an Australian cartoon series called *Arthur!*

ARTHUR, GEORGE K. (1899–   ) (G. K. A. Brest). Small but gamy hero of the British silent screen, popular in such films as *Kipps* (21), *A Dear Fool* (22). Went to Hollywood and was popular for a while: *Madness of Youth* (23), *Lights of Old Broadway* (25), *The Salvation Hunters* (25), *Irene* (26), *The Boy Friend* (26), *Rookies* (first of a series of comedies with Karl Dane) (27), *Baby Mine* (28), *The Last of Mrs Cheyney* (29), *Chasing Rainbows* (30), *Oliver Twist* (33), *Riptide* (34), *Vanessa* (last to date) (35). Became a financier and distributor of art shorts.

ARTHUR, JEAN (1905–) (Gladys Greene). Squeaky-voiced American leading actress who entered films at fifteen and scored her greatest success as determined feminist heroine of social comedies in the 30s and 40s. *Cameo Kirby* (23), *Horseshoes* (27), *The Mysterious Dr Fu Manchu* (29), *The Lawyer's Secret* (31), *The Whole Town's Talking* (34), *Diamond Jim* (35), *The Ex Mrs Bradford* (35), *Mr Deeds Goes to Town* (36), *History Is Made at Night* (37), *Easy Living* (37), *You Can't Take It with You* (38), *Mr Smith Goes to Washington* (39), *Only Angels Have Wings* (39), *Arizona* (40), *My Two Husbands* (40), *The Devil and Miss Jones* (41), *Talk of the Town* (42), *The More the Merrier* (43), *The Impatient Years* (44), *A Foreign Affair* (48), *Shane* (53), many others. After retirement punctuated by stage appearances, made a TV comeback in 1966 with *The Jean Arthur Show*: it was regrettably shortlived.

ARTHUR, ROBERT (1909–) (R. A. Feder). American producer, mainly with Universal. *Buck Privates Come Home* (46), *Abbott and Costello Meet Frankenstein* (49), *The Big Heat* (53), *Man of a Thousand Faces* (57), *The Great Impostor* (60), *Lover Come Back* (60), *That Touch of Mink* (62), *Father Goose* (64), *Shenandoah* (65), *Blindfold* (66), *Hellfighters* (68), many others.

ARTHUR, ROBERT (1925–) (Robert Arthaud). American actor, former radio announcer, in general supporting roles since 1945. *Roughly Speaking* (45), *Twelve O'clock High* (49), *Ace in the Hole* (51), *Young Bess* (54), *Top of the World* (55), *Hellcats* (57), *Young and Wild* (58), others.

ARUNDELL, DENIS (1898–). British character actor (radio's *Dr Morelle*). Sporadic film roles include *The Show Goes On* (35), *The Return of Carol Deane* (38), *Pimpernel Smith* (41), *Colonel Blimp* (43), *Carnival* (46), *The History of Mr Polly* (49), *Something Money Can't Buy* (52).

ARZNER, DOROTHY (1900–). American editor of *Blood and Sand* (22), *The Covered Wagon* (25), etc. Became Hollywood's only woman director of the 30s. *The Wild Party* (29), *Alias French Gertie* (31), *Lost Squadron* (32), *Merrily We Go to Hell* (33), *Christopher Strong* (33), *Nana* (35), *Craig's Wife* (35), *The Bride Wore Red* (37), *Dance Girl Dance* (40), *First Comes Courage* (43), etc.

A.S.C. Often seen on credit titles behind the names of cinematographers, these initials stand for the American Society of

59

Cinematographers, a professional association, membership of which is by invitation only. Its aims since its foundation in 1918 have been 'to advance the art and science of cinematography'.

ASHCROFT, DAME PEGGY (1907–). Distinguished British stage actress who has appeared in films only occasionally. *The Wandering Jew* (33), *The Thirty-nine Steps* (35), *Rhodes of Africa* (36), *Quiet Wedding* (40), *The Nun's Story* (58), *Secret Ceremony* (68), etc.

ASHER, JACK (1916–). British cinematographer, brother of director Robert Asher. *Jassy* (47), *Lili Marlene* (52), *The Good Die Young* (53), *The Young Lovers* (54), *Reach for the Sky* (56), *Dracula* (58), *She'll Have to Go* (also co-p) (61), *The Intelligence Men* (65), *The Early Bird* (65), *That Riviera Touch* (66), many others.

ASHER, JANE (1946–). British leading lady, former child performer in films from 1951. *Mandy* (52), *The Greengage Summer* (60), *The Girl in the Headlines* (63), *The Masque of the Red Death* (64), *Alfie* (66), etc. Also on TV.

ASHER, ROBERT (c. 1917–). British director: *Follow a Star* (59), *Make Mine Mink* (60), *On the Beat* (62), *A Stitch in Time* (63), *The Intelligence Men* (65), etc. With his brother Jack Asher, wrote, produced and directed *She'll Have To Go* (61).

ASHER, WILLIAM (c. 1919–). American director with TV experience. *Shadow on the Window* (57), *Beach Party* (63), *Muscle Beach Party* (64), *Johnny Cool* (64), *Bikini Beach* (65), etc.

ASHERSON, RENEE (1920–). British stage actress who played Katharine in *Henry V* (44); also in *The Way Ahead* (44), *The Way to the Stars* (44), *The Small Back Room* (49), *The Cure for Love* (50), *The Day the Earth Caught Fire* (62), *Rasputin the Mad Monk* (65), etc. Also on TV. Was married to the late Robert Donat.

ASHLEY, EDWARD (1904–) (E. A. Cooper). British leading man who went to Hollywood but never did better than third leads. *Men of Steel* (Br) (33), *Underneath the Arches* (Br) (37), *Spies of the Air* (Br) (39), *Pride and Prejudice* (40), *Bitter Sweet* (41), *The Black Swan* (43), *Nocturne* (46), *Macao* (52), *The Court Jester* (as The Fox) (56), etc.

ASHLEY, ELIZABETH (1939–). American leading lady, notable in *The Carpetbaggers* (64), *Ship of Fools* (65), *The Third Day* (65). Married George Peppard.

ASKEY, ARTHUR (1900–). Diminutive (5′ 2″) British comedian with music hall experience; gained fame as 'Big Hearted Arthur' in radio shows. Films include *Band Wagon* (38), *Charley's Big-hearted Aunt* (40), *The Ghost Train* (41), *Miss London Ltd* (42), *King Arthur*

Was a Gentleman (42), *Bees in Paradise* (44). Later turned to music hall and TV, but made a comeback in *The Love Match* (54), *Make Mine a Million* (58), *Friends and Neighbours* (59), etc.

ASKIN, LEON (c. 1920–   ). Rotund American supporting actor who often plays sinister or comic Russians. *Road to Bali* (52), *Knock on Wood* (54), *Son of Sindbad* (55), *My Gun Is Quick* (58), *The Maltese Bippy* (69). Often on TV.

ASLAN, GREGOIRE (1908–   ) (Kridor Aslanian). Franco-Turkish character actor, usually in comic or villainous roles. *Sleeping Car to Trieste* (48), *Occupe-Toi D'Amélie* (49), *Last Holiday* (50), *Cage of Gold* (50), *Confidential Report* (53), *He Who Must Die* (56), *Roots of Heaven* (56), *The Criminal* (60), *Cleopatra* (62), *Paris When It Sizzles* (64), *The High Bright Sun* (65), *Moment to Moment* (65), *Our Man in Marrakesh* (66), *Lost Command* (66), *A Flea in Her Ear* (68), many others.

aspect ratio. Relative breadth and height of screen. Before 1953 this was 4:3 or 1.33:1. 'Standard' wide screen varies from 1.66:1 to 1.85:1. Anamorphic processes are wider: SuperScope 2:1, CinemaScope and most others 2.35:1 (or 2.55:1 with magnetic stereophonic sound). VistaVision, a printing process, was shot in 1.33:1 but recommended for screening at up to 2:1, i.e. with top and bottom cut off and the rest magnified. The TV screen is fixed at 1.33:1, therefore all wide-screen films lose something when played on it.

THE ASPHALT JUNGLE (US 1950). W. R. Burnett's crime melodrama about a plan that failed was nimbly directed by John Huston; also notable for Sam Jaffe's performance and a brief but telling appearance by the young Marilyn Monroe. There have been two disguised remakes (*The Badlanders* [58], *Cairo* [62]) and a TV series based on the original.

†ASQUITH, ANTHONY (1902–68). British director, son of Lord Oxford and Asquith, nicknamed 'Puffin'. His first film, *Shooting Stars* (28), used revolutionary methods and effects, as to a lesser extent did *Underground* (30) and *A Cottage on Dartmoor* (30); but his later films, while always civilized and usually entertaining, tended to lack a vital spark. *The Runaway Princess* (30), *Tell England* (31), *Dance Pretty Lady* (31), *Lucky Number* (33), *Unfinished Symphony* (34), *Moscow Nights* (35), *Pygmalion* (co-d) (38), *French without Tears* (39), *Freedom Radio* (40), *Quiet Wedding* (40), *Cottage To Let* (41), *Uncensored* (42), *We Dive at Dawn* (43), *The Demi-Paradise* (43), *Welcome to Britain* (doc.) (43), *Two Fathers* (Fr.) (44), *Fanny by Gaslight* (44), *The Way to the Stars* (45), *While the Sun Shines* (46), *The Winslow Boy* (48), *The Woman in Question* (50), *The Browning Version* (50), *The Importance of Being Earnest* (51), *The Net* (53), *The Final Test* (53),

The Young Lovers (54), *Carrington V.C.* (55), *Orders To Kill* (58), *Libel* (60), *The Millionairess* (61), *Guns of Darkness* (62), *Two Living One Dead* (62), *The V.I.P.s* (63), *The Yellow Rolls-Royce* (64).

assistant director. More properly 'assistant to the director', being concerned with details of administration rather than creation.

associate producer. Usually the actual producer or supervisor of the film, the title of 'executive producer' having been taken by the head of the studio.

Associated British is the only British complex of companies comparable with the power of the Rank Organization (qv). Its history is tied up with Elstree Studios, originally owned by British Instructional Pictures, which after many mergers emerged as Associated British in 1933. The men involved in the story are producer Herbert Wilcox, John Maxwell, a lawyer who turned film distributor and later founded the ABC cinema chain, and J. D. Williams, a wealthy exhibitor. Distribution was arranged through Pathé Pictures, which became a powerful partner. Elstree was the first British studio to wire for sound (*Blackmail*) and the first to produce a bilingual talkie (*Atlantic*). Throughout the 30s it turned out fifteen films a year, usually unambitious but competent, and unmistakably British. In 1940 a great number of shares were sold to Warner Brothers, and in 1956 the distribution arm became known as Warner-Pathé. Other associated companies include Pathé News, Pathé Laboratories, Pathé Equipment, and ABC Television. In 1969, after several years of comparative inactivity, the complex was taken over by E.M.I.

Association of Cinematograph, Television and Allied Technicians. ACTT: the film-makers' union. Founded 1931.

ASTA. A wire-haired fox-terrier who appeared (impersonated by several dogs) in *The Thin Man* and other films between 1934 and 1947.

†ASTAIRE, FRED (1899–   ) (Frederick Austerlitz). American dancing star. From childhood was teamed with his sister Adèle as a vaudeville team; she retired in 1932 and he came to Hollywood for a small role in *Dancing Lady* (33). In the same year he was teamed for the first time with Ginger Rogers in *Flying Down to Rio*, which began their famous series of light musicals: *The Gay Divorce* (34), *Roberta* (34), *Top Hat* (35), *Follow the Fleet* (36), *Swing Time* (36), *Shall We Dance?* (37), *Carefree* (38) and *The Story of Vernon and Irene Castle* (39), with a less successful reunion in 1949 (*The Barkeleys of Broadway*). Astaire's musicals with other partners have been of variable quality apart from his own always impeccable solo

numbers. *A Damsel in Distress* (37), *Broadway Melody of 1940*, *Second Chorus* (40), *You'll Never Get Rich* (41), *You Were Never Lovelier* (42), *Holiday Inn* (42), *The Sky's the Limit* (42), *Ziegfeld Follies* (44), *Yolanda and the Thief* (45), *Blue Skies* (which he insisted for a while would be his last film) (46), *Easter Parade* (48), *Three Little Words* (50), *Let's Dance* (50), *Royal Wedding* (52), *The Belle of New York* (53), *Bandwagon* (53), *Daddy Longlegs* (55), *Funny Face* (56), *Silk Stockings* (57), *Finian's Rainbow* (68). In later years he emerged as a straight actor: *On the Beach* (59), *The Pleasure of His Company* (61), *Notorious Landlady* (62), *The Midas Run* (69). Published autobiography 1960: *Steps in Time*. Gained Academy Award 1949 'for his unique artistry and his contribution to the techniques of motion pictures'. This contrasts amusingly with the studio report on his first screen test: 'Can't act; can dance a little.'

ASTHER, NILS (1897–   ). Suave Swedish-born leading man, in Hollywood from the mid-20s. *Sorrell and Son* (27), *Wild Orchids* (28), *Our Dancing Daughters* (28), *Letty Lynton* (31), *The Bitter Tea of General Yen* (32), *Abdul the Damned* (GB) (35), *Make Up* (GB) (37), *The Night of January 16th* (41), *The Man in Half Moon Street* (44), *Jealousy* (45), *That Man from Tangier* (53), many others.

ASTIN, JOHN (1930–   ). American comic actor with stage experience. In *West Side Story* (61), *That Touch of Mink* (62); then became familiar in TV series *I'm Dickens He's Fenster* and *The Addams Family*. Recently: *Candy* (68).

ASTOR, MARY (1906–   ) (Lucille Langehanke). American actress who despite a stormy private life remained a star from the mid-20s to the mid-40s and stayed in demand for character roles, especially on TV. *The Beggar Maid* (20), *Beau Brummell* (23), *Don Juan* (26), *Behind Office Doors* (30), *Red Dust* (32), *The Man with Two Faces* (33), *Dodsworth* (36), *The Prisoner of Zenda* (37), *Turnabout* (40), *The Great Lie* (AA) (41), *The Palm Beach Story* (42), *Meet Me in St Louis* (44), *Claudia and David* (46), *Cass Timberlane* (47), *Little Women* (49), *Act of Violence* (49), *A Kiss Before Dying* (56), *Return to Peyton Place* (61), *Hush Hush Sweet Charlotte* (64), many others. Published autobiography 1959: *My Story*.

ASTRUC, ALEXANDRE (1923–   ). French director, former film critic. *The Crimson Curtain* (51), *Les Mauvaises Rencontres* (54), *Une Vie* (56), *La Proie pour L'Ombre* (61), *L'Education Sentimentale* (61), *La Longue Marche* (65).

L'ATALANTE (France 1934). Strange dreamlike film by Jean Vigo about a honeymoon on a barge, with Dita Parlo, Jean Daste, and Michel Simon as the skipper. Music by Maurice Jaubert, photography Boris Kaufmann.

ATES, ROSCOE (1892–1962). American comic actor with well-known nervous stutter. Many films include *The Champ* (31), *Alice in Wonderland* (33), *Gone with the Wind* (39), *Captain Caution* (40), *The Errand Boy* (61).

ATLANTIC (GB 1929). Directed by E. A. Dupont, this early talkie was also the first to be made in two language versions (English and German, with different leading actors). There is now very little intrinsic interest in its melodramatics set on the sinking *Titanic*.

THE ATONEMENT OF GOSTA BERLING (Sweden 1924). Remembered chiefly for introducing Greta Garbo to the screen, this is a strong Scandinavian brew about a clergyman, unfrocked for alcoholism, who dissipates his talents in high society. Solidly well directed by Mauritz Stiller from Selma Lagerlöf's novel; with Lars Hanson.

ATTENBOROUGH, RICHARD (1923–   ). British actor, trained at R.A.D.A. Entered films 1942 as cowardly seaman in *In Which We Serve* and promptly became typecast in similar roles (*Journey Together* (44), *The Man Within* (46), *Morning Departure* (50), etc.) Has determinedly sought fresh characterizations. *Brighton Rock* (as vicious hoodlum) (47), *London Belongs to Me* (48), *The Guinea Pig* (as 13-year-old schoolboy) (49), *The Lost People* (49), *Boys in Brown* (50), *The Gift Horse* (52), *Father's Doing Fine* (53), *Eight O'Clock Walk* (54), *Private's Progress* (55), *The Baby and the Battleship* (56), *Brothers in Law* (57), *The Scamp* (58), *Dunkirk* (58), *The Man Upstairs* (58), *Danger Within* (58), *I'm All Right, Jack* (59), *The Angry Silence* (also produced) (59), *The League of Gentlemen* (also produced) (59), *Only Two Can Play* (61), *Whistle down the Wind* (produced but did not appear) (62), *The Dock Brief* (62), *The Great Escape* (63), *Seance on a Wet Afternoon* (also produced) (64), *Guns at Batasi* (BFA) (64), *The Third Secret* (64), *The Flight of the Phoenix* (65), *The Sand Pebbles* (66), *Dr Dolittle* (67), *The Bliss of Mrs Blossom* (68), *Oh What a Lovely War* (co-produced and directed only) (69), *David Copperfield* (69), *A Severed Head* (69), others.

ATWILL, LIONEL (1885–1946). British stage actor who went to Hollywood in 1932 to play leading role in *The Silent Witness*; stayed to play long succession of supporting parts, especially Teutonic villains, mad doctors and burgomasters. *The Mystery of the Wax Museum* (32), *Song of Songs* (33), *Nana* (34), *Captain Blood* (35), *The High Command* (36), *The Great Waltz* (38), *Son of Frankenstein* (39), *The Hound of the Baskervilles* (39), *Man Made Monster* (41), *The Mad Doctor of Market Street* (41), *Sherlock Holmes and the Secret Weapon* (42), *House of Dracula* (45), *Lost City of the Jungle* (serial) (46), many others.

AUBERT, LENORE (c. 1918–   ). Jugoslavian actress in Hollywood from the late 30s. *Bluebeard's Eighth Wife* (38), *They Got Me Covered* (42), *Action in Arabia* (44), *Wife of Monte Cristo* (46), *Return of the Whistler* (48), *Abbott and Costello Meet Frankenstein* (49), *Abbott and Costello Meet the Killer* (50), etc. Retired.

AUBREY, ANNE (1937–   ). British leading lady of a few comedies and adventures in the late fifties. *No Time To Die* (*Tank Force*) (58), *The Bandit of Zhobe* (59), *Idle on Parade* (59), *Let's Get Married* (60), *The Hellions* (61), etc.

AUBRY, CECILE (1929–   ) (Anne-José Benard). Petite French actress. *Manon* (49), *The Black Rose* (50), *Bluebeard* (51), *La Ironia* (54); later films unremarkable. Married a Moroccan prince.

AUCLAIR, MICHEL (1922–   ) (Vladimir Vujovic). French leading man. *La Belle et La Bête* (45), *Les Maudits* (47), *Manon* (48), *Justice Est Faite* (50), *Henriette* (52), *Funny Face* (US) (56), *The Fanatics* (57), *Rendezvous de Minuit* (61), etc.

AUDLEY, MAXINE (1923–   ). British stage actress who has made occasional film appearances. *The Sleeping Tiger* (54), *The Barretts of Wimpole Street* (57), *The Vikings* (58), *Our Man in Havana* (59), *The Trials of Oscar Wilde* (60), *Hell is a City* (60), *Here We Go Round the Mulberry Bush* (67), *Frankenstein Must Be Destroyed* (69), etc.

AUDRY, JACQUELINE (1908–   ). French director. *Gigi* (49), *L'Ingénue Libertine* (50), *Olivia* (51), *Huis Clos* (54), *In Six Easy Lessons* (57), *Les Petits Matins* (62), *Soledad* (66), etc.

AUER, JOHN H. (1909–   ). Hungarian-born director, in Hollywood from early 30s. *Smuggled Cargo* (39), *Citadel of Crime* (41), *Gangway for Tomorrow* (44), *Pan-Americana* (45), *City That Never Sleeps* (also produced) (53), *Hell's Half Acre* (also produced) (54), *Johnny Trouble* (also produced) (56), etc. Recently inactive.

AUER, MISCHA (1905–1967) (Mischa Ounskowsky). Lanky Russian with prominent eyes; after the revolution found himself on Broadway stage; in 1928 went to Hollywood and played small roles until his impersonation of a gorilla in *My Man Godfrey* (36) brought him into demand, usually for broken English noble idiot roles. Best remembered in *One Hundred Men and a Girl* (37), *You Can't Take It with You* (38), *Destry Rides Again* (39), *Seven Sinners* (40), *Trail of the Vigilantes* (40), *Hellzapoppin* (42), *Twin Beds* (43), *Around the World* (43), *Cracked Nuts* (43), *Up in Mabel's Room* (44), *Lady in the Dark* (44), *Czarina* (45), *Ten Little Niggers* (*And So There Were None*) (45), *Sentimental Journey* (46). Returned to Europe: *Sofia* (48), *Song of Paris* (GB) (52), *Confidential Report* (53), *We Joined the Navy* (GB) (62), *Arrivederci Baby* (GB) (66), etc.

AUGER, CLAUDINE (1942–   ). French leading lady, seen abroad as heroine of *Thunderball* (65), *Triple Cross* (66), *Jeu Massacre* (67), *The Devil in Love* (67), *The Bastard* (68).

AUGUST, JOSEPH (1890–1947). American cinematographer. *The Silent Man* (17), *Lightnin'* (25), *Two Arabian Knights* (27), *The Beloved Rogue* (27), *Men Without Women* (30), *Man's Castle* (33), *Twentieth Century* (34), *The Informer* (35), *Mary of Scotland* (37), *The Plough and the Stars* (37), *Gunga Din* (39), *The Hunchback of Notre Dame* (40), *All That Money Can Buy* (41), *They Were Expendable* (45), *Portrait of Jennie* (48), many others.

AULT, MARIE (1870–1951) (M. Cragg). British character actress of stage and screen, usually in dialect comedy roles. *The Lodger* (26), *Hobson's Choice* (31), *Major Barbara* (40), *Love on the Dole* (41), *We Dive at Dawn* (43), *I See a Dark Stranger* (46), *Madness of the Heart* (49), many others.

AUMONT, JEAN-PIERRE (1909–   ) (J.-P. Salomons). French leading man, in films since 1931, Hollywood from 1941. *Jean de la Lune* (32), *Drôle de Drame* (36), *Hôtel du Nord* (38), *The Cross of Lorraine* (42), *Assignment in Brittany* (43), *Heartbeat* (46), *Song of Scheherazade* (48), *The First Gentleman* (GB) (48), *Charge of the Lancers* (53), *Lili* (53), *The Seventh Sin* (57), *Five Miles to Midnight* (63), *Castle Keep* (69), etc.

AURENCHE, JEAN (1904–   ). French writer who with PIERRE BOST (1901–   ) wrote many well-known films: *Sylvie et la Fantome* (45), *La Symphonie Pastorale* (46), *Le Diable au Corps* (46), *Occupe-Toi d'Amélie* (49), *Dieu A Besoin des Hommes* (50), *The Red Inn* (51), *Les Jeux Interdits* (51), *Ripening Seed* (53), *Gervaise* (56), *En Cas de Malheur* (57), *L'Affaire d'Une Nuit* (60), etc. Aurenche alone worked on the screenplay of *Woman in White* (65).

AURIC, GEORGES (1899–   ). French composer. *Le Sang d'un Poète* (30) *A Nous la Liberté* (31), *Lac aux Dames* (34), *L'Alibi* (37), *L'Eterne Retour* (43), *Dead of Night* (45), *Caesar and Cleopatra* (45), *La Belle et la Bête* (46), *It Always Rains on Sunday* (47), *Corridor of Mirrors* (48), *Passport to Pimlico* (49), *Orphée* (49), *Belles de Nuit* (52), *Roman Holiday* (53), *The Wages of Fear* (53), *Father Brown* (54), *Rififi* (55), *The Witches of Salem* (56), *Gervaise* (56), *The Picasso Mystery* (56), *Heaven Fell That Night* (58), *Bonjour Tristesse* (59), *La Chambre Ardente* (62), many others.

AURTHUR, ROBERT ALAN (1922–   ). American novelist and TV playwright/producer. Film scripts include *Edge of the City* (*A Man Is Ten Feet Tall*) (56), *Warlock* (59), *Lilith* (65), *For Love of Ivy* (68).

AUTANT-LARA, CLAUDE (1903–   ). French director, usually of

66

stylish romantic dramas; former assistant to René Clair. *Ciboulette* (33), *L'Affair du Courier de Lyons* (37), *Fric Frac* (39), *Lettres de l'Amour* (42), *Douce* (43), *Sylvie et la Fantome* (46), *Le Diable au Corps* (46), *Occupe-Toi d'Amélie* (49), *The Red Inn* (51), *Ripening Seed* (53), *Le Rouge et le Noir* (54), *Marguérite de la Nuit* (55), *La Traversée de Paris* (56), *En Cas de Malheur* (57), *The Green Mare's Nest* (59), *Le Bois des Amants* (60), *The Count of Monte Cristo* (61), *Le Meurtrier* (62), *Thou Shalt Not Kill* (62), *The Woman in White* (65), etc.

authenticator. Studio researcher responsible for establishing accuracy of all script details, ensuring use of 'clear' telephone numbers, etc.

automobiles with enough personality to figure in movie titles include *Genevieve*, *The Fast Lady*, *La Belle Americaine*, *The Yellow Rolls Royce*, *Chitty Chitty Bang Bang*, *The Gnome-Mobile* and *The Love Bug*. Other cars with individuality were James Bond's tricksy Aston Martin in *Goldfinger*; the Flying Wombat in *The Young in Heart*; the gadget-filled limousine in *Only Two Can Play*; the flying Model T in *The Absent-minded Professor*.

Multitudes of strange vehicles were featured in *It's a Mad Mad Mad Mad World*, *The Great Race*, *Monte Carlo or Bust* (*Those Daring Young Men in Their Jaunty Jalopies*). Of hundreds of car chases, the best was certainly that in *Bullitt*.

See also: *motor racing.*

AUTRY, GENE (1907–   ). Easy-going Texan who made innumerable minor Westerns 1934–54 as singing cowboy, usually with his horse Champion. *Carolina Moon* (40), *Back in the Saddle* (41), *Sunset in Wyoming* (42), *Range War* (46), *Guns and Saddles* (49), *Goldtown Ghost Riders* (53), many others.

AVALON, FRANKIE (1939–   ) (Francis Avallone). American pop singer, former trumpeter. *Guns of the Timberland* (60), *The Alamo* (61), *Voyage to the Bottom of the Sea* (62), *Beach Blanket Bingo* (65), *Sergeant Deadhead* (66), *Fireball 500* (66), *Pajama Party in a Haunted House* (66), etc.

avant-garde. An adjective generally used to describe artists 'in advance of their time'; especially used of French surrealists in the 20s, e.g. Kirsanoff, Bunuel, Germaine Dulac.

AVEDON, DOE (1928–   ). American leading lady who had a very short career before retiring to marry: *The High and the Mighty* (54), *Deep in My Heart* (55), *The Boss* (56).

AVERBACK, HY (c. 1925–   ). American director with much TV experience, especially in comedy series. *Where Were You When the Lights Went Out?* (68), *I Love You Alice B. Toklas* (68), *The Great Bank Robbery* (69), etc.

AVERY, TEX (1918–   ). American animator, best known for Tom and Jerry cartoons which combined savagery with hilarity.

L'AVVENTURA (Italy 1960). Here at great length we see the search for a girl lost on an island; gradually the searchers become pre-occupied with their own problems, and the girl is never found. Highbrow reaction was so favourable to this rather bewildering film by Michelangelo Antonioni that he has since been able to continue exploring life's irrationalities and enigmas, without always communicating his purpose to the audience. Photographed by Aldo Scavarda; with Gabrielle Ferzetti, Monica Vitti.

THE AWFUL TRUTH (US 1937). This sophisticated crazy comedy, about a couple who decide to get divorced and then change their minds, was a trend-setter of its day and won an Academy Award for director Leo McCarey, who also write it. Cary Grant and Irene Dunne were the stars. In 1953 the script was reshot to less effect by Alexander Hall as *Let's Do It Again*, with Ray Milland and Jane Wyman.

AXELROD, GEORGE (1922–   ). American comedy writer. Plays filmed include *The Seven Year Itch* (55), *Will Success Spoil Rock Hunter* (57), *Goodbye Charlie* (65). Other scripts: *Phffft* (54), *Breakfast at Tiffany's* (61), *The Manchurian Candidate* (62), *How to Murder Your Wife* (also produced) (65), *Lord Love a Duck* (also produced and directed) (66), *The Secret Life of an American Wife* (also produced and directed) (68), etc.

AYLMER, FELIX (1889–   ) (Felix Edward Aylmer Jones). Dis-tinguished British stage character actor, a respected industry figure who since 1950 has been president of Equity, the actors' trade union. In films has mainly played schoolmasters, bankers, bishops, etc.; starred once as *Mr Emmanuel* (44), but has normally been found at head of supporting cast. *The Wandering Jew* (33), *The Iron Duke* (35), *Tudor Rose* (36), *As You Like It* (36), *Victoria the Great* (37), *The Citadel* (38), *Saloon Bar* (40), *The Ghost of St Michael's* (41), *Henry V* (44), *The Ghosts of Berkeley Square* (47), *Hamlet* (as Polonius) (48), *Edward My Son* (49), *Quo Vadis* (51), *Knights of the Round Table* (54), *The Angel Who Pawned Her Harp* (54), *Saint Joan* (57), *Separate Tables* (58), *Never Take Sweets from a Stranger* (60), *The Chalk Garden* (64), *Becket* (64), *Decline and Fall* (68), *Hostile Witness* (68), scores of others.

AYRES, AGNES (1896–1940) (Agnes Hinkle). American leading lady of the silent screen. *Forbidden Fruit* (19), *The Affairs of Anatol* (20), *The Sheik* (21), *Racing Hearts* (23), *Tess of the Storm Country* (23), *When a Girl Loves* (24), *Morals for Men* (25), *Her Market Value* (26), *Son of the Sheik* (26), *Eve's Love Letters* (29), many others. Retired when sound came.

AYRES, LEW (1908–   ) (Lewis Ayer). Boyish-looking American leading man of the 30s, a former dance band musician who made good use of a Los Angeles booking by winning a small part in a silent film; stardom quickly followed. *The Kiss* (opposite Garbo) (29), *All Quiet on the Western Front* (30), *East Is West* (30), *The Iron Man* (31), *Penalty of Fame* (32), *State Fair* (33), *Holiday* (38), *Young Dr Kildare* (and subsequent series) (39), *The Golden Fleecing* (40), etc.; war service; *The Dark Mirror* (46), *The Unfaithful* (47), *Johnny Belinda* (48), *The Capture* (49), *New Mexico* (52), *No Escape* (53), *Donovan's Brain* (53), *Advise and Consent* (61), *The Carpetbaggers* (63), etc. Much TV work as guest star.

AYRES, ROBERT (1914–1968). Canadian actor of strong silent types, resident in Britain. *They Were Not Divided* (49), *Cosh Boy* (52), *Contraband Spain* (55), *It's Never Too Late* (55), *A Night to Remember* (57), *The Sicilians* (63), innumerable second features and TV.

AZNAVOUR, CHARLES (1924–   ) (C. Aznavurjan). French leading man of the small but rugged school. *La Tête contre les Murs* (58), *Shoot the Pianist* (60), *Passage du Rhin* (61), *Cloportes* (65), *Candy* (68), *The Adventurers* (69), *The Games* (69), etc.

B

BABES IN ARMS (US 1939). Made immediately after *The Wizard of Oz*, this lively teenage musical directed by Busby Berkeley not only established Judy Garland as one of the brightest stars in the MGM sky but was the first of several teaming her with the irrepressible Mickey Rooney: *Strike Up The Band* (40), *Babes on Broadway* (41), *Girl Crazy* (43).

BABES IN TOYLAND. The Victor Herbert operetta was filmed by Hal Roach in 1934 as a vehicle for Laurel and Hardy. In 1961 Jack Donohue made a lavish but empty version with Ray Bolger as the villain; Laurel and Hardy, curiously, were closely impersonated by Henry Calvin and Gene Sheldon.

babies who have achieved screen stardom include Baby Parsons and Baby Peggy in silent days, Baby Le Roy in the early 30s and Baby Sandy in the early 40s. Shirley Temple and the Our Gang cast were scarcely weaned when they hit the big time. Other films about particular babies include *Bachelor Mother*, *Bobbikins*, and *A Diary for Timothy*.

There was a shortlived TV series about a talking baby called *Happy*; and Lucille Ball worked her own confinement into her weekly half-hour.

BABY DOLL (US 1956). Tennessee Williams wrote and Elia Kazan directed this deliberately shocking comedy about a child-wife of a 'poor white' southerner. Starring Eli Wallach, Karl Malden and Carroll Baker, it is not generally remembered with affection but did its bit towards loosening the Hollywood production code, which had been far too restrictive.

†BACALL, LAUREN (1924–   ) (Betty Perske). American leading lady who after stage experience made her film debut opposite Humphrey Bogart in *To Have and Have Not* (44); she subsequently married him, and changed her sultry siren image to that of a cool and resourceful woman of the world. *Confidential Agent* (45), *The Big Sleep* (46), *Dark Passage* (47), *Key Largo* (48), *Young Man with a Horn* (50), *Bright Leaf* (50), *How To Marry a Millionaire* (53), *Woman's World* (54), *Blood Alley* (55), *The Cobweb* (56), *Written on the Wind* (56), *Designing Woman* (57), *The Gift of Love* (59), *Northwest Frontier* (GB) (59), *Shock Treatment* (64), *Sex and the Single Girl* (64), *Harper* (*The Moving Target*) (66).

BACCALONI, SALVATORE (1900–1969). Italian opera singer who played some comedy roles in American films. *Full of Life* (56), *Merry Andrew* (58), *Rock a Bye Baby* (59), *Fanny* (61), *The Pigeon That Took Rome* (62), etc.

BACHELOR MOTHER (US 1939). A light, bright, romantic comedy showing Hollywood talents at the top of their accomplished form and introducing a new one in the shape of writer-director Garson Kanin who managed to give a fresh aspect to a collection of farcical misunderstandings over a foundling baby. Ginger Rogers, David Niven and Charles Coburn all performed nimbly. The film was reshot in 1955 as *Bundle of Joy*, but without the essential sparkle.

THE BACHELOR PARTY (US 1957). A straight filming of Paddy Chayevsky's TV play, this not only showed Hollywood's willingness to learn and profit from its hated rival but was a measure of how adult it had become in a very few years. Nothing, theoretically, could have been more anti-box-office than this study of the thwarted lives of New York office workers—a tragedy presented as comedy. The scene showing the men's reactions to a pornographic film—not the film itself—was banned in the UK. With Don Murray, Jack Warden, E. G. Marshall, Carolyn Jones; directed by Delbert Mann.

back projection. A method of producing 'location' sequences in the studio: the players act in front of a translucent screen on which the scenic background is projected.

BACK STREET. Fannie Hurst's tearful novel has been filmed three times since sound: in 1932 with John Boles and Irene Dunne, directed by John M. Stahl; in 1941 with Charles Boyer and Margaret Sullavan, directed by Robert Stevenson; and in 1961 with Susan Hayward and John Gavin, directed by David Miller. The story of the married man and the woman who sacrificed all for him has worked at the box office every time.

BACKUS, JIM (1913–   ). American character actor with long experience in stock, vaudeville and radio; achieved world fame as the voice of Mr Magoo in UPA cartoons. Played second lead in long-running TV series *I Married Joan* (53–55); subsequently had his own show, *Hot off the Wire* (60). Other film appearances, among many, include *The Great Lover* (47), *Father Was a Fullback* (49), *His Kind of Woman* (51), *Androcles and the Lion* (53), *Rebel Without a Cause* (55), *Meet Me in Las Vegas* (56), *It's a Mad Mad Mad Mad World* (63), *Billie* (65), *Hurry Sundown* (67). Later TV series: *Gilligan's Island* (64–67), *Blondie* (68).

BACLANOVA, OLGA (1899–   ). Russian ballerina who played leads in a few American films: *Street of Sin* (27), *Docks of New York* (28), *Freaks* (32), *Billion Dollar Scandal* (33), *Claudia* (43), etc.

BACON, IRVING (1893–1965). American character actor in films from 1920, often as not-so-dumb country type or perplexed official. *Million Dollar Legs* (32), *Sing You Sinners* (38), *Meet John Doe* (41), *Pin Up Girl* (44), *Monsieur Verdoux* (47), *Room for One More* (52), *A Star Is Born* (54), *Fort Massacre* (58), many others.

BACON, LLOYD (1890–1955). American director long under contract to Warners; former actor in Chaplin silent shorts. Competent rather than brilliant, he nevertheless handled a dozen or so memorable films among the scores of routine ones. *The Singing Fool* (28), *Moby Dick* (30), *42nd Street* (33), *A Slight Case of Murder* (38), *Boy Meets Girl* (39), *Brother Orchid* (40), *Action in the North Atlantic* (43), *The Sullivans* (44), *Sunday Dinner for a Soldier* (44), *Captain Eddie* (45), *Don't Tell Your Husband* (48), *The Good Humour Man* (50), *Golden Girl* (51), *Walking My Baby Back Home* (53), *The French Line* (54), *The Great Sioux Uprising* (54), etc.

THE BAD AND THE BEAUTIFUL (US 1952). A moderately caustic Hollywood self-exposé, this entertaining if ultimately cliché-ridden melodrama was well acted by Kirk Douglas as a talented heel, and smoothly written and directed by Charles Schnee (AA) and Vincente Minnelli. Gloria Grahame won an Oscar for her supporting performance as did Robert Surtees for his cinematography. Ten years later Douglas played a similar role in a not dissimilar film, *Two Weeks in Another Town*, about a Hollywood film crew in Rome: it even used clips from *The Bad and the Beautiful* to illustrate the character's previous career.

BAD DAY AT BLACK ROCK (US 1955). Classic suspense melodrama hingeing on race hatred, with Spencer Tracy as the one-armed stranger who defies violence to prove that the townsfolk of a midwestern settlement were communally guilty of an old murder. Written by Millard Kaufmann, directed by John Sturges.

bad language. It now seems impossible that in 1938 the phrase 'not bloody likely' in Shaw's *Pygmalion* could have caused a minor sensation; or that in 1942 the seamen in *In Which We Serve* could not say 'Hell' or 'damn' in front of American audiences. But these things happened. Perhaps it was in 1953 that the rot really set in, when Otto Preminger accepted a Legion of Decency 'C' rating and the loss of a production seal for his film of *The Moon Is Blue* rather than rob it of the words 'virgin' and 'mistress'. Three years later, Mickey Shaughnessy in *Don't Go Near the Water* was allowed to mouth obscenities while the sound track amusingly bleeped them out. By the time *Pygmalion* was remade in 1964 as *My Fair Lady* the phrase originally so shocking would have no dramatic effect; it was replaced by 'Move your bloomin' arse'. In 1967–68 the floodgates really opened. *Poor Cow* and *Who's Afraid of Virginia Woolf* were the first to allow 'bugger'. In *Here We Go Round the Mulberry Bush* Maxine Audley reproaches her husband as follows: 'Darling, you've got him pissed again'. And in *A Flea in Her Ear* Rex Harrison unchivalrously instructs Rosemary Harris to 'piss off'. That still-notorious four-letter word beginning with F was first uttered by Marianne Faithful in *I'll Never Forget Whatshisname*, and second by Elizabeth Taylor in *Boom*. And the slang word for defecation has so far been uttered in *In Cold Blood*, *Boom*, *Rosemary's Baby* and *Secret Ceremony*. In general, the effect of such words on the big screen has merely been to show how meaningless, harmless and stupid they are.

BADDELEY, ANGELA (1900–   ). British stage character actress, sister of Hermione Baddeley. Few films include *The Speckled Band* (31), *The Ghost Train* (32), *Quartet* (48).

BADDELEY, HERMIONE (1906–   ). British character comedienne, adept at blowsy roles. Long stage experience before film debut in *The Guns of Loos* (28). Sporadic appearances since in *Caste* (30), *Kipps* (41), *Brighton Rock* (47), *Quartet* (48), *Scrooge* (51), *Pickwick Papers* (52), *The Belles of St Trinian's* (54), *Room at the Top* (59), *The Unsinkable Molly Brown* (64), *Mary Poppins* (64), etc. TV series: *Camp Runamuck*.

BADEL, ALAN (1923–   ). British stage and screen actor of considerable sensitivity, not easy to cast in leading roles. Notable in *The Stranger Left No Card* (53), *Three Cases of Murder* (55), *Magic Fire* (56), *This Sporting Life* (63), *Children of the Damned* (64), *Arabesque* (66), *Otley* (69), *Where's Jack?* (69).

BADHAM, MARY (1952–   ). American teenage actress. *To Kill a Mockingbird* (63), *This Property Is Condemned* (66), *Let's Kill Uncle* (66).

BAER, BUDDY (1915–   ) (Jacob Henry Baer). American heavyweight, brother of Max. In several films: *Africa Screams* (59), *Quo Vadis* (51), *Jack and the Beanstalk* (52), *Slightly Scarlet* (56), etc.

BAER, MAX (1909–1959). American boxer who made several films: *The Prizefighter and the Lady* (33), *Over She Goes* (58), *The Iron Road* (44), *Riding High* (50), *The Harder They Fall* (56), etc.

BAGGOTT, KING (c. 1874–1948). American actor: tall, powerful star of silent adventure dramas. Made a few early talkies, then retired. *Lady Audley's Secret* (12), *Ivanhoe* (12), *Dr Jekyll and Mr Hyde* (13), *The Corsican Brothers* (15), many others; then took to directing, including William S. Hart in *Tumbleweeds* (25); talkies include *Once a Gentleman* (31), *Scareheads* (32), *Romance in the Rain* (34).

BAILEY, PEARL (1918–   ). American Negro entertainer. Film appearances include *Variety Girl* (47), *Isn't It Romantic* (48), *Carmen Jones* (54), *That Certain Feeling* (55), *St Louis Blues* (57), *Porgy and Bess* (59), *All the Fine Young Cannibals* (60), *The Landlord* (69).

BAILEY, RAYMOND (c. 1907–   ). American character comedian. now most familiar as Mr Drysdale in TV's *The Beverly Hillbillies* (62–69). Films include *Secret Service of the Air* (39), *Tidal Wave* (40), *Picnic* (56), *The Incredible Shrinking Man* (57), *Al Capone* (59), *From the Terrace* (60).

BAILEY, ROBIN (1919–   ). British character actor, usually in deferential or ineffectual roles. *School for Secrets* (46), *Private Angelo* (49), *His Excellency* (51), *For Better for Worse* (55), *Hell Drivers* (57), *The Spy with a Cold Nose* (66), *The Whisperers* (67), etc.

BAINTER, FAY (1892–1968). American actress who, after stage experience, came to films in 1934 and specialized in sympathetic matrons. *Jezebel* (AA) (38), *White Banners* (39), *The War Against Mrs Hadley* (42), *Mrs Wiggs of the Cabbage Patch* (42), *The Human Comedy* (43), *Cry Havoc* (43), *Dark Waters* (44), *State Fair* (45), *The Virginian* (45), *The Secret Life of Walter Mitty* (47), *June Bride* (48), *The President's Lady* (53), *The Children's Hour* (*The Loudest Whisper*) (62), many others.

BAIRD, TEDDY (c. 1900–   ). British producer, in films since 1928 after journalistic experience. Films include *The Browning Version* (51), *The Importance of Being Earnest* (52), *Carrington V.C.* (56), *Two Living One Dead* (62), etc.

BAKALEINIKOFF, CONSTANTIN (1898–1966). Russian music director, long in US. With RKO 1941–52. Own scores include *Notorious* (46), *Mourning Becomes Electra* (47), *Mr Blandings Builds His Dream House* (48), *The Conqueror* (56), many others.

BAKER, CARROLL (1932–   ). Blonde American actress who began as night club dancer, then attended the Actors' Studio. Sensational impact as thumb-sucking child wife in *Baby Doll* (56) led to her being typed as sex symbol in mainly routine films. *But Not for Me* (59), *Bridge to the Sun* (60), *Something Wild* (62), *Station Six Sahara* (63), *The Carpetbaggers* (64), *Harlow* (65), *Sylvia* (65), *Mister Moses* (65), *Jack of Diamonds* (67), *The Sweet Body of Deborah* (68), etc.

BAKER, DIANE (c. 1940–   ). American leading lady. *The Diary of Anne Frank* (debut) (58), *Journey to the Centre of the Earth* (59), *The Best of Everything* (59), *Nine Hours to Rama* (63), *The Prize* (63),

Stolen Hours (63), *Straitjacket* (64), *Marnie* (64), *Mirage* (65), *The Horse in the Grey Flannel Suit* (68), *Krakatoa* (68), etc.

BAKER, GEORGE (1931–). British leading man, also on stage and TV. *The Intruder* (52), *The Dam Busters* (55), *A Hill in Korea* (56), *The Woman for Joe* (56), *The Moonraker* (57), *Tread Softly Stranger* (58), *Lancelot and Guinevere* (63), *Curse of the Fly* (65), *Mr Ten Per Cent* (67), *Justine* (69), etc.

BAKER, KENNY (1912–). American crooner, popular in the late 30s but little heard of in recent years. *King of Burlesque* (36), *The Goldwyn Follies* (38), *The Mikado* (GB: as Nanki Poo) (39), *52nd Street* (39), *At the Circus* (39), *Hit Parade of 1941*, *Silver Skates* (43), *Doughboys in Ireland* (43), *The Harvey Girls* (46), etc.

BAKER, ROBERT S. (1916–). British producer: co-founder with Monty Berman of Tempean Films, which since 1948 has produced many co-features, also *The Saint* (TV series).

BAKER, ROY (1916–). British director. Served apprenticeship at Gainsborough 1934–39, then war service. *The October Man* (47), *The Weaker Sex* (48), *Morning Departure* (50), *The House in the Square* (US) (51), *Inferno* (US) (52), *Don't Bother to Knock* (US) (52), *Passage Home* (54), *Jacqueline* (56), *Tiger in the Smoke* (56), *The One That Got Away* (57), *A Night to Remember* (58), *The Singer Not the Song* (also produced) (60), *Flame in the Streets* (also produced) (61), *The Valiant* (61), *Two Left Feet* (64), *Quatermass and the Pit* (67), *The Anniversary* (68), *Moon Zero Two* (69), etc. Has directed many TV episodes.

BAKER, STANLEY (1927–). Tough-looking Welsh leading man who started in films at the age of fourteen and rose to stardom after years in lesser roles projecting strength and sometimes villainy. *Undercover* (41); war service; *All over the Town* (48), *Home to Danger* (51), *The Cruel Sea* (53), *The Red Beret* (53), *Hell below Zero* (54), *Knights of the Round Table* (54), *The Good Die Young* (54), *Alexander the Great* (55), *A Hill in Korea* (56), *Richard III* (as Henry Tudor) (56), *Child in the House* (56), *Checkpoint* (57), *Campbell's Kingdom* (57), *Violent Playground* (57), *Hell Drivers* (57), *Sea Fury* (58), *The Angry Hills* (59), *Blind Date* (60), *Yesterday's Enemy* (60), *Hell Is a City* (60), *The Criminal* (60), *The Guns of Navarone* (61), *Sodom and Gomorrah* (62), *A Prize of Arms* (62), *Eve* (France) (62), *In the French Style* (63), *Zulu* (also co-produced) (63), *Dingaka* (65), *Sands of the Kalahari* (also co-produced) (65), *Accident* (66), *Robbery* (also co-produced) (67), *Where's Jack* (68), *The Games* (69), *Grigsby* (69).

BALABAN, BURT (1922–1965). American director. *Lady of Vengeance* (57), *High Hell* (58), *Murder Inc.* (60), etc.

BALASZ, BELA (1884–1949). Hungarian writer who worked on *Die Dreigroschenoper* (30) and *The Blue Light* (31); later wrote book, 'Theory of the Film'.

BALCHIN, NIGEL (1908–   ). British novelist: books filmed include *Mine Own Executioner*, *The Small Back Room*, *Suspect* ('A Sort of Traitors'). Has also adapted other people's work for the screen: *The Barbarian and the Geisha*, *The Blue Angel* (remake), etc.

BALCON, JILL (1925–   ). British actress, daughter of Sir Michael Balcon. *Nicholas Nickleby* (47), *Good Time Girl* (48), *Highly Dangerous* (50), etc.

BALCON, SIR MICHAEL (1896–   ). British executive producer. During a long and distinguished career has headed Gainsborough, Gaumont-British, MGM-British, Ealing, Bryanston and his own production companies. Has been directly responsible for the planning and production of such famous films as *The Thirty-nine Steps* (35), *Goodbye Mr Chips* (38), *Next of Kin* (41), *Dead of Night* (45), *Kind Hearts and Coronets* (49), *The Blue Lamp* (50), *Saturday Night and Sunday Morning* (60), *Tom Jones* (63), and many others. Published autobiography 1969: *A Lifetime of Films*.

BALDERSTON, JOHN (1889–1954). Anglo-American screenwriter (former journalist) with a penchant for romantic and fantastic themes. Worked on *Frankenstein* (31), *The Mummy* (32), *Smilin' Through* (32 and 41), *Berkeley Square* (33), *The Mystery of Edwin Drood* (35), *Lives of a Bengal Lancer* (35), *Bride of Frankenstein* (35), *Beloved Enemy* (36), *The Prisoner of Zenda* (37), *Victory* (40), *Tennessee Johnson* (42), *Gaslight* (44), *Red Planet Mars* (52), others.

BALFOUR, BETTY (1903–   ). British comedienne of silent days, a popular favourite of the 20s as pert heroine of *Cinders*, *Love Life and Laughter* and the *Squibs* series. Has made occasional talkies including *The Brat* (30), *The Vagabond Queen* (30), *Paddy the Next Best Thing* (33), *Squibs* (remake) (36), *29 Acacia Avenue* (45).

BALFOUR, MICHAEL (1918–   ). American character actor in British films who usually plays dumb gangsters, cabbies, etc. *No Orchids for Miss Blandish* (48), *Venetian Bird* (53), *The Steel Key* (55), *Breakaway* (56), many others.

BALIN, INA (1937–   ) (Ina Rosenberg). American leading lady, with stage experience. *Compulsion* (58), *The Black Orchid* (59), *The Comancheros* (62), *The Patsy* (64), *The Greatest Story Ever Told* (65), *Run Like a Thief* (68), *Charro* (69), etc.

BALIN, MIREILLE (1909–1968). French leading lady of *Don Quixote* (33), *Pepe le Moko* (36), *Guerde d'Amour* (38), etc.

BALL, LUCILLE (1910–   ). Vivacious American comedienne who from modelling went into the chorus and was chosen as a Goldwyn Girl for *Roman Scandals* (33). From then on she enlivened a great many films, mostly inferior; but TV in 1950 gave her her biggest opportunity in the long-running *I Love Lucy* series in which she starred with her then husband Desi Arnaz. She has more recently been successful solo in *The Lucy Show*, and is executive president of Desilu Studios. Generally acknowledged to be the greatest female clown in the business; her occasional recent features have not suited her talents. Films include *Roberta* (35), *Stage Door* (37), *Room Service* (39), *The Marines Fly High* (40), *The Navy Steps Out* (41), *Valley of the Sun* (41), *The Big Street* (42), *Seven Days' Leave* (42), *Dubarry Was a Lady* (43), *Best Foot Forward* (44), *Ziegfeld Follies* (44), *Without Love* (45), *Easy to Wed* (45), *The Dark Corner* (46), *Her Husband's Affairs* (47), *Lured (Personal Column)* (47), *Sorrowful Jones* (48), *Miss Grant Takes Richmond* (49), *Fancy Pants* (49), *The Fuller Brush Girl* (50), *The Magic Carpet* (as villainess) (51), *The Long, Long Trailer* (54), *Forever Darling* (56), *The Facts of Life* (60), *Critic's Choice* (63), *Yours, Mine and Ours* (68).

BALL, SUZAN (1933–1955). American leading lady of the early fifties. *Untamed Frontier* (52), *City beneath the Sea* (53), *War Arrow* (54), *Chief Crazy Horse* (55), etc.

BALLAD OF A SOLDIER (Russia 1959). Pleasant, sentimental, and technically very skilled, this piece of romantic hokum served to show that Soviet film-makers could beat Hollywood at its own game. The simple plot details the mishaps which prevent a soldier from spending his leave in the way he intended before returning to the front and probable death. The leading role is played by Vladimir Ivashov, but the real stars are director Grigori Chukrai and photographers Vladimir Nikolayev and Era Savaleva.

BALLARD, KAYE (1926–   ) (Catherine Balotta). American comedienne with stage experience. Films include *The Girl Most Likely* (56), *A House is Not a Home* (64). TV series: *The Mothers-in-Law* (67–68).

BALLARD, LUCIEN (1908–   ). American cinematographer: *Morocco* (30), *The Devil Is a Woman* (33), *Crime and Punishment* (36), *The Lodger* (44), *This Love of Ours* (45), *The House on Telegraph Hill* (50), *New Faces* (54), *A Kiss before Dying* (56), *The Killing* (56), *Anna Lucasta* (58), *Al Capone* (59), *Desire in the Dust* (60), *Wives and Lovers* (63), *The Sons of Katie Elder* (65), *Nevada Smith* (66), *Will Penny* (67), *How Sweet It Is* (68), *The Wild Bunch* (69), *True Grit* (69); many others.

ballet sequences have been a boon to many indifferent films, permitting a brief glimpse into a world that is strange, alarming, but graceful and glamorous. From the time of *The Goldwyn Follies* (38), any Hollywood musical with aspirations had to have a ballet sequence, some of the most memorable being in *The Pirate*, *On the Town*, *An American in Paris*, *Singing in the Rain*, and *The Band Wagon*. The custom died out in the fifties, since when there has been an over-abundance of unimaginatively presented full-length stage ballets with famous dancing stars. These, filmed at low cost, have found a market, but expensive film ballets like *Tales of Hoffman*, *Invitation to the Dance* and *Black Tights* had tougher going. Dramatic films set in the ballet world have included *La Mort du Cygne* (remade in Hollywood as *The Unfinished Dance*), *The Red Shoes* and *The Spectre of the Rose*; lighter stories in which the heroine is a ballerina (usually a novice) include *Waterloo Bridge*, *Carnival*, *Dance Pretty Lady*, *On Your Toes* amd *St Martin's Lane*. Several comedians have found themselves pursued by plot complications on to a stage and forced to take part clumsily in the ballet in progress: Jack Buchanan in *That's a Good Girl*, Danny Kaye in *Knock on Wood*, Morecambe and Wise in *The Intelligence Man*; while even Laurel and Hardy donned tutus in *The Dancing Masters*.

BALL OF FIRE (US 1941). A zany comedy written by Charles Brackett and Billy Wilder, directed by Howard Hawks. Its plot is cheerfully derived from 'Snow White', the seven dwarfs having become professors writing an encyclopaedia, and Snow White a strip-teaser on the run from gangsters. In view of the talent involved, the fun now seems somewhat slow and obvious despite Gary Cooper, Barbara Stanwyck and a first-rate cast. In 1948 a musical version, *A Song is Born*, became an unsuccessful vehicle for Danny Kaye.

ballyhoo. An expressive term, allegedly Irish in origin, used in show business to denote the kind of wild publicity that has nothing to do with the merits, or indeed the actual contents, of the film in question.

BALSAM, MARTIN (1919–   ). American character actor with stage and TV experience. Many parts in last ten years include *On the Waterfront* (debut) (54), *Twelve Angry Men* (57), *Time Limit* (57), *Marjorie Morningstar* (58), *Al Capone* (59), *Middle of the Night* (59), *Psycho* (60), *Breakfast at Tiffany's* (61), *Cape Fear* (62), *The Carpetbaggers* (63), *Seven Days in May* (64), *The Bedford Incident* (65), *A Thousand Clowns* (AA) (65), *After the Fox* (66), *Hombre* (67), *The Good Guys and the Bad Guys* (69), *Little Big Man* (70).

BAMBI (US 1942). One of Disney's best-loved feature cartoons, virtually excluding the human element from its sentimentalized but charming story of the life of a forest deer, based on the book by Felix Salten.

BANCROFT, ANNE (1931–   ) (Anne Italiano). American leading

actress who after TV experience was signed in 1952 as heroine
of a number of inferior Hollywood films: *Don't Bother to Knock* (52),
Treasure of the Golden Condor (53), *Gorilla at Large* (54), *New York
Confidential* (55), *Walk the Proud Land* (56), *The Girl in Black Stockings*
(57), etc. She returned to the Broadway stage and did not film
again until she repeated her Broadway triumph as Annie Sullivan
in *The Miracle Worker* (AA; BFA) (62). Next, in England, *The
Pumpkin Eater* (BFA) (64); then *Seven Women* (66), *The Slender
Thread* (66), *The Graduate* (68).

BANCROFT, GEORGE (1882–1956). American actor who after a period
in the Navy became popular in Broadway musicals and straight
plays. Went to Hollywood in the 20s and found his strong masculine
personality much in demand for tough or villainous roles, almost
always in run-of-the-mill films; best remembered are probably
Pony Express (25), *Underworld* (27), *White Gold* (27), *Docks of New
York* (28), *Ladies Love Brutes* (30), *Scandal Sheet* (31), *Lady and Gent*
(33), *Mr Deeds Goes to Town* (36), *Angels with Dirty Faces* (38),
Stagecoach (39), *Each Dawn I Die* (39), *Young Tom Edison* (40),
Syncopation (last film) (41).

BAND, ALBERT (1924–   ). French-born director, in Hollywood
since the 40s. *The Young Guns* (56), *I Bury the Living* (also produced)
(58), *The Tramplers* (also produced) (66), etc.

THE BANDIT (O CANGACEIRO) (Brazil 1953). The only Brazilian film
to achieve world-wide commercial success, a fact attributable less
to writer-director Lima Barreto's routine outlaw story than to the
theme music by G. Migliori.

THE BAND WAGON. 1. British farce of 1939, based on radio show, with
Arthur Askey and Richard Murdoch. 2. Hollywood musical of
1953 notable for 'Girl Hunt' ballet, lively Dietz/Schwarz music and
lyrics, and star performance of Jack Buchanan.

†BANKHEAD, TALLULAH (1902–1968). American stage and screen
actress, daughter of eminent politician; titillated Broadway and
London in the 20s by her extravagant performances on stage and
off. Films never really managed to contain her, but her personality
had more or less full rein in *Tarnished Lady* (31), *The Devil and the
Deep* (32), *Thunder Below* (32), *Lifeboat* (43), *Czarina* (*A Royal
Scandal*) (45), *Fanatic* (*Die Die My Darling*) (65).

BANK HOLIDAY (GB 1938). Low-budget 'slice of life' melodrama
generally agreed to show the first flowering of Carol Reed's
directorial talent. Still enjoyable, in its dated way, for its picture
of Brighton on a pre-war summer's day.

BANKS, LESLIE (1890–1952). Distinguished British stage actor who after
unsuccessful experiments in home-grown silent films went to Hollywood and was a great success as the villain in *The Hounds of Zaroff*
(*The Most Dangerous Game*) (32). Later in British films: *The Fire-
Raisers* (33), *Night of the Party* (33), *The Man Who Knew Too Much*
(34), *The Tunnel* (35), *Sanders of the River* (35), *Fire over England*
(36), *Farewell Again* (37), *Twenty-one Days* (39), *Jamaica Inn* (39),
The Door with Seven Locks (40), *Neutral Port* (40), *Ships with Wings*
(41), *Cottage to Let* (41), *The Big Blockade* (42), *Went the Day Well*
(42), *Henry V* (as Chorus) (44), *Mrs Fitzherbert* (47), *The Small Back
Room* (48), *Madeleine* (49), *Your Witness* (50), etc.

BANKS, MONTY (1897–1950) (Mario Bianchi). Italian comic dancer
who appeared in many silent two-reel comedies of the 20s. Moved
to Britain and played in *Atlantic* (30), *Weekend Wives* (31), etc.;
then turned director; *Almost a Honeymoon* (31), *Tonight's the Night*
(32), *No Limit* (35), *We're Going to Be Rich* (38), *Great Guns* (US) (41),
many others. Was for a time married to Gracie Fields.

BANKY, VILMA (1903–   ) (Vilma Lonchit). Austro-Hungarian star
of American silents, discovered by Sam Goldwyn during a European holiday. Popular in the twenties but could not make the
transition to sound. *The Eagle* (25), *Son of the Sheik* (26), *The Dark
Angel* (26), *The Winning of Barbara Worth* (28), etc.

BANNEN, IAN (1928–   ). British stage actor who has been effective
in several films, including *Private's Progress* (55), *The Birthday Present*
(57), *Carlton Browne of the F.O.* (58), *Macbeth* (59), *A French Mistress*
(60), *Suspect* (60), *On Friday at Eleven* (61), *Station Six Sahara* (63),
Rotten to the Core (65), *The Hill* (65), *The Flight of the Phoenix* (US)
(65), *Sailor from Gibraltar* (66), *Penelope* (67), *Lock Up Your Daughters*
(69), *Too Late the Hero* (69), etc.

BANNER, JOHN (1910–   ). American character actor of Austrian
origin; usually plays explosive Europeans. *Once upon a Honeymoon*
(42), *The Fallen Sparrow* (44), *Black Angel* (47), *My Girl Tisa* (48),
The Juggler (53), *The Rains of Ranchipur* (56), *The Story of Ruth* (60),
etc. TV series: *Hogan's Heroes* (65–69).

BANNON, JIM (1911–   ). American actor with radio experience:
played second feature leads in the 40s and starred in a Western
series as 'Red Ryder' in the 50s. *The Missing Juror* (44), *I Love a
Mys'ery* (45), *The Thirteenth Hour* (47), *Daughter of the Jungle* (49),
The Man from Colorado (49), *Rodeo* (53), *Chicago Confidential* (58),
Madame X (65), many others. TV series: *Champion* (55).

BAR, JACQUES (1921–   ). French producer, often in association
with American companies. *Where the Wind Blows* (60), *Vie Privée*

(61), *A Monkey in Winter* (62), *Joy House* (64), *Once a Thief* (65), *The Guns of San Sebastian* (67), etc.

BARA, THEDA (1890–1955) (Theodosia Goodman). American actress, the first to be called a 'vamp' (because of her absurdly vampirish, man-hungry screen personality). An extra in 1915, she was whisked to stardom on some highly imaginary publicity statistics (she was the daughter of an Eastern potentate, her name was an anagram of 'Arab death', etc.). Her first starring film, *A Fool There Was* (16), is remembered for its classic sub-title, 'Kiss Me, My Fool!' Later films included *Romeo and Juliet* (16), *Under Two Flags* (17), *Camille* (17), *Du Barry* (17), *Cleopatra* (17), *Salome* (18), *Kathleen Mavourneen* (19); in 1919, her popularity waning, she forsook Hollywood for the Broadway stage, and when she returned in 1925 was forced to accept parts burlesquing her former glories, e.g. *Madame Mystery* (26). Wisely, she soon retired.

BARATIER, JACQUES (1918–   ). French director of shorts and occasional features: *Paris la Nuit* (55), *Goha* (57), *La Poupée* (62), *Dragées au Poivre* (63), *L'Or du Duc* (65), etc.

BARBERA, JOE: see HANNA, WILLIAM

BARBIER, GEORGE (1865–1945). American character actor remembered in talkies as a blustery but essentially kindly old man. *The Smiling Lieutenant* (30), *One Hour With You* (32), *The Crusades* (35), *On the Avenue* (37), *Sweethearts* (39), *The Man Who Came to Dinner* (41), *Song of the Islands* (42), *Yankee Doodle Dandy* (42), many others.

BARDEM, JUAN-ANTONIO (1922–   ). Spanish director: *Welcome Mr Marshall* (52), *Death of a Cyclist* (54), *Calle Mayor* (56), *Vengeance* (57), *Los Pianos Mecanicos* (64), etc.

BARDOT, BRIGITTE (1934–   ). French 'pin-up' girl who, given world publicity as a 'sex kitten', was able to make some inferior films very profitable. Most typical: *The Light Across the Street* (55), *And God Created Woman* (56), *Heaven Fell That Night* (57), *Parisienne* (57), *The Devil is a Woman* (58), *Babette Goes to War* (59), *Please Not Now* (61), *The Truth* (61), *Vie Privée* (62), *Contempt* (64), *Dear Brigitte* (65), *Viva Maria* (65), *Two Weeks in September* (67), *Shalako* (68).

BARE, RICHARD (c. 1909–   ). American director. *Smart Girls Don't Talk* (48), *Flaxy Martin* (48), *Return of the Frontiersman* (51), *Prisoners of the Casbah* (53), *Shoot-Out at Medicine Bend* (57), etc.; went into TV and has directed hundreds of episodes of *Cheyenne*, *Maverick*, *Twilight Zone*, *The Virginian*, *Green Acres*, etc.

BARI, LYNN (1916–   ) (Marjorie Bitzer). American actress who usually played 'the other woman'. After drama school was chosen for the chorus in *Dancing Lady* (33); then featured in a long line of fairly routine movies. *Stand Up and Cheer* (33), *Mr Moto's Gamble* (37), *Return of the Cisco Kid* (38), *City of Chance* (39), *Kit Carson* (40), *Charter Pilot* (40), *Blood and Sand* (41), *The Magnificent Dope* (42), *Orchestra Wives* (42), *Hello Frisco Hello* (43), *The Bridge of San Luis Rey* (44), *Captain Eddie* (45), *Shock* (46), *Margie* (47), *Nocturne* (47), *On the Loose* (51), *Abbott and Costello Meet the Keystone Kops* (54), etc. Retired apart from minor recent comebacks in *Trauma* (64), *The Young Runaways* (68).

BARKER, ERIC (1912–). British character comedian long popular on radio with his wife Pearl Hackney. Successful film debut in *Brothers In Law* (57); subsequently in great demand for comedy cameos. *Happy Is the Bride* (58), *Blue Murder at St Trinian's* (58), *Carry On Sergeant* (58), *Left, Right and Centre* (59), *Carry On Constable* (60), *Heavens Above* (63), *The Bargee* (65), *The Great St Trinian's Train Robbery* (66), *Maroc 7* (67), etc.

BARKER, JESS (1914–). Lightweight American leading man of minor forties films. *Cover Girl* (44), *Keep Your Powder Dry* (44), *This Love of Ours* (45), *Take One False Step* (49), *Shack out on 101* (56), etc.

BARKER, LEX (1919–). Blond, virile-looking American actor who in 1948 was signed to play Tarzan. After five films the role passed to another actor and Barker's stock slumped, but he continued to make routine action adventures. *Battles of Chief Pontiac* (52), *The Price of Fear* (56), *Jungle Heat* (57), *The Girl in the Kremlin* (57), *Victim Five* (63), *Kali-Yug, Goddess of Vengeance* (64), *A Place Called Glory* (66), etc.

BARKER, WILL C. (1867–1951). Pioneer British producer. *Henry VIII* (11), *Sixty Years a Queen* (13), *East Lynne* (13), *Jane Shore* (15), etc.

BARNARD, IVOR (1887–1953). British character actor of stage and screen, often of henpecked or nosey parker types. *Storm in a Teacup* (37), *Pygmalion* (38), *The Saint's Vacation* (41), *Hotel Reserve* (44), *The Wicked Lady* (45), *Great Expectations* (46), *Oliver Twist* (48), *Beat the Devil* (his last and best role, as a vicious killer) (53), many others.

BARNES, BARRY K. (1906–1965). Stylish British stage actor whose first film, *The Return of the Scarlet Pimpernel* (38), led to his popularity as a crime reporter in *This Man Is News* (39) and the series which followed. Other films include *Prison without Bars* (39), *The Ware Case* (39), *The Midas Touch* (40), *Bedelia* (46), *Dancing with Crime* (47); after this returned to stage work.

BARNES, BINNIE (1906–). British actress who was farm girl, nurse, rope-spinner and ballroom dancer before her role in *The Private Life of Henry VIII* (32) won her a Hollywood contract. Played mainly friends of the heroine and wisecracking comedy relief, usually in undistinguished films. *The Private Life of Don Juan* (GB) (34), *Three Smart Girls* (36), *The Adventures of Marco Polo* (38), *Holiday* (38), *Tight Shoes* (41), *Call Out the Marines* (41), *Three Girls around Town* (41), *The Man from Down Under* (43), *It's in the Bag* (*The Fifth Chair*) (45), *If Winter Comes* (47), *Shadow of the Eagle* (GB) (50), *Fugitive Lady* (51), *Decameron Nights* (GB) (53), etc. Married Columbia executive Mike Frankovich and was not on screen for thirteen years; comeback in *The Trouble with Angels* (66), *Where Angels Go Trouble Follows* (68).

BARNES, GEORGE (1893–1953). American cinematographer. *The Eagle* (25), *Son of the Sheik* (26), *Sadie Thompson* (28), *Our Dancing Daughters* (28), *Street Scene* (31), *In Caliente* (35), *Jesse James* (39), *Rebecca* (AA) (40), *Meet John Doe* (41), *Jane Eyre* (43), *None But the Lonely Heart* (44), *Spellbound* (45), *From This Day Forward* (45), *Sindbad the Sailor* (46), *Mourning Becomes Electra* (47), *The Boy with Green Hair* (48), *Force of Evil* (48), *The Emperor Waltz* (48), *Samson and Delilah* (49), *The Greatest Show on Earth* (52), etc.

BARNES, JOANNA (1934–). American actress occasionally seen in cool supporting roles. *Home Before Dark* (58), *Spartacus* (60), *The Parent Trap* (61), *Goodbye Charlie* (64), *The War Wagon* (67), etc.

BARNETT, VINCE (1902–). American character actor, usually of minor gangsters or downtrodden little men. *Scarface* (32), *I Cover the Waterfront* (35), *A Star Is Born* (37), *No Leave, No Love* (42), *The Killers* (46), *Brute Force* (47), *The Human Jungle* (54), many others.

BARNEY OLDFIELD'S RACE FOR LIFE. This oft-quoted film is a twenty-minute Mack Sennet short of 1916, parodying the old railroad melodramas. Mabel Normand and Ford Sterling starred.

BARON MUNCHAUSEN (Czechoslovakia 1962). Karel Zeman's stylish if slightly arid semi-animated fantasy is the last of a longish line of movies about the tall-story teller. Melies made a version in 1911, Emile Cohl in 1913; Hans Albers starred in a German version of 1943. The real Munchausen (1720–97) was a German army officer, but the collection of stories written by Rudolf Raspe (first published in English in 1785) included much material from other sources.

BARR, PATRICK (1908–). British stage and screen actor who has been playing solid, dependable types since the 30s. Achieved great popularity on TV during 50s. Latest films include *The Longest Day* (63), *Ring of Spies* (64).

BARRAT, ROBERT (1891–). American character actor in films from silent days, usually as heavy Western villain. *The Picture*

Snatcher (33), *Devil Dogs of the Air* (35), *Last of the Mohicans* (36), *The Buccaneer* (38), *Go West* (41), *The Adventures of Mark Twain* (44), *Magnificent Doll* (47), *Joan of Arc* (48), *Tall Man Riding* (55), many others.

BARRAULT, JEAN-LOUIS (1910–). Celebrated French stage actor whose most rewarding film roles have been in *Mademoiselle Docteur* (36), *Drôle de Drame* (36), *La Symphonie Fantastique* (42), *Les Enfants du Paradis* (44), *D'Homme à Hommes* (48), *La Ronde* (50), *Le Testament du Docteur Cordelier* (59), *The Longest Day* (62).

BARRETO, LIMA (1905–). Brazilian director responsible for his country's best-known film, *O'Cangaceiro* (*The Bandit*) (53).

BARRETT, JAMES LEE (1929–). American screenwriter. *The D.I.* (58), *The Greatest Story Ever Told* (co-w) (65), *The Truth About Spring* (65), *Shenandoah* (65), *Bandolero* (68), *The Green Berets* (68), *The Cheyenne Social Club* (also produced) (70), etc.

BARRETT, JANE (1923–1969). British leading lady. *The Captive Heart* (45), *Eureka Stockade* (48), *Time Gentlemen Please* (52), *The Sword and the Rose* (53), etc.

THE BARRETTS OF WIMPOLE STREET. Rudolph Besier's play about the wooing by Robert Browning of Elizabeth Barrett against her tyrannical father's opposition was twice filmed by MGM. The 1934 version with Norma Shearer, Fredric March and Charles Laughton was a resounding success; the 1957 version with Jennifer Jones, Bill Travers and John Gielgud was a failure. The play was later turned into a musical, *Robert and Elizabeth*, and a film has been promised.

BARRIE, AMANDA (1939–) (Amanda Broadbent). British leading lady with TV experience. *Carry On Cleo* (64), *I Gotta Horse* (65), etc.

BARRIE, SIR J. M. (1860–1937). British playwright whose work usually had a recognizable fey quality. Plays filmed include *The Admirable Crichton* (qv), *Peter Pan* (24 and 53), *The Little Minister* (34), *What Every Woman Knows* (34), *Quality Street* (37), *Darling How Could You* ('Alice Sit by the Fire') (51), *Forever Female* ('Rosalind') (53), etc.

BARRIE, MONA (1909–) (M. Smith). Australian actress in Hollywood from early 30s. *The House of Connelly* (34), *A Message to Garcia* (36), *I Met Him in Paris* (37), *When Ladies Meet* (41), *Storm over Lisbon* (44), *I Cover Big Town* (47), *Strange Fascination* (52), *Plunder of the Sun* (54), others. Recently inactive.

BARRIE, WENDY (1912–) (Wendy Jenkins). Pert British leading lady who went to Hollywood on the strength of her performance in *The Private Life of Henry VIII* (32), but made only mediocre pictures despite her attractive personality. *It's a Boy* (GB) (32), *A Feather in Her Hat* (35), *The Hound of the Baskervilles* (39), *Five Came Back* (39), *The Saint Takes Over* (40), *Who Killed Aunt Maggie* (40), *The Gay Falcon* (41), *Eyes of the Underworld* (42), *Women in War* (42), *Forever and a Day* (43), *It Should Happen to You* (guest appearance) (53), etc. Had her own TV show in 1948; recently active on local American radio stations.

BARRIER, EDGAR (1906–1964). American character actor with stage experience. *Flesh and Fantasy* (44), *A Game of Death* (46), *Macbeth* (48), *To the Ends of the Earth* (48), *Cyrano de Bergerac* (50), *Princess of the Nile* (54), *Irma la Douce* (63), many others.

barring clause. The part of an exhibitor's contract with a renter preventing him from showing new films before other specified cinemas in the area. The showing of a film in London may thus prevent its exhibition elsewhere within a radius of fifty miles or more.

BARRY, DON (c. 1916–   ) (Donald Barry d'Acosta). Rugged American actor, in Hollywood from 1939 after stage experience and immediately popular as hero of second feature Westerns. Also in *Remember Pearl Harbour* (42), *Jesse James' Women* (also directed) (53), *I'll Cry Tomorrow* (55), *Fort Utah* (66), *Bandolero* (68), *Shalako* (68), etc.

BARRY, GENE (1921–   ) (Eugene Klass). Debonair American actor and entertainer, with experience in stock and Broadway musicals. In Hollywood sporadically from 1950 in such films as *The War of the Worlds* (53), *Red Garters* (54), *Soldier of Fortune* (56), *Thunder Road* (58); now known to millions through TV series *Bat Masterson* (59–61), *Burke's Law* (63–65), and *The Name of the Game* (68–69). Recent Movies: *Maroc 7* (67), *Subterfuge* (69).

BARRY, IRIS (c. 1894-1969). Founder-member of the London Film Society (1925); director of New York Museum of Modern Art Film Library from 1935; president of the International Federation of Film Archives 1946; author of books on the film. Now retired.

BARRY, JOHN (1933–   ). British composer. *Beat Girl* (59), *The Amorous Prawn* (62), *Dr No* (62), *The L-shaped Room* (62), *From Russia with Love* (63), *Zulu* (63), *The Man in the Middle* (64), *Goldfinger* (64), *The Ipcress File* (65), *The Knack* (65), *Thunderball* (65), *King Rat* (65), *The Chase* (66), *Born Free* (66), *The Wrong Box* (66), *The Quiller Memorandum* (66), *Petulia* (68), *Boom* (68), *Deadfall* (68), *The Lion in Winter* (AA) (68), *Midnight Cowboy* (69), etc.

BARRY, PHILIP (1896–1949). American playwright, several of whose sophisticated comedies have been filmed: *The Animal Kingdom* (32) (remade as *One More Tomorrow* [46]), *Holiday* (38), *The Philadelphia Story* (40), *Without Love* (45).

BARRYMORE, DIANA (1921–1960). This daughter of John Barrymore made a few rather unsuccessful films in the early forties: *Nightmare* (42), *Between Us Girls* (42), *Eagle Squadron* (43), etc. She later wrote her autobiography *Too Much Too Soon*, filmed in 1958 with Dorothy Malone (and Errol Flynn as John Barrymore).

BARRYMORE, ETHEL (1879–1959) (Ethel Blythe). Distinguished American actress, on stage from 1894. Made some early silents: *The Divorcee* (09), *The Nightingale* (14), *Kiss of Hate* (16), *Our Miss McChesney* (18). Did not film again until *Rasputin and the Empress* (32), in which she starred with her brothers John and Lionel; then nothing again until *None But the Lonely Heart* (AA) (44). After this she stayed in Hollywood to play an assortment of crotchety old ladies with hearts of gold: *The Spiral Staircase* (46), *The Farmer's Daughter* (47), *Moss Rose* (47), *Night Song* (47), *The Paradine Case* (48), *Moonrise* (48), *Portrait of Jennie* (48), *The Great Sinner* (49), *That Midnight Kiss* (49), *The Red Danube* (49), *Pinky* (49), *Kind Lady* (51), *The Secret of Convict Lake* (51), *It's a Big Country* (51), *Deadline USA* (52), *Just for You* (52), *The Story of Three Loves* (53), *Main Street to Broadway* (53), *Young at Heart* (54), *Johnny Trouble* (57). Published autobiography 1956: *Memories*. (†Sound films complete.)

BARRYMORE, JOHN (1882–1942) (John Blythe). Celebrated American actor, brother of Ethel and Lionel Barrymore. Famous for his 'great profile' and his stage *Hamlet*, he became a romantic movie idole of the 20s but later squandered his talents in inferior comedies caricaturing his own debauchery and alcoholism. *Are You a Mason?* (13), *An American Citizen* (13), *The Man from Mexico* (14), *The Dictator* (15), *The Incorrigible Dukane* (15), *The Lost Bridegroom* (16), *The Red Widow* (16), *Raffles* (17), *Here Comes the Bride* (18), *On the Quiet* (18), *Test of Honour* (19), *Sherlock Holmes* (20), *Dr Jekyll and Mr Hyde* (20), *The Lotus Eater* (21), *Beau Brummell* (24), *The Sea Beast* (25), *The Beloved Rogue* (26), *Don Juan* (26), *When a Man Loves* (26), *Tempest* (28), *Eternal Love* (28), *Show of Shows* (first talkie: reciting *Richard III*) (28), *General Crack* (29), *The Man from Blankley's* (30), *Moby Dick* (30), *The Mad Genius* (31), *Svengali* (31), *A Bill of Divorcement* (32), *Arsène Lupin* (32), *Grand Hotel* (32), *Rasputin and the Empress* (32), *Dinner at Eight* (33), *Reunion in Vienna* (33), *Counsellor at Law* (33), *Topaze* (33), *Twentieth Century* (34), *Long Lost Father* (34), *Romeo and Juliet* (as Mercutio) (36), *Night Club Scandal* (37), *Maytime* (37), three *Bulldog Drummond* films (as the inspector) (37–38), *Spawn of the North* (38), *True Confession* (38), *Marie Antoinette* (38), *Hold that Co-ed* (38), *The Great Man Votes* (38), *The Great Profile* (40), *Invisible Woman* (40), *Playmates* (42), etc. Published autobiography 1926: *Confessions of an Actor*. The best biography is Gene Fowler's *Good Night Sweet Prince* (44).

BARRYMORE, JOHN JNR (JOHN DREW BARRYMORE) (1932–   ). American actor, son of John Barrymore and Dolores Costello. Debut *The Sundowners* (50). Played weakling in films like *The Big Night* (51), *Thunderbirds* (52), *While the City Sleeps* (56); later found more favour in European costume melodramas: *The Boatmen* (59), *Nights of Rasputin* (61), *War of the Zombies* (63), etc.

BARRYMORE, LIONEL (1878–1954) (Lionel Blythe). Celebrated American character actor, brother of Ethel and John Barrymore; his career was mainly devoted to films and from the early 30s he was a familiar and well-loved member of the MGM payroll, playing sentimental grandpas or churlish millionaires. *Friends* (09), *Fighting Blood* (11), *Judith of Bethulia* (11), *The New York Hat* (12), *The Exploits of Elaine* (15), *The Brand of Cowardice* (16), *His Father's Son* (17), *The Copperhead* (20), *Jim the Penman* (21), *The Great Adventure* (21), *Face in the Fog* (22), *Enemies of Women* (23), *America* (24), *The Wrongdoers* (25), *The Bells* (26), *Drums of Love* (27), *Love* (27), *Sadie Thompson* (28), *Madame X* (directed only) (29), *A Free Soul* (AA) (30), *The Rogue Song* (directed only) (31), *The Yellow Ticket* (31), *Arsène Lupin* (32), *Mata Hari* (32), *Rasputin and the Empress* (32), *Dinner at Eight* (33), *Night Flight* (33), *Carolina* (34), *Treasure Island* (34), *David Copperfield* (as Dan Peggotty) (34), *Mark of the Vampire* (34), *The Little Colonel* (35), *The Return of Peter Grimm* (35), *Ah Wilderness* (35), *The Voice of Bugle Ann* (36), *The Devil Doll* (36), *The Gorgeous Hussy* (36), *Camille* (36), *Captains Courageous* (37), *A Family Affair* (as Judge Hardy: first of series) (37), *Saratoga* (37), *A Yank at Oxford* (38), *Test Pilot* (38), *You Can't Take It With You* (38), *Young Dr Kildare* (as Dr Gillespie in this and fourteen subsequent films) (38), *Let Freedom Ring* (38), *On Borrowed Time* (39), *The Penalty* (41), *The Man on America's Conscience* (41), *A Guy Named Joe* (43), *Since You Went Away* (44), *The Valley of Decision* (45), *Duel in the Sun* (46), *Three Wise Fools* (46), *It's a Wonderful Life* (46), *The Secret Heart* (46), *Key Largo* (48), *Down to the Sea in Ships* (49), *Malaya* (50), *Right Cross* (50), *Bannerline* (51), *Lone Star* (52), *Main Street to Broadway* (53), others. From 1938, the results of arthritis and a bad fall forced him to act from a wheelchair.

BART, LIONEL (1930–   ) (L. Begleiter). London-born lyricist and composer who can't read music but has been phenomenally successful with West End musicals such as *Fings Ain't What They Used To Be*, *Oliver*, *Blitz* and *Maggie May*. Has written songs and scores for films since 1957. *Oliver* was filmed in 1968.

BARTHELMESS, RICHARD (1895–1963). American actor who went straight from college into silent pictures. Signed by D. W. Griffith who used him memorably in *Broken Blossoms* (19), *Way Down East* (20), etc. Formed his own company; had great success in *Tol'able David* (21) and was popular through the 20s in *The Fighting Blade* (23), *The Patent Leather Kid* (26), *The Amateur Gentleman* (27), *Dawn Patrol* (30); but the talkies made his innocent image seem old-fashioned and he turned to rather dull character roles, usually villainous. *A Modern Hero* (34), *Only Angels Have Wings* (39), *The Man Who Talked Too Much* (41), *The Spoilers* (last role) (42), etc.

BARTHOLOMEW, FREDDIE (1924–   ). British child actor who gained world fame in the title role of *David Copperfield* (34). Other films included *Anna Karenina* (35), *Lloyds of London* (37), *Little Lord Fauntleroy* (37), *Captains Courageous* (37), *The Boy from Barnado's* (39), *Tom Brown's Schooldays* (39), *The Swiss Family Robinson* (40), *A Yank at Eton* (42), *Junior Army* (43), *The Town Went Wild* (45), *St Benny the Dip* (51). Retired from acting to become an advertising executive.

BARTLETT, HALL (1922–   ). American producer: *Navajo* (52), *Unchained* (also wrote and directed) (54), *Drango* (also wrote and directed) (56), *Zero Hour* (directed only) (57), *All the Young Men* (also directed) (59), *A Global Affair* (63), *The Caretakers* (*Borderlines*) (also directed) (63), *Sol Madrid* (*The Heroin Gang*) (68), etc.

BARTLETT, SY (1909–   ) (Sacha Baraniev). American writer. *Road to Zanzibar* (41), *The Princess and the Pirate* (44), *12 O'Clock High* (49), *The Big Country* (57), many others. Produced *Pork Chop Hill* (59), *Cape Fear* (62), *Che* (69), etc.

BARTOK, EVA (1926–   ) (Eva Sjöke). Hungarian actress who has decorated a number of British and American films including *A Tale of Five Cities* (51), *Venetian Bird* (52), *The Crimson Pirate* (52), *Break in the Circle* (55), *Ten Thousand Bedrooms* (57), *Operation Amsterdam* (59), *Beyond the Curtain* (60), *Blood and Black Lace* (64), etc. Many European films. Published autobiography 1959: *Worth Living For*.

BARTON, CHARLES (1902–   ). American director of routine entertainments. *Wagon Wheels* (34), *Babies for Sale* (40), *Two Latins from Manhattan* (41), *What's Buzzin' Cousin* (43), *The Beautiful Cheat* (also produced) (45), *Abbott and Costello Meet Frankenstein* (49), *Free for All* (49), *The Milkman* (50), *Ma and Pa Kettle at the Fair* (52), *The Shaggy Dog* (59), *Toby Tyler* (59), many others, also TV films.

BARTON, JAMES (1890–1962). American character actor, veteran of Broadway and burlesque. Film appearances, usually as grizzled, hard-drinking type, include *Captain Hurricane* (35), *Shepherd of the*

Hills (41), *The Time of Your Life* (48), *Yellow Sky* (48), *Wabash Avenue* (50), *Here Comes the Groom* (51), *Golden Girl* (51), *The Naked Hills* (56), *Quantez* (58).

BARTOSCH, BERTHOLD (1893–   ). Austro-Hungarian animator, best known for his symbolic *L'Idée* (34).

BARZMAN, BEN (1911–   ). Canadian writer with Hollywood experience; in Britain from early 50s. *True to Life* (42), *The Boy With Green Hair* (48), *He Who Must Die* (56), *Time Without Pity* (57), *Blind Date* (59), *The Ceremony* (63), *The Heroes of Telemark* (65), *The Blue Max* (66), etc.

baseball has been the subject for occasional films ever since 1906, when *How the Office Boy Saw the Ball Game* was made. Several biopics have been produced about the game's leading personalities: *The Stratton Story* (James Stewart), *The Babe Ruth Story* (William Bendix), *Pride of the Yankees* (Gary Cooper as Lou Gehrig), *The Winning Team* (Ronald Reagan as Grover Cleveland Alexander), *The Jackie Robinson Story*, *The Pride of St Louis* (Dan Dailey as Dizzy Dean), *Fear Strikes Out* (Anthony Perkins as Jim Piersall), etc. Comedies on the subject have included *Casey at the Bat* (Wallace Beery), *Fast Company* (Jack Oakie), *Elmer the Great* and *Alibi Ike* (Joe E. Brown), *Rhubarb* (about a millionaire cat that owns a baseball team) and *It Happens Every Spring*. Baseball musicals are led by *Take Me Out to the Ball Game* and *Damn Yankees*. Serious drama has hardly had a look in, but one might mention *The Bush Leaguer* of 1917 and *The Big Leaguer* of 1953; there was even *Angels in the Outfield*, in which a team had heaven on its side. Finally, baseball stadiums have provided memorable scenes in films on other subjects: *The FBI Story*, *Beau James*, *The Satan Bug*, *Experiment in Terror*.

BASEHART, RICHARD (1919–   ). American leading man, equally adept at portraying honesty, villainy and mental disturbance. Experience in radio, newspapers and local politics before Broadway success and film debut in *Cry Wolf* (46). Later: *He Walked by Night* (48), *Reign of Terror* (*The Black Book*) (49), *The House on Telegraph Hill* (51), *Decision before Dawn* (51), *The Stranger's Hand* (53), *Titanic* (53), *La Strada* (Italy) (54), *The Good Die Young* (GB) (54), *Il Bidone* (*The Swindlers*) (Italy) (55), *Moby Dick* (56), *The Intimate Stranger* (*Finger of Guilt*) (56), *Time Limit* (57), *The Brothers Karamazov* (58), *Portrait in Black* (60), *Hitler* (title role) (63), *Kings of the Sun* (63), *The Satan Bug* (65), etc. TV series: *Voyage to the Bottom of the Sea*.

BASS, ALFIE (1920–   ). Pint-sized British character comedian, adept at Cockney/Jewish roles. *Johnny Frenchman* (debut) (45), *Holiday Camp* (47), *It Always Rains on Sunday* (47), *The Hasty Heart* (49), *The Lavender Hill Mob* (51), *The Bespoke Overcoat* (55), *A Kid for Two Farthings* (55), *A Tale of Two Cities* (57), *I Only Arsked* (59), *The Millionairess* (60), *Alfie* (66), *The Fearless Vampire Killers* (67), etc. Became a national figure as 'Excused Boots' Bisley in the long-running TV series *The Army Game* and *Bootsie and Snudge*.

BASS, SAUL (1920–   ). American title designer whose ingenious credits have enlivened such films as *Carmen Jones*, *The Shrike*, *The Man with the Golden Arm*, *Around the World in Eighty Days*, *Vertigo*, *The Big Country*, *Bonjour Tristesse*, *North by Northwest*, *Psycho*, *Ocean's Eleven*, *A Walk on the Wild Side*, *It's a Mad Mad Mad Mad World*, *Bunny Lake Is Missing*, many others.

BASSERMAN, ALBERT (1867–1952). Distinguished German stage actor who came to Hollywood as refugee in 1939 and played sympathetic roles in *Dr Ehrlich's Magic Bullet* (40), *This Man Reuter* (40), *Foreign Correspondent* (40), *Escape* (40), *The Great Awakening* (41), *The Moon and Sixpence* (42), *Once Upon a Honeymoon* (42), *Madame Curie* (43), *Since You Went Away* (44), *Rhapsody in Blue* (45), *The Searching Wind* (46), *Bel Ami* (47), *The Red Shoes* (GB) (48), etc.

BASSLER, ROBERT (1903–   ). American producer, in Hollywood from 1924. *The Black Swan* (43), *The Lodger* (44), *The Snake Pit* (50), *Beyond the Twelve Mile Reef* (53), *Suddenly* (54), etc. Much TV work.

THE BAT. The spooky house melodrama by Mary Roberts Rinehart was first filmed in 1926 with Louise Fazenda and Emily Fitzroy. In 1930 came a sound variation known as *The Bat Whispers*, with Grayce Hampton and some splendid over-acting from Chester Morris. In 1959 there was a somewhat spiritless remake with Agnes Moorehead and Vincent Price.

LA BATAILLE DU RAIL (France 1944–45). A remarkable documentary, directed by René Clement, shot in occupied France during World War II to show the railwaymen's resistance to the Nazis.

BATCHELOR, JOY (1914–   ). British animator, wife of John Halas and co-founder of Halas and Batchelor Cartoon Films.

BATES, ALAN (1930–   ). British stage and TV actor who has played leading roles in *A Kind of Loving* (61), *Whistle Down the Wind* (62), *The Caretaker* (63), *The Running Man* (63), *Nothing But the Best* (64), *Zorba the Greek* (65), *Georgy Girl* (66), *King of Hearts* (French) (67), *Far From the Madding Crowd* (67), *The Fixer* (US) (68), *Women in Love* (69), *Three Sisters* (70), etc.

BATES, BARBARA (1925–1969). American leading lady, former model and ballet dancer. *This Love of Ours* (45), *The Fabulous Joe* (48), *The Inspector General* (49), *Cheaper by the Dozen* (49), *All About Eve* (50), *Belles on Her Toes* (52), *Rhapsody* (54), *House of Secrets* (GB) (56), *Town on Trial* (GB) (57), *Apache Territory* (58), etc.

BATES, FLORENCE (1888–1954) (Florence Rabe). American businesswoman and lawyer persuaded by Hitchcock to play the snobbish and domineering Mrs Van Hopper in *Rebecca* (40); subsequently in many similar roles including *Road Show* (41), *The Moon and Sixpence* (42), *Claudia and David* (46), *The High Window* (47), *I Remember Mama* (47), *The Secret Life of Walter Mitty* (47), *Belle of Old Mexico* (50), *County Fair* (51), *Paris Model* (53).

BATES, MICHAEL (1929–   ). British character actor who specializes in stupid policemen. *Carrington V.C.* (55), *I'm All Right Jack* (59), *Bedazzled* (67), *Here We Go Round the Mulberry Bush* (67), *Salt and Pepper* (68), etc.

bathtubs, though especially associated with Cecil B. DeMille, have been a favourite Hollywood gimmick from early silent days. But DeMille undressed his heroines with the most showmanship, whether it was Gloria Swanson in *Male and Female,* Claudette Colbert in her asses' milk in *The Sign of the Cross* (emulated years later by Frances Day in *Fiddlers Three*) or Paulette Goddard in *Unconquered.* Other ladies who have bathed spectacularly include Joan Crawford in *The Women,* Deanna Durbin in *Can't Help Singing,* Jean Harlow in *Red Dust,* Phyllis Haver in *The Politic Flapper,* Gina Lollobrigida in *Belles de Nuit,* Carroll Baker in *Harlow* and Sophia Loren (who had Gregory Peck hiding in her shower) in *Arabesque.* Not that the men have had it all their own way: Roger Livesey in *Colonel Blimp* and Gary Cooper in *Love in the Afternoon* suffered in the steamroom; and all the actors who have played coal miners, including Trevor Howard in *Sons and Lovers* and Donald Crisp in *How Green Was My Valley,* know how it feels to be scrubbed all over. The most bathed male star is probably Cary Grant, who had a tub in *The Howards of Virginia,* a shower in *Mr Blandings Builds His Dream House,* another shower, fully clothed this time, in *Charade,* and a Japanese geisha bath in *Walk, Don't Run.* And Hitchcock, with *Psycho,* still takes the prize for the most memorable shower scene.

THE BATTLE OF THE SOMME. In 1915 a feature-length British war documentary was released under this title. In 1927 H. Bruce Woolfe (qv) made it the subject of the first of his famous series of reconstructions of famous battles (*Ypres, Mons, The Battle of the Coronel and Falkland Islands*); in these newsreel material was mingled with restaged sequences to brilliant effect, and *The Battle of the Somme* is probably the most striking of them.

THE BATTLESHIP POTEMKIN (USSR 1925). A historical reconstruction of an incident at Odessa in the revolution of 1905. Eisenstein, directing his second film, used the theme not merely as propaganda but as a means to develop his cinematic technique. The editing of

Baur, Henry

the massacre sequence on the steps is justly famous and has been frequently copied. Photographed by Edouard Tisse; assistant to Eisenstein, Grigori Alexandrov.

BAUR, HARRY (1881–1941). Celebrated French actor of stage and screen. *Shylock* (10), *La Voyante* (23), *David Golder* (31), *Poil de Carotte* (32), *Golgotha* (34), *Moscow Nights* (35), *Crime and Punishment* (35), *Taras Bulba* (35), *Un Carnet de Bal* (37), *The Rebel Son* (38), *Volpone* (39), etc.

BAVA, MARIO (1914–   ). Italian director of period muscle-man epics and imitation-British horror stories, revered by the *cognoscenti* for his tongue-in-cheek attitude to some of them. Former cinematographer. *Black Sunday* (w, ph, d) (60), *Hercules in the Centre of the earth* (w, ph, d) (61), *The Evil Eye* (w, ph, d) (62), *Blood and Black Lace* (w, ph, d) (64), *Dr Goldfoot and the Girl Bombs* (d) (66), *Curse of the Dead* (w, d) (66), *Diabolik* (w, d) (68), etc.

BAXTER, ALAN (1908–   ). American leading man of second features in the 40s; now playing colonels and tough executives. *Mary Burns, Fugitive* (35), *The Last Gangster* (38), *Rags to Riches* (41), *Submarine Base* (43), *Winged Victory* (45), *The Devil's Weed* (49), *The Set-Up* (49), *End of the Line* (GB) (56), *The Mountain Road* (60), many others.

BAXTER, ANNE (1923–   ). American actress, trained for the stage but starring in Hollywood at 17. Equally at home in shy or scheming roles. *The Great Profile* (40), *Charley's American Aunt* (42), *The Pied Piper* (42), *The Magnificent Ambersons* (42), *North Star* (43), *Sunday Dinner for a Soldier* (44), *The Sullivans* (44), *Guest in the House* (44), *The Eve of St Mark* (44), *Czarina (A Royal Scandal)* (45), *Angel on My Shoulder* (46), *The Razor's Edge* (AA) (46), *Blaze of Noon* (47), *You're My Everything* (49), *All About Eve* (50), *The Outcasts of Poker Flat* (51), *My Wife's Best Friend* (52), *I Confess* (53), *The Blue Gardenia* (53), *The Carnival Story* (53), *Bedevilled* (55), *The Spoilers* (56), *The Ten Commandments* (56), *Chase a Crooked Shadow* (GB) (57), *Summer of the Seventeenth Doll* (60), *Cimarron* (61), *Mix Me a Person* (GB) (61), *A Walk on the Wild Side* (62), *The Family Jewels* (guest appearance) (65), *Frontier Woman* (66), *The Busy Body* (67), others.

BAXTER, BERYL (1926–   ) (B. Ivory). British leading lady who was groomed for stardom but appeared in only one film, and that notoriously poor: *Idol of Paris* (46).

BAXTER, JANE (1909–   ) (Feodora Forde). Gentle-mannered British actress of stage and screen. *The Constant Nymph* (32), *The Clairvoyant* (34), *We Live Again* (US) (35), *The Ware Case* (39), *Ships with Wings* (41), *The Flemish Farm* (43), *Death of an Angel* (51), etc. Recently inactive.

92

BAXTER, JOHN (1896–   ). British producer-director with experience as actor, manager and casting director. Made early talkie realist films such as *Doss House* (32) and had a good period during World War II with *Love on the Dole* (40), *The Common Touch* (41), *Let the People Sing* (42), *When We Are Married* (43). Later: *The Second Mate* (50), *Judgment Deferred* (51), *Ramsbottom Rides Again* (56), other modest regional comedies.

BAXTER, STANLEY (1928–   ). Scottish comedian, popular since 1959 on British stage, TV and films. Latter include *Very Important Person* (61), *Crooks Anonymous* (62), *The Fast Lady* (63), *Joey Boy* (65); but films have not as yet given full scope to his talent for mimicry.

BAXTER, WARNER (1892–1951). American leading man with stage experience. Popular hero of silent melodramas: survived transition to talkies. *Her Own Money* (23), *Alimony* (24), *Aloma of the South Seas* (26), *The Great Gatsby* (26), *Ramona* (28), *In Old Arizona* (AA) (29), *West of Zanzibar* (30), *The Cisco Kid* (31), *Stand Up and Cheer* (33), *Forty-second Street* (33), *Grand Canary* (34), *Broadway Bill* (34), *Robin Hood of Eldorado* (36), *King of Burlesque* (36), *Slave Ship* (37), *Prisoner of Shark Island* (37), *Kidnapped* (38), *Earthbound* (40), *Adam Had Four Sons* (41), *The Crime Doctor* (and subsequent series) (43–48), *Lady in the Dark* (44), *State Penitentiary* (50), others.

BAYES, NORA (1880–1928) (Dora Goldberg). American vaudeville singer, impersonated by Ann Sheridan in the biopic *Shine On Harvest Moon* (44).

BAYLDON, GEOFFREY (c. 1929–   ). British character actor with a leaning to eccentric comedy; much on TV. *The Stranger Left No Card* (53), *Dracula* (58), *Libel* (60), *The Webster Boy* (62), *King Rat* (65), *Sky West and Crooked* (65), *To Sir With Love* (66), *Otley* (69), etc.

BAZIN, ANDRÉ (1918–1958). French critic who wrote books on Welles, de Sica and Renoir: 'the spiritual father of the New Wave'. Founded 'Cahiers du Cinema'.

BEAL, JOHN (1909–   ) (Alexander Bliedung). American stage actor whose look of boyish innocence made him ideal casting for *The Little Minister* (35). Infrequent appearances since include *Les Misérables* (35), *The Cat and the Canary* (39), *The Great Commandment* (43), *Alimony* (49), *Messenger of Peace* (50), *My Six Convicts* (52), *Remains To Be Seen* (53), *That Night* (57), *The Vampire* (60), *Ten Who Dared* (61), etc.

BEAN, JUDGE ROY (1823–1902). American western badman, a self-appointed lawmaker who kept himself in whisky from his fines.

Played by Walter Brennan in *The Westerner* (40) and by Edgar Buchanan in a TV series, *Judge Roy Bean* (56).

THE BEATLES. This phenomenally popular Liverpudlian singing group consists of JOHN LENNON (1940–   ), GEORGE HARRISON (1943–   ), PAUL MCCARTNEY (1942–   ) and RINGO STARR (Richard Starkey) (1940–   ). *A Hard Day's Night* (64), *Help!* (65). Lennon also appeared solo in a 'straight' role in *How I Won the War* (67), and Starr was in *Candy* (68).

BEATON, CECIL (1902–   ). British photographer and designer who has advised on many films, his greatest achievements probably being *Gigi* (58) and *My Fair Lady* (64).

BEATTY, ROBERT (1909–   ). Rugged Canadian actor long resident in Britain. Films since 1942 mainly routine crime dramas, but include *San Demetrio, London* (43), *Appointment with Crime* (46), *Odd Man Out* (46), *Against the Wind* (47), *Counterblast* (48), *Captain Horatio Hornblower RN* (51), *The Square Ring* (53), *Albert RN* (53), *Something of Value* (57), *Tarzan and the Lost Safari* (58), *The Amorous Prawn* (62), *2001: A Space Odyssey* (68), *Where Eagles Dare* (69). TV series: *Dial 999*.

†BEATTY, WARREN (1937–   ) (Warren Beaty). American leading man, brother of Shirley MacLaine. *Splendour in the Grass* (61), *The Roman Spring of Mrs Stone* (61), *All Fall Down* (62), *Lilith* (65), *Mickey One* (65) *Promise Her Anything* (66), *Kaleidoscope* (66), *Bonnie and Clyde* (also produced) (67), *The Only Game in Town* (69).

BEAUDINE, WILLIAM (1892–   ). American director since 1909: a prolific creator of second features in his later years. *Penrod and Sam* (23), *Little Annie Rooney* (25), *Sparrows* (26), *Misbehaving Ladies* (30), *Make Me a Star* (32), *Hey Hey USA* (GB) (36), *Broadway Big Shot* (42), *The Mystery of the Thirteenth Guest* (43), *Kidnapped* (48), *Westward Ho the Wagons* (56), *Lassie's Great Adventure* (63), *Billy the Kid versus Dracula* (66), many episodes of *The Bowery Boys*, hundreds of others.

BEAU GESTE. P. C. Wren's romantic novel of a missing gem, a debt of honour, and savagery in the Foreign Legion, was filmed in 1926 with Ronald Colman as Beau and Noah Beery as the sadistic sergeant. The 1939 version had Gary Cooper and Brian Donlevy; 1966 saw Guy Stockwell and Telly Savalas in the roles (and much of the plot missing).

BEAUMONT, CHARLES (1930–1967). American writer, chiefly of science fiction. *Queen of Outer Space* (58), *The Intruder* (61), *Night of the Eagle* (62), *The Haunted Palace* (63), *Seven Faces of Dr Lao* (64), *Mr Moses* (65), etc.

BEAUMONT, HARRY (1893–1966). American director in Hollywood from early silent days. Most memorable for *Babbitt* (28), *Our Dancing Daughters* (28), *Broadway Melody* (28), *When Ladies Meet* (33). Retired in 1934 apart from a few 40s films: *Maisie Goes to Reno* (44), *The Show-off* (46), etc.

BEAUMONT, HUGH (1909–). American leading man of second features. *South of Panama* (51), *The Seventh Victim* (44), *Objective Burma* (45), *Railroaded* (49), *Mr Belvedere Rings the Bell* (52), *The Mole People* (57), etc.; also appeared brifly as Michael Shayne and the Falcon. TV series: *Leave It to Beaver* (57–60).

BEAUMONT, SUSAN (1936–) (Susan Black). British leading lady of a few fifties films. *Jumping for Joy* (55), *High Tide at Noon* (57), *Innocent Sinners* (58), *Carry On Nurse* (59), *Web of Suspicion* (59), etc.

LE BEAU SERGE (France 1958). Sometimes claimed as the first 'nouvelle vague' film, this is a quiet, unsensational story about a young man who returns to his native village and tries to help an unhappy friend. Almost too life-like to be dramatic. Director: Claude Chabrol.

BEAVERS, LOUISE (1902–1962). American Negro actress who played scores of cheerful housekeepers. Seized one major acting chance in *Imitation of Life* (34). Also in *Safety in Numbers* (debut) (31), *Blonde Bombshell* (33), *Bullets or Ballots* (36), *Brother Rat* (39), *Reap the Wild Wind* (42), *Delightfully Dangerous* (45), *Mr Blandings Builds His Dream House* (48), *I Dream of Jeannie* (52), *You Can't Run Away from It* (56), *All the Fine Young Cannibals* (60), etc. TV series: *Beulah* (60).

BECKER, JACQUES (1906–1960). French director, mainly of civilized comedies. *Goupi Mains Rouges* (42), *Falbalas* (44), *Antoine et Antoinette* (49), *Rendezvous de Juillet* (49), *Edouard et Caroline* (50), *Casque d'Or* (51), *Rue de L'Estrapade* (52), *Touchez Pas au Grisbi* (53), *Ali Baba* (55), *The Adventures of Arsène Lupin* (56), *Montparnasse 19* (57), *The Hole* (60), etc.

BECKER, JEAN (1933–). French director, son of Jacques Becker. *Echappement Libre* (62), *Pas de Caviare pour Tante Olga* (64), *Tendre Voyou* (66), etc.

BECKET (GB 1964). Based on Jean Anouilh's unhistorical but witty play, this interesting but talkative film was determinedly sold as a sex-and-action epic. An intellectual rather than a visual experience, stagily directed by Peter Glenville and surprisingly produced by Hollywood veteran Hal Wallis, its box-office success was an indication of the adult fare now saleable to the mass audience. Stars Richard Burton and Peter O'Toole naturally helped.

BECKETT, SCOTTY (1929–1968). American child actor of the 30s, one-time member of 'Our Gang'. Also: *Dante's Inferno* (35), *Marie*

Walewska (38), *The Bluebird* (40), *Kings Row* (42), *The Jolson Story* (46), *Battleground* (50), *Corky* (51), *Three for Jamie Dawn* (57), etc.

BECKWITH, REGINALD (1908–1965). British actor-writer. Made scores of cameo appearances, usually as butler, civil servant, or harassed little man: memorable in *Scott of the Antarctic* (48), *Genevieve* (53), *The Runaway Bus* (54), *The Captain's Table* (58), *The Thirty-Nine Steps* (59), *The Password Is Courage* (62), *Never Put It in Writing* (64), *Mister Moses* (65), etc. Wrote successful plays, e.g. 'Boys in Brown', 'A Soldier For Christmas'.

BECKY SHARP (US 1935). The first full-length Technicolor feature, a version of 'Vanity Fair'. Directed by Rouben Mamoulian, with Miriam Hopkins as Becky.

BEDDOE, DON (1891–). American character actor with genial, sometimes startled, look; in hundreds of films, often as sheriff, reporter, cop. *Golden Boy* (39), *The Face behind the Mask* (41), *O.S.S.* (46), *The Best Years of Our Lives* (46), *The Farmer's Daughter* (47), *Carrie* (51), *Night of the Hunter* (55), *Saintly Sinners* (lead role) (61), *Jack the Giant Killer* (as a leprechaun) (62), *Texas across the River* (66), *The Impossible Years* (68), etc.

BEDFORD, BRIAN (1935–). British stage actor who has been in a few films: *Miracle in Soho* (58), *The Angry Silence* (59), *The Punch and Judy Man* (63), *The Pad* (66), *Grand Prix* (67), etc.

BEDOYA, ALFONSO (1904–1957). Smiling Mexican actor who made Hollywood debut as the bandit in *Treasure of Sierra Madre* (48). Also in *The Streets of Laredo* (49), *The Black Rose* (50), *Sombrero* (52), *Ten Wanted Men* (55), *The Big Country* (58), etc.

BEEBE, FORD (1888–). American writer-director of low-budget Westerns, second features and serials, most notably *Flash Gordon Goes to Mars* (37), *Riders of Death Valley* (41), *The Invisible Man's Revenge* (44), *Enter Arsène Lupin* (45), *Bomba the Jungle Boy* (49).

BEECHER, JANET (1884–1955) (J. B. Meysenburg). American character actress usually seen in ladylike roles. *Gallant Lady* (34), *The Dark Angel* (36), *Bitter Sweet* (40), *Reap the Wild Wind* (42), *Mrs Wiggs of the Cabbage Patch* (43), *Henry Gets Glamour* (43), etc. Retired 1943.

BEERY, NOAH (1884–1946). American character actor, brother of Wallace Beery and one of the silent screen's most celebrated villains. *The Mormon Maid* (18), *The Mark of Zorro* (20), *Tolable David* (21), *The Spoilers* (22), *The Coming of Amos* (25), *Beau Geste* (26), *Don Juan* (26), *Beau Sabreur* (27), *The Four Feathers* (29), *Noah's Ark* (29), *The Drifter* (31), *Out of Singapore* (32), *She Done Him*

Wrong (33), *King of the Damned* (GB) (35), *Our Fighting Navy* (GB) (37), *The Girl of the Golden West* (38), *Isle of Missing Men* (42), *This Man's Navy* (45), many others.

BEERY, NOAH JNR (1913–   ). American character actor, son of Noah Beery. Started as child actor, and later played easy-going country cousins. *The Mark of Zorro* (20), *Heroes of the West* (26), *Father and Son* (29), *Jungle Madness* (31), *The Road Back* (37), *Only Angels Have Wings* (39), *Of Mice and Men* (40), *Riders of Death Valley* (41), *Prairie Chickens* (43), *Gung Ho* (44), *Red River* (48), *Destination Moon* (50), *White Feather* (55), *Inherit the Wind* (60), *The Seven Faces of Dr Lao* (64), *Incident at Phantom Hill* (65), many others. TV series: *Crocus Boy* (57–59), *Custer* (67).

BEERY, WALLACE (1889–1949). American actor with circus and musical comedy experience. Started in silent comedies as grotesque female impersonator; later graduated to star parts at MGM, his usual character being tough, ugly but easy-going. Memorable in *Teddy at the Throttle* (16), *The Four Horsemen of the Apocalypse* (21), *Robin Hood* (as Richard the Lionheart) (24), *The Lost World* (as Professor Challenger) (25), *The Sea Hawk* (25), *The Last of the Mohicans* (27), *We're in the Navy Now* (27) (and other comedies with Raymond Hatton), *Chinatown Nights* (30), *The Big House* (31), *Jenny Lind* (31), *Min and Bill* (31), *The Champ* (AA) (32), *Grand Hotel* (32), *Tugboat Annie* (33), *The Bowery* (33), *Viva Villa* (34), *Treasure Island* (as Long John) (34), *The Mighty Barnum* (35), *China Seas* (35), *Bad Man of Brimstone* (36), *Slave Ship* (37), *Stand Up and Fight* (38), *Two-Gun Cupid* (40), *Barnacle Bill* (41), *Jackass Mail* (42), *Rationing* (43), *Barbary Coast Gent* (44), *The Mighty McGurk* (46), *A Date with Judy* (48), *Big Jack* (49), many others.

THE BEGGAR'S OPERA. Several attempts have been made to film John Gay's 17th-century operetta of the London underworld. 1. *Die Dreigroschenoper* (Germany 1931) starred Rudolph Forster as Macheath and had music by Kurt Weill. (French version, with Albert Prejean, known as *L'Opéra de Quatr'Sous*.) 2. *The Beggar's Opera* (GB 1952) was a straight version with Laurence Olivier, directed by Peter Brook. 3. *The Threepenny Opera* (Germany/US 1965) stars Curt Jurgens and Sammy Davis Jnr.

BEGLEY, ED (1901–   ). American stage and radio actor who came late in life to films. Often plays the flustered, self-important man with something to hide. *Boomerang* (47), *The Street with No Name* (48), *Tulsa* (49), *The Great Gatsby* (49), *Backfire* (50), *Wyoming Mail* (50), *Deadline USA* (52), *Patterns of Power* (56), *Twelve Angry Men* (57), *Odds Against Tomorrow* (59), *Sweet Bird of Youth* (AA) (62), *The Unsinkable Molly Brown* (64), *The Oscar* (66), *Warning Shot*

Behrman, S. N.

(67), *Firecreek* (67), *Billion Dollar Brain* (67), *Wild in the Streets* (68), *Hang 'Em High* (68), *The Violent Enemy* (69), etc.

BEHRMAN, S. N. (1893–   ). American playwright of urbane comedies. Works filmed include *Biography*, *No Time for Comedy*, *The Second Man*, *Me and the Colonel*, *Fanny*. Also scripted *Queen Christina* (33), *Cavalcade* (33), *Anna Karenina* (35), *Conquest* (38), *Quo Vadis* (51), etc.

BEICH, ALBERT (1919–   ). American radio and film writer, one of the 'Hollywood Ten' who defied the McCarthy witch-hunt in 1947. *Girls in Chains* (44), *The Perils of Pauline* (47), *The Bride Goes Wild* (48), *Key to the City* (50), *The Lieutenant Wore Skirts* (55), etc.

BEKASSY, STEPHEN (c. 1915–   ). Hungarian stage actor who came to Hollywood in the 40s. *A Song to Remember* (as Lizst) (45), *Arch of Triumph* (48), *Black Magic* (49), *Fair Wind to Java* (53), *Hell and High Water* (54), *Interrupted Melody* (55), *The Light in the Forest* (58), etc.

BELAFONTE, HARRY (1927–   ). American Negro singer who has acted in several films. *Carmen Jones* (55), *Island in the Sun* (57), *The World, the Flesh and the Devil* (58), *Odds Against Tomorrow* (59), *The Angel Levine* (69), etc.

BELASCO, LEON (1902–   ). Wiry Russian-born small-part player of excitable ballet-masters, head waiters, landlords, etc. *The Best People* (debut) (26), *Topper Takes a Trip* (39), *The Mummy's Hand* (40), *Nothing But the Truth* (41), *Pin-up Girl* (44), *Call Me Madam* (53), many others. TV series: *My Sister Eileen*.

BEL GEDDES, BARBARA (1922–   ) (Barbara Geddes Lewis). American stage actress who makes occasional films, e.g. *I Remember Mama* (47), *The Long Night* (47), *Caught* (49), *Panic in the Streets* (50), *Fourteen Hours* (51), *Vertigo* (58), *The Five Pennies* (59), *By Love Possessed* (61).

BELITA (1924–   ) (Gladys Jepson-Turner). British ice-skating and dancing star who made a few Hollywood films: *Ice Capades* (41), *Silver Skates* (43), *Suspense* (46), *The Hunted* (47), *Never Let Me Go* (53), *Invitation to the Dance* (56), *Silk Stockings* (57), etc.

BELL, JAMES (1891–   ). American character actor, usually in benevolent roles. *I Am a Fugitive from a Chain Gang* (32), *I Walked with a Zombie* (42), *The Spiral Staircase* (45), *The Violent Hour* (50), *The Glenn Miller Story* (54), *The Lonely Man* (57), many others.

BELL, MARIE (1900–   ) (Marie-Jeanne Bellon-Downey). Distinguished French actress who appeared in a few well-remembered films: *Le Grand Jeu* (34), *La Garconne* (35), *Carnet de Bal* (37), *La Charette Fantome* (40), *Colonel Chabert* (43), *La Bonne Soupe* (64), etc.

BELL, MONTA (1891–1958). American director. Worked with Chaplin on *A Woman of Paris* (23). Later: *The Torrent* (27), *After Midnight* (28), *East Is West* (30), *Men in White* (33), *West Point of the Air* (35), etc. Left show business.

BELL, REX (1905–1962) (George F. Beldam). American cowboy star of the thirties: left Hollywood to become Lieut.-Governor of Nevada.

BELL, TOM (1934–   ). Gaunt British leading man, ex-Theatre Workshop. *Payroll* (61), *The L-Shaped Room* (62), *A Prize of Arms* (63), *Ballad in Blue* (65), *He Who Rides a Tiger* (66), *The Long Day's Dying* (68), *In Enemy Country* (US) (68), *Lock Up Your Daughters* (69), etc.

BELLAMY, EARL (1917–   ). American director with much TV experience, now directing Westerns for Universal. *Fluffy* (65), *Incident at Phantom Hill* (66), *Gunpoint* (66), *Munster Go Home* (66), etc.

BELLAMY, RALPH (1904–   ). American stage and screen leading man who during the 30s became typecast as the simple-minded good guy who never got the girl: parodied himself in *His Girl Friday* (41). More recently a leader of Actors Equity and a noted Broadway star. *Surrender* (29), *The Secret Six* (31), *The Narrow Corner* (33), *The Wedding Night* (35), *The Crime of Dr Hallett* (36), *The Awful Truth* (37), *Carefree* (38), *Boy Meets Girl* (38), *Ellery Queen* series (39–42), *His Girl Friday* (41), *The Wolf Man* (41), *Ghost of Frankenstein* (42), *The Great Impersonation* (42), *Guest in the House* (44), *Lady on a Train* (45), then to Broadway stage; recent appearances include *The Court Martial of Billy Mitchell* (55), *Sunrise at Campobello* (as Franklin D. Roosevelt) (60), *The Professionals* (66), *Rosemary's Baby* (68). TV series: *The Eleventh Hour* (63), *The Survivors* (69).

BELLAVER, HARRY (1905–   ). American character actor, often seen as cop, small-time gangster, or cabby. *Another Thin Man* (40), *The House on 92nd Street* (46), *No Way Out* (50), *Miss Sadie Thompson* (54), *Slaughter on Tenth Avenue* (57), *One Potato Two Potato* (64), *A Fine Madness* (66), *Madigan* (67), etc. TV series: *Naked City* (58–63).

LA BELLE ET LA BÊTE (France 1946). Jean Cocteau wrote and directed this imaginative film version of the 18th-century fairy tale. There are no plot surprises, but Berard's décor is uniquely beautiful, and Henri Alekan's photography has exactly the right sense of mystery. With Josette Day, Jean Marais, Michel Auclair.

BELMONDO, JEAN-PAUL (1933–   ). French leading actor with 'new wave' qualifications. *A Double Tour* (59), *A Bout de Souffle* (59), *Moderato Cantabile* (60), *La Viaccia* (60), *Leon Morin, Priest* (61), *Two Women* (61), *Cartouche* (62), *Un Singe en Hiver* (*It's Hot in Hell*) (62), *That Man from Rio* (64), *Weekend in Dunkirk* (65), *Pierrot le Fou* (65), *Is Paris Burning?* (66), *Tendre Voyou* (66), *Le Voleur* (67), *The Brain* (68), *The Mississippi Mermaid* (69), *A Man I Like* (69), etc.

BELMORE, BERTHA (1882–1953). British character comedienne, whose dignity was all too inevitably shattered in farce: the British Margaret Dumont. *Going Gay* (34), *In the Soup* (36), *Over She Goes* (38), *Yes Madam* (39), etc.

BELOIN, EDMUND (1910–   ). American comedy writer with radio experience. *Because of Him* (45), *The Great Lover* (also produced) (48), *A Yankee at King Arthur's Court* (49), *The Sad Sack* (57), *G.I. Blues* (60), etc.

THE BELOVED ROGUE: see IF I WERE KING.

BENCHLEY, ROBERT (1889–1945). American humorist who appeared in many films as an amiable bumbler, usually trying to explain something complicated or control a patently unmanageable situation. Did a memorable series of short 'scientific' lectures for MGM and Paramount between 1928 and 1942: won AA for one of them, *How to Sleep* (35). Applied similar technique to feature, *Road to Utopia* (45). Also memorable in *Dancing Lady* (33), *Foreign Correspondent* (40), *Bedtime Story* (41), *The Major and the Minor* (42), *I Married a Witch* (42), *See Here Private Hargrove* (44), *Kiss and Tell* (45), *It's in the Bag* (*The Fifth Chair*) (45), *Janie Gets Married* (46), etc. A biography, *Robert Benchley*, was published in 1946 by his son Nathaniel; and several volumes of Benchleys own writings are still in print.

BENDIX, WILLIAM (1906–1964). American character actor, usually the tough guy with the heart of gold. Sprang to stardom after a meaty role in *The Glass Key* (42); his broken nose and Brooklyn accent later sustained many a mediocre film as well as adding to the flavour of good ones. *Woman of the Year* (41), *The McGuerins from Brooklyn* (42), *Hostages* (43), *Lifeboat* (43), *The Hairy Ape* (leading role) (44), *Abroad with Two Yanks* (44), *The Blue Dahlia* (45), *A Bell for Adano* (45), *The Dark Corner* (46), *Blaze of Noon* (47), *The Web* (47), *The Time of Your Life* (48), *A Yankee in King Arthur's Court* (49), *Kill the Umpire* (50), *Detective Story* (51), *Macao* (51), *A Girl in Every Port* (51), *Dangerous Mission* (54), *The Deep Six* (57), *The Rough and the Smooth* (GB) (59), *Johnny Nobody* (62), *Law of the Lawless* (63), *Young Fury* (64), many others. TV series: *The Life of Riley* (53–58), *Overland Stage* (60).

BENEDEK, LASLO (1907–   ). Hungarian photographer, writer and editor who in 1948 got a chance to direct in Hollywood but whose output has been surprisingly meagre. *The Kissing Bandit* (48), *Port of New York* (49), *Death of a Salesman* (52), *The Wild One* (54), *Bengal Rifles* (54), *Kinder Mutter und Ein General* (Ger.) (55), *Affair in Havana* (57), *Moment of Danger* (GB) (58), *Namu the Killer Whale* (also produced) (66), *The Daring Game* (68), etc.

BENEDICT, BILLY (1917–   ). American character actor who in his youth was one of the original 'Bowery Boys'; now plays cabbies, bartenders, etc. *The Clock Struck Eight* (35), *King of the Newsboys* (38), *Call a Messenger* (40) (the first of the 'Bowery Boys' series which ran until 1953), *The Hallelujah Trail* (65), many others.

BENEDICT, RICHARD (c. 1920–   ). American leading man, usually in second features; sometimes plays the heavy. *Till the End of Time* (46), *Crossfire* (47), *City across the River* (49), *State Penitentiary* (50), *Ace in the Hole* (51), *Okinawa* (52), *The Juggler* (53), *Hoodlum Empire* (55), *The Shrike* (55), etc.

BEN HUR. There were several silent versions of Lew Wallace's semi-biblical adventure novel. Best-known is MGM's lavish spectacular of 1927, directed by Fred Niblo with Ramon Navarro and Francis X. Bushman; it was reissued with sound effects in 1931. In 1959–60 it was remade by MGM (AA) and William Wyler, with Charlton Heston and Stephen Boyd: the greatest praise went to the chariot race sequence directed by Andrew Marton.

BENJAMIN, ARTHUR (1893–   ). British composer. *The Man Who Knew Too Much* (34), *The Scarlet Pimpernel* (34), *Turn of the Tide* (35), *Under the Red Robe* (36), *Master of Bankdam* (47), etc.

BENNET, SPENCER GORDON (1893–   ). American silent actor and stunt man who became a famous director of serials, of which he made 52 in all. *Rogue of the Rio Grande* (30), *Mysterious Pilot* (37), *Arizona Bound* (42), *Batman and Robin* (48), *Atom Man Versus Superman* (50), *Adventures of Sir Galahad* (51). Still directs occasional features: *Brave Warrior* (52), *The Bounty Killer* (65).

BENNETT, ARNOLD (1867–1931). British novelist, little of whose work has been filmed. *Buried Alive* has, however, been seen in several versions, under its own title, as *The Great Adventure*, as *His Double Life*, and as *Holy Matrimony*. British studios filmed *The Card* with Alec Guinness, and less successfully *Dear Mr Prohack* with Cecil Parker.

BENNETT, BARBARA (1902–1958). American leading lady of a few silent films: retired before sound came. Sister of Constance and Joan Bennett, daughter of Richard.

BENNETT, BELLE (1891–1932). American actress of the silent screen. Best remembered for *Stella Dallas* (25); also in *A Soul in Trust* (18), *Mother Machree* (27), *The Way of All Flesh* (28), *Their Own Desire* (29), *The Iron Mask* (30), etc.

BENNETT, BRUCE (1909–) (Herman Brix). American leading man who under his real name played Tarzan in an early talkie version made in Guatemala (*Tarzan and the Green Goddess*). Later became well-known in Hollywood, usually playing sympathetic executive types and friends of the family: *A Stolen Life* (47), *Nora Prentiss* (48), *Dream Wife* (53), *Strategic Air Command* (55), *The Outsider* (61), etc.

BENNETT, CHARLES (1899–). British screenwriter who worked on some of Hitchcock's British thrillers and later did sporadic work in Hollywood. *Blackmail* (30), *The Man Who Knew Too Much* (34), *The Thirty-nine Steps* (35), *Secret Agent* (36), *Foreign Correspondent* (40), *Ivy* (US) (47), *Madness of the Heart* (also directed) (49), *Black Magic* (US) (49), *The Green Glove* (52), *No Escape* (US) (also directed) (53), *Night of the Demon* (57), *Five Weeks in a Balloon* (US) (62), etc.

BENNETT, COMPTON (1900–). British director, former editor for Korda. The success of *The Seventh Veil* (46) and *The Years Between* (46), took him to Hollywood, but after *My Own True Love* (48), *The Forsyte Saga* (49), and *King Solomon's Mines* (50), he returned to England and has directed more routine films and TV episodes. *So Little Time* (52), *The Gift Horse* (52), *It Started in Paradise* (52), *Desperate Moment* (53), *That Woman Opposite* (57), *The Flying Scot* (57), *Beyond the Curtain* (60), etc.

BENNETT, CONSTANCE (1905–1965). American actress adept at sophisticated roles. Daughter of Richard Bennett, sister of Joan. Made a few silents in the 20s: *Cytharea* (20), *The Forbidden Way* (24), *The Goose Woman* (26), *Should a Woman Tell* (26), etc. Retired to marry but soon made a talkie comeback: *The Common Law* (31), *Sin Takes a Holiday* (31), *What Price Hollywood* (32), *Moulin Rouge* (34), *The Affairs of Cellini* (34), *After Office Hours* (35), *Topper* (37), *Tailspin* (39), *Two-Faced Woman* (41), *Escape to Glory* (41), *Madame Spy* (42), *Sin Town* (42), *Madame Pimpernel* (also produced) (45), *Centennial Summer* (46), *The Unsuspected* (47), *Smart Woman* (48), *As Young as You Feel* (51), etc.; then long absence until *Madame X* (66).

BENNETT, HYWEL (1944–). Welsh TV and film player of sensitive roles. *The Family Way* (66), *Twisted Nerve* (68), *The Virgin Soldiers* (69), *Buttercup Chain* (70).

BENNETT, JILL (1930–). British stage, screen and TV actress whose unusual features allow her to play the more determined or neurotic type of heroine. *Hell Below Zero* (54), *Lust for Life* (56), *The Criminal* (60), *The Skull* (65), *The Nanny* (65), *Inadmissible Evidence* (68), *Julius Caesar* (70), etc.

BENNETT, JOAN (1910–). American actress, daughter of Richard Bennett, sister of Constance. On her stage debut with her father was offered a Hollywood contract and appeared in *Bulldog Drummond* (29); was constantly busy in Hollywood for the next 25 years, progressing from heroines through sluts to mothers. *Disraeli* (30), *Moby Dick* (30), *Smiling Through* (31), *Wild Girl* (32), *Little Women* (33), *Private Worlds* (34), *The Man Who Broke the Bank at Monte Carlo* (35), *Big Brown Eyes* (36), *Vogues of 1938*, *Trade Winds* (38), *The Texans* (39), *Green Hell* (40), *Man Hunt* (41), *Confirm or Deny* (41), *Twin Beds* (42), *A Yank in Dutch* (42), *Margin for Error* (43), *The Woman in the Window* (44), *Scarlet Street* (45), *Nob Hill* (45), *The Woman on the Beach* (46), *The Macomber Affair* (47), *The Reckless Moment* (49), *Father of the Bride* (50), *Father's Little Dividend* (51), *Highway Dragnet* (52), *We're No Angels* (55), *There's Always Tomorrow* (56), *Desire in the Dust* (60), many others. Makes TV guest appearances and has leading role in daily soap opera *Dark Shadows* (66–69).

BENNETT, RICHARD (1873-1944). American stage actor, small and precise, father of Constance and Joan Bennett. Occasional films include *Damaged Goods* (15), *The Eternal City* (24), *This Reckless Age* (27), *Arrowsmith* (32), *Nana* (34), *The Magnificent Ambersons* (42), *Journey into Fear* (43).

BENNETT, RICHARD RODNEY (1936–). British composer whose film work includes *Interpol* (57), *Indiscreet* (58), *Only Two Can Play* (61), *Billy Liar* (63), *One Way Pendulum* (64), *The Nanny* (65), *Far from the Madding Crowd* (67).

BENNY, JACK (1894–) (Joseph Kubelsky). Famous American radio, TV and film comedian. Was violinist, doorman and props manager before a talent scout spotted him in burlesque. First film: *Hollywood Revue of 1929*. Long-running radio and TV shows have limited his film appearances, but he was memorable in *Artists and Models* (38), *Love Thy Neighbour* (40), *Charley's American Aunt* (41), *George Washington Slept Here* (42), *To Be or Not To Be* (a first-rate comedy performance) (42), *The Meanest Man in the World* (43), *The Horn Blows at Midnight* (45), *It's in the Bag* (*The Fifth Chair*) (45); briefly glimpsed in *It's a Mad Mad Mad Mad World* (63), *A Guide for the Married Man* (67). His trade marks are his indignant put-upon look and his pretence of meanness. He is married to his radio leading lady Mary Livingstone (Sadye Marks).

Benoit-Levy, Jean

BENOIT-LEVY, JEAN (1888–1959). French producer-director, author of books on cinema. Best-known films: *La Maternelle* (33), *La Mort du Cygne* (38).

BENSON, GEORGE (1911–). British character actor of stage, screen and TV, the nervous 'little man' of countless films including *Keep Fit* (37), *The October Man* (48), *The Man in the White Suit* (51), *The Captain's Paradise* (53), *Doctor in the House* (54), *Value for Money* (56), *A Home of Your Own* (65).

BENSON, MARTIN (1918–). British character actor often seen as a smooth foreign-looking crook. *The King and I* (US) (56), *Windom's Way* (58), *The Three Worlds of Gulliver* (60), *Cleopatra* (62), *Behold a Pale Horse* (64), *Goldfinger* (64), *The Secret of My Success* (65), many others. Also story editor and documentary producer.

BENTINE, MICHAEL (1922–). Anglo-Peruvian comedian, popular on stage and TV, who has made several unsuccessful attempts to film his goonish style of humour, most recently in *The Sandwich Man* (66).

BENTLEY, JOHN (1916–). British leading man who left the stage in 1946 to play in innumerable low-budget crime dramas, including series about Paul Temple and The Toff. TV series: *African Patrol*. Films include *Hills of Donegal* (47), *Calling Paul Temple* (48), *The Happiest Days of Your Life* (49), *The Lost Hours* (51), *The Scarlet Spear* (53), *Golden Ivory* (55), *Istanbul* (US) (58), *The Singer Not the Song* (60), *Mary Had a Little* (61), *The Fur Collar* (63).

BENTLEY, THOMAS (c. 1880–195*). British director, former Dickensian impersonator, who began in films by making silent versions of several Dickens novels. Later: *Young Woodley* (30), *Hobson's Choice* (31), *The Scotland Yard Mystery* (33), *Those Were the Days* (34), *The Old Curiosity Shop* (35), *Music Hath Charms* (35), *Marigold* (38), *The Middle Watch* (39), *Lucky to Me* (39), *Old Mother Riley's Circus* (41), scores of others.

BERG, GERTRUDE (1899–1966) (G. Edelstein). Plump American character actress famous on TV and radio as Molly of the Goldberg family. She appeared in a film version, *Molly* (51), also in another TV series, *Mrs G Goes to College* (61).

BERGEN, CANDICE (1946–). American leading actress, daughter of Edgar Bergen. *The Group* (66), *The Sand Pebbles* (66), *The Day the Fish Came Out* (67), *Vivre Pour Vivre* (67), *The Magus* (68), *The Plot* (70).

BERGEN, EDGAR (1903–). American ventriloquist of Swedish descent. Won Special AA in 1937 for appearances in musicals and shorts with his famous dummies Charlie McCarthy and Mortimer

Snerd: *Letter of Introduction* (38), *The Goldwyn Follies* (38), *You Can't Cheat an Honest Man* (39), *Charlie McCarthy, Detective* (41), *Here We Go Again* (42), etc. Later played straight character roles, usually as inoffensive little man: *I Remember Mama* (47), *The Hanged Man* (64), *One-Way Wahine* (66), *Don't Make Waves* (67), *Rogues Gallery* (68), etc.; also on TV.

BERGEN, POLLY (1929–). American stage/radio/TV singer and actress with pleasing quiet personality. Has made occasional films including *At War with the Army* (50), *Warpath* (51), *That's My Boy* (51), *Escape from Fort Bravo* (53), *Cape Fear* (62), *Borderlines* (*The Caretakers*) (63), *Move Over Darling* (63), *Kisses for My President* (64).

BERGER, LUDWIG (1892–) (L. Bamberger). German director who made some international films. *Ein Glas Wasser* (22), *Waltz Dream* (26), *The Woman from Moscow* (US) (28), *The Vagabond King* (US) (30), *La Guerre des Valses* (Fr.) (33), *The Thief of Bagdad* (co-d) (GB/US) (40), *Ballerina* (Fr.) (50), etc.

BERGER, NICOLE (1934–1967). French leading lady whose films include *Juliette* (52), *Game of Love* (54), etc.

BERGER, SENTA (1941–). Viennese leading lady, with stage experience; recently in Hollywood. *The Secret Ways* (debut) (61), *The Victors* (63), *Major Dundee* (65), *The Glory Guys* (65), *Cast a Giant Shadow* (66), *The Quiller Memorandum* (66), *The Ambushers* (67), *De Sade* (69), etc.

BERGERAC, JACQUES (1927–). French actor, former lawyer. Went to Hollywood 1953, married Ginger Rogers. Played mainly supporting roles in routine films: *Les Girls* (57), *Thunder in the Sun* (59), *The Hypnotic Eye* (60), *Taffy and the Jungle Hunter* (65), etc.

BERGHOF, HERBERT (1909–). Austrian character actor long on American stage. Rare films include *Assignment Paris* (52), *Five Fingers* (52), *Red Planet Mars* (52), *Fraulein* (58), *Cleopatra* (62).

BERGMAN, INGMAR (1918–). Swedish writer-director who divides his time between stage and film. His films have had considerable world-wide impact because of their bravura presentation and semimystic treatment of serious themes; he also makes light sex comedies. Most important titles: *Thirst* (49), *Summer Interlude* (51), *Waiting Women* (52), *Summer with Monika* (53), *Sawdust and Tinsel* (54), *Smiles of a Summer Night* (55), *The Seventh Seal* (56), *Wild Strawberries* (58), *The Face* (*The Magician*) (59), *The Virgin Spring* (60), *The Devil's Eye* (60), *Winter Light* (61), *Through a Glass Darkly* (62), *The Silence* (63), *Now About These Women* (64), *Persona* (65), *Hour of the Wolf* (67), *The Shame* (68).

†BERGMAN, INGRID (1915–   ). Swedish leading actress who went t Hollywood in 1938 and stayed to become an international star. In 1948 her affair with Rossellini caused a return to Europe where she has appeared in mainly inferior films, but made significant stage and TV appearances. Ten Swedish films including *Intermezzo* (36), *Die Vier Gesellen* (Ger.) (38), *Intermezzo* (US version, also called *Escape to Happiness*) (39), *Rage in Heaven* (41), *Adam Had Four Sons* (41), *Dr Jekyll and Mr Hyde* (41), *Casablanca* (42), *For Whom the Bell Tolls* (43), *Gaslight* (AA) (44), *The Bells of St Mary* (45), *Spellbound* (45), *Saratoga Trunk* (45), *Notorious* (46), *Arch of Triumph* (48), *Joan of Arc* (48), *Under Capricorn* (GB) (49), *Stromboli* (It.) (50), *Europa* (It.) (51), *We the Women* (It.) (53), *Journey to Italy* (It.) (54), *Joan at the Stake* (It.) (54), *Fear* (It.) (54), *Anastasia* (AA) (56), *Paris Does Strange Things* (Fr.) (57), *Indiscreet* (GB) (58), *The Inn of the Sixth Happiness* (GB) (58), *Goodbye Again* (Fr.) (61), *The Visit* (Fr./It.) (64), *The Yellow Rolls-Royce* (GB) (65), *Stimulantia* (Sw.) (67), *Cactus Flower* (US) (69), *A Walk in the Spring Rain* (US) (69).

BERGNER, ELISABETH (1900–   ). Austrian actress who in the 30s made several popular films in Britain: *Catherine the Great* (34), *Escape Me Never* (35), *As You Like It* (36), *Dreaming Lips* (37), *A Stolen Life* (39), *Paris Calling* (US) (41), etc. Now lives privately in London with director husband Paul Czinner (qv); plans 1970 comeback in *Cry of The Banshee*.

BERKE, WILLIAM (1904–1958). American director of second features. *Minesweeper* (43), *The Falcon in Mexico* (44), *Splitface* (46), *Jungle Jim* (48), *Deputy Marshal* (49), *Zamba the Gorilla* (49), *I Shot Billy the Kid* (also produced) (50), *Four Boys and a Gun* (also produced) (55), *Cop Hater* (also produced) (57), etc.

BERKELEY, BALLARD (1904–   ). British light actor of stage and screen. *The Chinese Bungalow* (30), *London Melody* (35), *The Outsider* (38), *In Which We Serve* (42), *They Made Me a Fugitive* (47), *The Long Dark Hall* (51), *Three Steps to the Gallows* (56), *See How They Run* (57), *Star* (68), etc.

BERKELEY, BUSBY (1895–   ) (William Berkeley Enos). American dance director who left Broadway for Hollywood soon after the coming of sound and developed the kaleidoscopically cinematic girlie numbers that were a feature of (especially) Warner musicals in the thirties. *Whoopee* (31), *Palmy Days* (32), *Roman Scandals* (33), *42nd Street* (33), *Footlight Parade* (33), *Dames* (34), *Fashions* (34), *Wonder Bar* (34), and the *Gold Diggers* series (33–37). Later directed complete movies: *Go into Your Dance* (36), *Stage Struck* (36), *Hollywood Hotel* (37), *Men Are Such Fools* (38), *They Made Me a Criminal* (39), *Babes in Arms* (39), *Babes on Broadway* (40), *Strike Up the Band* (40), *For Me and My Gal* (42), *The Gang's All Here* (44), *Cinderella*

Jones (45), *Take Me Out to the Ball Game (Everybody's Cheering)* (48), *Rose Marie* (numbers only) (54), *Jumbo* (numbers only) (62), etc.

BERKELEY SQUARE. The romantic/macabre play by John Balderston, about a man who enters his own past and falls in love with a girl of two hundred years ago, was delicately filmed in 1933 by Frank Lloyd, with Leslie Howard in the lead. The 1951 remake with Tyrone Power, alternatively known as *The House on the Square* and *I'll Never Forget You,* is best forgotten.

BERLANGA, LUIS (1921–). Spanish director; *Welcome Mr Marshall* (52), *Calabuch* (56), *The Executioner* (63), etc.

BERLE, MILTON (1908–) (Milton Berlinger). American vaudeville and TV comedian who has made occasional films: *Margin for Error* (43), *Always Leave Them Laughing* (his autobiography) (49), *It's a Mad Mad Mad Mad World* (63), *The Oscar* (65), *Who's Minding the Mint* (67), *The Happening* (67), *Heironymus Merkin* (69), etc. Between 1948 and 1956 his zany TV shows were so popular that he was generally known as 'Mr Television', but later attempts at a comeback failed.

Berlin has seemed to film makers a grim grey city, and history provides obvious reasons for this. Standard attitudes are shown in *The Murderers Are Amongst Us, Germany Year Zero, Four Men in a Jeep, Hotel Berlin, Berlin Express, The Man Between, Night People, The Big Lift, I Am a Camera, The Spy Who Came in from the Cold, The Man Who Finally Died, A Prize of Gold* and *Funeral in Berlin.* But some people have found fun there, notably Billy Wilder in *People on Sunday, A Foreign Affair* and *One Two Three*; and in 1928 Walter Ruttman's stylishly kaleidoscopic documentary, *Berlin: Symphony of a Great City,* showed the place and its people to be just as sympathetic as anywhere else once they are understandingly portrayed.

BERLIN, IRVING (1888–) (Israel Baline). Prolific American composer and writer of popular songs. Began as a singing waiter in New York. Among the films for which he has written songs are *The Awakening* (28), *The Cocoanuts* (29), *Hallelujah* (29), *Putting on the Ritz* (30), *Mammy* (30), *Reaching for the Moon* (31), *Kid Millions* (34), *Top Hat* (35), *Follow the Fleet* (36), *On the Avenue* (37), *Alexander's Ragtime Band* (38), *Carefree* (38), *Second Fiddle* (39), *Louisiana Purchase* (42), *Holiday Inn* (42), *This Is the Army* (in which he also appeared and sang 'Oh How I Hate to Get Up in the Morning') (43), *Blue Skies* (46), *Easter Parade* (47), *Annie Get Your Gun* (50), *Call Me Madam* (53), *There's No Business Like Show Business* (54), *White Christmas* (54), *Sayonara* (57). A biopic under the title *Say It with Music* is on MGM's schedule.

BERLINGER, WARREN (1937–   ). American light actor, usually as chubby innocent. Mostly on stage: films include *Teenage Rebel* (56), *Blue Denim* (59), *The Wackiest Ship in the Army* (60), *All Hands on Deck* (61).

BERMAN, MONTY (1913–   ). British producer, former cinematographer. Co-founder of Tempean Films (1948); films mainly second feature crime subjects, with occasional more ambitious projects such as *Jack the Ripper* (56), *The Flesh and the Fiends* (59), *Sea of Sand* (59), *Blood of the Vampire* (60), *The Hellfire Club* (61). TV series: *The Saint*.

BERMAN, PANDRO S. (1905–   ). American producer, with RKO in the 30s, later MGM. *Morning Glory* (32), *The Gay Divorce* (34), *Top Hat* (35), *The Hunchback of Notre Dame* (40), *The Picture of Dorian Gray* (44), *The Three Musketeers* (48), *Father of the Bride* (50), *The Blackboard Jungle* (55), *The Brothers Karamazov* (58), *Sweet Bird of Youth* (62), *A Patch of Blue* (66), many others.

BERMAN, SHELLEY (1926–   ). American entertainer and monologuist. Film appearances: *The Best Man* (64), *Divorce American Style* (67), *The St Valentine's Day Massacre* (67).

BERN, PAUL (1889–1932) (Paul Levy). MGM executive whose tragic death soon after his marriage to Jean Harlow is still a subject of controversy.

BERNARD, JAMES (1925–   ). British composer with a predilection for horror themes. *The Quatermass Experiment* (55), *Dracula* (58), *Windom's Way* (58), *The Hound of the Baskervilles* (59), *The Gorgon* (64), *The Plague of the Zombies* (65), etc. Co-authored film script, *Seven Days to Noon* (50).

BERNARDI, HERSCHEL (1923–   ). American general purpose actor often seen as cop or gangster. *A Cold Wind in August* (61), *The Honey Pot* (67), etc. Much on TV.

BERNDS, EDWARD (*   –   ). American director of second features, former sound effects man for the Three Stooges. *Harem Girl* (also wrote) (52), *Spy Chasers* (55), *World Without End* (also wrote) (56), *Quantrill's Raiders* (58), *The Return of the Fly* (also wrote) (59), *The Three Stooges in Orbit* (62), etc.

BERNHARDT, CURTIS (or KURT) (1899–   ). German director, in Hollywood since 1940. *The Beloved Vagabond* (GB) (38), *Lady with Red Hair* (41), *Million Dollar Baby* (41), *Juke Girl* (42), *Devotion* (43), *My Reputation* (44), *Conflict* (45), *A Stolen Life* (46), *Possessed* (48), *High Wall* (48), *Payment on Demand* (also wrote) (51), *The Blue Veil* (51), *The Merry Widow* (53), *Miss Sadie Thompson* (54), *Beau*

Brummell (54), *Interrupted Melody* (56), *Gaby* (56), *Kisses for My President* (also produced) (64), etc.

BERNHARDT, SARAH (1844–1923) (Rosalie Bernard). Famous French stage tragedienne who lent dignity if nothing else to early silent films: *La Dame aux Camélias* (10), *Queen Elizabeth* (12), etc.

BERNSTEIN, ELMER (1922–   ). American composer-conductor. Film scores include *Saturday's Hero* (51), *Sudden Fear* (52), *Cat Women of the Moon* (53), *The Man with the Golden Arm* (55), *The Ten Commandments* (56), *The Sweet Smell of Success* (57), *The Tin Star* (57), *God's Little Acre* (58), *The Buccaneer* (59), *The Magnificent Seven* (60), *A Walk on the Wild Side* (62), *To Kill a Mockingbird* (62), *Baby the Rain Must Fall* (65), *The Sons of Katie Elder* (65), *The Reward* (65), *Return of the Seven* (66), *Thoroughly Modern Millie* (AA) (67).

BERNSTEIN, LEONARD (1918–   ). American concert musician, conductor and composer. *On the Town* (49), *On the Waterfront* (54), *West Side Story* (61).

BERNSTEIN, SIDNEY (1899–   ). British executive and producer, founder and chairman of Granada Group, including an ITV programme company and a theatre group. Films adviser to Ministry of Information and SHAEF during World War II. Produced three films with Alfred Hitchcock as director: *Rope* (48), *Under Capricorn* (49), *I Confess* (53). Founder member of the Film Society (1924). First to institute Saturday morning shows for children and to investigate audience likes and dislikes (via the Bernstein Questionnaire).

BERRI, CLAUDE (1934–   ) (C. Langmann). French director. *The Two of Us* (*Le Vieil Homme et l'Enfant*) (also wrote) (66), *Le Mariage* (68), *Le Pistonné* (70).

†BERRY, JOHN (1917–   ). American director with stage experience. *Cross My Heart* (45), *From This Day Forward* (46), *Miss Susie Slagle's* (46), *Casbah* (48), *Tension* (49), *He Ran All the Way* (51), *Ca Va Barder* (French) (55), *The Great Lover* (*Don Juan*) (French) (55), *Tamango* (57), *Oh Que Mambo* (It.) (59), *Maya* (66).

BERRY, JULES (1883–1951) (Jules Paufichet). French actor most memorable as the villain of *Le Jour Se Lève* (39) and the devil in *Les Visiteurs du Soir* (42).

BEST, EDNA (1900–   ). British leading actress, once married to Herbert Marshall; went to Hollywood 1939 and stayed; still plays occasional character roles. *A Couple of Down and Outs* (23), *Escape* (30), *Tilly of Bloomsbury* (30), *The Calendar* (31), *Michael and Mary* (32), *The Faithful Heart* (32), *The Man Who Knew Too Much* (34), *South Riding* (38), *Escape to Happiness* (39), *The Swiss Family Robinson*

(40), *This Man Reuter* (40), *The Late George Apley* (46), *The Iron Curtain* (48), etc.

BEST, JAMES (1926–   ). American actor, mostly in Westerns, who can project slyness or virility. Much on TV. *Winchester 73* (50), *The Caine Mutiny* (54), *Come Next Spring* (56), *The Killer Shrews* (59), *The Mountain Road* (60), *Three on a Couch* (66), *Firecreek* (67), etc.

THE BEST MAN (US 1964). Biting political comedy, a film version by Franklin Schaffner of Gore Vidal's successful play about presidential nominations. Lee Tracy and Henry Fonda on top form, but stage origins not quite disguised.

BEST, WILLIE (1916–1962). American Negro comedian, memorable as the frightened manservant in *The Ghost Breakers* (41) and other thrillers. Known for a time as 'Sleep'n Eat'. Films include *The Monster Walks* (32), *The Nitwits* (35), *Nothing But the Truth* (41), *A Haunting We Will Go* (42), *The Bride Wore Boots* (46), *The Hidden Hand* (49).

THE BEST YEARS OF OUR LIVES (US 1946: AA). On its original release, this film about the resettlement of ex-servicemen in a small American town seemed like an enduring classic. Twenty years later the mood of the time is impossible to recapture and much of the film seems humdrum. But it was an important step in Hollywood's development towards maturity, presented by a highly talented group: director William Wyler (AA), cinematographer Gregg Toland, writer Robert E. Sherwood (AA), from a novel by Mackinlay Kantor. The cast included Fredric March (AA), Myrna Loy, Dana Andrews, Teresa Wright, and a handless veteran, Harold Russell (AA), whose only film this was.

BESWICK, MARTINE (1941–   ). British fashion model now appearing in films. *From Russia With Love* (63), *Thunderball* (65), *One Million Years B.C.* (66), etc.

LA BÊTE HUMAINE (France 1938). Jean Renoir's steamy emotional melodrama with a railway setting, released in Britain as *Judas Was a Woman*, starred Jean Gabin and Simone Simon, with photography by Curt Courant and music by Joseph Kosma. It was remade (US 1954) by Fritz Lang as *Human Desire*, with Glenn Ford and Broderick Crawford. The script was by Renoir from a novel by Zola.

BETTGER, LYLE (1915–   ). American screen actor who started in 1946 as leading man but seemed more at home in villainous roles. *No Man of Her Own* (49), *Union Station* (50), *The First Legion* (51), *All I Desire* (53), *The Greatest Show on Earth* (53), *The Sea Chase* (55),

Gunfight at the OK Corral (57), *Guns of the Timberland* (60), *Town Tamer* (65), *Nevada Smith* (66), etc. TV series: *Grand Jury* (58–59).

BETTY BOOP. Doll-like cartoon creation, a wide-eyed gold-digging flapper created by Max Fleischer in 1915 and popular throughout the twenties.

BETZ, CARL (1920–). American actor who established himself on TV as hubby in *The Donna Reed Show* (57–64), and in *Judd* (67). Films include *The President's Lady* (52), *Dangerous Crossing* (52), *Inferno* (53), *Spinout* (66), *The Girl From Peking* (70).

BEVAN, BILLY (1887–1957) (William Bevan Harris). Moustachioed silent comedian of British origin, with Mack Sennett in the 20s; later became a bit player and was often seen as a bewildered policeman. *Journey's End* (30), *Cavalcade* (33), *The Lost Patrol* (34), *Dracula's Daughter* (36), *Captain Fury* (39), *The Lodger* (44), *Cluny Brown* (46), *The Black Arrow* (48), many others.

BEVANS, CLEM (1880–1963). American actor, long-faced and latterly white-haired, who played 'pop' parts, doorkeepers, oldest inhabitants, etc., in countless films. Debut in *Way Down East* (35) after thirty years in vaudeville.

BEY, TURHAN (1920–) (Turhan Selahattin Sahultavy Bey). Turkish leading man who had a good run in Hollywood during World War II in the absence of more established faces. *Footsteps in the Dark* (41), *Drums of the Congo* (41), *Arabian Nights* (42), *The Mad Ghoul* (43), *White Savage* (43), *Dragon Seed* (44), *Bowery to Broadway* (44), *The Climax* (44), *Sudan* (45), *A Night in Paradise* (46), *Out of the Blue* (47), *Adventures of Casanova* (48), *Prisoners of the Casbah* (53), *Stolen Identity* (produced only) (53), etc. Now lives in Vienna as a photographer.

BEYMER, RICHARD (1939–). American child actor of the fifties: *So Big* (52), *Indiscretion of an American Wife* (54), *Johnny Tremaine* (57), etc. Later became juvenile lead: *The Diary of Anne Frank* (59), *Bachelor Flat* (61), *West Side Story* (61), *Hemingway's Adventures of a Young Man* (62), *Five Finger Exercise* (62), *The Stripper* (63), etc.

BEZZERIDES, A. I. (* –). American writer. *They Drive By Night* (40), *Thieves Highway* (49), *On Dangerous Ground* (51), *Beneath the Twelve Mile Reef* (53), *Track of the Cat* (54), *Kiss Me Deadly* (55), *The Jayhawkers* (59), etc.

BIANCHI, DANIELA (1942–). Italian leading lady seen abroad as heroine of *From Russia With Love* (63).

BIBERMAN, ABNER (1909–). American character actor who is equally convincing as Red Indian, Latin-American or Italian gangster. Stage experience before film debut in 1939. *Gunga Din* (39), *Each Dawn I Die* (39), *His Girl Friday* (40), *The Bridge of San Luis Rey* (44), *Captain Kid* (45), *Back to Bataan* (50), *Elephant Walk* (53), *Above All Things* (57), many others. Also directed: *The Price of Fear* (56), *Gun for a Coward* (57), etc.

BIBERMAN, HERBERT J. (1900–). American director whose career has been influenced by his political convictions. *Meet Nero Wolfe* (36), *The Master Race* (also wrote) (45), *Abilene Town* (produced only) (46), *Salt of the Earth* (53), *Slaves* (69), etc. Married to Gale Sondergaard.

THE BIBLE. The extravaganza which claimed to be the 'film of the book' was conceived by Dino de Laurentiis as a nine-hour survey by several directors. It turned up in 1966 as a slow plod through Genesis by and with John Huston. Of the hundreds of films which have been inspired by the Old Testament stories, some of the most memorable are *The Private Life of Adam and Eve*, *Sodom and Gomorrah*, *Green Pastures*, *A Story of David*, *David and Bathsheba*, *Samson and Delilah*, *The Prodigal*, *The Ten Commandments* (two versions), *Salome*, *Esther and the King* and *The Story of Ruth*. For the New Testament, see under CHRIST; the immediate effects of whose life have been treated in such assorted films as *The Robe*, *Demetrius and the Gladiators*, *The Sign of the Cross*, *The Big Fisherman*, *Quo Vadis*, *Ben Hur*, *Spartacus*, *Fabiola*, *Barabbas*, *The Silver Chalice*, and *The Fall of the Roman Empire*.

BICKFORD, CHARLES (1889–1967). American stage and screen actor, one of the great Hollywood dependables: he effortlessly projected men of rugged and thoughtful sincerity, but could be equally convincing in stubborn or unscrupulous roles. *Dynamite* (debut) (29), *Anna Christie* (31), *Little Miss Marker* (35), *Mutiny in the Big House* (39), *Of Mice and Men* (39), *Reap the Wild Wind* (42), *The Song of Bernadette* (43), *Captain Eddie* (45), *Duel in the Sun* (46), *The Farmer's Daughter* (47), *Woman on the Beach* (47), *Brute Force* (47), *Johnny Belinda* (48), *Treason* (50), *Man of Bronze* (52), *A Star Is Born* (54), *Prince of Players* (55), *The Court Martial of Billy Mitchell* (55), *Not as a Stranger* (55), *You Can't Run Away from It* (56), *Mister Cory* (56), *The Big Country* (58), *The Unforgiven* (59), *Days of Wine and Roses* (62), *A Big Hand for the Little Lady* (66), many others. Published autobiography 1965: *Bulls, Balls, Bicycles and Actors*. TV series: *The Virginian* (64–66).

BICYCLE THIEVES (Italy 1947). Hailed as the fount of Italian post-war realism, this simple tale of a billposter's quest for the bicycle essential to his job was actually in a well-established Italian tradition. It was nevertheless an absorbing and brilliant film which influenced film-making in every country where it was seen.

Vittorio de Sica directed from Cesare Zavattini's script, and the non-professional performances of Lamberto Maggiorani (the man) and Enzo Staiola (his son) were outstanding.

bicycling. A trade term for the sharing, usually illegally, of one print between two theatres: the manager had to make frequent bicycle trips!

big business was beyond the ken of silent movie-makers, but in the 30s it became a useful villain for the comedies and dramas of social conscience, and was usually personified by Edward Arnold. A switch was made in *Dodsworth*, in which the businessman became an innocent abroad. Not till the 50s did Hollywood think it worth while to probe into the lives of those who occupy the corridors of power. Then in quick succession we had *Executive Suite, Woman's World, Patterns of Power,* and *The Power and the Prize.* The inevitable knocking process began as early as *The Man in the White Suit* and continued with *The Man in the Grey Flannel Suit, Patterns of Power, The Solid Gold Cadillac, Cash McCall, The Apartment* and *The Wheeler Dealers.*

bigamists have not frequently been idolized by film-makers. Perhaps it is significant that although the Italian film called *The Bigamist* is a comedy, the American one of the same title is a solemn affair However, the last ten years or so have been sympathetic times for people like Alec Guinness in *The Captain's Paradise,* Clifton Webb in *The Remarkable Mr Pennypacker,* Leo McKern in *Decline and Fall* and Jean-Claude Drouot in *Le Bonheur.*

BIGGERS, EARL DERR (1884–1953). American crime novelist, the creator of Charlie Chan (qv).

THE BIG CARNIVAL: see ACE IN THE HOLE.

THE BIG HEAT (US 1953). A gangster film directed by Fritz Lang showing the new violence required and permitted in the 50s (one girl is exploded, another disfigured by scalding coffee). What made it worse was that the characters were recognizably human rather than mere film types.

THE BIG PARADE (US 1925). King Vidor's film of 'the average guy who went to war' cost a quarter of a million dollars and grossed fifteen million in two years, thus establishing its makers, MGM, as a top company. Photographed by John Arnold, from a play by Lawrence Stallings, it also established John Gilbert as a big star.

BIKEL, THEODORE (1924–   ). Heavily-built Viennese actor, guitarist and singer; can play most nationalities. International stage, TV, cabaret and film work. *The African Queen* (51), *The Love Lottery* (54),

The Pride and the Passion (57), *The Defiant Ones* (58), *The Blue Angel* (59), *A Dog of Flanders* (60), *My Fair Lady* (64), *Sands of the Kalahari* (65), *The Russians Are Coming, The Russians Are Coming* (66), *My Side of the Mountain* (68), etc.

BILL, TONY (1940–   ). American light leading man. *Come Blow Your Horn* (63), *None But the Brave* (65), *Marriage on the Rocks* (66), *Ice Station Zebra* (68), *Castle Keep* (69), *Nobody Loves Flapping Eagle* (70), etc.

billing. The official credits for a film, usually stating the relative sizes of type to be accorded to title, stars, character actors, etc.

BILLINGTON, KEVIN (1933–   ). British director, from TV. *Interlude* (68), *The Rise and Rise of Michael Rimmer* (70).

A BILL OF DIVORCEMENT. Clemence Dane's play about the return of a deranged father from a mental institution was made into a topical film in 1932, with Katharine Hepburn in her film debut playing opposite John Barrymore. It was directed by George Cukor. By the time of John Farrow's scene-for-scene remake in 1940 the material seemed artificial and old-fashioned; Maureen O'Hara lacked Hepburn's intensity, though Adolphe Menjou was surprisingly good as the father.

Billy the Kid, the historical, homicidal Western gunslinger, has frequently been turned by the movies into some kind of hero. A favourite character of the silents, he has been seen also in numerous talkie versions. Johnny Mack Brown played him on the wide screen in *Billy the Kid* (30); pious Roy Rogers was the star of *Billy the Kid Returns* (39); in 1940 Robert Taylor was *Billy the Kid*; and in 1943 (or so) came *The Outlaw*, with a happy ending for Jack Buetel who played Billy. In 1949 Audie Murphy played Billy in *The Kid from Texas*; 1950 brought *I Shot Billy the Kid* with Don Barry; 1954 *The Law Versus Billy the Kid* with Scott Brady; 1955 *The Parson and the Outlaw* with Anthony Dexter; 1958 *The Left-handed Gun* with Paul Newman; and in 1966 we were even offered *Billy the Kid Meets Dracula*. There were also scores of second features in the 30s and 40s, with Bob Steele or Buster Crabbe as Billy; whose real name incidentally was William Bonney and who died in 1881 at the age of 21.

BING, HERMAN (1889–1947). German comedy actor, former assistant to F. W. Murnau. In Hollywood from 1929, usually in excitable roles. *The Guardsman* (32), *Dinner at Eight* (33), *Call of the Wild* (34), *Rose Marie* (36), *The Great Ziegfeld* (36), *Sweethearts* (38), *Bitter Sweet* (41), *Where Do We Go From Here* (45), *Rendezvous 24* (46), etc.

BINYON, CLAUDE (1905–   ). American writer-director. *Arizona* (w) (40), *Suddenly It's Spring* (w) (44), *The Saxon Charm* (w, d) (48),

Family Honeymoon (w, d) (49), *Mother Didn't Tell Me* (w) (50), *Stella* (w, d) (50), *Aaron Slick from Punkin Crick* (w, d) (52), *Dreamboat* (w, d) (52), *You Can't Run Away From It* (w) (56), *North to Alaska* (w) (60), *Kisses for My President* (w) (64), etc.

Biograph. 1. An old name for a cinema projector. 2. Britain's first public cinema, near Victoria Station, London. Opened 1905, still operating. 3. The name of D. W. Griffith's New York studios, 1903–1910.

biopic. A contraction of 'biographical picture', i.e. a film about the life of a real person. For examples see under *Composers, Courtesans, Explorers, Entertainers, Inventors, Kings and Queens, Painters, Politicians, Scientists, Soldiers, Spies, Sportsmen, Writers.*

BIRD, NORMAN (c. 1920–   ). British character actor, usually of underdogs. *An Inspector Calls* (54), *The League of Gentlemen* (59), *Victim* (62), *The Hill* (65), *Sky West and Crooked* (65), *The Wrong Box* (66), many others.

BIRD, RICHARD (1894–   ). British light actor who played genial middle-aged roles in the 30s. *Guy of Bloomsbury* (31), *Mimi* (35), *Sensation* (37), *The Terror* (also directed) (38), *The Door with 7 Locks* (40), *Halfway House* (44), *Forbidden* (49), many others.

birds fit nicely into the glamorous romantic backgrounds of which Hollywood used to be so fond, but a few particular examples have been malevolent, including *The Vulture*, the owner of *The Giant Claw*, the carnivorous birds which nearly pecked *Barbarella* to death, and of course *The Birds* which turned on the human race in Hitchcock's 1964 movie. (In the various versions of Edgar Allan Poe's *The Raven*, the title character has been almost irrelevant.) Other notable birds have been seen in *Treasure Island, Birdman of Alcatraz, The Pigeon that Took Rome, Run Wild Run Free, The Bluebird* and *Bill and Coo*; and in the cartoon field one must remember with affection Donald and Daffy Duck, Tweetie Pie and an assortment of other feathered friends.

BIRELL, TALA (1908–   ) (Natalie Bierle). Polish-Austrian leading lady who appeared in some international films of the thirties. *Men in a Cage* (GB) (30), *Doomed Battalion* (US) (31), *Crime and Punishment* (US) (36), *Josette* (US) (38), *The Purple Heart* (US) (43), *The House of Tao Ling* (US) (47), etc.

BIRKETT, MICHAEL (1929–   ). British producer, mainly of specialized entertainments: *The Caretaker* (63), *The Soldier's Tale* (64), *Modesty Blaise* (associate) (66), *The Marat/Sade* (66), *A Midsummer Night's Dream* (68), etc.

BIRO, LAJOS (1880–1948). Hungarian screenwriter with Hollywood experience in the 20s followed by much work for Korda in Britain. *Forbidden Paradise* (24), *The Last Command* (27), *The Way of All Flesh* (38), *Service for Ladies* (32), *The Private Life of Henry VIII* (32), *Catherine the Great* (34), *The Scarlet Pimpernel* (34), *Sanders of the River* (35), *The Divorce of Lady X* (37), *The Drum* (38), *The Four Feathers* (39), *The Thief of Baghdad* (40), etc.; mostly in collaboration.

BIROC, JOSEPH F. (1903–). American cinematographer. *It's a Wonderful Life* (46), *Magic Town* (47), *Roughshod* (49), *Without Warning* (52), *The Tall Texan* (53), *Down Three Dark Streets* (54), *Nightmare* (56), *Run of the Arrow* (56), *Attack* (57), *The Ride Back* (57), *The Amazing Colossal Man* (57), *Home Before Dark* (58), *Hitler* (61), *Bye Bye Birdie* (63), *Bullet for a Badman* (64), *Hush Hush Sweet Charlotte* (64), *I Saw What You Did* (65), *The Flight of the Phoenix* (65), *The Russians Are Coming, The Russians Are Coming* (66), *The Killing of Sister George* (68), *Whatever Happened to Aunt Alice?* (69), etc.

BIRT, DANIEL (1907–1955). British director, former editor: busy in late 40s. *The Three Weird Sisters* (48), *No Room at the Inn* (49), *The Interrupted Journey* (49), *Circumstantial Evidence* (52), *Background* (53), etc.

THE BIRTH OF A NATION (US 1914). D. W. Griffith's monumental melodrama of the American Civil War and its aftermath, supposedly the biggest money-maker of all time (allowing for rising costs), has become something of an embarrassment to Hollywood in view of its anti-Negro bias. It remains exciting to watch, especially during the battle sequences and the final 'heroic' rescue charge of the Ku Klux Klan; and it abounds in technical innovations which became current usage. Various versions have been reissued with sound effects. Written by Griffith and Frank Woods from Thomas Dixon's novel 'The Clansman'; photographed by Billy Bitzer.

BISCHOFF, SAMUEL (1890–). American producer, with Warners in 30s (*The Charge of the Light Brigade* [36,] *A Slight Case of Murder* [38], etc.); Columbia 1941–46 (*You'll Never Get Rich* [41], *A Night to Remember* [43], etc.); subsequently worked independently. *Macao* (51), *The Phoenix City Story* (55), *The Big Bankroll* (59), *Operation Eichmann* (60), etc.

BISHOP, JOEY (1919–) (Joseph Abraham Gottlieb). American TV comedian who has made few film appearances. *Sergeants Three* (63), *Texas across the River* (66), *A Guide for the Married Man* (67), *Who's Minding the Mint* (67). TV series: *The Joey Bishop Show* (61–64).

BISHOP, JULIE (1917–   ). American leading lady of routine films; also known as Jacqueline Wells. *Alice in Wonderland* (33), *The Bohemian Girl* (36), *The Nurse's Secret* (41), *Rhapsody in Blue* (45), *Sands of Iwo Jima* (49), *Westward the Women* (52), *The High and the Mighty* (54), many others.

BISHOP, TERRY (1912–   ). British director: *You're Only Young Twice* (52), *Model for Murder* (58), *Cover Girl Killer* (59), *The Unstoppable Man* (61), etc. Much TV work.

BISHOP, WILLIAM (1918–1959). American leading man, mostly in routine features. *Pillow to Post* (46), *The Romance of Rosy Ridge* (47), *Anna Lucasta* (49), *Cripple Creek* (52), *The Boss* (56), *The Oregon Trail* (59), etc.

BISSELL, WHIT (c. 1914–   ). American character actor who plays anything from attorneys to garage attendants. *Holy Matrimony* (43), *Another Part of the Forest* (47), *It Should Happen to You* (53), *The Young Stranger* (57), *Teenage Frankenstein* (58), *The Time Machine* (60), *Hud* (63), *Seven Days in May* (64), many others.

BISSET, JACQUELINE (1944–   ). British leading lady in American films. *The Detective* (68), *Bullitt* (68), *You Don't Need Pajamas at Rosie's* (69), *L'Echelle Blanche* (Fr.) (69), *Airport* (69), *The Grasshopper* (70), etc.

BITTER SWEET. Noel Coward's operetta was filmed twice: with Anna Neagle and Fernand Gravet (GB 1933) and with Jeanette Mac-Donald and Nelson Eddy (US 1940).

BITZER, BILLY (1874–1944). American cameraman who worked with D. W. Griffith on his most important films and is credited with several major photographic developments. *The New York Hat* (12), *Judith of Bethulia* (13), *Birth of a Nation* (14), *Intolerance* (15), *Hearts of the World* (18), *Broken Blossoms* (19), *Way Down East* (21), *America* (24), *The Struggle* (30), many others.

BIXBY, BILL (1934–   ). American leading man, in TV series *My Favourite Martian* (63–65), *The Courtship of Eddie's Father* (69). Films include *Lonely Are the Brave* (62), *Irma la Douce* (63), *Under the Yum Yum Tree* (64), *Spinout* (67).

BJORK, ANITA (1923–   ). Swedish actress who was internationally acclaimed for *Miss Julie* (51); subsequent films have been little seen outside Sweden apart from *Night People* (US) (54).

BJORNSTRAND, GUNNAR (1909–   ). Swedish character actor, prominent in *Frenzy* (44), *Waiting Women* (52), *Sawdust and Tinsel* (53), *Smiles of a Summer Night* (55), *The Seventh Seal* (56), *Through a Glass Darkly* (61), *Winter Light* (62), *Loving Couples* (65), *Persona* (66), *The Red Mantle* (67), etc.

THE BLACK CAT. Two of the best-known films under this title had nothing whatever to do with the Poe story on which they were allegedly based. They were the 1934 film about devil worshippers, with Karloff and Lugosi, and the 1941 thunderstorm mystery with Basil Rathbone. The Poe story was more faithfully treated in *The Living Dead* (Ger.) (33), *Tales of Terror* (US) (62), and *The Black Cat* (US) (67).

black comedy derives humour from serious matters such as death, murder, neurosis, sex perversion. It is enjoyed chiefly by those with sophisticated tastes. Notable black comedies since sound have included *Bondu Sauvé des Eaux*, *The Front Page*, the various Laurel and Hardy sequences involving physical distortion, *The Old Dark House*, *Bride of Frankenstein*, *Drôle de Drame*, *A Slight Case of Murder*, *Here Comes Mr Jordan*, *Kind Hearts and Coronets*, *The Criminal Life of Archibaldo de la Cruz*, *The Naked Truth*, *A Comedy of Terrors*, *She'll Have to Go*, *The Wrong Box*, *The Loved One*, *Who's Afraid of Virginia Woolf*, *The Fearless Vampire Killers*, *The Honey Pot*, *The Anniversary*, *The Assassination Bureau*. Elements of black comedy are found in many modern films, notably the James Bond series and the films of Billy Wilder, John Huston, Alfred Hitchcock and Joseph L. Mankiewicz.

Black Maria. In the history of film this evocative phrase for a police van has a secondary meaning, being the nickname given to Edison's first portable studio.

BLACK ORPHEUS (France 1959). The myth of Orpheus and Eurydice was given a Negro setting in this visually splendid but dramatically unsatisfactory piece written and directed by Marcel Camus. With Marpessa Dawn, Breno Mello.

BLACK, NOEL (1937–). American director of short films (*Skaterdater*, etc.). Graduated to features with *Pretty Poison* (68), *Run Shadow Run* (69).

BLACK, STANLEY (1913–). British bandleader and composer. responsible for scoring nearly 200 films during the last thirty years. *Rhythm Racketeers* (36), *Mrs Fitzherbert* (47), *It Always Rains on Sunday* (47), *Laughter in Paradise* (50), *The Trollenberg Terror* (57), *Hell Is a City* (60), *The Young Ones* (61), *Summer Holiday* (63), etc.

THE BLACKBOARD JUNGLE (US 1955). A classroom melodrama which (*a*) shocked by its revelation of America's teenage hoodlum problem, (*b*) introduced 'Rock Around the Clock' which was played over the credits by Bill Haley and the Comets. Directed by Richard Brooks, with Glenn Ford as the harassed teacher.

BLACKMAIL (GB 1930). The first British sound film, shot by Alfred

Hitchcock as a silent and partially remade when sound came in. The story is still told mainly of visual terms, with many typical Hitchcock touches. The voice in Anny Ondra, who played the heroine, was too foreign-sounding and had to be dubbed.

THE BLACK PIRATE (US 1926). A typical Douglas Fairbanks silent swashbuckler, involving an experimental use of colour. Directed by Albert Parker, photographed by Henry Sharp.

BLACKMAN, HONOR (1926–   ). British leading lady, a Rank 'charm school' product submerged in 'English rose' roles from 1946 until the TV series 'The Avengers' fitted her up with kinky suits and judo tactics. *Fame Is the Spur* (47), *Quartet* (48), *Diamond City* (49), *So Long at the Fair* (50), *The Rainbow Jacket* (53), *Breakaway* (55), *The Square Peg* (58), *A Matter of Who* (61), *Goldfinger* (64), *The Secret of My Success* (65), *Life at the Top* (65), *Moment to Moment* (65), *A Twist of Sand* (68), *Shalako* (68), *Captain Nemo* (69), *Grigsby* (69), *The Virgin and the Gypsy* (70), etc.

BLACKMER, SIDNEY (1898–   ). American character actor of stage and screen: has often played smooth crook or politician. *A Most Immoral Lady* (29), *Little Caesar* (30), *The Count of Monte Cristo* (34), *Wife, Doctor and Nurse* (37), *In Old Chicago* (38), *Gallant Lady* (42), *Quiet Please, Murder* (43), *Duel in the Sun* (46), *My Girl Tisa* (as Teddy Roosevelt) (48), *People Will Talk* (50), *The High and the Mighty* (54), *High Society* (56), *Tammy and the Bachelor* (57), *How to Murder Your Wife* (65), *Covenant with Death* (67), *Rosemary's Baby* (68), many others.

BLACKTON, J. STUART (1868–1941). British-born film pioneer who worked with Edison. Later produced (and usually directed) *Raffles* (05), *The Life of Moses* (10), *Womanhood* (16), *The Glorious Adventure* (in Prizmacolour) (21), *Gypsy Cavalier* (24), *The Redeeming Sin* (25), *Bride of the Storm* (30), others.

BLACKWELL, CARLYLE (1888–1955). American matinée idol who was in successful film version of *Uncle Tom's Cabin* (09) and remained in demand throughout the 20s. *The Key to Yesterday* (14), *The Restless Sex* (20), *Sherlock Holmes* (22), *The Beloved Vagabond* (23), *Bulldog Drummond* (23), *She* (25), *The Wrecker* (29), *The Crooked Billet* (30), etc. His declamatory style could scarcely survive the coming of sound.

BLAIN, GERARD (1930–   ). French leading man. *Les Fruits Sauvages* (53), *Crime et Chatiment* (55), *Desire Takes the Men* (56), *Les Mistons* (57), *Le Beau Serge* (58), *Les Cousins* (58), *Hatari* (62), etc.

BLAINE, VIVIAN (1921–   ) (Vivienne Stapleton). American leading lady and singer who made a pleasant but hardly memorable impression in 40s musicals like *Jitterbugs* (42), *Greenwich Village* (44),

Blair, Betsy

Nob Hill (45), *Three Little Girls in Blue* (46). Became a Broadway star but made only three other films: *Skirts Ahoy* (52), *Guys and Dolls* (55), *Public Pigeon Number One* (57).

BLAIR, BETSY (1923–   ) (Betsy Boger). American leading actress who has often played plain or nervous women. *Another Part of the Forest* (48), *The Snake Pit* (48), *Kind Lady* (51), *Marty* (BFA) (55), *Calle Mayor* (*Grand Rue*) (Spain) (56), *Il Grido* (*The Cry*) (Italian) (57), *The Halliday Brand* (57), *All Night Long* (GB) (61), etc.

BLAIR, GEORGE (1906–1970). American director of second features. *Duke of Chicago* (48), *Flaming Fury* (49), *Daughter of the Jungle* (49), *Insurance Investigator* (51), *Jaguar* (55), *The Hypnotic Eye* (60), etc.

BLAIR, JANET (1921–   ). American leading lady of the 40s. *Three Girls About Town* (42), *Broadway* (42), *My Sister Eileen* (43), *Once Upon A Time* (44), *The Fabulous Dorseys* (47), *I Love Trouble* (48), then on stage; *Night of the Eagle* (GB) (62), *Boys' Night Out* (62), etc.

BLAKE, AMANDA (c. 1931–   ) (Beverly Louise Neill). American leading lady, notably seen as Kitty in long-running TV series *Gunsmoke* (56–69). Films include *Battleground* (50), *Lili* (53), *About Mrs Leslie* (54), *High Society* (56).

BLAKE, ROBERT (1934–   ). American character actor. *Battle Flame* (59), *In Cold Blood* (leading role) (67), etc. TV series: *The Richard Boone Show* (64).

BLAKELY, COLIN (1930–   ). British stage actor, in occasional films. *This Sporting Life* (62), *The Informers* (63), *The Long Ships* (64), *The Spy with a Cold Nose* (67), *Charlie Bubbles* (67), *The Day the Fish Came Out* (67), *The Vengeance of She* (68), *Decline and Fall* (68), *The Private Life of Sherlock Holmes* (as Watson) (69), *Alfred the Great* (69), etc.

BLAKELEY, JOHN E. (1889–1958). British producer-director of low-budget Lancashire comedies. *Somewhere in England* (40), *Somewhere in Camp* (42), *Demobbed* (44), *Home Sweet Home* (46), *Cup Tie Honeymoon* (48), *It's a Grand Life* (53), etc.

BLAKELEY, TOM (1918–   ). British producer of second features. *Love's a Luxury* (58), *Tomorrow at Ten* (62), *Devils of Darkness* (65), *Island of Terror* (66), etc.

BLANC, MEL (1908–   ). The voice of Warner Brothers' cartoon characters, including Bugs Bunny, Sylvester and Tweetie Pie. Makes occasional cameo appearances in films.

BLANCHAR, PIERRE (1892–1963). Distinguished French screen and stage actor, remembered abroad chiefly for *Un Carnet de Bal* (37). Also in *Jocelyn* (23), *L'Atlantide* (31), *Le Diable en Bouteille* (34),

Crime and Punishment (35), *Mademoiselle Docteur* (36), *L'Affaire du Courrier de Lyon* (37), *Pontcarral* (42), *La Symphonie Pastorale* (46), *Rififi Chez les Femmes* (58), etc.

BLANCHARD, MARI (1927–   ). American leading lady prominent in Universal co-features of the 50s: *Veils of Bagdad* (53), *Destry* (54), *The Crooked Web* (56), *The Return of Jack Slade* (56), *Jungle Heat* (57), *McLintock* (63), etc.

BLANDICK, CLARA (1881–1962). American character actress usually seen as no-nonsense aunt or sensible servant. *The Wizard of Oz* (39), *Rings on Her Fingers* (42), *Life With Father* (47), *Key to the City* (50), many others from 1929.

BLANKE, HENRY (1901–   ). German-American producer long associated with Warner Brothers. Films include *A Midsummer Night's Dream* (35), *Green Pastures* (37), *The Life of Emile Zola* (38), *The Adventures of Robin Hood* (38), *The Maltese Falcon* (41), *The Treasure of the Sierra Madre* (48), *Room for One More* (52), *Young at Heart* (54), *The Nun's Story* (58), *Hell Is for Heroes* (62), etc.

BLASETTI, ALESSANDRO (1900–   ). Italian director mainly associated with comedy and spectaculars. *Sole* (29), *Nero* (30), *Resurrection* (31), *The Old Guard* (33), *The Countess of Parma* (37), *Four Steps in the Clouds* (42), *A Day of Life* (46), *Fabiola* (48), *First Communion* (50), *Altri Tempi (Infidelity)* (52), *Europe by Night* (59), *I Love You Love* (61), many others.

BLATT, EDWARD A. (1905–   ). American director who worked for Warners in the 40s. *Between Two Worlds* (44), *Escape in the Desert* (45), *Smart Woman* (48), etc. Returned to stage and TV.

BLAUSTEIN, JULIAN (1913–   ). American producer with wide show business experience. *Broken Arrow* (50), *Désirée* (54), *Storm Centre* (56), *Bell Book and Candle* (58), *The Four Horsemen of the Apocalypse* (62), *Khartoum* (66), etc.

BLIER, BERNARD (1916–   ). French actor who makes a virtue of his plumpness and baldness. Memorable in *Hôtel du Nord* (38), *Quai des Orfèvres* (47), *Dédée d'Anvers* (47), *L'École Buissonière* (48), *Manèges (The Wanton)* (49), *Souvenirs Perdus* (50), *Les Misérables* (57), *Les Grandes Familles* (58), *Le Cave Se Rebiffe* (61), *Les Saintes Nitouches* (63), *A Question of Honour* (Italy) (66), *Breakdown* (also directed) (67), etc.

blimp. A soundproof cover fixed over a camera during shooting to absorb running noise.

BLIND HUSBANDS (US 1919). The start of Erich von Stroheim's short-lived but spectacular career as a Hollywood actor-writer-director, this bitterly ironic study of a military seducer had all the savage wit for which he is remembered as well as hints of the extravagance which caused his downfall.

Blindness, a tragic affliction in real life, has on the whole been treated by movie-makers with discretion, often to provide irony, as in *Bride of Frankenstein*, when the blind hermit innocently makes a friend of the monster and lives happily with him until sighted people come on the scene. In *Tread Softly Stranger* a murderer gives himself away through fear of the only witness—who turns out to be blind. In *Silent Dust* a blind man wins a battle in the dark with the villain; and in *Faces in the Dark* a blind man successfully traps his would-be murderers. Edward Arnold played a blind detective, Duncan McLain, in an MGM series of the 40s, and Herbert Marshall as a blind pianist in *The Enchanted Cottage* gave advice to those otherwise handicapped. Dick Powell was blinded by cordite fumes in *Farewell My Lovely*; and Esmond Knight, while genuinely blinded by a war injury, played a normal-sighted role in *The Silver Fleet*. Serious, and mainly sentimental, blind roles have been played by Irene Dunne (later Jane Wyman) in *Magnificent Obsession*, by Ronald Colman (later Fredric March) in *The Dark Angel*, by Arthur Kennedy in *Bright Victory*, by Jean-Louis Barrault in *La Symphonie Pastorale*, by Michael Wilding in *Torch Song*, by Elizabeth Hartman in *A Patch of Blue*, by Virginia Cherrill in *City Lights*, by Van Johnson in *23 Paces to Baker Street*, by Ronald Colman in *The Light That Failed*, by John Garfield in *Pride of the Marines*, by O. P. Heggie in *Bride of Frankenstein*, by Hilton Edwards in *Victim*, by Patricia Neal in *Psyche '59*, by the genuinely blind pianist Ray Charles in *Ballad in Blue*, and by Nicol Williamson in *Laughter in the Dark*. Two terrified blind heroines were Patricia Dainton in *Witness in the Dark* and Audrey Hepburn in *Wait Until Dark*.

BLISS, SIR ARTHUR (1891–   ). British composer whose major work for the cinema has been the score for *Things to Come* (36). Also composed for *Christopher Columbus* (49).

BLITHE SPIRIT (GB 1945). The nearest British films have come to cocktail comedy, this smooth and glossy version of Noel Coward's ghostly farce was directed by David Lean, photographed in Technicolor by Ronald Neame, and starred Rex Harrison, Kay Hammond, Margaret Rutherford and Constance Cummings.

BLOCH, ROBERT (1917–   ). American novelist and screenwriter associated exclusively with horror themes. *Psycho* (60), *The Cabinet of Dr Caligari* (62), *Straitjacket* (63), *The Night Walker* (64), *The Psychopath* (66), *The Deadly Bees* (66), *The Torture Garden* (67), etc. TV series: *Thriller, Alfred Hitchcock Presents*.

BLOCKER, DAN (c. 1930–   ). Heavyweight American character actor well known as Hoss in TV series *Bonanza* (59–69). Film appearances: *Come Blow Your Horn* (63), *Lady in Cement* (68).

block booking. A system supposedly illegal but still practised, whereby a renter forces an exhibitor to book a whole group of mainly mediocre films in order to get the one or two he wants.

BLOCKADE (US 1938). A rare indication (in its period) of Hollywood's awareness of the world outside. Walter Wanger produced this melodrama of the Spanish Civil War, but despite good intentions it wasn't easy to tell whose side the film was on. Henry Fonda and Madeleine Carroll starred.

BLOMFIELD, DEREK (1920–1964). British boy actor of the 30s. *Emil and the Detectives* (35), *Turn of the Tide* (35), *The Ghost of St Michael's* (41), *Alibi* (42), *Night and the City* (50), *Hobson's Choice* (54), *Carry On Admiral* (57), etc.

BLONDELL, JOAN (1909–   ). American comedienne who played the slightly dizzy friend of the heroine in many 30s musicals; later graduated to character roles. *Sinner's Holiday* (30), *Night Nurse* (32), *Miss Pinkerton* (32), *The Greeks Had a Word for Them* (32), *Footlight Parade* (32), *Gold Diggers of 1933*, *Three on a Match* (33), *Dames* (34), *Bullets or Ballots* (36), *Gold Diggers of 1937*, *The Perfect Specimen* (37), *Stand In* (37), *Good Girls Go to Paris* (39), *Model Wife* (40), *Topper Returns* (41), *Three Girls about Town* (41), *Lady for a Night* (41), *Cry Havoc* (43), *A Tree Grows in Brooklyn* (45), *Adventure* (46), *Christmas Eve* (47), *Nightmare Alley* (48), *The Blue Veil* (51), *The Opposite Sex* (56), *The Desk Set* (*His Other Woman*) (56), *Lizzie* (59), *Angel Baby* (60), *The Cincinatti Kid* (65), *Ride Beyond Vengeance* (65), *Waterhole Three* (67), *Stay Away Joe* (68), etc. TV series: *Here Come the Brides* (68).

BLONDIE. Chic Young's comic strip about family man Dagwood Bumstead and his pretty wife was first filmed in 1938 by Columbia, with Arthur Lake and Penny Singleton, also Jonathan Hale as Mr Dithers, Larry Simms as Baby Dumpling (later Alexander) and a dog (called Daisy) with star quality. It was so successful that Columbia produced an average of one Blondie film every six months for the next ten years; most of them were directed by Frank Strayer or Abby Berlin. All had 'Blondie' in the title except *The Boss Said No* (42), *A Bundle of Trouble* (42), and *Henpecked* (46); the last of all was *Blondie's Hero* (50). Lake and Pamela Britton appeared in a TV series in the early fifties, and the project was revived in 1968 with Will Hutchins and Patricia Harty.

BLOOD AND SAND. This tragic novel of the bullring by Vicente Blasco Ibanez has twice been filmed in Hollywood. In 1922, directed by

Bloom, Claire

Fred Niblo, it became one of Rudolph Valentino's most popular vehicles, with Lila Lee and Nita Naldi as co-stars. In the 1941 colour version directed by Rouben Mamoulian, the leading roles were filled by Tyrone Power, Linda Darnell and Rita Hayworth.

BLOOM, CLAIRE (1931–). British leading lady who came to the screen via the Old Vic. *The Blind Goddess* (48), *Limelight* (52), *Innocents in Paris* (52), *The Man Between* (53), *Richard III* (56), *Alexander the Great* (56), *The Brothers Karamazov* (58), *Look Back in Anger* (59), *The Buccaneer* (59), *The Chapman Report* (61), *The Wonderful World of the Brothers Grimm* (63), *The Haunting* (63), *The Outrage* (64), *The Spy Who Came in from the Cold* (66), *Charly* (68), *Three into Two Won't Go* (69), *The Illustrated Man* (69), *A Severed Head* (69).

bloop. To cover a join in the sound track, usually with thick 'blooping ink'.

BLORE, ERIC (1887–1959). British comic actor with stage experience; went to Hollywood in 1934 and played unctuous/insulting butlers and other eccentric types in many films. *The Gay Divorce* (34), *Top Hat* (35), *Michael Strogoff* (37), *A Gentleman's Gentleman* (39), *The Lone Wolf* series (40–47), *Sullivan's Travels* (41), *The Moon and Sixpence* (42), *Holy Matrimony* (43), *Kitty* (46), *Fancy Pants* (50), *Love Happy* (50), *Babes in Baghdad* (52), etc.

BLOW-UP (GB 1967). Michelangelo Antonioni's first film in English and his most successful practical joke to date, a fashionably decorated but empty anecdote in which, as usual, many questions are posed but none answered. David Hemmings plays a selfish photographer who thinks he has witnessed a murder but never finds out whether he imagined the whole thing; the theme is dislocated by irrelevant sex sequences. Carlos di Palma's photography is exquisite and a general sense of style prevents total boredom.

blow up. To magnify an image, either a photograph for background purposes, or a piece of film (e.g. from 16mm to 35mm).

THE BLUE ANGEL (Germany 1930). This heavy melodrama, with Emil Jannings as a professor ignobly infatuated with a tawdry night club singer, was made in both German and English. The latter version made an international star of Marlene Dietrich, whose throaty rendering of 'Falling In Love Again' became a cinema landmark. Sombrely Teutonic in mood and setting, with tirelessly tricksy direction by Joseph von Sternberg, the film still packs a punch for patient audiences. It was written by Karl Zuckmayer from a novel by Heinrich Mann, with music by Frederick Hollander. Remade (unsuccessfully) in Hollywood in 1959, with Curt Jurgens and May Britt.

BLUE, BEN (1900–   ). American rubber-limbed comedian with vaudeville experience: also night-club owner. Films occasionally from 1926 include *College Rhythm* (33), *High, Wide and Handsome* (38), *For Me and My Gal* (42), *Thousands Cheer* (43), *My Wild Irish Rose* (47), *It's a Mad Mad Mad Mad World* (63), *The Russians Are Coming, The Russians Are Coming* (66), *Where Were You When the Lights Went Out* (68).

THE BLUEBIRD (US 1940). Maurice Maeterlinck's rather eerie child-fantasy, with its moral that happiness is to be found in one's own back-yard, made one of Hollywood's more successful excursions into the supernatural, moving gracefully from the land of the dead to the land of those unborn; but it appealed less widely than its brasher rival *The Wizard of Oz*. Filmed in soft colour, it was directed by Walter Lang with Shirley Temple, Gale Sondergaard and Eddie Collins heading the cast. There had been a silent version in 1916, with Robin MacDougall and Tula Belle.

THE BLUE LAMP (GB 1950). This documentary-style crime story about the work of the London police is said to have done a great deal of good to the police image. It certainly produced many imitators, and the policeman played by Jack Warner, though killed in the film, was revived on BBC for the long-running series *Dixon of Dock Green*. Directed by Basil Dearden; BFA best British film.

BLUE, MONTE (1890–1963). American actor, originally a lumberjack, who was in most of Griffith's great silents and later became a popular tough hero. Talkies relegated him to bit parts but he never retired. *Intolerance* (15), *Till I Come Back to You* (18), *The Affairs of Anatol* (20), *Orphans of the Storm* (22), *The Marriage Circle* (24), *One-Round Hogan* (27), *White Shadows of the South Seas* (28), *The Flood* (31), *Lives of a Bengal Lancer* (35), *Souls at Sea* (37), *Dodge City* (39), *The Mask of Dimitrios* (44), *The Tomahawk Trail* (50), *Apache* (54), many others.

BLUM, DANIEL (1900–1965). American writer, editor and collector; annually produced *Theatre World* and *Screen World* annuals.

BLYSTONE, JOHN G. (1892–1938). American director, former actor. *The Sky Hawk* (21), *Seven Chances* (25), *Mother Knows Best* (28), *Tolable David* (30), *Charlie Chan's Chance* (32), *Jubilo* (32), *Change of Heart* (34), *Blockheads* (38), many others.

BLYTH, ANN (1928–   ). American leading lady who originally trained for opera. Began her film career in Donald O'Connor musicals, then graduated to dramatic roles with occasional musicals. *Chip Off the Old Block* (43), *The Merry Monahans* (44), *Babes on Swing Street* (45), *Mildred Pierce* (a momentous role as the evil daughter) (45), *Brute Force* (47), *A Woman's Vengeance* (48), *Mr Peabody and the Mermaid* (48), *Top o' the Morning* (49), *Our Very Own* (50), *The Great Caruso* (51), *The House on the Square* (51), *One Minute to Zero* (52), *Sally and Saint Anne* (52), *All the Brothers Were Valiant* (53), *Rose Marie* (54), *The Student Prince* (54), *Kismet* (55), *The Helen Morgan Story (Both Ends of the Candle)* (57), *The Buster Keaton Story* (57), etc. Retired to private life but is occasionally seen on TV.

BLYTHE, BETTY (1893–) (Elizabeth Blythe Slaughter). American leading lady of silent films, many made in Britain. Still plays occasional bit parts. *Queen of Sheba* (21), *Chu Chin Chow* (23), *She* (25), *The Girl from Gay Paris* (27), *Eager Lips* (30), *Tom Brown of Culver* (32), *The Gorgeous Hussy* (36), *Misbehaving Husbands* (40), *Jiggs and Maggie in Society* (47), *My Fair Lady* (64), many others.

BLYTHE, JOHN (1921–). British character actor, often of spiv types. *This Happy Breed* (44), *Holiday Camp* (48), *Vote for Huggett* (49), *Worms Eye View* (51), *The Gay Dog* (54), *Foxhole in Cairo* (60), *A Stitch in Time* (64), many others.

BOARDMAN, ELEANOR (1898–). American leading lady of the silents. *The Stranger's Banquet* (23), *Three Wise Fools* (23), *Wife of a Centaur* (25), *Memory Lane* (26), *The Crowd* (28), *The Squaw Man* (31), etc. Retired.

BOCHNER, LLOYD (1924–). Canadian leading man, mainly on TV. Films include *The Night Walker* (64), *Sylvia* (65), *Tony Rome* (67), *Point Blank* (67), *The Detective* (68).

BODARD, MAG (c. 1928–). French producer, a rare example of a woman in this job. *The Umbrellas of Cherbourg* (64), *Les Demoiselles de Rochefort* (66), *Le Bonheur* (66), *Mouchette* (67), *Benjamin* (67), *La Chinoise* (68), etc.

BODEEN, DE WITT (1908–). American screenwriter. *The Seventh Victim* (43), *The Curse of the Cat People* (44), *The Enchanted Cottage* (44), *I Remember Mama* (47), *Twelve to the Moon* (58), *Billy Budd* (co-w) (62), etc.

THE BODY SNATCHER (US 1945). Generally felt to be the most successful of Val Lewton's highly-regarded horror films for RKO, this version of the R. L. Stevenson story had excellent sets of old Edinburgh and a first-class performance by Henry Daniell. The subject matter has, of course, been used in several other films. Directed by Robert Wise.

BOEHM, KARL or CARL (1928–   ). German leading man who has been in international films. *Peeping Tom* (GB) (59), *Too Hot to Handle* (GB) (60), *The Magnificent Rebel* (as Beethoven) (60), *The Four Horsemen of the Apocalypse* (US) (62), *The Wonderful World of the Brothers Grimm* (US) (63), *Come Fly With Me* (US) (63), *Venetian Affair* (66), etc.

BOEHM, SYDNEY (1908–   ). American screen writer. *High Wall* (48), *Union Station* (50), *The Atomic City* (52), *The Big Heat* (53), *Six Bridges to Cross* (54), *The Tall Men* (55), *Violent Saturday* (55), *The Revolt of Mamie Stover* (56), *Harry Black* (58), *A Woman Obsessed* (also produced) (59), *Seven Thieves* (59), *Sylvia* (65), *Rough Night in Jericho* (co-w) (68), etc.

BOETTICHER, BUDD (1916–   ) (Oscar Boetticher). American director, former bullfighter. Has not risen above co-features, but some of them are highly regarded by cineastes. *The Missing Juror* (44), *Assigned to Danger* (47), *The Bullfighter and the Lady* (also produced and co-wrote) (51), *Bronco Buster* (52), *East of Sumatra* (53), *Wings of the Hawk* (53), *The Magnificent Matador* (also wrote) (55), *Seven Men from Now* (56), *Decision at Sundown* (57), *The Rise and Fall of Legs Diamond* (60), *A Time for Dying* (69), etc.

boffins are research scientists working on hush-hush government projects. Their problems have been dramatized in such films as *The Small Back Room, School for Secrets, Suspect, The Man in the Moon* and *The Satin Bug*.

BOGARDE, DIRK (1920–   ) (Derek Van Den Bogaerd). British leading actor of Dutch descent, who after stage experience was put under contract by Rank in 1947. Debut in *Esther Waters* (47); since then has managed to keep and enlarge his following by shrewdly varied choice of roles. *Quartet* (48), *The Blue Lamp* (50), *Hunted* (52), *Doctor in the House* (53), *The Spanish Gardener* (56), *Ill Met by Moonlight* (57), *Campbell's Kingdom* (58), *A Tale of Two Cities* (58), *The Doctor's Dilemma* (58), *Libel* (59), *Song without End* (as Liszt) (US) (60), *The Angel Wore Red* (US) (60), *The Singer Not the Song* (60), *Victim* (61), *HMS Defiant* (62), *The Password Is Courage* (62), *I Could Go On Singing* (63), *The Mind Benders* (63), *The Servant* (BFA) (63), *Hot Enough for June* (64), *King and Country* (64), *The High Bright Sun* (65), *Darling* (BFA) (65), *Modesty Blaise* (66), *Accident* (67), *Our Mother's House* (67), *Mr Sebastian* (67), *The Fixer* (68), *The Damned* (69). *Justine* (69), etc.

†BOGART, HUMPHREY (1899–1957). American leading actor who became one of Hollywood's imperishable personalities. Had naval and business experience before Broadway stage. Played minor film roles from 1930: *A Devil with Women* (30), *Up the River* (30), *Body*

and Soul (30), *Bad Sister* (31), *Women of All Nations* (31), *A Holy Terror* (31), *Love Affair* (32), *Big City Blues* (32), *Three on a Match* (32), *Midnight* (34). Returned to Broadway: his big Hollywood break came when he recreated his stage role of gangster Duke Mantee in *The Petrified Forest* (36). Four years of mainly heavy roles followed, but by 1941 he had established himself as an entirely acceptable hero for the *films noirs* of the period. *Two Against the World* (36), *Bullets or Ballots* (36), *China Clipper* (36), *Isle of Fury* (36), *The Great O'Malley* (37), *Black Legion* (37), *San Quentin* (37), *Marked Woman* (37), *Kid Galahad* (37), *Dead End* (37), *Stand In* (37), *Men Are Such Fools* (38), *Swing Your Lady* (38), *Crime School* (38), *The Amazing Dr Clitterhouse* (38), *Racket Busters* (38), *King of the Underworld* (38), *Angels with Dirty Faces* (38), *You Can't Get Away with Murder* (39), *Dark Victory* (39), *The Return of Dr X* (as a vampire) (39), *The Oklahoma Kid* (39), *The Roaring Twenties* (39), *Invisible Stripes* (39), *Virginia City* (40), *It All Came True* (40), *Brother Orchid* (40), *They Drive by Night* (40), *High Sierra* (41), *The Wagons Roll at Night* (41), *The Maltese Falcon* (41), *All Through the Night* (41), *The Big Shot* (42), *Across the Pacific* (42), *Casablanca* (42), *Action in the North Atlantic* (43), *Thank Your Lucky Stars* (43), *Sahara* (43), *Conflict* (43), *Passage to Marseilles* (44), *To Have and Have Not* (44), *The Big Sleep* (46), *The Two Mrs Carrolls* (47), *Dark Passage* (47), *Dead Reckoning* (47), *The Treasure of the Sierra Madre* (48), *Key Largo* (48), *Knock on Any Door* (49), *Tokyo Joe* (49), *Chain Lightning* (50), *In a Lonely Place* (51), *The Enforcer (Murder Inc.)* (51), *Sirocco* (51), *The African Queen* (AA) (GB) (51), *Deadline USA* (51), *Battle Circus* (52), *Beat the Devil* (53), *The Caine Mutiny* (54), *Sabrina Fair* (54), *The Barefoot Contessa* (54), *We're No Angels* (55), *The Desperate Hours* (55), *The Left Hand of God* (55), *The Harder They Fall* (56). Several biographies have been published.

BOGEAUS, BENEDICT (1904–1968). American independent producer, formerly in real estate; his films have been mildly interesting though eccentric. *The Bridge of San Luis Rey* (44), *The Diary of a Chambermaid* (45), *Christmas Eve* (47), *The Macomber Affair* (47), *Johnny One Eye* (49), *Passion* (54), *Slihgtly Scarlet* (56), *The Most Dangerous Man Alive* (61), etc.

BOHNEN, ROMAN (1894–1949). American character actor usually found in honest-working-man parts. *Vogues of 1938, Of Mice and Men* (39), *The Song of Bernadette* (43), *The Hitler Gang* (44), *None but the Lonely Heart* (44), *A Bell for Adano* (45), many others.

BOIS, CURT (c. 1900–   ). Dapper German-American comedy-actor, often seen as head waiter, pompous clerk, etc. *Tovarich* (38), *Boom Town* (41), *My Gal Sal* (42), *The Woman in White* (48), *The Great Sinner* (49), *The Fortunes of Captain Blood* (50), many others. In

Germany in the mid-fifties, starred in *Herr Puntila and His Servant Matti*.

BOLAND, MARY (1880–1965). American stage tragedienne who after a few early silents (*The Edge of the Abyss* [16], *His Temporary Wife* [18], etc.) returned to Broadway. When she reappeared in Hollywood in the 30s, it was in fluttery comedy roles. *Secrets of a Secretary* (32), *Six of a Kind* (33), *Ruggles of Red Gap* (34), a series of domestic comedies with Charlie Ruggles, *The Women* (39), *New Moon* (40), *Pride and Prejudice* (as Mrs Bennett) (40), *The Right to Live* (45), *Julia Misbehaves* (48), *Guilty Bystander* (last appearance) (50), many others.

BOLES, JOHN (1895–1969). American leading man and singer, popular in the early 30s. *So This Is Marriage* (25), *The Loves of Sunya* (26), *Rio Rita* (29), *The Desert Song* (30), *King of Jazz* (30), *Frankenstein* (31), *One Heavenly Night* (31), *Back Street* (32), *Only Yesterday* (33), *Stand Up and Cheer* (33), *Curly Top* (35), *Stella Dallas* (37), *Between Us Girls* (42), *Thousands Cheer* (43), etc. Only appearance since mid-40s: *Babes in Baghdad* (52).

BOLESLAWSKI, RICHARD (1889–1937) (Boleslaw Ryszart Srzednicki). Polish director, formerly with the Moscow Arts Theatre: came to Hollywood in 1930, and made a few stylish movies. *Three Meetings* (USSR 17), *Rasputin and the Empress* (32), *The Painted Veil* (34), *Clive of India* (35), *Les Misérables* (35), *The Garden of Allah* (36), *Theodora Goes Wild* (36).

†BOLGER, RAY (1904–). American eccentric dancer, a stage star who has made too few films. *The Great Ziegfeld* (36), *The Wizard of Oz* (as the Scarecrow) (39), *Sunny* (41), *The Harvey Girls* (46), *Look for the Silver Lining* (49), *Where's Charley* (52), *April in Paris* (53), *Babes in Toyland* (61), *The Daydreamer* (66).

BOLT, ROBERT (1924–). British playwright, whose *A Man for All Seasons* (AA) (67) is his first stage work to be filmed. Wrote screenplays for *Lawrence of Arabia* (62), *Doctor Zhivago* (AA) (65).

BOLTON, GUY (1885–). American humorous writer often associated with P. G. Wodehouse. Films include *The Love Parade* (30), *Rio Rita* (30), *Anything Goes* (36), *Anastasia* (56).

BONANOVA, FORTUNIO (1896–1969). Spanish opera singer and impresario who in the 30s brought his own repertory company to Broadway. Engaged by Orson Welles to play the temperamental singing teacher in *Citizen Kane* (41), he stayed in Hollywood to play scores of supporting roles. *The Black Swan* (42), *For Whom the Bell Tolls* (43), *Double Indemnity* (44), *The Red Dragon* (46), *September*

Bonaparte, Napoleon

Affair (51), *An Affair to Remember* (57), *Thunder in the Sun* (59), *The Running Man* (63), *The Million Dollar Collar* (67), etc.

BONAPARTE, NAPOLEON: *see* NAPOLEON BONAPARTE.

BOND, DEREK (1919–). British light leading man with varied experience including Grenadier Guards before film debut in *The Captive Heart* (46). Subsequently: *Nicholas Nickleby* (title role) (47), *Scott of the Antarctic* (48), *Marry Me* (49), *Love's a Luxury* (52), *Stranger from Venus* (54), *The Hand* (60), *Saturday Night Out* (64), *Wonderful Life* (64), *Press For Time* (66), etc. Also on TV and stage.

BOND, WARD (1904–1960). Burly American actor who distinguished himself in small roles from the coming of sound, notably in John Ford's films; in 1957 gained TV stardom as the wagonmaster in *Wagon Train*. *The Informer* (35), *The Oklahoma Kid* (37), *Tobacco Road* (41), *Hitler Dead or Alive* (43), *Dakota* (45), *Three Godfathers* (47), *Joan of Arc* (48), *The Quiet Man* (52), *Blowing Wild* (53), *Mr Roberts* (55), *The Searchers* (56), scores of others.

BONDARTCHUK, SERGEI (1920–). Russian actor and director, best known for *The Young Guards* (a) (48), *The Grasshopper* (a) (55), *Othello* (a) (56), *Destiny of a Man* (a, d) (59), *War and Peace* (a, d) (64), *Waterloo* (d) (69).

BONDI, BEULAH (1892–). American character actress who left stage for films in 1932 and has specialized in elderly ladies both sympathetic and grumpy. *Street Scene* (32), *Rain* (32), *Christopher Bean* (33), *The Good Fairy* (35), *The Trail of the Lonesome Pine* (36), *Maid of Salem* (37), *Make Way for Tomorrow* (37), *Of Human Hearts* (38), *On Borrowed Time* (39), *Our Town* (40), *One Foot in Heaven* (41), *Watch on the Rhine* (43), *The Southerner* (45), *It's a Wonderful Life* (46), *The Snake Pit* (48), *The Furies* (50), *Track of the Cat* (54), *Back from Eternity* (56), *The Big Fisherman* (59), *Tammy Tell Me True* (61), *The Wonderful World of the Brothers Grimm* (63), etc.

BONNIE AND CLYDE (US 1967). A retelling in sixties-style of the sordid story of two hoodlums of the American depression, the amoral Bonnie Parker and Clyde Barrow, who murdered scores of people in bank hold-ups before being shot down by police. The sympathy for these public enemies generated by the film is undeniable, but it is partly dissipated by the general treatment which finds comedy in the most outlandish situations, and by Burnett Guffey's crisp colour photography (AA). Warren Beatty (who also produced) and Faye Dunaway do everything possible with the lead roles, and Arthur Penn's direction is artful. For once, a 'cult' film worth cultivating.

boobs occur even in the best-regulated movies, and sometimes they pass the eagle eyes of editor and director and get into the official release version. Here are a few personal favourites:

In *Carmen Jones*, the camera tracks with Dorothy Dandridge down a street; and the entire camera crew is reflected in the shop windows. In *The Wrong Box*, the roofs of Victorian London are disfigured by TV aerials. In *Decameron Nights*, Louis Jourdan stands on the deck of his 14th-century pirate ship; and a white lorry trundles down the hill in the background. In *The Viking Queen*, set in the times of Boadicaea, a wrist watch is clearly visible on one of the leading characters. In *Camelot*, the character played by Lionel Jeffries first meets Arthur an hour into the film; but twenty minutes earlier he is one of the courtiers visible in a montage following the king's wedding.

boom. A 'long arm' extending from the camera unit and carrying a microphone to be balanced over the actors so that sound can be picked up in a semi-distant shot. A 'camera boom' is a high movable platform strong enough to support the entire camera unit.

BOOMERANG (US 1947). This who-done-it based on the murder of a priest in a small town set a new style in semi-documentary thrillers. Written by Richard Murphy, directed by Elia Kazan.

BOONE, DANIEL (1735–?1820). American pioneer and Indian scout who helped to open up Kentucky and Missouri. He has been frequently portrayed in films, notably by George O'Brien (*Daniel Boone*, 1936), David Bruce (*Young Daniel Boone*, 1950) and Bruce Bennett (*Daniel Boone, Trail Blazer*, 1956). In 1965 began a long-running TV series, *Daniel Boone*, starring Fess Parker.

BOONE, PAT (1934–   ). Gentle-mannered American pop singer whose trademark is his lack of private vices. Film debut *Bernardine* (57); subsequently *Journey to the Centre of the Earth* (59), *State Fair* (62), *The Horror of It All* (64), *Never Put It in Writing* (64), *Goodbye Charlie* (65), *The Perils of Pauline* (67), and a number of light musicals.

BOONE, RICHARD (1917–   ). Craggy American character actor, ex-Navy and Actors' Studio. *Halls of Montezuma* (debut) (51), *Rommel, Desert Fox* (51), *Red Skies of Montana* (52), *Way of a Gaucho* (53), *Vicki* (53), *The Robe* (53), *Dragnet* (54), *Battle Stations* (55), *Away All Boats* (56), *Lizzie* (57), *Garment Center* (57), *The Tall T* (57), *I Bury the Living* (58), *A Thunder of Drums* (61), *Rio Conchos* (64), *The War Lord* (65), *Hombre* (67), *Kona Coast* (68), *The Night of the Following Day* (69), *The Arrangement* (69), *Little Big Man* (70). TV series: *Medic* (54–56), *Have Gun Will Travel* (57–61), *The Richard Boone Show* (64).

†BOORMAN, JOHN (1933–   ). British director with TV experience. *Catch Us If You Can* (66), *Point Blank* (US) (67), *Hell in the Pacific* (US) (68).

BOOTH, ANTHONY (1937–   ). British general purpose actor. Small parts in *Mix Me a Person* (62), *The L-shaped Room* (62), etc.; went into TV and became famous as lazy son-in-law in *Till Death Do Us Part*, a role he repeated in the 1968 film version.

BOOTH, EDWINA (1909–   ) (Josephine Constance Woodruff). American leading lady who graduated from bit parts in the twenties to the lead in *Trader Horn* (30), during the filming of which she caught jungle fever. After appearing in two or three serials of the early thirties (*The Vanishing Legion*, *The Last of the Mohicans*) she disappeared from public view.

BOOTH, JAMES (1930–   ). British actor, adept at other ranks and shifty characters: trained at London's Theatre Workshop. Films include *The Trials of Oscar Wilde* (60), *The Hellions* (61), *In the Doghouse* (62), *Sparrows Can't Sing* (63), *French Dressing* (63), *Zulu* (64), *The Secret of My Success* (65), *Ninety Degrees in the Shade* (65), *Robbery* (67), *The Bliss of Mrs Blossom* (68), *The Man Who Had Power Over Women* (70).

BOOTH, SHIRLEY (1907–   ) (Thelma Ford Booth). American leading stage actress who came to the screen in middle-aged roles. *Come Back Little Sheba* (AA) (debut) (52), *About Mrs Leslie* (54), *Hot Spell* (57), *The Matchmaker* (59). TV series: *Hazel* (61–66).

BORCHERS, CORNELL (1925–   ). German leading actress in some international films. *The Big Lift* (US) (50), *The Divided Heart* (GB) (BFA) (55), *Never Say Goodbye* (US) (56), etc. Real name: Cornelia Bruch.

BORG, VEDA ANN (1915–   ). American actress who reliably played good-hearted tarts, gangsters' molls, etc., in scores of programmers since the mid-30s. *San Quentin* (37), *Bitter Sweet* (41), *Two Yanks in Trinidad* (42), *The Big Noise* (44), *What a Blonde* (45), *Big Town* (46), *Forgotten Women* (49), *Big Jim McLain* (52), *Guys and Dolls* (55), *The Naked Gun* (58), *The Alamo* (60), etc.

BORGIA, CESARE (1476–1507) and LUCRETIA (1480–1519). The son and daughter of Pope Alexander VI were suspected of several family murders. On screen they have been played as melodramatic figures, notably by MacDonald Carey and Paulette Goddard (*Bride of Vengeance*, 1949), Orson Welles (*Prince of Foxes*, 1949), Pedro Armendariz and Martine Carol (*Lucretia Borgia*, 1952), and France Fabrizi and Belinda Lee (*Nights of Lucretia Borgia*, 1959).

BORGNINE, ERNEST (1917–). Burly American character actor who after stage and TV work made film debut in *China Corsair* (51), and was at first typecast in heavy roles: *The Whistle at Eaton Falls* (51), *From Here to Eternity* (as the bullying sergeant) (53), *Johnny Guitar* (54), *Vera Cruz* (54), *Bad Day at Black Rock* (54), etc. Made a great hit as the gentle *Marty* (AA, BFA) (55); subsequently cast in a variety of leading roles, good suitable ones being hard to find. *The Last Command* (55), *Jubal* (56), *The Catered Affair (Wedding Breakfast)* (56), *The Best Things in Life Are Free* (56), *Three Brave Men* (57), *The Vikings* (58), *The Rabbit Trap* (59), *Pay or Die* (60), *Summer of the Seventeenth Doll* (60), *Barabbas* (62), *The Flight of the Phoenix* (65), *The Dirty Dozen* (66), *Chuka* (67), *The Split* (68), *Ice Station Zebra* (68), *The Wild Bunch* (69), *The Adventurers* (69), etc. TV series: *McHale's Navy* (62–65).

BORN FREE (GB 1965). A commercially successful though aesthetically cloying version of Joy Adamson's book about a tame lioness in Kenya. Indifferently directed by James Hill apart from a few animal sequences: Virginia McKenna and Bill Travers perpetuate the myth of the stiff upper lip.

BORRADAILE, OSMOND (c. 1892–). Canadian cinematographer, in Hollywood from 1914 and later in Britain, where he became well known for his work on such films as *The Drum* (38), *The Four Feathers* (39), *The Overlanders* (46). 1966: *The Trap* (second unit).

BORZAGE, FRANK (1893–1962). American director, former coalminer and actor; known for soft, sentimental, pictorial films. After early Westerns made a big hit with *Humoresque* (20); followed up with *Children of the Dust* (23), *Secrets* (24), *The Marriage Licence* (26), *Seventh Heaven* (AA) (27), *Street Angel* (28), *The River* (29), *Liliom* (30), *Young America* (31), *Bad Girl* (AA) (32), *A Farewell to Arms* (32), *Secrets* (33), *Man's Castle* (34), *Little Man What Now* (34), *Living on Velvet* (35), *Desire* (36), *The Green Light* (37), *History Is Made at Night* (37), *Big City* (38), *Mannequin* (38), *Three Comrades* (39), *Disputed Passage* (39), *Flight Command* (40), *Smiling Through* (41), *Stage Door Canteen* (43), *His Butler's Sister* (43), *Till We Meet Again* (44), *The Spanish Main* (45), *Magnificent Doll* (47), *Moonrise* (48), *China Doll* (58), *The Big Fisherman* (59), etc.

BOSE, LUCIA (1931–). Italian leading lady, former beauty queen. *No Peace among the Olives* (50), *Cronaca di un Amore* (51), *Girls of the Spanish Steps* (52), *Death of a Cyclist* (Sp.) (55), etc.

BOSLEY, TOM (1927–). American character actor with stage and TV experience. *The World of Henry Orient* (64), *Love with the Proper Stranger* (64), *The Secret War of Harry Frigg* (67), etc. TV series: *Debbie* (69).

Bost, Pierre

BOST, PIERRE; see under AURENCHE, JEAN.

Boston Blackie was an American comic strip character, a small-time crook with a weakness for helping people. The first film about his exploits, *Boston Blackie's Little Pal*, was made in 1919. In 1923 there were two Blackie adventures with William Russell. Between 1940 and 1948 the character was revived for nearly a dozen second features starring Chester Morris (with George E. Stone as 'the Runt'). And in 1951–53 Kent Taylor appeared in a TV series.

BOSUSTOW, STEPHEN (1911–   ). Founder of UPA cartoons (1943) after working as artist for Disney and others. Later won Academy Awards for creation of Gerald McBoing Boing and Mr Magoo.

BOSWORTH, HOBART (1867–1943). American character actor, on stage from 1885, films from 1909. *The Country Mouse* (14), *Joan the Woman* (16), *Oliver Twist* (16), *The Border Legion* (19), *Captain January* (24), *The Blood Ship* (27), *Lady for a Day* (33), *The Crusades* (35), *Sin Town* (42), etc.

BOUCHIER, CHILI (1909–   ) (Dorothy Bouchier). British leading lady, mainly on stage. *Shooting Stars* (28), *Carnival* (31), *Get off My Foot* (36), *The Mind of Mr Reeder* (39), *The Laughing Lady* (47), *Old Mother Riley's New Venture* (49), *The Boy and the Bridge* (59), others

BOUCHET, BARBARA (1943–   ). German-American glamour girl whose film appearances include *In Harm's Way* (65), *Casino Royale* (67), *Danger Route* (68).

BOUCHEY, WILLIS (c. 1895–   ). American character actor with stage experience; in films from 1951, often as judge or sheriff. *Elopement* (51), *Suddenly* (54), *Johnny Concho* (56), *The Sheepman* (58), *Sergeant Rutledge* (60), *Support Your Local Sheriff* (69), many others.

BOUDU SAUVE DES EAUX (France 1932). Written and directed by Jean Renoir, this wry little piece could qualify as the screen's first black comedy. Michel Simon appears as a morose individual who proceeds to make a family very sorry they saved him from drowning.

BOULE DE SUIF. The chief versions of Guy de Maupassant's story, about the effects of a prostitute on a band of travellers during the 1870s, were by Mikhail Romm in 1934, Robert Wise (as *Mademoiselle Fifi*, with Simone Simon) in 1944, and Christian-Jaque (with Micheline Presle) in 1945. John Ford's *Stagecoach* (39) is based on a very similar situation.

BOULTING, JOHN and ROY (both 1913–   ). Twin Britishers who were determined to work in films. After varied experience founded Charter Films 1937 and made some modest successes: *Consider*

Your Verdict (37), *Pastor Hall* (39), *Thunder Rock* (42). After World War II (during which John made *Journey Together* and Roy co-directed *Desert Victory*) they broadened their range: *Fame Is the Spur* (46), *Brighton Rock* (47), *The Guinea Pig* (49), *Seven Days to Noon* (50). (They produced and directed alternately.) In 1955, after a barren period, they made *Private's Progress* and henceforth were known for realistic comedies pillorying national institutions: *Brothers in Law* (56), *Lucky Jim* (57), *I'm All Right, Jack* (59), *Heavens Above* (63), *Rotten to the Core* (65), *The Family Way* (66), etc. Roy also directed *Run for the Sun* (56) in Hollywood. Both are now directors of British Lion Films. Their would-be shocker *Twisted Nerve* (68) was a poor effort.

BOURGUIGNON, SERGE (1928–   ). French director chiefly known for *Sundays and Cybele* (AA) (62). Went to Hollywood to make *The Reward* (65). 1967: *Two Weeks in September* (*A Coeur Joie*). 1969: *The Picasso Summer*.

BOURVIL (1917–   ) (André Raimbourg). Diminutive French comedian, seen abroad chiefly in *La Ferme du Pendu* (45), *La Traversée de Paris* (56), *Tout l'Or du Monde* (62), *Heaven Sent* (63), *The Secret Agents* (65), *The Big Spree* (66), *The Sucker* (66), *Don't Look Now* (67), *The Brain* (68), *Monte Carlo or Bust* (69), etc.

BOW, CLARA (1905–1965). American actress, the 'IT' girl of the 20s Her films depicted the gay young generation and her wide-eyed vivacity was enormously popular. *Down to the Sea in Ships* (23), *Kid Boots* (26), *Dancing Mothers* (26), *It* (27), *The Plastic Age* (27), *Rough House Rosie* (29), *The Saturday Night Kid* (29), *Call Her Savage* (32), *Hoopla* (33), etc. Retired in the early 30s.

BOWER, DALLAS (1907–   ). British producer. Originally sound recordist, editor and writer, he became director of BBC TV 1936–1939, supervisor of Ministry of Information film production 1940–42. Associate producer *As You Like It* (36), *Henry V* (44), etc.; produced *Sir Lancelot*, TV series. Directed French puppet version of *Alice in Wonderland* (50), *The Second Mrs Tanqueray* (52), *Doorway to Suspicion* (57).

BOWERS, WILLIAM (1916–   ). American scenarist, usually in collaboration. *The Wistful Widow* (47), *Black Bart* (48), *The Sheepman* (57), *Alias Jesse James* (58), *Imitation General* (58), *Advance to the Rear* (64), *Support Your Local Sheriff* (69), many others.

THE BOWERY (US 1933). Wallace Beery and George Raft are the brawling but good-natured protagonists of this rumbustious comedy-melodrama which marked Hollywood's breakaway forever from the static early talkie style. Raoul Walsh's direction abounds in vigour, the screenplay by Howard Estabrook and James Gleason is crisply funny, and the whole production brings to vivid life the teeming side-streets of New York at the turn of the century. It was the first production of Darryl Zanuck's Twentieth Century company, which the following year merged with Fox.

THE BOWERY BOYS. One of the splinter groups from the original Dead End Kids (the other was the East Side Kids, but they overlap), this team of young Brooklyn 'roughnecks' turned themselves into slapstick comedians. Led by Leo Gorcey and Huntz Hall, they made scores of popular second features during the 40s and 50s.

BOWIE, JIM (1796–1836). American folk-hero who died at the Alamo; invented the Bowie knife. Played by Alan Ladd in *The Iron Mistress*, Sterling Hayden in *The Last Command*, Jeff Morrow in *The First Texan*, Richard Widmark in *The Alamo*.

BOWMAN, LEE (1910–   ). American stage leading man who made film debut in *Three Men in White* (36). A pleasant actor of playboy and 'other man' roles, his films include *I Met Him in Paris* (37), *Love Affair* (39), *Florian* (40), *We Were Dancing* (42), *The Impatient Years* (44), *Tonight and Every Night* (44), *The Walls Came Tumbling Down* (46), *A Woman Destroyed (Smash-Up)* (48), *There's a Girl in My Heart* (49), *Double Barrel Miracle* (55), *Youngblood Hawke* (64); but since 1949 he has worked mainly on Broadway.

BOX, BETTY (1920–   ). Sister of Sydney Box and former assistant to him; became producer at Islington Studios, then Pinewood. Turns out comedies and dramas with box-office appeal but little cinematic flavour; *Doctor in the House* (53), *The Iron Petticoat* (56), *A Tale of Two Cities* (58), *The Thirty-nine Steps* (59), *No Love for Johnnie* (61), *The High Bright Sun* (65), *Deadlier than the Male* (66), *Some Girls Do* (68), etc.

BOX, JOHN (1920–   ). British production designer. *Lawrence of Arabia* (AA) (62), *Dr Zhivago* (AA) (65), *A Man for All Seasons* (AA) (66), *Oliver!* (AA) (68).

BOX, MURIEL (1905–   ). British director, wife of Sydney Box. Entered films 1927; collaborated with him on script of *The Seventh Veil* (46); later directed *The Beachcomber* (54), *Simon and Laura* (55), *Subway in the Sky* (58), *Rattle of a Simple Man* (64), etc.

BOX, SYDNEY (1907–   ). British writer-producer-director. After varied industry experience, including production of wartime propaganda films, formed his own company and had great success with *The Seventh Veil* (46). Later productions include *The Man Within* (47), *Quartet* (48), *The Prisoner* (55), *The Truth About Women* (59), many others. Still an active behind-the-scenes figure.

boxing. Actual prizefighters whose lives have been fictionalized on film include Jim Corbett (Errol Flynn in *Gentleman Jim*), John L. Sullivan (Greg McClure in *The Great John L.*), Joe Louis (Coley Wallace in *The Joe Louis Story*) and Rocky Graziano (Paul Newman in *Somebody Up There Likes Me*). Most other boxing films have tended to emphasize the corruption of the fight game: they include *The Champ, The Crowd Roars, Kid Galahad, Kid Nightingale, Body and Soul, The Set-Up, Champion, Golden Boy, The Square Ring, No Way Back, Run with the Wind,* and *The Harder They Fall.* Central Europe has latterly taken up the theme with *Fists in the Pocket* and *Boxer.* Boxing comedy is rare, but most comedians have taken part in boxing sequences: Chaplin in *The Champion*, Lloyd in *The Miky. Way*, Danny Kaye in *The Kid from Brooklyn*, Abbott and Costello in *Meet the Invisible Man*, Leon Errol in the *Joe Palooka* series, etc.

BOYD, STEPHEN (1928–   ) (William Millar). Irish-born, now American, leading man; former child performer and radio actor. *An Alligator Named Daisy* (55), *The Man Who Never Was* (a scene-stealing performance as the German spy) (56), *A Hill in Korea* (56), *Island in the Sun* (56), *Les Bijoutiers du Clair de Lune* (*Heaven Fell That Night*) (57), *Seven Thunders* (57), *The Best of Everything* (58), *Ben Hur* (as Messala) (59), *The Big Gamble* (60), *The Inspector* (*Lisa*) (62), *Jumbo* (62), *The Fall of the Roman Empire* (64), *The Third Secret* (64), *Genghis Khan* (65), *The Oscar* (66), *Fantastic Voyage* (66), *The Bible* (66), *Caper of the Golden Bulls* (67), *Assignment K* (68), *Shalako* (68), *Slaves* (69), etc.

BOYD, WILLIAM (1898–   ). American actor, in films since 1919. World-famous since 1935 as cowboy hero Hopalong Cassidy, in which role he has made scores of minor Westerns; also TV series. Other films include *Why Change Your Wife* (19), *Lady of the Pavements* (24), *Skyscraper* (26), *King of Kings* (27), *The Volga Boatmen* (27), *Two Arabian Knights* (28), *Yankee Clipper* (28).

BOYD, WILLIAM 'STAGE' (1890–1935). American actor so known to distinguish him from his 'Hopalong Cassidy' namesake. Chief film appearance as Bill Sikes in *Oliver Twist* (33).

BOYER, CHARLES (1899–   ). French stage and film actor who went to Hollywood first in 1929. In the later 30s his name became a household word as the screen's 'great lover'. Films include *La Ronde Infernale* (27), *Barcarolle d'Amour* (30), *The Battle* (34), *Mayerling* (34), *Caravan* (35), *Private Worlds* (35), *Break of Hearts* (35), *The Garden of Allah* (36), *History Is Made at Night* (37), *Tovarich* (37), *Marie Walewska* (*Conquest*) (as Napoleon) (38), *Algiers* (as Pepe le Moko) (38), *Love Affair* (39), *When Tomorrow Comes* (39), *All This and Heaven Too* (40), *Back Street* (41), *Hold Back the Dawn* (41), *Tales of Manhattan* (42), *Flesh and Fantasy* (43), *Gaslight* (*The Murder*

E*

in Thornton Square) (44), *The Constant Nymph* (44), *Together Again* (44), *Confidential Agent* (45), *Cluny Brown* (46), *Arch of Triumph* (48), *A Woman's Vengeance* (48), *The Thirteenth Letter* (51), *The First Legion* (51), *The Happy Time* (52), *Madame De* (53), *Nana* (55), *The Cobweb* (55), *Parisienne* (57), *Paris Palace Hotel* (59), *Fanny* (61), *The Four Horsemen of the Apocalypse* (62), *Love Is a Ball* (63), *Adorable Julia* (63), *A Very Special Favour* (65), *Is Paris Burning* (66), *How to Steal a Million* (66), *Casino Royale* (66), *Barefoot in the Park* (67), *The Mad Woman of Chaillot* (69), *The April Fools* (69), others including un-exported French films. Co-founder of Four Star TV; appeared in *The Rogues* series.

'B' picture. A low-budget production usually designed as a co-feature.

BOYS' TOWN (US 1938). MGM's highly successful sentimentalized biography of Father Flanagan and his work among juvenile semi-delinquents. Set the Hollywood fashion in boys and priests for years. Spencer Tracy (AA) and Mickey Rooney starred; Norman Taurog directed. The sequel, *Men of Boys' Town*, was less interesting.

BRABIN, CHARLES (1883–1957). British-born director, former actor; with the Edison company from 1908. *Stella Maris* (18), *The Bridge of San Luis Rey* (29), *Beast of the City* (32), *The Mask of Fu Manchu* (32), *Wicked Woman* (34), etc. Retired 1934.

BRABOURNE, JOHN (1924–   ) (Lord Brabourne). British producer, in films from 1950. *Harry Black* (58), *Sink the Bismarck* (60), *HMS Defiant* (62), etc.

BRACKEN, EDDIE (1920–   ). American actor, in films from 1940, usually as shy and stuttering hayseed. Made best films for Preston Sturges: *The Miracle of Morgan's Creek* (43), *Hail the Conquering Hero* (44). Other appearances include *The Fleet's In* (41), *Caught in the Draft* (41), *Sweater Girl* (42), *Happy Go Lucky* (43), *Star-Spangled Rhythm* (43), *Rainbow Island* (44), *Bring on the Girls* (45), *Hold that Blonde* (45), *Out of This World* (46), *Fun on a Weekend* (47), *Two Tickets to Broadway* (51), *We're Not Married* (52), *A Slight Case of Larceny* (53), etc. Recently inactive apart from occasional TV and stage appearances.

BRACKETT, CHARLES (1892–1969). American writer-producer, in films since 1937. Co-wrote *Ninotchka* (39), *Arise My Love* (40), *Ball of Fire* (41); co-wrote and produced *Five Graves to Cairo* (43), *Double Indemnity* (44), *The Lost Weekend* (AA) (45), *A Foreign Affair* (48), *Sunset Boulevard* (AA) (50), etc. Long association with Billy Wilder was severed when he joined Fox as producer: *Titanic* (AA) (53), *The King and I* (56), *Ten North Frederick* (57), *Journey to the Centre of the Earth* (57), *State Fair* (61), etc.

BRADBURY, RAY (1920–   ). American writer of imaginative science fiction. Direct film career began with scenario of *Moby Dick* (56), though one of the first 3-D films, *It Came from Outer Space* (53), was based on one of his stories; his book *The Martian Chronicles* is constantly being adapted for the screen, though no film has yet resulted; his *Fahrenheit 451*, however, has been filmed by Truffaut, and *The Illustrated Man* by Jack Smight.

BRADEN, BERNARD (1916–   ). Canadian radio and TV personality resident in Britain since 1938 and recently TV host of *On the Braden Beat*. Film appearances include *Love in Pawn* (52), *The Full Treatment* (60), *The Day the Earth Caught Fire* (62), *The War Lover* (63).

BRADNA, OLYMPE (1920–   ). American leading lady, former circus bareback rider. *Three Cheers for Love* (36), *Souls at Sea* (37), *Say It in French* (38), *South of Pago Pago* (40), *The Knockout* (41), *International Squadron* (41), etc. Retired.

BRADY, ALICE (1893–1939). American stage actress who appeared in many films from 1914 on, latterly as fluttery society matrons. *La Bohème* (16), *Betsy Ross* (17), *Woman and Wife* (18), *A Dark Lantern* (19), etc.; returned to stage during 20s but came back in talkies: *When Ladies Meet* (33), *False Faces* (34), *The Gay Divorce* (34), *My Man Godfrey* (36), *Three Smart Girls* (37), *In Old Chicago* (AA) (38), *Young Mr Lincoln* (39), etc.

BRADY, SCOTT (1924–   ) (Gerald Tierney). Tough-looking American leading man, mainly in second features; brother of Lawrence Tierney. *Canon City* (debut) (48), *Undercover Girl* (50), *Bronco Buster* (52), *Perilous Journey* (53), *Johnny Guitar* (54), *Gentlemen Marry Brunettes* (55), *Mohawk* (56), *Battle Flame* (59), *Destination Inner Space* (66), *Castle of Evil* (66), etc.

†BRAHM, JOHN (1893–   ) (Hans Brahm). German director who in 1936 went via Britain to Hollywood and made competent routine pictures. *Scrooge* (GB) (35), *The Last Journey* (GB) (35), *Broken Blossoms* (GB) (36), *Counsel for Crime* (37), *Penitentiary* (38), *Girls School* (38), *Let Us Live* (39), *Rio* (39), *Escape to Glory* (40), *Wild Geese Calling* (41), *The Undying Monster* (42), *Tonight We Raid Calais* (42), *Wintertime* (43), *The Lodger* (44), *Hangover Square* (44), *Guest in the House* (44), *The Locket* (46), *The Brasher Doubloon* (*The High Window*) (47), *Singapore* (47), *The Thief of Venice* (51), *The Miracle of Fatima* (52), *The Diamond Queen* (53), *The Mad Magician* (54), *Die Goldene Pest* (Ger.) (54), *Special Delivery* (55), *Bengazi* (55), *Hot Rods to Hell* (57). Also made many TV films.

BRAMBELL, WILFRID (1912–   ). Dublin-born character actor, famous in Britain as Old Steptoe in the TV series *Steptoe and Son*.

Bramble, A. V.

Has played cameo roles in many films, notably *Dry Rot* (56), *Serious Charge* (59), *What a Whopper* (61), *In Search of the Castaways* (62), *The Three Lives of Thomasina* (64), *A Hard Day's Night* (64), *Crooks in Cloisters* (64), *Where the Bullets Fly* (66), *Witchfinder General* (68).

BRAMBLE, A. V. (c. 1880– *). British director, former actor. *Fatal Fingers* (16), *Wuthering Heights* (18), *Shooting Stars* (co-d) (28), *The Will* (39), etc.

BRAND, MAX (1892–1944) (Frederick Faust). American popular novelist whose major bequests to Hollywood were 'Destry Rides Again' and the Dr Kildare books.

BRAND, NEVILLE (1920–). Thick-set American actor with stage and TV experience; often seen as Red Indian or gangster. In films from 1948 after ten years in the US Army: he was the fourth most decorated soldier. *D.O.A.* (49), *Halls of Montezuma* (51), *Stalag 17* (53), *Riot in Cell Block Eleven* (54), *Mohawk* (55), *The Tin Star* (57), *Cry Terror* (58), *Five Gates to Hell* (59), *The Scarface Mob* (as Al Capone) (60), *Huckleberry Finn* (60), *Birdman of Alcatraz* (62), *That Darn Cat* (65), *The Desperados* (68), many others. TV series: *Laredo* (65).

BRANDO, JOCELYN (c. 1920–). American stage actress, sister of Marlon Brando. Rare films include *The Big Heat* (53), *China Venture* (53), *The Ugly American* (63), *Bus Riley's Back in Town* (65), *The Chase* (66).

†BRANDO, MARLON (1924–). American leading man, much publicized for his mumbling accent and his 'method' technique. After stage experience, made film debut in *The Men* (50), but his next role as Kowalski in *A Streetcar Named Desire* (52) typed him as a primitive male. Later: *Viva Zapata* (BFA) (52), *Julius Caesar* (BFA) (as Mark Antony) (53), *The Wild One* (54), *On the Waterfront* (AA, BFA) (54), *Désirée* (as Napoleon) (54), *Guys and Dolls* (55), *The Teahouse of the August Moon* (56), *Sayonara* (57), *The Young Lions* (58), *One-Eyed Jacks* (also directed) (60), *The Fugitive Kind* (60), *Mutiny on the Bounty* (62), *The Ugly American* (63), *Bedtime Story* (64), *The Saboteur, Code Name Morituri* (65), *The Chase* (66), *The Appaloosa* (*Southwest to Sonora*) (66), *A Countess from Hong Kong* (66), *Reflections in a Golden Eye* (67), *Candy* (68), *The Night of the Following Day* (68).

BRASSELLE, KEEFE (1923–). American light leading man whose best chance was the title role of *The Eddie Cantor Story* (53). Other films routine: *Fairy Tale Murder* (45), *Not Wanted* (49), *A Place in the Sun* (51), *Bannerline* (51), *Skirts Ahoy* (52), *Mad at the World* (55), *Battle Stations* (56), etc. Now TV executive producer.

BRASSEUR, PIERRE (1903–   ). Distinguished French stage actor, in occasional films from 1925. *Claudine à l'École* (28), *Café de Paris* (33), *Quai des Brumes* (38), *Lumière d'Été* (42), *Les Enfants du Paradis* (44), *Les Portes de la Nuit* (46), *Julie de Carneilhan* (50), *Bluebeard* (51), *Porte des Lilas* (55), *Il Bell'Antonio* (60), *Deux Heures à Tuer* (65), *A New World* (66), etc.

BRAY, ROBERT (c. 1920–   ). American actor of the strong silent type. *Blood on the Moon* (49), *Warpath* (52), *Bus Stop* (56), *The Wayward Bus* (57), *My Gun Is Quick* (as Mike Hammer) (58), *Never So Few* (60), etc. TV series: *Man from Blackhawk* (54), *Stagecoach West* (60), *Lassie* (61–68).

BRAZZI, ROSSANO (1916–   ). Italian romantic actor who apart from local work has made several internationally popular films: *Little Women* (49), *Three Coins in the Fountain* (54), *The Barefoot Contessa* (54), *Summertime (Summer Madness)* (55), *The Story of Esther Costello* (57), *A Certain Smile* (58), *South Pacific* (58), *The Light in the Piazza* (62), *The Battle of the Villa Fiorita* (65), *The Bobo* (67), *Krakatoa* (68), *The Italian Job* (69), etc.

break figure. A specified amount of takings after which an exhibitor pays a greater percentage to the renter. For the protection of both parties many contracts are on a sliding scale, with the exhibitor paying anything from 25% to 50% of the gross according to the business he does.

breakaway furniture is specially constructed from balsa wood for those spectacular saloon brawls in which so much damage is apparently done to stars and stunt men.

BREAKSTON, GEORGE (1922–   ). French-born producer who as a child went to Hollywood and acted in *Great Expectations* (34), *Mrs Wiggs of the Cabbage Patch* (34), *Jesse James* (39), etc. Later went to Africa and turned out many heavy-handed adventure films and TV series, usually with British backing. *Urubu* (48), *The Scarlet Spear* (54), *Golden Ivory* (55), *Escape in the Sun* (56), *Woman and the Hunter* (57), *Shadow of Treason* (also directed) (63), *The Boy Cried Murder* (also directed) (66), etc.

BREATHLESS (À BOUT DE SOUFFLE) (France 1959). The first film of Jean-Luc Godard, with François Truffaut's story providing a somewhat less anarchic narrative than one finds in Godard's later solo efforts. In the vanguard of the 'new wave', it had an improvised plot apparently dedicated to the proposition that life is just one damned thing after another with death as the end; superficially it was about a small-time gangster's busy life with pauses for sex. Dedicated to Monogram Pictures. With Jean-Paul Belmondo, Jean Seberg.

BRECHER, IRVING (1914–   ). American radio writer who moved on to Hollywood. *At the Circus* (39), *Meet Me in St Louis* (co-w) (44), *Summer Holiday* (co-w) (47), *The Life of Riley* (also directed) (49), *Somebody Loves Me* (also directed) (52), *Cry for Happy* (60), *Sail a Crooked Ship* (also directed) (61), etc. TV series: *The People's Choice.*

BRECHT, BERTOLT (1898–1956). German poet and playwright whose 'alienation method' (by which audiences are forced by various theatrical devices to remember that they are watching a play) has been influential on films from *Citizen Kane* to *Alfie*. His *Dreigroschenoper*, based on *The Beggar's Opera*, has been twice filmed.

BREEN, BOBBY (1927–   ). American boy singer of the 30s. *Rainbow on the River* (37), *Make a Wish* (38), *Way Down South* (39), *Johnny Doughboy* (43), etc. Later in night clubs.

BREEN, JOSEPH (1890–1965). American executive, for many years administrator of the Production Code. (See CENSORSHIP.)

BREEN, RICHARD L. (1919–1967). American scenarist: *A Foreign Affair* (co-author) (48), *Miss Tatlock's Millions* (49), *The Model and the Marriage Broker* (51), *Niagara* (53), *Titanic* (AA) (53), *Dragnet* (54), *Pete Kelly's Blues* (55), *Stopover Tokyo* (57), *Wake Me When It's Over* (60), *Captain Newman* (63), *Do Not Disturb* (65), *Tony Rome* (67), many others. Former president of Screenwriters' Guild.

BREMER, LUCILLE (c. 1923–   ). American dancer groomed for stardom by MGM in the 40s. *Meet Me in St Louis* (44), *Ziegfeld Follies* (44), *Yolanda and the Thief* (45), *Till the Clouds Roll By* (46), *Cynthia's Secret* (47), *Ruthless* (48), etc. Retired.

BRENDEL, EL (1891–1964). Mild-mannered American comedian with vaudeville experience and an attractive way of fracturing the English language. *The Campus Flirt* (26), *Wings* (27), *Just Imagine* (30), *Jubilo* (32), *Happy Landing* (38), *If I Had My Way* (40), *Captain Caution* (40), *Machine Gun Mama* (44), *The Beautiful Blonde from Bashful Bend* (49), *The She Creature* (56), many others.

BRENNAN. MICHAEL (1912–   ). British 'tough guy' supporting actor, in films from 1932. Recently: *Moll Flanders* (65), *Thunderball* (65).

BRENNAN, WALTER (1894–   ). American character actor, in films since 1923. Can be comic, tragic, evil, sympathetic, shrewd or countrified. Won three Academy Awards as supporting actor. *King of Jazz* (30), *Barbary Coast* (35) *Come and Get It* (AA) (36), *Banjo on My Knee* (37), *The Buccaneer* (38), *Kentucky* (AA) (38), *The Adventures of Tom Sawyer* (38), *Stanley and Livingstone* (39), *Northwest Passage* (40), *The Westerner* (AA) (as Judge Roy Bean) (41), *Sergeant York* (41), *Meet John Doe* (41), *Pride of the Yankees*

(42), *North Star* (43), *The Princess and the Pirate* (44), *To Have and Have Not* (44), *Dakota* (45), *Centennial Summer* (46), *My Darling Clementine* (as Old Man Clanton) (46), *Red River* (48), *Task Force* (49), *Curtain Call at Cactus Crick* (50), *Best of the Badmen* (51), *Sea of Lost Ships* (53), *Bad Day at Black Rock* (54), *Glory* (56), *God Is My Partner* (57), *Rio Bravo* (58), *Those Calloways* (65), *The Oscar* (66), *Who's Minding the Mint* (67), *The Gnome-Mobile* (67), *The One and Only Genuine Original Family Band* (68), *Support Your Local Sheriff* (69), others. Recently spent five years in TV series *The Real McCoys* (57–63), and later *Tycoon* (64), *The Guns of Will Sonnett* (67–68).

BRENON, HERBERT (1880–1958). Irish director, in Hollywood after stage experience: a big name of the 20s. *Ivanhoe* (13), *The Kreuter Sonata* (15), *War Brides* (16), *The Passing of the Third Floor Back* (18), *The Sign on the Door* (21), *The Spanish Dancer* (23), *Peter Pan* (24), *A Kiss for Cinderella* (24), *Beau Geste* (26), *Sorrell and Son* (GB) (27), *The Great Gatsby* (27), *The Rescue* (29), *Beau Ideal* (29), *Oliver Twist* (33), *The Housemaster* (GB) (38), *At the Villa Rose* (GB) (38), *Yellow Sands* (GB) (38), *The Flying Squadron* (GB) (40), etc.

BRENT, EVELYN (1899–   ) (Mary Elizabeth Riggs). American leading lady of the silent screen, little seen in talkies. *The Shuttle of Life* (GB) (20), *Sybil* (GB) (21), *Married to a Mormon* (GB) (22), *Silk Stocking Sal* (24), *Queen of Diamonds* (26), *Underworld* (27), *Beau Sabreur* (28), *The Woman Trap* (29), *Madonna of the Streets* (30), *The World Gone Mad* (33), etc. Retired apart from small roles in *The Seventh Victim* (43), *Bowery Champs* (44), *The Golden Eye* (48).

BRENT, GEORGE (1904–   ) (George Nolan). Irish leading man who went to Hollywood in silent days and after years as he-man developed into useful foil for strong dramatic actresses, especially Bette Davis. *Charlie Chan Carries On* (31), *So Big* (32), *Life Begins* (32), *Forty-second Street* (33), *The Painted Veil* (34), *Special Agent* (35), *Front Page Woman* (35), *God's Country and the Woman* (36), *Jezebel* (38), *Dark Victory* (39), *The Rains Came* (39), *South of Suez* (40), *The Great Lie* (41), *International Lady* (41), *In This Our Life* (42), *Twin Beds* (42), *Silver Queen* (43), *Experiment Perilous* (44), *The Spiral Staircase* (45), *The Affairs of Susan* (45), *Tomorrow Is Forever* (45), *Temptation* (46), *Slave Girl* (47), *Christmas Eve* (47), *The Corpse Came C.O.D.* (47), *Luxury Liner* (48), *Bride for Sale* (49), *The Last Page* (GB) (50), *Montana Belle* (52), *Mexican Manhunt* (53) (last to date), etc. Subsequently made some TV films; inactive since about 1958.

BRENT, ROMNEY (1902–   ) (Romulo Larralde). Dapper Mexican actor in British films in the 30s, later elsewhere. *East Meets West* (36), *Dreaming Lips* (37), *School for Husbands* (37), *Dinner at the Ritz*

(38), *Let George Do It* (40), *The New Adventures of Don Juan* (48), *The Virgin Queen* (55), *The Sign of Zorro* (58), etc.

BREON, EDMUND (1882–c. 1951) (E. MacLaverty). British stage actor often seen in films as an amiable bumbler. *The Dawn Patrol* (30), *Three Men in a Boat* (33), *The Scarlet Pimpernel* (34), *Keep Fit* (37), *A Yank at Oxford* (38), *Goodbye Mr Chips* (39), then to US; *The Murder in Thornton Square* (44), *The Woman in the Window* (45), *Sherlock Holmes and the Secret Code* (46), *Forever Amber* (48), *Sons of the Musketeers* (51), others.

BRESLER, JERRY (1912–   ). American independent producer. *Another Part of the Forest* (47), *The Flying Missile* (50), *The Vikings* (58), *Diamond Head* (63), *Love Has Many Faces* (65), *Major Dundee* (65), many others.

BRESSART, FELIX (1890–1949). German stage actor who went to Hollywood 1938 and played sympathetic comedy roles: memorable in *Ninotchka* (39), *The Shop Around the Corner* (40), *Escape* (41), *Blossoms in the Dust* (41), *To Be or Not To Be* (42), *Concerto* (47), *Portrait of Jennie* (48), *Take One False Step* (49), etc.

BRESSLAW, BERNARD (1934–   ). British comedian who sprang to fame as giant-size dope in TV series *The Army Game*. Made a few films, e.g. *I Only Arsked* (57), *Too Many Crooks* (58), *The Ugly Duckling* (59), etc. Recently in smaller roles: *Morgan* (66), *Carry On Screaming* (66).

†BRESSON, ROBERT (1907–   ). French writer-director of austere introspective, almost mystical films: *Les Anges du Péché* (43), *Les Dames du Bois de Boulogne* (44), *Le Journal d'un Curé de Campagne* (50), *Un Condamné à Mort S'Est Echappé* (56), *Pickpocket* (59), *The Trial of Joan of Arc* (62), *Au Hazard Balthazar* (66), *Mouchette* (67), *Une Femme Douce* (68).

BRETHERTON, HOWARD (1896–1969). American director of second features, in Hollywood from 1914. *The Redeeming Sin* (24), *Ladies They Talk About* (31), *Chasing Trouble* (39), *The Girl Who Dared* (44), *Prince of Thieves* (48), *Whip Law* (50), many others.

BRETT, JEREMY (1935–   ) (Jeremy Huggins). British light leading man. *War and Peace* (56), *The Wild and the Willing* (61), *The Very Edge* (63), *My Fair Lady* (64), etc.

BREWSTER'S MILLIONS. Originally a novel (by George McCutcheon) about a young man bound by a legacy to spend millions of pounds within twenty-four hours (in order to inherit yet more money) and who has trouble doing it. This was turned into a popular stage farce and has been filmed at least four times: in 1921 with Fatty

Arbuckle, in 1935 with Jack Buchanan, in 1945 with Dennis O'Keefe, and in 1961 (as *Three on a Spree*) with Jack Watling.

BRIALY, JEAN-CLAUDE (1933–   ). French leading man. *Éléna et les Hommes* (56), *Lift to the Scaffold* (57), *Le Beau Serge* (58), *The Four Hundred Blows* (59), *Tiré au Flanc* (61), *La Chambre Ardente* (62), *The Devil and Ten Commandments* (62), *La Ronde* (64), *Un Homme de Trop* (67), *King of Hearts* (67), *Le Roje et le Noir* (70), etc.

BRIAN, DAVID (1914–   ). American actor: former song-and-dance man who came to Hollywood 1949 for *Flamingo Road* and was used mainly in ruthless or upstanding roles. *Beyond the Forest* (49), *Intruder in the Dust* (49), *The Damned Don't Cry* (50), *The Great Jewel Robber* (51), *Inside the Walls of Folsom Prison* (51), *This Woman Is Dangerous* (52), *Springfield Rifle* (52), *The High and the Mighty* (54), *Timberjack* (55), *The First Travelling Saleslady* (56), *The Rabbit Trap* (59), *How the West Was Won* (62), *The Rare Breed* (66), *The Destructors* (67), *Childish Things* (69), etc. TV series: *Mr District Attorney* (54–55).

BRIAN, MARY (1908–   ) (Louise Dantzler). American leading lady of the 20s. *Peter Pan* (as Wendy) (24), *Beau Geste* (27), *Shanghai Bound* (28), *The Virginian* (30), *The Front Page* (31), *Ever Since Eve* (34), *The Amazing Quest of Ernest Bliss* (36), *Navy Bound* (37), etc.; then retired apart from one second feature, *The Dragnet* (48).

BRICE, FANNY (1891–1951) (Fanny Borach). American entertainer who made a virtue of her plainness. Three films have been based on her life: *Broadway Thro' a Keyhole* (33), *Rose of Washington Square* (38) and *Funny Girl* (68). Rare screen appearances include *My Man* (28), *The Great Ziegfeld* (36), *Ziegfeld Follies* (44).

BRICUSSE, LESLIE (1931–   ). British lyricist and composer. *Charley Moon* (56), *Stop the World I Want to Get Off* (65), *Doctor Dolittle* (67), *Goodbye Mr Chips* (69), etc.

THE BRIDE OF FRANKENSTEIN (US 1935). At once the best of the horror films and a gentle mockery of them, this elegant Gothic piece with its eighteenth-century prologue is full of wry humour and pictorial delights. Its reputation rests on James Whale's direction and the script by John Balderston and Anthony Veiller; but Karloff as the monster, Elsa Lanchester as Mary Shelley and Ernest Thesiger as Dr Praetorius are gloriously grotesque.

THE BRIDGE ON THE RIVER KWAI (GB 1957). Carefully directed by David Lean (AA), adapted by Carl Foreman from Pierre Boulle's novel, this ambitious anti-heroic war film had an intriguing plot and fascinating performances from Alec Guinness (AA) and Sessue Hayakawa. Despite these assets and its great visual beauty, the climax was unforgivably confusing.

THE BRIDGE OF SAN LUIS REY. Thornton Wilder's fatalistic novel, tracing the lives of five people who happened to be on a Peruvian rope bridge when it collapsed, was filmed in 1929 by Charles Brabin and in 1944 by Rowland V. Lee.

BRIDGES, ALAN (1927–   ). British director, from TV. *An Act of Murder* (65), *Invasion* (66).

BRIDGES, LLOYD (1913–   ). American general purpose actor, a stalwart of melodramas and Westerns for many years; has recently achieved some TV eminence. *Here Comes Mr Jordan* (41), *A Walk in the Sun* (46), *Canyon Passage* (46), *Secret Service Investigator* (48), *Home of the Brave* (49), *Rocketship XM* (50), *The Whistle at Eaton Falls* (51), *The Sound of Fury* (51), *High Noon* (52), *Plymouth Adventure* (52), *The Tall Texan* (53), *The Limping Man* (GB) (54), *Apache Woman* (55), *The Rainmaker* (57), *The Goddess* (58), *Around the World under the Sea* (66), *The Daring Game* (68), etc. TV series include *Sea Hunt* (57–61), *The Lloyd Bridges Show* (62), *The Loner* (65).

BRIEF ENCOUNTER (GB 1946). One of the great post-war British films, this understated romance about middle-aged people both comfortably married to other partners now seems badly out of 60s fashion but will certainly be rediscovered in a more tender age. Mainly played against railway station settings, it was photographed by Robert Krasker and directed by David Lean from a Noël Coward play. Celia Johnson and Trevor Howard starred.

BRIERS, RICHARD (1934–   ). British light comedian, usually in dithery roles. *A Matter of Who* (62), *The Girl on the Boat* (62), *Fathom* (67), etc. Most familiar on TV, especially in *The Marriage Lines* series.

BRIGHTON ROCK (GB 1946). Graham Greene worked on the screen play of his tough 'entertainment' about a racetrack gang run by a vicious adolescent. The Boulting Brothers produced it in bravura fashion, with a softened ending which was criticized; the film was acclaimed for its new realism and attacked for its new viciousness. Both it and Richard Attenborough's performance now seem rather tame.

BRINGING UP BABY (US 1938). A classic example of 30s crazy comedy, this was full of upper-bracket people behaving in a ridiculous and even anti-social manner in pursuit of an escaped pet leopard, a dog and a dinosaur bone. Delightfully written, directed (Howard Hawks) and played (Katharine Hepburn, Cary Grant, Charles Ruggles, May Robson). It hasn't dated at all.

BRISSON, CARL (1895–1958) (Carl Pedersen). Danish leading man who made films in Britain. *The Ring* (28), *The Manxman* (29),

The American Prisoner (29), *Song of Soho* (30), *All the King's Horses* (35), etc.

BRISSON, FREDERICK (c. 1915–   ). Danish producer with long experience in Britain (pre-39) and Hollywood. Films include *The Pajama Game* (57), *Under the Yum Yum Tree* (64). Married Rosalind Russell and subsequently masterminded her appearances.

the British Empire has provided a useful background for innumerable movies: some comic, some tragic, but most of them plain adventurous. The Elizabethan adventurers roistered through films like *The Sea Hawk, The Virgin Queen* and *Seven Seas to Calais*; the westward voyage occupied *Plymouth Adventure*; Australia provided the canvas for *Under Capricorn, Robbery Under Arms*, and *Botany Bay*; *Mutiny on the Bounty* showed the British in the South Seas; Africa was the subject of *Zulu, The Four Feathers, Khartoum, Sundown, Rhodes of Africa, The Sun Never Sets* and (for the anti-British view) *Ohm Kruger*; and, favourite of all far-flung outposts, India provided splendid terrain for such adventures as *The Drum, Northwest Frontier, Gunga Din, King of the Khyber Rifles, The Rains Came, Charge of the Light Brigade* and *Lives of a Bengal Lancer*. When the Empire was at its height, one could view the British influence as benevolent (*Pacific Destiny*), maiden-auntish (*Sanders of the River*), or merely acquisitive (*Victoria the Great*).

The inevitable break-up was rather less well covered. Even American independence has been played down by Hollywood producers with an eye on the British market, though of course it comes into such films as *Last of the Mohicans, Lafayette, Daniel Boone,* and even Disney's *Ben and Me.* Emergent Africa was the theme of *Men of Two Worlds* as long ago as 1946, but between that and the independent state depicted in *Guns at Batasi* came the Mau Mau period shown in *Simba, Safari* and *Something of Value. The High Bright Sun* dealt with Cyprus; *The Planter's Wife* and *The Seventh Dawn* with Malaya; *Exodus, Judith* and *Cast a Giant Shadow* with Israel; scores of films with the Irish troubles; *Bhowani Junction* and *Nine Hours to Rama* with India. But the emergence of new states is a painful business as a rule, and most of these films give the impression of so much tasteless picking at sore points.

British Film Academy. Organization founded 1946 'for the advancement of the film'. Since 1959 amalgamated with the Society of Film and Television Arts. Its award statuette is known as Stella, and is noted in this book by the letters BFA.

British Film Institute. Partly government-subsidized organization founded 1933 'to encourage the use and development of cinema as a means of entertainment and instruction'. Includes the National Film Archive (founded 1935) and the National Film Theatre (founded after the 1951 Festival of Britain). Also library, information section, stills collection, film distribution agency, lecture courses, etc. Chief publications: Monthly Film Bulletin, Sight and Sound.

BRITT, MAY (1933–   ) (Maybritt Wilkens). Swedish leading lady who made a few American films (*The Young Lions* [58], *The Blue Angel* [59], etc.) and married Sammy Davis Jnr.

BRITTON, BARBARA (1920–   ) (Barbara Brantingham Czukor). American leading lady of the 40s; went to Hollywood straight from college. *Secret of the Wastelands* (debut) (40), *Louisiana Purchase* (41), *Wake Island* (42), *Reap the Wild Wind* (42), *So Proudly We Hail* (43), *Till We Meet Again* (first leading role) (44), *The Story of Dr Wassell* (44), *A Man Called Sullivan* (45), *Captain Kidd* (45), *The Virginian* (46), *The Fabulous Suzanne* (47), *Millie's Daughter* (47), *Champagne for Caesar* (49), *Bandit Queen* (50), *The Raiders* (52), *Ain't Misbehaving* (55), *Night Freight* (55), etc. Recently on stage. TV series: *Mr and Mrs North* (52).

BRITTON, TONY (1925–   ). British stage, screen and TV actor of quiet and polished style. *Salute the Toff* (52), *Loser Take All* (57), *The Birthday Present* (57), *Operation Amsterdam* (58), *The Rough and the Smooth* (59), *Suspect* (60), *Stork Talk* (61), *The Horsemasters* (61), *The Break* (63), *Dr Syn* (63), etc.

BROADWAY BILL (US 1934). A typically hard-boiled but soft-centred racetrack comedy directed with great verve by Frank Capra from a script by Mark Hellinger. Starring Warner Baxter and Myrna Loy, it was released in the UK as *Strictly Confidential*. In 1949 Capra remade it as a semi-musical, *Riding High*, with Bing Crosby and Nancy Olson.

BROADWAY MELODY (US 1929: AA). Early sound musical which, imitated, improved and expanded, set the style for the 30s. Harry Beaumont directed; Anita Page, Bessie Love and Charles King starred. MGM later used the title but not the plot for *Broadway Melody of 1936* and followed with *Broadway Melody of 1938* and *Broadway Melody of 1940*; there was to have been one for 1944 but the title was changed to *Broadway Rhythm*.

BROCCOLI, ALBERT R. (1909–   ). American producer resident in England since early 50s when with Irving Allen he founded Warwick Pictures (*Cockleshell Heroes* (56), *Zarak* (57), *Fire Down Below* (58), etc.). Now co-producer with Harry Saltzman of the James Bond films for Eon Productions. 1968: *Chitty Chitty Bang Bang*.

BRODERICK, HELEN (1890–1959). Wry-faced American stage comedienne, mother of Broderick Crawford. Enlivened many 30s comedies, but was little seen in later years. *Fifty Million Frenchmen* (51), *Top Hat* (35), *Swing Time* (37), *The Rage of Paris* (38), *No No Nanette* (40), *Nice Girl* (41), *Her Primitive Man* (44), *Because of Him* (46), etc.

BRODIE, STEVE (1919–   ) (John Stevens). Tough-looking American leading man and character actor, mainly in second features. *This Man's Navy* (45), *Trail Street* (47), *Home of the Brave* (49), *Winchester 37* (50), *Only the Valiant* (51), *The Beast from Twenty Thousand Fathoms* (53), *The Caine Mutiny* (54), *Gun Duel in Durango* (57), *Three Came to Kill* (60), etc.

BRODINE, NORBERT (c. 1895–   ). American cinematographer, in Hollywood from 1919. Films include *The Sea Hawk* (24), *Beast of the City* (32), *Little Man What Now* (33), *Topper* (37), *Of Mice and Men* (39), *The House on 92nd Street* (46), *13 Rue Madeleine* (46), *Kiss of Death* (47), *Boomerang* (47), *I Was a Male War Bride* (49), *Thieves Highway* (49), *Five Fingers* (52). Retired.

BRODNEY, OSCAR (1905–   ). American comedy writer, former lawyer. With Universal since the 40s, working mainly on routine series and light costume dramas. *Are You With It* (48), *Francis* (50), *Yes, Sir, That's My Baby* (52), *Little Egypt* (53), *The Glenn Miller Story* (54), *Lady Godiva* (55), *Tammy and the Bachelor* (57), *Bobbikins* (GB; also produced) (59), *Tammy and the Doctor* (63), *The Brass Bottle* (64), *I'd Rather Be Rich* (65), etc.

BRODSZKY, NICHOLAS (1905–   ). Russian-born composer, long in Britain. *French Without Tears* (39), *Quiet Wedding* (40), *The Way to the Stars* (45), *A Man About the House* (47), others.

BROKEN ARROW (US 1950). Hollywood Western which does not wear well as entertainment but is significant for its sympathetic attitude to the Indians and its depiction of their chief Cochise as an honourable man. Starred James Stewart, Jeff Chandler; Delmer Daves directed.

BROKEN BLOSSOMS. It suited D. W. Griffith's rather Victorian outlook to make this highly sentimental tale of a gentle Chinaman and an innocent waif in a highly imaginary Limehouse, and his 1919 version, being played for every last tear by Richard Barthelmess and Lillian Gish, was a great success. In 1936 Griffith was assigned to do a British remake with Emlyn Williams and Dolly Haas, but he resigned during preparation and Hans (John) Brahm took over. By now the tale was too outmoded for popular success, but it was interestingly done in the arty manner.

BROMBERG, J. EDWARD (1903–1951). Hungarian actor, in America from infancy. *Under Two Flags* (36), *Jesse James* (39), *The Mark of Zorro* (40), *The Devil Pays Off* (42), *Halfway to Shanghai* (42),

Phantom of the Opera (43), *A Voice in the Wind* (45), *A Song Is Born* (48), others.

BROMBERGER, HERVE (1918–   ). French director. *Identité Judiciaire* (51), *Les Fruits Sauvages* (54), *Les Loups dans la Bergerie* (60), *Mort Ou Est Ta Victoire* (64), etc.

BROMFIELD, JOHN (1922–   ) (Farron Bromfield). American leading man, mainly in second features. *Harpoon* (48), *Paid in Full* (50), *The Furies* (50), *Ring of Fear* (53), *Crime Against Joe* (55), *Hot Cars* (57), etc. TV series, *Sheriff of Cochise*, etc.

BRON, ELEANOR (c. 1939–   ). British revue and TV player. *Help* (65), *Alfie* (66), *Two for the Road* (67), *Women in Love* (69).

BRONSON, BETTY (1907–   ). American leading lady of the silent screen. *Peter Pan* (24), *A Kiss for Cinderella* (25), *Are Parents People?* (24), *The Cat's Pajamas* (27), *Ben Hur* (27), *The Singing Fool* (28), *Medicine Man* (30), etc.; last appearance in *The Yodelling Kid from Pine Ridge* (37).

BRONSON, CHARLES (1922–   ) (Charles Buchinsky). American actor, a former wrestler whose deeply-etched features and tough manner can deal with any nationality from Russian to Red Indian. Started as a villain, but has recently had more sympathetic roles, also his own TV series *Meet McGraw*. Films include *Red Skies of Montana* (51), *Pat and Mike* (52), *House of Wax* (53), *Drumbeat* (54), *Vera Cruz* (54), *Jubal* (56), *Machine Gun Kelly* (57), *Never So Few* (60), *A Thunder of Drums* (61), *The Sandpiper* (65), *Battle of the Bulge* (65), *This Property Is Condemned* (66), *The Dirty Dozen* (67), *Once Upon a Time in the West* (69), *Twinky* (69), *Dubious Patriots* (70); etc.

BRONSTON, SAMUEL (c. 1910–   ). Russian-born independent producer, in Hollywood for many years: *Jack London* (43), *A Walk in the Sun* (46), etc. Later became president of Samuel Bronston Productions, centred in Madrid, making films on epic scale for world markets: *King of Kings* (60), *El Cid* (61), *Fifty-five Days at Peking* (62), *The Fall of the Roman Empire* (64), *The Magnificent Showman* (*Circus World*) (64). Financial difficulties have caused a temporary withdrawal.

BRONTË, CHARLOTTE (1816–55). British novelist whose *Jane Eyre* has been frequently filmed, most recently in 1934 with Virginia Bruce and Colin Clive and in 1943 with Joan Fontaine and Orson Welles. Its central situation, of a governess in the house of a mysterious but romantic tyrant, has also been frequently plagiarized.

BRONTË, EMILY (1818–48). British novelist, sister of Charlotte Brontë, and author of *Wuthering Heights* (qv), much filmed in Britain before the definitive 1939 version. A somewhat romantic film about the sisters was filmed in 1943 under the title *Devotion*, with Olivia de Havilland as Charlotte and Ida Lupino as Emily.

BROOK, CLIVE (1887–   ) (Clifford Brook). Distinguished British leading man of stage and screen; for forty years a perfect gentleman (or, very occasionally, a cad). Many silent films in Britain and Hollywood include *A Debt of Honour* (19), *Woman to Woman* (21), *The Royal Oak* (23), *Seven Sinners* (25), *Underworld* (27), *The Four Feathers* (28); talkies include *Slightly Scarlet* (28), *The Return of Sherlock Holmes* (29), *East Lynne* (31), *Shanghai Express* (32), *Cavalcade* (33), *For the Love of a Queen* (35), *Action for Slander* (37), *The Ware Case* (39), *Convoy* (40), *Breach of Promise* (41), *On Approval* (also produced and directed) (43), *The Shipbuilders* (44), etc.; returned to stage. Only recent film appearance: *The List of Adrian Messenger* (63).

BROOK, FAITH (1922–   ). British actress of stage, screen and TV; daughter of Clive Brook. *Jungle Book* (42), *Uneasy Terms* (48), *Wicked as They Come* (56), *Chase a Crooked Shadow* (57), *The Thirty-nine Steps* (59), *To Sir With Love* (66), etc.

BROOK, LESLEY (1916–   ). British leading lady of a few sentimental dramas of the 40s. *The Vulture* (37), *Rose of Tralee* (41), *Variety Jubilee* (42), *I'll Walk Beside You* (43), *The Trojan Brothers* (46), *House of Darkness* (48), etc.

BROOK, LYNDON (1926–   ). British actor of stage, screen and TV; son of Clive Brook. *Train of Events* (49), *The Purple Plain* (54), *Reach for the Sky* (56), *Innocent Sinners* (58), *Song Without End* (US) (60), *Invasion* (66), etc.

†BROOK, PETER (1925–   ). British stage producer who has directed some ambitious but not wholly successful films: *The Beggar's Opera* (52), *Moderato Cantabile* (60), *Lord of the Flies* (63), *The Marat/Sade* (66), *Tell Me Lies* (67), *King Lear* (69).

BROOKE, HILLARY (c. 1916–   ). Well-groomed American leading lady of co-features in the 40s. *New Faces of 1937*, *The Adventures of Sherlock Holmes* (39), *The Ministry of Fear* (43), *The Woman in Green* (44), *Big Town* (46), *Africa Screams* (49), *Vendetta* (50), *Confidence Girl* (52), *Abbott and Costello Meet Captain Kidd* (53), *Invaders from Mars* (54), *The Man Who Knew Too Much* (56), etc.

BROOK-JONES, ELWYN (1911–1962). Thick-set British character actor usually seen in villainous roles. *Dangerous Moonlight* (40), *Tomorrow We Live* (42), *Odd Man Out* (46), *The Three Weird Sisters* (48), *I'll Get You For This* (50), *Beau Brummell* (54), etc.

Brooks, Geraldine

BROOKS, GERALDINE (1925–) (Geraldine Stroock). American leading lady most at home in intense roles. *Cry Wolf* (47), *Possessed* (47), *This Side of the Law* (48), *Embraceable You* (48), *The Reckless Moment* (49), *Volcano* (It.) (50), *The Green Glove* (52), *Street of Sinners* (56), etc. More recently on stage and TV.

BROOKS, JEAN (1921–). Stylish-looking American leading lady who worked briefly for RKO in the 40s. *The Seventh Victim* (43), *The Leopard Man* (43), *The Falcon and the Co-Eds* (44), *Two O'clock Courage* (46), etc.

BROOKS, LESLIE (1922–) (Leslie Gettman). American leading lady of the 40s. *Undercover Agent* (42), *Nine Girls* (44), *Tonight and Every Night* (45), *The Cobra Strikes* (48), etc.

BROOKS, LOUISE (1900–). American actress who made several films in Germany (*Pandora's Box* [29], *Diary of a Lost Girl* [30], etc.) and has remained an attractive enigma to specialist critics. Retired 1938 after routine Hollywood roles.

BROOKS, PHYLLIS (1915–) (Phyllis Seiller). American leading lady of the 30s. *I've Been Around* (35), *Rebecca of Sunnybrook Farm* (38), *In Old Chicago* (38), *The Shanghai Gesture* (41), *The Unseen* (45), etc.

BROOKS, RAND (1918–). American leading man, usually in minor films. *Gone with the Wind* (39), *Florian* (40), *Son of Monte Cristo* (41), *Joan of Arc* (47), *The Steel Fist* (52), *Man from the Black Hills* (56), *Comanche Station* (60), etc.

BROOKS, RAY (1942–). British juvenile leading man with repertory experience. *HMS Defiant* (62), *Play it Cool* (62), *Some People* (63), *The Knack* (65), *Daleks Invasion Earth 2150 AD* (66), etc. TV series: *Taxi*.

†BROOKS, RICHARD (1912–). American writer-director. *White Savage* (w) (42), *Cobra Woman* (w) (44), *Brute Force* (w) (47), *Crossfire* (w; from his own novel) (47), *Crisis* (w, d) (50), *The Light Touch* (w, d) (51), *Deadline USA* (w, d) (52), *Battle Circus* (w, d) (52), *The Last Time I Saw Paris* (w, d) (54), *Take the High Ground* (d) (54), *The Flame and the Flesh* (d) (54), *The Blackboard Jungle* (w, d) (55), *The Last Hunt* (w, d) (56), *The Catered Affair* (d) (56), *Something of Value* (w, d) (57), *The Brothers Karamazov* (w, d) (58), *Cat on a Hot Tin Roof* (w, d) (58), *Elmer Gantry* (w, d) (AA screenplay) (60), *Sweet Bird of Youth* (w, d) (62), *Lord Jim* (w, d, p) (65), *The Professionals* (w, d, p) (66), *In Cold Blood* (w, d, p) (67), *The Happy Ending* (w, d, p) (69). (List *as director* complete.)

BROPHY, ED (1895–1960). American character actor, often seen as a tough, cigar-smoking little man in a bowler hat, who could be a gangster or an odd kind of valet. In hundreds of films since 1919;

best roles in *The Champ* (32), *Wonder Man* (45), *The Last Hurrah* (58), and the 'Falcon' series in which he played Goldie the valet.

Brothels were fairly prevalent in American silent movies, but the Hays Code banished them and for many years one had to look to the French for such revelations as he could be found in *Le Plaisir* and *Hungry for Love*. In recent years however the doors have opened. *Lady L* showed the funny side of brothel life, *Ulysses* the vulgar, *House of a Thousand Dolls* the fantastic, *How Sweet It Is* the charming, *The Balcony* the expressionist; while *A Walk on the Wild Side* concentrated on the miserable aspects and even sported a lesbian madam. Nowadays every western has one, notably *Waterhole 3*, *Five Card Stud* and *Hang 'Em High*.

BROTHER ORCHID (US 1939). The virtual end of the 30s gangster cycle was marked by this warm comedy in which Edward G. Robinson plays a gangster who, left for dead after being 'taken for a ride', is cared for by monks and literally sees the light. Directed by Lloyd Bacon.

THE BROTHERS KARAMAZOV, Dostoievsky's nineteenth-century novel of Russian family life was filmed by Robert Wiene in Germany in 1921, with Emil Jannings; the same country produced the next version, *The Murder of Dmitri Karamazov*, in 1930 with Fritz Kortner under the direction of Fedor Ozep. In 1957 Richard Brooks made a Hollywood version with Yul Brynner, and the Russian director Pyriev completed a Russian film of the book in 1967.

BROUGH, MARY (1863–1934). British character comedienne long associated with the Aldwych farce company of the 20s and in some of their early talking films: *Rookery Nook* (30), *Tons of Money* (32), *Turkey Time* (32), *Thark* (33). Usually a battleaxe or suspicious landlady.

BROWN, CHARLES D. (1887–1948). American supporting actor who played scores of detectives, officials and executives. *It Happened One Night* (34), *Algiers* (38), *The Grapes of Wrath* (40), *Roxie Hart* (42), *The Big Sleep* (46), etc.

BROWN, CLARENCE (1890–   ). American director, former electrical engineer. Has made many big but sensitive films, usually notable for soft pictorial quality. *The Eagle* (25), *Flesh and the Devil* (27), *Trail of '98* (28), *Romance* (30), *Anna Christie* (30), *A Free Soul* (31), *Emma* (32), *Letty Lynton* (32), *Night Flight* (33), *Chained* (35), *Anna Karenina* (35), *Ah Wilderness* (35), *The Gorgeous Hussey* (36), *Marie Walewska (Conquest)* (37), *Idiot's Delight* (39), *The Rains Came* (39), *Edison the Man* (40), *Come Live with Me* (41), *The Human Comedy* (43), *The White Cliffs of Dover* (43), *National Velvet* (44), *The Yearling*

(46), *Song of Love* (47), *Intruder in the Dust* (49), *To Please a Lady* (50), *When in Rome* (52), *Plymouth Adventure* (52), *Never Let Me Go* (produced only) (53), many others. Retired.

BROWN, GEORGE (1913–). British producer, former production manager. *Sleeping Car to Trieste* (48), *The Chiltern Hundreds* (50), *The Seekers* (54), *Jacqueline* (56), *Dangerous Exile* (57), *Tommy the Toreador* (60), *Murder at the Gallop* (63). *Guns at Batasi* (64), *The Trap* (66), *Finders Keepers* (66), etc.

BROWN, HARRY (1917–). American novelist and screenwriter, mainly on war themes. *The True Glory* (co-w) (45), *A Walk in the Sun* (46), *Arch of Triumph* (48), *Sands of Iwo Jima* (49), *A Place in the Sun* (51), *Bugles in the Afternoon* (52), *The Sniper* (co-w) (52), *Eight Iron Men* (52), *All the Brothers Were Valiant* (co-w) (53), *D-Day Sixth of June* (co-w) (56), *Between Heaven and Hell* (co-w) (57), *El Dorado* (co-w) (66), etc.

BROWN, HARRY JOE (1892–). American producer with long experience in all branches of show business. *Captain Blood* (35), *Alexander's Ragtime Band* (38), *The Rains Came* (39), *Western Union* (41), *Knickerbocker Holiday* (also directed) (44), many others; more recently has turned out innumerable Westerns, mostly starring Randolph Scott.

BROWN, JIM (1936–). American Negro leading man, former athlete. *Rio Conchos* (64), *The Dirty Dozen* (67), *Dark of the Sun* (68), *The Split* (68), *Riot* (68), *100 Rifles* (69), *The Grasshopper* (70), etc.

BROWN, JOE (1941–). British pop singer who appears with a group called The Bruvvers. In several light variety films; also lead in *What a Crazy World* (63), *Three Hats for Lisa* (65).

BROWN, JOE E. (1892–). Wide-mouthed American star comedian with background in circus, basketball and vaudeville. Screen debut 1928. *Crooks Can't Win* (28), *On with the Show* (29), *Sally* (30), *Local Boy Makes Good* (31), *The Tenderfoot* (32), *You Said a Mouthful* (33), *A Midsummer Night's Dream* (35), *Wide Open Faces* (37), *Beware Spooks* (39), *Shut My Big Mouth* (41), *The Daring Young Man* (42), *Pin-Up Girl* (43), *The Tender Years* (straight role) (49), *Showboat* (51), *Some Like It Hot* (59), *A Comedy of Terrors* (63), many others. Published autobiography 1959: 'Laughter is a Wonderful Thing'.

BROWN, JOHNNY MACK (1904–). American actor, former footballer; a popular star of low-budget Westerns in the 30s and 40s. *The Bugle Call* (debut) (26), *Our Dancing Daughters* (28), *Billy the Kid* (31), *The Last Flight* (31), *The Vanishing Frontier* (33), *Riding the Apache Trail* (36), *Bad Man from Red Butte* (40), *Ride 'Em Cowboy*

(41), *The Right to Live* (45), etc. Recent comeback in *The Bounty Killer* (65), *Apache Uprising* (65).

BROWN, NACIO HERB (1896–1964). American light composer who usually supplied the music for Arthur Freed's lyrics: 'Broadway Melody', 'Singing in the Rain', 'Good Morning', 'You Are My Lucky Star', many others.

BROWN, PAMELA (1917–   ). British stage actress who has been in occasional films, usually in haughty or eccentric roles: *One of Our Aircraft Is Missing* (42), *I Know Where I'm Going* (45), *Tales of Hoffman* (51), *The Second Mrs Tanqueray* (52), *Personal Affair* (53), *Richard III* (56), *The Scapegoat* (59), *Becket* (64), *Secret Ceremony* (68), etc.

BROWN, ROBERT (c. 1918–   ). Burly British actor of stage, TV and film, *Helen of Troy* (55), *A Hill in Korea* (56), *Campbell's Kingdom* (57), *Ben Hur* (59), *Sink the Bismarck* (60), *The Masque of the Red Death* (64), *One Million Years BC* (66), etc.

BROWN, ROWLAND V. (1901–1963). American director acclaimed for *Quick Millions* (31). Career waned oddly after only two other notable films, *Blood Money* (33), *The Devil Is a Sissy* (37).

BROWN, TOM (1913–   ). American leading man of the 'boy next door' type. *Queen High* (31), *Tom Brown of Culver* (32), *Three-Cornered Moon* (33), *Judge Priest* (34), *Maytime* (37), *In Old Chicago* (38), *Margie* (41), *The Pay-Off* (43), *Duke of Chicago* (49), *The Quiet Gun* (57), etc.

BROWN, VANESSA (1928–   ) (Smylla Brind). American leading lady, usually in demure roles. *Youth Runs Wild* (45), *The Late George Apley* (47), *The Secret of St Ives* (49), *Three Husbands* (50), *The Bad and the Beautiful* (52), etc. Retired but reappeared in *Rosie* (67). TV series: *My Favourite Husband* (54).

BROWNE, CORAL (1913–   ). Australian actress long in high comedy roles on British stage. Films: *Auntie Mame* (US) (58), *The Roman Spring of Mrs Stone* (61), *Dr Crippen* (63), *The Killing of Sister George* (68).

BROWNING, RICOU (1930–   ). American actor and stunt man who played the title role in *The Creature from the Black Lagoon*; later became specialist in underwater direction for Ivan Tors and worked on the *Flipper* series, *Around the World under the Sea*, *Thunderball*, *Lady in Cement*, etc.

BROWNING, TOD (1882–1962). American director known principally for horror films of early 30s. Films since 1918 include *The Brazen Beauty* (18), *Virgin of Stamboul* (20), *Under Two Flags* (22), *The*

White Tiger (23), *The Unholy Three* (25), *The Mystic* (25), *The Road
to Mandalay* (26), *The Unknown* (27), *London after Midnight* (27),
West of Zanzibar (28), *Where East Is East* (29), *The Thirteenth Chair*
(29), *Outside the Law* (30), *The Unholy Three* (sound remake) (30),
Dracula (30), *Freaks* (32), *Fast Workers* (33), *Mark of the Vampire* (35),
The Devil Doll (36), *Miracles for Sale* (last film) (39), etc.

BROWNLOW, KEVIN (1938–). British producer-director who made
his first film, *It Happened Here*, on a shoestring budget over seven
years. It was released in 1966. Published 1969 *The Parade's Gone By*,
a collection of interviews with silent stars.

BRUCE, BRENDA (1918–). British screen and stage actress, often in
comedy roles. *Millions Like Us* (43), *They Came to a City* (45), *The
Final Test* (53), *Nightmare* (63), *The Uncle* (65), etc.

BRUCE, DAVID (1914–) (Marden McBroom). American light
leading man familiar in Universal films during World War II.
The Sea Hawk (40), *Singapore Woman* (42), *The Mad Ghoul* (43),
Salome Where She Danced (45), *Lady on a Train* (45), *Prejudice* (48),
Masterson of Kansas (55), etc.

BRUCE, NIGEL (1895–1953). British comedy actor, on stage from 1920,
screen from 1930 (mainly in Hollywood); usually played upper-
class benevolent buffoons. Best remembered as Dr Watson to Basil
Rathbone's Sherlock Holmes in fourteen films beginning with *The
Hound of the Baskervilles* in 1939 and ending with *Terror by Night*
in 1946. Other appearances include *I Was a Spy* (33), *Treasure Island*
(34), *Becky Sharp* (35), *She* (35), *The Last of Mrs Cheyney* (37), *The
Rains Came* (39), *Rebecca* (40), *The Bluebird* (40), *Suspicion* (41),
The Chocolate Soldier (41), *This Above All* (42), *Lassie Come Home* (43),
Frenchman's Creek (44), *The Corn Is Green* (45), *The Two Mrs Carrolls*
(46), *The Exile* (47), *Hong Kong* (51), *Limelight* (53).

BRUCE, VIRGINIA (1910–) (Helen Virginia Briggs). American
leading lady of the 30s, often in scheming roles; once a Goldwyn
Girl. *The Love Parade* (30), *Downstairs* (32), *Jane Eyre* (title role)
(34), *Metropolitan* (35), *The Great Ziegfeld* (36), *Let Freedom Ring* (39),
Invisible Woman (40), *Careful Soft Shoulder* (43), *Night Has a Thousand
Eyes* (48), *The Reluctant Bride* (GB) (52), *Strangers When We Meet*
(60), many others.

BRUCKMAN, CLYDE (1894–1955). American writer-director of many
silent comedies, including *The General* and *Feet First*. Often collaborated with such stars as Keaton, Lloyd and Laurel and Hardy.

BRUMMELL, BEAU (1778–1840). A famous British dandy and politician
who has been the subject of two biopics: in 1924 with John
Barrymore (directed by Harry Lachman) and in 1954 with
Stewart Granger (directed by Curtis Bernhardt).

BRUNEL, ADRIAN (1892–1958). British director mainly eminent in silent days. Co-founded Minerva Films with Leslie Howard in 1920 and made humorous shorts such as *Bookworms* and *The Bump*; was founder member of the London Film Society; later directed *The Man without Desire* (23), *Crossing the Great Sagrada* (short) (24), *Blighty* (27), *The Constant Nymph* (27), *The Vortex* (28), *While Parents Sleep* (35), *The City of Beautiful Nonsense* (36), *Prison Breaker* (36), *The Girl Who Forgot* (40), etc. Wrote autobiography, 'Nice Work'.

BRUNIUS, JACQUES (1906–1967). French critic, once assistant to Clair, Renoir and Brunel. Acted in *Partie de Campagne* (37). Subsequently worked in Britain with C.O.I. and B.B.C.

BRUTE FORCE (US 1947). A confected, violent but harrowingly exciting prison melodrama which marked Jules Dassin's debut as a notable director. Photographed by William Daniels, written by Richard Brooks, with powerful performances by Burt Lancaster, Charles Bickford and Hume Cronyn.

BRYAN, DORA (1923–) (Dora Broadbent). British stage and film comedienne, specializing in warm-hearted tarts of the cockney or northern variety. *Odd Man Out* (debut) (46), *The Fallen Idol* (48), *The Cure for Love* (48), *The Blue Lamp* (50), *High Treason* (51), *Lady Godiva Rides Again* (51), *Mother Riley Meets the Vampire* (52), *Time, Gentlemen, Please* (53), *Fast and Loose* (54), *See How They Run* (55), *Cockleshell Heroes* (56), *The Green Man* (57), *Desert Mice* (59), *The Night We Got the Bird* (60), *A Taste of Honey* (BFA: leading role) (61), *The Great St Trinian's Train Robbery* (66), *The Sandwich Man* (66), *Two a Penny* (68), etc.

BRYAN, JANE (1918–) (Jane O'Brien). American leading lady of the late 30s. *Marked Woman* (36), *A Slight Case of Murder* (38), *The Sisters* (39), *Each Dawn I Die* (39), *We Are Not Alone* (39), *Invisible Stripes* (40), etc. Retired.

BRYAN, JOHN (1911–1969). British production designer (*Great Expectations* [AA] [46], *Pandora and the Flying Dutchman* [51], etc.) and producer: *The Card* (52), *The Purple Plain* (54), *Windom's Way* (57), *The Horse's Mouth* (58), *There Was a Crooked Man* (60), *Tamahine* (62), *After the Fox* (66), *The Touchables* (68), etc.

BRYANT, NANA (1888–1955). American character actress with stage experience; usually played middle-class mothers. *The Unsuspected* (47), *The Lady Gambles* (49), *Harvey* (51), *Geraldine* (53), *The Private War of Major Benson* (55), many others.

†BRYNNER, YUL (1916–). Russian-American leading actor, the only bald-headed romantic star in the business. Film debut in

Port of New York (49) interrupted long Broadway and TV experience; returned to Hollywood 1956 to repeat stage success in *The King and I* (AA). Later roles include *The Ten Commandments* (56), *Anastasia* (56), *The Brothers Karamazov* (58), *The Journey* (58), *Solomon and Sheba* (59), *Once More with Feeling* (59), *The Magnificent Seven* (60), *Surprise Package* (60), *Taras Bulba* (62), *Escape to Zahrain* (62), *Flight from Ashiya* (63), *Kings of the Sun* (63), *Invitation to a Gunfighter* (64), *The Saboteur, Code Name Morituri* (65), *Cast a Giant Shadow* (guest appearance) (66), *Return of the Seven* (66), *Triple Cross* (66), *The Double Man* (67), *The Long Duel* (67), *Villa Rides* (68), *The Madwoman of Chaillot* (69), *The File of the Golden Goose* (69), *The Battle of Neretva* (70).

B.S.C. British Society of Cinematographers, a professional society founded in the 50s, similar in aims to the A.S.C. (qv).

BUCHAN, JOHN (1875–1940). British adventure novelist oddly neglected by the cinema apart from *The 39 Steps*, neither version of which bears much resemblance to the original; and a 1927 version of *Huntingtower*.

BUCHANAN, EDGAR (1902–). American character actor, often in Westerns as crooked judge, comic side-kick or out-and-out villain. *The Richest Man in Town* (41), *The Desperadoes* (42), *The Bandit of Sherwood Forest* (45), *The Best Man Wins* (leading role) (48), *Cheaper by the Dozen* (50), *The Big Trees* (52), *Shane* (53), *Human Desire* (54), *Destry* (55), *Come Next Spring* (56), *The Sheepman* (58), *Chartroose Caboose* (60), *Cimarron* (61), *A Ticklish Affair* (63), *Move Over Darling* (63), *Welcome to Hard Times* (67), many others. TV series: *Hopalong Cassidy, Judge Roy Bean, Petticoat Junction*.

BUCHANAN, JACK (1891–1957). British song-and-dance man, a major stage personality of the 20s with his good looks, long legs, nasal voice and immaculate debonair appearance. Films include *Bulldog Drummond's Third Round* (25), *Toni* (27), *Show of Shows* (US) (29), *Monte Carlo* (US) (30), *Goodnight Vienna* (31), *Brewster's Millions* (33), *That's a Good Girl* (also directed) (34), *This'll Make You Whistle* (35), *When Knights Were Bold* (36), *Break the News* (36), *The Sky's the Limit* (38), *The Gang's All Here* (39), *Bulldog Sees It Through* (40), *The Band Wagon* (US) (53), *As Long As They're Happy* (54), *Josephine and Men* (55).

BUCHHOLZ, HORST (1933–). German leading man with wider reputation after *Tiger Bay* (59), *The Magnificent Seven* (60), *Fanny* (61), *One Two Three* (61), *Nine Hours to Rama* (63), *The Empty Canvas* (64), *Marco the Magnificent* (65), *Cervantes* (66), *l'Astragale* (68), etc.

BUCHMAN, SIDNEY (1902–). American writer (*The Sign of the Cross* (32). *Theodora Goes Wild* (36), *Mr Smith Goes to Washington* (38),

Here Comes Mr Jordan (AA) (41), *The Talk of the Town* (42), etc.) and producer: *A Song to Remember* (also co-wrote) (45), *Jolson Sings Again* (also co-wrote) (50), *Boots Malone* (also co-wrote) (51), *The Group* (66), etc.

BUCK, FRANK (1888–). American explorer who made several animal films. *Bring 'Em Back Alive* (32), *Fang and Claw* (36), *Jungle Menace* (37), *Jacare, Killer of the Amazon* (42), etc. Appeared in *Africa Screams* (50).

BUCK, JULES (1917–). American producer, associate on *Brute Force* (47), *Naked City* (48). As solo producer his films have been more routine until his association with Peter O'Toole as co-founder of Keep Films: *The Day They Robbed the Bank of England* (61), *Becket* (64), *Great Catherine* (68).

BUCK, PEARL (1892–). American novelist and missionary. Two of her novels on China, *The Good Earth* and *Dragon Seed*, were filmed.

BUCKNER, ROBERT (1906–). American screenwriter. *Gold Is Where You Find It* (37), *Jezebel* (38), *Dodge City* (39), *Virginia City* (39), *Santa Fe Trail* (40), *Yankee Doodle Dandy* (42), *Gentleman Jim* (also produced) (43), *The Desert Song* (also produced) (43), *The Gang's All Here* (44), *Rogue's Regiment* (also produced) (48), *Sword in the Desert* (also produced) (49), *Bright Victory* (also produced) (51), *Safari* (56), *From Hell to Texas* (58), *Return of the Gunfighter* (67), *etc.*

BUCQUET, HAROLD S. (1891–1946). English-born director, in Hollywood from mid-30s. *Dr Kildare* series; also *On Borrowed Time* (39), *The Adventures of Tartu* (GB) (43), *Dragon Seed* (44), *Without Love* (45), others.

BUETEL, JACK (1917–). American leading man who made a highly publicized debut as Billy the Kid in *The Outlaw* (43), but was subsequently little seen: *Best of the Badmen* (51), *The Half Breed* (52), *Jesse James' Women* (54), etc.

BUGS BUNNY. Warners' famous cartoon character, the wise-cracking Brooklynesque rabbit who maintains his aplomb in all situations. Voiced since 1936 by Mel Blanc.

BUJOLD, GENEVIEVE (1942–). French-Canadian leading lady. *French Cancan* (56), *La Guerre Est Finie* (63), *Isabel* (67), *Anne of the Thousand Days* (70).

BULL, PETER (1912–). Portly British character actor often in haughty, aggressive or explosively foreign roles. *Sabotage* (37) *The Ware Case* (39), *The Turners of Prospect Road* (47), *Oliver Twist* (48), *Saraband for Dead Lovers* (48), *The African Queen* (51), *The Malta Story* (53), *Footsteps in the Fog* (55), *Tom Jones* (63), *Dr*

Bulldog Drummond

Strangelove (63), *The Old Dark House* (63), *Dr Dolittle* (67), *Lock Up Your Daughters* (69), many others. Has written several semi-autobiographical books including *I Know the Face But* and *Not On Your Telly.*

BULLDOG DRUMMOND. 'Sapper' (Hector McNeil) created this famous character, an amateur James Bond of the 20s with old-fashioned manners. First portrayed on screen by Carlyle Blackwell in 1922; later by Jack Buchanan (1925), Ronald Colman (1928 and 1934), Kenneth McKenna (1930), Ralph Richardson (1934), Atholl Fleming, in Jack Hulbert's *Bulldog Jack* (1935), John Lodge (1937), Ray Milland (1937), John Howard, in eight films (1937–39), Ron Randell, in two films (1947), Tom Conway, in two films (1948), Walter Pidgeon in *Calling Bulldog Drummond* (1951) and Richard Johnson in *Deadlier than the Male* (1966).

bullfights have understandably not been a popular ingredient of English-speaking films; apart from the romanticism of the two versions of *Blood and Sand* and the cynicism of *The Last Flight* (31) and *The Sun Also Rises*. Several continental films, including *The Moment of Truth*, have tried to convey the mystique of bullfighting, but it has more often been seen as a background for suspense films (*The Caper of the Golden Bulls*) and comedy (*The Kid from Spain*, Laurel and Hardy in *The Bullfighters*, *Tommy the Toreador*, Abbott and Costello in *Mexican Hayride*, Peter Sellers in *The Bobo*, etc.). The two American attempts to make a serious drama on the subject, *The Brave Bulls* and *The Magnificent Matador*, were notably unpopular.

BUNNY, JOHN (1863–1915). British actor who became the funny fat man of early American silent comedy; made more than 150 shorts, usually with Flora Finch.

†BUNUEL, LUIS (1900–   ). Spanish writer-director who worked in France in the 20s and 30s, made many films in Mexico 1945–60, then returned to Europe. A once-notorious surrealist, his later films have mocked hypocrisy and the shows of religion. *Un Chien Andalou* (28), *L'Age d'Or* (30), *Land Without Bread* (32), *Grand Casino* (46), *El Gran Calavera* (49), *Los Olividados* (50), *Suzana la Perverse* (50), *La Hija del Engano* (51), *Una Mujer Sin Amor* (51), *Subida ad Cielo* (51), *The Brute* (52), *Wuthering Heights* (52), *Robinson Crusoe* (52), *El* (53), *La Illusion Viaja en Tranvia* (53), *El Rio y la Muerte* (54), *The Criminal Life of Archibaldo de la Cruz* (55), *La Mort en ce Jardin* (56), *La Fievre Monte a El Pao* (59), *Nazarin* (59), *La Jeune Fille* (60), *Viridiana* (61), *The Exterminating Angel* (62), *Diary of a Chambermaid* (64), *Belle de Jour* (66), *Simon of the Desert* (66), *The Milky Way* (69).

BUONO, VICTOR (1938–   ). 300-lb American actor who moved from amateur theatre to TV. *Whatever Happened to Baby Jane* (63), *The Strangler* (64), *Hush Hush Sweet Charlotte* (64), *The Greatest Story Ever Told* (65), *Young Dillinger* (65), *The Silencers* (66), *Who's Minding the Mint* (67), *Beneath the Planet of the Apes* (69), *etc.*

BURDEN, HUGH (1913–   ). British character actor of diffident roles. *One of Our Aircraft Is Missing* (41), *The Way Ahead* (44), *Fame Is the Spur* (46), *Sleeping Car to Trieste* (48), *No Love for Johnnie* (61), *Funeral in Berlin* (66), others; also on stage and TV.

BURGE, STUART (1918–   ). British director, from TV. *There Was a Crooked Man* (60), *Othello* (66), *The Mikado* (67), *Julius Caesar* (70).

BURKE, ALFRED (1918–   ). British stage, screen and TV actor usually in cold, unsympathetic or other-worldly roles. Notable in *The Angry Silence* (59), *Children of the Damned* (64). TV series: *Public Eye.*

BURKE, BILLIE (1885–   ) (Mary William Ethelbert Appleton Burke). American actress on stage since childhood and in films since 1916, latterly as fluttery matrons. Widow of Florenz Ziegfeld. *Peggy* (16), *Gloria's Romance* (16), *The Land of Promise* (17), *The Misleading Widow* (19), *Let's Get a Divorce* (24), *A Bill of Divorcement* (32), *Dinner at Eight* (33), *Craig's Wife* (34), *Becky Sharp* (35), *Parnell* (36), *Topper* (37), *The Young in Heart* (39), *The Wizard of Oz* (39), *The Man Who Came to Dinner* (41), *They All Kissed the Bride* (42), *Hi Diddle Diddle* (43), *So's Your Uncle* (lea dingrole) (44), *The Cheaters* (45), *Bachelor Girls* (47), *Father of the Bride* (50), *Three Husbands* (50), *The Young Philadelphians* (59), *Sergeant Rutledge* (60) (last to date), many others. Was played by Myrna Loy in *The Great Ziegfeld* (36).

BURKE, JOHNNY (1908–1964). American songwriter who often supplied lyrics for Jimmy Van Heusen's music. 'Pennies from Heaven', 'Moonlight Becomes You', 'Swinging on a Star' (AA 44), many others.

BURKE, MARIE (1894–   ) (Marie Holt). British actress, mostly on stage. Films include *After the Ball* (33), *Odette* (50), *The Constant Husband* (55), *The Snorkel* (58).

BURKE, PAUL (1926–   ). American leading man, in TV series *Noah's Ark* (60), *Naked City* (60–63), *Twelve O'clock High* (65). Films include *Valley of the Dolls* (67), *The Thomas Crown Affair* (68), *Daddy's Gone a-Hunting* (69).

BURKE, PATRICIA (1917–   ). British actress, daughter of Marie Burke. Films include *The Lisbon Story* (45), *The Trojan Brothers* (45),

Burks, Robert

Love Story (46), *While I Live* (47), *Forbidden* (49), *The Happiness of Three Women* (54), *Spider's Web* (60), *The Day the Fish Came Out* (67).

BURKS, ROBERT (1910–1968). American cinematographer. *Arsenic and Old Lace* (44), *Night and Day* (46), *The Unsuspected* (47), *Key Largo* (48), *The Fountainhead* (49), *Beyond the Forest* (49), *The Glass Menagerie* (50), *Strangers on a Train* (51), *Room for One More* (52), *I Confess* (53), *To Catch a Thief* (AA) (55), *The Trouble with Harry* (55), *The Wrong Man* (56), *Vertigo* (58), *North by Northwest* (59), *The Music Man* (61), *The Birds* (63), *Marnie* (64), *Once a Thief* (65), *A Patch of Blue* (66), *Waterhole Three* (67), many others.

burlesque. A word of Italian origin which came to mean an acted 'spoof' of a serious subject. In America it was applied to what the British would call music hall or variety, and eventually connoted striptease and low comedians. It died out as an institution in the thirties: Mamoulian's film *Applause* (29) gives a vivid picture of its latter days. George Watters and Arthur Hopkins' play *Burlesque*, popular in the twenties, concerns a comedian who leaves his long-suffering wife for other women and the demon rum. It was filmed three times, most recently as *When My Baby Smiles at Me* (48), with Betty Grable and Dan Dailey. The heyday of burlesque was also evoked in *The Night They Raided Minsky's* (68).

THE BURMESE HARP (Japan 1956). Kon Ichikawa's long, savage epic of the Burmese campaign of 1943–44 centres on a soldier who after horrifying adventures sees that his vocation is to bury the unknown dead. Lead played by Shoji Yasui; written by Natto Wada.

BURNABY, DAVY (1881–1949). Heavyweight, monocled British light entertainer. *The Co-optimists* (29), *Three Men in a Boat* (33), *Are You a Mason?* (34), *Boys Will Be Boys* (35), *Feather Your Nest* (37), *Many Tanks Mr Atkins* (39), etc.

BURNESS, PETE (1910–   ). American animator who worked his way through *The Little King* and *Tom and Jerry* to *U.P.A.* and *Bullwinkle*.

BURNETT, CAROL (1934–   ). American revue star and comedienne whose only film appearance to date has been in *Who's Been Sleeping In My Bed* (63).

BURNETT, W. R. (1899–   ). American writer of gangster novels and screenplays which have been influential: *Little Caesar* (30), *Scarface* (32), *Dr Socrates* (35), *High Sierra* (40), *Crash Dive* (43), *Nobody Lives Forever* (46), *The Asphalt Jungle* (50), *Captain Lightfoot* (54), *Sergeants Three* (62), etc.

BURNETTE, SMILEY (1911–67). Tubby American character actor, for many years Gene Autry's comic side-kick in low-budget Westerns. Recently in TV series *Petticoat Junction*.

BURNS, BOB ('Bazooka') (1893–1946). Folksy American comedian and humorist who after radio success appeared in several light films. *The Big Broadcast of 1937, Waikiki Wedding* (37), *Wells Fargo* (37), *Your Arkansas Traveller* (38), *Tropic Holiday* (38), *Our Leading Citizen* (39), *Belle of the Yukon* (44), etc.

BURNS, DAVID (1902–   ). American character actor who often played the hero's buddy, the villain's henchman, or a fast-talking agent. *The Queen's Affair* (GB) (34), *The Sky's the Limit* (GB) (38), *A Girl Must Live* (GB) (38), *Knock On Wood* (54), *Deep In My Heart* (55), *Let's Make Love* (60), etc.

BURNS, GEORGE (1896–   ) (Nathan Birnbaum). American vaudeville comedian who married his partner Gracie Allen (qv) and spent many successful years on radio and TV, puffing philosophically at his cigar as he suffered her hare-brained schemes. Films include *The Big Broadcast* (32), *International House* (32), *Love in Bloom* (33), *We're Not Dressing* (34), *The Big Broadcast* (38), *Many Happy Returns* (39). TV series: *The Burns and Allen Show* (50–58), *The George Burns Show* (59–60), *Wendy and Me* (64).

BURNS, MARK (1937–   ) British leading man. *The Charge of the Light Brigade* (67), *The Adventures of Gerard* (69), *A Day on the Beach* (70), etc.

BURR, RAYMOND (1917–   ). Solidly-built Canadian actor who played Hollywood heavies for years before becoming TV's long-running Perry Mason. *Desperate* (47), *Pitfall* (48), *Fort Algiers* (50), *His Kind of Woman* (51), *A Place in the Sun* (51), *Bride of the Gorilla* (51), *The Return of the Corsican Brothers* (53), *Rear Window* (54), *Godzilla* (54), *Serpent of the Nile* (as Mark Antony) (54), *Count Three and Pray* (55), *Great Day in the Morning* (56), *Crime of Passion* (57), *Desire in the Dust* (60), *P.J.* (*New Face in Hell*) (67), many others. TV series: *Perry Mason* (57–66), *Ironside* (67–68).

BURROUGHS, EDGAR RICE (1875–1950). American novelist, the creator (in 1914) of *Tarzan of the Apes* (qv).

BURROWS, ABE (1910–   ). American librettist: *Guys and Dolls, How to Succeed in Business*, etc.

†BURTON, RICHARD (1925–   ) (Richard Jenkins). Welsh stage actor whose dark brooding good looks did not bring him immediate success on his film debut in *The Last Days of Dolwyn* (48). Since going to Hollywood in 1952, however, he has slowly climbed to the crest of popularity, assisted to some extent by his well-publicized romance with Elizabeth Taylor, now his wife. *Now Barabbas Was a Robber* (49), *Waterfront* (50), *The Woman with No Name* (51), *Green Grow the Rushes* (51), then to US; *My Cousin*

Rachel (53), The Robe (53), The Desert Rats (53), Prince of Players (54), The Rains of Ranchipur (55), Alexander the Great (56), Seawife (57), Bitter Victory (58), Look Back in Anger (GB) (59), The Bramble Bush (60), Cleopatra (62), The VIPs (63), Becket (64), The Night of the Iguana (64), The Spy Who Came In From the Cold (65), The Sandpiper (65), Who's Afraid of Virginia Woolf (66), The Taming of the Shrew (67), Dr Faustus (also co-directed) (67), The Comedians (67), Boom (68), Where Eagles Dare (68), Candy (68), Staircase (69), Anne of the Thousand Days (70).

BUSCH, MAE (1897–1946). American leading lady of silent films; her roles usually had a sinister edge. The Grim Game (19), The Devil's Passkey (20), Foolish Wives (21), The Christian (GB) (23), Broken Barriers (24), Fazil (27), The Beauty Shoppers (28), etc. In sound films she is best remembered as a foil for Laurel and Hardy in some of their two-reelers of the 30s, e.g. Oliver the Eighth, in which she was the homicidal widow.

BUSCH, NIVEN (1903–   ).   American novelist and screenwriter: In Old Chicago (38), The Westerner (40), Duel in the Sun (46), Pursued (47), The Furies (50), The Moonlighter (52), Treasure of Pancho Villa (56), etc.

buses have often provided a dramatic background for film plots. Man-Made Monster and The October Man began with bus accidents, and one of the stories in Dead of Night ended with one. Strangers met in a bus in Friday the Thirteenth, It Happened One Night, San Diego I Love You (in which Buster Keaton defied regulations by driving his bus along the seashore), Bus Stop and The Wayward Bus. Parting at the bus station was featured in Orchestra Wives, Dark Passage, Two Tickets to Broadway, and Rattle of a Simple Man; romances were conducted on a bus in Violent Playground and Underground; a trap was set for a criminal in a bus station in Down Three Dark Streets. Passengers on buses broke into song in Keep Your Seats Please, Ride 'Em Cowboy and Summer Holiday. As for comedy effects using buses, there was the little boy whose head stuck in the bus wheel in Monsieur Hulot's Holiday, Will Hay driving a bus round a race-track in Ask a Policeman, Bob Hope wrecking an Irish bus outing in My Favourite Blonde, Frankie Howerd losing his way in the fog in The Runaway Bus, Richard Burton escorting his matrons on a bus tour in The Night of the Iguana, and Laurel and Hardy driving a bus on to a roller coaster in The Dancing Masters . . . among others.

BUSHELL, ANTHONY (1904–   ). British leading man of the 30s who started his career in Hollywood. Disraeli (30), Journey's End (30), Five Star Final (32), Sally Bishop (GB) (33), Soldiers of the King (GB) (33), The Scarlet Pimpernel (GB) (34), Dark Journey (GB) (37), Farewell Again (GB) (37), Dusty Ermine (GB) (37), The Lion Has

Wings (GB) (39), etc. After war service, turned to production: *Hamlet* (co-p) (48), *The Angel with the Trumpet* (a, d) (49), *The Long Dark Hall* (a, p, d) (51), *High Treason* (a) (51), *The Purple Plani* (a) (54), *Richard III* (co-p) (56), *The Wind Cannot Read* (a) (57), etc.; recently acting in, producing and directing episodes of TV series.

BUSHMAN, FRANCIS X (1883–1966). Heavily-built American leading man of the silent era: *The Magic Wand* (12), *The Spy's Defeat* (13), *Romeo and Juliet* (16), many others, then stage work until *Ben Hur* (27). Later played small roles in talkies: *Hollywood Boulevard* (36), *David and Bathsheba* (51), *Sabrina Fair* (54), *The Ghost in the Invisible Bikini* (66), etc.

BUSSIERES, RAYMOND (1907–   ). Mournful-looking French character actor. *Nous les Gosses* (41), *Les Portes de la Nuit* (46), *Quai des Orfèvres* (47), *Porte des Lilas* (55), *Fanny* (60), many others.

BUTCHER, ERNEST (1885–1965). British character actor who spent a lifetime playing mild little men. *Variety Jubilee* (42), *Tawny Pipit* (43), *My Brother Jonathan* (48), many others.

BUTLER, DAVID (1894–   ). American director of mainly routine light entertainments. *Sunny Side Up* (29), *Bottoms Up* (34), *The Little Colonel* (35), *Kentucky* (38), *If I Had My Way* (40), *You'll Find Out* (41), *Caught in the Draft* (41), *Road to Morocco* (42), *Shine On Harvest Moon* (44), *The Princess and the Pirate* (44), *San Antonio* (45), *My Wild Irish Rose* (47), *It's a Great Feeling* (49), *Lullaby of Broadway* (51), *Where's Charley* (52), *Calamity Jane* (53), *King Richard and the Crusaders* (54), *Glory* (also produced) (56), many others.

BUTLER, FRANK (1890–1967). British-born writer, long in Hollywood. *College Humour* (33), *Babes in Toyland* (34), *Strike Me Pink* (36), *Road to Singapore* (40), *Road to Morocco* (42), *Going My Way* (AA) (44), *Incendiary Blonde* (45), *The Perils of Pauline* (47), *Whispering Smith* (49), *Strange Lady in Town* (55), many others.

butlers. Hollywood has always been fascinated by butlers, especially those who give an impression of British imperturbability. Actors notably benefiting from this penchant include Arthur Treacher (who played Jeeves on film in the 30s), Robert Greig, Charles Coleman, Aubrey Mather, Melville Cooper, Halliwell Hobbes and Eric Blore (whose butlers usually had a kind of suppressed malevolence). The catch-phrase 'the butler did it' was however seldom true of murder mysteries, though Bela Lugosi played some very sinister servants in the 40s, Richard Haydn was guilty of at least one murder in *Ten Little Niggers*, and the butler in *The Hound of the Baskervilles* certainly had something to hide. Another villainous 'man's man' was Philip Latham in *Dracula Prince of*

Butterworth, Charles

Darkness: he lured the count's victims. Comedy butlers are led by Edward Brophy, who often played an American imitation of the real thing, Richard Hearne in *The Butler's Dilemma*, Edward Rigby in *Don't Take It to Heart*, and Laurel and Hardy, who in *A Chump at Oxford* took literally an instruction to 'serve the salad undressed'. Jack Buchanan pretended to be his own butler in *Lord Richard in the Pantry*, and William Powell and David Niven, who both played *My Man Godfrey*, had their own reasons for going into service.

BUTTERWORTH, CHARLES (1897–1946). American comedian who from 1931 played the balding, shy, upper-class bachelor, always immaculately turned out but never getting the girl. Typical roles in *Love Me Tonight* (32), *Ruggles of Red Gap* (34), *Baby Face Harrington* (lead) (35), *The Moon's Our Home* (36), *Every Day's a Holiday* (37), *Road Show* (41), *This Is the Army* (43).

BUTTERWORTH, DONNA (1956–). American child actress. *The Family Jewels* (65), *Paradise Hawaiian Style* (66).

BUTTERWORTH, PETER (c. 1923–). British comedian usually seen as well-meaning bumbler. *William Comes to Town* (49), *Penny Princess* (51), *Mr Drake's Duck* (52), *Carry On* series (58–69), many others.

BUTTONS, RED (1919–) (Aaron Schwatt). American vaudeville and TV comic, in occasional films. *Sayonara* (AA) (57), *Five Weeks in a Balloon* (62), *Hatari* (62), *A Ticklish Affair* (63), *Harlow* (65), *Up from the Beach* (65), *Stagecoach* (66), *They Shoot Horses Don't They* (69), etc. TV: *The Red Buttons Show* (52), *The Double Life of Henry Phyfe* (66).

BUZZELL, EDWARD (1897–). American musical comedy star who became Hollywood actor and later a competent but not very individual director. *The Big Timer* (32), *False Witness* (34), *The Luckiest Girl in the World* (36), *Honolulu* (38), *The Marx Brothers at the Circus* (39), *The Marx Brothers Go West* (40), *Ship Ahoy* (41), *The Omaha Trail* (42), *Best Foot Forward* (43), *Keep Your Powder Dry* (44), *Song of the Thin Man* (45), *Three Wise Fools* (46), *Neptune's Daughter* (49), *A Woman of Distinction* (50), *Confidentially Connie* (53), *Ain't Misbehaving* (55), *Mary Had a Little* (GB) (61), many others.

BWANA DEVIL (US 1953). A poor jungle adventure which has some historical interest as the first feature film to be produced in 3-D. As written, produced and directed by Arch Oboler, it had little else to offer; Robert Stack and Nigel Bruce led the struggling cast.

BYGRAVES, MAX (1922–). British entertainer who has played in several films: *Skimpy in the Navy* (49), *Tom Brown's Schooldays* (50), *Charley Moon* (53), *A Cry from the Streets* (57), *Bobbikins* (59), *Spare the Rod* (61), etc.

BYINGTON, SPRING (1893–   ). American stage actress who has been in Hollywood since she went to play Marmee in *Little Women* (33). Usually plays pleasant maternal types, sometimes a little scatter-brained: *Jones Family* series (36–40), *You Can't Take It With You* (38), *The Bluebird* (40), *When Ladies Meet* (41), *The Devil and Miss Jones* (41), *Roxie Hart* (42), *Heaven Can Wait* (43), *I'll Be Seeing You* (44), *The Enchanted Cottage* (44), *Dragonwyck* (45), *Little Mister Jim* (46), *The Rich Full Life* (47), *It Had To Be You* (48), *Louisa* (leading role) (50), *According to Mrs Hoyle* (leading role) (51), *The Rocket Man* (54), *Please Don't Eat the Daisies* (60), many others. TV series: *December Bride* (54–58), *Laramie* (60–62).

BYRD, RALPH (1909–1952). Tough-looking American leading man, mainly in second features. *Hell Ship Morgan* (31), *Dick Tracy* (38), *Desperate Cargo* (41), *Guadalcanal Diary* (43), *Mark of the Claw* (47), etc.

BYRNE, EDDIE (1911–   ). Irish character actor, in British films since 1946. *Odd Man Out* (46), *The Gentle Gunman* (52), *Time, Gentlemen, Please* (leading role) (53), *A Kid for Two Farthings* (55), *The Admirable Crichton* (57), *The Mummy* (59), *The Bulldog Breed* (60), *Devils of Darkness* (65), *Island of Terror* (66), many others.

BYRNES, EDD (1933–   ) (Edward Breitenberger). American juvenile TV lead of the fifties, popular as 'Kookie' in *77 Sunset Strip*. Films include *Darby's Rangers* (58), *Marjorie Morningstar* (58), *Up Periscope* (59), *The Secret Invasion* (64).

BYRON, KATHLEEN (1922–   ). British leading actress of the 40s; on stage and screen. *The Young Mr Pitt* (41), *The Silver Fleet* (43), *A Matter of Life and Death* (46), *Black Narcissus* (as mad nun) (46), *The Small Back Room* (48), *Madness of the Heart* (49), *The Reluctant Widow* (50), *Four Days* (51), *The Gambler and the Lady* (54), *Hand In Hand* (60), *Night of the Eagle* (62), etc. Recently on TV.

C

CAAN, JAMES (c. 1938–). American leading man. *Lady in a Cage* (64), *Red Line 7000* (65), *El Dorado* (67), *Countdown* (67), *Journey to Shiloh* (68), *The Rain People* (69), *Man Without Mercy* (69), *Rabbit, Run* (70), etc.

CABANNE, CHRISTY (1888–1950). American director of many silent films; worked for D. W. Griffith and Douglas Fairbanks. Later directed second features. *Enoch Arden* (15), *Flirting with Fate* (16), *Reckless Youth* (22), *Altars of Desire* (27), *The Girl of the Limberlost* (32), *The Last Outlaw* (36), *The Mummy's Hand* (40), *Keep 'Em Slugging* (43), *Scared to Death* (46), *Robin Hood of Monterey* (47), *Back Trail* (48), many others.

THE CABINET OF DR CALIGARI (Germany 1919). Classic horror film, valued not only for its expressionist sets and clever story finally revealed to have been told by a madman, but for its unmistakable influence on German film-making for ten years after. Werner Krauss, Conrad Veidt and Lil Dagover starred, Robert Wiene directed from a script by Carl Mayer and Hans Janowitz; Willi Hameister was photographer. Allowing for certain primitive aspects, it still has power to thrill; certainly more so than the inferior American remake of 1962, which used the gimmicks but little else.

CABIN IN THE SKY (US 1943). This all-Negro film, though a musical, was an important step forward in Hollywood's treatment of coloured people. (*Hallelujah* (29) and *Green Pastures* (36) had both tended to be patronizing.) Directed by Vincente Minnelli, with Eddie Anderson, Lena Horne and Ethel Waters.

CABIRIA (Italy 1913). A famous silent spectacle set in Caesarean Rome and concerning the romantic adventures of a lively lady saved as an infant from sacrifice to Baal. Her strong-man servant is one Maciste, who has reappeared as hero of scores of Italian adventure films since. Directed by Pastrone from a scenario by himself and Gabriele d'Annunzio. With Lidia Quaranta, Bartolomeo Pagano. The original film ran over four hours: a condensed sound version was issued in 1930 and in 1950 came a rather poor remake. Fellini's *Nights of Cabiria* (Italy 1957) is something else again, a wry modern comedy about the ill-luck of a cheerful prostitute, starring Giulietta Masina. This emerged again in 1969 as the Hollywood musical *Sweet Charity*, with Shirley Maclaine.

cable cars have added excitement to the climax of many a film adventure, notably *Night Train to Munich*, *The Trollenberg Terror*, *Edge of Eternity*, *Second Chance*, *Where Eagles Dare* and *Hannibal Brooks*.

CABOT, BRUCE (1904–) (Jacques de Bujac). Tough American leading man of the 30s, the hero of *King Kong* (33). Still seen in second feature Westerns and on TV. *The Roadhouse Murder* (32), *Don't Gamble with Love* (35), *The Last of the Mohicans* (36), *Dodge City* (39), *Captain Caution* (40), *The Flame of New Orleans* (41), *Sundown* (41), *Divorce* (45), *Fancy Pants* (50), *Kid Monk Baroni* (52), *The Quiet American* (58), *Hatari* (62), *McLintock* (63), *Town Tamer* (65), *In Harm's Way* (65), *The Chase* (66), *The War Wagon* (67), *The Green Berets* (68), etc.

CABOT, SEBASTIAN (1918–). Heavily-built British character actor with stage experience; lately bearded. *Secret Agent* (36), *Love on the Dole* (41), *Pimpernel Smith* (41), *The Agitator* (45), *They Made Me a Fugitive* (47), *Dick Barton Strikes Back* (48), *Old Mother Riley's Jungle Treasure* (50), *Ivanhoe* (52), *Romeo and Juliet* (54), *Kismet (US)* (55), *Terror in a Texas Town (US)* (58), *The Time Machine (US)* (60), *Twice Told Tales* (63), *The Family Jewels (US)* (65), etc. TV series: *Checkmate* (59–62), *A Family Affair* (66–69).

CABOT, SUSAN (1927–). American leading lady of the 50s. *Flame of Araby* (51), *Battle at Apache Pass* (52), *Duel at Silver Creek* (53), *Ride Clear of Diablo* (54), etc.

CACOYANNIS, MICHAEL (1922–). Greek director, trained in England. *Windfall in Athens* (53), *Stella* (54), *A Girl in Black* (55), *A Matter of Dignity* (57), *One Last Spring* (59), *The Wastrel* (61), *Electra* (62), *Zorba the Greek* (65), *The Day the Fish Came Out* (67).

CADELL, JEAN (1884–1967). Scottish actress, sometimes cast as acidulous spinster or dowager. On stage and screen since 1906. *The Loves of Robert Burns* (30), *David Copperfield (US)* (34), *Pygmalion* (38), *Quiet Wedding* (40), *Dear Octopus* (43), *Whisky Galore* (49), *Madeleine* (50), *The Late Edwina Black* (51), *Rockets Galore* (56), *A Taste of Money* (leading role) (60), many others.

CAESAR AND CLEOPATRA (GB 1945). Notorious as Britain's most expensive picture, this entertaining version of Shaw's comedy was produced with unnecessary elaboration and recklessness by Gabriel Pascal. Did not do particularly well at the box office but has strong entertainment value mainly deriving from Shaw and the performances of Claude Rains and Vivien Leigh.

CAESAR, SID (1922–   ). American comedian, a big hit on TV (49–58). Occasional films include *Tars and Spars* (44), *It's a Mad Mad Mad Mad World* (63), *A Guide for the Married Man* (67), *The Busy Body* (67).

†CAGNEY, JAMES (1904–   ). American leading actor, one of the great Hollywood stars of the 30s and 40s. Was a vaudeville dancer before a talent scout took him to Hollywood, where his cocky walk and punchy personality as gangster, cop, or song-and-dance man: he even had a shot at Shakespeare. *Sinner's Holiday* (30), *Doorway to Hell* (30), *Other Men's Women* (31), *The Millionaire* (31), *Public Enemy* (31), *Smart Money* (31), *Blonde Crazy* (31), *Taxi* (32), *The Crowd Roars* (32), *Winner Takes All* (32), *Hard to Handle* (33), *The Picture Snatcher* (33), *Mayor of Hell* (33), *Footlight Parade* (33), *Lady Killer* (34), *Jimmy the Gent* (34), *He Was Her Man* (34) *Here Comes the Navy* (34), *St Louis Kid* (34), *Devil Dogs of the Air* (35), *The Irish in Us* (35), *The Frisco Kid* (35), *G-Men* (35), *A Midsummer Night's Dream* (as Bottom) (35), *Ceiling Zero* (35), *Great Guy* (36), *Something to Sing About* (37), *Angels with Dirty Faces* (38), *Boy Meets Girl* (38), *The Oklahoma Kid* (39), *Each Dawn I Die* (39), *The Roaring Twenties* (39), *The Fighting 69th* (40), *Torrid Zone* (40), *City for Conquest* (40), *Strawberry Blonde* (41), *The Bride Came C.O.D.* (41), *Captains of the Clouds* (42), *Yankee Doodle Dandy* (AA) (as George M. Cohan) (42), *Johnny Come Lately* (43), *Blood on the Sun* (45), *13 Rue Madeleine* (46), *The Time of Your Life* (48), *White Heat* (49), *West Point Story* (50), *Kiss Tomorrow Goodbye* (50), *Come Fill the Cup* (51), *Starlift* (guest) (51), *What Price Glory* (52), *A Lion Is in the Streets* (53), *Run for Cover* (55), *Love Me or Leave Me* (55), *Mister Roberts* (55), *The Seven Little Foys* (guest) (55), *Tribute to a Bad Man* (56), *These Wilder Years* (56), *Man of a Thousand Faces* (as Lon Chaney) (57), *Never Steal Anything Small* (59), *The Gallant Hours* (60), *One Two Three* (61). Directed *Short Cut to Hell* (58).

CAGNEY, JEANNE (1919–   ). American actress, sister of James Cagney. Occasional films include *Golden Gloves* (40), *Yankee Doodle Dandy* (42), *The Time of Your Life* (49), *A Lion Is in the Streets* (55), *Town Tamer* (65).

CAHN, EDWARD L. (1899–1963). American director of second features. *Homicide Squad* (31), *Law and Order* (32) (his best film, with Walter Huston as Wyatt Earp), *Confidential* (35), *Main Street After Dark* (44), *The Checkered Coat* (48), *Prejudice* (48), *Experiment Alcatraz* (also produced) (51), *The Creature with the Atom Brain* (55), *Girls in Prison* (56), *Curse of the Faceless Man* (58), *Guns, Girls and Gangsters* (58), *It, The Terror from Beyond Space* (58), *Riot in a Juvenile Prison* (61), *Beauty and the Beast* (62), *Incident in an Alley* (63), many others.

CAHN, SAMMY (1913–   ). American lyricist who has written many film songs, usually with James Van Heusen. *Tonight and Every Night* (44), *Anchors Aweigh* (45), *Wonder Man* (45), *West Point Story* (50), *April in Paris* (53), *The Court Jester* (55), etc. Won Academy Awards for four songs: 'Three Coins in the Fountain', High Hopes', 'All the Way' and 'Call Me Irresponsible'.

CAIN, JAMES M. (1892–   ). American author of the tough school. Books filmed include *Double Indemnity* (44), *Mildred Pierce* (45), *The Postman Always Rings Twice* (46), *Serenade* (56).

CAINE, MICHAEL (1933–   ) (Maurice Micklewhite). British leading man with mild manner and cockney origins. Played in several second features before gaining attention. *Zulu* (63), *The Ipcress File* (65), *Alfie* (66), *The Wrong Box* (66), *Gambit* (US) (66), *Funeral in Berlin* (66), *Hurry Sundown* (US) (67), *Billion Dollar Brain* (67), *Deadfall* (68), *The Magus* (68), *Play Dirty* (68), *The Italian Job* (69), *The Battle of Britain* (69), *Too Late the Hero* (US) (69).

THE CAINE MUTINY (US 1954). Produced by Stanley Kramer and directed by Edward Dmytryk, this well-made film retained most of the values of the book by Herman Wouk about the mental breakdown of the disciplinarian captain of a naval destroyer. There were interesting performances by Humphrey Bogart and Jose Ferrer, and the film makes a good example of the more adult themes explorable in the fifties.

CALAMITY JANE (c. 1848–1903) (Muriel Jane Cannaray). This rootin' tootin' shootin' woman of the old west has been glamorized many times for the movies, notably by Jean Arthur in *The Plainsman* (36), Frances Farmer in *Badlands of Dakota* (41), Jane Russell in *The Paleface* (48), Yvonne de Carlo in *Calamity Jane and Sam Bass* (49), Evelyn Ankers in *The Texan Meets Calamity Jane* (51), Doris Day in *Calamity Jane* (53), Judi Merdith in *The Raiders* (64), and Abby Dalton in *The Plainsman* (66).

CALDWELL, ERSKINE (1903–   ). American novelist who attacked social injustice in several novels which by their sensationalism earned him a fortune. *Tobacco Road* was filmed as a farce; *God's Little Acre* had to be taken straight.

CALHERN, LOUIS (1895–1956) (Carl Vogt). Distinguished American stage actor, in films occasionally from silent days and latterly under contract to MGM. *The Blot* (21), *Stolen Heaven* (31), *Duck Soup* (33), *The Life of Émile Zola* (37), *Heaven Can Wait* (43), *Up In Arms* (44), *The Bridge of San Luis Rey* (44), *Notorious* (46), *Arch of Triumph* (48), *Annie Get Your Gun* (50), *The Asphalt Jungle* (50), *The Magnificent Yankee* (51), *The Prisoner of Zenda* (52), *Confidentially*

Connie (53), *Julius Caesar* (title role) (53), *Executive Suite* (54), *The Blackboard Jungle* (55), *High Society* (56), etc.

CALHOUN, RORY (1922–) (Francis Timothy Durgin). American leading man with easy manner; has not quite reached the front rank. *Something for the Boys* (debut) (44), *The Red House* (46), *Sand* (49), *The Way of a Gaucho* (52), *How to Marry a Millionaire* (53), *River of No Return* (54), *Dawn at Socorro* (54), *Red Sundown* (56), *The Spoilers* (56), *Utah Blaine* (57), *The Hired Gun* (57), *Marco Polo* (It.) (61), *A Face in the Rain* (62), *The Gun Hawk* (64), *Black Spurs* (65), *Apache Uprising* (65), *Finger on the Trigger* (67), *Dayton's Devils* (68), etc. TV series: *The Texan* (58–60).

CALLAN, MICHAEL (1935–) (Martin Caliniff). American leading man, former dancer. *They Came to Cordura* (58), *Bon Voyage* (62), *The Interns* (63), *The Victors* (63), *Cat Ballou* (65), *You Must Be Joking* (65), etc. TV series: *Occasional Wife* (66).

CALLEIA, JOSEPH (1897–) (Joseph Spurin-Calleja). Maltese character actor who toured the world as a singer before settling in Hollywood in the mid-30s, usually in sinister roles. *Public Hero Number One* (35), *After the Thin Man* (36), *Marie Antoinette* (38), *Algiers* (38), *Golden Boy* (39), *Five Came Back* (39), *Wyoming* (40), *The Monster and the Girl* (41), *Jungle Book* (42), *The Glass Key* (42), *For Whom the Bell Tolls* (43), *The Conspirators* (44), *Gilda* (46), *Deadline at Dawn* (47), *Noose* (GB) (48), *They Passed This Way* (48), *Vendetta* (50), *Valentino* (51), *Underwater* (55), *Serenade* (56), *Touch of Evil* (58), *Wild Is the Wind* (58), *The Alamo* (60), *Johnny Cool* (63), etc. Has also recently acted on stage.

CALLOWAY, CAB (1907–) (Cabell Calloway). High-spirited American Negro entertainer and band leader. Occasional film appearances include *The Big Broadcast* (32), *International House* (33), *Stormy Weather* (43), *Sensations of 1945*, *St Louis Blues* (58), *A Man Called Adam* (66).

CALTHROP, DONALD (1888–1940). British stage actor who played several screen roles, usually as nervy little villains. *The Gay Lord Quex* (debut) (18), *Nelson* (19), *Shooting Stars* (27), *Blackmail* (30), *Elstree Calling* (30), *Atlantic* (30), *Murder* (31), *The Bells* (31), *The Ghost Train* (32), *Almost a Honeymoon* (32), *Rome Express* (32), *Friday the Thirteenth* (33), *Broken Blossoms* (36), *Dreaming Lips* (37), *Major Barbara* (40), etc.

CALVERT, PHYLLIS (1915–) (Phyllis Bickle). British leading lady, on stage as a child. *They Came by Night* (film debut) (40), *Let George Do It* (40), *Kipps* (41), *The Young Mr Pitt* (41), *Uncensored* (42), *The Man in Grey* (43), *Fanny by Gaslight* (43), *Two Thousand Women* (44), *Madonna of the Seven Moons* (44), *They Were Sisters* (45),

Men of Two Worlds (46), *The Magic Bow* (46), *The Root of All Evil* (47), *Time Out of Mind* (US) (47), *Broken Journey* (48), *My Own True Love* (US) (48), *Appointment with Danger* (US) (49), *The Woman with No Name* (50), *Mr Denning Drives North* (51), *Mandy* (52), *The Net* (53), *It's Never Too Late* (55), *Child in the House* (56), *Indiscreet* (58), *Oscar Wilde* (60), *The Battle of the Villa Fiorita* (65), *Twisted Nerve* (68), *Oh What a Lovely War* (69), *The Walking Stick* (69), etc. Also on stage and TV.

CALVET, CORINNE (1925–) (Corinne Dibos). French leading lady, a statuesque blonde who had some success in Hollywood in the early 50s. *La Part de l'Ombre* (45), *Rope of Sand* (49), *When Willie Comes Marching Home* (50), *On the Riviera* (51), *What Price Glory* (52), *Flight to Tangier* (53), *The Far Country* (54), *So This Is Paris* (55), *The Plunderers of Painted Flats* (58), *Bluebeard's Ten Honeymoons* (60), *Hemingway's Adventures of a Young Man* (62), *Apache Uprising* (65), etc.

CAMBRIDGE, GODFREY (c. 1929–). American Negro comedian of cynical humour. Film appearances include *The Biggest Bundle of Them All* (67), *The President's Analyst* (68).

CAMELOT (US 1967). A deliberately sober version of the Arthurian myth, this overlong film by Joshua Logan of the Lerner and Loewe stage musical might, if successful, have marked a new departure for Hollywood's handling of fantasy. In fact much of it seemed rather dull, and the wit of T. H. White's original saga *The Once and Future King* was sadly missing. Richard Harris and Vanessa Redgrave were perhaps the last non-singers to be entrusted with major singing roles; both acted well, but were upstaged by John Truscott's set designs. See also under: ARTHUR.

CAMERINI, MARIO (1895–). Italian director, from 1920. Best-known films abroad include *I Promessi Sposi* (41), *Molti Sogni Per Le Strade* (48), *Il Brigante Musolino* (50), *Wife for a Night* (50), *Honeymoon Deferred* (51), *Kali-Yug Goddess of Vengeance* (63), etc.

CAMERON, EARL (1925–). Jamaican actor seen in many British films: *Pool of London* (50), *Emergency Call* (51), *The Heart of the Matter* (53), *Simba* (55), *Safari* (56), *Sapphire* (59), *Flame in the Streets* (61), *Thunderball* (65), etc. Many TV appearances.

CAMERON, ROD (1910–) (Rod Cox). Rugged Canadian star of many a Hollywood second feature; originally labourer, engineer, and stand-in for Fred Macmurray. *Christmas in July* (40), *Northwest Mounted Police* (40), *The Monster and the Girl* (41), *The Remarkable Andrew* (42), *Wake Island* (42), *Gung Ho* (43), *Boss of Boom Town* (44), *Salome Where She Danced* (45), *The Runaround* (46), *The Bride Wasn't Willing* (46), *The Plunderers* (48), *The Sea Hornet* (51), *Ride the Man Down* (53), *Escapement* (GB) (57), *The Bounty Killer* (65), *Old Firehand* (Ger.) (66), many others. TV series: *City Detective* (53–55), *Coronado 9* (59), *State Trooper* (60).

CAMILLE. The Dumas *fils* tearjerker about a courtesan dying of tuberculosis has been a favourite vehicle for many actresses. On screen, Bernhardt did it in 1912, Clara Kimball Young in 1915, Theda Bara in 1917, Nazimova (with Rudolph Valentino) in 1920, Norma Talmadge (with Gilbert Roland) in 1927 and Garbo (with Robert Taylor) in 1936. In post-war years many producers must have eyed it longingly before deciding that it belongs to a bygone age.

CAMPANELLA, JOSEPH (1927–). American character actor with stage experience. *Murder Incorporated* (61), *Young Lovers* (64). TV series: *Mannix* (66).

CAMPBELL, BEATRICE (1923–). British leading lady. *Wanted for Murder* (46), *Things Happen at Night* (48), *Last Holiday* (50), *Laughter in Paradise* (51), *Grand National Night* (53), *Cockleshell Heroes* (55), etc.

CAMPBELL, ERIC (c. 1870–1917). Scottish actor who played the bearded heavy in some of Chaplin's most famous two-reelers. 1916–1917: *Easy Street*, *The Cure*, *The Adventurer*, etc.

CAMPBELL, JUDY (1916–) (Judy Gamble). British leading lady of stage and TV; film appearances infrequent. *Saloon Bar* (40), *Breach of Promise* (41), *The World Owes Me a Living* (44), *Bonnie Prince Charlie* (48), etc.

CAMPBELL, MRS PATRICK (1865–1940) (Beatrice Tanner). British leading actress, the original Eliza in Shaw's *Pygmalion*. Spent her last years in America and played heavy dowagers in a few films: *Riptide* (34), *One More River* (34), *Crime and Punishment* (35), etc.

CAMPBELL, PATRICK (1907–). British humorist and screenplay writer, the latter usually with Vivienne Knight. *Captain Boycott* (47), *Helter Skelter* (50), *The Oracle* (54), *Lucky Jim* (57), *Go to Blazes* (62), *The Girl in the Headlines* (63), etc.

CAMPBELL, WILLIAM (1926–). American actor, often seen as personable villain or friend of the hero. *The Breaking Point* (50), *The People Against O'Hara* (52), *Escape from Fort Bravo* (53), *The High and the Mighty* (54), *Man without a Star* (55), *Cell 2455 Death Row* (as Caryl Chessman) (55), *Backlash* (56), *Eighteen and Anxious* (57), *The Naked and the Dead* (58), *The Young Racers* (63), *The Secret Invasion* (64), *Hush Hush Sweet Charlotte* (64), etc.

CAMUS, MARCEL (1912–   ). French director, chiefly known for *Black Orpheus* (58).

CANALE, GIANNA MARIA (1927–   ). Italian leading lady, seen abroad in *Theodora, Slave Empress* (54), *I Vampiri* (57), *The Silent Enemy* (GB) (58), *The Whole Truth* (GB) (58), etc.

CANNON, J. D. (1922–   ). Cold-eyed American character actor. *An American Dream* (66), *Cool Hand Luke* (67), etc.

CANNON, ROBERT (1901–64). American animator, a leading figure at UPA during the formative period and the designer of simplified, witty cartoons like *Gerald McBoing Boing* and *Christopher Crumpet*.

CANOVA, JUDY (1916–   ). American comedienne whose homely knockabout and hillbilly yodelling brightened a number of programmers of the 40s; more recently on radio and TV. *In Caliente* (36), *Scatterbrain* (40), *The Queen of Spies* (42), *Singin' in the Corn* (46), *Honeychile* (51), *Untamed Heiress* (54), *The Adventures of Huckleberry Finn* (60), etc.

CANTINFLAS (1913–   ) (Mario Moreno). Mexican clown, acrobat and bullfighter who had been making unambitious local comedies for years when Mike Todd signed him to play Passepartout in *Around the World in Eighty Days* (56). Although *Pepe* (59) was constructed around him, it failed and he returned to Mexico.

†CANTOR, EDDIE (1892–1964) (Edward Israel Isskowitz). American entertainer, on stage from New York childhood and a Ziegfeld star from 1916. His rolling eyes, sprightly movement and inimitable singing voice took him to Hollywood for film version of his show *Kid Boots* (26), but his real movie success came with sound (though his films do not wear well). *Special Delivery* (27), *Whoopee* (30), *Palmy Days* (31), *The Kid from Spain* (32), *Roman Scandals* (33), *Kid Millions* (34), *Strike Me Pink* (35), *Ali Baba Goes to Town* (38), *40 Little Mothers* (40), *Thank Your Lucky Stars* (43), *Show Business* (44), *If You Knew Susie* (48), etc. Many series in radio and TV. A biopic, *The Eddie Cantor Story*, was made in 1953, and he was given a special Academy Award in 1956 'for distinguished service to the film industry'. Published autobiographical books: *Take My Life* (57), *The Way I See It* (59), *As I Remember Them* (62).

CANUTT, YAKIMA (1895–   ). Famous half-Indian stunt man of American silent films; later became a director of low-budget Westerns. Directed second unit on *The Fall of the Roman Empire* (64).

CAPELLANI, ALBERT (1870–1931). French director of silent films, in Hollywood from 1915. *Camille* (15), *La Vie de Bohème* (16), *Daybreak* (17), *The Red Lantern* (19), *The Fortune Teller* (20), *The Young Diana* (22), etc.

CAPONE, AL (1899–1947). Italian-American gangster, the king of Chicago during the roaring twenties. Has been impersonated many times on screen, notably by Paul Muni (*Scarface*), Edward G. Robinson (*Little Caesar*), Rod Steiger (*Al Capone*), Neville Brand (*The Scarface Mob*), Jason Robards (*The St Valentine's Day Massacre*).

CAPOTE, TRUMAN (1925–   ). American novelist. Works filmed include *Breakfast at Tiffany's*, *In Cold Blood*. Contributed to scripts of *Beat the Devil*, *The Innocents*.

CAPRA, FRANK (1897–   ). Italian-American director, in Hollywood from 1921. Responsible for Harry Langdon's most successful silent comedies: *The Strong Man*, *Long Pants*, *Tramp Tramp Tramp*, etc. His early talkies are an interesting mixed bag: *Ladies of Leisure* (30), *Dirigible* (31), *Platinum Blonde* (32), *American Madness* (32), *The Bitter Tea of General Yen* (32), *Broadway Bill* (33). Then he hit on the vein of benevolent social comedy showing how nice everybody can be if you give them a chance: *Lady for a Day* (33), *It Happened One Night* (AA) (34), *Mr Deeds Goes to Town* (AA) (36), *Lost Horizon* (a disguised restatement of the same theme) (37), *You Can't Take It With You* (AA) (38), *Mr Smith Goes to Washington* (39), *Meet John Doe* (41). During war service he directed the brilliant series of 'Why We Fight' documentaries (qv), but on his return to Hollywood there were signs of a falling-off in *Arsenic and Old Lace* (44), *It's a Wonderful Life* (also produced) (46), *State of the Union* (also produced) (48), *Riding High* (50), *Here Comes the Groom* (51). He retired for eight years before his two latest films, *A Hole in the Head* (59) and *A Pocketful of Miracles* (61). (†Talkies complete.)

CAPTAIN BLOOD. Swashbuckling melodrama from Rafael Sabatini's novel, filmed in 1925 with J. Warren Kerrigan, in 1935 with Errol Flynn. In 1962 Flynn's son Sean starred in an Italian-made *Son of Captain Blood*; and, during the early 50s, Louis Hayward starred in *The Fortunes of Captain Blood* and *Captain Blood Fugitive*.

CAPUCINE (1933–   ) (Germaine Lefebvre). French actress and model who has made several films: *Song Without End* (60), *A Walk on the Wild Side* (62), *The Pink Panther* (63), *The Seventh Dawn* (64), *What's New Pussycat* (65), *The Honey Pot* (67), *The Queens* (67), etc.

CARDIFF, JACK (1914–   ). British cinematographer who did notable work on many colour films including *Wings of the Morning* (37), *The Four Feathers* (39), *Western Approaches* (44), *Caesar and Cleopatra* (45), *A Matter of Life and Death* (46), *Black Narcissus* (AA) (46), *The Red Shoes* (48), *Pandora and the Flying Dutchman* (51), *The Barefoot Contessa* (54), *War and Peace* (56), *The Vikings* (58). Became director: *Intent to Kill* (58), *Beyond This Place* (59), *Scent of Mystery* (*Holiday in Spain*) (60), *Sons and Lovers* (60), *My Geisha* (62), *The Lion* (62), *The Long Ships* (64), *Young Cassidy* (65), *The Liquidator*

(65), *Dark of the Sun* (*The Mercenaries*) (67), *Girl on a Motorcycle* (also produced and co-wrote) (68), etc.

CARDINALE, CLAUDIA (1939–   ). Italian leading lady who has been selected for Hollywood star treatment. *Persons Unknown* (*I Soliti Ignoti*) (58), *Upstairs and Downstairs* (GB) (58), *Il Bell'Antonio* (59), *Rocco and His Brothers* (60), *Cartouche* (61), *The Leopard* (62), *Eight and a Half* (63), *The Pink Panther* (63), *Circus World* (*The Magnificent Showman*) (64), *Vaghe Stella Dell'Orsa* (*Of a Thousand Delights*) (65), *Blindfold* (65), *Lost Command* (66), *The Professionals* (66), *Don't Make Waves* (67), *The Queens* (67), *Day of the Owl* (It.) (68), *Once Upon a Time in the West* (69), *A Fine Pair* (69), etc.

CARERE, CHRISTINE (1930–   ). French actress (*Olivia* [50], *Les Collégiennes* [57], etc.) who went to Hollywood in 1957 to play the lead in *A Certain Smile*; returned to France after *Mardi Gras* (58) and *A Private Affair* (59). 1966: *I Deal in Danger*.

CARETTE, JULIEN (1897–1966). Dapper French character actor, seen abroad in *L'Affaire Est dans le Sac* (32), *La Grande Illusion* (37), *La Marseillaise* (38), *La Règle du Jeu* (39), *Adieu Léonard* (43), *Les Portes de la Nuit* (46), *Occupe-Toi d'Amélie* (49), *The Red Inn* (51), *Elena et les Hommes* (55), *Archimède le Clochard* (58), many others.

CAREWE, EDWIN (1883–1940). American director of silent films noted for their pictorial beauty. *The Final Judgment* (15), *The Trail to Yesterday* (18), *Shadow of Suspicion* (19), *Rio Grande* (20), *Son of the Sahara* (24), *Resurrection* (27), *Ramona* (28), *Evangeline* (29), etc.

CAREY, HARRY (1878–1947). American leading man of silent films, later character actor. Was making Westerns as early as 1911. Later: *The Outcasts of Poker Flat* (19), *Desperate Trails* (20), *The Fox* (24), *Trail of '98* (27), *Trader Horn* (30), *Barbary Coast* (35), *Kid Galahad* (36), *Prisoner of Shark Island* (37), *Mr Smith Goes to Washington* (39), *Shepherd of the Hills* (41), *The Spoilers* (42), *Happy Land* (43), *Duel in the Sun* (46), *Red River* (48), many others.

CAREY, HARRY JNR (1921–   ). American light actor, son of Harry Carey; in supporting roles. *She Wore a Yellow Ribbon* (49), *Wagonmaster* (50), *Gentlemen Prefer Blondes* (53), *Mister Roberts* (55), *The Great Impostor* (60), *Bandolero* (68), etc.

CAREY, JOYCE (1898–   ) (Joyce Lawrence). British stage actress, daughter of Lilian Braithwaite. Appeared in a few silent films including *God and the Man, Because, and the Newcomes*; did not film again until the 40s. *In Which We Serve* (42), *Blithe Spirit* (45), *The Way to the Stars* (45), *Brief Encounter* (47), *The October Man* (48), *London Belongs to Me* (48), *Cry the Beloved Country* (52), *The End of the Affair* (55), *The Eyes of Annie Jones* (63), *A Nice Girl Like Me* (69), etc.

CAREY, MACDONALD (1913–). American leading man, usually the sympathetic good guy in routine romantic comedy-dramas. *Dr Broadway* (debut) (42), *Wake Island* (42), *Shadow of a Doubt* (43), war service, *Suddenly It's Spring* (46), *Dream Girl* (47), *East of Java* (49), *Copper Canyon* (50), *Let's Make It Legal* (51), *My Wife's Best Friend* (52), *Stranger at My Door* (56), *Blue Denim* (59), *The Damned* (GB) (62), *Tammy and the Doctor* (63), *Broken Sabre* (65), etc. TV series: *Dr Christian* (56), *Lock Up* (59–61).

CAREY, PHIL (1925–). American leading man of the good-humoured rugged type, in films since 1951 (*Operation Pacific*). Mostly routine action dramas: best parts in *Pushover* (54), *Wicked As They Come* (56). Star of TV series *77th Bengal Lancers* and *Philip Marlowe*. Recently: *The Time Travellers* (64), *Dead Ringer* (*Dead Image*) (64), *The Great Sioux Massacre* (65).

CAREY, TIMOTHY (c. 1925–). Heavy-eyed American character actor, often a loathsome villain. *Hellgate* (52), *Alaska Seas* (54), *The Killing* (56), *Paths of Glory* (57), *One-Eyed Jacks* (59), *Reprieve* (62), *Bikini Beach* (64), *Waterhole Three* (67), etc.

CARGILL, PATRICK (1918–). British comedy actor, mainly on stage. Films include *The Cracksman* (60), *This Is My Street* (63), *A Stitch in Time* (64), *A Countess from Hong Kong* (66), *Inspector Clouseau* (68).

CARLISLE, KITTY (1915–) (Catherine Holzman). American leading lady, briefly with MGM in the 30s. *Murder at the Vanities* (34), *Here Is My Heart* (34), *A Night at the Opera* (35), etc.; glimpsed in *Hollywood Canteen* (45).

CARLISLE, MARY (1912–). American leading lady of the 30s. *Justice for Sale* (32), *College Humour* (33), *One Frightened Night* (35), *Dr Rhythm* (38), *Call a Messenger* (40), *Baby Face Morgan* (last to date) (42), etc.

CARLO-RIM (1905–) (Jean-Marius Richard). French writer-director, mainly of Fernandel comedies. *L'Armoire Volante* (47), *Les Truands* (*Lock Up the Spoons*) (56), *Le Petit Prof* (59), etc.

CARLSON, RICHARD (1912–). American leading man who played the diffident juvenile until he outgrew it. *The Young in Heart* (debut) (39), *The Ghost Breakers* (40), *No No Nanette* (40), *Back Street* (41), *West Point Widow* (41), *The Little Foxes* (41), *White Cargo* (42), *My Heart Belongs to Daddy* (42), *Presenting Lily Mars* (43), *So Well Remembered* (GB) (47), *King Solomon's Mines* (50), *The Blue Veil* (51), *Valentino* (51), *Whispering Smith Hits London* (GB) (52),

It Came from Outer Space (53), *Riders to the Stars* (also directed) (54), *Bengazi* (55), *Four Guns to the Border* (directed only) (56), *The Saga of Hemp Brown* (directed only) (58), *Kid Rodelo* (also directed) (66), *The Valley of Gwangi* (69), etc. TV series: *Mackenzie's Raiders* (58).

CARLSON, VERONICA (1945–   ). British leading lady. *Dracula Has Risen From the Grave* (68), *Frankenstein Must Be Destroyed* (69).

CARMEN. Prosper Mérimée's high-romantic tale of a fatal gypsy was promptly turned by Bizet into an opera, which has been filmed many times, notably as *Carmen Jones* (54). The straight dramatic story has also been popular. There was a French version in 1909 and Spanish ones in 1910 and 1914. Theda Bara was in an American version of 1915 which inspired Chaplin's *Burlesque on Carmen*; there was also a rival version with Geraldine Farrar. In 1942 Vivianne Romance starred in a French version, and in 1948 it was Rita Hayworth's turn in *The Loves of Carmen*.

CARMICHAEL, HOAGY (1899–   ) (Hoaglund Howard Carmichael). American song composer and lyricist, best known for 'Stardust' and 'In the Cool, Cool, Cool of the Evening' (AA 1951). Also a slow-speaking actor of light supporting roles, usually involving his singing at the piano. *To Have and Have Not* (44), *Canyon Passage* (46), *The Best Years of Our Lives* (46), *Young Man with a Horn* (50), *Belles on Their Toes* (52), *Timberjack* (55), etc. TV series: *Laramie* (59–63).

CARMICHAEL, IAN (1920–   ). British light leading man, adept at nervous novices; long experience in revue. *Meet Mr Lucifer* (54), *The Colditz Story* (54), *Storm over the Nile* (55), *Simon and Laura* (in his stage role, a notable success) (55), *Private's Progress* (leading role) (55), *Brothers in Law* (57), *Lucky Jim* (57), *Happy Is the Bride* (57), *The Big Money* (57), *Left, Right and Centre* (59), *School for Scoundrels* (59), *I'm All Right, Jack* (59), *Light Up the Sky* (60), *Double Bunk* (61), *The Amorous Prawn* (62), *Hide and Seek* (63), *Heavens Above* (63), *Smashing Time* (67), etc.; latterly on West End stage. TV series: *The World of Wooster*.

CARMINATI, TULLIO (1894–   ). Italian nobleman who became an actor in Europe before going to Hollywood for *The Bat* (26). Foreign-accented hero of several sound films including *One Night of Love* (34), *The Three Maxims* (36); still plays character roles, e.g. *The Cardinal* (63).

†CARNE, MARCEL (1903–   ). Certainly the most brilliant of French directors 1937–45; his career has more recently suffered a semi-eclipse. *Jenny* (36), *Drôle de Drame* (37), *Quai des Brumes* (38), *Hôtel du Nord* (38), *Le Jour Se Lève* (39), *Les Visiteurs du Soir* (42), *Les Enfants du Paradis* (44), *Les Portes de la Nuit* (46), *La Marie du Port* (48), *Juliette ou La Clef des Songes* (51), *Thérèse Raquin* (53), *L'Air*

de Paris (54), *Le Pays D'Ou Je Viens* (56), *Les Tricheurs* (58), *Terrain Vague* (60), *Du Mouron pour les Petits Oiseaux* (62), *Three Rooms in Manhattan* (65), *The Young Wolves* (68).

UN CARNET DE BAL (France 1937). A romantic film which gave its director Julien Duvivier a world-wide reputation. Its connection of several stories by means of an inanimate object (here a dance programme, in later films a tail coat, a Rolls-Royce, etc.) was influential. As an entertainment it now seems rather lacking in substance despite its star cast. In America in 1941, Duvivier directed what amounted to a remake: *Lydia*.

CARNEY, ALAN (1911–   ). American comedy supporting actor, often with WALLY BROWN (qv). *Mr Lucky* (43), *Step Lively* (44), *Genius at Work* (46), *Zombies on Broadway* (46), many others in bit roles.

CARNEY, ART (1918–   ). American TV performer: in *The Yellow Rolls-Royce* (64).

CARNEY, GEORGE (1887–1947). British character actor of stage and screen. *Say It With Flowers* (34), *Father Steps Out* (title role) (37), *Love on the Dole* (41), *The Common Touch* (41), *Tawny Pipit* (44), *I Know Where I'm Going* (45), etc.

CARNOVSKY, MORRIS (1898–   ). Distinguished American stage actor who has appeared in occasional films: *The Life of Emile Zola* (37), *Tovarich* (37), *Address Unknown* (44), *Rhapsody in Blue* (as Gershwin Snr) (45), *Our Vines Have Tender Grapes* (45), *Dead Reckoning* (47), *Saigon* (48), *Thieves' Highway* (49), *Cyrano de Bergerac* (51), etc.

CAROL, MARTINE (1922–1967) (Maryse Mourer). French leading lady popular in undressed roles in the early 50s. *Caroline Chérie* (50), *A Night with Caroline* (52), *Lucrezia Borgia* (52), *The Bed* (53), *The Beach* (54), *Nana* (55), *Lola Montes* (55), *Action of the Tiger* (57), *Ten Seconds to Hell* (59), *Le Cave Se Rebiffe* (61), *Hell Is Empty* (66), etc.

CAROL, SUE (1907–   ) (Evelyn Lederer). American leading lady of the 30s. *Is Zat So* (27), *Girls Gone Wild* (29), *Dancing Sweeties* (30), *Graft* (31), *Secret Sinners* (34), *A Doctor's Diary* (last to date) (37), etc.

CARON, LESLIE (1931–   ). French leading lady and dancer, chosen by Gene Kelly for lead in *An American in Paris* (51). Subsequent roles, including dramatic and comedy parts, include *Man with a Cloak* (51), *Glory Alley* (52), *The Story of Three Loves* (52), *Lili* (BFA) (53), *The Glass Slipper* (54), *Daddy Longlegs* (55), *Gaby* (56), *Gigi* (58), *The Doctor's Dilemma* (58), *The Man Who Understood Women* (58), *The Subterraneans* (60), *Fanny* (61), *Guns of Darkness* (62),

The L-shaped Room (BFA) (62), *Father Goose* (64), *A Very Special Favour* (65), *Promise Her Anything* (66), *Is Paris Burning?* (66).

CARPENTER, CARLETON (1926–   ). American light leading man groomed by MGM in the early 50s. *Lost Boundaries* (48), *Father of the Bride* (50), *Summer Stock* (51), *Fearless Fagan* (53), *Sky Full of Moon* (53), *Take the High Ground* (54), etc. Left show business.

CARPENTER, PAUL (1921–1964). Canadian leading man long in Britain as hero of scores of second features. *School for Secrets* (46), *Albert RN* (53), *The Sea Shall Not Have Them* (55), *Fire Maidens from Outer Space* (56), *The Iron Petticoat* (56), *Jet Storm* (59), etc.

THE CARPETBAGGERS (US 1963). From Harold Robbins' rather salacious best-seller, producer Joe Levine and director Edward Dmytryk fashioned a long and basically old-fashioned movie about a Howard Hughes-type mogul and a Jean Harlow-type star in thirties Hollywood. It did have plot and pace, which made it pretty unusual for its year; and on the whole it entertained. Note for British audiences: carpetbaggers were rapacious Yankees who moved into the southern states after the Civil War to make money out of hardship. Legally to gain entrance they had to bring property with them, and this often consisted of a hastily-packed carpet bag. In 1965 Levine produced *Nevada Smith*, with Steve McQueen going through the unlikely early life of one of the *Carpetbaggers* characters.

CARR, JANE (1909–1957) (Rita Brunstrom). British leading lady, in occasional films. *Taxi to Paradise* (33), *Lord Edgware Dies* (37), *Lilac Domino* (37), *The Lady from Lisbon* (37), *It's Not Cricket* (48), *36 Hours* (54), etc.

CARR, THOMAS (1907–   ). American director, mainly of second feature Westerns. *West of the Brazos* (50), *Captain Scarlett* (52), *Superman* (54), *Three for Jamie Dawn* (57), *Dino* (57), *Tall Stranger* (58), *Cast a Long Shadow* (59), many others. Went into TV and has turned out hundreds of Western episodes for *Rawhide*, etc.

CARRADINE, DAVID (1940–   ). American actor son of John Carradine. Played lead in TV series *Shane* (66). Also in film *The Violent Ones* (67), *Young Billy Young* (69).

CARRADINE, JOHN (1906–   ) (Richmond Reed Carradine). Gaunt American Shakespearean actor who on screen has lately dissipated his talent in conventional horrific roles. *Bride of Frankenstein* (35), *Les Misérables* (36), *Captains Courageous* (37), *Alexander's Ragtime Band* (38), *Stagecoach* (39), *The Grapes of Wrath* (40), *The Black Swan* (42), *Hitler's Madman* (as Heydrich) (43), *Gangway for Tomorrow* (44), *The Invisible Man's Revenge* (44), *Gangway for Tomorrow* (44),

Bluebeard (44), *It's in the Bag* (*The Fifth Chair*) (45), *House of Frankenstein* (as Dracula) (45), *House of Dracula* (45), *The Mummy's Ghost* (46), *The Private Affairs of Bel Ami* (47), *C-Man* (49), *The Egyptian* (54), *Casanova's Big Night* (54), *The Court Jester* (55), *The Black Sleep* (56), *The Cosmic Man* (59), *The Man Who Shot Liberty Valance* (62), *Cheyenne Autumn* (64), *Billy the Kid versus Dracula* (65), *Munster Go Home* (66), *The Good Guys and the Bad Guys* (69), many others.

CARRERAS, JAMES (1910–   ). British production executive, former exhibitor; founder of Hammer Films.

CARRERAS, MICHAEL (1927–   ). British writer-producer-director, a co-director of Hammer Films. Directed: *Maniac* (62), *What a Crazy World* (63), *The Curse of the Mummy's Tomb* (64). Produced: *She* (65), *One Million Years BC* (66), etc.

CARRICK, EDWARD (1905–   ) (Edward Anthony Craig). British art director, son of Edward Gordon Craig. In films from 1927. *Autumn Crocus* (34), *Jump for Glory* (36), *Captain Boycott* (47), *The Divided Heart* (54), *Tiger Bay* (59), *What a Crazy World* (63), *The Nanny* (65), many others. Author of 'Art and Design in the British Film'.

CARRILLO, LEO (1880–1961). American character actor of Spanish descent; usually played amiably talkative fellows in broken English. *Hell Bound* (debut) (31), *City Streets* (32), *Viva Villa* (34), *The Gay Desperado* (36), *History Is Made at Night* (37), *Bad Man of Wyoming* (40), *Horror Island* (41), *Riders of Death Valley* (41), *Top Sergeant* (43), *Pancho Villa Returns* (50), many others.

CARROLL, DIAHANN (1935–   ). American Negro entertainer and actress. *Goodbye Again* (60), *Paris Blues* (61), *Hurry Sundown* (67), *The Split* (68), etc. TV series: *Julia* (68–69).

CARROLL, JOHN (1908–   ) (Julian la Faye). American singing leading man, mostly in second-string musicals of the 40s. *Susan and God,* (40), *Marx Brothers Go West* (41), *Rio Rita* (42), *Flying Tigers* (43), *Bedside Manner* (44), *Fiesta* (47), *The Flame* (48), *Hit Parade of 1951* *The Reluctant Bride* (GB) (52), *Decision at Sundown* (57), *The Plunderers of Painted Flats* (59), etc.

CARROLL, LEO G. (1892–   ). Distinguished British stage and screen character actor long based in Hollywood; usually plays doctors, academics, and lately spies. *The Barretts of Wimpole Street* (34), *Clive of India* (35), *Wuthering Heights* (39), *Rebecca* (40), *Waterloo Bridge* (41), *The House on 92nd Street* (45), *Spellbound* (45), *Forever Amber* (47), *The Paradine Case* (47), *Enchantment* (47), *The Happy Years* (50), *Father of the Bride* (50), *The First Legion* (51), *Strangers on a Train* (51), *Rommel, Desert Fox* (51), *The Bad and the Beautiful* (52), *Young Bess* (54), *We're No Angels* (55), *Tarantula* (55), *The Swan*

(56), *North by Northwest* (59), *The Prize* (63), etc. TV series: *Topper* (53–55), *Going My Way* (62), *The Man from U.N.C.L.E.* (64–67).

CARROLL, LEWIS (1832–1898) (C. L. Dodgson). British writer, an Oxford lecturer in mathematics who wrote *Alice in Wonderland* (qv).

CARROLL, MADELEINE (1906–   ). British leading lady with gentle, well-bred personality; once a teacher. *The Guns of Loos* (debut) (28), *The First Born* (28), *Atlantic* (30), *The W Plan* (30), *Young Woodley* (30), *French Leave* (31), *I Was a Spy* (33), *The World Moves On* (US) (34), *The Thirty-Nine Steps* (35), *Loves of a Dictator* (35), *Secret Agent* (36), *The General Died at Dawn* (US) (37), *Lloyds of London* (US) (37), *On the Avenue* (US) (37), *The Prisoner of Zenda* (US) (37), *Blockade* (US) (38), *Café Society* (US) (39), *Northwest Mounted Police* (US) (40), *One Night in Lisbon* (US) (41), *Bahama Passage* (US) (41), *My Favourite Blonde* (US) (42), *White Cradle Inn* (46), *Don't Trust Your Husband* (US) (48), *Lady Windermere's Fan* (US) (49), etc. Retired.

CARROLL, NANCY (1906–1965). American star of early talkie musicals and straight dramas: *Abie's Irish Rose* (debut) (28), *Shopworn Angel* (29), *Paramount on Parade* (30), *Laughter* (30), *Broken Lullaby* (32), *The Kiss before the Mirror* (33), etc. Retired after *That Certain Age* (38). Real name: Anna la Hiff.

CARRY ON, SERGEANT (GB 1958). The first of a series of ramshackle low comedies made on a shoestring budget by producer Peter Rogers and director Gerald Thomas. Their blue jokes and zany gags made them surprisingly popular in America as well as Britain. The comedians most likely to be found in them are Kenneth Williams, Kenneth Connor, Sidney James, Jim Dale and Joan Sims; and the titles so far include *Carry On Nurse, Carry On Teacher, Carry On Constable, Carry On Regardless, Carry On Cruising, Carry On Cabby, Carry On Jack, Carry On Spying, Carry On Cleo, Carry On Cowboy, Carry On Screaming, Carry On Doctor, Carry On Up the Khyber, Carry On Camping* and *Carry On Again Doctor*. Other very similar comedies by the same team have included *Watch Your Stern, Raising the Wind, Follow that Camel* and *Don't Lose Your Head*. The level of invention is not high.

CARSON, CHARLES (1885–   ). British character actor of stage and screen, seen latterly as distinguished old gentlemen. *Leap Year* (32), *Dark Journey* (37), *Quiet Wedding* (40), *Pink String and Sealing Wax* (45), *Cry the Beloved Country* (52), *Reach for the Sky* (56), *The Trials of Oscar Wilde* (60), many others.

CARSON, JACK (1910–1963). Beefy American comedy actor, previously in vaudeville; usually played 'smart guys' who were really dumb. *Stage Door* (debut) (37), *Carefree* (38), *Destry Rides Again* (39),

Strawberry Blonde (40), *The Male Animal* (42), *The Hard Way* (42), *Princess O'Rourke* (43), *Shine On Harvest Moon* (44), *Make Your Own Bed* (as star) (44), *Arsenic and Old Lace* (44), *Roughly Speaking* (45), *Mildred Pierce* (45), *One More Tomorrow* (46), *Royal Flush* (47), *April Showers* (48), *It's a Great Feeling* (49), *The Groom Wore Spurs* (51), *Dangerous When Wet* (52), *Red Garters* (54), *Phfft* (54), *A Star Is Born* (54), *Ain't Misbehaving* (55), *Cat on a Hot Tin Roof* (58), *The Bramble Bush* (60), *Sammy the Way-Out Seal* (62), etc.

CARSON, JEANNIE (1928–   ) (Jean Shufflebottom). Vivacious British entertainer who retired for some years at the peak of her success. Her few films include *Love in Pawn* (51), *As Long As They're Happy* (52), *An Alligator Named Daisy* (56), *Rockets Galore* (57), *Seven Keys* (62). TV series: *Hey Jeannie* (in US) (56).

CARSON, KIT (1809–1868). American western frontiersman and guide who became a legendary figure and has been portrayed in several films, notably *Kit Carson* (39) in which he was played by Jon Hall.

CARSTAIRS, JOHN PADDY (1918–   ). British director, in films since 1937. Subjects and treatment generally light-hearted. *Night Ride* (39), *Spare a Copper* (40), *He Found a Star* (40), war service, *Dancing with Crime* (46), *Sleeping Car to Trieste* (48), *The Chiltern Hundreds* (49), *Made in Heaven* (52), *Trouble in Store* (53), *Up to His Neck* (54), *Up in the World* (56), *Just My Luck* (57), *The Square Peg* (58), *Tommy the Toreador* (59), *Sands of the Desert* (60), *Weekend with Lulu* (61), many others; latterly directing TV films. Also writes comic novels and paints; has collaborated on several screenplays.

CARTER, HELENA (1923–   ) (Helen Rickerts). American leading lady of second features in the 40s; former model. *Time Out of Mind* (46), *River Lady* (47), *Double Crossbones* (49), *Invaders from Mars* (53), etc. Retired.

CARTER, JANIS (1921–   ) (J. Dremann). American leading lady of minor films in the 40s; former radio experience. *Cadet Girl* (41), *Notorious Lone Wolf* (43), *Paula* (44), *I Love Trouble* (47), *The Woman on Pier 13* (49), *My Forbidden Past* (51), *The Half-Breed* (52), etc. Retired.

CARTER, MRS LESLIE (1862–1937). American stage actress, a protégé of David Bealasco. Rare films include *The Heart of Maryland* (15), *The Vanishing Pioneer* (34), *Rocky Mountain Mystery* (35). She was played by Miriam Hopkins in a 1941 biopic, *Lady With Red Hair*.

cartoon. A film composed of animated drawings.

CARUSO, ANTHONY (c. 1913–   ). American character actor, usually seen as menace. *Johnny Apollo* (40), *Objective Burma* (45), *Wild Harvest* (47), *Bride of Vengeance* (49), *The Iron Mistress* (52),

Phantom of the Rue Morgue (54), *Hell on Frisco Bay* (56), *The Bad-landers* (58), *Young Dillinger* (65), *Nobody Loves Flapping Eagle* (70), many others.

CASABLANCA (AA) (US 1943). A romantic spy melodrama full of cynical conversations, this very professional entertainment hit the headlines accidentally, being released a week before the Casablanca conference. Deserved and kept its fame for tense and witty script (Julius J. and Philip G. Epstein and Howard Koch: AA), polished direction (Michael Curtiz: AA), and lustrous star and supporting performances (Humphrey Bogart, Ingrid Bergman, Claude Rains, Conrad Veidt, Dooley Wilson).

CASARES, MARIA (1922–   ) (Maria Casares Quiroga). Dark-eyed Franco-Spanish actress, memorable as Death in *Orpheus* (49). Also in *Les Enfants du Paradis* (44), *Les Dames du Bois de Boulogne* (45), *La Chartreuse de Parme* (47), *Bagarres* (48), *Le Testament d'Orphée* (59), etc.

case histories from medical files, which would once have been considered pretty dull plot material, have recently been presented quite starkly to paying audiences who appear to have relished them. In the 40s, *Lady in the Dark* was a richly decorated trifle, and even *The Snake Pit* and *Mandy* had subsidiary love interest, but in recent years we have had such unvarnished studies as *El* (paranoiac jealousy), *Pressure Point* (fascist tendencies), *A Child Is Waiting* (mentally handicapped children), *Life Upside Down* (withdrawal), *The Collector* (sex fantasies), *Repulsion* and *The Boston Strangler* (homicidal mania), *Bigger Than Life* (danger from drugs), *The Three Faces of Eve* and *Lizzie* (split personality), *Marnie* (frigidity), and *Morgan* (infantile regression). At least the pretence of studying a case history relieves writers of the responsibility of providing a dramatic ending.

See also: *dreams; fantasy; amnesia.*

CASINO ROYALE (GB 1966). At once the ultimate in spy kaleidoscope and the folly that killed off the fashion, this huge shapeless romp is living proof that all the money and talent in the world won't necessarily make a good movie . . . not, at least, when the script seems to have been put together with paste at a late-night party. If the distinguished directors and actors who made it had fun, they failed to communicate it to the audience.

CASPARY, VERA (1904–   ). American novelist, several of whose crime stories have been filmed: *Laura* (44), *Bedelia* (47), etc. Also wrote screen plays from 1937, including *Letter to Three Wives* (49), *Three Husbands* (50), *I Can Get It for You Wholesale* (51), *The Blue Gardenia* (53), *Les Girls* (57).

CASQUE D'OR (GOLDEN MARIE) (France 1952). The flavour and detail of French low-life in the 90s are subtly caught by director Jacques Becker in this much-admired melodrama starring Simone Signoret and Serge Reggiani.

CASS, HENRY (1902–). British director with stage experience as actor and producer. *Lancashire Luck* (37), *Acacia Avenue* (45), *The Glass Mountain* (48), *No Place for Jennifer* (49), *Last Holiday* (50), *Young Wives' Tale* (51), *Windfall* (55), *Blood of the Vampire* (60), *The Hand* (60), etc.

CASS, MAURICE (1884–1954). American character actor of Russian origin; often played old men. *Two for Tonight* (35), *Charlie Chan at the Opera* (37), *Son of Monte Cristo* (40), *Blood and Sand* (41), *Charley's Aunt* (42), *Up in Arms* (44), *Spoilers of the North* (47), *We're Not Married* (52), etc.

CASSAVETES, JOHN (1929–). American actor-director with stock and radio experience. As actor: *Taxi* (54), *The Night Holds Terror* (55), *Edge of the City (A Man Is Ten Feet Tall)* (57), *Saddle the Wind* (58), *The Dirty Dozen* (67), *Rosemary's Baby* (68), etc. TV series: *Johnny Staccato* (59). As director: *Shadows* (60), *Too Late Blues* (61), *A Child Is Waiting* (62), *Faces* (68), *The Husbands* (69).

CASSEL, JEAN-PIERRE (1932–). French leading man. *Les Jeux de l'Amour* (60), *L'Amant de Cinq Jours* (61), *The Vanishing Corporal* (62), *La Ronde* (64), *Those Magnificent Men in Their Flying Machines* (65), *Les Fetes Galantes* (65), *Is Paris Burning?* (66), *Jeu de Massacre* (67), etc.

CASTELLANI, RENATO (1913–). Italian director. *Un Colpo di Pistola* (41), *My Son the Professor* (46), *E Primavera* (50), *Due Soldi di Speranza* (51), *Romeo and Juliet* (GB) (54), *Nella Citta l'Inferno* (59), *Il Brigante* (61), *Mare Matto* (62), etc.

CASTLE, DON (1919–1966). American leading man of second features in the 40s.

CASTLE, IRENE and VERNON (Irene Foote, Vernon Blythe). A dancing team who were highly popular in American cabaret 1912–17. Irene (1893–1968) was American, Vernon (1885–1918) was British. Apart from some 1914 shorts, their only feature together was *The Whirl of Life* (15); but Irene alone made a number of dramatic films, especially after Vernon's death in an air crash: *Patria* (17), *The Hillcrest Mystery* (18), *The Invisible Bond* (19), *The Broadway Bride* (21), *No Trespassing* (22), etc. In 1939 Fred Astaire and Ginger Rogers appeared in *The Story of Vernon and Irene Castle*, and in 1958 Irene published an autobriography, *Castles in the Air*.

CASTLE, MARY (1931–   ). American leading lady. *Criminal Lawyer* (51), *Eight Iron Men* (52), *The Lawless Breed* (53), etc.

CASTLE, NICK (1910–1968). American dance director. *Hellzapoppin* (42), *Royal Wedding* (47), *Red Garters* (54), others.

CASTLE, PEGGIE (1927–   ). American 'B' picture heroine of the 50s. *The Long Wait* (54), *The Counterfeit Plan* (56), *Miracle in the Rain* (56), *Hell's Crossroads* (57), *Seven Hills of Rome* (58), etc. TV series: *Lawman* (58–62).

CASTLE, WILLIAM (1914–   ). American screen actor (1937–40), director of second features (1941–57) and producer-director of gimmicky horror films involving give-away insurance policies, mobile skeletons, tingling seats, etc. *The Whistler* (44), *When Strangers Marry* (44), *Johnny Stool Pigeon* (49), *Undertow* (50), *Fort Ti* (53), *The Americano* (55), *Masterson of Kansas* (56), *Macabre* (58), *The House on Haunted Hill* (59), *The Tingler* (59), *Homicidal* (61), *Mr Sardonicus* (62), *The Old Dark House* (63), *The Night Walker* (64), *I Saw What You Did* (65), *Let's Kill Uncle* (66), *The Spirit Is Willing* (67), *Rosemary's Baby* (produced only) (68), *Project X* (68), *Riot* (produced only) (68), many others.

THE CAT AND THE CANARY. An eccentric will read at midnight in a spooky house, with secret panels behind which a maniac lurks, are the ingredients of John Willard's stage thriller of 1922, which prompted a host of Hollywood imitations as well as being itself filmed three times. Paul Leni's 1927 version was a semi-surrealist send-up, with Creighton Hale and Laura la Plante. Rupert Julian's sound remake of 1930 was retitled *The Cat Creeps*, and featured Helen Twelvetrees and Raymond Hackett. In 1939 came Elliott Nugent's very satisfactory comedy vehicle for Bob Hope and Paulette Goddard, with Gale Sondergaard as the sinister house-keeper and some elegant photography by Charles Lang.

CAT BALLOU (US 1965). A spoof western directed with some but not quite enough flair by Eliot Silverstein from a joky script by Walter Newman and Frank Pierson. An amusing ballad by Nat King Cole and Stubby Kaye effectively linked disparate threads of story, and Lee Marvin collected an Oscar for guying a dual role.

CATHERINE THE GREAT, 'mother of all the Russias', has been played on screen by, among others, Pola Negri (*Forbidden Paradise* [24]), Elizabeth Bergner (*Catherine the Great* [34]), Marlene Dietrich (*The Scarlet Empress* [34]), Tallulah Bankhead (*A Royal Scandal/Czarina* [46]), Viveca Lindfors (*Tempest* [58]), Jeanne Moreau (*Great Catherine* [68]), and Bette Davis (*John Paul Jones* [59]). What a pity Mae West's play *Catherine Was Great* never reached the screen!

CATLETT, WALTER (1889–1960). American comedian and character actor with long vaudeville experience. Used flustered mannerisms not unlike those of Will Hay; played supporting roles in innumerable films from the early 30s. *Palmy Days* (31), *A Tale of Two Cities* (35), *Mr Deeds Goes to Town* (36), *Come Up Smiling* (37), *Bringing Up Baby* (38), *Horror Island* (41), *His Butler's Sister* (43), *Ghost Catchers* (44), *Riverboat Rhythm* (46), *Look for the Silver Lining* (49), *The Inspector General* (49), *Father Takes the Air* (51), *Davy Crockett and the River Pirates* (56), many others.

CAT PEOPLE (US 1943). Much-praised low-budget thriller produced by Val Lewton and directed by Jacques Tourneur, notable for suspenseful set-pieces on a lonely street and in a darkened swimming bath. The first monster film to refrain from showing its monster.

CATTO, MAX (1907–). Popular British adventure novelist. Novels filmed include *Daughter of Darkness* ('They Walk Alone') (48), *A Prize of Gold* (54), *A Hill in Korea* (56), *Trapeze* (56).

CAULFIELD, JOAN (1922–). American leading lady, a demure decoration of 40s films. *Miss Susie Slagle's* (debut) (46), *Blue Skies* (46), *Monsieur Beaucaire* (46), *Welcome Stranger* (56), *Dear Ruth* (47), *The Unsuspected* (47), *Dear Wife* (49), *Girl of the Year* (50), *The Lady Said No* (52), *The Rains of Ranchipur* (55), *Guns of Wyoming* (*Cattle King*) (63), *Red Tomahawk* (66), etc. TV series: *My Favourite Husband* (53).

CAVALCADE (US 1933: AA). Noel Coward's patriotic twentieth-century pageant was brought to the screen by Frank Lloyd (AA) in a spectacular if rather lifeless Hollywood version, with a mainly British cast led by Clive Brook and Diana Wynyard. Art direction by William Darling (AA).

CAVALCANTI, ALBERTO (1897–). Brazilian director who made his reputation in Paris with 'realistic' films like *Rien que les Heures* (26), *En Rade* (27). Joined British GPO Film Unit to make documentaries, e.g. *North Sea* (38), *Men of the Lightship* (41). Joined Ealing Studios to direct entertainment features: *Went the Day Well* (42), *Champagne Charlie* (45), *Dead of Night* (part) (45), *Nicholas Nickleby* (47), *They Made Me a Fugitive* (47), *The First Gentleman* (48), *For Them That Trespass* (49), etc. Never managed a British masterpiece; returned to Brazil and has made several films there, also in Europe. *O Canto do Mar* (53), *Herr Puntila* (Ger.) (55), *La Prima Notte* (It.) (58), *Yerma* (It.) (62), etc.

CAVANAUGH, HOBART (1886–1950). Mild-mannered American character actor often seen as clerk, nervous husband or frightened caretaker. *Mayor of Hell* (33), *I Cover the Waterfront* (35), *Captain*

Blood (35), *Cain and Mabel* (37), *Horror Island* (as the villain) (41), *Kismet* (44), *Black Angel* (46), *You Gotta Stay Happy* (48), many others.

CAVANAUGH, PAUL (1895–196*). Suave British actor who went to Hollywood in the early 30s and spent the rest of his career playing villains and murder victims. *The Runaway Princess* (29), *Grumpy* (31), *A Bill of Divorcement* (32), *Tarzan and His Mate* (34), *Romance in Flanders* (37), *Crime over London* (38), *Captains of the Clouds* (42), *Shadows on the Stairs* (43), *The Scarlet Claw* (45), *Rogues of Sherwood Forest* (50), *House of Wax* (53), *Diane* (57), *The Four Skulls oj Jonathan Drake* (59), many others.

CAYATTE, ANDRÉ (1909–). French lawyer who became writer-director of films with something to say: *Justice Est Faite* (50), *Nous Sommes Tous les Assassins* (52), *An Eye for an Eye* (56), *The Mirror Has Two Faces* (57), *The Crossing of the Rhine* (62), *La Vie Conjugale* (63), *A Trap for Cinderella* (65), etc.

CELI, ADOLFO (1922–). Italian character actor with long stage career in Brazil. Films include *That Man from Rio* (64), *Thunderball* (65), *Von Ryan's Express* (65), *El Greco* (66), *Grand Prix* (67), *The Honey Pot* (67), *The Bobo* (67), *Fragment of Fear* (69).

CELLIER, FRANK (1884–1948). British stage actor who usually played unsympathetic types. Many screen appearances since 1930 in supporting roles: *Soldiers of the King* (33), *Sixty Glorious Years* (38), *The Ware Case* (38), *Quiet Wedding* (40), *Love on the Dole* (41), *Give Us the Moon* (44), *Quiet Weekend* (46), *The Blind Goddess* (48), etc.

censorship. Each country has found it necessary to apply its own rules for film producers; in Britain and America at least these rules were drawn up and enforced at the request of the industry itself. The British Board of Film Censors was founded in 1912. For many years films were classified as 'U' (for universal exhibition), 'A' (adults and accompanied children only) or (from 1933) 'H' (horrific; prohibited for persons under 16). In 1951, with the growing emphasis on sex, 'H' was replaced by 'X', which includes sex *and* horror. In America, the Arbuckle scandal of 1921 precipitated the founding of the 'Hays Office' (named after its first paid president) by the Motion Picture Producers and Distributors of America. The first Production Code was issued in 1930 and has undergone constant amendment, especially since *The Moon Is Blue* (53), and very rapidly indeed since *Room at the Top* (59); in 1966 *Who's Afraid of Virginia Woolf* almost swamped it completely and a revised, broadened code was issued. The independent and very strict Catholic Legion of Decency was founded in 1934 and issues its own classifications; it recently changed its name to the National Catholic Office for Motion Pictures.

CERVI, GINO (1901–   ). Italian actor with long experience. Best known as the communist mayor in the *Don Camillo* films (51–55); also in *Frontier* (34), *Four Steps in the Clouds* (42), *Fabiola* (47), *Maddalena* (53), many others.

CHABROL, CLAUDE (1930–   ). French director credited with starting the 'nouvelle vague'. *Le Beau Serge* (58), *Les Cousins* (59), *A Double Tour* (59), *Les Bonnes Femmes* (60), *Ophelia* (62), *Landru* (62), *Le Tigre Aime la Chair Fraiche* (65), *La Scandale* (*The Champagne Murders*) (67), *The Road to Corinth* (68), *Les Biches* (68), *The Beast Must Die* (69), etc.

CHAFFEY, DON (1917–   ). British director; started in art department at Gainsborough in the early 40s. *Time Is My Enemy* (53), *The Girl in the Picture* (56), *The Flesh Is Weak* (57), *A Question of Adultery* (58), *The Man Upstairs* (59), *Danger Within* (59), *Dentist in the Chair* (60), *Greyfriars Bobby* (60), *Nearly a Nasty Accident* (60), *A Matter of Who* (61), *The Prince and the Pauper* (62), *Jason and the Argonauts* (63), *A Jolly Bad Fellow* (64), *One Million Years B.C.* (66), *The Viking Queen* (67), *A Twist of Sand* (68), etc.; many episodes of TV series.

CHAGRIN, FRANCIS (1905–   ). Russian-born composer in films (mostly British) from 1934; has composed over 200 scores. Recently: *Last Holiday* (50), *An Inspector Calls* (54), *The Colditz Story* (55), *The Snorkel* (58), *Danger Within* (59), *Greyfriars Bobby* (60), *In the Cool of the Day* (63), etc.

CHAKIRIS, GEORGE (1933–   ). American actor-dancer, in films from 1951. *Two and Two Make Six* (GB) (60), *West Side Story* (AA) (61), *Diamondhead* (63), *Flight from Ashiya* (63), *Kings of the Sun* (63), *633 Squadron* (64), *The High Bright Sun* (GB) (65), *Is Paris Burning?* (66), *The Young Girls of Rochefort* (67), *The Big Cube* (69), etc.

CHALIAPIN, FEDOR (1873–1938). Russian operatic bass whose film roles included Massenet's *Don Quixote* (33).

CHALLIS, CHRISTOPHER (1919–   ). British cinematographer. *The Small Back Room* (48), *The Elusive Pimpernel* (50), *Tales of Hoffman* (51), *Genevieve* (53), *The Story of Gilbert and Sullivan* (53), *The Flame and the Flesh* (54), *The Adventures of Quentin Durward* (55), *The Battle of the River Plate* (56), *Blind Date* (59), *Sink the Bismarck* (60), *HMS Defiant* (62), *The Victors* (63), *The Long Ships* (64), *Return from the Ashes* (65), *Arabesque* (66), *Two for the Road* (67), *Chitty Chitty Bang Bang* (68), *Staircase* (69), *The Private Life of Sherlock Holmes* (70), etc.

CHAMBERLAIN, CYRIL (1909–   ). British small-part player often seen as average man, policeman or dull husband. *This Man in Paris*

(39), *London Belongs to Me* (48), *Trouble in Store* (53), *Blue Murder at St Trinians* (58), *Carry On Constable* (60), many others.

CHAMBERLAIN, RICHARD (1935–   ). Boyish-looking American leading man, neglected by Hollywood until he became TV's *Dr Kildare* (61–65). Films include *A Thunder of Drums* (62), *Twilight of Honour* (63), *Joy in the Morning* (65), *Petulia* (68), *The Madwoman of Chaillot* (69), *Julius Caesar* (70).

THE CHAMP (US 1931). A sentimental tale about a boozy boxer and his small son, this affectionately-remembered movie won an Academy Award for Wallace Beery in the lead and for scriptwriter Frances Marion; it also confirmed the stardom of boy actor Jackie Cooper.

CHAMPION (US 1949). One of the first anti-boxing films, and Stanley Kramer's first big success as producer. Written by Carl Foreman, starring Kirk Douglas, Arthur Kennedy, Lola Albright.

CHAMPION, MARGE (1925–   ), and GOWER (1921–   ). American husband-wife dance team who appeared in several MGM musicals of the early 50s: *Showboat* (51), *Lovely to Look At* (52), *Give a Girl a Break* (53), *Three for the Show* (55), *Jupiter's Darling* (55), etc. Gower had previously appeared solo, e.g. in *Till the Clouds Roll By* (46); he has lately turned to direction: *My Six Loves* (63). Marge has played small roles in *The Summer* (67) and *The Party* (68).

CHANDLER, CHICK (1905–   ). Wiry American hero of many a 40s second feature. *Melody Cruise* (33), *Alexander's Ragtime Band* (38), *Swanee River* (40), *Hot Spot* (41), *Seven Doors to Death* (44), *Lost Continent* (47), *Family Honeymoon* (49), *Battle Cry* (55), *The Naked Gun* (58), *It's a Mad Mad Mad Mad World* (63), over 100 others, often in bit parts. TV series: *Soldiers of Fortune* (55).

CHANDLER, GEORGE (1902–   ). American character actor, an ex-vaudevillian who specialized in sly or cringing roles. *Fury* (36), *Nothing Sacred* (37), *Jesse James* (39), *The Return of Frank James* (41), *It Happened Tomorrow* (44), *Dead Reckoning* (47), *The Paleface* (48), *Hans Christian Andersen* (52), *The High and the Mighty* (54), *Gunsight Ridge* (58), many others.

CHANDLER, HELEN (1909–1968). American leading lady of the early thirties: her early retirement robbed films of an interesting personality. *The Music Master* (28), *Dracula* (30), *Outward Bound* (30), *The Last Flight* (31), *Christopher Strong* (33), *Long Lost Father* (34), *Midnight Alibi* (GB) (34), *It's a Bet* (GB) (35), etc.

CHANDLER, JEFF (1918–1961) (Ira Grossel). American leading man with the unusual attraction of prematurely grey hair. Stage and radio experience. *Johnny O'clock* (46), *Sword in the Desert* (47),

Chandler, John Davis

Broken Arrow (a great hit as Cochise) (50), *Iron Man* (51), *Battle at Apache Pass* (52), *Sign of the Pagan* (54), *The Female on the Beach* (55), *Away All Boats* (56), *Pay the Devil* (57), *Drango* (57), *Stranger in My Arms* (59), *Ten Seconds to Hell* (59), *The Jayhawkers* (59), *The Plunderers* (60), *Return to Peyton Place* (61), *Merrill's Marauders* (61), others.

CHANDLER, JOHN DAVIS (c. 1940–). American player who seems to have taken over from Elisha Cook the mantle of the screen's most neurotic, twitching villain. *The Young Savages* (61), *Major Dundee* (65), *Once a Thief* (65), etc.

CHANDLER, RAYMOND (1889–1959). American thriller-writer to whom literary acclaim came late in life. Successful films were made of *Farewell My Lovely* (44), *The Big Sleep* (46), *The Lady in the Lake* (48); he also collaborated on screenplays of *Double Indemnity* (44), *Strangers on a Train* (51), etc. In 1969 came the long-promised film of *The Little Sister*, rechristened *Marlowe*. There was also a TV series called *Philip Marlowe* (59), with Phil Carey.

CHANEY, LON (1883–1930). American star character actor, famous for elaborate make-up in macabre roles; known as the man of a thousand faces. *Where the Forest Ends* (14), *Triumph* (18), *Riddle Gawne* (18), *The Miracle Man* (19), *The Unholy Three* (19), *The Penalty* (20), *Treasure Island* (20), *Oliver Twist* (21), *Quincey Adams Sawyer* (22), *A Blind Bargain* (23), *The Hunchback of Notre Dame* (23), *He Who Gets Slapped* (24), *The Phantom of the Opera* (25). *Tell It to the Marines* (26), *The Unknown* (27), *Mr Wu* (27), *West of Zanzibar* (28), *Laugh Clown Laugh* (28), *Where East Is East* (29), *The Unholy Three* (sound remake) (30), etc. A biopic, *Man of a Thousand Faces*, was made in 1957 starring James Cagney.

CHANEY, LON JNR (1907–) (some sources say 1905) (Creighton Chaney). Heavily-built American character actor who mainly followed his father's type of role in progressively inferior films. *Bird of Paradise* (32), *Lucky Devils* (33), *Wife, Doctor and Nurse* (37), *Of Mice and Men* (best performance, as Lennie) (39), *The Wolf Man* (40), *Billy the Kid* (41), *Ghost of Frankenstein* (as the monster) (41), *Man Made Monster* (*The Electric Man*) (41), *Calling Dr Death* (42), *Son of Dracula* (43), *Frankenstein Meets the Wolf Man* (43), *The Mummy's Ghost* (44), *The Frozen Ghost* (45), *House of Frankenstein* (45), *House of Dracula* (45), *My Favourite Brunette* (47), *Abbott and Costello Meet Frankenstein* (49), *Inside Straight* (51), *High Noon* (52), *Black Castle* (52), *The Cyclops* (53), *I Died a Thousand Times* (55), *The Black Sleep* (56), *The Indestructible Man* (56), many others. Now plays small parts in Westerns, leads in horror films: *The Haunted Palace* (63), *Black Spurs* (65), *Witchcraft* (GB) (65). TV series: *The Last of the Mohicans* (as Chingachgook) (56).

CHANG (US 1927). Famous documentary by Merian Cooper and Ernest Schoedsack telling how a tribesman of Siam guards his family against the terrors of the encroaching jungle. Originally ended with a stampede of elephants on the 'Magnascope', an early form of giant screen.

change-over. Transition from one reel of film to another during projection. A reel originally lasted ten minutes but most 35mm projectors now take 20 or 30 minutes. Change-over cues are given in the form of dots which appear on the top right-hand corner of the screen a standard number of seconds before the end of the reel.

CHANNING, CAROL (1921–   ). American stage comedienne who has so far demonstrated her vivacity in only two films: *The First Travelling Saleslady* (56), *Thoroughly Modern Millie* (67).

CHAPLIN, CHARLES (1889–   ). A legendary figure in his own lifetime despite a comparatively limited output, this British pantomimist went to the US in 1910 with Fred Karno's troupe and was invited to join the Keystone company; later also worked for Essanay and Mutual, and these early two-reelers are held by many to be superior to the later, more pretentious features which he produced himself. *Kid Auto Races at Venice* (not only his first film but the one in which he first wore the improvised tramp costume in which he later became famous) (13), *Tillie's Punctured Romance* (14), *Dough and Dynamite* (15), *The Tramp* (15), *Charlie at the Show* (15), *The Vagabond* (16), *The Adventurer* (16), *Easy Street* (16), *The Cure* (16), *The Immigrant* (17), *A Dog's Life* (18), *Shoulder Arms* (18), many others. †Features: *The Kid* (20), *The Pilgrim* (23), *A Woman of Paris* (directed only) (23), *The Gold Rush* (24), *The Circus* (AA) (28), *City Lights* (31), *Modern Times* (36), *The Great Dictator* (40), *Monsieur Verdoux* (47), *Limelight* (52), *A King in New York* (GB) (57), *A Countess from Hong Kong* (GB) (66). The later films have tended to sacrifice humour, rather unsatisfactorily, for sentiment and philosophy.

CHAPLIN, GERALDINE (1944–   ). Actress daughter of Charles Chaplin. *Doctor Zhivago* (65), *Stranger in the House* (67), *I Killed Rasputin* (68), *The Hawaiians* (70).

CHAPLIN, SAUL (1912–   ). American songwriter and musical director. Arranger of *An American in Paris* (AA) (51), *Seven Brides for Seven Brothers* (AA) (54). Associate producer *Can Can* (59), *West Side Story* (61), *The Sound of Music* (65), *Star* (67).

CHAPLIN, SYD (1885–1965). British comedian, elder brother of Charles Chaplin; became popular in America in the 20s. Many two-reelers, also *Shoulder Arms* (18), *King Queen Joker* (21), *Her Temporary Husband* (23), *The Perfect Flapper* (24), *Charley's Aunt* (26), *The*

Chaplin, Sydney

Better 'Ole (27), *The Missing Link* (27), *A Little Bit of Fluff* (GB) (28), etc. Retired on coming of sound.

CHAPLIN, SYDNEY (1926–). Actor son of Charles Chaplin; made debut in *Limelight* (52) but subsequent appearances have been unexciting: *Confession* (55), *Follow That Man* (61), *A Countess from Hong Kong* (66), etc.

CHAPMAN, EDWARD (1901–). British character actor, former bank clerk. On stage from 1924, films from 1929 (*Juno and the Paycock*); subsequently played Yorkshire aldermen, mild villains and ordinary chaps in scores of films, e.g. *Things to Come* (35), *Rembrandt* (37), *The Proud Valley* (39), *The Briggs Family* (40), *They Flew Alone* (42), *The October Man* (47), *It Always Rains on Sunday* (47), *Mr Perrin and Mr Traill* (49), *The Card* (52), *A Day to Remember* (54), *X the Unknown* (56), *The Square Peg* (58), *School for Scoundrels* (60), *Oscar Wilde* (as the Marquis of Queensberry) (60), *A Stitch in Time* (63), *Joey Boy* (65), many others. TV series: *Champion House* (67–68).

CHAPMAN, MARGUERITE (1916–). Dependable American heroine of many 40s co-features. *Parachute Nurse* (42), *Destroyer* (43), *One Way to Love* (46), *Mr District Attorney* (47), *Coroner Creek* (48), *Kansas Raiders* (50), *Flight to Mars* (51), *The Seven Year Itch* (55), *The Amazing Transparent Man* (59), etc.

CHARADE (US 1963). A richly decorated spy spoof with Cary Grant and Audrey Hepburn, mixing sex, black comedy and high camp in a way that became briefly fashionable in other similarly titled movies (*Arabesque*, *Kaleidoscope*, etc.) which relied more on stars, sets and exciting scenes than on a logical plot. *Charade* succeeded pretty well by virtue of Peter Stone's script and Charles Lang's photography.

THE CHARGE OF THE LIGHT BRIGADE. The 1936 film of this name was directed by Michael Curtiz for Warners and had a completely fictitious story which took place largely in India; the last half-hour took us to the Crimea and a spectacular piece of self-sacrifice by Errol Flynn and a great many horses and extras. As a piece of Hollywood stunting expertise this sequence has seldom been surpassed. Tony Richardson's 1968 film has a script by Charles Wood which attempts in wry fashion to tell the true story of the charge. Dull characters and muddled direction kill the climax, but the first half has many rewarding moments of Victoriana and some splendid bridging animation, in the manner of political cartoons of the period, by Richard Williams.

CHARISSE, CYD (1923–) (Tula Finklea). Long-legged American dancer and leading lady, in many MGM musicals. *Ziegfeld Follies* (44), *The Harvey Girls* (46), *Till the Clouds Roll By* (46), *Fiesta* (47),

The Unfinished Dance (47), *On an Island with You* (48), *Words and Music* (48), *East Side West Side* (50), *Mark of the Renegade* (51), *Singing in the Rain* (52), *Sombrero* (53), *Band Wagon* (53), *Easy to Love* (53), *Brigadoon* (54), *It's Always Fair Weather* (55), *Meet Me in Las Vegas* (56), *Silk Stockings* (56), *Party Girl* (58), *Black Tights* (61), *Two Weeks in Another Town* (63), *The Silencers* (66), *Maroc 7* (66), etc. Married to Tony Martin.

CHARLESWORTH, JOHN (1935–1960). British teenage actor of the 50s, *Tom Brown's Schooldays* (51), *Scrooge* (51), *John of the Fair* (54). *Yangtse Incident* (57), *The Angry Silence* (59), etc.

CHARLEY'S AUNT. Brandon Thomas' Victorian farce has been filmed many times, notably with Syd Chaplin in 1926, Charles Ruggles in 1931, Arthur Askey in 1940, Jack Benny in 1942, and Ray Bolger (musical version, *Where's Charley*) in 1952. Danny La Rue is scheduled for a 1970 reprise.

CHARLIE BUBBLES (GB 1967). A small but pleasing bitter comedy about the horrors of being a very rich author with a working-class background. Albert Finney, director, extracts a perfect performance from Albert Finney, actor; he also handles comic set-piece scenes with great bravura and accuracy of mood. Billie Whitelaw (BFA) is a splendidly shrewish ex-wife, and the whole adds up to a fine sardonic comment on the affluent society.

CHARLIE CHAN. The polite oriental detective created by Earl Derr Biggers was first featured by Hollywood in a serial (1926) in which he was played by George Kuwa. Kamiyama Sojin played him once in 1928, E. L. Park once in 1929, Warner Oland sixteen times (1931–37), Sidney Toler twenty-two times (1938–47) and Roland Winters six times (1948–52). J. Carroll Naish then played the role in 39 TV films (57).

CHARTERS, SPENCER (1878–1943). American character actor who usually played rural fellow who may have been deaf but not too dumb to outsmart the city slicker. *Whoopee* (31), *Twenty Thousand Years in Sing Sing* (32), *The Raven* (35), *Libelled Lady* (36), *Banjo on My Knee* (37), *In Old Chicago* (38), *Jesse James* (39), *Maryland* (40), *Tobacco Road* (42), *Juke Girl* (42), many others.

the chase has always been a standard ingredient of film-making, providing a convenient and not too expensive way of rounding off a comedy or thriller in good style. In silent days it was necessary to almost every comedian, from Buster Keaton to the Keystone Kops; while Westerns invariably concluded with the goodies chasing the baddies. Sound comedies used the chase more sparingly, but René Clair's *Le Million* was a superb early example of the fuller orchestration now possible, and sophisticated comedies like *It Happened One Night*, *Sullivan's Travels* and *The Runaround* did not disdain the basic theme: nor, of course, did comics like Abbott and Costello and W. C. Fields. Later, the Ealing comedies dusted off the device and used it brilliantly in *Whisky Galore*, *The Man in the White Suit*, *A Run for Your Money* and others. A recent marathon chase extravaganza was *It's a Mad Mad Mad Mad World*, and *The Great Race* has its share of similar excitements; and *A Funny Thing Happened on the Way to the Forum* has a final chariot chase into which as many old gags as possible are crammed. Car chases seem to be a speciality of Peter Yates, who stages a cracking one for *Robbery* and then excelled it in *Bullitt*.

The best-established serious use of the chase is in the much remade *Les Misérables*, which has also sparked off no fewer than four television series: *The Fugitive*, *Run for Your Life*, *Branded* and *Run, Buddy, Run*. Chases made neat climaxes for innumerable location crime thrillers, of which the best is perhaps *The Naked City*. Hitchcock has used the chase brilliantly in such films as *Saboteur*, *The Thirty-nine Steps* and *North by Northwest*; John Ford gave it dignity in Westerns like *Stagecoach* and *She Wore a Yellow Ribbon*; and it seems doubtful whether its uses will ever be exhausted while Hollywood can come up with twists like *The Chase* itself, where pursuit is used allegorically as the basis of a downbeat modern social melodrama.

CHASE, BORDEN (* –). American writer. *Blue, White and Perfect* (41), *Flame of the Barbary Coast* (43), *Red River* (48), *Winchester 73* (50), *Lone Star* (51), *Bend of the River* (52), *The World in His Arms* (52), *Sea Devils* (53), *Vera Cruz* (54), *Man without a Star* (55), *Backlash* (56), *Night Passage* (57), many others.

CHASE, CHARLIE (1893–1940). American comedian who made innumerable two-reel farces from c. 1925, usually as henpecked husband. Real name Charles Parrott; brother of James Parrott, comedy director of the 20s and 30s.

CHASE, ILKA (1900–). American stage and occasionally film actress; also journalist. Films include *Paris Bound* (29), *Soak the Rich* (36), *Now Voyager* (42), *Miss Tatlock's Millions* (50), *The Big Knife* (55), *Ocean's Eleven* (60), etc.

CHATTERTON, RUTH (1893–1961). American actress on stage from 1909, films from 1928. *Sins of the Fathers* (28), *Madame X* (29), *The Laughing Lady* (30), *Unfaithful* (31), *The Rich Are Always with Us* (32), *Frisco Jenny* (33), *Female* (33), *Dodsworth* (36), *The Rat* (GB) (38), *A Royal Divorce* (38), etc. Later became successful novelist.

CHAUVEL, CHARLES (1897–1959). Australian writer-producer-director. *In the Wake of the Bounty* (33), *Forty Thousand Horsemen* (42), *The*

Rats of Tobruk (48), *The Rugged O'Riordans* (48), *Jedda* (53), many others.

CHAYEFSKY, PADDY (1923–   ). American writer whose TV plays made successful movies: *Marty* (AA) (55), *The Bachelor Party* (56), *Middle of the Night* (58), etc. Wrote screenplays: *The Goddess* (57), *The Americanization of Emily* (64), *Paint Your Wagon* (69).

CHEAPER BY THE DOZEN (US 1950). A very popular film about the life of Frank Gilbreth, a slightly eccentric efficiency expert and father of twelve children. Clifton Webb and Myrna Loy played Mr and Mrs Gilbreth, and two years later came a sequel called *Belles on Their Toes*, about the problems of Mrs Gilbreth as a widow. Comedies about large families have more recently been popular again: *Yours, Mine and Ours* (68), *With Six You Get Egg Roll* (68).

THE CHEAT (US 1915). This melodrama by Hector Turnbull was a huge commercial success in its day, with Sessue Hayakawa as the wily Japanese who loans money to a foolish society dame, illtreats her when she will not succumb to his lascivious desires, and is killed by her husband. Cecil B. de Mille directed; the film was remade by George Abbott in 1923 and 1931, and in 1937 (in France) by Marcel L'Herbier.

CHEKHOV, MICHAEL (1891–1955). Russian actor who formed drama schools in London and New York, also appeared in Hollywood films from 1943. *Song of Russia* (43), *Cross My Heart* (45), *Spellbound* (45), *Spectre of the Rose* (46), *Abie's Irish Rose* (46), *Arch of Triumph* (47), *Holiday for Sinners* (52), *Rhapsody* (55), etc.

CHENAL, PIERRE (1903–   ) (P. Cohen). French director. *Crime and Punishment* (35), *Alibi* (37), *Le Dernier Tournant* (39), *Clochemerle* (48), *Native Son* (US) (51), etc.; little of note in recent years.

CHERKASSOV, NICOLAI (1903–66). Russian actor of epic hero stature. *Peter the Great* (38), *Alexander Nevsky* (39), *Ivan the Terrible* (44–48), *Don Quixote* (56), etc.

CHERRILL, VIRGINIA (1908–   ). American leading lady of the 30s, a society girl who was persuaded by Chaplin to play the blind flower-seller in *City Lights* (31). Later: *Delicious* (32), *Charlie Chan's Greatest Case* (33), *What Price Crime* (35), *Troubled Waters* (last appearance) (36), etc.

CHERRY, HELEN (1915–   ). Aristocratic-looking British actress, wife of Trevor Howard. Mostly on stage. *The Courtneys of Curzon Street* (47), *Adam and Evelyn* (49), *Morning Departure* (50), *Young Wives' Tale* (51), *Castle in the Air* (52), *High Flight* (57), *Flipper and the Pirates* (64), etc.

Chester, Hal E.

CHESTER, HAL E. (1921–). American producer: former 'Dead End Kid'-type actor. Producer *Joe Palooka* series 1946–50; *The Highwayman* (53), *The Bold and the Brave* (55), *Night of the Demon* (GB) (57), *School for Scoundrels* (GB) (60), *Hide and Seek* (GB) (62), *The Comedy Man* (GB) (64), *The Double Man* (67), etc.

CHEVALIER, MAURICE (1887–). Celebrated French singing entertainer, 'the man in the straw hat'. Widely varied early experience; became famous in Mistinguett's Paris revues of the 20s. Went to Hollywood for *Innocents of Paris* (29); later films include *The Love Parade* (30), *One Hour with You* (32), *The Smiling Lieutenant* (32), *Love Me Tonight* (32), *The Merry Widow* (34), *The Man from the Folies Bergères* (35), *The Beloved Vagabond* (GB) (36), *Break the News* (GB) (37), *Pièges* (39); then several years on stage; *Le Silence Est d'Or* (46), *Ma Pomme* (50), *Le Roi* (51), *I Have Seven Daughters* (54), *Love in the Afternoon* (56), *Gigi* (58), *Can-Can* (59), *Fanny* (61), *Jessica* (61), *In Search of the Castaways* (62), *I'd Rather Be Rich* (64), *Monkeys Go Home* (66), etc. Special Academy Award 1958 'for his contributions to the world of entertainment for more than half a century'. Published autobiography 1960: *With Love*.

CHIARI, MARIO (1909–). Italian production designer. *Miracle in Milan* (51), *The Golden Coach* (54), *Neapolitan Fantasy* (54), *I Vitelloni* (54), *The Sea Wall* (56), etc.

CHIARI, WALTER (1924–) (W. Annichiarico). Italian comic actor, in films from 1947; seen abroad in *OK Nero* (51), *Chimes at Midnight* (66), *They're a Weird Mob* (66), etc.

LA CHIENNE (France 1931). Written and directed by Jean Renoir from a novel by La Fouchardiere, this bitter melodrama had Michel Simon as an unhappy man who takes up with a prostitute (Janie Mareze), kills her, and allows another man to be condemned in his place. It was remade by Fritz Lang in Hollywood in 1945, as *Scarlet Street*, with Edward G. Robinson and Joan Bennett. Heavy and unconvincing, this version was important as the first American film in which justice was not seen to be done after a crime . . . though Robinson was shown years later, tortured by remorse.

A CHILD IS WAITING (US 1963). From Abby Mann's script, Stanley Kramer produced and John Cassavetes directed this most delicate of problem pictures, exploring the world of mentally handicapped children. Over-tactfulness rendered it rather obvious as a motion picture, but its sincerity is as obvious as its professional polish, and that such a film should have come from Hollywood at all is encouraging. Burt Lancaster, Judy Garland, and Bruce Ritchey as a withdrawn child, give excellent performances.

child stars have been popular with every generation of filmgoers. Throughout the 20s Mary Pickford stayed at the top by remaining a child as long as, and after, she could; with only slight competition from Baby Peggy, Madge Evans, Dawn O'Day (later Anne Shirley) and Wesley Barry. Stronger competitors, perhaps, were Junior Coghlan and, around 1930, Junior Durkin; strongest of all was Jackie Coogan, immortalized by Chaplin as *The Kid* in 1921 and subsequently cast in all the standard juvenile roles. The child comedians who composed *Our Gang* for Hal Roach started in the 20s and went on, with cast changes, into the 40s: best remembered of them are Joe Cobb, Jean Darling, Johnny Downs, Mickey Daniels, Farina, Spanky Macfarland, Alfalfa Switzer, Darla Hood and Buckwheat Thomas.

Jackie Cooper also started in *Our Gang* but became a star in his own right after starring in *The Champ* and *Skippy*. In the early 30s his main rival was Dickie Moore, a lad of somewhat gentler disposition. Soon both were displaced in popular favour by Freddie Bartholomew in *David Copperfield*; but no boy could hold a candle to the multi-talented prodigy Shirley Temple, a star in 1933 at the age of five. She captivated a generation in a dozen or more hurriedly-produced sentimental comedies, and neither the angelic British Binkie Stuart nor the mischievous Jane Withers could cast the same spell.

Noting a splendid performance by twelve-year-old Robert Lynen in the French *Poil de Carotte*, we next encounter the still irrepressible Mickey Rooney, who popped up variously as Puck, Andy Hardy or a one-man-band. Then in 1937, the year that the Mauch twins appeared in *The Prince and the Pauper*, an MGM short called *Every Sunday* introduced two singing teenage girls, Deanna Durbin and Judy Garland, who went on to achieve enormous popularity in maturing roles until both were overtaken by personal difficulties. Another child who went on to musical stardom was vaudeville-bred Donald O'Connor, first seen in *Sing You Sinners*. But little more was seen of Tommy Kelly, who played *Tom Sawyer*, or Anne Gillis, or Terry Kilburn, or even Roddy McDowall until he re-emerged as a leading man twenty-five years later.

The early 40s saw Edith Fellowes as a good girl and Virginia Weidler, so marvellous in *The Philadelphia Story*, as a bad one. Baby Sandy appeared in a few comedies, as had Baby Le Roy ten years earlier; neither was seen on screen after the toddler stage. Two infant Dead-End Kids, Butch and Buddy, roamed mischievously through several Universal comedies. Margaret O'Brien and Peggy Ann Garner were two truly remarkable child actresses who never quite managed the transition to adult stardom. Teenagers Ann Blyth and Peggy Ryan partnered Donald O'Connor in many a light musical. Other child actors of the period were

Ted Donaldson, Diana Lynn, Darryl Hickman and Sharyn Moffett, while Skippy Homeier gave an electrifying performance as the young Nazi in *Tomorrow the World*. In the post-war years Europe contributed Ivan Jandl in *The Search*; Britain had George Cole and Harry Fowler for cockney roles, Jeremy Spenser for well-bred ones, Antony Wager and Jean Simmons in *Great Expectations*, and very memorable performances from Bobby Henrey in *The Fallen Idol* and John Howard Davies in *Oliver Twist*. Hollywood responded with thoughtful Claude Jarman, tearful Bobs Watson, spunky Bobby Driscoll and Tommy Rettig, and pretty little misses Gigi Perreau and Natalie Wood.

The 50s brought William (now James) Fox in *The Magnet*, Brigitte Fossey and Georges Poujouly in *Les Jeux Interdits*, Mandy Miller in *Mandy*, Vincent Winter and Jon Whiteley in *The Kidnappers*, and Patty McCormack as the evil child in *The Bad Seed*. In 1959 Hayley Mills embarked on a six-year reign (somewhat outshone in *Whistle Down the Wind* by Alan Barnes); the similar and equally capable American actress Patty Duke confined herself principally to stage and TV apart from *The Miracle Worker*. Then there have been Disney's over-wholesome Tommy Kirk and Annette Funicello, Fergus McClelland in *Sammy Going South*, Jean-Pierre Léaud in *The Four Hundred Blows*, William Dix in *The Nanny*, Matthew Garber and Karen Dotrice in *Mary Poppins*, Deborah Baxter in *A High Wind in Jamaica*, Mark Lester and Jack Wild in *Oliver* . . . and more moppets are doubtless waiting in the wings.

THE CHILDHOOD OF MAXIM GORKI (USSR 1938). Mark Donskoi's trilogy—the later sections are *Out in the World* and *My Universities*—subordinate propaganda to a highly pictorial evocation of old Russia. They are perhaps the most humane and personal of Soviet films.

CHILDREN OF HIROSHIMA (Japan 1953). Written and directed by Kaneto Shindo, this strikingly stylish semi-documentary begins with an unforgettable impressionistic montage of the dropping of the first A-bomb, then continues on a more soberly journalistic note as it follows a young schoolmistress round the stricken city seven years later.

Children's Film Foundation. British company formed in 1951 to produce and distribute specially-devised entertainment films for children's Saturday matinées. Sponsored by trade organizations.

CHIN, TSAI (c. 1938–   ). Chinese leading lady in international films. *The Face of Fu Manchu* (65), *Invasion* (66), *The Brides of Fu Manchu* (66), etc.

THE CHINESE BUNGALOW. A popular British stage melodrama of the 20s, by Marian Osmond and James Corbett, this was first filmed in 1926 by Sinclair Hill, with Matheson Lang repeating his stage performance as the sinister oriental who covets an English rose. He also appeared in the 1930 sound version, with Anna Neagle as his victim: J. B. Williams directed. In 1940 the tale was remade with Paul Lukas and Kay Walsh, directed by George King.

CHODOROV, EDWARD (1904–   ). American writer. *The World Changes* (33), *The Story of Louis Pasteur* (co-w) (35), *Yellow Jack* (38), *The Hucksters* (47), *Roadhouse* (48), etc.

CHODOROV, JEROME (1911–   ). American writer, usually with JOSEPH FIELDS. *Louisiana Purchase* (41), *My Sister Eileen* (42), *Junior Miss* (45), *Happy Anniversary* (59) (all from their plays), etc.

CHOUREAU, ETCHIKA (1923–   ). French leading lady of the 50s. *Children of Love* (53), *The Fruits of Summer* (55), *Lafayette Escadrille* (US) (57), *Darby's Rangers* (US) (58), etc.

CHRETIEN, HENRI (1879–1956). French inventor of the anamorphic lens subsequently used in CinemaScope and allied processes.

CHRIST on the screen was for many years a controversial subject: film-makers have usually preferred to imply his presence by a hand, a cloak, or simply reactions of onlookers. However, even in the first ten years of cinephotography there were several versions of his life, and in 1912 Robert Henderson played the role in a 'super' production of *From the Manger to the Cross*. In 1915 came *Civilisation*, with George Fisher as Christ on the battlefields, and in the same year *Intolerance*, in which Howard Gaye was Jesus. In 1924 Cecil B. de Mille's *King of Kings* had H. B. Warner in the role; any offence was minimized by having his first appearance a misty fade-in as the blind girl regains her sight. In 1932 Divivier made *Golgotha*, with Robert le Vigan; twenty years then went by before Christ's next appearance on the screen, played by a non-professional, Robert Wilson, in a sponsored movie called *Day of Triumph*. In 1961 Jeffrey Hunter appeared as Christ in *King of Kings*, which was unfortunately tagged by the trade *I Was a Teen-Age Jesus*. George Stevens' disappointing 1965 colossus, *The Greatest Story Ever Told*, cleverly cast Swedish Max von Sydow in the part; in the same year came Pasolini's *The Gospel According to St Matthew*, with Enrique Irazoqui; and in 1969 Bunuel cast Bernard Verley as Christ in *The Milky Way*. Christ-like figures of various kinds have been found in such films as *The Passing of the Third Floor Back*, *The Fugitive*, *Strange Cargo* and *The Face*; while films about the direct influence of Christ's life include *Quo Vadis*, *The Last Days of Pompeii*, *Ben Hur*, *Barabbas* and *The Wandering Jew*.

CHRISTENSEN, BENJAMIN (1879–1959). Swedish director whose career faded after a sojourn in Hollywood. *The Mysterious X* (13), *The Night of Revenge* (15), *Haxan (Witchcraft through the Ages)* (21), *Seine Frau Die Unbekannte* (23), *The Devil's Circus* (25), *Mockery* (27), *The Hawk's Nest* (28), *Seven Footprints to Satan* (29), others.

CHRISTIAN-JAQUE (1904–   ) (Christian Maudet). French writer-director, former journalist. *Les Disparus de Saint-Agil* (38), *La Symphonie Fantastique* (42), *Sortilèges* (44), *Un Revenant* (46), *D'Homme à Hommes* (48), *Souvenirs Perdus* (50), *Bluebeard* (51), *Fanfan la Tulipe* (51), *Lucrezia Borgia* (52), *Adorables Creatures* (52), *Nana* (54), *Si Tous les Gars du Monde (Race for Life)* (55), *Babette Goes to War* (59), *Madame Sans Gêne* (61), *The Black Tulip* (63), *The Secret Agents (The Dirty Game)* (co-director) (66), *The Saint Versus . . .* (66), *Two Tickets to Mexico (Dead Run)* (67), etc.

CHRISTIAN, LINDA (1923–   ) (Blanca Rosa Welter). Actress of mixed nationalities, Mexican-born, who married into European nobility. *Holiday in Mexico* (46), *Tarzan and the Mermaids* (48), *The Happy Time* (52), *Athena* (54), *Thunderstorm* (56), *How to Seduce a Playboy* (Austrian) (66), etc.

CHRISTIANS, MADY (1900–1951) (Margarethe Marie Christians) Austrian-born stage actress in occasional Hollywood films. *The Runaway Princess* (GB) (29), *Escapade* (36), *Seventh Heaven* (37), *Heidi* (38), *Address Unknown* (44), *All My Sons* (48), *Letter from an Unknown Woman* (48), etc.

CHRISTIE, AGATHA (1891–   ). British best-selling mystery writer, curiously neglected by the screen. Her detective Hercule Poirot was played by Austin Trevor in some second features of the early 30s, and guyed by Tony Randall in *The Alphabet Murders* (65); otherwise the screen is indebted to her only for *Ten Little Niggers/ Indians* (45 and 65), *Witness for the Prosecution* (58), *Spider's Web* (60) and four Miss Marple films with Margaret Rutherford.

CHRISTIE, AL (1886–1951). American comedy producer, mainly of two-reelers, in Hollywood from 1914 and a rival of Mack Sennett. Features include *Tillie's Punctured Romance* (15), *Up in Mabel's Room* (26); produced and directed *Charley's Aunt* (25).

CHRISTIE, HOWARD (1912–   ). American producer: *Lady on a Train* (44), *Abbott and Costello Meet the Invisible Man* (50), *The Purple Mask* (55), *Away All Boats* (56), *Gunfight at Abilene* (60), other routine films.

CHRISTIE, JULIE (1941–   ). British leading lady: *Billy Liar* (63), *Young Cassidy* (64), *Darling* (AA) (65), *Dr Zhivago* (66), *Fahrenheit*

451 (66), *Far from the Madding Crowd* (67), *Petulia* (68), *In Search of Gregory* (69), etc.

CHRISTINE, VIRGINIA (1917–). American character actress. *Edge of Darkness* (42), *The Mummy's Curse* (45), *The Killers* (46), *Cyrano de Bergerac* (50), *Not as a Stranger* (55), *Nightmare* (56), *Invasion of the Body Snatchers* (56), *The Careless Years* (58), *Guess Who's Coming to Dinner* (67), etc.

Christmas has provided a favourite sentimental climax for many a film. Films wholly based on it include *The Holly and the Ivy, Tenth Avenue Angel, Miracle on 34th Street, White Christmas, Christmas Eve, Christmas in Connecticut, The Bishop's Wife, I'll Be Seeing You,* and the many versions of *Scrooge*. There were happy Christmas scenes in *The Bells of St Mary, The Inn of the Sixth Happiness, The Man Who Came to Dinner, Holiday Inn, Since You Went Away, Three Godfathers, Meet Me in St Louis, On Moonlight Bay, Little Women, The Cheaters, Desk Set* and *Young at Heart* among others; while unhappy Christmases were spent in *Things to Come, Full House* ('The Gifts of the Magi'), *The Apartment, Meet John Doe, The Glenn Miller Story,* and *The Victors*. (Nor was there much for the characters in *The Lion in Winter* to celebrate at their Christmas court of 1189.)

Santa Claus himself put in an appearance in *Miracle on 34th Street* (played by Edmund Gwenn), *The Lemon Drop Kid* (played by Bob Hope), *The Light at Heart* (played by Monty Woolley), and *Robin and the Seven Hoods* (played by the Sinatra clan). Disney featured him in *Babes in Toyland* and a short cartoon, *The Night Before Christmas*; and in their 1934 version of *Babes in Toyland* Laurel and Hardy found him an irate employer.

Christmas was celebrated in unlikely settings in *Knights of the Round Table, Conquest of Space, Scott of the Antarctic, Encore* ('Winter Cruise'), *Destination Tokyo* (in a submarine), *The Nun's Story* (in a Congo mission), and *Black Narcissus* (in an Indian nunnery).

CHUKRAI, GRIGORI (1920–). Russian director. *The Forty First* (56), *Ballad of a Soldier* (59), *Clear Sky* (61), *There Was an Old Man and an Old Woman* (65), etc.

churches have provided a setting for many pretty secular-minded films, from the various versions of *The Hunchback of Notre Dame* to the use of a church as refuge during a flood in *When Tomorrow Comes*. Other memorable moments include Bogart confessing the plot of *Dead Reckoning* to a priest; Robert Donat's sermon in *Lease of Life* and Orson Welles' in *Moby Dick*; the scandalous confessions in *Jeux Interdits* and the dramatic one in *I Confess*; the murder of *Becket*; the bombed but well-used churches in *Mrs Miniver* and *Sundown*; the thing in the rafters of Westminster Abbey in *The Quatermass Experiment*; the attempted murder in Westminster

Cathedral in *Foreign Correspondent* and the fall from the church tower in *Vertigo*; the arrest of *Pastor Hall*; Arturo de Cordova going mad during a service in *El*; the church-tower climax of *The Stranger*; the Russian services in *Ivan the Terrible* and *We Live Again*; Cagney dying on the church steps in *The Roaring Twenties*; the church used as refuge against the Martians in *The War of the Worlds*; the church used for a town meeting in *High Noon*; the Turkish mosque and espionage rendezvous in *From Russia with Love*; the comic rifling of offertory boxes in *Heaven Sent*; the finale of *Miracle in the Rain* in the church porch; the meeting in church of the protagonists of *The Appaloosa* (*Southwest to Sonora*); the churches swept away by the elements in *The Hurricane* and *Hawaii*; and all the many films in which the protagonists are *priests, monks* and *nuns* (qv).

CHURCHILL, BERTON (1876–1940). Canadian character actor of stage and (in later years) screen; usually seen as unsympathetic bosses and stern fathers. *Scandal for Sale* (32), *I Am a Fugitive from a Chain Gang* (32), *Madame Butterfly* (33), *Judge Priest* (34), *Dimples* (36), *Sweethearts* (38), *Stagecoach* (as the absconding banker) (39), etc.

CHURCHILL, DIANA (1913–). British stage actress, widow of Barry K. Barnes. Occasional films include *School for Husbands* (36), *The Housemaster* (37), *House of the Arrow* (40), etc.

CHURCHILL, DONALD (1930–). British light actor, usually of callow or nervous young men. *Victim* (62), *The Wild Affair* (64), etc.; also TV playwright.

CHURCHILL, MARGUERITE (1910–). American leading lady. *The Valiant* (29), *The Big Trail* (31), *Riders of the Purple Sage* (31), *The Walking Dead* (36), *Dracula's Daughter* (last to date) (36), etc.

CHURCHILL, SARAH (1914–). British actress, daughter of Sir Winston. Films include *He Found a Star* (40), *All over the Town* (47), *Royal Wedding* (US) (51), *Serious Charge* (59).

CHURCHILL, WINSTON (1874–1965). British statesman and author who has been the subject of a major documentary, *The Finest Hours* (64) and a TV series, *The Valiant Years* (60). He was impersonated by Dudley Field Malone in *Mission to Moscow* (43), by Patrick Wymark in *Operation Crossbow* (65) and by a number of Russian actors in various propaganda pieces.

CIANNELLI, EDUARDO (1887–1969). Italian character actor, former doctor and opera singer. Long in Hollywood, usually in sinister roles. *Reunion in Vienna* (33), *The Scoundrel* (34), *Winterset* (37), *Gunga Din* (39), *The Mummy's Hand* (40), *Foreign Correspondent* (40), *They Got Me Covered* (42), *For Whom the Bell Tolls* (43), *The Conspirators* (44), *Dillinger* (45), *The Creeper* (48), *The People Against*

O'Hara (51), *Mambo* (55), *Houseboat* (59), *The Visit* (64), *Mackenna's Gold* (68), *The Brotherhood* (68), many others. TV series: *Johnny Staccato* (59).

CICOGNINI, ALESSANDRO (1906–   ). Italian composer. *Four Steps in the Clouds* (42), *Shoeshine* (46), *I Miserabili* (48), *Tomorrow Is Too Late* (50), *Miracle in Milan* (51), *Don Camillo* (52), *Umberto D* (52), *Due Soldi di Speranza* (52), *Gold of Naples* (54), *Ulysses* (54), *Summer Madness* (55), *The Black Orchid* (58), *Yesterday, Today and Tomorrow* (63), etc.

CILENTO, DIANE (1933–   ). Blonde British leading lady, wife of Sean Connery. Her talent has never been fully used on screen: *The Angel Who Pawned Her Harp* (54), *The Passing Stranger* (54), *Passage Home* (55), *The Woman for Joe* (56), *The Admirable Crichton* (57), *Jet Storm* (59), *The Full Treatment* (60), *The Naked Edge* (61), *I Thank a Fool* (63), *Tom Jones* (63), *The Third Secret* (64), *Rattle of a Simple Man* (64), *The Agony and the Ecstasy* (65), *Hombre* (66), *Negatives* (69).

CIMARRON (US 1931). Famous Western, written by Howard Estabrook from Edna Ferber's novel, directed by Wesley Ruggles, with Richard Dix and Irene Dunne. AA best picture. Remade 1961 to little effect, with Glenn Ford and Maria Schell.

cinemas have only rarely provided a background for film situations. A Hollywood première and a sneak preview were shown in *Singing in the Rain*, and *The Oscar* revealed all about the Academy Awards ceremony. Characters in *Sherlock Junior*, *Borderlines* (*The Caretakers*) and *Merton of the Movies* (Red Skelton version) clambered on to the stage while a film was showing. Projectionists were featured in *Clash by Night*, *The Blob*, *The Great Morgan*, and *Hellzapoppin*; also in *The Smallest Show on Earth*, the only film concerned with the running of a cinema as its main plot. Fred Allen in *The Fifth Chair* (*It's in the Bag*) had a terrible time trying to find a seat in a full house; Dillinger was killed coming out of a cinema in *The F.B.I. Story*; Bogart was nearly shot in a Chinese cinema in *Across the Pacific*, and Anthony Perkins met Valli in a Siamese one in *This Angry Age* (*The Sea Wall*). A cinema was used as a rendezvous for spies in *The Traitors* and *Sabotage*; a church was used as a cinema in *Sullivan's Travels* when chain-gang convicts watched Mickey Mouse. Mark Stevens and Joan Fontaine in *From This Day Forward* visited a news cinema but were too much in love to heed the warnings of impending war. Louis Jourdan and Linda Christian watched Valentino at the local in *The Happy Time*, and astronauts watched Bob Hope in a space station in *Conquest of Space*. Deanna Durbin got a murder clue in a cinema in *Lady on a Train*; and in *Bullets or Ballots* Humphrey Bogart took Barton Maclane to see a documentary about his nefarious career. Linda Hayden in *Baby Love* was accosted in a cinema. Robert Cummings in *Saboteur* started a riot in Radio City Music Hall. In *Brief Encounter*, Celia Johnson and Trevor Howard thought the organist was the best part of the programme. Polly Bergen in *The Caretakers* went crazy and climbed up in front of the screen. *Bonnie and Clyde* found time between robberies to see a *Gold Diggers* movie. In *Eye Witness* a cinema manager was killed during the Saturday night performance; and in *Targets* a killer is apprehended by Boris Karloff at a drive-in. Home movies figured most notably in *Rebecca* and *Adam's Rib*. See *excerpts*.

CinemaScope. Wide-screen process copyrighted by Fox in 1953; invented many years earlier by Henri Chretien. Other companies either adopted it or produced their own trade name: WarnerScope, SuperScope, Panavision, etc. Basically, the camera contains an anamorphic lens which 'squeezes' a wide picture on to a standard 4x3 35mm frame. This, when projected through a complementary lens, gives a picture ratio on screen of 2.55:1 with stereophonic magnetic sound, or 2.35:1 with optical sound. Directors found the new shape awkward to compose for, the easiest way of handling it being to park the camera and let the actors move, a reversion to early silent methods. Although wide screens are said to have helped the box office, they have effectively prevented the full use of cinematic techniques. Oddly enough Fox in the mid-60s quietly dropped their own system and moved over to Panavision.

Cinematograph Exhibitors' Association. The British theatre-owners' protective association, founded in 1912 with 10 members. In 1922 there were 2000, in 1950 4000.

cinematographer. Lighting cameraman or chief photographer.

cinema vérité. A fashionable term of the 60s for what used to be called candid camera. A TV-style technique of recording life and people as they are, in the raw, using handheld cameras, natural sound and the minimum of rehearsal and editing. Chiefly applied to *Chronique d'une Été* (61), *Le Joli Mai* (62), and the documentaries of Richard Leacock and the Maysles brothers.

Cinerama. Extra-wide-screen system, invented by Fred Waller. Three projectors, electronically synchronized, were used to put the picture on the screen in three sections: this gave a disturbing wobble at the joins, though the range of vision was sometimes magnificently wide, as in the aerial shots and roller coaster sequence in *This Is Cinerama* (52). After ten years of scenic but cinematically unremarkable travelogues (*Cinerama Holiday, Seven Wonders of the World, Search for Paradise*, etc.), the first story film in the process, *How the West Was Won*, was made in 1962. Shortly afterwards the three-camera system was abandoned in favour of 'single-lens Cinerama' which is virtually indistinguishable from CinemaScope except for the higher definition resulting from using wider film.— 'Cinemiracle', a similar process, was short-lived.

circuit. A chain of cinemas under the same ownership, often playing the same release programme.

circuses, according to the cinema, are full of drama and passion behind the scenes. So you would think if you judged from *Variety, Freaks, The Wagons Roll at Night, The Greatest Show on Earth, Sawdust and Tinsel. Circus of Horrors, Tromba, Four Devils, The Three Maxims, Trapeze, Captive Wild Woman, Ring of Fear, Charlie Chan at the Circus, A Tiger Walks. Circus World (The Magnificent Showman), The Trojan Brothers, Circus of Fear, Berserk, The Dark Tower, He Who Gets Slapped, Flesh and Fantasy, Pagliacci* and *Far from the Madding Crowd.* But there is a lighter side, as evidenced by *Doctor Dolittle, Yo Yo, Life Is a Circus, The Marx Brothers at the Circus, Three Ring Circus,* Chaplin's *The Circus, The Great Profile, You Can't Cheat an Honest Man,* and *Road Show.* TV series have included *Circus Boy, Frontier Circus* and *The Greatest Show on Earth.*

THE CISCO KID. This ingratiating Latin rogue was first played by Warner Baxter in Irving Cummings' 1931 film. In 1937 Cesar Romero played him in the first of a series; the role was taken over in 1945 by Duncan Renaldo, who has also been in a TV series. The Kid's side-kicks have included Leo Carrillo and Chris-Pin Martin.

THE CITADEL (GB 1938). Masterly film version of Cronin's novel about a doctor's rise from Welsh slums to Harley Street, directed by King Vidor for MGM-British, with Robert Donat and Ralph Richardson.

CITIZEN KANE (US 1941). Often acclaimed as the best film of all time: certainly none has used the medium with more vigour and enthusiasm. Herman J. Mankiewicz' script paralleled the career of newspaper magnate William Randolph Hearst, making the point that money isn't everything. Orson Welles, the boy wonder of American radio, produced and directed it as a cinematic box of tricks, often somewhat obscuring the story of a journalist's quest for the truth after Kane's death; nevertheless there isn't a dull scene in the film's 119 minutes. Cameraman Gregg Toland and composer Bernard Herrmann contributed massively to the general effect of a new joyous era in film-making, and many of Welles' Mercury company of theatre actors launched new careers for themselves: Joseph Cotten, Everett Sloane, Agnes Moorehead, George Coulouris, Ray Collins, Paul Stewart, and Welles himself as Kane. After thirty years the film seems scarcely to have faded at all.

CITY LIGHTS (US 1931). Chaplin's depression-period comedy in which the tramp meets a drunken millionaire and a blind flower girl. Comedy over-flooded with sentiment, but some brilliant moments.

CIVILISATION (US 1915). One of the few films of its time which can stand beside the work of Griffith, Thomas Ince's film is a painstaking anti-war allegory intended to keep America neutral in the 14–18 war: Christ returns to earth in human form to work for peace. A very fluent piece of film-making.

CLAIR, RENÉ (1898–   ) (René Chomette). French comedy director with a nimble touch, an optimistic outlook, and no malice. *Paris Qui Dort* (23) and *Entr'acte* (24) are early experiments, *Sous les Toits de Paris* (29) is now heavy going; but the following comedies defy the passage of time: *An Italian Straw Hat* (28), *Le Million* (31), *A Nous La Liberté* (31), *Le Quatorze Juillet* (34), *The Ghost Goes West* (GB) (35), *I Married a Witch* (US) (42), *It Happened Tomorrow* (US) (44), *Ten Little Niggers* (US) (45), *Le Silence Est d'Or* (46), *La Beauté du Diable* (49), *Les Belles de Nuit* (52). More recent films show a slight falling-off: *Les Grandes Manoeuvres* (55), *Porte des Lilas* (56), *Tout l'Or du Monde* (60), *Les Fêtes Galantes* (65).

CLAIRE, INA (1892–   ) (Ina Fagan). American stage actress who made occasional films: *The Puppet Crown* (15), *Polly with a Past* (20), *The Awful Truth* (29), *The Royal Family of Broadway* (31), *Rebound* (32), *The Greeks Had a Word for Them* (32), *Ninotchka* (39), *Claudia* (42), etc.

clairvoyance on the screen seems to have caused a remarkable amount of suffering to Edward G. Robinson: he was haunted by the effects of a prophecy in *Flesh and Fantasy, Nightmare* and *Night Has a Thousand Eyes*. Other frightened men for similar reasons were Claude Rains in *The Clairvoyant*, Dick Powell in *It Happened Tomorrow*, George Macready in *I Love a Mystery* and Mervyn Johns in *Dead of Night*.

clapperboard. A hinged board recording film details. At the beginning of each 'take' it is held before the camera for identification and then 'clapped' to make a starting point in the sound track. This point is then synchronized with the image of the closed board.

CLARE, MARY (1894–   ). British stage actress, latterly in formidable matron roles. On stage since 1910, occasional films from mid-20s. *Becket* (24), *Hindle Wakes* (31), *The Constant Nymph* (33), *The Clairvoyant* (34), *The Passing of the Third Floor Back* (35), *Young and Innocent* (37), *The Lady Vanishes* (38), *A Girl Must Live* (39), *Old Bill and Son* (40), *Mrs Pym of Scotland Yard* (title role) (40), *Next of Kin* (42), *The Night Has Eyes* (42), *The Hundred-Pound Window* (44),

The Three Weird Sisters (48), *Oliver Twist* (48), *Moulin Rouge* (53), *Mambo* (55), *The Price of Silence* (59), many others. Retired.

CLARENCE, O. B. (1870–1955). Distinguished British stage actor who came to films in silent days and became familiar in benevolent doddering roles. *The Scarlet Pimpernel* (34), *Pygmalion* (38), *Inspector Hornleigh Goes to It* (41), *A Place of One's Own* (44), *Great Expectations* (46), *Uncle Silas* (47), many others.

CLARK, DANE (1913–   ) (Bernard Zanville). Pint-sized American tough-guy leading man of the 40s; later declined to second features. *Tennessee Johnson* (*The Man on America's Conscience*) (debut) (42), *Destination Tokyo* (43), *The Very Thought of You* (44), *God Is My Co-Pilot* (first leading role) (45), *A Stolen Life* (46), *Deep Valley* (47), *Moonrise* (48), *Without Honour* (49), *Highly Dangerous* (GB) (50), *Never Trust a Gambler* (51), *Go Man Go* (53), *Port of Hell* (54), *The Toughest Man Alive* (55), *Murder by Proxy* (GB) (55), etc. TV series: *Wire Service* (57).

CLARK, ERNEST (1912–   ). British stage and screen actor, usually in cold, tight-lipped roles. *Private Angelo* (49), *Doctor in the House* (53), *The Dam Busters* (55), *A Tale of Two Cities* (58), *Sink the Bismarck* (60), *Arabesque* (66), many others.

CLARK, FRED (1914–1968). Bald-headed, explosive American character comedian whose many films include *Ride the Pink Horse* (48), *Sunset Boulevard* (50), *Dreamboat* (52), *How to Marry a Millionaire* (53), *Abbott and Costello Meet the Keystone Kops* (54), *Daddy Longlegs* (55), *How To Be Very Very Popular* (55), *The Court Martial of Billy Mitchell* (55), *The Solid Gold Cadillac* (56), *Don't Go Near the Water* (56), *Joe Butterfly* (57), *The Mating Game* (59), *Bells Are Ringing* (60), *The Curse of the Mummy's Tomb* (GB) (64), *Sergeant Deadhead* (65), *The Horse in the Gray Flannel Suit* (68), *Skidoo* (68). TV series: *The Double Life of Henry Phyfe* (66).

CLARK, JAMES B. (* –   ). American director, mainly of films for children. *The Big Show* (60), *Misty* (61), *Flipper* (63), *And Now Miguel* (66), *My Side of the Mountain* (68), etc.

CLARK, MARGUERITE (1883–1940). American heroine of the silent screen, a rival for Mary Pickford in waif-like and innocent roles. *Wildflower* (14), *The Goose Girl* (15), *Molly Make-Believe* (16), *Snow White* (17), *Prunella* (18), *Mrs Wiggs of the Cabbage Patch* (18), *Girls* (19), *All-of-a-Sudden Peggy* (20), *Scrambled Wives* (21). Retired 1921.

CLARK, PETULA (1932–   ). British singer, former child actress, First film *Medal for the General* (44); first major role *London Town* (46). Also in the Huggett family films (48–51), *Vice Versa* (48),

Clark, Robert

The Card (52), *The Runaway Bus* (54), etc. After international cabaret and TV success, appeared in *Finian's Rainbow* (68).

CLARK, ROBERT (1905–). British executive, longtime director (resigned 1969) of Associated British Picture Corpn. Former lawyer; producer of many ABPC films including *The Hasty Heart*, *The Dam Busters*, etc.

CLARKE, MAE (1910–). American leading lady of the 30s; from musical comedy. *Big Time* (29), *The Front Page* (30), *Waterloo Bridge* (31), *Frankenstein* (31), *Public Enemy* (31), *Night World* (32), *Lady Killer* (34), *Women in War* (40), etc.; later played bit parts in *Not as a Stranger* (55), *Come Next Spring* (56), *Big Hand for a Little Lady* (66), etc.

CLARKE, SHIRLEY (1925–). American director of the New York *cinema vérité* school. *The Connection* (60), *Cool World* (63), etc.

CLARKE, T. E. B. (1907–). British screenwriter, former journalist; associated with the heyday of Ealing comedy. *Hue and Cry* (46), *Passport to Pimlico* (48), *The Blue Lamp* (50), *The Lavender Hill Mob* (51), *The Titfield Thunderbolt* (53), *Barnacle Bill* (57), *Sons and Lovers* (60), *The Horse Without a Head* (63), etc.

CLARKE-SMITH, D. A. (1888–1959). British character actor, mainly on stage. *Atlantic* (30), *The Ghoul* (33), *Warn London* (34), *Sabotage* (36), *The Flying Fifty-Five* (39), *Frieda* (47), *The Baby and the Battleship* (56), etc.

CLAUDIA (US 1943). Rose Franken's whimsical book about a child-wife who matures when she hears that her mother is dying was filmed in 1943 with Dorothy McGuire (who played the role on Broadway) and Robert Young. Three years later came a sequel, *Claudia and David*, with the same stars.

CLAVELL, JAMES (1922–). Australian writer of Anglo-Irish descent. *The Fly* (58), *Five Gates to Hell* (also produced and directed) (58), *Walk Like a Dragon* (also produced and directed) (60), *The Sweet and the Bitter* (w, p, d) (Can.) (62), *The Great Escape* (63), *The Satan Bug* (65), *King Rat* (novel only) (65), *To Sir With Love* (also produced and directed) (66), *Where's Jack* (also produced and directed) (69), etc.

CLAYTON, JACK (1921–). British producer-director who worked his way up through the industry. *The Bespoke Overcoat* (p, d) (55), *Three Men in a Boat* (p) (56), *Room at the Top* (d) (58), *The Innocents* (d) (61), *The Pumpkin Eater* (d) (64), *Our Mother's House* (d) (67).

CLEMENS, WILLIAM (1905–). American director of second features. *The Case of the Velvet Claws* (36), *Calling Philo Vance* (39), *The Night of January 16th* (41), *Sweater Girl* (42), *Crime by Night* (43), *The Thirteenth Hour* (47), etc.

CLEMENT, DICK (1937–   ). British writer who with Ian La Frenais wrote for TV *The Likely Lads* (66–67) and for films *The Jokers* (67), *Otley* (69). Clement also directed *Otley*, and *A Severed Head* (69).

CLEMENT, RENE (1913–   ). French director whose international reputation dates from *Bataille du Rail* (43). *Les Maudits* (46), *Les Jeux Interdits* (51), *Knave of Hearts* (GB) (53), *Gervaise* (55), *The Sea Wall* (*This Angry Age*) (56), *Plein Soleil* (59), *The Love Cage* (*Joy House*) (65), *Is Paris Burning?* (66), etc.

CLEMENTS, JOHN (1910–   ). Distinguished British actor-manager on stage from 1930. Films (from 1934) include *Ticket of Leave* (35), *Things to Come* (35), *Rembrandt* (36), *Knight Without Armour* (36), *South Riding* (38), *The Housemaster* (39), *The Four Feathers* (39), *Convoy* (40), *This England* (41), *Ships with Wings* (41), *Tomorrow We Live* (42), *Undercover* (42), *They Came to a City* (45), *Call of the Blood* (also wrote, produced and directed) (47), *The Silent Enemy* (57), *The Mind Benders* (63), *Oh What a Lovely War* (69), etc.

CLEMENTS, STANLEY (1926–   ). American actor familiar in the 40s as tough teenager. *Tall, Dark and Handsome* (41), *Going My Way* (44), *Salty O'Rourke* (45), *Bad Boy* (49), *Jet Job* (52), *Robbers Roost* (55), *Up In Smoke* (59), *Saintly Sinners* (61), many others.

CLEO DE 5 A 7 (France 1961). A highly personal film by Agnes Varda, about a young woman who thinks she is dying and sees the world around her with heightened perception. With Corinne Marchand; photographed by Jean Rabier.

CLEOPATRA (69–30 BC). The sultry Egyptian queen has been portrayed in many films, notably in a Melies trick film of 1899; by unspecified American actresses in 1908 and 1909; by Helen Gardner in 1911; by Theda Bara in 1917; by Claudette Colbert in the de Mille version of 1934; by Vivien Leigh in Pascal's 1945 *Caesar and Cleopatra*; by Elizabeth Taylor in the well-publicized 1962 version; and by Amanda Barrie in a spoof, *Carry On, Cleo*, in 1963. There seems to be something about the lady that encourages waste, for the Leigh version was Britain's most expensive film and the Taylor version the world's; in neither case did the money show on the screen.

CLEVELAND, GEORGE (1886–1965). American character actor, in many films as grizzled, kindly old man. In Hollywood from 1904. *Ghost Town Riders* (38), *The Spoilers* (42), *Sunbonnet Sue* (45), *The Wistful Widow* (48), *Trigger Junior* (52), *Untamed Heiress* (54), many others. TV series: *Lassie* (55–65).

cliffhanger

cliffhanger. Trade name for a serial, especially an episode ending in an unresolved situation which keeps one in suspense till next time.

†CLIFT, MONTGOMERY (1920–1966). Romantic American leading actor of stage and screen, usually in introspective roles; his career was jeopardized in 1957 by a car accident which somewhat disfigured him. *The Search* (48), *Red River* (48), *The Heiress* (49), *The Big Lift* (50), *A Place in the Sun* (51), *I Confess* (53), *From Here to Eternity* (53), *Indiscretion of an American Wife (Stazione Termini)* (54), *Raintree County* (57), *The Young Lions* (58), *Lonelyhearts* (59), *Suddenly Last Summer* (59), *Wild River* (60), *The Misfits* (60), *Judgment at Nuremberg* (60), *Freud* (63), *The Defector* (66).

CLIFTON, ELMER (c. 1893–1949). American director mainly of second features; started as actor with D. W. Griffith, in *Birth of a Nation* and *Intolerance*. Directed *Down to the Sea in Ships* (22), *The Wreck of the Hesperus* (27), *Virgin Lips* (28), *Six-Cylinder Love* (31), many Buck Jones Westerns, *Seven Doors to Death* (44), *Not Wanted* (49), etc.

CLINE, EDWARD (1892–1961). American comedy director who started with Mack Sennett bathing beauties. *Summer Girls* (18), *Three Ages* (23), *Sherlock Junior* (26), *Ladies' Night in a Turkish Bath* (26), *Broadway Fever* (29), *Million Dollar Legs* (32), *Peck's Bad Boy* (35), *The Villain Still Pursued Her* (40), *My Little Chickadee* (40), *The Bank Dick* (41), *Never Give a Sucker an Even Break* (41), *Crazy House* (43), *See My Lawyer* (44), *Jiggs and Maggie in Society* (48), many others.

CLIVE, COLIN (1898–1937) (Clive Greig). British stage actor who went to Hollywood in 1930 to film *Journey's End*, and stayed; generally typecast in fraught, serious roles. *Frankenstein* (title role) (31), *The Stronger Sex* (GB) (31), *Lily Christine* (GB) (32), *Christopher Strong* (33), *Jane Eyre* (34), *Bride of Frankenstein* (35), *Clive of India* (35), *The Hands of Orlac* (35), *History Is Made at Night* (37), etc.

CLIVE, E. E. (1879–1940). British character actor who came late in life to Hollywood and played mainly sour-faced but amiable butlers. *The Invisible Man* (33), *The Mystery of Edwin Drood* (35), *The Bride of Frankenstein* (as the burgomaster) (35), *The Charge of the Light Brigade* (36), *Camille* (36), Bulldog Drummond series (as Tenny) (37–39), *Raffles* (39), etc.

CLOCHE, MAURICE (1907–   ). French director, in films (as documentarist) from 1933. *La Vie Est Magnifique* (38), *Monsieur Vincent* (37), *Cage aux Filles* (48), *Né de Père Inconnu* (50), *Les Filles de la Nuit* (57), *Coplan, Secret Agent* (64), etc.

CLOONEY, ROSEMARY (1928–   ). Blonde American singer who makes occasional film appearances: *Red Garters* (54), *White Christmas* (54), *Deep in My Heart* (55), etc. Married to Jose Ferrer.

CLOSELY OBSERVED TRAINS (Czechoslovakia 1966). Jiri Menzel's oddly likeable little tragi-comedy won the 1968 Academy Award for the best foreign film. Apart from a strangely downbeat ending, it consists of a number of amusing scenes and character set in a country railway station during World War II.

close-up. Generally applied to a head-and-shoulders shot of a person, or any close shot of an object. The first close-up is said to be that of Fred Ott sneezing in an Edison experimental film of 1900. See *long shot*.

CLOTHIER, WILLIAM H. (* –). American cinematographer. *Track of the Cat* (54), *The Deadly Companions* (61), *The Man Who Shot Liberty Valance* (62), *A Distant Trumpet* (64), *Shenandoah* (65), *The Way West* (67), *The War Wagon* (67), *Firecreek* (67), *The Devil's Brigade* (68), *Hellfighters* (68), etc.

CLOUTIER, SUZANNE (1927–). French-Canadian leading lady. *Temptation* (US) (46), *Au Royaume des Cieux* (47), *Juliette ou la Clef des Songes* (50), *Othello* (51), *Derby Day* (GB) (51), *Romanoff and Juliet* (US) (61), etc.

CLOUZOT, HENRI-GEORGES (1907–). French writer-director, noted for suspense melodramas. *Un Soir de Rafle* (w) (31), *Le Dernier des Six* (w) (41), *Les Inconnus dans la Maison* (w) (42), *L'Assassin Habite Au 21* (w, d) (42), *Le Corbeau* (w, d) (43), *Quai des Orfèvres* (w, d) (47), *Manon* (w, d) (49), *Retour à la Vie* (w, d) (49), *The Wages of Fear* (w, d) (53), *Les Diaboliques* (w, d) (55), *The Picasso Mystery* (w, d) (56), *Les Espions* (w, d) (57), *The Truth* (w, d) (AA) (60), etc.

CLOUZOT, VERA (1921–1960). French actress, wife of H. G. Clouzot. *The Wages of Fear* (53), *Les Diaboliques* (54), *Les Espions* (57), etc.

CLUNES, ALEC (1912–). British stage actor who has made occasional films: *Convoy* (40), *Saloon Bar* (41), *Melba* (53), *Quentin Durward* (55), *Richard III* (56), *Tomorrow at Ten* (62), etc.

CLURMAN, HAROLD (1901–). American stage director chiefly associated with New York's Group Theatre of the 30s. Directed one very pretentious film: *Deadline at Dawn* (46).

CLUTE, CHESTER (1891–1956). American character comedian. The inimitable henpecked husband or harassed clerk of innumerable films.

CLYDE, ANDY (1892–1967). Acrobatic Scottish-born comedian who made scores of knockabout two-reelers in the 30s and supplied comedy relief in the Hopalong Cassidy Westerns. Usually appeared as grizzled old men. Recently in TV series *No Time for Sergeants*.

coal mines and the bravery of the men who work in them formed a theme which commanded the respect of cinema audiences for many years. Apart from *Kameradschaft* (the French-German border) and *Black Fury* (US) all the major films on this subject have been about Britain: *The Proud Valley*, *The Stars Look Down*, *How Green Was My Valley*, *The Citadel*, *The Corn Is Green*, *The Brave Don't Cry*, *Sons and Lovers*, *Women in Love*.

COBB, LEE J. (1911–   ) (Leo Jacob). Distinguished, heavily-built American character actor who forsook the stage for the screen. *North of the Rio Grande* (debut) (37), *Danger on the Air* (38), *Golden Boy* (in his stage role) (39), *This Thing Called Love* (40), *Men of Boys' Town* (41), *The Moon Is Down* (43), *The Song of Bernadette* (43), *Winged Victory* (44), *Anna and the King of Siam* (46), *Johnny O'clock* (46), *Boomerang* (47), *Captain from Castile* (48), *Call Northside 777* (48), *The Dark Past* (49), *Thieves' Highway* (49), *The Man Who Cheated Himself* (50), *Sirocco* (51), *The Tall Texan* (53), *On the Waterfront* (54), *Gorilla at Large* (54), *The Left Hand of God* (55), *The Man in the Grey Flannel Suit* (56), *Twelve Angry Men* (57), *The Garment Jungle* (57), *The Brothers Karamazov* (58), *Party Girl* (59), *Exodus* (61), *The Four Horsemen of the Apocalypse* (62), *Come Blow Your Horn* (63), *Our Man Flint* (66), *Coogan's Bluff* (68), *Mackenna's Gold* (69), *Lord Byron Jones* (70), etc. TV series: *The Virginian* (62–69).

COBORN, CHARLES (1852–1945) (Colin McCallum). British music hall artiste famous for his rendering of 'The Man Who Broke the Bank at Monte Carlo', performed in *Variety Jubilee* (43). Also appeared in *Say It With Flowers* (34).

COBURN, CHARLES (1877–1961). Distinguished American actor, a star of stage for many years; came to the screen as an elderly man and exuded crusty benevolence for twenty years. *Of Human Hearts* (38), *Vivacious Lady* (38), *Idiot's Delight* (39), *Stanley and Livingstone* (39), *Road to Singapore* (39), *Bachelor Mother* (39), *Edison the Man* (40), *The Devil and Miss Jones* (41), *The Lady Eve* (41), *H. M. Pulham Esq.* (41), *King's Row* (42), *In This Our Life* (42), *The More the Merrier* (AA) (43), *The Constant Nymph* (43), *Heaven Can Wait* (43), *My Kingdom for a Cook* (43), *Knickerbocker Holiday* (44), *Wilson* (44), *The Impatient Years* (44), *A Royal Scandal* (Czarina) (45), *Colonel Effingham's Raid* (45), *Over 21* (45), *The Green Years* (46), *Man of the Hour* (46), *The Paradine Case* (47), *B.F.'s Daughter* (Polly Fulton) (48), *Personal Column* (49), *Louisa* (50), *Mr Music* (51), *The Highwayman* (52), *Monkey Business* (52), *Gentlemen Prefer Blondes* (53), *The Long Wait* (54), *How To Be Very Very Popular* (55), *Around the World in Eighty Days* (56), *Town on Trial* (GB) (57), *How To Murder a Rich Uncle* (GB) (57), *John Paul Jones* (59), many others.

COBURN, JAMES (1928–   ). American leading man with easy grin and lithe movement. *Ride Lonesome* (59), *Face of a Fugitive* (59), *The Magnificent Seven* (60), *Hell Is for Heroes* (62), *Charade* (63), *A High Wind in Jamaica* (65), *Major Dundee* (65), *Our Man Flint* (66), *What Did You Do in the War, Daddy?* (66), *Dead Heat on a Merry-go-round* (66), *In Like Flint* (67), *Waterhole 3* (67), *The President's Analyst* (68), *Hard Contract* (69), *Blood Kin* (69), etc. TV series: *Klondyke* (60), *Acapulco* (60).

COCA, IMOGEN (1909–   ). American TV and revue comedienne whose rare screen appearances include *Under the Yum Yum Tree* (64). TV series: *Grindl* (63).

COCHISE (c. 1818–1874). Peace-loving Apache Indian chief who became a prominent cinema character after Jeff Chandler played him in *Broken Arrow* (50), and later in *Battle at Apache Pass* (52) and *Taza Son of Cochise* (53). John Hodiak took over for *Conquest of Cochise* (53).

COCHRAN, STEVE (1917–1965). American screen actor, usually a good-looking heavy. *Wonder Man* (45), *The Best Years of Our Lives* (46), *The Chase* (46), *The Damned Don't Cry* (50), *Storm Warning* (51), *Tomorrow Is Another Day* (51), *Operation Secret* (52), *She's Back on Broadway* (53), *Carnival Story* (54), *Come Next Spring* (56), *Il Grido* (It.) (57), *I Mobster* (59), *The Beat Generation* (60), *The Deadly Companions* (61), *Of Love and Desire* (63), etc.

COCTEAU, JEAN (1889–1963). Fanciful French poet and writer who occasionally dabbled in cinema with effective if slightly obscure results. *Le Sang d'un Poète* (w, d) (30), *La Comédie du Bonheur* (w) (40), *L'Éternel Retour* (w) (43), *Le Belle et La Bête* (w, co-d) (46), *L'Aigle A Deux Têtes* (w, d) (48), *Les Parents Terribles* (w, d) (48), *Les Enfants Terribles* (w) (50), *Orphée* (w, d) (50), *Le Testament d'Orphée* (59), etc.

CODEE, ANN (1890–1961). American character actress who played a variety of middle-aged roles for many years. *Hi Gaucho* (35), *Captain Caution* (40), *Old Acquaintance* (44), *The Other Love* (47), *On the Riviera* (51), *Kiss Me Kate* (53), *Daddy Long Legs* (55), *Can Can* (59), etc.

CODY, LEW (1884–1934) (Louis Joseph Coté). American leading man of silent films. *Comrade John* (15), *The Demon* (18), *Don't Change Your Wife* (19), *The Sign on the Door* (21), *Within the Law* (23), *Rupert of Hentzau* (23), *Man and Maid* (25), *On Ze Boulevard* (27), *Beau Broadway* (28), *Dishonoured* (31), *I Love That Man* (33), etc.

CODY, WILLIAM FREDERICK (BUFFALO BILL) (c. 1846–c. 1916). American guide, Indian scout, bison hunter and carnival showman. He has been played in movies by James Ellison in *The Plainsman* (36),

Coe, Fred

Joel McCrea in *Buffalo Bill* (42), Louis Calhern in *Annie Get Your Gun* (50), Charlton Heston in *Pony Express* (52), Clayton Moore in *Buffalo Bill in Tomahawk Territory* (53), Gordon Scott in *Buffalo Bill* (Germ.) (64) and Guy Stockwell in *The Plainsman* (66). He was a favourite hero of silent movies.

COE, FRED (1914–   ). American director with stage and TV background. *A Thousand Clowns* (66), *Me Natalie* (69).

COE, PETER (1929–   ). British director with stage experience. First film: *Lock Up Your Daughters* (69).

co-feature. A moderate-budget production designed (or fated) to form equal half of a double bill.

COGHLAN, JUNIOR (1916–   ) (Frank Coghlan). American boy star of the 20s; previously played baby roles. *Slide, Kelly, Slide* (26), *The Country Doctor* (27), *River's End* (31), *Penrod and Sam* (32), *Boys Reformatory* (39), *Henry Aldrich for President* (41), *The Adventures of Captain Marvel* (serial) (50), other appearances in declining roles. 1966: *The Sand Pebbles*.

COHAN, GEORGE M. (1878–1942). Dapper American actor-dancer-author-composer of the Broadway stage. Songs include *Mary's a Grand Old Name*, *Give My Regards to Broadway*, *Over There*, *Yankee Doodle Dandy*; plays include the much-filmed *Seven Keys to Baldpate* (qv). Film appearances: *Broadway Jones* (16), *Hit-the-Trail Holiday* (18), *The Phantom President* (32), *Gambling* (34), etc. Was impersonated by James Cagney in a biopic, *Yankee Doodle Dandy* (42), and in *The Seven Little Foys* (55).

COHEN, HERMAN (c. 1928–   ). American producer and director of low-budget horror films: *I Was a Teenage Werewolf* (57), *Konga* (61), *Black Zoo* (63), *Berserk* (68), *Crooks and Coronets* (69), *Trog* (70), etc.

COHEN, NORMAN (c. 1936–   ). Irish director. *The London Nobody Knows* (68), *Till Death Us Do Part* (68).

THE COHENS AND THE KELLYS. This series of domestic farces about a Jew and an Irishman, played by George Sidney and Charlie Murray, began in 1926 (title as shown). Subsequent adventures were: (*The Cohens and Kellys*) *in Paris* (28), *in Scotland* (30), *in Africa* (31), *in Hollywood* (33), *in Trouble* (33), etc.

COHL, EMILE (1857–1938) (Emile Courte). Pioneer French cartoonist of the 1908–18 period. *Fantasmagorie* (08), *Les Allumettes Animées* (09), *Don Quichotte* (09), *Aventures d'une Bout de Papier* (11), *Monsieur Stop* (13), *Snookums* (series) (US) (13–15), *Les Pieds Nickelés* (18), many others.

COHN, HARRY (1891–1958). American executive, chief of Columbia Pictures (qv) for many years; a former song-plugger and vaudevillian who built the company in 1924, reputedly from the profits of his sales of a film called *Traffic in Souls*. Biography published 1967: *King Cohn*, by Bob Thomas.

cokuloris. A palette with random irregular holes, placed between lights and camera to prevent glare and give a better illusion of real-life light and shadow.

COLBERT, CLAUDETTE (1905–   ) (Claudette Cauchoin). French actress who went to America as a child and became a popular star of the 30s. *For the Love of Mike* (debut) (27), *The Hole in the Wall* (29), *Manslaughter* (30), *The Smiling Lieutenant* (31), *The Sign of the Cross* (as Poppea) (33), *Three-Cornered Moon* (33), *It Happened One Night* (AA) (34), *Cleopatra* (34), *I Cover the Waterfront* (35), *Imitation of Life* (35), *Private Worlds* (35), *Under Two Flags* (36), *I Met Him in Paris* (37), *Tovarich* (38), *Bluebeard's Eighth Wife* (38), *Midnight* (38), *Zaza* (39), *Drums Along the Mohawk* (40), *Arise My Love* (40), *Boom Town* (40), *Remember the Day* (41), *The Palm Beach Story* (42), *No Time for Love* (43), *So Proudly We Hail* (43), *Since You Went Away* (44), *Practically Yours* (44), *Guest Wife* (45), *Tomorrow Is Forever* (45), *Without Reservations* (46), *The Egg and I* (47), *Sleep My Love* (48), *Bride for Sale* (49), *Three Came Home* (50), *The Secret Fury* (50), *Let's Make It Legal* (51), *Bonaventure* (*Thunder on the Hill*) (51), *The Planter's Wife* (GB) (52), *Texas Lady* (55), *Parrish* (61), etc.

the Cold War has occupied the cinema right from Churchill's Fulton speech in 1948. For three years diehard Nazis had been the international villains par excellence, but a change was required, and Russians have been fair game ever since, in films like *The Iron Curtain, Diplomatic Courier, I Was a Communist for the FBI, I Married a Communist, The Big Lift, Red Snow, The Red Danube, Red Menace, Red Planet Mars, The Journey, From Russia With Love* and innumerable pulp spy thrillers. Rather surprisingly none of these caused much escalation of tension between the nations, and more recently cooler feelings have permitted comedies like *One Two Three, Dr Strangelove* and *The Russians Are Coming, The Russians Are Coming*; while such terrifying panic-button melodramas as *Fail Safe* and *The Bedford Incident* are probably our best guarantee that the dangers are realized on both sides.

COLE, GEORGE (1925–   ). British comedy actor who made film debut in his stage role as a cockney evacuee in *Cottage to Let* (41). Usually plays the befuddled innocent. *Henry V* (44), *Quartet* (48), *Morning Departure* (50), *Laughter in Paradise* (50), *Lady Godiva Rides Again* (51), *Scrooge* (51), *Top Secret* (51), *Will Any Gentleman?* (52), *Happy Ever After* (53), *Our Girl Friday* (53), *The Belles of St Trinian's*

(54), *A Prize of Gold* (55), *The Weapon* (56), *It's a Wonderful World* (56), *The Green Man* (57), *Blue Murder at St Trinian's* (58), *Too Many Crooks* (58), *The Bridal Path* (59), *The Pure Hell of St Trinian's* (60), *Cleopatra* (62), *Dr Syn* (63), *One-Way Pendulum* (64), *The Legend of Young Dick Turpin* (65), *The Great St Trinian's Train Robbery* (66), etc. Radio and TV series: *A Life of Bliss*.

COLE, NAT KING (1919–1965). American Negro pianist and singer who made occasional film appearances. *The Blue Gardenia* (53), *St Louis Blues* (as W. C. Handy) (58), *The Night of the Quarter Moon* (59), *Cat Ballou* (65), etc.

COLEMAN, CHARLES (1885–1951). Australian actor who from 1932 played innumerable and indistinguishable butler roles in Hollywood.

COLEMAN, NANCY (1917–). American leading lady of the 40s, usually in timid roles. *Dangerously They Live* (42), *Kings Row* (42), *The Gay Sisters* (42), *Devotion* (45), *Her Sister's Secret* (47), *Mourning Becomes Electra* (48), *That Man from Tangier* (53), *Slaves* (68), etc.

COLETTE (Gabriel-Sidonie Colette) (1873–1954). French writer, usually on sex themes. Films of her work include *Claudine à l'Ecole* (38), *Gigi* (48 and 58), *Julie de Carnelihan* (50), *L'Ingénne Libertine* (51), *Ripening Seed* (54).

COLIN, JEAN (1905–). British leading lady who makes sporadic appearances still. *Compromising Daphne* (30), *The Mikado* (as Yum Yum) (39), *Bob's Your Uncle* (41), *Laxdale Hall* (54), etc.

COLLEANO, BONAR (1924–1959) (Bonar Sullivan). Wise-cracking American actor, from family of acrobats; worked chiefly in Britain. *The Way to the Stars* (debut) (45), *A Matter of Life and Death* (46), *While the Sun Shines* (46), *Good Time Girl* (47), *One Night With You* (48), *Pool of London* (50), *A Tale of Five Cities* (52), *Eight Iron Men* (US) (52), *The Sea Shall Not Have Them* (55), *Interpol* (57), *No Time To Die* (58), etc.

COLLIER, CONSTANCE (1878–1955) (Laura Constance Hardie). Distinguished British stage actress who made occasional Hollywood films, latterly portraying slightly fey great ladies. *Intolerance* (15), *Bleak House* (20), *Dinner at Eight* (33), *Girls' Dormitory* (36), *Wee Willie Winkie* (37), *Stage Door* (37), *Susan and God* (40), *Kitty* (45), *Monsieur Beaucaire* (46), *The Perils of Pauline* (47), *An Ideal Husband* (GB) (47), *Rope* (49), *Whirlpool* (49), etc.

COLLIER, JOHN (1901–). British writer of polished macabre stories, whose screen work has been sporadic: *Sylvia Scarlett* (35), *The Story of Three Loves* (53), *I Am a Camera* (55), etc.

COLLIER, WILLIAM (1866–1944). American stage actor, usually of comedy character roles: moved to Hollywood in 1929. *Six Cylinder Love* (31), *The Cheater* (34), *Josette* (38), *Thanks for the Memory* (38), *Invitation to Happiness* (39), *There's Magic in Music* (41), many others.

COLLINGE, PATRICIA (1894–). Irish-American stage actress who made occasional film appearances and is particularly remembered as Birdie in *The Little Foxes* (41). Also: *Shadow of a Doubt* (43), *Casanova Brown* (44), *Teresa* (51), *The Nun's Story* (58), etc.

COLLINS, JOAN (1933–). London-born leading lady whose sultry good looks quickly won her star parts: *I Believe In You* (52), *Our Girl Friday* (53), *The Good Die Young* (54), *Land of the Pharaohs* (US) (55), *The Virgin Queen* (US) (55), *The Girl in the Red Velvet Swing* (US) (55), *The Opposite Sex* (US) (56), *Island in the Sun* (US) (56), *Sea Wife* (US) (57), *Stopover Tokyo* (US) (57), *Rally Round the Flag, Boys* (US) (58), *Seven Thieves* (US) (59), *Esther and the King* (US) (60), etc. Recent comeback in *Warning Shot* (66), *Can Hieronymus Merkin Forget Mercy Humpe and Find True Happiness* (69), *The Executioner* (69). Married Anthony Newley.

COLLINS, RAY (1890–1965). American stage actor who joined Orson Welles' Mercury Players and made film debut in *Citizen Kane* (41). Later in demand for kindly uncle roles. *The Magnificent Ambersons* (42), *The Seventh Cross* (44), *Bachelor Knight* (*The Bachelor and the Bobbysoxer*) (47), *The Heiress* (49), *Francis* (50), *The Reformer and the Redhead* (51), *I Want You* (51), *Dreamboat* (52), *Rose Marie* (54), *The Desperate Hours* (55), *Never Say Goodbye* (56), many others. TV series: *Perry Mason* (as Lieut. Tragg) (58–65).

COLLINS, RUSSELL (1897–1965). Hardened-looking American character actor whose films include *Shockproof* (49), *Niagara* (53), *Bad Day at Black Rock* (55), *Soldier of Fortune* (56), *The Enemy Below* (57), etc.

COLLINSON, PETER (1938–). British director who began with pretentiously 'angry' themes. *The Penthouse* (67), *Up the Junction* (68), *The Long Day's Dying* (68), *The Italian Job* (69), *The Iron Outlaws* (70).

COLLYER, JUNE (1907–1968) (Dorothy Heermance). American leading lady in a few light films of the early 30s; married Stuart Erwin. *Woman Wise* (27), *East Side West Side* (28), *Charley's Aunt* (31), etc.

COLMAN, RONALD (1891–1958). Distinguished British romantic actor whose polished manner and good looks thrilled two generations. Originally office boy and clerk, he turned to acting after being wounded in World War I. On stage in Britain from 1916, America from 1920. Played small parts in British silents; starred in his first Hollywood film, *The White Sister* (22). Other silents: *Beau Geste* (26), *Stella Dallas* (27), *The Winning of Barbara Worth* (28), etc. Sound: *Bulldog Drummond* (29), *Condemned* (30), *Raffles* (31), *Arrowsmith* (32), *Cynara* (33), *The Masquerader* (33), *Clive of India* (35), *A Tale of Two Cities* (36), *Under Two Flags* (36), *Lost Horizon* (37), *The Prisoner of Zenda* (37), *If I Were King* (38), *Talk of the Town* (42), *Random Harvest* (43), *The Late George Apley* (47), *A Double Life* (AA) (48), *Champagne for Caesar* (50), *The Story of Mankind* (57), etc. TV series: *Halls of Ivy*.

COLONNA, JERRY (1904–   ). American comic with strong, high-pitched voice, walrus moustache and bulging eyes. *College Swing* (38), *Little Miss Broadway* (38), *Road to Singapore* (39), *Sis Hopkins* (41), *True to the Army* (42), *Star-Spangled Rhythm* (43), *Ice Capades* (42), *Atlantic City* (44), *The Fifth Chair* (*It's in the Bag*) (45), *Road to Rio* (47), *Kentucky Jubilee* (51), *Meet Me in Las Vegas* (56), *Andy Hardy Comes Home* (58), etc.

colour. Colour movies of a kind were made as long ago as 1898. During the next few years many films were hand-coloured by stencil, and two unsatisfactory processes, KinemaColor and Gaumontcolor, were tried out. D. W. Griffith in *The Birth of a Nation* (14) developed the French practice of tinting scenes for dramatic effect: blue for night, orange for sunshine, etc. In 1918 red-and-green Technicolor was tried out along with half a dozen other processes. 1921: Prizmacolour was used for the British historical film *The Great Adventure*. 1923: de Mille used a colour sequence in *The Ten Commandments*. 1926: *The Black Pirate* was shot in two-colour Technicolor. 1932: first three-colour Technicolor film, Disney cartoon *Flowers and Trees* (AA). 1934: colour used in dramatic sequences of *La Cucaracha*. 1935: first feature film entirely in colour, *Becky Sharp*. 1938: first British Technicolor feature, *Wings of the Morning*. 1939: two-colour Cinecolor, very cheap, becomes popular for low-budget Westerns. 1942: Technicolor introduces monopack process, using one negative instead of three and making equipment less cumbersome and more flexible. 1948: Republic adopts Trucolor. 1949: Anscocolor, later to become Metrocolor, used on *The Man on the Eiffel Tower*. 1951: Supercinecolor (3 colours) adopted by Columbia in *Sword of Monte Cristo*. 1952: Eastmancolour used in *Royal Journey*; Warners adopt it as Warnercolor. 1954: Fox adopt De Luxe Colour.

Today, with new colours springing up all the time, effectiveness seems to depend not on the trademark but on how well the film is shot, processed and printed.

colour sequences in otherwise black-and-white movies were used at first experimentally (see above) but have also been employed for dramatic effect. Early examples include *The Ten Commandments* (23), *The Wedding March* (28), *The Desert Song* (29), *Chasing Rainbows* (30); many of the early sound musicals went into colour for their final number, and this went on as late as *Kid Millions* (35). *Victoria the Great* (37) had colour for the final 'Empress of India' scenes. *The Wizard of Oz* (39) had the Oz scenes in colour and the Kansas scenes in sepia. *Irene* (40) went into colour for the 'Alice Blue Gown' number—which made the second half of the film anti-climactic. *The Moon and Sixpence* (42) blazed into colour for the fire at the end . . . and the same director, Albert Lewin, used a similar trick whenever the picture was shown in *The Picture of Dorian Gray* (44). *A Matter of Life and Death* (45) had earth in colour, heaven in a rather metallic monochrome. *Task Force* (49) went into colour for its final battle reels, most of which consisted of blown-up 16mm war footage. *The Secret Garden* (49) played the same trick as *The Wizard of Oz*. *The Solid Gold Cadillac* (56) had a few final feet of colour to show off the irrelevant car of the title. In 1958 *I Was a Teenage Frankenstein* revived the old dodge of colour for the final conflagration. And *Is Paris Burning?* (66) used colour for the climactic victory sequence, having been forced into black-and-white for the rest of the movie by the necessity of using old newsreel footage. In few of the above cases has reissue printing maintained the original intention: printing short sequences in colour is time-consuming. See also: *tinting*.

COLPI, HENRI (1921–   ). French editor (*Hiroshima Mon Amour* [59], *Last Year in Marienbad* [61], etc.); director (*Une Aussi Longue Absence* [61], *Codine* [62]).

Columbia Pictures. American production and distribution company long considered one of the 'little two' (the other being Universal) against the 'big five' (MGM, RKO, Fox, Warner and Paramount). Columbia originated with one man, Harry Cohn, who founded it in 1924 after a career as a salesman and shorts producer. Throughout the 30s and 40s he turned out competent co-features and second features, apart from prestige pictures such as the Capra comedies and an ill-fated Kramer deal; he was also prepared to spend big money on certainties such as Rita Hayworth and *The Jolson Story*. From the late 40s, with films like *All the King's Men*, *Born Yesterday* and *From Here to Eternity*, the company began to pull itself into the big-time, and when Cohn died in 1958 it was one of the leaders of international co-production, with such major films to its credit as *On the Waterfront* and *The Bridge on the River Kwai*, with *Lawrence of Arabia* and *A Man for All Seasons* to come. It also produces and distributes TV films through its subsidiary Screen Gems.

COLUMBO, RUSS (1908–1934) (Ruggerio de Rudolpho Columbo). American violinist, vocalist, songwriter and bandleader who appeared in a few films: *Wolf Song* (29), *The Street Girl* (29), *Hellbound* (31), *Broadway through a Keyhole* (33), *Wake Up and Dream* (34), etc.

COLVIG, VANCE (1892–1967). American actor who spent most of his career at the Disney studio and became the voice for Pluto and Goofy. He was also co-author of the song 'Who's Afraid of the Big Bad Wolf?'

combined print. One on which both sound and picture (always produced separately) have been 'married', i.e. a standard print as shown in cinemas. See *double-headed print.*

COMDEN, BETTY (1919–   ) (Elizabeth Cohen). American screen-writer who has collaborated with Adolph Green on books and lyrics of many Broadway shows and films. *On the Town* (49), *Singing in the Rain* (52), *Band Wagon* (54), *Auntie Mame* (58), *What a Way to Go* (64), etc.

comedy. See *comedy teams; crazy comedy; light comedians; satire; sex; social comedy; slapstick.*

comedy teams in the accepted sense began in vaudeville, but, depending so much on the spoken word, could make little headway in films until the advent of the talkies. Then they all tried, and many (Amos 'n Andy, Gallagher and Shean, Olsen and Johnson) didn't quite make it, at least not immediately. Laurel and Hardy, who had been successful in silents by the use of mime, adapted their methods very little and remained popular; during the 30s they were really only challenged by Wheeler and Wolsey, whose style was more frenetic. From 1940 the cross-talking Abbott and Costello reigned supreme, with an occasional challenge from Hope and Crosby and the splendid *Hellzapoppin* from Olsen and Johnson. Then came Martin and Lewis, who didn't appeal to everybody, Rowan and Martin, who in 1957 didn't appeal to anybody, and, latest of all, Allen and Rossi, about whose success we must wait and see. In Britain, comedy teams were popular even in poor films: the best of them were Jack Hulbert and Cicely Courtneidge, Tom Walls and Ralph Lynn, Lucan and MacShane ('Old Mother Riley'), Arthur Askey and Richard Murdoch, and the Crazy Gang, a bumper fun bundle composed of Flanagan and Allen, Naughton and Gold, and Nervo and Knox. Morecambe and Wise, the latest recruits to the fold, are having trouble adapting their talent to the big screen, but will undoubtedly succeed in due course. One should also mention Basil Radford and Naunton Wayne, not cross-talkers but inimitable caricaturists of the Englishman abroad.

Of larger groups, among the most outstanding are Our Gang, the Keystone Cops, the Marx Brothers, the Three Stooges, Will

Hay with Moore Marriott and Graham Moffatt, the 'Carry On' team, and one supposes the Beatles.

See also: *romantic teams*.

COMENCINI, LUIGI (1916–   ). Italian director. *Bambini in Citta* (46), *Proibito Rubare* (48), *The Mill on the Po* (co-writer only) (49), *La Citta Si Difende* (co-writer only) (51), *Persiane Chiuse* (51), *Bread, Love and Dreams* (also wrote) (53), *Bread, Love and Jealousy* (54), *Mariti in Citta* (58), *Bebo's Girl* (63), etc.

COMER, ANJANETTE (c. 1941–   ). American leading lady. *Quick Before It Melts* (65), *The Loved One* (65), *The Appaloosa* (*Southwest to Sonora*) (66), *Banning* (66), *Rabbit, Run* (70), etc.

COMFORT, LANCE (1908–1966). British director, formerly cameraman. *Penn of Pennsylvania* (41), *Hatter's Castle* (41), *When We Are Married* (42), *Old Mother Riley, Detective* (42), *Daughter of Darkness* (also produced) (45), *Great Day* (45), *Silent Dust* (48), *Portrait of Clare* (50), *Eight O'clock Walk* (54), *At the Stroke of Nine* (57), *Make Mine a Million* (58), *The Ugly Duckling* (59), *Touch of Death* (62), *Tomorrow at Ten* (62), *Devils of Darkness* (65), others. Directed many episodes of TV series, especially *Douglas Fairbanks Presents* which he also co-produced.

comic strips in newspapers have always been avidly watched by film producers with an eye on the popular market. Among films and series so deriving are the following:

Gertie the Dinosaur (cartoon series) (19); *The Gumps* (two-reelers) (23–28); *Bringing Up Father* (16) (drawn), (20) (two-reeler), (28) (feature with J. Farrell Macdonald and Marie Dressler), (45) (series of 'Jiggs and Maggie' features with Joe Yule and Renee Riano); *The Katzenjammer Kids* (cartoon series) (17 and 38); *Krazy Kat* (various cartoons 16–38); *Ella Cinders* (with Colleen Moore) (22); *Tillie the Toiler* (with Marion Davies) (27); *Skippy* (with Jackie Cooper) (30); *Little Orphan Annie* (32) (with Mitzi Green) and (38) (with Ann Gillis); *Joe Palooka* (34) (with Stu Erwin) and (47–51) (with Joe Kirkwood); *Blondie* (with Penny Singleton) (38–48); *Gasoline Alley* (with James Lydon) (51); *Lil Abner* (qv); *Popeye* (qv); *Jungle Jim* (49–54); *Prince Valiant* (54), *Up Front* (51–53); *Felix the Cat* (qv); *Old Bill* (GB) (40); *Dick Barton* (GB) in various personifications; *Jane* (GB) in an abysmal 1949 second feature; and, of course, *Modesty Blaise* (66), *Batman* (66), and *Barbarella* (68).

Strip characters whose adventures were turned into Hollywood serials during the 30s and 40s include *Tailspin Tommy, Buck Rogers, Mandrake the Magician, Don Winslow of the Navy, Jet Jackson Flying Commando, Flash Gordon, Batman, Buck Rogers* ('in the 25th century'),

Brick Bradford ('in the centre of the earth'), *Chandu, Superman, Dick Tracy* (also in 40s features), *The Lone Ranger* and *Red Ryder.*

COMINGORE, DOROTHY (1918–   ). American actress who played the second wife in *Citizen Kane* (41) and has been little seen since: *The Hairy Ape* (44), *Any Number Can Play* (49), *The Big Night* (52), etc.

COMING THRU THE RYE (GB 1924). A sentimental Victorian love story directed by Cecil Hepworth. Slow-moving but pleasantly photographed, it is valued as an example of the 'superior' British silent film of its time. Starred Alma Taylor and James Carew. (Miss Taylor had also starred with Stewart Rome in an earlier 1916 version, also directed by Hepworth.)

communism has always been treated by Hollywood as a menace. In the 30s one could laugh at it, in *Ninotchka* and *He Stayed for Breakfast*. Then in World War II there was a respite during which the virtues of the Russian peasantry were extolled in such films as *Song of Russia* and *North Star*. But with the cold war, every international villain became a commie instead of a Nazi, and our screens were suddenly full of dour dramas about the deadliness of 'red' infiltration: *I Married a Communist, I Was a Communist for the FBI, The Red Menace, The Iron Curtain, Trial, My Son John, Walk East on Beacon, The Red Danube, Red Snow, Red Planet Mars, Blood Alley, Big Jim McLain, The Manchurian Candidate*. In the early 60s a documentary compilation of red aggression was released under the title *We'll Bury You*. The British never seemed to take the peril seriously, though the agitator in *The Angry Silence* was clearly labelled red.

COMO, PERRY (1912–   ). Italian-American crooner with deceptively relaxed manner which in recent years made him a popular TV star. Appeared in a few musical films of the 40s: *Something for the Boys* (44), *Doll Face* (45), *If I'm Lucky* (46), *Words and Music* (48), etc.

compilation films have become commonplace on TV through such series as *Twentieth Century, Men of Our Time* and *The Valiant Years*, all using library material to evoke a pattern of the past. Thanks to the careful preservation of original documentary material, film-makers have been able, over the last thirty years or so, to give us such films on a wide variety of subjects and to develop an exciting extra dimension of film entertainment which also serves a historical need.

The first outstanding efforts in this direction were made by H. Bruce Woolfe in his 20s documentaries of World War I, mixing newsreel footage with reconstructed scenes. In 1940 Cavalcanti assembled his study of Mussolini, *Yellow Caesar*; and in 1942 Frank Capra, working for the US Signal Corps, gave a

tremendous fillip to the art of the compilation film with his 'Why
We Fight' series. Paul Rotha's *World of Plenty* (43) was a clever
study of world food shortages, all kinds of film material including
animated diagrams and acted sequences. In 1945 Carol Reed
and Garson Kanin, in *The True Glory*, gave the story of D-Day to
Berlin an unexpected poetry, and in 1946 Don Siegel in his short
Hitler Lives showed all too clearly what a frightening potential
the compilation form had as propaganda. Nicole Vedres in 1947
turned to the more distant past and in *Paris 1900* produced an
affectionate portrait of a bygone age; Peter Baylis followed this
with *The Peaceful Years*, covering the period between the two wars.
In 1950 Stuart Legg's *Powered Flight* traced the history of aviation.

The Thorndikes, working in East Germany, started in 1956
their powerful series *The Archives Testify*, attributing war crimes
to West German officials; this aggressive mood was followed in
their *Du Und Mancher Kamerad* ('The German Story') and *The
Russian Miracle*, though in the latter case they seemed somewhat
less happy in praising than in blaming. In 1959 George Morrison's
Mise Eire graphically presented the truth of the much-fictionalized
Irish troubles; and in 1960 came the first of the films about Hitler,
Erwin Leiser's *Mein Kampf*, to be sharply followed by Rotha's *The
Life of Adolf Hitler* and Louis Clyde Stoumen's rather fanciful
Black Fox. Jack Le Vien, producer of the last-named, went on to
make successful films about Churchill (*The Finest Hours*) and the
Duke of Windsor (*A King's Story*). Now every year the compilations
come thick and fast. From France, *Fourteen-Eighteen*; from BBC-TV,
twenty-six half-hours of *The Great War*; from Granada TV, *The
Fanatics* (suffragettes), *The World of Mr Wells* (H.G., that is) and
a long-running weekly series, *All Our Yesterdays*, which consists
entirely of old newsreels; from Associated-British, *Time to Remember*,
a series devoting half an hour to each year of the century; from
Italy, *Allarmi Siam' Fascisti*, a history of the fascist movement;
from Japan, *Kamikaze*, about the suicide pilots; from France,
Rossif's *Mourir à Madrid* and *The Fall of Berlin*. The list will be
endless, because even though every foot of old newsreel were used
up, one could begin again, using different editing, juxtapositions
and commentary to achieve different effects.

See also: *documentary*.

composers have frequently been lauded on cinema screens, though the
stories used usually bore little relation to their real lives and the
films were not often box office. Here are some of the subjects of
musical biopics:

George Frederick Handel (1685–1759): Wilfred Lawson, *The
Great Mr Handel* (42).

Wolfgang Amedeus Mozart (1756–91): Gino Cervi, *Eternal
Melody* (39); *Whom the Gods Love* (43).

225

composers

Ludwig van Beethoven (1770–1827): Johann Holzmeister, *Eroica* (49); Carl Boehm, *The Magnificent Rebel* (60).

Niccolo Paganini (1782–1840): Stewart Granger, *The Magic Bow* (47).

Franz Schubert (1797–1828): Nils Asther, *Love Time* (34); Richard Tauber, *Blossom Time* (34); Hans Jaray, *Unfinished Symphony* (35); Alan Curtis, *New Wine* (41); Tino Rossi, *La Belle Meunière* (47); Claude Laydu, *Symphony of Love* (54).

Vincenzo Bellini (1801–35): Phillips Holmes, *The Divine Spark* (35).

Hector Berlioz (1803–69): Jean-Louis Barrault, *La Symphonie Fantastique* (40).

Frederic Chopin (1810–49): Jean Servais, *Adieu* (35); Cornel Wilde, *A Song to Remember* (44); Czeslaw Wollejko, *The Young Chopin* (52).

Robert Schumann (1810–56): Paul Henried, *Song of Love* (47).

Franz Liszt (1811–86): Stephen Bekassy, *A Song to Remember* (44); Henry Daniell, *Song of Love* (47); Dirk Bogarde, *Song Without End* (60).

Richard Wagner (1813–83): Alan Badel, *Magic Fire* (56).

Johann Strauss Jnr (1825–99): Esmond Knight, *Waltzes from Vienna* (33); Anton Walbrook, *Vienna Waltzes* (34); Fernand Gravet, *The Great Waltz* (38); Kerwin Matthews, *The Waltz King* (60).

Stephen Foster (1826–64): Don Ameche, *Swanee River* (39); Ray Middleton, *I Dream of Jeannie* (52).

Johannes Brahms (1833–97): Robert Walker, *Song of Love* (47).

W. S. Gilbert (1836–1911) and Arthur Sullivan (1842–1900): Robert Morley and Maurice Evans, *The Story of Gilbert and Sullivan* (53).

Peter Ilich Tchaikovsky (1840–93): Frank Sundstrom, *Song of My Heart* (47); Innokenti Smoktunovsky, *Tchaikovsky* (69).

Nikolai Rimsky-Korsakov (1844–1908): Jean-Pierre Aumont, *Song of Scheherezade* (47).

John Philip Sousa (1854–1932): Clifton Webb, *Stars and Stripes Forever* (52).

Victor Herbert (1859–1924): Walter Connolly, *The Great Victor Herbert* (39).

Leslie Stuart (1866–1928): Robert Morley, *You Will Remember* (40).

W. C. Handy (1873–1948): Nat King Cole, *St Louis Blues* (57).

Jerome Kern (1885–1945): Robert Walker, *Till the Clouds Roll By* (47).

Sigmund Romberg (1887–1951): Jose Ferrer, *Deep in My Heart* (54).

Irving Berlin (1888–   ): Tyrone Power, *Alexander's Ragtime Band* (38).

Cole Porter (1892–1964): Cary Grant, *Night and Day* (45).

George Gershwin (1898–1937): Robert Alda, *Rhapsody in Blue* (45).

The list of biopics of lesser modern composers would be long indeed.

composite print: see *combined print*.

COMPSON, BETTY (1897–   ). American leading lady of the 20s, in Christie comedies from 1915. *The Miracle Man* (19), *Love Call* (22), *Woman to Woman* (GB) (23 and 29), *The Enemy Sex* (24), *The Fast Set* (26), *Docks of New York* (28), *The Great Gabbo* (29), *On with the Show* (30), *Laughing Irish Eyes* (GB) (36), *A Slight Case of Murder* (38), *Strange Cargo* (40), *Claudia and David* (46), *Hard-Boiled Mahoney* (48), etc.

COMPTON, FAY (1894–   ). British stage actress who has made occasional film appearances. *One Summer's Day* (17), *A Woman of No Importance* (21), *Mary Queen of Scots* (22), *Robinson Crusoe* (27), *Fashions in Love* (US) (29), *Tell England* (31), *Autumn Crocus* (34), *The Mill on the Floss* (35), *The Prime Minister* (41), *Odd Man Out* (46), *London Belongs to Me* (48), *Laughter in Paradise* (50), *Othello* (52), *Aunt Clara* (54), others.

COMPTON, JOYCE (1907–   ) (Eleanor Hunt). American light leading lady of the 30s. *Three Rogues* (31), *Only Yesterday* (33), *Magnificent Obsession* (35), *The Toast of New York* (37), *Balalaika* (39), *City for Conquest* (40), *Blues in the Night* (42), *Pillow to Post* (45), *Grand Canyon* (51), etc.

concentration camps, until long after World War II, were thought too harrowing a subject for film treatment; but a few serious reconstructions have emerged, notably *The Last Stage* (Poland [48]), *Kapo* (Italy [60]), and *Passenger* (Poland [61]), while the shadow of Auschwitz hangs over *The Diary of Anne Frank* (59). An alleged British concentration camp in South Africa was depicted in the Nazi film *Ohm Kruger* (42), and we are still being promised a film version of Mackinlay Kantor's novel *Andersonville*, which shows an American one in the Civil War period.

concerts of serious music naturally figure largely in films about the lives of *composers* (qv), and also in those concerned to show off living musicians: *They Shall Have Music, Music for Millions, Battle for Music, Tonight We Sing, Carnegie Hall, A Hundred Men and a Girl*. In the 40s a string of romantic films were centred on classical musicians and had concert climaxes: *Dangerous Moonlight, Love Story, The Seventh Veil, Intermezzo, The Great Lie*; this style has recently returned in *Interlude*. Other dramatic and comic concerts were featured in *Unfaithfully Yours, Tales of Manhattan, The Man Who Knew Too Much, The World of Henry Orient, The Bride Wore Black* and *Deadfall*. The most influential film concert was certainly *Fantasia*, and the most poignant probably Myra Hess's recital in the blitz-beset National Gallery in *Listen to Britain*.

CONFESSIONS OF A NAZI SPY (US 1939). First of the anti-Hitler films made in Hollywood before World War II began. This Warner melodrama, blending fact with fiction, toned in well with the company's social and biographical output and was often exciting in its own right. While its innovations of technique have since become standard, and its propaganda content now seems naïve, it remains an important landmark pointing the way to *The House on 92nd Street, Boomerang*, etc. Anatole Litvak directed a cast including Edward G. Robinson as the G-man and Francis Lederer and Paul Lukas as spies.

confidence tricksters have figured as minor characters in hundreds of films, but full-length portraits of the breed are few and choice. Harry Baur in *Volpone* and Rex Harrison in *The Honey Pot*; Roland Young, Billie Burke, Janet Gaynor and Douglas Fairbanks Jnr in *The Young in Heart*; Gene Tierney, Laird Cregar and Spring Byington in *Rings on Her Fingers*; Mai Zetterling in *Quartet*; Paul Newman in *The Hustler*; Charles Coburn and Barbara Stanwyck in *The Lady Eve*; David Niven and Marlon Brando in *Bedtime Story*; George C. Scott in *The Flim Flam Man*; Richard Attenborough and David Hemmings in *Only When I Larf*.

CONGRESS DANCES (Germany 1931). This handsome historical romance, shot in three languages, showed a new face of German film-making and made world stars of Lilian Harvey and Conrad Veidt. Directed by Erik Charell, with music by Werner Heymann.

CONKLIN, CHESTER (1888–   ). American silent comedian of Keystone and Sennett knockabout farces; former circus clown. Later seen in *Greed* (23), *Modern Times* (36), *The Great Dictator* (40), *The Perils of Pauline* (47), etc.

CONLIN, JIMMY (1885–1962). Bird-like little American character comedian, in many films, notably those of Preston Sturges, from 1932. *College Rhythm* (33), *Sullivan's Travels* (41), *The Palm Beach Story* (42), *Ali Baba and the Forty Thieves* (44), *Mad Wednesday* (47), *The Great Rupert* (50), *Anatomy of a Murder* (59), many others.

A CONNECTICUT YANKEE AT THE COURT OF KING ARTHUR. Three American versions have been made of this Mark Twain fantasy: 1920 with Harry Myers, 1931 with Will Rogers, and 1949 with Bing Crosby.

CONNERY, SEAN (1930–   ). Virile-looking Scots leading man who after a variety of small screen roles shot to international fame as James Bond in a series of films from the Ian Fleming spy stories. *No Road Back* (55), *Time Lock* (56), *Hell Drivers* (57), *Darby O'Gill and the Little People* (58), *Tarzan's Greatest Adventure* (59), *The Frightened City* (60), *On the Fiddle* (as a dumb army private) (61), *Doctor No* (62), *From Russia with Love* (63), *Woman of Straw* (64), *Marnie* (64), *Goldfinger* (64), *The Hill* (65), *Thunderball* (65), *A Fine Madness* (66), *You Only Live Twice* (67), *Shalako* (68), *The Red Tent* (69), etc.

CONNOLLY, WALTER (1887–1940). American stage actor who came to films in *The Bitter Tea of General Yen* (32), stayed to play rasping, choleric millionaires, executives and editors. Perhaps best remembered in *Nothing Sacred* (37) as the editor who threatened to take out Fredric March's heart and 'stuff it—like an olive!' Last film: *Fifth Avenue Girl* (40).

CONNOR, EDRIC (1915–1968). British West Indian actor and singer. *Cry the Beloved Country* (52), *Moby Dick* (56), *Fire Down Below* (57), *Four for Texas* (63), *Nobody Runs Forever* (68), many others.

CONNOR, KENNETH (1918–   ). British radio and TV comedian adept at nervous or shy roles. A mainstay of the *Carry On* film series. *There Was a Young Lady* (53), *The Black Rider* (55), *Davy* (57), *Carry On Sergeant* (58), *Carry On Nurse* (59), *Dentist in the Chair* (60), *Carry On Constable* (60), *What a Carve-up* (61), *Gonks Go Beat* (65), etc.

CONNORS, CHUCK (1921–   ) (Kevin Joseph Connor). Tough-guy American leading man—and sometimes villain, his smile being adaptable to friendship or menace. Became a star through television. *Pat and Mike* (52), *South Sea Woman* (53), *The Human Jungle* (55), *Tomahawk Trail* (57), *Geronimo* (62), *Flipper* (63), *Move Over Darling* (63), *Broken Sabre* (65), *Ride Beyond Vengeance* (66), *Captain Nemo* (69), etc. TV series: *Rifleman* (57–62), *Arrest and Trial* (63), *Branded* (64–65).

CONNORS, MICHAEL (1925–   ) (Kreker Ohanian). American leading man, in Hollywood from mid-50s. *Where Love Has Gone* (64), *Situation Hopeless But Not Serious* (65), *Harlow* (65), *Stagecoach* (66), *Kiss the Girls and Make Them Die* (67), etc. TV series: *Tightrope* (59), *Mannix* (67–69).

CONRAD, JESS (1940–   ). British pop singer and lightweight actor. *Too Young to Love* (59), *Konga* (61), *The Boys* (62), *The Golden Head* (65), *Hell Is Empty* (67), *The Assassination Bureau* (69), etc.

CONRAD, JOSEPH (1857–1924) (Teodor Josef Konrad Korzeniowski). Polish/Ukrainian novelist, former seaman, who settled in Britain.

Conrad, William

Films based on his books include *Lord Jim* (26 and 65), *Sabotage* (37), *Victory* (30 and 40), *An Outcast of the Islands* (52), *Laughing Anne* (53).

CONRAD, WILLIAM (1920–). Heavily-built American radio writer and actor who came to films to play unpleasant villains: *The Killers* (46), *Sorry, Wrong Number* (48), *The Racket* (51), *Cry Danger* (51), *Johnny Concho* (56), *The Ride Back* (57), etc. Lately producing and directing: *Two on a Guillotine* (p, d) (64), *My Blood Runs Cold* (p, d) (65), *Brainstorm* (p, d) (65), *Chamber of Horrors* (p) (66), *An American Dream* (p) (66), *Covenant with Death* (p) (67), etc.

CONRIED, HANS (1917–). Tall, weedy American comic actor with precise diction and a richly variable voice. *Dramatic School* (37), *Crazy House* (43), *Mrs Parkington* (44), *The Senator Was Indiscreet* (47), *My Friend Irma* (49), *The Twonky* (53), *The Five Thousand Fingers of Doctor T* (53), *Bus Stop* (56), *Rockabye Baby* (58), *The Patsy* (64), many others; also does voices for cartoons. TV series: *Fractured Flickers*.

CONROY, FRANK (1890–1964). British stage actor who went to Hollywood in the early 30s: generally played domestic tyrants. *The Royal Family of Broadway* (30), *Grand Hotel* (32), *Call of the Wild* (35), *Wells Fargo* (37), *The Ox-Bow Incident* (42), *Naked City* (48), *The Last Mile* (59), etc.

THE CONSTANT NYMPH. Margaret Kennedy's popular sentimental novel about the Sanger family and the handsome tutor has been filmed three times: in 1927 with Ivor Novello and Mabel Poulton, directed by Adrian Brunel; in 1933 with Brian Aherne and Victoria Hopper, directed by Basil Dean (co-author of the play version); and in 1944 with Charles Boyer and Joan Fontaine, directed by Edmund Goulding.

CONSTANTINE, EDDIE (1917–). Tough American actor popular in France where he plays Peter Cheyney heroes in crime films. British films include *SOS Pacific* (59), *Treasure of San Teresa* (60). Recently seen in *Alphaville* (65).

CONTE, RICHARD (1915–). Italian-American actor on Broadway from 1936, films from 1936, often playing gangsters or jaded heroes. *The Purple Heart* (44), *A Walk in the Sun* (46), *Somewhere in the Night* (46), *The Other Love* (47), *Call Northside 777* (48), *House of Strangers* (49), *Thieves Highway* (49), *Whirlpool* (49), *The Sleeping City* (50), *Hollywood Story* (51), *The Fighter* (52), *Desert Legion* (53), *The Blue Gardenia* (53), *Slaves of Babylon* (53), *New York Confidential* (55), *The Big Combo* (55), *Bengazi* (56), *Little Red Monkey* (GB) (57), *I'll Cry Tomorrow* (57), *The Brothers Rico* (57), *Full of Life* (57), *They Came to Cordura* (59), *Ocean's Eleven* (61), *Who's Been Sleeping in My Bed* (63), *The Greatest Story Ever Told* (65), *Synanon* (65), *Stay Tuned for Terror* (66), *Assault on a Queen* (66), *Hotel* (67), *Tony Rome* (67), *Lady in Cement* (68), etc. TV series: *The Four Just Men* (59).

continuity. The development of cinematic narrative from beginning to end of a film. If continuity is good the audience will be carried smoothly from one scene to another without disturbing breaks or lapses of detail.

CONWAY, JACK (1887–1952). American director, former actor. Launched in Hollywood by D. W. Griffith: first directed *The Old Armchair* (12). Long with MGM, for whom his films include *Our Modern Maidens* (28), *New Moon* (30), *The Unholy Three* (30), *Arsène Lupin* (32), *Hell Below* (33), *Viva Villa* (34), *A Tale of Two Cities* (35), *Libelled Lady* (36), *A Yank at Oxford* (38), *Too Hot to Handle* (39), *Boom Town* (40), *Honky Tonk* (41), *Crossroads* (42), *Assignment in Brittany* (43), *Dragon Seed* (co-d) (44), *High Barbaree* (47), *The Hucksters* (47), *Julia Misbehaves* (48).

CONWAY, GARY (1938–   ) (Gareth Carmody). American leading man. Films include *Teenage Frankenstein* (as the monster) (57), *Young Guns of Texas* (59), Later successful in TV: *Burke's Law* (63–65), *Land of the Giants* (68–69).

CONWAY, TOM (1904–1967) (Thomas Sanders). British actor, long in America; had widely varied experience before his first Hollywood film, *Sky Murder* (40). In 1942 took over from his brother, George Sanders, as hero of the 'Falcon' series. Roles dwindled during the 50s, but he made some second features in England. *Cat People* (42), *I Walked with a Zombie* (43), *Two O'clock Courage* (45), *Whistle Stop* (46), *One Touch of Venus* (48), *Park Plaza 505* (GB) (53), *Barbados Quest* (GB) (55), *Operation Murder* (GB) (56), *The Last Man to Hang* (GB) (56), *The She-Creature* (56), *Rocket to the Moon* (59), *What a Way To Go* (unbilled) (64), many others. TV series: *Mark Saber* (52–54).

CONYERS, DARCY (1919–   ). British director, former actor. *Ha'penny Breeze* (also acted and produced) (52), *The Devil's Pass* (also wrote and produced) (56), *The Night We Dropped a Clanger* (60), *Nothing Barred* (61), *In the Doghouse* (62), etc.

COOGAN, JACKIE (1914–   ). Former American child actor who achieved world fame opposite Chaplin in *The Kid* (20). Popular throughout silent period: *Peck's Bad Boy* (21), *Oliver Twist* (21), *My Boy* (22), *Daddy* (23), *Old Clothes* (25), *The Bugle Call* (27), many others. Made a few early sound films, such as *Tom Sawyer* (30), *Sooky* (30), *Huckleberry Finn* (31); then retired to emerge as a less appealing adult in minor films: *College Swing* (38), *Kilroy Was Here*

Cook, Donald

(47), *Outlaw Woman* (52), *Lost Women* (56), *High School Confidential* (58), *A Fine Madness* (66), *The Shakiest Gun in the West* (68), etc. Made a comic hit, grotesque and bald, in TV series *The Addams Family* (64–65).

COOK, DONALD (1900–1961). American stage leading man who never quite made it in Hollywood. *The Unfaithful* (32), *Viva Villa* (34), *The Spanish Cape Mystery* (37), *Patrick the Great* (44), *Bowery to Broadway* (44), *Our Very Own* (51), many others.

COOK, ELISHA JNR (1902–   ). Slightly-built American character actor with stage background; adept at neurotics, such as Wilmer the 'gunsel' in *The Maltese Falcon* (41). Also: *Hot Spot* (41), *Hellzapoppin* (41), *Phantom Lady* (44), *Dillinger* (45), *The Big Sleep* (46), *The Great Gatsby* (49), *Don't Bother to Knock* (51), *Shane* (53), *I the Jury* (53), *The Indian Fighter* (55), *The Killing* (56), *Baby Face Nelson* (57), *The House on Haunted Hill* (59), *Day of the Outlaw* (59), *One-Eyed Jacks* (61), *The Haunted Palace* (64), *Rosemary's Baby* (68), many others.

COOK, FIELDER (1923–   ). American TV director who makes occasional films: *Patterns of Power* (56), *Home Is the Hero* (Eire) (59), *Big Hand for a Little Lady* (66), *How to Save a Marriage* (67), *Prudence and the Pill* (68).

COOK, PETER (1937–   ). British cabaret comedian and writer. Film appearances: *The Wrong Box* (66), *Bedazzled* (67), *Monte Carlo or Bust* (69), *The Bed Sitting Room* (69).

COOP, DENYS (1920–   ). British cameraman: *A Kind of Loving* (61), *Billy Liar* (63), *This Sporting Life* (63), *One-Way Pendulum* (64), *King and Country* (65), *Bunny Lake Is Missing* (65), *The Double Man* (67), *My Side of the Mountain* (68), etc.

†COOPER, GARY (1901–1961) (Frank J. Cooper). Slow-speaking, deep-thinking American leading man, a long-enduring Hollywood star who always projected honest determination. Was cowboy and cartoonist before becoming a film extra; progressed to two-reelers and became a star in his first feature, *The Winning of Barbara Worth* (26). Then: *It* (27), *Children of Divorce* (27), *Arizona Bound* (27), *Wings* (27), *Nevada* (27), *The Last Outlaw* (27), *Beau Sabreur* (28), *Legion of the Condemned* (28), *Doomsday* (28), *Half a Bride* (28), *Lilac Time* (28), *The First Kiss* (28), *Shopworn Angel* (28), *Wolf Song* (29), *The Betrayal* (29), *The Virginian* (29), *Only the Brave* (29), *The Texan* (29), *Seven Days' Leave* (30), *A Man from Wyoming* (30), *The Spoilers* (30), *Morocco* (30), *Fighting Caravans* (31), *I Take This Woman* (31), *His Woman* (31), *The Devil and the Deep* (32), *A Farewell to Arms* (32), *City Streets* (32), *If I Had a Million* (32), *One Sunday Afternoon* (33), *Alice in Wonderland* (as the White Knight) (33),

Today We Live (33), *Design for Living* (34), *Peter Ibbetson* (34), *Operator Thirteen* (34), *The Wedding Night* (35), *Lives of a Bengal Lancer* (35), *Now and Forever* (35), *Desire* (36), *Mr Deeds Goes to Town* (36), *The General Died at Dawn* (36), *The Plainsman* (37), *Souls at Sea* (37), *The Adventures of Marco Polo* (38), *Bluebeard's Eighth Wife* (38), *The Cowboy and the Lady* (39), *Beau Geste* (39), *The Real Glory* (39), *The Westerner* (40), *Northwest Mounted Police* (40), *Meet John Doe* (41), *Sergeant York* (AA) (41), *Ball of Fire* (41), *Pride of the Yankees* (42), *For Whom the Bell Tolls* (43), *The Story of Dr Wassell* (44), *Saratoga Trunk* (44), *Casanova Brown* (44), *Along Came Jones* (also produced) (45), *Cloak and Dagger* (46), *Unconquered* (47), *Good Sam* (48), *The Fountainhead* (49), *Task Force* (49), *Bright Leaf* (50), *Dallas* (50), *You're in the Navy Now* (51), *Distant Drums* (51), *Springfield Rifle* (52), *High Noon* (AA) (52), *Return to Paradise* (52), *Blowing Wild* (53), *Garden of Evil* (54), *Vera Cruz* (54), *The Court Martial of Billy Mitchell* (55), *Friendly Persuasion* (56), *Love in the Afternoon* (56), *Ten North Frederick* (58), *Man of the West* (58), *They Came to Cordura* (59), *The Hanging Tree* (59), *The Wreck of the Mary Deare* (59), *The Naked Edge* (GB) (61). Special Academy Award 1960 'for his many memorable screen performances and for the international recognition he, as an individual, has gained for the film industry'.

COOPER, GEORGE A. (c. 1913–   ). British character actor of vengeful types. *Miracle in Soho* (56), *Violent Playground* (58), *Tom Jones* (63), *Life at the Top* (65), *The Strange Affair* (68), etc.

COOPER, GLADYS (1888–   ). Distinguished British stage actress who appeared in a few early silents (*Masks and Faces* [17], *The Bohemian Girl* [22], etc.) but essentially began her film career in Hollywood in *Rebecca* (40). She subsequently aired her warm aristocratic personality in many roles, few of them worthy. *The Gay Falcon* (41), *The Black Cat* (41), *Lady Hamilton* (41), *This Above All* (42), *Now Voyager* (AA) (42), *Forever and a Day* (43), *Mr Lucky* (43), *The Song of Bernadette* (43), *The White Cliffs of Dover* (44), *Mrs Parkington* (44), *The Valley of Decision* (45), *Love Letters* (45), *The Green Years* (46), *Beware of Pity* (GB) (46), *Green Dolphin Street* (47), *The Pirate* (48), *Homecoming* (48), *Madame Bovary* (49), *The Secret Garden* (50), *Sons of the Musketeers* (52), *The Man Who Loved Redheads* (GB) (54), *Separate Tables* (58), *My Fair Lady* (64), *The Happiest Millionaire* (67), *A Nice Girl Like Me* (69), etc. TV series: *The Rogues* (64). Published autobiography 1953: *Without Veils*.

COOPER, JACKIE (1921–   ). American child actor of the 30s, famous for his 'spunky' performances in 'Our Gang' shorts, *Movietone Follies* (28), *Sunny Side Up* (29), *Skippy* (30), *Sooky* (30), *The Champ* (31), *When a Fellow Needs a Friend* (31), *Lumpy* (31), *Lost* (32), *The Bowery* (33), *Treasure Island* (34), *O'Shaughnessy's Boy* (35), etc.

His appeal waned as he approached manhood: *The Devil Is a Sissy* (36), *Gangster's Boy* (38), *Seventeen* (40), *Gallant Sons* (40), *Her First Beau* (41), *Syncopation* (42), *Stork Bites Man* (47), *Kilroy Was Here* (47), etc. Film appearances grew increasingly rare, his last being in *Everything's Ducky* (61); but he became popular on TV in *The People's Choice* and *Hennessey*, and is now a powerful TV executive producer.

COOPER, JAMES FENIMORE (1789–1851). American adventure novelist whose 'westerns' include *The Last of the Mohicans, The Pathfinder* and *The Deerslayer*, all frequently filmed.

COOPER, MELVILLE (1896–   ). British character actor, in Hollywood since 1936. Best film part as Mr Collins in *Pride and Prejudice* (40); also in *The Scarlet Pimpernel* (35), *Rebecca* (40), *Holy Matrimony* (43), *13 Rue Madeleine* (47), *Enchantment* (47), *Father of the Bride* (50), *Moonfleet* (55), *The King's Thief* (56), *The Story of Mankind* (57), etc.

COOPER, MERIAN C. (1893–   ). American executive producer associated with such outstanding films as *Grass* (25), *Chang* (27), *King Kong* (33), *The Last Days of Pompeii* (35), *She Wore a Yellow Ribbon* (49), *The Quiet Man* (52), *The Searchers* (56), etc. Special Academy Award 1952 'for his many innovations and contributions to the art of the motion picture'.

COOPER, VIOLET KEMBLE (1886–1961). British stage actress who appeared in a few Hollywood films in the 30s. *Our Betters* (33), *Vanessa* (34), *David Copperfield* (as Miss Murdstone) (35), *The Invisible Ray* (36), *Romeo and Juliet* (36), etc.

COOPER, WILKIE (1911–   ). British cinematographer, once a child actor. *The Rake's Progress* (45), *Green for Danger* (46), *Captain Boycott* (47), *London Belongs to Me* (48), *Stage Fright* (50), *The Admirable Crichton* (57), *Jason and the Argonauts* (63), *One Million Years BC* (66), etc.

COOTE, ROBERT (1909–   ). British stage character actor who has filmed mainly in Hollywood; familiar in amiable silly-ass roles. *Sally in Our Alley* (31), *A Yank at Oxford* (38), *Gunga Din* (US) (39), *You Can't Fool Your Wife* (US) (40), *The Commandos Strike at Dawn* (US) (43), *A Matter of Life and Death* (46), *The Ghost and Mrs Muir* (US) (47), *Forever Amber* (US) (47), *Bonnie Prince Charlie* (48), *The Elusive Pimpernel* (49), *Rommel, Desert Fox* (US) (51), *The Prisoner of Zenda* (US) (52), *The Constant Husband* (55), *Othello* (as Roderigo) (55), *The Swan* (US) (56), *Merry Andrew* (US) (58), *The League of Gentlemen* (59), *The Golden Head* (65), *A Man Could Get Killed* (US) (66), *The Swinger* (US) (66), *Prudence and the Pill* (68), etc. TV series: *The Rogues* (64).

COPE, KENNETH (1931–   ). British TV actor, usually of Liverpudlian types. Films include *The Criminal* (60), *The Damned* (62), *Genghis Khan* (65), *Dateline Diamonds* (65).

COPLAND, AARON (1900–   ). American composer. *The City* (39), *Of Mice and Men* (39), *Our Town* (40), *North Star* (43), *The Red Pony* (48), *The Heiress* (AA) (49), *Something Wild* (61), etc.

COPLEY, PETER (1915–   ). British stage actor who makes occasional film appearances, usually in quiet, downtrodden or slightly sinister roles. *The Golden Salamander* (49), *The Card* (52), *The Sword and the Rose* (53), *Victim* (61), etc.

†COPPOLA, FRANCIS FORD (1939–   ). American writer-director who graduated from nudie movies. *Dementia* (*The Haunted and the Hunted*) (Eire) (63), *This Property Is Condemned* (w) (65), *Is Paris Burning?* (w) (66), *You're a Big Boy Now* (w, d) (67), *Finian's Rainbow* (d) (68), *The Rain People* (w, d) (69).

CORBETT, HARRY H. (1925–   ). British stage actor who played tough guys, regional types and maniacs in an assortment of films before gaining great TV popularity in *Steptoe and Son*; subsequently starred in a number of unsatisfactory comedy vehicles. *Floods of Fear* (57), *Nowhere To Go* (58), *Cover Girl Killer* (60), *Sammy Going South* (62), *What a Crazy World* (63), *Ladies Who Do* (63), *The Bargee* (64), *Rattle of a Simple Man* (64), *Joey Boy* (65), *The Sandwich Man* (66), *Carry On Screaming* (66), *Crooks and Coronets* (69), etc.

CORBETT, LEONORA (1907–1960). British stage actress who made few films. *Heart's Delight* (32), *The Constant Nymph* (33), etc.

CORBY, ELLEN (1913–   ). American actress specializing in prissy spinsters, nosey neighbours, etc. Memorable as one of the aunts in *I Remember Mama* (48); recently in *The Strangler* (64), *Night of the Grizzly* (66).

CORD, ALEX (1931–   ) (Alexander Viespi). American leading man with stage and TV experience. *Synanon* (*Get Off My Back*) (65), *Stagecoach* (66), *The Brotherhood* (68), *Stiletto* (69), *Grigsby* (69).

CORDY, RAYMOND (1898–1956) (R. Cordiaux). French comedy actor, especially seen in René Clair's films. *Le Million* (31), *À Nous la Liberté* (31), *Le Quatorze Juillet* (33), *Le Dernier Milliardaire* (34), *Ignace* (37), *Les Inconnus dans la Maison* (42), *Le Silence Est d'Or* (46), *La Beauté du Diable* (49), *Les Belles de Nuit* (52), *Les Grandes Manœuvres* (55), etc.

CORDAY, MARA (1932–   ) (Marilyn Watts). American leading lady of the 50s. *Sea Tiger* (52). *So This Is Paris* (54), *Man without a Star* (55), *The Quiet Gun* (57), *The Black Scorpion* (57), etc.

Corday, Paula

CORDAY, PAULA (1924–) (also known as Paule Croset and Rita Corday). Anglo-Swiss leading lady who went to Hollywood in the 40s. *The Falcon Strikes Back* (43), *The Body Snatcher* (45), *The Exile* (47), *Sword of Monte Cristo* (51), *Because You're Mine* (52), *The French Line* (54), etc.

COREY, JEFF (1914–). American supporting actor with stage experience; seen as policeman, convict, gangster, etc. *All That Money Can Buy* (film debut) (41), *The Killers* (46), *Fourteen Hours* (51), *New Mexico* (62), *The Balcony* (63), *Lady in a Cage* (64), *Once a Thief* (65), *Mickey One* (65), *The Cincinnati Kid* (65), *Seconds* (66), *The Boston Strangler* (69), many others.

COREY, WENDELL (1914–1968). American stage and screen actor, in films since 1947, usually as solid dependable type. *Desert Fury* (47), *I Walk Alone* (48), *No Sad Songs for Me* (50), *The Furies* (50), *Harriet Craig* (51), *Carbine Williams* (52), *Laughing Anne* (GB) (53), *Hell's Half Acre* (54), *Rear Window* (54), *The Big Knife* (55), *The Killer Is Loose* (56), *The Rainmaker* (57), *Alias Jesse James* (59), *Prehistoric Planet Women* (65), *Broken Sabre* (65), *Waco* (66), *Red Tomahawk* (66), others. TV series: *Harbour Command* (57), *The Eleventh Hour* (62).

CORFIELD, JOHN (1893–). British producer in films from 1929; co-founder of British National Films with Lady Yule and J. Arthur Rank. *Turn of the Tide* (35), *Laugh It Off* (40), *Gaslight* (40), *Headline* (42), *Bedelia* (46), *The White Unicorn* (47), *My Sister and I* (48), etc.

CORMAN, ROGER (1926–). American writer-producer-director, who made so many cheap horror films in the late 50s that he became known as King of the Bs. First sign of real talent appeared in his series of colourful Poe adaptations: *The Fall of the House of Usher* (60), *The Pit and the Pendulum* (61), *The Masque of the Red Death* (64), *The Tomb of Ligeia* (64), etc. Also: *The Stranger* (*The Intruder*) (61), *Tower of London* (62), *The Secret Invasion* (64), *The Wild Angels* (66), *The St Valentine's Day Massacre* (67), *The Trip* (67), *Bloody Mama* (70).

†CORNELIUS, HENRY (1913–1958). British director, former editor, whose first film *Passport to Pimlico* (48) was a great comedy success. Topped it with the classic *Genevieve* (53), but his other films were comparatively disappointing: *The Galloping Major* (also wrote) (51), *I Am a Camera* (55), *Next to No Time* (57).

CORNFIELD, HUBERT (1929–). American director. *Sudden Danger* (56), *Lure of the Swamp* (57), *Plunder Road* (59), *The Third Voice* (59), *Pressure Point* (62), *Night of the Following Day* (68), etc.

CORRI, ADRIENNE (1930–). Red-headed British actress whose film appearances alternate between stage and TV. *The River* (debut)

(51), *Quo Vadis* (51), *The Kidnappers* (53), *Devil Girl from Mars* (54), *Lease of Life* (54), *Make Me an Offer* (54), *The Feminine Touch* (55), *Three Men in a Boat* (56), *Corridors of Blood* (58), *The Rough and the Smooth* (59), *The Hellfire Club* (61), *The Tell-Tale Heart* (61), *A Study in Terror* (65), *Bunny Lake Is Missing* (65), *The Viking Queen* (67), *Moon Zero Two* (69), etc.

CORRIGAN, LLOYD (1900–1969). Chubby, jovial American character actor, former screenwriter and director (1930–37). Many cameo appearances. *High School* (39), *The Ghost Breakers* (41), *Mantrap* (leading role) (42), *Hitler's Children* (43), *Since You Went Away* (44), *The Bandit of Sherwood Forest* (45), *The Big Clock* (48), *Cyrano de Bergerac* (51), *The Bowery Boys Meet the Monsters* (54), *Hidden Guns* (57), *The Manchurian Candidate* (62), etc.

THE CORSICAN BROTHERS. The romantic adventure novel by Dumas *père* presents a splendid dual role for an actor. Dustin Farnum starred in a film version in 1919, followed by Douglas Fairbanks Jnr in 1940. *The Return of the Corsican Brothers* (or *Bandits of Corsica*), starring Richard Greene, followed in 1953; and the original was remade in France in 1960, with Geoffrey Toone.

CORTESA, VALENTINA (1924–   ). Italian romantic actress who gained wider fame in *The Glass Mountain* (48). Went to Hollywood and subsequently appeared in several international films before settling again in Italy. *Thieves' Highway* (US) (49), *The Secret People* (GB) (51), *Shadow of the Eagle* (GB) (51), *The House on Telegraph Hill* (US) (51), *The Barefoot Contessa* (US) (54), *Le Amiche* (55), *Magic Fire* (US) (56), *Barabbas* (61), *The Visit* (64), *Juliet of the Spirits* (It.) (65), *The Legend of Lylah Clare* (68), many others.

CORTEZ, RICARDO (1899–   ) (Jack Kranz). American leading man of Viennese origin, developed in the 20s as a Latin lover in the Valentino mould. Later developed outside interests and quit movies after a sojourn in routine roles. *Sixty Cents an Hour* (debut) (23), *Pony Express* (24), *The Torrent* (26), *The Sorrows of Satan* (27), *The Private Life of Helen of Troy* (27), *Behind Office Doors* (28), *Ten Cents a Dance* (31), *Melody of Life* (32), *The Phantom of Crestwood* (33), *Wonder Bar* (34), *Special Agent* (35), *The Walking Dead* (36), *Talk of the Devil* (GB) (36), *Mr Moto's Last Warning* (38), *World Premiere* (40), *I Killed That Man* (42), *Make Your Own Bed* (44), *The Locket* (46), *Blackmail* (47), *The Last Hurrah* (58), many others. Also directed a few films including *City Girl* (38), *Free Blonde and Twenty-one* (40), *The Girl in 313* (40).

CORTEZ, STANLEY (1908–   ) (Stanley Kranz). Viennese-American cinematographer, brother of Ricardo Cortez; in Hollywood from silent days. *The Black Cat* (41), *The Magnificent Ambersons* (42), *Since You Went Away* (44), *Flesh and Fantasy* (44), *Captain Kidd* (45),

The Secret Beyond the Door (48), *The Man on the Eiffel Tower* (50), *Riders to the Stars* (54), *Night of the Hunter* (55), *Man from Del Rio* (56), *The Three Faces of Eve* (57), *Back Street* (61), *Shock Corridor* (63), *Nightmare in the Sun* (64), *The Navy Versus the Night Monsters* (66), *Blue* (68), etc.

COSSART, ERNEST (1876-1951). Portly British actor, inevitably cast by Hollywood in butler roles. *The Scoundrel* (34), *The Great Ziegfeld* (36), *The Light That Failed* (39), *Charley's American Aunt* (42), *Casanova Brown* (44), *John Loves Mary* (49), many others.

COSTA-GAVRAS (1933–   ). Russo-Greek director, in France from childhood. *The Sleeping Car Murders* (65), *Un Homme de Trop* (67), *Shock Troops* (69), '*Z*' (69).

COSTELLO, DOLORES (1905–   ). Gentle, blonde American actress, daughter of actor Maurice Costello, wife of John Barrymore. Played small parts before being cast opposite Barrymore in *The Sea Beast*. Then starred in *Bride of the Storm* (26), *When a Man Loves* (27), *Noah's Ark* (28), *The Redeeming Sin* (29), *Expensive Woman* (31), *Little Lord Fauntleroy* (36), *King of the Turf* (39), *The Magnificent Ambersons* (42), *This Is the Army* (43), etc.

COSTELLO, LOU (1906-1959) (Louis Cristillo). Dumpy American comedian, the zanier half of Abbott and Costello. For films, see BUD ABBOTT. Costello finally made one on his own, *The Thirty-Foot Bride of Candy Rock* (59).

COSTELLO, MAURICE (1877-1950). American matinée idol, in films from 1907. *A Tale of Two Cities* (11), *The Night Before Christmas* (12), *Human Collateral* (20), *Conceit* (21), *Glimpses of the Moon* (23), *The Mad Marriage* (25), *Camille* (27), *Hollywood Boulevard* (36), *Lady from Louisiana* (41), others.

COTTAFAVI, VITTORIO (1914–   ). Italian director, mainly of cut-rate spectaculars like *Revolt of the Gladiators* (58), *The Legions of Cleopatra* (59), *The Vengeance of Hercules* (60), *Hercules Conquers Atlantis* (61). Has won critical approval for stylish handling of some of them.

†COTTEN, JOSEPH (1905–   ). Tall, quiet American leading man, former drama critic and Broadway stage star. Brought to Hollywood by Orson Welles for *Citizen Kane* (41), *The Magnificent Ambersons* (42), *Journey into Fear* (42). Rapidly developed into useful romantic lead. *Lydia* (41), *Shadow of a Doubt* (43), *Hers to Hold* (43), *Gaslight* (44), *Since You Went Away* (44), *Love Letters* (45), *I'll Be Seeing You* (45), *Duel in the Sun* (46), *The Farmer's Daughter* (47), *Portrait of Jennie* (48), *Under Capricorn* (49), *Beyond the Forest* (49), *The Third Man* (49), *Two Flags West* (50), *Walk Softly Stranger* (50),

September Affair (50), *Half Angel* (51), *Man with a Cloak* (51),
Peking Express (52), *Untamed Frontier* (52), *The Steel Trap* (52),
Niagara (52), *Blueprint for Murder* (53), *Special Delivery* (54), *The
Bottom of the Bottle* (55), *The Killer is Loose* (56), *The Halliday
Brand* (56), *From the Earth to the Moon* (58), *The Angel Wore
Red* (60), *The Last Sunset* (61), *Hush Hush Sweet Charlotte* (64),
The Money Trap (65), *The Great Sioux Massacre* (65), *The Tramplers*
(66), *The Oscar* (67), *The Hellbenders* (67), *Jack of Diamonds* (67),
Petulia (68). Much on TV as guest star; also host of *Hollywood and
the Stars* (63).

COULOURIS, GEORGE (1903–   ). British character actor, in New
York from 1929. Briefly in films (33) then back to Broadway;
returned to Hollywood (41) with Orson Welles to play Walter
Parks Thatcher in *Citizen Kane*; subsequently in *For Whom the Bell
Tolls* (43), *None But the Lonely Heart* (45), *Sleep My Love* (48), many
others. Returned to England 1950 and has remained active: *An
Outcast of the Islands* (51), *Doctor in the House* (53), *The Runaway Bus*
(54), *King of Kings* (61), *The Skull* (65), countless others.

THE COUNT OF MONTE CRISTO. This popular adventure yarn by
Alexandre Dumas was filmed in 1912 with Hobart Bosworth, and
again in the same year with James O'Neill. John Gilbert starred
in the 1923 silent film, but the best-remembered version is the
1934 talkie remake with Robert Donat, directed by Rowland V.
Lee. Oddly enough it has never since been remade in English,
though a French version in 1961 starred Louis Jourdan and there
have been over a dozen films using the name Monte Cristo to cover
a multitude of plots, some of them present-day: *Sword of Monte
Cristo*, *Wife of Monte Cristo*, *Monte Cristo's Revenge*, etc.

COURANT, CURT (c. 1895–   ). German cinematographer who did
his best work elsewhere. *Quo Vadis* (24), *Woman in the Moon* (29),
Perfect Understanding (GB) (33), *Amok* (34), *The Man Who Knew
Too Much* (GB) (34), *The Iron Duke* (GB) (35), *Broken Blossoms*
(GB) (36), *La Bête Humaine* (38), *Louise* (39), *Le Jour Se Lève* (39),
De Mayerling à Sarajevo (40), *Monsieur Verdoux* (US) (47), etc.

COURCEL, NICOLE (1930–   ) (Nicole Andrieux). French leading
lady of warm personality. *La Marie du Port* (49), *Versailles* (53), *La
Sorcière* (55), *The Case of Dr Laurent* (56), etc.

COURT, HAZEL (1926–   ). Red-headed British leading lady, in films
since 1944. *Dear Murderer* (46), *My Sister and I* (48), *It's Not Cricket*
(48), many second features. Since *The Curse of Frankenstein* (56)
has been associated with horror films: *The Man Who Could Cheat
Death* (59), *Doctor Blood's Coffin* (60), *The Premature Burial* (US)
(62), *The Masque of the Red Death* (64), etc. TV series: *Dick and the
Duchess* (57).

Courtenay, Tom

COURTENAY, TOM (1937–   ). Lean young British actor specializing in under-privileged roles. Originally Albert Finney's stage under-study in *Billy Liar*, he played the lead in the film version (63). Also: *The Loneliness of the Long Distance Runner* (62), *Private Potter* (62), *King and Country* (64), *Operation Crossbow* (65), *King Rat* (65), *Doctor Zhivago* (65), *The Night of the Generals* (66), *The Day the Fish Came Out* (67), *A Dandy in Aspic* (68), *Otley* (69).

courtesans have always been viewed by the cinema through rose-coloured glasses. There have been innumerable films about Madame du Barry, Madame Sans Gene and Nell Gwynne; Garbo played Camille and Marie Walewska as well as Anna Christie; even Jean Simmons had a shot at Napoleon's *Désirée*, and Vivien Leigh was a decorative Lady Hamilton. Martine Carol played Lola Montes in the Max Ophuls film, Yvonne de Carlo in *Black Bart* (in which she became involved in Western villainy during an American tour).
See also: *prostitutes*.

COURTLAND, JEROME (1926–   ). Gangling young American actor of 40s comedies. *Kiss and Tell* (45), *Battleground* (49), *The Barefoot Mailman* (52), *The Bamboo Prison* (55), others. TV series: *Tales of the Vikings* (60).

COURTNEIDGE, CICELY (1893–   ). Australian comedienne long resident in Britain; wife of Jack Hulbert. On stage from 1901, her great vitality made her a musical comedy favourite. Films include *The Ghost Train* (32), *Jack's the Boy* (32), *Soldiers of the King* (33), *Aunt Sally* (34), *Me and Marlborough* (36), *The Imperfect Lady* (US) (37), *Take My Tip* (38), *Under Your Hat* (40), then concentrated for a long period on stage work; *The L-shaped Room* (62), *Those Magnificent Men in Their Flying Machines* (65), *The Wrong Box* (66), etc. Makes occasional TV appearances. Published autobiography 1953: *Cicely*.

courtroom scenes have been the suspenseful saving grace of more films than can be counted; and they also figure in some of the best films ever made.
British courts best preserve the ancient aura of the law; among the films they have figured in are *London Belongs to Me*, *The Paradine Case*, *Eight o'Clock Walk*, *Life for Ruth*, *Twenty-one Days*, *Brothers in Law*, *The Winslow Boy*, *Witness for the Prosecution*, *The Blind Goddess* and *The Dock Brief*. The last four are based on stage plays, as are the American *Madame X*, *Counsellor at Law*, and *The Trial of Mary Dugan*. Other American films depending heavily on courtroom denouements include *They Won't Believe Me*, *The Unholy Three*, *The Mouthpiece*, *Boomerang*, *They Won't Forget*, *The Missing Juror*, *Trial*, *The Young Savages*, *The Criminal Code*, *To Kill*

a Mockingbird, *Criminal Lawyer*, *The People Against O'Hara*, **The Lady**
from Shanghai, *Twilight of Honour*, *An American Tragedy* (and its
remake *A Place in the Sun*), the several Perry Mason films, and *Young
Mr Lincoln*. These, even the last-named, were fictional: genuine cases
were reconstructed in *I Want to Live*, *Cell 2555 Death Row*, *Compulsion*,
Inherit the Wind, *Dr Ehrlich's Magic Bullet*, *The Witches of Salem*, *The
Trials of Oscar Wilde*, *Judgment at Nuremberg*, *The Life of Emile Zola*,
Dr Crippen, *Captain Kidd*, *Landru* and *The Case of Charles Peace*.
Comedy courtroom scenes have appeared in *I'm No Angel*, *Mr
Deeds Goes to Town*, *You Can't Take It With You*, *Roxie Hart*, *My
Learned Friend*, *Adam's Rib*, *Pickwick Papers*, *Brothers in Law*, *Star*, and
A Pair of Briefs.

Films in which special interest has centred on the jury include
Twelve Angry Men, *Murder* (*Enter Sir John*), *Perfect Strangers* (*Too
Dangerous to Love*), *Justice Est Faite* and *The Monster and the Girl*
(in which the criminal brain inside the gorilla murders one by
one the jurors at his trial). Ghostly juries figured in *All That
Money Can Buy* and *The Remarkable Andrew*. The judge has been the
key figure in *Indian Summer* (*The Judge Steps Out*), *Talk of the Town*,
The Bachelor and the Bobbysoxer, and *Destry Rides Again*; and we are
constantly being promised a film of Henry Cecil's *No Bail for the
Judge*. *Anatomy of a Murder* remains the only film in which a real
judge (Joseph E. Welch) has played a fictional one. A lady
barrister (Anna Neagle) had the leading role in *The Man Who
Wouldn't Talk*.

Specialized courts were seen in *M* (convened by criminals),
Saint Joan and *The Hunchback of Notre Dame* (church courts), *Black
Legion* (Ku Klux Klan), *The Devil's Disciple* (18th-century military
court), *Kind Hearts and Coronets* (a court of the House of Lords),
The Wreck of the Mary Deare (mercantile), *Cone of Silence* (civil
aviation), *A Tale of Two Cities* and *The Scarlet Pimpernel* (French
Revolutionary courts). Courts in other countries were shown in
The Lady in Question, *The Count of Monte Cristo*, *Crack in the Mirror*,
A Flea in Her Ear, *La Verité*, and *Can Can* (French); *The Purple
Heart* (Japanese); *The Fall of the Roman Empire* (ancient Roman);
The Spy Who Came in from the Cold (East German); and *Shoeshine*
(Italian). Coroners' courts were featured in *Inquest*, *My Learned
Friend* and *Rebecca*.

Courts martial figured largely in *The Caine Mutiny*, *Time Limit*,
The Man in the Middle, *Across the Pacific*, *The Rack*, *Carrington VC* and
The Court Martial of Billy Mitchell. There is also a TV series called
Court Martial (*Counsellors at War* in the US).

Heavenly courts were convened in *A Matter of Life and Death*,
Outward Bound and *The Flight That Disappeared*; while other fantasy
courts appeared in *Rashomon*, *Morgan*, *One-Way Pendulum*, *Alice in
Wonderland*, *The Balcony*, *The Wonderful World of the Brothers Grimm*,
The Trial, *All That Money Can Buy*, and *The Remarkable Andrew*. The

Cousteau, Jacques-Yves

court in *Planet of the Apes* is perhaps best classed as prophetic, along with that in *1984*.

TV series based on trials and lawyers include *The Law and Mr Jones, Harrigan and Son, Sam Benedict, The Trials of O'Brien, Perry Mason, Arrest and Trial, The Defenders* and *The Verdict Is Yours*. In Britain, *Boyd Q.C., On Trial* and *In Court Today* were also popular.

COUSTEAU, JACQUES-YVES (1910–). French underwater explorer and documentarist: *The Silent World* (56), *World Without Sun* (64), etc.

COUTARD, RAOUL (1924–). French cinematographer. *Ramuntcho* (50), *À Bout de Souffle* (59), *Shoot the Pianist* (60), *Lola* (60), *Jules et Jim* (61), *Vivre Sa Vie* (61), *Les Carabiniers* (63), *Silken Skin* (63), *Pierrot Le Fou* (65), *Made in USA* (66), *Sailor from Gibraltar* (66), *The. Bride Wore Black* (67), etc.

THE COVERED WAGON (US 1923). A big-scale pioneer Western which, though it now seems tame, did much to establish the form. Directed by James Cruze, photographed by Karl Brown, edited by Dorothy Arzner, written by Jack Cunningham from a novel by Emerson Hough.

COVER GIRL (US 1944). A zippy Technicolor entertainment which, it is sometimes claimed, heralded the rebirth of the American musical; it certainly gave Gene Kelly his biggest step forward. With Rita Hayworth, Phil Silvers; directed by Charles Vidor.

COWAN, JEROME (1897–). American character actor with an easy manner. In films from 1936 (*Beloved Enemy*: out of character as a fanatic Irishman). Has played hundreds of supporting roles, typically in *The Maltese Falcon* (41) as the detective killed while searching for the mysterious Floyd Thursby; played the lead in *Crime by Night* (43), *Find the Blackmailer* (44). Recently graduated from jealous rivals to executives, from lawyers to judges. *Claudia and David* (46), *The Unfaithful* (47), *Miracle on 34th Street* (48), *June Bride* (48), *The Fountainhead* (49), *Young Man with a Horn* (50), *Dallas* (51), *The System* (53), *Visit to a Small Planet* (60), *Frankie and Johnny* (65), *The Gnome-Mobile* (67), many others. Latterly much on TV, especially in series *The Tab Hunter Show* (60), *Tycoon* (64).

COWAN, LESTER (c. 1905–). American producer from 1934. *My Little Chickadee* (39), *Ladies in Retirement* (41), *The Story of G.I. Joe* (44), *Main Street to Broadway* (52), etc.

COWAN, MAURICE (c. 1900–). British producer of mainly routine films: *Derby Day* (52), *Turn the Key Softly* (55), *The Gypsy and the Gentleman* (57), etc. Former journalist.

COWARD, NOËL (1899–   ). British actor-writer-composer-director, the bright young man of the 20s show business world. First film appearance in *Hearts of the World* (18), next *The Scoundrel* (34) (in Hollywood). Later acted in *In Which We Serve* (42) (also w, p, d), *The Astonished Heart* (50), *Our Man in Havana* (59), *Surprise Package* (61), *Paris When It Sizzles* (63), *Bunny Lake Is Missing* (65), *The Italian Job* (69), etc. Films which have been made from his plays include *Cavalcade, Bitter Sweet, Private Lives, Design for Living, Blithe Spirit, This Happy Breed, Brief Encounter*, etc. Special Academy Award 1941 'for his outstanding production achievement *In Which We Serve*'.

COWL, JANE (1890–1950). American leading stage actress who made very few film appearances: *The Garden of Lies* (15), *The Spreading Dawn* (17), *Once More My Darling* (49), *No Man of Her Own* (49), *The Secret Fury* (50), *Payment on Demand* (50).

COX, VIVIAN (1915–   ). British producer. *Father Brown* (54), *The Prisoner* (55), *Bachelor of Hearts* (58), etc. Has also written screenplays.

COX, WALLY (1924–   ). American comic actor, usually seen as the bespectacled, weedy character he played in the TV series *Mr Peepers* (52–55) and *Hiram Holliday* (56). Films include *Spencer's Mountain* (62), *Fate Is the Hunter* (64), *Morituri* (65), *The Bedford Incident* (65), *A Guide for the Married Man* (67).

CRABBE, BUSTER (1907–   ) (Clarence Linden Crabbe). American athlete who became leading man of 'B' pictures. *King of the Jungle* (33), *Nevada* (36), *Flash Gordon's Trip to Mars* (38), *Buck Rogers* (39), *Queen of Broadway* (43), *Caged Fury* (48), *Gunfighters of Abilene* (59), *Arizona Raiders* (65), many others. TV series: *Captain Gallant* (55). Now markets swimming pools.

CRABTREE, ARTHUR (1900–   ). British director, former cameraman. *Madonna of the Seven Moons* (44), *They Were Sisters* (45), *Dear Murderer* (46), *Caravan* (46), *The Calendar* (48), *Lili Marlene* (50), *Hindle Wakes* (52), *The Wedding of Lili Marlene* (53), *West of Suez* (57), *Morning Call* (58), *Horrors of the Black Museum* (59), etc. Since 1954 has been directing TV films.

CRAIG, JAMES (1912–   ) (James Meador). American leading man, usually the good-natured but tough outdoor type. Varied early experience. *Thunder Trail* (debut) (37), *The Buccaneer* (38), *The Man They Could Not Hang* (39), *Zanzibar* (40), *Kitty Foyle* (40), *All That Money Can Buy* (the 'Faust' role, and his best) (41), *Valley of the Sun* (41), *The Omaha Trail* (42), *The Human Comedy* (43), *Lost Angel* (43), *Kismet* (44), *Our Vines Have Tender Grapes* (45), *Boys' Ranch* (45), *Little Mister Jim* (46), *Northwest Stampede* (48),

Craig, Michael

> *Side Street* (50), *Drums in the Deep South* (51), *Hurricane Smith* (52), *Fort Vengeance* (53), *While the City Sleeps* (56), *Four Fast Guns* (59), *The Hired Gun* (67), many others.

CRAIG, MICHAEL (1928–) (Michael Gregson). British light leading man, a former crowd artist groomed by the Rank Organization; latterly attempting more ambitious roles. *Malta Story* (53), *The Love Lottery* (54), *Yield to the Night* (55), *House of Secrets* (56), *High Tide at Noon* (57), *Campbell's Kingdom* (58), *The Silent Enemy* (58), *Nor the Moon by Night* (58), *Sea of Sand* (59), *Sapphire* (59), *Upstairs and Downstairs* (59), *The Angry Silence* (59), *Cone of Silence* (60), *Doctor in Love* (60), *Mysterious Island* (61), *Payroll* (61), *A Pair of Briefs* (62), *Life for Ruth* (62), *The Iron Maiden* (62), *Stolen Hours* (63), *Of a Thousand Delights* (*Vaghe Stella Dell'Orsa*) (65), *Life at the Top* (65), *Modesty Blaise* (66), *Star* (68), *The Royal Hunt of the Sun* (69), etc.

CRAIG, WENDY (1934–). British stage actress who has filmed in *The Mind Benders* (63), *The Servant* (63), *The Nanny* (65), *Just Like a Woman* (66), *I'll Never Forget Whatshisname* (67), etc. TV series: *Not in Front of the Children* (67–69).

CRAIGIE, JILL (1914–). British documentary director: *The Way We Live* (46), *Blue Scar* (48), etc. Scenarist: *The Million Pound Note* (51), *Windom's Way* (57), etc.

CRAIN, JEANNE (1925–). American leading lady, former model. *Home in Indiana* (debut) (44), *In the Meantime, Darling* (44), *Winged Victory* (44), *State Fair* (45), *Leave Her to Heaven* (45), *Centennial Summer* (46), *Margie* (47), *A Letter to Three Wives* (48), *Lady Windermere's Fan* (49), *Pinky* (49), *Cheaper by the Dozen* (50), *Take Care of My Little Girl* (51), *The Model and the Marriage Broker* (51), *People Will Talk* (51), *Belles on Their Toes* (52), *Full House* (52), *Vicki* (52), *Duel in the Jungle* (54), *Man without a Star* (55), *The Second Greatest Sex* (55), *Gentlemen Marry Brunettes* (55), *The Fastest Gun Alive* (56), *The Joker Is Wild* (57), *Guns of the Timberland* (60), *Madison Avenue* (61), *It Started in Tokyo* (*Twenty Plus Two*) (62), *Queen of the Nile* (It.) (63), *Fifty-two Miles to Terror* (66), etc.

crane shot. A high-angle shot in which the camera travels up, down or laterally while mounted on a travelling crane.

THE CRANES ARE FLYING (USSR 1957). The simple but moving story of a wartime Moscow romance, distinguished by Mikhail Kalatozov's direction, Urusevsky's mobile camerawork, and the performance of Tatiana Samoilova.

CRAVAT, NICK (1911–). Small, agile American actor, once Burt Lancaster's circus partner. Appeared with him in *The Flame and the Arrow* (51), *The Crimson Pirate* (52), *Run Silent, Run Deep* (59);

also in *King Richard and the Crusaders* (54), *Three-Ring Circus* (55), *Kiss Me Deadly* (55), *Davy Crockett* (56), *The Scalphunters* (68), etc.

CRAVEN, FRANK (1875–1945). American stage character actor and playwright, most memorable on screen as the kindly 'stage manager' in *Our Town* (40) (his stage role). Also in *Barbary Coast* (35), *Miracles for Sale* (39), *City for Conquest* (40), *The Richest Man in Town* (41), *Keeper of the Flame* (43), *Through Different Eyes* (43), *The Right to Live* (45), etc.

CRAWFORD, ANDREW (1917–   ). Scottish actor, in films from 1946 (*The Brothers*) as hearty, good-humoured young chaps. After a gap in the 50s, came back as character actor: occasional films (e.g. *Shadow of the Cat* [61]) but more usually TV.

CRAWFORD, ANNE (1920–1956) (Imelda Crawford). British leading lady with gentle, humorous personality. *They Flew Alone* (debut) (42), *The Peterville Diamond* (42), *The Dark Tower* (42), *The Hundred-Pound Window* (43), *Millions Like Us* (43), *Two Thousand Women* (44), *They Were Sisters* (45), *Caravan* (46), *Bedelia* (46), *Master of Bankdam* (47), *Daughter of Darkness* (48), *The Blind Goddess* (48), *It's Hard To Be Good* (49), *Tony Draws a Horse* (49), *Bonaventure* (US) (50), *Street Corner* (52), *Knights of the Round Table* (53), *Mad about Men* (54), etc.

CRAWFORD, BRODERICK (1910–   ). Beefy American character actor, son of Helen Broderick; began by playing comic stooges and gangsters, with acting performances coming later; after a long spell in TV his popularity waned. *Woman Chases Man* (debut) (37), *The Real Glory* (39), *Eternally Yours* (39), *When the Daltons Rode* (40), *The Black Cat* (41), *Butch Minds the Baby* (42), *Broadway* (42), *Sin Town* (42), etc.; war service; *The Runaround* (46), *Slave Girl* (47), *The Flame* (47), *The Time of Your Life* (48), *Anna Lucasta* (49), *All the King's Men* (AA) (50), *Born Yesterday* (51), *Lone Star* (52), *Scandal Sheet* (52), *Last of the Comanches* (52), *Stop You're Killing Me* (52), *Night People* (54), *Human Desire* (54), *Down Three Dark Streets* (54), *New York Confidential* (55), *Il Bidone* (*The Swindlers*) (55), *Not as a Stranger* (55), *The Fastest Gun Alive* (56), *The Decks Ran Red* (58), *Up from the Beach* (65), *The Oscar* (66), *The Texican* (66), *Red Tomahawk* (66), etc. TV series: *Highway Patrol* (55–59), *King of Diamonds* (64).

†CRAWFORD, JOAN (1904–   ) (Lucille le Sueur; known for a time as Billie Cassin). American leading lady; one of Hollywood's most durable stars, first as a flapper of the jazz age and later as the personification of the career girl and the repressed older woman. Few of her films have been momentous, but she has always been 'box office', especially with women fans, who liked to watch her suffering in mink. *Pretty Ladies* (debut) (25), *The Only Thing* (25),

Crawford, Michael

Old Clothes (25), *Sally, Irene and Mary* (25), *The Boob* (25), *Paris* (25), *Tramp Tramp Tramp* (26), *The Taxi Dancer* (27), *Winners of the Wilderness* (27), *The Understanding Heart* (27), *The Unknown* (27), *Twelve Miles Out* (27), *Spring Fever* (27), *West Point* (28), *Rose Marie* (28), *Across to Singapore* (28), *The Law of the Range* (28), *Four Walls* (28), *Our Dancing Daughters* (28), *Dream of Love* (28), *The Duke Steps Out* (29), *Our Modern Maidens* (29), *Hollywood Revue* (29), *Untamed* (29), *Montana Moon* (30), *Our Blushing Brides* (30), *Paid* (30), *Dance Fools Dance* (31), *Laughing Sinners* (31), *This Modern Age* (31), *Possessed* (31), *Letty Lynton* (32), *Grand Hotel* (32), *Rain* (32), *Today We Live* (33), *Dancing Lady* (33), *Sadie McKee* (34), *Chained* (34), *Forsaking All Others* (34), *No More Ladies* (35), *I Live My Life* (35), *The Gorgeous Hussy* (36), *Love on the Run* (36), *The Last of Mrs Cheyney* (37), *The Bride Wore Red* (37), *Mannequin* (38), *The Shining Hour* (38), *Ice Follies* (39), *The Women* (39), *Strange Cargo* (40), *Susan and God* (40), *A Woman's Face* (41), *When Ladies Meet* (41), *They All Kissed the Bride* (42), *Reunion in France* (42), *Above Suspicion* (43), *Hollywood Canteen* (44), *Mildred Pierce* (AA) (45), *Humoresque* (46), *Possessed* (47), *Daisy Kenyon* (47), *Flamingo Road* (49), *The Damned Don't Cry* (50), *Harriet Craig* (50), *Goodbye My Fancy* (51), *This Woman Is Dangerous* (52), *Sudden Fear* (52), *Torch Song* (53), *Johnny Guitar* (54), *The Female on the Beach* (55), *Queen Bee* (55), *Autumn Leaves* (56), *The Story of Esther Costello* (GB) (57), *The Best of Everything* (59), *Whatever Happened to Baby Jane* (62), *The Caretakers* (63), *Straitjacket* (64), *I Saw What You Did* (65), *The Karate Killers* (67), *Berserk* (GB) (67), *Trog* (70). Published autobiography 1962: *A Portrait of Joan.*

CRAWFORD, MICHAEL (1942–   ). Lively young British leading man, also on stage and TV. Appeared as juvenile in children's films such as *Soap Box Derby* and *Blow Your Own Trumpet.* Later: *Two Living, One Dead* (62), *The War Lover* (63), *Two Left Feet* (63), *The Knack* (65), *A Funny Thing Happened on the Way to the Forum* (66), *The Jokers* (66), *How I Won the War* (67), *Hello Dolly* (69), *The Games* (69), *Hello and Goodbye* (70), etc. TV series: *Sir Francis Drake* (62).

crazy comedy has two distinct meanings in the cinema. On one hand it encompasses the Marx Brothers, *Hellzapoppin* and custard pies; for this see *Slapstick.* On the other it means the new kind of comedy which came in during the 30s, with seemingly adult people behaving in what society at the time thought was a completely irresponsible way. The Capra comedies, for instance, are vaguely 'agin' the government', upholding Mr Deeds' right to give away his money and play the tuba, the Vanderhofs' right not to work, and Mr Smith's right to be utterly honest. This endearing eccentricity permeated many of the funniest and most modern comedies of the period. William Powell and Myrna Loy in *The Thin Man* were a married couple who upheld none of the domestic virtues. In *Libelled Lady* four top stars behaved like low comedians. In *My Man Godfrey* a rich man pretended to be a tramp and so reformed a party of the idle rich who found him during a 'scavenger hunt'. *Theodora Goes Wild*, *I Met Him in Paris* and *Easy Living* had what we would now call 'kooky' heroines. In *True Confession* Carole Lombard confessed to a murder she hadn't done, and was told by John Barrymore that she would 'fry'; in *Nothing Sacred* she pretended to be dying of an obscure disease and was socked on the jaw by Fredric March. Hal Roach introduced comedy ghosts, played by two of Hollywood's most sophisticated stars, in *Topper*, and followed it up with two sequels as well as three individual and endearingly lunatic comedies called *The House-keeper's Daughter* (a battle of fireworks), *Turnabout* (a husband and wife exchange bodies) and *Road Show* (an asylum escapee runs a travelling circus). *The Awful Truth* had no respect for marriage; *You Can't Take It With You* had no respect for law, business, or the American way of life. A film called *Bringing Up Baby* turned out to be about a leopard and a brontosaurus bone; *Boy Meets Girl* was a farcical send-up of Hollywood; and *A Slight Case of Murder* had more corpses than characters. *The Women* had its all-female cast fighting like tiger-cats. *Road to Singapore* began as a romantic comedy but degenerated into snippets from Joe Miller's gag-book; and any Preston Sturges film was likely to have pauses while the smart and witty hero and heroine fell into a pool. In *Here Comes Mr Jordan* the hero was dead after five minutes or so and spent the rest of the film trying to get his body back.

The genre was by this time well-established, and although America's entry into the war modified it somewhat it has remained fashionable and popular ever since. A 1966 film like *Morgan* may seem rather startling, but in fact it goes little further in its genial anarchy than *You Can't Take It With You*; only the method of expression is different. What modern crazy comedies lack is the clear pattern which produced so many little masterpieces within a few years.

THE CRAZY GANG. Three pairs of British music hall comedians made up this famous group which was enormously popular on stage from 1935 till 1962. Bud Flanagan (qv) and Chesney Allen (qv); Jimmy Nervo (1890–) and Teddy Knox (c. 1898–); Charlie Naughton (1887–) and Jimmy Gold (1886–1967). The Crazy Gang films (apart from a few in which the teams appeared separately) were: *OK for Sound* (37), *Alf's Button Afloat* (38), *The Frozen Limits* (39), *Gasbags* (40), *Life Is a Circus* (54).

THE CREATURE FROM THE BLACK LAGOON (US 1954). A poor horror film which spawned one of Universal's more inept monsters, a chap in a rubber suit who was called the gill man but remained singularly unimpressive and restricted in two sequels: *Revenge of the Creature* (55) and *The Creature Walks Among Us* (56).

credits. Titles at beginning or end of film (nowadays very often five minutes *after* beginning) listing the names of the creative talents concerned.

creeping title. One which moves up (or sometimes across) the screen at reading pace. Also known as *roller title*.

†CREGAR, LAIRD (1916–1944). American character actor who had a tragically brief but impressive career in a rich variety of roles: *Hudson's Bay* (40), *Hot Spot* (41), *This Gun for Hire* (42), *Charley's Aunt* (42), *Joan of Paris* (42), *Rings on Her Fingers* (42), *Ten Gentlemen from West Point* (42), *The Black Swan* (43), *Hello Frisco Hello* (43), *Heaven Can Wait* (as the devil) (43), *Holy Matrimony* (43), *The Lodger* (as Jack the Ripper) (44), *Hangover Square* (44).

CREHAN, JOSEPH (1884–1966). American character actor, often as sheriff or cop. *Identity Parade* (34), *Boulder Dam* (36), *Happy Landing* (38), *Stanley and Livingstone* (39), *Texas* (42), *Phantom Lady* (44), *The Foxes of Harrow* (48), *Red Desert* (54), many others.

CRENNA, RICHARD (1926–   ). American leading man, formerly boy actor on radio and TV. *Red Skies of Montana* (52), *It Grows on Trees* (52), *Over Exposed* (56), *John Goldfarb Please Come Home* (64), *Made in Paris* (65), *The Sand Pebbles* (66), *Wait Until Dark* (67), *Star* (68), *Marooned* (69), etc. TV series: *Our Miss Brooks* (52–55), *The Real McCoys* (57–63), *Slattery's People* (64–65).

CREWS, LAURA HOPE (1880–1942). American stage actress who played character parts in several films. *New Morals for Old* (32), *Escapade* (35), *Camille* (36), *Thanks for the Memory* (38), *Gone with the Wind* (as Aunt Pittypat) (39), *The Bluebird* (40), *One Foot in Heaven* (42), etc.

CRIBBINS, BERNARD (1928–   ). British comedy character actor and recording star. Played light support roles in several films: *Two Way Stretch* (60), *The Girl on the Boat* (62), *The Wrong Arm of the Law* (62), *Carry On Jack* (63), *Crooks in Cloisters* (64), *She* (65), *The Sandwich Man* (66), *Daleks' Invasion Earth 2150 A.D.* (66), etc.

CRICHTON, CHARLES (1910–   ). British director, former editor. *For Those in Peril* (44), *Dead of Night* (part) (45), *Painted Boats* (45), *Hue and Cry* (47), *Against the Wind* (47), *Another Shore* (48), *Train of Events* (49), *Dance Hall* (50), *The Lavender Hill Mob* (51), *Hunted* (52), *The Titfield Thunderbolt* (53), *The Love Lottery* (54), *The Divided Heart* (54), *The Man in the Sky* (56), *Law and Disorder* (57), *Floods of*

Fear (also wrote) (58), *The Battle of the Sexes* (59), *The Boy Who Stole a Million* (60), *The Third Secret* (63), *He Who Rides a Tiger* (65), etc. Latterly directed many episodes of TV series.

CRIME DOES NOT PAY. A series of 48 two-reelers, made by MGM between 1935 and 1948 in a very imitable but entertaining hard-hitting style. The first, called *Buried Loot*, introduced Robert Taylor; other budding stars were featured later, and the series proved a valuable training ground for directors, including Jules Dassin and Fred Zinnemann.

criminals—real-life ones—whose careers have been featured in films include Burke and Hare (*The Flesh and the Fiends*), Cagliostro (*Black Magic*), Al Capone (*Little Caesar, The Scarface Mob, Al Capone*), Caryl Chessman (*Cell 2455 Death Row*), Crippen (*Dr Crippen*), John Wilkes Booth (*Prince of Players*), Jack the Ripper (*The Lodger, A Study in Terror, Jack the Ripper,* many others), Landru (*Landru, Bluebeard, Monsieur Verdoux, Bluebeard's Ten Honeymoons*), Leopold and Loeb (*Rope* and *Compulsion*), Charlie Peace (*The Case of Charles Peace*), Dick Turpin (qv), Jesse James (qv), Vidocq (*A Scandal in Paris*), Robert Stroud (*Birdman of Alcatraz*), Barbara Graham (*I Want To Live*), Rasputin (qv), Eddie Chapman (*Triple Cross*), and the various American public enemies of the 30s: *Bonnie and Clyde, Dillinger, Baby Face Nelson,* etc. The clinical 60s also brought accounts of the motiveless murderers of *In Cold Blood* and of *The Boston Strangler*. Criminal movements have been very well explored in fictional films, especially the Mafia, the Thugs, Murder Inc. and the racketeers and bootleggers of the 20s.

THE CRIME DOCTOR. The hero of this Hollywood-concocted series was a criminal restored by a brain operation to the sober pursuance of his former profession as a doctor. That was in 1943: once the series got under way the premise was forgotten and Warner Baxter was simply a psychiatrist whose involvement in and solution of various complicated crimes was both unlikely and (usually) accidental. The series died with Baxter in 1951.

THE CRIME OF MONSIEUR LANGE (France 1935). An influential satirical fantasy, written by Jacques Prevert and others, directed by Jean Renoir; about workers who take over a factory when the boss absconds.

CRIME WITHOUT PASSION (US 1934). A melodrama made in New York by writer-directors Ben Hecht and Charles Macarthur, who had hopes of founding a new school of film-making; but the result, despite Claude Rains, was a plain and uncommercial though well-made account of an advocate who murders a young girl and suffers the consequences.

CRISP, DONALD (1882–   ). Distinguished British screen actor, in America from 1906. Worked as assistant to D. W. Griffith and others; later directed many silents including *The Mark of Zorro*, *Don Q Son of Zorro* and *The Black Pirate*. As actor: *Home Sweet Home* (14), *The Birth of a Nation* (14), *Broken Blossoms* (19), *Don Q Son of Zorro* (25), *The Viking* (28), *The Return of Sherlock Holmes* (29), *Burnt Offering* (32), *The Little Minister* (34), *Mutiny on the Bounty* (35), *Parnell* (37), *Jezebel* (38), *Wuthering Heights* (39), *How Green Was My Valley* (AA) (41), *Dr Jekyll and Mr Hyde* (41), *Lassie Come Home* (43), *The Uninvited* (44), *National Velvet* (44), *The Valley of Decision* (45), *Ramrod* (47), *Challenge to Lassie* (49), *Bright Leaf* (50), *Prince Valiant* (54), *The Man from Laramie* (55), *A Dog of Flanders* (60), *Greyfriars Bobby* (60), *Spencer's Mountain* (63), many others.

CRISTAL, LINDA (1936–   ) (Victoria Maya). Mexican leading lady, in Hollywood from 1956. *Comanche* (56), *The Fiend Who Walked the West* (58), *The Perfect Furlough* (58), *Cry Tough* (59), *The Alamo* (60), *Panic in the City* (68), etc. TV series: *The High Chaparral* (67–69).

CROCKETT, DAVY (1786–1836). American trapper and Indian scout who became a legendary hero and a politician before dying at the Alamo (qv). He has been portrayed on film by George Montgomery (*Indian Scout*), Fess Parker (*Davy Crockett, Davy Crockett and the River Pirates*), Arthur Hunnicutt (*The Last Command*) and John Wayne (*The Alamo*), among others.

CROMWELL, JOHN (1888–   ). Distinguished American director, former stage actor and producer, in Hollywood from the late 20s. *The Racket* (28), *Burlesque* (30), *Street of Chance* (31), *Rich Man's Folly* (32), *Ann Vickers* (33), *Of Human Bondage* (34), *Little Lord Fauntleroy* (36), *The Prisoner of Zenda* (37), *Algiers* (38), *Abe Lincoln in Illinois* (39), *So Ends Our Night* (41), *Son of Fury* (42), *Since You Went Away* (44), *The Enchanted Cottage* (44), *Anna and the King of Siam* (46), *Dead Reckoning* (47), *Caged* (50), *The Racket* (51), *The Company She Keeps* (51), *The Goddess* (58), others.

CROMWELL, RICHARD (1910–1960) (Roy Radebaugh). American leading man, gentle hero of early sound films, including *Tol'able David* (31), *Emma* (32), *Tom Brown of Culver* (33), *Lives of a Bengal Lancer* (35), *Poppy* (36), *Jezebel* (38), *Young Mr Lincoln* (39), *Riot Squad* (42), *Baby Face Morgan* (42), *Bungalow 13* (48), etc.

CRONIN, A. J. (1896–   ). British novelist, former doctor. Works filmed include *Grand Canary* (34), *The Citadel* (38), *The Stars Look Down* (39), *Shining Victory* (41), *Hatter's Castle* (41), *The Keys of the Kingdom* (44), *The Green Years* (46), *The Spanish Gardener* (56). TV series: *Dr Finlay's Casebook*.

CRONJAGER, EDWARD (1904–1960). American cinematographer. *The Quarterback* (26), *The Virginian* (30), *Cimarron* (31), *Roberta* (35), *The Gorilla* (39), *Hot Spot* (41), *Heaven Can Wait* (43), *Canyon Passage* (46), *The House by the River* (50), *Treasure of the Golden Condor* (53), *Beyond the Twelve-Mile Reef* (53), many others.

CRONYN, HUME (1911–   ). Slightly-built Canadian actor, long on American stage and screen. Married to Jessica Tandy. *Shadow of a Doubt* (film debut) (43), *Lifeboat* (43), *The Seventh Cross* (44), *The Green Years* (46), *Brute Force* (47), *People Will Talk* (50), *Sunrise at Campobello* (60), *Cleopatra* (62), *There Was a Crooked Man* (69), etc.

CROSBY, BING (1904–   ) (Harry Lillis Crosby). American crooner, popular throughout the 30s, 40s and 50s. First sang with bands: film debut *King of Jazz* (30). Later: *The Big Broadcast of 1932*, *College Humour* (33), *We're Not Dressing* (34), *Mississippi* (35), *Anything Goes* (36), *Rhythm on the Range* (37), *Pennies from Heaven* (38), *Doctor Rhythm* (38), *Sing You Sinners* (38), *East Side of Heaven* (39), *Paris Honeymoon* (39), *Road to Singapore* (beginning his amiable feud with Bob Hope) (39), *If I Had My Way* (40), *Rhythm on the River* (40), *Road to Zanzibar* (41), *Birth of the Blues* (41), *Road to Morocco* (42), *Holiday Inn* (42), *Dixie* (43), *Star-Spangled Rhythm* (43), *Going My Way* (AA) (44), *The Bells of St Mary* (45), *Road to Utopia* (45), *Blue Skies* (46), *Welcome Stranger* (47), *Road to Rio* (47), *The Emperor Waltz* (48), *A Yankee at King Arthur's Court* (49), *Mr Music* (50), *Riding High* (50), *Here Comes the Groom* (51), *Just for You* (52), *Road to Bali* (52), *Little Boy Lost* (53), *White Christmas* (54), *The Country Girl* (first dramatic role) (55), *High Society* (56), *Man on Fire* (57), *Say One for Me* (59), *High Time* (60), *Road to Hong Kong* (GB) (62), *Stagecoach* (66), others. TV series: *The Bing Crosby Show* (64). Published autobiography 1953: *Call Me Lucky*.

CROSBY, BOB (1913–   ). American band leader, brother of Bing. Has appeared as guest in many films.

CROSBY, FLOYD (c. 1900–   ). American cinematographer who has worked on everything from documentary to horror thrillers. *Tabu* (AA) (31), *The River* (37), *Of Men and Music* (50), *Man in the Dark* (53), *The Naked Street* (55), *Shack Out on 101* (55), *Naked Paradise* (56), *The Screaming Skull* (58), *The Fall of the House of Usher* (60), *The Pit and the Pendulum* (61), *Pajama Party* (65), *Fireball 500* (66), etc.

CROSET, PAULE: see under CORDAY, PAULA.

CROSLAND, ALAN (1894–1936). American director, in films from 1914. Mainly remembered for *Don Juan* (26) (first film with synchronized music) and *The Jazz Singer* (27) (first film with talking and songs). Also: *Under the Red Robe* (24), *The Beloved Rogue* (27), *On with the*

Show (29), *General Crack* (30), *Weekends Only* (32), *Massacre* (34), *The Great Impersonation* (35), etc.

CROSS, ERIC (1902–   ). British cinematographer. *Make Up* (37), *Song of Freedom* (38), *The First of the Few* (42), *Don't Take It To Heart* (44), *The Chance of a Lifetime* (49), *Hunted* (52), *The Kidnappers* (53), *Private's Progress* (55), *The One That Got Away* (57), *Behind the Curtain* (60), many others.

cross cutting. Interlinking fragments of two or more separate sequences so that they appear to be taking place at the same time.

CROSSFIRE (US 1947). First of the American racialist dramas, a tough adult thriller about the murder of a Jew. (In Richard Brooks' original novel it was a homosexual.) Adapted by John Paxton, directed by Edward Dmytryk, with Robert Ryan as the anti-Semite and Robert Young as the patient cop.

THE CROWD (US 1928). King Vidor directed and co-wrote this early experiment in social realism, an account of the drab life of a city clerk. James Murray and Eleanor Boardman starred. In 1933 Vidor made a sequel, *Our Daily Bread*, showing his couple leaving the town for a farming community: Tom Keene and Karen Morley were the stars.

CROWLEY, PAT (1933–   ). American leading lady of the 50s, former child model. *Forever Female* (debut) (53), *Red Garters* (54), *Hollywood or Bust* (56), *There's Always Tomorrow* (57), *The Scarface Mob* (60), etc. TV series: *Please Don't Eat the Daisies* (65–66).

CRUICKSHANK, ANDREW (1907–   ). Scottish stage actor who has appeared in a number of films, usually as doctor or judge. Debut *Auld Lang Syne* (37); later in *The Mark of Cain* (47), *Paper Orchid* (49), *Your Witness* (50), *The Cruel Sea* (53), *Richard III* (56), *Innocent Sinners* (58), *Kidnapped* (60), *There Was a Crooked Man* (60), *El Cid* (61), *Murder Most Foul* (64), etc. A national figure on TV as Dr Cameron in *Dr Finlay's Casebook*.

CRUTCHLEY, ROSALIE (1921–   ). Striking, lean-featured British stage actress who makes occasional film appearances. *Take My Life* (debut) (47), *Give Us This Day* (49), *Quo Vadis* (51), *Make Me an Offer* (55), *The Spanish Gardener* (56), *A Tale of Two Cities* (58), *Beyond This Place* (59), *Sons and Lovers* (60), *Freud* (62), *The Girl in the Headlines* (63), *Behold a Pale Horse* (64), etc.

CRUZE, JAMES (1884–1942) (Jens Cruz Bosen). Danish-American director best remembered for *The Covered Wagon* (23). His other films include *Dr Jekyll and Mr Hyde* (12), *Million Dollar Mystery* (14), *Valley of the Giants* (19), *Ruggles of Red Gap* (23), *Pony Express* (25), *Old Ironsides* (26), *The Great Gabbo* (29), *If I Had a Million* (part) (32), *David Harum* (34), *I Cover the Waterfront* (35), *Sutter's Gold* (37), *Gangs of New York* (38), etc.

CUGAT, XAVIER (c. 1900–   ). Spanish bandleader and caricaturist, a feature of many MGM musicals of the 40s.

†CUKOR, GEORGE (1899–   ). American director, from the Broadway stage; proved to be one of Hollywood's most reliable handlers of high comedy and other literate material. *Tarnished Lady* (30), *Girls About Town* (31), *The Royal Family of Broadway* (31), *One Hour with You* (with Lubitsch) (32), *What Price Hollywood* (32), *A Bill of Divorcement* (32), *Rockabye* (32), *Our Betters* (33), *Dinner at Eight* (33), *Little Women* (33), *David Copperfield* (34), *Sylvia Scarlett* (35), *Romeo and Juliet* (36), *Camille* (36), *Holiday* (37), *Zaza* (39), *The Women* (39), *Susan and God* (40), *The Philadelphia Story* (40), *A Woman's Face* (41), *Two-Faced Woman* (41), *Her Cardboard Lover* (42), *Keeper of the Flame* (43), *Gaslight* (44), *Winged Victory* (44), *Desire Me* (co-d) (47), *A Double Life* (47), *Adam's Rib* (49), *Edward My Son* (GB) (49), *A Life of Her Own* (50), *Born Yesterday* (50), *The Model and the Marriage Broker* (52), *The Marrying Kind* (52), *Pat and Mike* (52), *The Actress* (53), *It Should Happen to You* (53), *A Star Is Born* (54), *Bhowani Junction* (56), *Les Girls* (57), *Written on the Wind* (57), *Heller in Pink Tights* (59), *Let's Make Love* (61), *My Fair Lady* (AA) (64), *Justine* (69).

CULP, ROBERT (c. 1930–   ). American leading man. *P.T.109* (62), *Bob and Carol and Ted and Alice* (69), *Laurie Lee* (70). TV series: *Trackdown* (57), *I Spy* (66–68).

CULVER, ROLAND (1900–   ). British stage actor of impeccably English types, usually comic. *77 Park Lane* (32), *Nell Gwyn* (34), *Paradise for Two* (37), *French Without Tears* (his stage role) (39), *Quiet Wedding* (40), *Night Train to Munich* (40), *Talk about Jacqueline* (42), *On Approval* (43), *Dear Octopus* (43), *Dead of Night* (45), *Wanted for Murder* (46), *To Each His Own* (US) (47), *Down to Earth* (US) (47), *The Emperor Waltz* (US) (48), *Trio* (as Somerset Maugham) (50), *The Holly and the Ivy* (54), *The Man Who Loved Redheads* (55), *Touch and Go* (57), *Bonjour Tristesse* (58), *The Yellow Rolls-Royce* (64), *A Man Could Get Killed* (65), *Fragment of Fear* (69), others.

CUMMINGS, CONSTANCE (1910–   ) (Constance Halverstadt). American stage actress, long resident in England. In films from 1931: *Movie Crazy* (US) (32), *Channel Crossing* (32), *Glamour* (34), *Looking for Trouble* (34), *Busman's Honeymoon* (40), *This England* (41), *The Foreman Went to France* (42), *Blithe Spirit* (45), *John and Julie* (55), *The Intimate Stranger* (56), *The Battle of the Sexes* (59), *Sammy Going South* (*A Man Ten Feet Tall*) (62), etc.

CUMMINGS, IRVING (1888–1959). American director, former actor; in films from 1909. *The Johnstown Flood* (26), *The Brute* (27), *In Old Arizona* (28), *Cameo Kirby* (29), *The Cisco Kid* (31), *Man Against Woman* (32), *Grand Canary* (34), *Curly Top* (35), *Girls' Dormitory* (36), *Vogues of 1938*, *Hollywood Cavalcade* (39), *The Story of Alexander Graham Bell* (39), *Lilian Russell* (40), *Down Argentine Way* (40), *That Night in Rio* (41), *Belle Starr* (41), *Louisiana Purchase* (42), *The Impatient Years* (44), *The Dolly Sisters* (45), *Double Dynamite* (51), many others.

CUMMINGS, JACK (c. 1900–   ). American producer, with MGM since 1934. Films include many musicals, e.g. *Kiss Me Kate* (53), *Seven Brides for Seven Brothers* (54).

CUMMINGS, ROBERT (1908–   ). Ever-young American light comedian and leading man. Varied stage experience: once pretended to be British actor named Blade Stanhope Conway. *So Red the Rose* (film debut) (35), *Souls at Sea* (37), *Three Smart Girls Grow Up* (39), *Spring Parade* (40), *Moon Over Miami* (41), *It Started with Eve* (41), *Saboteur* (42), *Kings Row* (serious role) (42), *You Came Along* (45), *The Lost Moment* (47), *Dial M for Murder* (54), *How to be Very Very Popular* (55), *The Carpetbaggers* (64), *Stagecoach* (66), *Promise Her Anything* (66), *Five Golden Dragons* (67), many others. Star of TV series *The Bob Cummings Show* (54–61), *My Living Doll* (64).

CUMMINS, PEGGY (1925–   ). British leading lady, former teenage star. Films include *Dr O'Dowd* (debut) (39), *The Late George Apley* (47), *Escape* (48), *My Daughter Joy* (50), *Who Goes There?* (52), *To Dorothy a Son* (54), *The March Hare* (55), *Night of the Demon* (57), *Dentist in the Chair* (60), *In the Doghouse* (62), etc.

CUNY, ALAIN (1908–   ). Tall, imposing French actor, in occasional films: *Les Visiteurs du Soir* (42), *Il Cristo Proibito* (50), *The Hunchback of Notre Dame* (56), *Les Amants* (58), *The Milky Way* (68), etc.

CURRIE, FINLAY (1878–1968). Veteran Scottish actor with stage and music-hall experience. *The Case of the Frightened Lady* (film debut) (32), *Rome Express* (32), *Edge of the World* (38), *The Bells Go Down* (42), *Great Expectations* (as Magwitch) (46), *Sleeping-Car to Trieste* (48), *Trio* (50), *Treasure Island* (50), *The Mudlark* (as John Brown) (51), *Quo Vadis* (51), *People Will Talk* (52), *Ivanhoe* (52), *Rob Roy* (53), *The End of the Road* (leading role) (54), *Make Me an Offer* (55), *Dangerous Exile* (57), *Ben Hur* (US) (59), *Kidnapped* (60), *The Fall of the Roman Empire* (64), *Who Was Maddox?* (leading role) (64), *The Battle of the Villa Fiorita* (65), many others.

CURTIS, ALAN (1909–1953) (Harold Neberroth). American leading man, and sometimes villain, of many 'B' pictures of the 40s. *Winterset* (36), *Mannequin* (38), *Hollywood Cavalcade* (39), *Buck*

Privates (Rookies) (40), *The Great Awakening* (41), *Two Tickets to London* (43), *Hitler's Madman* (43), *Phantom Lady* (44), *The Invisible Man's Revenge* (44), *The Naughty Nineties* (45), *Philo Vance's Gamble* (48), *The Masked Pirate* (50), etc.

CURTIS, TONY (1925–   ) (Bernard Schwarz). Bouncy American leading man whose range broadened considerably in the late 50s. *City Across the River* (debut) (49), *Winchester 73* (50), *The Prince Who Was a Thief* (51), *Son of Ali Baba* (52), *Houdini* (53), *The Black Shield of Falworth* (54), *So This Is Paris* (54), *The Purple Mask* (55), *Trapeze* (56), *The Midnight Story* (56), *Mister Cory* (56), *Sweet Smell of Success* (57), *The Vikings* (58), *The Defiant Ones* (58), *Some Like It Hot* (59), *Operation Petticoat* (59), *Spartacus* (60), *Who Was That Lady* (60), *The Great Impostor* (61), *The Outsider* (61), *Taras Bulba* (62), *Forty Pounds of Trouble* (63), *Wild and Wonderful* (63), *Captain Newman* (63), *Sex and the Single Girl* (64), *Goodbye Charlie* (64), *The Great Race* (65), *Boeing Boeing* (66), *Arrivederci Baby* (66), *Not with My Wife You Don't* (66), *Don't Make Waves* (67), *The Chastity Belt* (It.) (68), *The Boston Strangler* (68), *Monte Carlo or Bust* (69), *The Dubious Patriots* (70), others.

CURTIZ, MICHAEL (1888–1962) (Mihaly Kertesz). Hungarian-American director, in Hollywood since 1928 and responsible for some highly polished entertainments. *Noah's Ark* (28), *Mammy* (30), *The Mad Genius* (31), *Cabin in the Cotton* (32), *The Mystery of the Wax Museum* (32), *Twenty Thousand Years in Sing Sing* (32), *Female* (33), *British Agent* (34), *Black Fury* (35), *Captain Blood* (35), *The Walking Dead* (36), *The Charge of the Light Brigade* (36), *Kid Galahad* (37), *Four Daughters* (38), *The Adventures of Robin Hood* (co-director) (38), *Angels with Dirty Faces* (38), *Dodge City* (39), *Elizabeth and Essex* (39), *The Sea Hawk* (40), *Virginia City* (40), *Sante Fe Trail* (40), *The Sea Wolf* (41), *Mission to Moscow* (42), *Yankee Doodle Dandy* (42), *Casablanca* (AA) (42), *This Is the Army* (43), *Passage to Marseilles* (44), *Mildred Pierce* (45), *Night and Day* (46), *Life with Father* (47), *The Unsuspected* (47), *Romance on the High Seas* (48), *Young Man with a Horn* (50), *The Breaking Point* (51), *I'll See You in My Dreams* (52), *The Jazz Singer* (52), *Trouble Along the Way* (53), *The Egyptian* (54), *White Christmas* (54), *We're No Angels* (55), *The Vagabond King* (56), *The Best Things in Life Are Free* (56), *King Creole* (58), *The Adventures of Huckleberry Finn* (60), *Francis of Assisi* (60), *The Comancheros* (62), others.

CURZON, GEORGE (1896–   ). British stage actor, in occasional films from early 30s, usually in aristocratic or sinister roles. *The Impassive Footman* (32), *Lorna Doone* (35), *Young and Innocent* (37), *Sexton Blake and the Hooded Terror* (38), *Uncle Silas* (47), *Harry Black* (58), etc.

CUSACK, CYRIL (1910–   ). Diminutive Irish actor with 14 years' Abbey Theatre experience. Film debut as child 1917; as man *Odd*

Man Out (47). Later: *The Blue Lagoon* (48), *The Elusive Pimpernel* (49), *The Blue Veil* (US) (51), *Soldiers Three* (US) (51), *The Man Who Never Was* (56), *Jacqueline* (56), *The Spanish Gardener* (56), *Ill Met by Moonlight* (57), *Floods of Fear* (58), *Shake Hands with the Devil* (59), *A Terrible Beauty* (59), *The Waltz of the Toreadors* (62), *Eighty Thousand Suspects* (63), *The Spy Who Came In from the Cold* (65), *I Was Happy Here* (66), *Fahrenheit 451* (66), *The Taming of the Shrew* (67), *Oedipus the King* (67), *Galileo* (It.) (68), *David Copperfield* (69), many others.

CUSHING, PETER (1913–   ). British character actor of stage, TV and screen. His slightly fussy manner at first confined him to mild roles, but since allying himself with the Hammer horror school he has dealt firmly with monsters of all kinds. *Vigil in the Night* (US) (39), *A Chump at Oxford* (US) (40), *Hamlet* (as Osric) (48), *The Black Knight* (54), *The End of the Affair* (55), *The Curse of Frankenstein* (56), *Violent Playground* (58), *Dracula* (58), *The Mummy* (59), *The Hound of the Baskervilles* (as Sherlock Holmes) (59), *Brides of Dracula* (60), *Captain Clegg* (62), *The Gorgon* (64), *Cash On Demand* (64), *She* (65), *Dr Who and the Daleks* (65), *The Skull* (65), *The Torture Garden* (67), *Corruption* (68), *Frankenstein Must Be Destroyed* (69), many others. TV series: *Sherlock Holmes* (68).

custard pies as a comic weapon were evolved at the Keystone studio around 1915, and most silent comedians relied heavily on them. In the 30s Mack Sennett staged a splendid one for a nostalgic farce called *Keystone Hotel*. Other notable pie fighters have included Laurel and Hardy in *The Battle of the Century* (28); the whole cast of *Beach Party* (63); and most of the cast of *The Great Race* (64).

cut. Noun: abrupt transition from one shot to another, the first being instantaneously replaced by the second (as opposed to a wipe or a dissolve). Verb: to edit a film, or (during production) to stop the camera moving on a scene.

CUSTER, GEORGE ARMSTRONG (1839–1876). American major-general whose romantic eccentricities and foolish death at Little Big Horn have been favourite screen fodder. The screen Custers include Dustin Farnum in *Flaming Frontier* (26), Frank McGlynn in *Custer's Last Stand* (36), Ronald Reagan in *Santa Fe Trail* (40), Addison Richards in *Badlands of Dakota* (41), Errol Flynn in the large-scale Custer biopic *They Died with Their Boots On* (41), James Millican in *Warpath* (51), Sheb Wooley in *Bugles in the Afternoon* (52) Britt Lomond in *Tonka* (58), Phil Carey in *The Great Sioux Massacre* (65), and Robert Shaw in *Custer of the West* (67). There has also been a TV series, *The Legend of Custer*, with Wayne Maunder.

CUTHBERTSON, ALLAN (c. 1921–   ). British actor adept at supercilious roles: *Room at the Top* (59), *Tunes of Glory* (60), *Term of Trial*

(62), *The Informers* (63), *The Seventh Dawn* (64), *Life at the Top* (65), *Press For Time* (66), many others.

cutting copy. The first print assembled from the 'rushes'. When this is deemed satisfactory, the negative will be cut to match it, and release prints made.

CUTTS, GRAHAM (1885–1958). British director, eminent in silent days: *Flames of Passion* (24), *Woman to Woman* (26), *The Rat* (27), *The Sign of Four* (32), *Aren't Men Beasts* (37), *Just William* (39), etc.

CUTTS, PATRICIA (1926–   ). British leading lady who had a brief film career. *Just William's Luck* (49), *Your Witness* (50), etc. Daughter of Graham Cutts.

CYBULSKI, ZBIGNIEW (1927–67). Polish leading-actor. *A Generation* (54), *Ashes and Diamonds* (58), *He, She or It* (*La Poupée*) (62), *To Love* (64), *Manuscript Found in Saragossa* (65), etc.

CYRANO DE BERGERAC. Edmond Rostand's nineteenth-century play about the mock-heroic cavalier with the romantic yearnings and the unfortunately long nose was filmed in Italy in 1909 and 1922, and in France in 1946. In 1950 came Stanley Kramer's American version, directed by Michael Gordon, starring Jose Ferrer (AA); a fair exam crib of the play, it was not much of a motion picture. In 1964 Abel Gance directed a French pastiche, *Cyrano et D'Artagnan*. Charles Laughton, incidentally, played a famous actor in *Because of Him* (45), and at one point was seen as Cyrano. The original Cyrano lived 1619–55 and was a French writer of comedies: whether he had a long nose is uncertain.

Czechoslovakian films were almost unknown in Western countries until recently, when the gentle realistic comedies of Milos Forman (*Peter and Pavla, A Blonde in Love*) began winning festival prizes. Other notable Czech films of the last few years include Pavel Juracek's *Josef Kilian*, Jan Kadar and Elmar Klos's *The Shop on the High Street*, and Jan Nemec's *Diamonds of the Night*.

CZINNER, PAUL (1890–   ). Hungarian producer-director, long in Britain: husband of Elizabeth Bergner. Films directed include *Der Traumende Mund* (32), *Catherine the Great* (33), *Escape Me Never* (35), *As You Like It* (36), *Dreaming Lips* (37), *Stolen Life* (39). Since 1955 has concentrated on films of opera and ballet, using multiple cameras.

D

DA COSTA, MORTON (1914–   ) (Morton Tecosky). American director of stage musicals and three films: *Auntie Mame* (58), *The Music Man* (61), *Island of Love* (64).

DADE, STEPHEN (1909–   ). British cinematographer, in films from 1927. *We'll Meet Again* (42), *Caravan* (46), *The Brothers* (47), *Snowbound* (49), *A Question of Adultery* (57), *Bluebeard's Ten Honeymoons* (60), *Zulu* (64), *City under the Sea* (65), *The Viking Queen* (66), many others.

DADDY LONGLEGS. Jean Webster's sentimental novel about a January-May romance against an orphanage setting was filmed in 1919 with Mary Pickford and Mahlon Hamilton; in 1930 with Janet Gaynor and Warner Baxter; and in 1955, as a musical, with Leslie Caron and Fred Astaire.

D'AGOSTINO, ALBERT S. (1893–   ). American art director, in Hollywood from early silent days; with RKO 1936–58. *The Raven* (35), *Mr and Mrs Smith* (41), *The Enchanted Cottage* (44), *Notorious* (46), *The Woman on the Beach* (47), *Mourning Becomes Electra* (48), *Clash by Night* (51), *Androcles and the Lion* (53), *Back from Eternity* (56), many others.

DAGOVER, LIL (1897–   ) (Marta Maria Liletts). German actress seen abroad in *The Cabinet of Dr Caligari* (19), *Congress Dances* (31), etc. Still active in German films.

DAGUERRE, LOUIS (1787–1851). French pioneer of photography; his copper-plated prints were known as *daguerrotypes*.

DAHL, ARLENE (1924–   ). Red-headed American leading lady, former model and beauty columnist. *My Wild Irish Rose* (debut) (47), *Woman's World* (54), *Wicked As They Come* (56), *Journey to the Centre of the Earth* (59), *Kisses for My President* (64), many others.

DAHLBECK, EVA (1921–   ). Swedish actress, often in Ingmar Bergman's films: *Waiting Women* (52), *Smiles of a Summer Night* (55), *So Close to Life* (61), *Now About These Women* (64), *Loving Couples* (64), *Les Creatures* (65), *The Red Mantle* (67), etc.

DAILEY, DAN (1915–   ). Lanky American actor-dancer with wide experience in vaudeville and cabaret. *The Mortal Storm* (film debut), *Dulcy* (40), *Ziegfeld Girl* (41), *Moon over Her Shoulder* (41), *Lady Be*

Good (41), *Panama Hattie* (42), *Give Out Sisters* (42), etc.; war service; *Mother Wore Tights* (47), *Give My Regards to Broadway* (48), *You Were Meant for Me* (48), *When My Baby Smiles at Me* (48), *Chicken Every Sunday* (49), *My Blue Heaven* (50), *When Willie Comes Marching Home* (50), *I Can Get It for You Wholesale* (51), *Call Me Mister* (51), *Pride of St Louis* (51), *What Price Glory* (52), *Meet Me at the Fair* (53), *There's No Business Like Show Business* (54), *It's Always Fair Weather* (55), *Meet Me in Las Vegas* (56), *The Wings of Eagles* (56), *Oh Men, Oh Women* (57), *The Wayward Bus* (57), *Pepe* (60), *Hemingway's Adventures of a Young Man* (62), others. TV series: *The Four Just Men* (59), *The Governor and J.J.* (69).

dailies: see *rushes*.

DAINTON, PATRICIA (1930–   ). British leading lady who started as a teenager. *Don't Ever Leave Me* (49), *The Dancing Years* (50), *Castle in the Air* (52), *Operation Diplomat* (54), *The Passing Stranger* (57), *Witness in the Dark* (60), etc.

DALBY, AMY (c. 1888–1969). British character actress who normally on screen played ageing spinsters. Recently had good parts in *The Lamp in Assassin Mews* (62), *The Secret of My Success* (65), *Who Killed the Cat?* (66).

DALE, JIM (1935–   ). British pop singer turned light comedian and member of the 'Carry On' team. *Carry On Spying* (64), *Carry On Cleo* (65), *The Big Job* (65), *Carry On Cowboy* (66), *Carry On Screaming* (66), *Lock Up Your Daughters* (69), etc.

DALE, ESTHER (1886–1961). American character actress, usually a motherly soul, nurse, or grandma. *Crime without Passion* (34), *Dead End* (37), *The Mortal Storm* (40), *Back Street* (41), *North Star* (43), *Stolen Life* (47), *No Man of Her Own* (50), *Ma and Pa Kettle at the Fair* (52), many others.

DALEY, CASS (1915–   ) (Catherine Dailey). American comedienne whose shouted songs and acrobatic contortions were a feature of several light musicals of the 40s. *The Fleet's In* (41), *Star-Spangled Rhythm* (43), *Crazy House* (43), *Out of This World* (45), *Ladies' Man* (46), *Red Garters* (54), *The Spirit Is Willing* (67), etc.

DALI, SALVADOR (1904–   ). Spanish surrealist painter who collaborated with Luis Bunuel in making two controversial films: *Un Chien Andalou* (29) and *L'Age D'Or* (30).

DALIO, MARCEL (1900–   ). Dapper French comedy actor, frequently in Hollywood. *La Grande Illusion* (37), *La Règle du Jeu* (39), *The Song of Bernadette* (43), *Temptation Harbour* (GB) (46), *On the Riviera* (51), *The Happy Time* (52), *The Snows of Kilimanjaro* (52), *Lucky Me* (54), *Sabrina Fair* (54), *Miracle in the Rain* (56), *Pillow Talk* (59),

Can Can (59), *Wild and Wonderful* (63), *Lady L* (65), *The 25th Hour* (67), *How Sweet It Is* (68), many others.

DALL, EVELYN (c. 1914–   ). American night-club singer who appeared in some British film extravaganzas of the 40s. *He Found a Star* (41), *King Arthur Was a Gentleman* (42), *Miss London Ltd* (43), *Time Flies* (44), etc.

DALL, JOHN (1918–   ) (John Jenner Thompson). American leading actor who had some good film roles in the late 40s but has been little seen in recent years. *The Corn Is Green* (as Morgan Evans) (45), *Something in the Wind* (46), *Another Part of the Forest* (47), *Rope* (49), *The Man Who Cheated Himself* (51), *Spartacus* (60), etc.

DALRYMPLE, IAN (1903–   ). British producer. Editor 1923–36, writer 1936–40. Wrote and produced *The Lion Has Wings* (39), then with Crown Film Unit throughout World War II. Formed Wessex Films (46): *Once a Jolly Swagman* (46), *The Wooden Horse* (50), *The Heart of the Matter* (52), *The Admirable Crichton* (57), *A Cry from the Streets* (58), etc.

DALTON, AUDREY (1934–   ). British leading lady in US from 1951 (*The Girls from Pleasure Island*). *Titanic* (53), *Separate Tables* (58), *Mr Sardonicus* (62), *The Bounty Killer* (65), many other routine films.

DALY, JAMES (1918–   ). American stage actor who has appeared in only four films: *The Court Martial of Billy Mitchell* (55), *The Young Stranger* (57), *I Aim at the Stars* (60), *The Five Man Army* (69). TV series: *Medical Center* (69).

DALY, MARK (1887–1957). British character actor, on stage from 1906, screen from 1930, often as cheerful tramp. *The Private Life of Henry VIII* (32), *A Cuckoo in the Nest* (33), *The Ghost Goes West* (36), *Next of Kin* (42), *Bonnie Prince Charlie* (49), *Lease of Life* (54), *The Shiralee* (57), many others.

DAMAGED GOODS. Eugene Brieux's propaganda play about venereal disease has been popular 'under the counter' fare since it was written in 1903. The chief film versions were in 1919 (British), 1937 (American) and 1961 (American).

LES DAMES DU BOIS DE BOULOGNE (France 1944). Robert Bresson's cold, talky film has over the years become something of a cult. It updates a story by Diderot about a jealous woman's revenge on her lover; but its style is so refined and thin as to be almost the antithesis of cinema. Maria Casares has a splendid stab at the leading role.

DAMITA, LILI (1901–   ) (Lilliane Carré). French leading lady who made a few American films and married Errol Flynn. *The Rescue* (28), *The Bridge of San Luis Rey* (29), *The Cockeyed World* (30),

The Match King (31), *This Is the Night* (32), *L'Escadrille de la Chance* (Fr.) (36), etc.

DAMON, STUART (1937–) (Stuart M. Zonis). American stage and TV leading man. TV series: *The Champions* (68).

DAMONE, VIC (1929–) (Vito Farinola). American light leading man and dancer. *Rich, Young and Pretty* (51), *The Strip* (51), *Athena* (53), *Deep in My Heart* (55), *Kismet* (55), *Hell to Eternity* (60), etc.

DAMPIER, CLAUDE (1885–1955) (Claude Cowan). British comedian noted for nasal drawl and country yokel characterization. Long on stage and music hall. *Boys Will Be Boys* (35), *Mr Stringfellow Says No* (37), *Riding High* (39), *Don't Take It to Heart* (44), *Meet Mr Malcolm* (53), etc.

DANA, LEORA (1923–). American general purpose actress. *Three-Ten to Yuma* (57), *Kings Go Forth* (58), *Pollyanna* (60), *A Gathering of Eagles* (63), etc.

DANA, VIOLA (1897–) (Violet Flugrath). American silent screen actress, usually in light comedy and fashionable drama. *Molly the Drummer Boy* (14), *Rosie O'Grady* (17), *A Chorus Girl's Romance* (20), *Open All Night* (24), *Merton of the Movies* (24), *Winds of Chance* (25), *The Sisters* (29), etc.

DANDRIDGE, DOROTHY (1923–1965). American Negro leading lady, former child actress, e.g. in *A Day at the Races* (37). Adult roles include *Jungle Queen* (51), *Bright Road* (53), *Carmen Jones* (54), *Island in the Sun* (56), *Tamango* (58), *The Decks Ran Red* (58), *Porgy and Bess* (59), *Moment of Danger* (60).

DANE, KARL (1886–1934). Lanky Danish actor, one-time studio carpenter in Hollywood, who scored a hit in *The Big Parade* (25) and was henceforth cast as a comedian, often with George K. Arthur. Sound ended his career.

DANGEROUS MOONLIGHT (GB 1941). The film which featured Richard Addinsell's 'Warsaw Concerto' and by its success started the crop of concerto movies which finally proved so tiresome in the 40s. Basically a romantic melodrama of the Polish Air Force, with Anton Walbrook and Sally Gray; directed by Brian Desmond Hurst.

DANIELL, HENRY (1894–1963). British stage actor with incisive voice, cold eyes and manner; popular since 1913 in London and on Broadway. From 1929 was much in Hollywood playing character roles. *Camille* (37), *The Sea Hawk* (40), *The Philadelphia Story* (41), *Sherlock Holmes in Washington* (42), *Jane Eyre* (44), *The Body Snatcher* (leading role) (45), *Hotel Berlin* (45), *The Man in the Grey Flannel*

Daniels, Bebe

Suit (56), *The Chapman Report* (62), many others. 1961–63: several appearances in TV series *Thriller*. Died during rehearsals for *My Fair Lady* (64), in which he can be glimpsed.

DANIELS, BEBE (1901–) (Virginia Daniels). American leading lady of the silent screen. Film debut at seven; played opposite Harold Lloyd and became a popular star; later married Ben Lyon, moved to Britain and appeared with their family on radio and TV. *Male and Female* (19), *Pink Gods* (21), *Unguarded Women* (24), *She's a Sheik* (27), *Rio Rita* (29), *Alias French Gertie* (30), *Reaching for the Moon* (31), *The Maltese Falcon* (31), *Forty-second Street* (33), *Counsellor at Law* (33), *The Return of Carol Deane* (35), *Hi Gang* (GB) (40), *Life with the Lyons* (GB) (53), *The Lyons in Paris* (GB) (55), etc.

DANIELS, WILLIAM (1895–). American cinematographer. *Foolish Wives* (21), *Greed* (23), *Flesh and the Devil* (27), *Anna Christie* (30), *Grand Hotel* (32), *Queen Christina* (33), *Dinner at Eight* (33), *Camille* (36), *Ninotchka* (39), *Brute Force* (47), *Naked City* (AA) (48), *Harvey* (50), *Winchester 73* (50), *When in Rome* (52), *The Glenn Miller Story* (53), *The Shrike* (55), *Cat on a Hot Tin Roof* (58), *Can Can* (59), *Jumbo* (62), *Robin and the Seven Hoods* (also produced) (64), *Von Ryan's Express* (65), *Assault on a Queen* (also produced) (66), *Valley of the Dolls* (67), *The Impossible Years* (68), *The Maltese Bippy* (69), many others.

DANIELY, LISA (c. 1929–). Anglo-French leading lady. *Lili Marlene* (50), *Hindle Wakes* (51), *The Wedding of Lili Marlene* (53), *Tiger by the Tail* (55), *The Vicious Circle* (57), *An Honourable Murder* (60), *The Lamp in Assassin Mews* (62), etc.

DANISCHEWSKY, MONJA (1911–). Russian writer-producer, in Britain since 30s. Publicist and writer for Ealing 1938–48. Produced *Whisky Galore* (48), *The Galloping Major* (50), *The Battle of the Sexes* (61), etc. Screenplay, *Topkapi* (64). Published autobiography 1966: *White Russian, Red Face*.

the Danish cinema was one of the first to start production. Nordisk studios were founded in 1906 and from 1910 to 1915 Danish films were as internationally popular as those of any country in the world. But the talent was all drained away, first by the merger with Germany's UFA studios in 1917 and later by a steady trek to Hollywood. Carl Dreyer, one of the wanderers, later returned to Denmark and made there such major films as *Day of Wrath* and *Ordet*; but no Danish school ever emerged again.

DANKWORTH, JOHNNY (1927–). British bandleader who has written scores for *The Criminal* (60), *Saturday Night and Sunday Morning* (60), *The Servant* (64), *Return from the Ashes* (65), etc.

DANOVA, CESARE (1926–). Italian leading man, recently in Hollywood. *The Captain's Son* (47), *The Three Corsairs* (52), *Don Juan* (55), *The Man Who Understood Women* (59), *Cleopatra* (62), *Viva Las Vegas* (64), *Chamber of Horrors* (66), *Che* (69), etc.

DANTE, MICHAEL (1931–) (Ralph Vitti). American 'second lead' with a screen tendency to villainy. *Fort Dobbs* (58), *Westbound* (59), *Seven Thieves* (60), *Kid Galahad* (62), *The Naked Kiss* (64), *Harlow* (65), etc.

DANTINE, HELMUT (1918–). Good-looking Austrian actor, in US from 1938. *International Squadron* (debut) (41), *Mrs Miniver* (41), *Passage to Marseilles* (44), *Hotel Berlin* (45), *Escape in the Desert* (45), *Northern Pursuit* (45), *Shadow of a Woman* (46), *Whispering City* (48), *Call Me Madam* (53), *Stranger from Venus* (GB) (54), *War and Peace* (56), *Fraulein* (57), *Thundering Jets* (directed only) (58), *Operation Crossbow* (65), etc. Latterly an executive with the Joseph M. Schenk organization.

DANTON, RAY (1931–). Tall, dark American leading man with radio experience. *Chief Crazy Horse* (52), *The Spoilers* (56), *I'll Cry Tomorrow* (57), *Too Much Too Soon* (58), *The Rise and Fall of Legs Diamond* (59), *The George Raft Story* (61), *The Chapman Report* (62), *The Longest Day* (62), *Sandokan the Great* (It.) (63), *Tiger of Terror* (It.) (64), *The Spy Who Went into Hell* (Ger.) (65), etc.

THE DANZIGER BROTHERS (Edward and Harry). American producers who after making *Jigsaw* (46) and two or three other films came to England, set up New Elstree Studios and spent fifteen years producing hundreds of second features and TV episodes, hardly any worth recalling.

DARC, MIREILLE (1940–). French leading lady. *Tonton Flingeurs* (64), *Galia* (65), *Du Rififi a Paname* (66), *Weekend* (67), *Jeff* (68), etc.

DARCEL, DENISE (1925–) (Denise Billecard). French leading lady, in Hollywood from 1947. *To the Victor* (debut) (48), *Tarzan and the Slave Girl* (50), *Battleground* (50), *Westward the Women* (51), *Dangerous When Wet* (52), *Flame of Calcutta* (53), *Vera Cruz* (54), etc.; recently appearing in night clubs.

D'ARCY, ALEX (1908–) (Alexander Sarruf). Egyptian light actor who has appeared in films of many nations. *Champagne* (GB) (28), *A Nous la Liberté* (France) (31), *La Kermesse Héroïque* (France) (35), *The Prisoner of Zenda* (US) (37), *Marriage Is a Private Affair* (US) (44), *How to Marry a Millionaire* (US) (53), *Soldier of Fortune* (US) (56), *Way Way Out* (66), *The St Valentine's Day Massacre* (67), etc.

DARIN, BOBBY (1936–) (Robert Walden Cassotto). American pop singer who alternates lightweight appearances with more serious roles. *Come September* (debut) (60), *Too Late Blues* (61), *Pressure Point* (62), *That Funny Feeling* (65), *Gunfight at Abilene* (67), *Stranger in the House* (67), *The Happy Ending* (69), etc.

THE DARK ANGEL. Guy Bolton's melodramatic play about a romantic triangle and war blindness was filmed by George Fitzmaurice in 1925, with Ronald Colman, Vilma Banky and Wyndham Standing; Sidney Franklin remade it in 1935 with Fredric March, Merle Oberon and Herbert Marshall.

DARK VICTORY (US 1939). Romantic drama which began a trend towards unhappy endings: Bette Davis played a socialite dying of a brain tumour. Directed by Edmund Goulding. Remade 1963 as *Stolen Hours*, with Susan Hayward; but the time was past and it did not appeal.

DARLING (GB 1965). A scathing but ultimately pointless attack on some worthless members of the affluent society, in particular a selfish girl who gets through men at a rate of knots and leaves despair in her wake. John Schlesinger's direction keeps it interesting in a repellent way. With Julie Christie (AA, BFA), Dirk Bogarde (BFA); from a script by Frederic Raphael (AA, BFA); art direction by Ray Simm (BFA).

DARNBOROUGH, ANTHONY (1913–   ). British producer: *The Calendar* (47), *Quartet* (48), *The Net* (52), *The Baby and the Battleship* (56), etc.

DARNELL, LINDA (1923–1965) (Manetta Eloisa Darnell). American leading lady of the 40s. *Hotel for Women* (debut) (39), *Brigham Young* (40), *The Mark of Zorro* (40), *Chad Hanna* (40), *Blood and Sand* (41), *Rise and Shine* (41), *The Loves of Edgar Allan Poe* (42), *The Song of Bernadette* (as the Virgin Mary) (43), *Buffalo Bill* (44), *It Happened Tomorrow* (44), *Summer Storm* (44), *Sweet and Lowdown* (44), *The Great John L* (45), *Fallen Angel* (45), *Hangover Square* (45), *Anna and the King of Siam* (46), *Centennial Summer* (46), *My Darling Clementine* (46), *Forever Amber* (47), *A Letter to Three Wives* (48), *No Way Out* (50), *The Thirteenth Letter* (51), *The Guy Who Came Back* (51), *Island of Desire (Saturday Island)* (52), *Night Without Sleep* (52), *Blackbeard the Pirate* (53), *Second Chance* (53), *This Is My Love* (54), *Zero Hour* (57), *Black Spurs* (65), etc. From 1953 more on stage and TV than in Hollywood.

DARREN, JAMES (1936–   ) (James Ercolani). American leading man whose appeal seems to have waned with maturity. *Rumble on the Docks* (debut) (56), *Operation Mad Ball* (57), *Gidget* (59), *Let No Man Write My Epitaph* (60), *The Guns of Navarone* (61), *Diamondhead* (63), *For Those Who Think Young* (64), etc. TV series: *Time Tunnel* (66).

DARRIEUX, DANIELLE (1917–   ). Vivacious French leading lady, in films since 1931. Her role in *Mayerling* (36) took her to Hollywood for *The Rage of Paris* (38), but she quickly returned home and stayed there with very occasional excursions. *Battement de Cœur* (39), *Premier Rendezvous* (44), *Occupe-Toi d'Amélie* (49), *La Ronde* (50), *Le Plaisir* (51), *Rich, Young and Pretty* (US) (51), *Five Fingers* (US) (52), *Adorables Créatures* (52), *Madame De* (53), *Alexander the Great* (US) (55), *Marie Octobre* (58), *Lady Chatterley's Lover* (59), *Murder at 45 RPM* (61), *L'Or du Duc* (65), *Le Dimanche de la Vie* (66), *The Young Girls of Rochefort* (67), *L'Homme a la Buick* (67), many others.

DARRO, FRANKIE (1917–   ) (Frank Johnson). Tough-looking little American actor, former child and teenage player; star of many second features. *The Cowboy Cop* (26), *The Mad Genius* (32), *Racing Blood* (37), *Chasing Trouble* (39), *Laughing at Danger* (40), *Freddie Steps Out* (45), *Heart of Virginia* (48), *Across the Wide Missouri* (51), *Operation Petticoat* (59), many others.

DARROW, CLARENCE (1857–1938). Celebrated American defence lawyer, impersonated by Orson Welles in *Compulsion* (58) and by Spencer Tracy in *Inherit the Wind* (60).

DARVI, BELLA (1928–   ) (Bella Wegier). Polish-French leading lady, in a few Hollywood films after being discovered by Darryl Zanuck. *Hell and High Water* (54), *The Egyptian* (54), etc.; then back to French films.

DARWELL, JANE (1880–1967) (Patti Woodward). American character actress, usually in warm-hearted motherly roles. *Rose of the Rancho* (14), *Brewster's Millions* (20), *Back Street* (32), *Design for Living* (34), *Life Begins at Forty* (35), *Captain January* (36), *Slave Ship* (37), *Three Blind Mice* (38), *Jesse James* (39), *The Rains Came* (39), *Gone with the Wind* (39), *The Grapes of Wrath* (AA: as the indomitable Ma Joad) (40), *All That Money Can Buy* (41), *Private Nurse* (41), *The Impatient Years* (44), *Captain Tugboat Annie* (title role) (46), *My Darling Clementine* (46), *Three Godfathers* (48), *Wagonmaster* (50), *Caged* (50), *The Lemon Drop Kid* (51), *Fourteen Hours* (51), *We're Not Married* (52), *The Sun Shines Bright* (52), *Hit the Deck* (55), *The Last Hurrah* (58), *Mary Poppins* (64), many others.

DA SILVA, HOWARD (1909–   ) (Harold Silverblatt). American character actor with stage experience. Graduated from bit parts to a peak in the late 40s, then subsided into routine. *Abe Lincoln in Illinois* (39), *The Sea Wolf* (41), *The Big Shot* (43), *The Lost Weekend* (45), *The Blue Dahlia* (46), *Blaze of Noon* (47), *Unconquered* (47), *They Live by Night* (48), *Three Husbands* (50), *Fourteen Hours* (51), *M* (51), then returned to stage for several years; *David and Lisa* (62), *The Outrage* (65), *Nevada Smith* (66), etc.

†DASSIN, JULES (1911–   ). American director, former radio writer and actor. Joined MGM 1941 to direct shorts (including a two-reel version of *The Tell-Tale Heart*); moved to features; left for Europe during the McCarthy witch hunt of the late 40s. *Nazi Agent* (42), *The Affairs of Martha* (42), *Reunion in France* (42), *Young Ideas* (43), *The Canterville Ghost* (44), *A Letter for Evie* (44), *Two Smart People* (46), *Brute Force* (47), *Naked City* (48), *Thieves' Highway* (49), *Night and the City* (GB) (50), *Rififi* (also acted, as Perlo Vita) (54), *He Who Must Die* (56), *Where the Hot Wind Blows* (58), *Never on Sunday* (also acted) (60), *Phaedra* (62), *Topkapi* (64), *10.30 p.m. Summer* (66), *Survival* (68), *Uptight* (68). Has helped to write most of these.

DAUGHERTY, HERSCHEL (* –   ). American director, from TV. *The Light in the Forest* (58), *The Raiders* (63), etc.

DAUPHIN, CLAUDE (1903–   ) (Claude Franc-Nohain). French actor of stage and screen: in films from 1930. *Entrée des Artistes* (38), *Battement de Cœur* (39), *Les Deux Timides* (42), *English Without Tears* (GB) (44), *Deported* (US) (50), *Le Plaisir* (51), *Casque d'Or* (52), *Little Boy Lost* (US) (53), *Innocents in Paris* (GB) (54), *Phantom of the Rue Morgue* (US) (54), *The Quiet American* (US) (58), *The Full Treatment* (60), *Lady L* (65), *Two for the Road* (67), *Hard Contract* (69), many others.

DAVENPORT, HARRY (1866–1949). American character actor, in films from 1935 as white-haired, benevolent, wise old man. Previously a stage actor at six; film director for a period from 1912. Memorable in *You Can't Take It With You* (as judge) (38), *Gone with the Wind* (39), *The Hunchback of Notre Dame* (a key role as King Francis) (40), *All This and Heaven Too* (40), *The Ox-Bow Incident* (42), *Meet Me in St Louis* (44), *Too Young To Know* (45), *Adventure* (46), *The Enchanted Forest* (46), *The Bachelor and the Bobbysoxer* (47), *The Forsyte Saga* (49), many others.

DAVENPORT, NIGEL (1928–   ). British general purpose actor, much on TV. *Peeping Tom* (59), *In the Cool of the Day* (63), *A High Wind in Jamaica* (65), *Sands of the Kalahari* (65), *Where the Spies Are* (66), *A Man for All Seasons* (67), *Red and Blue* (67), *Play Dirty* (68), *Sinful Davey* (69), *The Virgin Soldiers* (69), *The Royal Hunt of the Sun* (69), etc.

DAVES, DELMER (1904–   ). American writer-producer-director with highly miscellaneous experience. Writer with MGM from 1933, writer-director with Warners from 1943. *Destination Tokyo* (w, d) (43), *The Red House* (w, d) (47), *Dark Passage* (w, d) (47), *Broken Arrow* (d) (50), *Bird of Paradise* (w, d) (51), *Never Let Me Go* (d) (53), *Demetrius and the Gladiators* (d) (54), *Jubal* (w, d) (56), *The Last Wagon* (w, d) (56), *3.10 to Yuma* (d) (57), *Cowboy* (w, d) (58), *The Hanging Tree* (d) (59), *Parrish* (w, d) (61), *Spencer's*

Mountain (w, p, d) (62), *Youngblood Hawke* (w, d) (64), *The Battle of Villa Fiorita* (w, p, d) (65), many others.

DAVID COPPERFIELD (US 1934). Probably the most successful and satisfactory 'Hollywood classic', an impeccable costume narrative, richly acted, with the true Dickens flavour. George Cukor directed; Hugh Walpole worked on the screenplay (and played the vicar). Cast included W. C. Fields (Micawber), Freddie Bartholomew (young David), Frank Lawton (David as a man), Edna May Oliver (Aunt Betsy), Basil Rathbone (Mr Murdstone), Roland Young (Uriah Heep), Lionel Barrymore (Dan Peggotty), Jessie Ralph (Nurse Peggotty), etc. The 1969 all-star remake is intended for TV in the States, theatres elsewhere.

DAVIES, BETTY ANN (1910–1955). British stage actress, usually in tense roles; occasional films from early 30s. *Chick* (34), *Kipps* (41), *It Always Rains on Sunday* (47), *The History of Mr Polly* (49), *Trio* (50), *Cosh Boy* (52), *Grand National Night* (53), *The Belles of St Trinians* (54), etc.

DAVIES, JACK (1913–). British comedy scriptwriter, busy since 1932 on Will Hay and Norman Wisdom comedies, 'Doctor' series, etc.; also *Laughter in Paradise* (51), *Top Secret* (52), *An Alligator Named Daisy* (56), *Very Important Person* (61), *The Fast Lady* (62), *Those Magnificent Men in Their Flying Machines* (65), many others.

DAVIES, JOHN HOWARD (1939–). British child actor who played *Oliver Twist* (48). Appeared in a few other films (*The Rocking-Horse Winner* [50], *Tom Brown's Schooldays* [51], etc.) then left the industry. Now a BBC TV director.

DAVIES, MARION (1898–1961) (Marion Douras). American leading lady famous less for her rather mediocre films than for being the protégée of William Randolph Hearst the newspaper magnate, who was determined to make a star of her. She enjoyed moderate success 1917–36, then retired. *Runaway Romance* (17), *The Dark Star* (19), *The Restless Sex* (21), *Little Old New York* (23), *Yolanda* (24), *The Red Mill* (25), *Show People* (28), *Hollywood Revue of 1929* (29), *Polly of the Circus* (32), *Peg o' My Heart* (33), *Operator 13* (34), *Page Miss Glory* (35), many others.

DAVIES, RUPERT (c. 1913–). British character actor, formerly in small roles, then famous as TV's *Maigret*. Films include *The Uncle* (65), *The Spy Who Came In from the Cold* (65), *Brides of Fu Manchu* (66), *House of a Thousand Dolls* (67), *Witchfinder General* (68).

DAVION, ALEXANDER (1929–). Anglo-French leading man, mostly on stage and American TV. *Song Without End* (as Chopin) (60),

Davis, Bette

Paranoiac (63), *Valley of the Dolls* (67), *The Royal Hunt of the Sun* (69), etc. TV series: *Gideon's Way* (64), *Custer* (67).

†DAVIS, BETTE (1908–   ) (Ruth Elizabeth Davis). American dramatic actress and Hollywood star of long standing; in a series of intense melodramas for women she was box-office queen from 1936 until after World War II; she later played eccentric roles. *Bad Sister* (debut) (31), *Seed* (31), *Waterloo Bridge* (31), *Way Back Home* (31), *The Menace* (32), *Hell's House* (32), *The Man Who Played God* (32), *So Big* (32), *The Rich Are Always with Us* (32), *The Dark Horse* (32), *Cabin in the Cotton* (32), *Twenty Thousand Years in Sing Sing* (32), *Three on a Match* (32), *Parachute Jumper* (32), *The Working Man* (32), *Ex Lady* (33), *Bureau of Missing Persons* (33), *Fashions* (34), *The Big Shakedown* (34), *Jimmy the Gent* (34), *Fog over Frisco* (34), *Of Human Bondage* (as Mildred: the performance that made her a star) (34), *Housewife* (34), *Bordertown* (34), *The Girl from Tenth Avenue* (34), *Dangerous* (AA) (35), *Front Page Woman* (35), *Secret Agent* (35), *The Petrified Forest* (36), *Golden Arrow* (36), *Satan Met a Lady* (36), *Marked Woman* (36), *Kid Galahad* (37), *It's Love I'm After* (37), *That Certain Woman* (37), *Jezebel* (AA) (38), *The Sisters* (38), *Dark Victory* (39), *Juarez* (39), *The Old Maid* (39), *Elizabeth and Essex* (39), *All This and Heaven Too* (40), *The Letter* (40), *The Great Lie* (41), *The Bride Came C.O.D.* (41), *The Little Foxes* (41), *The Man Who Came to Dinner* (41), *In This Our Life* (42), *Now Voyager* (42), *Watch on the Rhine* (43), *Old Acquaintance* (43), *Thank Your Lucky Stars* (43), *Mr Skeffington* (44), *The Corn Is Green* (45), *Stolen Life* (46), *Deception* (46), *Winter Meeting* (48), *June Bride* (48), *Beyond the Forest* (49), *All About Eve* (50), *Payment on Demand* (51), *Another Man's Poison* (GB) (51), *Phone Call from a Stranger* (52), *The Star* (52), *The Virgin Queen* (55), *Storm Centre* (56), *The Catered Affair* (*Wedding Breakfast*) (56), *The Scapegoat* (59), *John Paul Jones* (59), *Whatever Happened to Baby Jane* (62), *Where Love Has Gone* (64), *The Empty Canvas* (It.) (64), *Hush Hush Sweet Charlotte* (64), *The Nanny* (GB) (65), *The Anniversary* (GB) (67), *Connecting Rooms* (GB) (69). Published autobiography 1962: *The Lonely Life*.

†DAVIS, DESMOND (1927–   ). British director, former cameraman. *Girl with Green Eyes* (64), *The Uncle* (65), *I Was Happy Here* (66), *Smashing Time* (67), *A Nice Girl Like Me* (69).

DAVIS, JAMES (or JIM) (1915–   ). American actor whose first leading role, after small parts from 1942, was opposite Bette Davis in *Winter Meeting* (48). Did not survive as a star but subsequently played the tough hero of many low-budget Westerns. Recently: *Fort Utah* (66).

DAVIS, JOAN (1908–1961). Rubber-faced American comedienne, in show business from infancy, who enlivened many routine musicals of the 30s and 40s. *On the Avenue* (37), *Wake Up and Live* (37), *My Lucky Star* (38), *Tailspin* (39), *Sun Valley Serenade* (41), *Hold That Ghost* (42), *Sweetheart of the Fleet* (42), *Around the World* (44), *She Gets Her Man* (44), *Show Business* (44), *George White's Scandals* (45), *If You Knew Susie* (48), *The Travelling Saleswoman* (49), *Harem Girl* (52), etc. Later became very popular on TV in the series *I Married Joan* (53–55).

DAVIS, JOHN (1906–   ). British executive, a former accountant, who became chairman of the Rank Organization. After the artistic extravagance of the mid-40s, he imposed financial stability; but subsequent film production was comparatively routine and in the late 60s dwindled to nothing as the group was diversified into other fields.

DAVIS, NANCY (c. 1926–   ). American leading lady of a few 50s films. *Shadow on the Wall* (50), *The Doctor and the Girl* (50), *Night into Morning* (51), *It's a Big Country* (53), *Donovan's Brain* (53), *Crash Landing* (57), *Hellcats of the Navy* (59), etc.

DAVIS, OSSIE (1917–   ). American Negro actor of massive presence. *No Way Out* (50), *The Joe Louis Story* (53), *Gone Are the Days* (63) (also wrote), *The Hill* (GB) (66), *The Scalphunters* (68), *Sam Whiskey* (69), *Slaves* (69).

DAVIS, SAMMY JNR (1925–   ). American singer and entertainer, a bundle of vitality who describes himself as a 'one-eyed Jewish Negro'. *Anna Lucasta* (59), *Porgy and Bess* (59), *Ocean's Eleven* (61), *Sergeants Three* (63), *Robin and the Seven Hoods* (64), *The Threepenny Opera* (65), *A Man Called Adam* (66), *Salt and Pepper* (68), *Sweet Charity* (68), *Man Without Mercy* (69). Published autobiography 1966: *Yes I Can.*

DAVIS, STRINGER (c. 1899–   ). Gentle-mannered British character actor, always to be found playing small roles in the films of his wife Margaret Rutherford. Has played larger parts in her 'Miss Marple' series: *Murder She Says* (63), *Murder Most Foul* (64), etc.

DAWN PATROL (US 1930). Famous melodrama of World War I flyers, directed by Howard Hawks, starring Richard Barthelmess and Douglas Fairbanks Jnr. Retailored 1937 for Errol Flynn, using much of the same footage and exactly the same script (by John Monk Saunders).

DAWSON, ANTHONY (1916–   ). Lean-faced British character actor. *The Way to the Stars* (45), *The Queen of Spades* (48), *The Long Dark Hall* (51), *Dial M for Murder* (US) (54), *Midnight Lace* (US) (60), *Seven Seas to Calais* (US) (63), etc. The 'Anthony Dawson' who directs Italian costume epics is in fact the nom-de-film of Antonio Margheriti.

DAY, DORIS (1924–   ) (Doris Kappelhoff). Vivacious American singer and comedienne who achieved instant popularity in her first film *It's Magic* (*Romance on the High Seas*) (48), and seventeen years later was still big box-office after a carefully nurtured career culminating in a series of comedies about a working girl's efforts to protect her maidenhood. Formerly a dance band singer. Films include *Young Man with a Horn* (50), *Storm Warning* (51), *West Point Story* (51), *Lullaby of Broadway* (51), *I'll See You in My Dreams* (52), *April in Paris* (53), *Calamity Jane* (53), *Young at Heart* (55), *Love Me or Leave Me* (55), *The Man Who Knew Too Much* (55), *Julie* (56), *The Pajama Game* (57), *Teacher's Pet* (58), *Pillow Talk* (59), *Midnight Lace* (60), *That Touch of Mink* (61), *Jumbo* (62), *Move Over Darling* (63), *Send Me No Flowers* (64), *Do Not Disturb* (65), *The Glass Bottom Boat* (66), *Caprice* (67), *The Epic of Josie* (67), *Where Were You When the Lights Went Out?* (68), *With Six You Get Egg Roll* (68), others. TV series: *The Doris Day Show* (68–69).

DAY, FRANCES (1908–   ). Revue star of German and Russian origin, long resident in Britain. *The Price of Divorce* (27), *The First Mrs Fraser* (32), *The Girl from Maxim's* (34), *Who's Your Lady Friend* (37), *The Girl in the Taxi* (38), *Room for Two* (40), *Fiddlers Three* (as Poppea) (44), *Tread Softly* (52), *There's Always a Thursday* (57), etc.

DAY, JILL (1932–   ). British pop singer: appeared in films *Always a Bride* (54), *All for Mary* (56).

DAY, JOSETTE (1914–   ). French leading lady. *Allo Berlin, Ici Paris* (32), *La Fille du Puisatier* (40), *Le Belle et la Bete* (45), *Les Parents Terribles* (48), *Four Days' Leave* (50), etc.

DAY, LARAINE (1920–   ) (Laraine Johnson). American leading lady of the 40s, with stage experience. *Stella Dallas* (debut) (37), *Border G-Men* (38), *Young Dr Kildare* (and others in the series) (39), *My Son, My Son* (40), *Foreign Correspondent* (40), *The Trial of Mary Dugan* (41), *Unholy Partners* (41), *Fingers at the Window* (41), *Journey for Margaret* (42), *Mr Lucky* (43), *The Story of Dr Wassell* (43), *Bride by Mistake* (44), *Those Endearing Young Charms* (45), *Keep Your Powder Dry* (45), *The Locket* (46), *Tycoon* (47), *I Married a Communist* (49), *Without Honour* (49), *The High and the Mighty* (54), *Toy Tiger* (56), *Three for Jamie Dawn* (57), *The Third Voice* (last to date) (59), etc. Makes occasional TV appearances.

DAY OF WRATH (Denmark 1943). Carl Dreyer's horrifying drama of a medieval witch-hunt, uncannily photographed by Karl Andersson so that every scene looks like a Rembrandt painting. A sombre classic. Written by Dreyer and others from a novel by Wiers Jenssens; music by Paul Schierbeck; cast headed by Lisbeth Movin, Thorkild Roose.

DAY, RICHARD (c. 1905–   ). American production designer. *The Dark Angel* (AA) (35), *Dodsworth* (36), *The Little Foxes* (41), *How Green Was My Valley* (41), *A Streetcar Named Desire* (51), *On the Waterfront* (54), *Exodus* (60), *The Greatest Story Ever Told* (65), *The Chase* (66), *Valley of the Dolls* (67), etc.

DAY, ROBERT (1922–   ). British director, former cameraman. *The Green Man* (57), *Grip of the Strangler* (58), *First Man into Space* (58), *Corridors of Blood* (59), *Bobbikins* (59), *Two-Way Stretch* (60), *The Rebel* (61), *Operation Snatch* (62), *Tarzan's Three Challenges* (64), *She* (65), *Tarzan and the Valley of Gold* (66), *Tarzan and the Great River* (69), etc.; also many episodes of TV film series.

DEACON, RICHARD (1923–   ). Bald, bespectacled American character actor who usually plays comic snoops. *Abbott and Costello Meet the Mummy* (55), *The Power and the Prize* (56), *The Remarkable Mr Pennypacker* (58), *Blackbeard's Ghost* (68), many others. TV series include *Leave It to Beaver* (57–63), *Dick Van Dyke* (61–66), *Mothers-in-Law* (67–68).

DEAD END (US 1937). Set-bound but powerful melodrama from Sidney Kingsley's play about New York slums. Its success led Hollywood to produce more social dramas; it provided an important part for Humphrey Bogart as the returning gangster; and it introduced the Dead End Kids. As entertainment, despite Gregg Toland's photography and William Wyler's direction, it has dated.

DEAD OF NIGHT (GB 1945). An Ealing omnibus of ghost stories, almost the first serious British treatment of the supernatural. Quality varies, but the Michael Redgrave sequence about a deranged ventriloquist has lost none of its power, and the linking story about an architect caught up in an endless series of recurring dreams is neatly underplayed until its phantasmagoric climax and brilliant trick ending. Directors: Cavalcanti ('Christmas Party' and 'Ventriloquist'), Basil Dearden ('Hearse Driver' and linking story), Charles Crichton ('Golf') and Robert Hamer ('Haunted Mirror').

deaf mutes have been movingly portrayed by Jane Wyman in *Johnny Belinda*, Mandy Miller in *Mandy*, Dorothy McGuire in *The Spiral Staircase*, Harry Bellaver in *No Way Out*, and Alan Arkin in *The Heart Is a Lonely Hunter*.

DEAN, BASIL (1888–   ). British stage producer who also directed several important films for Associated Talking Pictures, which he founded. *The Impassive Footman* (32), *The Constant Nymph* (also co-wrote) (33), *Java Head* (34), *Sing As We Go* (34), *Lorna Doone* (35), *Twenty-one Days* (39), etc.

DEAN, EDDIE (c. 1908–   ) (Edgar D. Glossup). American star of Western second features in the 30s and 40s. *Renegade Trail* (39),

Dean, Isabel

Sierra Sue (41), *Romance of the West* (47), *Hawk of Powder River* (50), many others.

DEAN, ISABEL (1918–   ) (I. Hodgkinson). British stage actress, usually in upper-class roles; very occasional film appearances. *The Passionate Friends* (47), *Twenty-four Hours of a Woman's Life* (52), *The Story of Gilbert and Sullivan* (53), *Out of the Clouds* (55), *Virgin Island* (58), *The Light in the Piazza* (62), *A High Wind in Jamaica* (65), *Inadmissible Evidence* (68), etc.

†DEAN, JAMES (1931–1955). American actor who after a brief stage career was acclaimed for his performance as the moody, restless son in *East of Eden* (54). *Rebel Without a Cause* (55) further identified him with turbulent youth, and his death in a car crash before *Giant* (55) was released caused an astonishing outburst of emotional necrophilia from fans all over the world. A biopic, *The James Dean Story*, was patched together in 1957. Real name: James Byron.

DEAN, JULIA (1878–1952). American stage actress who made a few movies after she retired to California. *Curse of the Cat People* (44), *O.S.S.* (46), *Nightmare Alley* (48), *People Will Talk* (51), *Elopement* (52), etc.

DEAR RUTH (US 1947). Norman Krasna's play, about a teenager who writes love letters to a service man using her elder sister's name and photograph, was pleasantly if unremarkably filmed by William D. Russell with a cast including William Holden, Joan Caulfield, Mona Freeman, Edward Arnold and Billy de Wolfe. So successful was it that two sequels were called for: *Dear Wife* (49), *Dear Brat* (51).

DEARDEN, BASIL (1911–   ). British director, in films from 1937. Co-director of Will Hay's last comedies for Ealing. On his own: *The Bells Go Down* (42), *The Halfway House* (43), *Dead of Night* (part) (45), *Frieda* (47), *The Blue Lamp* (50), *The Gentle Gunman* (52), *The Smallest Show on Earth* (57), *Sapphire* (58), *The League of Gentlemen* (59), *Victim* (62), *Masquerade* (65), *Khartoum* (67), *The Assassination Bureau* (68), many others. Since 1955 has normally worked with Michael Relph as producer-director team (often writer also), with alternating responsibility.

death has always fascinated film-makers, though the results have often looked somewhat undergraduatish, as fantasy tends to look when brought down to a mass-appeal level. Death has been personified in *Death Takes a Holiday* by Fredric March, in *On Borrowed Time* by Cedric Hardwicke, in *Here Comes Mr Jordan* by Claude Rains, in *Orphée* by Maria Casares, in *The Seventh Seal* by Bengt Ekerot, by Richard Burton in *Boom*, and by several actors

272

in *The Masque of the Red Death*. In *Devotion*, Ida Lupino as Emily Brontë dreamed of death on horseback coming to sweep her away; in *The Bluebird* Shirley Temple ventured into the land of the dead to see her grandparents. Most of the characters in *Thunder Rock*, and all in *Outward Bound* (remade as *Between Two Worlds*) were already dead at the start of the story. Other films to involve serious thought about death include *Dark Victory*, *Jeux Interdits*, *All the Way Home*, *Sentimental Journey*, *No Sad Songs for Me*, *One Way Passage*, *Paths of Glory* and *Wild Strawberries*.

'Black' comedies, i.e. taking death lightly, have included *A Slight Case of Murder*, *Kind Hearts and Coronets*, *The Trouble with Harry*, *Too Many Crooks*, *The Criminal Life of Archibaldo de la Cruz*, *Send Me No Flowers*, *The Assassination Bureau*, *The Loved One*, *The Wrong Box*, *Arrivederci Baby*, and *Kiss the Girls and Make Them Die*.

DEATH OF A CYCLIST (Spain 1954). A rare Spanish success in the film world. Directed and co-written by Juan-Antonio Bardem, it tells of the effect of a road accident on the relationship of two lovers. With Alberto Closas, Lucia Bose.

DEATH OF A SALESMAN (US 1953). Produced by Stanley Kramer and directed by Laslo Benedek, this screen adaptation of Arthur Miller's play about the tragedy of an American 'good guy' for whom life turns sour had an air of being done on the cheap; but Fredric March's performance was peerless and the time-transitions were effected with skill and simplicity.

DE BANZIE, BRENDA (1915–   ). British actress, in films since 1935 but not given her big chance until *Hobson's Choice* (54), in which she starred. Soon reverted to character roles: *What Every Woman Wants* (54), *A Kid for Two Farthings* (55), *The Thirty-nine Steps* (59), *Flame in the Streets* (61), *The Pink Panther* (63), *Pretty Polly* (67), many others.

DE BRAY, YVONNE (1889–1954). French character actress, in films from 1943. *Gigi* (48), *Les Parents Terribles* (best role) (49), *Olivia* (50), *Caroline Chérie* (50), *Nous Sommes Tous des Assassins* (52), etc.

DE BROCA, PHILIPPE (1933–   ). French director. *Les Jeux de l'Amour* (60), *L'Amant de Cinq Jours* (61), *Cartouche* (62), *That Man from Rio* (63), *Un Monsieur de Compagnie* (64), *Tribulations Chinoise en Chine* (65), *King of Hearts* (67), *Give Her the Moon* (70), etc.

DE BRULIER, NIGEL (1878–1948). British actor in Hollywood: career waned with sound. *Intolerance* (16), *The Four Horsemen of the Apocalypse* (21), *The Three Musketeers* (21), *Salome* (23), *The Hunchback of Notre Dame* (23), *Ben Hur* (26), *Wings* (27), *Noah's Ark* (29), *The Iron Mask* (29), *Moby Dick* (31), *Rasputin and the Empress* (32), *Mary of Scotland* (36), *The Garden of Allah* (36), *The Hound of the*

Baskervilles (39), *One Million B.C.* (40), *The Adventures of Captain Marvel* (48), many others.

DEBUCOURT, JEAN (1894–1958). French character actor with long stage experience. *Le Petit Chose* (22), *La Chute de la Maison Usher* (28), *Douce* (43), *Le Diable au Corps* (46), *Occupe-Toi d'Amélie* (49), etc.

DECAE, HENRI (1915–   ). Distinguished French cinematographer, *Le Silence de la Mer* (49), *Les Enfants Terribles* (49), *Crève-Cœur* (52), *Bob le Flambeur* (55), *Lift to the Scaffold* (57), *Le Beau Serge* (58), *Les Quatre Cents Coups* (59), *Les Cousins* (59), *Les Bonnes Femmes* (60), *Plein Soleil* (59), *Léon Morin, Priest* (61), *Sundays and Cybele* (62). *Dragées au Poivre* (63), *Viva Maria* (65), *Weekend at Dunkirk* (65), *Night of the Generals* (66), *The Comedians* (67), *Castle Keep* (69), etc.

DE CAMP, ROSEMARY (c. 1914–   ). American actress specializing in elder sisters and motherly types. Film debut *Cheers for Miss Bishop* (41); since in scores of films including *Yankee Doodle Dandy* (43), *The Merry Monahans* (44), *Rhapsody in Blue* (45), *Nora Prentiss* (48), *Strategic Air Command* (55), etc. On TV in *The Bob Cummings Show*, etc.

DE CARLO, YVONNE (1922–   ) (Peggy Yvonne Middleton). Canadian leading lady of the 40s; trained as dancer. In 1944 won lead in *Salome Where She Danced* by submitting photo in contest. Followed with exotic adventure films, Westerns and comedies; recently made comeback in character roles. *The Bride Wasn't Willing* (45), *Song of Scheherazade* (46), *Brute Force* (47), *Slave Girl* (47), *River Lady* (48), *Black Bart Highwayman* (as Lola Montes) (48), *Casbah* (48), *Criss Cross* (49), *The Gal Who Took the West* (50), *Calamity Jane and Sam Bass* (50), *Hotel Sahara* (GB) (51), *Scarlet Angel* (51), *The San Francisco Story* (52), *Sombrero* (53), *Sea Devils* (GB) (53), *The Captain's Paradise* (GB) (53), *Passion* (54), *Magic Fire* (56), *The Ten Commandments* (56), *Death of a Scoundrel* (56), *Band of Angels* (58), *A Global Affair* (63), *Law of the Lawless* (64), *Munster Go Home* (66), *Hostile Guns* (67), etc. Played Vampira in TV series *The Munsters* (64–66).

DE CASALIS, JEANNE (1896–1966). British revue comedienne and character actress, best known as radio's 'Mrs Feather' in dithery telephone monologues. Published autobiography 1953: *Things I Don't Remember*. Films include *Nell Gwyn* (34), *Cottage to Let* (41), *Those Kids from Town* (42), *Medal for the General* (44), *This Man Is Mine* (46), *Woman Hater* (48), etc.

DECKER, DIANA (1926–   ). Bright, blonde, American leading lady, in Britain from 1939; became known through toothpaste commercials ('Irium, Miriam?'). Films include *Fiddlers Three* (44),

Meet Me at Dawn (48), *Murder at the Windmill* (49), *Devils of Darkness* (65), etc.

DECKERS, EUGENE (1917–   ). French character actor who has played continental types in British films since 1946. *Sleeping Car to Trieste* (48), *The Elusive Pimpernel* (50), *The Lavender Hill Mob* (51), *Father Brown* (54), *Port Afrique* (56), *Northwest Frontier* (59), *Lady L* (66), *The Limbo Line* (68), many others.

DECOIN, HENRI (1896–1969). French director, in films since 1929. *Abus de Confiance* (37), *Les Inconnus dans la Maison* (42), *La Fille du Diable* (46), *Three Telegrams* (50), *The Truth about Bebe Donge* (52), *The Lovers of Toledo* (53), *Razzia sur la Chnouf* (55), *Charmants Garçons* (57), *The Face of the Cat* (58), *Outcasts of Glory* (64), many others.

DE CORDOBA, PEDRO (1881–1950). American stage actor, lean and often sinister, in many silent and sound films. *Carmen* (15), *Maria Rosa* (16), *Runaway Romany* (20), *Young Diana* (22), *The Crusades* (35), *Anthony Adverse* (36), *The Light That Failed* (39), *The Ghost Breakers* (40), *The Mark of Zorro* (40), *Son of Fury* (42), *For Whom the Bell Tolls* (43), *The Beast with Five Fingers* (47), *When the Redskins Rode* (50), etc.

DE CORDOVA, ARTURO (1908–   ) (Arturo Garcia). Mexican leading man with flashing grin and impudent eyes. Popular in Mexico since 1935; made a few Hollywood films in the 40s. *For Whom the Bell Tolls* (43), *Hostages* (43), *Frenchman's Creek* (44), *Incendiary Blonde* (44), *A Medal for Benny* (45), *Masquerade in Mexico* (45), *The Flame* (47), *New Orleans* (47), *The Adventures of Casanova* (48), *El* (Mexican) (51), *Kill Him for Me* (53), etc.

DE CORDOVA, FREDERICK (1910–   ). American director with stage experience. *Too Young to Know* (45), *The Countess of Monte Cristo* (47), *Bedtime for Bonzo* (51), *Column South* (53), etc.; then to TV as producer, director and executive. 1965: *I'll Take Sweden*.

DE CORSIA, TED (1906–   ). American character actor with long vaudeville experience; usually plays surly villains. *The Lady from Shanghai* (47), *Naked City* (48), *Murder Inc* (*The Enforcer*) (51), *Vengeance Valley* (51), *Man In The Dark* (53), *Twenty Thousand Leagues Under The Sea* (54), *The Big Combo* (55), *Slightly Scarlet* (56), *The Killing* (56), *Baby Face Nelson* (57), *Gunfight at the O.K. Corral* (57), *Blood on the Arrow* (61), *The Quick Gun* (64), *Nevada Smith* (66), many others.

DE COURVILLE, ALBERT (1887–1960). British stage director who directed a few film comedies: *Things Are Looking Up* (34), *The Case of Gabriel Perry* (35), *Crackerjack* (38), etc.

Dee, Frances

DEE, FRANCES (1908–) (Jean Dee). American leading lady of the 30s, long married to Joel McCrea; a former extra, she was chosen by Chevalier to play opposite him in her first speaking role. *Playboy of Paris* (31), *An American Tragedy* (31), *Becky Sharp* (35), *So Ends Our Night* (41), *Meet the Stewarts* (42), *I Walked with a Zombie* (43), *Happy Land* (43), *Bel Ami* (48), *They Passed This Way* (48), *Gypsy Colt* (54), etc.

DEE, RUBY (1924–). (Ruby Ann Wallace). American Negro actress. *No Way Out* (50), *Tall Target* (51), *Go Man Go* (53), *Edge of the City* (*A Man is Ten Feet Tall*) (57), *Take a Giant Step* (59), *A Raisin in the Sun* (61), *The Balcony* (62), etc.

DEE, SANDRA (1942–) (Alexandra Zuck). American leading lady, former model. *Until They Sail* (57), *The Reluctant Debutante* (58), *Gidget* (59), *Imitation of Life* (59), *A Summer Place* (59), *Portrait in Black* (60), *Romanoff and Juliet* (62), *Come September* (62), *Tammy and the Doctor* (63), *Take Her She's Mine* (64), *That Funny Feeling* (65), *A Man Could Get Killed* (66), *Doctor, You've Got to be Kidding* (67), etc.

DE FILLIPPO, EDUARDO (1900–). Italian actor-writer-director, mainly on stage. *Tre Uomini in Frac* (a) (32). *Il Cappello a tre Punte* (a) (34), *Napoli Milionaria* (a, w, d), (50), *Questi Fantasmi* (w, d) (54), *Gold of Naples* (a) (54), *Fortunella* (a, co-w) (58) etc.

DEFOE, DANIEL (c.1660–1731). English writer whose work included the oft-filmed *Robinson Crusoe* (qv); also *Moll Flanders*, which the 1965 film resembled but slightly.

DEFORE, DON (1917–). American actor who played the 'good guy' or dumb hearty westerner in dozens of forgettable films in the 40s and 50s. *The Affairs of Susan* (45), *You Came Along* (45), *It's Magic* (48), *Dark City* (50), *Jumping Jacks* (52), *Battle Hymn* (57), *The Facts of Life* (60), etc.

DE FOREST, LEE (1873–1961). American inventor, pioneer of many developments in wireless telegraphy, also the De Forest Phonofilm of the 20s, an early experiment in synchronized sound.

DE FUNES, LOUIS (1908–). French character comedian. *Lock up the Spoons* (56), *Femmes de Paris* (58), *Taxi* (59), *A Pied a Cheval et en Spoutnik* (60), *The Sucker* (65), *Don't Look Now* (67), many others.

DE GRASSE, ROBERT (1900–). American cinematographer, with RKO from 1934. *Break of Hearts* (35), *Stage Door* (37), *The Story of Vernon and Irene Castle* (39), *Kitty Foyle* (40), *Forever and a Day* (43), *Step Lively* (44), *The Body Snatcher* (45), *The Miracle of the Bells* (48), *Home of the Brave* (49), *The Men* (50), *Chicago Calling* (52), many others.

DE GRUNWALD, ANATOLE (1910–67). British writer-producer, in films since 1939. Wrote scripts for *French Without Tears* (39), *Quiet Wedding* (40), *The First of the Few* (41), etc. Produced *The Demi-Paradise* (42), *The Way to the Stars* (45), *The Winslow Boy* (48), *The Holly and the Ivy* (54), *The Doctor's Dilemma* (58), *Libel* (61), *Come Fly with Me* (62), *The VIPs* (63), *The Yellow Rolls-Royce* (64), *Stranger in the House* (67), others.

DE GRUNWALD, DMITRI (C. 1913–   ). British producer: *The Dock Brief* (62), *Connecting Rooms* (69), *Grigsby* (69), etc. Brother of Anatole de Grunwald.

DE HAVEN, GLORIA (1925–   ). American soubrette, in films since 1940: mostly light musicals of no enduring quality. *Thousands Cheer* (43), *Two Girls and a Sailor* (44), *The Thin Man Goes Home* (45), *Summer Holiday* (48), *Scene of the Crime* (49), *Three Little Words* (50), *Two Tickets to Broadway* (51), *The Girl Rush* (55), etc. Recently in cabaret and TV shows.

†DE HAVILLAND, OLIVIA (1916–   ). British-born leading lady, sister of Joan Fontaine. Transferred from stage to film version of Reinhardt's *A Midsummer Night's Dream* (35), was quickly established as a heroine for Warner costume dramas, and spent twenty busy years in Hollywood, mainly as a provider of sweetness and light. *Alibi Ike* (35), *Captain Blood* (35), *Anthony Adverse* (36), *The Charge of the Light Brigade* (36), *Call It a Day* (36), *The Great Garrick* (36), *It's Love I'm After* (37), *Gold Is Where You Find It* (37), *Four's a Crowd* (38), *The Adventures of Robin Hood* (38), *Hard To Get* (38), *Wings of the Navy* (39), *Dodge City* (39), *Gone with the Wind* (39), *Elizabeth and Essex* (39), *Raffles* (40), *My Love Came Back* (40), *Sante Fe Trail* (40), *Strawberry Blonde* (41), *Hold Back the Dawn* (41), *They Died with Their Boots On* (41), *The Male Animal* (42), *In This Our Life* (42), *Government Girl* (43), *Devotion* (as Charlotte Bronte) (43), *Princess O'Rourke* (43), *The Well-Groomed Bride* (45), *The Dark Mirror* (46), *To Each His Own* (AA) (46), *The Snake Pit* (47), *The Heiress* (AA) (49), *My Cousin Rachel* (52), *That Lady* (55), *Not as a Stranger* (55), *The Ambassador's Daughter* (56), *The Proud Rebel* (58), *Libel* (GB) (60), *The Light in the Piazza* (62), *Lady in a Cage* (64), *Hush Hush Sweet Charlotte* (64), *The Adventurers* (69), *Waterloo* (69). Published semi-autobiographical book 1960: *Every Frenchman Has One*.

DEHN, PAUL (1912–   ). British screen writer, former film critic. *Seven Days to Noon* (51), *Orders to Kill* (58), *Goldfinger* (64) (co-author), *The Spy Who Came In from the Cold* (65), *The Deadly Affair* (66), *The Taming of the Shrew* (67), *Fragment of Fear* (also produced) (69), etc.

DEHNER, JOHN (1915–   ). American character actor, usually as sympathetic smart alec or dastardly villain. *Captain Eddie* (45),

Dekker, Albert

The Secret of St Ives (49), *Last of the Buccaneers* (50), *Lorna Doone* (51), *Scaramouche* (52), *Apache* (54), *Carousel* (56), *The Left-Handed Gun* (as Pat Garrett) (58), *Timbuktu* (59), *The Chapman Report* (62), *Youngblood Hawke* (64), *Stiletto* (69), etc. TV series: *The Roaring Twenties*.

DEKKER, ALBERT (1905–1968). Dutch-American stage actor of long experience. First notable on screen as *Dr Cyclops* (39); also *Among the Living* (41), *In Old Oklahoma* (43), *Woman of the Town* (44), *The French Key* (46), *Gentlemen's Agreement* (48), *The Furies* (50), *As Young as You Feel* (51), *Wait Till the Sun Shines, Nellie* (53), *East of Eden* (54), *Kiss Me Deadly* (55), *Illegal* (56), *Suddenly Last Summer* (59), *The Wild Bunch* (69), etc.

DELAIR, SUZY (1916–). Vivacious French entertainer, in several films including *Quai des Orfèvres* (47), *Lady Paname* (49), *Robinson Crusoeland* (50), *Gervaise* (55), *Rocco and his Brothers* (60).

DE LA MOTTE, MARGUERITE (1903–1950). American leading lady of silent films: *The Mark of Zorro* (20), *The Three Musketeers* (21), *The Iron Mask* (28), etc. Rare talkies include *Woman's Man* (34), *Reg'lar Fellers* (42).

DE LANE LEA, WILLIAM (1900–1964). British executive, pioneer of sound dubbing processes.

DELANNOY, JEAN (1908–). French director, formerly journalist and cutter. *L'Eternel Retour* (43), *Les Jeux Sont Faits* (47), *Dieu a Besoin des Hommes* (49), *Le Garçon Sauvage* (51), *The Moment of Truth* (52), *Marie Antoinette* (56), *Notre Dame de Paris* (56), *Maigret Sets a Trap* (57), *Le Soleil des Voyous* (67), many others.

DE LA PATELLIERE, DENYS (1921–). French director. *Le Défroque* (wrote only) (52), *Les Aristocrates* (56), *Retour de Manivelle* (57), *Les Grandes Familles* (59), *Marco the Magnificent* (65), *Du Rififi a Paname* (66), *Black Sun* (66), etc.

DE LAURENTIIS, DINO (1919–). Italian producer: *Bitter Rice* (48), *Ulysses* (52), *La Strada* (54), *Barabbas* (62), *The Bible* (65), *Kiss the Girls and Make Them Die* (67), *Anzio* (68), *Barbarella* (68), *Waterloo* (69) etc.

DELERUE, GEORGES (1924–). French composer: *Hiroshima Mon Amour* (58), *Les Jeux de l'Amour* (60), *Une Aussi Longue Absence* (61), *Shoot the Pianist* (61), *Jules et Jim* (61), *Silken Skin* (63), *The Pumpkin Eater* (64), *Viva Maria* (65), *The 25th Hour* (67), *Interlude* (68), etc.

DELEVANTI, CYRIL (1887–). British-born stage actor who has been playing aged gentlemen for many years. Recently: *Mary Poppins* (64), *Night of the Iguana* (64), *The Greatest Story Ever Told* (65), *Counterpoint* (67), *The Killing of Sister George* (68).

DEL GIUDICE, FILIPPO (1892–1961). Italian producer who settled in England and became managing director of Two Cities Films. *French without Tears* (39), *In Which We Serve* (42), *Henry V* (44), *The Way Ahead* (44), *Blithe Spirit* (45), *Odd Man Out* (47), *The Guinea Pig* (48), many others. 1958: retired to a monastery.

DELL, JEFFREY (1904–   ). British comedy writer, author in the 30s of *Nobody Ordered Wolves*, a satirical novel of the film industry. *Sanders of the River* (co-w) (35), *The Saint's Vacation* (41), *Thunder Rock* (co-w) (42), *Don't Take it to Heart* (also directed) (44), *It's Hard to be Good* (also directed) (48), *The Dark Man* (also directed) (50), *Brothers-in-Law* (co-w) (56), *Lucky Jim* (co-w) (58), *Carlton-Browne of the F.O.* (also co-directed) (59), *A French Mistress* (co-w) (61), *Rotten to the Core* (co-w) (65), *The Family Way* (co-w) (66), etc.

DELLUC, LOUIS (1892–1924). Pioneer French director of the 20s associated with the impressionist school. *Fièvre* (21), *La Femme de Nulle Part* (24), etc.

DELON, ALAIN (1935–   ). French leading man, best known abroad for *Plein Soleil* (59), *Rocco and His Brothers* (60), *The Eclipse* (61), *The Leopard* (62), *The Big Snatch* (63), *The Black Tulip* (64), *The Yellow Rolls-Royce* (64), *The Love Cage* (*Joy House*) (US) (65), *Once a Thief* (US) (65), *Lost Command* (66), *Is Paris Burning?* (66), *Texas across the River* (66), *Les Aventuriers* (66), *Histoires Extraordinaires* (67), *Girl on a Motorcycle* (67), *La Pisane* (68), *Jeff* (68), etc.

DELORME, DANIELE (1926–   ) (Gabrielle Girard). French leading lady best remembered in the non-musical version of *Gigi* (48). Other films fairly routine: *La Cage aux Filles* (49), *Sans Laisser d'Adresse* (51), *Tempi Nostri* (54), *Prisons de Femmes* (58), etc. Produced *La Guerre des Boutons* (62) (directed by her husband Yves Robert).

DEL RIO, DOLORES (1905–   ) (Lolita Dolores de Martinez). Mexican leading lady with aristocratic background; beautiful and popular star of the 20s and 30s. Has continued to make very occasional appearances. *Joanna* (debut) (25), *High Stepper* (26), *What Price Glory?* (27), *The Loves of Carmen* (27), *Resurrection* (28), *Evangeline* (29), *The Bad One* (30), *The Dove* (31), *Bird of Paradise* (32), *Flying down to Rio* (33), *Wonder Bar* (34), *Madame Du Barry* (34), *Lancer Spy* (37), *Journey into Fear* (42), *Portrait of Maria* (45), *The Fugitive* (47), *Cheyenne Autumn* (64), *Once upon a Time* (67), many others.

DEL RUTH, ROY (1895–1961). American director, former gag writer for Mack Sennett. *Wolf's Clothing* (27), *Lady Killer* (34), *Kid Millions* (35), *Broadway Melody of 1936*, *On the Avenue* (37), *The Chocolate Soldier* (41), *Topper Returns* (41), *Broadway Rhythm* (44), *It Happened on Fifth Avenue* (47), *Always Leave Them Laughing* (49), *Stop, You're*

Killing Me (52), *Phantom of the Rue Morgue* (54), *The Alligator People* (59), *Why Must I Die?* (60), many others.

DEMAREST, WILLIAM (1892–   ). American character actor, an 'old pro' with vast vaudeville experience before film debut in 1927. *The Jazz Singer* (27), *Fingerprints* (27); did not film again till 1936, then became Hollywood resident. *Wedding Present* (36), *Rosalie* (38), *Mr Smith Goes to Washington* (39), *Tin Pan Alley* (40), *The Great McGinty* (40), *Sullivan's Travels* (41), *The Palm Beach Story* (42), *Hail the Conquering Hero* (43), *The Miracle of Morgan's Creek* (as Officer Kockenlocker) (43), *Once upon a Time* (44), *Pardon My Past* (45), *Along Came Jones* (45), *The Jolson Story* (one of his best roles, as the old vaudevillian who becomes Jolson's manager) (46), *The Perils of Pauline* (47), *On Our Merry Way* (49), *Jolson Sings Again* (50), *The First Legion* (51), *Riding High* (51), *Dangerous When Wet* (52), *Escape from Fort Bravo* (53), *Jupiter's Darling* (54), *The Rawhide Years* (56), *Son of Flubber* (63), *It's a Mad Mad Mad Mad World* (63), *That Darn Cat* (65), over a hundred others. TV series: *Wells Fargo*, *Love and Marriage*.

DE MARNEY, DERRICK (1906–   ). Good-looking British actor with stage experience. *Things to Come* (film debut) (35), *Young and Innocent* (37), *Victoria the Great* (as Disraeli) (37), *Blonde Cheat* (US) (38), *The Spider* (39), *The Lion Has Wings* (40), *Dangerous Moonlight* (40), *The First of the Few* (42), etc.; war service; *Latin Quarter* (also co-produced) (46), *Uncle Silas* (47), *Sleeping Car to Trieste* (48), *She Shall Have Murder* (also produced) (50), *Meet Mr Callaghan* (also produced) (54), *Private's Progress* (55), *Doomsday at Eleven* (62), *The Projected Man* (66), etc. Recently involved in production deals rather than acting.

DE MARNEY, TERENCE (1909–   ). British actor with stage experience, brother of Derrick de Marney. *The Mystery of the Marie Celeste* (36), *I Killed the Count* (38), *Dual Alibi* (46), *No Way Back* (49), *Uneasy Terms* (as Peter Cheyney's Slim Callaghan) (49), *The Silver Chalice* (US) (55), *Death Is a Woman* (66). *All Neat in Black Stockings* (69), etc. Has also played on American TV.

DE MAUPASSANT, GUY (1850–93). French short story writer. Works filmed include *Diary of a Madman*, *Une Vie*, *Le Rosier de Madame Husson*, and many versions of *Boule de Suif*.

DEMICH, IRINA (1937–   ). Franco-Russian leading lady in international films. *The Longest Day* (62), *Those Magnificent Men in Their Flying Machines* (65), *Up From The Beach* (65), *Cloportes* (65), *Prudence and the Pill* (68), etc.

DE MILLE, CECIL B. (1881–1959). American producer-director, in films since 1913, when he directed *The Squaw Man*. Later noted for society sex dramas, bathtub scenes, and pseudo-biblical spectacles. Played himself in *Sunset Boulevard* (50). Films include *Carmen* (15), *Male and Female* (19), *Forbidden Fruit* (21), *The Ten Commandments* (23), *King of Kings* (27), *The Sign of the Cross* (32), *Cleopatra* (34), *Union Pacific* (39), *Northwest Mounted Police* (40), *Reap the Wild Wind* (42), *Unconquered* (47), *Samson and Delilah* (49), *The Greatest Show on Earth* (53), *The Ten Commandments* (56), *The Buccaneer* (59). Published *An Autobiography* in 1959.

DE MILLE, KATHERINE (1911–   ) (Katherine Lester). American leading lady of the 30s. *Viva Villa* (34), *Call of the Wild* (35), *Ramona* (36), *Banjo on My Knee* (37), *Blockade* (38), *Unconquered* (47), *The Gamblers* (50), etc.

DE MILLE, WILLIAM (1878–1955). Elder brother of Cecil B. de Mille, with theatrical background. Directed *Nice People* (22), *Craig's Wife* (28), *The Emperor Jones* (33), others. Produced *The Warrens of Virginia* (15), *Carmen* (16), *Why Change Your Wife* (19), *Captain Fury* (39), etc.

DEMONGEOT, MYLENE (1936–   ). Blonde French leading lady, briefly flaunted as sex symbol. *The Witches of Salem* (56), *Bonjour Tristesse* (57), *Upstairs and Downstairs* (GB) (59), *The Giant of Marathon* (60), *Gold for the Caesars* (62), *Uncle Tom's Cabin* (Ger) (65), *Fantomas* (66), *The Vengeance of Fantomas* (67), *The Private Navy of Sgt O'Farrell* (68), etc.

DEMPSTER, CAROL (1902–   ). American leading lady of the silent screen, especially for D. W. Griffith. *Scarlet Days* (19), *The Love Flower* (20), *Dream Street* (21), *One Exciting Night* (22), *America* (24), *Isn't Life Wonderful* (24), *That Royal Girl* (26), etc.; retired to marry.

†DEMY, JACQUES (1931–   ). French director. *Lola* (60), *La Baie des Anges* (62), *Les Parapluies de Cherbourg* (64), *The Young Girls of Rochefort* (67), *The Model Shop* (US) (60).

DENCH, JUDI (1934–   ). British stage actress now beginning a film career : *He Who Rides a Tiger* (66), *Four in the Morning* (BFA) (66), *A Midsummer Night's Dream* (68).

DENEUVE, CATHERINE (1943–   ). French leading lady, sister of Françoise Dorleac. *Les Parapluies de Cherbourg* (64), *Repulsion* (GB) (65), *Das Liebeskarussel (Who Wants to Sleep?)* (65), *Les Créatures* (66), *The Young Girls of Rochefort* (67), *Belle de Jour* (67), *Benjamin* (68), *Manon 70* (68), *Mayerling* (68), *The April Fools* (US) (69), *The Mississippi Mermaid* (69), etc.

DENHAM, MAURICE (1909–   ). British character actor with stage experience from 1934; popular as Dudley Davenport in radio's 'Much Binding' show in 40s. First sizeable film part in *It's Not*

Cricket (48); subsequently much in demand for eccentric cameo roles. *London Belongs to Me* (48), *The Spider and the Fly* (50), *The Million Pound Note* (54), *Simon and Laura* (55), *Checkpoint* (56), *Night of the Demon* (57), *Our Man in Havana* (59), *Sink the Bismarck* (60), *HMS Defiant* (62), *The Seventh Dawn* (64), *Hysteria* (65), *The Alphabet Murders* (65), *After the Fox* (66), *The Midas Run* (69), *The Virgin and the Gypsy* (70), many others.

DENISON, MICHAEL (1915–   ). British leading man with firm but gentle manner. On stage from 1938, films from 1940; married to Dulcie Gray. *Hungry Hill* (44), *My Brother Jonathan* (47), *The Glass Mountain* (47), *Angels One Five* (51), *The Importance of Being Earnest* (53), *Faces in the Dark* (61), many others. TV series: *Boyd Q.C.*

DENNER, CHARLES (c. 1933–   ). French leading actor, so far most notable in two eccentric roles: *Landru* (62), *Life Upside Down* (63).

DENNING, RICHARD (1916–   ) (Louis A. Denninger). American leading man who from 1937 played light romantic roles and manly athletes. *Hold 'Em Navy* (37), *Persons in Hiding* (38), *Union Pacific* (39), *Golden Gloves* (40), *Adam Had Four Sons* (41), *Beyond the Blue Horizon* (42), *The Glass Key* (42), etc.; war service; *Seven Were Saved* (46), *Black Beauty* (46), *Caged Fury* (48), *No Man of Her Own* (48), *Weekend with Father* (50), *Scarlet Angel* (51), *Hangman's Knot* (53), *The Creature from the Black Lagoon* (54), *Assignment Redhead* (GB) (56), *The Black Scorpion* (57), many others, mainly second features. TV series: *Mr and Mrs North* (53–54), *The Flying Doctor* (59), *Michael Shayne* (60). Married Evelyn Ankers.

DENNIS, SANDY (1937–   ). American leading actress. *Splendour in the Grass* (61), *Who's Afraid of Virginia Woolf* (66), *Up the Down Staircase* (67), *Sweet November* (68), *The Fox* (68), *The Out-of-Towners* (69), *A Touch of Love* (69), *That Cold Day in the Park* (69), etc.

DENNY, REGINALD (1891–1967) (Reginald Leigh Daymore). British actor, on stage from childhood. From 1919 starred in many Hollywood comedies and when sound came in began to play amiable stiff-upper-lip Britishers. More or less retired after 1950 to devote time to his aircraft company. *49 East* (20), *Footlights* (21), *The Leather Pushers* (22), *The Abysmal Brute* (23), *Skinner's Dress Suit* (25), *Oh Doctor* (26), *California Straight Ahead* (27), *Embarrassing Moments* (29), *Madame Satan* (30), *Private Lives* (32), *Anna Karenina* (35), *Romeo and Juliet* (36), several *Bulldog Drummond* films (37–38) (as Algy), *Rebecca* (as Frank Crawley) (40), *Sherlock Holmes and the Voice of Terror* (42), *Love Letters* (45), *The Secret Life of Walter Mitty* (47), *Mr Blandings Builds His Dream House* (as Mr Simms) (48), *Abbott and Costello Meet Dr Jekyll and Mr Hyde* (53), *Around the World in Eighty Days* (56), *Fort Vengeance* (59), *Cat Ballou* (65), *Batman* (66), many others.

dentists are seldom popular chaps, but Preston Sturges made a film about one of them, the inventor of laughing gas: *The Great Moment*. Sinister dentists were found in *The Man Who Knew Too Much* (original version), *The Secret Partner*, and *Footsteps in the Dark*, and a comic one, in the person of Bob Hope, in *The Paleface*. W. C. Fields once made a film of his sketch *The Dentist*; and Laurel and Hardy in *Leave 'Em Laughing* were overcome by laughing gas.

DENVER, BOB (1935–). American TV comedian. Films: *For Those Who Think Young* (64), *Who's Minding the Mint* (67). TV series: *Dobie Gillis* (59–62), *Gilligan's Island* (64–66).

department stores have usually been a background for comedy. New York store backgrounds have often shown the native superiority of the working girl to snobbish shopwalkers and obtuse management, as in *Bachelor Mother* and its remake *Bundle of Joy*, *The Devil and Miss Jones* and the 1924 *Manhandled*. Broader comedy elements were to the fore in *Miracle on 34th Street*, *The Big Store*, *Who's Minding the Store*, *Fitzwilly* and *How To Save a Marriage*. British comedies with store settings include *Kipps*, *The Crowded Day*, *Laughter in Paradise*, *Keep Fit*, and *Trouble in Store*.

DE PUTTI, LYA (1901–1931). Hungarian leading lady of the 20s. *The Phantom* (Ger.) (25), *Variety* (Ger.) (25), *The Sorrows of Satan* (US) (26), *The Heart Thief* (US) (27), *Buck Privates* (28), *The Informer* (GB) (29), etc.

DEREK, JOHN (1926–). American leading man who made film debut in *Knock on Any Door* (49). Subsequently in routine action pictures: *Mask of the Avenger* (51), *The Adventures of Hajji Baba* (54), *The Flesh Is Weak* (55), *The Ten Commandments* (56), *Exodus* (58), *Nightmare in the Sun* (64), *Once Before I Die* (66), *Childish Things* (69), many others.

DE ROCHEMONT, LOUIS (1899–). American producer, from the world of newsreel. Devised *The March of Time* (34); later produced semi-documentaries like *The House on 92nd Street* (47), *Boomerang* (47), *Martin Luther* (53), and was involved in many ventures including Cinerama and Cinemiracle.

DERR, RICHARD (1917–). American leading man, usually in minor films. *Ten Gentlemen from West Point* (42), *Tonight We Raid Calais* (43), *The Secret Heart* (47), *Joan of Arc* (48), *When Worlds Collide* (51), *Something To Live For* (52), *Terror is a Man* (59), *Three in the Attic* (68), etc.

DESAILLY, JEAN (1920–). French leading man. *Le Voyageur de la Toussaint* (42), *Sylvie et la Fantôme* (45), *Occupe Toi d'Amélie* (49), *Les Grandes Manoeuvres* (55), *Maigret Sets a Trap* (59), *Le Doulos* (62), *Le Peau Douce* (64), *The Twenty-Fifth Hour* (66), etc.

DE SANTIS, GIUSEPPE (1917–   ). Italian director. *Caccia Tragica* (47), *Bitter Rice* (49), *No Peace among the Olives* (50), *Rome Eleven O'clock* (51), *A Husband for Anna* (53), *Men and Wolves* (56), *La Garconnière* (60), etc.

DE SANTIS, JOE (1909–   ). American character actor who often plays Italianate gangsters. *Slattery's Hurricane* (49), *Man with a Cloak* (51), *The Last Hunt* (56), *Tension at Table Rock* (57), *And Now Miguel* (66), *The Professionals* (66), *Blue* (68), etc.

DE SARIGNY, PETER (1911–   ). South African-born producer, in Britain from 1936. *The Malta Story* (53), *Simba* (55), *True as a Turtle* (56), *Never Let Go* (60), *Waltz of the Toreadors* (62), etc.

desert islands have provided the locale of many a film adventure. *Robinson Crusoe* has been filmed several times, with two recent variations in *Robinson Crusoe on Mars* and *Lt. Robin Crusoe USN*. *Treasure Island* too has survived three or four versions, to say nothing of imitations like *Blackbeard the Pirate* and parodies such as *Abbott and Costello Meet Captain Kidd* and *Old Mother Riley's Jungle Treasure*. *The Admirable Crichton* (qv) is perhaps the next most overworked desert island story, with *The Swiss Family Robinson* following on. Dorothy Lamour found a few desert islands in films like *Typhoon* and *Aloma of the South Seas*; Cary Grant had one nearly to himself in *Father Goose*; Joan Greenwood and co. were marooned on a rather special one in *Mysterious Island*. *Our Girl Friday* played the theme for sex; *Dr Dolittle* found educated natives on one; Cary Grant lived on one as a reluctant spy in *Father Goose*. *Sea Wife*, *Lord of the Flies* and *The Day the Fish Came Out* were three recent but not very successful attempts to take the theme seriously: *Hell in the Pacific* was one that did work.

A comic TV series on the subject was *Gilligan's Island* (64–66); a serious one, *The New People* (69).

deserts have figured in many a western, from *Tumbleweed* to *Mackenna's Gold*. Other films which have paid particularly respectful attention to the dangers that too much sand can provide include *The Sheik* and *Son of the Sheik*, *Greed*, *The Lost Patrol*, *The Garden of Allah*, *Sahara*, *Five Graves to Cairo*, *Ice Cold in Alex*, *Sea of Sand*, *Desert Rats*, *Play Dirty*, *The Sabre and the Arrow*, *Legend of the Lost*, *The Ten Commandments*, *She*, *Lawrence of Arabia*, *The Black Tent*, *Oasis*, *Sands of the Kalahari* and *The Flight of the Phoenix*.

THE DESERT SONG. The popular operetta by Sigmund Romberg, Otto Harbach and Oscar Hammerstein was filmed in 1929, with John Boles and Carlotta King; in 1943, with Dennis Morgan and Irene Manning, and in 1952, with Gordon Macrae and Kathryn Grayson.

DE SETA, VITTORIO (1923–). Italian director, mainly of shorts until *Bandits at Orgosolo* (62).

DE SICA, VITTORIO (1902–). Italian actor and director, in the latter respect an important and skilful realist. Well known in Italy in the 30s, but not elsewhere until after World War II. *Teresa Venerdi* (d) (41), *I Bambini ci Guardino* (d) (42), *Shoeshine* (d) (46), *Bicycle Thieves* (AA) (d) (48), *Miracle in Milan* (d) (50), *Umberto D* (d) (52), *Madame De* (a) (52), *Stazione Termini (Indiscretion)* (d) (52), *Bread, Love and Dreams* (a, d) (53), *Gold of Naples* (d) (54), *A Farewell to Arms* (a) (57), *Il Generale della Rovere* (a) (59), *Two Women* (d) (61), *The Condemned of Altona* (d) (63), *A New World* (d) (66), *The Biggest Bundle of them All* (a) (66), *After the Fox* (d) (66), *Woman Times Seven* (d) (67), *The Shoes of the Fisherman* (a) (68), *A Place for Lovers* (d) (69), *Sunflower* (d) (70), etc. TV series as actor: *The Four Just Men* (Br) (59).

DESMOND, FLORENCE (1905–) (F. Dawson). British dancer and impersonator, seen in many stage revues but few films. *Sally in Our Alley* (31), *No Limit* (35), *Keep Your Seats Please* (37), *Hoots Mon* (40), *Three Came Home* (US) (50), *Charley Moon* (56), *Some Girls Do* (68), etc.

DESMOND, WILLIAM (1878–1949). Irish leading man of the American silent screen, mostly in westerns: *The Sunset Trail* (24), *Blood and Steel* (26), *Tongues of Scandal* (29), *Hell Bent for Frisco* (31), *Flying Fury* (33), *Arizona Days* (36), etc.

DESMONDE, JERRY (1908–67). British character actor with long music-hall experience, a perfect foil for comedians from Sid Field to Norman Wisdom. *London Town* (46), *Cardboard Cavalier* (48), *Follow a Star* (59), *A Stitch in Time* (63), *The Early Bird* (65), many others. Also TV quizmaster and panellist.

DESNI, TAMARA (1913–). Russian-born, British-resident leading lady. *Jack Ahoy* (34), *Fire over England* (36), *The Squeaker* (37), *Traitor Spy* (40), *Send for Paul Temple* (46), *Dick Barton at Bay* (50), etc.

DESNY, IVAN (1922–). Continental leading man, in films from 1948. *Madeleine* (GB) (50), *La Putain Respectueuse* (52), *Lola Montes* (55), *The Mirror Has Two Faces* (58), *The Magnificent Rebel* (60), *Das Liebeskarussel (Who Wants to Sleep?)* (65), *The Mystery of Thug Island* (66), *I Killed Rasputin* (68), *Mayerling* (68), etc.

DE SOUZA, EDWARD (1933–). British leading man, mostly on stage. *The Roman Spring of Mrs Stone* (film debut) (61), *The Phantom of the Opera* (62), *Kiss of the Vampire* (63), etc. TV series: *The Marriage Lines*.

Destry Rides Again

DESTRY RIDES AGAIN (US 1939). Tragi-comic Western based on Max
Brand's story of the diffident hero who finally buckles on his guns.
(Filmed several times, the latest being *Destry* [55] with Audie
Murphy.) This version has become a classic for several reasons:
Marlene Dietrich's brilliant comeback performance as Frenchy,
with songs like 'See What the Boys in the Back Room Will Have';
George Marshall's crisply professional direction; and a near-
perfect cast including James Stewart, Mischa Auer, Charles
Winninger, Samuel S. Hinds, Brian Donlevy and Una Merkel
(whose on-screen fight with Dietrich caused a mild censorship
problem at the time).

DE TOTH, ANDRE (c. 1900–   ). Hungarian-American director, in
films since 1931, Hollywood since 1940. Films competent but
routine, the most memorable being *House of Wax* (53), the first
3-D films from a major studio; de Toth, having only one eye,
couldn't see the effect. *Dark Waters* (44), *Passport to Suez* (45),
The Other Love (47), *Ramrod* (47), *Pitfall* (48), *Slattery's Hurricane*
(49), *Springfield Rifle* (52), *The City is Dark* (54), *The Indian Fighter*
(55), *Monkey on My Back* (57), *The Two-Headed Spy* (GB) (58),
Day of the Outlaw (59), *Morgan the Pirate* (61), *Gold for the Caesars*
(62), *Play Dirty* (GB) (68), etc.

DEUTSCH, DAVID (1926–   ). British producer, in films from 1949,
Blind Date (59), *Nothing But the Best* (64), *Catch Us If You Can* (65),
Lock Up Your Daughters (69), etc.

THE DEVIL has made frequent appearances in movies. There were
versions of *Faust* in 1900, 1903, 1904, 1907, 1909, 1911, 1921 and
1925, the last of these featuring Emil Jannings as Mephistopheles.
Later variations on this theme include *The Sorrows of Satan* (27)
with Adolphe Menjou; *All That Money Can Buy* (41), with Walter
Huston as Mr Scratch; *Alias Nick Beal* (49), with Ray Milland;
La Beauté du Diable (50) with Gérard Philippe; *Damn Yankees* (58)
with Ray Walston; *Bedazzled* (67) with Peter Cook; and *Doctor
Faustus* (68) with Andreas Teuber. In other stories, Satan was
played by Helge Nissen in *Leaves From Satan's Book* (20), Jules Berry
in *Les Visiteurs du Soir* (42), Alan Mowbray in *The Devil with Hitler*
(42), Laird Cregar in *Heaven Can Wail* (43), Claude Rains in *Angel
on My Shoulder* (46), Stanley Holloway in *Meet Mr Lucifer* (53),
Mel Welles in *The Undead* (57), Vincent Price in *The Story of Mankind*
(57), Cedric Hardwicke in *Bait* (54), Vittorio Gassman in *The
Devil in Love* (67), Stig Järrel in *The Devil's Eye* (60), Pierre Clement
in *The Milky Way* (68). In the Swedish *Witchcraft through the
Ages* (21) the devil was played by the director, Benjamin Christensen. Devil worship has been the subject of *The Black Cat* (34), *The
Seventh Victim* (43), *Night of the Demon* (57), *Back from the Dead* (57),

The Witches (66), *Eye of the Devil* (66), *The Devil Rides Out* (68), *Rosemary's Baby* (68).

DEVILLE, MICHEL (1931–   ). French director. *Ce Soir ou Jamais* (60), *L'Appartement de Filles* (63), *Benjamin* (67), *Bye Bye Barbara* (69), etc.

Devil's Island, the French penal colony, has intermittently fascinated film-makers. Apart from the versions of the Dreyfus case (*Dreyfus*, *The Life of Emile Zola*, *I Accuse*), there have been Ronald Colman in *Condemned to Devil's Island*, Boris Karloff in *Devil's Island*, Clark Gable in *Strange Cargo*, Humphrey Bogart in *Passage to Marseilles*, and Eartha Kitt in *Saint of Devil's Island*.

DEVINE, ANDY (1905–   ). Fat, husky-voiced American character comedian seen in scores of Westerns from the 20s on. Best roles in *Stagecoach* (39), *The Red Badge of Courage* (51). More recently on TV, especially *Wild Bill Hickock* series. Recently: *The Man Who Shot Liberty Valance* (62), *How the West Was Won* (62), *Zebra in the Kitchen* (65), *The Epic of Josie* (67).

DEVON, LAURA (c. 1939–   ). American leading lady from TV. *Goodbye Charlie* (65), *Red Line 7000* (66), *Gunn* (67).

DE WILDE, BRANDON (1942–   ). Former American child actor, on stage when seven years old in 'The Member of the Wedding'. Played same role in film version (53), then *Shane* (53), *Blue Jeans* (59), *Hud* (63), *Those Calloways* (65), *In Harm's Way* (65), others.

DE WOLFE, BILLY (1907–   ) (William Andrew Jones). Toothy, moustachioed American comedy actor, formerly dancer, with vaudeville and night club experience. (Famous act: a lady taking a bath.) Spasmodically on screen: *Dixie* (43), *Blue Skies* (46), *Dear Ruth* (47), *Lullaby of Broadway* (51), *Call Me Madam* (53), *Billie* (65), etc. TV series: *The Pruitts of Southampton* (67), *The Queen and I* (69).

DEXTER, ANTHONY (1919–   ) (Walter Fleischmann). American leading man with stage experience. Cast as *Valentino* (51), he never lived down the tag, and his subsequent roles have been in small-scale action dramas and science-fiction quickies. *The Brigand* (52), *Captain John Smith and Pocahontas* (53), *Captain Kidd and the Slave Girl* (54), *Fire Maidens from Outer Space* (GB) (54), *He Laughed Last* (56), *The Parson and the Outlaw* (as Billy the Kid) (57), *Twelve to the Moon* (59), *Thoroughly Modern Millie* (67), etc.

DEXTER, BRAD (1922–   ). American character actor often seen as tough hoodlum. *Bus Riley's Back in Town* (64), *Von Ryan's Express* (65), *Blindfold* (66), many others. Produced *The Naked Runner* (67).

DEXTER, MAURY (c. 1928–   ). American producer-director of second features (*Harbour Lights* [62], *House of the Damned* [63], etc.) which were praised for their old-fashioned pacy professionalism. 1965: *The Outlaw of Red River*. 1966: *The Naked Brigade*.

DHERY, ROBERT (1921–   ) (Robert Foullcy; born Hery). French cabaret comedian and pantomimist. Films include *Les Enfants du Paradis* (44), *Sylvie et la Fantôme* (45), *La Patronne* (directed only) (49), *Ah, Les Belles Bacchantes* (*Femmes de Paris*) (also wrote and directed) (54), *La Belle Américaine* (also wrote and directed) (61), *Allez France* (also wrote and directed) (64), *Le Petit Baigneur* (also wrote and directed) (67).

LE DIABLE AU CORPS (France 1946). A tragic love story of World War I, written by Aurenche and Bost, directed by Claude Autant-Lara, with Gerard Philipe and Micheline Presle. Its international success was a boost for the post-war French cinema.

LES DIABOLIQUES (THE FIENDS) (France 1954). Suspense thriller which has become a minor classic partly because of the twists of its Boileau-Narcejac plot (frequently copied since), partly because of the acting of Simone Signoret and Vera Clouzot, but chiefly because of Henri-Georges Clouzot's spellbinding direction.

DIAMOND, I. A. L. (* –   ). American writer. *Murder in the Blue Room* (44), *Never Say Goodbye* (46), *Always Together* (48), *The Girl from Jones Beach* (49), *Let's Make It Legal* (51), *Love Nest* (51), *Something for the Birds* (52), etc.; later began collaboration with Billy Wilder in scripting *Some Like It Hot* (59), *The Apartment* (60), *Kiss Me Stupid* (64), etc. 1969: *Cactus Flower*.

DIARY OF A CHAMBERMAID. Octave Mirabeau's eccentric novel of the decadent French squirearchy was filmed rather unsatisfactorily by Jean Renoir in America in 1943, with Paulette Goddard, Francis Lederer and Burgess Meredith. Luis Bunuel directed a French remake in 1964, with Jeanne Moreau and a more sympathetic cast.

A DIARY FOR TIMOTHY (GB) (1945). One of World War II's most brilliantly-assembled documentaries, a picture of Britain in the war's last months, looking to the future through the eyes of four men and a baby. Written by E. M. Forster, produced by Basil Wright, directed by Humphrey Jennings, with commentary by Michael Redgrave. Fifteen years later Granada TV mounted a programme to trace what had happened to the characters in the film.

DICK, DOUGLAS (1920–   ). Innocent-looking American 'second lead'. *The Searching Wind* (46), *Saigon* (47), *Home of the Brave* (49),

The Red Badge of Courage (51), *The Gambler from Natchez* (55), *The Oklahoman* (57), etc.

DICKENS, CHARLES (1812–1870). Prolific British novelist whose gusto in characterization and plot-weaving made his books ideal cinema material until the last decade when producers seem to have thought them old-fashioned. Most filmed has perhaps been *A Christmas Carol*, usually personified as *Scrooge* (qv); but *Oliver Twist* (qv) runs it a close second. There had been several early silent versions of *David Copperfield* before Cukor's splendid 1934 version (qv), and *The Old Curiosity Shop* was popular as the basis of one-reelers before the most recent version (GB 1934) with Hay Petrie as Quilp. *A Tale of Two Cities* had been a popular stage play under the title 'The Only Way'; after many early versions it was directed as a spectacular by Frank Lloyd in 1917, with William Farnum; as a British silent in 1926, with Martin Harvey; as a vehicle for Ronald Colman in 1935; and in a rather uninspired British version of 1958 starring Dirk Bogarde. A 1969 all-star version of *David Copperfield* was primarily intended for American TV.

Other Dickens novels less frequently filmed include *The Mystery of Edwin Drood*, once as an early British silent and again in Hollywood in 1935, with Claude Rains as John Jasper; *Great Expectations*, which had two silent versions, a rather dull Hollywood remake of 1934 and the magnificent David Lean version of 1946 (qv); *Dombey and Son*, under the title *Rich Man's Folly*, starring George Bancroft in 1931; *Nicholas Nickleby*, the only picturization of which was the patchy Ealing version of 1947; and *The Pickwick Papers*, seen in various potted versions in silent days and in Noel Langley's superficial version of 1952.

Dickens' novels which were filmed in the silent period but not since sound include *The Cricket on the Hearth*, *Martin Chuzzlewit*, *Little Dorrit*, *Our Mutual Friend* and *Barnaby Rudge*.

DICKINSON, ANGIE (1931–). American leading lady, former beauty contest winner, in films from 1954: *Lucky Me* (54), *Rio Bravo* (59), *The Sins of Rachel Cade* (61), *Jessica* (62), *Captain Newman* (63), *The Art of Love* (65), *The Chase* (66), *Cast a Giant Shadow* (66), *Pistolero* (67), *Point Blank* (68), *Sam Whiskey* (68), *Fuzz* (69), etc.

DICKINSON, DESMOND (1902–). British cinematographer. *Men of Two Worlds* (45), *Fame is the Spur* (46), *Hamlet* (47), *The History of Mr Polly* (49), *Morning Departure* (50), *The Browning Version* (52), *The Importance of Being Earnest* (53), *Carrington VC* (55), *Orders to Kill* (58), *City of the Dead* (60), *Sparrows Can't Sing* (63), *A Study in Terror* (65), *Circus of Blood* (67), *Decline and Fall* (68), etc.

DICKINSON, THOROLD (1903–). British director, in films since 1925. *The High Command* (36), *Gaslight* (39), *Next of Kin* (41), *The Queen of Spades* (48), *The Secret People* (50), etc. Now teaches film theory at Slade School, London.

DICKSON, DOROTHY (1902–   ). American musical comedy star who spent most of her career in Britain. Films include *Money Mad* (17), *Channel Crossing* (32), *Danny Boy* (34), *Sword of Honour* (39).

DICKSON, PAUL (1920–   ). British director, hailed for documentaries *The Undefeated* (49), *David* (51). His feature films have been less distinguished: *Satellite in the Sky* (56), *The Depraved* (57), many second features and TV episodes.

DIERKES, JOHN (c. 1906–   ). Gaunt supporting actor who has played small parts in many films since 1950. *The Red Badge of Courage* (51), *The Naked Jungle* (54), *Jubal* (56), *The Left-handed Gun* (58), etc.

DIETERLE, WILLIAM (1893–   ). Distinguished German-American director of great pictorial style. (Formerly an actor in such films as Paul Leni's *Waxworks*.) In Hollywood from 1930. *The Last Flight* (31), *Grand Slam* (32), *Fog over Frisco* (34), *A Midsummer Night's Dream* (co-d) (35), *Dr Socrates* (35), *The Story of Louis Pasteur* (35), *Satan Met a Lady* (36), *The White Angel* (36), *The Life of Émile Zola* (37), *Blockade* (38), *Juarez* (39), *The Hunchback of Notre Dame* (40), *Dr Ehrlich's Magic Bullet* (40), *This Man Reuter* (41), *All That Money Can Buy* (also produced) (41), *Syncopation* (also produced) (42), *Tennessee Johnson* (43), *Kismet* (44), *Love Letters* (45), *I'll Be Seeing You* (45), *The Searching Wind* (46), *Portrait of Jennie* (48), *Rope of Sand* (49), *September Affair* (50), *Dark City* (50), *Volcano* (It.) (50), *Red Mountain* (51), *Boots Malone* (52), *Salome* (53), *Elephant Walk* (54), *Magic Fire* (55), *Omar Khayyam* (57), etc.

†DIETRICH, MARLENE (1902–   ) (Maria Magdalena von Losch). German singer/actress long in America, a living legend of glamour despite many poor films and her domination in the 30s by the heavy style of Josef von Sternberg. *The Tragedy of Love* (23), *Manon Lescaut* (26), *I Kiss Your Hand Madame* (28), *The Blue Angel* (30), all in Germany, then to Hollywood: *Morocco* (30), *Dishonoured* (31), *Shanghai Express* (32), *Blonde Venus* (32), *Song of Songs* (33), *The Scarlet Empress* (34), *The Devil Is a Woman* (35), *Desire* (36), *The Garden of Allah* (36), *Knight Without Armour* (GB) (37), *Angel* (37), *Destry Rides Again* (39), *Seven Sinners* (40), *The Flame of New Orleans* (41), *Manpower* (41), *The Lady Is Willing* (42), *The Spoilers* (42), *Pittsburgh* (42), *Follow the Boys* (44), *Kismet* (44), *Martin Roumagnac* (Fr.) (46), *Golden Earrings* (47), *A Foreign Affair* (48), *Stage Fright* (GB) (50), *No Highway* (GB) (51), *Rancho Notorious* (52), *Witness for the Prosecution* (57), *Touch of Evil* (58), *Judgment at Nuremberg* (61). Since 1950 an international success in cabaret.

DIETZ, HOWARD (1896–   ). American librettist and writer, with MGM from its inception. Best film score: *The Band Wagon* (53).

DIFFRING, ANTON (1918–   ). German actor, in British films from 1951; often the villainous Nazi or the protagonist of a horror film. *State Secret* (50), *Albert RN* (53), *The Sea Shall Not Have Them* (55), *The Colditz Story* (55), *I Am a Camera* (56), *The Man Who Could Cheat Death* (59), *Circus of Horrors* (60), *Incident at Midnight* (63), *The Heroes of Telemark* (65), *Fahrenheit 451* (66), *The Double Man* (67), *Counterpoint* (US) (67), *Where Eagles Dare* (68), etc.

DIGGES, DUDLEY (1879–1947). Irish character actor, with Abbey Theatre experience; played a variety of good roles in Hollywood in the 30s. *Outward Bound* (30), *Condemned to Devil's Island* (30), *The Maltese Falcon* (31), *The Invisible Man* (33), *China Seas* (35), *Mutiny on the Bounty* (35), *The General Died at Dawn* (36), *Raffles* (39), *Son of Fury* (42), *The Searching Wind* (46), etc.

DIGHTON, JOHN (1909–   ). British writer, in films from 1935. *Nicholas Nickleby* (47), *Saraband for Dead Lovers* (48), *Kind Hearts and Coronets* (49), *The Happiest Days of Your Life* (from his own play) (49), *Roman Holiday* (53), *Summer of the Seventeenth Doll* (60), many others including comedies for Will Hay and Max Miller.

DIGNAM, BASIL (1909–   ). British character actor, in innumerable small parts, often as barrister or other professional man. Recently: *Room at the Top* (59), *The Silent Partner* (61), *Life for Ruth* (63), *Victim* (63), etc. Also on stage and TV.

DIGNAM, MARK (c. 1907–   ). British character actor, brother of Basil Dignam. Also plays professional men. Recently: *Sink the Bismarck* (60), *No Love for Johnnie* (62), *Hamlet* (69), etc. Also on stage and TV.

DILLER, PHYLLIS (1917–   ). Zany, grotesque American comedienne who has had trouble adapting her TV style to movies. *Boy Did I Get a Wrong Number* (66), *Eight on the Lam* (67), *The Private Navy of Sergeant O'Farrell* (68), *Did You Hear the One about the Travelling Saleslady?* (68), *The Adding Machine* (GB) (69). TV series: *The Pruitts of Southampton* (66), *The Beautiful Phyllis Diller Show* (68).

DILLMAN, BRADFORD (1930–   ). American actor: *A Certain Smile* (58), *Compulsion* (59), *Circle of Deception* (61), *Francis of Assisi* (61), *A Rage to Live* (65), *The Helicopter Spies* (67), *The Bridge at Remagen* (69), etc. TV series: *Court Martial* (GB) (65).

DINEHART, ALAN (1886–1944). American supporting actor who played many bluff-business-man roles. *Wicked* (32), *Lawyer Man* (33), *Dante's Inferno* (35), *This Is My Affair* (37), *Hotel for Women* (39), *Girl Trouble* (43), *Minstrel Man* (44), many others.

DINGLE, CHARLES (1887–1956). American stage actor who made notable screen debut as one of the wicked uncles in *The Little Foxes* (41). Later: *Johnny Eager* (41), *Talk of the Town* (42), *The Song of Bernadette* (43), *Duel in the Sun* (46), *The Beast with Five Fingers* (47), *State of the Union* (48), *Call Me Madam* (53), *The Court Martial of Billy Mitchell* (55), etc.

DINNER AT EIGHT (US 1933). The cynical society drama by Edna Ferber and George Kaufman was filmed in 1933 by George Cukor, with an all-star cast including the two Barrymore brothers, Marie Dressler, Wallace Beery and Jean Harlow.

director. Normally the most influential creator of a film, who may not only shoot scenes on the studio floor but also supervise script, casting, editing, etc., according to his standing. In more routine films these functions are separately controlled.

directors' appearances in films are comparatively few. Hitchcock remains the unchallengeable winner, with moments in over thirty of his fifty-odd films, including the confined *Rope* (in which his outline appears on a neon sign) and *Lifeboat* (in which he can be seen in a reducing ad. in a newspaper). Preston Sturges can be glimpsed in *Sullivan's Travels*, and in *Paris Holiday*, as a French resident, gets a whole scene to himself. John Huston, uncredited, plays a tourist in *The Treasure of the Sierra Madre* and a master of foxhounds in *The List of Adrian Messenger*; he has more recently begun to take sizeable credited roles, e.g. in *The Cardinal* and *The Bible*. The Paramount lot became a familiar scene in many 40s pictures, with notable guest appearances by Mitchell Leisen in *Hold Back the Dawn* and Cecil B. de Mille in *Sunset Boulevard*, *The Buster Keaton Story*, *Star-Spangled Rhythm*, *Variety Girl*, *Son of Paleface* and others. Jean Cocteau played an old woman in *Orphée* and appeared throughout *The Testament of Orphée*. Nicholas Ray was the American Ambassador in *55 Days in Peking*. Jules Dassin played major roles in *Rififi* (as Perlo Vita) and *Never on Sunday*, as did Jean Renoir in *La Règle du Jeu*. Hugo Fregonese was a messenger in *Decameron Nights*, Samuel Fuller a Japanese cop in *House of Bamboo*. Others who can be glimpsed in their own work include Tony Richardson in *Tom Jones*, Michael Winner in *You Must Be Joking*, George Marshall in *The Crime of Dr Forbes*, Frank Borzage in *Jeanne Eagels*, Robert Aldrich in *The Big Night*, Ingmar Bergman in *Waiting Women*, King Vidor in *Our Daily Bread*, William Castle (producer) in *Rosemary's Baby*, Claude Chabrol in *Les Biches* and *the Road to Corinth*, and Joseph Losey in *The Intimate Stranger* (which he made under the name of Joseph Walton).

disguise has featured in many hundreds of films, and was in the 20s the perquisite of Lon Chaney, all of whose later films featured it.

Lon Chaney Jnr has also had a tendency to it, as had John Barrymore; while most of the Sherlock Holmes films involved it. Other notable examples include Henry Hull in *Miracles for Sale*; Donald Wolfit in *The Ringer*; Marlene Dietrich in *Witness for the Prosecution*; Jack Lemmon and Tony Curtis in *Some Like It Hot*; Tony Randall in *The Seven Faces of Dr Lao*; and practically the entire cast of *The List of Adrian Messenger*. Extensions of disguise are the split personality films, from *Dr Jekyll and Mr Hyde* to *The Three Faces of Eve*.

See also: *transvestism; multiple roles.*

DISKANT, GEORGE E. (1907–1965). American cinematographer. *Riff Raff* (47), *The Narrow Margin* (50), *On Dangerous Ground* (51), *The Bigamist* (53), others.

DISNEY, WALT (1901–1966). American animator and executive whose name is a household word all over the world. Formerly a commercial artist, he produced his first Mickey Mouse cartoon in 1928, using his own voice; also Silly Symphonies, one of which (*Flowers and Trees* [33]) was first film in full Technicolor. Donald Duck first appeared in 1936. First full-length cartoon: *Snow White and the Seven Dwarfs* (37), followed by *Pinocchio* (39), *Fantasia* (40), *Dumbo* (41), *Bambi* (43), *The Three Caballeros* (combining cartoon and live action) (44), *Cinderella* (50), *Alice in Wonderland* (51), *Peter Pan* (53), *Lady and the Tramp* (56), *One Hundred and One Dalmatians* (61), *The Sword in the Stone* (63), *Winnie the Pooh and the Honey Tree* (66), *The Jungle Book* (67), etc. First live-action feature *Treasure Island* (50), followed by a plentiful supply including Westerns (*Westward Ho the Wagons, The Nine Lives of Elfego Baca*), adventure classics (*Kidnapped, Dr Syn*), animal yarns (*Greyfriars Bobby, Old Yeller, The Incredible Journey*), cosy fantasies with music (*In Search of the Castaways, Mary Poppins*), trick comedies (*The Absent-minded Professor, Son of Flubber*) and plain old-fashioned family fun (*Bon Voyage, The Ugly Dachshund*). The patchiness of these films has meant that although the Disney label is still a sure sign of suitability for children, it no longer necessarily indicates quality of any other kind. In 1948 began the irresistible series of 'True-Life Adventures' (cleverly jazzed-up animal documentaries containing much rare footage) and in 1953 came the first feature of this kind, *The Living Desert*; the series has unfortunately died out.

Disney's long list of Academy Awards are all for shorts, apart from 'special awards' for *Snow White, Fantasia, The Living Desert* and *The Vanishing Prairie*. They include a special award for creating Mickey Mouse (32), *Three Little Pigs* (33), *The Tortoise and the Hare* (34), *Three Orphan Kittens* (35), *The Old Mill* (37), *Ferdinand the Bull* (38), *The Ugly Duckling* (39), *Lend a Paw* (41), *Der Fuhrer's Face* (42), *Seal Island* (48), *Beaver Valley* (50), *Nature's Half Acre* (51),

Disraeli, Benjamin

Water Birds (52), *Toot Whistle Plunk and Boom* (53), *Bear Country* (53), *The Alaskan Eskimo* (53), *Men against the Arctic* (55), *The Wetback Hound* (57), *White Wilderness* (58), *Ama Girls* (58), *The Horse with the Flying Tail* (60), *Winnie the Pooh and the Blustery Day* (68), etc. A biography, *Walt Disney*, was published in 1958 by his daughter Diane, and in 1968 came Richard Schickel's iconoclastic *The Disney Version*.

DISRAELI, BENJAMIN (1804–1881), novelist and prime minister, has been notably portrayed on screen by George Arliss in 1921 and 1930 (in each case his wife Florence Arliss played Mrs Disraeli), by Derrick de Marney in *Victoria the Great* (37) and *Sixty Glorious Years* (38), by John Gielgud in *The Prime Minister* (40); and by Alec Guinness in *The Mudlark* (50).

dissolve (or mix). A change of scene accomplished by gradually exposing a second image over the first while fading the first away.

distributor (or renter). A company which, for a percentage of the profits or a flat fee, undertakes to rent a film to exhibitors on the producing company's behalf. Originally major producers like MGM, Warner and Paramount distributed their own films exclusively, but with the rise of independent producers the situation has become much more fluid, with distributors bidding for the films they consider most likely to succeed at the box office and tying up successful producers to long-term contracts.

DI VENANZO, GIANNI (1920–1966). Italian cinematographer, in films from 1941. *Amore in Citta* (53), *Le Amiche* (55), *Il Grido* (57), *I Soliti Ignoti* (58), *Salvatore Giuliano* (61), *La Notte* (61), *L'Éclisse* (62), *Eva* (62), *Eight and a Half* (63), *Juliet of the Spirits* (65), etc.

DIX, RICHARD (1894–1949) (Ernest Brimmer). American leading man of 20s and 30s, a stern-looking but good-hearted hero of films like *The Sin Flood* (20), *The Christian* (GB) (23), *The Ten Commandments* (23), *Icebound* (24), *Manhattan* (24), *The Vanishing American* (24), *Say It Again* (25), *The Quarterback* (26), *Paradise for Two* (27). Started well in sound films but by the mid-30s was playing in co-features. *Seven Keys to Baldpate* (29), *Cimarron* (31), *The Arizonian* (33), *The Tunnel* (GB) (35), *Once a Hero* (37), *Man of Conquest* (39), *The Round-Up* (41), *Eyes of the Underworld* (42), *The Iron Road* (43), *The Ghost Ship* (44), etc.; also from 1943 played the lead in the 'Whistler' series.

DIX, WILLIAM (1956–   ). British child actor. *The Nanny* (65), *Doctor Dolittle* (67).

DIXON, THOMAS (1864–1946). American baptist minister who wrote the anti-Negro novel *The Clansman*, on which Griffith's *The Birth of a Nation* was based.

†DMYTRYK, EDWARD (1908–   ). American director, in films from 1923. After years of second features he gained a reputation as a stylist with some tough adult thrillers of the 40s; but after years of exile due to the McCarthy witch-hunt his more ambitious recent films have seemed impersonal. *The Hawk* (35), *Television Spy* (39), *Emergency Squad* (40), *Golden Gloves* (40), *Mystery Sea Raider* (40), *Her First Romance* (40), *The Devil Commands* (41), *Under Age* (41), *Sweetheart of the Campus* (41), *Blonde from Singapore* (41), *Confessions of Boston Blackie* (41), *Secrets of the Lone Wolf* (41), *Counter Espionage* (42), *Seven Miles from Alcatraz* (42), *Hitler's Children* (43), *The Falcon Strikes Back* (43), *Behind the Rising Sun* (43), *Captive Wild Woman* (43), *Tender Comrade* (44), *Murder My Sweet* (*Farewell My Lovely*) (44), *Back to Bataan* (45), *Cornered* (46), *Till the End of Time* (46), *Crossfire* (47), *So Well Remembered* (GB) (47), *Obsession* (GB) (48), *Give Us This Day* (GB) (49), *Mutiny* (Fr.) (52), *The Sniper* (52), *Eight Iron Men* (52), *The Juggler* (53), *The Caine Mutiny* (54), *Broken Lance* (54), *The End of the Affair* (GB) (54), *Soldier of Fortune* (55), *The Left Hand of God* (55), *The Mountain* (also produced) (56), *Raintree County* (57), *The Young Lions* (58), *Warlock* (59), *The Blue Angel* (59), *The Reluctant Saint* (It.) (61), *A Walk on the Wild Side* (62), *The Carpetbaggers* (63), *Where Love Has Gone* (64), *Mirage* (65), *Alvarez Kelly* (66), *Anzio* (68), *Shalako* (68).

DOBIE, ALAN (1932–   ). British leading actor, usually in astringent roles on stage or TV. Films include *Seven Keys* (62), *The Comedy Man* (64), *The Long Day's Dying* (68), *Alfred the Great* (69).

DOCKS OF NEW YORK (US 1928). A late silent melodrama directed by Josef von Sternberg in a manner realistic for 20s Hollywood, pretentious in retrospect; from a script by Jules Furthman about a coal stoker who rescues and marries a would-be suicide. With George Bancroft, Betty Compson, Olga Baclanova.

Dr Christian was the kindly country doctor hero, played by Jean Hersholt, of a number of unambitious little films which came out between 1938 and 1940, based on a radio series. In 1956 Macdonald Carey featured in a TV series of the same name, but he played the nephew of the original Dr Christian.

DR CYCLOPS (US 1939). Horror film marking a notable advance in colour trick photography. Albert Dekker was the mad scientist who reduced the rest of the cast to midgets.

DOCTOR DOLITTLE (US 1967). An expensive illustration of the fact that talent, expense, colour and wide-screen will get you nowhere without style. Under Richard Fleischer's flat direction, Hugh Lofting's famous character (who talks to animals and travels the world in search of the pink sea snail) seems quite charmless; Leslie

Bricusse's songs and script are thin; and despite the miscast presence of Rex Harrison the movie could appeal only to indulgent tots.

DR EHRLICH'S MAGIC BULLET (US 1940). One of the Warner biographical series which also included Pasteur, Zola, Juarez and Reuter, this engrossing production has Edward G. Robinson bearded and unrecognizable as the German research chemist who discovered a cure for syphilis. Directed with great accomplishment by William Dieterle, and splendidly produced and acted.

DOCTOR IN THE HOUSE (GB 1953). First in a long and still expanding series of comedies adapted from Richard Gordon's collections of anecdotes about a doctor's life. All have been lucrative, but only the first had genuine vitality.

DR JEKYLL AND MR HYDE. Robert Louis Stevenson's classic thriller of split personality has become one of the screen's most popular and oft-borrowed themes. There was a Selig version in 1908 and a Danish one in 1909. James Cruze directed a Universal version in 1912, and in 1913 King Baggott appeared in a rival production. 1919 brought Sheldon Lewis as the doctor (copies still exist) and in 1921 John Barrymore gave a brilliant portrayal in the role, with very little use of trick photography or make-up. Meanwhile in Germany in 1920 Conrad Veidt, directed by Murnau, had had an equally splendid shot at the character. In 1932 Fredric March won an Academy Award for his performance in Rouben Mamoulian's version, which was remade in 1941 with Spencer Tracy. Louis Hayward suffered the fatal dose in *Son of Dr Jekyll* (51); Boris Karloff (as well as Lou Costello and Reginald Denny) underwent the transformation in *Abbott and Costello Meet Dr Jekyll and Mr Hyde* (53); Gloria Talbott was *Daughter of Dr Jekyll* (57); and in 1958 Sylvester the cartoon cat was 'translated' in *Dr Jekyll's Hide*. In 1959 Bernard Bresslaw was in a funny version, *The Ugly Duckling*, and in 1960 the same studio, Hammer, had Paul Massie in a serious version called *The Two Faces of Dr Jekyll*, in which for the first time the evil side of the character was handsomer than the good. The latest comic version is Jerry Lewis's *The Nutty Professor* (63).

DR MABUSE. The master criminal hero-villain of two films directed in Germany by Fritz Lang: *Dr Mabuse the Gambler* (23) and *The Testament of Dr Mabuse* (32). The latter was blatant anti-Nazi propaganda and caused Lang to hurry to Hollywood. In the late 50s the character was revived by Lang and others, but to less effect.

DR NO (GB 1962). First of the James Bond spy adventures from the books by Ian Fleming, marking a new advance in sex and sadism on the screen, though played strictly for laughs. Further episodes,

From Russia with Love (63), *Goldfinger* (64), *Thunderball* (65), *You Only Live Twice* (67), *On Her Majesty's Secret Service* (69), have been increasingly successful, to the consternation of moral reformers.

DR STRANGELOVE (GB/US 1963). The first nuclear comedy, full of black laughter about what might happen if a madman pressed *that* button. Directed by Stanley Kubrick (from Peter George's novel 'Red Alert') to great critical acclaim; but cinematically disappointing and even dull once one knew what it was about. Full credit, however, to the sets of Ken Adam and to Peter Sellers in his three roles. Won three BFA awards: best film, best British film, and United Nations Award.

DR SYN. Russell Thorndyke's novel about the smuggling vicar of Dymchurch was filmed in 1938 with George Arliss, in 1961 (as *Captain Clegg*) with Peter Cushing, and in 1963 with Patrick McGoohan.

DOCTOR ZHIVAGO (US 1965). MGM insist on 'Doctor' being spelt out, and this may serve as a key to the pretentiousness of this would-be epic from Boris Pasternak's novel of modern Russia. The story has been simplified until there is almost nothing of it and Zhivago is a nonentity; what's left plays like a thin variant on 'Gone with the Wind'. The chief demerit is Robert Bolt's tortuous screenplay, which has characters making inexplicable appearances and disappearances; but David Lean's direction is self-indulgent, wasting time on inessentials, and only Frederick Young's cinematography (AA) emerges with full credit. Maurice Jarre (AA) wrote the score.

doctors (in the medical sense) have been crusading heroes of many movies: fictional epics that come readily to mind include *Arrowsmith, The Citadel, Magnificent Obsession, Private Worlds, Men in White, The Green Light, Disputed Passage, Yellow Jack, The Last Angry Man, Not as a Stranger, So Bright the Flame, The Crime of Dr Forbes, The Interns, The New Interns, The Young Doctors, Behind the Mask, Doctor Zhivago,* and *White Corridors.* A few have even commanded whole series to themselves: *Dr Kildare, Dr Christian, Dr Gillespie, The Crime Doctor.* Living doctors have received the accolade of a Hollywood biopic: *The Story of Louis Pasteur, Dr Ehrlich's Magic Bullet, The Story of Dr Wassell, Il Est Minuit Dr Schweizer.* Many less single-minded films have had a background of medicine and doctors as leading figures: *The Nun's Story, Kings Row, No Way Out, People Will Talk.* More or less villainous doctors were found in *The Flesh and the Fiends, Frankenstein, Dr Socrates, Dr Jekyll and Mr Hyde, Green for Danger, Dr Cyclops, Dr Goldfoot,* and *The Amazing Dr Clitterhouse.* TV series on medical subjects have included *Medic* (54–55), *Ben Casey* (60–65), *Dr Kildare* (61–65), *Dr Christian* (56), *Dr Hudson's*

Secret Journal (55–56), *The Nurses* (62–63), *The Doctors and the Nurses* (64), *Marcus Welby M.D.* (69).

documentary was not coined as a word until 1929, but several famous films, including Ponting's *With Scott to the Antarctic*, Lowell Thomas's *With Allenby in Palestine*, and Flaherty's *Nanook of the North*, had before 1921 brought an attitude to their reportage which made them more than mere travel films. In Britain during the 20s, H. Bruce Woolfe made a series of painstaking and still evocative reconstructions of the battles of World War I; while Cooper and Schoedsack went even further afield for the exciting material in *Grass* and *Chang*. 1928 brought Eisenstein's *The General Line*, a brilliant piece of farming propaganda, and Turin's *Turksib*, a showy account of the building of the Turko-Siberian railway. John Grierson, who invented the term 'documentary', made in 1929 a quiet little two-reeler about Britain's herring fleet, and called it *Drifters*; for the next ten years Britain's official and sponsored film units produced such brilliant results as *Shipyard*, *Coalface*, *Housing Problems*, *Song of Ceylon*, *North Sea* and *Night Mail*. In 1931 Vigo made his satirical documentary *A Propos de Nice*, and shortly afterwards Eisenstein was at work on his never-finished *Thunder over Mexico*, brilliant fragments of which survive as *Time in the Sun*. Travel films by explorers like the Martin Johnsons proliferated during the 30s; Flaherty spent two uncomfortable years off the Irish coast to make his *Man of Aran*, and later produced in India the semi-fictional *Elephant Boy*. Pare Lorenz produced cinematic poetry out of America's geographical problems in *The Plow that Broke the Plains* and *The River*.

World War II stimulated documentarists to new urgency and new techniques, brilliantly exemplified by Frank Capra's *Why We Fight* series for the US Signal Corps, turning unpleasant facts into breathtaking entertainment. With a predictably understated approach the British units produced a more sober but equally stirring series of reports on the war (*Western Approaches*, *Desert Victory*, *Target for Tonight*) and the home front (*Listen to Britain*, *Fires Were Started*, *A Diary for Timothy*), many of them directed by Britain's first documentary poet, Humphrey Jennings. The two countries combined resources to present a brilliant, high-flying compilation film about the last year of war, *The True Glory*.

Since 1945 the use of documentary for advertising (often very subtly) and teaching has so proliferated that no simple line of development can be shown. Television has relentlessly explored and elaborated every technique of the pioneers, with special attention to 'action stills', compilation films, and hard-hitting popular journalist approaches such as NBC's White Paper series and Granada's *World in Action*. Entertainment films devised a popular blend of fact and fiction in such neo-classics as *Boomerang*,

The House on 92nd Street and *Naked City*. At last documentary was accepted as an agreeable blend of instruction and pleasure; and in the changed environment Flaherty's lyrical *Louisiana Story* seemed slow and solemn.

DODSWORTH (US 1936). William Wyler made a remarkably adult and intelligent film of Sinclair Lewis' novel about a dull but sincere businessman who tried to preserve his marriage to a selfish woman. With Walter Huston, Ruth Chatterton.

DOLAN, ROBERT EMMETT (1908–). American composer, in Hollywood from 1941. Scores include *Birth of the Blues* (41), *Going My Way* (44), *The Bells of St Mary's* (45), *My Son John* (51), etc. Produced *White Christmas* (54), *Anything Goes* (56), etc.

LA DOLCE VITA (Italy 1959). Federico Fellini's 'exposé' of 'the sweet life', a sprawling, persuasive, orgiastic movie assumed by many to have contributed to a decline in standards because it reported without condemning.

DOLEMAN, GUY (1923–). Australian character actor, in British films. *Phantom Stockade* (53), *The Shiralee* (57), *The Ipcress File* (65), *Thunderball* (65), *The Idol* (66), etc.

DOLENZ, GEORGE (1908–1963). Trieste-born leading man who played leads in some Hollywood films from 1941. *Unexpected Uncle* (41), *Enter Arsène Lupin* (45), *Vendetta* (50), *My Cousin Rachel* (53), *The Purple Mask* (55), *The Four Horsemen of the Apocalypse* (62), others.

dolly. A trolley on which a camera unit can be soundlessly moved about during shooting: can usually be mounted on rails. A 'crab dolly' will move in any direction.

DOMERGUE, FAITH (1925–). American leading lady, launched in 1950 with a publicity campaign which misfired. However, she played competently in a number of films, including *Vendetta* (50), *Where Danger Lives* (50), *This Island Earth* (55), *California* (63), etc.

DONAHUE, TROY (1937–) (Merle Johnson). American leading man who has not yet amounted to more than beefcake despite good roles in *A Summer Place* (59), *The Crowded Sky* (60), *Parrish* (61), (65), etc. TV series: *Surfside Six* (60–62).

DONALD DUCK. Belligerent Disney cartoon character who was introduced in 1936 in *Orphans' Benefit*, was quickly streamlined and became more popular than Mickey Mouse. Still going strong.

DONALD, JAMES (1917–). British stage actor who has been in occasional films since 1941 (*The Missing Million*). Usually plays a

299

man of conscience rather than action. *In Which We Serve* (42), *The Way Ahead* (44), *Broken Journey* (47), *The Small Voice* (47), *Trottie True* (49), *White Corridors* (51), *Brandy for the Parson* (51), *The Gift Horse* (52), *The Pickwick Papers* (52), *The Net* (53), *Beau Brummell* (54), *Lust for Life* (56), *The Bridge on the River Kwai* (57), *The Vikings* (58), *The Great Escape* (63), *King Rat* (65), *Cast a Giant Shadow* (66), *The Jokers* (67), *Hannibal Brooks* (69), *David Copperfield* (69), *The Royal Hunt of the Sun* (69), etc.

DONALDSON, TED (1933–   ). American child star of the 40s. *Once Upon a Time* (44), *A Tree Grows in Brooklyn* (45), *For the Love of Rusty* (47) (and others in this series), *The Decision of Christopher Blake* (48), etc.

†DONAT, ROBERT (1905–1958). Distinguished British stage actor with an inimitably melodious voice; he made some impressive films despite asthma which blighted his career. *Men of Tomorrow* (32), *That Night in London* (32), *Cash* (32), *The Private Life of Henry VIII* (32), *The Count of Monte Cristo* (34), *The Thirty-nine Steps* (35), *The Ghost Goes West* (36), *Knight without Armour* (37), *The Citadel* (38), *Goodbye Mr Chips* (AA) (39), *The Young Mr Pitt* (42), *The Adventures of Tartu* (43), *Perfect Strangers* (45), *Captain Boycott* (guest appearance) (47), *The Winslow Boy* (48), *The Cure for Love* (also directed) (50), *The Magic Box* (50), *Lease for Life* (55), *Inn of the Sixth Happiness* (58). A biography by J. C. Trewin was published in 1968.

DONATH, LUDWIG (1900–1967). Austrian actor busy in Hollywood since the 30s. *The Strange Death of Adolf Hitler* (43), *The Jolson Story* (46), *Cigarette Girl* (47), *Jolson Sings Again* (50), *The Great Caruso* (51), *Sins of Jezebel* (53), *Torn Curtain* (66), many others.

DONEHUE, VINCENT J. (1916–1966). American stage director who came to Hollywood to make *Lonelyhearts* (59), *Sunrise at Campobello* (60).

DONEN, STANLEY (1924–   ). American director, trained as dancer. With Gene Kelly, co-directed *Anchors Aweigh* (45), *On the Town* (49), *Singing in the Rain* (52), etc.; continued on his own and later branched out from musicals to sophisticated comedies and thrillers. *Fearless Fagan* (51), *Give a Girl a Break* (51), *Wedding Bells* (52), *Seven Brides for Seven Brothers* (54), *Deep in My Heart* (55), *It's Always Fair Weather* (55), *Funny Face* (57), *The Pajama Game* (57), *Kiss Them for Me* (57), *Indiscreet* (58), *Damn Yankees* (58), *Once More with Feeling* (59), *Surprise Package* (60), *The Grass Is Greener* (61), *Charade* (63), *Arabesque* (66), *Two for the Road* (67), *Bedazzled* (67), *Staircase* (69), etc.

DONIGER, WALTER (1917–   ). American writer. *Mob Town* (41), *Red Sundown* (49), *Cease Fire* (52), *The Steel Jungle* (also directed) (56), etc.

DON JUAN. The amorous adventures of this legendary rascal, a heartless seducer created in stories by Gabriel Tellez (1571–1641), have been filmed several times, notably with John Barrymore in 1927, Douglas Fairbanks Snr in 1934, Errol Flynn in 1948 and (of all people) Fernandel in 1955. Versions of the opera, *Don Giovanni*, are legion.

DONLAN, YOLANDE (1920–   ). American leading lady who had great success on the British stage as the dumb blonde in 'Born Yesterday', settled in England and married Val Guest. Film debut *Turnabout* (41); later, *Miss Pilgrim's Progress* (50), *Mr Drake's Duck* (50), *Penny Princess* (51), *They Can't Hang Me* (55), *Expresso Bongo* (59), *Jigsaw* (62), *Eighty Thousand Suspects* (63), etc.

DONLEVY, BRIAN (1899–   ). Irish-American leading man, later character actor, in Hollywood from the 20s after stage experience; characteristically in fast-talking tough roles with soft centres. *Mother's Boy* (28), *Barbary Coast* (35), *In Old Chicago* (38), *We're Going To Be Rich* (GB) (38), *Jesse James* (39), *Beau Geste* (as the evil sergeant) (39), *Destry Rides Again* (39), *The Great McGinty* (best leading role) (40), *Brigham Young* (40), *The Great Man's Lady* (40), *A Gentleman after Dark* (41), *Billy the Kid* (41), *The Remarkable Andrew* (41), *Wake Island* (42), *The Glass Key* (42), *Nightmare* (42), *Hangmen Also Die* (43), *The Miracle of Morgan's Creek* (43), *An American Romance* (44), *Two Years before the Mast* (44), *The Virginian* (45), *The Trouble with Women* (46), *The Beginning or the End* (47), *Kiss of Death* (47), *The Lucky Stiff* (48), *Shakedown* (50), *Hoodlum Empire* (52), *The Woman They Almost Lynched* (53), *The Big Combo* (55), *The Quatermass Experiment* (GB) (55), *A Cry in the Night* (56), *Quatermass II* (GB) (57), *Cowboy* (58), *Never So Few* (59), *The Errand Boy* (61), *Curse of the Fly* (GB) (65), *How to Stuff a Wild Bikini* (65), *The Fat Spy* (66), *Waco* (66), *Rogues' Gallery* (67), etc.

DONNELL, JEFF (1921–   ). Pert American actress who played the heroine's friend in many routine comedies of the 40s, now plays mothers. *A Night to Remember* (43), *He's My Guy* (45), *In a Lonely Place* (50), *Thief of Damascus* (52), *Sweet Smell of Success* (57), *Gidget Goes Hawaiian* (61), *The Iron Maiden* (GB) (62), many others.

DONNELLY, DONAL (1932–   ). Irish stage actor, in occasional films. *The Rising of the Moon* (57), *Shake Hands with the Devil* (59), *Young Cassidy* (65), *The Knack* (65), *Up Jumped a Swagman* (65), etc.

DONNELLY, RUTH (1896–   ). American character actress, a wisecracking girl friend in the 30s, latterly in mother roles. *Transatlantic* (31), *Wonder Bar* (34), *Mr Deeds Goes to Town* (36), *Holiday* (37), *A Slight Case of Murder* (38), *Mr Smith Goes to Washington* (39), *Thank Your Lucky Stars* (43), *The Snake Pit* (48), *The Spoilers* (55), *The Way to the Gold* (57), etc.

†DONNER, CLIVE (1920–   ). British director, former editor, in films since 1942. *The Secret Place* (56), *Heart of a Child* (57), *A Marriage of Convenience* (59), *The Sinister Man* (60), *Some People* (62), *The Caretaker* (63), *Nothing But the Best* (63), *What's New Pussycat* (65), *Luv* (67), *Here We Go Round the Mulberry Bush* (67), *Alfred the Great* (69).

DONNER, JÖRN (1933–   ). Finnish writer-director. *To Love* (65), *Black on White* (67), etc.

DONOHUE, JACK (1912–   ). American dance director, former Ziegfeld Follies dancer. Worked on several MGM musicals; also directed *The Yellow Cab Man* (50), *Watch the Birdie* (51), *Calamity Jane* (dances only) (53), *Lucky Me* (54), then back to stage and TV; *Babes in Toyland* (61), *Marriage on the Rocks* (65), *Assault on a Queen* (66), etc.

DONOVAN, KING (c. 1919–   ). American general purpose actor, usually in support roles; a frequent TV guest star. *Murder Inc.* (51), *The Beast from Twenty Thousand Fathoms* (53), *Invasion of the Body Snatchers* (56), *The Hanging Tree* (59), many others.

DON QUIXOTE. There have been many screen versions of Cervantes' picaresque novel about the adventures of the addled knight and his slow but faithful lieutenant Sancho Panza . . . but none have been entirely successful because the genius of the book is a purely literary one. There was a French production in 1909; an American one in 1916 directed by Edward Dillon; a British one in 1923 directed by Maurice Elvey and starring Jerrold Robertshaw. In 1933 Pabst made a British film of the story with Chaliapin and (again) George Robey; meanwhile a Danish director, Lau Lauritzen, had done one in 1926. The next batch of Quixotes began in 1947 with Rafael Gil's Spanish version; but the Russian production of 1957, directed by Kozintsev with Cherkassov in the title role, was probably the best of all. Since 1958 Orson Welles has been filming sections of his own version, which it looks as though we may never see; a Jugoslavian cartoon version appeared in 1961; and in 1962 Finland, of all nations, contributed its own Quixote, directed by Eino Ruutsalo. The popular stage musical *Man of la Mancha*, currently due for filming, is based on the life of Miguel de Cervantes (1547–1616).

DONSKOI, MARK (1897–   ). Russian director celebrated for his 'Maxim Gorki trilogy' 1938–40.

DOONAN, PATRICK (1927–1958). British stage and screen actor, usually in honest, put-upon roles. Son of comedian George Doonan. *Once a Jolly Swagman* (48), *The Blue Lamp* (50), *The Gentle Gunman* (52),

Seagulls over Sorrento (54), *Cockleshell Heroes* (55), many second features.

dope sheet. A list of the contents of a piece of film, usually applied to newsreel libraries.

DORAN, ANN (1914–   ). American character actress, often a friend of the heroine. *Penitentiary* (38), *Blondie* (38), *Blue, White and Perfect* (42), *The More the Merrier* (43), *Fear in the Night* (46), *The Snake Pit* (48), *Rebel without a Cause* (55), *The Man Who Turned to Stone* (58), *The Rawhide Trail* (60), *Rosie* (67), many others.

DORLEAC, FRANCOISE (1941–1967). French leading lady, killed in car crash. *Payroll* (GB) (61), *That Man from Rio* (64), *Genghis Khan* (65), *Where the Spies Are* (65), *Cul de Sac* (GB) (66), *The Young Girls of Rochefort* (67), etc.

DORN, DOLORES (1935–   ) (D. Dorn-Heft). American stage actress briefly in Hollywood. *Phantom of the Rue Morgue* (54), *Uncle Vanya* (58), *Underworld USA* (60), *13 West Street* (62), etc.

DORN, PHILIP (1905–   ) (Fritz van Dungen). Dutch stage actor who went to Hollywood 1940 and was used mainly in sincere refugee or thoughtfully professional roles. *Ski Patrol* (40), *Escape* (40), *Ziegfeld Girl* (41), *Tarzan's Secret Treasure* (41), *Calling Dr Gillespie* (41), *Random Harvest* (42), *Reunion in France* (42), *Chetniks* (43), *Passage to Marseilles* (44), *Blonde Fever* (44), *Escape in the Desert* (45), *Concerto* (46), *I Remember Mama* (48), *Panther's Moon* (49), *Sealed Cargo* (51), etc. Returned to Holland.

DORNE, SANDRA (1925–   ). British 'platinum blonde', often in tawdry roles. *Eyes That Kill* (45), *Once a Jolly Swagman* (48), *The Beggar's Opera* (51), *Roadhouse Girl* (54), *The Gelignite Gang* (56), *The Iron Petticoat* (57), etc.

DORO, MARIE (1882–1956) (Marie Stewart). American leading lady of the silent screen, one of Zukor's 'Famous Players'. *Oliver Twist* (title role) (16), *The Morals of Marcus* (15), *The White Pearl* (15), *The Heart of Nora Flynn* (16), *The Wood Nymph* (16), *The Mysterious Princess* (19), *Twelve Ten* (19), *Maid of Mystery* (20), etc.

DORS, DIANA (1931–   ) (Diana Fluck). British 'blonde bombshell' who has been playing a good-time girl since the mid-40s. *The Shop at Sly Corner* (46), *Holiday Camp* (47), *Oliver Twist* (48), *Good Time Girl* (48), *The Calendar* (49), *Here Come the Huggetts* (49), *Dance Hall* (50), *Lady Godiva Rides Again* (51), *The Weak and the Wicked* (52), *Is Your Honeymoon Really Necessary* (52), *It's a Grand Life* (53), *A Kid for Two Farthings* (55), *Miss Tulip Stays the Night* (55), *As Long as They're Happy* (55), *Yield to the Night* (56), *I Married a Woman* (US) (56), *The Unholy Wife* (US) (56), *The Long Haul* (57),

Tread Softly, Stranger (58), *Passport to Shame* (59), *On the Double* (US) (60), *Mrs Gibbons' Boys* (62), *West Eleven* (63), *The Sandwich Man* (66), *Berserk* (67), *Baby Love* (69), etc.

D'ORSAY, FIFI (1907–   ). Vivacious Canadian leading lady of Hollywood films in the early 30s. Still plays small roles. *Hot for Paris* (30), *Just Imagine* (31), *Silk Stockings* (32), etc.; then support roles in *Accent on Youth* (45), *Wild and Wonderful* (63), *The Art of Love* (65), others.

DORSEY, JIMMY (1904–1957) and TOMMY (1905–1956). American bandleaders and brothers; individually they decorated many musicals of the 40s, and came together in a biopic, *The Fabulous Dorseys* (46).

DOSTOIEVSKY, FYODOR (1821–1881). Russian writer, chiefly of doom-laden novels, of which the most frequently-filmed is *Crime and Punishment*; there have also been attempts at *The Idiot*, *The Brothers Karamazov*, *White Nights*, *The Great Sinner*, *Pyriev* and others.

DOTRICE, KAREN (1955–   ). British child actress. *The Three Lives of Thomasina* (63), *Mary Poppins* (64), *The Gnomobile* (67).

DOTRICE, ROY (1923–   ). British stage actor with a strong line in senile impersonation. Films include *The Heroes of Telemark* (65), *A Twist of Sand* (68), *Lock Up Your Daughters* (69).

DORZIAT, GABRIELLE (1880–   ) (G. Moppert). French character actress. *Mayerling* (36), *La Fin du Jour* (39), *Premier Rendezvous* (41), *Les Parents Terribles* (48), *Manon* (49), *Act of Love* (54), *Les Espions* (57), *Germinal* (63), etc.

double exposure. This occurs when two or more images are recorded on the same piece of film. Used for trick shots when two characters played by the same actor have to meet; also for dissolves, dream sequences, etc.

double-headed print. One in which sound and picture are recorded on separate pieces of film, usually at cutting copy stage or before OK is received to make combined negative.

DOUBLE INDEMNITY (US 1944). The 40s are a pretty dated era at present, but this tawdry crime story, about a man who murders his mistress's husband for his insurance money, still packs a punch by virtue of Billy Wilder's direction and a witty script in which Wilder and Raymond Chandler had a hand. Fred MacMurray and Edward G. Robinson are in good form: Barbara Stanwyck's *femme fatale* has worn less well. From a novel by James Cain; photographed by John Seitz with music by Miklos Rozsa.

A DOUBLE LIFE (US 1947). The film for which Ronald Colman belatedly won an Oscar was an arrant piece of nonsense about an actor who got his Othello mixed up with his private life. Neither Garson Kanin's script nor George Cukor's direction could save it.

DOUGLAS, DONALD (1905–1945) (Douglas Kinleyside). Quiet-spoken American actor, usually seen as smooth villain or 'good loser'. *Men in White* (34), *Alexander's Ragtime Band* (38), *Whistling in the Dark* (41), *The Crystal Ball* (43), *Show Business* (44), *Farewell My Lovely* (44), *Club Havana* (45), etc.

DOUGLAS, GORDON (1909–). American director, former comedy writer for Hal Roach. Work has grown in importance but talent remains routine. *Saps at Sea* (40), *Broadway Limited* (41), *The Devil with Hitler* (43), *Zombies on Broadway* (45), *If You Knew Susie* (48), *The Doolins of Oklahoma* (49), *Kiss Tomorrow Goodbye* (50), *Only the Valiant* (51), *I Was a Communist for the FBI* (51), *Come Fill the Cup* (51), *Mara Maru* (52), *The Iron Mistress* (53), *The Grace Moore Story* (53), *The Charge at Feather River* (53), *Them* (54), *Young at Heart* (54), *Sincerely Yours* (55), *The Big Land* (56), *Bombers B-52* (58), *Yellowstone Kelly* (59), *The Sins of Rachel Cade* (60), *Gold of the Seven Saints* (61), *Follow That Dream* (62), *Call Me Bwana* (63), *Robin and the Seven Hoods* (64), *Rio Conchos* (64), *Sylvia* (65), *Harlow* (65), *Stagecoach* (66), *Way Way Out* (66), *In Like Flint* (67), *Chuka* (67), *Tony Rome* (67), *The Detective* (68).

†DOUGLAS, KIRK (1916–) (Issur Danielovitch Demsky). American leading actor with stage experience; started playing weaklings and gangsters but graduated to tense, virile, intelligent heroes in films of many kinds. *The Strange Love of Martha Ivers* (debut) (46), *Out of the Past (Build My Gallows High)* (47), *I Walk Alone* (47), *Mourning Becomes Electra* (47), *The Walls of Jericho* (48), *A Letter to Three Wives* (48), *Champion* (49), *Young Man with a Horn* (50), *The Glass Menagerie* (51), *Ace in the Hole* (51), *Along the Great Divide* (51), *Detective Story* (51), *The Big Trees* (52), *The Big Sky* (52), *The Bad and the Beautiful* (52), *The Story of Three Loves* (53), *The Juggler* (53), *Act of Love* (54), *Ulysses* (It.) (54), *Twenty Thousand Leagues under the Sea* (54), *Man without a Star* (55), *The Racers* (55), *The Indian Fighter* (55), *Lust for Life* (as Van Gogh) (56), *Top Secret Affair* (57), *Gunfight at the OK Corral* (as Doc Holliday) (57), *Paths of Glory* (57), *The Vikings* (58), *Last Train from Gun Hill* (58), *The Devil's Disciple* (59), *Spartacus* (60), *Town Without Pity* (61), *Lonely Are the Brave* (62), *Two Weeks in Another Town* (62), *The List of Adrian Messenger* (63), *For Love or Money* (63), *Seven Days in May* (64), *In Harm's Way* (65), *The Heroes of Telemark* (65), *Cast a Giant Shadow* (66), *Is Paris Burning?* (66), *The Way West* (67), *The War Wagon* (67), *A Lovely Way to Go* (68), *The Brotherhood* (68), *The Arrangement* (69), *There Was a Crooked Man* (69).

Douglas, Lloyd C.

DOUGLAS, LLOYD C. (1877–1951). American best-selling novelist: a doctor who did not begin writing till in his fifties. Films of his books include *The Green Light, Magnificent Obsession, The Robe, White Banners, Disputed Passage, The Big Fisherman.*

DOUGLAS, MELVYN (1901–   ) (Melvyn Hesselberg). Suave, polished American leading man of 30s and 40s, now character actor; also Broadway stage star. *Tonight or Never* (debut) (31), *As You Desire Me* (32), *The Old Dark House* (32), *The Vampire Bat* (33), *Dangerous Corner* (34), *She Married Her Boss* (35), *The Gorgeous Hussy* (36), *Theodora Goes Wild* (36), *I Met Him in Paris* (37), *Fast Company* (38), *That Certain Age* (38), *The Shining Hour* (39), *Ninotchka* (39), *My Two Husbands* (40), *He Stayed for Breakfast* (40), *Married But Single* (40), *That Uncertain Feeling* (41), *A Woman's Face* (41), *Our Wife* (41), *Two-Faced Woman* (41), *We Were Dancing* (42), *They All Kissed the Bride* (42), *Three Hearts for Julia* (42), etc.; war service; *Sea of Grass* (47), *The Guilt of Janet Ames* (47), *My Own True Love* (47), *Mr Blandings Builds His Dream House* (48), *The Great Sinner* (49), *On the Loose* (51), then ten years on stage; *Billy Budd* (61), *Hud* (AA) (63), *The Americanization of Emily* (64), *Rapture* (65), *Hotel* (67), etc. TV series: *Hollywood Confidential.*

DOUGLAS, PAUL (1907–1959). Burly American actor, on stage and radio from 1930. Notable film debut in *A Letter to Three Wives* (49); later in *Love That Brute* (50), *Fourteen Hours* (51), *Clash by Night* (52), *When in Rome* (52), *The Maggie* (GB) (53), *Executive Suite* (54), *Green Fire* (54), *Joe Macbeth* (GB) (55), *The Leather Saint* (56), *The Solid Gold Cadillac* (56), *The Mating Game* (58), etc.

DOUGLAS, ROBERT (1909–   ) (Robert Douglas Finlayson). British stage leading man who made some home-grown films during the 30s; moved to Hollywood after the war and played mainly suave villains in routine melodramas. *P.C. Josser* (31), *The Blarney Stone* (34), *The Street Singer* (36), *The Challenge* (38), *Over the Moon* (39), etc; war service; *The End of the River* (47), *The Decision of Christopher Blake* (48), *The New Adventures of Don Juan* (48), *Sons of the Musketeers* (51), *Ivanhoe* (52), *The Prisoner of Zenda* (52), *Fair Wind to Java* (53), *King Richard and the Crusaders* (54), *The Virgin Queen* (55), *The Scarlet Coat* (56), etc. Moved into TV and directed many episodes of series including *77 Sunset Strip*. In 1964 directed film in GB: *Night Train to Paris.*

DOVE, BILLIE (1900–   ) (Lilian Bohny). American leading lady of the 20s. *Beyond the Rainbow* (22), *Polly of the Follies* (22), *Wanderer of the Wasteland* (24), *The Black Pirate* (26), *One Night at Susie's* (28), *Painted Angel* (30), *Blondie of the Follies* (32), etc.; could not adapt to sound. Played a small part in *Diamond Head* (62).

DOVZHENKO, ALEXANDER (1894–1956). Russian writer-director, former teacher; in films since 1925. *Arsenal* (29), *Earth* (30), *Ivan* (32), *Aerograd* (35), *Life in Blossom* (47), etc.

DOW, PEGGY (1928–   ) (Peggy Varnadow). American leading lady who made a strong impression in several Universal films, especially *Undertow* (49), *Harvey* (50), *Bright Victory* (51), *I Want You* (51), before retiring to marry.

DOWLING, CONSTANCE (1923–1969). American leading lady who flowered briefly in the 40s. *Knickerbocker Holiday* (44), *Up in Arms* (44), *The Flame* (47), *Gog* (54), etc.

DOWLING, DORIS (1921–   ). American leading lady, sister of Constance Dowling. Briefly in Hollywood character roles, then moved to Italy. *The Lost Weekend* (45), *The Blue Dahlia* (46), *Bitter Rice* (48), *Othello* (51), etc.

DOWLING, JOAN (1929–1954). British teenage actress who failed to get mature roles. *Hue and Cry* (46), *No Room at the Inn* (48), *Landfall* (49), *Pool of London* (51), *Woman of Twilight* (52), etc.

DOWNS, CATHY (1924–   ). American leading lady of a few 40s films. *Diamond Horseshoe* (45), *My Darling Clementine* (46), *The Noose Hangs High* (48), *Short Grass* (50), *Gobs and Gals* (52), etc.

DOWNS, JOHNNY (1913–   ). American light leading man and dancer, former member of 'Our Gang'. *The Clock Strikes Eight* (35), *Melody Girl* (40), *All-American Co-ed* (41), *Harvest Melody* (44), *The Right to Love* (45), *Cruising Down the River* (53), many others.

DOYLE, SIR ARTHUR CONAN (1859–1930). British novelist and creator of Sherlock Holmes (qv). His other chief bequest to the screen is the twice-filmed *The Lost World*.

DOZIER, WILLIAM (1908–   ). American producer, former talent agent. With RKO, Columbia and Goldwyn in 40s; independently made *Two of a Kind* (51), *Harriet Craig* (53); then into TV. Latest series: *Batman*, *The Green Hornet*.

DRACULA. The Transylvanian vampire count created by Bram Stoker in his novel published 1897 has been on the screen in many manifestations. Max Schreck played him in Murnau's German silent *Nosferatu* (23). Bela Lugosi first donned the cloak for Universal's *Dracula* (31), was not in *Dracula's Daughter* (36) but reappeared in *Return of the Vampire* (44) and *Abbott and Costello Meet Frankenstein* (48). Lon Chaney starred in *Son of Dracula* (43); John Carradine took over in *House of Frankenstein* (45) and *House of Dracula* (46); Francis Lederer had a go in *The Return of Dracula* (*The Fantastic Disappearing Man*) (58). Also in 1958 came the British remake of the original *Dracula* (*Horror of Dracula*) with Christopher Lee; David Peel was one of the count's disciples in *Brides of Dracula* (60) and Noel Willman another in *Kiss of the Vampire* (63); while Lee ingeniously reappeared in 1965 as *Dracula Prince of Darkness*, and in 1968 in *Dracula Has Risen from the Grave*. Meanwhile Hollywood in 1957 produced a lady vampire (Sandra Harrison) in *Blood of Dracula*, and in 1965 *Billy the Kid Meets Dracula*. Polanski's failed satire of 1967, *The Fearless Vampire Killers*, had Ferdy Mayne as Von Krolock, who was Dracula in all but name. It seems that the Count, though officially dead, is unlikely ever to lie down for long.

DRAKE, ALFRED (1914–) (Alfredo Capurro). Italian-American singer-dancer popular in Broadway shows; his only film has been *Tars and Spars* (44).

DRAKE, BETSY (1923–). American leading lady, formerly on stage; married for a time to Cary Grant, opposite whom she appeared in *Every Girl Should Be Married* (48), *Room for One More* (52). Also in *Pretty Baby* (50), *Ellen* (*The Second Woman*) (51), *Clarence the Cross-Eyed Lion* (65), etc.

DRAKE, CHARLES (1914–) (Charles Ruppert). American actor usually found in dullish, good-natured 'second leads'. In films from early 40s: *Dive Bomber* (41), *The Man Who Came to Dinner* (41), *Yankee Doodle Dandy* (42), *Air Force* (43), *You Came Along* (44), *Conflict* (45), *A Night in Casablanca* (45), *Whistle Stop* (46), *Tarzan's Magic Fountain* (49), *Harvey* (50), *Gunsmoke* (52), *It Came from Outer Space* (53), *The Glenn Miller Story* (53), *All That Heaven Allows* (55), *The Price of Fear* (56), *The Third Day* (65), *Valley of the Dolls* (67), *The Swimmer* (68), others. TV series: *Rendezvous* (GB).

DRAKE, CHARLIE (1925–). Diminutive British TV comedian with high-pitched voice and tendency to acrobatic slapstick. *Sands of the Desert* (60), *Petticoat Pirates* (61), *The Cracksman* (63), *Mister Ten Per Cent* (66).

DRAKE, DONA (1920–) (Rita Novella). Mexican singer, dancer and general livewire, former band vocalist as Rita Rio. *Aloma of the South Seas* (41), *Road to Morocco* (42), *Salute for Three* (43), *The House of Tao Ling* (47), *So This Is New York* (48), *Beyond the Forest* (49), *Valentino* (51), *Princess of the Nile* (54), etc.

DRAKE, FABIA (1904–) (F. D. McGlinchy). British stage and screen character actress: usually plays battleaxes. *Meet Mr Penny* (38), *All over the Town* (48), *Young Wives' Tale* (51), *Fast and Loose* (54), *The Good Companions* (57), many others.

DRAKE, TOM (1919–) (Alfred Alderdice). American actor, the 'boy next door' of many a 40s film. *Two Girls and a Sailor* (44), *Meet*

Me in St Louis (44), *The Green Years* (46), *I'll Be Yours* (47), *Master of Lassie* (48), *Never Trust a Gambler* (51), *Sudden Danger* (55), *The Sandpiper* (65), *Red Tomahawk* (66), etc.

DRAPER, PETER (1925–). British playwright and screenwriter: *The System* (63), *I'll Never Forget Whatshisname* (67), *The Buttercup Chain* (70), etc.

DRAYTON, ALFRED (1881–1949) (Alfred Varick). Bald British actor who in later life often played comedy villains in stage farces co-starring Robertson Hare. On stage from 1908, films from early 20s. *A Scandal in Bohemia* (25), *Friday the Thirteenth* (33), *Jack Ahoy* (34), *The Crimson Circle* (36), *So This Is London* (38), *A Spot of Bother* (40), *The Big Blockade* (42), *They Knew Mr Knight* (44), *The Halfway House* (44), *Nicholas Nickleby* (as Squeers) (47), *Things Happen at Night* (48), etc.

dreams, with their opportunities for camera magic and mystery, are dear to Hollywood's heart. The first film with dream sequences followed by a psychological explanation was probably Pabst's *Secrets of a Soul*; the trick caught on very firmly in such later pictures as *Lady in the Dark*, *A Matter of Life and Death*, *Spellbound*, *Dead of Night*, *Fear in the Night*, *Farewell My Lovely*, *The Secret Life of Walter Mitty*, *Possessed*, *Dream Girl*, *Three Cases of Murder* and *The Night Walker*. In *Vampyr* the hero dreamed of his own funeral; and in *Devotion* Ida Lupino dreamed of death as a man on horseback coming across the moor to sweep her away. Recently, flashbacks have become less fashionable than a story told as in a series of daydreams by the main character, the past mingling with the present, as in *Death of a Salesman* and *I Was Happy Here*. *Roman Scandals*, *A Connecticut Yankee at the Court of King Arthur*, *Ali Baba Goes to Town*, *Fiddlers Three* and *Dreaming* are but five examples of the many comedies in which a character has been knocked on the head and dreams himself back in some distant time.

In the mid-40s such films as *The Woman in the Window*, *The Strange Affair of Uncle Harry* and *The Horn Blows at Midnight* set the fashion for getting the hero out of some impossible situation by having him wake up and find he'd been dreaming. This was scarcely fair in adult films, though it had honourable origins in *Alice in Wonderland* and *The Wizard of Oz*. Nor is there much excuse for the other favourite script trick of having one's cake and eating it, as in *Portrait of Jennie* and *Miracle in the Rain*, when some ghostly occurrence to the hero is passed off as a dream until he finds some tangible evidence—a scarf or a coin—that it was real.

The closest a film dream came to coming true was in *The Night My Number Came Up*, when the foreseen air crash was narrowly averted. In the brilliantly clever frame story of *Dead of Night*, the hero dreams he will commit a murder, and does, only to wake up and find the whole sequence of events beginning again: he is caught in an endless series of recurring nightmares.

See also *fantasy* and *psychological drama*.

DREIER, HANS (1884–1966). German art director, primarily associated with Lubitsch and, like him, long in Hollywood. *The Hunchback of Notre Dame* (23), *Forbidden Paradise* (24), *The Love Parade* (29), *Dr Jekyll and Mr Hyde* (32), *Trouble in Paradise* (32), *Cleopatra* (34), *Desire* (36), *Bluebeard's Eighth Wife* (38), *Dr Cyclops* (39), *Reap the Wild Wind* (42), *For Whom the Bell Tolls* (43), *Lady in the Dark* (43), *Incendiary Blonde* (45), *The Emperor Waltz* (48), *Samson and Delilah* (49), *Sunset Boulevard* (50), *A Place in the Sun* (51), many others.

DREIFUSS, ARTHUR (1908–   ). German-born American director of second features, former child conductor and choreographer. *Baby Face Morgan* (42), *The Pay Off* (43), *Eadie Was a Lady* (45), *There's a Girl in My Heart* (also produced) (49), *Secret File USA* (also produced) (55), *The Last Blitzkrieg* (58), *Juke Box Rhythm* (59), *The Quare Fellow* (GB) (62), *Riot on Sunset Strip* (67), *The Young Runaways* (68), etc.

DREISER, THEODORE (1871–1945). Serious American novelist, a social realist who was popular in the early part of the century. Films of his books include *An American Tragedy* (remade as *A Place in the Sun*), *Jennie Gerhardt* and *Carrie*.

DRESDEL, SONIA (1909–   ) (Lois Obee). British stage actress usually cast in masterful roles. *The World Owes Me a Living* (film debut) (42), *While I Live* (47), *This Was a Woman* (47), *The Fallen Idol* (48), *The Clouded Yellow* (50), *The Third Visitor* (51), *Now and Forever* (54), *The Trials of Oscar Wilde* (60), etc.

DRESSER, LOUISE (1882–1965) (Louise Kerlin). American character actress of the 30s, former vaudevillian. *The Eagle* (25), *Not Quite Decent* (27), *Mammy* (30), *State Fair* (33), *The Scarlet Empress* (34), *Maid of Salem* (37), etc.

DRESSLER, MARIE (1869–1934) (Leila Kerber). Kindly, heavyweight American comedienne of silents and early talkies, formerly in opera, vaudeville and burlesque. *Tillie's Punctured Romance* (debut) (14), *Anna Christie* (30), *Min and Bill* (AA) (31), *Emma* (32), *Tugboat Annie* (32), *Dinner at Eight* (33), etc.

DREVILLE, JEAN (1906–   ). French director. *Cage aux Rossignols* (43), *La Ferme du Pendu* (46), *Le Visiteur* (47), *Operation Swallow* (*The Battle for Heavy Water*) (47), *Les Casse-Pieds* (48), *Horizons Sans Fin* (53), *A Pied A Cheval et en Spoutnik* (58), *Normandie-Niemen* (60), *Lafayette* (61), *The Sleeping Sentry* (66), etc.

DREW, ELLEN (1915–   ) (Terry Ray). American leading lady of the 40s, popular in many light movies: *Sing You Sinners* (debut) (38), *French without Tears* (39), *Christmas in July* (40), *The Monster and the Girl* (41), *Our Wife* (42), *Isle of the Dead* (45), *The Swordsman* (47), *The Great Missouri Raid* (51), *The Outlaw's Son* (57), etc.

DREW, MR and MRS SIDNEY (*   –   ). American stage actors who between 1917 and 1922 appeared in a number of very popular middle-class domestic comedies: *Duplicity, Her Obsession, Hypochondriacs, Henry's Ancestors, Her First Game, His Deadly Calm*, etc.

†DREYER, CARL (1889–1968). Celebrated Danish director whose later works were few but notable. *Præsidenten* (20), *Leaves from Satan's Book* (20), *Præsteenken* (21), *Elsker Hverandre* (22), *Once Upon a Time* (22), *Michael* (24), *Du Skal Aere Din Hustru* (25), *Glomsdal Bruden* (26), *The Passion of Joan of Arc* (28), *Vampyr* (32), *Day of Wrath* (43), *Tva Manniskor* (45), *Ordet* (55), *Gertrud* (64). Plus several shorts, mainly for the Danish government.

DREYFUS, ALFRED (1859–1935). The French officer unjustly sentenced to Devil's Island, but reprieved by Zola's advocacy, has been played on screen by Cedric Hardwicke in *Dreyfus* (GB 1930), by Joseph Schildkraut in *The Life of Émile Zola* (US 1937) and by Jose Ferrer in *I Accuse* (GB 1957).

DRIFTERS (GB 1929). John Grierson's first documentary, a study of North Sea herring fishers which now seems dull but on its first screening was a new departure and a revelation.

DRISCOLL, BOBBY (1936–   ). American child actor of the 40s and 50s. *Lost Angel* (debut) (43), *From This Day Forward* (45), *Song of the South* (46), *The Window* (48), *So Dear to My Heart* (49), *Treasure Island* (50), *The Happy Time* (52), etc. The voice of Disney's *Peter Pan* (54). AA 1949: best juvenile actor.

drive-in. A cinema in the open air, with loudspeakers relaying the sound track into your car. There are 6–7,000 in the USA alone.

DROLE DE DRAME (France 1937). Intellectual crazy comedy written by Jacques Prevert (from J. Storer Clouston's 'The Lunatic at Large') and directed by Marcel Carne, with a star cast headed by Françoise Rosay, Jean-Louis Barrault, Michel Simon and Louis Jouvet. Made with great vigour, but considerably ahead of its time.

DRU, JOANNE (1923–   ) (Joanne la Cock). American leading lady, formerly model and showgirl. *Abie's Irish Rose* (debut) (46), *Red River* (48), *She Wore a Yellow Ribbon* (49), *All the King's Men* (50), *Wagonmaster* (51), *Three Ring Circus* (55), *September Storm* (60), *Sylvia* (65), others. TV series: *Guestward Ho*.

drug addiction

drug addiction, long forbidden by the Hays Code, even in Sherlock Holmes films, has recently been the subject of many intense reforming movies such as *The Man with the Golden Arm, A Hatful of Rain, Monkey on My Back* and *Synanon. Confessions of an Opium Eater,* on the other hand, is a throwback to the Hollywood films of the 20s, when almost every adventure involved a chase through a Chinatown opium den. The addiction has provided plots for many thrillers about the tireless efforts of agents of the US Narcotics Bureau.

drunk scenes have been the delight of many actors as well as audiences. Who can judge between the delights of the following? Greta Garbo in *Ninotchka*; Robert Montgomery in *June Bride*; Jean Arthur in *Mr Smith Goes to Washington*; Laurel and Hardy in *The Bohemian Girl* and *Scram*; Albert Finney in *Saturday Night and Sunday Morning*; Alan Bates in *A Kind of Loving*; Bette Davis in *Dark Victory*; Claudia Cardinale in *The Pink Panther*; Charles Laughton in *Hobson's Choice*; Katharine Hepburn in *The Philadelphia Story* and *State of the Union*; Lucille Ball in *Yours Mine and Ours*; Arthur Askey in *The Love Match*; Dan Dailey in *It's Always Fair Weather*; Julie Andrews in *Star!*; Dean Martin and Tony Curtis in *Who Was That Lady?* Martin indeed has deliberately built himself an off-screen alcoholic reputation, as did W. C. Fields.

See also: *alcoholics.*

DRURY, JAMES (1934–). American leading man who, after an ineffective start in movies (*Blackboard Jungle* [55], *Diane* [55], *Love Me Tender* [56]), moved to TV and played the title role in the long-running series *The Virginian* (64–69).

dry ice. A chemical substance which in water produces carbon dioxide gas and gives the effect of a low-hanging white ground mist, very effective in fantasy sequences.

DRYHURST, EDWARD (1904–). British producer, former writer, in films from 1920. *So Well Remembered* (47), *Master of Bankdam* (48), *Noose* (48), *While I Live* (49), *Castle in the Air* (52), etc.

dubbing has several shades of meaning. It can be the process of adding sound (effects, music, dialogue) to pictures already shot; or, re-recording; or, replacing original language dialogue by a translation.

DUCK SOUP (US 1933). Probably the most perfect, zany and absolute of the vintage Marx Brothers romps, a Ruritanian spy send-up with Margaret Dumont and Louis Calhern as butts. Gags by various hands including Nat Perrin and Arthur Sheekman; music by Bert Kalmar and Harry Ruby.

DUEL IN THE SUN (US 1946). When first released this was the longest film since *Gone with the Wind*; it became notorious for its emphasis on violence and for casting Gregory Peck and Jennifer Jones as no-good villains who finally shot each other to death. The screenplay, by Niven Busch and producer David O. Selznick, was tasteless and King Vidor's direction, despite some good Western action sequences, unremarkable.

duels are fought in hundreds of low-budget action dramas, but the well-staged ones are rare enough to be recounted. Basil Rathbone fought Errol Flynn in *The Adventures of Robin Hood* (and later spoofed the occasion in *The Court Jester*). He also lost to Tyrone Power in *The Mark of Zorro*. Flynn also encountered Rathbone in *Captain Blood* and Henry Daniell in *The Sea Hawk*. Douglas Fairbanks Snr fought duels in *The Thief of Baghdad*, *The Black Pirate* and others; Douglas Fairbanks Jnr was a memorable opponent for Ronald Colman in *The Prisoner of Zenda* (later restaged for James Mason and Stewart Granger) and duelled again in *The Corsican Brothers* and *Sindbad the Sailor*. Granger also duelled with Mason in *Fanny by Gaslight*, but used pistols this time; it was back to foils again for *Scaramouche* and *Swordsman of Siena*. John Barrymore fought splendid duels in his silent films, notably *Don Juan* and *General Crack*, later opposing Rathbone in *Romeo and Juliet*. In the 40s Cornel Wilde became fencer in chief, in such films as *Bandit of Sherwood Forest*, *Forever Amber* and *Sons of the Musketeers*. All the versions of *The Three Musketeers* involved duelling, but Gene Kelly turned it into a splendid series of acrobatic feats. In more serious films Ferrer duelled in *Cyrano de Bergerac* and Olivier in *Hamlet*.

DUFF, HOWARD (1917–). American actor with stage experience; usually plays good-looking but shifty types. *Brute Force* (debut) (47), *Naked City* (48), *All My Sons* (48), *Calamity Jane and Sam Bass* (50), *Woman in Hiding* (50), *Shakedown* (50), *Steel Town* (52), *Women's Prison* (54), *While the City Sleeps* (56), *Boys' Night Out* (62), *Sardanapalus the Great* (It.) (63), etc. TV series: *Mr Adams and Eve* (56–57), *Dante* (60), *The Felony Squad* (66–68). Married Ida Lupino.

DUGAN, TOM (1889–1958). American burlesque comic, in films from 1927. *The Hot Heiress* (31), *Sing You Sinners* (38), *To Be or Not to Be* (best role) (42), *Up in Arms* (44), *The Lemon Drop Kid* (51), *Andy Hardy Comes Home* (58), hundreds of others.

DUGGAN, ANDREW (1923–). American character actor of stalwart types. *Patterns* (56), *The Bravados* (58), *The Chapman Report* (62), *FBI Code 98* (66), *The Secret War of Harry Frigg* (67), etc. TV series: *Bourbon Street Beat* (59), *Room for One More* (61), *Lancer* (68–69).

DUGGAN, PAT (1910–). American producer, former performer and writer. *Red Garters* (54), *The Search for Bridey Murphy* (57), *The Young Savages* (61), etc.

DUKE, IVY (1895–). Star of British silent screen; married to Guy Newall. *The Garden of Resurrection* (18), *The Lure of Crooning Water* (20), *The Persistent Lover* (22), etc.

DUKE, PATTY (1946–). American teenage actress who made her name on the stage and TV (*The Patty Duke Show*). Films include *The Goddess* (57), *The Miracle Worker* (AA) (62), *Billie* (65), *Me Natalie* (69).

DULAC, GERMAINE (1882–1942) (G. Saisset-Schneider). French woman director. *Ames de Fous* (18), *Le Diable dans la Ville* (24), *The Seashell and the Clergyman* (26), *Theme and Variations* (30), etc.

DULLEA, KEIR (c. 1939–). American leading actor usually in tense roles. *The Hoodlum Priest* (61), *David and Lisa* (62), *Bunny Lake Is Missing* (65), *2001: A Space Odyssey* (67), *De Sade* (69), etc.

DUMAS, ALEXANDRE, père (1802–1870). Highly industrious French novelist, mainly of swashbuckling adventures. Films resulting include several versions of *The Count of Monte Cristo* and *The Three Musketeers*, *The Man in the Iron Mask*, *The Fighting Guardsman* and *The Black Tulip*.

DUMAS, ALEXANDRE, fils (1824–1895). French novelist best known for *Camille*, which has been filmed several times.

DU MAURIER, DAPHNE (1907–). Best-selling British novelist, of whose works *Rebecca*, *Jamaica Inn*, *Frenchman's Creek*, *The Years Between*, *Hungry Hill*, *My Cousin Rachel*, *The Scapegoat*, and *The Birds* have been filmed.

DUMBRILLE, DOUGLAS (c. 1893–). American character actor with stage experience; the perfect well-dressed suave villain of many a 'B' picture and a foil for many comedians. *His Woman* (debut) (31), *Lives of a Bengal Lancer* (35), *Mr Deeds Goes to Town* (36), *Crime and Punishment* (36), *A Day at the Races* (37), *The Firefly* (38), *The Three Musketeers* (39), *The Big Store* (41), *Gypsy Wildcat* (44), *Christmas Eve* (47), *Abbott and Costello in the Foreign Legion* (50), *Son of Paleface* (52), *Julius Caesar* (53), *The Ten Commandments* (56), scores of others. TV series: *The Phil Silvers Show* (63), *Petticoat Junction* (64–65).

DUMONT, MARGARET (1890–1965). American actress, the stately butt of many a comedian including Groucho Marx. Memorable in *The Coconuts* (29), *Duck Soup* (33), *A Night at the Opera* (35), *Anything Goes* (36), *A Day at the Races* (37), *At the Circus* (39), *Up in Arms* (44), *Stop, You're Killing Me* (53), *What a Way to Go* (64), many others.

ance.ance

DUNA, STEFFI (1913–   ) (Stephanie Berindey). Hungarian dancer who appeared in some dramatic roles in the 30s. *The Indiscretions of Eve* (31), *La Cucaracha* (35), *The Dancing Pirate* (36), *Anthony Adverse* (36), *Pagliacci* (37), *Waterloo Bridge* (40), *Rivers End* (41), etc.

†DUNAWAY, FAYE (1941–   ). American leading acress. *The Happening* (67), *Bonnie and Clyde* (67), *The Thomas Crown Affair* (68), *A Place for Lovers* (69), *Little Big Man* (70).

DUNCAN, ARCHIE (1914–   ). Burly Scottish actor, the 'Little John' of TV's *Robin Hood* series. Film debut 1947; has played scores of cameo roles. *Operation Diamond* (47), *The Bad Lord Byron* (48), *The Gorbals Story* (51), *Robin Hood* (53), *The Maggie* (53), *Laxdale Hall* (54), *Johnny on the Run* (56), *Harry Black* (58), *Lancelot and Guinevere* (63), *Ring of Bright Water* (69), etc.

DUNING, GEORGE (1908–   ). American composer. *The Corpse Came C.O.D.* (46), *The Dark Past* (49), *The Man from Laramie* (55), *Picnic* (56), *Cowboy* (57), *3.10 to Yuma* (57), *The World of Suzie Wong* (61), *Toys in the Attic* (63), *Dear Brigitte* (65), etc.

DUNN, EMMA (1875–1966). British character actress, long in Hollywood: *The Man I Killed* (32), *The Crusades* (35), *The Great Dictator* (40), *I Married a Witch* (42), *The Bridge of San Luis Rey* (44), many others.

DUNN, JAMES (1905–1967). American actor, formerly on stage. Popular in early 30s in good-natured roles: *Bad Girl* (31), *Stand Up and Cheer*, etc. Made comeback in *A Tree Grows in Brooklyn* (AA)(44) but his later appearances have been in low-budget crime dramas and Westerns.

DUNN, MICHAEL (1935–   ) (Gary Neil Miller). Dwarf (3′ 10″) American actor who made a big impression in *Ship of Fools* (65); since on TV. 1967: *You're a Big Boy Now*. 1969: *Justine*.

DUNNE, IRENE (1904–   ). American leading lady of the 30s, usually seen as sensible, well-bred woman. Formerly in musical comedy. *Present Arms* (debut) (30), *Cimarron* (31), *Back Street* (32), *Roberta* (34), *Magnificent Obsession* (35), *Showboat* (36), *Theodora Goes Wild* (36), *High, Wide and Handsome* (37), *The Awful Truth* (37), *Joy of Living* (38), *Love Affair* (39), *When Tomorrow Comes* (39), *My Favourite Wife* (40), *Penny Serenade* (41), *Unfinished Business* (41), *Lady in a Jam* (42), *A Guy Named Joe* (43), *The White Cliffs of Dover* (44), *Together Again* (45), *Over Twenty-one* (45), *Anna and the King of Siam* (46), *Life with Father* (47), *I Remember Mama* (48), *Never a Dull Moment* (50), *The Mudlark* (as Queen Victoria) (GB) (51), *It Grows on Trees* (last to date) (52), many others.

DUNNE, PHILIP (1908–   ). American writer-director. *How Green Was My Valley* (w) (42), *The Robe* (w) (53), *Prince of Players* (p, d) (54), *Three Brave Men* (w, d) (56), *Ten North Frederick* (w, d) (58), *Blue Denim* (w, d) (59), *Lisa* (*The Inspector*) (d) (62), *Blindfold* (w, d) (65), many others.

DUNNOCK, MILDRED (c. 1900–   ). American character actress, formerly on stage. *The Corn Is Green* (debut) (45), *Kiss of Death* (50), *Death of a Salesman* (51), *Viva Zapata* (52), *The Trouble with Harry* (56), *Cat on a Hot Tin Roof* (58), *Something Wild* (62), *Youngblood Hawke* (64), *Seven Women* (66), *Whatever Happened to Aunt Alice?* (69), etc.

dupe negative. One made from the original negative (via a lavender print) to protect it from wear by producing too many copies.

duping print (*or lavender print*). A high quality print made from the original negative. From it dupe negatives can be made.

DUPONT, E. A. (Ewald André) (1891–1956). German director who moved with unhappy results to Britain and Hollywood. *Baruh* (23), *Variety* (26), *Love Me and the World Is Mine* (27), *Moulin Rouge* (28), *Piccadilly* (28), *Atlantic* (30), *Ladies in Love* (33), *The Bishop Misbehaves* (35), *Forgotten Faces* (36), *Hell's Kitchen* (39), *The Scarf* (also wrote) (50), *The Neanderthal Man* (53), *Return to Treasure Island* (54), etc.

DUPREE, MINNIE (1873–1947). American stage actress whose best film role was as the not-so-helpless victim of confidence tricksters in *The Young in Heart* (39).

DUPREZ, JUNE (1918–   ). British leading lady. *The Crimson Circle* (36), *The Spy in Black* (38), *The Four Feathers* (39), *The Thief of Baghdad* (41), *None But the Lonely Heart* (US) (44), *Ten Little Niggers* (US) (45), *Calcutta* (US) (46), *That Brennan Girl* (US) (47), *The Kinsey Report* (US) (61), etc.

DUPUIS, PAUL (1916–   ). French-Canadian leading man popular in British films in the late 40s. *Johnny Frenchman* (45), *The White Unicorn* (47), *Sleeping Car to Trieste* (48), *Passport to Pimlico* (49), etc.

DURANTE, JIMMY 'SCHNOZZLE' (1893–   ). Well-loved, long-nosed American comedian with long career in vaudeville, night clubs and musical comedy. In films since 1929, with only mild success (*Cuban Love Song* [32], *The Passionate Plumber* [32], *Land without Music* [GB] [38]) until the 40s, when he made guest appearances in MGM musicals, doing his old routines: 'Umbriago', 'The Lost Chord', 'Ink-a-dink-a-doo', etc. *You're in the Army Now* (41), *The Man Who Came to Dinner* (41), *Two Girls and a Sailor* (44), *This Time for Keeps* (46), *It Happened in Brooklyn* (46), *On an Island with You* (47), *The*

Milkman (50), *Jumbo* (62), etc. A biography by Gene Fowler, *Schnozzola*, was published in 1952.

DURAS, MARGUERITE (1914–   ). French novelist. Works filmed: *The Sea Wall, Hiroshima Mon Amour, Moderato Cantabile* and *Sailor from Gibraltar*. 1966: directing *La Musica*.

†DURBIN, DEANNA (1921–   ) (Edna Mae Durbin). Canadian girl singer who won instant world-wide success as a teenage star; her career faltered after ten years when weight problems added to a change in musical fashion and brought about her premature retirement. *Three Smart Girls* (36), *One Hundred Men and a Girl* (37), *Mad about Music* (38), *That Certain Age* (38), *Three Smart Girls Grow Up* (38), *First Love* (39), *It's a Date* (39), *Spring Parade* (40), *Nice Girl* (40), *It Started with Eve* (41), *The Amazing Mrs Holliday* (42), *Hers to Hold* (43), *His Butler's Sister* (43), *Christmas Holiday* (44), *Can't Help Singing* (44), *Lady on a Train* (45), *Because of Him* (45), *I'll Be Yours* (46), *Something in the Wind* (47), *Up in Central Park* (47), *For the Love of Mary* (47). Special Academy Award 1938 'for bringing to the screen the spirit and personification of youth'.

DURFEE, MINTA (1897–   ). American leading lady of knockabout comedies 1914–16, including some with Chaplin. Married Roscoe Arbuckle and retired.

DURKIN, JUNIOR (1915–1935) (Trent Durkin). American juvenile player who was Huck Finn in *Tom Sawyer* (30) and *Huckleberry Finn* (31).

DURYEA, DAN (1907-1968). Laconic, long-faced American actor type-cast in villainous roles since he repeated his stage success as the evil cousin Leo in *The Little Foxes* (41). Has been prominent ever since, usually but not always in villainous roles; in addition to films, is a frequent TV guest star. *Ball of Fire* (41), *Pride of the Yankees* (42), *Sahara* (43), *Mrs Parkington* (44), *The Woman in the Window* (44), *The Great Flamarion* (44), *The Valley of Decision* (45), *Lady on a Train* (45), *Scarlet Street* (45), *Along Came Jones* (45), *White Tie and Tails* (46), *Black Angel* (47), *Black Bart Highwayman* (48), *Another Part of the Forest* (48), *Winchester 73* (50), *Underworld Story* (50), *Chicago Calling* (51), *Thunder Bay* (53), *Sky Commando* (53), *World for Ransom* (53), *Silver Lode* (54), *Foxfire* (55), *Storm Fear* (56), *Battle Hymn* (57), *Kathy 'O* (59), *Rich, Young and Deadly* (60), *Taggart* (64), *The Flight of the Phoenix* (65), others.

DUSE, ELEONORA (1858–1924). Eminent Italian tragedienne whose one film appearance was in *Cenere* (16).

DUVALL, ROBERT (1931–   ). American actor, usually seen as nervous villain. *The Chase* (65), *Countdown* (66), *Bullitt* (68), *The Rain People* (69), *True Grit* (69), etc.

317

DUVIVIER, JULIEN (1896–1967). Celebrated French director of the 30s whose touch seemed to falter after a wartime sojourn in Hollywood. *Hacadelma* (19), *Poil de Carotte* (25 and 32), *David Golder* (30), *Maria Chapdelaine* (33), *Le Golem* (35), *La Belle Equipe* (36), *Pepe Le Moko* (37), *Un Carnet de Bal* (37), *The Great Waltz* (US) (38), *La Fin du Jour* (39), *La Charette Fantôme* (39), *Lydia* (US) (41), *Tales of Manhattan* (US) (42), *Flesh and Fantasy* (US) (43), *The Impostor* (US) (44), *Panique* (46), *Anna Karenina* (GB) (48), *Au Royaume des Cieux* (49), *Sous le Ciel de Paris* (51), *Don Camillo* (52), *La Fete à Henriette* (54), *L'Affaire Maurizius* (54), *Voici le Temps des Assassins* (55), *The Man in the Raincoat* (57), *Pot-Bouille* (57), *Marie Octobre* (59), *La Femme et le Pantin* (59), *La Grande Vie* (61), *La Chambre Ardente* (62), *Chair de Poule* (63), etc.

DVORAK, ANN (1912–   ) (Ann McKim). American leading lady of the 30s. *Scarface* (debut) (32), *The Crowd Roars* (33), then many routine pictures. In Britain during the war for *Squadron Leader X* (41), *This Was Paris* (42); then *Escape to Danger* (43), *Flame of the Barbary Coast* (44), *The Long Night* (47), *Bel Ami* (48), *A Life of Her Own* (50), *I Was an American Spy* (51), *The Secret of Convict Lake* (last to date) (52), etc.

DWAN, ALLAN (1885–   ). Veteran American director, former writer; has competently handled commercial movies of every type. *Wildflower* (14), *The Good Bad Man* (15), *Manhattan Madness* (16), *A Modern Musketeer* (18), *Luck of the Irish* (20), *Robin Hood* (22), *Big Brother* (23), *Zaza* (23), *Manhandled* (24), *Wicked* (25), *Stage Struck* (25), *While Paris Sleeps* (27), *The Iron Mask* (29), *Man to Man* (31), *Mayor of Hell* (33), *Human Cargo* (36), *Heidi* (37), *Suez* (38), *The Three Musketeers* (Ritz Brothers version) (39), *Trail of the Vigilantes* (40), *Rise and Shine* (41), *Abroad with Two Yanks* (44), *Up in Mabel's Room* (44), *Brewster's Millions* (45), *Getting Gertie's Garter* (46), *Angel in Exile* (48), *Sands of Iwo Jima* (49), *The Wild Blue Yonder* (51), *Montana Belle* (52), *The Woman They Almost Lynched* (53), *Silver Lode* (54), *Tennessee's Partner* (55), *Hold Back the Night* (56), *Slightly Scarlet* (56), *The River's Edge* (57), *The Most Dangerous Man Alive* (61), scores of others.

DWYER, LESLIE (1906–   ). Plump cockney character actor, in films from childhood. *The Fifth Form at St Dominic's* (21), *The Flag Lieutenant* (31), *The Goose Steps Out* (41), *The Way Ahead* (44), *Night Boat to Dublin* (46), *When the Bough Breaks* (48), *The Calendar* (48), *Midnight Episode* (50), *Laughter in Paradise* (51), *Hindle Wakes* (52), *Where There's a Will* (53), *Act of Love* (54), *Left, Right and Centre* (59), *I've Gotta Horse* (64), many others.

DYALL, VALENTINE (1908–   ). Gaunt British actor with resounding voice, famous as radio's wartime 'Man in Black'. Film debut *The*

Life and Death of Colonel Blimp (43); later in many supporting roles, notably *Henry V* (44), *Caesar and Cleopatra* (45), *Brief Encounter* (46), *Vengeance Is Mine* (48), *City of the Dead* (60), *The Haunting* (63), *The Horror of It All* (65), etc. Son of stage actor FRANKLIN DYALL (1874–1950), whose few films included *Atlantic* (30), *F.P.1* (33), *Fire Over England* (36).

Dynamic Frame. A concept invented in 1955 by an American, Glenn Alvey: the screen was to be the maximum size, i.e. CinemaScope, but individual scenes were to be masked down to whatever ratio suited them best, e.g. rather narrow for a corridor. Only one experimental British film, a version of H. G. Wells' *The Hole in the Wall*, was made in Dynamic Frame, which proved distracting and has in any case been overtaken by the multiscreen experiments of the 60s.

E

EADY, DAVID (1924–   ). British director. *The Bridge of Time* (documentary) (52), *Three Cases of Murder* (one story) (55), *In the Wake of a Stranger* (58), *Faces in the Dark* (60), etc. Much TV work.

EAGELS, JEANNE (1894–1929). American theatrical and screen personality with a highly-publicized private life. *Man, Woman and Sin* (27), *The Letter* (29), *Jealousy* (29), etc. Kim Novak starred in a biopic of her in 1957.

EARP, WYATT (1848–1928). American frontier marshal, the most famous lawman of the wild west. Screen impersonations of him include Walter Huston in *Law and Order* (31); Jon Hall in *Frontier Marshal* (39); Richard Dix in *Tombstone* (42); Henry Fonda in *My Darling Clementine* (46); Joel McCrea in *Wichita* (55); Burt Lancaster in *Gunfight at the OK Corral* (57); James Stewart in *Cheyenne Autumn* (64); James Garner in *Hour of the Gun* (67). There was also a long-running TV series starring Hugh O'Brian.

EARTH (USSR 1930). Dovzhenko's epic drama on the relation of man to the soil. Written by the director, photographed by Daniel Demutski.

EASDALE, BRIAN (1909–   ). British composer: GPO Film Unit shorts (34–38), *Ferry Pilot* (42), *Black Narcissus* (46), *The Red Shoes* (AA) (48), *An Outcast of the Islands* (51), *The Battle of the River Plate* (56), etc.

EASON, B. REEVES (1886–1956). American second unit director, famous for chariot race sequence in *Ben Hur* (27). Also directed *Moon Riders* (20), *The Galloping Ghost* (31), many second features up to *Rimfire* (49).

EAST LYNNE. Mrs Henry Wood's heavy-going Victorian novel, in which mother and baby are literally cast out into the cold, cold snow, was a favourite silent film subject. There were British versions in 1912 and 1921, and an American one in 1925; but the 1930 sound remake, with Ann Harding, was not a success.

EAST OF EDEN (US 1955). Notable for introducing the young James Dean as a teenage rebel of yesteryear, this version by Elia Kazan of John Steinbeck's novel about father-son relationships in agricultural California before World War I had emotional power to make up for its rather sluggish pace and inflated biblical parallels. Raymond Massey and Jo Van Fleet (AA) were the mainstays of a film which at least treated its audience as adults.

EASTMAN, GEORGE (1854–1952). American pioneer of cinematography: invented the roll film, which made him a millionaire.

EASTWOOD, CLINT (1930–   ). American leading man who had some success in TV, then went to Italy and became enormously popular as the vengeful leading man of a series of violent imitative westerns. *The First Travelling Saleslady* (55), *A Fistful of Dollars* (64), *For a Few Dollars More* (66), *The Good, the Bad and the Ugly* (67), *Hang 'Em High* (back in Hollywood) (68), *Coogan's Bluff* (68), *Where Eagles Dare* (68), *Paint Your Wagon* (69), *Two Mules for Sister Sara* (69), *The Warriors* (70). TV series: *Rawhide* (60–65).

EASY STREET (US 1917). Perhaps Chaplin's most notable two-reeler, a deft combination of farce and social documentary, with jokes about the Salvation Army, overcrowded slums and drug addiction. Still poignant and funny.

EATON, SHIRLEY (1936–   ). Pneumatic British blonde who has decorated many comedies since 1954; unsuccessfully played American in *The Girl Hunters* (63), and was encased in gold by *Goldfinger* (64). *Rhino* (65), *Ten Little Indians* (65), *Around the World under the Sea* (66), *Eight on the Lam* (67), *Sumuru* (68), etc.

EBSEN, BUDDY (1908–   ) (Christian Rudolf Ebsen). 'Countryfied' American actor-dancer, a reliable second string in many 30s musicals: *Broadway Melody of 1936*, *Captain January* (36), *Banjo on My Knee* (37), *Four Girls in White* (38), *My Lucky Star* (39), etc. Barely glimpsed in the 40s, he later emerged as a character actor: *Thunder in God's Country* (51), *Red Garters* (54), *Davy Crockett* (56), *Attack* (56), *Breakfast at Tiffany's* (61), *West of Montana* (*Mail Order Bride*) (63). Latterly a great success as star of the long-running TV series: *The Beverly Hillbillies* (62–69).

EBURNE, MAUDE (1875–1960). Small-built American character actress; usually played wry or waspish matrons. *The Bat Whispers* (31), *The Guardsman* (32), *Ruggles of Red Gap* (34), *The Suspect* (44), *Bowery to Broadway* (44), *Arson Inc* (50), many others.

ECSTASY: see EXTASE

EDDY, NELSON (1901–67). American actor-singer, former commercial artist, reporter and opera star. Famous for series of 30s musicals with Jeanette MacDonald: *Naughty Marietta* (35), *Rose Marie* (36), *Maytime* (37), *The Girl of the Golden West* (38), *Sweethearts* (38), *New Moon* (40), *Bitter Sweet* (40), *I Married an Angel* (42). Also in *Rosalie* (38), *Balalaika* (39), *The Chocolate Soldier* (41),

Phantom of the Opera (43), *Knickerbocker Holiday* (44), *Make Mine Music* (voice only) (46), *End of the Rainbow* (47), etc. Subsequently toured night clubs.

EDEN, BARBARA (1934–) (B. Huffman). American leading lady, former chorine. *Back from Eternity* (56), *Twelve Hours to Kill* (60), *Voyage to the Bottom of the Sea* (61), *The Wonderful World of the Brothers Grimm* (63), *The Brass Bottle* (64), *The Seven Faces of Dr Lao* (64), etc. TV series: *How to Marry a Millionaire* (58), *I Dream of Jeannie* (65–69).

EDENS, ROGER (1905–). American musical supervisor who has moulded many MGM musicals, often as associate to producer Arthur Freed. Academy Awards for *Easter Parade* (48), *On the Town* (49), *Annie Get Your Gun* (50). Produced *Deep in My Heart* (55), *Funny Face* (56), *Hello Dolly* (69), etc.

EDESON, ARTHUR (1891–1970). American cinematographer. *Wild and Woolly* (17), *Robin Hood* (23), *The Thief of Baghdad* (24), *The Lost World* (25), *The Bat* (26), *The Patent Leather Kid* (27), *In Old Arizona* (28), *All Quiet on the Western Front* (30), *Frankenstein* (31), *The Big Trail* (31), *The Old Dark House* (32), *The Invisible Man* (33), *Mutiny on the Bounty* (35), *Sergeant York* (41), *The Maltese Falcon* (41), *Casablanca* (42), *The Mask of Dimitrios* (44), *The Fighting O'Flynn* (48), many others.

EDGAR, MARRIOTT (1880–1951). British comedy scenarist, in films from 1935. Worked on many of the best vehicles of Will Hay and the Crazy Gang: *Good Morning Boys* (36), *Oh Mr Porter* (38), *Alf's Button Afloat* (38), *The Frozen Limits* (39), *The Ghost Train* (41), many others; later on children's films. Also author of the 'Sam Small' and 'Albert' monologues made famous by Stanley Holloway.

edge numbers. Serial numbers printed along the edge of all film material to assist identification when re-ordering sections.

EDISON, THOMAS ALVA (1847–1931). American inventor of the phonograph and the incandescent lamp, among over a thousand other devices including the kinetoscope, a combined movie camera and projector. Biopics: *Young Tom Edison* (39) with Mickey Rooney; *Edison the Man* (40) with Spencer Tracy.

editor. Technician who assembles final print of film from various scenes and tracks available; works closely under director's control except in routine pictures.

EDOUARD ET CAROLINE (France 1950). Jacques Becker's slight but charming comedy of a tiff between a young married couple was highly influential on later styles. Anne Vernon and Daniel Gelin starred.

EDOUART, FARCIOT (* –). American special effects man, with Paramount for many years. *Alice in Wonderland* (33), *Lives of a Bengal Lancer* (35), *Sullivan's Travels* (41), *Reap the Wild Wind* (42), *Unconquered* (47), *Ace in the Hole* (51), *The Mountain* (56), many others.

†EDWARDS, BLAKE (1922–) (William Blake McEdwards). American writer-producer-director with a leaning for all kinds of comedy. Radio experience. *Panhandle* (w) (47), *All Ashore* (w) (53), *Cruising down the River* (w) (53), *Drive a Crooked Road* (w) (54), *Sound Off* (w) (54), *Bring Your Smile Along* (w, d) (55), *My Sister Eileen* (w) (55), *He Laughed Last* (w, d) (55), *Mr Cory* (w, d) (56), *Operation Mad Ball* (w) (57), *This Happy Feeling* (w, d) (58), *The Perfect Furlough* (w, d) (58), *Operation Petticoat* (d) (59), *High Time* (d) (60), *Breakfast at Tiffany's* (d) (61), *Experiment in Terror* (*The Grip of Fear*) (d) (62), *Notorious Landlady* (w) (62), *Days of Wine and Roses* (w) (62), *The Pink Panther* (w, d) (63), *A Shot in the Dark* (w, p, d) (64), *The Great Race* (w, p, d) (64), *What Did You Do in the War, Daddy?* (w, p, d) (66), *Waterhole Three* (p) (67), *Gunn* (p, d) (67), *The Party* (w, p, d) (68), *Darling Lili* (w, p, d) (69). TV series: *Richard Diamond, Dante, Peter Gunn* (all as creator).

EDWARDS, CLIFF (1895–). American light entertainer known as 'Ukelele Ike'. *Hollywood Revue* (29), *George White's Scandals* (35), *Saratoga* (37), *Gone with the Wind* (39), *His Girl Friday* (40), *She Couldn't Say No* (45), *The Avenging Rider* (53), others.

EDWARDS, HENRY (1882–1952). Popular British stage actor, author and manager, equally popular in films from 1915. *Broken Threads* (18), *The Amazing Quest of Ernest Bliss* (22), *A Lunatic at Large* (24), *The Flag Lieutenant* (26), *Fear* (27), *Three Kings* (28), *Call of the Sea* (31), *The Flag Lieutenant* (talkie version) (31), *General John Regan* (33), many others; often appeared with his wife Chrissie White. Directed many films including *The Barton Mystery* (32), *Discord* *Driven* (33), *Juggernaut* (37), *Spring Meeting* (41). Later came back as character actor: *Green for Danger* (46), *Oliver Twist* (48), *London Belongs to Me* (48), *The Long Memory* (52), etc.

EDWARDS, JAMES (1922–1970). American Negro actor, on stage from 1945. *The Set-Up* (film debut) (49), *Home of the Brave* (49), *The Member of the Wedding* (52), *The Caine Mutiny* (54), *The Phenix City Story* (55), *Men in War* (57), *The Sandpiper* (65), etc.

EDWARDS, JIMMY (1920–). Moustachioed British comedian of stage, radio and TV. Occasional films include *Treasure Hunt* (48), *Three Men in a Boat* (55), *Bottoms Up* (60), *Nearly a Nasty Accident* (62).

EDWARDS, MEREDITH (1917–). Balding Welsh character actor with stage experience. Debut in leading role in *A Run for Your Money*

(50); since frequently seen in cameos. *The Blue Lamp* (50), *Girdle of Gold* (53), *The Cruel Sea* (53), *The Long Arm* (56), *The Trials of Oscar Wilde* (60), *Only Two Can Play* (61), *This Is My Street* (64), etc.

EDWARDS, VINCE (1928–   ). American leading man of the tough/sincere kind. *Hiawatha* (52), *City of Fear* (58), *Murder by Contract* (59), *The Victors* (63), *The Devil's Brigade* (68), *Hammerhead* (68), *The Desperadoes* (69), etc. TV series: *Ben Casey* (60–65).

EGAN, RICHARD (1921–   ). American leading man with varied experience before film debut 1949. Once thought likely successor to Clark Gable but has been mainly confined to Westerns and action dramas. *The Damned Don't Cry* (debut) (49), *Undercover Girl* (50), *Split Second* (52), *Demetrius and the Gladiators* (54), *Wicked Woman* (54), *Gog* (54), *Underwater* (55), *Untamed* (55), *Violent Saturday* (55), *The View from Pompey's Head* (55), *Seven Cities of Gold* (55), *Love Me Tender* (56), *Tension at Table Rock* (56), *These Thousand Hills* (58), *A Summer Place* (59), *Pollyanna* (60), *Esther and the King* (60), *The 300 Spartans* (62), *The Destructors* (66), *Chubasco* (68), *The Big Cube* (69), etc. TV series: *Empire*, *Redigo*.

EGGAR, SAMANTHA (1940–   ). British leading lady. *The Wild and the Willing* (61), *Dr Crippen* (63), *Psyche 59* (63), *The Collector* (65), *Return from the Ashes* (65), *Walk, Don't Run* (66), *Doctor Dolittle* (67), *The Molly Maguires* (69), *The Walking Stick* (69), *The Lady in the Car* (70), etc.

EIGHT AND A HALF (Italy 1963). Fellini's beautiful, irresponsible, mainly incomprehensible but highly cinematic extravaganza for our times, about a film director with doubts. Superbly photographed by Gianni de Venanzo, with a fine central part for Marcello Mastroianni. AA 1963: best foreign film.

EILERS, SALLY (1908–   ). American leading lady of the late 20s and early 30s. *The Cradle Snatchers* (28), *Quick Millions* (31), *Over the Hill* (32), *State Fair* (33), *Alias Mary Dow* (34), *Strike Me Pink* (36), *I Was a Prisoner on Devil's Island* (41), *Lost Stage Valley* (51), many others.

EISENSTEIN, SERGEI (1898–1948). Russian director, one of the cinema giants. Used the camera more vividly and purposefully than almost anyone else. *Strike* (24), *The Battleship Potemkin* (25), *October* (*Ten Days That Shook the World*) (27), *The General Line* (28), *Que Viva Mexico* (unfinished: sections later released under this title and as *Time in the Sun*) (32), *Alexander Nevsky* (38), *Ivan the Terrible* (42–46). Books published include *Film Form*, *The Film Sense*, *Notes of a Film Director*. He virtually invented 'montage'.

EISINGER, JO (* –   ). American screen writer. *The Spider* (45), *Gilda* (46), *The Sleeping City* (50), *Night and the City* (51), *The System* (53), *Bedevilled* (55), *The Poppy is Only a Flower* (*Danger Grows Wild*) (66), many others.

EISLER, HANNS (1898–1963). German composer who in 40s scored some Hollywood films (*None But the Lonely Heart*, *The Woman on the Beach*, etc.). In Germany, *Aktion J* (61), many others.

EKBERG, ANITA (1931–   ). Statuesque Swedish blonde who has decorated a number of films in various countries. *The Golden Blade* (53), *Blood Alley* (55), *Artists and Models* (55), *Back from Eternity* (56), *War and Peace* (56), *Zarak* (56), *Interpol* (*Pickup Alley*) (57), *Sign of the Gladiator* (58), *La Dolce Vita* (59), *Boccaccio 70* (61), *Call Me Bwana* (63), *Four for Texas* (63), *The Alphabet Murders* (65), *Who Wants to Sleep* (*Das Liebeskarussel*) (65), *Way Way Out* (66), *The Glass Sphinx* (67), etc.

EKLAND, BRITT (1942–   ). Swedish leading lady once married to Peter Sellers. In *After the Fox* (66), *The Bobo* (67), *The Night They Raided Minsky's* (68), *Stiletto* (69).

EKMAN, GOSTA (1887–1937). Swedish leading actor. *Charles XII* (24), *Faust* (26), *Intermezzo* (36), etc.

EL (Mexico 1953). A haunting psychological melodrama written and directed by Luis Bunuel, with Arturo de Cordova as a happily married man who unaccountably goes mad with jealousy.

ELAM, JACK (1916–   ). Laconic, swarthy American character actor, often seen as western villain or sinister comic relief. *Rawhide* (50), *Kansas City Confidential* (52), *The Moonlighter* (53), *Vera Cruz* (54), *Moonfleet* (55), *Kiss Me Deadly* (55), *Gunfight at the OK Corral* (57), *Baby Face Nelson* (57), *Edge of Eternity* (59), *The Comancheros* (62), *The Rare Breed* (66), *The Way West* (67), *Firecreek* (67), *Once Upon a Time in the West* (69), etc. TV series: *The Dakotas* (62), *Temple Houston* (63).

ELDREDGE, JOHN (1904–1960). Mild-looking American actor usually cast as weakling brother or bland schemer. *The Man with Two Faces* (34), *Persons in Hiding* (38), *Blossoms in the Dust* (41), *The French Key* (47), *The First Travelling Saleslady* (56), many others.

ELDRIDGE, FLORENCE (1901–   ) (Florence McKechnie). Distinguished American stage actress, wife of Fredric March. Occasional film appearances: *Six-Cylinder Love* (23), *The Story of Temple Drake* (32), *Mary of Scotland* (36), *An Act of Murder* (47), *Another Part of the Forest* (48), *Christopher Columbus* (GB) (49), *Inherit the Wind* (60), etc.

ELDRIDGE, JOHN (1917–   ). British documentary and feature director. *Waverley Steps* (47), *Three Dawns to Sydney* (49), *Brandy for the Parson* (51), *Laxdale Hall* (53), *Conflict of Wings* (54), etc.

ELEPHANT BOY (GB 1937). Directed by Robert Flaherty and Zoltan Korda, this adaptation of Kipling's 'Toomai of the Elephants' had the air of a fictionalized travel film but was a great commercial success because of the popularity of the boy Sabu, who became a star and went to Hollywood. Its Indian backgrounds were charming and authentic.

elephants have come closest to starring roles in *Zenobia*, *Elephant Boy* and *Hannibal Brooks*; but they were the subject of concern in *Where No Vultures Fly*, *Elephant Walk* and *Roots of Heaven*, and Tarzan and Dorothy Lamour (in her jungle days) usually had one around as a pet.

elevators: see *lifts*.

ELG, TAINA (c. 1931–   ). Finnish leading lady, in a few Hollywood and British films: *The Prodigal* (55), *Gaby* (56), *Les Girls* (57), *The Thirty-nine Steps* (59), etc.

ELIZABETH I, queen of England (1533–1603), has been notably played by Flora Robson in *Fire over England* (36) and *The Sea Hawk* (40); by Bette Davis in *Elizabeth and Essex* (39) and *The Virgin Queen* (55); by Sarah Bernhardt in *Queen Elizabeth* (12), and by Irene Worth in *Seven Seas to Calais* (63). Jean Simmons played the young queen in *Young Bess* (54).

ELLERY QUEEN. The fictional American detective was played by four actors between 1935 and 1943: Donald Cook, Eddie Quillan, Ralph Bellamy and William Gargan. The name is a pseudonym for two authors: Frederick Dannay (1905–   ) and Manfred Lee (1905–   ).

ELLIOTT, DENHOLM (1922–   ). British stage and screen actor, often of well-mannered ineffectual types, latterly in more sophisticated roles. *The Sound Barrier* (52), *The Cruel Sea* (53), *The Heart of the Matter* (53), *They Who Dare* (54), *The Night My Number Came Up* (55), *Pacific Destiny* (56), *Scent of Mystery* (*Holiday in Spain*) (59), *Station Six Sahara* (63), *Nothing But the Best* (64), *The High Bright Sun* (65), *You Must Be Joking* (65), *King Rat* (65), *Alfie* (66), *The Spy with a Cold Nose* (67), *Maroc 7* (67), *Here We Go Round the Mulberry Bush* (67), *The Night They Raided Minsky's* (68), *Too Late the Hero* (69), etc.

ELLIOTT, 'WILD BILL' (1906–1965) (Gordon Elliott). Burly American leading man of the 20s who later appeared in many second feature Westerns and mysteries. *The Private Life of Helen of Troy* (27),

Broadway Scandals (28), *The Great Divide* (31), *Wonder Bar* (34), *False Evidence* (40), *Blue Clay* (42), *The Plainsman and the Lady* (46), *The Fabulous Texan* (48), *The Longhorn* (51), *Dial Red O* (55), etc.

ELLIS, EDWARD (1872–1952). American stage character actor. Made a few talkies usually as judge or white-haired father. *I Was a Fugitive from a Chain Gang* (32), *The Thin Man* (34), *Winterset* (36), *Fury* (36), *Maid of Salem* (37), *Man of Conquest* (39), *The Omaha Trail* (42), etc.

ELLIS, MARY (1900–   ) (Mary Elsas). American leading lady and singer famous in British stage musicals, especially those of Ivor Novello. Films include *Bella Donna* (34), *Paris Love Song* (35), *All the King's Horses* (35), *Glamorous Night* (36), *The Three Worlds of Gulliver* (61).

ELLISON, JAMES (1910–   ) (James Ellison Smith). Genial American leading man, mainly seen in routine Westerns. *The Play Girl* (32), *Hopalong Cassidy* (35), *The Plainsman* (as Buffalo Bill) (36), *Vivacious Lady* (38), *Fifth Avenue Girl* (39), *Ice Capades* (41), *Charley's American Aunt* (41), *I Walked with a Zombie* (43), *The Ghost Goes Wild* (46), *Calendar Girl* (47), *Last of the Wild Horses* (48), *The Undying Monster* (48), *Lone Star Lawman* (50), *Dead Man's Trail* (52), etc. Recently inactive.

ELMER GANTRY (US 1960). In this lengthy version written (AA) and directed by Richard Brooks, Sinclair Lewis's novel about old-time revivalist religion has its emotions compromised and its satire blunted; but the flavour of the book often filters through, and the film benefits from John Alton's colour photography and the broad, beaming, zestful performance of Burt Lancaster (AA) as the hymn and hellfire salesman.

ELMES, GUY (1920–   ). British writer. *The Planter's Wife* (co-w) (51), *The Stranger's Hand* (53), *Across the Bridge* (co-w) (57), *Swordsman of Siena* (62), *A Face in the Rain* (63), *El Greco* (66), etc.

ELSOM, ISOBEL (1893–   ) (Isobel Reed). British stage actress who starred in over 60 British silent romantic dramas beginning with *A Debt of Honour* (19). Moved to Hollywood in the 30s and stayed there as character actress. *Dick Turpin's Ride to York* (22), *The Sign of Four* (23), *The Wandering Jew* (23), *The Love Story of Aliette Brunon* (24), *Stranglehold* (30), *Illegal* (31), *Ladies in Retirement* (41), *Of Human Bondage* (46), *Monsieur Verdoux* (47), *Désirée* (54), *Twenty-three Paces to Baker Street* (57), *My Fair Lady* (64), many others.

ELTINGE, JULIAN (1882–1941) (William J. Dalton). American female impersonator who appeared in a few silent films: *The Countess Charming* (17), *Over the Rhine* (18), *Madame Behave* (24), etc.

Elton, Sir Arthur

ELTON, SIR ARTHUR (1906–). British producer especially associated with documentary; GPO Film Unit 34–37, Ministry of Information 37–45, Shell Film Unit 45 on. Founder Film Centre, governor BFI, etc.

ELVEY, MAURICE (1887–1967) (William Folkard). Veteran British director of over 300 features. *Maria Marten* (12), *Comradeship* (18), *Nelson* (19), *At the Villa Rose* (20), *The Elusive Pimpernel* (20), *The Hound of the Baskervilles* (21), *Dick Turpin's Ride to York* (22), *The Love Story of Aliette Brunon* (24), *The Flag Lieutenant* (26), *Hindle Wakes* (27), *Balaclava* (28), *High Treason* (30), *The School for Scandal* (30), *Sally in Our Alley* (31), *In a Monastery Garden* (31), *The Water Gypsies* (32), *The Lodger* (32), *The Wandering Jew* (33), *The Clairvoyant* (34), *The Tunnel* (34), *Heat Wave* (35), *The Return of the Frog* (37), *For Freedom* (39), *Room for Two* (39), *Under Your Hat* (40), *The Lamp Still Burns* (43), *The Gentle Sex* (co-d) (43), *Medal for the General* (44), *Salute John Citizen* (44), *Beware of Pity* (46), *The Third Visitor* (51), *My Wife's Lodger* (52), *Fun at St Fanny's* (55), *Dry Rot* (56), etc.

EMERSON, FAYE (1917–). American socialite leading lady popular for a time in 40s: *Between Two Worlds* (44), *The Mask of Dimitrios* (44), *Hotel Berlin* (45), etc. Left Hollywood for stage and TV roles: guest spot in *A Face in the Crowd* (57).

EMERSON, HOPE (1897–1960). Brawny 6′ 2″ American character actress, in films from early 30s, for whom a typical part was that of the circus strongwoman in *Adam's Rib* (49). Also: *Cry of the City* (48), *Caged* (50), *Casanova's Big Night* (54), *The Day They Gave Babies Away* (56), *Rock a Bye Baby* (58), many others. TV series: *Peter Gunn* (58–60).

EMERTON, ROY (1892–1944). Long-nosed Canadian character actor in British films: an eminently hissable villain. *The Sign of Four* (32), *Java Head* (34), *Lorna Doone* (as Carver) (35), *Doctor Syn* (38), *The Drum* (38), *Busman's Honeymoon* (40), *The Thief of Bagdad* (41), *The Man in Grey* (43), *Henry V* (44), etc.

EMERY, GILBERT (1889–1945). American character actor with stage experience. *Cousin Kate* (21), *The Sky Hawk* (30), *Gallant Lady* (also wrote) (33), *Dracula's Daughter* (36), *The Life of Emile Zola* (37), *Nurse Edith Cavell* (39), *Return of the Vampire* (43), *The Brighton Strangler* (45), etc.

EMERY, JOHN (1905–1964). American stage and screen actor of suave and sometimes Mephistophelean types. *Here Comes Mr Jordan* (41), *Spellbound* (45), *Blood on the Sun* (45), *The Woman in White* (48), *The Gay Intruders* (48), *Let's Live Again* (49), *The Mad Magician* (54), *Ten North Frederick* (57), *Youngblood Hawke* (64), many others.

EMHARDT, ROBERT (c. 1901–). American character actor, short and tubby; once understudied Sidney Greenstreet. *The Iron Mistress* (52), *Three-Ten to Yuma* (57), *Underworld USA* (60), *The Stranger* (61), *Kid Galahad* (62), *The Group* (66), *Where Were You When the Lights Went Out?* (68), etc.

EMIL AND THE DETECTIVES. Erich Kastner's German novel of school-boys who track down a thief has been filmed five times: in 1932 (Germany) by Gerhardt Lamprecht; in 1935 (GB) by Milton Rosmer; in 1954 (Germany) by R. A. Stemmle; in 1956 in Japan; and in 1963 (US) by Peter Tewkesbury for Walt Disney.

EMMER, LUCIANO (1918–). Italian director. Art documentaries 1942–54. Features: *Domenica d'Agosto* (50), *The Girls of the Spanish Steps* (52), *The Bigamist* (56), etc.

EMMETT, E. V. H. (1902–). British commentator, for many years the voice of Universal News. Producer of occasional documentaries.

EMNEY, FRED (1900–). Heavyweight British comedian, charac-terized by a growl, a cigar, and a top hat. Occasional films: *Brewster's Millions* (35), *Yes Madam* (39), *Just William* (40), *Let the People Sing* (42), *Fun at St Fanny's* (56), *San Ferry Ann* (65), *The Sandwich Man* (66), *Lock Up Your Daughters* (69), etc.

EN CAS DE MALHEUR (LOVE IS MY PROFESSION) (France 1958). A melo-drama of adultery, very big at the French box-office, notable for its bringing together of an extraordinary collection of talent. Written by Aurenche and Bost; directed by Claude Autant-Lara; with Jean Gabin, Brigitte Bardot, Edwige Feuillere.

the end of the world has been fairly frequently considered in movies, and not only in the recent crop of panic button dramas like *Dr Strangelove*, *The Bedford Incident* and *Fail Safe*. Movement of the earth was stopped in *The Day the Earth Stood Still* and (by Roland Young) in *The Man Who Could Work Miracles*. Plague very nearly ended everything in *Things to Come*. Danger from other planets looming perilously close was only narrowly averted in *Red Planet Mars*, while in *When Worlds Collide* and *The Day the Earth Caught Fire* the worst happened. Another kind of danger was met in *Crack in the World*. The Martians nearly got us in *The War of the Worlds*. In *Five* there were only five people left alive, in *The World, the Flesh and the Devil* only three, and in *On the Beach* none at all.

ENDFIELD, CY (1914–). American director, in films since 1942. Made second features until 1951; thereafter resident in Britain. *Gentleman Joe Palooka* (47), *Stork Bites Man* (also wrote) (47), *The Argyle Secrets* (also wrote) (48), *Underworld Story* (50), *The Sound of*

Fury (51), *Tarzan's Savage Fury* (52), *The Search* (55), *Child in the House* (56), *Hell Drivers* (57), *Sea Fury* (58), *Jet Storm* (59), *Mysterious Island* (61), *Zulu* (63), *Sands of the Kalahari* (65), *De Sade* (69), etc. Sometimes calls himself Cyril Endfield or C. Raker Endfield.

LES ENFANTS DU PARADIS (France 1944). A superbly evocative and pictorial romance of Paris's 'theatre street' in the 1830s. Jacques Prevert's script mingles fact and fiction, farce and tragedy; Marcel Carne directs with superb control of the rich detail. The fine cast includes Arletty, Jean-Louis Barrault, Pierre Brasseur and Marcel Herrand. Photography by Roger Hubert and Marc Fossard, music by Joseph Kosma and Maurice Thiriet.

ENGEL, MORRIS (1918–   ). American producer-director of off-beat semi-professional features: *The Little Fugitive* (53), *Lovers and Lollipops* (55), *Weddings and Babies* (58).

ENGEL, SAMUEL (1904–   ). American producer. *My Darling Clementine* (46), *Sitting Pretty* (48), *Rawhide* (50), *Belles on Their Toes* (52), *Daddy Long Legs* (55), *Boy on a Dolphin* (57), *The Story of Ruth* (60), *The Lion* (62), others.

ENGLUND, GEORGE H. (1926–   ). American producer-director. *The World, the Flesh and the Devil* (p) (59), *The Ugly American* (p, d) (62), *Signpost to Murder* (d) (64), *Captain Cook* (p) (project) (67), *Dark of the Sun* (p) (67), etc.

ENGLUND, KEN (1914–   ). American writer, in films from 1938. *Good Sam* (47), *The Secret Life of Walter Mitty* (48), *The Caddy* (53), *The Vagabond King* (56), etc.

ENOCH ARDEN was a character in a Tennyson poem who came back to his family after having been long supposed dead. Films with an 'Enoch Arden' theme include *Tomorrow Is Forever* (with Orson Welles), *The Years Between* (with Michael Redgrave), *My Two Husbands* (with Fred MacMurray) and its remake *Three for the Show* (with Jack Lemmon), *My Favourite Wife* (with Irene Dunne) and its remake *Move Over Darling* (with Doris Day), *Piccadilly Incident* (with Anna Neagle), *Return from the Ashes* (with Ingrid Thulin), *Desire Me* (with Robert Mitchum), and *The Man from Yesterday* (with Clive Brook). D. W. Griffith in 1910 and 1911 made short versions of the original story.

ENRICO, ROBERT (1931–   ). French director. *Incident at Owl Creek* (64), *Au Coeur de la Vie* (65), *La Belle Vie* (65), *Les Aventuriers* (67), *Zita* (67), etc.

ENRIGHT, RAY (1896–1965). American director, former editor and Sennett gagman. Rin-Tin-Tin silents, scores of routine sound Westerns and musicals. *Dames* (34), *The Wagons Roll at Night* (41),

The Spoilers (42), *Sin Town* (42), *Gung Ho* (44), *Man Alive* (46), *Coroner Creek* (48), *Return of the Bad Men* (49), *Kansas Raiders* (50), *Flaming Feather* (51), etc.

entertainers have been the subject of many biopics, with *The Jolson Story* and *Jolson Sings Again* perhaps topping the box office list thanks to Al Jolson's voice and Larry Parks' impersonation of the Jolson manner. Other subjects from the vaudeville stage and musical were James Cagney as George M. Cohan in *Yankee Doodle Dandy*, Frank Sinatra as Joe E. Lewis in *The Joker Is Wild*, Tommy Trinder as *Champagne Charlie* (Charles Leybourne), Ann Sheridan as Nora Bayes in *Shine On Harvest Moon*, Betty Grable and June Haver as *The Dolly Sisters*, Milton Berle as himself in *Always Leave Them Laughing*, Keefe Brasselle in *The Eddie Cantor Story*, Betty Hutton as Texas Guinan in *Incendiary Blonde*, Ann Blyth as Helen Morgan in *Both Ends of the Candle*, Susan Hayward as Jane Froman in *With a Song in My Heart*, Tony Curtis as *Houdini*, Danny Kaye as Red Nichols in *The Five Pennies*, June Haver as Marilyn Miller in *Look for the Silver Lining*, Will Rogers Jnr in *The Story of Will Rogers*, Bob Hope as Eddie Foy in *The Seven Little Foys*, Doris Day as Ruth Etting in *Love Me or Leave Me*, Pat Kirkwood as Vesta Tilley in *After the Ball*, Alice Faye as *Lillian Russell*, Kirk Douglas as Bix Beiderbecke in *Young Man with a Horn*, Mitzi Gaynor as Eva Tanguay in *The I Don't Care Girl*, Natalie Wood as Gypsy Rose Lee in *Gypsy*, James Stewart in *The Glenn Miller Story*, Eleanor Parker as Marjorie Laurence in *Interrupted Melody*, Kathryn Grayson as Grace Moore in *So This Is Love*, Patrice Munsel in *Melba*, Mario Lanza in *The Great Caruso*, Julie Andrews as Gertrude Lawrence in *Star!*, and Barbra Streisand as Fanny Brice in *Funny Girl*. If impresarios are counted, there's William Powell in *The Great Ziegfeld* and David Wayne as Sol Hurok in *Tonight We Sing*. Straight actors have understandably attracted less attention, but Anna Neagle played Peg Woffington in *Peg of Old Drury*, Richard Burton was Edwin Booth in *Prince of Players*, Miriam Hopkins had a field day as Mrs Leslie Carter in *Lady with Red Hair* (with Claude Rains as David Belasco), Errol Flynn was John Barrymore in *Too Much Too Soon*, with Dorothy Malone as Diana, and Jimmy Cagney was Lon Chaney in *Man of a Thousand Faces*.

EPHRON, HENRY (1912–   ) and **PHOEBE** (1914–   ). American husband-wife writing team. *The Jackpot* (50), *There's No Business Like Show Business* (54), *Daddy Longlegs* (55), *Take Her She's Mine* (63), etc. He alone has also produced: *Twenty-three Paces to Baker Street* (56), *Carousel* (56), etc.

epidemics featured memorably in *Jezebel*, *Yellow Jack*, *Arrowsmith*, *The Rains Came*, *Forever Amber*, *Panic in the Streets*, *The Killer That Stalked New York*, and *Eighty Thousand Suspects*,

episodic films

episodic films in a sense have always been with us—*If I Had a Million*, after all, came out in 1932, and *Intolerance* in 1915—but it was in the 40s, possibly spurred by the all-star variety films intended to help the war effort, that they achieved their greatest popularity. *Tales of Manhattan* was linked by a tail coat, *Flesh and Fantasy* by the ramblings of a club bore, *Forever and a Day* by a house. Then came the author complex: *Quartet* (Somerset Maugham), *Le Plaisir* (Maupassant), *Meet Me Tonight* (Noël Coward). The French took over with films like *The Seven Deadly Sins*, *The Devil and Ten Commandments*, *Life Together*; and the Italians are still at it with *Four Kinds of Love*, *Made in Italy* and *The Queens*. But for English-speaking markets the form was killed in the mid-50s by the advent of the half-hour tele-play.

EPSTEIN, JEAN (1897–1953). French director since 1922; also wrote books on film theory. *Coeur Fidèle* (23), *The Fall of the House of Usher* (28), *Finis Terrae* (28), *Mor Vran* (30). His sister MARIE EPSTEIN (1899–   ) often worked with him, and herself directed *La Maternelle* (33), *La Mort du Cygne* (38), etc.

EPSTEIN, JULIUS J. (1909–   ) and PHILIP G. (1912–   ). American brothers who write as team. Many play adaptations, also *Casablanca* (AA) (42), *My Foolish Heart* (48), *The Last Time I Saw Paris* (54), etc.

L'EQUIPAGE. Directed by Maurice Tourneur in 1927, this was a popular silent drama of a triangular love affair in which the male participants were airmen during World War I. Anatole Litvak remade it in 1935 (with Charles Vanel, Annabella and Jean Pierre Aumont); then went to Hollywood and in 1937 made an English version, *The Woman I Love* (with Paul Muni, Miriam Hopkins and Louis Hayward).

ERDMAN, RICHARD (1925–   ). American actor who began playing callow youths and now takes rather crustier roles. *Thunder across the Pacific* (44), *Objective Burma* (45), *The Men* (50), *The Happy Time* (52), *Benghazi* (55), *Bernardine* (57), *Saddle the Wind* (58), *Namu the Killer Whale* (66), others. TV series: *The Tab Hunter Show*.

ERICKSON, LEIF (1911–   ) (William Anderson). American 'second lead', former singer. In unspectacular roles since 1935. Also on stage and TV. *Wanderer of the Wasteland* (35), *College Holiday* (36), *Ride a Crooked Mile* (38), *Nothing But the Truth* (41), *Eagle Squadron* (42), *Sorry, Wrong Number* (48), *Fort Algiers* (50), *Carbine Williams* (52), *On the Waterfront* (54), *The Fastest Gun Alive* (56), *Tea and Sympathy* (57), *Straitjacket* (63), *Mirage* (65), many others. TV series: *High Chaparral* (67–69).

ERICSON, JOHN (1927–   ) (Joseph Meibes). German-born leading man, long in America. *Teresa* (debut) (51), *Rhapsody* (54), *Green*

Fire (54), *Bad Day at Black Rock* (54), *The Return of Jack Slade* (55), *Forty Guns* (57), *Pretty Boy Floyd* (59), *The Seven Faces of Dr Lao* (64), *The Destructors* (66), *Operation Bluebook* (67), etc.

EROICA (Poland 1957). A pardonably propagandist saga of heroism during the Warsaw uprising and in a POW camp; directed by Andrzej Munk from a script by J. Stavinski.

EROTIKON. There are two films of this title, both dealing with sexual experience and adultery. 1. Sweden 1920, written and directed by Mauritz Stiller, about a scientist who takes up with his niece when his wife proves unfaithful. 2. Czechoslovakia 1929, written and directed by Gustav Machaty, about a poor girl who takes a rich lover.

ERROL, LEON (1881–1951). Australian-born comedian who in 1910 left medicine for Broadway musical comedy and vaudeville. The prototype henpecked husband, his bald pate, nervous twitches and frantic gestures were a staple of farcical two-reelers from silent days. Also memorable as 'Lord Epping' in the *Mexican Spitfire* features of the early 40s; and in *One Heavenly Night* (30), *Her Majesty Love* (32), *We're Not Dressing* (34), *What a Blonde* (43), *Mama Loves Papa* (45), *Joe Palooka, Champ* (46), *Joe Palooka in the Big Fight* (49), many others.

ERSKINE, CHESTER (1905–   ). American writer-producer-director. *Call It Murder* (p, d), 34, *The Egg and I* (w, p, d) (47), *All My Sons* (w, p), (48), *Take One False Step* (co-w, p, d) (49), *Androcles and the Lion* (w, d) (53), *Witness to Murder* (w, p) (57), *The Wonderful Country* (p) (59), etc.

ERWIN, STUART (1903–1967). American character comedian, often the hero's timid, slow-thinking friend; or just Mr Average. *Mother Knows Best* (also directed) (28), *International House* (32), *Viva Villa* (34), *Three Men on a Horse* (35), *Hollywood Cavalcade* (39), *The Great Mike* (44), *Heaven Only Knows* (48), many others. TV series: *The Trouble with Father* (53), *The Greatest Show on Earth* (63), *The Bing Crosby Show* (65).

ESCAPE. There are several films under this title. 1. D. W. Griffith 1914; from a play by Paul Armstrong about sex problems in the slums; with Blanche Sweet. Remade 1928 with Virginia Valli. 2. The play by John Galsworthy, about a man on the run from Dartmoor, was filmed by Basil Dean in 1930, with Gerald du Maurier, and by Joseph L. Mankiewicz in 1948, with Rex Harrison. 3. Ethel Vance's novel about an ingenious extrication of the hero's mother from a concentration camp was filmed by Mervyn le Roy in 1940, with Robert Taylor, Nazimova, Norma Shearer and Conrad Veidt.

ESCAPE ME NEVER. The two films under this title have no connection. In 1935 Paul Czinner directed Elizabeth Bergner in a tale of an unwed mother and a struggling musician; in 1946 Peter Godfrey had Errol Flynn as a composer torn between two women.

ESMOND, CARL (1905–) (Willy Eichberger). Austrian actor in Britain from 1933; later moved to Hollywood. *Blossom Time* (34), *Dawn Patrol* (38), *The Story of Dr Wassell* (43), *Ministry of Fear* (43), *Experiment Perilous* (44), *A Woman Destroyed (Smash-Up)* (49), *The Desert Hawk* (51), *The World in His Arms* (53), *Thunder in the Sun* (59), *Agent for H.A.R.M.* (66), etc.

ESSEX, HARRY (1910–). American writer. *Boston Blackie and the Law* (43), *He Walked by Night* (48), *The Killer That Stalked New York* (50), *Kansas City Confidential* (52), *It Came from Outer Space* (53), *I The Jury* (also directed) (55), *Mad at the World* (also directed) (56), *The Lonely Man* (57), *The Sons of Katie Elder* (co-w) (64), others; also many TV episodes.

establishing shot. Opening shot of sequence, showing location of scene or juxtaposition of characters in action to follow.

ESTABROOK, HOWARD (1894–). American writer. *The Four Feathers* (28), *Hell's Angels* (30), *Cimarron* (AA) (31), *A Bill of Divorcement* (32), *The Masquerader* (33), *David Copperfield* (34), *International Lady* (39), *The Bridge of San Luis Rey* (44), *The Human Comedy* (45), *The Girl from Manhattan* (48), *Lone Star* (51), *The Big Fisherman* (59), others.

ESTRIDGE, ROBIN (1920–). British screenwriter. *Above Us the Waves* (54), *The Young Lovers* (54), *Campbell's Kingdom* (57), *Northwest Frontier* (59).

ETAIX, PIERRE (1928–). French mime comedian, former circus clown and assistant to Tati. *Rupture* (short) (61), *Happy Anniversary* (short) (61), *The Suitor* (62), *Yo Yo* (65), *As Long As You Have Your Health* (67), *Le Grand Amour* (69).

L'ETERNEL RETOUR (France 1943). Jean Cocteau wrote and co-directed (with Jean Delannoy) this modernized, freewheeling but sombre version of the Tristan and Isolde legend. The Nazi occupiers approved its Teutonic appearance, but the French saw in it a message of hope. With Jean Marais, Madeleine Sologne.

EVANS, BARRY (1945–). British juvenile lead who made a big hit in *Here We Go Round the Mulberry Bush* (67).

EVANS, CLIFFORD (1912–). Welsh actor with stage experience. In films from 1936, at first as leading man and latterly as character actor. *Ourselves Alone* (36), *The Mutiny on the Elsinore* (37), *The Luck of the Navy* (39), *The Proud Valley* (39), *His Brother's Keeper* (39), *The Saint Meets the Tiger* (40), *Love on the Dole* (41), *Penn of Pennsylvania* (41), *Suspected Person* (42), *The Foreman Went to France* (42), war service, *The Silver Darlings* (47), *While I Live* (48), *Valley of Song* (52), *The Gilded Cage* (55), *Passport to Treason* (56), *Violent Playground* (58), *SOS Pacific* (60), *Curse of the Werewolf* (62), *Kiss of the Vampire* (63), *The Long Ships* (64), etc. TV series: *Stryker of the Yard, The Power Game,* etc.

EVANS, DALE (1912–   ) (Frances Butts). American actress, formerly singer; co-star of numerous Roy Rogers westerns and TV shows from late 30s. Married to Roy Rogers.

†EVANS, DAME EDITH (1888–   ). Distinguished British stage actress who makes occasional films. *The Queen of Spades* (debut) (48), *The Last Days of Dolwyn* (48), *The Importance of Being Earnest* (53), *Look Back in Anger* (59), *The Nun's Story* (59), *Tom Jones* (63), *The Chalk Garden* (64), *Young Cassidy* (65), *The Whisperers* (BFA) (67), *Fitzwilly* (US) (68), *Prudence and the Pill* (68), *Crooks and Coronets* (69), *David Copperfield* (69).

EVANS, GENE (1922–   ). Stocky American actor in demand for heavy roles since 1947. *Berlin Express* (48), *Donovan's Brain* (53), *The Golden Blade* (53), *Hell and High Water* (54), *The Sad Sack* (57), *Operation Petticoat* (59,) *Apache Uprising* (65), *Support Your Local Sheriff* (69), etc.

EVANS, JOAN (1934–   ) (Joan Eunson). American actress who played teenage roles in the early 50s. *Our Very Own* (50), *On the Loose* (51), *Roseanna McCoy* (51), *Skirts Ahoy* (52), *Edge of Doom* (54), *The Fortune Hunter* (*The Outcast*) (54), *The Flying Fontaines* (60), etc.

EVANS, MADGE (1909–   ). American actress, a child star of silent days, pretty heroine of mainly unremarkable films in the 30s. *The Sign of the Cross* (14), *The Burglar* (16), *Classmates* (24), *Son of India* (29), *Lovers Courageous* (30), *The Greeks Had a Word for Them* (32), *Hallelujah I'm a Bum* (33), *Dinner at Eight* (33), *Grand Canary* (34), *David Copperfield* (34), *The Tunnel* (GB) (35), *Piccadilly Jim* (37), *The Thirteenth Chair* (37), etc. Retired: married playwright Sydney Kingsley.

EVANS, MAURICE (1901–   ). Eloquent Welsh actor who, long in America, distinguished himself on the Broadway stage. Occasional films include *White Cargo* (30), *Raise the Roof* (30), *Wedding Rehearsal* (32), *Scrooge* (GB) (35), *Kind Lady* (51), *The Story of Gilbert and Sullivan* (as Sullivan) (53), *Androcles and the Lion* (as Caesar) (53), *Macbeth* (title role) (59), *The War Lord* (65), *Jack of Diamonds* (67), *Planet of the Apes* (67), *Rosemary's Baby* (68).

EVANS, RAY (1915–   ). American songwriter: 'Buttons and Bows' (AA 48), 'Che Sera Sera' (AA 56), many others.

EVANS, REX (1903–1969). British character actor in Hollywood. Often played stately butlers, as in *The Philadelphia Story* (40). Other appearances include *Camille* (36), *It Should Happen to You* (53), *The Matchmaker* (58). Ran an art gallery in his spare time.

EVANS, ROBERT (1930–   ). American child actor, mostly on radio. Went to Hollywood and played in *The Man of a Thousand Faces* (57), *The Sun Also Rises* (57), *The Fiend Who Walked the West* (title role) (58), *The Best of Everything* (59). Became a producer, and in 1966 went to Paramount as vice-president in charge of production.

EVEIN, BERNARD (1929–   ). French art director. *Les Amants* (57), *Les Jeux de l'Amour* (60), *Zazie dans le Métro* (61), *Lola* (61), *Cleo de 5 à 7* (62), *La Baie des Anges* (62), *Le Feu Follet* (63), *The Umbrellas of Cherbourg* (64), *Do You Like Women* (64), *Viva Maria* (65), *The Young Girls of Rochefort* (67), *Woman Times Seven* (67), etc.

EVELYN, JUDITH (1913–1967) (J. E. Allen). American stage actress; often seen as neurotic woman. Films include *The Egyptian* (54), *Rear Window* (54), *Hilda Crane* (56), *The Tingler* (59).

EVEREST, BARBARA (1891–1967). British stage actress who appeared in many films, latterly in motherly roles. *Lily Christine* (31), *The Wandering Jew* (33), *The Passing of the Third Floor Back* (35), *He Found a Star* (40), *Mission to Moscow* (US) (43), *Jane Eyre* (US) (43), *The Uninvited* (US) (44), *The Valley of Decision* (US) (45), *Wanted for Murder* (46), *Frieda* (47), *Madeleine* (49), *Tony Draws a Horse* (51), etc.

EVERGREEN (GB 1935). Nostalgic Jessie Matthews vehicle often quoted as Britain's best musical. Victor Saville directed, with script contribution by Emlyn Williams.

EWELL, TOM (1909–   ) (S. Yewell Tomkins). American comic actor with wide stage experience. *Adam's Rib* (49), *Mr Music* (50), *Finders Keepers* (51), *Up Front* (51), *Abbott and Costello Lost in Alaska* (52), *The Seven-Year Itch* (55), *The Lieutenant Wore Skirts* (56), *The Girl Can't Help It* (57), *Tender Is the Night* (61), *State Fair* (61), etc. TV series: *The Tom Ewell Show* (60).

excerpts from films are sometimes incorporated into other films in which characters go to a cinema or watch television. So in *Hollywood Cavalcade* Don Ameche watched a rough-cut of *The Jazz Singer*, just as ten years later Larry Parks in *Jolson Sings Again* watched a rough cut of himself in *The Jolson Story*; an unidentified silent comedy was being played in the room below when the first murder took place in *The Spiral Staircase*; Linda Christian and Louis Jourdan saw *Son of the Sheik* at their local in *The Happy Time,* and Fredric March and Martha Scott watched a William S. Hart film in *One Foot in Heaven.* Prisoners watched *Wings of the Navy* during *Each Dawn I Die* and *The Egg and I* during *Brute Force*; and the chain gang in *Sullivan's Travels* roared with laughter at a Mickey Mouse cartoon. Footage from *Phantom of the Opera* was shown in *Hollywood Story,* from *Comin' thru' the Rye* in *The Smallest Show on Earth,* from *Tolable David* in *The Tingler,* from *Queen Kelly* in *Sunset Boulevard,* from *Camille* in *Bridge to the Sun,* from *Destination Tokyo* in *Operation Pacific,* and from *Boom Town* in *Watch the Birdie.* Other movies shown in 'cinemas' in later films include: *Uncle Tom's Cabin* (27) in *Abbott and Costello Meet the Keystone Kops*; *Gold Diggers of 1933* in *Bonnie and Clyde*; *Crossroads* in *The Youngest Profession*; *Casablanca* in *First to Fight*; *The Walking Dead* in *Ensign Pulver*; *Caprice* in *Caprice* (Doris Day went to the movies, saw herself on the screen, and didn't like it). In *Two Weeks in Another Town,* which had a plot pretty close to that of *The Bad and the Beautiful,* Kirk Douglas watched himself in—*The Bad and the Beautiful*! The Bette Davis character in *Whatever Happened to Baby Jane* was criticized as a bad actress on the strength of clips from early Bette Davis movies, *Ex-Lady* and *Parachute Jumper.* In the same film Joan Crawford watched herself on TV in *Sadie McKee*; and in *Walk Don't Run* there was a flash of James Stewart dubbed in Japanese in *Two Rode Together.* Finally the cosmonauts on their space station in *Conquest of Space* were entertained by a showing of *Here Come the Girls* . . . thus showing, as one critic remarked, that in 50 years' time TV will still be relying on old movies!

Other uses for old footage in new films include such gags as Bob Hope in *Road to Bali* meeting up with Humphrey Bogart in *The African Queen*; and economy dictates such measures as the ten-minute chunk of *The Mummy* at the beginning of *The Mummy's Hand* and the use in *Singin' in the Rain,* as part of a 'new' picture in production, of sequences from Gene Kelly's version of *The Three Musketeers.* Great chunks of the *Joan of Arc* battles turned up in *Thief of Damascus,* as did *The Black Knight* in *Siege of the Saxons* and *The Four Feathers* in *Storm Over the Nile* and *East of Sudan.* Universal's *Sword of Ali Baba* used so much footage from their *Ali Baba and the Forty Thieves* that one actor had to be engaged to replay his original part! It was however wit rather than economy that persuaded Preston Sturges to open *Mad Wednesday* with the last reel of *The Freshman.*

exchange. An American enterprise: a middleman business which for a commission deals with the small exhibitors of an area on behalf of major renters.

EXECUTIVE SUITE (US 1954). In the 50s, Hollywood took a sudden interest in big business, notably in this all-star adaptation of

Cameron Hawley's novel about a boardroom struggle for power. Script by Ernest Lehman, directed by Robert Wise; with Barbara Stanwyck and Fredric March heading an all-star cast. The film's success provoked a rash of boardroom melodramas including *Patterns of Power*, *The Power and the Prize* and *Cash McCall*.

EXODUS (US 1961). Otto Preminger's marathon film of the birth of Israel, from the book by Leon Uris. Seldom exciting, it was a good solid plod, with Paul Newman and Ralph Richardson leading a good cast. Irresistible is the story that Mort Sahl at a Hollywood preview stood up after three hours, turned to the director, and said: 'Otto: let my people go.'

exploitation. A trade word covering all phases of publicity, public relations and promotion, especially in the case of 'exploitation pictures' which have no discernible merit apart from the capability of being sensationalized.

explorers have inspired many documentaries but surprisingly few features except wholly fictitious ones like *Trader Horn, She* and *The Lost World*. *Marco Polo* has twice been dealt with, and *Christopher Columbus* got the full Rank treatment as well as featuring in the satirical *Where Do We Go From Here?* The Pilgrim Fathers were the heroes of *Plymouth Adventure*, and Drake of *Seven Seas to Calais*. *Scott of the Antarctic* was played by John Mills, and a biopic of Nansen is promised. *Penn of Pennsylvania* and *Stanley and Livingstone* were in the practical sense explorers, though driven by other motives.

expressionism. A term indicating the fullest utilization of cinematic resources to give dramatic larger-than-life effect, as in *Citizen Kane* or, in a different way, *The Cabinet of Dr Caligari*.

EXTASE (Czechoslovakia 1933). Gustav Machaty directed this mildly experimental, symbol-crammed erotic drama, widely publicized on account of Hedy Lamarr's nude swimming sequence.

THE EXTERMINATING ANGEL (Mexico 1962). An enigmatic but fascinating film exercise, written and directed by Luis Bunuel, in which a group of dinner guests find themselves psychologically incapable of going home despite attacks of sickness and violent death. Though it is packed with apparent clues, Bunuel himself says there is 'no rational explanation'.

extra. A crowd player with no lines to speak.

EYTHE, WILLIAM (1918–1947). American leading man of the 40s: *The Ox-Bow Incident* (42), *The Song of Bernadette* (43), *The Eve of St Mark* (44), *Czarina* (45), *The House on 92nd Street* (45), *Meet Me at Dawn* (47), etc.

F

FABIAN (1942–   ) (Fabian Forte Bonaparte). American teenage idol, singer and guitarist. *The Hound Dog Man* (debut) (59), *North to Alaska* (60), *Mr Hobbs Takes a Vacation* (62), *Dear Brigitte* (65), *Ten Little Indians* (65), *Fireball 500* (66), *The Devil's Eight* (68), etc.

FABRAY, NANETTE (1922–   ) (Nanette Fabares). American comedy actress and singer, former child star of 'Our Gang' comedies. Adult films: *Elizabeth and Essex* (39), *Band Wagon* (53), etc. Frequently on TV.

FABRI, ZOLTAN (1917–   ). Hungarian director: *Professor Hannibal* (56), *The Last Goal* (61), *Twenty Hours* (65), etc.

FABRIZI, ALDO (1905–   ). Italian character actor, known abroad chiefly for *Open City* (45), *Vivere in Pace* (47), *First Communion* (50), *Cops and Robbers* (54), *Altri Tempi* (55), *The Birds the Bees and the Italians* (65), *Made in Italy* (68).

A FACE IN THE CROWD (US 1957). Directed by Elia Kazan from a Budd Schulberg story, this was a potent attack on the cult of personality in TV. Andy Griffith made a strong impression as the brash hick intoxicated by his own success; so did Patricia Neal as his mentor who finally destroys him.

fade in. Gradual emergence of a scene from blackness to full definition; opposite of *fade out.*

FAHRENHEIT 451 (GB 1966). A pale but oddly haunting version by François Truffaut of Ray Bradbury's cynically prophetic vision of a society where books are outlawed and firemen start fires (of literature) rather than putting them out. Ultimately quite moving, it could have been more cinematically paced. Nicholas Roeg's photography gleams; Oskar Werner's performance is a major asset.

FAIRBANKS, DOUGLAS (1883–1939) (Julius Ullman). American actor, the swashbuckling, acrobatic, ever-smiling hero of many silent spectaculars and modern comedies. *The Lamb* (debut) (14), *His Picture in the Papers* (15), *Reggie Mixes In* (16), *The Americano* (16), *Manhattan Madness* (16), *Down to Earth* (17), *In Again Out Again* (17), *Wild and Woolly* (17), *Reaching for the Moon* (17), *Bound in Morocco* (18), *Heading South* (18), *The Knickerbocker Buckaroo* (19), *A Modern Musketeer* (19), *Matrimaniac* (19), *His Majesty the American* (19), *The Mollycoddle* (20), *The Mark of Zorro* (21), *The Three Musketeers* (21),

Fairbanks, Douglas Jnr

Robin Hood (22), *The Thief of Baghdad* (24), *Don Q, Son of Zorro* (25), *The Black Pirate* (26), *The Gaucho* (27), *The Taming of the Shrew* (28), *The Iron Mask* (29), *Reaching for the Moon* (30), *Around the World in Eighty Minutes* (31), *Mr Robinson Crusoe* (32), *The Private Life of Don Juan* (GB) (last film) (34), etc. Was forced to retire because his romantic zestful image could not fight middle-age spread. He had a famous marriage with Mary Pickford, and they were joint founders in 1919, with Charlie Chaplin and D. W. Griffith, of United Artists Film Corporation. A biography, *The Fourth Musketeer*, was published in 1953. Posthumous AA 1939 for his 'unique and outstanding contribution to the international development of the motion picture'.

FAIRBANKS, DOUGLAS JNR (1907–). American leading man, resident in Britain since World War II. On screen from 1923; more lithe and debonair than his father, he spent more film time in drawing-rooms than on castle battlements. *Stephen Steps Out* (23), *Stella Dallas* (25), *Is Zat So* (27), *Dead Man's Curve* (28), *Our Modern Maidens* (29), *Woman of Affairs* (29), *Little Caesar* (30), *Dawn Patrol* (31), *It's Tough To Be Famous* (31), *Parachute* (32), *The Narrow Corner* (33), *Catherine the Great* (GB) (34), *Mimi* (35), *The Amateur Gentleman* (GB) (36), *Jump for Glory* (GB) (37), *The Prisoner of Zenda* (37), *Joy of Living* (38), *Gunga Din* (39), *The Sun Never Sets* (39), *Green Hell* (40), *Angels over Broadway* (40), *The Corsican Brothers* (41), etc.; war service; *Sindbad the Sailor* (47), *The Exile* (47), *That Lady in Ermine* (49), *The Fighting O'Flynn* (also wrote and produced) (49), *State Secret* (GB) (50), *Mr Drake's Duck* (GB) (53), etc. In Britain during the later 50s, produced and sometimes played in innumerable TV film playlets under the title *Douglas Fairbanks Presents*. A biography by Brian Connell, *Knight Errant*, was published in 1955.

FAIRBROTHER, SYDNEY (1873–1941) (S. Tapping). British character actress, in films occasionally from 1916. *Iron Justice* (16), *The Third String* (31), *Chu Chin Chow* (33), *The Crucifix* (34), *The Last Journey* (36), *King Solomon's Mines* (as Gagool) (37), *Little Dolly Daydream* (38), etc.

FAIRCHILD, WILLIAM (1918–). British film writer (*Morning Departure* [50], *Outcast of the Islands* [52], *The Silent Enemy* [58], etc.) and director (*John and Julie* [54], *The Silent Enemy* [58], *The Horsemasters* [61], etc.).

FAIRHURST, LYN (1920–). British writer. *Band of Thieves* (62), *Touch of Death* (63), *Be My Guest* (64), *Devils of Darkness* (65), etc.

fairy tales; see *fantasy.*

FAITH, ADAM (1940–   ) (Terence Nelhams). British pop singer who has made guest appearances in films, also acted straight roles in *Never Let Go* (60), *Mix Me a Person* (62), etc.

FAITHFULL, GEOFFREY (1894–   ). British cinematographer, with Hepworth from 1908. Recently: *The Lavender Hill Mob* (51), *Corridors of Blood* (59), *Village of the Damned* (60), *On the Beat* (62), etc.

FAITHFULL, MARIANNE (1947–   ). British leading lady. *I'll Never Forget Whatshisname* (67), *Girl on a Motorcycle* (68), *Hamlet* (69).

THE FALCON was a Robin Hood of crime who appeared in many second features of the 40s, originally inspired by a Michael Arlen character. At RKO, George Sanders appeared in *The Gay Falcon, A Date with the Falcon, The Falcon Takes Over* and *The Falcon's Brother*, in which he was 'killed' and his role assumed by his real-life brother, Tom Conway, who proceeded to make nine more Falcon features of declining merit. In nearly all these films Edward Brophy appeared as Goldie, the bumbling valet. Around 1950 John Calvert made a couple of very inferior Falcon movies for a small independent company.

FALCONETTI (1901–1946). French stage actress, unforgettable in her only film, *The Passion of Jeanne d'Arc* (28).

FALK, PETER (1927–   ). American actor from off-Broadway stage, often seen in Brooklynesque parts. *Wind Across the Everglades* (58), *Murder Inc.* (60), *A Pocketful of Miracles* (61), *Pressure Point* (62), *It's a Mad Mad Mad Mad World* (63), *The Balcony* (64), *Robin and the Seven Hoods* (64), *The Great Race* (65), *Penelope* (66), *Luv* (67), *Anzio* (68), *Castle Keep* (69), etc. TV series: *The Trials of O'Brien* (65).

FALKENBURG, JINX (1919–   ) (Eugenia Falkenburg). Tall, good-looking American model who made a few light comedies and musicals in the 40s. *Two Latins from Manhattan* (42), *Sing for Your Supper* (42), *Lucky Legs* (43), *Tahiti Nights* (44), *Talk about a Lady* (46), etc. Later became TV personality.

THE FALLEN IDOL (GB 1948). One of Carol Reed's most subtle and successful films, from Graham Greene's story about a boy who sees what he thinks is a murder and tries to cover up for his friend. With Ralph Richardson, Michele Morgan, Bobby Henrey; music by William Alwyn. BFA (best British film).

THE FALL OF THE HOUSE OF USHER. This grisly tale by Edgar Allan Poe was filmed by Jean Epstein in 1928, by British semi-professionals in 1950, and by Roger Corman in 1960.

falling is, of all man's inherited fears, the one most spectacularly played on by Hollywood, where the shot of the villain's hand slipping away from the hero's frenzied grasp, followed by a quick-fading scream, has become a screen stereotype. Harold Lloyd's skyscraper comedies played on this fear, as did the films of many comedians since; in *The Horn Blows at Midnight*, for instance, Jack Benny is only one of six people hanging on to each other's coat-tails from the top of a high building. All circus films, and that includes *The Marx Brothers at the Circus*, base one or two of their thrills on trapeze acts that might go wrong. And whenever a villain starts climbing upwards, as Ted de Corsia did in *Naked City*, or along a ledge, as the same accident-prone Ted de Corsia did in *The Enforcer*, the audience grits its teeth and waits for the inevitable. The whole action of *Fourteen Hours* was based on the question whether a potential suicide would or would not jump from a ledge.

Some of the screen's most spectacular falls include Walter Abel's in *Mirage*, the key to the whole action; Agnes Moorehead's (through a window) in *Dark Passage*; Charlotte Henry's in *Alice in Wonderland*; Cedric Hardwicke's in *Hunchback of Notre Dame*; W. C. Fields' (from an aeroplane) in *Never Give a Sucker an Even Break*; Alan Ladd's (through a roof) in *The Glass Key*; and *King Kong's* (from the top of the Empire State Building). To Alfred Hitchcock falls are a speciality: Edmund Gwenn fell from Westminster Cathedral in *Foreign Correspondent*, Norman Lloyd from the torch of the Statue of Liberty in *Saboteur*, while *Vertigo* not only boasted three falls but based its entire plot on the hero's fear of heights. Falls under trains and buses are legion, but in *The Well* a little girl fell down an old mineshaft, in *The List of Adrian Messenger* a victim fell to his death in a lift, in Somerset Maugham's *Encore* an acrobat hoped to fall safely into a water tank; and an unnamed gentleman was pushed out of *The High Window* by Florence Bates.

the family is the centre of most people's lives, so naturally there have been many memorable film families. Those popular enough to have warranted a series include the Joneses, the Hardys, the Huggetts, the Wilkinses of *Dear Ruth*, *The Cohens and the Kellys*, the Bumsteads of *Blondie* and the *Four Daughters* saga. World War II brought a sentimental attachment to the family which in Hollywood expressed itself in *Happy Land*, *The Human Comedy*, *Our Town*, *Since You Went Away*, *Meet Me in St Louis*, *A Genius in the Family*, *The Sullivans* and *The Best Years of Our Lives*; in Britain, *Salute John Citizen*, *Dear Octopus*, *Quiet Wedding*, *This Man is Mine*. Semi-classical treatments of the theme include *Cavalcade*, *The Swiss Family Robinson*, *Pride and Prejudice*, *Little Women*, *Scrooge* and *Whiteoaks*. Odd families, ranging from the merely sophisticated to the downright bizarre, were seen in *Three Cornered Moon*, *The*

Old Dark House, The Royal Family of Broadway, My Man Godfrey, You Can't Take It With You, The Young in Heart, The Little Foxes, Tobacco Road, The Bank Dick, House of Strangers, An Inspector Calls, Sweethearts, Treasure Hunt, Holiday, The Philadelphia Story, The Anniversary, and *The Lion in Winter.* Vaudeville families were seen in *Yankee Doodle Dandy, The Merry Monahans, The Seven Little Foys, The Buster Keaton Story.* There has recently been a fashion for the large family, started by *Cheaper by the Dozen* and *Chicken Every Sunday* in 1949 and reprised by *With Six You Get Egg Roll* and *Yours Mine and Ours* in 1968 and a TV series *The Brady Bunch* in 1969. Other charming families have included those in *Our Vines Have Tender Grapes, Background, The Happy Family, Four Sons, The Holly and the Ivy, Made in Heaven, 29 Acacia Avenue* and *My Wife's Family*; but the most memorable family of all is likely to remain the Joads in *The Grapes of Wrath.*

FANNY. Originally one of Marcel Pagnol's 1932–34 trilogy (the others: *Marius* and *César*) about the Marseilles waterfront, this tale of a girl left pregnant by a sailor was almost unrecognizable in the MGM version *Port of Seven Seas* (38). The film was subsequently turned into a stage musical, and in 1960 Joshua Logan filmed this—but deleted the songs! The stars were Leslie Caron, Maurice Chevalier and Charles Boyer.

FANTASIA (US 1940). Disney's ambitious concert sequence of cartoons caused dissension at first but seems to have established its reputation and its popularity after thirty years. Despite lapses of inventiveness and taste, three of its eight pieces are extremely well done: the Bach Toccata and Fugue, Stravinsky's Rite of Spring and Mussorgsky's Night on the Bare Mountain. Leopold Stokowski conducted the Philadelphia Symphony Orchestra.

fantasy has always been a popular form of cinema entertainment because the camera can lie so well, and trick work is most easily used in an unrealistic or fanciful story. The early films of Méliès and his innumerable imitators set a high standard and were still popular when the sombre German classics of the 20s—*The Golem, Nosferatu, Faust, Warning Shadows, The Niebelungen Saga, Metropolis*— awakened filmgoers to the possibilities of the medium for sustaining impossible situations throughout a whole serious feature.

Although Ince's *Civilisation* showed Christ on the battlefields, and the 20s brought such films as *The Four Horsemen of the Apocalypse, The Lost World* and *The Sorrows of Satan,* Hollywood did not fully explore the possibilities of fantasy until sound. Then in quick succession picturegoers were startled by *Outward Bound, Dracula, Frankenstein, Berkeley Square, King Kong* and *The Invisible Man. The Scoundrel,* with Noel Coward, was the forerunner of the few serious ghost films: *The Uninvited, The Ghost and Mrs Muir, Portrait of Jennie,*

The Haunting, etc. Comic ghosts have, of course, been legion, notably in the *Topper* films, *The Ghost Breakers*, *I Married a Witch*, *The Canterville Ghost*, *The Man in the Trunk*, *The Remarkable Andrew*, *Thirteen Ghosts*, *The Spirit Is Willing*, *Blackbeard's Ghost*, *Wonder Man*, and so on. Britain's contributions to the genre were few but choice: *The Ghost Goes West*, *Blithe Spirit*, *Things to Come*, *The Man Who Could Work Miracles*, *A Matter of Life and Death*, *Dead of Night*.

In 1936 *Green Pastures* showed the Negro view of Heaven, and *On Borrowed Time* three years later paved the way for the heavenly comedies of the 40s; *Here Comes Mr Jordan*, *That's the Spirit*, *A Guy Named Joe*, *Heaven Can Wait*, *Down to Earth*, *The Horn Blows at Midnight*, *You Never Can Tell*, even *Ziegfeld Follies* (in which Ziegfeld's shade wrote in his diary 'Another *heavenly* day . . .'). For many years the last in this vein was *Carousel* (56); but 1968 brought *Barbarella* with its slightly tarnished angel. Meanwhile objects with magical properties were well served in *Alf's Button Afloat*, *A Thousand and One Nights*, *The Thief of Baghdad*, *Turnabout* and *The Picture of Dorian Gray*.

Among the many fairy tales filmed are *The Bluebird*, *The Wizard of Oz*, *Alice in Wonderland*, *The Glass Slipper*, *Tom Thumb*, *Mary Poppins* and a selection in *Hans Christian Andersen* and *The Wonderful World of the Brothers Grimm*. Disney's cartoon versions included *Pinocchio*, *Dumbo*, *The Sleeping Beauty*, *Cinderella*, *Peter Pan*, and, of course, *Snow White and the Seven Dwarfs*, which was cannily adapted for grown-ups by Billy Wilder as *Ball of Fire*. *Lost Horizon* was a kind of grown-up fairy tale too; and *The Red Shoes* as shown was certainly not for children. Original fairy tales for both categories were *The Luck of the Irish*, with Cecil Kellaway as a leprechaun, and *Miracle on 34th Street*, with Edmund Gwenn as Santa Claus.

In France during the occupation Marcel Carné made *Les Visiteurs du Soir*, a medieval fantasy with allegorical overtones, and after the war poet Jean Cocteau once again turned his attention to the cinema with such results as *La Belle et la Bête*, *Love Eternal*, *Orphée*, and *The Testament of Orphée*. More recently Albert Lamorisse has produced fantasies like *Crin Blanc* and *The Red Balloon*. Japan electrified the world with *Rashomon* and other strange, fanciful, stylized entertainments; Russia contributed many solidly-staged versions of old legends like *Sadko* and *Epic Hero and the Beast* (*Ilya Muromets*).

Since 1950, when in Hollywood Dick Powell played an Alsatian dog in *You Never Know* and James Stewart in *Harvey* had a white rabbit six feet high which the script could never quite categorize as a fact or a hallucination, fantastic elements have been infiltrating into supposedly realistic films to such an extent that it is now difficult to separate them, especially in the films of Fellini, Antonioni, Tony Richardson and Richard Lester.

See also: *dreams; horror; time; prophecy; science fiction.*

FANTOMAS (France 1913–1914). Famous thriller serial in five parts, about the exploits of a character reminiscent of Robin Hood, Raffles and the Ringer. Directed by Louis Feuillade (qv). Subsequent versions were made in 1932 by Paul Fejos, 1947 by Jean Sacha, 1949 by Robert Vernay, and 1964 by André Hunebelle.

FANTONI, SERGIO (1930–   ). Italian leading man now in Hollywood films: *Esther and the King* (60), *The Prize* (63), *Kali-Yug Goddess of Vengeance* (63), *Von Ryan's Express* (65), *Do Not Disturb* (65), *What Did You Do in the War, Daddy?* (66), etc.

FAPP, DANIEL (* –   ). American cinematographer. *Kitty* (45), *Golden Earrings* (47), *Bride of Vengeance* (49), *Union Station* (50), *Knock on Wood* (54), *Living It Up* (54), *Desire under the Elms* (58), *One, Two, Three* (61), *West Side Story* (AA) (61), *I'll Take Sweden* (65), *Our Man Flint* (66), *Lord Love a Duck* (66), *Sweet November* (67), *Ice Station Zebra* (68), many others.

A FAREWELL TO ARMS. Hemingway's tough-romantic anti-war novel has twice been filmed: in 1933 by Frank Borzage, with Gary Cooper and Helen Hayes, and in 1958 by Charles Vidor, with Rock Hudson and Jennifer Jones. Neither version was a triumph artistically, but the first proved more popular than the second, which was badly inflated by David O. Selznick into a pseudo-epic.

FARMER, FRANCES (1914–   ). American leading lady of the late 30s. *Too Many Parents* (36), *Come and Get It* (36), *Ebb Tide* (38), *Badlands of Dakota* (41), *Son of Fury* (42), etc. Retired through ill-health. In *The Party Crashers* (58).

THE FARMER'S DAUGHTER (US 1947). A lightweight political comedy from a screenplay by Allen Rivkin and Laura Kerr, directed by H. C. Potter, this romantic fable gained an Academy Award for Loretta Young as the Swedish maid who influences her congressman employer. Joseph Cotten, Ethel Barrymore and Charles Bickford were strong in support. In 1963–65 there followed a popular TV series on the subject, with Inger Stevens, William Windom and Cathleen Nesbitt.

FARNON, ROBERT (1917–   ). Canadian composer whose many scores include *Captain Hornblower*, *The Little Hut*, *Road to Hong Kong*, etc.

FARNUM, DUSTIN (1874–1929). Brother of William Farnum. American cowboy star of silent days: *The Squaw Man* (13), *The Virginian* (14), *The Scarlet Pimpernel* (17), *The Corsican Brothers* (19), *Flaming Frontier* (26), etc.

FARNUM, FRANKLYN (1876–1961). American leading man of the silent screen, especially westerns; appeared in more than 1,000 films.

345

FARNUM, WILLIAM (1876–1953). American leading man of the silent screen. *The Spoilers* (14), *Les Misérables* (18), *The Lone Star Ranger* (19), *If I Were King* (20), etc.; later slipped into character bit parts and was frequently on screen until *Jack and the Beanstalk* (53).

FARR, DEREK (1912–   ). British leading man of stage and screen, married to Muriel Pavlow; former schoolmaster. *The Outsider* (40), *Spellbound* (40), *Quiet Wedding* (40), etc.; war service; *Quiet Weekend* (46), *Wanted for Murder* (46), *Teheran* (47), *Bond Street* (48), *Noose* (48), *Silent Dust* (49), *Man on the Run* (49), *Young Wives' Tale* (51), *Reluctant Heroes* (52), *The Dam Busters* (55), *Town on Trial* (56), *Doctor at Large* (57), *The Truth About Women* (58), *Attempt to Kill* (61), *The Projected Man* (66), *Thirty is a Dangerous Age Cynthia* (68), etc.

FARR, FELICIA (1932–   ). American leading lady. *Timetable* (56), *Jubal* (56), *3.10 to Yuma* (57), *Hell Bent for Leather* (60), *Kiss Me Stupid* (64), *The Venetian Affair* (67), etc. Married to Jack Lemmon.

FARRAR, DAVID (1908–   ). Tall, virile-looking British leading man whose career faltered when he went to Hollywood and played villains. Repertory experience. *The Sheepdog of the Hills* (debut) (41), *Suspected Person* (41), *Danny Boy* (42), *The Night Invader* (42), *The Dark Tower* (43), *They Met in the Dark* (44), *The World Owes Me a Living* (44), *Meet Sexton Blake* (title role) (44), *The Echo Murder* (45), *The Lisbon Story* (46), *The Trojan Brothers* (46), *Black Narcissus* (46), *Frieda* (47), *Mr Perrin and Mr Traill* (48), *The Small Back Room* (48), *Diamond City* (49), *Night Without Stars* (51), *The Golden Horde* (US) (51), *Gone to Earth* (52), *Duel in the Jungle* (54), *The Black Shield of Falworth* (US) (54), *Lilacs in the Spring* (55), *The Sea Chase* (US) (55), *Lost* (56), *I Accuse* (57), *Solomon and Sheba* (US) (59), *John Paul Jones* (US) (59), *Beat Girl* (60), *The 300 Spartans* (62). Published autobiography 1948: *No Royal Road*.

FARRAR, GERALDINE (1882–1967). American operatic star who, unexpectedly, appeared for Samuel Goldwyn as heroine of *silent* films. *Carmen* (15), *Maria Rosa* (16), *The Devil Stone* (17), *Flame of the Desert* (19), *The Riddle Woman* (20), etc.

FARREBIQUE (France 1947). A slow-moving drama of peasant life in 1830, marked by a tremendous feeling for the land and for life. Written and directed by Georges Rouquier, photographed (with much use of time-lapse) by André Danton, with music by Henri Languet.

FARRELL, CHARLES (1901–   ). Gentle-mannered American leading man well-known for series of silent romances with Janet Gaynor: *Seventh Heaven* (27), *Sunny Side Up* (29), etc. Other films include *The Ten Commandments* (23), *The Princess and the Plumber* (30), *Tess of the Storm Country* (36), *Moonlight Sonata* (GB) (37), *Tailspin* (39), *The Deadly Game* (42). Latterly inactive in Hollywood; has been mayor of Palm Springs since 1947. TV series: *My Little Margie* (52–55), *The Charlie Farrell Show* (56).

FARRELL, CHARLES (1901–). Irish character actor who has been playing bit parts in British films since childhood. *Creeping Shadows* (31), *Meet Mr Penny* (38), *Meet Sexton Blake* (44), *Night and the City* (50), *The Sheriff of Fractured Jaw* (58), etc.

FARRELL, GLENDA (1904–). American leading lady and comedienne of the 30s, often seen as wisecracking reporter. Made a comeback in the 50s as character actress. *Little Caesar* (debut) (30), *Three on a Match* (31), *I Am a Fugitive from a Chain Gang* (32), *The Mystery of the Wax Museum* (32), *Hi Nellie* (33), *Gold Diggers of 1935*, *In Caliente* (36), *Torchy Blane in Chinatown* (and ensuing series) (39), *Johnny Eager* (41), *A Night for Crime* (42), *Heading for Heaven* (47), *I Love Trouble* (48), *Apache War Smoke* (52), *Girls in the Night* (52), *Susan Slept Here* (54), *The Girl in the Red Velvet Swing* (55), *The Middle of the Night* (59), *Kissing Cousins* (64), *The Disorderly Orderly* (65), many others.

FARROW, JOHN (1904–1963). Australian writer-director, former research scientist; in Hollywood from the mid-30s. *War Lord* (w, d) (37), *Five Came Back* (w, d) (39), *A Bill of Divorcement* (d) (40), etc.; war service; *Wake Island* (d) (42), *The Commandos Strike at Dawn* (w, d) (43), *The Hitler Gang* (w, d) (44), *You Came Along* (d) (44), *Two Years before the Mast* (w, d) (45), *California* (d) (46), *Blaze of Noon* (d) (47), *The Big Clock* (d) (47), *Night Has a Thousand Eyes* (d) (48), *Alias Nick Beal* (d) (49), *Copper Canyon* (d) (50), *His Kind of Woman* (w, d) (51), *Botany Bay* (d) (53), *Hondo* (d) (54), *Plunder of the Sun* (d) (54), *The Sea Chase* (w, d) (55), *Around the World in Eighty Days* (co-w) (56), *John Paul Jones* (w, d) (59), many others.

FARROW, MIA (1945–). American leading lady, daughter of John Farrow and Maureen O'Sullivan. *Guns at Batasi* (64), *A Dandy in Aspic* (67), *Rosemary's Baby* (68), *Secret Ceremony* (68), *John and Mary* (69). TV series: *Peyton Place.*

fast motion. See *accelerated motion.*

FATHER BROWN (GB 1954). The only British attempt to film the adventures of G. K. Chesterton's tubby detective-priest was a civilized comedy with all concerned on the same wavelength. A quietly witty script by Thelma Schnee, polished direction by Robert Hamer, and high comedy acting by Alec Guinness, Peter Finch, Joan Greenwood and Ernest Thesiger made it a film with a rare flavour. Known in US as *The Detective*. In 1934 Walter

Father of the Bride

Connolly played the role in a Hollywood second feature, *Father Brown Detective*.

FATHER OF THE BRIDE (US 1950). The American domestic comedy *par excellence*, taken from Edward Streeter's book and starring Spencer Tracy as the harassed pa. A sequel, *Father's Little Dividend* (51), was somewhat less effective. Leon Ames later played the role in a TV series.

FAULKNER, WILLIAM (1897–1964). Distinguished American novelist. Works filmed include *Sanctuary, Intruder in the Dust, The Sound and the Fury*; also collaborated on screenplays of *Road to Glory* (36), *To Have and Have Not* (44), *The Big Sleep* (46), *Land of the Pharaohs* (55), etc.

FAUST, JOHANN (1488–1541). These at least are the approximate dates of a German conjurer, the scanty details of whose wandering life were the basis of plays by Marlowe and later Goethe which turned into classics. The theme of the man who sells his soul to the devil in exchange for a rich full life has been seen in innumerable film versions, including many musical ones based on Gounod's opera, and a puppet one from Czechoslovakia. The first straight version was made in France in 1905; the most famous silent version is Murnau's of 1926, with Emil Jannings and Gosta Ekman. 1941 brought Dieterle's *All That Money Can Buy*, from Stephen Vincent Benet's *The Devil and Daniel Webster*; René Clair's version, *La Beauté du Diable*, followed in 1949, Autant-Lara's *Marguerite de la Nuit* in 1955 and Richard Burton's *Dr Faustus* in 1967. There were modernized versions in France (63), USA (64) and Rumania (66), and a Spanish version of 1957, *Faustina*, in which the hero becomes a heroine. The latest variation on the theme is *Bedazzled* (67), a comic extravaganza with Peter Cook as the tempter and Dudley Moore as the tempted.

FAYE, ALICE (1912–) (Alice Leppert). American leading lady and singer, once with Rudy Vallee's band. In films since 1934, at first as unsympathetic other women, later as heroine. *George White's Scandals* (34), *She Learned about Sailors* (35), *King of Burlesque* (35), *Poor Little Rich Girl* (36), *Stowaway* (36), *On the Avenue* (37), *Wake Up and Live* (38), *In Old Chicago* (38), *Sally, Irene and Mary* (38), *Alexander's Ragtime Band* (38), *Tailspin* (39), *Rose of Washington Square* (39), *Hollywood Cavalcade* (39), *Lilian Russell* (40), *Tin Pan Alley* (40), *That Night in Rio* (41), *Weekend in Havana* (41), *Hello Frisco Hello* (43), *The Gang's All Here* (*The Girls He Left Behind*) (44), *Four Jills in a Jeep* (44), *Fallen Angel* (45), etc. Retired to marry Phil Harris; made solitary reappearance in *State Fair* (61).

FAYLEN, FRANK (c. 1907–). American character actor with stage experience. Played scores of bartenders, gangsters, sheriffs, cops, etc., from 1936. *Bullets or Ballots* (36), *The Grapes of Wrath* (40), *Top Sergeant Mulligan* (42), *The Lost Weekend* (his best role, as the male nurse) (45), *Blue Skies* (46), *Road to Rio* (47), *Detective Story* (51), *Riot in Cell Block Eleven* (54), *Killer Dino* (58), *The Monkey's Uncle* (65), *Funny Girl* (68), many others.

FAZENDA, LOUISE (1895–1962). American silent comedienne with vaudeville experience. Mack Sennett bathing beauty, later in slapstick farces and, in the 30s, as character comedienne. *Abraham Lincoln* (25), *The Terror* (27), *Cuban Love Song* (32), *Alice in Wonderland* (33), *Colleen* (36), *The Old Maid* (last film) (39). Married Hal Wallis.

feature film. Normally accepted to mean a (fictional) entertainment film of more than 3000 feet in length (approx. 34 minutes). Anything less than this is technically a 'short'. NB. In journalism and television a 'feature' usually means a *non*-fiction article or documentary.

featured players. Those next in importance to the stars; usually billed after the title.

Federation of Film Societies. British organization which issues information and arranges screenings for film societies; also publishes magazine, 'Film'.

FEGTE, ERNST (1900–   ). German production designer, in Hollywood from the early 30s. *The General Died at Dawn* (36), *The Palm Beach Story* (42), *I Married a Witch* (42), *Five Graves to Cairo* (43), *Frenchman's Creek* (44), *Concerto* (47), *Angel and the Badman* (47), etc.

FEIST, FELIX E. (1910–1965). American director, at first of short subjects including Pete Smith Specialties; in Hollywood from 1928. *This Is the Life* (44), *George White's Scandals* (45), *The Devil Thumbs a Ride* (also wrote) (47), *The Threat* (49), *Treason* (50), *The Man Who Cheated Himself* (51), *The Big Trees* (52), *This Woman Is Dangerous* (52), *Donovan's Brain* (54), *Pirates of Tripoli* (55), etc.; then into TV.

FEJOS, PAUL (1893–1963). Hungarian director, in America from 1923. *The Last Moment* (27), *Lonesome* (28), *Erik the Great* (29), *The Big House* (co-d) (30), *Marie* (Hung.) (32), *The Golden Smile* (Dan.) (35), *A Handful of Rice* (Swedish) (38). Went into scientific research.

FELD, FRITZ (1900–   ). German character actor, once stage director for Max Reinhardt, in America since c. 1928. Usually plays temperamental head waiters, etc. Memorable as psychiatrist in *Bringing Up Baby* (38), Anatole of Paris in *The Secret Life of Walter Mitty* (48), waiter in *The Patsy* (64), scores of others. 1967: *Barefoot in the Park*.

349

FELDMAN, CHARLES K. (1904–1968) (C. Gould). American producer, former lawyer and talent agent. *Pittsburgh* (42), *Follow the Boys* (44), *To Have and Have Not* (44), *The Big Sleep* (46), *Red River* (48), *The Red Pony* (49), *A Streetcar Named Desire* (51), *The Seven Year Itch* (54), *North to Alaska* (59), *A Walk on the Wild Side* (62), *The Seventh Dawn* (64), *What's New Pussycat* (65), *The Group* (66), *Casino Royale* (67), etc.

FELIX (THE CAT). Cartoon creation of Pat Sullivan, a perky and indestructible character highly popular in the 20s; recently revived for TV by other hands in more streamlined style.

FELIX, MARIA (1915–   ). Mexican actress of strong personality. *The Devil Is a Woman* (52), *French Can Can* (53), *Les Héros Sont Fatigués* (55), many Mexican films.

FELIX, SEYMOUR (1892–1961). American dance director, in films since 1929. *The Great Ziegfeld* (AA) (36), *Alexander's Ragtime Band* (38), *Cover Girl* (44), *The I Don't Care Girl* (52), many others.

†FELLINI, FEDERICO (1920–   ). Fashionable and influential Italian director, formerly cartoonist. Film actor and writer from 1941. Directed: *Lights of Variety* (50), *I Vitelloni* (53), *La Strada* (54). *Il Bidone* (55), *Notti di Cabiria* (57), *La Dolce Vita* (59), *Boccaccio 70* (part) (62), *Eight and a Half* (63), *Juliet of the Spirits* (65), *Histoires Extraordinaires* (part) (68), *Satyricon* (69).

FELLOWES, EDITH (1923–   ). American teenage star of the 30s. *Riders of Death Valley* (32), *Jane Eyre* (34), *Pennies from Heaven* (36), *Five Little Peppers* (38), *Five Little Peppers in Trouble* (41), *Girls Town* (42), *Her First Romance* (47), etc.

FELLOWS, ROBERT (1903–1969). American producer. *Virginia City* (39), *They Died with Their Boots On* (41), *The Spanish Main* (45), *A Yankee in King Arthur's Court* (49), *Hondo* (54), *The High and the Mighty* (54), etc.

FELTON, VERNA (1890–1966). American character actress, often seen as neighbour or busybody. *The Gunfighter* (50), *New Mexico* (52), *Picnic* (55), *Little Egypt* (55), etc. TV series: *December Bride* (54–59), *Pete and Gladys* (60).

female impersonation: see transvestism.

LA FEMME DU BOULANGER (*The Baker's Wife*) (France 1938). Like all Marcel Pagnol's films, this peasant comedy about a baker whose bread suffers when his wife leaves him has little cinematic merit but survives by virtue of Pagnol's warm script, Raimu's acting and the affectionate regard for village life.

FENTON, FRANK (1906–1957). American general purpose supporting actor. *Lady of Burlesque* (42), *Buffalo Bill* (44), *Magic Town* (46), *Red River* (48), *Island in the Sky* (53), *Emergency Hospital* (56), *Hellbound* (58), many others.

FENTON, LESLIE (1902–   ). British-born director of Hollywood 'B' pictures. (Former actor in many silent films and early talkies including *What Price Glory, The Man I Love, Broadway, Public Enemy, F.P.1,* etc.) *Night Flight* (33), *Lady Killer* (34), *Star of Midnight* (35), *The Casino Murder Case* (37), *Tell No Tales* (39), *The Golden Fleecing* (40), *The Saint's Vacation* (GB) (41), etc.; war service; *There's a Future in It* (GB) (43), *Tomorrow the World* (also produced) (44), *Pardon my Past* (45), *Saigon* (47), *Whispering Smith* (48), *The Streets of Laredo* (50), *The Redhead and the Cowboy* (51), etc. Recently inactive.

FERBER, EDNA (1887–   ). American novelist. Works filmed include *Showboat* (29, 35 and 51), *The Royal Family of Broadway* (31), *Cimarron* (31 and 61), *So Big* (32 and 53), *Dinner at Eight* (33), *Come and Get It* (36), *Saratoga Trunk* (43), *Giant* (56), *Ice Palace* (59).

FERGUSON, ELSIE (1883–1961). American leading lady of silent melodramas about the upper classes. Popular 1918–27, then retired. *Barbary Sheep* (17), *The Lie* (18), *Song of Songs* (18), *A Society Exile* (19), *His House in Order* (20), *Sacred and Profane Love* (21), *Outcast* (22), etc.

FERGUSON, FRANK (c. 1899–   ). Toothy American character actor, often in comic bit parts. *This Gun For Hire* (42), *The Miracle of the Bells* (48), *Abbott and Costello Meet Frankenstein* (49), *Elopement* (51), *Johnny Guitar* (54), *Andy Hardy Comes Home* (58), *Raymie* (60), many others. TV series: *Peyton Place* (65–69).

FERNANDEL (1903–1971) (Fernand Contandin). Rubber-faced French comedian with toothy grin and music-hall background. Films since 1930, usually 'naughty but nice', include *Regain (Harvest)* (37), *Un Carnet de Bal* (37), *Fric Frac* (39), *La Fille du Puisatier* (40), *The Red Inn* (51), *Forbidden Fruit* (52), the *Don Camillo* series from 1952, *The Sheep Has Five Legs* (54), *Paris Holiday* (57), *The Cow and I* (59), *Croesus* (60), *La Cuisine au Beurre* (63), *Le Voyage du Père* (66), *L'Homme a la Buick* (67), etc.

FERNANDEZ, EMILIO (1904–   ). Prolific Mexican director, few of whose films have been seen abroad. *Isle of Passion* (41), *Maria Candelaria* (44), *The Pearl* (45), *Rio Escondido* (47), *Maclovia* (48), *The Torch* (50), etc.

FERRER, JOSE (1912–   ) (Jose Vincente Ferrer Otero y Cintron) Distinguished American stage and screen actor of Puerto Rican

Ferrer, Mel

origin. *Joan of Arc* (debut; as the dauphin) (48), *Crisis* (49), *Whirl-pool* (49), *Cyrano de Bergerac* (AA) (50), *Anything Can Happen* (52), *Moulin Rouge* (GB; as Toulouse Lautrec) (53), *Miss Sadie Thompson* (54), *The Caine Mutiny* (54), *Deep in My Heart* (as Sigmond Romberg) (54), *The Shrike* (also directed) (55), *Cockleshell Heroes* (GB) (55), *The Great Man* (also directed and co-scripted) (56), *I Accuse* (also directed) (57), *The High Cost of Loving* (58), *Return to Peyton Place* (directed only) (61), *State Fair* (directed only) (61), *Lawrence of Arabia* (62), *Nine Hours to Rama* (63), *The Greatest Story Ever Told* (65), *Ship of Fools* (65), *Enter Laughing* (67), *Cervantes* (Sp.) (67).

FERRER, MEL (1917–). Sensitive-looking American leading man, former radio writer and producer; married to Audrey Hepburn. *Lost Boundaries* (45), *The Secret Fury* (director only) (50), *The Brave Bulls* (51), *Scaramouche* (52), *Lili* (53), *Knights of the Round Table* (54), *Oh Rosalinda* (GB) (55), *War and Peace* (56), *The Sun Also Rises* (57), *The Vintage* (57), *The World, the Flesh and the Devil* (59), *Blood and Roses* (Fr.) (62), *El Greco* (Sp.) (65), *Every Day Is a Holiday* (also wrote, produced and directed) (Sp.) (67), etc.

FERRERI, MARCO (1928–). Italian director. *El Pisito* (Sp.) (56), *The Wheelchair* (Sp.) (60), *Queen Bee* (63), *The Bearded Lady* (64), *Wedding March* (65), *Dillinger Is Dead* (68), etc.

FERRIS, BARBARA (1941–). British leading lady. *Catch Us If You Can* (66), *Interlude* (68), *A Nice Girl Like Me* (69).

FERZETTI, GABRIELE (1925–) (Pasquale Ferzetti). Italian leading man. *William Tell* (48), *Cuore Ingrato* (51), *Three Forbidden Stories* (52), *Puccini* (54), *Le Amiche* (55), *Donatello* (56), *L'Avventura* (59), *Torpedo Bay* (64), *The St Valentine's Day Massacre* (US) (67), *Once Upon a Time in the West* (69), etc.

festivals. Since World War II a great many cities round the world have derived excellent publicity from annual film festivals. Producers, distributors and actors in search of accolades now diligently trek each year to Cannes, Venice, Berlin, Mar del Plata, Cork, Edinburgh, Karlovy Vary, San Sebastian, Moscow, etc., while London and New York offer résumés in October.

FETCHIT, STEPIN (1902–) (Lincoln Perry). Gangly, slow-moving American Negro comedian, popular in films of the 30s. *In Old Kentucky* (29), *Stand Up and Cheer* (33), *Steamboat Round the Bend* (35), *On the Avenue* (37), *Elephants Never Forget* (39), *Bend of the River* (52), *The Sun Shines Bright* (53), many others.

LE FEU FOLLET (*A Time to Live and a Time to Die*) (France 1963). An example of the downbeat themes possible in the 60s: the step-by-step story of a successful suicide. Written and directed by Louis Malle, starring Maurice Ronet.

FEUILLADE, LOUIS (1873–1925). Newly-rediscovered and feted French director who made marathon silent serials about master criminals: *Fantomas* (13), *Les Vampires* (15), *Judex* (16–17) (remade by Franju 63), *Tih Minh* (18), *Parisette* (21), etc.

FEUILLERE, EDWIGE (1907–   ) (Edwige Cunati). Distinguished French actress, a leading member of the Comédie Française. *Le Cordon Bleu* (30), *Topaze* (32), *I Was An Adventuress* (38), *Sans Lendemain* (40), *La Duchesse de Langeais* (42), *L'Idiot* (46), *L'Aigle a Deux Têtes* (47), *Woman Hater* (GB) (48), *Olivia* (50), *Adorable Creatures* (52), *Le Blé en Herbe* (53), *The Fruits of Summer* (54), *En Cas de Malheur* (*Love Is My Profession*) (57), *Crime Doesn't Pay* (62), *Do You Like Women?* (64), etc.

FEYDEAU, GEORGES (1862–1921). French writer of stage farces, many of which have become classics and are often filmed, the best cinematic examples being *Occupe toi d'Amelie* (49) and *Hotel Paradiso* (66).

FEYDER, JACQUES (1888–1948) (Jacques Frederix). French director, former actor; married Françoise Rosay. *L'Atalantide* (21), *Crainquebille* (22), *Thérèse Raquin* (28), *Les Nouveaux Messieurs* (29), *The Kiss* (US) (29), *Le Grand Jeu* (34), *La Kermesse Héroïque* (36), *Knight without Armour* (GB) (37), *Les Gens du Voyage* (38), *Une Femme Disparait* (41), *Macadam* (supervised only) (45), etc.

F.I.D.O. The Film Industry Defence Organization, a body formed by British renters and exhibitors to prevent old feature films being sold to television. It collapsed in 1964 after five years during which no renter dared sell his product for fear of reprisals.

FIELD, BETTY (1918–   ). American stage actress who has played occasional film roles, at first as neurotic girls, later as cosy mums. *Of Mice and Men* (39), *Victory* (40), *Are Husbands Necessary?* (41), *King's Row* (41), *Blues in the Night* (41), *Flesh and Fantasy* (43), *The Great Moment* (43), *Tomorrow the World* (44), *The Southerner* (45), *The Great Gatsby* (49), *Picnic* (56), *Middle of the Night* (59), *Birdman of Alcatraz* (62), *Seven Women* (66), *How to Save a Marriage* (67), *Coogan's Bluff* (68), etc.

FIELD, MARY (1896–1968). British executive long associated with films specially made for children. From 1926 worked as continuity girl, editor, etc., also directed some instructional films, including the *Secrets of Life* series. Well-known writer and lecturer on social aspects of film.

FIELD, RACHEL (1894–1942). American novelist. Books filmed include *All This and Heaven Too*, *And Now Tomorrow*.

M   353

Field, Sally

FIELD, SALLY (1946–   ). Diminutive American actress who played
the lead in TV series *Gidget* (65), *The Flying Nun* (67–68). Film
debut: *The Way West* (67).

FIELD, SHIRLEY ANN (1938–   ). British leading lady with stage
experience; career has waned somewhat after a promising start.
Once More with Feeling (59), *The Entertainer* (59), *Saturday Night and
Sunday Morning* (60), *The Man in the Moon* (60), *The Damned* (61),
The War Lover (62), *Lunch Hour* (63), *Kings of the Sun* (US) (63),
Doctor in Clover (66), *Alfie* (66), etc.

FIELD, SID (1904–50). British comedian who after years in music hall
became West End star in 1943. First film, *London Town* (46), valuable as record of his sketches; second and last, *Cardboard Cavalier*
(48), an unhappy historical farce.

FIELD, VIRGINIA (1917–   ) (Margaret Cynthia Field). British-born
second-lead of Hollywood films in the 40s. *The Primrose Path* (GB)
(35), *Lloyds of London* (37), *Lancer Spy* (38), *Waterloo Bridge* (40),
Hudson's Bay (41), *The Perfect Marriage* (46), *The Violent Hour* (50),
The Big Story (58), *The Earth Dies Screaming* (65), others.

FIELDING, FENELLA (c. 1930–   ). Anglo-Rumanian leading lady,
usually in outrageously exaggerated roles on stage and TV. Films
include *In the Doghouse* (62), *The Old Dark House* (63), *Doctor in
Clover* (66), *Carry on Screaming* (66), *Arrivederci Baby* (66), *Lock Up
Your Daughters* (69).

FIELDING, MARJORIE (1892–1956). British stage actress who usually
played strict but kindly gentlewomen. Repeated her stage role in
Quiet Wedding (40) and was subsequently in many films, e.g. *The
Demi-Paradise* (43), *Quiet Weekend* (46), *Spring in Park Lane* (47),
The Conspirator (49), *The Chiltern Hundreds* (49), *The Franchise Affair*
(50), *The Lavender Hill Mob* (51), *Mandy* (52), *Rob Roy* (53), etc.

FIELDS, GRACIE (1898–   ) (Grace Stansfield). British singer and
comedienne whose Lancashire humour helped to carry working-
class audiences through the 30s depression. On stage from 1911.
Sally in Our Alley (31), *Looking on the Bright Side* (32), *Sing As We Go*
(34), *Queen of Hearts* (36), *The Show Goes On* (37), *Shipyard Sally*
(40), *Holy Matrimony* (US) (43), *Molly and Me* (US) (44), *Madame
Pimpernel* (US) (45), etc. Published autobiography 1960: *Sing As
We Go*.

FIELDS, STANLEY (c. 1880–1941) (Walter L. Agnew). American
character actor, former prizefighter and vaudevillian. *Mammy* (30),
Little Caesar (30), *Island of Lost Souls* (32), *Kid Millions* (35), *Way Out
West* (37), *New Moon* (40), etc.

354

FIELDS, W. C. (1879–1946) (William Claude Dukinfield). Red-nosed, bottle-hitting, misogynist American comedian around whose gravel voice, intolerance and dubious habits many legends have been built. After a hard life as an eccentric juggler his off-beat personality found a niche in silent films, and he continued until 1941 to make unpredictable appearances in films often written by himself on the back of an envelope or made up as he went along. (Pen-names: Mahatma Kane Jeeves, Otis Criblecoblis, etc.) Surprisingly successful as Micawber in *David Copperfield* (34); but purer moments of Fields are to be found in *Pool Sharks* (debut) (15), *Janice Meredith* (24), *Sally of the Sawdust* (25), *So's Your Old Man* (26), *Poppy* (27), *Tillie's Punctured Romance* (28), *Her Majesty Love* (30), *Million Dollar Legs* (32), *If I Had a Million* (32), *Alice in Wonderland* (33), *International House* (33), *The Man on the Flying Trapeze* (33), *Tillie and Gus* (34), *Six of a Kind* (34), *It's a Gift* (34), *Mrs Wiggs of the Cabbage Patch* (34), *Mississippi* (35), *Poppy* (36), *You Can't Cheat an Honest Man* (39), *My Little Chickadee* (40), *The Bank Dick* (41), *Never Give a Sucker an Even Break* (41), *Sensations of 1945*, etc. A biography by Robert Lewis Taylor, *W. C. Fields, His Follies and Fortunes*, was published in 1949.

FIGUEROA, GABRIEL (1907–   ). Mexican cinematographer who worked in Hollywood with Gregg Toland and on Luis Bunuel's Mexican films. Also: *The Fugitive* (47), *MacLovia* (50), *Night of the Iguana* (64), etc.

film society. A club formed to show high quality revivals and new films not normally found in public cinemas.

LA FIN DU JOUR (France 1939). A delightful comedy-drama set in a home for old actors, with subtle direction by Julien Duvivier and effortlessly effective performances from Michel Simon, Louis Jouvet and Victor Francen.

FINCH, FLORA (1869–1940). British-born actress, formerly on stage; famous as John Bunny's partner in early film comedies. After his death in 1915 she formed her own production company and was in many silent films of the 20s.

FINCH, PETER (1916–   ) (William Mitchell). Australian actor who came to London in the late 40s and quickly became a star. *Mr Chedworth Steps Out* (Austr.) (38), *Rats of Tobruk* (Austr.) (44), *Eureka Stockade* (Br./Austr.) (47), *Train of Events* (49), *Robin Hood* (as Sheriff) (51), *The Story of Gilbert and Sullivan* (as Rupert D'Oyly Carte) (53), *Elephant Walk* (US) (53), *Father Brown* (54), *Make Me an Offer* (54), *The Dark Avenger* (55), *Passage Home* (55), *Simon and Laura* (55), *The Battle of the River Plate* (as Langsdorff) (55), *A Town Like Alice* (BFA) (56), *The Shiralee* (56), *Robbery under Arms* (57), *Windom's Way* (57), *The Nun's Story* (US) (58), *Operation Amsterdam*

(59), *Kidnapped* (60), *The Sins of Rachel Cade* (US) (60), *The Trials of Oscar Wilde* (title role) (BFA) (60), *No Love for Johnnie* (BFA) (61), *I Thank a Fool* (62), *In the Cool of the Day* (63), *Girl with Green Eyes* (64), *The Pumpkin Eater* (64), *Judith* (US) (65), *The Flight of the Phoenix* (US) (65), *10.30 p.m. Summer* (67), *Far from the Madding Crowd* (67), *The Legend of Lylah Clare* (68).

fine grain print. One of high quality stock (avoiding the coarseness of silver salt deposit); used for making dupe negatives.

FINKLEHOFFE, FRED F. (1911–). American writer-producer. *Brother Rat* (co-w, also co-w original stage play) (39), *For Me and My Gal* (co-w) (42), *Meet Me in St Louis* (w) (44), *The Egg and I* (c-w, p) (47), *At War with the Army* (co-w, p) (50), etc.

FINLAY, FRANK (1926–). British stage actor who has made tentative screen appearances. *Life for Ruth* (62), *The Informers* (63), *Othello* (as Iago) (65), *Robbery* (67), *Inspector Clouseau* (68), *Twisted Nerve* (68), *Cromwell* (69), etc.

FINLAYSON, JAMES (1887–1953). Scottish-born comedian who went to Hollywood in early silent days and became popular comic butt or villain in Mack Sennett and Hal Roach comedies in which his 'double take' and pop eyes were used to great advantage; e.g. with Laurel and Hardy in *Big Business* (31), *Fra Diavolo* (33), *Way Out West* (36). Best other film *Dawn Patrol* (30); last seen in *Grand Canyon Trail* (51).

†FINNEY, ALBERT (1936–). British stage actor whose few films to date have been both controversial and popular. *The Entertainer* (59), *Saturday Night and Sunday Morning* (60), *Tom Jones* (63), *The Victors* (63), *Night Must Fall* (63), *Two for the Road* (67), *Charlie Bubbles* (also as director) (67), *The Picasso Summer* (69), etc.

fire is a standard part of the melodramatist's equipment, whether it be used for disposing of country houses with too many memories (*Dragonwyck*, *Rebecca*, *The Lost Moment*, *The Fall of the House of Usher*, *The Tomb of Ligeia*, *Brides of Dracula*) or whole cities (*Forever Amber*, *In Old Chicago*, *Quo Vadis*). Sometimes, as in *House of Wax*, it makes a splendid starting point; though to judge from *She* one can't rely on its life-prolonging qualities. Its use in realistic films is rare, though cases of arson were seriously studied in *On the Night of the Fire* and *Violent Playground*. The fires of hell were most spectacularly re-created in the 1935 version of *Dante's Inferno*. Comedies about firemen include *Where's That Fire?* (Will Hay), *Fireman Save My Child*, *Harvey Middleman Fireman*, and *Go to Blazes* (Dave King); and firemen who start fires instead of putting them out are prophesied in *Fahrenheit 451*. Oil fires were spectacularly depicted in *Tulsa*, *Wildcat*, and *Hellfighters*. The classic study of conventional firemen remains *Fires Were Started*. Finally fire was always a splendid aid for serial producers, as the oft-used title 'Next Week: Through the Flames' may suggest.

See also: *forest fires*.

FIRE OVER ENGLAND (GB 1936). A charade of the Spanish Armada, produced by Alexander Korda with an eye to repeating his 'Henry VIII' success. Directed by William K. Howard. Now chiefly remembered for its gallery of star talents: Flora Robson, Leslie Banks, Laurence Olivier, Vivien Leigh, Raymond Massey, etc.

FIRES ON THE PLAIN (NOBU) (Japan 1959). Kon Ichikawa's horrifying film about World War II from the Japanese angle is remarkable for the ferocity of its images and of Natto Wada's script, in which the hero resorts finally to cannibalism.

FIRES WERE STARTED (GB 1943). Humphrey Jennings' documentary about the Auxiliary Fire Service during the London blitz is slower and slighter than one might expect from an official tribute, but the treatment gives it an almost poetic quality, and all its people—real firemen—live in the memory.

firing squads have figured chiefly in films about World War I (*Paths of Glory, King and Country*) or those telling the lives of spies, (*Mata Hari, Nurse Edith Cavell, Carve Her Name With Pride*). Other uses have been in *Dishonoured, The Fugitive, Custer of the West, The Long Ride Home, Reach for Glory* and *The Ceremony*; and firing squads were given a comic effect in *The Captain's Paradise, Casino Royale, Morgan* and *The Ambushers*.

THE FIRST OF THE FEW (GB 1942). Leslie Howard wrote and directed this gentle, cinematically unremarkable but moving film about R. J. Mitchell, inventor of the Spitfire plane. It proved to be one of World War II's most inspirational films, typifying the idealist attitude.

FISCHER, GUNNAR (1911–). Swedish cinematographer who has worked on most of Ingmar Bergman's films. *Smiles of a Summer Night* (55), *The Seventh Seal* (57), *Wild Strawberries* (58), *The Face* (58), *The Devil's Eye* (60), etc.

FISCHER, O. W. (1915–). Leading German actor, in films since 1936 but hardly known abroad. *Sommerliebe* (42), *Heidelberger Romanze* (51), *El Hakim* (57), *Uncle Tom's Cabin* (65), many others.

FISHER, EDDIE (1928–). American night-club singer and actor. *Bundle of Joy* (56), *Butterfield 8* (60), etc.

FISHER, GERRY (1926–). British cinematographer. *The Devil's Disciple* (59), *Suddenly Last Summer* (60), *The Millionairess* (61),

Night Must Fall (63), *Guns at Batasi* (64), *Modesty Blaise* (66), *Accident* (67), *Sebastian* (68), *Interlude* (68), etc.

FISHER, TERENCE (1904–). British director, former editor, in films from 1933. Work mainly routine; latterly associated with Hammer horror. *To the Public Danger* (47), *Portrait from Life* (48), *Marry Me* (49), *The Astonished Heart* (49), *So Long at the Fair* (50), *Home to Danger* (51), *Kill Me Tomorrow* (55), *The Curse of Frankenstein* (56), *Dracula* (57), *The Hound of the Baskervilles* (58), *Brides of Dracula* (59), *The Two Faces of Dr Jekyll* (60), *The Phantom of the Opera* (62), *The Gorgon* (64), *Dracula, Prince of Darkness* (65), *Island of Terror* (66), *The Devil Rides Out* (68), etc. Also worked for TV, especially *Douglas Fairbanks Presents*.

FISZ, BENJAMIN (1922–). Polish-born independent producer, long in England. *Hell Drivers* (57), *Sea Fury* (58), *On the Fiddle* (61), *Heroes of Telemark* (co-p) (65), *The Battle of Britain* (co-p) (69), etc.

FITZGERALD, BARRY (1888–1961) (William Shields). Diminutive Irish actor long popular at Dublin's Abbey Theatre. Went to Hollywood 1936 to play stage role in *The Plough and the Stars*; stayed to play irascible or whimsical 'Oirish' roles. *Ebb Tide* (37), *Bringing Up Baby* (38), *Four Men and a Prayer* (38), *The Long Voyage Home* (40), *The Sea Wolf* (41), *How Green Was My Valley* (42), *The Amazing Mrs Holliday* (43), *Going My Way* (AA) (44), *Incendiary Blonde* (44), *Two Years Before the Mast* (45), *Ten Little Niggers* (45), *The Stork Club* (45), *Easy Come, Easy Go* (46), *Welcome Stranger* (46), *Naked City* (48), *Top o' the Morning* (49), *Union Station* (50), *The Quiet Man* (52), *Happy Ever After* (54), *The Catered Affair* (56), *Rooney* (GB) (57), *Broth of a Boy* (Irish) (59), others.

FITZGERALD, F. SCOTT (1896–1940). American novelist and chronicler of 'the jazz age'; was played by Gregory Peck in a biopic, *Beloved Infidel* (59). Works filmed include *The Great Gatsby* (48), *Tender is the Night* (61).

FITZGERALD, GERALDINE (1914–). Irish leading lady who played in British films from 1935; went to Hollywood in 1939 but had rather disappointing roles. *Turn of the Tide* (35), *The Mill on the Floss* (36), *Dark Victory* (39), *Wuthering Heights* (39), *Till We Meet Again* (40), *Flight from Destiny* (41), *The Gay Sisters* (42), *Watch on the Rhine* (43), *Ladies Courageous* (44), *Wilson* (44), *Uncle Harry* (45), *Three Strangers* (46), *O.S.S.* (46), *Nobody Lives Forever* (47), *So Evil My Love* (GB) (48), then long absence; *Ten North Frederick* (58), *The Fiercest Heart* (61), *The Pawnbroker* (65), etc.

FITZGERALD, WALTER (1896–) (Walter Bond). British character actor, on stage from 1922, films from 1930. *Murder at Covent Garden* (30), *This England* (40), *Squadron Leader X* (41), *Strawberry Roan* (45),

Mine Own Executioner (47), *Treasure Island* (50), *Pickwick Papers* (52), *Personal Affair* (53), *Lease of Life* (54), *Cockleshell Heroes* (55), *Something of Value* (57), *Third Man on the Mountain* (59), *HMS Defiant* (62), others.

FITZMAURICE, GEORGE (1885–1940). French stage director long in America; his films had some reputation for style in the late 20s and early 30s. *Bella Donna* (23), *The Dark Angel* (25), *Son of the Sheik* (26), *Lilac Time* (28), *The Devil to Pay* (30), *One Heavenly Night* (51), *Mata Hari* (32), *Live, Love and Learn* (37), *Adventure in Diamonds* (39), etc.

FITZPATRICK, JAMES A. (1902–). American documentarist, who from 1925 produced and narrated innumerable travel shorts ('Fitzpatrick Traveltalks'), invariably concluding 'And so we leave . . .' Wrote, produced and directed one feature, *Song of Mexico* (45).

FIVE FINGERS (US 1952). L. C. Moyzich's book *Operation Cicero*, about the British Ambassador in Ankara's valet, who during World War II sold secrets to the Germans, can be credited with the postwar reawakening of interest in spying which led eventually to the Bond spoofs. In Joseph L. Mankiewicz' film, Cicero was played by James Mason. There was a TV series of the same name (59) with David Hedison.

FIVE GRAVES TO CAIRO (US 1943). Spy story set in the African desert in 1943 and using Rommel as a chief character; a remarkable illustration of writer-director Billy Wilder's penchant for turning headlines into entertainment. Also boasts an ingenious plot and a fascinating performance by Erich Von Stroheim.

FIVE STAR FINAL (US 1932). A famous melodrama of the hardboiled newspaperman school, about a ruthless editor whose probing of a long-dead scandal drives two people to suicide. Directed by Mervyn le Roy, from a play by Louis Weitzenkorn; with Edward G. Robinson.

FIX, PAUL (1902–). American character actor with wry, lugubrious features. Has played hundreds of cameos since 1922; among latest, *To Kill a Mockingbird* (63), *Mail Order Bride* (*West of Montana*) (63), *Shenandoah* (65).

THE FLAG LIEUTENANT. The stiff-upper-lip stage melodrama by W. P. Drury and Lee Trevor, about the intrepid exploits of a naval officer in an outpost of empire, was filmed as a silent in 1919 with George Wynn, and in 1926 with Henry Edwards. In 1932 Edwards appeared in a sound remake, his leading lady being Anna Neagle.

Flagstad, Kirsten

FLAGSTAD, KIRSTEN (1895–1962). Norwegian operatic soprano whose only film appearance was, surprisingly, in *The Big Broadcast of 1938*.

FLAHERTY, ROBERT (1884–1951). American documentary pioneer, originally explorer. *Nanook of the North* (20), *Moana* (26), *White Shadows of the South Seas* (28), *Tabu* (29), *Man of Aran* (34), *Elephant Boy* (37), *Louisiana Story* (48), etc. A biography, *The Innocent Eye*, was published in 1963 by Arthur Calder-Marshall.

FLANAGAN, BUD (1896–1968) (Robert Winthrop). Genial British comedian, long teamed with Chesney Allen (qv for list of films); they formed part of the Crazy Gang. Wrote and sang catchy, sentimental songs: 'Hometown', 'Underneath the Arches', 'Umbrella Man', 'Strolling'.

FLASH GORDON. American newspaper strip hero whose exploits were featured in three famous Hollywood serials starring Buster Crabbe. In the original *Flash Gordon* (36) our hero and his friends saved the earth from collision with another planet at the cost of being stranded there at the mercy of the wicked Emperor Ming. *Flash Gordon's Trip to Mars* (38) and *Flash Gordon Conquers the Universe* (40) were compounded of similar elements. The directors respectively were Frederick Stephani; Ford Beebe and Robert Hill; and Ray Taylor.

flashback. A break in chronological narrative during which we are shown events of past time which bear on the present situation. The device is as old as the cinema: you could say that *Intolerance* was composed of four flashbacks. As applied to more commonplace yarns, however, with the flashback narrated by one of the story's leading characters, the convention soared into popularity in the 30s until by 1945 or so a film looked very dated indeed if it was not told in retrospect. In the 50s flashbacks fell into absolute disuse, but are now creeping back into fashion again. Some notable uses are:
    The Power and the Glory (33), which was advertised as being in 'Narratage' because Spencer Tracy spoke a commentary over the action. *Bride of Frankenstein* (35), which was narrated by Elsa Lanchester as Mary Shelley; the gag was that she also played the monster's mate. *The Great McGinty* (40), in which the flashback construction revealed the somewhat corrupt leading figures finally as penniless, thus mollifying the Hays Office. *Rebecca* (40), in which the introductory narrative, while revealing that Manderley was to go up in flames, also comforted in the knowledge that the hero and heroine would be saved. *Citizen Kane* (41), the complex structure of which was so influential that a whole host of pictures followed in which we tried to get at the truth about a character already dead, by questioning those who knew him: cf. *The Killers*, *The Rake's Progress*, *The Moon and Sixpence*, *The Bridge of San Luis Rey*,

The Woman in Question, Letter from an Unknown Woman, Rashomon, The Great Man, even *Doctor Zhivago. Hold Back the Dawn* (41), in which Charles Boyer as a penniless refugee visited Paramount Studios and sold his story to Mitchell Leisen. *The Mummy's Hand* (41), in which the ten-minute chunk telling how the mummy came to be buried alive was lifted straight from the 1932 film *The Mummy.* (Such economies have become commonplace.) *Roxie Hart* (42), in which George Montgomery told a twenty-year-old tale about a notorious lady who at the end of the film was revealed as the mother of his large family. *Ruthless* (48), a tortuous Zachary Scott melodrama reviewed as follows by the British critic C. A. Lejeune:

> Beginning pictures at the end
> Is, I'm afraid, a modern trend;
> But I'd find *Ruthless* much more winning
> If it could end at the beginning.

Road to Utopia (45), in which Hope and Lamour appeared as old folks telling the story; as a pay-off their 'son' appeared, looking just like Crosby, and Hope told the audience: 'We adopted him.' *Passage to Marseilles* (44), a complex melodrama ranging from Devil's Island to war-torn Britain; it had flashbacks within flashbacks *within flashbacks.* In *Dead of Night* (45), all the characters told supernatural experiences to a psychiatrist, who was then murdered by one of them; the murderer then woke up with no recollection of his nightmare, and proceeded to meet all the other characters again as though for the first time, being caught in an endless series of recurring dreams. *Enchantment* (47), and later *Death of a Salesman* (52), and many films up to *I Was Happy Here* (66), in which characters walk straight out of the present into the past, dispensing with the boring 'I remember' bit. *Edward My Son* (49) and *Teahouse of the August Moon* (56), in which characters step out of the play to tell the story to the audience. *Dead Reckoning* (47), in which Humphrey Bogart confesses the entire plot to a priest. *Kind Hearts and Coronets* (49), in which the story springs from the memoirs of a murderer being written on the night before his execution. *An Inspector Calls* (54), in which a supernatural figure visits a family to make them remember their harsh treatment of a girl who has committed suicide. *Repeat Performance* (47), in which a desperate husband relives the events of the year, leading up to his predicament and gets a chance to change the outcome.

If the format is to catch on again it will have to be more deftly used than in two recent films: *Ride Beyond Vengeance,* with its completely irrelevant framing story about a census-taking, and *Lady L,* in which the framing story with the characters as old folks is only marginally less inept than the basic one. Two big-scale musicals, *Star!* and *Funny Girl,* have used flashbacks with style but little purpose.

Flavin, James

FLAVIN, JAMES (1906–). Irish-American supporting actor, usually as genial or bewildered cop. *Cloak and Dagger* (46), *Desert Fury* (47), *Mighty Joe Young* (50), *Fighter Attack* (53), *Mister Roberts* (55), *The Last Hurrah* (58), *It's a Mad Mad Mad Mad World* (63), *Cheyenne Autumn* (64), *Bullwhip Griffin* (67), many others.

fleapit. An affectionate British term for the kind of tatty little cinema in which, it was sometimes alleged, the management loaned a hammer with each ticket.

FLEISCHER, MAX (1889–). Austrian-born cartoonist and producer, long in Hollywood. Created Betty Boop, Koko, Out of the Inkwell series, Popeye the Sailor, etc. Feature cartoons: *Gulliver's Travels* (39), *Mr Bug Goes to Town* (41). His brother DAVE FLEISCHER (1894–) has worked as his administrative head.

†FLEISCHER, RICHARD (1916–). American director, son of Max Fleischer; former shorts producer. His films usually sound more interesting than they prove to be. *Child of Divorce* (46), *Banjo* (47), *So This Is New York* (49), *Make Mine Laughs* (49), *Trapped* (49), *Follow Me Quietly* (49), *The Clay Pigeon* (49), *The Armoured Car Robbery* (50), *The Narrow Margin* (51), *The Happy Time* (52), *Arena* (53), *Twenty Thousand Leagues under the Sea* (54), *Violent Saturday* (55), *The Girl in the Red Velvet Swing* (55), *Bandido* (56), *Between Heaven and Hell* (56), *The Vikings* (57), *These Thousand Hills* (58), *Compulsion* (58), *Crack in the Mirror* (60), *The Big Gamble* (61), *Barabbas* (62), *Fantastic Voyage* (66), *Doctor Dolittle* (67), *The Boston Strangler* (68), *Che!* (69), *Tora! Tora! Tora!* (69).

FLEMING, ERIC (1924–1966). Gaunt, taciturn American leading man well known on TV as the trailmaster in *Rawhide*. Few films include *Conquest of Space* (55), *Fright* (57), *Curse of the Undead* (59), *The Glass Bottom Boat* (66).

FLEMING, IAN (1906–1964). Creator of James Bond, whose exploits have been so successfully filmed from the novels.

FLEMING, IAN (1888–). Australian-born character actor, long in British films as doctors, civil servants, solicitors, etc. A memorable Dr Watson in the 30s series starring Arthur Wontner as Sherlock Holmes.

FLEMING, RHONDA (1923–) (Marilyn Louis). Red-haired American leading lady of the 40s and 50s. *When Strangers Marry* (43), *Spellbound* (45), *The Spiral Staircase* (45), *Adventure Island* (46), *Out of the Past (Build My Gallows High)* (47), *A Yankee in King Arthur's Court* (49), *Cry Danger* (50), *The Redhead and the Cowboy* (51), *The Great Lover* (51), *Little Egypt* (52), *The Golden Hawk* (52), *Serpent of the Nile* (53), *Inferno* (53), *Yankee Pasha* (54), *The Killer Is Loose*

362

(56), *Slightly Scarlet* (56), *Gunfight at the OK Corral* (57), *Gun Glory* (57), *Home Before Dark* (58), *Alias Jesse James* (59), *The Big Circus* (59), *Run For Your Wife* (66), etc.

FLEMING, VICTOR (1883–1949). American director, former cameraman. *The Clouds Roll By* (19), *The Way of All Flesh* (27), *The Virginian* (29), *Red Dust* (32), *The White Sister* (33), *Treasure Island* (34), *Captains Courageous* (37), *Test Pilot* (38), *The Wizard of Oz* (39), *Gone with the Wind* (AA) (39), *Dr Jekyll and Mr Hyde* (41), *Tortilla Flat* (42), *A Guy Named Joe* (43), *Adventure* (46), *Joan of Arc* (48), many others.

FLEMYNG, GORDON (1934–   ). British director, from TV. *Great Catherine* (68), *The Split* (68), *Grigsby* (69).

FLEMYNG, ROBERT (1912–   ). British actor who usually plays attractive professional men. On stage from 1931, films from 1936 (*Head Over Heels*). Later: *The Guinea Pig* (49), *The Blue Lamp* (50), *The Holly and the Ivy* (52), *The Man Who Never Was* (55), *Funny Face* (US) (56), *Windom's Way* (57), *A Touch of Larceny* (59), *The Terror of Dr Hichcock* (It.) (63), *The Deadly Affair* (66), *The Spy with a Cold Nose* (67), etc.

FLESH AND FANTASY (US 1943). One of the earliest compendiums of short stories, linked only by the ramblings of a club bore. In this case, unfortunately, the stories were poorly chosen, and Julien Duvivier's direction somewhat flavourless. The form did not achieve any popularity until 1948 with Somerset Maugham's *Quartet*, and then after three or four years of all-star casts in tenuously linked anecdotes, the advent of television playlets killed the idea stone dead. See also: TALES OF MANHATTAN.

FLETCHER, BRANWELL (1904–   ). British light leading man of the 30s. *Chick* (30), *To What Red Hell* (30), *Raffles* (US) (31), *Svengali* (US) (31), *The Mummy* (US) (32), *The Scarlet Pimpernel* (34), *Random Harvest* (US) (42), *White Cargo* (US) (42), *The Immortal Sergeant* (US) (42), *Night Monster* (US) (last to date) (45), etc.

FLETCHER, CYRIL (1913–   ). British comedian and entertainer who has made appearances in a few films: *Yellow Canary* (43), *Nicholas Nickleby* (47), *A Piece of Cake* (48), etc.

FLICKER, THEODORE J. (c. 1929–   ). American director, former Greenwich Village satirist. *The Troublemaker* (64), *The President's Analyst* (68).

FLIPPEN, JAY C. (c. 1898–   ). American character actor with vaudeville and stage experience; usually seen as sheriff, sergeant or cop. *A Woman's Secret* (debut) (49), *Flying Leathernecks* (51), *Thunder Bay* (53), *The Wild One* (54), *The Killing* (56), *Cat Ballou* (65), *Firecreek* (67), *Hellfighters* (68), many others.

FLOREY, ROBERT (1900–   ). French-born director, in Hollywood since 1921. *The Romantic Age* (27), *The Coconuts* (29), *The Murders in the Rue Morgue* (32), *Ex Lady* (33), *The Woman in Red* (34), *Hollywood Boulevard* (36), *Hotel Imperial* (38), *The Face Behind the Mask* (40), *Lady Gangster* (42), *Dangerously They Live* (43), *God Is My Co-Pilot* (44), *The Beast with Five Fingers* (46), *Monsieur Verdoux* (co-d) (47), *Rogues' Regiment* (48), *Outpost in Morocco* (48), *Johnny One Eye* (49), *The Gangster We Made* (50), many second features; latterly directed hundreds of TV films. Also wrote several scripts, including work on *Frankenstein* (31).

THE FLY (US 1958). An unpleasant horror film given big studio treatment in lieu of taste and style, based on an unfortunate mix-up during transmission through space of human and insect atoms. David (then Al) Hedison was the unfortunate victim. There were two sequels: *Return of the Fly* (60), *Curse of the Fly* (64).

FLYING DOWN TO RIO (US 1933). The musical that started the Astaire-Rogers cycle; also notable for a brilliantly-photographed finale with chorus girls on the wings of flying aeroplanes. Nominal stars Dolores del Rio and Gene Raymond; directed by Thornton Freeland.

†FLYNN, ERROL (1909–1959). Irish-American leading man who led an adventurous life on and off screen and by his handsome impudence maintained a world-wide following for nearly twenty years before hard living got the better of him. *Murder at Monte Carlo* (GB) (34), *The Case of the Curious Bride* (GB) (34), *Don't Bet on Blondes* (35), *Captain Blood* (35), *The Charge of the Light Brigade* (36), *The Green Light* (36), *The Prince and the Pauper* (37), *Another Dawn* (37), *The Perfect Specimen* (37), *The Adventures of Robin Hood* (37), *Four's a Crowd* (38), *The Sisters* (38), *The Dawn Patrol* (38), *Dodge City* (39), *Elizabeth and Essex* (39), *Virginia City* (39), *The Sea Hawk* (40), *Santa Fe Trail* (40), *Footsteps in the Dark* (41), *Dive Bomber* (41), *They Died with Their Boots On* (41), *Desperate Journey* (42), *Gentleman Jim* (42), *Edge of Darkness* (43), *Northern Pursuit* (43), *Thank Your Lucky Stars* (43), *Uncertain Glory* (44), *Objective Burma* (45), *San Antonio* (45), *Never Say Goodbye* (45), *Cry Wolf* (46), *Escape Me Never* (47), *Silver River* (47), *The New Adventures of Don Juan* (48), *The Forsyte Saga* (as Soames) (49), *Montana* (50), *Rocky Mountain* (50), *Kim* (51), *The Adventures of Captain Fabian* (also wrote) (51), *Mara Maru* (52), *Against All Flags* (52), *The Master of Ballantrae* (GB) (53), *Crossed Swords* (It.) (53), *Lilacs in the Spring* (GB) (55), *The Dark Avenger* (GB) (55), *King's Rhapsody* (GB) (56), *The Big Boodle* (56), *Istanbul* (57), *The Sun Also Rises* (57), *Too Much Too Soon* (as John Barrymore) (58), *Roots of Heaven* (58), *Cuban Rebel Girls* (59). Wrote two autobiographical books, *Beam Ends* (34) and *My Wicked Wicked Ways* (59).

FOCH, NINA (1924–   ). Cool, blonde, Dutch-born actress, long in America. *The Return of the Vampire* (debut) (43), *Nine Girls* (43), *Cry of the Werewolf* (44), *Shadows in the Night* (44), *A Song to Remember* (44), *I Love a Mystery* (44), *Prison Ship* (45), *My Name Is Julia Ross* (46), *Johnny O'clock* (46), *The Guilt of Janet Ames* (48), *The Dark Past* (49), *Undercover Man* (50), *An American in Paris* (51), *Young Man with Ideas* (51), *Scaramouche* (52), *Fast Company* (53), *Sombrero* (53), *Executive Suite* (54), *You're Never Too Young* (55), *Illegal* (55), *The Ten Commandments* (56), *Three Brave Men* (57), *Spartacus* (60), *Cash McCall* (60), etc.; recently on stage and TV.

fog has been a godsend to many a cinematic entertainment, whether it's the genuine pea-souper inseparable from Hollywood's idea of London, or the ankle-high white mist which used to distinguish heaven and dream sequences. Fog can provide a splendid dramatic background, especially in horror-thrillers like *Dracula*, *The Wolf Man* and *The Cat and the Canary*; but too often it is simply imposed on a film to force a particular atmosphere, as in *Footsteps in the Fog*, *Fog over Frisco*, *Fog Island*, *Winterset*, *Out of the Fog* and *The Notorious Landlady*. *Barbary Coast* seemed to be permanently enveloped in fog, as did the village in *Sherlock Holmes and the Scarlet Claw*: while in *The Adventures of Sherlock Holmes* London had fog in May! Fog was dramatically used in *The VIPs* and *The Divorce of Lady X* (for bringing people together in a hotel); in *The Runaway Bus* (for bringing people together in an abandoned village); in *Midnight Lace* (for masking the identity of the voice threatening Doris Day); in *Twenty-three Paces to Baker Street* (for hampering the villain but not the blind hero); in *Alias Nick Beal* (as a background for the devil's materialization); in *The Lost Continent* (as a nauseous yellow for the weird community); in *Random Harvest* (as a means for the hero's escape); and in the various versions of *The Sea Wolf* (for causing the accident that brings hero and heroine together on Wolf Larsen's boat). Even comedies find it useful: the chase through fog in *After the Fox* results in happy confusion.

FOLSEY, GEORGE J. (c. 1900–   ). American cinematographer. *Applause* (29), *The Smiling Lieutenant* (31), *Reckless* (35), *The Great Ziegfeld* (36), *The Shining Hour* (38), *Meet Me in St Louis* (44), *A Guy Named Joe* (44), *Under the Clock* (45), *Green Dolphin Street* (47), *State of the Union* (48), *Take Me Out to the Ball Game* (48), *The Great Sinner* (49), *Adam's Rib* (49), *Man with a Cloak* (51), *Executive Suite* (54), *Seven Brides for Seven Brothers* (55), *The Fastest Gun Alive* (56), *Imitation General* (58), etc.

†FONDA, HENRY (1905–   ). American leading actor who used to play gauche young fellows and graduated to roles of amiable wisdom. Long stage experience; father of Jane and Peter Fonda. *The Farmer Takes a Wife* (35), *Way Down East* (35), *I Dream Too*

Much (36), *The Trail of the Lonesome Pine* (36), *The Moon's Our Home* (36), *Spendthrift* (36), *Wings of the Morning* (GB) (37), *You Only Live Once* (37), *Slim* (37), *That Certain Woman* (37), *I Met My Love Again* (37), *Jezebel* (38), *Blockade* (38), *Spawn of the North* (38), *The Mad Miss Manton* (38), *Jesse James* (39), *Let Us Live* (39), *The Story of Alexander Graham Bell* (39), *Young Mr Lincoln* (39), *Drums Along the Mohawk* (39), *The Grapes of Wrath* (40), *Lilian Russell* (40), *The Return of Frank James* (40), *Chad Hanna* (40), *The Lady Eve* (41), *Wild Geese Calling* (41), *You Belong to Me* (41), *The Male Animal* (42), *Rings on Her Fingers* (42), *The Ox-Bow Incident* (42), *The Big Street* (42), *Tales of Manhattan* (42), *The Magnificent Dope* (42), *The Immortal Sergeant* (42); war service; *My Darling Clementine* (as Wyatt Earp) (46), *The Long Night* (47), *The Fugitive* (47), *Daisy Kenyon* (47), *On Our Merry Way* (48), *Fort Apache* (48); long absence on stage; *Mister Roberts* (55), *The Wrong Man* (56), *War and Peace* (56), *Twelve Angry Men* (BFA) (also produced) (57), *Stage Struck* (57), *The Tin Star* (57), *Warlock* (59), *The Man Who Understood Women* (59), *Advise and Consent* (61), *Spencer's Mountain* (63), *The Best Man* (64), *Fail Safe* (64), *Sex and the Single Girl* (64), *The Battle of the Bulge* (65), *In Harm's Way* (65), *Big Hand for a Little Lady* (66), *Welcome to Hard Times* (67), *Firecreek* (67), *Madigan* (68), *Yours, Mine and Ours* (68), *The Boston Strangler* (68), *Once upon a Time in the West* (69), *There Was a Crooked Man* (69), *The Cheyenne Social Club* (70), TV series: *The Deputy* (59–60).

FONDA, JANE (1937–   ). American leading lady, daughter of Henry Fonda. Stage and modelling experience. *Tall Story* (debut) (60), *Walk on the Wild Side* (61), *The Chapman Report* (62), *Period of Adjustment* (62), *In the Cool of the Day* (63), *Sunday in New York* (63), *La Ronde* (64), *Joy House* (*The Love Cage*) (65), *Cat Ballou* (65), *The Chase* (66), *Any Wednesday* (66), *The Game is Over* (Fr.) (66), *Hurry Sundown* (67), *Barefoot in the Park* (67), *Barbarella* (68), *They Shoot Heroes Don't They* (69).

FONDA, PETER (1939–   ). American actor, son of Henry Fonda. *Tammy and the Doctor* (63), *The Victors* (63), *Lilith* (64), *The Wild Angels* (66), *Easy Rider* (also produced) (69).

†FONTAINE, JOAN (1917–   ) (Joan de Havilland; sister of Olivia) British-born leading actress, in America from childhood. Became typed as a shy English rose; later made efforts to play sophisticated roles. *No More Ladies* (35), *Quality Street* (37), *You Can't Beat Love* (37), *Music for Madame* (37), *A Damsel in Distress* (38), *Blonde Cheat* (38), *The Man Who Found Himself* (38), *The Duke of West Point* (38), *Sky Giant* (38), *Gunga Din* (39), *Man of Conquest* (39), *The Women* (39), *Rebecca* (40), *Suspicion* (AA) (41), *This Above All* (42), *The Constant Nymph* (43), *Jane Eyre* (43), *Frenchman's Creek* (44), *The Affairs of Susan* (45), *From This Day Forward* (46), *Ivy* (47), *The*

Emperor Waltz (48), *Kiss the Blood off My Hands* (48), *Letter from an Unknown Woman* (48), *You Gotta Stay Happy* (48), *Born To Be Bad* (50), *September Affair* (50), *Darling How Could You?* (51), *Something To Live For* (52), *Ivanhoe* (52), *Decameron Nights* (GB) (53), *Flight to Tangier* (53), *The Bigamist* (53), *Casanova's Big Night* (54), *Serenade* (56), *Beyond a Reasonable Doubt* (56), *Island in the Sun* (56), *Until They Sail* (57), *A Certain Smile* (58), *Tender Is the Night* (61), *Voyage to the Bottom of the Sea* (61), *The Devil's Own* (*The Witches*) (GB) (66).

†FONTANNE, LYNN (1887–   ). Celebrated British-born stage actress, long in America and the wife of Alfred Lunt. Never really took to the screen: *Second Youth* (26), *The Guardsman* (32), *Stage Door Canteen* (43).

FOOLISH WIVES (US 1922). Most typical of Erich Von Stroheim's extravagant, over-charged sex dramas, this tragi-farce is set on the Riviera where a family of swindlers prey on rich women. Stroheim wrote, directed, and gives a rapacious performance. Photographer: William Daniels.

footage. Length of a film expressed in feet.

FORAN, DICK (1910–   ). Burly American leading man of countless comedies and westerns since 1934; often the good guy who doesn't get the girl. *Stand Up and Cheer* (34), *The Perfect Specimen* (38), *Horror Island* (41), *Guest Wife* (44), *Atomic Submarine* (60), *Taggart* (65), many others.

FORBES, BRYAN (1926–   ) (Brian Clarke). British actor turned writer and executive. *The Small Back Room* (debut) (48), *The Wooden Horse* (52), *An Inspector Calls* (54), *Cockleshell Heroes* (w) (55), *Quatermass II* (56), *House of Secrets* (w) (57), *The Angry Silence* (w, co-p) (59), *The League of Gentlemen* (a, w) (59), *Whistle Down the Wind* (d) (61), *The L-shaped Room* (w, d) (62), *Seance on a Wet Afternoon* (w, d) (64), *King Rat* (w, d) (65), *The Wrong Box* (co-w, d) (66), *The Whisperers* (w, d) (66), *Deadfall* (w, d) (67), *The Madwoman of Chaillot* (d) (69), etc. 1969: appointed head of production for Associated British.

FORBES, MARY (1880–1964). American character actress in Hollywood, usually as haughty society lady. *A Farewell to Arms* (32), *Blonde Bombshell* (33), *Les Misérables* (35), *Wee Willie Winkie* (37), *Always Goodbye* (38), *The Adventures of Sherlock Holmes* (40), *This Above All* (42), *The Picture of Dorian Gray* (44), *Ivy* (47), *You Gotta Stay Happy* (48), *The Ten Commandments* (56), many others.

FORBES, MERIEL (1913–   ) (M. Forbes-Robertson). British stage actress, wife of Sir Ralph Richardson. Film appearances include *Borrow a Million* (35), *Young Man's Fancy* (39), *The Gentle Sex* (43), *The Captive Heart* (46), *Home at Seven* (52).

Forbes, Ralph

FORBES, RALPH (1902–1951). British leading man who became a Hollywood star in the late 20s. *The Fifth Form at St Dominics* (GB) (21), *Beau Geste* (26), *Mr Wu* (29), *The Trail of '98* (30), *Bachelor Father* (31), *Smilin' Through* (32), *The Barretts of Wimpole Street* (33), *The Three Musketeers* (36), *Romeo and Juliet* (36), *If I Were King* (39), *Elizabeth and Essex* (last appearance) (39), etc.

FORBIDDEN PLANET (US 1956). One of the few science-fiction romps to win critical acclaim, this lively futuristic comic strip, directed by Fred M. Wilcox, was actually a reworking of *The Tempest*, with Walter Pidgeon as Morbius/Prospero fighting monsters from his own *id*. His tame robot Robby also appeared in *The Invisible Boy* (57).

FORD, ALEXANDER (1908–). Polish director who has been making films since 1930. Best known abroad: *The Young Chopin* (51), *Five Boys from Barska Street* (53), *Knights of the Teutonic Order* (60).

FORD, CECIL (1911–). Former Irish actor who turned production manager on some notable films: *Moby Dick* (56), *Around the World in Eighty Days* (57), *The Bridge on the River Kwai* (57), *The Inn of the Sixth Happiness* (58). Produced *The Guns of Navarone* (61), *633 Squadron* (64), others.

FORD, FRANCIS (1883–1953) (Francis Feeney). American character actor, often seen as grizzled, cheerly westerner. In silents; also *Charlie Chan's Greatest Case* (33), *The Informer* (35), *Prisoner of Shark Island* (36), *In Old Chicago* (38), *Drums across the Mohawk* (39), *Lucky Cisco Kid* (40), *The Ox-Bow Incident* (42), *The Big Noise* (44), *My Darling Clementine* (46), *Wagonmaster* (50), *The Sun Shines Bright* (52), many others.

FORD, GLENN (1916–) (Gwyllyn Ford). Stocky Canadian-born leading man, once married to Eleanor Powell. Stage experience before Hollywood debut; has become adept at tortured heroes. *Heaven with a Barbed Wire Fence* (debut) (40), *Convicted Woman* (40), *The Lady in Question* (40), *Blondie Plays Cupid* (40), *So Ends Our Night* (41), *Texas* (41), *Go West Young Lady* (41), *The Adventures of Martin Eden* (42), *Flight Lieutenant* (42), *The Desperadoes* (43), *Destroyer* (43); war service; *A Stolen Life* (46), *Gilda* (46), *Gallant Journey* (47), *The Man from Colorado* (48), *The Loves of Carmen* (48), *Undercover Man* (49), *Lust for Gold* (49), *The Flying Missile* (50), *The Redhead and the Cowboy* (51), *Follow the Sun* (52), *The Green Glove* (52), *Affair in Trinidad* (52), *Plunder of the Sun* (53), *The Big Heat* (53), *Human Desire* (54), *The Americano* (54), *The Violent Men* (55), *The Blackboard Jungle* (55), *Interrupted Melody* (55), *Trial* (55), *Ransom* (56), *The Fastest Gun Alive* (56), *Jubal* (56), *The Teahouse of the August Moon* (56), *Don't Go Near the Water* (56), *Cowboy* (57), *The Sheepman* (58), *Torpedo Run* (58), *The Gazebo* (59), *It Started with* a Kiss (60), *Cimarron* (61), *Pocketful of Miracles* (61), *The Four Horse-men of the Apocalypse* (62), *Experiment in Terror* (*The Grip of Fear*) (62), *Love Is a Ball* (63), *The Courtship of Eddie's Father* (63), *The Rounders* (65), *Dear Heart* (65), *Is Paris Burning?* (66), *Rage* (66), *Pistolero* (67), *Heaven with a Gun* (69), *Smith!* (69), others.

FORD, JOHN (1895–) (Sean O'Fearna). Distinguished Irish-American director who since 1917 has made nearly 200 features. At his best, makes incomparable outdoor films with strong feeling for characters and scenery. *The Tornado* (also wrote and acted) (17), *A Woman's Fool* (18), *Bare Fists* (19), *The Wallop* (21), *Silver Wings* (22), *The Face on the Bar-Room Floor* (23), *The Iron Horse* (24), *Lightnin'* (25), *Three Bad Men* (26), *Four Sons* (28), *Men Without Women* (30), *Up the River* (30), *Arrowsmith* (31), *Flesh* (32), *The World Moves On* (33), *The Lost Patrol* (34), *Judge Priest* (34), *Steamboat Round the Bend* (35), *The Informer* (AA) (35), *The Whole Town's Talking* (35), *Prisoner of Shark Island* (36), *Mary of Scotland* (36), *The Plough and the Stars* (36), *Wee Willie Winkie* (37), *The Hurricane* (37), *Four Men and a Prayer* (38), *Submarine Patrol* (38), *Stagecoach* (39), *Young Mr Lincoln* (39), *Drums along the Mohawk* (39), *The Grapes of Wrath* (AA) (40), *The Long Voyage Home* (40), *Tobacco Road* (41), *How Green Was My Valley* (41); war service (during which he produced the *Why We Fight* series); *They Were Expendable* (45), *My Darling Clementine* (46), *The Fugitive* (47), *Three Godfathers* (48), *Fort Apache* (48), *She Wore a Yellow Ribbon* (49), *Wagonmaster* (50), *When Willie Comes Marching Home* (50), *Rio Grande* (51), *What Price Glory* (52), *The Quiet Man* (52), *The Sun Shines Bright* (53), *Mogambo* (53), *The Long Gray Line* (54), *Mister Roberts* (co-d) (55), *The Searchers* (56), *The Wings of Eagles* (57), *The Last Hurrah* (58), *The Horse Soldiers* (59), *Gideon's Day* (GB) (59), *Sergeant Rutledge* (60), *Two Rode Together* (61), *The Man Who Shot Liberty Valance* (62), *Donovan's Reef* (63), *Cheyenne Autumn* (64), *Seven Women* (65), etc. (†Sound films complete.)

FORD, PAUL (1901–). American character actor best known on TV as the harassed colonel in the *Bilko* series and star of *The Baileys of Balboa*. Films include *Lust for Gold* (49), *Too Dangerous To Love* (*Perfect Strangers*) (50), *The Teahouse of the August Moon* (56), *The Matchmaker* (58), *Advise and Consent* (61), *Never Too Late* (65), *Big Hand for a Little Lady* (66), *The Russians Are Coming, The Russians Are Coming* (66), *The Spy with a Cold Nose* (GB) (67), *The Comedians* (67), etc.

FORD, WALLACE (1897–1966) (Sam Grundy). British general purpose actor who went to Hollywood in the early 30s and after a few semi-leads settled into character roles. *Freaks* (32), *Lost Patrol* (34), *The Informer* (35), *OHMS* (GB) (36), *The Mummy's Hand* (40), *Inside the Law* (42), *Shadow of a Doubt* (43), *The Green Years* (46),

Forde, Eugene

Embraceable You (48), *Harvey* (50), *The Nebraskan* (53), *Destry* (55), *Johnny Concho* (56), *The Last Hurrah* (58), *A Patch of Blue* (66), many others.

FORDE, EUGENE (1898–). American director of second features, former silent screen actor. *Charlie Chan in London* (33), *Buy Me That Town* (41), *Berlin Correspondent* (42), *Jewels of Brandenberg* (46), many others for Fox and Paramount.

FORDE, WALTER (1896–). British director, formerly a popular slapstick comedian of the silents: *Wait and See, Would You Believe It*, many shorts, one of which was featured in *Helter Skelter* (49). Directed some high-speed farces and several thrillers and melodramas: *The Silent House* (28), *Lord Richard in the Pantry* (30), *The Ghost Train* (31), *Jack's the Boy* (32), *Rome Express* (32), *Orders Is Orders* (33), *Jack Ahoy* (34), *Chu Chin Chow* (34), *Bulldog Jack* (35), *King of the Damned* (35), *Land Without Music* (36), *The Gaunt Stranger* (38), *The Four Just Men* (39), *Inspector Hornleigh on Holiday* (39), *Saloon Bar* (40), *Sailors Three* (40), *The Ghost Train* (41), *Atlantic Ferry* (41), *Charley's Big-Hearted Aunt* (41), *It's That Man Again* (42), *Time Flies* (44), *Master of Bankdam* (47), *Cardboard Cavalier* (48), many others.

FOREIGN CORRESPONDENT (US 1940). Hitchcock's first American thriller, a welcome return to his best form apart from the final message: 'Don't let the lights go out all over Europe!' Splendid moments in a Dutch windmill, a crashing aeroplane, and Westminster Cathedral.

the Foreign Legion has been taken reasonably seriously in the three versions of *Beau Geste*; the two versions of *Le Grand Jeu*; *Beau Sabreur*; *Rogues' Regiment*; *Ten Tall Men*; and *The Legion's Last Patrol*. It was sent up something wicked by Laurel and Hardy in *Beau Hunks* and *The Flying Deuces*; by Abbott and Costello *In the Foreign Legion*; and by the Carry On gang in *Follow That Camel*.

FOREMAN, CARL (1914–). American writer-producer-director. *So This Is New York* (w) (48), *The Clay Pigeon* (w) (49), *Home of the Brave* (w) (49), *Champion* (w) (49), *The Men* (w) (50), *Cyrano de Bergerac* (w) (50), *High Noon* (w) (52), *The Bridge on the River Kwai* (w) (57), *The Key* (w, p) (58), *The Guns of Navarone* (w, p) (61), *The Victors* (w, p, d) (63), *Born Free* (p) (65), *Mackenna's Gold* (p) (68), *The Virgin Soldiers* (69), etc. Now resident in Britain.

FOREST, MARK (1933–) (Lou Degni). American athlete and gymnast who has appeared in many Italian muscle-man epics: *The Revenge of Hercules, Maciste in the Valley of Kings, Goliath and the Giant*, etc.

forest fires have made a roaring climax for many films including *The Blazing Forest, Red Skies of Montana, Guns of the Timberland, The Big Trees* and *Ring of Fire*. None was more dramatic than the cartoon version in *Bambi*.

FORESTER, C. S. (1899–1966). British adventure novelist. Works filmed include *Captain Horatio Hornblower, The African Queen, Payment Deferred, The Pride and the Passion* ('The Gun').

FOREVER AND A DAY (US 1942). Originally conceived as a World War II charity appeals film called *Let the Rafters Ring*, this all-star production finally consisted of episodes in the life of an English family (and their house) from 1804 to 1942. Many hands were involved in the script, and there was a different director for each episode: René Clair, Edmund Goulding, Cedric Hardwicke, Frank Lloyd, Victor Saville, Robert Stevenson, Herbert Wilcox. Almost every Hollywood-based actor with English connections took part.

†FORMAN, MILOS (1932–   ). Czech director of realistic comedies: *Peter and Pavla* (64), *A Blonde in Love* (65), *The Firemen's Ball* (68)

†FORMBY, GEORGE (1905–1961). Lancashire comedian with a toothy grin and a ukelele, long popular in music halls. *Boots Boots* (debut) (33), *On the Dole* (34), *No Limit* (35), *Keep Your Seats Please* (36), *Feather Your Nest* (37), *Keep Fit* (37), *I See Ice* (38), *It's in the Air* (38), *Trouble Brewing* (39), *Come On, George* (39), *Let George Do It* (40), *Spare a Copper* (41), *Turned Out Nice Again* (41), *South American George* (dual role) (42), *Much Too Shy* (42), *Get Cracking* (43), *Bell-Bottom George* (43), *He Snoops To Conquer* (44), *I Didn't Do It* (45), *George in Civvy Street* (last film) (46). In 1939 was Britain's top box office star.

FORREST, SALLY (1928–   ) (Katharine Scully Feeney). American leading lady of the early 50s. *Not Wanted* (49), *Mystery Street* (50), *Excuse My Dust* (51), *The Strange Door* (51), *The Strip* (51), *Son of Sindbad* (55), *Ride the High Iron* (57), etc.

FORREST, STEVE (1924–   ) (William Forrest Andrews). American leading man, brother of Dana Andrews. *The Bad and the Beautiful* (52), *Phantom of the Rue Morgue* (54), *Prisoner of War* (54), *Bedevilled* (55), *The Living Idol* (57), *Heller in Pink Tights* (60), *The Yellow Canary* (63), *Rascal* (69), etc. TV series: *The Baron* (65).

FORSTER, RUDOLPH (1884–1968). German leading actor of heavy personality, seen abroad chiefly in *Die Dreigroschenoper* (*The Threepenny Opera*; as Macheath) (32).

FORSYTH, ROSEMARY (1944–   ). American leading actress. *Shenandoah* (debut) (65), *The War Lord* (65), *Texas Across the River* (66), *Fuzz* (69), *Where It's At* (69), *Whatever Happened to Aunt Alice?* (69).

FORSYTHE, JOHN (1918–   ) (John Freund). Smooth American leading man with Broadway experience. *Destination Tokyo* (43), *Captive City* (52), *Escape from Fort Bravo* (53), *The Trouble with Harry* (56), *The Ambassador's Daughter* (56), *Kitten with a Whip* (65), *Madame X* (66), *In Cold Blood* (67), *Topaz* (69), *The Happy Ending* (69), etc. TV series: *Bachelor Father* (57–62), *The John Forsythe Show* (65), *To Rome with Love* (69).

FORTY-NINTH PARALLEL (GB 1941). Producer-director team Michael Powell and Emeric Pressburger made this impressive all-star pro-paganda piece about a stranded submarine-load of Nazis on the run through Canada. Laurence Olivier, Leslie Howard and Anton Walbrook starred as assorted democrats; Eric Portman leapt to stardom as the chief Nazi.

FORTY-SECOND STREET (US 1933). Classic 'putting-on-a-show' musical from Hollywood's 'golden age', with a genuine backstage atmos-phere and a fairly caustic script. Music by Al Dubin and Harry Warren; directed by Lloyd Bacon with a cast including Warner Baxter, Ruby Keeler, Dick Powell, Ginger Rogers and Bebe Daniels.

FOR WHOM THE BELL TOLLS (US 1943). Ernest Hemingway's nove about an American living with guerrillas during the Spanish civil war, and sacrificing his life for their cause, was made by Sam Wood into a disappointingly tedious and self-satisfied film in which the whole cast struck unconvincing attitudes, mostly in broken English. Katina Paxinou won an Oscar for her performance; Gary Cooper and Ingrid Bergman seemed to wish they were else-where. The basic situation, incidentally, was borrowed ten years later by a Sterling Hayden second feature called *Fighter Attack*.

†FOSSE, BOB (1927–   ). American dancer who became a Broadway director. *Give a Girl a Break* (52), *Kiss Me Kate* (53), *My Sister Eileen* (also choreographed) (55), *The Pajama Game* (choreographed only) (57), *Sweet Charity* (directed and choreographed) (68).

FOSTER, BARRY (1931–   ). British actor, usually figuring as comic relief. *Sea of Sand* (56), *Yesterday's Enemy* (59), *King and Country* (64), *The Family Way* (66), *Robbery* (67), *Twisted Nerve* (68), etc. Much on TV.

FOSTER, DIANNE (1928–   ) (D. Laruska). Canadian leading lady who has made British and American films. *The Quiet Woman* (GB) (51), *Isn't Life Wonderful* (GB) (53), *Drive a Crooked Road* (US) (54), *The Kentuckian* (US) (55), *The Brothers Rico* (US) (57), *Gideon's Day* (GB) (58), *The Last Hurrah* (US) (58), *King of the Roaring Twenties* (61), etc.

FOSTER, JULIA (1941–   ). British leading lady, *The Small World of Sammy Lee* (63), *Two Left Feet* (63), *The System* (64), *The Bargee* (64), *One-Way Pendulum* (64), *Alfie* (66), *Half a Sixpence* (67), etc.

FOSTER, LEWIS (1900–   ). American director, former Hal Roach gag writer. *The Lucky Stiff* (also wrote) (48), *Manhandled* (also wrote) (49), *Captain China* (49), *The Eagle and the Hawk* (also wrote) (49), *Crosswinds* (51), *Those Redheads from Seattle* (also wrote) (53), *Top of the World* (55), *The Bold and the Brave* (56), *Tonka* (also wrote) (58), etc.

FOSTER, NORMAN (1900–   ) (Norman Hoeffer). American leading man of the early 30s: *Reckless Living* (31), *Steady Company* (32), *State Fair* (33), *Elinor Norton* (35), many others. Acted in and directed *I Cover Chinatown* (36); thereafter remained a director, with a rather patchy career. *Mr Moto's Last Warning* (38), *Ride, Kelly, Ride* (40), *Scotland Yard* (41), *Journey into Fear* (with Orson Welles) (42), *Rachel and the Stranger* (47), *Kiss the Blood off My Hands* (48), *Tell It to the Judge* (49), *Father Is a Bachelor* (50), *Woman on the Run* (50), *Navajo* (51), *Sky Full of Moon* (also wrote) (52), *Sombrero* (also wrote) (52), *Davy Crockett* (56), *The Nine Lives of Elfego Baca* (59), *Indian Paint* (64), *Brighty* (67), etc.

FOSTER, PRESTON (1902–   ). Handsome American leading man of the 30s, former shipping clerk and singer. *Nothing But the Truth* (debut) (30), *Life Begins* (31), *Two Seconds* (32), *Wharf Angel* (34), *The Informer* (35), *The Last Days of Pompeii* (35), *Annie Oakley* (36), *The Plough and the Stars* (37), *First Lady* (38), *News Is Made at Night* (38), *Geronimo* (39), *Moon over Burma* (40), *Northwest Mounted Police* (40), *Unfinished Business* (41), *Secret Agent of Japan* (42), *My Friend Flicka* (43), *The Bermuda Mystery* (44), *The Valley of Decision* (45), *The Last Gangster* (45), *The Harvey Girls* (46), *Ramrod* (47), *Green Grass of Wyoming* (48), *Tomahawk* (49), *The Tougher They Come* (51), *The Big Night* (52), *Kansas City Confidential* (53), *I the Jury* (55), *Destination 60,000* (58), *Advance to the Rear* (64), *The Time Travellers* (65), *Chubasco* (68), many others. TV series: *Waterfront* (54–56), *Gunslinger* (60).

FOSTER, STEPHEN (1826–1864). American songwriter of popular sentimental ballads: 'Old Folks at Home', 'Beautiful Dreamer', etc. Impersonated on screen by Dennis Morgan in *Harmony Lane* (35), Don Ameche in *Swanee River* (39), Bill Shirley in *I Dream of Jeannie* (52).

FOSTER, SUSANNA (1924–   ) (Suzan Larsen). American operatic singer and heroine of several 40s films. *The Great Victor Herbert* (40), *There's Magic in Music* (41), *Hearts in Springtime* (42), *Top Man* (43), *Phantom of the Opera* (43), *The Climax* (44), *Bowery to Broadway* (44), *This Is the Life* (44), *Frisco Sal* (45), *That Night with You* (45), etc.

FOULGER, BYRON (c. 1902–   ). American small-part actor, the prototype of the worried, bespectacled clerk. *The Prisoner of Zenda* (37), *Edison the Man* (40), *Sullivan's Travels* (41), *Since You Went Away* (44), *Champagne for Caesar* (49), *The Magnetic Monster* (53), *The Long Hot Summer* (59), *The Gnome-Mobile* (67), innumerable others.

FOUR DAUGHTERS. The three Lane sisters and Gale Page appeared as Claude Rains' musical daughters in this dollop of sweetness and light which despite its computerized script was a big hit in 1938. It can be credited with introducing the angry-young-man hero, and at the same time a new actor, John Garfield. All these components were reproduced the following year in a film called *Daughters Courageous* which however dealt with different people in a different milieu; the original characters then reappeared in *Four Wives* (39) and *Four Mothers* (40). *Four Sons* (40) was something else again, an anti-Nazi propaganda piece about the break-up of a German family. In 1955 the original *Four Daughters* was remade as a semi-musical, *Young at Heart*, with Doris Day and Frank Sinatra.

THE FOUR FEATHERS. A. E. W. Mason's novel of the old Empire, with heroism and cowardice in the Sudan after General Gordon's death, was magnificently filmed by Alexander Korda in 1939, with John Clements and Ralph Richardson. Much of the same footage reappeared in Zoltan Korda's 1955 remake *Storm over the Nile*, stretched into CinemaScope and not improved thereby. (The action scenes have also been used in several other films, e.g. *Zarak* [57], *Master of the World* [61], *East of Sudan* [64].) There was a British silent version in 1921 starring Harry Ham and Cyril Perceval, and a Hollywood one in 1928 starring Richard Arlen and Clive Brook.

THE FOUR HORSEMEN OF THE APOCALYPSE. In 1921 Rex Ingram directed a spectacular version of Ibanez' novel about love, war and death, notable for introducing Rudolph Valentino as a star. Vincente Minnelli remade it in 1962 with Glenn Ford and an updated script, but by now the entire conception seemed to belong to a Victorian novelette.

THE FOUR HUNDRED BLOWS (France 1958). This influential 'new wave' film, written and directed by François Truffaut, was basically a moving account of a small boy's adventures in the big city while on the run from an unhappy home and school life. Henri Decae's location photography was masterly.

FOUR STEPS IN THE CLOUDS (Italy 1942). A still enjoyable and historically significant step forward in Italian light realist comedy; a film full of sunshine and joie de vivre with little relation to the war then raging. Gino Cervi plays a young commuter who by a series of mischances spends twenty-four hours in complicated excitements before returning to his wife and family. Written by Giuseppe Amato, directed by Alessandro Blasetti.

FOURTEEN HOURS (US 1951). This suspenser based on the real case of a man who stood on a ledge threatening suicide and defied police to come and get him, was well written (John Paxton from an article by Joel Sayre) and directed (Henry Hathaway); it seemed at the time to point to new profitable combinations of actuality and entertainment, though there was some over-dramatization and a happy outcome was substituted for the real tragic one. Richard Basehart was in his element as the unfortunate central figure.

FOWLER, HARRY (1926–). British cockney actor on screen since the early 40s, often in cameo roles. *Those Kids from Town* (42), *Champagne Charlie* (44), *Hue and Cry* (46), *For Them That Trespass* (48), *I Believe in You* (52), *Pickwick Papers* (53), *Home and Away* (56), *Idle on Parade* (59), *Ladies Who Do* (63), *Doctor in Clover* (66), many others. TV series: *The Army Game, Our Man at St Mark's*.

FOWLEY, DOUGLAS (1911–). American character actor, in hundreds of films since 1932. Usually plays nervous gangster: best role probably the Hollywood director in *Singing in the Rain* (52). Produced and directed *Macumba Love* (59). TV series: *Pistols and Petticoats* (67).

FOX, JAMES (1939–). British leading man, who usually plays a weakling. Once a child actor, notable in *The Magnet* (50). *The Servant* (63), *Those Magnificent Men in Their Flying Machines* (65), *King Rat* (65), *The Chase* (65), *Thoroughly Modern Millie* (67), *Duffy* (68), *Isadora* (68), *Arabella* (69).

FOX, WILLIAM (1879–1952) (W. Friedman). Hungarian-American pioneer and executive, the Fox of 20th Century Fox. Moved from the garment industry into exhibition, production and distribution. *Upton Sinclair Presents William Fox*, a biography, was published in 1933.

FOXWELL, IVAN (1914–). British producer, in films since 1933. *No Room at the Inn* (47), *The Intruder* (51), *The Colditz Story* (54), *Manuela* (56), *A Touch of Larceny* (59), *Tiara Tahiti* (62), *The Quiller Memorandum* (66), *Decline and Fall* (also wrote) (68), etc.

FOY, BRYAN (1900–). American producer since 1924, mainly of low-budget co-features, among the most notable being *House of Wax* (53). Wrote the song 'Mr Gallagher and Mr Shean'.

FOY, EDDIE JNR (1905–). American vaudeville entertainer, son of another and one of the 'seven little Foys'. Occasional film appearances include *Fugitive from Justice* (40), *The Farmer Takes a Wife* (53), *Lucky Me* (54), *The Pajama Game* (57), *Bells Are Ringing* (60), *Thirty Is a Dangerous Age, Cynthia* (67), etc. TV series: *Fair Exchange*. Eddie Foy Snr (1854–1928) made no film appearances but was impersonated by Eddie Foy Jnr in *Yankee Doodle Dandy* and Bob Hope in *The Seven Little Foys*.

frame. A single picture on a strip of film. At normal sound projection speed, 24 frames are shown each second.

France's national film history falls into a pattern of clearly-defined styles. First of note was that of Louis Feuillade, whose early serials had tremendous panache. In the 20s came René Clair, with his inimitable touch for fantastic comedy, and a little later Jean Renoir, whose view of the human comedy was wider but equally sympathetic. Sacha Guitry contributed a series of rather stagey but amusing high comedies; Jean Vigo in his brief career introduced surrealism. Marcel Pagnol made a number of self-indulgent regional comedies which were hugely enjoyable but had little to do with cinema. Then beginning in the 30s came an unsurpassed group of adult entertainments from the writer-director team of Jacques Prevert and Marcel Carné; these were widely copied by less talented hands and the resulting stream of sex dramas, seldom less than competent, preserved the legend of the naughty French. Other notable directors were Julien Duvivier, the romantic; Jacques Becker, at his happiest in comedy; and Jacques Feyder, who generally made melodramas with flashes of insight. Henri-Georges Clouzot developed into the French Hitchcock, and Cocteau's art films reached a wide public. In the 40s Robert Bresson, Rene Clement and Jacques Tati all begun to make themselves felt. The 50s were in danger of becoming a dull period, with no new talent of note, when the 'new wave' (qv) changed the whole direction of French film-making and made some of the older hands look suddenly and undeservedly old-fashioned.

Among French male stars of note are Raimu, Michel Simon, Harry Baur, Fernandel, Louis Jouvet, Jean Gabin, Pierre Fresnay, Jean-Louis Barrault, Gérard Philippe and Jean-Paul Belmondo. Of the women, the most influential have been Ginette Leclerc, Michele Morgan, Danielle Darrieux, Arletty, Simone Signoret, Brigitte Bardot, and Jeanne Moreau.

FRANCE, C. V. (1868–1949). British stage character actor, most typically seen in films as dry lawyer or ageing head of household. *Lord Edgware Dies* (35), *Scrooge* (35), *Victoria the Great* (37), *A Yank at Oxford* (38), *If I Were King* (US) (39), *Night Train to Munich* (40), *Breach of Promise* (41), *The Halfway House* (44), etc.

FRANCEN, VICTOR (1888–   ). Belgian stage actor, occasionally in French films from 1920, but most familiar in Hollywood spy dramas during World War II. *Crepuscule d'Epouvante* (21), *Après l'Amour* (31), *Nuits de Feu* (36), *Le Roi* (36), *J'Accuse* (38), *Sacrifice d'Honneur* (38), *La Fin du Jour* (39), *Tales of Manhattan* (42), *Mission to Moscow* (43), *Devotion* (43), *The Mask of Dimitrios* (44), *The Conspirators* (44), *Passage to Marseilles* (44), *Confidential Agent* (45), *The Beast with Five Fingers* (46), *Le Nuit s'Acheve* (49), *The Adventures of Captain Fabian* (51), *Hell and High Water* (54), *Bedevilled* (55), *A Farewell to Arms* (58), *Fanny* (61), *Top-Crack* (66), many others.

FRANCIOSA, ANTHONY or TONY (1928–   ) (Anthony Papaleo). Italian-American leading actor with lithe movement and ready grin. *A Face in the Crowd* (debut) (57), *This Could Be the Night* (57), *A Hatful of Rain* (his stage role) (57), *Wild Is the Wind* (58), *The Long Hot Summer* (58), *The Naked Maja* (59), *Career* (59), *The Story on Page One* (59), *Go Naked in the World* (60), *Period of Adjustment* (62), *Rio Conchos* (64), *The Pleasure Seekers* (65), *A Man Could Get Killed* (65), *Assault on a Queen* (66), *The Swinger* (66), *Fathom* (GB) (67), *The Sweet Ride* (68), *In Enemy Country* (68), *A Man Called Gannon* (68), etc. TV series: *Valentine's Day* (61), *The Name of the Game* (68–69).

FRANCIS. The talking mule of several Universal comedies (1950–56) was the direct ancestor of TV's talking palomino *Mister Ed*, also produced by Arthur Lubin. Francis' first master was Donald O'Connor, but later Mickey Rooney took over the reins.

FRANCIS, ANNE (1932–   ). American leading lady of several 50s films: formerly model, with radio and TV experience. *Summer Holiday* (debut) (48), *So Young So Bad* (50), *Elopement* (52), *Susan Slept Here* (54), *Bad Day at Black Rock* (54), *The Blackboard Jungle* (55), *Forbidden Planet* (56), *Don't Go Near the Water* (57), *Girl of the Night* (60), *The Satan Bug* (65), *Funny Girl* (68), *The Love God* (69), etc. TV series: *Honey West* (64).

FRANCIS, CONNIE (1938–   ) (Constance Franconero). American pop singer who has had some light films built around her: *Where the Boys Are* (63), *Follow the Boys* (64), *Looking for Love* (65).

FRANCIS, FREDDIE (1917–   ). British cinematographer: *Mine Own Executioner* (47), *Time Without Pity* (57), *Room at the Top* (59), *Sons and Lovers* (AA) (60), *The Innocents* (61), many others. Latterly turned to direction with less distinguished results: *Two and Two Make Six* (61), *Paranoiac* (63), *The Evil of Frankenstein* (63), *Dr Terror's House of Horrors* (65), *The Skull* (65), *The Psychopath* (66), *Dracula Has Risen from the Grave* (68), etc.

FRANCIS, KAY (1899–1968) (Katharine Gibbs). 'Ladylike' American star popular in 30s. After stage experience: *The Coconuts* (29), *Raffles* (30), *Street of Chance* (30), *One-Way Passage* (32), *Trouble in Paradise* (32), *Cynara* (32), *I Loved a Woman* (33), *Wonder Bar* (34),

British Agent (34), *Living on Velvet* (35), *The White Angel* (36), *First Lady* (37), *In Name Only* (39), *It's a Date* (40), *The Feminine Touch* (41), *Little Men* (41), *Always in My Heart* (42), *Four Jills in a Jeep* (44), *Divorce* (45), *Wife Wanted* (last film) (46), etc.

FRANCIS, ROBERT (1930–1955). American leading man whose budding career was cut short by an air crash. *The Caine Mutiny* (54), *The Long Gray Line* (55), etc.

FRANCISCUS, JAMES (1934–   ). American leading man. *Four Boys and a Gun* (56), *I Passed for White* (60), *The Outsider* (61), *The Miracle of the White Stallions* (63), *Youngblood Hawke* (64), *The Valley of Gwangi* (69), *Marooned* (69), *Beneath the Planet of the Apes* (69), etc. TV series: *Naked City* (58), *Mr Novak* (63–64).

FRANCKS, DON (1932–   ). Canadian singer whose first notable film role was in *Finian's Rainbow* (68).

FRANJU, GEORGES (1912–   ). French director, former set designer. Co-founder of Cinémathèque Française. Best-known documentaries: *Le Sang des Bêtes* (49), *Hôtel des Invalides* (51), *Le Grand Melies* (51). Features: *La Tête contre les Murs (The Keepers)* (58), *Eyes without a Face* (59), *Spotlight on a Murderer* (61), *Thérèse Desqueyroux* (62), *Judex* (63).

FRANK, CHARLES (1910–   ). British director, former dubbing expert. *Uncle Silas* (47), *Intimate Relations* (53), etc.

FRANK, HARRIET: see RAVETCH, IRVING.

FRANK, MELVIN (c. 1917–   ). American comedy scriptwriter since 1942, often in collaboration with Norman Panama (*Star-Spangled Rhythm* [43], *Road to Utopia* [46], *Mr Blandings Builds His Dream House* [48], *Knock On Wood* [54], etc.). More recently they have produced their own films: *Road to Hong Kong* (62), *Strange Bedfellows* (65), etc. Frank alone produced and co-wrote *A Funny Thing Happened on the Way to the Forum* (66), *Buona Sera Mrs Campbell* (also directed) (68).

FRANKAU, RONALD (1894–1951). British stage and radio comedian with an 'idle rich' characterization. Occasional film appearances include *The Calendar* (31), *His Brother's Keeper* (39), *Double Alibi* (46), *The Ghosts of Berkeley Square* (47).

FRANKEL, BENJAMIN (1906–   ). British composer. Scores include *The Seventh Veil* (46), *Mine Own Executioner* (47), many others.

FRANKEL, CYRIL (1921–   ). British director, former documentarist with Crown Film Unit. *Devil on Horseback* (54), *Make Me an Offer* (55), *It's Great To Be Young* (56), *No Time for Tears* (57), *She Didn't Say No* (58), *Alive and Kicking* (58), *Never Take Sweets from a Stranger*

(61), *Don't Bother To Knock* (61), *On the Fiddle* (61), *The Very Edge* (63), *The Witches* (*The Devil's Own*) (66), *The Trygon Factor* (67), etc. Also directs TV films.

†FRANKENHEIMER, JOHN (1930–   ). Ebullient American director, formerly in TV. *The Young Stranger* (57), *The Young Savages* (61), *All Fall Down* (61), *The Manchurian Candidate* (62), *Birdman of Alcatraz* (62), *Seven Days in May* (64), *The Train* (64), *Seconds* (66), *Grand Prix* (67), *The Extraordinary Seaman* (68), *The Fixer* (68), *The Gypsy Moths* (69), *An Exile* (70).

FRANKENSTEIN. The 1931 Hollywood film, written by Robert Florey and directed by James Whale, borrowed as much from Wegener's *The Golem* (22) as from Mary Shelley's early 18th-century novel; but despite censorship problems the elements jelled, with Boris Karloff a great success as the monster, and a legend was born. Sequels included *Bride of Frankenstein* (35), *Son of Frankenstein* (39), *Ghost of Frankenstein* (41), *Frankenstein Meets the Wolf Man* (43), *House of Frankenstein* (45), *House of Dracula* (46), *Abbott and Costello Meet Frankenstein* (49); among those who took over from Karloff were Lon Chaney, Bela Lugosi and Glenn Strange. In 1956 the original story was remade in Britain's Hammer Studios under the title *The Curse of Frankenstein*; colour and gore were added, and sequels, with various monsters, came thick and fast: *The Revenge of Franken-stein* (58), *The Evil of Frankenstein* (63), *Frankenstein Created Woman* (67), *Frankenstein Must Be Destroyed* (69). A variation on the original monster make-up was used by Fred Gwynne in the TV comedy series. *The Munsters* (64–65). There have also been several recent American attempts to cash in on the name of Frankenstein in cheap exploitation pictures: *I Was a Teenage Frankenstein* (57), *Frankenstein 1970* (58), *Frankenstein Versus the Space Monsters* (65), etc. 1966 brought the Japanese *Frankenstein Conquers the World*.

FRANKLIN, PAMELA (1949–   ). British juvenile actress. *The Innocents* (61), *The Lion* (62), *Our Mother's House* (67), *The Night of the Follow-ing Day* (68), *The Prime of Miss Jean Brodie* (69), *Sinful Davey* (69), *David Copperfield* (69), etc.

FRANKLIN, SIDNEY (1893–   ). American producer-director, in Hollywood since leaving school. *Martha's Vindication* (d) (16), *Heart o' the Hills* (d) (19), *Dulcy* (d) (23), *Beverly of Graustark* (d) (26), *The Last of Mrs Cheyney* (d) (29), *Private Lives* (d) (31), *The Guardsman* (d) (32), *Smiling Through* (d) (32), *Reunion in Vienna* (d) (33), *The Barretts of Wimpole Street* (d) (33), *The Dark Angel* (d) (35), *The Good Earth* (d) (37), *On Borrowed Time* (p) (39), *Waterloo Bridge* (p) (40), *Mrs Miniver* (p) (42), *Random Harvest* (p) (42), *The White Cliffs of Dover* (p) (44), *The Yearling* (p) (46), *The Miniver Story* (p)

(50), *Young Bess* (p) (54), *The Barretts of Wimpole Street* (d) (57), many others. Gained Academy Award 1942 'for consistent high achievement'.

FRANKOVICH, MIKE (1910–   ). American screenwriter who turned producer and during the 50s ran Columbia's British organization; in 1963 was made head of world production. His personal productions include *Decameron Nights* (53), *Footsteps in the Fog* (55), *Joe Macbeth* (55), *Marooned* (69), *Cactus Flower* (69).

FRANZ, ARTHUR (1920–   ). American leading man, latterly character actor; radio, stage and TV experience. *Jungle Patrol* (debut) (48), *Sands of Iwo Jima* (49), *Abbott and Costello Meet the Invisible Man* (51), *The Sniper* (52), *Eight Iron Men* (52), *The Caine Mutiny* (54), *The Unholy Wife* (57), *Running Target* (58), *Hellcats of the Navy* (59), *Alvarez Kelly* (66), *Anzio* (68), etc.

FRANZ, EDUARD (1905–   ). American actor, usually of Jewish or foreign roles. *The Iron Curtain* (48), *The Magnificent Yankee* (51), *Dream Wife* (53), *White Feather* (55), *Man Afraid* (57), *The Four Skulls of Jonathan Drake* (59), *The Story of Ruth* (60), many others. TV series: *The Breaking Point*.

FRASER, BILL (1907–   ). British comic character actor, TV's 'Snudge'. Wide stage experience; film parts since 1938 usually bits till recently: *The Americanization of Emily* (65), *Joey Boy* (65), *Masquerade* (65), *I've Gotta Horse* (65), etc.

FRASER, JOHN (1931–   ). British juvenile lead with stage experience, sporadically in films since 1953. *Tunes of Glory* (59), *The Trials of Oscar Wilde* (60), *El Cid* (61), *Fury at Smugglers Bay* (61), *The Waltz of the Toreadors* (62), *Repulsion* (65), *Operation Crossbow* (65), *Isadora* (68), etc.

FRASER, LIZ (1933–   ). British character actress specializing in dumb cockney blondes. *Wonderful Things* (58), *I'm All Right, Jack* (59), *Two-Way Stretch* (60), *The Rebel* (61), *Double Bunk* (61), *Carry On Regardless* (61), *The Painted Smile* (leading role) (61), *Live Now Pay Later* (63), *The Americanization of Emily* (64), *The Family Way* (66), *Up the Junction* (68), etc.

FRASER, MOYRA (1923–   ). Australian comedienne in British stage and TV. Occasional films: *Here We Go Round the Mulberry Bush* (67), *Prudence and the Pill* (68), etc.

FRASER, RICHARD (1913–   ). Scottish-born leading man of some American second features in the 40s. *How Green Was My Valley* (41), *The Picture of Dorian Gray* (44), *Fatal Witness* (46), *The Cobra Strikes* (48), *Alaska Patrol* (51), etc. Now a TV sales executive.

FRASER, RONALD (1930–   ). Stocky British character actor, in films and TV since 1954. *The Sundowners* (59), *The Pot Carriers* (62), *The Punch and Judy Man* (63), *Crooks in Cloisters* (64), *The Beauty Jungle* (64), *The Flight of the Phoenix* (65), *The Killing of Sister George* (68), *Sinful Davey* (69), *Too Late the Hero* (69), etc.

FRATERNALLY YOURS: see SONS OF THE LEGION.

FRAWLEY, WILLIAM (1887–1966). American character actor with long vaudeville experience. In mainly comic roles as cigar-chewing gangsters, drunks, incompetent cops, etc. *Moonlight and Pretzels* (debut) (33), *Bolero* (33), *The Lemon Drop Kid* (34), *The General Died at Dawn* (36), *High, Wide and Handsome* (38), *One Night in the Tropics* (40), *Roxie Hart* (42), *Going My Way* (44), *Mother Wore Tights* (47), *Kiss Tomorrow Goodbye* (50), *The Lemon Drop Kid* (51), *Rancho Notorious* (52), hundreds of others. Latterly achieved greater fame in TV series; from 1951–60 in *I Love Lucy* and from 1960–63 in *My Three Sons*.

FRAZEE, JANE (c. 1919–   ) (Mary Jane Frahse). Vivacious American singer and leading lady of minor musicals in the 40s. *Rookies* (41), *Moonlight in Havana* (42), *Swing and Sway* (44), *Incident* (48), *Rhythm Inn* (last to date) (51), etc.

FREAKS (US 1932). Tod Browning's macabre drama set in a circus enjoyed a greater reputation than it deserved because it was unseen for thirty years owing to a censor's ban. Now it seems interesting but unsatisfactory.

FREDA, RICCARDO (1909–   ). Italian director who brings some style to exploitation pictures; former art critic. *Les Misérables* (46), *Theodora, Slave Express* (54), *I Vampiri* (57), *The Giant of Thessaly* (61), *The Terror of Dr Hichcock* (62), *The Spectre* (63), *Coplan FX 18 Casse Tout* (*The Exterminators*) (65), etc.

FREDERICK, PAULINE (1883–1938). American leading lady, in films from 1915. *Madame X, Bella Donna, Smouldering Fires*, etc. Later had small roles in sound films until *Thank You, Mr Moto* (37).

FREDERICKS, ELLSWORTH (* –   ). American cinematographer. *Invasion of the Body Snatchers* (55), *The Friendly Persuasion* (56), *Sayonara* (57), *High Time* (60), *Seven Days in May* (64), *Pistolero* (66), *The Power* (67), *Mister Buddwing* (67), etc.

free cinema. A term applied to their own output by a group of British documentarists of the 50s, e.g. Lindsay Anderson, Karel Reisz. Their aim was to make 'committed' films which cared about the individual and the significance of the everyday. The resulting films were not always better than those produced by professional units with more commercial intent. The most notable were *O Dreamland*,

Momma Don't Allow, *The March to Aldermaston*, *Every Day Except Christmas* and *We Are the Lambeth Boys*, the two latter films being sponsored by commercial firms.

FREED, ARTHUR (1894–   ) (Arthur Grossman). American lyricist of popular songs, usually with music by Nacio Herb Brown. Long associated with MGM as producer of musicals: *Cabin in the Sky* (43), *Meet Me in St Louis* (44), *On the Town* (49), *An American in Paris* (51), *Singing in the Rain* (with a score consisting entirely of his own songs) (52), *Band Wagon* (53), *Gigi* (58), others.

FREELAND, THORNTON (1898–   ). American director (from 1929), former cameraman. Mainly routine films include *Whoopee* (30), *Flying Down to Rio* (33), *Brewster's Millions* (GB) (35), *The Amateur Gentleman* (GB) (36), *Jericho* (GB) (37), *The Gang's All Here* (GB) (39), *Over the Moon* (GB) (39), *Too Many Blondes* (41), *Meet Me at Dawn* (47), *The Brass Monkey* (*Lucky Mascot*) (GB) (48), *Dear Mr Prohack* (GB) (49), etc.

FREEMAN, EVERETT (1911–   ). American writer, usually in collaboration. *Larceny Inc* (42), *Thank Your Lucky Stars* (43), *The Secret Life of Walter Mitty* (47), *Million Dollar Mermaid* (52), *My Man Godfrey* (57), *The Glass Bottom Boat* (66), *Where Were You When the Lights Went Out?* (also co-produced) (68), many others.

FREEMAN, HOWARD (1899–1967). American character actor, usually in comic roles as businessman on the make. *Pilot Number Five* (43), *Once Upon a Time* (44), *Take One False Step* (49), *Scaramouche* (52), *Remains To Be Seen* (53), *Dear Brigitte* (65), many others.

FREEMAN, KATHLEEN (c. 1919–   ). American character actress. *Bonzo Goes to College* (49), *Full House* (52), *Athena* (54), *The Fly* (58), *The Ladies' Man* (61), *The Disorderly Orderly* (65), etc.

FREEMAN, MONA (1926–   ). American leading lady of the 40s and 50s, specializing in teenage roles. *Till We Meet Again* (debut) (44), *Black Beauty* (46), *Dear Ruth* (47), *The Heiress* (49), *Streets of Laredo* (50), *Dear Brat* (51), *Jumping Jacks* (52), *Battle Cry* (55), *Before I Wake* (GB) (55), *Dragoon Wells Massacre* (57), *The World Was His Jury* (58), others.

FREEMAN, ROBERT (c. 1935–   ). British director, former fashion director and title artist (*A Hard Day's Night*, *Help*). *The Touchables* (68), *World of Fashion* (short) (68), *L'Echelle Blanche* (69).

FREEMAN, Y. FRANK (1890–   ). American executive, v.p. of Paramount in charge of the studio from 1938 until his retirement.

freeze frame. A printing device whereby the action appears to 'freeze' into a still, this being accomplished by printing one frame many times.

FREGONESE, HUGO (1908–   ). Argentine-born director, former journalist, in Hollywood from 1945. *One-Way Street* (50), *Saddle Tramp* (51), *Apache Drums* (51), *Mark of the Renegade* (52), *My Six Convicts* (52), *Decameron Nights* (53), *Blowing Wild* (54), *The Man in the Attic* (54), *The Raid* (53), *Black Tuesday* (54), *Seven Thunders* (GB) (57), *Harry Black* (58), *Marco Polo* (61), *Apaches Last Battle (Old Shatterhand)* (Ger.) (64), *Savage Pampas* (Sp.) (66), etc.

FRENCH, HAROLD (1897–   ). British stage actor and producer, in films since 1931. Directed *The House of the Arrow* (39), *Jeannie* (41), *Unpublished Story* (42), *The Day Will Dawn* (42), *Secret Mission* (42), *Dear Octopus* (43), *English Without Tears* (44), *Mr Emmanuel* (44), *Quie Weekend* (46), *My Brother Jonathan* (47), *The Blind Goddess* (48), *Quartet* (part) (48), *The Dancing Years* (49), *Trio* (part) (50), *Encore* (part) (51), *The Hour of 13* (52), *Isn't Life Wonderful* (53), *Rob Roy* (53), *Forbidden Cargo* (54), *The Man Who Loved Redheads* (55), etc.

FRENCH, VALERIE (1931–   ). British actress, in occasional Hollywood films. *Jubal* (56), *Garment Center* (57), *Decision at Sundown* (57), *The Four Skulls of Jonathan Drake* (59), *Shalako* (68), etc.

FREND, CHARLES (1909–   ). British director. *The Foreman Went to France* (42), *San Demetrio, London* (43), *Johnny Frenchman* (45), *Scott of the Antarctic* (48), *The Cruel Sea* (52), *Lease of Life* (55), *Barnacle Bill* (57), *Cone of Silence* (60), *Torpedo Bay* (It.) (62), many TV films, etc.

FRENZY (Sweden 1944). Written by Ingmar Bergman and directed by Alf Sjöberg, this melodrama about a sadistic schoolmaster reawakened interest in Swedish cinema after a lapse of nearly twenty years. With Stig Jarrel, Mai Zetterling, Alf Kjellin.

FRESNAY, PIERRE (1897–   ) (Pierre Laudenbach). Distinguished French stage actor who has made several films: *Marius* (debut) (31), *Fanny* (32), *César* (34), *The Man Who Knew Too Much* (GB) (34), *La Grande Illusion* (37), *Le Corbeau* (43), *Monsieur Vincent* (47), *God Needs Men* (50), *The Fanatics* (57), others.

FREUD (US 1962). A biographical film written by Charles Kaufman and Wolfgang Reinhardt, directed by John Huston in the actual Viennese locations, with a cast including Montgomery Clift, Susannah York and Larry Parks; but to little avail in terms of public response despite the sensational incidents depicted. Significant as a contrast to the Warner biographical films of the late 30s, which were very similar but hugely successful.

FREUD, SIGMUND (1856–1939). Viennese physician who became the virtual inventor of psycho-analysis and the discoverer of sexual inhibition as a mainspring of human behaviour; a gentleman, therefore, to whom Hollywood has every reason to be grateful.

FREUND, KARL (1890–1969). Czech-born cinematographer, famous for his work in German silents like *The Last Laugh* (24), *Metropolis* (26), *Variety* (26), *Berlin* (27), etc. Since in USA: *The Mummy* (33), (also directed), *Moonlight and Pretzels* (33) (directed only), *Madame Spy* (33) (directed only), *Mad Love* (35) (directed only), *Camille* (36), *The Good Earth* (AA) (37), *Marie Walewska* (38), *Pride and Prejudice* (40), *The Seventh Cross* (44), *Key Largo* (48), many others. Recently worked on TV series including *I Love Lucy*.

FRIEDHOFER, HUGO (1902–   ). American composer. Scores include *The Adventures of Marco Polo* (38), *China Girl* (42), *The Lodger* (44), *The Woman in the Window* (45), *The Best Years of Our Lives* (AA) (46), *Joan of Arc* (48), *Ace in the Hole* (51), *Above and Beyond* (52), *Vera Cruz* (54), *The Rains of Ranchipur* (55), *One-Eyed Jacks* (59), *The Secret Invasion* (64), etc.

FRIEDKIN, WILLIAM (1939–   ). American director, from TV. *The Night They Raided Minsky's* (68), *The Boys in the Band* (70).

FRIEND, PHILIP (1915–   ). British leading man with stage experience. *Pimpernel Smith* (41), *Next of Kin* (42), *The Flemish Farm* (43), *Great Day* (45), *My Own True Love* (US) (48), *Panthers Moon* (US) (50), *The Highwayman* (US) (51), *Background* (53), *Son of Robin Hood* (59), etc.

FRIESE-GREENE, WILLIAM (1855–1921). Pioneer British inventor who built the first practical movie camera in 1889. Died penniless; his life was the subject of *The Magic Box* (51).

FRINGS, KETTI (*   –   ) (Catherine Frings). American scenarist. *Hold Back the Dawn* (also original novel) (41), *Guest in the House* (44), *The Accused* (48), *Dark City* (50), *Because of You* (52), *Come Back Little Sheba* (53), *Foxfire* (55), etc.

FRITSCH, WILLY (1901–   ). Popular German leading man, in films since 1921. *The Spy* (28), *Congress Dances* (31), *Drei Von Der Tankstelle* (31) (and 55), *Amphitryon* (35), *Film Ohne Titel* (47), many others.

FROBE, GERT (1912–   ). German character actor first seen abroad as the downtrodden little man of *Berliner Ballade* (48); later put on weight and emerged in the 60s as an international semi-star, usually as villain. *The Heroes Are Tired* (55), *He Who Must Die* (56), *The Girl Rosemarie* (58), *The Testament of Dr Mabuse* (64), *Goldfinger* (64), *Those Magnificent Men in Their Flying Machines* (65), *Is Paris Burning?* (66), *De Rififi a Paname* (67), *Rocket to the Moon* (68), *Monte Carlo or Bust* (69), etc.

FROHLICH, GUSTAV (1902–   ). German actor (from *Metropolis* [26]) and director (*The Sinner* [51], etc.). Few of his films have been exported.

FROM HERE TO ETERNITY (US 1953: AA). A seething melodramatic attack on the US Army, this over-sexed, over-sentimentalized and thoroughly unattractive picture, from James Jones' 'realistic' novel, was extremely well directed by Fred Zinneman (AA) from a scenario by Daniel Taradash (AA). Photography by Burnett Guffey (AA), with solid performances from Burt Lancaster, Frank Sinatra (AA), Deborah Kerr, Montgomery Clift, Donna Reed (AA) and Ernest Borgnine.

FROM THIS DAY FORWARD (US 1945). An early example of American romantic realism, a simple love story shot on the streets of New York. Written by Hugo Butler; photographed by George Barnes; directed by John Berry; with Joan Fontaine and Mark Stevens.

THE FRONT PAGE. Ben Hecht and Charles MacArthur's tough, hard-boiled Broadway comedy was first filmed in 1930 by Lewis Milestone, with Lee Tracy as the fast-talking reporter who shields an escaped murderer, and Adolphe Menjou as his scheming editor. In 1940 Howard Hawks remade it as *His Girl Friday*, with a sex switch: Rosalind Russell played the reporter and Cary Grant her boss.

frost on movie windows is usually produced from a mixture of epsom salts and stale beer.

FRYE, DWIGHT (1899–1943). American character actor who made a corner in crazed hunchbacks. *Dracula* (30), *Frankenstein* (31), *The Vampire Bat* (33), *Bride of Frankenstein* (35), *Something to Sing About* (38), *Son of Monte Cristo* (41), *Frankenstein Meets the Wolf Man* (43), etc.

FRYER, ROBERT (c. 1919–   ). American producer, former casting director. *The Boston Strangler* (68), *The Prime of Miss Jean Brodie* (69), *Myra Breckenridge* (69), *The Salzburg Connection* (70).

THE FUGITIVE. Under this title there have been at least two silent adventures, two second feature westerns, one Polish and one Indian film. John Ford's *The Fugitive* (47) is deservedly the best known of these, a pictorially beautiful if depressing account of the last struggles of a 'whisky priest' in Mexico, from Graham Greene's book *The Power and the Glory*.

FULLER, LESLIE (1889–1948). Beefy British concert-party comedian who was popular in broad comedy films of the 30s. *Not So Quiet on the Western Front* (31), *Kiss Me, Sergeant* (31), *The Pride of the Force*

(33), *The Stoker* (35), *Captain Bill* (36), *Two Smart Men* (40), *The Middle Watch* (40), *Front Line Kids* (42), etc.

†FULLER, SAMUEL (1911–   ). American writer-director who has also produced most of his own pictures; which have normally been violent melodramas on topical subjects. *I Shot Jesse James* (49), *The Baron of Arizona* (50), *Fixed Bayonets* (51), *The Steel Helmet* (51), *Park Row* (52), *Pickup on South Street* (52), *Hell and High Water* (54), *House of Bamboo* (55), *Run of the Arrow* (55), *China Gate* (56), *Forty Guns* (57), *Verboten* (58), *The Crimson Kimono* (59), *Underworld USA* (60), *Merrill's Marauders* (62), *Shock Corridor* (64), *The Naked Kiss* (66).

FULTON, JOHN P. (1902–   ). American special effects photographer, responsible for the tricks in most of the *Invisible Man* series and other fantasy movies.

FU MANCHU. Sax Rohmer's oriental master-criminal featured in a series of British two-reelers in the 20s. Warner Oland played him in *The Mysterious Fu Manchu* (29), Boris Karloff in *Mask of Fu Manchu* (32), and Henry Brandon in *Drums of Fu Manchu* (41); otherwise he was oddly neglected until the current series starring Christopher Lee, beginning with *The Face of Fu Manchu* (65) and *Brides of Fu Manchu* (66).

funerals provided a starting point for *The Third Man*, *Frankenstein*, *The Great Man*, *Death of a Salesman* and *The Bad and the Beautiful*; figured largely in *The Premature Burial*, *The Mummy*, *The Egyptian*, *The Fall of the House of Usher*, *The Glass Key*, *I Bury the Living*, *Miracle in Milan*, *Doctor Zhivago* and *Hamlet*; and formed a climax for *Our Town*. In *Vampyr* the hero dreamed of his own funeral; and in *Holy Matrimony* Monty Woolley attended his own funeral, having arranged to have his valet's body mistaken for his. Funerals were taken lightly in *I See a Dark Stranger*, *Little Caesar*, *Kind Hearts and Coronets*, *Too Many Crooks*, *A Comedy of Terrors*, *Charade*, *The Wrong Box*, *I Love You Alice B. Toklas*, and above all *The Loved One*.

funfairs have provided fascinating settings for many a bravura film sequence. *The Wagons Roll at Night*, *Nightmare Alley* and Hitchcock's *The Ring* were set almost entirely on fairgrounds. Tawdry or 'realistic' funfairs were shown in *Jeanne Eagels*, *Saturday Night and Sunday Morning*, *Picnic*, and *Inside Daisy Clover*; glamorized or sentimentalized ones cropped up in *The Wolf Man*, *My Girl Tisa*, *Roseanna McCoy*, *The Great Ziegfeld* and *Mr and Mrs Smith*. Musicals like *On the Town*, *On the Avenue*, *Coney Island*, *Centennial Summer*, *State Fair* and *Down to Earth* had funfair sequences, and they are also used to excellent advantage in thrillers: *Brighton Rock*, *Spider Woman*, *The Third Man*, *Lady from Shanghai*, *Strangers on a Train*. Naturally funfairs are also marvellous places for fun: though not for Eddie Cantor in *Strike Me Pink*, Laurel and Hardy in *The Dancing Masters*, or Bob Hope (fired from a cannon) in *Road to Zanzibar*. The star who made the most of a funfair sequence was undoubtedly Mae West as the carnival dancer in *I'm No Angel*, in which she delivered her famous line: 'Suckers!' *The Beast from 20,000 Fathoms* was finally cornered in a funfair; *Dr Caligari* kept his cabinet in one.

FUNICELLO, ANNETTE (1942–   ). American leading lady, former juvenile actress; was host of Disney's TV Mickey Mouse Club, and in his films is known simply as 'Annette'. *Babes in Toyland* (61), *The Misadventures of Merlin Jones* (63), *Bikini Beach* (64), *The Monkey's Uncle* (65), *Fireball 500* (66), etc.

FUNNY FACE (US 1956). Slight but fashionable 50s musical with sophisticated design and colour effects by Richard Avedon. Directed by Stanley Donen, with Fred Astaire, Audrey Hepburn, Kay Thompson; tunes by Gershwin.

†FURIE, SIDNEY J. (1933–   ). Canadian director with a restless camera; came to Britain 1959, Hollywood 1966. *A Dangerous Age* (57), *A Cool Sound from Hell* (58), *The Snake Woman* (60), *Doctor Blood's Coffin* (61), *During One Night* (61), *Three on a Spree* (61), *The Young Ones* (62), *The Boys* (62), *The Leather Boys* (63), *Wonderful Life* (64), *The Ipcress File* (65), *The Appaloosa* (66), *The Naked Runner* (67). TV series: *Hudson's Bay* (59).

FURNEAUX, YVONNE (1928–   ). French leading lady in British films. *Meet Me Tonight* (52), *The Dark Avenger* (55), *Lisbon* (56), *The Mummy* (59), *La Dolce Vita* (59), *Enough Rope* (French) (63), *The Scandal* (French) (66), etc.

FURSE, JUDITH (1912–   ). British character actress who often plays District Nurses, matrons, heavy schoolmistresses, etc. Film debut *Goodbye Mr Chips* (39); later in *English Without Tears* (44), *Black Narcissus* (46), *The Man in the White Suit* (51), *Doctor at Large* (57), *Serious Charge* (59), etc.; also on stage.

FURSE, ROGER (1903–   ). British stage designer. *Henry V* (costumes only) (44), *The True Glory* (45), *Odd Man Out* (47), *Hamlet* (47), *Ivanhoe* (52), *Richard III* (56), *The Prince and the Showgirl* (57), *Saint Joan* (57), *Bonjour Tristesse* (58), *The Roman Spring of Mrs Stone* (61), *Road to Hong Kong* (62), etc.

FURTHMAN, JULES (1888–1966). American writer, usually in collaboration. *Treasure Island* (20), *The Way of All Flesh* (27), *Shanghai Express* (32), *Mutiny on the Bounty* (35), *Spawn of the North* (38), *Only Angels Have Wings* (39), *The Outlaw* (43), *To Have and Have Not* (44), *The Big Sleep* (46), *Nightmare Alley* (48), *Jet Pilot* (50) (released 57), *Peking Express* (51), many others.

FURY (US 1936). Fritz Lang's first and best American film, an indictment of lynch law, but with a happy ending. Important and influential, coming two years before *They Won't Forget*, it was also highly commercial, with a suspenseful plot and a star performance from Spencer Tracy as the man unjustly accused. Written by Lang and Bartlett Cormack from a novel by Norman Krasna; photographed by Joseph Ruttenberg, with music by Franz Waxman.

FUSCO, GIOVANNI (1906–   ). Italian composer, especially associated with Antonioni. *Cronaca di un Amore, Le Amiche, Il Grido, Hiroshima Mon Amour, L'Avventura, The Eclipse, The Red Desert, The War is Over*, etc.

FYFFE, WILL (1884–1947). Pawky Scots comedian, famous on the halls for his song 'I Belong to Glasgow'. Many films include *Happy* (34), *Annie Laurie* (36), *Cotton Queen* (37), *Owd Bob* (38), *The Mind of Mr Reeder* (39), *For Freedom* (40), *Neutral Port* (40), *Heaven Is Round the Corner* (44), *The Brothers* (47).

G

GAAL, FRANCESKA (1909–   ) (Fanny Zilveritch). Hungarian leading lady who made three American films: *The Buccaneer* (38), *Paris Honeymoon* (39), *The Girl Downstairs* (39).

GABEL, MARTIN (1912–   ). American character actor of stage and screen. *Fourteen Hours* (51), *M* (51), *The Thief* (52), *Tip on a Dead Jockey* (57), *Marnie* (64), *Divorce American Style* (66), *Lady in Cement* (68), etc. Also directed one film, *The Lost Moment* (48).

GABIN, JEAN (1904–   ) (Alexis Moncourge). Distinguished French actor, former Folies Bergère extra, cabaret entertainer, etc. His stocky virility and world-weary features have kept him a star from the early 30s. *Les Bas Fonds* (36), *Pepe Le Moko* (36), *La Grande Illusion* (37), *Quai des Brumes* (38), *La Bête Humaine* (38), *Le Jour Se Lève* (39), *Martin Roumagnac* (45), *Au delà des Grilles* (48), *Touchez Pas au Grisbi* (53), *French Can Can* (54), *Crime and Punishment* (56), *Les Grandes Familles* (58), *Le President* (60), *Le Cave Se Rebiffe* (61), *Le Baron de l'Ecluse* (62), *The Big Snatch* (*Melodie en Sous-Sol*) (62), *Maigret Voit Rouge* (63), *Monsieur* (64), *De Rififi à Paname* (66), *Le Jardinier d'Argenteuil* (66), *Le Soleil des Voyous* (67), *Le Tatoué* (68), *Fin de Journée* (69), many others.

†GABLE, CLARK (1901–1960). American leading man who kept his popularity for nearly thirty years, and was known as the 'king' of Hollywood. His big ears were popular with caricaturists; his impudent grin won most female hearts. *The Painted Desert* (30), *The Easiest Way* (31), *Dance Fools Dance* (31), *A Free Soul* (31), *The Finger Points* (31), *The Secret Six* (31), *Laughing Sinners* (31), *Night Nurse* (31), *Sporting Blood* (31), *Susan Lenox* (32), *Possessed* (32), *Hell's Divers* (32), *Polly of the Circus* (32), *Red Dust* (32), *Strange Interlude* (32), *No Man of Her Own* (32), *The White Sister* (32), *Dancing Lady* (33), *Hold Your Man* (33), *Night Flight* (33), *It Happened One Night* (AA) (34), *Men in White* (34), *Manhattan Melodrama* (34), *Chained* (34), *After Office Hours* (35), *Forsaking All Others* (35), *Mutiny on the Bounty* (35), *China Seas* (35), *Call of the Wild* (35), *Wife Versus Secretary* (36), *San Francisco* (36), *Cain and Mabel* (36), *Love on the Run* (37), *Parnell* (37), *Saratoga* (37), *Test Pilot* (38), *Too Hot to Handle* (38), *Idiot's Delight* (39), *Gone with the Wind* (39), *Strange Cargo* (40), *Boom Town* (40), *Comrade X* (40), *They Met in Bombay* (41), *Honky Tonk* (41), *Somewhere I'll Find You* (41); war service; *Adventure* (45), *The Hucksters* (47), *Homecoming* (48), *Command Decision*

(48), *Any Number Can Play* (49), *Key to the City* (50), *To Please a Lady* (50), *Across the Wide Missouri* (51), *Lone Star* (52), *Never Let Go* (GB) (53), *Mogambo* (53), *Betrayed* (54), *The Tall Men* (55), *Soldier of Fortune* (55), *The King and Four Queens* (56), *Band of Angels* (57), *Teacher's Pet* (58), *Run Silent Run Deep* (58), *But Not for Me* (59), *It Started in Naples* (59), *The Misfits* (60). Several biographies have been published, including one by his wife.

GABOR, EVA (1921–). Hungarian leading lady, sister of Zsa Zsa. *Forced Landing* (US) (41), *Song of Surrender* (US) (49), *Captain Kidd and the Slave Girl* (US) (54), *The Truth about Women* (GB) (58), etc. TV series: *Green Acres.* Published autobiography 1954: *Orchids and Salami.*

GABOR, ZSA ZSA (1919–) (Sari Gabor). Exotic international lead-ing lady, Miss Hungary of 1936, who has decorated films of many nations. *Lovely To Look At* (US) (52), *Lili* (US) (53), *Moulin Rouge* (GB) (53), *Public Enemy Number One* (Fr.) (54), *Diary of a Scoundrel* (US) (56), *The Man Who Wouldn't Talk* (GB) (57), *Touch of Evil* (US) (58), *Queen of Outer Space* (US) (59), *A New Kind of Love* (US) (63), *Arrivederci Baby* (66), *Picture Mommy Dead* (US) (66), etc. Published autobiography 1961: *My Story.*

GALEEN, HENRIK (c. 1882– *). Dutch writer-director, a leading figure of the German silent cinema. *The Student of Prague* (w, d) (12 and 26), *The Golem* (w, d) (14 and 20), *Nosferatu* (w) (22), *Waxworks* (w) (25), *Alraune* (w, d) (27), etc.

GALLAGHER, SKEETS (Richard) (c. 1902–1955). Cheerful American vaudevillian, in some films of the early talkie period. *The Racket* (28), *It Pays to Advertise* (31), *Merrily We Go to Hell* (32), *Riptide* (34), *Polo Joe* (37), *Zis Boom Bah* (42), *The Duke of Chicago* (50), etc.

GALLONE, CARMINE (1886–). Veteran Italian director, in films since 1913. Specialist in cinema opera, but came down to *Carthage in Flames* (59).

GALLU, SAMUEL (1918–). American director, former opera singer. *Theatre of Death* (66), *The Man Outside* (67), *The Limbo Line* (68).

GALSWORTHY, JOHN (1867–1933). British novelist who wrote about the upper middle class. Works filmed include *Escape* (30 and 48), *The Skin Game* (31), *Loyalties* (34), *Twenty-one Days* (39), *The Forsyte Saga* (49), etc.

GALTON, RAY (1930–). British comedy writer; with Alan Simp-son, co-author of successful TV series, e.g. *Hancock's Half-Hour*, *Steptoe and Son*; films include *The Rebel* (61), *The Wrong Arm of the Law* (62), *The Bargee* (64), *The Spy with a Cold Nose* (67), etc.

GALVANI, DINO (1890–1960). Distinguished-looking Italian actor, in films (mainly British) from 1908. *Atlantic* (30), *In a Monastery Garden* (32), *Midnight Menace* (35), *Mr Satan* (38), *It's That Man Again* (as Signor So-So) (42), *Sleeping Car to Trieste* (48), *Father Brown* (54), *Checkpoint* (57), *Bluebeard's Ten Honeymoons* (60), many others.

GAM, RITA (1928–   ). American stage leading lady who made film debut in the no-dialogue film *The Thief* (52); later in *Sign of the Pagan* (54), *Night People* (54), *Magic Fire* (55), *Mohawk* (56), *King of Kings* (61), etc.

gambling, in the indoor sport sense, is quite a preoccupation of film-makers. Gregory Peck in *The Great Sinner* played a man who made a great career of it, and in *The Queen of Spades* Edith Evans learnt the secret of winning at cards from the devil himself. Other suspenseful card games were played in *The Cincinnati Kid* and *Big Hand for a Little Lady*; snooker pool was the game in *The Hustler*; old-time Mississippi river-boats were the setting for *Mississippi Gambler*, *The Naughty Nineties*, *Frankie and Johnny* and a sequence in *The Secret Life of Walter Mitty*. Roulette, however, is the most spectacular and oft-used film gambling game, seen in *Robin and the Seven Hoods*, *Ocean's Eleven*, *The Big Snatch*, *Doctor No*, *La Baie des Anges*, *Quartet* (the 'Facts of Life' sequence), *Seven Thieves*, *The Las Vegas Story*, *The Big Sleep*, *Gilda*, *Kaleidoscope*, and many others. Second features with such titles as *Gambling House*, *Gambling Ship* and *Gambling on the High Seas* were especially popular in the 40s. Musically, the filmic high-point was undoubtedly the 'biggest floating crap game in the world' number in *Guys and Dolls*.

GANCE, ABEL (1889–   ). French producer-director, in films since 1910. Pioneer of wide-screen techniques, in *Napoleon* (26), etc. Also *Barberousse* (16), *J'Accuse* (19 and 37), *La Roue* (21), *La Fin du Monde* (31), *Lucrezia Borgia* (35), *Un Grand Amour de Beethoven* (36), *Paradis Perdu* (39), *La Tour de Nesle* (54), *The Battle of Austerlitz* (60), etc.

gangsters, a real-life American menace of the 20s, provided a new kind of excitement for early talkies like *Little Caesar* and *Public Enemy*, which told how their heroes got into criminal activities but didn't rub in the moral very hard. The pace of the action, however, made them excellent movies, and critics defended them against religious pressure groups. *Quick Millions*, *Scarface*, *Lady Killer*, *The Little Giant* and *Public Enemy's Wife* were among the titles which followed; then Warner Brothers cleverly devised a way of keeping their thrills while mollifying the protesters: they made the policeman into the hero, in films like *G-Men*, *I Am the Law*, *Bullets or Ballots*. By 1938 it seemed time to send up the whole genre in *A Slight Case of Murder*, with its cast of corpses, and in the later *Brother Orchid* the gangster-in-chief became a monk; yet in 1940 the heat had cooled off sufficiently to allow production of *The Roaring Twenties*, one of the most violent gangster movies of them all. The war made gangsters old-fashioned, but in the late 40s Cagney starred in two real psychopathic toughies, *White Heat* and *Kiss Tomorrow Goodbye*. After that the fashion was to parody gangsterism, in *Party Girl*, *Some Like It Hot*, and a couple of Runyon movies; but the success of a TV series called *The Untouchables* left the field wide open for redevelopment, and recent successes in the field included *Bonnie and Clyde* and *The St Valentine's Day Massacre*.

GARBER, MATTHEW (1956–   ). British child actor. *The Three Lives of Thomasina* (63), *Mary Poppins* (64), *The Gnomobile* (67).

GARBO, GRETA (1905–   ) (Greta Gustafson). One of the screen's greatest star personalities: whether or not she was a great actress, her beautiful features in close-up were enough to give her the stature almost of a goddess. Films in her native Sweden include *The Atonement of Gosta Berling* (24); after *Joyless Street* in Germany (25) she was taken to Hollywood by director Mauritz Stiller, and Louis B. Mayer rapidly built her into a legend. *Torment* (26), *Flesh and the Devil* (27), *Love* (27), *The Divine Woman* (28), *The Kiss* (29), *Anna Christie* ('Garbo Talks!') (30), *Susan Lenox* (31), *As You Desire Me* (32), *Romance* (32), *Mata Hari* (32), *Grand Hotel* (32–33), *Queen Christina* (33), *The Painted Veil* (34), *Anna Karenina* (35), *Camille* (36), *Marie Walewska* (38), *Ninotchka* (39), *Two-Faced Woman* (41), etc. After the comparative failure of the last-named, she retired and has not filmed again. Special Academy Award 1954 'for her unforgettable screen performances'. A biography, *Garbo*, by John Bainbridge, was published in 1955. (†Sound film list complete.)

THE GARDEN OF ALLAH. Robert Hichens' novel about a sophisticated woman whose husband turns out to be an escaped Trappist monk was filmed as a silent in 1917, with Tom Santschi and Helen Ware, and again in 1927 with Ivan Petrovitch and Alice Terry. The 1936 sound remake had excellent early colour, direction by Richard Boleslawski, and exotic performances from Charles Boyer and Marlene Dietrich.

GARDINER, REGINALD (1903–   ). British actor who perfected the amiable silly ass type. After stage experience played leads in early talkies: *The Lovelorn Lady* (32), *Borrow a Million* (34), etc. To Hollywood (36), and has remained there, playing supporting roles. *Born to Dance* (36), *Everybody Sing* (37), *Marie Antoinette* (38), *Sweethearts* (39), *The Great Dictator* (40), *My Life with Caroline* (41), *The Man Who Came to Dinner* (41), *Captains of the Clouds* (42), *The Immortal Sergeant* (43), *Molly and Me* (44), *Christmas in Connecticut*

(45), *Cluny Brown* (46), *Fury at Furnace Creek* (48), *Wabash Avenue* (50), *Halls of Montezuma* (51), *The Black Widow* (54), *Ain't Misbehaving* (55), *The Birds and the Bees* (56), *Mr Hobbs Takes a Vacation* (62), *Do Not Disturb* (65), many others. TV series: *The Pruitts of Southampton* (65).

GARDNER, AVA (1922–   ) (Lucy Johnson). American leading lady, once voted the world's most beautiful woman. *We Were Dancing* (debut) (40), *Highway to Freedom* (41), *Kid Glove Killer* (42), *Hitler's Madman* (43), *Ghosts on the Loose* (43), *Three Men in White* (44), *She Went to the Races* (45), *Whistle Stop* (46), *The Killers* (46), *The Hucksters* (47), *Singapore* (47), *One Touch of Venus* (48), *The Bride* (48), *The Great Sinner* (49), *East Side West Side* (50), *My Forbidden Past* (51), *Showboat* (51), *Pandora and the Flying Dutchman* (GB) (51), *Lone Star* (52), *The Snows of Kilimanjaro* (52), *Ride Vaquero* (53), *Mogambo* (53), *Knights of the Round Table* (54), *The Barefoot Contessa* (54), *Bhowani Junction* (56), *The Little Hut* (57), *The Naked Maja* (58), *On the Beach* (59), *The Angel Wore Red* (60), *Fifty-five Days at Peking* (62), *Seven Days in May* (64), *The Night of the Iguana* (64), *The Bible* (66), *Mayerling* (68), etc. Married at various times to Artie Shaw, Mickey Rooney, Frank Sinatra. A biography, *Ava*, by David Hanna, was published in 1960.

GARDNER, JOAN (1914–   ). British leading lady of the 30s who married Zoltan Korda. *Men of Tomorrow* (32), *Catherine the Great* (34), *The Scarlet Pimpernel* (35), *The Man Who Could Work Miracles* (36), *Dark Journey* (39), *The Rebel Son* (last to date) (39), etc.

GARFEIN, JACK (1930–   ). American stage and screen director, married to Carroll Baker. *End as a Man* (57), *Something Wild* (62).

†GARFIELD, JOHN (1913–1952) (Julius Garfinkle). American leading actor, usually in aggressive or embittered roles; formerly a star of New York's leftish Group Theatre. *Four Daughters* (38), *Blackwell's Island* (38), *They Made Me a Criminal* (39), *Juarez* (39), *Daughters Courageous* (39), *Dust Be My Destiny* (39), *Saturday's Children* (40), *Castle on the Hudson* (40), *Flowing Gold* (40), *The Sea Wolf* (41), *Out of the Fog* (41), *Tortilla Flat* (42), *Dangerously They Live* (42), *Air Force* (43), *The Fallen Sparrow* (43), *Thank Your Lucky Stars* (43), *Between Two Worlds* (44), *Destination Tokyo* (44), *Pride of the Marines* (45), *Nobody Lives Forever* (46), *The Postman Always Rings Twice* (46), *Humoresque* (46), *Body and Soul* (47), *Gentleman's Agreement* (48), *We Were Strangers* (48). *Force of Evil* (49), *Under My Skin* (50), *The Breaking Point* (50), *He Ran All the Way* (51).

GARGAN, ED (1902–1964). American character actor, brother of William Gargan; often seen as comedy cop or prizefighter's manager. *Gambling Ship* (34), *My Man Godfrey* (36), *Thanks for the*

Memory (38), *We're in the Army Now* (40), *A Haunting We Will Go* (42), *Wonder Man* (45), *Gallant Bess* (50), *Cuban Fireball* (last appearance) (52), etc.

GARGAN, WILLIAM (1905–). American leading man of the 30s, usually in 'good guy' roles; latterly character actor. Retired when left voiceless after operation. *Rain* (32), *The Story of Temple Drake* (33), *The Milky Way* (36), *You're a Sweetheart* (38), *They Knew What They Wanted* (40), *Cheers for Miss Bishop* (41), *Miss Annie Rooney* (42), *Till the End of Time* (46), *Strange Impersonation* (48), *The Argyle Secrets* (48), *Miracle in the Rain* (56), many others. TV series: *Martin Kane* (57). Brother of Ed Gargan.

GARLAND, BEVERLY (1926–) (Beverly Campbell). Pert leading lady of some Hollywood films; more successful later in TV. *D.O.A.* (49), *The Glass Web* (53), *The Desperate Hours* (55), *The Joker Is Wild* (57), *The Alligator People* (59), *Twice Told Tales* (63), *Pretty Poison* (68), *The Mad Room* (69), etc.

†GARLAND, JUDY (1922–1969) (Frances Gumm). American entertainer and leading lady who for many years in the 40s seemed to radiate the soul of show business. The child of vaudeville performers, on stage from five years old, she seemed later unable to stand the pace of her own success; but her resultant personal difficulties only accentuated the loyalty of her admirers. *Every Sunday* (short) (36), *Pigskin Parade* (36), *Broadway Melody of* 1938, *Thoroughbreds Don't Cry* (38), *Everybody Sing* (38), *Listen Darling* (38), *Love Finds Andy Hardy* (38), *The Wizard of Oz* (39), *Babes in Arms* (39), *Andy Hardy Meets a Debutante* (39), *Strike Up the Band* (40), *Little Nellie Kelly* (40), *Ziegfeld Girl* (41), *Life Begins for Andy Hardy* (41), *Babes on Broadway* (41), *For Me and My Gal* (42), *Presenting Lily Mars* (42), *Girl Crazy* (42), *Thousands Cheer* (guest) (43), *Meet Me in St Louis* (44), *Ziegfeld Follies* (44), *Under the Clock* (45), *The Harvey Girls* (46), *Till the Clouds Roll By* (guest) (46), *The Pirate* (47), *Easter Parade* (48), *Words and Music* (guest) (48), *In the Good Old Summertime* (49), *Summer Stock* (50), *A Star Is Born* (54), *Judgment at Nuremberg* (60), *A Child Is Waiting* (62), *I Could Go On Singing* (GB) (63). Special Academy Award 1939 'for her outstanding performance as a screen juvenile'.

GARMES, LEE (1897–). Distinguished American cinematographer, in Hollywood from 1916. Films include *The Grand Duchess and the Waiter* (26), *The Private Life of Helen of Troy* (27), *Disraeli* (29), *Lilies of the Field* (30), *Whoopee* (30), *Morocco* (30), *Dishonoured* (31), *City Streets* (31), *An American Tragedy* (31), *Shanghai Express* (AA) (32), *Scarface* (32), *Smilin' Through* (32), *Zoo in Budapest* (33), *Crime without Passion* (34), *The Scoundrel* (34), *Dreaming Lips* (GB) (37), *Angels over Broadway* (40), *Lydia* (41), *Jungle Book* (42), *Guest in the House*

(44), *Since You Went Away* (44), *Love Letters* (45), *Duel in the Sun* (46), *The Spectre of the Rose* (also co-produced) (46), *The Secret Life of Walter Mitty* (47), *The Paradine Case* (48), *Our Very Own* (50), *Detective Story* (51), *Actors and Sin* (also co-directed) (52), *The Desperate Hours* (55), *Land of the Pharaohs* (55), *The Big Fisherman* (59), *Hemingway's Adventures of a Young Man* (62), *Lady in a Cage* (64), *Big Hand for a Little Lady* (66), *How to Save a Marriage* (68).

GARNER, JAMES (1928–   ) (James Baumgarner). American leading man, usually in good-humoured roles. *Brink of Hell* (*Towards the Unknown*) (56), *Sayonara* (57), *Darby's Rangers* (58), *Up Periscope* (59), *Cash McCall* (60), *The Children's Hour* (*The Loudest Whisper*) (62), *The Great Escape* (63), *The Thrill of It All* (63), *Move Over, Darling* (63), *The Americanization of Emily* (64), *The Art of Love* (65), *A Man Could Get Killed* (66), *Duel at Diablo* (66), *Mister Buddwing* (66), *The Law and Tombstone* (67), *Grand Prix* (67), *The Pink Jungle* (67), *How Sweet It Is* (68), *Support Your Local Sheriff* (68), *Marlowe* (69), etc. TV series: *Maverick* (57–61), *Cheyenne* (62).

GARNER, PEGGY ANN (1931–   ). Former American child star: *In Name Only* (39), *The Pied Piper* (43), *Jane Eyre* (44), *A Tree Grows in Brooklyn* (44), *Junior Miss* (45), *Nob Hill* (45), *Home Sweet Homicide* (46), *Bob, Son of Battle* (47), *Sign of the Ram* (48), *The Loveable Cheat* (49), *Bomba the Jungle Boy* (49), *Teresa* (51), *Black Widow* (54), *Black Forest* (Ger.) (56), *The Cat* (67). Special Academy Award 1945 as 'outstanding child actress'. Recently has been seen on TV with her husband Albert Salmi.

GARNETT, TAY (1898–   ). American director, in films since 1920. Silent films include *The Spieler, Celebrity, Officer O'Brien*. Since sound: *Her Man* (also wrote) (30), *One-Way Passage* (also wrote) (32), *China Seas* (also wrote) (34), *Slave Ship* (36), *Joy of Living* (38), *Trade Winds* (also wrote) (38), *Slightly Honourable* (also wrote) (39), *Cheers for Miss Bishop* (also wrote) (41), *My Favourite Spy* (42), *Bataan* (43), *The Cross of Lorraine* (44), *Mrs Parkington* (44), *The Valley of Decision* (45), *Wild Harvest* (46), *The Postman Always Rings Twice* (46), *A Yankee in King Arthur's Court* (49), *Cause for Alarm* (also wrote) (51), *One Minute to Zero* (52), *Main Street to Broadway* (52), *The Black Knight* (GB) (54), *A Terrible Beauty* (*Night Fighters*) (GB) (60), *Cattle King* (*Guns of Wyoming*) (63), etc. Much TV work.

GARRETT, BETTY (1919–   ). Peppy American singer and actress with musical comedy experience. *Big City* (debut) (46), *Take Me Out to the Ball Game* (48), *On the Town* (49), *My Sister Eileen* (55), *The Shadow on the Window* (57), etc. Married to Larry Parks.

GARRICK, DAVID (1717–1779). Famous English actor who has been impersonated on screen by Cedric Hardwicke in *Peg of Old Drury* (34) and Brian Aherne in *The Great Garrick* (37).

GARRICK, JOHN (1902–   ) (Reginald Doudy). British stage actor of the 20s and 30s; made some film appearances, usually as 'the other man'. *The Lottery Bride* (US) (31), *Chu Chin Chow* (33), *Rocks of Valpre* (35), *Sunset in Vienna* (37), *The Great Victor Herbert* (US) (39), etc.

GARRISON, SEAN (1937–   ). American leading man. *Moment to Moment* (66), *Banning* (67), etc. TV series: *Dundee and the Culhane* (67).

†GARSON, GREER (1908–   ). Red-haired Anglo-Irish leading lady who after stage experience was cast as Mrs Chipping in *Goodbye Mr Chips* (39) and promptly went to Hollywood, where her gentle aristocratic good looks enabled her to reign as a star for ten years. *Remember* (39), *Pride and Prejudice* (40), *Blossoms in the Dust* (41), *When Ladies Meet* (41), *Mrs Miniver* (AA) (42), *Random Harvest* (42), *Madame Curie* (43), *Mrs Parkington* (44), *The Valley of Decision* (45), *Adventure* (45), *Desire Me* (47), *Julia Misbehaves* (48), *The Forsyte Saga* (49), *The Miniver Story* (50), *The Law and the Lady* (51), *Scandal at Scourie* (52), *Julius Caesar* (53), *Her Twelve Men* (53), *Strange Lady in Town* (54), *Sunrise at Campobello* (as Eleanor Roosevelt) (60), *The Singing Nun* (66), *The Happiest Millionaire* (67).

GASLIGHT. Patrick Hamilton's stage suspense thriller, about a Victorian wife being driven deliberately insane by her murderous husband, was perfectly filmed in Britain in 1939 by Thorold Dickinson with Anton Walbrook, Diana Wynyard and Frank Pettingell. MGM promptly bought and destroyed the negative, and in 1943 produced an opulent and inferior remake with Charles Boyer, Ingrid Bergman (AA) and Joseph Cotten, directed by George Cukor. In Britain this version was known as *The Murder in Thornton Square*; prints of the original version did survive and have been shown in America as *Angel Street*.

GASSMAN, VITTORIO (1922–   ). Italian actor and matinée idol, in occasional films since 1946. *Bitter Rice* (48), *Sombrero* (US) (53), *Rhapsody* (US) (54), *War and Peace* (56), *Tempest* (57), *The Love Specialist* (60), *Barabbas* (62), *The Devil in Love* (66), *Woman Times Seven* (67), etc.

GASTONI, LISA (1935–   ). Italian leading lady in British films. *The Runaway Bus* (54), *Man of the Moment* (55), *The Baby and the Battleship* (56), *Intent to Kill* (58), *Hello London* (59), etc.

GATE OF HELL (JIGOKUMON) (Japan 1953). Known principally for its outstanding use of Eastmancolour, this medieval legend was directed by Teinosuke Kinugasa and photographed by Kohei Suziyama. Academy Award 1954: 'best foreign film'.

GATES, LARRY (1915–   ). American character actor, often seen as small town merchant or middle-aged good guy. *Has Anybody Seen My Gal* (52), *The Girl Rush* (54), *Invasion of the Body Snatchers* (56), *Jeanne Eagels* (57), *Cat on a Hot Tin Roof* (58), *One Foot in Hell* (60), others.

GATES, NANCY (1926–   ). American leading lady of the 40s and 50s. *The Great Gildersleeve* (42), *The Spanish Main* (45), *The Atomic City* (52), *The Member of the Wedding* (53), *Suddenly* (54), *The Search for Bridey Murphy* (56), *The Brass Legend* (56), *Death of a Scoundrel* (56), *Some Came Running* (59), etc.

GAUDIO, TONY (1885–   ). Italian cinematographer, long in Hollywood. *The Mark of Zorro* (20), *The Temptress* (25), *Hell's Angels* (30), *All Quiet on the Western Front* (30), *Sky Devils* (32), *Bordertown* (35), *The Story of Louis Pasteur* (35), *Anthony Adverse* (AA) (36), *The Life of Emile Zola* (37), *The Adventures of Robin Hood* (38), *Juarez* (39), *The Letter* (40), *The Constant Nymph* (43), *The Red Pony* (49), many others.

GAUGE, ALEXANDER (1914–1960). Heavyweight British actor, Friar Tuck in TV's *Robin Hood* series. *The Interrupted Journey* (debut) (49), *Murder in the Cathedral* (51), *Pickwick Papers* (52), *Fast and Loose* (54), *Martin Luther* (55), *The Iron Petticoat* (56), *The Passing Stranger* (57), etc.

GAUMONT, LEON (1864–1946). Pioneer French inventor, producer and exhibitor. Founder of Gaumont Studios at Shepherds Bush, also Gaumont circuit, both later sold to Rank.

GAVIN, JOHN (1934–   ). American leading man. *A Time To Live and a Time To Die* (58), *Imitation of Life* (59), *Spartacus* (60), *A Breath of Scandal* (61), *Back Street* (61), *Romanoff and Juliet* (62), etc.; then after an absence, *Thoroughly Modern Millie* (67), *The Madwoman of Chaillot* (69). TV series: *Convoy* (65).

GAWTHORNE, PETER (1884–1962). Splendidly pompous-looking British stage actor, often seen as general, admiral or chief constable in comedies of the 30s. *Sunny Side Up* (US) (29), *Charlie Chan Carries On* (US) (31), *Jack's the Boy* (32), *The Iron Duke* (35), *Wolf's Clothing* (36), *Alf's Button Afloat* (38), *Ask a Policeman* (39), *Much Too Shy* (42), *The Case of Charles Peace* (49), *Five Days* (54), many others.

GAXTON, WILLIAM (1894–1963). American entertainer who made a few film appearances: *Fifty Million Frenchmen* (31), *Something to Shout About* (42), *Best Foot Forward* (43), *Tropicana* (44), *Diamond Horseshoe* (45), etc.

GAYNOR, JANET (1907–   ) (Laura Gainer). American leading lady of the 20s and 30s, immensely popular in simple sentimental films, especially when teamed with Charles Farrell. Played in many short comedies and Westerns; then *The Johnstown Flood* (26), *Seventh Heaven* (AA) (27), *Sunrise* (27), *Street Angel* (28), *Lucky Star* (29), *Sunny Side Up* (29), *High Society Blues* (30), *Daddy Longlegs* (31), *Delicious* (31), *Merely Mary Ann* (31), *Tess of the Storm Country* (32), *State Fair* (33), *Paddy the Next Best Thing* (33), *Carolina* (34), *The Farmer Takes a Wife* (35), *Ladies in Love* (36), *A Star Is Born* (37), *Three Loves Has Nancy* (38), *The Young in Heart* (39), etc.; retired 1939 apart from a mother role in *Bernardine* (57).

GAYNOR, MITZI (1930–   ) (Francesca Mitzi Marlene de Charney von Gerber). American leading lady of Hungarian descent, trained for opera and ballet, *My Blue Heaven* (debut) (50), *Take Care of My Little Girl* (51), *Golden Girl* (51), *The I Don't Care Girl* (52), *Bloodhounds of Broadway* (53), *There's No Business Like Show Business* (54), *Anything Goes* (56), *The Birds and the Bees* (56), *The Joker Is Wild* (57), *South Pacific* (58), *Surprise Package* (60), *For Love or Money* (63), etc.

GAYSON, EUNICE (1931–   ). British leading lady, also on stage. *Dance Hall* (50), *Street Corner* (53), *Out of the Clouds* (54), *Zarak* (57), *The Revenge of Frankenstein* (58), etc.

GAZZARA, BEN (1931–   ). American stage and TV actor. Films include *End as a Man* (57), *Anatomy of a Murder* (59), *Reprieve* (62), *The Young Doctors* (62), *A Rage to Live* (65), *The Bridge at Remagen* (69). TV series: *Arrest and Trial* (63), *Run for Your Life* (65–67).

GEER, WILL (1902–   ). American character actor with a penchant for sinister old men. *Lust for Gold* (49), *Broken Arrow* (50), *Tall Target* (51), etc.; then on stage for years. Recently, *Seconds* (66), *Bandolero* (68).

GEESINK, JOOP (1913–   ). Dutch puppeteer who in the late 30s made several shorts under the general heading of 'Dollywood'.

GEESON, JUDY (1950–   ). British leading lady who started with sexy teenage roles. *Berserk* (67), *To Sir With Love* (67), *Here We Go Round the Mulberry Bush* (67), *Prudence and the Pill* (68), *Hammerhead* (68), *Three into Two Won't Go* (69), *The Executioner* (69), etc.

GELIN, DANIEL (1921–   ). French leading man with stage experience. In films since 1941: *Rendezvous de Juillet* (49), *Edouard et Caroline* (50), *La Ronde* (50), *Les Mains Sales* (51), *Rue de l'Estrapade* (53), *Les Amants du Tage* (*The Lovers of Lisbon*) (54), *The Man Who Knew Too Much* (US) (55), *Charmants Garçons* (57), *There's Always a Price Tag* (58), *Carthage in Flames* (60), *The Season for Love* (65), *Black Sun* (66), many others.

THE GENERAL (US 1926). Famous Buster Keaton silent comedy-adventure with a Civil War setting and a train as co-hero. Basically a succession of impeccably-timed gags devised by Keaton himself.

The story was used by Walt Disney in somewhat more serious vein for *The Great Locomotive Chase* (56).

THE GENERAL DIED AT DAWN (US 1936). A rather pretentious melodrama which gave the impression of being backed by political thought, concerning an idealistic American's fight against a Chinese warlord. It paved the way for Hollywood involvement in the Spanish Civil War. Directed by Lewis Milestone, with Gary Cooper, Madeleine Carroll and Akim Tamiroff.

THE GENERAL LINE (THE OLD AND THE NEW) (Russia 1928). A brilliant semi-documentary, photographed by Tissé and directed by Eisenstein, intended as propaganda to introduce the newest and most productive methods to Soviet peasant farmers.

A GENERATION (Poland 1954). Andrzej Wajda's famous trilogy (the other two titles being *Kanal* [56], *Ashes and Diamonds* [58]) gave a vivid picture of life in wartime Poland. Its impact is largely responsible for the resurgence of that country's film industry during the last few years.

GENEVIEVE (GB 1953). A sophisticated comedy, written by William Rose and directed by Henry Cornelius, which marked a turn away from Ealing's polished innocence towards a more realistic Chelsea-based robustness. Despite many imitations its freshness and *joie de vivre* have not been equalled. Larry Adler's harmonica score immensely assisted the frolicsome story of a vintage car race from London to Brighton, and there were made-to-measure parts for Kenneth More, Kay Kendall, Dinah Sheridan and John Gregson.

GENINA, AUGUSTO (1892–1957). Italian pioneer director. *La Gloria* (13), *The White Squadron* (35), *Bengasi* (42), *Heaven Over the Marshes* (49), *Three Forbidden Stories* (52), *Maddalena* (54), *Frou Frou* (55), many others.

GENN, LEO (1905–   ). Bland British character actor, formerly a practising barrister. *Jump for Glory* (debut) (37), *Kate Plus Ten* (38), *Contraband* (40), war service, *The Way Ahead* (44), *Henry V* (44), *Caesar and Cleopatra* (45), *Green for Danger* (46), *Mourning Becomes Electra* (US) (48), *The Velvet Touch* (US) (48), *The Snake Pit* (US) (48), *The Wooden Horse* (50), *The Miniver Story* (50), *Quo Vadis* (51), *Plymouth Adventure* (US) (52), *Personal Affair* (53), *The Green Scarf* (55), *Beyond Mombasa* (56), *Lady Chatterley's Lover* (Fr.) (56), *Moby Dick* (56), *I Accuse* (57), *No Time To Die* (58), *Too Hot To Handle* (60), *The Longest Day* (62), *Fifty-five Days at Peking* (62), *Ten Little Indians* (65), *Circus of Fear* (67), etc. Also on stage and TV.

GENTLEMAN'S AGREEMENT (US 1948) (AA). An earnest indictment of anti-Semitism, written by Moss Hart from Laura Hobson's novel, and directed by Elia Kazan, with Gregory Peck and John Garfield. Not very lively as a film, but immensely significant to Hollywood as the first of a series of anti-racialist pictures.

GENTLEMEN PREFER BLONDES. Anita Loos' comic novel about a gold-digging 20s chorus girl on the make in the millionaire set was filmed in 1928 by Mal St Clair, with Ruth Taylor and Alice White, then in 1953 by Howard Hawks with Marilyn Monroe and Jane Russell.

GEORGE, GLADYS (1902–1954) (Gladys Clare). American leading actress with stage experience. *Straight Is the Way* (35), *Valiant Is the Word for Carrie* (37), *Madame X* (title role) (37), *The House across the Bay* (41), *The Maltese Falcon* (41), *Christmas Holiday* (44), *Steppin' in Society* (45), *The Best Years of Our Lives* (46), *Millie's Daughter* (47), *Undercover Girl* (50), *Detective Story* (51), *It Happens Every Thursday* (53), etc.

GEORGE, MURIEL (1883–1965). Plump, motherly British character actress who often played charladies or landladies. Music-hall background. *His Lordship* (debut) (32), *Yes Mr Brown* (33), *Dr Syn* (37), *A Sister to Assist 'Er* (leading role) (38), *Quiet Wedding* (40), *Dear Octopus* (43), *The Dancing Years* (49), *Simon and Laura* (55), many others.

GEORGE, SUSAN (1950–   ). British leading lady. *Billion Dollar Brain* (67), *The Strange Affair* (68), *All Neat in Black Stockings* (69), *Spring and Port Wine* (69).

GEORGY GIRL (GB 1966). The dying fall of Britain's 'new wave', this eccentric comedy cast Lynn Redgrave as a plain Jane who envies her glamorous but selfish girl friend; she finally settles for adopting the friend's unwanted baby and marriage to a lecherous business-man. Touches of zany black comedy did not give the wanted illusion of freshness. With James Mason and Charlotte Rampling; directed by Silvio Narizzano from Peter Nichols' rather desperate screenplay.

GERALD, JIM (1889–1958) (Jacques Guenod). French actor, in occasional films from 1911. *An Italian Straw Hat* (27), *La Chant au Marin* (31), *French Without Tears* (as le professeur) (39), *Boule de Suif* (45), *The Crimson Curtain* (52), *Father Brown* (54), *Fric Frac en Dentelles* (57), etc.

GERALD MCBOING BOING (US 1951). The first Stephen Bosustow cartoon for UPA, whose spareness of line and sharpness of wit con-trasted happily with Disney's chocolate-box period. It concerned a little boy who could speak only sounds. There were a couple of less successful sequels.

GERAY, STEVE (1904–   ) (Stefan Gyergyay). Hungarian character actor of stage and screen, usually seen as mild-mannered little fellow. In London from 1934, Hollywood from 1941. *Dance Band* (34), *Inspector Hornleigh* (39), *Man at Large* (41), *The Moon and Sixpence* (as Dirk Stroeve: best role) (42), *Night Train from Chungking* (43), *The Mask of Dimitrios* (44), *So Dark the Night* (leading role) (46), *Gilda* (46), *I Love Trouble* (48), *The Big Sky* (52), *Call Me Madam* (53), *The Birds and the Bees* (56), *Count Your Blessings* (59), many others.

GERASIMOV, SERGEI (1906–   ). Russian director, best known abroad for *And Quiet Flows the Don* (57). Formerly an actor.

GERING, MARION (1901– *). Polish/Russian director with long stage experience; in America from 1925. *The Devil and the Deep* (32), *Madame Butterfly* (33), *Rumba* (35), *Lady of Secrets* (36), *Thunder in the City* (GB) (37), *She Married an Artist* (38), *Sarumba* (also co-p) (50), etc.

German cinema had its most influential period in the years following World War I, when depression and despair drove directors into a macabre fantasy world and produced films like *The Golem*, *The Cabinet of Dr Caligari*, *Nosferatu*, *Warning Shadows* and *Waxworks*; it is also notable that many of the makers of these films later went to Hollywood and exerted a strong influence there. G. W. Pabst was somewhat more anchored to reality apart from the stylish *Die Dreigroschenoper*; Fritz Lang seemed primarily interested in the criminal mentality though he produced masterworks of prophecy and Teutonic legend. With the advent of Hitler most of Germany's genuine creative talent was forced abroad; the main achievements of the 30s were Leni Riefenstahl's colossal propaganda pieces *Triumph of the Will* and *Olympische Spiele*. The anti-British wartime films have their interest, but the post-war German cinema has not been influential, producing competent thrillers and comedies for the homemarket. Notable German players include Werner Krauss, Conrad Veidt, Marlene Dietrich, Anton Walbrook and Gert Frobe.

GERMAINE, MARY (1933–   ). British leading lady of the 50s. *Laughter in Paradise* (51), *Where's Charley* (52), *Women of Twilight* (53), *The Green Buddha* (last to date) (54), etc.

GERMI, PIETRO (1904–   ). Italian director, in films since 1945. *In the Name of the Law* (49), *The Road to Hope* (50), *Man of Iron* (56), *Maledotto Imbroglio (A Sordid Affair)* (59), *Divorce Italian Style* (61), *Seduced and Abandoned* (63), *The Birds the Bees and the Italians* (65), many others.

GERONIMO (1829–1909). Apache Indian chief who dealt destruction to the whites. Memorably impersonated by Chief Thundercloud in *Geronimo* (38), Jay Silverheels in *The Battle at Apache Pass* (52), Chuck Connors in *Geronimo* (62).

GERRARD, GENE (1892–   ) (Eugene O'Sullivan). Bouncy British star of musical comedy and farce, in films occasionally from 1912. Since sound: *Let's Love and Laugh* (30), *My Wife's Family* (32), *Lucky Girl* (32), *Let Me Explain, Dear* (33), *No Monkey Business* (35), *Wake Up Famous* (37), etc. Retired 1945.

GERSHENSON, JOSEPH (1904–   ). Russian musician, long in US. In films from 1920; head of Universal music department from 1941.

GERSHWIN, GEORGE (1899–1937). American popular composer of scores of songs and concert pieces. Contributed to many films. His biography was told in *Rhapsody in Blue* (45), and his music was used exclusively in *An American in Paris* (51). Three hitherto unpublished songs were even used in *Kiss Me Stupid* (64).

GERSHWIN, IRA (1896–   ). American lyricist, brother of George Gershwin. Has written for stage since 1918, films since 1931: *Delicious* (31), *Goldwyn Follies* (39), *Cover Girl* (44), *An American in Paris* (51), *Kiss Me Stupid* (64), many others.

GERTIE THE DINOSAUR. Early American cartoon character created by Winsor McKay in 1909.

GERTSMAN, MAURY (c. 1910–   ). American cinematographer. *Strange Confession* (45), *Terror by Night* (46), *Singapore* (47), *Rachel and the Stranger* (48), *One Way Street* (50), *Meet Danny Wilson* (52), *The World in My Corner* (55), *Kelly and Me* (57), *Gunfight in Abilene* (66), many others.

GERVAISE (France 1956). Written by Jean Aurenche and Pierre Bost from Zola's novel, directed by René Clement, this seamy story presented a vivid picture of 19th-century Paris, comparable with David Lean's Dickens films. Delightfully acted by Maria Schell, François Perier and Suzy Delair.

THE GHOST BREAKER. This American stage thriller by Paul Dickey and Charles W. Goddard, about an heiress's voodoo-haunted castle, was filmed in 1915 with H. B. Warner and in 1922 (directed by Alfred E. Green) with Wallace Reid. In 1940 George Marshall directed a talkie version as a vehicle for Bob Hope, and the result was an oddly successful combination of laughs and horror, with contributions from Willie Best, Paulette Goddard and Paul Lukas. (The title, incidentally, was made plural.) In 1953 Marshall remade it, with remarkable fidelity to the 1940 script, as a vehicle for Martin and Lewis under the title *Scared Stiff*, with Lizabeth Scott and Carmen Miranda; the results were hardly stimulating.

THE GHOST GOES WEST (GB 1936). René Clair showed British films a lighter touch than they had known before in this fantasy of a gay Scottish ghost who follows his castle when it is moved stone by stone to America. Robert Donat shone in a dual role.

THE GHOST TRAIN. This hugely successful British stage comedy-thriller by Arnold Ridley, about stranded passengers at a lonely Cornish station being used by gun-runners, was first filmed in 1928, directed by C. Bolvary, with Guy Newall as the silly-ass hero who turns out to be a policeman. A talkie version followed in 1931 with Jack Hulbert, directed by Walter Forde, who also directed the 1941 remake in which the leading role was split between Arthur Askey and Richard Murdoch.

ghosts : see *fantasy.*

GIALLELIS, STATHIS (1939–   ). Greek actor who went to Hollywood to play the lead in *America America* (63). Since in *Blue* (67).

GIBBONS, CEDRIC (1895–1960). American art director; worked for Edison 1915–17. Goldwyn 1918–24, MGM 1924 on. Films include *The Bridge of San Luis Rey* (AA) (29), *Pride and Prejudice* (AA) (40), *Blossoms in the Dust* (AA) (41), *Gaslight* (AA) (44), *The Yearling* (AA) (46), *Little Women* (AA) (49), *An American in Paris* (AA) (51), hundreds of others. Co-directed one film, *Tarzan and His Mate* (34). Designed the 'Oscar' statuette.

GIBBS, GERALD (c. 1910–   ). British cinematographer. *Whisky Galore* (49), *Fortune Is a Woman* (57), *The Man Upstairs* (58), *The Leather Boys* (63), *A Jolly Bad Fellow* (64), *Mister Ten Per Cent* (67), etc.

GIBSON, HELEN (1892–   ) (Rose August Wenger). American leading lady of the silent screen; of Swiss descent; married to Hoot Gibson. Former stunt girl. *The Hazards of Helen* (serial) (15), *No Man's Woman* (20), *The Wolverine* (21), etc.; appeared in *Hollywood Story* (51).

GIBSON, HOOT (1892–1962). American cowboy hero of silent films; in Hollywood from 1911 after real cowpunching experience. Films good-humoured but not memorable. *The Hazards of Helen* (15), *The Cactus Kid* (19), *The Denver Dude* (22), *Surefire* (24), *Spirit of the West* (32), *Powdersmoke Range* (33), *The Marshal's Daughter* (53), *The Horse Soldiers* (59), *Ocean's Eleven* (61), hundreds of others. Real Christian name: Edward.

GIBSON, WYNNE (1899–   ). American leading lady, from the chorus. *Nothing But the Truth* (30), *Ladies of the Big House* (32), *I Give My Love* (34), *The Captain Hates the Sea* (34), *Gangs of New York* (38), *Café Hostess* (40), *The Falcon Strikes Back* (43), many others.

GIDDING, NELSON (c. 1915–   ). American scenarist. *I Want To Live* (58), *Odds against Tomorrow* (59), *Nine Hours to Rama* (61), *The Inspector* (62), *The Haunting* (64), *Lost Command* (66), etc.

GIDGET. American teenage heroine of a number of American surfing comedy-romances typical of the early 60s; also, in 1965, a TV series.

†GIELGUD, JOHN (1904–   ). Distinguished British stage actor who has made occasional films. *Insult* (32), *The Good Companions* (32), *Secret Agent* (36), *The Prime Minister* (as Disraeli) (40), *Julius Caesar* (53), *Richard III* (56), *The Barretts of Wimpole Street* (57), *Saint Joan* (57), *Becket* (64), *The Loved One* (65), *Chimes at Midnight* (66), *The Charge of the Light Brigade* (68), *Assignment to Kill* (68), *The Shoes of the Fisherman* (68), *Oh What a Lovely War* (69), *Julius Caesar* (70).

GIFFORD, ALAN (c. 1905–   ). American character actor in British films. *It Started in Paradise* (52), *Lilacs in the Spring* (54), *The Iron Petticoat* (56), *A King in New York* (57), *Too Young to Love* (60), *Carry On Cowboy* (66), *Arrivederci Baby* (66), etc. Much on TV.

GIFFORD, FRANCES (1922–   ). American leading lady of the 40s, trained as lawyer. *Hold That Woman* (40), *My Son Alone* (42), *Tarzan Triumphs* (43), *She Went to the Races* (45), *Little Mister Jim* (46), *Luxury Liner* (48), *Riding High* (49), *Sky Commando* (53), etc.; career subsequently halted by ill-health.

GIGI (US 1958) (AA). Colette's novel of a *fin-de-siècle* Parisian cocotte was filmed straight in the 40s with Daniele Delorme, but is now best known in the form of this American musical, directed by Vincente Minnelli (AA) with a Lerner and Loewe score (AA). Cecil Beaton's designs (AA) shared honours with Leslie Caron, Maurice Chevalier and Louis Jourdan. The film won 8 Academy Awards.

GIGLI, BENIAMINO (1890–1958). Famous Italian tenor who starred in several films: *Ave Maria* (37), *Pagliacci* (42), *Night Taxi* (50), etc.

GILBERT, BILLY (1894–   ). American character comedian usually seen as a fat, excitable Italian. In films since 1929, after vaudeville experience: a memorable stooge for Laurel and Hardy, the Three Stooges and the Marx Brothers. *Noisy Neighbours* (debut) (29), *The Music Box* (32), *Sutter's Gold* (37), *Snow White and the Seven Dwarfs* (as the voice of Sneezy) (37), *Blockheads* (38), *Destry Rides Again* (39), *The Great Dictator* (as Goering) (40), *His Girl Friday* (40), *Tin Pan Alley* (41), *Anchors Aweigh* (45), *Down Among the Sheltering Palms* (52), *Five Weeks in a Balloon* (62), many others.

GILBERT, JOHN (1895–1936) (John Pringle). American leading man of the 20s. From a theatrical family, he worked his way from bit parts to romantic leads, but sound revealed his voice to be less dashing than his looks. *Should a Woman Tell* (19), *Ladies in Love* (21), *The Count of Monte Cristo* (22), *A Man's Mate* (23), *Cameo Kirby* (23), *The Merry Widow* (25), *The Big Parade* (25), *La Bohème* (26), *Love* (27), *Flesh and the Devil* (27), *Man, Woman and Sin* (28), *The Cossacks* (28), *Desert Nights* (29), *Redemption* (30), *The Way of a Sailor* (32), *Queen Christina* (33), *The Captain Hates the Sea* (34), etc.

GILBERT, LEWIS (1920–   ). British director; originally child actor, later documentarist. *The Little Ballerina* (47), *Time Gentlemen Please* (52), *Albert RN* (53), *The Sea Shall Not Have Them* (54), *Reach for the Sky* (56), *The Admirable Crichton* (57), *Carve Her Name with Pride* (58), *Ferry to Hong Kong* (59), *Sink the Bismarck* (60), *The Greengage Summer* (61), *HMS Defiant* (62), *The Seventh Dawn* (64), *Alfie* (65), *You Only Live Twice* (67), *The Adventurers* (69), etc.

GILBERT, PAUL (1924–   ) (Paul MacMahon). American comedy dancer, former trapezist. *So This Is Paris* (55), *The Second Greatest Sex* (55), *You Can't Run Away from It* (56), *Women of the Prehistoric Planet* (66), etc.

GILCHRIST, CONNIE (1904–   ). American character actress of stage and screen. *Billy the Kid* (41), *The Hucksters* (47), *A Letter to Three Wives* (49), *The Man in the Grey Flannel Suit* (56), *Some Came Running* (58), *Auntie Mame* (59), *Say One For Me* (59), *A House Is Not a Home* (64), *Sylvia* (65), *Tickle Me* (65), *Fuzz* (69), etc. TV series: *Long John Silver* (56).

GILDA (US 1946). A highly professional example of the glossy *film noir* coming out of Hollywood in the somewhat dejected period following World War II, when victory had turned to ashes. Everyone in this tale is cynical and at least partly corrupt: George Macready as the nominal villain evokes more sympathy than hero (Glenn Ford) or heroine (Rita Hayworth). Charles Vidor's direction is showy but controlled, and Hayworth's song numbers (including 'Put the Blame on Mame') show her at her most torrid. Other films of this time and genre include *Till the End of Time*, *The Blue Dahlia*, *Johnny O'clock*, *Build My Gallows High* and *The Strange Love of Martha Ivers*.

GILLETTE, WILLIAM (1855–1937). American stage actor famous for his personification of *Sherlock Holmes*, which he played on film in 1916.

GILLIAT, LESLIE (1917–   ). British producer, brother of Sidney Gilliat, with whom he usually works.

GILLIAT, SIDNEY (1908–   ). British writer-producer-director, in films since 1927; worked on scripts of *Rome Express* (33), etc. Long association with Frank Launder began 1937; together they wrote *A Yank at Oxford* (37), *The Lady Vanishes* (38), *Night Train to Munich*

(40), *The Young Mr Pitt* (41) ; wrote, produced and directed *Millions Like Us* (43), *Two Thousand Women* (44), *Waterloo Road* (44), *I See a Dark Stranger* (45), *The Rake's Progress* (45), *Green for Danger* (47), *London Belongs to Me* (49), *State Secret* (50), *The Constant Husband* (55), *Only Two Can Play* (62), *Joey Boy* (65), many others including three 'St Trinians' films. A director of British Lion.

GILLIE, JEAN (1915–1949). British leading lady, former chorine. *School for Stars* (35), *Brewster's Millions* (35), *While Parents Sleep* (36), *Sweet Devil* (38), *Tilly of Bloomsbury* (40), *Sailors Don't Care* (40), *The Gentle Sex* (43), *Tawny Pipit* (44), *Decoy* (US) (47), *The Macomber Affair* (US) (47), etc.

GILLING, JOHN (1912–   ). British writer-director who has turned out dozens of crime and adventure pot-boilers since the war. *The Greed of William Hart* (w) (48), *The Man from Yesterday* (w, d) (49), *No Trace* (w, d) (50), *Mother Riley Meets the Vampire* (w, d) (52), *The Voice of Merrill* (d) (52), *The Gamma People* (w, d) (55), *Odongo* (w, d) (56), *Interpol* (w, d) (57), *High Flight* (d) (57), *The Man Inside* (w, d) (58), *Idle on Parade* (d) (59), *The Flesh and the Fiends* (w, d) (59), *The Challenge* (w, d) (60), *Fury at Smuggler's Bay* (w, d) (61), *Shadow of the Cat* (w, d) (62), *Pirates of Blood River* (w, d) (62), *The Scarlet Blade* (w, d) (63), *The Brigand of Kandahar* (w, d) (64), *The Plague of the Zombies* (w, d) (65), *The Mummy's Shroud* (67), many others.

GILLINGWATER, CLAUDE (1870–1939). American stage actor who came to films to play irascible old men. *Little Lord Fauntleroy* (21), *Dulcy* (23), *Daddies* (24), *Daddy Long Legs* (31), *The Captain Hates the Sea* (34), *Prisoner of Shark Island* (36), *Conquest* (37), *Café Society* (39), etc.

GILLIS, ANN (1927–   ) (Alma O'Connor). Former American child star (*The Garden of Allah* [36], *Tom Sawyer* [38], *Little Men* [39], *All This and Heaven Too* [40], etc.) ; adult films routine. Now resident in Britain ; frequently on TV.

GILLMORE, MARGALO (1897–   ). American stage actress in occasional films. *The Happy Years* (50), *High Society* (56), *Gaby* (56), etc.

GILMORE, LOWELL (1907–1960). American general purpose actor. *Calcutta* (47), *Dream Girl* (48), *Tripoli* (50), *Lone Star* (52), *Plymouth Adventure* (52), etc.

GINGOLD, HERMIONE (1897–   ). British revue comedienne who delights in grotesque characters. Occasional films include *Someone at the Door* (36), *Meet Mr Penny* (39), *The Butler's Dilemma* (43), *Cosh Boy* (52), *Pickwick Papers* (52), *Our Girl Friday* (53), *Bell, Book and Candle* (US) (58), *Gigi* (US) (58), *The Music Man* (US) (61),

I'd Rather Be Rich (US) (64), *Harvey Middlemann, Fireman* (US) (65), *Munster Go Home* (US) (66), etc.

GIRARD, BERNARD (c. 1929–   ). American director. *Green-Eyed Blonde* (57), *As Young As We Are* (58), *Dead Heat on a Merry-Go-Round* (66), *The Mad Room* (69), *Man Without Mercy* (69), etc. TV credits include *Medic, Hitchcock, Twilight Zone.*

GIRARDOT, ANNIE (1931–   ). French leading lady. *Thirteen at Table* (56), *Maigret Sets a Trap* (58), *Vivre pour Vivre* (67), *Les Gauloises Bleues* (68), *Dillinger Is Dead* (69), *A Man I Like* (69), etc.

GIRARDOT, ETIENNE (1856–1939). Dapper French character actor, in many American plays and films. *Twentieth Century* (34), *Clive of India* (35), *Go West Young Man* (37), *Professor Beware* (38), *The Hunchback of Notre Dame* (40), etc.

GIROTTI, MASSIMO (1918–   ). Italian leading man, seen abroad in *Obsession* (42), *Caccia Tragica* (47), *Fabiola* (47), *Bellissima* (51), *Aphrodite* (57), *Theorem* (68), etc.

GISH, DOROTHY (1898-1968) (Dorothy de Guiche). Famous American silent star, in films for D. W. Griffith from 1912: *Hearts of the World, Orphans of the Storm*, etc. 1928–44: on stage. Occasional films since: *Our Hearts Were Young and Gay* (44), *The Whistle at Eaton Falls* (51), *The Cardinal* (63), etc.

GISH, LILLIAN (1896–   ) (Lillian de Guiche). Famous American silent star, sister of Dorothy Gish, and also a D. W. Griffith discovery. *Birth of a Nation* (14), *Intolerance* (16), *Broken Blossoms* (18), *Way Down East* (20), *Orphans of the Storm* (22), *The Scarlet Letter* (26), etc. From mid-20s spent much time on stage, but filmed occasionally: *Annie Laurie* (27), *His Double Life* (34), *The Commandos Strike at Dawn* (43), *Miss Susie Slagle's* (46), *Duel in the Sun* (46), *Portrait of Jennie* (48), *Night of the Hunter* (55), *Orders to Kill* (58), *The Unforgiven* (59), *Follow Me Boys* (66), *The Comedians* (67), etc. Published autobiography 1969: *The Movies, Mr Griffith, and Me.*

GIVOT, GEORGE (1903–   ). American character actor, usually in hearty roles. *When's Your Birthday* (37), *Marie Walewska* (38), *Du Barry Was a Lady* (43), *Riff Raff* (46), *Captain Blood Fugitive* (52), *Miracle in the Rain* (56), etc.

glass shot. Usually a scenic shot in which part of the background is actually painted on a glass slide held in front of the camera and carefully blended with the action. In this way castles, towns, etc., may be shown on a location where none exist, without the expense of building them.

GLEASON, JACKIE (1916–   ). Chubby American entertainer, in night clubs from 1940, films (small roles) from 1941. Big TV success in 50s: *The Life of Riley*, *The Honeymooners*, *The Jackie Gleason Show*. Starred in films *The Hustler* (61), *Blood Money* (62), *Gigot* (63), *Requiem for a Heavyweight* (63), *Soldier in the Rain* (64), *Skidoo* (68), *How to Commit Marriage* (69), *Don't Drink the Water* (69), etc.

GLEASON, JAMES (1886–1959). American character actor noted for hard-boiled comedy roles, usually in Brooklynese. On stage from infancy; also wrote several plays. *A Free Soul* (30), *Orders Is Orders* (GB) (33), *Murder on the Bridle Path* (36), *The Higgins Family* (38), *On Your Toes* (39), *Meet John Doe* (41), *Here Comes Mr Jordan* (41), *A Guy Named Joe* (43), *Arsenic and Old Lace* (44), *Once Upon a Time* (44), *A Tree Grows in Brooklyn* (44), *Captain Eddie* (45), *Down to Earth* (47), *The Bishop's Wife* (48), *Come Fill the Cup* (51), *Suddenly* (54), *The Last Hurrah* (58), many others. His wife LUCILLE GLEASON (1886–1947) and son RUSSELL GLEASON (1908–1945) also appeared occasionally in films, and all three were together in *The Higgins Family* (38) and four subsequent episodes.

THE GLENN MILLER STORY (US 1953). Influential in giving a strong nostalgic twist to the aimless pop music of the 50s, this sentimental biography of the well-liked bandleader was otherwise a routine production, with a characteristic performance from James Stewart.

GLENNON, BERT (1893–1967). Distinguished American cinematographer. *The Ten Commandments* (23), *Woman of the World* (26), *Java Head* (34), *The Hurricane* (38), *Drums along the Mohawk* (39), *Stagecoach* (39), *They Died with Their Boots On* (41), *Destination Tokyo* (44), *The Red House* (47), *Wagonmaster* (50), *Operation Pacific* (50), *The Big Trees* (52), *House of Wax* (53), *Sergeant Rutledge* (60), many others.

GLENVILLE, PETER (1913–   ). British stage director who has made occasional films, usually of theatrical successes: *The Prisoner* (54), *Me and the Colonel* (58), *Summer and Smoke* (60), *Term of Trial* (61), *Becket* (64), *Hotel Paradiso* (66), etc.

THE GLORIOUS ADVENTURE (GB 1921). A restoration drama directed by J. Stuart Blackton, notable as the first British feature in a colour process (Prizmacolour). Not an artistic success.

GLOVER, JULIAN (1935–   ). British general purpose actor chiefly on stage and TV. *Tom Jones* (63), *Girl with Green Eyes* (64), *I Was Happy Here* (66), *Alfred the Great* (69), *The Adding Machine* (69), etc.

GLYN, ELINOR (1864–1943). Extravagant British romantic novelist whose 'daring' *Three Weeks* was filmed in Hollywood in 1924 and proved both sensational and influential.

GLYNNE, MARY (1898–1954). British stage actress of the well-bred school. Films include *The Cry of Justice* (19), *The Hundredth Chance*

(20), *The Good Companions* (as Miss Trant) (32), *Emil and the Detectives* (34), *Scrooge* (35), *The Heirloom Mystery* (last film) (37), etc.

G-MEN (US 1935). Following public outcry about glamorized gangster films, James Cagney went over to the law in this competent semi-documentary about J. Edgar Hoover's men. Directed by William Keighley, with a shoot-'em-up climax which is still rousing.

GOBEL, GEORGE (1920–). American TV comedian of 'little man' appeal. Made two films, *The Birds and the Bees* (remake of 'The Lady Eve') (56), *I Married a Woman* (57).

GODARD, JEAN-LUC (1930–). Semi-surrealist French writer-director of the 'new wave', his talent often muffled by incoherent narrative. *À Bout de Souffle* (*Breathless*) (60), *Une Femme Est Une Femme* (61), *Vivre Sa Vie* (62), *Le Petit Soldat* (63), *Les Carabiniers* (63), *Bande à Part* (64), *Une Femme Mariée* (64), *Alphaville* (65), *Pierrot Le Fou* (66), *Made in USA* (66), *Weekend* (67).

GODDARD, PAULETTE (1911–) (Marion Levy). Pert American leading lady; a former Goldwyn girl chosen by Chaplin to star opposite him in *Modern Times* (36). (She later married him.) A popular heroine of the 40s. *The Young in Heart* (39), *The Cat and the Canary* (39), *The Women* (39), *The Great Dictator* (40), *The Ghost Breakers* (40), *Northwest Mounted Police* (40), *Nothing But the Truth* (41), *Hold Back the Dawn* (41), *Reap the Wild Wind* (42), *The Lady Has Plans* (42), *The Crystal Ball* (43), *So Proudly We Hail* (43), *Standing Room Only* (44), *I Love a Soldier* (44), *Kitty* (45), *Diary of a Chambermaid* (45), *Suddenly It's Spring* (46), *Unconquered* (47), *My Favourite Brunette* (47), *An Ideal Husband* (GB) (47), *Hazard* (48), *On Our Merry Way* (48), *Bride of Vengeance* (49), *Anna Lucasta* (49), *Bandit General* (Mex.) (50), *Babes in Baghdad* (52), *Vice Squad* (53), *Sins of Jezebel* (53), *The Stranger Came Home* (GB) (54), *Time of Indifference* (66), etc.

GODFREY, BOB (1921–). British animator: shorts include *Polygamous Polonius, The Do-It-Yourself Cartoon Kit, The Plain Man's Guide to Advertising*, etc.

GODFREY, PETER (1899–). British stage actor and producer who in the 30s directed two quickies, subsequently went to Hollywood and remained to direct routine films. *Unexpected Uncle* (41), *Highways by Night* (42), *Hotel Berlin* (45), *Christmas in Connecticut* (45), *The Two Mrs Carrolls* (46), *Cry Wolf* (46), *Escape Me Never* (47), *The Decision of Christopher Blake* (48), *He's a Cockeyed Wonder* (50), *The Great Jewel Robber* (51), *Please Murder Me* (56), etc. Much TV work.

GODSELL, VANDA (c. 1919–   ). British character actress, usually in blowsy roles. *The Large Rope* (54), *Hour of Decision* (57), *Hell Is a City* (60), *This Sporting Life* (63), *The Earth Dies Screaming* (64), *Who Killed the Cat?* (66), etc.

GODZILLA. A Japanese monster creation first seen in the film of that name in 1955. Apparently closely related to *tyrannosaurus rex*, he has since suffered at the hands of King Kong and the Thing in inferior sequels.

GOETZ, BEN (1891–   ). American executive, long with MGM and in charge of their British studios in the 40s.

GOETZ, WILLIAM (1903–   ). American producer, in films since 1923, chiefly with Fox and Universal. As independent, has latterly produced *The Man from Laramie* (55), *Sayonara* (57), *They Came to Cordura* (58), *Me and the Colonel* (58), *Song Without End* (59), etc.

GOFF, IVAN (1910–   ). Australian-born screenwriter, in Hollywood from 1945. Has often collaborated with BEN ROBERTS (*White Heat* [49], *Captain Hornblower* [51], *The Rogues* [TV series], etc.).

GOING MY WAY (US 1944: AA). Produced and directed by Leo McCarey (AA) from his own story, this chunk of sweetness and light about a singing priest in a poor district was immensely popular and had several imitators. Bing Crosby (AA) and Barry Fitzgerald (AA) each won new laurels. A TV series of the same name, made in 1963, starred Gene Kelly, but he neither sang nor danced in it. *The Bells of St Mary* (45) also starred Crosby as Father O'Malley and was a kind of sequel.

GOLAN, GILA (c. 1940–   ). Hollywood leading lady of indeterminate background, being a European war orphan of probable Polish-Jewish parentage. *Ship of Fools* (65), *Our Man Flint* (66), *Three on a Couch* (66), *The Valley of Gwangi* (69), etc.

GOLAN, MENAHEM (1931–   ). Israeli director. *Sallah* (66), *Tevye and His Seven Daughters* (68), *What's Good for the Goose* (GB) (69), etc.

GOLD, ERNEST (1921–   ). Viennese-American composer. *Too Much Too Soon* (57), *On the Beach* (59), *Exodus* (AA) (60), *Judgment at Nuremberg* (60), *A Child Is Waiting* (62), *Pressure Point* (62), *It's a Mad Mad Mad Mad World* (63), *Ship of Fools* (65), *The Secret of Santa Vittoria* (69), etc.

GOLD, JACK (1930–   ). British TV director who moved into films with *The Bofors Gun* (68), *The Reckoning* (69).

GOLD, JIMMY: see THE CRAZY GANG.

GOLDBECK, WILLIS (* –). American director, former writer (co-author of *Freaks*). *Dr Gillespie's New Assistant* (42), *Between Two Women* (44), *She Went to the Races* (45), *Love Laughs at Andy Hardy* (46), *Johnny Holiday* (50), *Ten Tall Men* (51), etc.

THE GOLD DIGGERS. This Broadway play by Avery Hopwood, about a group of girls in search of millionaire husbands, was filmed in 1923 under its original title, in 1929 as *Gold Diggers of Broadway* and in 1951 as *Painting the Clouds with Sunshine*. It also figured largely in the plot of *The Greeks Had a Word for Them* (1932), which was the basis of *How to Marry a Millionaire* (53) and the resulting TV series of the latter title. *Gold Diggers of 1933* was the first of five annual Warner musicals loosely based on the theme, their lethargic plots being more or less compensated by Busby Berkeley's kaleidoscopic dance ensembles.

GOLDNER, CHARLES (1900–1955). Austrian character actor, in Britain from the 30s. *Room for Two* (40), *Brighton Rock* (47), *One Night With You* (48), *Third Time Lucky* (48), *Give Us This Day* (49), *Black Magic* (49), *Shadow of the Eagle* (50), *The Captain's Paradise* (54), etc.

THE GOLD RUSH (US 1924). Often accepted as Chaplin's greatest comedy, this sentimental farce played against a background of snow and ice has wonderfully-timed moments, though most of the fun is near the beginning and pathos takes over too firmly later on. Photographed by Rollie Totheroh.

GOLDONI, LELIA (c. 1938–). American actress who became well-known after *Shadows* (59), but made only *Hysteria* (64) afterwards.

GOLDSMITH, JERRY (* –). American composer. Recent scores include *The Manchurian Candidate* (62), *The Prize* (63), *Seven Days in May* (64), *Lilies of the Field* (64), *In Harm's Way* (65), *The Trouble with Angels* (66), *Stagecoach* (66), *The Blue Max* (66), *Seconds* (66), *The Sand Pebbles* (66), *In Like Flint* (67), etc.

GOLDSTONE, RICHARD (1912–). American producer since 1934. *The Set Up* (48), *The Tall Target* (52), *The Devil Makes Three* (52), etc. Later involved in Cinerama; also TV series *Adventures in Paradise*.

GOLDWYN, SAMUEL (1884–) (Samuel Goldfish). Polish-American producer, in Hollywood from 1910. Co-producer *The Squaw Man* (1913); a top producer ever since, with a high reputation for star-making; has always refused to make any but family films; famous for 'Goldwynisms' like 'Include me out', mostly invented. Films since sound include *Arrowsmith* (31), *Roman Scandals* (33), *Barbary Coast* (35), *Dodsworth* (36), *Dead End* (37), *The Adventures of Marco Polo* (38), *Wuthering Heights* (39), *The Westerner* (40), *The Little Foxes*

(41), *Up In Arms* (44), *The Best Years of Our Lives* (special AA) (46), *The Bishop's Wife* (48), *Hans Christian Andersen* (52), *Guys and Dolls* (55), *Porgy and Bess* (59), scores of others.

THE GOLEM (Germany 1920). This classic legend, filmed again many times in Europe, was written and directed by Henrik Galeen and Paul Wegener; the latter also played the clay monster brought to life by a rabbi to save the persecuted Jews. Brilliant Grimm-like medieval sets make the second part of the film still fresh, and both in detail and general development it was closely copied in *Frankenstein* (30). Photographed by Karl Freund.

GOMBELL, MINNA (c. 1900–   ) (also known as Winifred Lee and Nancy Carter). American character actress of the 30s and 40s, usually in hard-boiled roles. *Doctors' Wives* (debut) (31), *The Thin Man* (34), *Babbitt* (35), *Banjo on My Knee* (37), *The Great Waltz* (38), *The Hunchback of Notre Dame* (39), *Boom Town* (40), *A Chip Off the Old Block* (44), *Man Alive* (46), *Pagan Love Song* (51), *I'll See You in My Dreams* (52), etc.

GOMEZ, THOMAS (1905–   ). Bulky American stage character actor who became a familiar villain or detective in Hollywood films. *Who Done It* (42), *Phantom Lady* (44), *The Dark Mirror* (46), *Singapore* (47), *Ride the Pink Horse* (47), *Key Largo* (48), *Force of Evil* (49), *That Midnight Kiss* (rare comedy role) (49), *Anne of the Indies* (51), *Macao* (52), *Sombrero* (52), *Las Vegas Shakedown* (54), *The Magnificent Matador* (55), *The Conqueror* (55), *Trapeze* (56), *But Not for Me* (59), *John Paul Jones* (59), *Summer and Smoke* (61), *Stay Away Joe* (68), *Beneath the Planet of the Apes* (69), many others. Also on TV.

GONE WITH THE WIND (US 1939: AA). For many years the longest film (220 minutes) ever to be released in the Western Hemisphere, this enormously successful romance of the American Civil War, from Margaret Mitchell's novel, was a splendidly professional job. It starred Vivien Leigh (AA), Clark Gable, Leslie Howard and Olivia de Havilland; Victor Fleming (AA) directed most of it, with contributions from George Cukor and Sam Wood. Ernest Haller (AA) and Ray Rennahan (AA) were cinematographers, and the production was designed by William Cameron Menzies. The Technicolor which was so splendid at the time now seems less impressive. Producer David O. Selznick had to release through MGM in order to get Gable's services, and that company has reissued it many times with immense profit. In 1968 an 'adapted' negative was made for showing in 70 mm.

GOODBYE MR CHIPS (GB 1939). A highly successful product of MGM's short-lived British studio under Michael Balcon 1937–39, this sentimental biography of a schoolmaster, from James Hilton's novel, was impeccably produced, with a brilliant performance from

Robert Donat (AA). Directed by Sam Wood. Remade in 1969 as a semi-musical with Peter O'Toole, directed by Herbert Ross.

THE GOOD COMPANIONS (GB 1932). J. B. Priestley's sprawling comic novel of English life was filmed by Victor Saville in rather primitive style, but its very *naiveté* remains infectious, and there are attractive performances by Edmund Gwenn, Jessie Matthews, Max Miller and others. Remade by J. Lee-Thompson in 1957, with Eric Portman and Janette Scott, with only fair success.

GOODLIFFE, MICHAEL (1914–). British stage actor often cast as officer, professional man, diplomat, etc. *The Small Back Room* (debut) (48), *The Wooden Horse* (50), *Rob Roy* (53), *The Adventures of Quentin Durward* (55), *The Battle of the River Plate* (56), *A Night To Remember* (58), *Sink the Bismarck* (60), *The Trials of Oscar Wilde* (60), *Jigsaw* (62), *The Seventh Dawn* (64), many others.

GOODMAN, BENNY (1910–). American clarinettist and bandleader whose film appearances include *Hollywood Hotel* (38), *Hello Beautiful* (42), *The Gang's All Here* (44), *Sweet and Lowdown* (44), *A Song Is Born* (48). Provided the music for *The Benny Goodman Story* (55), in which he was portrayed by Steve Allen.

GOODRICH, FRANCES (* –). American screenwriter, almost always in collaboration with her husband ALBERT HACKETT. Scripts since 1933 include *Naughty Marietta* (35), *Another Thin Man* (38), *The Hitler Gang* (44), *It's a Wonderful Life* (46), *Summer Holiday* (47), *Father of the Bride* (50), *Seven Brides for Seven Brothers* (54), *The Diary of Anne Frank* (also stage play) (60), many others.

GOODWIN, BILL (1910–1959). American character actor, in films from 1941, who usually played friendly professional types, e.g. the impresario in *The Jolson Story* (46). Also: *Henpecked* (42), *Fairy Tale Murder* (45), *Jolson Sings Again* (50), *Lucky Me* (54), *Going Steady* (58), etc.

GOODWIN, HAROLD (c. 1924–). British character actor usually seen as cockney serviceman or small-time crook. *Dance Hall* (50), *The Card* (52), *The Cruel Sea* (53), *The Dam Busters* (55), *Sea of Sand* (58), *The Mummy* (59), *The Bulldog Breed* (61), *The Comedy Man* (63), *The Curse of the Mummy's Tomb* (64), *Frankenstein Must Be Destroyed* (69), many others.

GOODWIN, RON (* –). British composer. *I'm All Right, Jack* (59), *The Trials of Oscar Wilde* (60), *Postman's Knock* (62), *Lancelot and Guinevere* (63), *633 Squadron* (64), *Operation Crossbow* (65), *Those Magnificent Men in Their Flying Machines* (65), *The Alphabet Murders* (65), etc.

GOODWINS, LESLIE (1899–1969). British-born director, in Hollywood for many years. Films mainly routine second features, e.g. 'Mexican Spitfire' series (39–44), *Glamour Boy* (39), *Pop Always Pays* (40), *Silver Skates* (43), *Murder in the Blue Room* (44), *What a Blonde* (45), *The Mummy's Curse* (46), *Gold Fever* (52), *Fireman Save My Child* (54), *Paris Follies of* 1956.

GOOLDEN, RICHARD (1895–   ). British character actor, on stage and screen for many years, usually in henpecked or bewildered roles; created the radio character of Old Ebenezer the night watchman. *Whom the Gods Love* (38), *Meet Mr Penny* (38), *Mistaken Identity* (43), etc.

GORCEY, LEO (1915–1969). Pint-sized American actor, one of the original Dead End Kids. After *Dead End* (37) and several subsequent films featuring the gang, he headed the splinter group, The Bowery Boys, and made innumerable comedy second features through the 40s and early 50s, his screen personality being that of the tough, wisecracking, basically kindly Brooklyn layabout. His father BERNARD GORCEY (1888–1955), a vaudevillian who had been in *Abie's Irish Rose* (29), often appeared with him in these films.

GORDON, BERT I. (1922–   ). American producer of small independent trick films. *The Amazing Colossal Man* (57), *Cyclops* (also directed) (57), *The Magic Sword* (also directed) (62), etc.

GORDON, BRUCE (1919–   ). American character actor who played baddies for years, his best film role being in *Rider on a Dead Horse* (62); but his real fame came from playing Frank Nitti in TV's *The Untouchables* (59–63).

GORDON, C. HENRY (c. 1878–1940). American character actor, often seen as maniacally evil villain or Indian rajah. *Charlie Chan Carries On* (31), *Rasputin and the Empress* (32), *Mata Hari* (32), *Lives of a Bengal Lancer* (35), *Charge of the Light Brigade* (36), *The Return of the Cisco Kid* (38), *Kit Carson* (40), *Charlie Chan at the Wax Museum* (40), etc.

GORDON, COLIN (1911–   ). British light comedy actor, on stage from 1931; often seen as mildly cynical civil servant or schoolmaster. *Bond Street* (47), *The Winslow Boy* (48), *The Man in the White Suit* (51), *Folly To Be Wise* (52), *Escapade* (55), *The Safecracker* (58), *Please Turn Over* (59), *Night of the Eagle* (62), *The Pink Panther* (63), *The Family Way* (66), *Casino Royale* (67), many others.

GORDON, GALE (1906–   ). American comedy actor, internationally known as Mr Mooney in Lucille Ball's TV show. Other TV series include *My Favourite Husband* (51), *Our Miss Brooks* (52, 55), *The Brothers* (57), *Dennis the Menace* (62–64), Films: *A Woman of*

Distinction (50), *Rally Round the Flag Boys* (58), *Visit to a Small Planet* (62), *Speedway* (67), etc.

GORDON, GAVIN (1901–   ). American general purpose actor. *Romance* (lead) (30), *The Bitter Tea of General Yen* (32), *The Scarlet Empress* (34), *Bride of Frankenstein* (35), *Windjammer* (38), *Paper Bullets* (41), *Centennial Summer* (46), *Knock on Wood* (54), *The Bat* (59), etc.

GORDON, HAL (1894–   ). British comedy character actor, often seen as good-natured foil to star comedian. Former lawyer's clerk. *Adam's Apple* (31), *Happy* (34), *Captain Bill* (36), *Keep Fit* (37), *It's in the Air* (38), *Old Mother Riley, Detective* (43), *Give Me the Stars* (45) (last appearance), etc.

GORDON, LEO (1922–   ). Thick-set American character actor, usually in tough guy roles. *China Venture* (53), *Riot in Cell Block Eleven* (53), *Seven Angry Men* (55), *The Conqueror* (55), *The Man Who Knew Too Much* (56), *Cry Baby Killer* (also wrote) (57), *The Big Operator* (59), *The Stranger* (62), *The Haunted Palace* (64), *Beau Geste* (66), *Tobruk* (also wrote) (66), *The St Valentine's Day Massacre* (67), etc.

GORDON, MARY (1882–1963). Tiny Scottish character actress, long in Hollywood; best remembered as Mrs Hudson in the Basil Rathbone/Sherlock Holmes series 1939–46.

GORDON, MICHAEL (1909–   ). American director with stage experience. *Underground Agent* (42), *The Crime Doctor* (43), *The Web* (46), *Another Part of the Forest* (47), *An Act of Murder* (48), *The Lady Gambles* (49), *Woman in Hiding* (49), *Cyrano de Bergerac* (50), *I Can Get It For You Wholesale* (51), *The Secret of Convict Lake* (52), then back to stage for several years; *Pillow Talk* (58), *Portrait in Black* (60), *Boys' Night Out* (62), *Move Over Darling* (63), *A Very Special Favour* (65), *Texas Across the River* (66), *The Impossible Years* (68), etc.

GORDON, RUTH (1896–   ) (Ruth Jones). Distinguished American actress with wide stage experience. Occasional films include *Camille* (15), *The Wheel of Life* (16), *Abe Lincoln in Illinois* (39), *Dr Ehrlich's Magic Bullet* (40), *Two-faced Woman* (41), *Edge of Darkness* (43), *Inside Daisy Clover* (65), *Lord Love a Duck* (66), *Rosemary's Baby* (AA) (68), *Whatever Happened to Aunt Alice?* (69), etc. With her husband Garson Kanin has written several screenplays including *A Double Life* (48), *Adam's Rib* (49), *Pat and Mike* (52). Wrote original plays *Over 21* (filmed 45), *The Actress* (52).

GORING, MARIUS (1912–   ). British stage and screen actor adept at neurotic or fey roles. *Consider Your Verdict* (debut) (36), *Rembrandt* (37), *The Case of the Frightened Lady* (38), *A Matter of Life and Death* (45), *The Red Shoes* (48), *Mr Perrin and Mr Traill* (49), *So Little Time* (52), *Ill Met by Moonlight* (57), *The Inspector* (*Lisa*) (62), *Up From the Beach* (65), *Girl on a Motorcycle* (68), *Subterfuge* (69), *First Love* (70), etc. Frequently on TV and radio.

GORKY, MAXIM (1868–1936) (Alexei Maximovitch Petrov). Russian writer whose autobiography was filmed by Donskoi as *The Childhood of Maxim Gorky* (qv), *Out in the World* and *My Universities*. Other filmed works include *The Lower Depths* (many times) and *The Mother*.

GORSHIN, FRANK (c. 1932–   ). Wiry American character actor, popular as 'The Riddler' in TV's *Batman* series. *The True Story of Jesse James* (57), *Warlock* (59), *Studs Lonigan* (60), *Ring of Fire* (61), *The George Raft Story* (61), *Batman* (65), etc.

GOSHO, HEINOSUKE (1901–   ). Japanese director, best known for *Four Chimneys* (52), *Adolescence* (55), *When a Woman Loves* (59).

GOUDAL, JETTA (1898–   ). French leading lady of American silent films. *The Bright Shawl* (24), *Spanish Love* (25), *White Gold* (27), *Forbidden Woman* (28), etc.; only talkie, *Business and Pleasure* (32).

GOUGH, MICHAEL (1917–   ). Tall British stage (since 1936) and screen (since 1946) actor; has recently gone in for homicidal roles. *Blanche Fury* (debut) (46), *The Small Back Room* (48), *The Man in the White Suit* (51), *Richard III* (56), *Dracula* (57), *Horrors of the Black Museum* (58), *The Horse's Mouth* (59), *Konga* (61), *Black Zoo* (63), *Dr Terror's House of Horrors* (65), *Circus of Blood* (67), *Trog* (70) many others.

GOULDING, EDMUND (1891–1959). British stage actor who went to Hollywood in the 20s as writer; scripts include the original *Broadway Melody* (28). Turned to direction: *Love* (28), *The Trespasser* (29), *Reaching for the Moon* (30), *Grand Hotel* (32), *Riptide* (34), *That Certain Woman* (36), *Dawn Patrol* (38), *The Old Maid* (39), *Dark Victory* (39), *We Are Not Alone* (39), *The Great Lie* (41), *Claudia* (43), *The Constant Nymph* (43), *Of Human Bondage* (46), *The Razor's Edge* (46), *Nightmare Alley* (47), *Mister 880* (50), *We're Not Married* (52), *Teenage Rebel* (56), *Mardi Gras* (58), etc.

GOULET, ROBERT (1933–   ). Canadian singer and leading man, with experience mainly on TV. Films include *Honeymoon Hotel* (63), *I'd Rather Be Rich* (64), *Underground* (70).

governesses have most frequently been personified by Deborah Kerr: in *The King and I*, *The Innocents*, *The Chalk Garden*. Julie Andrews runs a close second with *Mary Poppins* and *The Sound of Music*; as does Bette Davis with *All This and Heaven Too* and *The Nanny*. Joan Fontaine's contribution to the gallery was *Jane Eyre*.

GOWLAND, GIBSON (1882– *). English character actor in mainly American films. *The Birth of a Nation* (14), *Blind Husbands* (19),

Greed (leading role) (23), *SOS Iceberg* (33), *The Secret of the Loch* (GB) (34), *The Mystery of the Marie Celeste* (GB) (36), *Cotton Queen* (GB) (last appearance) (37), etc.

GRABLE, BETTY (1916–   ). American song-and-dance girl, the leading forces' pin-up of World War II. In films from 1930; first good role in *The Gay Divorce* (34). Leading lady from 1939: *Million Dollar Legs* (39), *Down Argentine Way* (40), *Moon Over Miami* (41), *Hot Spot* (41), *Coney Island* (42), *Pin Up Girl* (43), *Diamona Horseshoe* (45), *Mother Wore Tights* (47), *Meet Me after the Show* (51), *How to Marry a Millionaire* (53), *How To Be Very Very Popular* (55), many others. Was for many years married to Harry James.

THE GRADUATE (US 1967). Set in the well-to-do suburbs of Los Angeles, and concerning an aimless young man whose protest at society takes the form of seducing one of his father's friends and then falling in love with her daughter, this beautifully photographed film (Robert Surtees) from a book by Charles Webb was filled with bitter hilarity and showed that a wide-screen film can still look good. Its enormous commercial success was presumably due to its comparative frankness on sexual matters; its direction (Mike Nichols: AA) and acting (Dustin Hoffman, Anne Bancroft) were impeccable.

GRAETZ, PAUL (1901–1966). Franco-Austrian independent producer whose best-known films are probably *Le Diable au Corps* (46), *Monsieur Ripois* (*Knave of Hearts*) (53), *Is Paris Burning* (66).

GRAHAM, MORLAND (1891–1949). Scottish character actor, on stage and screen from 20s. *The Scarlet Pimpernel* (35), *Jamaica Inn* (39), *Old Bill and Son* (as Old Bill) (40), *The Ghost Train* (41), *The Shipbuilders* (44), *The Brothers* (47), *Bonnie Prince Charlie* (48), *Whisky Galore* (48), etc.

GRAHAM, WILLIAM (c. 1930–   ). American director, from TV. *Waterhole Three* (67), *Submarine X-1* (68), *Change of Habit* (69).

GRAHAME, GLORIA (1924–   ) (Gloria Hallward). American leading lady, usually in offbeat roles. *Blonde Fever* (debut) (44), *Without Love* (45), *It's a Wonderful Life* (46), *Crossfire* (47), *Roughshod* (48), *A Woman's Secret* (48), *The Bad and the Beautiful* (AA) (52), *Prisoners of the Casbah* (53), *The Greatest Show on Earth* (53), *The Big Heat* (54), *The Good Die Young* (GB) (54), *Human Desire* (55), *The Man Who Never Was* (GB) (55), *Not as a Stranger* (55), *The Cobweb* (55), *Oklahoma* (56), *Odds Against Tomorrow* (59), *Ride Beyond Vengeance* (66), etc. Also on TV.

GRAHAME, MARGOT (1911–   ). British leading lady of the 30s, with stage experience. *Rookery Nook* (debut) (30), *Sorrell and Son* (34)

The Informer (US) (35), *The Three Musketeers* (US) (36), *Michael Strogoff* (US) (37), *The Shipbuilders* (44), *Broken Journey* (48), *The Romantic Age* (49), *Venetian Bird* (52), *Orders Are Orders* (55), *Saint Joan* (57), etc.

GRAINER, RON (c. 1925–   ). Australian composer in Britain. Film scores include *A Kind of Loving* (62), *Nothing But the Best* (64), *To Sir with Love* (67), *Lock Up Your Daughters* (68), many others.

GRAINGER, EDMUND (1906–   ). American producer and executive, long with RKO. Specialized in quality action pictures. *Diamond Jim* (35), *Sutter's Gold* (36), *International Squadron* (41), *Wake of the Red Witch* (48), *Sands of Iwo Jima* (49), *Flying Leathernecks* (50), *One Minute to Zero* (52), *Treasure of Pancho Villa* (55), *Green Mansions* (59), *Home from the Hill* (60), *Cimarron* (61), many others.

GRANACH, ALEXANDER (1890–1945). Polish character actor who went to Hollywood in the late 30s. *Ninotchka* (39), *Hangmen Also Die* (43), *The Hitler Gang* (44), *A Voice in the Wind* (45), etc.

LE GRAND JEU (France 1933). This melodrama by Charles Spaak and Jacques Feyder about the off-duty problems of Foreign Legionnaires was filmed by Feyder in 1933 and had memorable performances by Françoise Rosay and Marie Bell. Robert Siodmak's 1953 remake was flavourless despite the presence of Arletty and Gina Lollobrigida.

GRAND PRIX (US 1966). An absurdly cliché-ridden and poorly scripted motor-racing spectacular decorated by half a dozen brilliantly exciting race sequences directed by John Frankenheimer and photographed by Lionel Lindon with all the showmanship— and showing-off—they could muster. (These sequences were also notable for experimental use of multiscreen effects.) The actors paled into complete insignificance.

LA GRANDE ILLUSION (France 1937). Jean Renoir's great anti-war film, set in a German prison camp for officers in 1917, commanded by Erich Von Stroheim. A subtler piece than most of the recent variations on this theme, it was written by Charles Spaak and Renoir, with music by Joseph Kosma and photography by Christian Matras and Claude Renoir.

GRAND HOTEL (US 1932–33). The Hollywood all-star film *par excellence*, from Vicki Baum's novel; it allowed effective parts for Garbo, the Barrymore brothers, Joan Crawford and Wallace Beery. Not very cinematic, as directed by Edmund Goulding, but immensely popular. AA best picture of its year. More or less remade in 1945 as *Weekend at the Waldorf*, but with no impact whatever.

GRANGER, FARLEY (1925–   ). American leading man who began his film career straight from school. *North Star* (debut) (43), *They Live By Night* (47), *Rope* (48), *Strangers on a Train* (51), *Hans Christian Andersen* (52), *Senso* (Italian) (53), *The Girl in the Red Velvet Swing* (55), *Rogues' Gallery* (68), etc. More recently on TV.

GRANGER, STEWART (1913–   ) (James Stewart). British leading man, on stage from 1935. *So This Is London* (debut) (38), *The Man in Grey* (43), *The Lamp Still Burns* (43), *Fanny by Gaslight* (43), *Waterloo Road* (44), *Love Story* (44), *Madonna of the Seven Moons* (44), *Caesar and Cleopatra* (45), *Caravan* (46), *The Magic Bow* (as Paganini) (46), *Captain Boycott* (47), *Blanche Fury* (48), *Saraband for Dead Lovers* (as Koenigsmark) (48), *Woman Hater* (49), *Adam and Evelyne* (49), *King Solomon's Mines* (US) (50), *The Light Touch* (US) (51), *Scaramouche* (US) (52), *The Prisoner of Zenda* (US) (52), *Young Bess* (US) (53), *Salome* (US) (53), *All the Brothers Were Valiant* (US) (54), *Beau Brummell* (US) (54), *Green Fire* (US) (55), *Moonfleet* (US) (55), *Footsteps in the Fog* (55), *Bhowani Junction* (56), *The Last Hunt* (US) (56), *The Little Hut* (57), *The Whole Truth* (58), *Harry Black* (58), *North to Alaska* (US) (60), *The Secret Partner* (61), *Sodom and Gomorrah* (62), *Swordsman of Siena* (It.) (62), *The Legion's Last Patrol* (It.) (63), *Old Shatterhand* (Ger.) (63), *Among Vultures* (Ger.) (65), *The Trygon Factor* (67), *The Last Safari* (67), etc.

GRANGIER, GILLES (1911–   ). French director. *Le Cavalier Noir* (44), *L'Amour Madame* (52), *Archimède le Clochard* (58), *Le Cave Se Rebiffe* (61), *La Cuisine au Beurre* (63), *Train d'Enfer* (65), *L'Homme à la Buick* (67), *Fin de Journée* (69), etc.

GRANT, ARTHUR (* –   ). British cinematographer. *Hell Is a City* (60), *Jigsaw* (62), *Eighty Thousand Suspects* (63), *The Tomb of Ligeia* (64), etc.

†GRANT, CARY (1904–   ) (Archibald Leach). Debonair British-born leading man with a personality and accent all his own; varied theatrical experience before settling in Hollywood. *This Is the Night* (32), *Sinners in the Sun* (32), *Hot Saturday* (32), *Merrily We Go to Hell* (32), *Madame Butterfly* (33), *Blonde Venus* (33), *She Done Him Wrong* (33), *Alice in Wonderland* (as the Mock Turtle) (33), *The Eagle and the Hawk* (33), *Woman Accused* (33), *Gambling Ship* (33), *I'm No Angel* (33), *Thirty Day Princess* (34), *Born To Be Bad* (34), *Kiss and Make Up* (34), *Enter Madame* (34), *Ladies Should Listen* (34), *Wings in the Dark* (35), *The Last Outpost* (35), *Sylvia Scarlett* (35), *Big Brown Eyes* (35), *Suzy* (36), *Wedding Present* (36), *The Amazing Quest of Mr Ernest Bliss* (GB) (36), *When You're in Love* (36), *The Awful Truth* (37), *The Toast of New York* (37), *Topper* (37), *Bringing Up Baby* (38), *Holiday* (38), *Gunga Din* (39), *Only Angels Have Wings* (39), *In Name Only* (39), *My Favourite Wife* (40), *The Tree of Liberty*

Grant, James Edward

(40), *His Girl Friday* (40), *The Philadelphia Story* (40), *Penny Serenade* (41), *Suspicion* (41), *Talk of the Town* (42), *Once upon a Honeymoon* (42), *Destination Tokyo* (43), *Mr Lucky* (43), *Once upon a Time* (44), *None but the Lonely Heart* (44), *Arsenic and Old Lace* (44), *Night and Day* (as Cole Porter) (45), *Notorious* (46), *The Bachelor and the Bobbysoxer* (47), *The Bishop's Wife* (as an angel) (48), *Every Girl Should Be Married* (48), *Mr Blandings Builds His Dream House* (48), *I Was a Male War Bride* (49), *Crisis* (50), *People Will Talk* (51), *Monkey Business* (52), *Room for One More* (52), *Dream Wife* (53), *To Catch a Thief* (55), *The Pride and the Passion* (57), *An Affair to Remember* (57), *Kiss Them for Me* (57), *Indiscreet* (GB) (58), *Houseboat* (58), *North by Northwest* (59), *Operation Petticoat* (59), *The Grass Is Greener* (60), *That Touch of Mink* (62), *Charade* (63), *Father Goose* (64), *Walk Don't Run* (66).

GRANT, JAMES EDWARD (1902–1966). American writer. *Whipsaw* (35), *We're Going to Be Rich* (38), *Belle of the Yukon* (44), *The Great John L.* (45), *Angel and the Bad Man* (also directed) (46), *Sands of Iwo Jima* (49), *Big Jim McLain* (52), *Hondo* (54), *Ring of Fear* (co-w and directed) (54), *The Alamo* (60), *McLintock* (63), etc.

GRANT, KATHRYN (1933–   ) (Katherine Grandstaff). American leading lady who retired to marry Bing Crosby. *The Phoenix City Story* (55), *Mister Cory* (56), *Gunman's Walk* (58), *Operation Mad Ball* (58), *The Big Circus* (60), etc.

GRANT, KIRBY (1914–   ) (K. G. Horn). Dutch-Scottish-American leading man, former bandleader. *Red River Range* (39), *Ghost Catchers* (44), *The Lawless Breed* (47), *Trail of the Yukon* (50), *Snow Dog* (51), *Yukon Gold* (52), *One Man Mutiny* (*The Court Martial of Billy Mitchell*) (55), *Yukon Vengeance* (55), etc.

GRANT, LEE (1929–   ) (Lyova Rosenthal). American stage actress who scored a big hit in *Detective Story* (50) as the shoplifter, but did not film again for fourteen years. *The Balcony* (64), *In the Heat of the Night* (67), *Buona Sera Mrs Campbell* (68), *There Was a Crooked Man* (69).

GRANVILLE, BONITA (1923–   ). Former American child star, on stage from three years old. In films from 1932; notable as malicious schoolgirl in *These Three* (36); later in *The Life of Emile Zola* (37), *Gentleman after Midnight* (38), *Escape* (40), *H. M. Pulham Esquire* (41), *Now Voyager* (42), *The Glass Key* (42), *Hitler's Children* (43), *Youth Runs Wild* (44), *Senorita from the West* (45), *Suspense* (46), *The Guilty* (48), *Treason* (50), *The Lone Ranger* (57), etc.; also starred in the *Nancy Drew* detective series 1938–42. Retired to marry TV executive, but was associate producer of *Lassie* TV series and the 1963 feature *Lassie's Great Adventure*.

THE GRAPES OF WRATH (US 1940). John Ford's (AA) film of John Steinbeck's novel about the migration of poor workers from the midwestern dustbowl to the Californian fruit valleys is not only one of the earliest Hollywood exposés of social injustice but one of the most moving and beautiful films to come out of America. Gregg Toland's soft, warm photography, Alfred Newman's music and Nunnally Johnson's screenplay provide a perfect background for the performances of Henry Fonda, Jane Darwell (AA) and a fine cast.

GRAPEWIN, CHARLEY (1875–1956). American character actor with varied stage experience; in films from 1929. Best role: Jeeter Lester in *Tobacco Road* (41). Also: *Gold Dust Gertie* (31), *One Frightened Night* (35), *Captains Courageous* (37), *Three Comrades* (38), *The Wizard of Oz* (39), *Ellery Queen* series (as Inspector Queen) (40–43), *The Enchanted Valley* (47), *When I Grow Up* (51), many others.

GRASS (US 1925). Cooper and Schoedsack's feature-length documentary was shot among the Baktyari tribe of north-west Persia during their twice-yearly migration in search of grass. Though an impressive achievement at the time, it was less stirring than the same team's *Chang*, which followed in 1927.

GRAUMAN, WALTER (1922–   ). American director, from TV. *Lady in a Cage* (63), *633 Squadron* (64), *A Rage to Live* (65), *I Deal in Danger* (66), *The Last Escape* (69). TV series include *The Untouchables*, *Naked City*, *Route 66*, *The Felony Squad*.

GRAVES, PETER (1925–   ) (Peter Arness). American leading man, usually in 'B' action pictures; brother of James Arness. *Rogue River* (debut) (50), *Fort Defiance* (52), *Red Planet Mars* (52), *Stalag 17* (53), *Beneath the Twelve-Mile Reef* (53), *Black Tuesday* (55), *It Conquered the World* (56), *Wolf Larsen* (59), *A Rage to Live* (65), *The Ballad of Josie* (67), etc. TV series: *Fury* (55–59), *Whiplash* (60), *Court Martial* (*Counsellors at War*) (66), *Mission Impossible* (67–68).

GRAVES, PETER (1911–   ). British light leading man, tall and suave, usually in musical comedy. *Kipps* (debut) (41), *King Arthur Was a Gentleman* (42), *Bees in Paradise* (44), *I'll Be Your Sweetheart* (44), *Waltz Time* (45), *The Laughing Lady* (46), *Spring Song* (47), *Mrs Fitzherbert* (as the Prince Regent) (47), *Spring in Park Lane* (48), *Maytime in Mayfair* (50), *Derby Day* (52), *Lilacs in the Spring* (54), etc.; latterly in cameo roles, e.g. *The Wrong Box* (66).

GRAVET, FERNAND (1904–   ) (F. Martens). Debonair French leading man with some Hollywood experience. *Bitter Sweet* (33), *The Great Waltz* (38), *Fools for Scandal* (38), *Le Dernier Tournant* (38), *La Ronde* (50), *Short Head* (53), *How to Steal a Million* (66), *The Madwoman of Chaillot* (co-ph) (69), etc.

421

GRAY, CHARLES (1928–) (Donald M. Gray). British stage and TV actor usually seen in smooth unsympathetic roles. Films include *The Entertainer* (60), *The Man in the Moon* (61), *Masquerade* (65), *The Night of the Generals* (66), *The Secret War of Harry Frigg* (US) (67), *The Devil Rides Out* (68), *The File of the Golden Goose* (69), *Cromwell* (69).

GRAY, COLEEN (1922–) (Doris Jensen). American leading lady. *State Fair* (45), *Nightmare Alley* (48), *Red River* (48), *Riding High* (49), *Father Was a Bachelor* (50), *I'll Get You for This* (GB) (51), *That Kind of Girl* (54), *The Killing* (56), *Hell's Five Hours* (58), *Town Tamer* (65), etc.

GRAY, DOLORES (1924–). Statuesque American singer-dancer, on stage in musical comedy (played 'Annie Get Your Gun' in London). Films include *It's Always Fair Weather* (54), *Kismet* (55), *Designing Woman* (57).

GRAY, DONALD (1914–). One-armed British leading man, former radio actor and announcer; best known as TV's *Mark Saber*. Films include *Strange Experiment* (37), *The Four Feathers* (39), *Idol of Paris* (48), *Saturday Island* (*Island of Desire*) (52), *Timeslip* (55), *Satellite in the Sky* (56), etc.

GRAY, DULCIE (1919–) (Dulcie Bailey). Gentle-mannered British leading lady, married to Michael Denison. On stage from 1939, films from 1944. *A Place of One's Own* (44), *They Were Sisters* (45), *Mine Own Executioner* (47), *The Glass Mountain* (48), *Angels One Five* (51), etc. Recently on stage and TV. 1965: *A Man Could Get Killed.*

GRAY, GARY (1936–). American boy actor of the 40s. *A Woman's Face* (41), *Address Unknown* (44), *The Great Lover* (47), *Father Is a Bachelor* (49), *The Painted Hills* (51), others.

GRAY, GILDA (c. 1898–1959) (Marianna Michalska). Polish dancer who went to America and is credited with inventing the shimmy. *Aloma of the South Seas* (26), *The Devil Dancer* (28), *Rose Marie* (36), etc.

GRAY, NADIA (1923–) (Nadia Kujnir-Herescu). Russian-Roumanian leading lady, in European and British films. *The Spider and the Fly* (49), *Night without Stars* (51), *Valley of Eagles* (51), *Neapolitan Fantasy* (54), *Folies Bergère* (56), *The Captain's Table* (58), *Parisienne* (59), *Maniac* (63), *Two for the Road* (67), *The Naked Runner* (67), etc.

GRAY, SALLY (1916–) (Constance Stevens). Popular British screen heroine of 30s and 40s, with stage experience from 1925. *Cheer Up* (debut) (35), *The Saint in London* (38), *The Lambeth Walk* (38), *Dangerous Moonlight* (40), *Carnival* (46), *Green for Danger* (46), *They*

Made Me a Fugitive (47), *The Mark of Cain* (48), *Silent Dust* (49), *Obsession* (49), *Escape Route* (52), etc. Retired.

GRAYSON, KATHRYN (1922–   ) (Zelma Hedrick). American singing star in Hollywood from 1940 (as one of Andy Hardy's dates). Later: *The Vanishing Virginian* (41), *Rio Rita* (42), *Seven Sweethearts* (42), *Thousands Cheer* (43), *Ziegfeld Follies* (44), *Anchors Aweigh* (45), *Two Sisters from Boston* (45), *Till the Clouds Roll By* (46), *The Kissing Bandit* (48), *That Midnight Kiss* (49), *Showboat* (51), *Lovely To Look At* (52), *The Grace Moore Story* (*So This Is Love*) (53), *Kiss Me Kate* (53), *The Vagabond King* (55), etc.

Great Britain had been making films for more than fifty years when finally a 'British school' emerged capable of influencing world production. Hollywood films had invaded British cinemas during the first world war, and British audiences liked them; so the battle for power was won with only faint stirrings of resistance. British films were tepid, shoddy, stilted, old-fashioned in acting and production; and for many years they were kept that way by short-sighted government legislation, intended to help the industry, ensuring that at least a proportion (usually a third) of local product must be shown in every British cinema. Thus began the long list of 'quota quickies', deplorable B pictures whose producers knew they could not fail to get their money back. In the mid-thirties, Britain was producing 200 films a year, but they reflected nothing of life and offered little in the way of entertainment.

Exceptions to this general rule were the suspense thrillers of Alfred Hitchcock; a couple of promising dramas from Anthony Asquith; some well-produced entertainments from Victor Saville, such as *The Good Companions* and *South Riding*; Herbert Wilcox's popular view of such historical figures as Nell Gwyn and Queen Victoria; and the ambitious and often masterly, but not particularly British, productions of Alexander Korda, whose *Rembrandt* and *Things to Come* would still justify their inclusion in any list of the world's ten best. The British music-hall tradition also survived remarkably well in skilful low-budget productions with such stars as Gracie Fields, George Formby, Will Hay and the Crazy Gang; the two directors most concerned, Marcel Varnel and Walter Forde, had much to tell anyone who cared to listen about the art of screen comedy.

In 1939 MGM had produced three notable British productions—*A Yank at Oxford, Goodbye Mr Chips* and *The Citadel*—but the war swept away all plans and British studios started anew. Their renaissance began through the splendid official documentaries of Humphrey Jennings, Harry Watt and Basil Wright, graduates of the GPO Film Unit which had been turning out excellent short films in the 30s but failing to secure cinema bookings for them.

Great Britain

The strong feelings of national pride and urgency percolated to the fiction film, first in stories of social comment (*The Proud Valley*, *The Stars Look Down*, *Love on the Dole*), then in topical entertainments like Carol Reed's *Night Train to Munich* and Thorold Dickinson's *Next of Kin*. Noel Coward's *In Which We Serve* came as a revelation of style and substance, and what it did for the navy was done for the army by Reed's *The Way Ahead* and for the air force by Asquith's *The Way to the Stars*. The home front was covered with equal sensitivity by Launder and Gilliat's *Millions Like Us*, Leslie Howard's *The Gentle Sex*, and Coward's *This Happy Breed*.

Even non-war films had a fresh impetus. Gabriel Pascal made an excellent *Major Barbara* to follow the success of his 1938 *Pygmalion*. Dickinson's *Gaslight*, Reed's *Kipps*, Asquith's *Quiet Wedding* were all excellent of their kind. The new team of Michael Powell and Emeric Pressburger brought a fresh command and insight to some unlikely but ambitious themes in *The Life and Death of Colonel Blimp* and *A Matter of Life and Death*. Korda supplied *The Thief of Baghdad*, *Lady Hamilton* and *Perfect Strangers*. The Boulting Brothers followed up *Pastor Hall* with the thoughtful *Thunder Rock*. Launder and Gilliat followed the realistic *Waterloo Road* with sparkling comedy-dramas (*The Rake's Progress*, *I See a Dark Stranger*), and a classic who-done-it (*Green for Danger*). Gainsborough Studios turned out several competent costume-dramas on the Hollywood model. In 1945 the future of British films seemed bright indeed, with Olivier's *Henry V*, Coward and Lean's *Blithe Spirit*, and Ealing Studios' supernatural omnibus *Dead of Night* earning popular approval, and such films as *Brief Encounter* and *Odd Man Out* in the works.

In the next few years the industry was beset by financial problems and diminishing audiences. Then Britain's leading film magnate, J. Arthur Rank, set out to conquer by means which proved regrettable. Originally attracted to the cinema as a means for spreading the Methodist religion, he now determined to impress world markets by a series of enormously expensive and generally arty productions, few of which recovered their costs: *Caesar and Cleopatra* is the most notorious. The more modestly-budgeted pictures proved to have little to say now that the end of the war had removed their main subject; and with exceptions like *Mine Own Executioner*, *The Red Shoes*, and *The Third Man* the field was thin until the celebrated Ealing comedies (*Passport to Pimlico*, *Whisky Galore*, *The Man in the White Suit*, *Kind Hearts and Coronets*) began to attract world audiences. But these too had their day, and all through the 50s British studios were trying in vain to find subjects to replace them. During this period many stars found their way to Hollywood, and then gradually began to drift back as kingpins of international co-productions, ventures which seldom turned out very happily. It was not till the relaxed hand of censorship permitted *Room at the*

424

Top, Saturday Night and Sunday Morning, The Leather Boys, Tom Jones, James Bond and *Alfie* that British films at last set the world afire by showing just what you could get away with if you did it with sufficient skill and truth. Unfortunately even sex and violence must eventually pall . . . so what next?

THE GREAT CARUSO (US 1951). The film which confirmed Mario Lanza on his brief but triumphant career as a top singing star and also proved to a surprised Hollywood that opera can be big business if given the right sugar coating.

THE GREAT DICTATOR (US 1940). Chaplin's satire on Hitler has many moments of bitter hilarity but is marred by the sentimentality of the ghetto scenes. The first film in which Chaplin spoke coherently, and the last in which he used his famous tramp character.

GREAT EXPECTATIONS (GB 1946). Dickens' novel has been filmed several times, but never with such definition, pace and attention to detail as in this *de luxe* version directed by David Lean and photographed by Ronald Neame. Most outstanding in an excellent cast were John Mills, Jean Simmons, Alec Guinness, Finlay Currie and Martita Hunt; Guy Green (AA) was cinematographer and John Bryan (AA) was production designer. The best previous version was made in Hollywood in 1934, with Philips Holmes and Jane Wyatt.

THE GREAT IMPERSONATION. E. Phillips Oppenheim's cunningly-constructed spy thriller was filmed in 1921 with James Kirkwood; in 1935 with Edmund Lowe; and in 1942 with Ralph Bellamy.

THE GREAT MAN VOTES (US 1939). An early Garson Kanin comedy which provided John Barrymore with his last good part, as a night watchman whose vote turns out to be so crucial that he is able to blackmail the city into making him Schools Commissioner.

THE GREAT RACE (US 1965). A lavish and often splendid period comedy about a 1908 auto race from New York to Paris, this engaging Blake Edwards film was written by Arthur Ross with nods to Valentino, Laurel and Hardy and *The Prisoner of Zenda*. Some of the gags are prolonged, but the film is always good to look at, and the zany leading roles are comfortably filled by Tony Curtis, Jack Lemmon, Natalie Wood, Peter Falk and Ross Martin.

THE GREAT TRAIN ROBBERY (US 1903). An eleven-minute Western sometimes inaccurately hailed as the first story film; but it was the longest of its time, and it did have all the elements of its modern descendants, with careful editing and a sense of cinema showmanship. Directed by Edwin S. Porter.

The Great Ziegfeld

THE GREAT ZIEGFELD (US 1936). A mammoth musical drama of the 30s, running three hours and recounting the life story of Broadway's great showman. William Powell played the part, and Robert Z. Leonard directed. Academy Awards went to the film (best picture), to Luise Rainer, and to Seymour Felix for the dance direction of the closing number with its enormous revolving set.

THE GREATEST STORY EVER TOLD (US 1964). George Stevens' immensely long life of Christ (in Cinerama) was plainly a labour of love: he was quoted as hoping that it would still be showing 'at the end of the century and after'. But despite beautiful moments it was fatally compromised by the casting of stars in bit parts and by the heavy-handedness evident in all Stevens' later films. The publicity about deciding to shoot it in Utah (because Utah was 'more like Palestine than Palestine') didn't help; but Max von Sydow was an excellent Christ. At the box office, the picture died.

GRECO, JULIETTE (1927–). French singer who acted in several films both at home and abroad. *Au Royaume des Cieux* (49), *The Green Glove* (52), *The Sun Also Rises* (57), *Naked Earth* (58), *Roots of Heaven* (59), *Whirlpool* (59), *Crack in the Mirror* (60), etc.

GREED (US 1923). Originally an estimated nine hours long, cut by June Mathis to two, this realistic study of money as the root of all evil, set in contemporary American settings, was both Erich Von Stroheim's triumph and his downfall; for it made his extravagance a talking-point in Hollywood and a few years later he was forced to retire from directing. Here he also wrote the scenario, from Frank Norris's novel *McTeague*; his cinematographers were Ben Reynolds, William Daniels and Ernest Schoedsack and his leading actors Zasu Pitts, Gibson Gowland and Jean Hersholt.

GREEN, ADOLPH (1915–). American writer of books and lyrics for many Broadway shows and musical films, usually with Betty Comden (qv).

GREEN, ALFRED E. (1889–1960). American director of mainly routine but generally competent films; in Hollywood from 1912. *Little Lord Fauntleroy* (20), *Ella Cinders* (23), *Through the Back Door* (26), *The Green Goddess* (30), *Old English* (31), *Smart Money* (31), *Disraeli* (31), *The Rich Are Always with Us* (32), *Parachute* (33), *Dangerous* (35), *Duke of West Point* (38), *South of Pago Pago* (40), *Badlands of Dakota* (41), *Meet the Stewarts* (42), *A Thousand and One Nights* (44), *The Jolson Story* (46), *The Fabulous Dorseys* (47), *They Passed This Way* (48), *Invasion USA* (52), *The Eddie Cantor Story* (53), many others.

GREEN, DANNY (1903–). Heavyweight British character actor usually in cheerful—or sometimes menacing—cockney roles.

Appeared in some American silents. Later: *Crime over London* (37), *Fiddlers Three* (44), *The Man Within* (47), *No Orchids for Miss Blandish* (48), *Little Big Shot* (52), *A Kid for Two Farthings* (55), *The Lady Killers* (55), *Beyond This Place* (59), many others; also on TV.

GREEN, GUY (1913–). British cinematographer: *In Which We Serve* (42), *The Way Ahead* (44), *Great Expectations* (AA) (46), *Take My Life* (47), *Oliver Twist* (48), *Captain Horatio Hornblower* (50), *The Beggar's Opera* (52), *Rob Roy* (53), etc. Became director: *River Beat* (53), *Lost* (55), *House of Secrets* (56), *Sea of Sand* (58), *The Angry Silence* (59), *The Mark* (61), *The Light in the Piazza* (62), *Diamondhead* (US) (63), *A Patch of Blue* (US) (66), *The Magus* (68), *John Brown's Body* (69), *A Walk in the Spring Rain* (69), etc.

GREEN, HARRY (1892–1958). American comedian, primarily on stage; former lawyer. *Bottoms Up* (34), *The Cisco Kid and the Lady* (37), *Joe Macbeth* (GB) (55), *A King in New York* (GB) (57), etc.

GREEN, HUGHIE (1920–). Canadian actor in Britain, former juvenile, now popular TV quizmaster. *Little Friend* (34), *Midshipman Easy* (36), *Tom Brown's Schooldays* (US) (39), *If Winter Comes* (US) (48), *Paper Orchid* (49), etc.

GREEN, JANET (1914–). British screenwriter: *The Clouded Yellow* (49), *Cast a Dark Shadow* (54), *Lost* (55), *The Long Arm* (56), *Sapphire* (BFA) (59), *Midnight Lace* (60), *Life for Ruth* (62), *Seven Women* (66), etc.

GREEN, JOHNNY (1908–). American composer, bandleader, songwriter; in Hollywood from 1933. Scored *Easter Parade* (AA) (47), *An American in Paris* (AA) (51), many others.

GREEN, MITZI (1920–1969). American child performer of the 30s. *Honey* (30), *Tom Sawyer* (30), *Little Orphan Annie* (32), *Transatlantic Merry-Go-Round* (34), etc.; later appeared in *Lost in Alaska* (52), *Bloodhounds of Broadway* (52).

GREEN, NIGEL (1924–). Dominant British character actor with stage experience. *Reach for the Sky* (56), *Bitter Victory* (58), *The Criminal* (60), *Jason and the Argonauts* (63), *Zulu* (64), *The Ipcress File* (65), *The Face of Fu Manchu* (65), *The Skull* (66), *Let's Kill Uncle* (US) (66), *Deadlier than the Male* (66), *Tobruk* (US) (67), *Africa Texas Style* (67), *Play Dirty* (68), *Wrecking Crew* (US) (69), *The Kremlin Letter* (69), etc.

GREEN PASTURES (US 1936). A fairly lavish and sympathetic film version, directed by William Keighley, of the Marc Connelly play from Roark Bradford's stories showing the simple Negro interpretation of the Bible, with Heaven as a gigantic 'fish fry' and 'De

Green, Philip

Lawd' played by Rex Ingram as a dignified old Negro. The first film since *Hallelujah* (29) to give a fairly serious account of Negro thought, it did not entirely avoid a patronizing air.

GREEN, PHILIP (c. 1917–). British composer. *The March Hare* (54), *John and Julie* (55), *Rooney* (57), *Innocent Sinners* (58), *Operation Amsterdam* (59), *Sapphire* (59), *The Bulldog Breed* (61), *Victim* (62), *It's All Happening* (also co-produced) (63), *The Intelligence Men* (65), *Masquerade* (65), etc.

GREENE, CLARENCE (c. 1918–). American writer-producer, usually in collaboration with Russel Rouse. *The Town Went Wild* (45), *D.O.A.* (48), *The Well* (51), *New York Confidential* (55), *A House Is Not a Home* (64), *The Oscar* (66), *Caper of the Golden Bulls* (67), etc. TV series: *Tightrope* (59).

GREENE, DAVID (1924–). British director, former small-part actor; became a TV director in Canada and the U.S. Recent films: *The Shuttered Room* (66), *Sebastian* (68), *The Strange Affair* (68), *The Dolly Dolly Spy* (69), *I Start Counting* (also produced) (69).

GREENE, GRAHAM (1904–). Distinguished British novelist who has provided material for many interesting films: *Stamboul Train* (*Orient Express*) (34), *This Gun for Hire* (42), *The Ministry of Fear* (43), *Confidential Agent* (45), *The Man Within* (46), *Brighton Rock* (46), *The Fugitive* (48), *The Fallen Idol* (48), *The Third Man* (49), *The Heart of the Matter* (53), *The Stranger's Hand* (54), *The End of the Affair* (55), *The Quiet American* (58), *Our Man in Havana* (59), *The Comedians* (67), etc.

GREENE, LORNE (1915–). Canadian character actor, famous from TV series *Sailor of Fortune* (56), *Bonanza* (59–69). Films include *Autumn Leaves* (56), *The Gift of Love* (58), *The Buccaneer* (59).

GREENE, MAX (1896–1968). (Mutz Greenbaum). German cinematographer, long in Britain. *The Stars Look Down* (39), *Hatter's Castle* (41), *Spring in Park Lane* (48), *Maytime in Mayfair* (49), *Night and the City* (50), etc.

GREENE, RICHARD (1918–). British leading man with brief stage experience before film debut (*Four Men and a Prayer* [38]) resulted in Hollywood contract. *My Lucky Star* (38), *Submarine Patrol* (38), *Kentucky* (38), *The Little Princess* (39), *The Hound of the Baskervilles* (39), *Stanley and Livingstone* (39), *Little Old New York* (40), *Unpublished Story* (41), *Flying Fortress* (42), *Yellow Canary* (43), *Don't Take It to Heart* (44), *Gaiety George* (46), *Forever Amber* (47), *Lady Windermere's Fan* (49), *Now Barabbas* (50), *Shadow of the Eagle* (50), *Lorna Doone* (51), *The Black Castle* (52), *Captain Scarlett* (52), *The*

Return of the Corsican Brothers (53), *Contraband Spain* (55), *Beyond the Curtain* (60), *Sword of Sherwood Forest* (61), *Dangerous Island* (67), *Blood of Fu Manchu* (68), etc. Also starred in 165 TV episodes of *Robin Hood*.

GREENLEAF, RAYMOND (1892–1963). American character actor, usually seen as benevolent elderly man. *Storm Warning* (51), *Angel Face* (53), *Violent Saturday* (54), *When Gangland Strikes* (leading role) (56), *The Story on Page One* (60), many others.

†GREENSTREET, SIDNEY (1879–1954). British-born stage actor of immense presence who made no films until he played 'the fat man' in *The Maltese Falcon* (41), and at once became a household word. *They Died with Their Boots On* (42), *Across the Pacific* (42), *Casablanca* (42), *Background to Danger* (43), *Hollywood Canteen* (44), *Passage to Marseilles* (44), *Between Two Worlds* (44), *Devotion* (as Thackeray) (44), *The Conspirators* (44), *The Mask of Dimitrios* (44), *Conflict* (45), *Pillow to Post* (45), *Christmas in Connecticut* (45), *Three Strangers* (46), *The Verdict* (46), *That Way With Women* (47), *The Hucksters* (47), *The Woman in White* (as Count Fosco) (48), *The Velvet Touch* (48), *Ruthless* (48), *Flamingo Road* (49), *It's A Great Feeling* (49), *Malaya* (49).

GREENWOOD, CHARLOTTE (1893–   ). Tall American comedienne and eccentric dancer, on stage from 1905. Occasional films include *Jane* (18), *Baby Mine* (27), *Palmy Days* (32), *Down Argentine Way* (40), *Springtime in the Rockies* (43), *Up in Mabel's Room* (44), *Home in Indiana* (47), *Peggy* (50), *Dangerous When Wet* (52), *Glory* (55), *Oklahoma* (56), *The Opposite Sex* (56), etc.

GREENWOOD, JACK (1919–   ). British producer, responsible for second-feature crime series: Edgar Wallace, Scales of Justice, Scotland Yard, etc.

GREENWOOD, JOAN (1921–   ). Plummy-voiced leading lady, in films since 1941 after stage experience. *My Wife's Family* (41), *He Found a Star* (41), *The Gentle Sex* (43), *The Man Within* (46), *The October Man* (47), *Saraband for Dead Lovers* (48), *Kind Hearts and Coronets* (49), *The Man in the White Suit* (51), *The Importance of Being Earnest* (51), *Knave of Hearts* (51), *Father Brown* (54), *Moonfleet* (55), *Stage Struck* (57), *Mysterious Island* (61), *The Amorous Prawn* (62), *Tom Jones* (63), *The Moonspinners* (64), etc.

GREENWOOD, JOHN (1889–   ). British composer. *To What Red Hell* (30), *The Constant Nymph* (33), *Elephant Boy* (37), *Pimpernel Smith* (41), *San Demetrio, London* (44), *Frieda* (47), *Quartet* (48), others.

GREER, JANE (1924–   ). American leading lady of cool, intelligent roles; former night club singer. *Pan-Americana* (debut) (45), *Sindbad the Sailor* (46), *They Won't Believe Me* (47), *Build My Gallows High* (47), *The Big Steal* (48), *The Prisoner of Zenda* (52), *Run for the Sun* (56), *Man of a Thousand Faces* (58), *Where Love Has Gone* (64), *Billie* (65), etc.

GREGG, HUBERT (1914–   ). British songwriter, screenwriter, and light actor, married to Pat Kirkwood. On stage from 1933, films from 1942. *In Which We Serve* (42), *Acacia Avenue* (45), *Vote for Huggett* (49), *Robin Hood* (52), *The Maggie* (54), *Simon and Laura* (55), *Stars in My Eyes* (57), etc.

GREGORY, JAMES (1911–   ). American character actor with stage experience, a familiar Hollywood 'heavy' or senior cop. *Naked City* (47), *The Frogmen* (51), *The Scarlet Hour* (56), *The Young Stranger* (57), *Al Capone* (59), *Two Weeks in Another Town* (62), *The Manchurian Candidate* (62), *P.T.109* (63), *A Distant Trumpet* (64), *The Sons of Katie Elder* (65), *A Rage To Live* (65), *The Silencers* (66), *Clambake* (68), etc. TV series: *The Lawless Years* (59).

GREGORY, PAUL (c. 1905–   ) (Jason Lenhart). American impresario who teamed with Charles Laughton in 40s to present dramatized readings: also produced *Night of the Hunter* (55), which Laughton directed, and *The Naked and the Dead* (58).

GREGSON, JOHN (1919–   ). British leading man of the 50s, latterly character actor. *Scott of the Antarctic* (48), *Whisky Galore* (48), *Treasure Island* (50), *The Lavender Hill Mob* (51), *Angels One Five* (51), *The Brave Don't Cry* (52), *Venetian Bird* (53), *The Titfield Thunderbolt* (53), *Genevieve* (53), *To Dorothy a Son* (54), *Above Us the Waves* (54), *Value for Money* (55), *The Battle of the River Plate* (56), *Jacqueline* (56), *True as a Turtle* (57), *Rooney* (57), *The Captain's Table* (58), *Sea of Sand* (59), *SOS Pacific* (60), *Faces in the Dark* (60), *Hand in Hand* (61), *The Frightened City* (61), *The Longest Day* (62), *Live Now Pay Later* (63), *The Night of the Generals* (66), etc. TV series: *Gideon's Way*.

GREIG, ROBERT (1880–1958). Australian character actor, long in Hollywood; for many years the absolute doyen of portly butlers. *Animal Crackers* (30), *Trouble in Paradise* (32), *Clive of India* (35), *Rose Marie* (36), *Moon over Miami* (41), *Sullivan's Travels* (41), *The Moon and Sixpence* (42), *Unfaithfully Yours* (48), scores of others.

GREMILLON, JEAN (1902–1959). French director with limited but interesting output since 1929: *Remorques* (39), *Lumière d'Eté* (42), *Pattes Blanches* (48), etc.

GRENFELL, JOYCE (1910–   ) (Joyce Phipps). Angular British comedienne adept at refined gaucherie; a revue star and solo performer, on stage since 1939. Films include *The Demi-Paradise*

(42), *The Lamp Still Burns* (43), *While the Sun Shines* (46), *The Happiest Days of Your Life* (49), *Stage Fright* (50), *Laughter in Paradise* (51), *Genevieve* (53), *The Million Pound Note* (54), *The Belles of St Trinian's* (54), *Happy Is the Bride* (57), *Blue Murder at St Trinian's* (58), *The Pure Hell of St Trinian's* (60), *The Old Dark House* (63), *The Americanization of Emily* (64), etc.

GREVILLE, EDMOND (1906–   ). French director; assistant to Dupont on *Piccadilly* (30), to Clair on *Sous les Toits de Paris* (32). Solo: *Remous* (34), *Mademoiselle Docteur* (37), *L'Ile du Péché* (39), *Passionnelle* (46), *Noose* (GB) (48), *The Romantic Age* (GB) (49), *But Not In Vain* (also wrote and produced) (GB) (49), *Port du Désir* (56), *Guilty* (GB) (56), *Beat Girl* (GB) (60), *The Hands of Orlac* (GB) (61), *Les Menteurs* (61), etc.

GREY, NAN (1918–   ) (Eschal Miller). American leading lady of the late 30s. *Dracula's Daughter* (36), *Three Smart Girls* (36), *Three Smart Girls Grow Up* (38), *Tower of London* (39), *The Invisible Man Returns* (40), *Sandy Is a Lady* (41), etc. Retired.

GREY, VIRGINIA (1923–   ). American leading lady of minor 40s films. *Grand Central Murder* (42), *Grizzly's Millions* (45), *So This Is New York* (48), *Jungle Jim* (49), *Perilous Journey* (52), *Portrait in Black* (59), *Madame X* (65), *Rosie* (67), many others.

GREY, ZANE (1875–1939). American novelist whose Western yarns provided the basis of hundreds of silent and sound movies. He lacked sophistication, but as late as 1958 TV had its *Zane Grey Playhouse*.

GREYFRIARS BOBBY (US 1960). Elinor Atkinson's sentimental novel of old Edinburgh, about a dog who lies on his master's grave, was filmed agreeably enough by Disney. It had also been used as the plot of *Challenge to Lassie* (49).

GRIERSON, JOHN (1898–   ). Distinguished British documentarist. Founded Empire Marketing Board Film Unit (30), GPO Film Unit (33); Canadian Film Commissioner (39–45), etc. Produced *Drifters* (29), *Industrial Britain* (33), *Song of Ceylon* (34), *Night Mail* (36), etc. Since 1957 has had his own weekly TV show *This Wonderful World* showing excerpts from the world's best non-fiction films.

GRIES, TOM (1922–   ). American producer and co-writer with varied Hollywood experience from 1946. *Donovan's Brain* (p) (53), *Hell's Horizon* (w, d) (55), *Will Penny* (w, d) (67), *100 Rifles* (d) (69), *Number One* (d) (69), *The Hawaiians* (d) (70), etc.; also TV work.

GRIFFIES, ETHEL (1878–   ). British character actress of stage and screen who has spent many years in Hollywood. *Love Me Tonight*

(32), *Anna Karenina* (35), *Irene* (40), *Time to Kill* (43), *Jane Eyre* (43), *The Horn Blows at Midnight* (45), *Billy Liar* (GB) (63), many others.

GRIFFIN, JOSEPHINE (1928–   ). British leading lady. *The Weak and the Wicked* (54), *The Purple Plain* (54), *The Man Who Never Was* (56), *The Spanish Gardener* (last to date) (56), etc.

GRIFFITH, ANDY (1926–   ). Tall, slow-speaking American comic actor, adept at wily country-boy roles. *A Face in the Crowd* (debut), (57), *No Time for Sergeants* (58), *Onionhead* (58); then weekly TV series *The Andy Griffith Show.*

GRIFFITH, CORINNE (1898–   ). American silent screen star of *A Girl at Bay, Single Wives, Modern Madness, Syncopating Sue, The Divine Lady,* etc. Only talkie: *Lily Christine* (GB) (31).

GRIFFITH, D. W. (1875–1948). America's first major film director, who improved the cinema's image, developed many aspects of technique, made many stars, and was only flawed by his Victorian outlook which was largely responsible for his premature eclipse. *Rescued from an Eagle's Nest* (07), *Enoch Arden* (11), *Man's Genesis* (12), *The New York Hat* (12), *The Birth of a Nation* (14), *Intolerance* (16), *Hearts of a Nation* (18), *Broken Blossoms* (19), *Way Down East* (21), *Orphans of the Storm* (22), *One Exciting Night* (22), *America* (24), *Isn't Life Wonderful* (24), *Sally of the Sawdust* (25), *The Sorrows of Satan* (26), *Abraham Lincoln* (30), *The Struggle* (31), many others. Inactive from early 30s except for reputed contribution to Hal Roach's *One Million B.C.* (*Man and His Mate*) (41), a reworking of *Man's Genesis.*

GRIFFITH, EDWARD H. (1894– *). American director. *Garter Girl* (30), *No More Ladies* (31), *The Animal Kingdom* (32), *Biography of a Bachelor Girl* (34), *Café Society* (39), *Virginia* (40), *One Night in Lisbon* (41), *Bahama Passage* (41), etc.

GRIFFITH, HUGH (1912–   ). Flamboyant Welsh actor, former bank clerk. *Neutral Port* (debut) (40); war service; *The Three Weird Sisters* (48), *London Belongs to Me* (48), *The Last Days of Dolwyn* (48), *A Run for Your Money* (49), *Laughter in Paradise* (51), *The Galloping Major* (51), *The Beggar's Opera* (52), *The Titfield Thunderbolt* (53), *The Sleeping Tiger* (54), *Passage Home* (55), *Lucky Jim* (57), *Ben Hur* (AA) (59), *The Day They Robbed the Bank of England* (60), *Exodus* (61), *The Counterfeit Traitor* (62), *Tom Jones* (63), *The Bargee* (64), *Moll Flanders* (65), *Oh Dad, Poor Dad* (66), *Sailor from Gibraltar* (66), *How to Steal a Million* (66), *The Chastity Belt* (67), *Oliver* (68), *The Fixer* (68), others. Also on stage and TV.

GRIFFITH, KENNETH (1921–   ). Sharp-eyed Welsh actor of stage and screen, often the envious 'little man'. *Love on the Dole* (41), *The*

Shop at Sly Corner (45), *Bond Street* (48), *High Treason* (50), *Lucky Jim* (57), *I'm All Right, Jack* (59), *Circus of Horrors* (59), *Only Two Can Play* (61), *Rotten to the Core* (65), *The Bobo* (67), *The Whisperers* (67), many others.

GRIFFITH, RAYMOND (1896–1959). American silent comedian who after sound came retired from acting and became a producer and writer. *Fools First* (22), *Hands Up* (26), *You'd Be Surprised* (27), etc.

GRIGGS, LOYAL (* –). American cinematographer. *Shane* (AA) (53), *Elephant Walk* (54), *We're No Angels* (55), *The Ten Commandments* (56), *The Hangman* (59), *Walk Like a Dragon* (60), *The Slender Thread* (66), *Hurry Sundown* (67), *P.J.* (*New Face in Hell*) (68), others.

GRIMM, JAKOB (1785–1863) and WILHELM (1786–1859). German writers of philology and—especially—fairy tales. The latter are familiar throughout the world and have been the basis of many children's films by Walt Disney and others. A thin biopic, *The Wonderful World of the Brothers Grimm*, was made in 1962.

GRINDE, NICK (1894– *). American director, mainly of second features. *Riders of the Dark* (30), *The Bishop Murder Case* (32), *Ladies Crave Excitement* (35), *The Man They Could Not Hang* (39), *Behind the Door* (40), etc.

grip. A technician who builds or arranges the film set; a specialized labourer. The chief grip on a picture is usually credited as *Key Grip*.

GROCK (1880–1959) (Adrien Wettach). Swiss clown who made a few silent films in Britain, and later in Germany. A biopic, *Farewell Mr Grock*, was made in 1954.

THE GROUP (US 1966). A faithful and entertaining film version of Mary McCarthy's immensely detailed novel about the lives of some young women graduates in the thirties. Sidney Buchman's script and Sidney Lumet's direction keep the stories nicely contrasted. Of a cast of near-unknowns, impressive performances come from Joan Hackett, Jessica Walter, Elizabeth Hartman, Kathleen Widdoes and others.

Group 3. A British production company set up in 1951 by the National Film Finance Corporation. In charge were John Baxter, John Grierson and Michael Balcon, and their aim was to make low-budget films employing young talent. The venture was regarded with suspicion by the trade, and the results were not encouraging—a string of mildly eccentric comedies and thrillers lucky to get second feature circuit bookings. Some of the titles: *Judgement Deferred, Brandy for the Parson, The Brave Don't Cry, You're Only Young Twice, The Oracle, Laxdale Hall, Time Gentlemen Please*.

433

GUARESCHI, GIOVANNI (1908–1968). Italian author of the 'Don Camillo' stories about a parish priest's comic struggles with a communist mayor. Several have been filmed with Fernandel and Gino Cervi.

GUARDINO, HARRY (1925–   ). American leading actor, somewhat in the Brando mould; mostly on TV. *Houseboat* (58), *Pork Chop Hill* (59), *King of Kings* (61), *Hell Is for Heroes* (62), *Rhino* (65), *Bullwhip Griffin* (67), *Madigan* (68), etc. TV series: *The Reporter* (65).

GUESS WHO'S COMING TO DINNER (US 1967). A commercially successful sugar-coated race relations pill, showing the genteel and sympathetic reactions of an enlightened and wealthy couple to the news that their daughter is going to marry a distinguished negro. All bets are hedged, and the characters do little more than sit around and chat on a single set, but so much talent is involved that the effect is strangely enjoyable if traumatic. Spencer Tracy, whose last film this was, and Katharine Hepburn, who won an Academy Award for her performance, played the parents, with Sidney Poitier (who else?) as the bone of contention. William Rose (AA) wrote the screenplay; Stanley Kramer produced and directed with his usual bloodless competence.

GUEST, VAL (1911–   ). British writer-producer-director, former journalist. Worked on screenplays of 30s comedies for Will Hay, Arthur Askey, the Crazy Gang, etc. *Miss London Ltd* (d) (43), *Just William's Luck* (w, d) (47), *Mr Drake's Duck* (w, d) (50), *Penny Princess* (w, p, d) (51), *The Runaway Bus* (w, p, d) (54), *Quatermass II* (w, d) (56), *Hell Is a City* (w, d) (59), *The Day the Earth Caught Fire* (w, p, d) (62), *Jigsaw* (w, p, d) (62), *The Beauty Jungle* (w, p, d) (64), *Where the Spies Are* (w, p, d) (65), *Assignment K* (w, d) (67), *When Dinosaurs Ruled the Earth* (w, d), (69), many others. Married to Yolande Donlan.

GUETARY, GEORGES (1915–   ) (Lambros Worloou). Greek/Egyptian singer who became popular in French cabaret and musical comedy. Only American film: *An American in Paris* (51).

GUFFEY, BURNETT (1905–   ). Distinguished American cinematographer. *The Informer* (35), *Foreign Correspondent* (40), *Cover Girl* (44), *Johnny O'clock* (46), *Gallant Journey* (46), *The Reckless Moment* (48), *All the King's Men* (49), *In a Lonely Place* (50), *The Sniper* (52), *From Here to Eternity* (AA) (53), *Human Desire* (55), *The Harder They Fall* (56), *Edge of Eternity* (59), *Birdman of Alcatraz* (62), *King Rat* (65), *Bonnie and Clyde* (AA) (67), *The Madwoman of Chaillot* (69), etc.

GUILD, NANCY (1926–   ). American leading lady. *Somewhere in the Night* (46), *The High Window* (47), *Give My Regards to Broadway* (49), *Abbott and Costello Meet the Invisible Man* (51), *Francis Covers the Big Town* (54), etc.

GUILFOYLE, PAUL (1902–1961). American character actor usually in sly or sinister roles since his debut in *Special Agent* (36). *Sweetheart of Sigma Chi* (46), *Miss Mink of 1949*, *Mighty Joe Young* (50), *Torch Song* (52), *Julius Caesar* (53), *Valley of Fury* (55), many others. Directed *Captain Scarface* (53), *A Life at Stake* (54), *Tess of the Storm Country* (60).

GUILLERMIN, JOHN (1925–   ). British director; began work 1946 on French documentaries. *Torment* (49), *Two on the Tiles* (50), *The Crowded Day* (54), *Town on Trial* (56), *I Was Monty's Double* (58), *The Day They Robbed the Bank of England* (60), *Never Let Go* (60), *The Waltz of the Toreadors* (62), *Rapture* (65), *The Blue Max* (66), *P.J. (New Face in Hell)* (US) (68), *House of Cards* (US) (68), *The Bridge at Remagen* (69), others.

GUINNESS, SIR ALEC (1914–   ). Distinguished British actor, on stage from 1934. *Great Expectations* (debut, as Herbert Pocket) (46), *Oliver Twist* (as Fagin) (48), *Kind Hearts and Coronets* (eight roles) (49), *A Run for Your Money* (49), *Last Holiday* (50), *The Lavender Hill Mob* (51), *The Mudlark* (as Disraeli) (51), *The Man in the White Suit* (51), *The Card* (52), *The Malta Story* (53), *The Captain's Paradise* (53), *Father Brown* (54), *To Paris with Love* (54), *The Prisoner* (55), *The Ladykillers* (55), *The Swan* (US) (56), *The Bridge on the River Kwai* (AA, BFA) (57), *Barnacle Bill* (58), *The Scapegoat* (59), *The Horse's Mouth* (59), *Our Man in Havana* (59), *Tunes of Glory* (60), *A Majority of One* (US) (61), *HMS Defiant* (62), *Lawrence of Arabia* (as King Feisal) (62), *The Fall of the Roman Empire* (64), *Situation Hopeless But Not Serious* (65), *Doctor Zhivago* (66), *Hotel Paradiso* (66), *The Quiller Memorandum* (66), *The Comedians* (67), *Cromwell* (as Charles I) (69).

GUIOL, FRED (1898–   ). American director, mainly of second features. *Live and Learn* (30), *The Cohens and Kellys in Trouble* (33), *The Nitwits* (35), *Hayfoot* (41), *Here Comes Trouble* (48), many others; also worked as assistant on many of George Stevens' pictures.

GUITRY, SACHA (1885–1957). Distinguished French writer-director, in films occasionally over a long period. *Ceux de Chez Nous* (15), *Les Deux Couverts* (32), *Bonne Chance* (35), *Le Roman d'un Tricheur* (36), *Quadrille* (38), *Ils Etaient Neuf Célibataires* (39), *Donne-moi tes yeux* (43), *Le Comedien* (49), *Deburau* (51), *Versailles* (54), *Napoleon* (55), *La Vie à Deux* (57), many others.

GULLIVER'S TRAVELS (US 1939). Max Fleischer's full-length colour cartoon was the only serious rival to Disney; but his next attempt, *Mr Bug Goes to Town*, was less attractive and he made no more.

GUNFIGHT AT THE OK CORRAL (US 1957). A somewhat psychologically-motivated version of the celebrated if semi-legendary confrontation between Wyatt Earp and the Clanton gang in 1881 at Tombstone, Arizona. Here Burt Lancaster was Earp, with Kirk Douglas as Doc Holliday, roles played in *My Darling Clementine* (46) by Henry Fonda and Victor Mature. Jon Hall also played Earp in an earlier version, *Frontier Marshal* (39), and TV series *Wyatt Earp* starred Hugh O'Brian.

GUNGA DIN (US 1939). An exhilarating piece of high adventure and barrack-room comedy, very loosely based on Kipling's poem of the north-west frontier. Cary Grant, Douglas Fairbanks jnr and Victor McLaglen were the three rousing heroes, with Sam Jaffe as Gunga Din and Joan Fontaine as love interest. George Stevens in the director's chair kept things moving at a dauntless pace.

GUNN, GILBERT (c.1912–   ). British director, former documentarist. *The Elstree Story* (51), *The Strange World of Planet X* (57), *Girls At Sea* (58), *Operation Bullshine* (59), *What A Whopper* (62), etc.

GURIE, SIGRID (1911–1969) (S. G. Haukelid). American/Norwegian leading lady of the late 30s. *The Adventures of Marco Polo* (38), *Algiers* (38), *Rio* (40), *Three Faces West* (40), *Dark Streets of Cairo* (41), *A Voice in the Wind* (44), *Sword of the Avenger* (last to date) (48), etc.

GUTOWSKI, GENE (1925–   ). Polish producer with US TV experience. *Four Boys and a Gun* (56), *Station Six Sahara* (GB) (63), *Repulsion* (GB) (65), *Cul-de-Sac* (GB) (66), *The Vampire Killers* (GB) (66), etc.

GUY-BLACHE, ALICE (1873–1965). The first French woman director, at work in the early 1900s. *La Fée aux Choux* (00), *Le Voleur Sacrilège* (03), *Paris La Nuit* (04), *La Vie du Christ* (06), etc.

GWENN, EDMUND (1875–1959). Distinguished British character actor of stage and screen, on from 1896. *The Skin Game* (debut) (20), *How She Lied to Her Husband* (30), *Hindle Wakes* (31), *The Skin Game* (remake) (31), *The Good Companions* (as Jess Oakroyd) (32), *Channel Crossing* (32), *Friday the Thirteenth* (33), *Warn London* (34), *Java Head* (34), *The Bishop's Misadventures* (US) (34), *Laburnum Grove* (35), *Sylvia Scarlett* (US) (35), *Anthony Adverse* (US) (36), *Parnell* (US) (37), *A Yank at Oxford* (38), *South Riding* (38), *An Englishman's Home* (39), then to US to stay: *The Earl of Chicago* (40), *Pride and Prejudice* (40), *Foreign Correspondent* (40), *The Devil and Miss Jones* (41), *Cheers for Miss Bishop* (41), *Charley's American Aunt* (41), *A Yank at Eton* (42), *Lassie Come Home* (43), *Between Two Worlds* (44), *The Keys of the Kingdom* (44), *Of Human Bondage* (46), *Undercurrent* (46), *Bob, Son of Battle* (47), *The Big Heart* (*Miracle on 34th Street*) (as Santa Claus) (AA) (US) (47), *Life with Father* (47), *Mister 880* (50), *Pretty Baby* (52), *Peking Express* (52), *The Bigamist* (53), *Them* (54), *The Trouble with Harry* (55), *Calabuch* (Spanish) (58), etc.

GWYNN, MICHAEL (1916–   ). British stage actor in occasional films. *The Runaway Bus* (54), *The Secret Place* (57), *The Revenge of Frankenstein* (as the monster) (58), *Village of the Damned* (60), etc.

GWYNNE, ANNE (1918–   ) (Marguerite Gwynne Trice). American leading lady of the 40s, former model. *Sandy Takes a Bow* (39), *The Strange Case of Doctor RX* (42), *Weird Woman* (44), *House of Frankenstein* (45), *Fear* (46), *The Ghost Goes Wild* (46), *Dick Tracy Meets Gruesome* (48), *Call of the Klondike* (51), *Breakdown* (52), *The Meteor Monster* (57), etc.

GWYNNE, FRED (c. 1924–   ). Lanky, lugubrious American comic actor who appeared in TV series *Car 54 Where Are You* (61–62) and *The Munsters* (64–66). Film: *Munster Go Home* (66).

GYNT, GRETA (1916–   ) (Greta Woxholt). Norwegian leading lady, popular in British films of the 40s. *The Arsenal Stadium Mystery* (39), *Dark Eyes of London* (39), *Tomorrow We Live* (42), *It's That Man Again* (42), *Mr Emmanuel* (44), *London Town* (46), *Dear Murderer* (47), *Take My Life* (47), *The Calendar* (48), *Mr Perrin and Mr Traill* (48), *Shadow of the Eagle* (50), *Soldiers Three* (US) (51), *Forbidden Cargo* (54), *Bluebeard's Ten Honeymoons* (60), *The Runaway* (66), others.

H

HAANSTRA, BERT (1916–). Dutch documentarist: *Mirror of Holland* (50), *The Rival World* (55), *Rembrandt Painter of Man* (56), *Glass* (58), *Fanfare* (feature) (58), *Zoo* (62), *The Human Dutch* (64), etc.

HAAS, CHARLES (* –). American director. *Star in the Dust* (56), *Showdown at Abilene* (57), *Screaming Eagles* (57), *The Beat Generation* (59), etc.

HAAS, HUGO (1901–1968). Czech character actor long in Hollywood. After years in small roles, took to writing and directing low-budget melodramas as vehicles for himself: *Pick Up* (51), *Strange Fascination* (52), *Thy Neighbour's Wife* (53), *Hold Back Tomorrow* (55), *Lizzie* (57), *Night of the Quarter Moon* (59), etc.

HACKETT, ALBERT (1900–). American writer, usually with Frances Goodrich (qv).

HACKETT, BUDDY (1924–). Tubby American comedian with vaudeville experience: *God's Little Acre* (58), *The Music Man* (62), *It's a Mad Mad Mad Mad World* (63), *The Golden Head* (65), etc. TV series: *Stanley* (56).

HACKETT, JOAN (c. 1942–). American leading actress. *The Group* (66), *Will Penny* (67), *Support Your Local Sheriff* (69).

HACKETT, RAYMOND (1903–1958). American leading man who had brief popularity during the changeover from silent to sound. *The Loves of Sunya* (28), *Madame X* (29), *Our Blushing Brides* (29), *The Trial of Mary Dugan* (30), *The Cat Creeps* (31), *Seed* (31), etc.

HACKMAN, GENE (1930–). American character actor. *Lilith* (64), *Hawaii* (66), *Bonnie and Clyde* (67), *The Gypsy Moths* (69), etc.

HACKNEY, ALAN (1924–). British comedy writer. *Private's Progress* (55), *I'm All Right, Jack* (59), *Two-way Stretch* (co-wrote) (60), *Swordsman of Siena* (62), *You Must Be Joking* (65), etc.

HADDON, PETER (1898–1962) (Peter Tildsley). British light actor, usually in silly-ass roles. *Death at Broadcasting House* (34), *The Silent Passenger* (as Lord Peter Wimsey) (35), *Kate Plus Ten* (38), *Helter Skelter* (49), *The Second Mrs Tanqueray* (54), etc. Latterly theatrical manager.

HADEN, SARA (c. 1903–). American actress of quiet, well-spoken parts, best remembered as the spinster aunt of the Hardy family.

Spitfire (debut) (34), *Magnificent Obsession* (35), *First Lady* (38), *H. M. Pulham Esquire* (41), *Lost Angel* (43), *Mr Ace* (45), *Our Vines Have Tender Grapes* (45), *The Bishop's Wife* (48), *A Life of Her Own* (50), *A Lion Is in the Streets* (55), *Andy Hardy Comes Home* (58), etc.

HADLEY, REED (1911–   ) (Reed Herring). American 'second lead'. *Fugitive Lady* (38), *The Bank Dick* (41), *Guadalcanal Diary* (43), *Leave Her to Heaven* (46), *The Iron Curtain* (48), *Captain from Castile* (49), *Dallas* (51), *Big House USA* (55), etc.

HAGEN, JEAN (c. 1925–   ) (Jean Verhagen). American leading lady and sometimes character actress of 'dumb dames'. Broadway experience. *Adam's Rib* (debut) (49), *Singing in the Rain* (52), *The Big Knife* (55), *Panic in Year Zero* (62), *Dead Ringer* (64), others.

HAGGARD, SIR H. RIDER (1856–1925). British adventure novelist, whose most famous novel, *She*, has been filmed at least nine times. There have also been two versions of *King Solomon's Mines*.

HAIGH, KENNETH (1932–   ). British actor, the original stage hero of 'Look Back in Anger'. *My Teenage Daughter* (56), *High Flight* (56), *Saint Joan* (57), *Cleopatra* (62), *A Hard Day's Night* (64), *The Deadly Affair* (66), *A Lovely Way to Die* (US) (68), etc., but has remained mainly a stage performer.

HAINES, WILLIAM (1900–   ). American leading man of the silents. *Three Wise Fools* (23), *Tower of Lies* (24), *Tell It to the Marines* (27), *Alias Jimmy Valentine* (28), *Navy Blues* (30), *The Adventures of Get-Rich-Quick Wallingford* (31), *The Fast Life* (33), *The Marines Are Coming* (35), etc. Retired 1935.

HAKIM, ANDRE (1915–   ). Egyptian-born producer, long in US. *Mr Belvedere Rings the Bell* (52), *The Man Who Never Was* (56), etc.

HAKIM, ROBERT (1907–   ) and RAYMOND (1909–   ). Egyptian-born brothers who have been producing films since 1927. *Pepe Le Moko* (36), *La Bête Humaine* (38), *Le Jour Se Leve* (39), *The Southerner* (44), *Her Husband's Affairs* (47), *The Long Night* (47), *The Blue Veil* (52), *Belle de Jour* (67), *Isadora* (68), many others.

HALAS, JOHN (1912–   ). Hungarian-born animator, in films from 1928. In England from 1936, and with his wife JOY BATCHELOR formed Halas and Batchelor Ltd. They have produced a constant stream of short cartoons, mostly sponsored, one well-received feature (*Animal Farm* [54]) and several TV series. 1967: *Ruddigore*.

HALE, ALAN (1892–1950) (Rufus Alan McKahan). Jovial American actor, a hero of silent action films from 1911 and a familiar cheerful figure in scores of talkies. *The Cowboy and the Lady* (debut) (11), *The Four Horsemen of the Apocalypse* (20), *Robin Hood* (22), *The Covered Wagon* (23), *Main Street* (24), *She Got What She Wanted* (27),

Hale, Alan Jnr.

The Rise of Helga (30), *So Big* (32), *It Happened One Night* (34), *The Last Days of Pompeii* (35), *Jump for Glory* (GB) (36), *Stella Dallas* (37), *The Adventures of Robin Hood* (38), *Dodge City* (39), *The Man in the Iron Mask* (40), *The Sea Hawk* (40), *Tugboat Annie Sails Again* (41), *Strawberry Blonde* (41), *Manpower* (41), *Desperate Journey* (42), *Action in the North Atlantic* (43), *Destination Tokyo* (44), *Hotel Berlin* (45), *Escape to the Desert* (45), *Night and Day* (45), *My Wild Irish Rose* (47), *Pursued* (48), *The New Adventures of Don Juan* (48), *My Girl Tisa* (49), many others.

HALE, ALAN JNR (1918–   ). American character actor who bids fair to be his father's double. TV series: *Casey Jones, Gilligan's Island*. Films include *All American Co-ed* (42), *Sarge Goes to College* (47), *The Gunfighter* (51), *Sons of the Musketeers* (52), *Young at Heart* (54), *Destry* (55), *The Killer Is Loose* (56), others.

HALE, BARBARA (1922–   ). American leading lady, former model; in films from 1943, but roles mainly routine apart from *The Window* (47), *Jolson Sings Again* (50), *Lorna Doone* (51), *Airport* (69). Played Della in TV series *Perry Mason* (57–66).

HALE, BINNIE (1899–   ) (Bernice Hale Munro). British revue artist sister of Sonnie Hale. Rare films include *The Phantom Light* (35), *Hyde Park Corner* (36), *Love from a Stranger* (37), *Take a Chance* (37).

HALE, CREIGHTON (1882–1965) (Patrick Fitzgerald). Irish leading man of American films, sometimes in meek-and-mild roles. *The Exploits of Elaine* (15), *The Thirteenth Chair* (19), *Way Down East* (20), *The Marriage Circle* (24), *Trilby* (as Little Billee) (25), *The Cat and the Canary* (27), *Annie Laurie* (28), many other silents. Talkies, in gradually diminishing roles, include *Stage Whispers* (32), *The Masquerader* (33), *Death from a Distance* (35), *Crime by Night* (43), *Bullet Scars* (45).

HALE, JONATHAN (1892–1966) (J. Hatley). American character actor, former consular attaché, in films from 1934, usually as mildly exasperated business man or hero's boss. *Lightning Strikes Twice* (34), *Alice Adams* (35), *Bringing Up Baby* (38), the *Blondie* series (as Mr Dithers) (38–50), *Her Jungle Love* (39), *Johnny Apollo* (40), *Call Northside 777* (48), *The Steel Trap* (52), *The Night Holds Terror* (56), *Jaguar* (58), many others.

HALE, SONNIE (1902–1959) (Robert Hale Monro). British entertainer and light comedy stage star from 1920. Occasional films include *Tell Me Tonight* (32), *Friday the Thirteenth* (33), *Are You a Mason?* (34), *Evergreen* (35), *The Gaunt Stranger* (38), *Sailing Along* (also directed) (38), *Fiddlers Three* (44), *London Town* (46), etc. Directed but did not appear in three Jessie Matthews musicals of 1937–38: *Head Over Heels, Gangway, Sailing Along*.

HALE, WILLIAM (1928–   ). American director, from TV. *The Naked Hunt* (58), *Gunfight in Abilene* (66), *Journey to Shiloh* (67), etc.

Hale's Tours. In 1902 at the St Louis Exposition, George C. Hale, ex-chief of the Kansas City Fire Department, had the bright idea of shooting a film from the back of a train and screening the result in a small theatre decorated like an observation car. During the screening bells clanged, train whistles sounded and the "coach" rocked slightly. The idea was so successful that it toured for several years in the United States.

HALEY, JACK (1902–   ). American light comedian with diffident manner, in vaudeville and musical comedy from 1920. Films include *Follow Thru* (30), *Sitting Pretty* (33), *Mister Cinderella* (36), *Rebecca of Sunnybrook Farm* (38), *Alexander's Ragtime Band* (38), *The Wizard of Oz* (as the Tin Man) (39), *Higher and Higher* (42), *Scared Stiff* (44), *George White's Scandals* (45), *People Are Funny* (45), *Vacation in Reno* (47), etc. Came back from retirement for *Norwood* (70), directed by his son Jack Haley jnr.

HALL, ALEXANDER (1894–1968). American director from 1932, previously on Broadway. *Sinners in the Sun* (32), *Little Miss Marker* (35), *Limehouse Blues* (36), *Give Us This Night* (37), *The Doctor Takes a Wife* (40), *Married But Single* (41), *Here Comes Mr Jordan* (41), *Once Upon a Time* (44), *Down to Earth* (47), *The Great Lover* (49), *Love That Brute* (50), *Louisa* (50), *Willie and Joe Up Front* (51), *Because You're Mine* (52), *Let's Do It Again* (53), *Forever Darling* (56), etc.

HALL, CHARLES (1899–1959). American character actor, often in comedy two-reelers; memorable as the victim of many a Laurel and Hardy mishap culminating in a tit-for-tat disaster.

HALL, CHARLES D. (1899–   ). British-born production designer, long in Hollywood. *Frankenstein* (31), *Bride of Frankenstein* (35), *Diamond Jim* (35), *Showboat* (36), *Modern Times* (36), *Captain Fury* (39), *The Vicious Years* (51), etc.

HALL, CONRAD (1927–   ). American cinematographer. *Morituri* (65), *Harper* (66), *The Professionals* (66), *Cool Hand Luke* (67), *In Cold Blood* (67), *Hell in the Pacific* (69), *Butch Cassidy and the Sundance Kid* (69), etc.

HALL, HUNTZ (1920–   ) (Henry Hall). American actor, long-faced 'dumb-bell' second lead of the original Dead End Kids and later of the Bowery Boys. Innumerable films include *Angels with Dirty Faces* (38), *They Made Me a Criminal* (39), *A Walk in the Sun* (46), *Fighting Fools* (47), *Blues Busters* (48), *Private Eyes* (50), *The Bowery Boys Meet the Monsters* (54), *Bowery to Baghdad* (56), *Dig That Uranium* (56). Absent from screen after 1959 until *Gentle Ben* (67).

Hall, James

HALL, JAMES (1900–1940) (J. Brown). American hero of a few films at the end of the 20s, notably *Hell's Angels* (30). Later became a night club M.C. *Hotel Imperial* (27), *Rolled Stockings* (28), *Mother's Millions* (31), *Manhattan Tower* (33), etc.

HALL, JON (1913–   ) (Charles Locher). Athletic American leading man who after some stage experience was chosen as hero of *The Hurricane* (37). Later roles gradually diminished in stature: *South of Pago Pago* (39), *Kit Carson* (40), *The Tuttles of Tahiti* (41), *Eagle Squadron* (42), *Invisible Agent* (42), *Arabian Nights* (42), *White Savage* (43), *Cobra Woman* (44), *The Invisible Man's Revenge* (44), *Ali Baba and the Forty Thieves* (44), *San Diego I Love You* (44), *Lady in the Dark* (44), *Sudan* (45), *The Michigan Kid* (46), *The Vigilantes Return* (47), *Prince of Thieves* (48), *Hurricane Island* (50), *When the Redskins Rode* (51), *Last Train from Bombay* (52), *The Beachgirls and the Monster* (65), etc. TV series: *Ramar of the Jungle* (52–53). In recent years has been involved in non-film business activities.

HALL, JUANITA (1901–1968). American Negro character actress and singer, best remembered in the stages and screen versions of *South Pacific* (as Bloody Mary) and *Flower Drum Song*.

†HALL, PETER (1930–   ). British theatrical producer recently venturing into films. *Work is a Four-Letter Word* (68), *A Midsummer Night's Dream* (68), *Three Into Two Won't Go* (69), *Perfect Friday* (70),

HALL, PORTER (1888–1953). American character actor with stage experience before settling in Hollywood. *The Thin Man* (debut) (34), *The Story of Louis Pasteur* (36), *Mr Smith Goes to Washington* (39), *Sullivan's Travels* (41), *The Miracle of Morgan's Creek* (44), *Mad Wednesday* (47), *Intruder in the Dust* (49), *Ace in the Hole* (51), *The Half Breed* (52), *Pony Express* (53), *Return to Treasure Island* (53), many others.

HALL, THURSTON (1883–1958). American character actor adept at choleric executives. Long stage experience; ran his own touring companies. *Cleopatra* (as Mark Antony) (18), *Theodora Goes Wild* (36), *Professor Beware* (38), *The Great McGinty* (40), *He Hired the Boss* (43), *Brewster's Millions* (45), *The Secret Life of Walter Mitty* (47), *Affair in Reno* (56), scores of others.

HALL, WILLIS (1929–   ). British playwright and screenwriter (in collaboration with Keith Waterhouse). *The Long and the Short and the Tall* (61), *Whistle Down the Wind* (61), *A Kind of Loving* (62), *Billy Liar* (63), etc.

HALLATT, MAY (1882–   ). British character actress, mainly on stage. *No Funny Business* (33), *The Lambeth Walk* (39), *Painted Boats* (45), *Black Narcissus* (46), *The Pickwick Papers* (52), *Separate Tables* (her stage role) (58), *Make Mine Mink* (60), etc.

HALLELUJAH (US 1929). This famous film, directed by King Vidor, was probably the first serious screen treatment of Negro life, but despite an all-coloured cast it now seems exaggerated, patronizing and sentimental. The story concerns a Negro murderer who becomes a priest.

HALLER, DANIEL (* –). American art director, notably on Roger Corman's Poe films and *Diary of a Madman* (62). Recently produced *City under the Sea* (65), directed *Monster of Terror* (*Die, Monster, Die*) (66).

HALLER, ERNEST (1896–). Distinguished American cinematographer. *Stella Dallas* (25), *The Dawn Patrol* (31), *The Emperor Jones* (33), *Dangerous* (35), *Jezebel* (38), *Gone With The Wind* (AA) (39), *Dark Victory* (39), *All This and Heaven Too* (40), *Saratoga Trunk* (43), *Mr Skeffington* (44), *Rhapsody in Blue* (45), *Mildred Pierce* (45), *Humoresque* (46), *My Girl Tisa* (47), *The Flame and the Arrow* (50), *Rebel Without A Cause* (55), *Back From The Dead* (57), *God's Little Acre* (58), *Man of the West* (58), *The Third Voice* (59), *Whatever Happened to Baby Jane* (62), *Lilies of the Field* (64), *Dead Ringer* (64), many others.

HALLIDAY, JOHN (1880–1947). Suave Scottish actor, in Hollywood from silent days after considerable stage experience. Best roles: *Recaptured Love* (30), *The Impatient Maiden* (31), *Desirable* (34), *The Dark Angel* (36), *Desire* (36), *Hollywood Boulevard* (36), *That Certain Age* (38), *Escape to Happiness* (*Intermezzo*) (39), *The Philadelphia Story* (40), *Lydia* (41).

HALOP, BILLY (1920–). American actor, former leader of the Dead End Kids (1937–39) in such films as *Dead End, Crime School, Angels with Dirty Faces,* and *On Dress Parade*. When they became The Bowery Boys he left them for better roles which failed to materialize: *Tom Brown's Schooldays* (39), *Mug Town* (42), *Junior Army* (43), *Dangerous Years* (47), etc. Later in bit parts: *Fitzwilly* (68), etc.

HALPERIN, VICTOR (1895–). American director. *Party Girl* (29), *White Zombie* (32), *Supernatural* (33), *Revolt of the Zombies* (36), *I Conquer the Sea* (36), etc.

HALTON, CHARLES (1876–1959). American character actor, inimitable as a sour-faced bank clerk, professor or lawyer. *Dodsworth* (36), *Dr Cyclops* (39), *Jesse James* (39), *H. M. Pulham, Esq.* (41), *Tobacco Road* (41), *Up in Arms* (44), *The Best Years of Our Lives* (46), *Carrie* (51), *The Moonlighter* (53), many others.

†HAMER, ROBERT (1911–1963). British director, at his best impeccably stylish. *Dead of Night* (mirror episode) (45), *Pink String and Sealing*

Wax (45), *It Always Rains on Sunday* (48), *Kind Hearts and Coronets* (49), *The Spider and the Fly* (50), *Father Brown* (54), *To Paris With Love* (55), *The Scapegoat* (59), *School for Scoundrels* (60). Also wrote most of these, and the script for *A Jolly Bad Fellow* (64).

HAMILTON, GEORGE (1939–   ). American leading man, usually in serious roles. *Crime and Punishment USA* (debut) (58), *Home from the Hill* (60), *All the Fine Young Cannibals* (60), *Angel Baby* (61), *By Love Possessed* (61), *A Thunder of Drums* (61), *The Light in the Piazza* (62), *The Victors* (63), *Act One* (63), *Viva Maria* (65), *Your Cheating Heart* (65), *Doctor, You've Got To Be Kidding* (67), *The Long Ride Home* (67), *Jack of Diamonds* (67), *The Power* (67), etc. TV series: *The Survivors* (69).

†HAMILTON, GUY (1922–   ). British director, former assistant to Carol Reed. *The Ringer* (52), *The Intruder* (53), *An Inspector Calls* (54), *The Colditz Story* (54), *Charley Moon* (56), *Manuela* (57), *The Devil's Disciple* (58), *A Touch of Larceny* (59), *The Party's Over* (63), *The Man in the Middle* (64), *Goldfinger* (64), *Funeral in Berlin* (66), *The Battle of Britain* (69).

HAMILTON, MARGARET (1902–   ). American character actress, a former kindergarten teacher who came to films via Broadway and usually played hatchet-faced spinsters or maids. *Another Language* (33), *These Three* (36), *Nothing Sacred* (37), *The Wizard of Oz* (39), *Invisible Woman* (41), *Guest in the House* (44), *Mad Wednesday* (47), *State of the Union* (48), *The Great Plane Robbery* (50), etc.; then nothing until *Thirteen Ghosts* (60), *The Daydreamer* (66), *Rosie* (67).

HAMILTON, MURRAY (c. 1925–   ). American general purpose actor: *Lights Out (Bright Victory)* (50), *No Time for Sergeants* (58), *The FBI Story* (59), *Seconds* (66), *The Graduate* (67), *No Way to Treat a Lady* (68), *The Boston Strangler* (68), *If It's Tuesday This Must Be Belgium* (69), etc.

HAMILTON, NEIL (1899–   ). American leading man of silent days: still makes occasional appearances in character roles. *White Rose* (23), *America* (24), *Isn't Life Wonderful* (25), *Beau Geste* (26), *The Great Gatsby* (27), *Why Be Good* (28), *Keeper of the Bees* (29), *The Dawn Patrol* (30), *The Wet Parade* (31), *The Animal Kingdom* (32), *Tarzan the Ape Man* (32), *One Sunday Afternoon* (33), *Tarzan and His Mate* (34), *Federal Fugitives* (41), *The Little Shepherd of Kingdom Come* (61), *Madame X* (66), hundreds of others. TV series: *Batman* (65–68).

HAMLET (GB 1948). This, the most celebrated of the screen Hamlets (for others, see under Shakespeare), won Academy Awards as the best picture of its year, for Laurence Olivier's performance, for Roger Furse's art direction and costume design, and for Carmen

Dillon's set decoration. Those critics not overwhelmed by its prestige value, however, have often found it cold and empty, marred by injudicious text-cutting and a tendency to rove pointlessly and endlessly down corridors at the expense of action. Notable in the cast were Basil Sydney as Claudius, Eileen Herlie as Gertrude, Jean Simmons as Ophelia, Felix Aylmer as Polonius and Stanley Holloway as the gravedigger. Olivier produced and directed.

HAMMERSTEIN II, OSCAR (1895–1960). Immensely successful American lyricist who wrote many stage musicals, usually with RICHARD RODGERS (qv). *The King and I, South Pacific, The Sound of Music,* etc.

HAMMETT, DASHIELL (1894–1961). American writer of detective stories, of which the most filmed are *The Glass Key* (35 and 42), *The Maltese Falcon* (31 and 36 and 41), and *The Thin Man* (34) which resulted in a series unworthy of his original. Also wrote screenplays including *City Streets* (32).

HAMMOND, KAY (1909–   ) (Dorothy Standing). British stage leading lady with plummy voice, married to John Clements. In films occasionally from 1931 (*A Night in Montmartre*); most notably as Elvira in *Blithe Spirit* (45).

HAMMOND, PETER (1923–   ). British teenage player of the 40s (stage and film). *They Knew Mr Knight* (46), *Holiday Camp* (47), *Fly Away Peter* (48), *Vote for Huggett* (50), etc. Now a TV director (*The Avengers* and other series). 1969: directing *Spring and Port Wine*.

HAMPDEN, WALTER (1879–1955) (Walter Hampden Dougherty). American stage actor with a long career behind him when he came to Hollywood. *The Hunchback of Notre Dame* (debut) (40), *Reap the Wild Wind* (42), *All About Eve* (50), *Five Fingers* (52), *The Vagabond King* (55), etc.

HAMPSHIRE, SUSAN (1941–   ). 'Sweet' young British actress whose films include *During One Night* (61), *The Three Lives of Thomasina* (63), *Night Must Fall* (63), *Wonderful Life* (64), *The Trygon Factor* (67), *Monte Carlo or Bust* (69), *David Copperfield* (69), etc. TV series: *The Forsyte Saga.*

HANCOCK, SHEILA (1933–   ). British comic actress of stage and TV. *Light Up the Sky* (58), *The Girl on the Boat* (61), *Night Must Fall* (63), *The Anniversary* (67), etc.

HANCOCK, TONY (1924–1968). Popular British radio and TV comedian. *Orders Is Orders* (55), *The Rebel* (61), *The Punch and Judy Man* (63), *Those Magnificent Men in Their Flying Machines* (65), etc.

445

Hand, David

HAND, DAVID (1900–   ). American animator, formerly with Disney; came to Britain 1945 to found cartoon unit for Rank. Some pleasing results (*Musical Paintbox* series, etc.); but it was a financial failure and Hand returned to America in 1950.

HANDL, IRENE (1902–   ). Dumpy British comedienne, in films since 1938, often as maid or charlady. Memorable in *I'm All Right, Jack* (59), *Heavens Above* (63), *Morgan* (66).

HANDLEY, TOMMY (1902–49). British radio comedian most famous for his long-running, morale-building *Itma* series during World War II. Rare films include *Elstree Calling* (30), *Two Men in a Box* (38), *It's That Man Again* (42), *Time Flies* (43), *Tom Tom Topia* (short), (46).

THE HANDS OF ORLAC. This improbable thriller by Maurice Renard, about a pianist who loses his hands in an accident and has the hands of a murderer grafted on, has been the basis of three film versions: 1. Directed by Robert Wiene in 1924 (Germany); with Conrad Veidt and Werner Krauss. 2. Directed by Karl Freund in 1934 (US), with Colin Clive and Peter Lorre. 3. Directed by Edmond Greville in 1961 (GB), with Mel Ferrer and Donald Wolfit.

HANLEY, JIMMY (1918–1970). Former British child actor developed as 'the boy next door' type by Rank in the 40s. *Little Friend* (34), *Boys Will Be Boys* (35), *Night Ride* (37), *There Ain't No Justice* (39), *Salute John Citizen* (42), *For You Alone* (44), *The Way Ahead* (44), *Henry V* (44), *Acacia Avenue* (45), *The Captive Heart* (46), *Master of Bankdam* (47), *It Always Rains on Sunday* (48), *It's Hard To Be Good* (49), *Here Come the Huggetts* (and ensuing series 49–52), *The Blue Lamp* (50), *The Black Rider* (54), *The Deep Blue Sea* (56), etc. Latterly on stage and TV.

HANSON, LARS (1887–1965). Swedish stage actor who made silent films abroad but after the coming of sound remained in Sweden. *Ingeborg Holm* (debut) (13), *Dolken* (16), *Erotikon* (19), *The Atonement of Gosta Berling* (24), *The Scarlet Letter* (US) (26), *The Divine Woman* (US) (27), *The Wind* (US) (28), *The Informer* (GB) (28), etc.

HARAREET, HAYA (c. 1934–   ). Israeli leading lady. *Hill 24 Does Not Answer* (55), *Ben Hur* (59), *The Secret Partner* (61), etc.

HARDIN, TY (1930–   ). Brawny American leading man of TV series *Bronco*. Films include *Battle of the Bulge* (65), *Berserk* (GB) (67), *Custer of the West* (68).

HARDING, ANN (1902–   ) (Dorothy Gatley). American actress of gentlewoman roles, a popular leading lady of the 30s. *Paris Bound* (debut) (29), *East Lynne* (31), *Westward Passage* (31), *The Animal Kingdom* (32), *When Ladies Meet* (33), *The Life of Vergie Winters* (34), *Biography of a Bachelor Girl* (35), *Peter Ibbetson* (35), *The Witness Chair* (36), *Love from a Stranger* (GB) (37), then five years' absence; *Mission to Moscow* (42), *Eyes in the Night* (42), *North Star* (43), *Nine Girls* (44), *Those Endearing Young Charms* (45), *Christmas Eve* (47), *Two Weeks with Love* (50), *The Magnificent Yankee* (51), *The Man in the Grey Flannel Suit* (56), etc. Makes occasional TV appearances.

HARDING, LYN (1867–1952) (David Llewellyn Harding). British stage actor who made a splendid 'heavy' in some films of the 20s and 30s. *The Barton Mystery* (20), *When Knighthood Was in Flower* (as Henry VIII) (21), *The Speckled Band* (as Moriarty) (31), *The Triumph of Sherlock Holmes* (as Moriarty) (35), *Spy of Napoleon* (36), *Fire over England* (36), *Knight without Armour* (37), *Goodbye Mr Chips* (as Chips' first headmaster) (39), etc.

HARDWICKE, SIR CEDRIC (1893–1964). British stage and screen actor, too often given inferior material. *Dreyfus* (debut) (31), *Rome Express* (32), *The Ghoul* (33), *Nell Gwyn* (as Charles II) (34), *Jew Suss* (34), *Becky Sharp* (US) (35), *Things to Come* (35), *Peg of Old Drury* (35), *Les Misérables* (US) (35), *Tudor Rose* (36), *King Solomon's Mines* (37), then to US as resident: *The Green Light* (37), *Stanley and Livingstone* (as the latter) (39), *Tom Brown's Schooldays* (39), *On Borrowed Time* (as Death) (39), *The Hunchback of Notre Dame* (40), *The Invisible Man Returns* (40), *Suspicion* (41), *The Ghost of Frankenstein* (41), *The Moon Is Down* (43), *The Lodger* (44), *Wilson* (44), *The Keys of the Kingdom* (44), *Sentimental Journey* (45), *Beware of Pity* (GB) (46), *Nicholas Nickleby* (GB) (47), *Ivy* (47), *The Winslow Boy* (GB) (48), *A Yankee in King Arthur's Court* (49), *Rope* (49), *Rommel, Desert Fox* (51), *Salome* (53), *Diane* (55), *Richard III* (GB) (56), *Baby Face Nelson* (57), *Five Weeks in a Balloon* (62), *The Pumpkin Eater* (GB) (64), others. TV series: *Mrs G. Goes to College* (61). Published autobiography 1961: *A Victorian in Orbit*.

THE HARDY FAMILY. Between 1937 and 1947 fifteen highly successful modest-budget films were made by MGM about the vicissitudes of a 'typical family' in a small midwestern town: father just happened to be a judge who enjoyed man-to-man talks with his teenage son, the wildly untypical Mickey Rooney. Everyone was insufferably nice in these films: father Lewis Stone (Lionel Barrymore did the first episode), mother Fay Holden, daughter Cecilia Parker, aunt Sara Haden. Perhaps because of this they did not last into the post-war period, and an attempt to revive them in 1958 (*Andy Hardy Comes Home*) failed rather miserably. The series was given a special Academy Award in 1942 for 'furthering the American way of life'.

Hardy, Oliver

HARDY, OLIVER (1892–1957). American comedian, the fat half of the Laurel and Hardy team. Began film career 1913 in silent comedies; first teamed with Stan Laurel 1926 and quickly became familiar as a figure of genteel pomposity, frequently landed by his partner in 'another fine mess' climaxed by his long-suffering look at the camera. Of over fifty two-reelers, some of the most outstanding are *Putting Pants on Philip* (the first) (26), *The Battle of the Century* (27), *Leave 'Em Laughing* (28), *Two Tars* (28), *Double Whoopee* (29), *Big Business* (29), *Hog Wild* (30), *The Hoosegow* (30), *Laughing Gravy* (31), *Helpmates* (31), *The Music Box* (AA) (32), *County Hospital* (32), *Towed in a Hole* (33), *Dirty Work* (33), *Them Thar Hills* (34) and *Tit for Tat* (35). Their best features were *Pardon Us* (*Jailbirds*) (31), *Pack Up Your Troubles* (32), *Fra Diavolo* (33), *Sons of the Desert* (*Fraternally Yours*) (33), *Babes in Toyland* (34), *Bonnie Scotland* (35), *The Bohemian Girl* (36), *Our Relations* (36), *Way Out West* (37), *Swiss Miss* (38), *Blockheads* (38), *The Flying Deuces* (39), *A Chump at Oxford* (40), and *Saps at Sea* (40). Their later films, in which the material was out of their control, showed a falling-off: *Great Guns* (41), *A Haunting We Will Go* (42), *Air Raid Wardens* (42), *Jitterbugs* (43), *The Dancing Masters* (43), *The Big Noise* (44), *Nothing But Trouble* (44), *The Bullfighters* (45), *Atoll K* (*Robinson Crusoeland*) (50). A biography, *Mr Laurel and Mr Hardy*, was written in 1961 by John McCabe, and there have recently been three compilation films composed of excerpts from the early two-reelers: *Laurel and Hardy's Laughing Twenties*, *The Crazy World of Laurel and Hardy* and *The Further Perils of Laurel and Hardy*. Hardy solo made three talkie appearances: *Zenobia* (39), *The Fighting Kentuckian* (49) and *Riding High* (50).

HARE, LUMSDEN (1875–1964). Irish character actor, long in Hollywood. *Charlie Chan Carries On* (31), *Clive of India* (35), *She* (35), *Gunga Din* (39), *Rebecca* (40), *The Lodger* (44), *Challenge to Lassie* (49), *Julius Caesar* (53), *The Four Skulls of Jonathan Drake* (59), many others.

HARE, ROBERTSON (1891–   ). Bald-headed British comedian, the put-upon little man of the Aldwych farces of the 20s and 30s, transferred intact from stage to screen. *Rookery Nook* (30), *A Cuckoo in the Nest* (33), *Thark* (33), *Fishing Stock* (35), *Aren't Men Beasts* (38), *Banana Ridge* (41), etc. Later appearances include *He Snoops To Conquer* (45), *Things Happen at Night* (48), *One Wild Oat* (51), *Our Girl Friday* (53), *Three Men in a Boat* (56), *The Young Ones* (61).

HARKER, GORDON (1885–1967). British comic actor, the jutting-lipped Cockney of many a 30s comedy. On stage from 1903. Films: *The Ring* (debut) (27), *The Calendar* (31), *Rome Express* (33), *Friday the Thirteenth* (33), *Boys Will Be Boys* (35), *Millions* (37), *The Return of the Frog* (38), *Inspector Hornleigh* (40), *Saloon Bar* (41), *Warn That*

Man (43), *Acacia Avenue* (45), *Things Happen at Night* (48), *Her Favourite Husband* (50), *The Second Mate* (50), *Derby Day* (52), *Small Hotel* (58), *Left, Right and Centre* (59), etc.

hard ticket. A phrase used in the 60s to describe film exhibition of the type once called 'road show': separate performances, reserved seats, long runs and high prices.

HARLAN, RUSSELL (1903–   ). American cinematographer, former stunt man. *Red River* (48), *The Big Sky* (52), *Riot in Cell Block Eleven* (54), *The Blackboard Jungle* (55), *This Could Be the Night* (57), *Witness for the Prosecution* (57), *Run Silent Run Deep* (58), *King Creole* (58), *The Spiral Road* (62), *To Kill a Mockingbird* (62), *Quick Before It Melts* (65), *Tobruk* (66), etc.

HARLAN, KENNETH (1895–1967). American leading man of the silent screen. *Cheerful Givers* (17), *The Hoodlum* (19), *The Beautiful and the Damned* (22), *The Broken Wing* (23), *Bobbed Hair* (24), *Twinkletoes* (26), many others; small sound roles include *San Francisco* (36), *Paper Bullets* (41), *The Underdog* (44).

HARLAN, OTIS (1865–1940). Tubby American character actor with long stage experience. *What Happened to Jones* (25), *Lightnin'* (26), *Man to Man* (31), *The Hawk* (32), *Married in Haste* (34), *Diamond Jim* (35), *A Midsummer Night's Dream* (35), *Mr Boggs Steps Out* (38), many others.

HARLAN, VEIT (1899–1964). German director. *Kreutzer Sonata* (36), *Jew Suss* (40), *Der Grosse Konig* (41), *Offergang* (43), *Die Blaue Stunde* (52), *The Third Sex* (57), etc.

HARLINE, LEIGH (1907–1969). American screen composer. *Snow White and the Seven Dwarfs* (songs) (37), *Pinocchio* (songs) (AA) (39), *His Girl Friday* (40), *The More the Merrier* (43), *Road to Utopia* (45), *The Farmer's Daughter* (47), *The Big Steal* (49), *Monkey Business* (52), *Broken Lance* (54), *The Wayward Bus* (57), *Ten North Frederick* (58), etc.

HARLOW, JEAN (1911–1937) (Harlean Carpenter). American 'platinum blonde', Hollywood's most sensational star of the early 30s with a private life to suit her public image. *Hell's Angels* (30), *Public Enemy* (30), *Red Dust* (32), *Blonde Bombshell* (33), *Dinner at Eight* (33), *Suzy* (34), *Reckless* (34), *Libelled Lady* (36), *Saratoga* (37), others. The 1965 film biopic of her stars Carroll Baker; the 'electronovision' one Carol Lynley.

HARLOW, JOHN (1896–   ). British writer-director, former music-hall performer. *Spellbound* (d) (40), *Candles at Nine* (d) (43), *Meet Sexton Blake* (d) (44), *The Agitator* (d) (45), *Appointment with Crime* (w, d) (46), *Green Fingers* (w, d) (47), *While I Live (Dream of Olwen)* (w, d)

(48), *Old Mother Riley's New Venture* (d) (49), *Those People Next Door* (d) (52), etc.

HAROLDE, RALF (1899– *) (R. H. Wigger). American supporting actor often seen as thin-lipped crook. *Night Nurse* (32), *A Tale of Two Cities* (35), *Horror Island* (41), *Baby Face Morgan* (42), *Farewell My Lovely* (as the doctor) (44), *Alaska Patrol* (last film) (51), many others.

HARRINGTON, CURTIS (1928–   ). American director who made many experimental shorts before graduating to features: *Night Tide* (60), *Queen of Blood* (66), *Games* (67).

HARRIS, JAMES B. (1924–   ). American producer, associated with director Stanley Kubrick. *The Killing* (56), *Paths of Glory* (57), *Lolita* (62), *The Bedford Incident* (65) (also director), etc.

HARRIS, JONATHAN (c. 1919–   ). American character actor, popular in prissy roles in TV series *The Third Man* (59–61), *The Bill Dana Show* (63–64), *Lost in Space* (65–67). Films include *Botany Bay* (54), *The Big Fisherman* (59).

HARRIS, JULIE (c. 1922–   ). British costume designer. *The Naked Edge* (61), *Tamahine* (63), *The Chalk Garden* (64), *A Hard Day's Night* (64), *Help* (65), *Darling* (BFA) (65), *The Wrong Box* (66), etc.

HARRIS, JULIE (1925–   ). American stage actress, adept at fey roles. Occasional films: *Member of the Wedding* (52), *East of Eden* (54), *I Am a Camera* (GB) (55), *The Truth about Women* (GB) (58), *The Haunting* (63), *Harper* (*The Moving Target*) (66), *You're a Big Boy Now* (67), *Reflections in a Golden Eye* (67), *The Split* (68), etc.

HARRIS, PHIL (1906–   ). American bandleader and latterday comic actor; married to Alice Faye. In film musicals occasionally from 1933; dramatic role in *The High and the Mighty* (54). Recently: *The Wheeler Dealers* (*Separate Beds*) (63).

†HARRIS, RICHARD (1933–   ). Gaunt Irish leading actor, usually cast as a rebel, a part he tries to match in real life. *Alive and Kicking* (debut) (58), *Shake Hands with the Devil* (59), *A Terrible Beauty* (60), *The Long, the Short and the Tall* (61), *Guns of Navarone* (61), *Mutiny on the Bounty* (US) (62), *This Sporting Life* (63), *The Red Desert* (It.) (64), *Major Dundee* (US) (65), *The Heroes of Telemark* (65), *The Bible* (66), *Hawaii* (66), *Caprice* (66), *Camelot* (67), *The Molly Maguires* (69), *A Man Called Horse* (69), *Cromwell* (title role) (69).

HARRIS, ROBERT (1900–   ). British classical actor who has played occasional film roles. *How He Lied to Her Husband* (31), *The Life and Death of Colonel Blimp* (43), *The Bad Lord Byron* (48), *That Lady* (55), *Oscar Wilde* (60), *Decline and Fall* (68), etc.

HARRIS, ROBERT H. (c. 1909–   ). American character actor, usually in pompous comedy roles. *Bundle of Joy* (56), *How to Make a Monster* (58), *America America* (63), *Mirage* (65), *Valley of the Dolls* (67), etc.

HARRIS, ROSEMARY (1930–   ). British leading lady, chiefly on stage. Films include *Beau Brummell* (54), *The Shiralee* (55), *A Flea in Her Ear* (68).

HARRIS, VERNON (c. 1910–   ). British screenwriter. *Albert RN* (co-w) (53), *The Sea Shall Not Have Them* (co-w) (55), *Reach for the Sky* (56), *Ferry to Hong Kong* (57), *The Admirable Crichton* (57), *Light up the Sky* (61), *Oliver* (co-ow) (68), etc.

HARRISON, JOAN (1911–   ). British writer-producer, assistant for many years to Alfred Hitchcock. Screenplays: *Rebecca* (40), *Foreign Correspondent* (40), *Saboteur* (42); produced *Phantom Lady* (44), *Ride the Pink Horse* (48), etc. From 1958: produced TV series *Alfred Hitchcock Presents*.

HARRISON, KATHLEEN (1898–   ). British character actress, usually seen as a cockney but born in Lancashire. On stage from 1926; films have made her an amiable, slightly dithery but warm-hearted national figure. *Hobson's Choice* (debut) (31), *The Ghoul* (33), *Broken Blossoms* (36), *Night Must Fall* (US) (37), *Bank Holiday* (38), *The Outsider* (39), *The Ghost Train* (41), *Kipps* (41), *In Which We Serve* (42), *Dear Octopus* (43), *Great Day* (45), *Holiday Camp* (47), *Bond Street* (48), *Oliver Twist* (48), *Here Come the Huggetts* (and ensuing series) (49–52), *Waterfront* (50), *Scrooge* (51), *Pickwick Papers* (52), *Turn the Key Softly* (53), *Cast a Dark Shadow* (54), *Where There's a Will* (54), *Lilacs in the Spring* (54), *All for Mary* (55), *Home and Away* (56), *A Cry from the Streets* (58), *Alive and Kicking* (58), *Mrs Gibbons' Boys* (62), *West Eleven* (63), *Lock Up Your Daughters* (69), many others. Popular on radio and TV, especially as *Mrs Thursday*.

†HARRISON, REX (1908–   ) (Reginald Carey). Debonair British leading actor of pleasant if limited range, on stage since 1924; films have only occasionally given him the right material. *The Great Game* (30), *The School for Scandal* (30), *All at Sea* (34), *Men Are Not Gods* (36), *Storm in a Teacup* (37), *School for Husbands* (37), *St Martin's Lane* (38), *The Citadel* (38), *Over the Moon* (39), *The Silent Battle* (39), *Ten Days in Paris* (39), *Night Train to Munich* (40), *Major Barbara* (40); war service; *I Live in Grosvenor Square* (45), *Blithe Spirit* (45), *The Rake's Progress* (46), *Anna and the King of Siam* (US) (46), *The Ghost and Mrs Muir* (US) (47), *The Foxes of Harrow* (US) (47), *Unfaithfully Yours* (US) (48), *Escape* (48), *The Long Dark Hall* (51), *The Fourposter* (US) (52), *King Richard and the Crusaders* (as Saladin) (US) (54), *The Constant Husband* (55), *The Reluctant Debutante* (US) (58), *Midnight Lace* (US) (60), *The Happy Thieves* (US) (62),

Cleopatra (US) (62), *My Fair Lady* (AA) (US) (64), *The Yellow Rolls-Royce* (64), *The Agony and the Ecstasy* (US) (as a medieval pope) (65), *The Honey Pot* (US) (67), *Doctor Dolittle* (US) (67), *A Flea in Her Ear* (US/French) (68), *Staircase* (69).

HARRON, ROBERT (BOBBY) (1894–1920). American juvenile lead who joined D. W. Griffith's company almost from school. *Man's Genesis* (12), *The Birth of a Nation* (14), *Intolerance* (16), *Hearts of the World* (18), *True Heart Susie* (19), many others; died in shooting accident.

HARRYHAUSEN, RAY (c. 1920–   ). American trick film specialist and model maker; invented 'Superdynamation'. Worked on *Mighty Joe Young* (50), *It Came from Beneath the Sea* (52), *Twenty Million Miles to Earth* (57), *The Three Worlds of Gulliver* (60), *Jason and the Argonauts* (63), *The First Men in the Moon* (64), *One Million Years B.C.* (66), *The Valley of Gwangi* (69), etc.

HART, DOLORES (1938–   ). (D. Hicks). American lady of a few films in the late 50s. *Loving You* (56), *Wild is the Wind* (57), *Lonelyhearts* (59), *Sail a Crooked Ship* (60), *Lisa (The Inspector)* (62), etc.

HART, HARVEY (1928–   ). Canadian director, from TV, now in Hollywood. *Bus Riley's Back in Town* (65), *Sullivan's Empire* (67), *The Sweet Ride* (68).

HART, MOSS (1904–61). American author whose many scenarios and original plays to appear on the screen include *Once in a Lifetime* (32), *Broadway Melody of 1936*, *You Can't Take It with You* (with George Kaufman) (38), *The Man Who Came to Dinner* (with Kaufman) (41), *Winged Victory* (43), *Lady in the Dark* (44), *Gentlemen's Agreement* (48), *A Star Is Born* (54), etc. Also stage producer. A film was made of his autobiography: *Act One* (63).

HART, RICHARD (1915–1951). American leading man with a very brief Hollywood career. *Green Dolphin Street* (47), *Desire Me* (47), *B.F.'s Daughter* (48), *The Black Book* (49).

HART, WILLIAM S. (1870–1946). Solemn-faced Western hero of silent screen. *The Return of Draw Egan* (15), *Hell's Hinges* (16), *The Toll Gate* (18), *Wagon Tracks* (19), *Travellin' On* (21), *White Oak* (22), *Wild Bill Hickock* (23), *Tumbleweeds* (25), scores of others. The 'S' is variously reputed to have stood for 'Shakespeare' and 'Surrey'. Published autobiography 1929: *My Life East and West*.

HARTFORD-DAVIS, ROBERT (1923–   ). British producer-director, in films since 1939. *That Kind of Girl* (62), *The Yellow Teddybears* (63), *Saturday Night Out* (63), *Black Torment* (64), *Gonks Go Beat* (65), *The Sandwich Man* (66), *Corruption* (68), *The Smashing Bird I Used to Know* (69), etc.

HARTMAN, DON (1901–58). American director and screenwriter, mainly of light comedy. The *Road* films (w) (40–45), *Up In Arms* (w) (44), *Every Girl Should Be Married* (w, d) (48), many others. Executive producer for Paramount from 1951.

†HARTMAN, ELIZABETH (1945–   ). American leading actress. *A Patch of Blue* (66), *The Group* (66), *You're a Big Boy Now* (67).

HARTNELL, WILLIAM (1908–   ). British character actor, on stage from 1924, films from 1931. In late 40s was typed in sergeant-major roles; now more typically cast as TV's kindly *Dr Who*. *The Way Ahead* (first big hit) (44), *The Agitator* (44), *Murder in Reverse* (45), *Appointment with Crime* (46), *Brighton Rock* (46), *Odd Man Out* (47), *The Ringer* (52), *The Pickwick Papers* (53), *Private's Progress* (56), *The Mouse That Roared* (59), *Heavens Above* (63), many others.

HARVEY (US 1950). It was fashionable at the time to despise this as inferior to the stage play about a genial alcoholic who is accompanied by an invisible white rabbit six feet high. But James Stewart coped admirably with most of the googly lines; Josephine Hull was a positive delight as his much-abused sister; the supporting cast included gems from Cecil Kellaway, Wallace Ford, and Jesse White; and Henry Koster's direction, while not exciting, gave Mary Chase's script its full head.

HARVEY, ANTHONY (1931–   ). British editor: *Private's Progress* (55), *Tread Softly Stranger* (58), *I'm All Right, Jack* (59), *Lolita* (61), *Dr Strangelove* (63), *The Spy Who Came in from the Cold* (65), *The Whisperers* (67), many others. Turned director: *Dutchman* (66), *The Lion in Winter* (68),

HARVEY, FORRESTER (1890–1945). Irish character actor, long in Hollywood. *The White Sheik* (26), *Tarzan the Ape Man* (32), *Shanghai Express* (32), *The Invisible Man* (33), *David Copperfield* (34), *Lloyds of London* (37), *A Chump at Oxford* (40), *Dr Jekyll and Mr Hyde* (41), *Devotion* (44), many others.

HARVEY, FRANK (1912–   ). British playwright (*Saloon Bar*, filmed 1940; *The Poltergeist*, filmed 1948 as *Things Happen at Night*; etc.) and scriptwriter in collaboration (*Seven Days to Noon*, *Private's Progress*, *I'm All Right Jack*, *Heavens Above*, etc.).

HARVEY, LAURENCE (1928–   ) (Larushka Skikne). Lithuanian-born leading man who worked his way slowly from British second features to top Hollywood productions. Also on stage from 1947. *House of Darkness* (48), *The Scarlet Thread* (51), *Storm Over the Nile* (55), *Three Men in a Boat* (56), *The Silent Enemy* (58), *Room at the Top* (59), *Expresso Bongo* (59), *The Alamo* (60), *Butterfield 8* (61), *A Walk on the Wild Side* (62), *The Manchurian Candidate* (62), *The Running*

Man (63), *The Ceremony* (also producer-director) (63), *Of Human Bondage* (64), *The Outrage* (64), *Darling* (65), *Life at the Top* (65), *The Spy with a Cold Nose* (67), *He and She* (also produced) (69), *Hall of Mirrors* (70), etc.

HARVEY, LILIAN (1906–1968). British leading lady who in the 30s became star of German films. *Leidenschaft* (25), *Die Tolle Lola* (27), *Drei von der Tankstelle* (30), *Congress Dances* (31), *Happy Ever After* (32), *My Weakness* (US) (33), *I Am Suzanne* (US) (34), *Invitation to the Waltz* (GB) (35), *Capriccio* (38), *Serenade Eternelle* (French; last film) (39), etc.

HARVEY, PAUL (1884–1955). American character actor who often played the choleric executive or kindly father. *Advice to the Lovelorn* (34), *Rebecca of Sunnybrook Farm* (38), *Algiers* (38), *Stanley and Livingstone* (39), *Maryland* (40), *Pillow to Post* (45), *The Late George Apley* (47), *Father of the Bride* (50), *The First Time* (52), *Three for the Show* (55), hundreds of others.

HASKIN, BYRON (1899–   ). American director, former cameraman, in films from 1918; has a penchant for science fiction. *Ginsberg the Great* (26), *The Siren* (26), then spent many years as cameraman and special effects expert, returning to direction in the 40s. *I Walk Alone* (47), *Too Late for Tears* (49), *Treasure Island* (50), *Warpath* (51), *Silver City* (52), *The War of the Worlds* (53), *His Majesty O'Keefe* (54), *The Naked Jungle* (54), *Long John Silver* (55), *Conquest of Space* (55), *The Boss* (56), *From the Earth to the Moon* (58), *September Storm* (60), *Armoured Command* (61), *Captain Sindbad* (63), *Robinson Crusoe on Mars* (64), *The Power* (67), etc. Much TV work.

HASSO, SIGNE (1915–   ) (Signe Larsson). Swedish leading lady with stage and screen experience at home before going to America. *Journey for Margaret* (Hollywood debut) (42), *The Seventh Cross* (44), *The House on 92nd Street* (46), *To the Ends of the Earth* (47), *A Double Life* (48), etc.; more recently on stage and TV. 1966: *Picture Mommy Dead*.

HATFIELD, HURD (1918–   ). American leading man with stage experience before film debut in *Dragon Seed* (44) followed by title role in *The Picture of Dorian Gray* (44); then *The Diary of a Chambermaid* (45), *The Checkered Coat* (48), *Joan of Arc* (48), *The Unsuspected* (48), *Tarzan and the Slave Girl* (50), etc. Returned to stage; occasional recent appearances in *King of Kings* (61), *El Cid* (61), *Mickey One* (65), *The Boston Strangler* (68).

†HATHAWAY, HENRY (1898–   ). American director in films (as child actor) from 1907. Acted till 1932, then directed Westerns. Later became known as a capable handler of big action adventures and thrillers. *Wild Horse Mesa* (32), *Heritage of the Desert* (33),

Under the Tonto Rim (33), *Sunset Pass* (33), *Man of the Forest* (33), *To the Last Man* (33), *Come On Marines* (34), *The Last Round-up* (34), *Thundering Herds* (34), *The Witching Hour* (34), *Now and Forever* (34), *Lives of a Bengal Lancer* (35), *Peter Ibbetson* (35), *Trail of the Lonesome Pine* (36), *Go West Young Man* (36), *Souls at Sea* (37), *Spawn of the North* (38), *The Real Glory* (39), *Johnny Apollo* (40), *Brigham Young* (40), *Shepherd of the Hills* (41), *Sundown* (41), *Ten Gentlemen from West Point* (42), *China Girl* (43), *Home in Indiana* (44), *A Wing and a Prayer* (44), *Nob Hill* (45), *The House on 92nd Street* (45), *The Dark Corner* (46), *13 Rue Madeleine* (46), *Kiss of Death* (47), *Call Northside 777* (48), *Down to the Sea in Ships* (49), *The Black Rose* (50), *You're in the Navy Now* (51), *Rawhide* (51), *Fourteen Hours* (51), *Rommel, Desert Fox* (51), *Diplomatic Courier* (52), *Niagara* (52), *White Witch Doctor* (53), *Prince Valiant* (54), *Garden of Evil* (54), *The Racers* (54), *The Bottom of the Bottle* (55), *Twenty-three Paces to Baker Street* (56), *Legend of the Lost* (57), *From Hell to Texas* (58), *A Woman Obsessed* (59), *Seven Thieves* (60), *North to Alaska* (60), *How the West Was Won* (part) (62), *Circus World* (*The Magnificent Showman*) (64), *The Sons of Katie Elder* (65), *Nevada Smith* (66), *The Last Safari* (67), *5 Card Stud* (68), *True Grit* (69), *Airport* (69), etc.

HATTON, RAYMOND (1892–). American character actor in Hollywood from 1911. Played in hundreds of cowboy films, usually as comic sidekick, and was teamed with Wallace Beery 1926–29 in knockabout comedies such as *Behind the Front* and *We're in the Navy Now*. Also: *G-Men* (35), *Laughing Irish Eyes* (36), *Marked Woman* (37), *Operation Haylift* (50), *Shake, Rattle and Rock* (56), *In Cold Blood* (67), etc.

HATTON, RONDO (c. 1902–1946). American actor who suffered from facial and bodily deformity and was cast as a crazed or hypnotized killer in several minor thrillers of the 40s. *The Ox-Bow Incident* (42), *Pearl of Death* (44), *Spider Woman Strikes Back* (44), *House of Horror* (45), *The Creeper* (46), etc.

HAVELOCK-ALLAN, ANTHONY (1905–). British producer. *This Man Is News* (38), *In Which We Serve* (associate) (42), *Blithe Spirit* (45), *Brief Encounter* (46), *Great Expectations* (46), *Oliver Twist* (48), *The Small Voice* (49), *Never Take No for an Answer* (51), *The Young Lovers* (54), *Orders to Kill* (58), *The Quare Fellow* (61), *An Evening with the Royal Ballet* (64), *Othello* (65), *The Mikado* (67), etc.

HAVER, JUNE (1926–) (June Stovenour). American leading lady of the 40s, mostly in musicals; married Fred MacMurray. *Home in Indiana* (debut) (44), *Irish Eyes Are Smiling* (44), *Where Do We Go from Here* (45), *The Dolly Sisters* (45), *Three Little Girls in Blue* (46), *I Wonder Who's Kissing Her Now* (47), *Summer Lightning* (48), *Look for the Silver Lining* (as Marilyn Miller) (49), *The Daughter of Rosie O'Grady* (50), *Love Nest* (51), *The Girl Next Door* (53), etc. Retired.

HAVER, PHYLLIS (1899–1960). American leading lady of the silent screen, a former Sennett bathing beauty. *Small Town Idol* (20), *Temple of Venus* (23), *Fig Leaves* (25), *Up in Mabel's Room* (26), *The Way of All Flesh* (28), *Hard Boiled* (29), *Hell's Kitchen* (29), many others.

HAVOC, JUNE (1916–   ) (June Hovick). American leading lady, former child actress; sister of Gypsy Rose Lee. *Four Jacks and a Jill* (42), *Brewster's Millions* (45), *The Story of Molly X* (49), *Once a Thief* (50), *A Lady Possessed* (51), *Three for Jamie Dawn* (57), etc.

HAWKINS, JACK (1910–   ). Distinguished British leading man and character actor, on stage from 1923, films from 1932. *The Good Companions* (32), *Peg of Old Drury* (35), *The Frog* (37), *Next of Kin* (41); war service; *The Fallen Idol* (48), *The Small Back Room* (48), *The Elusive Pimpernel* (49), *No Highway* (50), *The Black Rose* (50), *State Secret* (50), *Angels One Five* (51), *Mandy* (52), *The Planter's Wife* (52), *The Cruel Sea* (53), *The Malta Story* (53), *The Intruder* (53), *Front Page Story* (54), *The Seekers* (54), *Land of the Pharaohs* (US) (55), *The Prisoner* (55), *Touch and Go* (55), *The Long Arm* (56), *The Man in the Sky* (56), *Fortune Is a Woman* (57), *The Bridge on the River Kwai* (57), *Gideon's Day* (58), *The Two-Headed Spy* (58), *Ben Hur* (US) (59), *The League of Gentlemen* (60), *Spinster* (61), *Five Finger Exercise* (62), *Lawrence of Arabia* (62), *Rampage* (63), *Zulu* (64), *Lord Jim* (65), *Masquerade* (65), *Judith* (65), etc. TV series: *The Four Just Men*. Retired from acting after operation on vocal cords, but played silent role in *Great Catherine* (67) and was dubbed in *Shalako* (68), *Monte Carlo or Bust* (69), *Waterloo* (70).

†HAWKS, HOWARD (1896–   ). American director, at his best an incomparable provider of professional comedies and action dramas. In films from 1918, at first as writer and editor. *Tiger Love* (wrote only) (24), *The Road to Glory* (also wrote) (26), *Fig Leaves* (also wrote) (26), *The Cradle Snatchers* (27), *Paid to Love* (27), *A Girl in Every Port* (also wrote) (28), *Fazil* (28), *The Air Circus* (28), *Trent's Last Case* (also wrote) (29), *The Dawn Patrol* (30), *The Criminal Code* (31), *The Crowd Roars* (32), *Scarface* (32), *Tiger Shark* (32), *Today We Live* (33), *Twentieth Century* (34), *Viva Villa* (part) (34), *Barbary Coast* (35), *Ceiling Zero* (36), *Road to Glory* (36), *Come and Get It* (co-d) (36), etc.; then produced all his subsequent pictures: *Bringing Up Baby* (38), *Only Angels Have Wings* (39), *His Girl Friday* (40), *Sergeant York* (41), *Ball of Fire* (41), *Air Force* (42), *To Have and Have Not* (44), *The Big Sleep* (46), *A Song Is Born* (48), *Red River* (48), *I Was a Male War Bride* (49), *The Thing from Another World* (produced only) (52), *The Big Sky* (52), *Monkey Business* (52),

Full House (one episode) (52), *Gentlemen Prefer Blondes* (53), *Land of the Pharaohs* (55), *Rio Bravo* (58), *Hatari* (62), *Man's Favourite Sport* (64), *Red Line 7000* (65), *El Dorado* (66).

HAWORTH, JILL (1945–   ). British leading lady. *Exodus* (60), *In Harm's Way* (65), *Curse of the Golem* (66), etc.

HAWTHORNE, NATHANIEL (1804–1864). American novelist whose books *The Scarlet Letter, Twice-Told Tales* and *The House of Seven Gables* have been much adapted for the screen.

HAWTREY, CHARLES (1914–   ) (Charles Hartree). British comic actor, spindle-shanked and often cast as ageing schoolboy in Will Hay comedies. On stage from 1929, films from 1930. Many good cameo roles; larger one in *You're Only Young Twice* (53); now one of the '*Carry On*' team.

HAY, ALEXANDRA (c. 1944–   ). American leading lady. *Skidoo* (68), *The Model Shop* (69), etc.

HAY, WILL (1888–1949). British character comedian who came to films in 1934 after many years on the music halls as an incompetent, seedy schoolmaster. *Those Were the Days* (34), *Boys Will Be Boys* (35), *Good Morning, Boys* (36), *Convict 99* (38), *Oh Mr Porter* (38), *Old Bones of the River* (39), *Ask a Policeman* (40), *Where's That Fire* (41), *The Black Sheep of Whitehall* (41), *The Goose Steps Out* (42), *The Ghost of St Michael's* (42), *My Learned Friend* (44), etc.

HAYAKAWA, SESSUE (1889–   ). Japanese actor, a popular star of American silents; more recently in occasional character roles. *The Typhoon* (14), *The Cheat* (15), *Forbidden Paths* (17), *The Tong Man* (19), *Daughter of the Dragon* (21), *Tokyo Joe* (49), *Three Came Home* (50), *The Bridge on the River Kwai* (57), *The Geisha Boy* (59), *The Swiss Family Robinson* (60), *Hell to Eternity* (61), etc.

HAYDEN, RUSSELL (1912–   ) (Pate Lucid). American 'second string' leading man, for many years Hopalong Cassidy's faithful side-kick. Now produces TV westerns. *Hills of Old Wyoming* (debut) (37), *Range War* (39), *Lucky Legs* (42), *'Neath Canadian Skies* (46), *Seven Were Saved* (47), *Silver City* (49), *Valley of Fire* (51), many others.

HAYDEN, STERLING (1916–   ). Tall American leading man, also globetrotter and explorer. *Virginia* (debut) (41), *Bahama Passage* (41), *Blaze of Noon* (47), *The Asphalt Jungle* (50), *Flaming Feather* (51), *So Big* (52), *The Star* (52), *Prince Valiant* (54), *Johnny Guitar* (54), *Suddenly* (54), *The Eternal Sea* (55), *The Last Command* (55), *The Killing* (56), *Terror in a Texas Town* (58), *Dr Strangelove* (63), *Hard Contract* (69), etc.

HAYDN, RICHARD (1905–   ). British revue star of 30s, in Hollywood from 1941, usually in adenoidal character cameos. *Ball of Fire* (debut) (41), *Charley's American Aunt* (41), *Forever and a Day* (43), *Ten Little Niggers* (45), *Cluny Brown* (46), *Sitting Pretty* (47), *Miss Tatlock's Millions* (also directed) (48), *Mr Music* (also directed) (49), *Dear Wife* (directed only) (50), *Jupiter's Darling* (54), *Please Don't Eat the Daisies* (60), *The Lost World* (60), *Mutiny on the Bounty* (62), *Five Weeks in a Balloon* (62), *The Sound of Music* (65), *Clarence the Cross-Eyed Lion* (65), *Bullwhip Griffin* (66), many others.

HAYE, HELEN (1874–1957) (Helen Hay). Distinguished British stage actress (debut 1898), in occasional films from mid-20s, usually as kindly dowager. *Atlantic* (30), *Congress Dances* (31), *The Spy in Black* (39), *Kipps* (41), *Dear Octopus* (43), *Anna Karenina* (48), *Richard III* (56), many others.

HAYERS, SIDNEY (1921–   ). British director, in films since 1942. Former editor and second unit director. *Violent Moment* (58), *The White Trap* (59), *Circus of Horrors* (59), *Echo of Barbara* (60), *Payroll* (61), *Night of the Eagle* (62), *This Is My Street* (63), *Three Hats for Lisa* (65), *The Trap* (66), *Finders Keepers* (66), *The Southern Star* (69).

HAYES, ALLISON (1930–   ) (Mary Jane Hayes). American leading lady of a few films in the 50s. *Francis Joins the WACS* (54), *The Purple Mask* (55), *The Blackboard Jungle* (55), *Mohawk* (56), *The Zombies of Mora Tau* (57), *Attack of the Fifty-foot Woman* (title role) (58), *Who's Been Sleeping in My Bed* (63), *Tickle Me* (65).

HAYES, GEORGE 'GABBY' (1885–   ). Bewhiskered American character actor, in Westerns since early silent days. Since 40s with Roy Rogers as comic relief; also had his own TV show 1956.

†HAYES, HELEN (1900–   ) (Helen Brown). Distinguished American stage actress who made few film appearances. *The Weavers of Life* (17), *Babs* (20), *The Sin of Madelon Claudet* (AA) (31), *Arrowsmith* (31), *A Farewell to Arms* (32), *The Son Daughter* (33), *The White Sister* (33), *Another Language* (33), *Night Flight* (33), *What Every Woman Knows* (34), *Vanessa* (35), *My Son John* (51), *Anastasia* (56), *Airport* (69).

HAYES, JOHN MICHAEL (1919–   ). American screenwriter. *Rear Window* (54), *To Catch a Thief* (55), *The Trouble with Harry* (56), *Peyton Place* (57), *The Carpetbaggers* (63), *Where Love Has Gone* (64), *Harlow* (65), *Judith* (66), *Nevada Smith* (66), etc.

HAYMES, DICK (1916–   ). Argentine-born crooner, former radio announcer. *Irish Eyes Are Smiling* (debut) (44), *Diamond Horseshoe* (45), *State Fair* (45), *Do You Love Me* (46), *The Shocking Miss Pilgrim*

(47), *Up in Central Park* (48), *One Touch of Venus* (48), *St Benny the Dip* (51), *All Ashore* (53), etc.

HAYS, WILL H. (1879–1954). American executive, for many years (1922–45) president of the Motion Picture Producers and Distributors Association of America, and author of its high-toned Production Code (1930), which for many years put producers in fear of 'the Hays office'. *The Memoirs of Will H. Hays* was published in 1955.

HAYTER, JAMES (1907–   ). Portly, jovial British character actor, on stage from 1925, films from 1936. *Sensation* (36), *Sailors Three* (41), *School for Secrets* (46), *Nicholas Nickleby* (as the Cheeryble twins) (47), *The Blue Lagoon* (48), *Trio* (50), *Tom Brown's Schooldays* (51), *Robin Hood* (as Friar Tuck) (52), *Pickwick Papers* (title role) (53), *The Great Game* (53), *A Day to Remember* (54), *Touch and Go* (56), *Port Afrique* (58), *The Thirty-nine Steps* (59), *Stranger in the House* (67), *Oliver* (68), *David Copperfield* (69), many others.

HAYTHRONE, JOAN (1915–   ) (Joan Haythornthwaite). British stage actress, usually in aristocratic roles. Few films include *School for Secrets* (46), *Jassy* (47), *Highly Dangerous* (50), *Svengali* (54), *The Weak and the Wicked* (54), *The Feminine Touch* (56), *Three Men in a Boat* (56), *Shakedown* (59), *So Evil So Young* (61).

HAYWARD, LELAND (1902–   ). American talent agent and stage producer. Recently produced films: *Mister Roberts* (55), *The Spirit of St Louis* (57), *The Old Man and the Sea* (58), etc.

HAYWARD, LOUIS (1909–   ) (Seafield Grant). South African-born leading man with stage experience; in Hollywood from 1935; latterly in character roles. *Chelsea Life* (GB) (33), *Sorrell and Son* (GB) (34), *The Flame Within* (35), *Anthony Adverse* (36), *The Luckiest Girl in the World* (36), *Midnight Intruder* (37), *The Rage of Paris* (38), *The Saint in New York* (38), *Duke of West Point* (39), *The Man in the Iron Mask* (39), *My Son, My Son* (39), *Son of Monte Cristo* (40), *Ladies in Retirement* (41); war service; *Ten Little Niggers* (45), *Monte Cristo's Revenge* (47), *Young Widow* (47), *Repeat Performance* (47), *The Black Arrow* (48), *Walk a Crooked Mile* (48), *The Fortunes of Captain Blood* (50), *Son of Dr Jekyll* (51), *Dick Turpin's Ride* (51), *Lady in the Iron Mask* (52), *The Saint's Return* (GB) (53), *Duffy of San Quentin* (54), *The Search for Bridey Murphy* (56), *Chuka* (67), etc.; recently on stage and TV. TV series: *The Lone Wolf* (54), *The Pursuers* (62), *The Survivors* (69).

†HAYWARD, SUSAN (1918–   ) (Edythe Marriner). Vivacious American leading lady, in films from 1938 after modelling experience: often in aggressive roles. *Girls on Probation* (38), *Our Leading Citizen* (39), *$1000 A Touchdown* (39), *Beau Geste* (39), *Adam Had Four Sons* (41), *Sis Hopkins* (41), *Among the Living* (41), *Reap the Wild Wind* (42),

The Forest Rangers (42), *I Married a Witch* (42), *Star Spangled Rhythm* (42), *Change of Heart* (43), *Jack London* (43), *Young and Willing* (43), *The Fighting Seabees* (44), *And Now Tomorrow* (44), *The Hairy Ape* (44), *Canyon Passage* (45), *Deadline at Dawn* (46), *Smash-Up* (*A Woman Destroyed*) (47), *They Won't Believe Me* (47), *The Lost Moment* (47), *Tap Roots* (48), *The Saxon Charm* (48), *Tulsa* (49), *My Foolish Heart* (49), *House of Strangers* (49), *I'd Climb the Highest Mountain* (50), *I Can Get It For You Wholesale* (51), *Rawhide* (51), *David and Bathsheba* (51), *With a Song in My Heart* (52), *The Lusty Men* (52), *The Snows of Kilimanjaro* (52), *The President's Lady* (53), *White Witch Doctor* (53), *Demetrius and the Gladiators* (54), *Garden of Evil* (54), *Untamed* (55), *Soldier of Fortune* (55), *The Conqueror* (55), *I'll Cry Tomorrow* (as Lilian Roth) (AA) (55), *Top Secret Affair* (57), *I Want To Live* (as Barbara Graham) (AA) (58), *A Woman Obsessed* (59), *Thunder in the Sun* (59), *The Marriage-Go-Round* (60), *Ada* (61), *Back Street* (61), *Stolen Hours* (GB) (63), *I Thank a Fool* (GB) (63), *Where Love Has Gone* (64), *The Honey Pot* (67), *Valley of the Dolls* (67).

HAYWORTH, RITA (1918–) (Marguerite Cansino). American star actress and dancer, on stage from six years old. *Dante's Inferno* (debut) (35), *Only Angels Have Wings* (39), *Strawberry Blonde* (41), *Blood and Sand* (41), *You'll Never Get Rich* (42), *Cover Girl* (44), *Tonight and Every Night* (45), *Gilda* (46), *Down to Earth* (47), *The Lady from Shanghai* (47), *The Loves of Carmen* (48), *Affair in Trinidad* (52), *Salome* (53), *Miss Sadie Thompson* (54), *Fire Down Below* (57), *Pal Joey* (57), *Separate Tables* (58), *They Came to Cordura* (59), *The Story on Page One* (61), *The Happy Thieves* (61), *Circus World* (*The Magnificent Showman*) (64), *The Money Trap* (65), *The Poppy is Also a Flower* (*Danger Grows Wild*) (66), *The Rover* (67), *Sons of Satan* (68), others.

HAZELL, HY (1920–) (Hyacinth Hazel O'Higgins). British revue and musical comedy artist. Films include *Meet Me at Dawn* (46), *Paper Orchid* (49), *Celia* (49), *The Lady Craved Excitement* (50), *The Night Won't Talk* (52), *Up in the World* (56), *The Whole Truth* (58).

HEAD, EDITH (1907–). American dress designer, in Hollywood since the 20s. First solo credit *She Done Him Wrong* (33); later won Academy Awards for *The Heiress* (49), *Samson and Delilah* (51), *A Place in the Sun* (52), etc. Published her autobiography, *The Dress Doctor*. Appears in *The Oscar* (66).

HEARNE, RICHARD (1908–). British acrobatic comedian, in music hall and circus practically from the cradle. Has made occasional films, often in his character of 'Mr Pastry'. *Dance Band* (35), *Millions* (37), *Miss London Ltd* (42), *The Butler's Dilemma* (43), *One Night with You* (48), *Helter Skelter* (49), *Captain Horatio Hornblower* (50), *Madame Louise* (51), *Miss Robin Hood* (52), *Something in the City* (53), *Tons of Trouble* (56), etc.

HEARST, WILLIAM RANDOLPH (1863–1951). American newspaper magnate thought to have been the original of *Citizen Kane*. Also noted for pushing his protégée Marion Davies (qv) to film stardom by buying a production company solely for her vehicles.

HEATHERTON, JOEY (1944–   ). American leading lady, former child stage performer. *Twilight of Honour* (64), *Where Love Has Gone* (64), *My Blood Runs Cold* (64), etc.

heaven; see *fantasy*.

HEAVENS ABOVE (GB 1963). The Boulting Brothers' long-awaited satire on the church turned out to be a long-drawn-out sentimental comedy which pulled its punches and drifted too often into tedious irrelevance. Peter Sellers made a dull fellow of the proletarian parson, but there were compensations in the contributions of Cecil Parker, Miles Malleson and Ian Carmichael as church dignitaries.

HEAVEN CAN WAIT (US 1943). One of the most charming, polished and unexpected comedies of Ernst Lubitsch, this half-forgotten film drew surprisingly warm performances from Don Ameche and Gene Tierney, the former as a lately-deceased gentleman describing his youthful follies to a sauve and sympathetic Satan in a very luxurious version of Hell. Script by Samson Raphaelson from Laslo Bus-Fekete's play *Birthday*. The period settings and fantasy endpapers, all in colour, made it a great success in the middle of World War II.

HECHT, BEN (1894–1964). American writer and critic with screenplay credits going back to silent days. *Underworld* (AA) (28), *The Great Garbo* (30), *The Front Page* (31), *Topaze* (33), *Viva Villa* (34), *Crime Without Passion* (34), *The Scoundrel* (AA) (35), *Nothing Sacred* (37), *Gunga Din* (38), *Wuthering Heights* (39), *Comrade X* (40), *Tales of Manhattan* (42), *The Black Swan* (42), *Spellbound* (45), *Notorious* (46), *The Spectre of the Rose* (also produced and directed) (46), *Kiss of Death* (47), *Whirlpool* (49), *Actors and Sin* (also produced and directed) (52), *Miracle in the Rain* (56), *Legend of the Lost* (58), many others; usually worked in collaboration with Charles MacArthur. Published his autobiography, *A Child of the Century*.

HECHT, HAROLD (1907–   ). American producer, formerly dance director and literary agent. From 1947 produced jointly with Burt Lancaster and later James Hill. *Vera Cruz* (54), *Marty* (55), *Trapeze* (56), *Separate Tables* (58), *Taras Bulba* (63), *Cat Ballou* (65), *The Way West* (67), many others.

HECKART, EILEEN (1919–   ). American character actress, mainly on stage. Films include *Miracle in the Rain* (56), *The Bad Seed* (56), *Somebody Up There Likes Me* (57), *Hot Spell* (57), *Heller in Pink Tights* (60), *Up the Down Staircase* (68), *No Way to Treat a Lady* (68).

461

HECKROTH, HEIN (1897–   ). German art director who has worked in Britain, mainly for Powell and Pressburger. *Caesar and Cleopatra* (45), *A Matter of Life and Death* (46), *The Red Shoes* (AA) (48), *Tales of Hoffman* (51), *The Story of Gilbert and Sullivan* (53), *The Battle of the River Plate* (56), *Torn Curtain* (US) (66), etc.

HEDISON, DAVID (formerly AL HEDISON) (1928–   ) (Ara Heditsian). American leading man, especially in TV series *Five Fingers* (59), *Voyage to the Bottom of the Sea* (63–67). Films include *The Enemy Below* (57), *The Fly* (58), *Son of Robin Hood* (59), etc.

HEDLEY, JACK (1933–   ). British leading man best remembered as TV's 'Tim Frazer'. Stage experience. *Room at the Top* (film debut) (59), *Make Mine Mink* (60), *Lawrence of Arabia* (62), *In the French Style* (63), *The Scarlet Blade* (63), *Of Human Bondage* (64), *Witchcraft* (65), *The Anniversary* (67), etc.

HEDREN, TIPPI (1935–   ). American leading lady, former TV model. *The Birds* (63), *Marnie* (64), *A Countess from Hong Kong* (66).

HEFLIN, VAN (1910–   ) (Emmett Evan Heflin). Purposeful American leading man with varied stage experience. *A Woman Rebels* (debut) (36), *Saturday's Heroes* (38), *Santa Fe Trail* (40), *The Feminine Touch* (41), *H. M. Pulham Esquire* (41), *Johnny Eager* (AA) (42), *Kid Glove Killer* (42), *Seven Sweethearts* (42), *Tennessee Johnson* (42), *Presenting Lily Mars* (42); war service; *The Strange Love of Martha Ivers* (46), *Till the Clouds Roll By* (46), *Possessed* (47), *Green Dolphin Street* (47), *B.F.'s Daughter* (48), *Act of Violence* (48), *The Three Musketeers* (48), *Tap Roots* (48), *Madame Bovary* (49), *The Prowler* (50), *Weekend with Father* (51), *My Son John* (51), *Shane* (53), *Woman's World* (54), *The Black Widow* (54), *Battle Cry* (55), *Count Three and Pray* (55), *Patterns of Power* (56), *3.10 to Yuma* (57), *Tempest* (58), *They Came to Cordura* (59), *Five Branded Women* (60), *Under Ten Flags* (61), *The Wastrel* (62), *Cry of Battle* (63), *Once a Thief* (65), *Stagecoach* (66), *The Man Outside* (GB) (67), *The Big Bounce* (68), *Airport* (69), others. A frequent TV guest star.

HEGGIE, O. P. (1879–1936). Scottish character actor of stage and, latterly, screen. *The Mysterious Dr Fu Manchu* (29), *East Lynne* (31), *Smiling Through* (32), *Midnight* (34), *Bride of Frankenstein* (as the blind hermit) (35), *Prisoner of Shark Island* (36), etc.

HEIFITS, JOSEPH (1904–   ). Russian director, from 1928. Known in 30s for *Baltic Deputy*, but did not come to Western notice again until *The Lady with the Little Dog* (59), *In the Town of S* (65).

HEINDORF, RAY (c. 1910–   ). American musical director. *Hard to Get* (38), *Strawberry Blonde* (41), *Yankee Doodle Dandy* (AA) (42),

Calamity Jane (53), *A Star is Born* (54), *The Music Man* (62), *Finian's Rainbow* (68), many others.

HEINZ, GERARD (1907–). German character actor, mainly in British movies. *Thunder Rock* (42), *Went the Day Well* (42), *Caravan* (46), *His Excellency* (51), *The Man Inside* (57), *House of the Seven Hawks* (59), *The Guns of Navarone* (61), *The Cardinal* (63), *The Dirty Dozen* (67), many others.

THE HEIRESS (US 1949). Oscars for best actress (Olivia de Havilland) and best art direction and costume design were won by this adaptation of the play by Ruth and Augustus Goetz from Henry James' novel *Washington Square*, about an unattractive spinster who finally turns the tables on her money-seeking suitor. With Montgomery Clift, Ralph Richardson; directed by William Wyler.

HEISLER, STUART (1894–). American director, in films since 1914. Former editor. *The Hurricane* (2nd unit) (37), *The Monster and the Girl* (40), *God Gave Him a Dog* (40), *Among the Living* (41), *The Remarkable Andrew* (42), *The Glass Key* (42); war service; *Along Came Jones* (45), *Blue Skies* (46), *Smash-Up* (47), *Tulsa* (49), *Tokyo Joe* (49), *Storm Warning* (50), *Chain Lightning* (50), *Journey into Light* (51), *Saturday Island* (52), *The Star* (53), *Beachhead* (54), *I Died a Thousand Times* (55), *The Burning Hills* (56), *Hitler* (61), etc. Much TV work.

helicopters, restricted in scope, have been put to sound dramatic use in two films about helicopter services, *Battle Taxi* and *Flight from Ashiya*; while their potential for thrill sequences was well explored in *The Bridges at Toko-Ri*, *Experiment in Terror*, *From Russia with Love*, *Arabesque*, *Caprice*, *You Only Live Twice*, *The Satan Bug*, *Fathom*, *Masquerade*, *Tarzan in the Valley of Gold*, *That Riviera Touch*, *The Wrecking Crew* and *Figures in a Landscape*. See also *airplanes*.

Hell has been used more figuratively than realistically in movies; but what passed for the real thing did appear in *Dante's Inferno*, *Heaven Can Wait*, *Hellzapoppin* and *Angel on My Shoulder*, not to mention a Sylvester cartoon called *Satan's Waitin'*.

HELLER, LUKAS (1930–). German-born screenwriter, associated chiefly with Robert Aldrich. *Whatever Happened to Baby Jane* (62), *Hush Hush Sweet Charlotte* (co-w) (64), *The Dirty Dozen* (co-w) (67), *The Killing of Sister George* (68), etc.

HELLER, OTTO (1896–1970). Czech-born cinematographer, in Britain since early 30s. Has more than 300 features to his credit: *The High Command* (36), *Tomorrow We Live* (42), *Mr Emmanuel* (44), *I Live in Grosvenor Square* (45), *The Queen of Spades* (48), *The Winslow Boy* (48), *Never Take No for an Answer* (51), *The Divided Heart* (54),

Manuela (57), *The Light in the Piazza* (62), *West Eleven* (63), *The Ipcress File* (65), *Alfie* (66), *Funeral in Berlin* (66), *Duffy* (68), etc.

HELLINGER, MARK (1903–1947). American journalist who scripted some films (e.g. *The Roaring Twenties* [40]) and later turned producer: *The Killers* (46), *Brute Force* (47), *Naked City* (47).

HELLMAN, LILLIAN (1905–). American playwright who has adapted much of her own work for the screen and also written other screenplays. *These Three* (36), *The Little Foxes* (41), *Watch on the Rhine* (43), *North Star* (43), *The Searching Wind* (46), *Another Part of the Forest* (48), *The Children's Hour* (*The Loudest Whisper*) (62), *Toys in the Attic* (63), *The Chase* (66), etc.

HELLMAN, MARCEL (1898–). Rumanian producer, long in Britain. *The Amateur Gentleman* (36), *Jeannie* (41), *Happy Go Lucky* (51), *Northwest Frontier* (59), *Moll Flanders* (65), many others.

HELL'S ANGELS (US 1927–30). Started as a silent and reshot for sound, this aerial spectacular of World War I, produced and directed by Howard Hughes, still survives by virtue of its highly dramatic combat scenes, including a zeppelin raid over London. The personal story is badly dated, though the scene in which Jean Harlow allures Ben Lyon by changing into 'something more comfortable' is not to be missed.

HELLZAPOPPIN (US 1942). Directed by H. C. Potter from the stage show starring Ole Olsen and Chic Johnson, this crazy farce now seems insufficiently daring: there's actually a plot and a love interest! Many of the gags, however, still work, and as a whole it was more successful in popularizing this kind of entertainment than the Marx Brothers had been.

HELM, BRIGITTE (1906–) (Gisele Eve Schittenhelm). German actress well-known in the 20s. *Metropolis* (debut) (26), *The Loves of Jeanne Ney* (27), *The Blue Danube* (32), *Gold* (34), etc. Retired.

HELPMANN, ROBERT (1909–). Australian ballet dancer and actor of stage and screen, in Britain since 1930. *One of Our Aircraft Is Missing* (42), *Henry V* (44), *The Red Shoes* (48), *Tales of Hoffman* (50), *55 Days in Peking* (62), *The Quiller Memorandum* (66), *Chitty Chitty Bang Bang* (68), others.

HELTON, PERCY (1894–). American character actor, a small round figure with a face which perfectly expresses surprise, bewilderment or dismay, and a high-pitched voice to match. *Miracle on 34th Street* (47), *My Friend Irma* (49), *A Star is Born* (54), innumerable others.

HEMINGWAY, ERNEST (1899–1961). Distinguished American novelist. Works filmed include *A Farewell to Arms* (32 and 57), *Spanish Earth* (original screenplay and production) (37), *The Killers* (46 and 64), *The Macomber Affair* (47), *The Snows of Kilimanjaro* (53), *The Sun Also Rises* (57), *The Old Man and the Sea* (58), *Adventures of a Young Man* (62), etc. *To Have and Have Not* was filmed three times (inaccurately); in 1944, 1951 (as *The Breaking Point*) and 1956 (as *The Gun Runner*).

HEMMINGS, DAVID (1942–   ). Slightly-built British leading man who after appearing in many second features suddenly seemed to have the acceptable image for the late 60s. *No Trees in the Street* (59), *The Wind of Change* (60), *Dateline Diamonds* (65), *Eye of the Devil* (66), *Blow Up* (66), *Camelot* (67), *The Charge of the Light Brigade* (68), *A Long Day's Dying* (68), *Only When I Larf* (68), *Barbarella* (68), *Alfred the Great* (69), *The Walking Stick* (69), *Fragment of Fear* (69), etc.

HENDRIX, WANDA (1928–   ). American leading lady. *Confidential Agent* (45), *Miss Tatlock's Millions* (48), *Prince of Foxes* (49), *Captain Carey USA* (50), *The Highwayman* (58), *The Last Posse* (53), *The Black Dakotas* (54), *Stage to Thunder Rock* (65), etc.

HENDRY, IAN (1931–   ). Virile British leading man, in TV from 1956. After small roles on screen, played leads in *Live Now, Pay Later* (62), *This Is My Street* (63), *The Beauty Jungle* (64), *Repulsion* (65), *The Hill* (65), *Doppelganger* (69), etc.

HENIE, SONJA (1912–1969). Norwegian skating star who went to Hollywood 1937, made several light musicals, and stayed. *One in a Million* (37), *Happy Landings* (38), *Second Fiddle* (40), *Sun Valley Serenade* (42), *It's a Pleasure* (44), *The Countess of Monte Cristo* (48), *Hello London* (61), etc. Later ran ice shows.

HENREY, BOBBY (1939–   ). British child actor, notable in *The Fallen Idol* (48). Retired after *The Wonder Kid* (50).

HENRIED, PAUL (1907–   ) (Paul von Hernreid). Austrian leading man of stage and film; came to Britain 1935 and was in *Goodbye Mr Chips* (39), *Night Train to Munich* (40). In Hollywood since 1941: *Now Voyager* (42), *Casablanca* (42), *Devotion* (43), *Between Two Worlds* (44), *Of Human Bondage* (46), *Deception* (46), *Rope of Sand* (49), *For Men Only* (also produced and directed) (52), *The Four Horsemen of the Apocalypse* (62), *Dead Ringer* (directed only) (64), *Ballad in Blue* (directed only) (65), *Operation Crossbow* (65), many others, also TV.

HENRY, CHARLOTTE (1916–   ). American juvenile actress of the early 30s. *Rebecca of Sunnybrook Farm* (32), *Alice in Wonderland* (33), *Babes in Toyland* (34), *Charlie Chan at the Opera* (37), *Stand and Deliver* (last to date) (41), etc.

Henry O.

HENRY, O. (1862–1910) (William Sydney Porter). American story writer who for the last ten years of his life wrote a weekly story for the *New York World*. A compendium of them was used in *O. Henry's Full House* (52), and there followed a TV series, *The O. Henry Playhouse* (56).

HENRY V (GB 1944). Laurence Olivier directed this Shakespearean spectacular, timed for victory, and also starred in it. The method of starting in the Globe Theatre, moving gradually into reality for the battle and then returning was controversial, but in general the production could not have been more splendid. Leslie Banks, Robert Newton and Leo Genn stood out in a remarkable cast, and the Agincourt charge sequence is justly famous. Photographed in Technicolor by Robert Krasker, with music by William Walton.

HENRY, WILLIAM (1918–). American leading man, former child actor, later in callow roles. *Lord Jim* (26), *The Thin Man* (34), *Tarzan Escapes* (36), *Four Men* (38), *Blossoms in the Dust* (41), *Women in Bondage* (44), *Federal Man* (49), *Jungle Moonmen* (54), *Mister Roberts* (55), *The Lone Ranger and the Lost City of Gold* (58), *How the West Was Won* (62), etc.

HENSON, GLADYS (1897–) (Gladys Gunn). Irish character actress often seen as plump, homely mum, or latterly grand-mum. On stage from 1910. *The Captive Heart* (45), *It Always Rains on Sunday* (47), *London Belongs to Me* (48), *The Blue Lamp* (50), *Lady Godiva Rides Again* (51), *Those People Next Door* (52), *Cockleshell Heroes* (55), *The Leather Boys* (63), etc.

HENSON, LESLIE (1891–1957). British stage comedian with bulging eyes; often in musical farces. Occasional films include *The Sport of Kings* (30), *It's a Boy* (33), *A Warm Corner* (34), *Oh Daddy* (35), *The Demi-Paradise* (43), *Home and Away* (56).

†HEPBURN, AUDREY (1929–) (Edda Hepburn van Heemstra) Belgian-born star actress of Irish-Dutch parentage. In England from 1948; rapid rise to Hollywood stardom as an elegant gamin. *Laughter in Paradise* (51), *The Lavender Hill Mob* (51), *Secret People* (51), *Roman Holiday* (AA, BFA) (53), *Sabrina Fair* (54), *War and Peace* (56), *Funny Face* (56), *Love in the Afternoon* (56), *Green Mansions* (58), *The Nun's Story* (BFA) (58), *The Unforgiven* (60), *Breakfast at Tiffany's* (61), *The Children's Hour* (*The Loudest Whisper*) (62), *Paris When It Sizzles* (63), *Charade* (BFA) (63), *My Fair Lady* (64), *How to Steal a Million* (66), *Two for the Road* (67), *Wait Until Dark* (67).

†HEPBURN, KATHARINE (1909–). American star actress with Bryn Mawr accent and dominant personality. Sporadically on stage, otherwise constantly in films from 1932. *A Bill of Divorcement* (32),

Christopher Strong (32), *Morning Glory* (AA) (33), *Little Women* (as Jo) (33), *Spitfire* (34), *The Little Minister* (34), *Alice Adams* (35), *Sylvia Scarlett* (35), *Break of Hearts* (35), *Mary of Scotland* (36), *A Woman Rebels* (36), *Quality Street* (37), *Stage Door* (37), *Bringing Up Baby* (38), *Holiday* (38), *The Philadelphia Story* (40), *Woman of the Year* (41), *Keeper of the Flame* (43), *Dragon Seed* (44), *Without Love* (45), *Undercurrent* (46), *Song of Love* (as Clara Schumann) (47), *Sea of Grass* (47), *State of the Union* (48), *Adam's Rib* (49), *The African Queen* (51), *Pat and Mike* (52), *Summertime* (*Summer Madness*) (54), *The Iron Petticoat* (GB) (56), *The Rainmaker* (56), *The Desk Set* (57), *Suddenly Last Summer* (59), *Long Day's Journey into Night* (62), *Guess Who's Coming to Dinner* (AA) (67), *The Lion in Winter* (AA) (BFA) (68), *The Madwoman of Chaillot* (69).

HEPWORTH, CECIL (1874–1953). Pioneer British film producer/ director, from 1899. Wrote the first book on cinema, 'Animated Photography' (1897). Later organized his own stock company of stars; and wrote his autobiography, 'Came the Dawn'. Most of his films were old-fashioned in appeal even in their day, but they include *Rescued by Rover* (05), *Blind Fate* (12), *Coming Thro' the Rye* (16 and 24). The 1924 version of the last-named was Hepworth's last film.

HERBERT, HOLMES (1882–1956) (Edward Sanger). British stage actor, on the Hollywood screen from 1917, usually in quiet British roles— butler, lawyer or clerk. *Gentlemen Prefer Blondes* (27), *Dr Jekyll and Mr Hyde* (32), *The Mystery of the Wax Museum* (33), *Mark of the Vampire* (35), *Lloyds of London* (37), *Stanley and Livingstone* (39), *This Above All* (42), *The Uninvited* (44), *Sherlock Holmes and the Secret Code* (*Dressed to Kill*) (46), *David and Bathsheba* (51), *The Brigand* (52), etc.

HERBERT, F. HUGH (1897–1958). Austrian-born playwright and screen- writer, in Hollywood from 1921. *The Great Gabbo* (32), *Kiss and Tell* (45), *Margie* (47), *Sitting Pretty* (47), *The Moon Is Blue* (51), many others. Wrote and directed *Summer Lightning* (48).

HERBERT, HUGH (1887–1952). American eccentric comedian, famous for 'woo woo' trademark, indicating whimsical nervousness. Debut in *Mind Your Business* (30); made many two-reelers in 30s, also *The Black Cat* (41), *Don't Get Personal* (41), *Hellzapoppin* (42), *Cracked Nuts* (42), *Mrs Wiggs of the Cabbage Patch* (42), *There's One Born Every Minute* (43), *Kismet* (44), *Men in Her Diary* (45), *Carnegie Hall* (46), *So This Is New York* (48), *A Song Is Born* (48), *Havana Rose* (51), many others.

HERBERT, PERCY (1925–). British character actor, usually seen as cockney rating or private. *The Baby and the Battleship* (56), *The Bridge on the River Kwai* (57), *Tunes of Glory* (61), *Mysterious Island*

(62), *Mutiny on the Bounty* (63), *One Million Years BC* (66), *Tobruk* (US) (66), *The Viking Queen* (67), *The Royal Hunt of the Sun* (69), etc. TV series: *Cimarron Strip* (67).

HERE COMES MR JORDAN (US 1941). This 'heavenly' comedy, from Harry Segal's play about a boxer who dies too early and is sent back to earth only to find that his body has been cremated, was a great success in wartime America and had several imitators. Directed by Alexander Hall, with Robert Montgomery, Claude Rains, Edward Everett Horton, James Gleason.

HERLIE, EILEEN (1919–   ) (Eileen Herlihy). Scottish stage actress who has made occasional films. *Hungry Hill* (debut) (47), *Hamlet* (48), *The Angel with the Trumpet* (49), *The Story of Gilbert and Sullivan* (53), *Isn't Life Wonderful* (53), *For Better For Worse* (54), *She Didn't Say No* (58), *Freud* (62), *The Seagull* (68).

HERNANDEZ, JUANO (1900–   ). Negro stage actor with powerful presence. Starred in his first film, *Intruder in the Dust* (48); later roles less impressive. *The Breaking Point* (50), *Young Man with a Horn* (50), *Kiss Me Deadly* (55), *Something of Value* (57), *The Pawnbroker* (64), *The Extraordinary Seaman* (68), etc.

HERRMAN, BERNARD (1911–   ). American composer and orchestral conductor. Film scores include *Citizen Kane* (41), *All That Money Can Buy* (AA) (41), *The Magnificent Ambersons* (42), *Jane Eyre* (43), *Hangover Square* (44), *Anna and the King of Siam* (46), *The Day the Earth Stood Still* (51), *The Snows of Kilimanjaro* (52), *Five Fingers* (52), *The Kentuckian* (55), *The Wrong Man* (56), *The Trouble with Harry* (56), *Vertigo* (58), *North by Northwest* (59), *Journey to the Centre of the Earth* (59), *Psycho* (60), *The Birds* (63), *Jason and the Argonauts* (64), *Marnie* (65), *Fahrenheit 451* (66), *The Bride Wore Black* (67), many others.

HERSHOLT, JEAN (1886–1956). Phlegmatic Danish character actor, in Hollywood films from the early 20s. *The Four Horsemen of the Apocalypse* (21), *Greed* (23), *Stella Dallas* (25), *The Secret Hour* (28), *Abie's Irish Rose* (29), *The Rise of Helga* (30), *Transatlantic* (31,) *Grand Hotel* (32), *The Mask of Fu Manchu* (32), *Mark of the Vampire* (35), *Seventh Heaven* (35), *Alexander's Ragtime Band* (38), *Meet Doctor Christian* (and ensuing series) (38–40), *They Meet Again* (41), *Stage Door Canteen* (43), *Dancing in the Dark* (49), *Run for Cover* (55), others.

HERVEY, IRENE (c. 1916–   ) (I. Herwick). American leading lady of light films in the 40s. *Three on a Honeymoon* (34), *East Side of Heaven* (39), *Destry Rides Again* (39), *Unseen Enemy* (42), *Half Way to Shanghai* (43), *My Guy* (44), *Mr Peabody and the Mermaid* (49), *Teenage Rebel* (56), *Going Steady* (59), *Cactus Flower* (69), etc. TV series: *Honey West* (64).

HESLOP, CHARLES (1884–1966). British comic actor, longtime star of stage farces. Rare screen appearances include *Waltzes from Vienna* (33), *The Lambeth Walk* (39), *Flying Fortress* (42), *The Late Edwina Black* (51), *Follow a Star* (59).

†HESTON, CHARLTON (1923–   ). Stalwart American leading actor with stage experience; for a time associated chiefly with epics. *Dark City* (debut) (50), *The Greatest Show on Earth* (52), *The Savage* (52), *Pony Express* (52), *Ruby Gentry* (53), *The President's Lady* (53), *Arrowhead* (53), *Bad For Each Other* (53), *The Naked Jungle* (54), *The Secret of the Incas* (54), *Lucy Gallant* (54), *The Far Horizons* (54), *The Private War of Major Benson* (55), *The Ten Commandments* (56), *Three Violent People* (56), *Touch of Evil* (57), *The Big Country* (58), *The Buccaneer* (58), *Ben Hur* (AA) (59), *The Wreck of the Mary Deare* (59), *The Pigeon That Took Rome* (61), *El Cid* (61), *55 Days in Peking* (62), *Diamond Head* (62), *The Greatest Story Ever Told* (65), *The Agony and the Ecstasy* (65), *Major Dundee* (65), *The War Lord* (65), *Khartoum* (as General Gordon) (66), *Planet of the Apes* (67), *Counterpoint* (67), *Will Penny* (67), *Number One* (69), *Julius Caesar* (70), *The Hawaiians* (70).

HEYDT, LOUIS JEAN (1905–1960). American character actor, often seen as a man with something to hide. *Test Pilot* (38), *Each Dawn I Die* (39), *Gone with the Wind* (39), *Dive Bomber* (41), *Our Vines Have Tender Grapes* (45), *The Furies* (50). *The Eternal Sea* (55), many others.

HEYER, JOHN (1916–   ). Australian documentarist, former cameraman. *The Back of Beyond* (54), *The Forerunner* (57), etc.

HEYES, DOUGLAS (1923–   ). American director, from TV. *Kitten With a Whip* (65), *Beau Geste* (67), etc.

HEYWOOD, ANNE (formerly Violet Pretty) (c. 1933–   ). British leading lady, former beauty contestant, married to Raymond Stross. *Checkpoint* (56), *Dangerous Exile* (57), *Violent Playground* (58), *Floods of Fear* (59), *A Terrible Beauty* (60), *The Very Edge* (62), *Ninety Degrees in the Shade* (66), *The Fox* (68), *The Most Dangerous Man in the World* (69), etc.

HIBBERT, GEOFFREY (1922–1969). British actor who played callow youths around 1940 but turned rather quickly into a character man. *Love on the Dole* (41), *The Common Touch* (42), *Next of Kin* (42); later *Orders to Kill* (58), *Crash Drive* (59), other small roles; much on TV.

HIBBS, JESSE (1906–   ). American director, mainly of routine 'B' features. *All American* (53), *Ride Clear of Diablo* (54), *Rails into Laramie* (54), *Black Horse Canyon* (55), *To Hell and Back* (55), *The Spoilers* (55), *The World in My Corner* (56), *Joe Butterfly* (57), *Ride A Crooked Trail* (58), etc. Directed scores of TV episodes.

HICKMAN, DARRYL (1931–   ). American juvenile actor who has more recently been seen in heavy roles. *The Grapes of Wrath* (40), *Hearts in Springtime* (41), *Boys' Ranch* (45), *Dangerous Years* (46), *Prisoner of War* (53), *Tea and Sympathy* (57), etc. TV series: *The Americans* (*The Blue and the Gold*).

HICKMAN, DWAYNE (1934–   ). American juvenile, former child actor. *Captain Eddy* (45), *The Return of Rusty* (46), *The Sun Comes Up* (49), *Rally Round the Flag Boys* (59), *Beach Party* (64), others. TV series: *The Affairs of Dobie Gillis* (59).

HICKOK, WILD BILL (1837–1876). American gunfighter of wild west days, played on screen by William S. Hart in *Wild Bill Hickok* (21), Gary Cooper in *The Plainsman* (37), Richard Dix in *Badlands of Dakota* (41), Forrest Tucker in *Pony Express* (52), Howard Keel in *Calamity Jane* (53), Don Murray in *The Plainsman* (66), and many others. Guy Madison had the lead in a popular TV series *Wild Bill Hickok* (51–57).

HICKS, RUSSELL (1895–1957). American character actor who almost always played executive types. Actor and director from silent days; in hundreds of films. *Laughing Irish Eyes* (36), *In Old Chicago* (38), *The Three Musketeers* (39), *The Big Store* (41), *His Butler's Sister* (43), *Bandit of Sherwood Forest* (46), *Bowery Battalion* (51), *Seventh Cavalry* (56), etc.

HICKS, SIR SEYMOUR (1871–1949). British stage farceur, also writer and producer. Occasional film appearances include *Always Tell Your Wife* (22), *Sleeping Partners* (26), *The Secret of the Loch* (34), *Vintage Wine* (35), *Scrooge* (35), *Pastor Hall* (39), *Busman's Honeymoon* (40), *Silent Dust* (48), etc.

HICKSON, JOAN (1906–   ). British character actress, on stage from 1927, films from 1934 (*Widow's Might*). In innumerable films since, usually as understanding wife or slightly dotty aunt: *I See a Dark Stranger* (45), *The Guinea Pig* (48), *Happy Is the Bride* (57), etc. TV series: *Our Man at St Marks*.

HIGH NOON (US 1952). A Western of classic economy, the action ranging over a few hours during which one man searches desperately for support against a gang of revengeful outlaws. Written by Carl Foreman, directed by Fred Zinnemann, with Gary Cooper and a first-rate cast. The ballad was written by Dmitri Tiomkin.

HIGH SIERRA (US 1941). Modish melodrama with Humphrey Bogart as a gangster on the run and Ida Lupino as the girl who befriends him too late. Gloomily directed by Raoul Walsh, from a script by W. R. Burnett; chiefly notable for its early example of an anti-hero. Remade 1955 by Stuart Heisler as *I Died a Thousand Times*, with Jack Palance, Shelley Winters, and no flair.

A HIGH WIND IN JAMAICA (GB 1965). A flawed but interesting attempt to put on film a plainly uncommercial literary work which finds good in pirates and evil in children who are virtually responsible for their martyrdom. Directed with insight and freshness by Alexander Mackendrick from Richard Hughes' book; photographed by Douglas Slocombe.

HILDYARD, JACK (c. 1915–). British cinematographer. *School for Secrets* (46), *While the Sun Shines* (46), *Vice Versa* (48), *Hobson's Choice* (54), *The Deep Blue Sea* (55), *The Bridge on the River Kwai* (AA) (57), *The Journey* (59), *Suddenly Last Summer* (59), *The Millionairess* (60), *55 Days at Peking* (62), *The VIPs* (63), *Battle of the Bulge* (66), *Casino Royale* (67), *The Long Duel* (67), *Villa Rides* (68), etc.

THE HILL (GB 1965). An engagingly arrant melodrama, played mostly for laughs, about brutalities in a North African prison camp during World War II. This raucous but stylish film unfortunately has pretensions which, coupled with poor sound recording, finally make it seem overblown and empty. But there are compensations in Sidney Lumet's direction, Oswald Morris's harsh photography, and the performances of Harry Andrews, Ian Hendry and Ossie Davis.

HILL, ARTHUR (1922–). Canadian actor, on British and American stage and screen. *Miss Pilgrim's Progress* (49), *Salute the Toff* (52), *Life with the Lyons* (54), *The Deep Blue Sea* (55), *The Ugly American* (63), *In the Cool of the Day* (63), *Moment to Moment* (65), *Harper* (*The Moving Target*) (66), *Petulia* (68), *The Most Dangerous Man in the World* (69), etc.

HILL, BENNY (1925–). British vaudeville comedian and mimic. Rare film appearances include *Who Done It* (55), *Light Up the Sky* (59), *Those Magnificent Men in Their Flying Machines* (65), *Chitty Chitty Bang Bang* (68), *The Italian Job* (69).

†HILL, GEORGE ROY (1922–). American director with New York stage background. *Period of Adjustment* (63), *Toys in the Attic* (63), *The World of Henry Orient* (64), *Hawaii* (66), *Thoroughly Modern Millie* (67), *Butch Cassidy and the Sundance Kid* (69).

HILL, JAMES (1919–). British director, former documentarist. *Journey for Jeremy* (47), *The Stolen Plans* (also wrote) (52), *The Clue of the Missing Ape* (also wrote) (53), *Giuseppina* (also wrote) (AA) (61), *The Kitchen* (62), *The Dock Brief* (62), *Every Day's a Holiday* (64), *A Study in Terror* (65), *Born Free* (66), *Captain Nemo* (69), etc.

HILL, JAMES (1916–). American producer: *Vera Cruz* (54), *The Kentuckian* (55), *Trapeze* (56), etc.

HILL, SINCLAIR (1894–1945). British director most eminent in the 20s. *The Tidal Wave* (20), *Don Quixote* (23), *Indian Love Lyrics* (23), *Boadicaea* (25), *Beyond the Veil* (25), *The King's Highway* (27), *A Woman Redeemed* (27), *The Guns of Loos* (28), *The Price of Divorce* (28), *The First Mrs Fraser* (30), *The Man from Toronto* (33), *My Old Dutch* (34), *Follow Your Star* (38), etc.

HILL, STEVEN (1924–   ) (Solomon Berg). American stage actor whose occasional films include *A Lady Without Passport* (50), *The Goddess* (58), *A Child is Waiting* (62), *The Slender Thread* (67). TV series: *Mission Impossible* (67).

hillbillies became a stereotype of the 30s cinema, and subsequently made infrequent appearances before the enormous success of the TV series *The Real McCoys* (57–63) and *The Beverly Hillbillies* (62–69). Notable hillbillies through the years include the Kettles, Lum and Abner, the Weaver Brothers and Elviry; the Ritz Brothers in *Kentucky Moonshine*; Annie in *Annie Get Your Gun*; and the characters in *Roseanna McCoy*, *Thunder Road*, *Lil Abner*, *Guns in the Afternoon* and *Coming Round the Mountain*; while the denizens of *Tobacco Road*, geographically not hillbillies, splendidly personified the image. Cartoon-wise, Elmer Fudd in the Bugs Bunny series is an old-fashioned hillbilly, and Disney produced a twenty-minute version of *The Martins and the Coys*.

HILLER, ARTHUR (c. 1924–   ). American director, from TV: *The Careless Years* (57), *The Flight of the White Stallions* (63), *The Americanization of Emily* (64), *Promise Her Anything* (66), *Tobruk* (66), *Penelope* (66), *The Tiger Makes Out* (67), *Popi* (69), *The Out-of-Towners* (69), etc.

HILLER, WENDY (1912–   ). Distinguished British stage actress, occasionally in films from 1937. *Lancashire Luck* (37), *Pygmalion* (38), *Major Barbara* (40), *I Know Where I'm Going* (45), *An Outcast of the Islands* (51), *Single Handed* (53), *Something of Value* (57), *Separate Tables* (AA) (58), *Sons and Lovers* (60), *Toys in the Attic* (63), *A Man for All Seasons* (66), *David Copperfield* (69), etc.

HILLIARD, HARRIET (1914–   ). American leading lady of 30s romantic comedies and musicals, e.g. *Follow the Fleet* (36), *She's My Everything* (38), *Sweetheart of the Campus* (41), *Canal Zone* (42), etc. Married Ozzie Nelson and for ten years from 1954 appeared with him in their weekly TV show *Ozzie and Harriet*; they also appeared with their family in the film *Here Come the Nelsons* (52).

HILLIER, ERWIN (1911–   ). British cinematographer. *The Lady from Lisbon* (41), *The Silver Fleet* (43), *Great Day* (45), *I Know Where I'm Going* (45), *London Town* (47), *The October Man* (48), *Mr Perrin and Mr Traill* (49), *Where's Charley?* (52), *The Dam Busters* (55),

Shake Hands with the Devil (59), *A Matter of Who* (62), *Sammy Going South* (63), *Operation Crossbow* (65), *Sands of the Kalahari* (65), *Eye of the Devil* (66), *The Quiller Memorandum* (66), *The Shoes of the Fisherman* (68), etc.

HILLYER, LAMBERT (1889–). American director of Westerns which have declined in stature since he used to write and direct for William S. Hart. *Travellin' On* (22), *White Oak* (23), *The Branded Sombrero* (28), *Dracula's Daughter* (36), *The Invisible Ray* (37), *Batman* (serial) (41), *Blue Clay* (42), *The Case of the Baby Sitter* (47), *Sunset Pass* (49), hundreds of others.

HILTON, JAMES (1900–1953). British novelist whose work was turned by himself and others into several highly successful films: *Knight Without Armour* (37), *Lost Horizon* (37), *Goodbye Mr Chips* (39), *We Are Not Alone* (39), *Random Harvest* (42), *The Story of Dr Wassell* (43), *So Well Remembered* (47), etc. Also worked as scenarist on other films, including *Mrs Miniver* (42).

HINDLE WAKES. This now-dated Lancashire drama by Stanley Houghton, about the mill-girl who gets pregnant by the boss's son, has been a staple of British films. There were silent versions in 1918 with Ada King and in 1926 with Estelle Brody; in 1931 Belle Chrystall starred in a sound remake, and as late as 1951 it was popular again with Lisa Daniely.

HINDS, ANTHONY (1922–). British producer, in films since 1946, latterly associated with Hammer's horror films. Also writes screenplays under the name 'John Elder'.

HINDS, SAMUEL S. (1875–1948). American character actor, formerly a lawyer for thirty-five years; specialized in kindly fathers and crooked lawyers. *Gabriel over the White House* (33), *She* (35), *Trail of the Lonesome Pine* (36), *Test Pilot* (38), *You Can't Take It with You* (38), *Destry Rides Again* (39), *The Strange Case of Doctor RX* (41), *The Spoilers* (42), *A Chip off the Old Block* (44), *The Boy with Green Hair* (48), scores of others.

HINES, JOHNNY (1895–). American comedian who after a vaudeville career became a silent star in such films as the *Torchy* series, *Alias Jimmy Valentine*, *The Crackerjack*, *The Brown Derby*, *Stepping Along*. Sound killed his appeal; had small roles in *Whistling in the Dark* (32), *Society Doctor* (35), *Too Hot to Handle* (38), etc.

HINGLE, PAT (1923–). American character actor with stage and TV experience. *On the Waterfront* (54), *End as a Man* (*The Strange One*) (57), *No Down Payment* (57), *Splendour in the Grass* (61), *The Ugly American* (63), *Invitation to a Gunfighter* (64), *Nevada Smith* (66), *Hang 'Em High* (68), etc.

Hird, Thora

HIRD, THORA (1914–   ). British character comedienne, of theatrical family. Mother of Janette Scott. *The Black Sheep of Whitehall* (debut) (41), *The Blind Goddess* (48), *Time, Gentlemen, Please* (53), *The Entertainer* (59), *A Kind of Loving* (62), many others. Frequently on stage; TV series *Meet the Wife, The First Lady*.

HIROSHIMA MON AMOUR (France/Japan 1959). Alain Resnais' cinematically explorative study of the effect of our wartorn past on the love affair of a Frenchwoman and a Japanese businessman. Original, influential, generally rewarding. Written by Marguerite Duras, with Emmanuele Riva, Eiji Okada.

HIRSCH, ROBERT (1929–   ). French character actor of the Comedie Française. *No Questions on Saturday* (64), *Kiss Me General* (66), etc.

HIS GIRL FRIDAY: see THE FRONT PAGE.

HISCOTT, LESLIE (1894–1968). British director, in films from 1919. *The Passing of Mr Quinn* (28), *Black Coffee* (32), *While London Sleeps* (33), *The Triumph of Sherlock Holmes* (35), *She Shall Have Music* (35), *Tilly of Bloomsbury* (40), *The Seventh Survivor* (41), *Welcome Mr Washington* (44), *The Time of His Life* (52), etc.; went into production management.

†HITCHCOCK, ALFRED (1899–   ). British director, in Hollywood since 1940. Former title artist; first film as director *The Pleasure Garden* (25). Subsequently made his name with stylish crime thrillers demonstrating his own special combination of suspense and impudence. *The Mountain Eagle* (26), *The Lodger* (26), *Downhill* (27), *Easy Virtue* (27), *The Ring* (27), *The Farmer's Wife* (28), *Champagne* (28), *The Manxman* (29), *Blackmail* (29), *Elstree Calling* (sketches) (30), *Juno and the Paycock* (30), *Murder* (30), *The Skin Game* (31), *Rich and Strange* (32), *Number Seventeen* (32), *Waltzes from Vienna* (33), *The Man Who Knew Too Much* (34), *The Thirty-nine Steps* (35), *Secret Agent* (36), *Sabotage* (37), *Young and Innocent* (37), *The Lady Vanishes* (38), *Jamaica Inn* (39), then to Hollywood; *Rebecca* (40), *Foreign Correspondent* (40), *Mr and Mrs Smith* (41), *Suspicion* (41), *Saboteur* (42), *Shadow of a Doubt* (43), *Lifeboat* (43), *Spellbound* (45), *Notorious* (46), *The Paradine Case* (47), *Rope* (48), *Under Capricorn* (49), *Stage Fright* (50), *Strangers on a Train* (51), *I Confess* (53), *Dial M for Murder* (54), *Rear Window* (54), *To Catch a Thief* (55), *The Trouble with Harry* (55), *The Man Who Knew Too Much* (56), *The Wrong Man* (57), *Vertigo* (58), *North by Northwest* (59), *Psycho* (60), *The Birds* (63), *Marnie* (64), *Torn Curtain* (66), *Topaz* (69). Also long-running TV series produced, introduced and occasionally directed by him: *Alfred Hitchcock Presents* (55–62) and *The Alfred Hitchcock Hour* (63–65).

HITLER, ADOLF (1889–1945). German dictator, the subject of many screen documentaries. In dramatic films he was impersonated by Ludwig Donath in *The Strange Death of Adolf Hitler* (43), by Robert Watson in *The Hitler Gang* (44), by Luther Adler in *The Magic Face* (51), and by Richard Basehart in *Hitler* (61). Watson in particular made a living from playing Hitler in gag walk-on roles during World War II.

HIVELY, JACK (* –). American director. *The Saint's Double Trouble* (40), *Anne of Windy Willows* (40), *Laddie* (40), *The Farmer Takes a Wife* (41), *Are You With It?* (48), etc.

HOBART, ROSE (1906–) (Rose Keefer). American actress, usually in character roles. *Dr Jekyll and Mr Hyde* (32), *Tower of London* (39), *Nothing But the Truth* (41), *Ziegfeld Girl* (41), *The Soul of a Monster* (44), *The Farmer's Daughter* (46), *Mickey* (last to date) (50), etc.

HOBBES, HALLIWELL (1877–1962). British character actor, long the impeccable butler, on stage from 1898, films from 1929 (since when he lived in Hollywood). *Charley's Aunt* (30), *Dr Jekyll and Mr Hyde* (32), *The Masquerader* (33), *Bulldog Drummond Strikes Back* (35), *Dracula's Daughter* (36), *You Can't Take It with You* (38), *Lady Hamilton* (41), *Sherlock Holmes Faces Death* (43), *If Winter Comes* (47), *The Forsyte Saga* (49), *Miracle in the Rain* (56), scores of others.

HOBBS, JACK (1893–). British actor on screen from silent days, usually in genial roles. *The Sin Game* (30), *Trouble in Store* (34), *No Limit* (35), *Millions* (37), *It's in the Air* (38), *Behind These Walls* (48), *Worm's Eye View* (51), etc.

HOBSON, VALERIE (1917–). British leading lady with 'upper-class' personality. *Path of Glory* (debut) (34), *The Bride of Frankenstein* (35), *The Mystery of Edwin Drood* (35), *The Great Impersonation* (36), *The Drum* (38), *This Man Is News* (38), *The Spy in Black* (39), *Contraband* (40), *The Adventures of Tartu* (42), *The Years Between* (46), *Great Expectations* (46), *The Small Voice* (48), *Kind Hearts and Coronets* (49), *The Card* (52), *The Voice of Merrill* (53), *Background* (53), etc. Retired from acting.

HOBSON'S CHOICE. This famous stage comedy by Harold Brighouse, set in industrial Salford at the turn of the century and showing how a heavy father gets his comeuppance, has been filmed three times in Britain. The 1920 version, directed by Percy Nash, with Joe Nightingale and Joan Ritz, was much improved on by the 1931 sound remake directed by Thomas Bentley, with Frank Pettingell and Viola Lyel. This was eclipsed, however, by David Lean's brilliant 1954 production, with Charles Laughton as the tyrant shoeseller, Brenda de Banzie as his stubborn daughter, and John Mills as her intended. The play has recently been turned into a stage musical called *Walking Happy*: this will presumably be filmed in due course.

HOCH, WINTON C. (c. 1908–   ). American cinematographer, former research physicist. *So Dear to My Heart* (48), *Joan of Arc* (co-ph) (AA) (48), *She Wore a Yellow Ribbon* (AA) (49), *Tulsa* (49), *Halls of Montezuma* (51), *The Quiet Man* (co-ph) (AA) (52), *Mr Roberts* (55), *The Searchers* (56), *Darby O'Gill and the Little People* (59), *The Lost World* (60), *Five Weeks in a Balloon* (62), *Robinson Crusoe on Mars* (64), *The Green Berets* (68), etc.

HODIAK, JOHN (1914–1955). American leading actor of Ukrainian descent. *Lifeboat* (43), *Marriage Is a Private Affair* (44), *Sunday Dinner for a Soldier* (44), *A Ball for Adano* (45), *The Harvey Girls* (46), *Somewhere in the Night* (46), *The Miniver Story* (50), *Night into Morning* (51), *The People against O'Hara* (51), *Battle Zone* (52), *Conquest of Cochise* (53), *On the Threshold of Space* (55), etc.

HOELLERING, GEORGE (c. 1900–   ). Austrian producer of *Hortobagy* long in Britain as specialized distributor and exhibitor; also producer of *Murder in the Cathedral* (51).

HOEY, DENNIS (1893–1960) (Samuel David Hyams). British actor, former singer, with stage experience from 1918, films from 1931 (mostly in Hollywood). *The Good Companions* (32), *Kitty* (46), *If Winter Comes* (47), many others; also played Inspector Lestrade in the Basil Rathbone-Sherlock Holmes series (39–45).

HOFFMAN, DUSTIN (1937–   ). American leading man with stage experience: leaped to fame as *The Graduate* (67), followed with *Midnight Cowboy* (69), *John and Mary* (69), *Little Big Man* (70).

HOGAN, JAMES V. (c. 1894–c. 1944). American director. *Last Train from Madrid* (37), *Ebb Tide* (38), *The Texans* (39), *Power Dive* (41), *The Mad Ghoul* (43), *The Strange Death of Adolf Hitler* (44), etc.

HOLBROOK, HAL (1925–   ). American character actor and Mark Twain impersonator. Films: *The Group* (66), *Wild in the Streets* (68).

HOLDEN, FAY (1895–   ) (Fay Hammerton). British actress who after stage experience went to Hollywood in 1935 and played character roles. Best remembered as mother in the Hardy Family series (1937–47); also in *Bulldog Drummond Escapes* (37), *Sweethearts* (38), *Bitter Sweet* (40), *Canyon Passage* (46), *The Baxter Millions* (46), *Whispering Smith* (49), *Samson and Delilah* (50), *Andy Hardy Comes Home* (58), etc.

HOLDEN, GLORIA (1908–   ). London-born leading lady, long in Hollywood. *Dracula's Daughter* (title role) (36), *The Life of Émile Zola* (37), *A Child Is Born* (40), *The Corsican Brothers* (41), *Behind the Rising Sun* (43), *The Hucksters* (47), *Dream Wife* (53), *The Eddy Duchin Story* (57), etc.

HOLDEN, WILLIAM (1918–   ) (William Beedle). Virile American leading man who went almost direct from college to Hollywood. *Golden Boy* (debut) (39), *Our Town* (40), *Arizona* (40), *Texas* (41), *The Fleet's In* (42), *Blaze of Noon* (47), *Dear Ruth* (47), *Sunset Boulevard* (50), *Born Yesterday* (51), *Stalag 17* (AA) (53), *The Moon Is Blue* (53), *Executive Suite* (54), *Sabrina Fair* (54), *Love is a Many-Splendoured Thing* (55), *Picnic* (56), *The Bridge on the River Kwai* (57), *The Key* (57), *The Horse Soldiers* (59), *The World of Suzie Wong* (61), *The Counterfeit Traitor* (62), *The Seventh Dawn* (64), *Alvarez Kelly* (66), *Casino Royale* (66), *The Devil's Brigade* (67), *The Wild Bunch* (69), etc.

HOLIDAY (US 1938). A slightly bitter comedy of manners, more refined than the crazy comedies of the 30s but in a similar mood, about a thinking man who marries into the idle rich, but at the last minute swaps his conventional intended for her eccentric sister. Directed by George Cukor from Philip Barry's play, with typically graceful performances from Katharine Hepburn and Cary Grant, and almost equally memorable contributions from Edward Everett Horton, Lew Ayres and Henry Kolker. In Britain the film was released as *Free To Live* and also (to someone's shame) as *Unconventional Linda*.

HOLLANDER, FREDERICK (1892–   ). German composer, long in America. Songs and scores include *The Blue Angel* (30), *Desire* (36), *The Man Who Came to Dinner* (42), *A Foreign Affair* (48), *The Five Thousand Fingers of Dr T* (53), etc.

HOLLES, ANTONY (1901–50). British actor who often played excitable foreigners. *The Lodger* (32), *Brewster's Millions* (35), *Dark Journey* (37), *Neutral Port* (41), *Warn That Man* (43), *Carnival* (46), *Bonnie Prince Charlie* (49), *The Rocking-Horse Winner* (50), others.

HOLLIDAY, DOC (1849–1885). American wild west character, a tubercular dentist and poker-player who oddly changed to the right side of the law when he teamed up with Wyatt Earp in Tombstone. Played inaccurately but picturesquely on screen by Cesar Romero in *Frontier Marshal* (39); Walter Huston in *The Outlaw* (41), Victor Mature in *My Darling Clementine* (46); Kirk Douglas in *Gunfight at the OK Corral* (56); Arthur Kennedy in *Cheyenne Autumn* (64); Jason Robards in *Hour of the Gun* (67).

HOLLIDAY, JUDY (1923–1965) (Judith Tuvim). American stage (revue) and screen star who shot to world fame as the not-so-dumb blonde in *Born Yesterday* (AA) (51). Also: *Winged Victory* (44), *Something for the Boys* (44) *Adam's Rib* (49), *The Marrying Kind* (52),

It Should Happen to You (54), *Phffft* (54), *The Solid Gold Cadillac* (56), *Full of Life* (58), *The Bells Are Ringing* (59), etc.

HOLLIMAN, EARL (1928–   ) (Anthony Numkena). American actor, often of simple Western roles. *Pony Soldier* (debut) (52), *Broken Lance* (54), *Forbidden Planet* (56), *Giant* (56), *The Rainmaker* (57), *Gunfight at the OK Corral* (57), *The Baited Trap* (58), *Armoured Command* (61), *Summer and Smoke* (61), *The Sons of Katie Elder* (65), *Covenant With Death* (67), *Anzio* (68), etc. TV series: *The Sundance Kid* (61), *The Wide Country* (62).

HOLLOWAY, STANLEY (1890–   ). British comic actor and singer with a long list of credits in revue, musical comedy and variety. *The Rotters* (debut) (21), *Sing As We Go* (34), *Squibs* (36), *Cotton Queen* (37), *The Vicar of Bray* (39), *Major Barbara* (40), *This Happy Breed* (44), *The Way Ahead* (44), *Champagne Charlie* (44), *Caesar and Cleopatra* (45), *Brief Encounter* (46), *Nicholas Nickleby* (47), *Hamlet* (as the gravedigger) (48), *Noose* (48), *Passport to Pimlico* (48), *Midnight Episode* (50), *The Lavender Hill Mob* (51), *One Wild Oat* (51), *Lady Godiva Rides Again* (51), *Meet Me Tonight* (52), *The Beggar's Opera* (52), *The Titfield Thunderbolt* (53), *Meet Mr Lucifer* (54), *Fast and Loose* (54), *An Alligator Named Daisy* (55), *Alive and Kicking* (58), *No Love for Johnnie* (61), *My Fair Lady* (his stage role as Dolittle) (64), *In Harm's Way* (65), *Ten Little Indians* (65), *The Sandwich Man* (66), *Mrs Brown You've Got A Lovely Daughter* (68), others. TV series: *Our Man Higgins* (62), *Thingumybob* (68).

HOLLOWAY, STERLING (1905–   ). Slow-speaking American comic actor, usually of yokels or hillbillies. Busiest in the 30s; latterly the voice of many Disney characters. *Casey at the Bat* (27), *Alice in Wonderland* (33), *Life Begins at Forty* (35), *Professor Beware* (38), *The Bluebird* (40), *A Walk in the Sun* (46), *The Beautiful Blonde from Bashful Bend* (49), *Shake, Rattle and Rock* (56), many others. TV series: *The Baileys of Balboa* (64).

HOLLYWOOD. The American film city, nominally a suburb of Los Angeles, was founded in 1912 when a number of independent producers headed west from New York to avoid the effects of a patents trust. The site was chosen because of its nearness to the Mexican border in case of trouble, and because the weather and location possibilities were excellent. By 1913 Hollywood was established as the film-maker's Mecca, and continued so for forty years. Several factors combined in the late 40s to affect its unique concentration. Actors forced themselves into independent producers and reduced the power of the 'front offices'; stars now made the films they liked instead of the ones to which they were assigned. The consequent break-up of many big studios, which now simply sold production space to independent outfits, weakened continuity of product. Each production now had to start from scratch; there was no longer a training ground for new talent, nor was the old production gloss always in evidence. The McCarthy witch-hunt unfortunately drove many leading talents to Europe, and many found they preferred Shepperton or Cinecitta to California. The coming of CinemaScope, a device to halt the fall in box-office returns which resulted from the beginning of commercial TV, meant that real locations were now necessary, as studio sets would show up on the big screen. So began the world-wide trekking now evident in American production: generally speaking only routine product and TV episodes are made in the film city itself, but each distribution set-up will have up to a dozen films being made in various parts of the globe.

HOLLYWOOD ON FILM has generally been shown as the brassy, gold-digging, power-conscious society which, in the nature of things, it can hardly fail to be. There was a somewhat sentimental period in the 20s and 30s, with *Ella Cinders, Hollywood Cavalcade*, and *Hollywood Boulevard*; but satire had already struck in such films as *The Last Command, Merton of the Movies, Lady Killer, Something to Sing About, Once in a Lifetime, Stardust, Hollywood Hotel, Stand In, A Star Is Born* and *Boy Meets Girl*. The moguls didn't seem to mind the film city being shown as somewhat zany, as in *The Goldwyn Follies*, Disney's *Mother Goose Goes Hollywood*, and *Hellzapoppin*; but they preferred the adulatory attitude best expressed in *The Youngest Profession*, which concerned the autograph hunters who lay in wait at the studio exits.

During the 40s Paramount was the studio most addicted to showing itself off, though front office can't have relished watching Preston Sturges bite the hand that fed him in *Sullivan's Travels*. The story of *Hold Back the Dawn* was supposedly told to sentimental Mitchell Leisen during a lunch break on the studio floor; Crosby and Hope based a score of gags on Paramount; and the studio was the setting for *Star Spangled Rhythm*, an all-star musical which encouraged other studios to emulate it, with Warner's *Thank Your Lucky Stars* and *It's a Great Feeling*, Universal's *Follow the Boys*, MGM's *Abbott and Costello in Hollywood*, the independent *Stage Door Canteen*, and later Paramount's less successful reprise, *Variety Girl*.

In 1950 *Sunset Boulevard* took a really sardonic look at the film city, and set a fashion for scathing movies like *The Star, The Bad and the Beautiful, The Barefoot Contessa* and *The Big Knife*. As though to atone, almost every studio threw in a light-hearted, nostalgic look at Hollywood's golden era: *Singin' in the Rain, The Perils of Pauline, Jolson Sings Again, The Eddie Cantor Story*. But in the last few years the only really affectionate review of Hollywood's past has been in the Cliff Richard musical *Wonderful Life*, though Jerry Lewis continued to paint zany pictures of studio life in *The Errand*

Boy, The Ladies' Man and *The Patsy*. The rest was all denunciation and bitterness: *The Goddess, Two Weeks in Another Town, The Carpetbaggers, Harlow, Inside Daisy Clover, The Loved One* and *The Oscar*. A 1969 TV series, *Bracken's World*, is set in a film studio (20th Century Fox) and sees it as a kind of valley of the dolls—and the studio scenes in *that* movie were none too convincing.

THE HOLLYWOOD TEN. Alvah Bessie, Herbert Biberman, Lester Cole, Edward Dmytryk, Ring Lardner Jnr, John Howard Lawson, Albert Maltz, Sam Ornitz, Adrian Scott and Dalton Trumbo were the famous band of writers, producers and directors who in 1947 refused to tell the Un-American Activities Committee whether they were or were not Communists. All served short prison sentences and had difficulty getting work in Hollywood for several years.

HOLM, CELESTE (1919–   ). American stage actress (from 1936), who in her screen appearances was typically cast in wisecracking roles. *Three Little Girls in Blue* (45), *Gentlemen's Agreement* (AA) (48), *The Snake Pit* (48), *Come to the Stable* (49), *All About Eve* (50), *Everybody Does It* (51), *The Tender Trap* (54), *High Society* (56), *Bachelor Flat* (61), *Doctor, You've Got To Be Kidding* (67).

HOLM, IAN (1932–   ). British stage actor recently emerging in films. *The Bofors Gun* (BFA) (68), *A Midsummer Night's Dream* (68), *A Severed Head* (69).

HOLMES, PHILLIPS (1909–1942). American juvenile lead who went straight from college to Hollywood; son of Taylor Holmes. His rather stiff personality soon lost its appeal. *The Return of Sherlock Holmes* (29), *The Criminal Code* (31), *An American Tragedy* (32), *The Man I Killed* (32), *State Fair* (33), *Nana* (34), *Great Expectations* (34), *The House of a Thousand Candles* (36), *The Housemaster* (GB) (38), etc.

HOLMES, TAYLOR (1872–1959). Veteran American character actor with long stage experience; latterly seen as amiably crooked politician or confidence trickster. On stage from 1899. *Efficiency Edgar's Courtship* (17), *Ruggles of Red Gap* (title role) (18), *One Hour of Love* (28), *The First Baby* (36), *Boomerang* (47), *Father of the Bride* (50), *The First Legion* (51), *Beware My Lovely* (52), *The Maverick Queen* (56), scores of others.

HOLT, CHARLENE (1939–   ). American leading lady, former star of TV commercials (and *The Tom Ewell Show*). Films include *Man's Favourite Sport* (64), *Red Line 7000* (66), *El Dorado* (66).

HOLT, JACK (1888–1951). Tough-looking American leading man of silent and sound action films. *A Cigarette—That's All* (14), *The*

Little American (16), *The Woman Thou Gavest Me* (18), *Held by the Enemy* (20), *Bought and Paid For* (22), *Empty Hands* (24), *Wanderer of the Wasteland* (25), *Vengeance* (28), *Hell's Island* (30), *Dirigible* (31), *War Correspondent* (32), *The Forgotten Man* (33), *The Littlest Rebel* (35), *San Francisco* (36), *Alien Sabotage* (40), *Holt of the Secret Service* (43), *They Were Expendable* (45), *Flight to Nowhere* (46), *Brimstone* (49), *Task Force* (49), *Across the Wide Missouri* (51), scores of others.

HOLT, PATRICK (1912–). British leading man formerly known as Patrick Parsons. On stage before small parts in 30s films. Later in *Hungry Hill* (47), *Master of Bankdam* (47), *The Mark of Cain* (48), *Portrait from Life* (49), *Marry Me* (49), *Guilt Is My Shadow* (50), *The Dark Avenger* (55), *Miss Tulip Stays the Night* (56), etc.; more recently in smaller roles, e.g. *Thunderball* (65), *Murderers' Row* (66).

†HOLT, SETH (1923–). British director, formerly editor and associate producer for Ealing. *Nowhere to Go* (58), *Taste of Fear* (61), *Station Six Sahara* (63), *The Nanny* (65), *Danger Route* (67), etc.

HOLT, TIM (1918–). American leading man, son of Jack Holt. In films from 1937, and was hero of many low-budget Westerns; also *History Is Made at Night* (37), *Stagecoach* (39), *The Swiss Family Robinson* (40), *The Magnificent Ambersons* (42), *Hitler's Children* (42), war service, *My Darling Clementine* (46), *The Treasure of the Sierra Madre* (47), *The Mysterious Desperado* (49), *His Kind of Woman* (51), *The Monster That Challenged the World* (57), etc. Has virtually retired to his ranch.

HOMEIER, SKIP (1929–). Former American child actor, notable as the young Nazi in *Tomorrow the World* (44) (also in stage play). Adult films, mainly 'B' Westerns, less exciting. *Boys' Ranch* (46), *The Gunfighter* (50), *Beachhead* (54), *Between Heaven and Hell* (56), *Comanche Station* (60), *The Ghost and Mr Chicken* (66), etc. TV series: *Dan Raven* (60).

HOMOKI-NAGY, ISTVAN (1914–). Hungarian naturalist who has made many films of wild life including *From Blossom Time Till Autumn Frost*.

HOMOLKA, OSCAR (1899–). Viennese-born character actor, a fine 'heavy'. On stage from 1918, international films from mid-30s. *Rhodes of Africa* (36), *Sabotage* (37), *Ebb Tide* (37), *Ball of Fire* (41), *Rage in Heaven* (41), *Mission to Moscow* (43), *The Shop at Sly Corner* (46), *I Remember Mama* (48), *Anna Lucasta* (49), *Top Secret* (52), *House of the Arrow* (53), *The Seven Year Itch* (55), *War and Peace* (56), *Tempest* (59), *Mr Sardonicus* (63), *The Long Ships* (63), *Joy in the Morning* (65), *Funeral in Berlin* (66), *The Happening* (67), *Jack of Diamonds* (67), *Billion Dollar Brain* (68), etc.

Un Homme et Une Femme

UN HOMME ET UNE FEMME (France 1966). A slight, sophisticated modern love story which achieved international box-office success because audiences were waiting for a reversion from the kitchen sink school and found it in this glossy accumulation of television commercial tricks. Critics busied themselves with theories as to why certain scenes were shot in colour and others in black and white, until director Claude Lelouch admitted that he ran out of funds and simply couldn't afford any more colour stock. Anouk Aimée and Jean-Louis Trintignant were the protagonists; Francis Lai's music helped immeasurably.

Homosexuality can now be said to have arrived as a fit subject for the western cinema, producers having toyed gingerly with it for thirty years or more. In 1941, Sidney Greenstreet's relationship to Elisha Cook Jnr in *The Maltese Falcon* could scarcely be inferred from the dialogue. Indeed, not until the last decade has advance been rapid. Germany's *The Third Sex* in 1957 was followed by the devious obscurities of *Suddenly Last Summer* and by the matter-of-factness of *Victim*, a thriller about the blackmail of homosexuals. *A Taste of Honey* featured a sympathetic homosexual, and the plots of both *Advise and Consent* and *The Best Man* hinged on allegations of homosexuality against an American politician. (*Cat on a Hot Tin Roof* [58] and *Spartacus* [60] were probably the last Hollywood movies to have homosexual inferences deliberately *removed* from their scripts.) *A Very Special Favour* was the first film to make fun of the subject; Rock Hudson made Leslie Caron think he was effeminate so that she would 'rescue' him. Other milestones since 1961 have been *A View from the Bridge*, with its male kiss; *The Leather Boys*; *Stranger in the House*; *The Fearless Vampire Killers*, with its young homosexual bloodsucker; *The Detective*, from which it appears that New York is almost entirely populated by homosexuals; and *The Lion in Winter*, which alleges homosexuality in—of all people—Richard the Lionheart. The last three films all appeared in 1968, quite a gay year when one considers its other productions involving homosexuality: *Reflections in a Golden Eye, The Sergeant, Riot, Midnight Cowboy, The Boston Strangler, If, Spitting Image* . . . and the announcement of *Myra Breckenridge*. See also: *Lesbianism*.

HONEGGER, ARTHUR (1892–1955). Swiss composer who worked on French and British pictures: *Les Misérables* (33), *Pygmalion* (38), *Pacific 231* (46), etc.

HOOKS, ROBERT (1937–   ). American Negro actor, seen in *Hurry Sundown* (67) and TV series *N.Y.P.D.* (67).

HOPALONG CASSIDY, the genial black-garbed hero of scores of Western second features since 1935, was created by novelist Clarence E.

Mulford. William Boyd has been his only screen and TV personification.

HOPE, BOB (1904–   ) (Leslie Townes Hope). Wisecracking American star comedian who after years in vaudeville and musical comedy made Hollywood debut in *The Big Broadcast of 1938* and has been busy ever since. *Thanks for the Memory* (38), *The Cat and the Canary* (39), *The Road to Singapore* (40), *The Ghost Breakers* (41), *Road to Zanzibar* (41), *My Favourite Blonde* (42), *Road to Morocco* (42), *Star-Spangled Rhythm* (43), *Road to Utopia* (45), *Monsieur Beaucaire* (46), *Road to Rio* (47), *The Paleface* (47), *Road to Bali* (52), *The Seven Little Foys* (55), *Paris Holiday* (57), *The Facts of Life* (60), *Call Me Bwana* (63), *Critic's Choice* (63), *A Global Affair* (63), *I'll Take Sweden* (65), *Boy, Did I Get a Wrong Number?* (66), *Eight on the Lam* (67), *The Private Navy of Sgt O'Farrell* (68), *How to Commit Marriage* (69), many others. Special Academy Awards in 1940, 1944 and 1952, mainly in consideration of his forces' entertainment and other charitable ventures. Has published two light-hearted chunks of autobiography, *Have Tux Will Travel* (*This Is on Me*) and *I Owe Russia Two Thousand Dollars*.

HOPE, VIDA (1918–1962). British character actress, usually in comic proletarian roles; also stage director. *English Without Tears* (44), *Nicholas Nickleby* (47), *It Always Rains on Sunday* (48), *The Man in the White Suit* (51), *Lease of Life* (54), *Family Doctor* (58), etc.

HOPKINS, MIRIAM (1902–   ). Pert American star of the 30s, previously a dancer. *Fast and Loose* (debut) (30), *Dr Jekyll and Mr Hyde* (32), *Trouble in Paradise* (32), *Design for Living* (34), *Becky Sharp* (35), *Barbary Coast* (35), *These Three* (36), *Woman Chases Man* (37), *The Old Maid* (39), *Virginia City* (40), *Lady with Red Hair* (41), *Old Acquaintance* (43), *The Heiress* (49), *The Mating Season* (50), *Carrie* (51), *The Outcasts of Poker Flat* (52), *The Children's Hour* (*The Loudest Whisper*) (62), *Fanny Hill* (64), *The Chase* (66), etc.

HOPPER, DENNIS (1936–   ). American 'second lead' and character actor. *Rebel Without a Cause* (55), *Giant* (56), *The Sons of Katie Elder* (65), *Cool Hand Luke* (67), *Easy Rider* (also directed) (69), etc.

HOPPER, HEDDA (1890–1966) (Elda Furry). American gossip columnist who vied with Louella Parsons for the strongest hold over Hollywood. Former screen actress, mainly in silent days. *Virtuous Wives* (19), *Has the World Gone Mad?* (23), *Free Love* (24), *Let Us Be Gay* (30), *As You Desire Me* (32), *The Women* (39), *That's Right You're Wrong* (39), *Reap the Wild Wind* (42), *Sunset Boulevard* (50), etc. Published two autobiographical books: *From Under My Hat* (1952) and *The Whole Truth and Nothing But* (1963).

HOPPER, JERRY (1907–   ). American director of routine action films and TV series. *The Atomic City* (52), *The Secret of the Incas* (54), *Naked Alibi* (54), *Never Say Goodbye* (55), *Toy Tiger* (56), *The Missouri Traveller* (58), etc. Much TV work.

HOPPER, VICTORIA (1909–   ). Canadian leading lady popular in British films of the 30s. *The Constant Nymph* (33), *Lorna Doone* (35), *Whom the Gods Love* (35), *The Mill on the Floss* (36), etc. No recent films.

HOPPER, WILLIAM (1915–   ). American actor, son of Hedda Hopper. Movie roles include *Rebel Without a Cause* (55), *The Bad Seed* (56), *Twenty Thousand Miles to Earth* (57); more famous as Paul Drake in TV's *Perry Mason* series (57–66).

HORDERN, MICHAEL (1911–   ). British character actor, on stage from 1937; film appearances usually as careworn official. *The Girl in the News* (debut) (39); war service; *School for Secrets* (46), *Mine Own Executioner* (47), *Good Time Girl* (48), *Passport to Pimlico* (48), *The Hour of Thirteen* (51), *The Heart of the Matter* (53), *The Baby and the Battleship* (55), *The Spanish Gardener* (56), *Sink the Bismarck* (60), *El Cid* (61), *The VIPs* (63), *Dr Syn* (63), *Genghis Khan* (65), *The Spy Who Came In from the Cold* (66), *Khartoum* (66), *A Funny Thing Happened on the Way to the Forum* (66), *The Taming of the Shrew* (67), *Where Eagles Dare* (68), *The Bed-Sitting Room* (69), *Anne of the Thousand Days* (70), others.

HORN, CAMILLA (1907–   ). German actress who had brief careers in Hollywood and Britain before retiring. *Faust* (26), *Tempest* (28), *The Return of Raffles* (32), *Luck of a Sailor* (GB) (34), etc.

HORNBLOW, ARTHUR JNR (1893–   ). American producer, in Hollywood from 1926. *Ruggles of Red Gap* (34), *The Cat and the Canary* (39), *The Murder in Thornton Square* (*Gaslight*) (43), *The Hucksters* (47), *The Asphalt Jungle* (50), *Witness for the Prosecution* (57), *The War Lover* (63), many others.

HORNE, DAVID (1898–   ). British character actor, mainly on stage; almost always in pompous roles. *General John Regan* (33), *The Mill on the Floss* (36), *The First of the Few* (42), *The Seventh Veil* (45), *The Rake's Progress* (45), *The Man Within* (46), *It's Hard To Be Good* (49), *Madeleine* (50), *Lust for Life* (56), *The Devil's Disciple* (59), many others.

HORNE, JAMES V. (1880–1942). American director, in Hollywood from 1911. Made some of Laurel and Hardy's best two-reelers; also *The Third Eye* (20), *American Manners* (24), *College* (27), *Bonnie Scotland* (35), *The Bohemian Girl* (36), *Way Out West* (37), *Holt of the Secret Service* (42), many others.

484

HORNE, LENA (1918-   ). Beautiful American Negro singer and actress who came to Hollywood from night clubs. *Cabin in the Sky* (43), *Stormy Weather* (43), *Two Girls and a Sailor* (44), *Till the Clouds Roll By* (45), many guest appearances in musicals. 1969: *Death of a Gunfighter*.

HORNE, VICTORIA (c. 1920-   ). American comedienne. *The Scarlet Claw* (44), *The Ghost and Mrs Muir* (47), *The Snake Pit* (48), *Abbott and Costello Meet the Killer* (49), *Harvey* (50), *Affair with a Stranger* (53), etc. Retired: married Jack Oakie.

HORNER, HARRY (1910-   ). Czech-born production designer with stage experience in Vienna and New York. *Our Town* (40), *The Little Foxes* (41), *A Double Life* (47), *The Heiress* (AA) (49), *Born Yesterday* (50), *The Hustler* (60), many others. Also director: *Beware My Lovely* (52), *Red Planet Mars* (52), *New Faces* (54), *A Life in the Balance* (55), *The Wild Party* (56), *Man from Del Rio* (56), etc.

horror as a staple of screen entertainment really emanates from Germany (although Edison shot a picture of *Frankenstein* as early as 1908). Before World War I Wegener had made a version of *The Golem*, which he improved on in 1920; it was this second version which directly influenced the Hollywood horror school stimulated by James Whale. What is surprising is that Hollywood took so long to catch on to a good idea, especially as the Germans, in depressed post-war mood, relentlessly turned out such macabre films as *The Cabinet of Dr Caligari* (with Veidt as a hypnotically-controlled monster), *Nosferatu* (Murnau's brilliantly personal account of Bram Stoker's 'Dracula'), *Waxworks* (Leni's three-part thriller about Ivan the Terrible, Haroun-al-Raschid and Jack the Ripper); *The Hands of Orlac* and *The Student of Prague*. Most of the talents involved were exported to Hollywood by 1927; but the only horror film directly resulting was Leni's *The Cat and the Canary*, which was a spoof. California did encourage Lon Chaney, but his films were grotesque rather than gruesome; and John Barrymore had already been allowed in 1921 to impersonate *Dr Jekyll and Mr Hyde* (a role to be played even more for horror by Fredric March in 1932). By the end of the 20s, the European horror film was played out except for Dreyer's highly individual *Vampyr*; the ball was in Hollywood's court.

In 1930 Tod Browning filmed the stage version of *Dracula*, using a Hungarian actor named Bela Lugosi; shortly after, Robert Florey wrote and James Whale directed a version of *Frankenstein* that borrowed freely from *The Golem*. Both films (see individual entries) were wildfire successes, and the studio involved, Universal, set out on a steady and profitable progress through a series of sequels. In 1932 Karloff appeared in *The Mummy*, and in 1933 Claude Rains was *The Invisible Man*; these characters were added

to the grisly band. In 1935 the studio made *Werewolf of London*,
which led five years later to *The Wolf Man* giving Lon Chaney Jnr
a useful sideline. By 1945, despite the upsurge in supernatural
interest during the war, these characters were thought to be played
out, and in the last two 'serious' episodes they appeared *en masse*.
In 1948 they began to meet Abbott and Costello, which one would
have thought might ensure their final demise; but more of that
later.

Meanwhile other landmarks had been established. Browning
made the outlandish *Freaks*, and in 1935 the spoof *Mark of the
Vampire*. James Whale in 1932 made *The Old Dark House*, an
inimitably entertaining mixture of disagreeable ingredients.
Warners in 1933 came up with *The Mystery of the Wax Museum*
(later remade as *House of Wax*) and later got some mileage out of
The Walking Dead and *Doctor X*. Paramount went in for mad
doctors, from *The Island of Dr Moreau* (*Island of Lost Souls*) to *Doctor
Cyclops*, and at the beginning of World War II produced scary
remakes of *The Cat and the Canary* and *The Ghost Breakers*. RKO
were busy with *King Kong* and *She*, MGM with *The Devil Doll*.
In the early 40s Universal began a listless anthology series under
the title *Inner Sanctum*, and later failed in *The Creature from the Black
Lagoon* to add another intriguing monster to their gallery. By far
the most significant extension of the genre was the small group
of depressive but atmospheric thrillers produced by Val Lewton at
RKO in 1942–45, the best of them being *The Body Snatcher*, *The
Cat People* and *I Walked with a Zombie*.

After the war, little was heard of horror until the advent of
science fiction in 1950. After this we heard a very great deal of
nasty visitors from other planets (*The Thing*, *Invasion of the Body
Snatchers*), mutations (*The Fly*, *This Island Earth*), robots (*The Day
the Earth Stood Still*, *Forbidden Planet*) and giant insects (*Them*,
Tarantula). To please the teenage audience, fly-by-night producers
thought up fantastic horror-comic variations and came up with
titles like *The Blob*, *I Married a Monster from Outer Space* and *I Was
a Teenage Werewolf*; such crude and shoddy productions cheapened
the genre considerably. The Japanese got into the act with stop-
motion monsters like *Godzilla* and *Rodan*; then, surprisingly, it
was the turn of the British. Hammer Films, a small independent
outfit with an old Thames-side house for a studio, persuaded
Universal to let them remake the sagas of Frankenstein, Dracula
et alia, and the results have been flooding the world's screens for
ten years now, marked by a certain bold style, lack of imagination,
and such excess of blood-letting that several versions have to be
made for each film (the bloodiest for Japan, the most restrained
for the home market). Britain also produced some commendable
screen versions of *The Quatermass Experiment* and other TV serials.

Since 1955 horror has been consistently in fashion, at least in the world's mass markets, and film-makers have been busy capping each other by extending the bounds of how much explicit physical shock and horror is permissible. (This, of course, does not make for good films.) If Franju was revolting in the detail of *Eyes Without a Face*, Hitchcock certainly topped him in *Psycho* and was himself outdone by William Castle in *Homicidal*. (*Psycho* also gave the screen an inventive horror-writing talent in Robert Bloch, who has since been kept as busy as he could wish.) And the cheapjack American nasties at least provided a training ground for producer-director Roger Corman, who between 1960 and 1964 made a series of Poe adaptations much admired for style and enthusiasm if not for production detail.

HORTON, EDWARD EVERETT (1887–   ). American comic actor with inimitable diffident manner. In theatre from 1908, films from 1916; talkies increased his popularity. *Beggar on Horseback* (25), *The Terror* (28), *The Front Page* (31), *Alice in Wonderland* (as Mad Hatter) (33), *It's a Boy* (34), *The Gay Divorce* (34), *Top Hat* (35), *The Man in the Mirror* (as star) (37), *Lost Horizon* (37), *Bluebeard's Eighth Wife* (38), *Here Comes Mr Jordan* (41), *The Magnificent Dope* (42), *Thank Your Lucky Stars* (43), *Summer Storm* (44), *Arsenic and Old Lace* (44), *Her Husband's Affairs* (47), many others; returned to stage, recent comeback on TV, also in films. *The Story of Mankind* (57), *A Pocketful of Miracles* (61), *Sex and the Single Girl* (64), *The Perils of Pauline* (67), *2000 Years Later* (69). TV series: *F Troop* (as a Red Indian!) (65–66).

HORTON, ROBERT (1924–   ). American leading man best known on TV for *Wagon Train* and *A Man Called Shenandoah*. Film appearances include *A Walk in the Sun* (46), *The Return of the Texan* (52), *Men of the Fighting Lady* (54), *This Man Is Armed* (56), *The Dangerous Days of Kiowa Jones* (66), *The Green Slime* (69).

HOSSEIN, ROBERT (1927–   ). French actor: *Rififi* (55), *The Wicked Go to Hell* (also directed) (55), *Girls Disappear* (58), *La Musica* (60), *Enough Rope* (63), *Marco the Magnificent* (65), *I Killed Rasputin* (also directed) (68).

hotels have frequently formed a useful setting for films wanting to use the 'slice of life' technique. Thus *Grand Hotel*, *Hotel for Women*, *Stage Door*, *Hotel Berlin*, *Weekend at the Waldorf*, *Separate Tables* and *Hotel* itself; while *Ship of Fools* is a variation on the same theme. The hotel background was a valuable dramatic asset to films as varied as *The Last Laugh*, *The October Man*, *Don't Bother to Knock*, *Hotel du Nord*, *Pushover*, *Honeymoon Hotel*, *Room Service* (and its remake *Step Lively*), *Hotel Reserve*, *Hotel Sahara*, *The Horn Blows at Midnight*, *Hotel for Women*, *Hollywood Hotel*, *Paris Palace Hotel*, *Bedtime Story*, *The Best Man*, *The Greengage Summer*, *A Hole in the*

Head, and *The Silence*. Hotel security did not prevent attempts on the hero's life in *Journey into Fear* and *Foreign Correspondent*. The most bewildering hotel was certainly that in *So Long at the Fair*; the most amusing hotel sequences may have been in *Ninotchka*, *The Bellboy*, *A Flea in Her Ear*, or *The Perfect Woman*. And hotels that have no accommodation left sparked off quite a few Hollywood comedies during the war, including *Government Girl*, *Standing Room Only*, and *The More the Merrier* (recently remade as *Walk Don't Run*).

HOUDINI, HARRY (1873–1926) (Ehrich Weiss). American escapologist and magician extraordinary, in films from 1918. *The Master Mystery* (serial) (18), *The Grim Game* (19), *Terror Island* (20), *The Man from Beyond* (21), *Haldane of the Secret Service* (23), etc. A biopic in 1953 starred Tony Curtis.

THE HOUNDS OF ZAROFF (US title: *The Most Dangerous Game*). This 1932 thriller, made by Merian Cooper and Ernest Schoedsack with Irving Pichel as co-director, was based on a story by Richard Connell about a mad sportsman who trapped human beings on his tropical island in order to hunt them. Brilliantly photographed by Henry Garrara, with a thumping Max Steiner score, it was a splendidly gruesome adventure story which became the most remade film in Hollywood history. In 1945 it was remade as *A Game of Death*, with Edgar Barrier replacing Leslie Banks as the villain; this version was directed by Robert Wise. In 1949 it turned up as *Johnny Allegro*, with George Macready shooting arrows at George Raft; *Kill Or Be Killed* in 1950 had George Coulouris menacing Lawrence Tierney; and in 1956 Trevor Howard used savage hounds to pursue Richard Widmark in *Run for the Sun*. 1966 found Cornel Wilde on the run from African headhunters in what is basically the same story, this time called *The Naked Prey*; and in the same year an exploitation item called *Blood Feast* borrowed the plot once more.

HOUSE OF WAX (US 1953). The film which seemed to gain public approval for 3-D (until CinemaScope proved the stronger card) was actually a remake of the old horror film *The Mystery of the Wax Museum* (32), with Vincent Price in Lionel Atwill's old part as the disfigured madman who creates a new wax face for himself.

THE HOUSE ON 92ND STREET (US 1946). Producer Louis de Rochemont here brought his March of Time technique to bear on a semi-fictional spy story with a clever mystery plot and a myriad of new documentary tricks. The brisk journalistic method was highly influential, and Henry Hathaway's direction neared his best.

HOUSEMAN, JOHN (1902–). American producer. After varied experience, helped Orson Welles to found his Mercury Theatre in New York 1937, later followed him to Hollywood. *The Blue Dahlia* (46), *Letter from an Unknown Woman* (48), *They Live by Night* (48), *The Bad and the Beautiful* (52), *Julius Caesar* (53), *Executive Suite* (54), *Lust for Life* (56), *Two Weeks in Another Town* (62), *This Property is Condemned* (66), etc.

houses have been the dramatic centre of many films: there was even one, *Enchantment*, in which the house itself told the story. The films of Daphne Du Maurier's novels usually have a mysterious old house at the crux of their plots, as in *Rebecca*, *Frenchman's Creek*, *Jamaica Inn*, *My Cousin Rachel*. So in *Dragonwyck*; so in *House of Fear*; so, of course, in *Jane Eyre* and *Wuthering Heights*. Both *Citizen Kane* and *The Magnificent Ambersons* are dominated by unhappy houses, as is *Gaslight*. Thrillers set in lonely houses full of secret panels and hidden menace are exemplified by *The Spiral Staircase*, *The Black Cat*, *Night Monster*, *The House on Haunted Hill*, *The Cat and the Canary*, *The Ghost Breakers*, *Ladies in Retirement* and *Ten Little Niggers*. Haunted houses are rarer, but those in *The Uninvited*, *The Unseen*, *The Innocents*, *The Enchanted Cottage* and *The Haunting* linger vividly in the memory. So for a different reason does the Bates house in *Psycho*. Happier houses of note include the rose-covered cottage in *Random Harvest*, the family mansions of *Forever and a Day* and *Enchantment*, the red-decorated Denver house in *The Unsinkable Molly Brown*, the laboriously built country seat of *Mr Blandings Builds His Dream House*, the broken-down houses of *George Washington Slept Here* and *Father Came Too*, and dear old *Rookery Nook*. And filmgoers have various reasons to remember *The House on 92nd Street*, *The House on Telegraph Hill*, *House of Strangers*, *House of Horrors*, *House of Bamboo*, *House of Numbers*, *House of the Damned*, *House of the Seven Hawks*, *House of Women*, *House by the River*, *House of Seven Gables*, *House of Dracula*, *House of Frankenstein*, *House of Wax*, *Sinister House*, *The Red House*, *Crazy House*, *The Old Dark House* and *The Fall of the House of Usher*.

HOUSMAN, ARTHUR: see under JACK NORTON.

HOUSTON, DONALD (1923–   ). Blond Welsh actor on stage from 1940, in films from 1941. *A Girl Must Live* (debut) (41), *The Blue Lagoon* (48), *Doctor in the House* (53), *The Man Upstairs* (59), *Room at the Top* (59), *Twice Round the Daffodils* (62), *A Study in Terror* (as Dr Watson) (65), *Don't You Cry* (70), many others; also on TV.

HOUSTON, GLYN (1926–   ). Welsh character actor, brother of Donald Houston. *The Blue Lamp* (50), *Payroll* (60), *Solo for Sparrow* (lead role) (62), *The Secret of Blood Island* (65), *Invasion* (66), etc. Much on TV.

HOUSTON, RENEE (1902–   ) (Katherina Houston Gribbin). British vaudeville and revue artiste, once teamed with her sister Billie,

later with Donald Stewart; more recently character actress of
screen and TV. *Mr Cinders* (34), *A Girl Must Live* (38), *Old Bill and
Son* (40), *Two Thousand Women* (44), *The Belles of St Trinians* (54),
A Town Like Alice (56), *Time Without Pity* (57), *The Horse's Mouth*
(59), *The Flesh and the Fiends* (60), *Three on a Spree* (61), etc.

HOVEY, TIM (1945–   ). American child actor of the mid-fifties.
The Private War of Major Benson (55), *Toy Tiger* (56), *Man Afraid*
(57), etc. Later on TV.

HOWARD, ARTHUR (1910–   ). British character actor, brother of
Leslie Howard, often seen as schoolmaster, clerk, etc. Best parts:
The Happiest Days of Your Life (49), *The Intruder* (53). TV series:
Whacko.

HOWARD, ESTHER (1893–1965). American character actress, usually
in blowsy roles. *Ready for Love* (35), *Serenade* (39), *Sullivan's Travels*
(41), *Farewell My Lovely* (44), *The Lady Gambles* (49), etc.

HOWARD, JOHN (1913–   ) (John Cox). American actor, hero of
many a 'B' picture in 30s and 40s, including Bulldog Drummond
series (37–39), *Lost Horizon* (37), *The Philadelphia Story* (40),
Invisible Woman (41), *Tight Shoes* (42), *Isle of Missing Men* (43),
Experiment Alcatraz (51), *The High and the Mighty* (54), *Unknown
Terror* (57), etc. TV series: *Dr Hudson's Secret Journal* (55–56),
Adventures of the Seahawk (58).

HOWARD, JOYCE (1922–   ). British leading lady of the 40s. *Love
on the Dole* (41), *The Gentle Sex* (43), *They Met in the Dark* (43),
Woman to Woman (46), *Mrs Fitzherbert* (47), *Shadow of the Past* (50),
etc.

†HOWARD, LESLIE (1893–1943) (Leslie Stainer). Distinguished British
actor whose screen image was that of the romantic intellectual.
Former bank clerk; turned to stage 1918; made short films 1920
but no features till 1930. *Outward Bound* (US) (30), *Never the Twain
Shall Meet* (US) (31), *A Free Soul* (US) (31), *Five and Ten* (US) (31),
Devotion (US) (31), *Smiling Through* (US) (32), *The Animal Kingdom*
(US) (32), *Secrets* (US) (33), *Captured* (US) (33), *Berkeley Square*
(US) (33), *The Lady Is Willing* (US) (34), *Of Human Bondage* (US)
(34), *British Agent* (US) (34), *The Scarlet Pimpernel* (34), *The Petrified
Forest* (US) (36), *Romeo and Juliet* (US) (36), *It's Love I'm After* (US)
(37), *Stand In* (US) (37), *Pygmalion* (also co-directed) (38), *Gone
with the Wind* (US) (39), *Intermezzo (Escape to Happiness)* (US) (39),
Pimpernel Smith (also produced) (41), *49th Parallel* (41), *The First
of the Few* (42), *The Gentle Sex* (produced only) (43), *The Lamp Still
Burns* (produced only) (43). His daughter later wrote a biography,
A Very Remarkable Father.

HOWARD, KATHLEEN (1879–1956). Canadian character actress, former opera singer; memorable as W. C. Fields' frequent screen wife. *Death Takes a Holiday* (34), *You're Telling Me* (34), *The Man on the Flying Trapeze* (35), *It's a Gift* (35), *Laura* (44), *The Late George Apley* (47), etc.

HOWARD, RONALD (1918–). British actor, son of Leslie Howard; formerly reporter. *While the Sun Shines* (debut) (46), *The Queen of Spades* (48), *Tom Brown's Schooldays* (51), *Drango* (56), *Babette Goes to War* (59), *Spider's Web* (60), *The Curse of the Mummy's Tomb* (64), *Africa Texas Style* (67), many others. TV series: *Sherlock Holmes* (made in Paris).

HOWARD, SIDNEY (1891–1939). American playwright whose chief contributions to Hollywood were *The Late Christopher Bean*, *They Knew What They Wanted*, *Yellow Jack*, and most of the script of *Gone with the Wind*.

HOWARD, SYDNEY (1885–1946). Plump British comedian famous for fluttering gestures. On stage from 1912, films from 1930. *French Leave* (debut) (30), *Up for the Cup* (33), *Splinters in the Navy* (34), *Night of the Garter* (36), *Chick* (36), *Shipyard Sally* (39), *Tilly of Bloomsbury* (40), *Once a Crook* (41), *When We Are Married* (42), *Flight from Folly* (45), etc.

†HOWARD, TREVOR (1916–). Distinguished British leading man, on stage from 1934; later concentrated on films. *The Way Ahead* (debut) (44), *The Way to the Stars* (45), *Brief Encounter* (46), *I See a Dark Stranger* (46), *Green for Danger* (46), *So Well Remembered* (47), *They Made Me a Fugitive* (47), *The Third Man* (49), *The Golden Salamander* (49), *Odette* (50), *The Clouded Yellow* (51), *An Outcast of the Islands* (52), *The Gift Horse* (52), *The Heart of the Matter* (53), *The Lovers of Lisbon* (Fr.) (54), *The Stranger's Hand* (54), *Cockleshell Heroes* (55), *Around the World in Eighty Days* (56), *Run for the Sun* (US) (56), *Interpol* (57), *Manuela* (57), *The Key* (BFA) (58), *Roots of Heaven* (59), *Moment of Danger* (50), *Sons and Lovers* (60), *Mutiny on the Bounty* (as Captain Bligh) (62), *The Lion* (62), *The Man in the Middle* (64), *Father Goose* (US) (64), *Von Ryan's Express* (US) (65), *Morituri* (US) (65), *The Liquidator* (65), *The Poppy is Also a Flower* (*Danger Grows Wild*) (66). *Triple Cross* (66), *The Long Duel* (67), *The Charge of the Light Brigade* (68), *The Battle of Britain* (69), *Twinky* (69), *Ryan's Daughter* (69).

HOWARD, WILLIAM K. (1899–1954). American director. *Border Legion* (24), *White Gold* (27), *Christina* (29), *Transatlantic* (31), *Sherlock Holmes* (32), *The Power and the Glory* (33), *Fire Over England* (GB) (36), *Johnny Come Lately* (43), *When the Lights Go On Again* (44), etc.

HOWE, JAMES WONG (1899–   ) (Wong Tung Jim). Distinguished Chinese cinematographer, in Hollywood from 1917. *Trail of the Lonesome Pine* (22), *Peter Pan* (24), *Sorrell and Son* (27), *Chandu the Magician* (32), *The Thin Man* (34), *Viva Villa* (34), *Mark of the Vampire* (35), *Fire Over England* (GB) (36), *The Prisoner of Zenda* (37), *The Adventures of Tom Sawyer* (37), *Algiers* (38), *Abe Lincoln in Illinois* (39), *Dr Ehrlich's Magic Bullet* (40), *King's Row* (41), *Yankee Doodle Dandy* (42), *Passage to Marseilles* (44), *Confidential Agent* (45), *Objective Burma* (45), *Body and Soul* (47), *Mr Blandings Builds His Dream House* (48), *The Brave Bulls* (51), *Come Back Little Sheba* (52), *The Rose Tattoo* (AA) (54), *Picnic* (55), *Diary of a Scoundrel* (56), *Sweet Smell of Success* (57), *Bell, Book and Candle* (58), *Song Without End* (59), *Hud* (62), *This Property Is Condemned* (66), *Hombre* (67), many others. Directed *Go Man Go* (52).

HOWELLS, URSULA (1922–   ). British actress, mainly on stage and TV. Film roles include *Flesh and Blood* (51), *The Constant Husband* (55), *They Can't Hang Me* (55), *The Long Arm* (56), *Dr Terror's House of Horrors* (65), etc.

HOWERD, FRANKIE (1921–   ). British eccentric comedian of stage and TV. Occasional films include *The Runaway Bus* (54), *Jumping for Joy* (55), *The Ladykillers* (55), *A Touch of the Sun* (56), *Further Up the Creek* (59), *The Cool Mikado* (63), *The Great St Trinian's Train Robbery* (66), *Carry On Doctor* (68), etc.

HOWES, BOBBY (1895–   ). Diminutive British revue comedian and musical comedy leading man; on stage from 1909. Occasional films from 1927: *Lord Babs* (32), *Yes, Madam* (38), *Bob's Your Uncle* (41), *The Good Companions* (57), etc.

HOWES, SALLY ANN (1930–   ). British stage and screen leading lady and singer, daughter of Bobby Howes. When 13 years old was chosen to star in *Thursday's Child* (43). Later films: *Halfway House* (44), *Dead of Night* (45), *Nicholas Nickleby* (47), *Anna Karenina* (48), *My Sister and I* (48), etc.; more recently on Broadway stage and TV. Recent films: *The Admirable Crichton* (58), *Chitty Chitty Bang Bang* (69).

HOW GREEN WAS MY VALLEY (US 1941: AA best picture). A stagey but oddly moving film version of Richard Llewellyn's novel about a Welsh mining family several decades ago. The elaborate village set was used again in other movies including *The Moon Is Down*. Directed by John Ford (AA); with Walter Pidgeon, Donald Crisp (AA) and Maureen O'Hara; photographed by Arthur Miller (AA).

HOWLETT, NOEL (1901–   ). British stage actor who has appeared in small film roles since 1936, often as solicitor, auctioneer or civil servant. *A Yank at Oxford* (46), *Corridor of Mirrors* (47), *The Blind Goddess* (49), *Father Brown* (54), *The Scapegoat* (59), etc.

HOWLIN, OLIN (1896–1959) (formerly known as OLIN HOWLAND). American character actor, in innumerable small film roles since the early talkies. *So Big* (32), *Nothing Sacred* (37), *This Gun for Hire* (42), *The Wistful Widow* (47), *Them* (54), *The Blob* (58), etc.

HOW THE WEST WAS WON (US 1962). Historically notable as the first story film—and almost the last—in three-lens Cinerama. (The single-lens system, almost indistinguishable from other wide-screen methods, was introduced in 1963.) A patchy Western directed by George Marshall, Henry Hathaway and John Ford, it has spectacular action sequences which dwarf the chatter of an all-star cast. Photographers: Charles Lang Jnr, William Daniels, Milton Krasner, Joseph la Shelle, Harold A. Wellman.

HOW TO MARRY A MILLIONAIRE (US 1953). The second film, and the first comedy, in CinemaScope. Showed no mastery of the technique but provided Marilyn Monroe with a good comedy part. Written by Nunnally Johnson, directed by Jean Negulesco.

HOYT, JOHN (1905–   ) (John Hoysradt). Incisive American character actor, sometimes cast as German officer or stylish crook. *O.S.S.* (46), *Rommel, Desert Fox* (51), *New Mexico* (52), *Androcles and the Lion* (53), *Julius Caesar* (53), *The Blackboard Jungle* (55), *The Conqueror* (56), *Six Inches Tall* (58), *Never So Few* (60), *Duel at Diablo* (66), many others.

HUBBARD, JOHN (1914–   ). American light leading man who starred in several Hal Roach comedies (*The Housekeeper's Daughter* [39], *Turnabout* [40], *Road Show* [41], etc.), later slid into character roles. TV series: *Don't Call Me Charlie*. Recently: *Gunfight at Comanche Creek* (63), *Fate Is the Hunter* (64), *Duel at Diablo* (66).

HUBER, HAROLD (1904–1959). American character actor, former lawyer; often seen as sly crook or dumb detective. *The Bowery* (33), *G-Men* (35), *Kit Carson* (40), *The Lady from Chungking* (43), *Let's Dance* (last film) (50), many others.

HUBLEY, JOHN (1914–   ). American animator, associated with the early days of UPA; a co-creator of Mr Magoo. Recently working on experimental documentary cartoons: *Of Stars and Men*, etc.

HUCKLEBERRY FINN. Mark Twain's lively Mississippi boy had film adventures in 1919, when he was played by Lewis Sargent; in 1931, by Junior Durkin; in 1939, by Mickey Rooney; and in 1960, by Eddie Hodges. He also turned up in several of the films about Tom Sawyer (qv).

493

HUD (US 1962). This realistic, ambling melodrama of a modern
Western ne'er-do-well was refreshingly off-beat for Hollywood.
Written by Irving Ravetch and Harriet Frank Jnr; directed by
Martin Ritt; photographed by James Wong Howe (AA); with
Paul Newman, Patricia Neal (AA), Melvyn Douglas (AA).

HUDD, WALTER (1898–1963). British character actor of stage and
screen; usually played aloof characters and in 1936 was cast as
T. E. Lawrence but the production was abandoned. *Rembrandt* (36),
Black Limelight (37), *Elephant Boy* (37), *The Housemaster* (38),
Major Barbara (40), *I Know Where I'm Going* (45), *Paper Orchid* (49),
Life For Ruth (62), etc.

HUDSON, ROCHELLE (1914–   ). American leading lady who played
ingénue roles in the 30s. *Laugh and Get Rich* (30), *She Done Him
Wrong* (33), *Les Misérables* (35), *Smuggled Cargo* (39), *Island of
Doomed Men* (40), *Meet Boston Blackie* (41), *Rubber Racketeers* (42),
Queen of Broadway (43), *Skyliner* (49), *Rebel without a Cause* (55),
The Night Walker (65), *Broken Sabre* (65), etc.

HUDSON, ROCK (1925–   ) (Roy Fitzgerald). Giant-sized American
leading man, latterly involved in sophisticated sex comedies.
Fighter Squadron (debut) (48), *Winchester 73* (50), *The Desert Hawk*
(50), *The Fat Man* (50), *Bend of the River* (52), *Scarlet Angel* (52),
Sea Devils (GB) (53), *Magnificent Obsession* (54), *Captain Lightfoot*
(54), *All That Heaven Allows* (54), *Never Say Goodbye* (55), *Giant* (56),
Written on the Wind (56), *Battle Hymn* (57), *Something of Value* (57),
The Tarnished Angels (58), *A Farewell to Arms* (58), *This Earth Is Mine*
(59), *Pillow Talk* (59), *The Last Sunset* (60), *Come September* (61),
Lover Come Back (62), *The Spiral Road* (62), *A Gathering of Eagles*
(63), *Man's Favourite Sport* (63), *Send Me No Flowers* (64), *Strange
Bedfellows* (65), *A Very Special Favour* (65), *Blindfold* (65), *Seconds*
(66), *Tobruk* (67), *Ice Station Zebra* (68), *A Fine Pair* (69), *Darling
Lili* (69), *The Hornet's Nest* (70), others.

HUE AND CRY (GB 1946). One of the first post-war Ealing comedies,
typical in its use of London bomb-site locations and its exhilarating
spoof of authority; basically a lively 'tuppenny blood' boys' adventure about crooks in Covent Garden. Written by T. E. B. Clarke,
directed by Charles Crichton; with Alastair Sim and Jack Warner,
Music George Auric; photography Douglas Slocombe.

HUGGINS, ROY (1914–   ). American writer-producer-director who
has had great success in TV with such series as *The Fugitive* and
Run for Your Life. Former industrial engineer. Film work includes
I Love Trouble (w) (48), *The Lady Gambles* (w) (49), *Hangman's
Knot* (w, d) (52), *Pushover* (w) (54), *A Fever in the Blood* (p) (59), etc.

HUGHES, HOWARD (1905–   ). American producer, executive and aviator of almost legendary habits and wealth. *Hell's Angels* (30), *The Front Page* (31), *Scarface* (32), *The Outlaw* (also directed) (44), *Jet Pilot* (52–56), etc.

HUGHES, KEN (1922–   ). British director, in films from 1937. *Wide Boy* (52), *Black Thirteen* (53), *The House Across the Lake* (54), *Little Red Monkey* (also wrote) (54), *The Brain Machine* (55), *Timeslip* (55), *Confession* (55), *Joe Macbeth* (also wrote) (55), *Wicked As They Come* (also wrote) (56), *Town on Trial* (also wrote) (57), *The Trials of Oscar Wilde* (also wrote) (60), *The Small World of Sammy Lee* (also wrote) (63), *Arrivederci Baby* (also wrote) (66), *Casino Royale* (part) (66), *Chitty Chitty Bang Bang* (also co-wrote) (68), *Cromwell* (also wrote) (69), etc.

HUGHES, MARY BETH (1919–   ). American leading lady of the 40s, mainly in second features. *These Glamour Girls* (39), *Lucky Cisco Kid* (40), *Orchestra Wives* (42), *The Ox-Bow Incident* (43), *I Accuse My Parents* (44), *Caged Fury* (47), *Gun Battle at Monterey* (57), etc.

HUGHES, RODDY (1891–   ). Welsh character actor in films from 1934, often in roly-poly comedy roles. *The Stars Look Down* (39), *The Ghost of St Michaels* (41), *Hatter's Castle* (41), *Nicholas Nickleby* (47), *Scrooge* (51), *Sea Wife* (57), etc.

HULBERT, CLAUDE (1900–1963). British 'silly ass' comedian, brother of Jack Hulbert, on stage from 1921, films from 1932. *Thark* (33), *Bulldog Jack* (36), *Wolf's Clothing* (36), *The Vulture* (38), *Sailors Three* (40), *The Ghost of St Michael's* (41), *The Dummy Talks* (43), *My Learned Friend* (44), *London Town* (46), *The Ghosts of Berkeley Square* (47), *Fun at St Fanny's* (55), etc.

HULBERT, JACK (1892–   ). Jaunty, long-chinned British comedian and light leading man; on stage from 1911, films from 1930. *Elstree Calling* (30), *The Ghost Train* (31), *Sunshine Susie* (32), *Jack's the Boy* (32), *Jack Ahoy* (34), *Bulldog Jack* (35), *Jack of All Trades* (36), *The Camels Are Coming* (37), *Under Your Hat* (40), etc. Recently in character roles: *Miss Tulip Stays the Night* (55), *Spider's Web* (60), etc. Still a stage star.

HULL, HENRY (1890–   ). Veteran American actor of stage and screen. *The Volunteer* (17), *For Woman's Favour* (24), *Great Expectations* (34), *Yellow Jack* (38), *Jesse James* (39), *Miracles for Sale* (39), *My Son, My Son* (40), *High Sierra* (41), *Lifeboat* (43), *Objective Burma* (45), *Mourning Becomes Electra* (47), *The Great Gatsby* (49), *Inferno* (53), *The Sheriff of Fractured Jaw* (58), *Master of the World* (61), *The Chase* (66), *Covenant with Death* (67), many others.

HULL, JOSEPHINE (1884–1957) (Josephine Sherwood). Distinguished American stage actress, best remembered in films as Aunt Abby in *Arsenic and Old Lace* (44) and as the harassed sister in *Harvey* (AA) (50). Also starred in *The Lady From Texas* (51).

HUMBERSTONE, H. BRUCE (1903–   ). American director, a competent craftsman of action films and musicals. *If I Had a Million* (part) (32), *The Crooked Circle* (32), *Pack Up Your Troubles* (32), *Charlie Chan in Honolulu* (37), *Lucky Cisco Kid* (40), *Tall, Dark and Handsome* (41), *Sun Valley Serenade* (41), *Hot Spot* (41), *To the Shores of Tripoli* (42), *Hello, Frisco, Hello* (43), *Wonder Man* (45), *Three Little Girls in Blue* (46), *Fury at Furnace Creek* (48), *East of Java* (49), *Happy Go Lovely* (GB) (51), *She's Working Her Way Through College* (52), *The Desert Song* (53), *The Purple Mask* (55), *Tarzan and the Lost Safari* (57), *Madison Avenue* (61), etc.

HUME, BENITA (1906–1967). British actress who made some films in the 30s, then retired to marry Ronald Colman. *High Treason* (29), *The Flying Fool* (32), *Lord Camber's Ladies* (33), *Jew Suss* (34), *The Garden Murder Case* (US) (36), *Tarzan Escapes* (US) (37), *Peck's Bad Boy with the Circus* (US) (39), etc.

HUME, KENNETH (1926–1967). British producer, former editor. *Cheer the Brave* (w, p, d) (50), *Hot Ice* (w, d) (51), *Sail into Danger* (w, d) (57), *Mods and Rockers* (p, d) (64), *I've Gotta Horse* (p, d) (65), etc.

THE HUNCHBACK OF NOTRE DAME. Victor Hugo's novel *Notre Dame de Paris* has been filmed three times under this title; in 1923 with Lon Chaney, in 1939 with Charles Laughton, and in 1956 with Anthony Quinn. The last of these was disappointing; the earlier two are considerable cinematic achievements, William Dieterle's 1939 version in particular standing out as a masterpiece of studio technique.

HUNNICUTT, ARTHUR (1911–   ). American actor of slow-speaking country characters. On stage for many years before film debut *Wildcat* (42). Later in *Lust for Gold* (49), *Broken Arrow* (50), *The Red Badge of Courage* (51), *The Big Sky* (52), *The French Line* (54), *The Last Command* (56), *The Kettles in the Ozarks* (56), *Apache Uprising* (65), *Cat Ballou* (65), *El Dorado* (66), others.

HUNNICUTT, GAYLE (1942–   ). American leading lady. *The Wild Angels* (66), *P.J.* (*New Face in Hell*) (68), *The Dolly Dolly Spy* (69), *Eye of the Cat* (69), *Fragment of Fear* (69), etc.

HUNT, MARSHA (1917–   ) (Marcia Hunt). American leading lady who usually plays gentle characters. *Virginia Judge* (debut) (35), *Hollywood Boulevard* (36), *The Hardys Ride High* (38), *These Glamour Girls* (39), *Pride and Prejudice* (40), *Blossoms in the Dust* (41), *Kid Glove Killer* (42), *Seven Sweethearts* (42), *The Human Comedy* (43), *Lost Angel* (43), *Cry Havoc* (44), *The Valley of Decision* (45), *A Letter for Evie* (45), *Carnegie Hall* (46), *Take One False Step* (49), *Mary Ryan, Detective* (50), *The Happy Time* (52), *No Place to Hide* (56), *Blue Denim* (59), etc.

HUNT, MARTITA (1900–1969). British stage and screen actress who graduated from nosy spinsters to *grandes dames. I Was a Spy* (debut) (33), *The Man in Grey* (43), *The Wicked Lady* (45), *Great Expectations* (as Miss Havisham) (46), *The Ghosts of Berkeley Square* (47), *My Sister and I* (48), *Lady Windermere's Fan* (US) (49), *Treasure Hunt* (52), *Melba* (53), *Three Men in a Boat* (56), *Anastasia* (56), *Brides of Dracula* (60), *The Unsinkable Molly Brown* (64), *Bunny Lake Is Missing* (65), others.

HUNT, PETER (1928–   ). British director, former editor. *On Her Majesty's Secret Service* (69).

HUNTER, EVAN (1926–   ). American novelist and scenarist. Novels filmed include *The Blackboard Jungle, Strangers When We Meet.* Also writes as *Ed McBain*: TV series *87th Precinct.*

HUNTER, IAN (1900–   ). British actor of dependable characters; on stage from 1919, films soon after. *Mr Oddy* (22), *Not for Sale* (24), *Confessions* (25), *The Ring* (27), *Something Always Happens* (31), *The Sign of Four* (as Dr Watson) (32), *Death at Broadcasting House* (34), *A Midsummer Night's Dream* (US) (35), *The White Angel* (US) (36), *Call It a Day* (US) (37), *52nd Street* (US) (38), *The Adventures of Robin Hood* (as King Richard) (US) (38), *Tower of London* (US) (39), *Strange Cargo* (US) (40), *Bitter Sweet* (US) (40), *Billy the Kid* (US) (41), *Dr Jekyll and Mr Hyde* (as Lanyon) (41), *A Yank at Eton* (US) (42), etc.; war service; *Bedelia* (46), *White Cradle Inn* (47), *The White Unicorn* (48), *Edward My Son* (49), *Appointment in London* (52), *Don't Blame the Stork* (53), *The Battle of the River Plate* (56), *Fortune Is a Woman* (57), *Northwest Frontier* (59), *The Bulldog Breed* (60), *Guns of Darkness* (63), many others.

HUNTER, JEFFREY (1927–1969) (Henry H. McKinnies). American leading man, in films from 1951 after radio experience. *Fourteen Hours* (debut) (51), *Red Skies of Montana* (52), *The Searchers* (56), *A Kiss Before Dying* (56), *The True Story of Jesse James* (57), *No Down Payment* (57), *The Last Hurrah* (57), *Hell to Eternity* (60), *King of Kings* (as Jesus) (61), *The Longest Day* (62), *Vendetta* (65), *Brainstorm* (65), *Custer of the West* (67), many others.

HUNTER, KIM (1922–   ) (Janet Cole). American leading lady who after brief stage experience was cast as lead in *The Seventh Victim* (43). Later: *A Matter of Life and Death* (45), *A Streetcar Named Desire* (AA) (51), *Deadline USA* (52), *Anything Can Happen* (53), *Storm Centre* (56), *The Young Stranger* (57), *Lilith* (64), *Planet of the*

Apes (68), *Beneath the Planet of the Apes* (69), etc; frequent Broadway appearances.

HUNTER, ROSS (1921–   ) (Martin Fuss). American producer, mainly of romantic dramas and glossy light entertainments for Universal. *Magnificent Obsession* (54), *Imitation of Life* (57), *Pillow Talk* (58), *Midnight Lace* (60), *Back Street* (61), *The Chalk Garden* (64), *Madame X* (66), *The Pad* (66), *Thoroughly Modern Millie* (67), *Airport* (69), many others. Was an actor, e.g. in *A Guy, a Gal and a Pal* (45), *Sweetheart of Sigma Chi* (47).

HUNTER, TAB (1931–   ) (Art Gelien). Athletic American leading man, a teenage rave of the 50s. *The Lawless* (debut) (48), *Saturday Island* (*Island of Desire*) (52), *Gun Belt* (53), *Return to Treasure Island* (53), *Track of the Cat* (54), *Battle Cry* (55), *The Sea Chase* (55), *The Burning Hills* (56), *The Girl He Left Behind* (57), *Gunman's Walk* (57), *Damn Yankees* (58), *That Kind of Woman* (59), *The Pleasure of His Company* (60), *The Golden Arrow* (It.) (62), *City under the Sea* (65), *Birds Do It* (66), etc.

HUNTER, T. HAYES (1896–1944). American director, in Britain in the 30s. *Desert Gold* (19), *Earthbound* (20), *The Triumph of the Scarlet Pimpernel* (29), *The Silver King* (29), *The Frightened Lady* (31), *Sally Bishop* (33), *The Ghoul* (33), etc.

HUNTINGTON, LAWRENCE (1900–1968). British director, mainly of routine thrillers. *Suspected Person* (also wrote) (41), *Night Boat to Dublin* (41), *Wanted for Murder* (46), *The Upturned Glass* (47), *When the Bough Breaks* (48), *Mr Perrin and Mr Traill* (48), *Man on the Run* (also wrote) (49), *The Franchise Affair* (also wrote) (51), *There Was a Young Lady* (also wrote) (53), *Contraband Spain* (also wrote) (55), *Stranglehold* (62), *The Fur Collar* (also wrote and produced) (63), etc. Much TV work.

HUNTLEY, RAYMOND (1904–   ). British character actor, often of supercilious types or self-satisfied businessmen; on stage from 1922, screen from 1934. *Rembrandt* (37), *Night Train to Munich* (40), *The Ghost of St Michael's* (42), *School for Secrets* (45), *Mr Perrin and Mr Traill* (49), *Trio* (50), *Room at the Top* (59), *Only Two Can Play* (62), *Rotten to the Core* (65), many others.

HURST, BRIAN DESMOND (1900–   ). Irish director who has made many varieties of film. *Sensation* (36), *Glamorous Night* (37), *Prison Without Bars* (39), *On the Night of the Fire* (40), *Dangerous Moonlight* (41), *Alibi* (42), *The Hundred Pound Window* (43), *Theirs Is the Glory* (45), *Hungry Hill* (47), *The Mark of Cain* (48), *Tom Brown's Schooldays* (51), *Scrooge* (51), *The Malta Story* (53), *Simba* (55), *The Black Tent* (56), *Dangerous Exile* (57), *Behind the Mask* (58), *His and Hers* (60), *The Playboy of the Western World* (62), etc.

HURST, DAVID (1925–   ). Austrian actor who played some comedy roles in British films. *The Perfect Woman* (49), *So Little Time* (52), *Mother Riley Meets the Vampire* (52), *As Long As They're Happy* (53), *The Intimate Stranger* (56), *After the Ball* (57), etc.

HURST, FANNIE (1889–1968). American popular novelist, several of whose romantic novels, usually with a tragic finale, have been filmed more than once: *Humoresque, Imitation of Life, Back Street*, etc.

HURST, PAUL (1889–1953). American character actor in hundreds of cameo roles from 1912, usually as gangster, bartender, outlaw or cop. *Tugboat Annie* (32), *Riff Raff* (34), *Gone With The Wind* (39), *Caught in the Draft* (41), *The Sun Shines Bright* (53), etc.

HURT, JOHN (1940–   ). Offbeat British stage and film leading man. *The Wild and the Willing* (62), *A Man for All Seasons* (66), *Before Winter Comes* (69), *Sinful Davey* (69).

HUSSEY, RUTH (1914–   ). American leading lady, on stage from 1931. Screen from 1937, usually in smart professional roles. *Fast and Furious* (38), *The Women* (39), *The Philadelphia Story* (40), *Our Wife* (41), *H. M. Pulham Esquire* (41), *The Uninvited* (44), *Bedside Manner* (45), *Diary of a Bride* (48), *Louisa* (50), *Mr Music* (50), *That's My Boy* (51), *Stars and Stripes Forever* (53), *The Facts of Life* (60), etc.

THE HUSTLER (US 1961; BFA best film). Robert Rossen wrote, produced and directed this unusual film from Walter Tevis's novel, with Paul Newman as a professional pool player who meets his match in Minnesota Fats, played by Jackie Gleason. Other key roles are cleverly played by George C. Scott and Myron McCormick, and the CinemaScope photography by Eugene Shuftan (AA), together with Harry Horner's (AA) art direction, adds immeasurably to the total effect. A tragic subplot involving Piper Laurie is less successful.

HUSTON, ANJELICA (1952–   ). American leading lady, daughter of John Huston. *Sinful Davey* (69), *A Walk With Love and Death* (69).

†HUSTON, JOHN (1906–   ). Unpredictable American director, writer and latterly actor; son of Walter Huston. In Hollywood from 1932 as writer: *The Murder in the Rue Morgue* (32), *The Amazing Dr Clitterhouse* (38), *Jezebel* (39), *High Sierra* (41), *Sergeant York* (41), *Three Strangers* (45), etc. Turned director with great success: *The Maltese Falcon* (still probably his best film) (41), *Across the Pacific* (43), *In This Our Life* (42); war service during which he made several official documentaries including *Report from the Aleutians* (43), *Let There Be Light* (45); *The Treasure of the Sierra Madre* (AA) (also wrote and acted) (47), *Key Largo* (48), *We Were Strangers*

(49), *The Asphalt Jungle* (also wrote) (50), *The Red Badge of Courage* (also wrote) (51), *The African Queen* (51), *Moulin Rouge* (53), *Beat the Devil* (54), *Moby Dick* (56), *Heaven Knows, Mr Alison* (57), *The Barbarian and the Geisha* (58), *Roots of Heaven* (58), *The Unforgiven* (59), *The Misfits* (60), *Freud* (63), *The List of Adrian Messenger* (also acted) (63), *The Cardinal* (acted only) (63), *Night of the Iguana* (64), *The Bible* (also acted) (66), *Casino Royale* (part) (67), *Reflections in a Golden Eye* (67), *Sinful Davey* (69), *A Walk With Love and Death* (69). A biography, *King Rebel*, by W. F. Nolan, was published in 1965.

†HUSTON, WALTER (1884–1950) (W. Houghston). Distinguished American character actor of stage and screen: latterly projected roguery and eccentricity with great vigour. *Gentlemen of the Press* (28), *The Lady Lies* (29), *The Virginian* (30), *The Bad Man* (30), *The Virtuous Sin* (30), *Abraham Lincoln* (30), *The Criminal Code* (31), *Star Witness* (31), *The Ruling Voice* (31), *A Woman from Monte Carlo* (31), *A House Divided* (32), *Law and Order* (as Wyatt Earp) (32), *Beast of the City* (32), *The Wet Parade* (32), *Night Court* (32), *American Madness* (32), *Kongo* (32), *Rain* (32), *Hell Below* (32), *Gabriel over the White House* (33), *The Prizefighter and the Lady* (33), *Storm at Daybreak* (33), *Ann Vickers* (33), *Keep 'Em Rolling* (33), *The Tunnel* (GB) (34), *Rhodes of Africa* (GB) (36), *Dodsworth* (36), *Of Human Hearts* (38), *The Light That Failed* (40), *All That Money Can Buy* (as the devil) (41), *Swamp Water* (41), *The Shanghai Gesture* (42), *Always in My Heart* (42), *Yankee Doodle Dandy* (42), *Mission to Moscow* (42), *Edge of Darkness* (42), *North Star* (43), *The Outlaw* (as Doc Holliday) (43), *Dragon Seed* (44), *Ten Little Niggers* (45), *Dragonwyck* (46), *Duel in the Sun* (46), *The Treasure of the Sierra Madre* (AA) (47), *Summer Holiday* (47), *The Great Sinner* (49), *The Furies* (50). He also played bit parts in his son John's first two films, as Captain Jacoby in *The Maltese Falcon* (41), and a bartender in *In This Our Life* (42). After his death his stage recording of 'September Song', played in *September Affair* (50), became a big hit.

HUTCHESON, DAVID (1905–   ). British light comedian who has often played monocled silly-asses, mainly on stage. *This'll Make You Whistle* (35), *Sabotage at Sea* (41), *Convoy* (42), *School for Secrets* (46), *Vice Versa* (48), *Sleeping Car to Trieste* (48), *The Elusive Pimpernel* (50), *The Evil of Frankenstein* (64), etc.

HUTCHINSON, JOSEPHINE (1904–   ). American actress who has usually played sweet or maternal types. *The Story of Louis Pasteur* (36), *Son of Frankenstein* (39), *Somewhere in the Night* (46), *Ruby Gentry* (52), *Miracle in the Rain* (56), *North By Northwest* (59), *Huckleberry Finn* (60), *Baby the Rain Must Fall* (64), *Nevada Smith* (66), etc.

HUTH, HAROLD (1892–1967). British leading man in silent films; later producer and director. *Busman's Honeymoon* (p) (39), *Bulldog Sees*

It Through (p, d) (39), *East of Piccadilly* (d) (40), *Love Story* (p) (44),
Night Beat (p, d) (46), *My Sister and I* (p, d) (48), *Look Before You
Love* (p, d) (48), *The Hostage* (p) (56), *The Bandit of Zhobe* (p) (57),
The Trials of Oscar Wilde (p) (60), *The Hellions* (p) (61), etc.

HUTTON, BETTY (1921–   ) (Betty Jane Thornburg). American
leading lady, blonde and vivacious heroine of many light enter-
tainments of the 40s. *The Fleet's In* (debut) (42), *The Miracle of
Morgan's Creek* (43), *Let's Face It* (43), *Here Come the Waves* (44),
And the Angels Sing (44), *Incendiary Blonde* (45), *The Stork Club* (46),
Cross My Heart (46), *The Perils of Pauline* (47), *Dream Girl* (48),
Annie Get Your Gun (50), *Let's Dance* (51), *Somebody Loves Me* (52),
The Greatest Show on Earth (53), *Spring Reunion* (57), etc. Recently in
night clubs and TV.

HUTTON, BRIAN G. (1935–   ). American director, from TV. *The
Pad* (66), *Sol Madrid* (67), *Where Eagles Dare* (68), *The Warriors* (70).

HUTTON, JIM (1938–   ). American leading man who usually
plays gangly types. *A Time to Love and a Time to Die* (58), *Bachelor
in Paradise* (61), *The Horizontal Lieutenant* (62), *Period of Adjustment*
(63), *The Hallelujah Trail* (65), *Never Too Late* (65), *Walk Don't
Run* (66), *The Green Berets* (68), *Hellfighters* (69), etc.

HUTTON, MARION (1920–   ) (Marion Thornburg). American singer,
with the Glenn Miller band; appeared in a few 40s musicals.
Sister of Betty Hutton. *Orchestra Wives* (42), *Crazy House* (44), *In
Society* (44), *Babes on Swing Street* (45), *Love Happy* (50), etc.

HUTTON, ROBERT (1920–   ) (Robert Bruce Winne). American
leading man of the 40s. *Destination Tokyo* (44), *Janie* (44), *Too Young
To Know* (45), *Time Out of Mind* (47), *Always Together* (48), *The
Steel Helmet* (51), *Casanova's Big Night* (54), *Invisible Invaders* (58),
Cinderfella (60), *The Slime People* (also produced and directed) (62),
The Secret Man (GB) (64), *Finders Keepers* (GB) (66), *They Came
from Beyond Space* (GB) (68), etc.

HYDE-WHITE, WILFRID (1903–   ). Impeccably British character
actor of stage and screen, mainly in comedy roles. *Murder by Rope*
(37), *The Third Man* (49), *The Story of Gilbert and Sullivan* (54),
See How They Run (55), *The Adventures of Quentin Durward* (56),
North-West Frontier (59), *Two-Way Stretch* (61), *My Fair Lady* (64),
John Goldfarb Please Come Home (64), *You Must Be Joking* (65), *Ten
Little Indians* (65), *The Liquidator* (65), *Our Man in Marrakesh* (66),
Chamber of Horrors (66), *You Only Live Twice* (67), etc.

HYER, MARTHA (1929–   ). American leading lady, in mainly
routine films from 1947. *Kelly and Me* (56), *Battle Hymn* (57), *Paris
Holiday* (57), *The Best of Everything* (59), *The Carpetbaggers* (64),

The First Men in the Moon (64), *The Sons of Katie Elder* (65), *Night of the Grizzly* (66), *The Chase* (66), *Picture Mommy Dead* (66), *The Happening* (67), *Crossplot* (GB) (69), etc.

HYLTON, JANE (1926–   ). British actress, in films since 1945. *When the Bough Breaks* (47), *Here Come the Huggetts* (49), *It Started in Paradise* (52), *The Weak and the Wicked* (53), *House of Mystery* (59), many others. Also on TV.

HYLTON, RICHARD (1921–1962). American actor with stage experience: films include *Lost Boundaries* (48), *The Secret of Convict Lake* (51), *Fixed Bayonets* (52).

HYMAN, KENNETH (1928–   ). American executive producer; formerly with AA and Seven Arts in Britain, now independent. *The Hound of the Baskervilles* (59), *The Roman Spring of Mrs Stone* (61), *Gigot* (62), *The Small World of Sammy Lee* (63), *The Hill* (65), *The Dirty Dozen* (66), etc.

HYMER, WARREN (1906–48). American character actor with stage experience; usually seen as dim-witted gangster. *Charlie Chan Carries On* (31), *Twenty Thousand Years in Sing Sing* (32), *Kid Millions* (35), *San Francisco* (36), *Tainted Money* (37), *Destry Rides Again* (39), *Meet John Doe* (41), *Baby Face Morgan* (42), *Joe Palooka Champ* (46), many others.

hypnosis on the screen has mainly been a basis for melodrama. *Svengali* was its most demonic exponent, but others who followed in his footsteps were Jacques Bergerac in *The Hypnotic Eye*, Boris Karloff in *The Climax*, Bela Lugosi in *Dracula*, Charles Gray in *The Devil Rides Out*, Erich von Stroheim in *The Mask of Diijon*, Orson Welles in *Black Magic*, and Jose Ferrer in *Whirlpool* (in which, immediately after major surgery, he hypnotized himself into leaving his bed and committing a murder). In *Fear in the Night* and its remake *Nightmare*, De Forrest Kelley and Kevin McCarthy were hypnotized into becoming murderers. Comic uses are legion, the perpetrators including Lugosi in *Abbott and Costello Meet Frankenstein*, Karloff in *The Secret Life of Walter Mitty*, Gale Sondergaard in *Road to Rio*, Alan Badel in *Will Any Gentleman*, and Pat Collins in *Divorce American Style*. The chief serious study of the subject has been *Freud*.

HYSON, DOROTHY (1915–   ). British leading lady of the 30s, with stage experience (mainly in Aldwych farces). *Soldiers of the King* (33), *The Ghoul* (33), *Turkey Time* (33), *Sing As We Go* (34), *A Cup of Kindness* (34), *Spare a Copper* (40), etc.

I

I AM A CAMERA (GB 1955). A tepid film version of John Van Druten's enjoyably theatrical play based on Christopher Isherwood's writings about Berlin in the early 30s. Julie Harris was somewhat miscast as the childishly naughty heroine Sally Bowles, and the production as a whole lacked spark. The elements however were vitalized into a successful 1966 Broadway musical called *Cabaret*, of which a spectacular film version is due.

I AM A FUGITIVE FROM A CHAIN GANG (US 1932). Arguably the first American social melodrama to urge actual reforms; also the first of Warner's 'prestige' films of the 30s. Paul Muni played the man forced against his will into a life of crime. Written by Sheridan Gibney and Brown Holmes; directed by Mervyn Le Roy.

IBBETSON, ARTHUR (1921–   ). British cinematographer. *The Horse's Mouth* (58), *The Angry Silence* (59), *The League of Gentlemen* (60), *Tunes of Glory* (61), *Whistle Down the Wind* (61), *The Inspector* (62), *Nine Hours to Rama* (63), *I Could Go On Singing* (63), *The Chalk Garden* (64), *Sky West and Crooked* (65), *A Countess from Hong Kong* (66), *Inspector Clouseau* (68), *Where Eagles Dare* (68), *The Walking Stick* (69), *Anne of the Thousand Days* (70), etc.

ICHIKAWA, KON (1915–   ). Distinguished Japanese director. *The Heart* (54), *The Punishment Room* (55), *The Burmese Harp* (55), *Odd Obsessions* (58), *Fires on the Plain* (59), *The Sin* (61), *An Actor's Revenge* (63), *Alone on the Pacific* (66), etc.

I, CLAUDIUS (GB 1937). Alexander Korda's ambitious epic of ancient Rome, based on Robert Graves' highly readable book, was never finished: star Merle Oberon was injured in a car crash and the production, which had presented Korda with many problems, was abandoned after two or three reels were in the can. Nearly thirty years later, in 1965, a television film, *The Epic That Never Was*, pieced the story together and made one wish that more had been shot, if only for the sake of George Perinal's photography and the performances of Charles Laughton and Emlyn Williams. Director Josef von Sternberg seemed less at home with the material. Tony Richardson will film a remake in 1970.

IDIOT'S DELIGHT (US 1939). Robert Sherwood's play marked Broadway's earliest reaction to the war clouds looming over Europe. This hasty film version, with Clark Gable as the eager hoofer and

Norma Shearer as the fake duchess, managed to be as false as its continental backcloths, despite Clarence Brown's direction, and probably made the danger seem remote instead of imminent to many Americans. In the early 60s a short-lived TV series called *Harry's Girls* borrowed the central character if little else.

IFIELD, FRANK (1936–   ). British-born ballad singer who grew up in Australia. Only film: *Up Jumped a Swagman* (65).

IF I HAD A MILLION (US 1933). Probably the first short story compendium; this one had the connecting link of a sudden windfall to a variety of people. The most quoted episode (each had a different director) is that in which Charles Laughton, as a downtrodden clerk, blows a raspberry to his boss.

IF I WERE KING. Justin McCarthy's play, a historical adventure about Francois Villon, was filmed in 1920 with William Farnum and in 1938 with Ronald Colman. On it was based Rudolf Friml's operetta *The Vagabond King*, filmed in 1930 with Dennis King and Jeanette Macdonald, and in 1955 with Oreste Kirkop and Kathryn Grayson.

IF WINTER COMES. A. S. M. Hutchinson's sentimental romance about the effect of malicious gossip in a village community was first filmed in 1923 with Percy Marmont and Ann Forrest, directed by Harry Millarde. In 1947 MGM unconvincingly up-dated it for Walter Pidgeon and Deborah Kerr, with direction by Victor Saville.

ILLING, PETER (1899–1966). German-born character actor, in British films since the 40s. *The End of the River* (46), *Eureka Stockade* (48), *I'll Get You for This* (51), *The Young Lovers* (54), *Zarak* (56), *Whirlpool* (59), *Sands of the Desert* (60), *The Twenty-fifth Hour* (66), many others.

IMAGE, JEAN (1911–   ). French animator, best known abroad for his cartoon feature *Johnny Lionheart* (*Jeannot L'Intrépide*) (50).

I'M ALL RIGHT, JACK (GB 1959). An ironic comedy on the serious subject of labour relations, with Peter Sellers as the Communist shop steward and Ian Carmichael as the innocent who precipitates a strike. The Boulting Brothers produced and directed from an enjoyable if uneven script by themselves and Frank Harvey.

I MARRIED A WITCH (US 1942). Generally considered René Clair's best American film, this gay fantasy starred Fredric March and Veronica Lake, with Cecil Kellaway as a most delightful old sorcerer. It directly inspired the recent TV series *Bewitched*.

IMITATION OF LIFE. Fannie Hurst's romantic novel, with its naïve but moving early depiction of a race problem (a black girl tries to pass

for white), was filmed in 1934 with Claudette Colbert, Warren
William and Louise Beavers; director John M. Stahl. In 1959 it was
glossily refashioned for Lana Turner, John Gavin and Juanita
Moore; director Douglas Sirk.

impresarios presented on film include Sol Hurok, by David Wayne
in *Tonight We Sing*; Rupert D'Oyly Carte, by Peter Finch in *The
Story of Gilbert and Sullivan*; Walter de Frece, by Laurence Harvey
in *After the Ball*; David Belasco, by Claude Rains in *Lady With
Red Hair*; Lew Dockstatter, by John Alexander in *The Jolson
Story*; Noël Coward by Daniel Massey, and Andre Charlot by
Alan Oppenheimer, in *Star!*; and Florenz Ziegfeld, by William
Powell in *The Great Ziegfeld* and by Walter Pidgeon in *Funny Girl*.
Of fictional impresarios, the most memorable were those played
by John Barrymore in *Maytime* and Anton Walbrook in *The Red
Shoes*.

impressionism. Generally understood to mean contriving an effect or
making a point by building up a sequence from short disconnected
shots or scenes.

INCE, RALPH (1887–1937). American stage actor who played leads in
many silent films. *The Sea Wolf* (26), *Not for Publication* (also
directed) (27), *Bigger Than Barnums* (also directed) (28), *Little
Caesar* (31), *The Honourable Mr Wong* (*The Hatchet Man*) (32), *No
Escape* (GB) (33), *The Perfect Crime* (37), etc.

INCE, THOMAS (1882–1924). American director, a contemporary of
D. W. Griffith and some say an equal innovator; he certainly
systematized production methods. Best remembered now for
Custer's Last Fight (12), *Civilization* (15), *Human Wreckage* (23).

India has provided the setting for English-speaking films mainly of
the military kind: *King of the Khyber Rifles*, *The Drum*, *Lives of a
Bengal Lancer*, *Gunga Din*, *Soldiers Three*, *The Charge of the Light
Brigade* (1936 version), *Bengal Brigade*. Civilian interests were the
concern of *They Met in Bombay*, *The Rains Came*, *Elephant Boy*,
Calcutta, *Thunder in the East*, *Northwest Frontier*, *Nine Hours to Rama*
and *The Guru*. Of native Indian films only a few have percolated
to Western cinemas, mostly directed by Mehboob, Satyajit Ray,
or James Ivory.

INESCORT, FRIEDA (1901–   ). Scottish-born actress of well bred
roles, once secretary to Lady Astor; on stage from 1922. Went to
Hollywood to begin film career. *If You Could Only Cook* (35), *Call
It a Day* (37), *Beauty for the Asking* (38), *Woman Doctor* (39), *Pride
and Prejudice* (40), *The Amazing Mrs Holliday* (43), *The Return of the
Vampire* (43), *The Judge Steps Out* (*Indian Summer*) (47), *Foxfire* (55),
The Crowded Sky (60), etc.

The Informer

THE INFORMER (US 1935). Despite, or perhaps because of, its murky expressionist studio look, this film of Liam O'Flaherty's novel about Dublin during the troubles was able to turn melodrama into something approaching a tragedy. It won Academy Awards for director John Ford, Max Steiner's music, Dudley Nichols' script, and Victor McLaglen's performance as the half-witted brute who betrays his friend for a handful of silver. Joseph H. August's photography was also notable. There was a previous British silent version in 1928, starring Lars Hanson; and in 1968 Jules Dassin made a Negro version called *Uptight*.

INGE, WILLIAM (1913–   ). American playwright much of whose work has been filmed: *Come Back, Little Sheba, Picnic, The Dark at the Top of the Stairs, The Stripper (A Loss of Roses)*, etc.

INGELS, MARTY (1936–   ). American character comedian, best known for TV series *I'm Dickens He's Fenster*. Films include *Ladies' Man* (60), *Armoured Command* (61), *Wild and Wonderful* (63).

INGRAM, REX (1892–1950) (Rex Fitchcock). Irish actor who went to Hollywood and became a noted director of silent spectaculars: *The Four Horsemen of the Apocalypse* (21), *The Arab* (22), *The Prisoner of Zenda* (22), *Scaramouche* (23), *Mare Nostrum* (26), *Belladonna* (27), etc.

INGRAM, REX (1895–   ). Impressive Negro actor, in films from 1919; former doctor. *The Ten Commandments* (23), *The Big Parade* (26), *The Four Feathers* (29), *The Emperor Jones* (33), *Captain Blood* (35), *Green Pastures* (as De Lawd) (36), *Huckleberry Finn* (38), *The Thief of Baghdad* (as the genie) (40), *Cabin in the Sky* (43), *Sahara* (43), *A Thousand and One Nights* (44), *God's Little Acre* (59), *Watusi* (59), *Hurry Sundown* (67), etc.

INGSTER, BORIS (c. 1913–   ). American writer-director. *The Last Days of Pompeii* (co-w) (35), *Happy Landings* (w) (38), *The Judge Steps Out* (w, d) (49), *Forgery* (d) (50), *Something for the Birds* (co-w) (52), etc.

INHERIT THE WIND (US 1960). Although essentially a filmed play, this is probably the most satisfactory cinematic example of Stanley Kramer's work as a producer-director. Based on Jerome Laurence and Robert E. Lee's dramatization of the Scopes 'monkey trial' of the 20s, when a schoolmaster in a God-fearing community was put in the dock for teaching evolution, the film benefits enormously from the performances of Spencer Tracy and Fredric March as defence and prosecution counsels (in real life Clarence Darrow and William Jennings Bryan). An absorbing entertainment, cleanly photographed by Ernest Laszlo.

in-jokes were especially frequent in films when Hollywood was a parochial society. The following are reasonably typical. In *The Black Cat* (34), Boris Karloff as a devil worshipper recites a Latin invocation, among whose phrases one can clearly hear: 'Reductio ad absurdum est' ('It is ridiculous'). In *Bride of Frankenstein*, Ernest Thesiger uses a line ('It's my only weakness') from his previous role in *The Old Dark House*. In *His Girl Friday*, Cary Grant refers to the execution of a fellow called Archie Leach: which is Grant's own real name. In *Hellzapoppin*, Olsen and Johnson see a sledge on a film set and remark: 'Orson Welles has been here' (a reference to *Citizen Kane*). In *The Maltese Falcon*, Walter Huston plays an uncredited bit part under his son John's direction. In *On the Town*, which stars Frank Sinatra, there is some good-natured joshing about Sinatra's real-life marriage to Ava Gardner. The *Road* films are full of intra-mural gags about anything from *Here Comes Mr Jordan* to the Paramount trade mark. In Warner films of the 30s, whenever a movie-house canopy was shown, it advertised a non-existent film called *Another Dawn*; in 1938 Warners were stuck for a title for a new Errol Flynn movie, so they casually and irrelevantly called it . . . *Another Dawn*. In *Song of the Thin Man*, William Powell picks up a razor blade and murmurs: 'Somerset Maugham has been here' (a reference to Maugham's then-popular novel *The Razor's Edge*). In *Some Like It Hot*, Tony Curtis is playing a character as a devastatingly accurate impersonation of Cary Grant, only to be told scathingly by Jack Lemmon: 'Nobody talks like that!' In the same movie, and also in *Singing in the Rain*, a gangster tossing a coin is a direct reference to a characterization created by George Raft in *Scarface*. In *One, Two, Three* James Cagney borrows Edward G. Robinson's famous *Little Caesar* line, 'Mother of mercy, is this the end of Rico?'; he also kids his own 30s image by threatening Horst Bucholz with a grapefruit. In *Caprice*, Doris Day as the heroine goes to a movie and sees on the screen . . . Doris Day. In *The Entertainer*, reference is made to a Sgt Ozzie Morris; Ozzie Morris was cinematographer on the movie. And in *Finian's Rainbow*, Fred Astaire has a chunk of dialogue which consists, with different emphasis, of the words of one of his old popular songs. See also: *uncredited appearances; directors' appearances*.

THE INN OF THE SIXTH HAPPINESS (GB 1958). A glamorized but generally successful version of the life of Gladys Aylward, an indomitable British missionary to China in the 30s. Ingrid Bergman, theoretically miscast, gave a commanding star performance; Robert Donat in his last film was most moving as a mandarin converted to Christianity. Directed by Mark Robson, photographed by Frederick Young, this was hailed as a reversion to 'family entertainment' after what seemed at the time a period of over-sophistication.

Inner Sanctum

Inner Sanctum. A series of second features made by Universal in the early 40s, starring Lon Chaney Jnr and offering apparently supernatural phenomena which are explained away in the last reel. Based on a radio series; introduced for no very clear reason by a spiel from a misshapen head within a crystal ball on a boardroom table! Titles include *Weird Woman, Pillow of Death, Dead Man's Eyes, The Frozen Ghost, Strange Confession.*

insanity in the cinema has usually been of the criminal kind: Robert Montgomery (and Albert Finney) in *Night Must Fall*, Keir Dullea in *Bunny Lake Is Missing*, Bette Davis in *Whatever Happened to Baby Jane* and *The Nanny*, Franchot Tone in *Phantom Lady*, Robert Mitchum in *Night of the Hunter*, Douglas Montgomery in *The Cat and the Canary*, Anthony Perkins in *Psycho*, Hywel Bennett in *Twisted Nerve*, Oliver Reed in *Paranoiac*, Brember Wills in *The Old Dark House* and hundreds of others. Indeed, most screen villains have been, if not psychopathic, at least subject to an *idée fixe*; and many a tortured hero has had a mad wife in the attic. Insanity has however been played quite frequently for comedy, notably in *Harvey, Miss Tatlock's Millions, The Criminal Life of Archibaldo de la Cruz* and *Drôle de Drame*. Serious studies of insanity and its effects are on the increase, not only through fictitious situations as shown in *A Bill of Divorcement, The Shrike, Suddenly Last Summer, Of Mice and Men* and *Cul de Sac*, but also in more clinical investigations such as *The Snake Pit, El, Labyrinth, La Tête contre les Murs, Morgan, Pressure Point, A Child Is Waiting* and *Repulsion*. A mixture of attitudes is found in the scientific fantasy of *Charly*; while *Bedlam* was a curious attempt at a horror film set entirely in an asylum. In *King of Hearts* the insane are shown to be wiser than the rest, like Mr Dick in *David Copperfield*.

insects on screen have generally been of the monstrous kind: *Tarantula, The Black Scorpion, The Wasp Woman, The Fly, Them,* and *The Monster That Challenged the World* come to mind. Of course, normal-sized ants can be monstrous enough if seen in quantity, as in *The Naked Jungle*, or if you are as small as *The Incredible Shrinking Man*. Giant spiders are perhaps the most popular breed: there was a particularly loathsome one in *The Thief of Baghdad*. Friendly insects have included those who went to the 'ugly bug ball' in *Summer Magic*; and the dancing caterpillar of *Once upon a Time*. The most symbolic insect was certainly the butterfly in *All Quiet on the Western Front*.

insert shot. One inserted into a dramatic scene, usually for the purpose of giving the audience a closer look at what the character on screen is seeing, e.g. a letter or a newspaper headline.

INTERMEZZO. A simple romantic tale, larded with classical music-this was originally filmed in Sweden in 1936 by Gustav Molander, with Gosta Ekman and Ingrid Bergman. In 1939 Bergman re-created the role in Hollywood opposite Leslie Howard; the film, known in Britain as *Escape to Happiness*, was directed by Gregory Ratoff.

IN THE HEAT OF THE NIGHT (US 1967; AA). Basically a rather uncon-vincing murder mystery set in a sweltering small town in the deep south, this screenplay by Sterling Silliphant (AA) benefited from fine colour photography by Haskell Wexler and splendid acting from Sidney Poitier and Rod Steiger (AA), whose conflict (as lazy local sheriff and arrogant Philadelphia detective) was intensified by race bitterness. Norman Jewison produced and directed.

INTOLERANCE (US 1916). D. W. Griffith's epic film, sub-titled 'Love's Struggle Through the Ages', is a sentimentally-conceived examina-tion of intolerance in four periods of history. The narrative moves constantly from one story to another, with frenzied cross-cutting at the climax. The spectacle of the Babylon sequence is on a massive scale, but the public were confused and the film was long considered a commercial failure. Written by Griffith, photographed by Billy Bitzer.

INVASION OF THE BODY SNATCHERS (US 1956). A catch-penny title obscures the most subtle film in the science-fiction cycle, with no visual horror whatever; about a small town whose population is taken over by 'duplicates' from outer space. Directed by Don Siegel; from Jack Finney's novel; with Kevin McCarthy and Dana Wynter.

inventors have been the subject of many screen biographies; indeed, Don Ameche had to live down his invention of the telephone in *The Story of Alexander Graham Bell* and of the sub-machine gun in *A Genius in the Family*. Mickey Rooney appeared as *Young Tom Edison* and Spencer Tracy as *Edison the Man*; James Stewart was *Carbine Williams*; Robert Donat played William Friese-Greene, inventor of the movie camera, in *The Magic Box*. Joel McCrea in *The Great Moment* invented laughing gas; *The Sound Barrier* covered Sir Frank Whittle's invention of the jet engine, and *The Dam Busters* has Michael Redgrave as the inventor of the bouncing bomb, Dr Barnes Wallis. That prolific inventor Galileo has yet to be covered on film; while Benjamin Franklin was portrayed not by an actor but by Disney's cartoonists in *Ben and Me*.

THE INVISIBLE MAN. The rights to H. G. Wells' tragi-comic fantasy novel were bought by Universal in 1933; the resulting film, directed by James Whale with splendid trick effects by Arthur Edeson, made a star of Claude Rains although his face was seen only briefly, in death. Universal later made a sporadic low-budget series alternating between farce and melodrama: *The Invisible*

Man Returns (Vincent Price) (40), *The Invisible Woman* (Virginia Bruce) (40), *Invisible Agent* (Jon Hall) (42), *The Invisible Man's Revenge* (Jon Hall) (44), *Abbott and Costello Meet the Invisible Man* (Arthur Franz) (51). Meanwhile invisibility had been put to excellent comic effect in the *Topper* series (qv) and many other movies. *Invisible Boy* (57) was something else again, a sequel to *Forbidden Planet*; but in the early 60s a new series of 'invisible man' movies emanated from Argentina and Mexico: and there was a TV series in 1958.

INVITATION TO THE DANCE (US/GB 1954). This ambitious ballet film in three parts was devised and directed by Gene Kelly, who also starred. Its lack of commercial success harmed his career, especially as it was not quite the masterpiece which had been anticipated. The cartoon sequence has been shown separately as *The Magic Lamp*.

IN WHICH WE SERVE (GB 1942). The first really important film about the Second World War, this was very much a Noel Coward enterprise. He surprised everyone at the time not only by producing, co-directing, and writing the script and music, but by his serious and effective performance as the captain of a doomed destroyer. The film was given a special Academy Award.

THE IPCRESS FILE (GB) (1965). A 'realistic' espionage picture which offered a useful corrective to the adventures of James Bond, this astringent movie was more coherent than the Len Deighton novel from which it sprang, but suffered from director Sidney Furie's apparent determination to smother it in weird camera angles. However, it clearly marked out Michael Caine for stardom; and it won BFA awards as the best British picture, also for Ken Adam's art direction and Otto Heller's photography.

Ireland to film makers has rather too often meant 'the troubles', which were celebrated in *Beloved Enemy, The Informer, The Gentle Gunman, Shake Hands with the Devil*, and the films of Sean O'Casey's plays, including *Juno and the Paycock* and *The Plough and the Stars*. (Rod Taylor played O'Casey, lightly disguised, in *Young Cassidy*.) More romantic or whimsical views of Eire were expressed in *The Luck of the Irish, The Rising of the Moon, Top of the Morning, Broth of a Boy, Home is the Hero, The Quiet Man, I See a Dark Stranger, Happy Ever After, Hungry Hill, The Search for Bridey Murphy, Jacqueline, Rooney, Never Put It In Writing* and *Ulysses*; realism was sought in *Odd Man Out, Parnell, Captain Boycott, No Resting Place, A Terrible Beauty*, and *Michael's Day*. The number of Irish characters on the screen is of course legion, the most numerous and memorable varieties being priests, drunks, New York cops, and Old Mother Riley.

IRELAND, JILL (1936–   ). British leading lady. *Oh Rosalinda* (55),
Three Men in a Boat (55), *Hell Drivers* (57), *Robbery under Arms* (57),
Carry On Nurse (59), *Raining the Wind* (61), *Twice Round the Daffodils*
(62), *Villa Rides* (US) (68), etc. Appeared in American TV series
Shane (66).

IRELAND, JOHN (1914–   ). Canadian leading man with stage
experience; a popular tough-cynical hero of the early 50s who
declined to second features. *A Walk in the Sun* (debut) (45), *My
Darling Clementine* (46), *Red River* (48), *All the King's Men* (50),
Vengeance Valley (51), *Hurricane Smith* (52), *Combat Squad* (53),
The Steel Cage (54), *The Good Die Young* (GB) (54), *Queen Bee* (55),
Hell's Horizon (56), *Gunfight at the OK Corral* (57), *Party Girl* (58),
Spartacus (60), *The Ceremony* (64), *The Fall of the Roman Empire* (as
the barbarian king) (64), *I Saw What You Did* (65), *Fort Utah* (66),
many others. A frequent TV guest star.

IRENE (1901–1962). American costume designer, with MGM for
many years.

iris. An adjustable diaphragm in the camera which opens or closes
from black like an expanding or contracting circle, giving a similar
effect on the screen. So called because it resembles the iris of the
human eye.

the Italian Cinema was an international force in the early years of the
century with spectaculars like *Cabiria* and *Quo Vadis*. It later
succumbed to the power of Hollywood and was little heard from
until the post-war realist movement brought de Sica to world
eminence. *Bicycle Thieves* was the high water mark of achievement;
afterwards came a slow slide into the commercialism of the 50s,
which however re-established Rome—and Cinecitta Studios—as
a world force in film making. Now many big Hollywood films are
made on Italian locations, as well as the familiar cut-rate spectaculars peopled by mythical strong-men.

AN ITALIAN STRAW HAT (UN CHAPEAU DE PAILLE D'ITALIE) (France
1928). Probably René Clair's most famous silent comedy, this
account of a hilariously impeded marriage, though now occasionally ponderous, set a new style in fast-paced yet stylish visual fun.
Written by Clair from a play by Eugene Labiche.

IT ALWAYS RAINS ON SUNDAY (GB 1947). A once-praised example
of early English realism which cannot now stand comparison with
the *Saturday Night and Sunday Morning* school. Basically a cliché-
ridden slice of hokum about an escaped convict in London's East
End, its often effective low-life atmosphere was chiefly attributable
to Douglas Slocombe's photography and to the cosy familiarity

of its long list of British players led by Jack Warner and Googie Withers.

IT HAPPENED HERE (GB 1957–63). A remarkable first film by two semi-professionals, Kevin Brownlow and Andrew Mollo, shot on a tiny budget over a period of seven years. In dramatically unwieldy but frequently vivid fashion it paints a grim picture of what might have happened if the Nazis had invaded London in 1942, and although sometimes let down by its dialogue sequences, the fake newsreel montages alone make it an achievement of more than mere cleverness.

IT HAPPENED ONE NIGHT (US 1934). This enormously successful romantic comedy was written by Robert Riskin (AA), directed by Frank Capra (AA), starred Claudette Colbert (AA) as a runaway heiress and Clark Gable (AA) as a wandering journalist. (It also won the Award for the best picture.) Its lively good humour and piquant dialogue endeared it to all comers; if today it seems on the slow side, it is infinitely preferable to the 1956 remake, *You Can't Run Away From It*, with June Allyson and Jack Lemmon.

IT'S A MAD MAD MAD MAD WORLD (US 1963). A marathon attempt to revive silent slapstick comedy and combine it with the modern taste for violence, all in colour and single-lens Cinerama. A large star cast played second fiddle to the stunt men; Stanley Kramer produced and directed from a script by William and Tania Rose.

ITURBI, JOSE (1895–). Spanish pianist and conductor who made American concert debut in 1929. Appeared as actor-performer in several MGM musicals of the 40s (*Thousands Cheer* [43], *Music for Millions* [44], *The Birds and the Bees* [48], etc.) and so helped to popularize classical music. His recording of a Chopin Polonaise for *A Song to Remember* (45) sold over a million copies.

IVENS, JORIS (1898–). Dutch writer-director best known for documentaries. *Rain* (29), *Zuidersee* (30), *New Earth* (34), *Spanish Earth* (37), *The 400 Millions* (39), *The Power and the Land* (40), *Song of the Rivers* (53), *The Threatening Sky* (66), etc.

IVAN, ROSALIND (1884–1959). American character actress, mainly on stage; made a hit as Laughton's nagging wife in *The Suspect* (44), and thereafter played in *Three Strangers* (46), *The Corn Is Green* (46), *Ivy* (47), *The Robe* (53), etc.

IVAN THE TERRIBLE (USSR 1942–46). Eisenstein's two-part historical film is full of splendidly grotesque imagery. Part One was released in 1942; Part Two was banned temporarily for political reasons and when eventually released proved somewhat disappointing because its colour experiments compared unfavourably with the brilliant black and white of Part One.

IVES, BURL (1909–   ) (Burl Icle Ivanhoe). American actor and ballad-singer, once itinerant worker and professional footballer. His paunchy figure, beard and ready smile are equally adaptable to villainous or sympathetic parts. *Smoky* (debut) (46), *East of Eden* (54), *Cat on a Hot Tin Roof* (57), *The Big Country* (AA) (58), *Our Man in Havana* (59), *The Brass Bottle* (64), *Rocket to the Moon* (67), etc. TV series: *O.K. Crackerby* (65), *The Bold Ones* (69).

IVORY, JAMES (1928–   ). American director who makes films in India. *The Householder* (62), *Shakespeare Wallah* (64), *The Guru* (69).

IWERKS, UB (1901–   ). American animator, long associated with Disney. Formed own company in 1930 to create Flip the Frog, with only mild success.

J

JACKS, ROBERT L. (1922–   ). American producer, long with Fox. *Man on a Tightrope* (53), *White Feather* (55), *A Kiss before Dying* (56), *Bandido* (57), *Roots of Heaven* (59), *Man in the Middle* (64), *Zorba the Greek* (65), *Bandolero* (68), many others.

JACKSON, ANNE (1925–   ). American stage actress, wife of Eli Wallach. Films include *The Tiger Makes Out* (67), *How to Save a Marriage* (68), *The Secret Life of an American Wife* (68).

JACKSON, FREDA (1909–   ). British character actress with a penchant for melodrama; on stage from 1934, films from 1942. *A Canterbury Tale* (42), *Henry V* (44), *Beware of Pity* (46), *Great Expectations* (46), *No Room at the Inn* (47), *Women of Twilight* (49), *The Crowded Day* (53), *Brides of Dracula* (60), *The Third Secret* (64), *The House at the End of the World* (65), etc.

JACKSON, GORDON (1923–   ). Scottish actor whose rueful expression got him typecast as a weakling; now getting more interesting roles. *The Foreman Went to France* (debut) (42), *Millions Like Us* (43), *Nine Men* (43), *San Demetrio, London* (44), *Pink String and Sealing Wax* (45), *The Captive Heart* (46), *Against the Wind* (47), *Eureka Stockade* (48), *Whisky Galore* (48), *The Lady with a Lamp* (51), *Meet Mr Lucifer* (54), *Pacific Destiny* (56), *Tunes of Glory* (60), *The Great Escape* (US) (62), *The Ipcress File* (65), *Cast a Giant Shadow* (US) (66), *The Fighting Prince of Donegal* (66), *The Prime of Miss Jean Brodie* (69), *Run Wild Run Free* (69), others.

JACKSON, PAT (1916–   ). British director, former editor; output rather sparse. *Western Approaches* (44), *The Shadow on the Wall* (US) (48), *White Corridors* (50), *The Feminine Touch* (55), *The Birthday Present* (57), *Virgin Island* (58), *Snowball* (60), *Don't Talk to Strange Men* (62), etc.

JACK THE RIPPER: see THE LODGER.

JACOBS, ARTHUR P. (1922–   ). American producer, head of APJAC productions; former publicist. *Doctor Dolittle* (67), *Planet of the Apes* (68), *The Most Dangerous Man in the World* (69), etc.

JACOBSSON, ULLA (1929–   ). Swedish leading lady best known abroad for *One Summer of Happiness* (51); recently in *Zulu* (64), *The Heroes of Telemark* (65), *The Double Man* (67).

JACOVES, FELIX (1907–). American dialogue director who directed *Homicide* (48), *Embraceable You* (49); later in TV.

JACQUES, HATTIE (1924–). Plump British comedienne, well known at the Players Theatre and on TV. In most of the 'Carry On' films, also *Oliver Twist* (48), *Trottie True* (49), *The Pickwick Papers* (52), *Make Mine Mink* (61), *In the Doghouse* (62), *The Bobo* (67), *Crooks and Coronets* (69), etc. TV series: *Sykes*.

JAECKEL, RICHARD (1926–). American actor, former Fox mail boy, who made a name playing frightened youths in war films. *Guadalcanal Diary* (43), *Jungle Patrol* (48), *Sands of Iwo Jima* (49), *The Gunfighter* (50), *Come Back Little Sheba* (52), *The Violent Men* (55), *Attack* (55), *3.10 to Yuma* (57), *The Gallant Hours* (60), *Time without Pity* (62), *Four for Texas* (63), *Town Tamer* (65), *The Dirty Dozen* (67), *The Devil's Brigade* (68), *The Green Slime* (69), many others.

JAFFE, CARL (1902–). Aristocratic-looking German actor, long in England. *Over the Moon* (39), *The Lion Has Wings* (40), *The Life and Death of Colonel Blimp* (43), *Gaiety George* (46), *Appointment in London* (53), *Operation Crossbow* (65), *The Double Man* (67), many others.

JAFFE, SAM (1897–). American character actor of eccentric appearance and sharp talent. On stage from 1916, films from 1933. *The Scarlet Empress* (34), *Lost Horizon* (37), *Gunga Din* (39), *Gentlemen's Agreement* (48), *The Asphalt Jungle* (50), *The Barbarian and the Geisha* (58), *Ben Hur* (59), *Guns for San Sebastian* (68), *The Kremlin Letter* (69), etc. Played Dr Zorba in TV series *Ben Casey* (60–64).

JAGGER, DEAN (1903–). American actor of sympathetic roles, on stage from 1933. *Woman from Hell* (debut) (29), *College Rhythm* (34), *Brigham Young* (40), *Western Union* (41), *I Live in Grosvenor Square* (GB) (44), *Twelve O'clock High* (AA) (49), *The Robe* (53), *Executive Suite* (54), *Bad Day at Black Rock* (54), *The Nun's Story* (58), *The Honeymoon Machine* (62), *Firecreek* (67), *Smith* (69), *The Kremlin Letter* (69), many others. TV series: *Mr Novak* (63–65).

JAMES BOND, the over-sexed one-man spy machine created by Ian Fleming, first came to the screen under the guise of Sean Connery in *Dr No* (62). Connery continued in *From Russia with Love* (63), *Goldfinger* (64), *Thunderball* (65), *You Only Live Twice* (67); George Lazenby took over for *On Her Majesty's Secret Service* (69).

JAMES, HARRY (1916–). American bandleader and trumpeter, married to Betty Grable. Made occasional guest appearances in musicals from 1941.

JAMES, JESSE (1847–1882). American wild west outlaw who has acquired the legend of a Robin Hood but in fact plundered ruthlessly as head of a gang which also included his sanctimonious elder brother FRANK JAMES (1843–1915). Among the many screen personifications of Jesse are Tyrone Power in *Jesse James* (39); Lawrence Tierney in *Badman's Territory* (46); Macdonald Carey in *The Great Missouri Raid* (52); Audie Murphy in *Kansas Raiders* (53); Willard Parker in *The Great Jesse James Raid* (53); Robert Wagner in *The True Story of Jesse James* (56); Ray Stricklyn in *Young Jesse James* (60); Chris Jones in a TV series *The Legend of Jesse James* (65).

JAMES, SID (or SIDNEY) (1913–). South African comedy actor, in Britain from 1946. A familiar face on TV and in scores of movies, including most of the 'Carry On' series (1958 to date). *Black Memory* (46), *Once a Jolly Swagman* (48), *The Man in Black* (49), *The Lavender Hill Mob* (51), *The Titfield Thunderbolt* (53), *Joe Macbeth* (55), *The Silent Enemy* (57), *Too Many Crooks* (58), *Tommy the Toreador* (59), *Double Bunk* (60), *What a Carve Up* (62), *The Big Job* (65), *Don't Lose Your Head* (67), many others. TV series include *Hancock's Half Hour*, *Citizen James*, *Taxi*, *George and the Dragon*.

JANCSO, MIKLOS (1921–). Hungarian director. *Cantata* (63), *My Way Home* (64), *The Round Up* (65), *The Red and the White* (67), etc.

JANE EYRE. Charlotte Brontë's romantic melodrama ('Reader, I married him') was screened in various silent versions, including one in 1913 with Ethel Grandin as Jane and Irving Cummings as the gloomy Mr Rochester; another in 1915 with Louise Vale and Alan Hale; and in 1921 with Mabel Ballin and Norman Trevor. Oddly enough there have been only two sound versions: in 1934 with Virginia Bruce and Colin Clive, and in 1943 with Joan Fontaine and Orson Welles.

JANIS, CONRAD (1926–). American teenage player of the 40s. *Snafu* (45), *Margie* (46), *The High Window* (46), *Beyond Glory* (48), *Keep it Cool* (58), etc.

JANIS, ELSIE (1889–1956) (Elsie Bierbauer). American musical comedy star who made a few silent movies such as *Betty in Search of a Thrill* and *A Regular Girl*; only talkie, *Women in War* (42).

JANNI, JOSEPH (1916–). Italian producer, in England from 1939. *The Glass Mountain* (48), *Romeo and Juliet* (53), *A Town Like Alice* (56), *A Kind of Loving* (62), *Darling* (65), *Modesty Blaise* (66), *Far From the Madding Crowd* (67), *Poor Cow* (68), etc.

JANNINGS, EMIL (1886–1950). Distinguished German actor, on stage from ten years old. Entered films through his friend Ernst Lubitsch. *Madame Dubarry* (18), *Peter the Great* (23), *The Last Laugh* (24), *Variety* (25), *Faust* (26), *The Way of All Flesh* (US) (AA) (28), *The*

Last Command (US) (28), *The Blue Angel* (30), *Ohm Kruger* (41), many others.

JANSSEN, DAVID (1930–   ) (David Meyer). American leading man, in routine films from 1951: *Yankee Buccaneer* (52), *Toy Tiger* (56), *Ring of Fire* (60), *Mantrap* (61), *King of the Roaring Twenties* (61), *Hell to Eternity* (61), *Belle Sommers* (62), *My Six Loves* (62), *The Warning Shot* (67), *The Green Berets* (68), *The Shoes of the Fisherman* (68), *Where It's At* (69), *Generation* (69), etc. TV: star of *Richard Diamond* (59), and *The Fugitive* (63–67).

JARMAN, CLAUDE, JNR (1934–   ). American boy actor of the 40s. *The Yearling* (special AA) (46), *High Barbaree* (47), *Intruder in the Dust* (49), *Rio Grande* (51), *Fair Wind to Java* (53), *The Great Locomotive Chase* (56), etc.

JARRE, MAURICE (1924–   ). French composer. *Hôtel des Invalides* (52), *La Tête contre les Murs* (59), *Eyes Without a Face* (59), *Crack in the Mirror* (60), *The Longest Day* (62), *Lawrence of Arabia* (AA) (62), *Weekend at Dunkirk* (65), *Dr Zhivago* (AA) (65), *Is Paris Burning?* (66), *The Professionals* (66), *The 25th Hour* (67), *Five Card Stud* (68), *Isadora* (68), *The Damned* (69), etc.

JASON, LEIGH (1904–   ). American director, mainly of second features. *The Mad Miss Manton* (38), *Lady for a Night* (39), *Model Wife* (41), *Three Girls About Town* (41), *Lost Honeymoon* (46), *Out of the Blue* (48), *Okinawa* (52), etc.

JASON, SYBIL (1929–   ). South African child actress of the 30s. *Barnacle Bill* (GB) (35), *Little Big Shot* (GB) (36), *The Singing Kid* (US) (36), *The Little Princess* (US) (39), *The Bluebird* (US) (40), etc.

JAUBERT, MAURICE (1900–1940). French composer. *L'Affaire Est dans le Sac* (32), *Le Quatorze Juillet* (33), *Zéro de Conduite* (33), *Drôle de Drame* (37), *Carnet du Bal* (37), *Quai des Brumes* (38), *Le Jour Se Lève* (39), *La Fin du Jour* (39), etc.

JAY, ERNEST (1894–1957). British stage character actor. Film appearances include *Tiger Bay* (34), *Broken Blossoms* (36), *Don't Take It to Heart* (44), *Vice Versa* (47), *The History of Mr Polly* (49), *Edward My Son* (49), *I Believe in You* (52), *Who Done It?* (55), *The Curse of Frankenstein* (56).

THE JAZZ SINGER (US 1927). The 'first talking film' has only a few patches of dialogue and some songs; but Al Jolson's personality is so vibrant that one can imagine the sensation he originally caused. The well-worn sentimental story is efficiently directed by Alan Crosland. There was a 1953 remake starring Danny Thomas.

JEAN, GLORIA (1928–   ) (Gloria Jean Schoonover). Former American child singer, on screen from 1939 as second feature rival to Deanna Durbin. *The Underpup* (39), *Pardon My Rhythm* (40), *If I Had My Way* (40), *Moonlight in Vermont* (41), *She's My Lovely* (42), *An Old-Fashioned Girl* (43), *I'll Remember April* (44), *Fairy Tale Murder* (45), *Copacabana* (47), *I Surrender, Dear* (48), *There's a Girl in My Heart* (49), etc. Retired, but appeared in *The Ladies' Man* (61).

JEANMAIRE, ZIZI (RENEE) (1924–   ). French leading lady and ballet dancer, in occasional films: *Hans Christian Andersen* (51), *Anything Goes* (56), *Folies Bergère* (56), *Charmants Garçons* (57), *Black Tights* (60), etc.

JEANS, ISABEL (1891–   ). British stage actress, invariably in aristo-cratic roles. Films include *The Rat* (25), *Downhill* (27), *Easy Virtue* (28), *Sally Bishop* (33), *Tovarich* (US) (38), *Suspicion* (US) (41), *Banana Ridge* (41), *Great Day* (45), *It Happened in Rome* (57), *Gigi* (58), *A Breath of Scandal* (60).

JEANS, URSULA (1906–   ) (Ursula McMinn). British stage actress, married to Roger Livesey; in occasional films. *The Gypsy Cavalier* (debut) (31), *Cavalcade* (33), *Dark Journey* (37), *Mr Emmanuel* (44), *The Woman in the Hall* (46), *The Weaker Sex* (48), *The Dam Busters* (55), etc.

JEANSON, HENRI (1900–   ). French writer. *Pepe le Moko* (37), *Carnet du Bal* (37). *Prison Without Bars* (38), *Carmen* (42), *Nana* (55), *L'Affaire d'une Nuit* (60), etc.

JEAYES, ALLAN (1885-1963). British stage actor of heavy presence; played supporting roles in many films including *The Impassive Footman* (32), *The Scarlet Pimpernel* (34), *Rembrandt* (37), *Elephant Boy* (37), *The Four Feathers* (39), *The Thief of Baghdad* (40), *The Man Within* (46), *Saraband for Dead Lovers* (48), *Waterfront* (50).

JEFFORD, BARBARA (1931–   ). British stage actress, more recently in films. *Ulysses* (67), *The Bofors Gun* (68), *A Midsummer Night's Dream* (68), *The Shoes of the Fisherman* (68).

JEFFREYS, ANNE (1923–   ). American leading lady of the 40s, formerly in opera. *I Married an Angel* (42), *Step Lively* (44), *Dillinger* (45), *Riff Raff* (47), *Return of the Badmen* (49), *Boys Night Out* (62), etc. Married Robert Sterling; appeared with him on TV, especially in series *Topper* (53), *Love That Jill* (58).

JEFFRIES, LIONEL (1926–   ). British character comedian, in films from 1952. *Windfall* (54), *The Baby and the Battleship* (55), *Law and Disorder* (57), *The Nun's Story* (58), *Idle on Parade* (59), *Two-Way Stretch* (60), *The Trials of Oscar Wilde* (60), *The Hellions* (61), *The Notorious Landlady* (61), *The Wrong Arm of the Law* (63), *Call Me Bwana* (63), *The Long Ships* (64), *The First Men in the Moon* (64),

The Truth about Spring (65), *The Secret of My Success* (65), *You Must Be Joking* (65), *Arrivederci Baby* (66), *The Spy with a Cold Nose* (67), *Rocket to the Moon* (67), *Camelot* (67), *Chitty Chitty Bang Bang* (68), etc.

JENKINS, ALLEN (1900–   ) (Al McGonegal). 'Tough guy' American comic actor who since his film debut in 1930 has played scores of cabbies, gangsters, managers, etc. TV series: *Hey Jeannie*. 1964: *Robin and the Seven Hoods, I'd Rather Be Rich.* 1967: *Doctor, You've got to be Kidding.*

JENKINS, JACKIE 'BUTCH' (1938–   ). Gravel-voiced American child star of the 40s. *The Human Comedy* (43), *National Velvet* (44), *Our Vines Have Tender Grapes* (45), *My Brother Talks to Horses* (47), *Summer Holiday* (47), etc. Retired in his teens.

JENKINS, MEGS (1917–   ). British actress of kindly or motherly roles, on stage from 1933, films from 1939. *The Silent Battle* (39), *Green for Danger* (46), *The Brothers* (47), *The Monkey's Paw* (48), *The History of Mr Polly* (49), *White Corridors* (51), *Ivanhoe* (52), *The Cruel Sea* (53), *The Gay Dog* (54), *John and Julie* (55), *The Man in the Sky* (56), *Conspiracy of Hearts* (59), *The Innocents* (61), *The Barber of Stamford Hill* (62), *Bunny Lake Is Missing* (65), *Stranger in the House* (67), *Oliver* (68), *David Copperfield* (69), etc.

JENKS, FRANK (1902–1962). American character comedian, usually seen as Runyonesque stooge, cop or valet. *When's Your Birthday* (37), *You Can't Cheat an Honest Man* (39), *Dancing on a Dime* (40), *Rogues Gallery* (45), *Loonies on Broadway* (46), *The She-Creature* (56), many others. TV series: *Colonel Flack.*

JENNINGS, HUMPHREY (1907–1950). Distinguished British documentarist, with the GPO Film Unit from 1934. Responsible for a fine World War II series of sensitive film records of the moods of the time: *The First Days* (co-d) (39), *London Can Take It* (co-d) (40), *Listen to Britain* (41), *The Silent Village* (43), *Fires Were Started* (43), *A Diary for Timothy* (45), etc.; also *The Cumberland Story* (47), *Dim Little Island* (49), *Family Portrait* (50), etc.

JENS, SALOME (1935–   ). American leading lady who played the title role in *Angel Baby* (61), but has since been little heard from.

JERGENS, ADELE (1922–   ). American leading lady, mainly in second features. *A Thousand and One Nights* (44), *Ladies of the Chorus* (48), *Blonde Dynamite* (50), *She Loves Me* (52), *Girls in Prison* (56), *The Lonesome Trail* (58), etc.

JERROLD, MARY (1877–1955) (Mary Allen). British character actress, mainly on stage; in films, played mainly sweet old ladies. *Alibi* (31), *Friday the Thirteenth* (33), *The Man at the Gate* (41), *The Way Ahead*

Jessel, George

(44), *The Queen of Spades* (48), *Mr Perrin and Mr Traill* (49), *Top of the Form* (52), etc.

JESSEL, GEORGE (1898–). American entertainer, in vaudeville from childhood. Star of very early talkie, *My Mother's Eyes* (*Lucky Boy*) (28), but never achieved film popularity equal to Al Jolson, whom he resembles in style. Made guest appearances in 40s, later produced several musicals for Fox. Published autobiography 1943: *So Help Me*. 1969: appeared as Death in *Heironymus Merkin*.

JESSEL, PATRICIA (1921–1968). British character actress, mostly on stage. Films include *Quo Vadis* (51), *City of the Dead* (61), *A Funny Thing Happened on the Way to the Forum* (66).

JESSUA, ALAIN (1932–). French writer-director of off-beat films. *Life Upside Down* (63), *Jeu de Massacre* (67).

JEUX INTERDITS (France 1952). A powerful anti-war film and a plea for innocence with a fresh angle: two children whose parents have been killed in an air raid are sheltered by peasants and invent their own game of death. Their world is shown as the only innocent one, all adults being in some way corrupt; but the world does not understand. Directed by René Clement from a novel by Françoise Boyer; with Brigitte Fossey and Georges Poujouly.

JEW SUSS (Germany 1940). This remake of the legend of a Jew who, inspired by a demoniacal Rabbi, takes over Wurtemberg but is finally toppled from power, was a natural theme for Nazi Germany, and Veit Harlan's film is said to have been dictated and supervised by Goebbels. There were earlier, more temperate versions, including a British one in 1934.

jewel thieves were fashionable with Hollywood film-makers in the 30s, the heyday of Raffles and Arsene Lupin; they were the subject of Lubitsch's best comedy, *Trouble in Paradise*. Recently they seem to be coming into their own again, with *To Catch a Thief*, *The Greengage Summer*, *Topkapi*, *The Pink Panther* and *Jack of Diamonds*.

JEWELL, ISABEL (1913–). American leading lady of the 30s, a minor 'platinum blonde' who graduated to character parts. *Blessed Event* (33), *A Tale of Two Cities* (36), *The Man Who Lived Twice* (37), *Marked Woman* (37), *Gone with the Wind* (39), *The Leopard Man* (43), *The Bishop's Wife* (48), *The Story of Molly X* (48), *Bernardine* (57), many others.

†JEWISON, NORMAN (c.1927–). American director, from TV: *Forty Pounds of Trouble* (63), *The Thrill of It All* (63), *Send Me No Flowers* (64), *The Art of Love* (65), *The Cincinnati Kid* (65), *The Russians Are Coming, The Russians Are Coming* (also produced) (66), *In the Heat of the Night* (p, d) (67), *The Thomas Crown Affair* (p, d) (68), *The*

Landlord (p) (69), *Gaily, Gaily* (p, d) (69), *Fiddler on the Roof* (p, d) (project) (71).

Jews and their plight in Europe under the Nazis were the subject of *So Ends Our Night, The Great Dictator, Professor Mamlock, Mr Emmanuel* and *The Diary of Anne Frank.* The problems of the new state of Israel were treated in *Sword in the Desert, Exodus, The Juggler, Judith* and *Cast A Giant Shadow*; while looking further back in history we find many versions of *Jew Suss* and *The Wandering Jew*, also *The Fixer* and *Fiddler on the Roof.* American films about Jews used to show them as warm-hearted comic figures: *Kosher Kitty Kelly, Abie's Irish Rose, The Cohens and the Kellys.* Gertrude Berg continued this tradition on TV in the 50s. Recently films set in Jewish milieus have treated their characters more naturally, if with a touch of asperity: *No Way to Treat a Lady, I Love You Alice B. Toklas, Bye Bye Braverman, Funny Girl, The Night They Raided Minsky's, Goodbye Columbus.* See also: *anti-semitism.*

JOAN OF ARC has had her story told several times on film. In 1916 Geraldine Farrar played her in *Joan the Woman.* Dreyer's classic *The Passion of Joan of Arc*, with Falconetti, came in 1928; and in 1930 Marco de Gastogne directed *Saint Joan the Maid* with Simone Genevois. In Germany, Angela Salloker had the role in 1935. The next two versions were Hollywood failures: Victor Fleming's *Joan of Arc* (48), with Ingrid Bergman, and Otto Preminger's *Saint Joan* (57), with Jean Seberg. Hedy Lamarr also made a brief appearance as Joan in *The Story of Mankind* (57). In 1962 Robert Bresson made his highly specialized *The Trial of Joan of Arc* with Florence Carrez.

JOE PALOOKA. The dumb boxer hero of the famous American comic strip was first on screen in 1934, played by Stuart Erwin. Ten years later Joe Kirkwood, an amateur golfer, played him in a Monogram series, with Leon Errol, later James Gleason, as his manager Knobby Walsh.

JOHN, ROSAMUND (1913–) (Nora R. Jones). Gentle-mannered British leading lady, also occasionally on stage. *The Secret of the Loch* (debut) (34), *The First of the Few* (42), *The Gentle Sex* (43), *The Lamp Still Burns* (43), *Tawny Pipit* (44), *The Way to the Stars* (45), *Green for Danger* (46), *The Upturned Glass* (47), *Fame Is the Spur* (47), *When the Bough Breaks* (48), *No Place for Jennifer* (49), *She Shall Have Murder* (50), *Never Look Back* (52), *Street Corner* (53), *Operation Murder* (56), etc. Retired.

JOHNS, GLYNIS (1923–). Husky-voiced British actress, on stage (as child) from 1935. *South Riding* (debut) (36), *Prison Without Bars* (38), *49th Parallel* (41), *Halfway House* (44), *Perfect Strangers* (45), *This Man Is Mine* (46), *Frieda* (47), *Miranda* (as a mermaid) (47),

An Ideal Husband (47), *State Secret* (50), *Appointment with Venus* (51), *The Card* (52), *The Sword and the Rose* (53), *Personal Affair* (53), *Rob Roy* (53), *The Weak and the Wicked* (54), *The Beachcomber* (55), *Mad About Men* (55), *The Court Jester* (US) (56), *The Day They Gave Babies Away* (US) (56), *Shake Hands with the Devil* (59), *The Sundowners* (60), *The Spider's Web* (61), *The Chapman Report* (US) (62), *Mary Poppins* (64), *Dear Brigitte* (65), *Don't Just Stand There* (US) (68), *Lock Up Your Daughters* (69), etc. Daughter of Mervyn Johns. TV series: *Glynis* (63).

JOHNS, MERVYN (1899–   ). Welsh character actor, on stage from 1923; usually plays mild-mannered roles. *Lady in Danger* (debut) (34), *Jamaica Inn* (39), *Saloon Bar* (40), *Next of Kin* (41), *Went the Day Well* (42), *Halfway House* (44), *My Learned Friend* (44), *Dead of Night* (45), *Pink String and Sealing Wax* (45), *Scrooge* (51), *The Intimate Stranger* (56), *No Love for Johnnie* (61), *80,000 Suspects* (63), *The Heroes of Telemark* (65), *Who Killed the Cat?* (66), many others.

JOHNSON, BEN (c. 1919–   ). American general purpose supporting actor, mainly in Westerns; former stunt rider. *She Wore a Yellow Ribbon* (49), *Mighty Joe Young* (50), *Wagonmaster* (50), *Shane* (53), *Slim Carter* (57), *Fort Bowie* (60), *Major Dundee* (65), *The Rare Breed* (66), etc.

†JOHNSON, CELIA (1908–   ). Distinguished British actress, on stage from 1928, usually in well-bred roles: films rare. *In Which We Serve* (debut) (42), *Dear Octopus* (42), *This Happy Breed* (44), *Brief Encounter* (46), *The Astonished Heart* (49), *I Believe In You* (52), *The Captain's Paradise* (53), *The Holly and the Ivy* (54), *A Kid for Two Farthings* (56), *The Good Companions* (57), *The Prime of Miss Jean Brodie* (69).

JOHNSON, CHIC (1891–1962). American vaudeville comedian (with partner Ole Olsen). Made early talkies (*Oh Sailor Behave* [30], *Fifty Million Frenchmen* [31], etc.) but their big success was in *Hellzapoppin* (42), from their stage show. Followed this with less effective comedies: *Crazy House* (43), *Ghost Catchers* (43), etc.

JOHNSON, KATIE (1878–1957). British character actress who after years in small roles made big hit in *The Ladykillers* (55); also *How to Murder a Rich Uncle* (56).

JOHNSON, NUNNALLY (1897–   ). American screenwriter, producer and director. *The House of Rothschild* (w), (34), *Cardinal Richelieu* (w) (35), *Jesse James* (w) (39), *The Grapes of Wrath* (w) (40), *Tobacco Road* (w) (41), *The Moon Is Down* (w, p) (43), *Holy Matrimony* (w, p) (43), *The Keys of the Kingdom* (w) (44), *The Dark Mirror* (w) (46), *The Gunfighter* (w, p) (50), *The Mudlark* (w, p) (51), *Rommel, Desert Fox* (w, p) (51), *How to Marry a Millionaire* (w, p) (53),

Night People (w, p, d) (54), *The Man in the Grey Flannel Suit* (w, d) (56), *Oh Men, Oh Women* (w, p, d) (57), *The Three Faces of Eve* (w, p, d) (57), *The Man Who Understood Women* (w, p, d) (59), *Take Her She's Mine* (w, p) (63), *The World of Henry Orient* (p) (64), many others.

JOHNSON, RAFER (1935–   ). American Negro actor, formerly Olympic athlete. *The Fiercest Heart* (61), *The Sins of Rachel Cade* (61), *Wild in the Country* (62), *The Lion* (63), etc.

JOHNSON, RICHARD (1927–   ). British leading man of stage and screen. *Captain Horatio Hornblower* (51), *Never So Few* (US) (59), *Cairo* (US) (62), *The Haunting* (63), *Eighty Thousand Suspects* (63), *The Pumpkin Eater* (64), *Operation Crossbow* (65), *Moll Flanders* (65), *Khartoum* (66), *Deadlier Than the Male* (as Bulldog Drummond) (66), *Danger Route* (67), *La Strega in Amore* (It.) (67), *Oedipus The King* (68), *A Twist of Sand* (68), *Lady Hamilton* (as Nelson) (German) (68), *Some Girls Do* (68), *Julius Caesar* (70).

JOHNSON, RITA (1912–1965). American actress who usually played 'the other woman'. *Serenade* (39), *Edison the Man* (40), *Here Comes Mr Jordan* (41), *Thunderhead, Son of Flicka* (44), *They Won't Believe Me* (47), *Family Honeymoon* (49), *Susan Slept Here* (54), *Emergency Hospital* (56), *The Day They Gave Babies Away* (57), etc.

JOHNSON, VAN (1916–   ). American light leading man, in films since 1941 after stage experience. *Murder in the Big House* (debut) (41), *Dr Gillespie's New Assistant* (42), *The Human Comedy* (43), *A Guy Named Joe* (43), *The White Cliffs of Dover* (44), *Two Girls and a Sailor* (44), *Thirty Seconds over Tokyo* (44), *Thrill of a Romance* (45), *Weekend at the Waldorf* (45), *Easy to Wed* (45), *No Leave, No Love* (45), *High Barbaree* (46), *The Romance of Rosy Ridge* (47), *State of the Union* (48), *The Bride Goes Wild* (48), *In the Good Old Summertime* (49), *Battleground* (50), *Go for Broke* (51), *When in Rome* (52), *Plymouth Adventure* (52), *The Caine Mutiny* (54), *Brigadoon* (55), *The Last Time I Saw Paris* (55), *The End of the Affair* (GB) (55), *Miracle in the Rain* (56), *Twenty-three Paces to Baker Street* (57), *Kelly and Me* (57), *Beyond This Place* (GB) (59), *Subway in the Sky* (GB) (60), *Wives and Lovers* (63), *Divorce American Style* (67), others.

JOHNSTON, ERIC A. (1895–1963). American executive, successor to Will H. Hays as President of the M.P.A.A. (Motion Picture Association of America) (1945–1963).

JOHNSTON, MARGARET (1917–   ). Australian actress who has made occasional films, notably in mid-40s. *The Prime Minister* (debut) (40), *The Rake's Progress* (45), *A Man About the House* (47), *Portrait of Clare* (50), *The Magic Box* (51), *Knave of Hearts* (53), *Night of the Eagle* (62), *Life at the Top* (65), *The Psychopath* (66), etc.

JOLSON, AL (c. 1880–1950) (Asa Yoelson). Celebrated Jewish-American entertainer, often in blackface. After years in vaudeville became a big Broadway attraction and starred in the first talking picture, *The Jazz Singer* (27). Popular through the 30s in such films as *The Singing Fool* (28), *Mammy* (30), *Wonder Bar* (33), *Hallelujah I'm a Bum* (34), *Go Into Your Dance* (36), *Rose of Washington Square* (39), *Swanee River* (40); made guest appearance in *Rhapsody in Blue* (45); in 1946 provided voice for Larry Parks in highly successful biopic *The Jolson Story*, followed in 1949 by *Jolson Sings Again*.

JONES, ALLAN (1908–). American singer and leading man of the 30s and 40s. *A Day at the Races* (37), *The Firefly* (38), *The Boys from Syracuse* (40), *One Night in the Tropics* (40), *True to the Army* (42), *When Johnny Comes Marching Home* (43), *Honeymoon Ahead* (45), etc. Retired for many years, then made TV appearances in small roles. Recent film: *Stage to Thunder Rock* (63).

JONES, BARRY (1893–). British character actor, usually in diffident roles; a well-known stage actor from 1921. Occasional films include *Arms and the Man* (as Bluntschli) (31), *Squadron Leader X* (42), *Dancing with Crime* (46), *Frieda* (47), *The Calendar* (48), *Seven Days to Noon* (leading role) (50), *White Corridors* (51), *Prince Valiant* (54), *Brigadoon* (55), *War and Peace* (56), *The Safecracker* (58), *A Study in Terror* (65).

JONES, BUCK (1889–1942) (Charles Jones). Popular American Western star of the 20s and 30s, mainly in second features. *Straight from the Shoulder* (20), *Skid Proof* (23), *Hearts and Spurs* (25), *Riders of the Purple Sage* (26), *The Flying Horseman* (27), *The Lone Rider* (30), *Border Law* (32), *The California Trail* (33), *When a Man Sees Red* (34), *Boss Rider of Gun Creek* (36), *Riders of Death Valley* (41), many others.

JONES, CAROLYN (1929–). American leading lady, usually in off-beat roles. *Road to Bali* (52), *The Big Heat* (53), *Invasion of the Body Snatchers* (55), *The Opposite Sex* (56), *The Bachelor Party* (57), *Last Train from Gun Hill* (58), *A Hole in the Head* (59), *Ice Palace* (60), *A Ticklish Affair* (63), etc. TV series: *The Addams Family* (as Morticia) (64–65).

JONES, CHRIS (1942–). American leading man. *Wild in the Streets* (67), *The Looking Glass War* (69), *Ryan's Daughter* (69). TV series: *The Legend of Jesse James* (65).

JONES, DEAN (1933–). American leading man who usually plays well-behaved fellows. *Handle with Care* (58), *Never So Few* (60), *Under the Yum Yum Tree* (64), *The New Interns* (64), *Two on a Guillotine* (64), *That Darn Cat* (65), *The Ugly Duckling* (66), *Any Wednesday*

(66), *Monkeys Go Home* (67), *Blackbeard's Ghost* (67), *The Love Bug* (69), etc. TV series: *Ensign O'Toole* (62).

THE JONES FAMILY. A popular series (15 between 1936 and 1940) depicting the life of an 'average' mid-western small town family in semi-farcical terms. Pa was Jed Prouty, Ma was Spring Byington.

JONES, EMRYS (1915–). British stage actor. Films include *One of Our Aircraft Is Missing* (42), *The Rake's Progress* (45), *The Wicked Lady* (46), *Nicholas Nickleby* (47), *The Small Back Room* (48), *Three Cases of Murder* (55), *Oscar Wilde* (60).

JONES, FREDDIE (1927–). British stage and TV character actor, now moving into films. *The Bliss of Mrs Blossom* (68), *Otley* (69), *Frankenstein Must Be Destroyed* (69).

JONES, GRIFFITH (1910–). British light leading man, on stage from 1930. *The Faithful Heart* (debut) (32), *Catherine the Great* (34), *The Mill on the Floss* (36), *A Yank at Oxford* (38), *The Four Just Men* (39), *Young Man's Fancy* (39), *Atlantic Ferry* (40), *This Was Paris* (41), etc.; war service; *Henry V* (44), *The Wicked Lady* (45), *The Rake's Progress* (45), *They Made Me a Fugitive* (47), *Good Time Girl* (48), *Miranda* (48), *Look Before You Love* (49), *Honeymoon Deferred* (51), *Star of My Night* (53), *The Sea Shall Not Have Them* (55), *Face in the Night* (57), *Kill Her Gently* (59), *Strangler's Web* (63), *Decline and Fall* (68), others; much on TV.

JONES, HARMON (1911–). Canadian director in Hollywood. *As Young As You Feel* (51), *Bloodhounds of Broadway* (52), *The Silver Whip* (52), *Gorilla at Large* (54), *A Day of Fury* (56), etc., then into TV. 1966: *Don't Worry We'll Think of a Title*.

JONES, HENRY (1912–). American character actor of stage, TV, and occasional films; usually plays the guy next door or the worm who turns. *The Lady Says No* (51), *The Bad Seed* (56), *The Girl Can't Help It* (57), *Vertigo* (58), *The Bramble Bush* (60), *Angel Baby* (60), *Never Too Late* (65), *Project X* (67), *Stay Away Joe* (68), *Support Your Local Sheriff* (69), etc.

†JONES, JENNIFER (1919–) (Phyllis Isley). American leading actress, in small film roles from 1939 (*Dick Tracy's G-Men* under her real name). Shot to fame in 1943 in *The Song of Bernadette* (AA). Subsequently: *Since You Went Away* (44), *Love Letters* (45), *Cluny Brown* (46), *Duel in the Sun* (46), *Portrait of Jennie* (48), *We Were Strangers* (49), *Madame Bovary* (49), *Carrie* (51), *Gone to Earth* (GB) (51), *Ruby Gentry* (52), *Indiscretion* (54), *Beat the Devil* (54), *Love Is a Many-Splendoured Thing* (55), *Good Morning, Miss Dove* (55), *The Man in the Grey Flannel Suit* (56), *The Barretts of Wimpole Street* (57),

Jones, Marcia Mae

A Farewell to Arms (58), *Tender Is the Night* (61), *The Idol* (GB) (66), *Angel Angel Down We Go* (69).

JONES, MARCIA MAE (1924–). American child actress of the 30s. *King of Jazz* (31), *These Three* (36), *Heidi* (37), *The Little Princess* (39), *Tomboy* (40), *Nice Girl* (41). *Nine Girls* (44), *Arson Inc.* (50), *Chicago Calling* (under the name of Marsha Jones) (52), *Rogue's Gallery* (68), etc.

JONES, PAUL (1901–1968). American producer, long with Paramount. *The Great McGinty* (40)? *Sullivan's Travels* (41), *Road to Morocco* (42), *The Virginian* (46), *Dear Ruth* (47), *Here Come the Girls* (53), *Living It Up* (54), *Pardners* (56), *The Disorderly Orderly* (64), many others.

JONES, PETER (1920–). British character comedian. *Fanny by Gaslight* (44), *The Yellow Balloon* (53), *Albert R.N.* (53), *Danger Within* (58), *Never Let Go* (61), *Romanoff and Juliet* (61), *Press for Time* (66), *Just Like a Woman* (66), etc. TV series: *The Rag Trade*.

JONES, SHIRLEY (1934–). American leading actress and singer. *Oklahoma* (55), *Carousel* (56), *Bobbikins* (GB) (59), *Elmer Gantry* (AA) (60), *Two Rode Together* (61), *The Music Man* (62), *A Ticklish Affair* (63), *Bedtime Story* (64), *The Secret of My Success* (65).

JONES, SPIKE (1912–1965) (Lindley Armstrong Jones). American bandleader ('Spike Jones and his City Slickers'), popular in the 40s for crazy variations on well-known songs. *Thank Your Lucky Stars* (43), *Bring on the Girls* (45), *Variety Girl* (47), *Fireman Save My Child* (55), etc.

JORY, VICTOR (1902–). Saturnine American actor, on stage from mid-20s. Usually a villain on screen. *Sailor's Luck* (debut) (32), *A Midsummer Night's Dream* (as Oberon) (35), *The Adventures of Tom Sawyer* (as Injun Joe) (38), *Gone with the Wind* (as the carpetbagger) (39), *Unknown Guest* (44), *The Gallant Blade* (48), *Canadian Pacific* (49), *Cat Women of the Moon* (53), *Valley of the Kings* (54), *Diary of a Scoundrel* (56), *The Man Who Turned to Stone* (58), *The Fugitive Kind* (60), *The Miracle Worker* (63), *Cheyenne Autumn* (64), *Mackenna's Gold* (narration only) (69), *A Time for Dying* (69), many others, especially second-string westerns. TV series: *Manhunt* (59–61).

JOSLYN, ALLYN (1905–). American character comedian whose crumpled features admirably portray bewilderment. On stage before films. *They Won't Forget* (debut) (37), *Bedtime Story* (41), *A Yank in Dutch* (42), *Heaven Can Wait* (43), *Bride by Mistake* (44), *Junior Miss* (45), *It Shouldn't Happen to a Dog* (47), *If You Knew Susie* (48), *As Young As You Feel* (51), *Titanic* (53), *The Fastest Gun Alive* (56), many others. Recently on TV (*The Addams Family, Don't Call Me Charlie*).

JOURDAN, LOUIS (1919–   ) (Louis Gendre). Smooth French leading man who has made films also in Britain and Hollywood. *Le Corsaire* (debut) (39), *The Paradine Case* (48), *Letter from an Unknown Woman* (48), *Madame Bovary* (49), *Bird of Paradise* (50), *Anne of the Indies* (51), *The Happy Time* (52), *Rue de l'Estrapade* (52), *Decameron Nights* (53), *Three Coins in the Fountain* (54), *The Swan* (56), *Julie* (56), *Gigi* (58), *Can-Can* (60), *The Count of Monte Cristo* (61), *The VIPs* (62), *Made in Paris* (65), *Peau d'Espion* (67), *A Flea in Her Ear* (68), etc. TV series: *Paris Precinct* (53).

JOUR DE FETE (France 1949). The first full-length comedy written and directed by Jacques Tati, who stars as the rural postman with sudden ambition to be efficient. The climactic sequence of visual gags is hilarious, but as in his later films Tati needs stronger control.

JOURNAL D'UN CURE DE CAMPAGNE (France 1950). Written and directed by Robert Bresson from Georges Bernanos' novel, this spare, ascetic film tells of a young priest's difficulties and early death in his first parish. Claude Laydu's withdrawn performance is exactly in keeping.

journalists: see *reporters*.

JOURNEY INTO FEAR (US 1942). Set up by Orson Welles before he fell out of favour with RKO, this tight little thriller from Eric Ambler's book bears unmistakable signs of his influence though allegedly directed by Norman Foster. Brilliantly atmospheric in its Constantinople settings, it provides excellent roles for Joseph Cotten, Dolores del Rio and Welles himself as Colonel Haki of the Turkish Secret Police. Its influence can be seen in *The Third Man*.

JOURNEY TO THE CENTRE OF THE EARTH (US 1959). Jules Verne's fantastic novel was here adapted by Charles Brackett and Walter Reisch, directed by Henry Levin and photographed by Leo Tover. Despite some cardboard sets, it successfully set a light whimsical trend in science fiction, with James Mason as an earnest professor and Arlene Dahl as a Victorian lady who makes tea several miles down.

JOURNEY'S END (GB/US 1930). This film version of R. C. Sheriff's play set in the World War I trenches was an early example of Anglo-American co-production. It was also the last major film of producer George Pearson, and it took to Hollywood two interesting talents: actor Colin Clive and director James Whale, both of whom were involved in these capacities in the London stage production.

LE JOUR SE LÈVE (France 1939). This memorable melodrama may have been over-praised because it was subsequently bought up and threatened with destruction to make way for an inferior American remake (*The Long Night* [47]). Nevertheless it drew great tension from Jacques Prevert's tragic story of a man who kills a girl's persecutor and, cornered by the police, commits suicide. Directed by Marcel Carne, with music by Maurice Jaubert and photography by Curt Courant; also first-rate performances by Jean Gabin, Arletty and Jules Berry.

JOUVET, LOUIS (1887–1951). Distinguished French actor of stage and screen. *Topaze* (32), *Doctor Knock* (33), *La Kermesse Héroïque* (35), *Les Bas Fonds* (36), *Un Carnet de Bal* (37), *Hôtel du Nord* (38), *La Fin du Jour* (38), *Volpone* (41), *Quai des Orfèvres* (47), *Retour à la Vie* (49), *Doctor Knock* (remake) (50), *Un Histoire d'Amour* (51), etc.

JOY, LEATRICE (1899–   ) (L. J. Zeidler). Vivacious American leading lady of the 20s: *Manslaughter* (22), *The Ten Commandments* (23), *Triumph* (24), *The Blue Danube* (28), etc. Later played character roles in talkies: *First Love* (40), *Love Nest* (52), etc.

JOYCE, ALICE (1889–1955). American leading lady of the silent screen. *Womanhood* (17), *The Lion and the Mouse* (19), *Cousin Kate* (21), *The Green Goddess* (23), *Daddy's Gone a-Hunting* (25), *Song o' My Heart* (30), etc.

JOYCE, BRENDA (1918–   ) (Betty Leabo). American leading lady, former model. Played innocent types in the 40s, then retired. *The Rains Came* (debut) (39), *Little Old New York* (40), *Maryland* (40), *Marry the Boss's Daughter* (41), *Whispering Ghosts* (42), *The Postman Didn't Ring* (42), *Little Tokyo USA* (43), *Strange Confession* (45), *The Enchanted Forest* (46), *Tarzan and the Huntress* (47), *Shaggy* (48), etc.

JOYLESS STREET (Germany 1925). Much-censored study of prostitution and other vices, a rare German film of the period to centre on squalid fact rather than romantic fantasy. Directed by G. W. Pabst, with a cast including Greta Garbo, Asta Nielsen and Werner Krauss.

JUDD, EDWARD (1932–   ). British actor who played supporting roles from 1951, starred in *The Day the Earth Caught Fire* (61), *Stolen Hours* (63), *The Long Ships* (63), *The First Men in the Moon* (64), *Strange Bedfellows* (65), *Island of Terror* (66), *Invasion* (66), *The Vengeance of She* (68), etc.

JUDEX (France 1916). A super-serial by Louis Feuillade, now enjoying belated recognition (in a six-hour version) as a primitive precursor of James Bond. A remake has been directed by Georges Franju (1963).

JUDGE, ARLINE (1912–   ). American general purpose leading lady. *Girl Crazy* (32), *Name This Woman* (35), *King of Burlesque* (36),

Valiant Is the Word for Carrie (37), *The Lady Is Willing* (42), *From This Day Forward* (45), *Two Knights in Brooklyn* (49), etc.

JUDGE PRIEST (US 1934). Directed by John Ford, this southern-state comedy-drama fairly oozed with local colour and provided a fat part for Will Rogers as a kindly old local judge. (Irvin S. Cobb, from whose writings it was taken, took over a couple of Will Rogers' roles after the actor died in an air crash in 1935.) In 1952 Ford remade the film as *The Sun Shines Bright*, with Charles Winninger.

JULES ET JIM (France 1961). François Truffaut's affectionate recreation of a period (pre-1914) and a curious triangular love affair has been enthusiastically adopted as a credo by sophisticated young people in many countries. Jeanne Moreau's performance transcends the lumpiness of the script, which ends in uneasy gloom.

JULIAN, RUPERT (1886– *). American director who seemed all set for the big time at Universal in the 20s, after finishing *Merry Go Round* for Stroheim and directing *The Phantom of the Opera* (26). Career oddly evaporated after a few routine films, the last of them *Love Comes Along* (30). Former stage and screen actor.

JULIET OF THE SPIRITS (Italy 1965). Federico Fellini wrote and directed, and his wife Giulietta Masina starred in, this long and gossamy but very stylish piece about a neurotic woman torn between reality and a dream world into which she has retreated from the fact of her husband's infidelity. Gianni di Venanzo's colour photography was a major asset.

JULIUS CAESAR (102–44 B.C.). The Roman emperor has been memorably portrayed by Claude Rains in *Caesar and Cleopatra*, Warren William in the 1934 *Cleopatra* and Rex Harrison in the 1962 remake. The Shakespeare play was filmed many times in silent days, but the only notable sound versions in English have been Joseph L. Mankiewicz's 1953 production with Louis Calhern as Caesar, James Mason as Brutus, and John Gielgud as Cassius, and the 1970 version with Gielgud as Caesar, Richard Johnson as Cassius, and Charlton Heston as Mark Antony. A British second feature of 1959, *An Honourable Murder*, brought the story up to date as a melodrama of boardroom intrigue.

jump-cutting. Moving abruptly from one scene to another to make a dramatic point, e.g. from cause to effect.

JUNE, RAY (c. 1908–). American cinematographer. *Arrowsmith* (32), *I Cover the Waterfront* (35), *The Hoodlum Saint* (46), *Crisis* (50), *The Reformer and the Redhead* (51), *The Court Jester* (55), *Funny Face* (56), etc.

JUNGE, ALFRED (1886–   ). German art director with long experience at UFA; in Britain from the 20s. *Piccadilly* (28), *The Good Companions* (32), *The Man Who Knew Too Much* (34), *Bulldog Jack* (35), *King Solomon's Mines* (37), *The Citadel* (38), *Goodbye Mr Chips* (39), *The Silver Fleet* (42), *The Life and Death of Colonel Blimp* (43), *I Know Where I'm Going* (45), *A Matter of Life and Death* (45), *Black Narcissus* (AA) (46), *Edward My Son* (49), *The Miniver Story* (50), *Ivanhoe* (52), *Mogambo* (53), *Invitation to the Dance* (56), *The Barretts of Wimpole Street* (57), *A Farewell to Arms* (58), many others.

JUNGLE JIM. This sub-Tarzan character began life as a comic strip, and in 1937 Ford Beebe directed a serial about his exploits. In 1948 began the rather tired series tossed off for Columbia, with a paunchy Johnny Weissmuller in the role: it started ineptly and quickly became ridiculous.

THE JUNGLE PRINCESS (US 1936). This Paramount programmer about a beautiful female Tarzan, directed by William Thiele, put Dorothy Lamour in a sarong for the first time and started her off on a series of similar exploits: *Her Jungle Love, Aloma of the South Seas, Typhoon, Beyond the Blue Horizon, Rainbow Island,* etc.

JURADO, KATY (1927–   ) (Maria Jurado Garcia). Mexican actress who has made Hollywood films: *The Bullfighter and the Lady* (51), *High Noon* (52), *Arrowhead* (53), *Broken Lance* (54), *Trial* (55), *Trapeze* (56), *One-Eyed Jacks* (59), *Barabbas* (61), *Smoky* (66), *Covenant With Death* (67), *Stay Away Joe* (68), etc.

JURAN, NATHAN (1907–   ). Austrian art director, long in the US. Won Academy Award for *How Green Was My Valley* (41). Later became a director of action films: *The Black Castle* (52), *The Golden Blade* (53), *Drums Across the River* (55), *The Crooked Web* (56), *The Seventh Voyage of Sinbad* (58), *The First Men in the Moon* (64), *The Day of the Landgrabber* (69), etc.

JURGENS, CURT (1915–   ). German stage leading man, in films from 1939; since the war has played internationally. *Les Héros Sont Fatigués* (55), *An Eye for an Eye* (56), *Without You It Is Night* (also directed) (56), *And Woman Was Created* (57), *Me and the Colonel* (57), *The Enemy Below* (57), *The Devil's General* (58), *Inn of the Sixth Happiness* (58), *The Blue Angel* (58), *Ferry to Hong Kong* (58), *I Aim at the Stars* (as Wernher von Braun) (59), *Tamango* (60), *Lord Jim* (64), *The Threepenny Opera* (65), *Das Liebeskarussel* (*Who Wants to Sleep*) (65), *The Assassination Bureau* (68), *The Battle of Neretva* (70), others.

JUROW, MARTIN (* –   ). American producer. *The Hanging Tree* (58), *The Fugitive Kind* (60), *Breakfast at Tiffany's* (61), *Soldier in the Rain* (63), *The Great Race* (65), etc.

JUSTICE EST FAITE (France 1950). Written and directed by André Cayatte, this study of a jury during a murder trial managed to provide entertaining drama while questioning points of law. Cayatte's subsequent films mostly followed a similar pattern, but not so successfully.

JUSTICE, JAMES ROBERTSON (1905–). Bearded Scottish actor and personality, former journalist and naturalist. In many British and American films. *Fiddlers Three* (debut) (44), *Scott of the Antarctic* (48), *Christopher Columbus* (49), *Whisky Galore* (49), *David and Bathsheba* (51), *Doctor in the House* (54), *Storm over the Nile* (55), *Land of the Pharaohs* (55), *Moby Dick* (56), *Campbell's Kingdom* (57), *Seven Thunders* (57), *Doctor at Large* (58), *Very Important Person* (61), *The Fast Lady* (62), *Crooks Anonymous* (62), *You Must Be Joking* (65), *Doctor in Clover* (66), *Mayerling* (68), *Chitty Chitty Bang Bang* (68), many others.

JUSTIN, JOHN (1917–). British leading man, on stage from 1933. *The Thief of Baghdad* (film debut) (40); war service; *The Gentle Sex* (43), *Journey Together* (45), *Call of the Blood* (47), *The Sound Barrier* (51), *Melba* (53), *Seagulls over Sorrento* (54), *The Man Who Loved Redheads* (55), *The Teckman Mystery* (55), *Safari* (56), *Island in the Sun* (56), *The Spider's Web* (61), *Candidate For Murder* (64), etc.

K

KADAR, JAN (1918–   ). Czech director who invariably works with writer ELMAR KLOS (1920–   ). *Kidnap* (56), *Death Is Called Engelchen* (58), *The Accused* (64), *A Shop on the High Street* (64), *The Angel Levine* (US) (69), etc.

KALMUS, HERBERT T. (1881–1963). American pioneer photographic expert, later president of Technicolor. His wife NATALIE KALMUS (1892–1965) was adviser on all Technicolor films from 1933.

KAMERADSCHAFT (Germany 1931). G. W. Pabst's most acclaimed film shows how a mine disaster in a French town near the German border breaks down the barriers of hatred between the two nations. The original version had a cynical ending. Photographed by Fritz Arno Wagner.

KANE, JOSEPH (1897–   ). American director since 1935, mainly of competent but unambitious Republic Westerns. *The Man from Music Mountain* (38), *The Man from Cheyenne* (42), *Flame of the Barbary Coast* (44), *The Cheaters* (45), *The Plainsman and the Lady* (46), *The Plunderers* (also produced) (48), *California Passage* (also produced) (50), *Hoodlum Empire* (also produced) *Jubilee Trail* (also produced) (53), *Spoilers of the Forest* (also produced) (57), many others. Some TV work.

KANIN, GARSON (1912–   ). American writer-producer-director with wide Broadway experience before *The Great Man Votes* (39), *Bachelor Mother* (39), *Tom, Dick and Harry* (40), etc. Married Ruth Gordon, and with her later wrote *A Double Life* (48), *Adam's Rib* (49), *Pat and Mike* (51), *Born Yesterday* (51), etc. Recently: creator-producer of TV series *Mr Broadway*. 1969: wrote and directed *Where It's At, Some Kind of Nut.*

KANIN, MICHAEL (1910–   ). American writer bro. of Garson Kanin; often works with his wife Fay. *Anne of Windy Poplars* (40), *Woman of the Year* (42), *The Cross of Lorraine* (44), *Centennial Summer* (46), *A Double Life* (47), *Rhapsody* (54), *The Opposite Sex* (56), etc.

KANN, LILY (c. 1898–   ). German character actress, long in England. *The Flemish Farm* (43), *Latin Quarter* (45), *Mrs Fitzherbert* (47), *A Tale of Five Cities* (51), *Betrayed* (US) (54), *A Kid for Two Farthings* (55), *No Trees in the Street* (59), many others.

KANTER, HAL (1918–). American writer-director with TV background. *I Married a Woman* (d) (55), *Loving You* (w, d) (56), *Once Upon a Horse* (w, d) (58), *Pocketful of Miracles* (co-w) (61), *Move Over Darling* (w) (63), *Dear Brigitte* (w) (65), etc.

KANTER, JAY (1927–). American executive responsible for Universal's somewhat unhappy European production programme 1965–69, when a number of erratic talents were apparently allowed to do exactly as they liked.

KANTOR, MACKINLAY (1904–). American popular writer full of sentiment and patriotism. Films of his works include *The Voice of Bugle Ann* (37), *Happy Land* (43), *The Best Years of Our Lives* (46), *The Romance of Rosy Ridge* (47) and *Follow Me Boys* (66).

KAPER, BRONISLAU (1902–). Polish composer now resident in US. Scores include *Gaslight* (*The Murder in Thornton Square*) (44), *Green Dolphin Street* (47), *The Forsyte Saga* (49), *The Red Badge of Courage* (51), *Lili* (AA) (53), *Them* (54), *The Swan* (56), *The Brothers Karamazov* (58), *Butterfield 8* (61), *Mutiny on the Bounty* (62), *Kisses for My President* (64), *Lord Jim* (64), *Tobruk* (66), *A Flea in Her Ear* (68), etc.

KARINA, ANNA (1940–) (Hanne Karin Beyer). Danish leading lady, mostly in French films, especially those of Jean-Luc Godard. *She'll Have To Go* (GB) (61), *Une Femme Est une Femme* (61), *Vivre Sa Vie* (62), *Le Petit Soldat* (63), *Bande à Part* (64), *Alphaville* (65), *Made in USA* (66), *The Magus* (68), *Before Winter Comes* (68), *Laughter in the Dark* (69), *Justine* (69), etc.

KARLIN, MIRIAM (1925–) (M. Samuels). Rasping-voiced British revue comedienne and character actress. Films include *The Deep Blue Sea* (55), *The Entertainer* (59), *On the Fiddle* (61), *The Small World of Sammy Lee* (63), *Heavens Above* (63), *The Bargee* (64), *Ladies Who Do* (64), etc.

KARLOFF, BORIS (1887–1969) (William Pratt). British character actor, on stage from 1910, films from 1919, mainly in US. Achieved world fame as the monster in *Frankenstein* (31), and became typed in horrific parts despite his gentle, cultured voice. *The Old Dark House* (32), *The Mask of Fu Manchu* (32), *Scarface* (32), *The Ghoul* (33), *The House of Rothschild* (34), *The Lost Patrol* (34), *The Black Cat* (34), *Bride of Frankenstein* (35), *The Raven* (35), *The Black Room* (35), *The Walking Dead* (36), *Mr Wong, Detective* (38), *The Man They Could Not Hang* (39), *Son of Frankenstein* (39), *Tower of London* (39), *Before I Hang* (40), *Behind the Door* (41), *Black Friday* (41), *The Devil Commands* (41), *The Boogie Man Will Get You* (42), *The Climax* (44), *The Body Snatcher* (45), *Isle of the Dead* (45), *House of Frankenstein* (45), *Bedlam* (46), *The Secret Life of Walter Mitty* (47), *Abbott and*

533

Costello Meet the Killer (49), *The Strange Door* (51), *The Black Castle* (52), *Abbott and Costello Meet Dr Jekyll and Mr Hyde* (53), *Sabaka* (55), *Grip of the Strangler* (57), *Frankenstein 1970* (58), *Corridors of Blood* (58), *The Raven* (62), *The Terror* (63), *A Comedy of Terrors* (64), *Black Sabbath* (64), *Monster of Terror* (66), *The Ghost in the Invisible Bikini* (66), *The Venetian Affair* (66), *The Sorcerers* (67), *Targets* (68), *Curse of the Crimson Altar* (68), many others.

KARLSON, PHIL (1908–   ). American director, in Hollywood from 1932. Mainly low-budget actioners until he suddenly gained stature in the 50s. *A Wave, a Wac and a Marine* (44), *Shanghai Cobra* (46), *Kilroy Was Here* (47), *Ladies of the Chorus* (48), *The Tomahawk Trail* (50), *Lorna Doone* (51), *The Brigand* (52), *They Rode West* (54), *Tight Spot* (55), *Five Against the House* (55), *The Phenix City Story* (55), *The Brothers Rico* (57), *Gunman's Walk* (58), *Hell to Eternity* (60), *The Secret Ways* (61), *The Young Doctors* (62), *Rampage* (63), *The Silencers* (66), *The Long Ride Home* (66), *Wrecking Crew* (68), etc.

KARNS, ROSCOE (1893–1970). American character actor, very active in the 30s, usually in hard-boiled comedy roles. *Beggars of Life* (28), *The Front Page* (30), *Undercover Man* (32), *Night After Night* (32), *It Happened One Night* (34), *Thanks for the Memory* (38), *They Drive by Night* (40), *His Butler's Sister* (43), *Will Tomorrow Ever Come* (47), *Inside Story* (48), *Onionhead* (58), many others. TV series: *Hennesey.*

KASKET, HAROLD (c. 1916–   ). British character actor of mixed descent, originally stage impressionist. *Hotel Sahara* (51), *Moulin Rouge* (53), *Interpol* (57), *Sands of the Desert* (60), *Arabesque* (66), etc.

KASTNER, ELLIOTT (1930–   ). American producer, former literary agent. *Bus Riley's Back in Town* (65), *Harper (The Moving Target)* (66), *Kaleidoscope* (66), *The Night of the Following Day* (68), *Where Eagles Dare* (68), *The Walking Stick* (69), etc.

KASTNER, PETER (1944–   ). Canadian actor who made a corner in frustrated adolescents. *Nobody Waved Goodbye* (Can.) (65), *You're a Big Boy Now* (US) (66). TV series: *The Ugliest Girl in Town* (68).

KASZNAR, KURT (1913–   ). Chubby Austrian character actor, in US from 1936. *The Light Touch* (debut) (51), *The Happy Time* (52), *Lili* (53), *Sombrero* (53), *My Sister Eileen* (55), *Anything Goes* (56), *A Farewell to Arms* (58), *For the First Time* (59), *Casino Royale* (66), *The King's Pirate* (67), *The Ambushers* (67), etc. Also on stage. TV series: *Land of the Giants* (68–69).

KATCH, KURT (1896–1958) (Isser Kac). Bald Polish character actor, in Hollywood from 1942. Memorable in *Ali Baba and the Forty*

Thieves (43), *The Mask of Dimitrios* (44); subsequent roles mainly routine. *Salome Where She Danced* (45), *The Mummy's Curse* (45), *Song of Love* (47), *The Secret of the Incas* (54), *Abbott and Costello Meet the Mummy* (55), *Pharaoh's Curse* (57), etc.

KATZMAN, SAM (1901–   ). American producer, chiefly of low-budget co-features including the *Jungle Jim* series, *Rock Around the Clock* (56), many others. 1965: *Get Yourself a College Girl, Harem Scarem, Girl Crazy*.

KAUFMAN, BORIS (c. 1906–   ). Polish cinematographer, in France from 1928 (with Vigo on *A Propos de Nice* [30], *Zéro de Conduite* [32], *L'Atalante* [34]). In US from 1942: *On the Waterfront* (AA) (54), *Baby Doll* (56), *Twelve Angry Men* (57), *Long Day's Journey into Night* (62), *The World of Henry Orient* (64), *The Pawnbroker* (64), *The Group* (66), *Up Tight* (68), many others.

KAUFMAN, GEORGE S. (1889–1961). American playwright who with Moss Hart wrote *Once in a Lifetime, You Can't Take It With You, The Man Who Came to Dinner* and other hits which were later filmed. Wrote and directed *The Senator Was Indiscreet* (47).

KAUFMAN, MILLARD (* –   ). American writer. *Bad Day at Black Rock* (54), *Raintree County* (57), *Never So Few* (60), *Reprieve* (also directed) (62), etc.

KAUFMANN, CHRISTINE (1944–   ). German leading lady, married to Tony Curtis. *Town without Pity* (61), *Taras Bulba* (62), *Wild and Wonderful* (64), etc.

KAUTNER, HELMUT (1908–   ). German director who had an unhappy experience in Hollywood in the 50s. *Kitty and the World Conference* (39), *Adieu Franciska* (41), *Romanze in Moll* (43), *Unter Den Brücken* (45), *In Jenen Tagen* (47), *Der Apfel Ist Ab* (48), *Epilog* (50), *The Last Bridge* (54), *Himmel Ohne Sterne* (55), *The Wonderful Years* (US) (58), *Stranger in my Arms* (US) (59), etc.

KAWALEROWICZ, JERZY (1922–   ). Polish director. *Gromada* (51), *Cien* (54), *The True End of the Great War* (57), *Pociag* (*Night Train*) (59), *Mother Jeanne of the Angels* (*The Devil and the Nun*) (60), *The Pharaoh* (64), etc.

†KAYE, DANNY (1913–   ). (David Daniel Kaminsky). American star entertainer of stage, screen and TV. After making several unpromising two-reelers in the 30s (later compiled as *The Danny Kaye Story*) he was given the big build-up by Sam Goldwyn and gained enormous popularity, though his recent films have been disappointing. *Up in Arms* (44), *Wonder Man* (45), *The Kid from Brooklyn* (46), *The Secret Life of Walter Mitty* (47), *A Song Is Born* (48), *The Inspector General* (49), *On the Riviera* (51), *Hans Christian Andersen* (52), *Knock*

on Wood (53), *White Christmas* (54), *Assignment Children* (UN short) (54), *The Court Jester* (56), *Me and the Colonel* (57), *Merry Andrew* (58), *The Five Pennies* (59), *On the Double* (62), *The Man from the Diners' Club* (63), *The Madwoman of Chaillot* (69). Special Academy Award in 1954 'for his unique talents, his service to the industry and the American people'.

KAYE, STUBBY (1918–). Rotund American comic actor who also spent some time in British plays and films. *Guys and Dolls* (55), *Lil Abner* (59), *40 Pounds of Trouble* (62), *Cat Ballou* (65), *Sweet Charity* (68), etc.

KAZAN, ELIA (1909–) (Elia Kazanjoglous). Distinguished American director of Greek/Turkish descent. In America from 1913; acted in New York's Group Theatre in the 30s, and later in several films: *Blues in the Night* (41), *City for Conquest* (41), etc. Returned to stage as director, then to Hollywood and made many cinematic, emotional 'problem pictures'. *A Tree Grows in Brooklyn* (44), *Sea of Grass* (47), *Boomerang* (47), *Gentleman's Agreement* (AA) (47), *Pinky* (49), *Panic in the Streets* (50), *A Streetcar Named Desire* (51), *Viva Zapata* (52), *Man on a Tightrope* (53), *On the Waterfront* (AA) (54), *East of Eden* (55), *Baby Doll* (56), *A Face in the Crowd* (57), *Wild River* (60), *Splendour in the Grass* (61), *America America* (*The Anatolian Smile*) (from his own novel) (63), *The Arrangement* (from his own novel) (69).

KEANE, ROBERT EMMETT (1883–). Toothbrush-moustached American character actor who played travelling salesmen and fall guys in scores of light comedies and dramas. *Men Call It Love* (31), *Boys' Town* (38), *We're in the Army Now* (40), *Tin Pan Alley* (41), *Jitterbugs* (43), *When My Baby Smiles at Me* (50), *When Gangland Strikes* (56), etc.

KEARTON, CHERRY (1871–1940). Pioneer British travel film producer whose success lasted from 1912 to the mid-30s.

KEATING, LARRY (1897–1964). American character comedian, typically cast as the cynical neighbour in TV's *Mister Ed* and *Burns and Allen* series. In radio, stage and film for many years in supporting roles. *Song of the Sarong* (45), *Come Fill the Cup* (51), *When Worlds Collide* (51), *A Lion Is in the Streets* (55), *The Buster Keaton Story* (57), etc.

KEATON, BUSTER (1895–1966) (Joseph Francis Keaton). One of America's great silent clowns, the unsmiling but game little fellow who always came out on top whatever the odds. Trained in vaudeville with family act. Did not easily survive sound, but later came back in featured roles and was gaining a fresh popularity at the time of his death. In two-reelers with Fatty Arbuckle from

1917, but soon began to shape his own material. *The Playhouse* (20), *Daydreams* (21), *Cops* (22), *Balloonatic* (23), *Our Hospitality* (23), *Sherlock Junior* (24), *The Navigator* (24), *Seven Chances* (25), *The General* (26), *Steamboat Bill Junior* (27), *The Cameraman* (28), *Hollywood Revue of 1929*, *Doughboys* (30), *Sidewalks of New York* (31), *The Passionate Plumber* (32), many two-reelers; *Hollywood Cavalcade* (39), *San Diego I Love You* (45), *God's Country* (47), *In the Good Old Summertime* (49), *Sunset Boulevard* (50), *Limelight* (52), *Huckleberry Finn* (60), *It's a Mad Mad Mad Mad World* (63), *How to Stuff a Wild Bikini* (65), *The Railrodder* (65), *Film* (65), *A Funny Thing Happened on the Way to the Forum* (66), many others. Published autobiography 1962: *My Wonderful World of Slapstick*. Special Academy Award 1959 'for his unique talents which brought immortal comedies to the screen'.

KEDROVA, LILA (c. 1918–   ). Russian-French character actress, known internationally for *Zorba the Greek* (AA) (64), *A High Wind in Jamaica* (65), *Torn Curtain* (66), *Penelope* (67), *The Kremlin Letter* (69).

KEEL, HOWARD (1919–   ) (Harold Keel). American singer and leading man, on stage in 'Oklahoma', etc. *The Small Voice* (debut) (48), *Annie Get Your Gun* (50), *Showboat* (51), *Lovely to Look At* (52), *Callaway Went Thataway* (52), *Ride Vaquero* (52), *Calamity Jane* (53), *Kiss Me Kate* (53), *Rose Marie* (54), *Seven Brides for Seven Brothers* (54), *Jupiter's Darling* (54), *Kismet* (55), *Floods of Fear* (58), *The Big Fisherman* (59), *Armoured Command* (61), *The Day of the Triffids* (62), *Waco* (66), *Red Tomahawk* (66), *The War Wagon* (67), *The Bushwackers* (67), etc.

KEELER, RUBY (1909–   ). Petite American singer-dancer, once wife of Al Jolson. Stage experience. *42nd Street* (debut) (33), *Dames* (34), *Go Into Your Dance* (36), *Mother Carey's Chickens* (38), etc.; retired 1941 after *Sweetheart of the Campus*.

KEEN, GEOFFREY (1918–   ). Incisive British character actor, son of Malcom Keen (stage actor). On stage from 1932, films from 1946. *His Excellency* (50), *Genevieve* (53), *The Long Arm* (56), *No Love for Johnnie* (61), *The Spiral Road* (62), *Live Now Pay Later* (63), *The Heroes of Telemark* (65), *Dr Zhivago* (65), *Born Free* (66), many others. Also on TV.

KEENE, RALPH (1902–63). British documentarist, in films from 1934. With Ministry of Information, British Transport, etc.; emphasis on animal studies. *Cyprus Is an Island, Crofters, Journey into Spring, Between the Tides, Winter Quarters, Under Night Streets*, etc.

KEENE, TOM (1896–1963) (also known at times as George Duryea and Richard Powers). American western star, mainly in second features of the 30s and 40s. *Golden Girl* (28), *The Dude Wrangler* (30), *Saddle Buster* (32), *Our Daily Bread* (33), *Where the Trails Divide* (37), *Dynamite Cargo* (41), *Up in Arms* (44), *If You Knew Susie* (48), *Red Planet Mars* (52), *Plan 9 from Outer Space* (56), many others.

KEIGHLEY, WILLIAM (1889–   ). American director with stage experience: made many highly polished entertainments for Warners. *The Match King* (32), *Big-Hearted Herbert* (33), *Babbitt* (34), *G-Men* (35), *Green Pastures* (36), *Bullets or Ballots* (36), *The Prince and the Pauper* (37), *The Adventures of Robin Hood* (co-d) (38), *Brother Rat* (39), *The Fighting 69th* (40), *Torrid Zone* (40), *No Time for Comedy* (40), *The Man Who Came to Dinner* (41), *George Washington Slept Here* (42), *The Bride Came C.O.D.* (42), *The Street with No Name* (48), *Close to My Heart* (51), *The Master of Ballantrae* (53), many others.

KEIR, ANDREW (c. 1910–   ). Scottish character actor, usually in stern roles. *The Lady Craved Excitement* (50), *The Brave Don't Cry* (52), *The Maggie* (54), *Heart of a Child* (57), *Pirates of Blood River* (60), *Dracula, Prince of Darkness* (65), *Daleks Invasion Earth* (66), *The Viking Queen* (67), *Quatermass and the Pit* (67), *The Royal Hunt of the Sun* (69), etc.

KEITH, BRIAN (1921–   ) (Robert Keith Jnr). American actor of easy-going types, understanding fathers and occasional villains. *Arrowhead* (debut) (52), *Alaska Seas* (53), *The Violent Men* (54), *Five Against the House* (55), *Storm Centre* (56), *Run of the Arrow* (57), *Sierra Baron* (58), *The Young Philadelphians* (59), *The Deadly Companions* (61), *The Parent Trap* (61), *Moon Pilot* (62), *Savage Sam* (63), *Those Calloways* (65), *The Hallelujah Trail* (65), *Nevada Smith* (66), *The Russians Are Coming* (66), *Reflections in a Golden Eye* (67), *With Six You Get Eggroll* (68), *Krakatoa* (68), etc. TV series: *Crusader* (56), *The Westerner* (63), *Family Affair* (64–68).

KEITH, IAN (1899–1960) (Keith Ross). American actor, latterly in character roles. Stage experience. *Manhandled* (24), *The Divine Lady* (27), *Abraham Lincoln* (31), *The Sign of the Cross* (32), *Queen Christina* (33), *The Crusades* (35), *The Three Musketeers* (as de Rochefort) (36), *The Sea Hawk* (40), *The Chinese Cat* (44), *Nightmare Alley* (48), *The Black Shield of Falworth* (54), *Prince of Players* (55), *The Ten Commandments* (as Rameses I) (56), many others.

KEITH, ROBERT (1896–1966). American character actor with concert and stage experience. Spent some time as a Hollywood writer in the 30s but did not act in films until the late 40s. *Boomerang* (47), *My Foolish Heart* (49), *Fourteen Hours* (51), *I Want You* (51), *Young at Heart* (54), *Guys and Dolls* (55), *Tempest* (58), *Cimarron* (61), etc.

KELLAWAY, CECIL (1893–   ). British character actor who was born in South Africa and spent many years acting in Australia; came to Hollywood in 1939 and became an endearing exponent of roguish benevolence. *Wuthering Heights* (39), *Intermezzo* (39), *I Married a Witch* (42), *My Heart Belongs to Daddy* (42), *The Good Fellows* (leading role) (43), *Practically Yours* (44), *Frenchman's Creek* (44), *Love Letters* (45), *Kitty* (as Gainsborough) (45), *Monsieur Beaucaire* (46), *The Postman Always Rings Twice* (46), *Unconquered* (47), *Portrait of Jennie* (48), *The Luck of the Irish* (as a leprechaun) (48), *Joan of Arc* (48), *Harvey* (50), *The Beast from 20,000 Fathoms* (53), *The Female on the Beach* (55), *The Shaggy Dog* (59), *The Cardinal* (63), *Hush Hush, Sweet Charlotte* (64), *Spinout (California Holiday)* (66), *Fitzwilly* (67), *Guess Who's Coming to Dinner* (67), many others.

KELLER, HARRY (1913–   ). American director. *Blonde Bandit* (49), *Rose of Cimarron* (52), *The Unguarded Moment* (56), *The Female Animal* (57), *Quantez* (58), *Voice in the Mirror* (58), *Six Black Horses* (61), *Tammy and the Doctor* (63), *Kitten with a Whip* (65), *In Enemy Country* (also produced) (68), etc.

KELLERMAN, ANNETTE (1888–   ). Australian dancer and swimming star who pioneered the one-piece bathing suit and appeared in two silent Hollywood movies, *Neptune's Daughter* (14) and *Daughter of the Gods* (16). Esther Williams played her in a biopic, *Million Dollar Mermaid* (52).

KELLEY, DE FORREST (1920–   ). American general purpose actor. *Fear in the Night* (leading role) (47), *Duke of Chicago* (50), *House of Bamboo* (55), *Gunfight* (57), *Warlock* (59), *Johnny Reno* (66), etc.

KELLINO, ROY (1912–1956). British director, former cinematographer (*The Phantom Light* [37], *The Last Adventurers* [38], *Johnny Frenchman* [45], etc.). Formed his own company, with his ex-wife Pamela Kellino and her then-husband James Mason, to make *I Met A Murderer* (38): later direction includes *Guilt is My Shadow* (49), *Lady Possessed* (co-d) (51), *Charade* (53), *The Silken Affair* (55).

KELLINO, PAMELA (1916–   ) (Pamela Ostrer). British actress, married first to Roy Kellino and then to James Mason. Now columnist and TV personality. *Jew Suss* (34), *I Met A Murderer* (38), *They Were Sisters* (45), *The Upturned Glass* (47), *Lady Possessed* (51), etc.

†KELLY, GENE (1912–   ). American actor-dancer-choreographer, one of Hollywood's great personalities in the 40s and 50s; danced on Broadway stage before coming to Hollywood. *For Me and My Gal* (debut) (42), *Pilot Number Five* (42), *Du Barry Was a Lady* (43), *Thousands Cheer* (43), *The Cross of Lorraine* (43), *Cover Girl* (44), *Christmas Holiday* (44), *Ziegfeld Follies* (44), *Anchors Aweigh* (45), *Living in a Big Way* (46), *The Pirate* (47), *The Three Musketeers* (48), *Words and Music* (48), *Take Me Out to the Ball Game* (49), *Black Hand* (49), *On the Town* (also co-d) (49), *Summer Stock* (50), *An American in Paris* (51), *Singing in the Rain* (also co-d) (52), *It's a Big Country*

Kelly, Grace

(53), *The Devil Makes Three* (53), *Brigadoon* (54), *Crest of the Wave* (*Seagulls over Sorrento*) (54), *It's Always Fair Weather* (also co-d) (55), *Invitation to the Dance* (also directed) (56), *The Happy Road* (also produced and directed) (56), *Les Girls* (57), *Marjorie Morningstar* (58), *The Tunnel of Love* (directed only) (58), *Inherit the Wind* (60), *Gigot* (directed only) (63), *What a Way To Go* (64), *The Young Girls of Rochefort* (67), *A Guide for the Married Man* (directed only) (67), *Hello Dolly* (directed only) (69), *The Cheyenne Social Club* (produced and directed) (70). TV series: *Going My Way* (62). Special Academy Award 1951 'in appreciation of his versatility as an actor, singer, director and dancer, and specially for his brilliant achievements in the art of choreography on film'.

KELLY, GRACE (1928–   ). American leading lady of 'iceberg' beauty who retired from the screen to become Princess of Monaco. *Fourteen Hours* (debut) (51), *High Noon* (52), *Dial M for Murder* (54), *Rear Window* (54), *The Country Girl* (AA) (55), *To Catch a Thief* (55), *The Swan* (56), *High Society* (56), etc.

KELLY, JACK (1927–   ). Irish-American actor who usually plays wryly humorous roles; notably in TV series *King's Row* and *Maverick*. *Where Danger Lives* (51), *Drive a Crooked Road* (54), *To Hell and Back* (56), *Hong Kong Affair* (58), *Love and Kisses* (65), *Young Billy Young* (69), etc. Brother of Nancy Kelly.

KELLY, JUDY (1913–   ). Australian leading lady, in British films. *His Night Out* (35), *Make Up* (37), *At the Villa Rose* (40), *Tomorrow We Live* (43), *The Butler's Dilemma* (43), *Dead of Night* (45), *Warning to Wantons* (last film to date) (48), etc.

KELLY, NANCY (1921–   ). American leading lady, former child model; in films 1938–47, then on Broadway stage. *Submarine Patrol* (38), *Tailspin* (38), *Jesse James* (39), *Stanley and Livingstone* (39), *Parachute Battalion* (41), *Tornado* (43), *Show Business* (44), *Woman in Bondage* (45), *Betrayal from the East* (45), *Friendly Enemies* (47), etc. Only recent films: *The Bad Seed* (56), *Crowded Paradise* (56).

KELLY, PATSY (1910–   ). Pert, homely, wisecracking American comedienne, familiar co-star of 30s farcical comedies, especially with Thelma Todd. Recently in cameo roles: *The Crowded Sky* (60), *Please Don't Eat the Daisies* (60), *The Ghost in the Invisible Bikini* (66), *Rosemary's Baby* (68). TV series: *Valentine's Day* (64).

KELLY, PAUL (1899–1956). Wiry American leading man of the 30s, Broadway star of the 50s; once known as 'king of the Bs'. *The New Klondike* (26), *Broadway through a Keyhole* (33), *The Silk Hat Kid* (35), *Parole Racket* (37), *The Missing Quest* (39), *Adventure in Sahara* (41), *Mystery Ship* (42), *Faces in the Fog* (44), *Spoilers of the North* (47), *Crossfire* (47), *Treason* (50), *Split Second* (52), *Storm Centre* (56), many others.

KELSALL, MOULTRIE (c. 1901–   ). Scottish character actor of stage and screen. *Landfall* (49), *The Lavender Hill Mob* (51), *The Master of Ballantrae* (53), *The Maggie* (54), *The Man Who Never Was* (56), *Violent Playground* (58), *The Battle of the Sexes* (60), etc.

KELTON, PERT (1907–1968). American character comedienne, seen occasionally in wisecracking roles, from *Sally* (29) to *Billy Bright* (69). Best part, perhaps, in *The Music Man* (62).

KEMBLE-COOPER, VIOLET (1889–1961). British stage actress, in Hollywood in the 30s. *Our Betters* (33), *David Copperfield* (34), *Romeo and Juliet* (36), etc.

KEMP, JEREMY (1934–   ) (Edmund Walker). British leading man who resigned from TV series *Z Cars* and has had some success in films: *Dr Terror's House of Horrors* (65), *Operation Crossbow* (65), *Cast A Giant Shadow* (66), *The Blue Max* (66), *Assignment K* (67), *The Strange Affair* (68), *Darling Lili* (69), *The Games* (69), etc.

KEMPSON, RACHEL (1910–   ). British actress, wife of Michael Redgrave. Rare films include *The Captive Heart* (46), *A Woman's Vengeance* (US) (48), *Georgy Girl* (66), *The Jokers* (66).

KEMP-WELCH, JOAN (1906–   ). British character actress who used to play shy girls and spinsters on stage and screen. *Once a Thief* (35), *The Girl in the Taxi* (37), *Busman's Honeymoon* (40), *Pimpernel Smith* (41), *Jeannie* (41) (last film to date). During the 50s emerged as a TV director of distinction.

KENDALL, SUZY (c. 1943–   ) (Frieda Harrison). British leading lady. *Circus of Fear* (67), *To Sir With Love* (67), *Penthouse* (67), *Up the Junction* (68), *Thirty is a Dangerous Age, Cynthia* (68), *The Betrayal* (69), etc.

KENDALL, HENRY (1897–1962). British entertainer, immaculate star of London revues in 30s and 40s. On stage from 1914: occasional films include *French Leave* (debut) (30), *Rich and Strange* (32), *King of the Ritz* (33), *Death at Broadcasting House* (34), *The Amazing Quest of Ernest Bliss* (36), *School for Husbands* (37), *The Butler's Dilemma* (43), *Acacia Avenue* (45), *The Voice of Merrill* (52), *An Alligator Named Daisy* (55), etc.

KENDALL, KAY (1927–1959). Vivacious British leading lady with brief stage experience before film success in *Genevieve* (53), *Doctor in the House* (53), *The Constant Husband* (55), *The Adventures of Quentin Durward* (56), *Les Girls* (57), *The Reluctant Debutante* (58), *Once More with Feeling* (59), etc.

KENNAWAY, JAMES (1928–1968). British novelist and screenwriter. *Tunes of Glory* (61), *The Mind Benders* (63), *The Shoes of the Fisherman* (co-w) (68), *The Battle of Britain* (co-w) (69), etc.

KENNEDY, ARTHUR (1914–   ). American leading actor of stage and screen: can play sincere or cynical. *Knockout* (41), *Strange Alibi* (41), *Devotion* (as Branwell Bronte) (43), *The Window* (48), *Champion* (49), *The Glass Menagerie* (50), *Impulse* (GB) (51), *Bright Victory* (51), *Rancho Notorious* (52), *Bend of the River* (52), *The Lusty Men* (52), *The Man from Laramie* (53), *The Rawhide Years* (54), *Trial* (55), *The Desperate Hours* (55), *Peyton Place* (57), *Some Came Running* (58), *Claudelle Inglish* (61), *Barabbas* (62), *Lawrence of Arabia* (62), *Cheyenne Autumn* (64), *Vendetta* (65), *Joy in the Morning* (65), *Nevada Smith* (66), *Fantastic Voyage* (66), *Anzio* (68), *Dead or Alive* (68), *Hail Hero* (69), etc. Much on TV.

KENNEDY, BURT (c. 1923–   ). American director, originally radio writer (from 1947), later TV writer-director (*Combat* series, etc.) *The Canadians* (w, d) (61), *Mail Order Bride* (w, d) (63), *The Rounders* (w, d) (64), *The Money Trap* (d) (65), *Return of the Seven* (66), *Welcome to Hard Times* (w, d) (67), *The War Wagon* (67), *Support Your Local Sheriff* (69), *Young Billy Young* (69), *The Good Guys and the Bad Guys* (69), *The Dubious Patriots* (70), etc.

KENNEDY, DOUGLAS (1915–   ) (formerly known as Keith Douglas). American leading man of action features, later character actor. *The Way of All Flesh* (40), *Women without Names* (41), war service, *Dark Passage* (47), *Chain Gang* (50), *I Was an American Spy* (51), *Ride the Man Down* (53), *Bomba and the Lion Hunters* (54), *The Amazing Transparent Man* (59), many others. TV series: *Steve Donovan Western Marshal*, etc.

KENNEDY, EDGAR (1890–1948). Bald, explosive American comedian with vaudeville experience. A former Keystone Kop, he continued in demand for supporting roles and also starred in innumerable domestic comedy two-reelers, his exasperated gestures being familiar the world over. *Tillie's Punctured Romance* (15), *The Leather Pushers* (22), *Midnight Patrol* (31), *Duck Soup* (33), *King Kelly of the USA* (34), *Captain Tugboat Annie* (46), *Unfaithfully Yours* (48), scores of others. His brother TOM KENNEDY (1885–1965), also a Keystone Kop, became a professional wrestler, and later played bit parts in movies and TV right up to his death.

KENNEDY, GEORGE (1925–   ). American character actor, usually seen as menace but graduating to sympathetic roles. Former TV producer. *Little Shepherd of Kingdom Come* (debut) (60), *Lonely Are the Brave* (62), *The Man from the Diner's Club* (63), *Charade* (63), *Strait-jacket* (64), *Mirage* (65), *Shenandoah* (65), *The Flight of the Phoenix* (65), *Hurry Sundown* (67), *The Dirty Dozen* (67), *Cool Hand Luke* (AA) (67), *Bandolero* (68), *The Boston Strangler* (68), *Guns of the Magnificent Seven* (69), *The Good Guys and the Bad Guys* (69), *Tick Tick Tick* (70), etc.

KENNEY, JAMES (1930–   ). British juvenile actor of the late 40s, son of vaudeville comedian Horace Kenney. *Circus Boy* (47), *Captain Horatio Hornblower* (50), *The Gentle Gunman* (52), *Cosh Boy* (53), *The Sea Shall Not Have Them* (54), *The Gelignite Gang* (56), *Son of a Stranger* (58), etc.

KENT, JEAN (1921–   ) (Joan Summerfield). British leading lady of the 40s, formerly in the Windmill chorus. *It's That Man Again* (debut) (43), *Fanny by Gaslight* (44), *Waterloo Road* (45), *The Rake's Progress* (45), *Caravan* (46), *Good Time Girl* (48), *Trottie True* (49), *The Woman in Question* (50), *The Browning Version* (52), *Please Turn Over* (60), etc. In TV plays, also series *Sir Francis Drake* (as Queen Elizabeth).

KENTON, ERLE C. (1896–   ). American director, from 1914. *Small Town Idol* (20), *The Leather Pushers* (22), *Street of Illusion* (25), *Father and Son* (27), *Isle of Lost Souls* (32), *Remedy for Riches* (39), *Petticoat Politics* (41), *North to the Klondike* (41), *Who Done It?* (42), *Frisco Lil* (42), *House of Frankenstein* (45), *House of Dracula* (45), *Should Parents Tell?* (49), *Killer with a Label* (50), etc.

KENYON, DORIS (1897–   ). American silent-screen leading lady who was married to Milton Sills. *The Pawn of Fate* (16), *A Girl's Folly* (17), *The Hidden Hand* (18), *The Ruling Passion* (22), *Monsieur Beaucaire* (24), *Blonde Saint* (26), *The Hawk's Nest* (28), *Alexander Hamilton* (31), *Voltaire* (33), *Counsellor at Law* (33), *The Man in the Iron Mask* (39), etc.

KERIMA (1925–   ). Algerian actress chosen for *An Outcast of the Islands* (51), later seen in *La Lupa* (52), *The Quiet American* (58), etc.

LA KERMESSE HEROIQUE (France 1935). Also known as 'Carnival in Flanders', this broad comedy about the occupation by Spanish troops of a 16th-century Flemish town seemed at the time delightfully spontaneous and had world-wide success unprecedented for a French film since sound. Written by Charles Spaak, directed by Jacques Feyder, photographed by Harry Stradling, with Françoise Rosay and Louis Jouvet.

KERN, JAMES V. (1909–1966). American director, former lawyer. *The Doughgirls* (w, d) (44), *Never Say Goodbye* (w, d) (46), *Stallion Road* (47), *April Showers* (48), *Two Tickets to Broadway* (52), etc.; then into TV.

KERN, JEROME (1885–1945). Celebrated American songwriter. Films using his music include *Roberta* (33), *Showboat* (36 and 51), *Swing Time* (36), *Cover Girl* (44), *Centennial Summer* (46), *Till the Clouds Roll By* (46). His Academy Award songs are 'The Way You Look Tonight' and 'The Last Time I Saw Paris'.

Kerr, Deborah

†KERR, DEBORAH (1921–   ) (Deborah Kerr-Trimmer). British leading lady usually cast in well-bred roles. On stage from 1938. *Major Barbara* (debut) (40), *Love on the Dole* (41), *Penn of Pennsylvania* (41), *Hatter's Castle* (41), *The Day Will Dawn* (42), *The Life and Death of Colonel Blimp* (43), *Perfect Strangers* (45), *I See a Dark Stranger* (45), *Black Narcissus* (46), then to Hollywood: *The Hucksters* (47), *If Winter Comes* (48), *Edward My Son* (49), *Please Believe Me* (49), *King Solomon's Mines* (50), *Quo Vadis* (51), *Thunder in the East* (51), *The Prisoner of Zenda* (52), *Dream Wife* (52), *Julius Caesar* (53), *From Here to Eternity* (53), *Young Bess* (53), *The End of the Affair* (55), *The King and I* (56), *The Proud and Profane* (56), *Tea and Sympathy* (56), *Heaven Knows Mr Alison* (56), *An Affair to Remember* (57), *Separate Tables* (58), *Bonjour Tristesse* (58), *Count Your Blessings* (59), *Beloved Infidel* (59), *The Sundowners* (60), *The Grass is Greener* (61), *The Innocents* (61), *The Naked Edge* (61), *The Chalk Garden* (63), *The Night of the Iguana* (64), *Marriage on the Rocks* (65), *Eye of the Devil* (66), *Casino Royale* (67), *Prudence and the Pill* (68), *The Gypsy Moths* (69), *The Arrangement* (69).

KERR, FREDERICK (1858–c. 1933) (F. Keen). British character actor of stage and, latterly, American screen; delightful as slightly doddering old man. *The Honour of the Family* (27), *Raffles* (29), *The Devil to Pay* (30), *Frankenstein* (as the old baron) (31), *Waterloo Bridge* (31), *The Midshipman* (32), *The Man from Toronto* (33), etc.

KERR, JOHN (1931–   ). American leading man, on Broadway in *Tea and Sympathy*, went to Hollywood for film version (56); also *South Pacific* (58), *The Pit and the Pendulum* (61), etc.

KERRIGAN, J. M. (1885–1965). Irish character actor who went with the Abbey players to Hollywood in 1935, and stayed there. *Little Old New York* (23), *Song of My Heart* (30), *The Informer* (35), *Laughing Irish Eyes* (36), *Little Orphan Annie* (39), *Captains of the Clouds* (42), *Black Beauty* (46), *The Wild North* (52), *The Fastest Gun Alive* (56), many others.

KERRIGAN, J. WARREN (1880–1947). American actor of the silent screen. *Samson* (13), *Landon's Legacy* (16), *A Man's Man* (18), *The Covered Wagon* (23), *Captain Blood* (24), etc. Played small roles in a few talkies.

KERRY, NORMAN (1889–1956) (Arnold Kaiser). American actor of the silent screen. *The Black Butterfly* (16), *Merry Go Round* (23), *The Hunchback of Notre Dame* (23), *Phantom of the Opera* (26), *The Unknown* (28), *Air Eagles* (last film) (31), many others.

KERSHNER, IRWIN (1923–   ). American director, formerly of documentaries. *Stakeout on Dope Street* (58), *The Hoodlum Priest* (61), *The Luck of Ginger Coffey* (64), *A Fine Madness* (66), *The Flim Flam Man* (67), etc.

THE KETTLES (MA and PA). Hillbilly couple played in *The Egg and I* (47), and in a subsequent long-running series of comedy second features, by Marjorie Main and Percy Kilbride. Highly successful in US, less so in Britain.

KEY LARGO (US 1948). Maxwell Anderson's preachy melodrama about gangsters hiding out in a remote Florida hotel was obviously intended to say something about the post-war human condition, and borrowed quite a bit from Sherwood's *The Petrified Forest*. But the film is remembered chiefly as a display of acting pyrotechnics, with Edward G. Robinson as the relentless baddie, Humphrey Bogart as the war veteran who realized that being good is not enough, and Lauren Bacall, Lionel Barrymore and Claire Trevor (AA) as assorted relevant attitudes. John Huston wrote (with Richard Brooks) and directed.

KEYES, EVELYN (1919–). American leading lady of 40s, originally dancer. *The Buccaneer* (debut) (38), *Gone with the Wind* (39), *Before I Hang* (40), *The Face behind the Mask* (41), *Here Comes Mr Jordan* (41), *Ladies in Retirement* (41), *Flight Lieutenant* (42), *The Desperadoes* (43), *Nine Girls* (44), *A Thousand and One Nights* (44), *The Jolson Story* (46), *Renegades* (46), *Johnny O'clock* (46), *The Mating of Millie* (46), *Enchantment* (47), *Mrs Mike* (48), *House of Settlement* (49), *The Killer That Stalked New York* (50), *Smugglers' Island* (51), *The Prowler* (51), *Rough Shoot* (GB) (52), *The Seven Year Itch* (54), etc.; since retired.

THE KEYSTONE KOPS. A troupe of slapstick comedians led by Ford Sterling who from 1912–20 under the inspiration of Mack Sennett at Keystone Studios, made innumerable violent comedies full of wild chases and trick effects. *Abbott and Costello Meet the Keystone Kops* (55) was a somewhat poor tribute.

KIBBEE, GUY (1882–1956). Bald-headed American character comedian, usually in flustered, shifty or genial roles. 25 years' stage experience before films. *Stolen Heaven* (debut) (31), *City Streets* (32), *Forty-second Street* (33), *Dames* (34), *Captain January* (35), *Mr Smith Goes to Washington* (39), *Chad Hanna* (41), *The Power of the Press* (43), *The Horn Blows at Midnight* (45), *Gentleman Joe Palooka* (47), *Fort Apache* (48), *Three Godfathers* (49), many others; also starred in the *Scattergood Baines* series in the early 40s.

KIBBEE, ROLAND (1914–). American radio, TV and screenwriter. *A Night in Casablanca* (45), *Angel on My Shoulder* (46), *Vera Cruz* (54), *Top Secret Affair* (57), *The Appaloosa* (*Southwest to Sonora*) (66), etc.

THE KID (US 1920). Chaplin's first feature-length film and one of his most effective, with young Jackie Coogan as his partner in crime in a slum-set comedy.

T

KID GALAHAD (US 1937). Thought at the time to be one of the best of boxing dramas, this was directed by Michael Curtiz, starred Edward G. Robinson and Bette Davis, and introduced Wayne Morris. It was remade in a disguised form as *The Wagons Roll at Night* (41), with Humphrey Bogart; then it turned up again in 1962 as an Elvis Presley vehicle, directed by Phil Karlson.

KIDD, MICHAEL (1919–   ). American dancer who appeared as co-star in *It's Always Fair Weather* (54). Choreographed *Where's Charley* (52), *Band Wagon* (53), *Seven Brides for Seven Brothers* (54), *Guys and Dolls* (55), *Merry Andrew* (also directed) (58), *Hello Dolly* (69), etc.

kidnapping has been the subject of a great number of films; apart from the various versions of Robert Louis Stevenson's *Kidnapped*, examples include *Nancy Steele is Missing, No Orchids for Miss Blandish, Ransom, The Kidnappers, A Cry in the Night, Cry Terror, Tomorrow at Ten, High and Low, Seance on a Wet Afternoon, The Collector, The Happening, Bunny Lake is Missing, Bonnie and Clyde* and *The Night of the Following Day.*

KIEPURA, JAN (1902–1966). Polish operatic tenor whose film appearances include *Farewell to Love* (GB) (30), *My Song for You* (GB) (31), *Be Mine Tonight* (GB) (32), *Give Us This Night* (US) (36), *Her Wonderful Lie* (It.) (50).

KILBRIDE, PERCY (1888–1964). American character actor of wily hayseed roles. On stage for many years before film debut in *George Washington Slept Here* (42). Subsequently in *Knickerbocker Holiday* (44), *She Wouldn't Say Yes* (45), *The Well-Groomed Bride* (45), etc.; then *The Egg and I* (47) set him off on the *Ma and Pa Kettle* series, of which he appeared in seven before retiring.

KILBURN, TERRY (c. 1927–   ). British boy actor of the 30s; never quite made it as an adult. *A Christmas Carol* (38), *The Boy from Barnardo's* (38), *Sweethearts* (39), *Goodbye Mr Chips* (as three generations of Colley) (39), *The Swiss Family Robinson* (40), *A Yank at Eton* (42), *National Velvet* (45), *Bulldog Drummond at Bay* (47), *Only the Valiant* (51), *The Fiend without a Face* (58), etc.

DR KILDARE. Max Brand's novels about a young intern were first filmed in 1938 with Joel McCrea in the leading role of a film called *Interns Can't Take Money*. In 1939 MGM made *Young Dr Kildare* starring Lew Ayres, the first of a popular series of nine films, with Lionel Barrymore as crusty old Dr Gillespie. In 1943 Ayres gave up his role and six films were made starring Barrymore only, with various interns including Van Johnson and Philip Dorn. No movies about Blair Hospital have been made since 1947, but in 1960 MGM revived the characters in a TV series starring Richard Chamberlain and Raymond Massey: it ran five years.

KILEY, RICHARD (1922–   ). American general purpose actor with stage experience: has latterly become a Broadway musical star. *The Mob* (51), *The Sniper* (52), *Pick Up on South Street* (52), *The Blackboard Jungle* (55), *The Phoenix City Story* (56), *Spanish Affair* (58), *Pendulum* (69), etc.

KILIAN, VICTOR (1891–   ). American character actor, usually as suspicious or downright villainous characters. *Air Hawks* (35), *Seventh Heaven* (36), *Dr Cyclops* (39), *Reap the Wild Wind* (42), *Spellbound* (45), *Gentleman's Agreement* (47), *The Flame and the Arrow* (50), *Tall Target* (51), etc.

THE KILLERS (US 1946). A brilliantly intricate and explosive crime melodrama elaborated by writer Anthony Veiller from a Hemingway sketch, photographed by Woody Bredell, and directed with tremendous verve by Robert Siodmak. It introduced Burt Lancaster to the screen and also had an excellent performance by Edmond O'Brien. In 1964 it was remade by Don Siegel in a version originally intended for colour TV had it not proved too violent; the star was Lee Marvin and the film had plenty of fashionable violence but little style.

KILLIAM, PAUL (1916–   ). American collector of silent movies, clips from which he introduces on TV in various series.

KIMMINS, ANTHONY (1901–1963). British writer-director-producer. In 30s adapted his own theatrical comedies for the screen (*While Parents Sleep*, etc.), and wrote scripts for George Formby. Later films include *Trouble Brewing* (d) (39), *Come On, George* (w) (39), then long break for war service; *Mine Own Executioner* (p, d) (47), *Bonnie Prince Charlie* (d) (48), *Flesh and Blood* (d) (51), *The Captain's Paradise* (w, p, d) (53), *Aunt Clara* (d) (54), *Smiley* (w, p, d) (56), *The Amorous Prawn* (w, p, d) (62).

KIND HEARTS AND CORONETS (GB 1949). Robert Hamer directed this witty comedy of Edwardian bad manners from a script by himself and John Dighton. Despite dull patches it remains supreme of its stylish kind, with Dennis Price as the most elegant of murderers and Alec Guinness as eight aristocratic victims.

A KIND OF LOVING (GB 1962). The first British film to take a genuinely realistic view of working-class life, without the sophistication of *Look Back in Anger* or the high good humour of *Saturday Night and Sunday Morning*. From a depressingly truthful novel by Stan Barstow, it had Alan Bates and June Ritchie as the young couple driven into a make-do-and-mend marriage; John Schlesinger directed as though it were a documentary.

Kinematograph Renters' Society

KINEMATOGRAPH RENTERS' SOCIETY (K.R.S.). This British organization was founded by film distributors in 1915 for their own protection and collective bargaining power, chiefly against exhibitors.

THE KING AND I: see ANNA AND THE KING OF SIAM.

KING, ANDREA (1915–) (Georgetta Barry). French-American leading lady with experience on the New York stage. *The Very Thought of You* (44), *Hotel Berlin* (45), *The Man I Love* (46), *Shadow of a Woman* (46), *The Violent Hour* (50), *The Lemon Drop Kid* (51), *Red Planet Mars* (53), *Band of Angels* (57), *Darby's Rangers* (58), *Daddy's Gone A-Hunting* (69), etc.

KING, ANITA (1889–1963). American leading lady of the silent screen, who came to fame in *The Virginian* (14).

KING ARTHUR: see ARTHUR.

KING, CHARLES (1894–1957). American leading man of the early talkies, with singing and dancing experience in the Ziegfeld Follies. *Broadway Melody* (28), *Hollywood Revue* (29), *Chasing Rainbows* (30), *Range Law* (32), *Mystery Ranch* (34), *O'Malley of the Mounted* (37), *Son of the Navy* (40), *Gunman from Bodie* (42), *Ghost Rider* (43), etc.

KING, DAVE (1929–). British comedian, much on TV but only rarely in films: *Pirates of Tortuga* (61), *Go to Blazes* (62). In *Strange Bedfellows* (65) is billed as DAVID KING.

KING, DENNIS (1897–) (Dennis Pratt). British-born opera singer who in the early 30s starred in two Hollywood films: *The Vagabond King* (30), *Fra Diavolo* (33).

KING, GEORGE (1900–1966). British producer-director, mainly of independent quota quickies and melodramas. *Too Many Crooks* (d) (31), *John Halifax Gentleman* (p) (36), *The Chinese Bungalow* (p) (39), *The Case of the Frightened Lady* (p, d) (40), *The Face at the Window* (p, d) (40), *The First of the Few* (p) (42), *Tomorrow We Live* (p, d) (42), *Candlelight in Algeria* (p, d) (44), *Gaiety George* (p, d) (45), *The Shop at Sly Corner* (p, d) (46), *Forbidden* (p, d) (48), *Eight O'clock Walk* (p) (54), etc.

KING, HENRY (1892–) (some sources say 1888). Veteran American director with experience in most branches of show business. In Hollywood, became a skilful exponent of the well-made expensive family entertainment, usually with a sentimental streak. *Who Pays* (16), *A Sporting Chance* (19), *Tol'able David* (21), *Romola* (24), *Stella Dallas* (25), *The Winning of Barbara Worth* (26), *Over the Hill* (31), *State Fair* (33), *Carolina* (34), *Marie Galante* (34), *Ramona* (36), *Seventh Heaven* (36), *Lloyds of London* (37), *In Old Chicago* (38),

Alexander's Ragtime Band (38), *Jesse James* (39), *Stanley and Livingstone* (39), *Little Old New York* (40), *Maryland* (40), *Chad Hanna* (40), *A Yank in the R.A.F.* (41), *The Black Swan* (42), *The Song of Bernadette* (43), *Wilson* (44), *A Bell for Adano* (45), *Margie* (46), *Captain from Castile* (47), *Prince of Foxes* (49), *Twelve O'clock High* (49), *The Gunfighter* (50), *I'd Climb the Highest Mountain* (51), *David and Bathsheba* (51), *Wait Till the Sun Shines Nellie* (52), *The Snows of Kilimanjaro* (52), *King of the Khyber Rifles* (53), *Love Is a Many-Splendoured Thing* (55), *Carousel* (56), *The Sun Also Rises* (57), *The Bravados* (58), *This Earth Is Mine* (59), *Tender Is the Night* (61), many others.

KING KONG (US 1932–33). The most famous of screen monsters remains after thirty years the most impressive. Willis H. O'Brien's trick photography has not been surpassed, and the film holds together as a splendid adventure for grown-up schoolboys; even the acting of Robert Armstrong and Fay Wray is delightfully of its period. Produced and directed by Merian Cooper and Ernest Schoedsack, with suitably throbbing music by Max Steiner. The production team made a further visit to the mysterious island for *Son of Kong* (34), but here the giant gorilla was played for laughs and the trick effects were skimpy. Other monsters animated by the stop-motion (qv) process include *Rodan* (a pterodactyl); *The Beast from Twenty Thousand Fathoms*, *Gorgo* and *Godzilla* (dinosaurs); *Tarantula*; *Them* (ants) and *The Black Scorpion*. There have also been several adventures of a Japanese King Kong.

KING, LOUIS (1898–1962). American director in films from 1919; brother of Henry King. Many low-budget westerns; also *Persons in Hiding* (38), *Typhoon* (40), *The Way of All Flesh* (40), *Moon over Burma* (41), *Thunderhead, Son of Flicka* (44), *Smoky* (46), *Bob, Son of Battle* (47), *Green Grass of Wyoming* (48), *Mrs Mike* (50), *The Lion and the Horse* (52), *Powder River* (53), *Dangerous Mission* (54), etc.

KING OF JAZZ (US 1930). A famous early revue directed by John Murray Anderson, produced by Carl Laemmle Jnr and photographed by Hal Mohr; with Paul Whiteman and his band and guest stars.

KING OF KINGS: see under *Christ*.

KING SOLOMON'S MINES. Rider Haggard's African adventure novel was more than adequately filmed in Britain in 1937, with Cedric Hardwicke as Allan Quartermain: the director was Robert Stevenson. MGM's 1951 remake with Stewart Granger was an unsatisfactory mishmash in which the plot thread was all but lost and there was so much spare location footage that a semi-remake, *Watusi*, used it up in 1959.

KING, WALTER WOOLF (c. 1899–   ). American actor, Broadway singing star who went to Hollywood and was gradually relegated to villain roles. *A Night at the Opera* (35), *Call It a Day* (37), *Swiss Miss* (38), *Balalaika* (39), *Marx Brothers Go West* (41), *Today I Hang* (42), *Tonight We Sing* (53), *Kathy 'O* (58), etc. Makes TV appearances in *Perry Mason*, etc.

KINGSFORD, WALTER (1882–1959). British character actor, in Hollywood from the 30s after long stage experience; usually played kindly professional men. Was Dr Carew in the *Kildare* series; also in *The Mystery of Edwin Drood* (35), *Captains Courageous* (37), *Algiers* (38), *Kitty Foyle* (40), *My Favourite Blonde* (42), *The Velvet Touch* (49), *Loose in London* (53), *Merry Andrew* (58), many others.

KINGSLEY, DOROTHY (c. 1908–   ). American scenarist, former radio writer for Bob Hope. *Neptune's Daughter* (49), *When In Rome* (52), *Kiss Me Kate* (53), *Seven Brides For Seven Brothers* (54), *Pal Joey* (57), *Can Can* (59), *Pepe* (60), *Half a Sixpence* (67), *Valley of the Dolls* (67), etc. Created TV series *Bracken's World* (69).

KINGSLEY, SIDNEY (1906–   ). American playwright. Works filmed include *Men in White* (35), *Dead End* (37), *Detective Story* (51).

Kings and Queens, of England at least, have been lovingly if not very accurately chronicled in the cinema. We still await an epic of the Norman Conquest, but in 1925 Phyllis Neilson-Terry went even further back to play *Boadicaea*. Henry II was a protagonist of *Becket* and *The Lion in Winter*. Richard I (Lionheart) was a shadowy figure in adventure films from *Robin Hood* to *King Richard and the Crusaders*, and John just as frequently was the villain of the piece. Edward IV made an appearance in *Tower of London* and *Richard III*, in each case as a pawn in the hands of Crookback. Henry IV is in *Chimes at Midnight*; Olivier played *Henry V*; Henry VIII is inseparably connected with Charles Laughton, who played him twice, and now Robert Shaw (*A Man for All Seasons*); Elizabeth I with Bette Davis and Florence Eldridge. *Mary of Scotland*, in film terms, was Katharine Hepburn. The early Stuarts were a dour lot, but Charles I appears in *Cromwell*; Charles II, the merry monarch, was impersonated by several actors from Cedric Hardwicke to George Sanders. The Hanoverians made little cinematic impact until Prinny, the Regent, came into view; he has been played notably by Cecil Parker and Peter Ustinov. Victoria to most people will always look like Anna Neagle; others who have played her on film include Fay Compton and Irene Dunne. And with her, for the moment, the record stops.

Foreign monarchs who have been notably filmed include Catherine the Great of Russia (Marlene Dietrich, Elizabeth Bergner, Tallulah Bankhead, Bette Davis), Peter the Great, Ivan the Terrible; Queen Christina of Sweden (Garbo); Philip II of Spain (Raymond Massey and Paul Scofield); Marie Antoinette of France (Norma Shearer).

KINGS ROW (US 1942). An unusually adult film to come from Hollywood in the middle of the war, this strong period drama from Henry Bellamann's novel of small town life was directed with bravura by Sam Wood and acted with relish by Claude Rains, Betty Field, Ann Sheridan, Charles Coburn, and Maria Ouspenskaya, with Ronald Reagan and Robert Cummings making surprisingly interesting heroes. Musical score by Erich Wolfgang Korngold. An undistinguished TV series of 1957 used the title and some of the characters.

KINNOCH, RONALD (c. 1911–). British producer, former scenarist and production manager. *Escape Route* (52), *How to Murder a Rich Uncle* (57), *The Secret Man* (also wrote and directed) (58), *Village of the Damned* (60), *Invasion Quartet* (61), *Cairo* (62), *The Ipcress File* (associate producer) (65), etc.

KINSKEY, LEONID (c. 1905–). Lanky Russian character actor, long in US. Was playing intense but not over-bright revolutionaries in 1932 (*Trouble in Paradise*) and still does it on TV. Also in *The Great Waltz* (38), *Down Argentine Way* (40), *Can't Help Singing* (44), *Monsieur Beaucaire* (46), *The Man with the Golden Arm* (55), many others.

KINNEAR, ROY (c. 1930–). Bulbous British character comedian whose perspiring bluster is a quickly overplayed hand. *Sparrows Can't Sing* (62), *The Heavens Above* (63), *French Dressing* (65), *The Hill* (65), *Help!* (66), *A Funny Thing Happened on the Way to the Forum* (67), *How I Won the War* (67), *Lock Up Your Daughters* (67), etc. Also on TV.

KINUGASA, TEINOSUKE (1896–). Japanese director. *Crossways* (28) *Joyu* (47), *Gate of Hell* (53), *The White Heron* (58), etc.

KIPLING, RUDYARD (1865-1936). British novelist who mainly concerned himself with the high days of the British in India. Films from his works include *Gunga Din*, *Soldiers Three*, *Elephant Boy*, *Wee Willie Winkie*, *Captains Courageous*, *The Light That Failed*, *The Jungle Book*, *Kim*.

KIPPS. H. G. Wells' comic-sentimental 'story of a simple soul' was first filmed in 1919 (GB) with George K. Arthur as the draper's assistant who comes into money and has an unhappy encounter with high society. In 1941 Carol Reed made a very stylish and satisfying sound version with Michael Redgrave; and 1967 brought the inevitable musical version, *Half a Sixpence*, with Tommy Steele vivacious but somewhat miscast in the lead.

KIRK, PHYLLIS (1930–) (Phyllis Kirkegaard). American leading lady of the 50s, former model and dancer. *Our Very Own* (50), *The Iron Mistress* (52), *House of Wax* (53), *Canyon Crossroads* (55), *That Woman Opposite* (GB) (58), etc. TV series; *The Thin Man* (57).

KIRK, TOMMY (1941–). American juvenile lead, former Disney child actor. *Old Yeller* (57), *The Shaggy Dog* (59), *The Swiss Family Robinson* (60), *The Absent-minded Professor* (60), *Babes in Toyland* (61), *Bon Voyage* (62), *Son of Flubber* (63), *The Misadventures of Merlin Jones* (63), *The Monkey's Uncle* (65), *How to Stuff a Wild Bikini* (65), etc.

KIRKOP, ORESTE (1926–). American operatic tenor whose sole film appearance to date has been in *The Vagabond King* (55).

KIRKWOOD, PAT (1921–). British leading lady and entertainer, in variety since her teens; married to Hubert Gregg. *Come On, George* (38), *No Leave No Love* (in Hollywood) (42), *Once a Sinner* (50), *After the Ball* (56), etc.

KIRSANOFF, DMITRI (1890–1957). Russian émigré film-maker in France; remembered for his avant-garde *Menilmontant* (26).

KISMET. Edward Knoblock's rather stolid Arabian Nights play has been filmed five times. In 1920 Louis Gesnier directed Otis Skinner; in 1931 (in Germany) William Dieterle directed Gustav Fröhlich; in 1931 Otis Skinner played in a talkie version directed by John Francis Dillon; in 1944 Dieterle had another crack at it, with Ronald Colman in the lead; and in 1955 the stage version with musical themes by Borodin was filmed by Vincente Minnelli, with Howard Keel.

KISS ME DEADLY (US 1955). A Mickey Spillane thriller directed by Robert Aldrich. Quite incomprehensible and extremely violent but with brilliantly entertaining moments. A phantasmagoria of Hollywood thriller clichés, its arty direction made it a considerable influence on Truffaut and the 'new wave'.

KISS ME KATE (US 1953). This film of the stage musical based on 'The Taming of the Shrew' was probably the best production shot in 3-D; it was, however, released 'flat'. Apart from its Cole Porter score it had lively performances from Howard Keel, Kathryn Grayson and Ann Miller; directed by George Sidney.

KISS OF DEATH (US 1947). A gangster thriller influential in its violence, despair and incisiveness; also notable for the first appearance of Richard Widmark in the role of a sadistic laughing killer. Written by Ben Hecht and Charles Lederer, photographed by Norbert Brodine, directed by Henry Hathaway. A disguised remake, *The Fiend Who Walked the West*, was issued in 1958 but had nothing to offer except blood-letting.

KITT, EARTHA (1928–   ). Negro night-club singer whose great theatrical impact has not been captured on film except in *New Faces* (54). *St Louis Blues* (57), *Anna Lucasta* (58), *The Saint of Devil's Island* (61), *Synanon* (65), etc.

KITZMILLER, JOHN (1913–1965). Negro character actor, in Italy from 1945 (after army service). *Paisa* (46), *To Live In Peace* (46), *Senza Pieta* (48), *The Naked Earth* (57), *Doctor No* (62), *Uncle Tom's Cabin* (title role) (Ger.) (65), etc.

KJELLIN, ALF (1920–   ). Swedish actor who after *Frenzy* (44) went to Hollywood but made few appearances: *My Six Convicts* (52), *The Iron Mistress* (52), *Ship of Fools* (65), *Assault on a Queen* (66), *Ice Station Zebra* (68), etc. Turned his talents to directing TV films, especially for *Alfred Hitchcock Presents*, then features: *The Midas Run* (69).

KLEIN, WILLIAM (1929–   ). American director, in Paris. *Far From Vietnam* (part) (66), *Qui Etes-vous Polly Magoo?* (67), *Mr Freedom* (68).

KLEINER, HARRY (1916–   ). American screenwriter. *Fallen Angel* (46), *The Street with No Name* (48), *Red Skies of Montana* (51), *Salome* (53), *Miss Sadie Thompson* (53), *Carmen Jones* (54), *The Garment Jungle* (also produced) (56), *Ice Palace* (60), *Fantastic Voyage* (66), etc.

KLEIN-ROGGE, RUDOLF (1889–1955). German actor who appeared in some of the most famous German films of the 20s. *Der Mude Tod* (21), *Dr Mabuse* (22), *Siegfried* (24), *Metropolis* (26), *The Testament of Dr Mabuse* (32), etc.

KLINE, HERBERT (1909–   ). American director, mainly of documentaries. Features include *The Forgotten Village* (also produced) (41), *The Fighter* (52).

KLINE, RICHARD (1926–   ). American cinematographer. *Camelot* (67), *The Boston Strangler* (68).

KLOS, ELMAR: see KADAR, JAN.

KLUGMAN, JACK (c. 1924–   ). American actor who can be comically henpecked, tragically weak, or just sinister. Films include *Twelve Angry Men* (57), *Days of Wine and Roses* (62), *Act One* (63), *Yellow Canary* (63), *The Detective* (68), *The Split* (68), *Goodbye Columbus* (69); seen more on TV, especially in series *Harris against the World*.

The Knack

THE KNACK (GB 1965). Richard Lester's free-wheeling film version of Ann Jellicoe's sex play was only dull while it stuck to the script; whereas the running gags and visually inventive interludes shot in London streets were almost undiluted joy. Photographed by David Watkin, with a spirited young cast, the film unfortunately encouraged less talented film makers to think that anything goes providing you keep moving.

KNEALE, NIGEL (1922–). Manx writer, best known for BBC TV serials about Professor Quatermass, two of which were filmed. Also scripted *Look Back in Anger* (59), *The Entertainer* (60), *The First Men in the Moon* (64), *The Devil's Own* (*The Witches*) (66), etc.

KNEF, HILDEGARDE: see NEFF, HILDEGARDE.

KNIGHT, CASTLETON (1894–). British newsreel producer (Gaumont British). Directed some films in the 30s, including *Kissing Cup's Race* and *The Flying Scotsman*; also various compilations such as *Theirs Is the Glory* and *Fourteenth Olympiad*.

KNIGHT, DAVID (1927–) (D. Mintz). American leading man, on London stage since 1953. *The Young Lovers* (debut) (55), *Lost* (57), *Across the Bridge* (57), *Battle of the V.1* (58), *Nightmare* (63), etc.

KNIGHT, ESMOND (1906–). Welsh actor, on stage since 1925, screen since 1931. Partially blinded during World War II. Notable in *The Silver Fleet* (42), *Henry V* (44), *End of the River* (47), *Hamlet* (47), *The Red Shoes* (48), *Richard III* (56), *Sink the Bismarck* (60), *Where's Jack?* (69), etc.

KNIGHT, FUZZY (1901–) (J. Forrest Knight). American night club musician who found himself a niche in Hollywood as comic relief in innumerable Westerns. *She Done Him Wrong* (33), *The Trail of the Lonesome Pine* (36), *Johnny Appollo* (40), *Trigger Trail* (44), *Down to the Sea in Ships* (50), *Topeka* (54), *These Thousand Hills* (59), *Waco* (66), etc.

KNIGHT, SHIRLEY (1937–). American leading actress, also on stage and TV. *The Dark at the Top of the Stairs* (60), *Sweet Bird of Youth* (62), *The Group* (66), *Dutchman* (67), *Petulia* (68), *The Rain People* (69), etc.

KNOPF, EDWIN H. (1899–). American producer, also sometimes writer and director. *Border Legion* (d) (30), *Bad Sister* (w) (31), *The Wedding Night* (w) (35), *Piccadilly Jim* (w) (36), *The Trial of Mary Dugan* (p) (41), *The Cross of Lorraine* (p) (44), *The Valley of Decision* (p) (45), *BF's Daughter* (p) (48), *Edward My Son* (p) (49), *The Law and the Lady* (d) (51), *Lili* (p) (53), *The Vintage* (p) (57), many others.

KNOTTS, DON (1924–   ). American 'nervous' comedian, from TV,
Films include *Wake Me Up When It's Over* (60), *The Last Time I Saw
Archie* (61), *The Incredible Mr Limpet* (62), *The Ghost and Mr Chicken*
(66), *The Reluctant Astronaut* (67), *The Shakiest Gun in the West* (68),
The Love God (69).

KNOWLES, BERNARD (1900–   ). British cinematographer: *The Good
Companions* (32), *Jew Suss* (34), *The Thirty-nine Steps* (35), *The
Mikado* (39), *Gaslight* (39), *Quiet Wedding* (40), many others.
Became director: *A Place of One's Own* (44), *The Magic Bow* (46),
A Man Within (46), *Jassy* (47), *Easy Money* (47), *The White Unicorn*
(48), *The Perfect Woman* (49), *The Lost People* (49), *The Reluctant
Widow* (50), *Spaceflight IC-1* (65), *Hell Is Empty* (68), etc. In the 50s,
made hundreds of TV films, especially for Douglas Fairbanks.

KNOWLES, PATRIC (1911–   ) (Reginald Knowles). British light
'second lead' who went to Hollywood in 1936 and stayed. *Irish
Hearts* (GB) (34), *Abdul the Damned* (GB) (34), *The Guvnor* (GB)
(35), *The Charge of the Light Brigade* (36), *The Adventures of Robin
Hood* (38), *Storm over Bengal* (39), *Anne of Windy Poplars* (40), *How
Green Was My Valley* (41), *The Wolf Man* (41), *Lady in a Jam* (42),
Eyes of the Underworld (42), *Frankenstein Meets the Wolf Man* (43),
Always a Bridesmaid (43), *Pardon My Rhythm* (44), *Kitty* (45), *Of
Human Bondage* (46), *Monsieur Beaucaire* (46), *Ivy* (47), *The Big Steal*
(49), *Three Came Home* (50), *Mutiny* (52), *Flame of Calcutta* (53),
Band of Angels (57), *Auntie Mame* (59), *The Devil's Brigade* (68), *In
Enemy Country* (68), others.

KNOX, ALEXANDER (1907–   ). Quiet-spoken Canadian actor, on
British stage from 1930, films from 1938; also in Hollywood. *The
Gaunt Stranger* (GB) (38), *The Sea Wolf* (40), *This Above All* (42),
None Shall Escape (43), *Wilson* (title role) (44), *Over Twenty-one* (45),
Sister Kenny (46), *The Judge Steps Out* (47), *The Sign of the Ram* (48),
I'd Climb the Highest Mountain (50), *Paula* (52), *The Sleeping Tiger*
(GB) (53), *The Divided Heart* (GB) (54), *Reach for the Sky* (GB) (56),
High Tide at Noon (GB) (57), *The Wreck of the Mary Deare* (GB) (59),
The Man in the Middle (GB) (64), *Crack in the World* (65), *Mister
Moses* (GB) (65), *The Psychopath* (GB) (66), *Accident* (GB) (66), *How
I Won the War* (GB) (67), *Villa Rides* (68), *Shalako* (68), others. Also
on TV.

KNOX, TEDDY: see THE CRAZY GANG.

KOBAYASHI, MASAKI (1916–   ). Japanese director: *Ningen No Joken*
(61), *Hara Kiri* (63), *Kwaidan* (64), *Rebellion* (67), etc.

KOCH, HOWARD (1902–   ). American screenwriter. *The Sea Hawk*
(co-w) (40), *The Letter* (co-w) (40), *Casablanca* (co-w) (AA) (42),
Mission to Moscow (co-w) (43), *Letter from an Unknown Woman* (47),

Koch, Howard W.

The Thirteenth Letter (51), *The War Lover* (63), *The Fox* (co-w, p) (68), many others.

KOCH, HOWARD W. (1916–   ). American executive, from 1965–66 Paramount's vice-president in charge of production. Former producer and director: films include *Big House USA* (d) (54), *Beachhead* (p) (55), *The Black Sleep* (p) (56), *Frankenstein 70* (d) (58), *Sergeants Three* (p) (62), *The Manchurian Candidate* (p) (62), *Come Blow Your Horn* (p) (63), *None But the Brave* (p) (65), *The Odd Couple* (p) (68).

KOHLMAR, FRED (1905–1969). American producer, in Hollywood from the early 30s, at first with Goldwyn. *That Night in Rio* (41), *The Glass Key* (42), *Kiss of Death* (47), *When Willie Comes Marching Home* (50), *It Should Happen to You* (53), *Picnic* (55), *Pal Joey* (57), *The Last Angry Man* (59), *The Notorious Landlady* (62), *How To Steal a Million* (66), *A Flea in Her Ear* (68), *The Only Game in Town* (69), many others.

KOHNER, SUSAN (1936–   ). American actress: *To Hell and Back* (55), *Imitation of Life* (58), *All the Fine Young Cannibals* (60), *Freud* (62), etc.

KOLB, CLARENCE (1875–1964). Veteran character actor, usually of explosive executive types; formerly in vaudeville. *Carefree* (38), *Nothing But the Truth* (41), *Hellzapoppin* (42), *True to Life* (43), *The Kid from Brooklyn* (46), *Christmas Eve* (47), *Adam's Rib* (49), *The Rose Bowl Story* (53), many others.

KOLKER, HENRY (1874–1947). American stage actor who played lawyers and heavy fathers in many films. *Dubarry* (31), *Wonder Bar* (34), *Now and Forever* (35), *Romeo and Juliet* (36), *Theodora Goes Wild* (37), *Holiday* (38), *A Woman's Face* (41), *Bluebeard* (45), etc.

KORDA, SIR ALEXANDER (1893–1956). Hungarian producer-director who worked in Paris, Berlin and Hollywood before settling in London 1930. More than any other man the saviour of the British film industry. Formed London Films and sealed its success with *The Private Life of Henry VIII* (32); built Denham Studios. Later produced *Catherine the Great* (33), *The Scarlet Pimpernel* (34), *Sanders of the River* (35), *Things to Come* (35), *The Ghost Goes West* (36), *Rembrandt* (p, d) (37), *Knight Without Armour* (37), *Elephant Boy* (37), *The Drum* (38), *The Four Feathers* (39), others; in Hollywood, *The Thief of Baghdad* (40), *Lady Hamilton* (p, d) (41), *Jungle Book* (42), etc.; back in Britain: *Perfect Strangers* (p, d) (45), *An Ideal Husband* (p, d) (47), *Anna Karenina* (48), *The Fallen Idol* (48), *The Third Man* (49), *Seven Days to Noon* (50), *The Sound Barrier* (51), *Hobson's Choice* (54), *Richard III* (56), etc.

KORDA, VINCENT (1896–   ). Hungarian art director who usually worked on the films of his brothers Alexander and Zoltan.

KORDA, ZOLTAN (1895–1961). Hungarian director, brother of Alexander Korda, spent most of his career in Britain and Hollywood. *Sanders of the River* (35), *The Drum* (38), *The Four Feathers* (39), *The Thief of Baghdad* (co-d) (40), *Sahara* (43), *The Macomber Affair* (47), *A Woman's Vengeance* (48), *Cry the Beloved Country* (51), etc.

KORJUS, MILIZA (1902–   ). Polish operatic soprano who settled in America but made only one film: *The Great Waltz* (38).

KORNGOLD, ERICH WOLFGANG (1897–1957). Czech composer-conductor, a child prodigy. To Hollywood in 1935 to work on *A Midsummer Night's Dream*; stayed with Warners. *Anthony Adverse* (AA) (36), *Green Pastures* (36), *The Adventures of Robin Hood* (AA) (38), *Kings Row* (42), *Deception* (46), etc.

KORRIS, HARRY (C. 1888–   ). British music-hall comedian who became popular on radio and made several slapdash film farces: *Somewhere in England* (40), *Somewhere in Camp* (41), *Happidrome* (43), etc.

KORTNER, FRITZ (1892–   ). German actor, in films of several nations since 1921. *Pandora's Box* (28), *Dreyfus* (30), *Abdul the Damned* (35), *The Hitler Gang* (45), *The High Window* (47), many others.

KORVIN, CHARLES (1907–   ) (Geza Karpathi). Czech-born leading man with varied experience before Hollywood debut. *Enter Arsène Lupin* (44), *This Love of Ours* (45), *Temptation* (47), *The Killer That Stalked New York* (50), *Lydia Bailey* (52), *Sangaree* (53), *Zorro the Avenger* (60), *Ship of Fools* (65), *The Man Who Had Power Over Women* (70), etc. TV series: *Interpol Calling* (59).

KOSCINA, SYLVA (1935–   ). Czech leading lady in international films. *Hot Enough for June* (GB) (63), *Juliet of the Spirits* (It.) (65), *Three Bites of the Apple* (US) (66), *Deadlier than the Male* (GB) (67), *A Lovely Way to Die* (68), *The Battle for Neretva* (70), etc.

KOSLECK, MARTIN (1907–   ) (Nicolai Yoshkin). Russian character actor with experience on the German stage; in America from mid-30s. *Confessions of a Nazi Spy* (as Goebbels) (39), *Nurse Edith Cavell* (39), *A Date with Destiny* (40), *Foreign Correspondent* (40), *North Star* (43), *The Hitler Gang* (as Goebbels) (44), *The Frozen Ghost* (44), *The Mummy's Curse* (45), *House of Horrors* (46), etc.; long interval on stage; *Hitler* (as Goebbels) (61), *Something Wild* (62), *Thirty-six Hours* (64), *Morituri* (65), *The Flesh Eaters* (67), etc.

KOSMA, JOSEPH (1905–1969). Hungarian composer, in France from 1933. *La Grande Illusion* (37), *La Bête Humaine* (38), *Partie de Campagne* (38), *La Règle du Jeu* (39), *Les Enfants du Paradis* (44), *Les Portes de la Nuit* (45), *Les Amants de Vérone* (48), *The Green Glove* (52),

Huis Clos (54), *Calle Mayor* (56), *The Doctor's Dilemma* (59), *Lunch on the Grass* (59), *La Poupée* (62), *In the French Style* (64), etc.

KOSSOFF, DAVID (1919–   ). British character actor and stage monologuist. *The Young Lovers* (55), *A Kid for Two Farthings* (56), *The Bespoke Overcoat* (57), *Freud* (62), *Ring of Spies* (64), many others. TV series: *The Larkins, A Little Big Business.*

KOSTAL, IRWIN (c. 1915–   ). American musician who has scored several films including *West Side Story* (AA) (61), *Mary Poppins* (64), *The Sound of Music* (AA) (65), *Half a Sixpence* (67).

KOSTER, HENRY (1905–   ) (Hermann Kosterlitz). German director, in Hollywood from mid-30s. *Peter* (Ger.) (33), *Marie Bashkirtzeff* (Ger.) (36), *Three Smart Girls* (36), *One Hundred Men and a Girl* (37) *The Rage of Paris* (38), *Three Smart Girls Grow Up* (38), *Spring Parade* (40), *It Started with Eve* (41), *Between Us Girls* (42), *Music for Millions* (44), *Two Sisters from Boston* (45), *The Unfinished Dance* (47), *The Bishop's Wife* (48), *Come to the Stable* (49), *The Inspector General* (49), *Harvey* (50), *No Highway* (GB) (51), *Mr Belvedere Rings the Bell* (52), *Stars and Stripes Forever* (52), *My Cousin Rachel* (52), *The Robe* (53), *Désirée* (54), *A Man Called Peter* (55), *Good Morning, Miss Dove* (55), *D-Day the Sixth of June* (56), *The Power and the Prize* (56), *My Man Godfrey* (57), *Fraulein* (58), *The Naked Maja* (59), *Flower Drum Song* (60), *Mr Hobbs Takes a Vacation* (62), *Take Her She's Mine* (63), *Dear Brigitte* (65), *The Singing Nun* (66), etc.

KOTCHEFF, TED (1931–   ). Canadian director resident in Britain; TV experience. *Tiara Tahiti* (62), *Life at the Top* (65).

KOVACK, NANCY (c. 1940–   ). American leading lady with stage and TV experience. *Strangers When We Meet* (60), *Diary of a Madman* (62), *Jason and the Argonauts* (63), *The Outlaws Is Coming* (65), *Frankie and Johnny* (66), *The Silencers* (66), *Tarzan and the Valley of Gold* (66), *Marooned* (69), etc.

†KOVACS, ERNIE (1919–1962). Big, cigar-smoking American comedian and TV personality. *Operation Mad Ball* (57), *Bell, Book and Candle* (58), *It Happened to Jane* (58), *Our Man in Havana* (60), *Wake Me When It's Over* (60), *Strangers When We Meet* (60), *North to Alaska* (60), *Pepe* (60), *Five Golden Hours* (61), *Sail a Crooked Ship* (62).

KOWALSKI, BERNARD (c. 1933–   ). American director, from TV. *Krakatoa East of Java* (69).

KOZINTSEV, GRIGORI (1905–   ). Russian director, in films since 1924. Best known abroad for *The Youth of Maxim* (35), *Don Quixote* (57), *Hamlet* (64).

KRAMER, STANLEY (1913–). American producer, with varied film experience before co-producing *So Ends Our Night* (41), *The Moon and Sixpence* (42); later as solo producer, made *Champion* (49), *Home of the Brave* (49), *The Men* (50), *Cyrano de Bergerac* (50), *High Noon* (52), etc. Contracted to produce quality low-budget films for Columbia, but only a few were satisfactory: *The Happy Time* (52), *Death of a Salesman* (52), *The Fourposter* (52), *The 5,000 Fingers of Dr T* (53), *The Member of the Wedding* (53). Back to big budgets: *Not as a Stranger* (p, d) (54), *The Caine Mutiny* (54), *The Pride and the Passion* (p, d) (56), *The Defiant Ones* (p, d) (58), *On the Beach* (p, d) (59), *Inherit the Wind* (p, d) (60), *Judgment at Nuremberg* (p, d) (61), *A Child Is Waiting* (p) (62), *Pressure Point* (p) (63), *It's a Mad Mad Mad Mad World* (p, d) (63), *Ship of Fools* (p, d) (65), *Guess Who's Coming to Dinner* (67), *The Secret of Santa Vittoria* (69), etc.

KRAMPF, GUNTER (1899–). German cinematographer, in Britain from 1931. *The Student of Prague* (24), *The Hands of Orlac* (24), *Pandora's Box* (28), *Rome Express* (32), *Little Friend* (34), *Latin Quarter* (45), *Fame is the Spur* (46), *Portrait of Clare* (50), *The Franchise Affair* (52), many others.

KRASKER, ROBERT (1913–). Australian cinematographer, long in Britain. *Dangerous Moonlight* (40), *Henry V* (44), *Caesar and Cleopatra* (45), *Brief Encounter* (46), *Odd Man Out* (47), *The Third Man* (AA) (49), *Romeo and Juliet* (53), *Trapeze* (56), *The Quiet American* (58), *The Criminal* (60), *El Cid* (61), *Billy Budd* (62), *The Running Man* (63), *The Fall of the Roman Empire* (64), *The Heroes of Telemark* (65), many others.

KRASNA, NORMAN (1909–). American playwright who has worked on many films since 1932, including adaptations of his own plays. *Fury* (36), *Bachelor Mother* (39), *The Flame of New Orleans* (41), *The Devil and Miss Jones* (41), *Princess O'Rourke* (AA) (also directed) (43), *The Big Hangover* (also produced and directed) (50), *The Ambassador's Daughter* (also directed) (56), *Indiscreet* (58), *Who Was That Lady* (also produced) (60), *Let's Make Love* (61), *Sunday in New York* (64), many others.

KRASNER, MILTON (c. 1898–). American cinematographer. *I Love That Man* (33), *The Crime of Dr Hallett* (36), *The House of the Seven Gables* (40), *The Woman in the Window* (44), *Scarlet Street* (45), *The Dark Mirror* (46), *The Farmer's Daughter* (47), *The Set Up* (49), *Rawhide* (50), *All About Eve* (50), *Monkey Business* (51), *Three Coins in the Fountain* (AA) (54), *The Rains of Ranchipur* (55), *Bus Stop* (56), *An Affair to Remember* (57), *The Four Horsemen of the Apocalypse* (62), *Two Weeks in Another Town* (62), *Love with the Proper Stranger* (64), *The Sandpiper* (65), *The Singing Nun* (66), *Hurry Sundown* (67), *The Epic of Josie* (67), *The St Valentine's Day Massacre* (68), *The Sterile Cuckoo* (69), etc.

559

KRAUSS, WERNER (1884–1959). Distinguished German actor remembered abroad for *The Cabinet of Dr Caligari* (19), *Waxworks* (24), *The Student of Prague* (25), *Secrets of a Soul* (26), *Jew Suss* (40), etc.

KREUGER, KURT (1917–   ). Swiss actor, former ski instructor, who appeared in many Hollywood films as smooth continental heartthrob or menace. *Sahara* (43), *The Moon Is Down* (43), *Mademoiselle Fifi* (44), *Madame Pimpernel* (45), *Unfaithfully Yours* (48), *The Enemy Below* (58), *What Did You Do in the War, Daddy?* (66), *The St Valentine's Day Massacre* (67), etc.

KRISH, JOHN (c. 1923–   ). British director, mainly of short documentaries for British Transport, etc.; also TV films. Features: *Unearthly Stranger* (61), *The Wild Affair* (65), *Decline and Fall* (68), *The Man Who Had Power Over Women* (70).

KRUGER, ALMA (1872–1960). American stage actress who made many films in later life and is specially remembered as the head nurse in the Dr Kildare series. Also: *These Three* (36), *One Hundred Men and a Girl* (37), *Marie Antoinette* (38), *Balalaika* (39), *Saboteur* (42), *A Royal Scandal* (46), *Forever Amber* (last film) (47), etc.

KRUGER, HARDY (1928–   ). German leading man who has filmed in Britain: *The One That Got Away* (57), *Bachelor of Hearts* (58), *Blind Date* (59). In France, *Sundays and Cybèle* (60). In Africa, *Hatari* (62). In America, *The Flight of the Phoenix* (65). In Germany, *The Defector* (66). In Italy, *The Secret of Santa Vittoria* (69).

KRUGER, OTTO (1885–   ). Suave American actor with long stage experience. *The Intruder* (debut) (32), *Chained* (34), *Springtime for Henry* (34), *Treasure Island* (35), *Dracula's Daughter* (36), *They Won't Forget* (37), *The Housemaster* (GB) (38), *Thanks for the Memory* (38), *Dr Ehrlich's Magic Bullet* (40), *This Man Reuter* (40), *The Big Boss* (41), *Escape in the Fog* (45), *Duel in the Sun* (46), *Smart Woman* (48), *Payment on Demand* (51), *High Noon* (52), *Magnificent Obsession* (54), *The Last Command* (56), *The Wonderful World of the Brothers Grimm* (63), *Sex and the Single Girl* (64), many others.

KRUSCHEN, JACK (1922–   ). American character comedian of stage and TV. Films include: *Red Hot and Blue* (49), *The Last Voyage* (60), *The Apartment* (60), *Lover Come Back* (62), *The Unsinkable Molly Brown* (64).

THE KU KLUX KLAN was sympathetically portrayed in Griffith's *The Birth of a Nation*, a fact which has never ceased to provoke controversy. The villainous actuality has, however, been displayed in *Black Legion* (36), *Legion of Terror* (37), *The Burning Cross* (47), *Storm Warning* (51), *The FBI Story* (59), and *The Cardinal* (63), among others. See also: *Lynch Law*.

KUBRICK, STANLEY (1928–   ). American writer-producer-director. After journalistic experience and semi-professional films, *The Killing* (w, d) (56), *Paths of Glory* (w, d) (58), *Spartacus* (d) (60), *Lolita* (d) (62), *Dr Strangelove* (co-w, d, p) (63), *2001: A Space Odyssey* (68).

KULIK, BUZZ (c. 1923–   ). American director, from TV. *The Explosive Generation* (61), *The Yellow Canary* (63), *Warning Shot* (also produced) (66), *Villa Rides* (68), *Riot* (68).

KURNITZ, HARRY (1907–1968). American writer, in Hollywood from 1938. *Fast and Furious* (38), *The Thin Man Goes Home* (44), *The Web* (47), *A Kiss in the Dark* (also produced) (48), *Pretty Baby* (49), *Melba* (53), *The Man Between* (53), *Land of the Pharaohs* (55), *How To Steal a Million* (66), many others.

KUROSAWA, AKIRA (1910–   ). Distinguished Japanese director whose best-known films abroad are *Tora-No-O* (45), *Rashomon* (50), *Living* (52), *Seven Samurai* (54), *The Lower Depths* (57), *Throne of Blood* (57), *The Hidden Fortress* (58), *High and Low* (62), *Redbeard* (64).

KWAN, NANCY (1938–   ). Chinese/English leading lady. *The World of Suzie Wong* (60), *Flower Drum Song* (61), *Tamahine* (63), *Fate Is the Hunter* (64), *The Wild Affair* (65), *Lt. Robin Crusoe* (65), *Arrivederci Baby* (66), *Nobody's Perfect* (67), *The Wrecking Crew* (68), *The Girl Who Knew Too Much* (69), etc.

KYDD, SAM (1917–   ). British character comedian whose sharp features have been seen in many films since 1945. TV series: *Crane*. *The Small Back Room* (48), *Treasure Island* (50), *The Cruel Sea* (53), *The Quatermass Experiment* (55), *I'm All Right, Jack* (59), *Follow That Horse* (60), *Island of Terror* (66), etc.

KYO, MACHIKO (1924–   ). Japanese actress. *Rashomon* (50), *Gate of Hell* (52), *The Teahouse of the August Moon* (56), *Ugetsu Monogatari* (58), etc.

KYSER, KAY (1897–   ). American bandleader who made a number of comedy films during World War II: *That's Right, You're Wrong* (39), *You'll Find Out* (40), *Playmates* (42), *Swing Fever* (43), *Carolina Blues* (44), *Around the World* (44), etc. Retired and became an active Christian Scientist.

L

LAAGE, BARBARA (1925–   ) (Claire Colombat). French leading
lady of several 50's films. *La Putain Respectueuse* (52), *L'Esclave
Blanche* (54), *Act of Love* (54), *Un Homme à Vendre* (58), etc.

labour relations is too downbeat a subject to be very popular on the
screen; but strikes have been treated with seriousness in *Strike,
The Crime of Monsieur Lange, Black Fury, How Green Was My Valley,
Love on the Dole, Chance of a Lifetime, The Whistle at Eaton Falls,* and
The Angry Silence; with humour in *A Nous la Liberté, Modern Times*
and *I'm All Right Jack.* The classic comical strike of women against
their husbands, led by Lysistrata, was depicted in the French
Love, Soldiers and Women and Americanized in *The Second Greatest
Sex.*

LA CAVA, GREGORY (1892–1949). American director, former cartoonist and writer: a delicate talent for comedy usually struggled
against unsatisfactory vehicles. *Womanhandled* (25), *Running Wild*
(27), *Feel My Pulse* (28), *Laugh and Get Rich* (31), *Symphony of Six
Million* (32), *The Half-Naked Truth* (32), *Gabriel over the White House*
(32), *Affairs of Cellini* (34), *What Every Woman Knows* (34), *Private
Worlds* (35), *She Married Her Boss* (35), *My Man Godfrey* (36), *Stage
Door* (37), *Fifth Avenue Girl* (39), *The Primrose Path* (40), *Unfinished
Business* (41), *Lady in a Jam* (42), *Living in a Big Way* (47), etc.

LACEY, CATHERINE (1904–   ). British stage and screen actress,
adept at sympathetic spinsters and eccentric types. *The Lady
Vanishes* (debut) (38), *Cottage to Let* (41), *I Know Where I'm Going*
(45), *The October Man* (47), *Whisky Galore* (49), *Rockets Galore* (56),
Crack in the Mirror (60), *The Fighting Prince of Donegal* (as Queen
Elizabeth I) (66), *The Sorcerers* (67), etc.

LADD, ALAN (1913–1964). American leading man of the 40s, poker-
faced and short of stature. Many bit parts (including *Citizen Kane*
[41]) before he achieved fame as the ruthless killer in *This Gun
for Hire* (42). Then: *The Glass Key* (42), *Lucky Jordan* (42) *Star
Spangled Rhythm* (43), *China* (43), *And Now Tomorrow* (44), *Salty
O'Rourke* (45), *Duffy's Tavern* (45), *Two Years Before the Mast* (46),
The Blue Dahlia (46), *O.S.S.* (46), *Calcutta* (47), *Wild Harvest* (47),
Saigon (48), *Beyond Glory* (48), *Whispering Smith* (48), *The Great
Gatsby* (48), *Chicago Deadline* (49), *Captain Carey U.S.A.* (50), *Branded*
(50), *Appointment with Danger* (51), *Red Mountain* (52), *The Iron*

Mistress (52), *Thunder in the East* (53), *Desert Legion* (53), *Shane* (53), *Botany Bay* (53), *The Red Beret* (GB) (54), *Saskatchewan* (54), *Hell Below Zero* (GB) (54), *The Black Knight* (GB) (54), *Drum Beat* (54), *The McConnell Story* (55), *Hell in Frisco Bay* (55), *Santiago* (56), *The Big Land* (57), *Boy on a Dolphin* (57), *The Deep Six* (58), *The Proud Rebel* (58), *The Badlanders* (58), *The Man in the Net* (59), *Guns of the Timberland* (59), *All the Young Men* (60), *One Foot in Hell* (60), *Duel of the Champions* (Italian) (61), *13 West Street* (62), *The Carpetbaggers* (64). (†Complete from 1942.)

THE LADY EVE (US 1941). Written and directed by Preston Sturges, this amusing trifle about a millionaire landed by the daughter of a confidence trickster was a sparkling example of the Sturges penchant for mixing sophisticated romance with pratfall farce. Henry Fonda, Barbara Stanwyck and Charles Coburn were the leads. In 1956 the plot was warmed over as a vehicle for George Gobel, with the assistance of Mitzi Gaynor and David Niven; but *The Birds and the Bees* was merely flat-footed.

LADY FOR A DAY (US 1933). Robert Riskin wrote, and Frank Capra directed, this Runyonesque fantasy about an old flower-seller who is helped by gangster friends to deceive her visiting daughter into thinking she is comfortably placed. Deftly handled, with a vigorous performance from May Robson, it was agreeable Hollywood moonshine. In 1961 Capra remade it as *A Pocketful of Miracles*, but it was now out of its period, and not even Bette Davis and a host of good character actors could save it from tedium, especially as its length was nearly doubled and Capra's direction seemed tired.

THE LADY FROM SHANGHAI (US 1948). The Orson Welles film which first showed his fatal fault as a solo director: inattention to detail. Even in this Hollywood-produced thriller the lighting is as murky as the plot and most of the dialogue is inaudible, with a dull performance from Welles himself. There are, however, some brilliantly-handled sequences, and the final shoot-up in a hall of mirrors has not been surpassed of its kind.

LADY HAMILTON (THAT HAMILTON WOMAN) (US 1941). Alexander Korda's historical romance about Nelson's mistress has the distinction of being Winston Churchill's favourite film. Laurence Olivier and Vivien Leigh were happily teamed; unfortunately the film was heavily cut on reissue, the 'endpapers' showing Lady Hamilton's decline being completely eliminated.

LADY IN THE DARK (US 1944). Moss Hart's now-dated stage play, with songs by Kurt Weill, was about a career girl who was psychologically going to pieces because she was torn between her work and three different men. The film version by Mitchell Leisen was good to look at but artificial, with dry-ice dream sequences largely replacing the songs. It did however mark the beginning of Hollywood's 40s interest in psychiatry, and its colour photography was coolly superior to anything we had seen before.

THE LADY IN THE LAKE (US 1946). The suspense and wit of Raymond Chandler's mystery novel were dissipated in this version by the experiment with subjective camera: the entire action was seen as through the hero's eyes, and he did not appear except in mirrors. Robert Montgomery played the role and also directed; but the film was not liked.

LADY KILLER (US 1933). Directed by Roy del Ruth, this Warner programmer marks an attempt to spoof gangster movies three years before *A Slight Case of Murder* and a year before the turnaround which put James Cagney on the side of the *G-Men*. Here he plays a cinema usher who turns con-man and gangster, then escapes his pursuers by becoming a Hollywood star. The pace is fast and furious, and the casting of Mae Clarke seems to indicate a direct aping of the *Public Enemy* image.

THE LADYKILLERS (GB 1955). An odd little black farce in which a fang-toothed Alec Guinness and his sinister gang move in on a little old lady who neatly parries their sinister designs and innocently brings about their doom. With Katie Johnson and many familiar British faces; directed by Alexander Mackendrick from a script by William Rose.

THE LADY VANISHES (GB 1938). Despite model sets and obvious back projection this remains the most likeable and probably the most entertaining of Hitchcock's films, a suspenseful comedy-thriller about a disappearing lady on a train. Scripted by Sidney Gilliat from a novel by Ethel Lina White, with a cast including Michael Redgrave, Margaret Lockwood, Dame May Whitty, Paul Lukas, Linden Travers, Mary Clare and Cecil Parker. Also notable as the film which introduced Basil Radford and Naunton Wayne as Charters and Caldicott, the Englishmen abroad *par excellence*.

THE LADY WITH A LITTLE DOG (USSR 1959). This highly pictorial love story, set at Yalta in the 90s, came as a mild revelation to Western audiences conditioned for years to Russian films stuffed with propaganda. Full of Chekhovian charm, it was directed by Josif Heifits and photographed by Andrej Moskvine.

LAEMMLE, CARL (1867–1939). German/American pioneer, in films from 1906; produced *Hiawatha* (09), founded Universal Pictures 1912. A biography by John Drinkwater was published in 1931.

LAEMMLE, CARL JNR (1908–). Son of Carl Laemmle; executive producer at Universal for many years. Credited with the success of *Frankenstein, Dracula*, and *All Quiet on the Western Front*.

LAFFAN, PATRICIA (1919–). British stage actress whose film appearances include *The Rake's Progress* (45), *Caravan* (46), *Quo Vadis* (as Poppea) (51), *Devil Girl from Mars* (54), *Twenty-three Paces to Baker Street* (56), etc.

LAHR, BERT (1895–1967) (Irving Lahrheim). American vaudeville, revue and radio comic who made very occasional film appearances without the expected impact: best remembered as the Cowardly Lion in *The Wizard of Oz* (39). Also: *Faint Heart* (debut) (31), *Josette* (38), *Zaza* (39), *Sing Your Worries Away* (42), *Meet the People* (44), *Always Leave Them Laughing* (49), *Rose Marie* (54), *The Second Greatest Sex* (55), *The Night They Raided Minsky's* (68), etc.

LAI, FRANCIS (c. 1933–). French film composer. *A Man and a Woman* (AA) (66), *Mayerling* (68), etc.

LAINE, FRANKIE (1913–) (Frank Paul Lo Vecchio). American pop singer who made several light musicals in the 50s: *When You're Smiling* (50), *The Sunny Side of the Street* (51), *Rainbow Round My Shoulder* (52), *Bring Your Smile Along* (55), *He Laughed Last* (56), etc.

LAIRD, JENNY (1917–). British actress. *Just William* (39), *The Lamp Still Burns* (43), *Black Narcissus* (46), *Painted Boats* (47), *The Long Dark Hall* (51), *Conspiracy of Hearts* (60), etc.

LAKE, ARTHUR (1905–) (Arthur Silverlake). American comedy character actor with circus background; best remembered as the harassed, over-domesticated Dagwood Bumstead in the *Blondie* series (37–47), and in the later TV series. Also: *Jack and the Beanstalk* (17), *Skinner's Dress Suit* (25), *On with the Show* (30), *Midshipman Jack* (34), *Topper* (37), *The Big Showoff* (44), *Sixteen Fathoms Deep* (48), etc.

LAKE, VERONICA (1919–) (Constance Ockleman). Petite American leading lady popular in 40s; distinguished by long blonde hair obscuring one eye (her 'peek-a-boo bang'). In films from 1939; overnight success in *I Wanted Wings* (41). Then: *Sullivan's Travels* (41), *This Gun For Hire* (42), *The Glass Key* (42), *I Married a Witch* (42), *Bring On the Girls* (44), *The Blue Dahlia* (46), *Ramrod* (47), *Saigon* (47), *Isn't It Romantic* (48), *Slattery's Hurricane* (49), *Stronghold* (51), etc. After many years of retirement, made *Footsteps in the Snow* (Can.) (66). Published autobiography 1968: *Veronica*.

LA MARR, BARBARA (1896–1926) (Reatha Watson). American leading lady of silent films from 1920. *The Prisoner of Zenda* (22), *The Eternal Struggle* (23), *Thy Name Is Woman* (24), *The Girl from Montmartre* (26), etc.

LAMARR, HEDY (1914–   ) (Hedwig Kiesler). Austrian leading lady of considerable beauty. In European films from 1931, including the notorious *Extase* (33) in which she appeared nude; went to Hollywood and became a household word for glamour. *Algiers* (38), *Lady of the Tropics* (39), *I Take This Woman* (39), *Comrade X* (40), *Boom Town* (40), *Come Live with Me* (41), *Ziegfeld Girl* (41), *H. M. Pulham Esquire* (41), *Tortilla Flat* (42), *Crossroads* (42), *White Cargo* (42), *The Heavenly Body* (43), *The Conspirators* (44), *Experiment Perilous* (44), *Her Highness and the Bellboy* (45), *The Strange Woman* (46), *Dishonoured Lady* (47), *Copper Canyon* (49), *Let's Live a Little* (49), *Samson and Delilah* (50), *My Favourite Spy* (51), *The Face That Launched a Thousand Ships* (It.) (54), *The Female Animal* (57). Published autobiography 1967: *Ecstasy and Me*.

LAMAS, FERNANDO (1917–   ). Argentinian leading man, in Hollywood from 1950 in routine musicals and comedies. *Rich, Young and Pretty* (51), *The Law and the Lady* (51), *The Merry Widow* (52), *The Girl Who Had Everything* (53), *Sangaree* (53), *Rose Marie* (54), *The Girl Rush* (55), *The Lost World* (60), *The Violent Ones* (also directed) (67), *100 Rifles* (69), etc.

LAMB, GIL (1906–   ). Rubber-boned American comic, seen in many 40s musicals. *The Fleet's In* (debut) (42), *Rainbow Island* (44), *Practically Yours* (44), *Humphrey Takes a Chance* (50), *Terror in a Texas Town* (58), *Blackbeard's Ghost* (67), others.

LAMBERT, GAVIN (1924–   ). British critic and novelist, in Hollywood since 1956. Scripts include *Bitter Victory* (57), *The Roman Spring of Mrs Stone* (61), *Inside Daisy Clover* (65), etc.

LAMBERT, JACK (1899–   ). Scottish character actor. *The Ghost Goes West* (36), *Nine Men* (43), *Hue and Cry* (46), *Eureka Stockade* (47), *The Brothers* (47), *The Lost Hours* (50), *The Sea Shall Not Have Them* (54), *Storm over the Nile* (56), *Reach for the Sky* (56), *Greyfriars Bobby* (60), *Modesty Blaise* (66), many others.

LAMBERT, JACK (c. 1922–   ). American character actor, usually an evil-eyed heavy. *The Cross of Lorraine* (43), *The Killers* (46), *The Unsuspected* (47), *The Enforcer* (51), *Scared Stiff* (53), *Kiss Me Deadly* (55), *Machine Gun Kelly* (57), *The George Raft Story* (61), *Four for Texas* (63), many others.

LAMBLE, LLOYD (1914–   ). Australian light actor who has been in many British films as detective, official, or other man. *The Story of Gilbert and Sullivan* (53), *The Belles of St Trinians* (54), *The Man Who Never Was* (56), *Quatermass II* (57), *Blue Murder at St Trinians* (58), *No Trees in the Street* (59), *The Trials of Oscar Wilde* (60), etc.

LAMONT, CHARLES (1898–   ). American director, in Hollywood from silent days. With Universal from mid-30s, making comedies featuring Abbott and Costello, the Kettles, etc. *Love, Honour and Oh Baby* (41), *The Merry Monahans* (44), *Bowery to Broadway* (44), *The Runaround* (46), *Slave Girl* (47), *Baghdad* (49), *Flame of Araby* (51), *Abbott and Costello Meet Dr Jekyll and Mr Hyde* (53), *Ma and Pa Kettle in Paris* (53), *Untamed Heiress* (54), *Abbott and Costello Meet the Mummy* (55), *Francis in the Haunted House* (56), *The Kettles in the Ozarks* (56), many others. Much TV work.

LAMONT, DUNCAN (1918–   ). Scottish actor with stage experience, in films since World War II. *The Golden Coach* (53), *The Adventures of Quentin Durward* (56), *Ben Hur* (59), *Mutiny on the Bounty* (62), *Murder at the Gallop* (63), *The Brigand of Kandahar* (65), *Arabesque* (65), many others.

LAMORISSE, ALBERT (1922–   ). French director known for short fantasy films: *Bim* (49), *Crin Blanc* (52), *The Red Balloon* (55), *Stowaway in the Sky* (61), *Fifi La Plume* (64), etc.

LAMOUR, DOROTHY (1914–   ) (Dorothy Kaumeyer). American leading lady. Miss New Orleans of 1931; starred in her first film, *The Jungle Princess* (36); became type-cast in sarong roles. *The Hurricane* (37), *Last Train from Madrid* (37), *Her Jungle Love* (38), *Spawn of the North* (38), *St Louis Blues* (39), *Disputed Passage* (39), *Road to Singapore* (and all subsequent 'Road' comedies) (39), *Johnny Apollo* (40), *Typhoon* (40), *Moon over Burma* (40), *Chad Hanna* (40), *Aloma of the South Seas* (41), *The Fleet's In* (41), *Beyond the Blue Horizon* (42), *They Got Me Covered* (42), *Dixie* (43), *And the Angels Sing* (43), *Rainbow Island* (44), *A Medal for Benny* (45), *Masquerdae in Mexico* (46), *Wild Harvest* (46), *My Favourite Brunette* (47), *Lulu Belle* (48), *The Girl from Manhattan* (49), *Manhandled* (49), *The Greatest Show on Earth* (53), etc.; retired 1953 apart from guest appearances in *Road to Hong Kong* (61), *Donovan's Reef* (63), *Pajama Party* (65).

†LANCASTER, BURT (1913–   ). Athletic American leading man and latterly distinguished actor. Former circus acrobat; acted and danced in soldier shows during World War II. *The Killers* (debut) (46), *Desert Fury* (47), *I Walk Alone* (47), *Brute Force* (47), *Sorry, Wrong Number* (48), *Kiss the Blood Off My Hands* (48), *All My Sons* (48), *Criss Cross* (49), *Rope of Sand* (49), *Mister 880* (50), *The Flame and the Arrow* (50), *Vengeance Valley* (51), *Ten Tall Men* (51), *Jim Thorpe, All-American* (51), *The Crimson Pirate* (52), *Come Back Little Sheba* (53), *South Sea Woman* (53), *From Here to Eternity* (53), *His Majesty O'Keefe* (54), *Apache* (54), *Vera Cruz* (54), *The Kentuckian* (also directed) (55), *The Rose Tattoo* (55), *Trapeze* (56), *The Rainmaker* (57), *Gunfight at the OK Corral* (as Wyatt Earp) (57), *Sweet Smell of Success* (57), *Separate Tables* (58), *The Devil's Disciple* (GB) (58), *Elmer Gantry* (AA) (60), *The Young Savages* (61), *Birdman of Alcatraz* (62), *A Child Is Waiting* (62), *The Leopard* (63), *Seven Days in May*

(64), *The Train* (64), *The Hallelujah Trail* (65), *The Professionals* (66), *The Swimmer* (67), *The Scalphunters* (68), *Castle Keep* (69), *The Gypsy Moths* (69), *Airport* (69).

LANCHESTER, ELSA (1902–   ) (Elizabeth Sullivan). British character actress, widow of Charles Laughton. On stage and screen in Britain before settling in Hollywood 1940. *Bluebottles* (28), *The Private Life of Henry VIII* (32), *David Copperfield* (35), *The Bride of Frankenstein* (35), *The Ghost Goes West* (36), *Rembrandt* (37), *Vessel of Wrath* (38), *Ladies in Retirement* (41), *Tales of Manhattan* (42), *The Spiral Staircase* (45), *End of the Rainbow* (47), *The Inspector-General* (49), *Androcles and the Lion* (53), *Bell, Book and Candle* (57), *Witness for the Prosecution* (57), *Mary Poppins* (64), *Blackbeard's Ghost* (67), *Me, Natalie* (69), many others.

LANDAU, ELY (1920–   ). American producer, former distributor *Long Day's Journey Into Night* (62), *The Pawnbroker* (64), etc.

LANDAU, MARTIN (1933–   ). Gaunt American actor often in sinister roles. *North by Northwest* (59), *The Gazebo* (59), *Cleopatra* (62), *The Hallelujah Trail* (65), *Nevada Smith* (66), etc. Much on TV, especially in series *Mission Impossible* (66–68).

LANDERS, LEW (1901–1962) (Lewis Friedlander). American director of 'B' pictures, especially Westerns, from silent days. *The Raven* (35), *The Man Who Found Himself* (37), *Canal Zone* (39), *Pacific Liner* (39), *The Boogie Man Will Get You* (42), *Return of the Vampire* (43), *The Enchanted Forest* (46), *State Penitentiary* (49), *Man in the Dark* (in 3-D) (53), *Captain Kidd and the Slave Girl* (53), *Hot Rod Gang* (58), *Terrified* (62), many others.

LANDI, ELISSA (1904–1948). Leading lady of the 30s, of aristocratic Austrian extraction. *Underground* (28), *The Yellow Ticket* (32), *The Sign of the Cross* (32), *The Masquerader* (33), *The Count of Monte Cristo* (34), *The Amateur Gentleman* (36), *The Thirteenth Chair* (37), *Corregidor* (44), etc.

LANDI, MARLA (c. 1937–   ). Italian leading lady and model: in British films. *Across the Bridge* (57), *First Man into Space* (58), *The Hound of the Baskervilles* (59), *Pirates of Blood River* (61), *The Murder Game* (65), etc.

LANDIS, CAROLE (1919–1948) (Frances Ridste). American leading lady, in films from 1937 (as extra). *Man and His Mate* (*One Million B.C.*) (40), *Turnabout* (40), *Road Show* (41), *Topper Returns* (41), *Hot Spot* (41), *Orchestra Wives* (42), *Wintertime* (43), *Having Wonderful Crime* (44), *Behind Green Lights* (45), *It Shouldn't Happen to a Dog* (46), *A Scandal in Paris* (46), *Out of the Blue* (47), *The Brass Monkey* (*Lucky Mascot*) (GB) (48), *Noose* (GB) (48), etc.

LANDIS, JESSIE ROYCE (1904–   ). American stage actress, occasionally in films, usually as fussy matron. *Derelict* (30), *My Foolish Heart* (50), *To Catch a Thief* (55), *The Swan* (56), *North by Northwest* (59), *Bon Voyage* (62), *Boys' Night Out* (63), etc.

LANDON, MICHAEL (1937–   ) (M. Orowitz). American leading man best known as Little Jo in TV series *Bonanza*. On screen, played the title role in *I Was a Teenage Werewolf* (57); also in *God's Little Acre* (58), *The Legend of Tom Dooley* (59), etc.

LANDONE, AVICE (1910–   ). British stage actress, usually in cool, unruffled roles. *My Brother Jonathan* (48), *The Franchise Affair* (51), *An Alligator Named Daisy* (55), *Reach for the Sky* (56), *Carve Her Name with Pride* (58), *Operation Cupid* (60), etc.

LANDRES, PAUL (1912–   ). American director, former editor. *Oregon Passage* (57), *The Miracle of the Hills* (58), *The Flame Barrier* (58), *The Vampire* (59), *Son of a Gunfighter* (65), etc.

LANE, ALLAN 'ROCKY' (c. 1901–   ) (Harry Albershart). American cowboy star of the 30s, former athlete. *Night Nurse* (32), *Maid's Night Out* (38), *The Dancing Masters* (44), *Trail of Robin Hood* (51), *The Saga of Hemp Brown* (58), *Hell Bent for Leather* (60), scores of second features. Supplies the voice for TV's talking horse *Mister Ed.*

LANE, CHARLES (1899–   ). American character actor seen since early 30s as comedy snoop, salesman or tax inspector. Latterly on TV as the villainous Mr Bedloe in *Petticoat Junction*. Films include *Mr Deeds Goes to Town* (36), *In Old Chicago* (38), *You Can't Take It With You* (38), *The Cat and the Canary* (39), *Hot Spot* (41), *Arsenic and Old Lace* (44), *Intrigue* (49), *The Juggler* (53), *Teacher's Pet* (58), *The Gnome-Mobile* (67), *What's So Bad About Feeling Good* (68), innumerable others.

LANE, LUPINO (1892–1959) (Henry George Lupino). Diminutive British stage comedian and tumbler who in the 20s made many clever comedy two-reelers, in one of which, *Only Me* (29), he played 24 parts. In 1939 filmed his stage show *Me and My Gal* (*The Lambeth Walk*). Also in *The Love Parade* (30), *The Deputy Drummer* (35), etc.

LANE, RICHARD (c.1898–   ). American supporting player frequently seen in the 40s as reporter, tough cop, of exasperated executive. Played the detective in the Boston Blackie series (40–48); also *Union Pacific* (39), *Hellzapoppin* (41), *What a Blonde* (45), *Gentleman Joe Palooka* (46), *Take Me Out to the Ball Game* (48), *I Can Get It For You Wholesale* (51), etc.

THE LANE SISTERS. American leading ladies, real name Mullican. Three of the five sisters (all actresses) had sizeable roles in Hollywood films: LOLA (1909–   ), ROSEMARY (1914–   ) and

PRISCILLA (1917–   ). They all appeared in the *Four Daughters* trilogy: *Four Daughters* (38), *Four Wives* (39), *Four Mothers* (40). Other appearances for Lola include *Speakeasy* (29), *Death from a Distance* (35), *Marked Woman* (37), *Zanzibar* (40), *Why Girls Leave Home* (46). Rosemary was in *Hollywood Hotel* (38), *The Oklahoma Kid* (38), *The Return of Dr X* (40), *Time Out for Rhythm* (42), *The Fortune Hunter* (45). Priscilla got the best parts: *Brother Rat* (39), *The Roaring Twenties* (40), *Blues in the Night* (41), *Saboteur* (42), *Arsenic and Old Lace* (44), *Fun on a Weekend* (46), *Bodyguard* (48), etc.

LANFIELD, SIDNEY (1900–   ). American director from 1932; former jazz musician. *Hat Check Girl* (32), *Sing Baby Sing* (36), *The Hound of the Baskervilles* (39), *Swanee River* (39), *You'll Never Get Rich* (41), *The Lady Has Plans* (41), *My Favourite Blonde* (42), *The Meanest Man in the World* (42), *Let's Face It* (43), *Standing Room Only* (44), *Bring on the Girls* (45), *The Well-Groomed Bride* (45), *Stations West* (47), *The Lemon Drop Kid* (50), *Follow the Sun* (51), *Skirts Ahoy* (52), etc. Recently inactive.

LANG, CHARLES (1915–   ). American writer. *The Magnificent Matador* (56), *Desire in the Dust* (62), etc.

LANG, CHARLES JNR (1902–   ). Distinguished American cinematographer. *Shopworn Angel* (29), *A Farewell to Arms* (AA) (33), *Lives of a Bengal Lancer* (35), *Desire* (36), *The Cat and the Canary* (39), *Nothing But the Truth* (41), *Practically Yours* (44), *A Foreign Affair* (47), *Ace in the Hole* (51), *Sudden Fear* (52), *The Big Heat* (53), *The Female on the Beach* (55), *The Man from Laramie* (55), *Autumn Leaves* (56), *The Solid Gold Cadillac* (56), *Gunfight at the OK Corral* (57), *Some Like It Hot* (59), *One-Eyed Jacks* (59), *The Facts of Life* (60), *Blue Hawaii* (61), *A Girl Named Tamiko* (62), *Charade* (63), *Inside Daisy Clover* (65), *How to Steal a Million* (66), *Not With My Wife You Don't* (66), *Hotel* (67), *The Flim Flam Man* (67), *Wait Until Dark* (67), *A Flea in Her Ear* (68), *Cactus Flower* (69), many others.

LANG, HAROLD (1923–   ). British actor and drama teacher. Occasional films include *Flood Tide* (49), *Cairo Road* (50), *Laughing Anne* (53), *The Quatermass Experiment* (55), *Carve Her Name with Pride* (58), *The Nanny* (65), etc.

†LANG, FRITZ (1890–   ). German director of distinguished silent films. Went to Hollywood 1934 and tended thereafter to make commercial though rather heavy-handed thrillers. *Halblut* (19), *Der Herr der Liebe* (19), *Die Spinnen* (19), *Der Goldene See* (19), *Hara Kiri* (19), *Das Brillanten Schiff* (20), *Das Wanderne Bild* (21), *Destiny* (21), *Vier um die Frau* (20), *Der Mude Tod* (21), *Dr Mabuse der Spieler* (22), *Inferno* (22), *Siegfried* (23), *Krimhild's Revenge* (24) *Metropolis* (26), *The Spy* (27), *Frau im Mond* (28), *M* (31), *The*

Testament of Dr Mabuse (32), *Gold* (33), *Liliom* (33), *Fury* (36), *You Only Live Once* (37), *You and Me* (38), *The Return of Frank James* (40), *Western Union* (41), *Man Hunt* (41), *Confirm or Deny* (part) (42), *Hangmen Also Die* (43), *The Woman in the Window* (44), *Ministry of Fear* (44), *Scarlet Street* (45), *Cloak and Dagger* (46), *The Secret Beyond the Door* (48), *House by the River* (49), *An American Guerrilla in the Philippines* (51), *Rancho Notorious* (52), *Clash by Night* (52), *The Blue Gardenia* (52), *The Big Heat* (53), *Human Desire* (54), *Moonfleet* (55), *While the City Sleeps* (55), *Beyond a Reasonable Doubt* (56), *Tigress of Bengal* (Ind.) (58), *Das Indische Grabmal* (Ger.) (58), *The Thousand Eyes of Dr Mabuse* (Ger.) (60).

LANG, JUNE (1917–   ) (June Vlasek). American leading lady, former dancer. *Chandu the Magician* (32), *Bonnie Scotland* (35), *Ali Baba Goes to Town* (38), *Redhead* (41), *Flesh and Fantasy* (44), *Lighthouse* (48), etc.

LANG, MATHESON (1879–1948). Scottish-Canadian stage actor, a London matinée idol of the 20s who made occasional films: *Mr Wu* (21), *Carnival* (21 and 31), *Dick Turpin's Ride to York* (22), *The Wandering Jew* (23), *The Chinese Bungalow* (25 and 30), *Beyond the Veil* (25), *Island of Despair* (26), *The Triumph of the Scarlet Pimpernel* (29), *Channel Crossing* (32), *Little Friend* (34), *Drake of England* (35), *The Cardinal* (36), etc.

LANG, WALTER (1896–   ). American director of competent but seldom outstanding films. *Satin Woman* (26), *Hell Bound* (31), *Meet the Baron* (34), *The Mighty Barnum* (36), *Wife, Doctor and Nurse* (38), *The Bluebird* (40), *Tin Pan Alley* (40), *Weekend in Havana* (41), *The Magnificent Dope* (42), *Coney Island* (43), *Greenwich Village* (44), *State Fair* (45), *Claudia and David* (46), *Mother Wore Tights* (47), *Sitting Pretty* (47), *When My Baby Smiles at Me* (48), *Cheaper by the Dozen* (49), *The Jackpot* (50), *On the Riviera* (51), *With a Song in My Heart* (52), *Call Me Madam* (53), *There's No Business Like Show Business* (54), *The King and I* (56), *But Not for Me* (59), etc.

LANGAN, GLENN (1917–   ). American light leading man, in films from the early 40s after stage experience. *Four Jills in a Jeep* (44), *Margie* (46), *Forever Amber* (47), *The Snake Pit* (48), *Treasure of Monte Cristo* (59), *Rapture* (Swedish) (50), *Hangman's Knot* (52), *99 River Street* (54), *The Amazing Colossal Man* (57), etc.

LANGDON, HARRY (1884–1944). Sad-faced American silent clown, formerly in vaudeville. Best films: *The Strong Man* (26), *Tramp Tramp Tramp* (26), *Long Pants* (27). Did not successfully survive sound, but appeared in *Hallelujah I'm a Bum* (34), *Elephants Never Forget* (39), *Misbehaving Husbands* (40), *House of Errors* (42), *Spotlight Scandals* (44), etc.

Lange, Hope

LANGE, HOPE (1931–   ). American leading lady, in films from 1956. *Bus Stop* (56), *Peyton Place* (57), *The Young Lions* (58), *A Pocketful of Miracles* (61), *Love Is a Ball* (*All This and Money Too*) (63), etc. TV series: *The Ghost and Mrs Muir* (68).

LANGFORD, FRANCES (1914–   ). American band singer, popular in 40s, mainly in guest spots. Appeared mainly in light musicals: *Every Night at Eight* (35), *Broadway Melody* (36), *Hollywood Hotel* (37), *Too Many Girls* (40), *Swing It, Soldier* (41), *The Girl Rush* (44), *The Bamboo Blonde* (45), *Beat the Band* (46), *No Time For Tears* (52), *The Glenn Miller Story* (54), etc.

LANGLEY, NOEL (1911–   ). South African playwright and screenwriter, in Britain and Hollywood from mid-30s. *Maytime* (co-w) (38), *The Wizard of Oz* (co-w) (39), *They Made Me a Fugitive* (47), *Tom Brown's Schooldays* (51), *Scrooge* (52), *The Pickwick Papers* (also directed) (53), *Our Girl Friday* (also directed) (54), *The Search for Bridey Murphy* (also directed) (56), others.

LANSBURY, ANGELA (1925–   ). British actress, in America since World War II evacuation. *Gaslight* (*The Murder in Thornton Square*) (44), *National Velvet* (44), *The Picture of Dorian Gray* (44), *The Harvey Girls* (45), *Till the Clouds Roll By* (46), *If Winter Comes* (47), *State of the Union* (48), *The Three Musketeers* (48), *The Red Danube* (49), *Samson and Delilah* (50), *Kind Lady* (51), *Mutiny* (52), *The Purple Mask* (55), *The Court Jester* (55), *The Long Hot Summer* (58), *Summer of the Seventeenth Doll* (59), *The Dark at the Top of the Stairs* (60), *All Fall Down* (61), *The Manchurian Candidate* (62), *The World of Henry Orient* (64), *Dear Heart* (64), *Harlow* (65), *Moll Flanders* (65), *Mister Buddwing* (66), others.

LANSING, ROBERT (c. 1926–   ) (Robert Howell Brown). American leading man, mainly on stage and TV. Films include: *A Gathering of Eagles* (63), *Under the Yum Yum Tree* (64). TV series: *87th Precinct* (61), *Twelve O'clock High* (64), *The Man Who Never Was* (66).

LANTZ, WALTER (1900–   ). American animator and cartoon producer; creator of Woody Woodpecker.

LANZA, MARIO (1921–1959) (Alfred Cocozza). American opera singer, popular in MGM musicals until overcome by weight problem. *That Midnight Kiss* (49), *The Great Caruso* (51), *Because You're Mine* (53), *Serenade* (56), *Seven Hills of Rome* (58), etc.

LA PLANTE, LAURA (1904–   ). American leading lady of the silent screen. *The Old Swimming Hole* (21), *Skinner's Dress Suit* (24), *The Cat and the Canary* (27), *Smouldering Fires* (28), *King of Jazz* (30), etc. Later played character parts: *Widow's Might* (35), *Little Mister Jim* (46), *Spring Reunion* (57), etc.

LA ROCQUE, ROD (1896–1969) (Roderick la Rocque de la Rour). Popular American leading man of the silent screen, in Hollywood from 1917 after circus experience. *Efficiency Edgar's Courtship* (17), *The Venus Model* (18), *The Ten Commandments* (23), *Forbidden Paradise* (25), *Resurrection* (26), *Our Modern Maidens* (28), *Let Us Be Gay* (29), *One Romantic Night* (30), *SOS Iceberg* (33), *Till We Meet Again* (36), etc.; later played small parts in *The Hunchback of Notre Dame* (40), *Dr Christian Meets the Women* (41), *Meet John Doe* (41), others.

LA RUE, DANNY (1928–) (Daniel Patrick Carroll). British revue star and female impersonator. Film debut: *Dear Sir or Madam* (70).

LA RUE, JACK (1903–) (Gaspare Biondolillo). Grim-faced American actor, typed as gangster since early 30s. Many supporting roles include *Lady Killer* (34), *Captains Courageous* (37), *Paper Bullets* (41), *Gentleman from Dixie* (a rare sympathetic part) (41), *Machine Gun Mama* (44), *No Orchids for Miss Blandish* (GB) (as the maniacal Slim Grisson) (48), *Robin Hood of Monterey* (49), *Ride the Man Down* (53), *Robin and the Seven Hoods* (64).

LA SHELLE, JOSEPH (1903–). American cinematographer. *Happy Land* (43), *Laura* (AA) (44), *Hangover Square* (44), *The Foxes of Harrow* (47), *Mister 880* (50), *Les Misérables* (52), *Marty* (55), *Storm Fear* (55), *The Bachelor Party* (57), *I Was a Teenage Werewolf* (57), *No Down Payment* (57), *The Naked and the Dead* (58), *The Apartment* (60), *Irma La Douce* (63), *The Fortune Cookie* (66), *Kona Coast* (68), many others.

LASKY, JESSE (1880–1958). American pioneer. Formed his first production company in 1914 and had big hit with *The Squaw Man*; in 1916 gained control of Famous Players and later Paramount. Later produced for Fox, Warner, RKO. His films include: *Sergeant York*, *The Adventures of Mark Twain*, *Rhapsody in Blue*, *The Miracle of the Bells*, *The Great Caruso*. In 1958 he published his autobiography, *I Blow My Own Horn*.

LASKY, JESSE JNR (1910–). American screenwriter, son of Jesse Lasky. *Union Pacific* (co-w) (39), *Reap the Wild Wind* (co-w) (42), *Unconquered* (co-w) (48), *Samson and Delilah* (co-w) (49), *The Thief of Venice* (50), *The Brigand* (52), *The Ten Commandments* (co-w) (56), *Seven Women from Hell* (co-w) (61), etc.

LASSALLY, WALTER (1926–). German cinematographer, long in Britain. *We Are the Lambeth Boys* (58), *A Taste of Honey* (61), *The Loneliness of the Long-Distance Runner* (62), *Tom Jones* (63), *Zorba the Greek* (AA) (65), *The Day the Fish Came Out* (67), *Oedipus the King* (67), *Joanna* (68), etc.

LASSIE. The first film featuring this intelligent collie (actually a laddie) was *Lassie Come Home* (42), based on Eric Knight's novel;

the dog, born in 1940, was called Pal, and continued his masquerade in several subsequent 'Lassie' adventures, though more recently different dogs have been used. The latest addition is *Lassie's Great Adventure* (62), and there has been a long-running TV series.

THE LAST CHANCE (Switzerland 1945). Almost the only Swiss film of international repute, this story of escape from Italy at the end of the 1943 campaign was directed by Leopold Lindtberg.

THE LAST DAYS OF POMPEII. Lord Lytton's novel climaxing in the catastrophic eruption of Vesuvius was filmed in Italy in 1912 ('10,000 people, 260 scenes'), 1925 and 1960. In 1935 Cooper and Schoedsack filmed it in Hollywood, with a cast including Basil Rathbone and Preston Foster.

THE LAST HURRAH (US 1958). Edwin O'Connor's amusing novel about the last days of a lovably roguish politician was turned by director John Ford into a sentimental reunion for a number of veteran character actors including Spencer Tracy, Edward Brophy, James Gleason, Basil Rathbone, John Carradine, Pat O'Brien, Donald Crisp, Ricardo Cortez, Wallace Ford, Frank McHugh, and Jane Darwell.

THE LAST LAUGH (DER LETZTE MANN) (Germany 1925). A silent drama dispensing entirely with sub-titles. Emil Jannings gave one of his most characteristic and clever performances as the lordly hotel porter degraded to washroom attendant; F. W. Murnau directed from a script by Karl Mayer; photography by Karl Freund.

THE LAST OF THE MOHICANS. Fenimore Cooper's adventure novel of American colonization was filmed in 1920 by Maurice Tourneur, with George Hackathorne; in 1936 by George Seitz, with Randolph Scott, and in 1952, as *The Last of the Redskins*, by George Sherman with Jon Hall. A Canadian TV series (56) starred John Hart.

LAST YEAR IN MARIENBAD (US 1961). Written by Alain Robbe-Grillet and directed by Alain Resnais, this curious film was hailed by many critics as a masterpiece, while others suspected a leg-pull. It had only three characters of note, but the problem for audiences was to find out how they were interrelated and what the film was about. Sacha Vierney's photography, in and around a baroque hotel, added its share of mystery.

LASZLO, ERNEST (c. 1905–   ). American cinematographer. *The Hitler Gang* (44), *Two Years Before the Mast* (44), *The Girl from Manhattan* (48), *Dead on Arrival* (49), *The Steel Trap* (52), *The Star* (52), *Stalag 17* (53), *Vera Cruz* (54), *The Big Knife* (55), *Judgment at Nuremberg* (60), *Inherit the Wind* (60), *It's A Mad Mad Mad Mad World* (63), *Ship of Fools* (AA) (65), *Fantastic Voyage* (66), *Star!* (68), *The First Time* (69), *Daddy's Gone A-Hunting* (69), many others.

LATHROP, PHILIP (* –). American cinematographer. *Experiment in Terror* (62), *Days of Wine and Roses* (63), *The Pink Panther* (63), *What Did You Do in the War, Daddy?* (66), *The Happening* (67), *Point Blank* (68), *Finian's Rainbow* (68), *I Love You Alice B. Toklas* (69).

LATIMER, JONATHAN (* –). American writer, usually in collaboration. *Topper Returns* (41), *They Won't Believe Me* (47), *Alias Nick Beal* (49), *Plunder of the Sun* (51), *Botany Bay* (54), *The Unholy Wife* (57), etc.

LATIMORE, FRANK (1925–) (F. Kline). American leading man with stage experience. *In the Meantime, Darling* (44), *Three Little Girls in Blue* (46), *Black Magic* (49), *Three Forbidden Stories* (Italian) (50), *John Paul Jones* (59), *The Sergeant* (68), etc.

LATTUADA, ALBERTO (1914–). Italian director: *The Mill on the Po* (48), *Without Pity* (48), *Lights of Variety* (co-d) (50), *Il Capotto* (52), *The Wolf* (53), *The Beach* (53), *Guendalina* (56), *Tempest* (58), *The Adolescents* (61), *La Steppa* (62), *The Mandrake* (65), *The Betrayal* (68), etc.

LAUDER, SIR HARRY (1870–1950). Scottish music-hall entertainer whose few films included *Huntingtower* (27), *Auld Lang Syne* (33), *Song of the Road* (36).

†LAUGHTON, CHARLES (1899–1962). Distinguished British character actor, on stage from 1926. His films of the 30s were masterly, but a tendency to ham became evident in the later Hollywood years. *Wolves* (27), *Bluebottles* (28), *Piccadilly* (29), *Comets* (30), *Down River* (30), *The Old Dark House* (US) (32), *The Devil and the Deep* (US) (32), *The Sign of the Cross* (as Nero) (US) (32), *Island of Lost Souls* (US) (32), *Payment Deferred* (US) (32), *If I Had a Million* (US) (32), *The Private Life of Henry VIII* (AA) (32), *White Woman* (US) (33), *The Barretts of Wimpole Street* (US) (34), *Les Misérables* (US) (35), *Ruggles of Red Gap* (US) (35), *Mutiny on the Bounty* (as Captain Bligh) (35), *Rembrandt* (36), *Vessel of Wrath* (37), *St Martin's Lane* (38), *Jamaica Inn* (39), *The Hunchback of Notre Dame* (US) (39), *They Knew What They Wanted* (US) (40), *It Started with Eve* (US) (41), *The Tuttles of Tahiti* (US) (41), *Tales of Manhattan* (US) (42), *Cargo of Innocents* (US) (42), *Forever and a Day* (US) (43), *This Land Is Mine* (US) (43), *The Man from Down Under* (US) (43), *The Canterville Ghost* (US) (44), *The Suspect* (US) (44), *Captain Kidd* (US) (45), *Because of Him* (US) (46), *The Paradine Case* (US) (47), *The Big Clock* (US) (47), *The Girl from Manhattan* (US) (48), *Arch of Triumph* (US) (48), *The Bribe* (US) (48), *The Man on the Eiffel Tower* (as Maigret) (Fr.) (50), *The Blue Veil* (US) (51), *The Strange Door* (US) (52), *Abbott and Costello Meet Captain Kidd* (US) (52), *Full House* (US) (53), *Young Bess* (as Henry VIII) (US) (53), *Salome* (US)

(53), *Hobson's Choice* (54), *Witness for the Prosecution* (US) (57), *Spartacus* (US) (60), *Under Ten Flags* (US) (60), *Advise and Consent* (US) (62). Directed one film: *Night of the Hunter* (55). Was long married to Elsa Lanchester, who wrote a book: *Charles Laughton and I.* Fragments of his performance in the unfinished *I Claudius* (37) leave one aching for more.

LAUNDER, FRANK (1907–   ). Half of the Launder-Gilliat writer-producer-director team. In films from 1930; for list see SIDNEY GILLIAT.

LAURA (US 1944). A superior mystery from a novel by Vera Caspary, this was notable for Otto Preminger's spare direction of his small cast, and for Clifton Webb's first star performance as the acidulous Waldo Lydecker. Cinematography: Joseph la Shelle (AA).

LAUREL, STAN (1890–1965) (Arthur Stanley Jefferson). British-born comedian, the thin half and gag deviser of the Laurel and Hardy team. Went to USA with Fred Karno's troupe, was in short comedies from 1915, teamed with Hardy 1926. He had director credit on some of their films and virtually directed many others. Special Academy Award 1960 'for his creative pioneering in the field of cinema comedy'. For list of films see OLIVER HARDY.

LAURENTS, ARTHUR (1918–   ). American playwright. Works filmed include *Caught* (original screenplay) (48), *Home of the Brave* (49), *Time of the Cuckoo* (as *Summer Madness*) (55); co-author of *West Side Story* (61).

LAURIE, JOHN (1897–   ). Scottish character actor, often in dour roles. On stage from 1921, screen from 1930 (*Juno and the Paycock*). Steadily in work ever since. *Red Ensign* (34), *The Thirty-nine Steps* (35), *Tudor Rose* (36), *As You Like It* (36), *Farewell Again* (37), *Edge of the World* (38), *Q Planes* (39), *Sailors Three* (40), *The Ghost of St. Michael's* (41), *Old Mother Riley Cleans Up* (41), *The Gentle Sex* (43), *Fanny by Gaslight* (43), *The Way Ahead* (44), *Henry V* (44), *I Know Where I'm Going* (45), *Caesar and Cleopatra* (35), *The Brothers* (47), *Uncle Silas* (47), *Bonnie Prince Charlie* (48), *Hamlet* (48), *Trio* (50), *Laughter in Paradise* (51), *The Fake* (53), *Hobson's Choice* (54), *The Black Knight* (55), *Campbell's Kingdom* (57), *Kidnapped* (60), *Siege of the Saxons* (63), *Mr Ten Per Cent* (66), etc. Recently on TV, especially as Algernon Blackwood in *Tales of Mystery*, and in *Dad's Army* series.

LAURIE, PIPER (1932–   ) (Rosetta Jacobs). Pert American leading lady of 50s costume charades: *Louisa* (debut) (49), *The Prince Who Was a Thief* (51), *Son of Ali Baba* (52), *The Golden Blade* (54), *Ain't Misbehavin'* (55), etc. Best role *The Hustler* (61).

LAVEN, ARNOLD (1922–   ). American director, former dialogue coach. *Without Warning* (52), *Down Three Dark Streets* (54), *The Rack* (56), *The Monster That Challenged the World* (57), *Slaughter on Tenth Avenue* (58), *Anna Lucasta* (58), *Geronimo* (also produced) (62), *The Glory Guys* (66), *Rough Night in Jericho* (67), *Sam Whiskey* (68), etc.

THE LAVENDER HILL MOB (GB 1950). One of the most affectionately-remembered Ealing comedies, a skit on *The Blue Lamp* with Alec Guinness and Stanley Holloway as unlikely gangsters almost getting away with the bullion. Lightly and amusingly scripted by T. E. B. Clarke, directed by Charles Crichton.

lavender print. A high quality, well-contrasted print, sometimes called a 'fine grain', struck from the original negative for the purpose of making duplicates.

LAVERICK, JUNE (1932–   ). British leading lady, groomed for star-dom by the Rank charm school of the 50s. *Doctor at Large* (56), *The Gypsy and the Gentleman* (57), *Son of Robin Hood* (58), *Follow a Star* (59), etc.; then lost to TV (*The Dickie Henderson Show*).

LAVI, DALIAH (c. 1940–   ). Israeli leading lady in international films. *Il Demonio* (Italian) (63), *Lord Jim* (65), *Ten Little Indians* (65), *The Silencers* (66), *The Spy with a Cold Nose* (67), *Nobody Runs Forever* (68), etc.

LAW, JOHN PHILIP (c. 1939–   ). American leading man. *The Russians Are Coming* (66), *Hurry Sundown* (67), *Barbarella* (68), *Skidoo* (68), *The Sergeant* (68), *Danger: Diabolik* (68), *The Hawaiians* (70), etc.

LAWFORD, PETER (1923–   ). British light leading man, former child actor, in Hollywood from 1938; recently a member of the Sinatra clan. *Poor Old Bill* (31), *The Boy from Barnardo's* (38), *Mrs Miniver* (42), *The White Cliffs of Dover* (44), *Cluny Brown* (46), *It Happened in Brooklyn* (47), *Easter Parade* (48), *Little Women* (49), *Royal Wedding* (52), *Exodus* (60), *Advise and Consent* (61), *Sylvia* (65), *Harlow* (65), *Dead Run* (Austria) (67), *Salt and Pepper* (GB) (68), *Buona Sera Mrs Campbell* (68), *The April Fools* (69), *One More Time* (70), etc. TV series: *Dear Phoebe* (55), *The Thin Man* (58).

LAWRANCE, JODY (1930–   ) (Josephine Lawrence Goddard). American leading lady. *Mask of the Avenger* (51), *Son of Dr Jekyll* (51), *The Brigand* (52), *Captain John Smith and Pocahontas* (53), *The Scarlet Hour* (55), etc.

LAWRENCE, BARBARA (1928–   ). American comedy actress, usually seen as wisecracking friend of the heroine. *Margie* (46), *You Were Meant for Me* (47), *Thieves Highway* (49), *Two Tickets to Broadway*

Lawrence, Delphi

(51), *Jesse James Versus the Daltons* (54), *Oklahoma* (55), *Joe Dakota* (57), etc.

LAWRENCE, DELPHI (c. 1927–   ). Anglo-Hungarian actress. In British films. *Blood Orange* (54), *Barbados Quest* (55), *It's Never Too Late* (56), *Too many Crooks* (59), *Cone of Silence* (60), *Farewell Performance* (63), *Pistolero* (US) (67), others.

LAWRENCE, FLORENCE (1886–1938). American leading lady of the silent screen; one of the industry's chief stars, she was known at first as 'the Biograph Girl'. *Miss Jones Entertains* (09), *Resurrection* (10), *A Singular Cynic* (14), *The Enfoldment* (20), many others. Retired in early 20s.

LAWRENCE, GERTRUDE (1898–1952) (Alexandre Dagmar Lawrence-Klasen). British revue and musical star, especially associated with Noël Coward. Her few films include *The Battle of Paris* (29), *No Funny Business* (32), *Mimi* (35), *Rembrandt* (36), *Men Are Not Gods* (37), *The Glass Menagerie* (50). Published autobiography 1949: *A Star Danced*. She was impersonated by Julie Andrews in *Star!* (68).

LAWRENCE, MARC (1910–   ). American character actor, former opera singer; usually seen as Italianate gangster. *White Woman* (33), *Dr Socrates* (35), *Penitentiary* (38), *The Housekeeper's Daughter* (39), *Johnny Apollo* (40), *The Monster and The Girl* (41), *Hold That Ghost* (42), *Dillinger* (45), *I Walk Alone* (47), *The Asphalt Jungle* (50), *My Favourite Spy* (51), *Helen of Troy* (55), *Kill Her Gently* (58), *Johnny Cool* (64), *Savage Pampas* (66), *Custer of the West* (67), *Krakatoa* (69), many others. Recently appeared in Italian spectaculars, directed a few; also wrote and directed *Nightmare in the Sun* (64).

LAWRENCE OF ARABIA (GB 1962). David Lean's epic account of a finally mysterious character: beautiful, careful, over-long. The supreme example of the modern multi-million-dollar international epic, several years in the making and shot on the actual locations. Peter O'Toole leads an all-star cast; production by Sam Spiegel, script by Robert Bolt. AA best picture, director, etc.

LAWRENCE, QUENTIN (c. 1923–   ). British director, from TV. *The Trollenberg Terror* (55), *Cash on Demand* (62), *The Man Who Finally Died* (63), *The Secret of Blood Island* (65), etc.

LAWSON, JOHN HOWARD (1886–   ). American writer with Marxist affiliations. *Heart of Spain* (37), *Algiers* (38), *Blockade* (38), *Five Came Back* (39), *Sahara* (43), *Counter Attack* (43), *Smash-Up* (47), etc.

LAWSON, WILFRID (1900–1966) (Wilfrid Worsnop). British character actor, on stage from 1916; revelled in eccentric parts. *Turn of the Tide* (film debut) (36), *Ladies in Love* (US) (36), *The Terror* (37),

The Gaunt Stranger (38), *Yellow Sands* (38), *Bank Holiday* (38), *Pygmalion* (as Dolittle) (38), *Stolen Life* (39), *Pastor Hall* (39), *The Long Voyage Home* (US) (40), *Tower of Terror* (41), *Hard Steel* (41), *The Night Has Eyes* (42), *Danny Boy* (42), *The Great Mr Handel* (42), *Thursday's Child* (43), *Fanny by Gaslight* (43), *The Turners of Prospect Road* (47), *The Prisoner* (55), *Tread Softly Stranger* (58), *Room at the Top* (59), *The Wrong Box* (66), etc.

LAWTON, FRANK (1904-1969). British leading man, on stage from 1923, screen from 1929 (*Young Woodley*). Married to Evelyn Laye. *Cavalcade* (33), *Friday the Thirteenth* (33), *David Copperfield* (34), *The Mill on the Floss* (36), *The Four Just Men* (39), *Went the Day Well* (42), *The Winslow Boy* (48), *Rough Shoot* (53), *A Night to Remember* (58), etc.

LAYDU, CLAUDE (1927–   ). Undernourished-looking French leading actor. *Diary of a Country Priest* (50), *Nous Sommes Tous les Assassins* (52), *Symphonie d'Amour* (55), *Le Dialogue des Carmelites* (59), etc.

LAYE, EVELYN (1900–   ). British leading lady of stage musicals since 1916. Made a few films in early 30s, notably *One Heavenly Night* (US) (31), *Waltz Time* (33), *Princess Charming* (34), *Evensong* (34); more recently appeared in *Make Mine a Million* (59). Married to Frank Lawton. Published autobiography 1958: *Boo to My Friends*.

LAZENBY, GEORGE (1939–   ). Australian leading man who made the big jump from TV commercials to playing James Bond in *On Her Majesty's Secret Service* (69).

LEACOCK, PHILIP (1917–   ). British director, in films from 1935. *The Brave Don't Cry* (52), *The Kidnappers* (53), *Escapade* (55), *The Spanish Gardener* (56), *High Tide at Noon* (57), *Innocent Sinners* (58), *The Rabbit Trap* (58), *Let No Man Write My Epitaph* (59), *The War Lover* (62), *Tamahine* (63), *Firecreek* (67) (produced only), etc.; TV series as producer and director include *Route 66, Cimarron Strip*.

LEACOCK, RICHARD (1921–   ). British-born cameraman and director, brother of Philip Leacock. Worked with Flaherty and is now associated with the 'cinema vérité' school; has made such shorts as *Primary, The Chair, Quins*, etc.

leader. Length of blank film joined to the beginning of a reel for lacing up in projector. 'Academy' leaders give a numbered countdown to the start of action.

†LEAN, DAVID (1908–   ). Distinguished British director, former editor, in films from 1928. *In Which We Serve* (co-d) (42), *This Happy Breed* (44), *Blithe Spirit* (45), *Brief Encounter* (46), *Great Expectations* (46), *Oliver Twist* (48), *The Passionate Friends* (48), *Madeleine* (49),

The Sound Barrier (also produced) (51), *Hobson's Choice* (also produced) (54), *Summer Madness* (55), *The Bridge on the River Kwai* (AA) (57), *Lawrence of Arabia* (AA) (62), *Doctor Zhivago* (66), *Ryan's Daughter* (69).

LEAVES FROM SATAN'S BOOK (Denmark 1921). A compendium of stories illustrating the work of the devil through the ages; written and directed by Carl Dreyer.

LEAVITT, SAM (* –). American cinematographer. *The Thief* (52), *A Star Is Born* (54), *Carmen Jones* (54), *The Man with the Golden Arm* (55), *The Defiant Ones* (58), *Anatomy of a Murder* (59), *Advise and Consent* (62), *Two on a Guillotine* (64), *Major Dundee* (65), *Brainstorm* (65), *An American Dream* (66), *Guess Who's Coming to Dinner* (67), *The Desperados* (68), etc.

LEBEDEFF, IVAN (1899–1953). Russian character actor, former diplomat, in US from 1925. *The Sorrows of Satan* (27), *Midnight Mystery* (30), *Blonde Bombshell* (33), *China Seas* (35), *History Is Made at Night* (37), *Hotel for Women* (39), *The Shanghai Gesture* (41), *They Are Guilty* (45), *The Snows of Kilimanjaro* (52), many others.

LE BORG, REGINALD (1902–). Austrian-born director, in Hollywood from 1937, at first as shorts director. Output mainly routine with occasional flashes of talent. *She's For Me* (42), *The Mummy's Ghost* (44), *Calling Dr Death* (44), *San Diego I Love You* (45), *Joe Palooka, Champ* (46), *Young Daniel Boone* (47), *Wyoming Mail* (49), *Bad Blonde* (51), *Sins of Jezebel* (53), *The Black Sleep* (56), *The Dalton Girls* (57), *The Flight That Disappeared* (61), *The Diary of a Madman* (62), many others.

LE BRETON, AUGUSTE (1915–). French writer. *Razzia sur la Chnouf* (54), *Rififi* (55), *Bob le Flambeur* (56), *Rafles sur la Ville* (57), etc.

LE CHANOIS, JEAN-PAUL (1909–) (J.-P. Dreyfus). French director. *L'École Buissonière* (48), *La Belle Que Voilà* (51), *Papa, Mama, the Maid and I* (54), *The Case of Dr Laurent* (56), *Les Misérables* (58), *Monsieur* (64), *Le Jardinier d'Argenteuil* (66), etc.

LECLERC, GINETTE (1912–). French stage and screen actress. Best-known films: *Prison sans Barreaux* (38), *La Femme du Boulanger* (38), *Le Corbeau* (43), *Le Plaisir* (51), *Les Amants du Tage* (54), *Gas-Oil* (55), *Le Cave Se Rebiffe* (61), etc.

LEDERER, CHARLES (c. 1906–). American writer, in Hollywood since 1931. *The Front Page* (31), *Kiss of Death* (48), *The Thing* (52), *It Started with a Kiss* (58), *Ocean's Eleven* (61), *Mutiny on the Bounty* (62), many others. Has directed occasionally: *Fingers at the Window* (42), *On the Loose* (51), *Never Steal Anything Small* (also wrote) (58), etc.

LEDERER, FRANCIS (1906–   ). Czech-born leading man, in Hollywood from 1933, after European stage and film experience. *Atlantic* (Ger.) (30), *The Bracelet* (Ger.) (32), *The Pursuit of Happiness* (34), *It's All Yours* (36), *The Lone Wolf in Paris* (37), *Midnight* (38), *Confessions of a Nazi Spy* (39), *The Man I Married* (40), *The Bridge of San Luis Rey* (44), *A Voice in the Wind* (45), *The Diary of a Chambermaid* (45), *Million Dollar Weekend* (48), *Captain Carey USA (After Midnight)* (49), *A Woman of Distinction* (50), *Stolen Identity* (53), *Lisbon* (56), *The Return of Dracula (The Fantastic Disappearing Man)* (58), *Terror Is a Man* (59), etc.

LEDERMAN, D. ROSS (1895–   ). American director, former prop man for Mack Sennett. Directed several Rin Tin Tin features. Later: *Riding Tornado* (32), *Glamour for Sale* (40), *The Body Disappears* (41), *Strange Alibi* (41), *Shadows on the Stairs* (43), etc.

LEE, ANNA (1914–   ) (Joanna Winnifrith). British leading lady, married to director Robert Stevenson; in US since 1939. *The Camels Are Coming* (36), *King Solomon's Mines* (37), *The Four Just Men* (39), *My Life with Caroline* (41), *Summer Storm* (44), *Fort Apache* (48), *Whatever Happened to Baby Jane* (62), *The Sound of Music* (65), *Seven Women* (65), *In Like Flint* (67), many others.

LEE, BELINDA (1935–1961). British leading lady who made film debut in *The Runaway Bus* (54) and was trained for stardom by Rank but given poor material (*Miracle in Soho* [57], *The Big Money* [58], etc.). Appeared in French and Italian spectacles and sex melodramas; died in car crash.

LEE, BERNARD (1908–   ). British character actor with solid, friendly personality, on stage from 1926. In films, often a sergeant or a superintendent . . . or 'M' in the James Bond films. *The River House Mystery* (35), *The Terror* (37), *Spare a Copper* (40), *Once a Crook* (41), etc.; war service; *The Courtneys of Curzon Street* (47), *The Fallen Idol* (48), *Quartet* (48), *The Third Man* (49), *The Blue Lamp* (50), *Appointment with Venus* (51), *The Gift Horse* (52), *The Purple Plain* (54), *Father Brown* (54), *The Battle of the River Plate* (56), *Dunkirk* (58), *Danger Within* (59), *The Angry Silence* (59), *The Secret Partner* (60), *Whistle Down the Wind* (61), *Dr No* (62), *Two Left Feet* (63), *From Russia with Love* (63), *Ring of Spies* (63), *Goldfinger* (64), *The Legend of Young Dick Turpin* (65), *Thunderball* (65), *The Spy Who Came In from the Cold* (65), *You Only Live Twice* (66), many others.

†LEE, CANADA (1907–1952) (Leonard Canegata). American Negro actor. *Lifeboat* (43), *Body and Soul* (47), *Lost Boundaries* (49), *Cry the Beloved Country* (52).

LEE, CHRISTOPHER (1922–   ). Gaunt British actor whose personality lends itself to sinister roles. In innumerable films, mostly second

Lee, Gypsy Rose

features and TV playlets, since 1947. *The Curse of Frankenstein* (56), *A Tale of Two Cities* (57), *Dracula* (57), *City of the Dead* (60), *The Virgin of Nuremberg* (63), *The Gorgon* (64), *She* (65), *The Face of Fu Manchu* (65), *Dracula, Prince of Darkness* (65), *Rasputin the Mad Monk* (66), *The Devil Rides Out* (68), *Dracula is Risen from the Grave* (68), *Julius Caesar* (70), etc.; also in German films as Sherlock Holmes.

LEE, GYPSY ROSE (1914–) (Louise Hovick). American burlesque artiste, on stage from six years old; her early life, glamourized, is recounted in *Gypsy* (62). Film appearances include *Ali Baba Goes to Town* (38), *My Lucky Star* (39), *Belle of the Yukon* (44), *Babes in Baghdad* (52), *Screaming Mimi* (57), *Wind Across the Everglades* (58), *The Stripper* (62), *The Trouble with Angels* (66). Wrote novel *The G-String Murders*, on which film *Lady of Burlesque* was based in 1942.

LEE, JACK (c. 1913–). British director, originally in documentaries. *Close Quarters* (44), *Children on Trial* (46), *The Woman in the Hall* (47), *The Wooden Horse* (co-d) (50), *Turn the Key Softly* (53), *A Town Like Alice* (56), *Robbery under Arms* (57), *The Captain's Table* (58), *Circle of Deception* (61), etc.

LEE, MICHELE (1942–) (M. Dusiak). American leading lady and singer, with stage experience. *How to Succeed in Business* (67), *The Love Bug* (69), *Billy Bright* (69).

LEE, PEGGY (1920–) (Norma Egstrom). American night-club singer, in occasional films: *Mr Music* (50), *The Jazz Singer* (53), *Pete Kelly's Blues* (55), etc. Sang and co-wrote songs for *Lady and the Tramp* (56).

LEE, ROWLAND V. (1891–). American director, in films from 1918. *Alice Adams* (26), *Barbed Wire* (26), *The Mysterious Dr Fu Manchu* (29), *Zoo in Budapest* (33), *The Count of Monte Cristo* (34), *Cardinal Richelieu* (35), *The Three Musketeers* (36), *Son of Frankenstein* (39), *Tower of London* (39), *Son of Monte Cristo* (41), *The Bridge of San Luis Rey* (44), *Captain Kidd* (45), etc.; inactive recently apart from producing *The Big Fisherman* (59). Former actor and director with Thomas Ince.

LEECH, RICHARD (1922–). British character actor, often as army or air force officer. *The Dam Busters* (55), *A Night to Remember* (57), *The Good Companions* (57), *Ice Cold in Alex* (59), *The Horse's Mouth* (59), *Tunes of Glory* (60), *The Wild and the Willing* (62), *I Thank a Fool* (63), *The Fighting Price of Donegal* (66), etc.

LEEDS, ANDREA (1914–) (Antoinette Lees). American leading lady, in several films of the late 30s. *Come and Get It* (36), *Stage Door* (37), *The Goldwyn Follies* (39), *Letter of Introduction* (39), *Swanee River* (39), etc.

LEEDS, HERBERT I. (* –). American director of second features. *Island in the Sky* (38), *The Cisco Kid and the Lady* (39), *Manila Calling* (42), *Time to Kill* (43), *Let's Live Again* (48), *Father's Wild Game* (51), etc.

†LEE-THOMPSON, J. (1914–). British director, former actor and playwright. *The Middle Watch* (w) (36), *For Them That Trespass* (w) (48), *Murder without Crime* (w, d) (50), *The Yellow Balloon* (w, d) (52), *The Weak and the Wicked* (w, d) (53), *As Long As They're Happy* (d) (54), *For Better For Worse* (d) (54), *An Alligator Named Daisy* (d) (55), *Yield to the Night* (d) (56), *The Good Companions* (co-p, d) (57), *Woman in a Dressing Gown* (d) (58), *Ice Cold in Alex* (d) (58), *No Trees in the Street* (d) (59), *Tiger Bay* (d) (59), *Northwest Frontier* (d) (59), *I Aim at the Stars* (d) (US) (60), *The Guns of Navarone* (d) (61), *Cape Fear* (d) (US) (62), *Taras Bulba* (d) (US) (62), *Kings of the Sun* (d) (US) (63), *What a Way To Go* (d) (US) (64), *John Goldfarb Please Come Home* (d) (US) (65), *Return from the Ashes* (p, d) (65), *Eye of the Devil* ('13') (p, d) (66), *Mackenna's Gold* (d) (US) (68), *Before Winter Comes* (d) (68), *The Most Dangerous Man in the World* (d) (69), *Country Dance* (d) (70).

LE GALIENNE, EVA (1899–). American stage actress whose only film appearance has been in *Prince of Players* (55).

LEGG, STUART (1910–). British documentarist and administrator. From 1932 with GPO Film Unit and Empire Marketing Board. 1939/45: National Film Board of Canada. 1953 on: director of Film Centre Ltd.

LEGGATT, ALISON (1904–). British character actress, mainly on stage. *This Happy Breed* (44), *Marry Me* (47), *The Card* (52), *Touch and Go* (55), *Never Take Sweets from a Stranger* (60), etc.

LEGRAND, MICHEL (1931–). French composer. *Lola* (61), *Eva* (62), *Vivre sa Vie* (62), *La Baie des Anges* (63), *The Umbrellas of Cherbourg* (64), *Bande a Part* (64), *Une Femme Mariée* (65), *Les Demoiselles de Rochefort* (67), *Ice Station Zebra* (68), etc.

LEHMAN, ERNEST (c. 1920–). American screenwriter. *Inside Story* (48), *Executive Suite* (54), *Sabrina* (54), *The Sweet Smell of Success* (57), *North by Northwest* (59), *The Prize* (63), *The Sound of Music* (65), *Who's Afraid of Virginia Woolf?* (also produced) (66), *Hello Dolly* (also produced) (69), *Portnoy's Complaint* (also produced and directed) (70), etc.

LEHMANN, CARLA (1917–). Canadian leading lady, in British films of the 40s. *So This Is London* (39), *Cottage to Let* (41), *Talk about Jacqueline* (42), *Acacia Avenue* (45), *Fame Is the Spur* (47), etc.

LEIBER, FRITZ (1883–1949). American Shakespearean actor who played many supporting roles in films. *A Tale of Two Cities* (35), *Anthony Adverse* (36), *The Hunchback of Notre Dame* (40), *Phantom of the Opera* (43), *Humoresque* (46), *Another Part of the Forest* (48), etc.

LEIGH, JANET (1927–   ) (Jeanette Morrison). American leading lady, in films from 1947. *The Romance of Rosy Ridge* (debut) (47), *Little Women* (49), *The Forsyte Saga* (49), *Two Tickets to Broadway* (51), *Prince Valiant* (54), *My Sister Eileen* (55), *Safari* (56), *The Vikings* (58), *Psycho* (60), *The Manchurian Candidate* (62), *Bye Bye Birdie* (63), *Wives and Lovers* (63), *Kid Rodelo* (65), *The Moving Target* (66), *Three on a Couch* (66), *An American Dream* (*See You in Hell, Darling*) (66), *Grand Slam* (67), *Hello Down There* (69), many others.

LEIGH, SUZANNA (1945–   ). British leading lady. *Boeing Boeing* (66), *Paradise Hawaiian Style* (66), *Deadlier Than the Male* (67).

†LEIGH, VIVIEN (1913–1967) (Vivien Hartley). Distinguished British leading lady whose stage and screen career was limited by delicate health; for many years the wife of Laurence Olivier. *Things Are Looking Up* (34), *The Village Squire* (35), *Gentleman's Agreement* (35), *Look Up and Laugh* (35), *Fire over England* (36), *Dark Journey* (37), *Storm in a Teacup* (37), *St Martin's Lane* (38), *Twenty-one Days* (38), *A Yank at Oxford* (38), *Gone with the Wind* (AA: as Scarlett O'Hara) (US) (39), *Waterloo Bridge* (US) (40), *Lady Hamilton* (US) (41), *Caesar and Cleopatra* (45), *Anna Karenina* (48), *A Streetcar Named Desire* (AA) (US) (51), *The Deep Blue Sea* (55), *The Roman Spring of Mrs Stone* (61), *Ship of Fools* (US) (65).

LEIGH-HUNT, RONALD (c. 1916–   ). Smooth British supporting actor. *Tiger by the Tail* (53), *Shadow of a Man* (55), *A Touch of Larceny* (59), *Sink the Bismarck* (60), *Piccadilly Third Stop* (61), *The Truth About Spring* (65), many others.

LEIGHTON, MARGARET (1922–   ). British leading lady, on stage since 1938. *Bonnie Prince Charlie* (debut) (48), *Under Capricorn* (49), *The Astonished Heart* (50), *The Holly and the Ivy* (54), *The Constant Husband* (55), *The Sound and the Fury* (58), *The Waltz of the Toreadors* (61), *The Best Man* (64), *Seven Women* (65), etc.

†LEISEN, MITCHELL (1898–   ). American director, former set designer; his films are mostly romantic trifles, but many have considerable pictorial style. *Cradle Song* (33), *Death Takes a Holiday* (34), *Murder at the Vanities* (34), *Behold My Wife* (35), *Four Hours to Kill* (35), *Hands across the Table* (35), *Thirteen Hours by Air* (36), *The Big Broadcast of 1937*), *Swing High Swing Low* (37), *Easy Living* (37), *The Big Broadcast of 1938*, *Artists and Models Abroad* (38), *Midnight* (39), *Remember the Night* (40), *Arise My Love* (40), *I Wanted Wings* (41), *Hold Back the Dawn* (41), *The Lady Is Willing* (42),

Take a Letter Darling (42), *No Time for Love* (also produced) (43), *Lady in the Dark* (also wrote) (44), *Frenchman's Creek* (44), *Practically Yours* (also produced) (44), *Kitty* (45), *Masquerade in Mexico* (45), *To Each His Own* (46), *Suddenly It's Spring* (46), *Golden Earrings* (47), *Dream Girl* (48), *Bride of Vengeance* (49), *Song of Surrender* (49), *Captain Carey USA* (50), *No Man of Her Own* (also wrote) (50), *The Mating Season* (51), *Darling How Could You* (51), *Young Man with Ideas* (52), *Tonight We Sing* (53), *Bedevilled* (55), *The Girl Most Likely* (57).

LEISER, ERWIN (1923–). Swedish documentarist. *Mein Kampf* (*Blodige Tiden*) (59), *Murder by Signature* (*Eichmann and the Third Reich*) (61), etc.

LEISTER, FREDERICK (1885–). British character actor, on stage from 1906, screen from 20s. Usually plays distinguished and kindly professional men. *Dreyfus* (30), *The Iron Duke* (35), *Goodbye Mr Chips* (39), *The Prime Minister* (41), *Dear Octopus* (43), *The Hundred Pound Window* (43), *The Captive Heart* (46), *Quartet* (48), *The End of the Affair* (54), *Left, Right and Centre* (59), many others.

†LELOUCH, CLAUDE (1937–). French director with lush visual style. *Le Propre de l'Homme* (60), *Une Fille et des Fusils* (63), *Un Homme et un Femme* (66), *Vivre Pour Vivre* (67), *A Man I Like* (69), *Le Rose et le Noir* (70).

LE MAY, ALAN (1899–). American writer. *Reap the Wild Wind* (42), *The Adventures of Mark Twain* (44), *Tap Roots* (48), *High Lonesome* (also directed) (50), *Thunder in the Dust* (51), *I Dream of Jeannie* (53), *The Searchers* (56), etc.

LE MESURIER, JOHN (1912–). British character actor. Usually plays bewildered professional men; a favourite for cameo roles since 1946. *Death in the Hand* (48), *Beautiful Stranger* (54), *Private's Progress* (55), *Happy Is the Bride* (57), *I Was Monty's Double* (58), *School for Scoundrels* (60), *Only Two Can Play* (61), *Invasion Quartet* (62), *The Pink Panther* (63), *The Moonspinners* (64), *Masquerade* (65), *Where the Spies Are* (65), *The Wrong Box* (66), *The Midas Run* (69), many others.

†LEMMON, JACK (1925–). American light comedy leading man with Broadway experience; lately typed in mildly lecherous or otherwise sex-fraught roles. *It Should Happen to You* (debut) (53), *Three for the Show* (53), *Phffft* (54), *My Sister Eileen* (55), *Mister Roberts* (AA) (55), *You Can't Run Away From It* (56), *Fire Down Below* (57), *Operation Mad Ball* (57), *Bell, Book and Candle* (58), *It Happened to Jane* (58), *Some Like It Hot* (59), *The Apartment* (60), *The Notorious Landlady* (62), *Days of Wine and Roses* (62), *Irma La Douce* (63), *Under the Yum Yum Tree* (64), *Good Neighbour Sam* (64), *How to Murder Your Wife* (65), *The Great Race* (65), *The Fortune*

Leni, Paul

Cookie (66), *Luv* (67), *The Odd Couple* (68), *The April Fools* (69), *The Out-of-Towners* (69).

LENI, PAUL (1885–1929). German director, former set designer. Best known for *Waxworks* (24), *The Cat and the Canary* (US) (27).

LENICA, JAN (1928–   ). Polish animator. *Once Upon a Time, Dom Labyrinth, Rhinosceros*, etc.

LENNART, ISABEL (c. 1914–   ). American screenwriter. *Lost Angel* (44), *Anchors Aweigh* (45), *East Side West Side* (49), *Skirts Ahoy* (52), *Latin Lovers* (54), *Inn of the Sixth Happiness* (58), *The Sundowners* (60), *Period of Adjustment* (62), *Funny Girl* (68), many others.

LENYA, LOTTE (1900–   ) (Caroline Blamauer). Austrian character actress; also inimitable singer of her late husband Kurt Weill's songs. *Die Dreigroschenoper* (31), *The Roman Spring of Mrs Stone* (61), *From Russia with Love* (63), *The Appointment* (69), etc.

LEONARD, ROBERT Z. (1889–1968). American director (former actor), in Hollywood from 1915. *The Waning Sex* (27), *The Demi-Bride* (27), *Adam and Evil* (28), *Tea for Three* (29), *Susan Lenox* (31), *Strange Interval* (32), *Dancing Lady* (33), *Peg o' My Heart* (33), *Outcast Lady* (34), *The Great Ziegfeld* (36), *Piccadilly Jim* (37), *Escapade* (37), *Maytime* (38), *The Firefly* (38), *New Moon* (also produced) (40), *Pride and Prejudice* (40), *Ziegfeld Girl* (41), *When Ladies Meet* (also produced) (41), *We Were Dancing* (42), *Stand By for Action* (42), *The Man from Down Under* (43), *Marriage Is a Private Affair* (44), *Weekend at the Waldorf* (45), *The Secret Heart* (46), *B.F.'s Daughter* (48), *The Bribe* (48), *In the Good Old Summertime* (49), *Nancy Goes to Rio* (49), *Duchess of Idaho* (50), *Everything I Have Is Yours* (52), *The Clown* (53), *The King's Thief* (55), *Kelly and Me* (56), *Beautiful But Dangerous* (It.) (56), others.

LEONARD, SHELDON (1907–   ) (Sheldon Bershad). American stage actor, on screen from 1939 in supporting roles, usually as comic Runyonesque gangster, e.g. *Lucky Jordan* (44), *Stop, You're Killing Me* (53), *Guys and Dolls* (55), *A Pocketful of Miracles* (61). Became powerful producer and director of TV series, including *I Spy* (65–68), *Gomer Pyle* (64–68), *My World and Welcome to It* (69).

LEONE, SERGIO (1921–   ). Italian director who has come to the fore internationally via his savage Westerns on the American pattern. *A Fistful of Dollars* (64), *For a Few Dollars More* (65), *The Good The Bad and The Ugly* (67), *Once Upon a Time in the West* (69), etc.

LEONTOVICH, EUGENIE (1894–   ). Russian stage actress whose rare film appearances include *Four Sons* (40), *Homicidal* (61).

THE LEOPARD (Italy 1963). An ambitious production based on Lampedusa's complex historical novel about Italian politics and noble life at the time of Garibaldi. Burt Lancaster made a somewhat unconvincing Italian, and the film in its international version was not popular; but Luchino Visconti's direction and Giuseppe Rotunno's cinematography were praised.

leprechauns have made rare but effective screen appearances in the persons of Cecil Kellaway (*Luck of the Irish*), Jimmy O'Dea (*Darby O'Gill and the Little People*), Don Beddoe (*Jack the Giant Killer*) and Tommy Steele (*Finian's Rainbow*).

LERNER, ALAN JAY (1918–). American composer and writer. Films using his work include: *An American in Paris* (w) (AA) (51), *Gigi* (score) (AA) (58), *My Fair Lady* (script and score in collaboration) (AA) (64), *Camelot* (script and score in collaboration) (67), *On a Clear Day You Can See Forever* (69), others.

LERNER, IRVING (1909–). American director, former cameraman, noted for short documentaries. *Muscle Beach* (co-ed) (48), *Man Crazy* (54), *Murder by Contract* (58), *Studs Lonigan* (60), *Cry of Battle* (63), *Custer of the West* (co-p only) (67), etc.

LE ROY, BABY (1932–) (Le Roy Winnebrenner). American toddler who appeared to general delight in *Bedtime Story* (33), *Alice in Wonderland* (33), *The Old-Fashioned Way* (34), *It's a Gift* (34), etc. The story goes that W. C. Fields, hating babies, mixed gin with his orange juice; anyway Baby Le Roy retired soon after their encounter.

LE ROY, MERVYN (1900–). American director, former actor, in Hollywood from 1924. *Hot Stuff* (27), *Top Speed* (28), *Broken Dishes* (29), *Little Caesar* (30), *Broadminded* (31), *Five Star Final* (32), *Three on a Match* (32), *I Am a Fugitive from a Chain Gang* (32), *Tugboat Annie* (32), *Gold Diggers of 1933*, *Hi Nellie* (33), *Oil for the Lamps of China* (33), *Page Miss Glory* (34), *I Found Stella Parish* (35), *Anthony Adverse* (36), *Three Men on a Horse* (36), *They Won't Forget* (37), *Fools for Scandal* (38), *Stand Up and Fight* (produced only) (38), *The Wizard of Oz* (produced only) (39), *At the Circus* (produced only) (39), *Waterloo Bridge* (40), *Escape* (40), *Blossoms in the Dust* (41), *Unholy Partners* (41), *Johnny Eager* (41), *Random Harvest* (42), *Madame Curie* (43), *Thirty Seconds over Tokyo* (44); war service: *Without Reservations* (47), *Homecoming* (48), *Little Women* (49), *Any Number Can Play* (49), *East Side West Side* (50), *Quo Vadis* (51), *Lovely To Look At* (52), *Million Dollar Mermaid* (53), *Rose Marie* (54), *Mister Roberts* (co-d) (55), *Strange Lady in Town* (also produced) (55), *The Bad Seed* (also produced) (56), *Toward the Unknown* (also produced) (56), *No Time for Sergeants* (also produced) (58), *Home*

Before Dark (also produced) (59), *The FBI Story* (also produced) (59), *A Majority of One* (also produced) (60), *The Devil at Four O'Clock* (also produced) (61), *Gypsy* (also produced) (62), *Mary Mary* (also produced) (63), *Moment to Moment* (also produced) (65), etc.

lesbianism has now come into its own with the filming of *The Killing of Sister George*; but for many years it was unthinkable as a screen subject. *These Three* in 1936 had to be so changed that it was almost unrecognizable as a version of *The Children's Hour*; and the matter was scarcely broached again until the 50s, when the French brought it up in *Olivia* and *The Girl with the Golden Eyes*. The first Hollywood film to bring the subject to our notice was *A Walk on the Wild Side* (62); since then there have been more or less discreet references in *The Haunting, The Balcony, Lilith, The Silence, La Religieuse, The Group, Tony Rome, The Fox, Therese and Isabelle, Baby Love* and *The Smashing Bird I Used to Know*; while *The Children's Hour* was filmed again, this time with its full force.

LESLEY, CAROLE (1935–   ). British leading lady briefly groomed for stardom. *Those Dangerous Years* (57), *Woman in a Dressing-Gown* (57), *No Trees in the Street* (59), *Doctor in Love* (60), *What a Whopper* (62), *The Pot Carriers* (62), etc. Retired.

LESLIE, BETHEL (1930–   ). American leading actress, mainly on TV (*The Richard Boone Show*). Films include *Captain Newman* (63), *A Rage to Live* (65).

LESLIE, JOAN (1925–   ) (Joan Brodell). Pert, pretty American leading lady of the 40s; in vaudeville from childhood. *Camille* (debut) (36), *Men with Wings* (38), *Foreign Correspondent* (40), *High Sierra* (41), *Sergeant York* (41), *The Male Animal* (42), *Yankee Doodle Dandy* (42), *The Hard Way* (42), *This Is the Army* (43), *Thank Your Lucky Stars* (43), *Hollywood Canteen* (44) *Rhapsody in Blue* (45), *Where Do We Go from Here?* (45), *Too Young to Know* (45), *Cinderella Jones* (46), *Royal Flush* (46), *Repeat Performance* (47), *Northwest Stampede* (49), *Born to Be Bad* (51), *The Toughest Man in Arizona* (52), *The Woman They Almost Lynched* (53), *Jubilee Trail* (54), *The Revolt of Mamie Stover* (last to date) (57), others. Has made some TV appearances.

LES MISERABLES. Film versions of Victor Hugo's classic novel about escaped convict Jean Valjean were made in 1909 (US), 1913 (France), 1918 (US), 1922 (GB), 1925 (France), 1934 (France), 1935 (US, with Fredric March and Charles Laughton), 1946 (Italy), 1952 (US, with Michael Rennie and Robert Newton) and 1957 (France, with Jean Gabin and Bernard Blier). The recent TV series, *The Fugitive*, acknowledges its indebtedness to the theme.

LESSER, SOL (1890–   ). American pioneer exhibitor of silent days, later producer: many Tarzan films, *Thunder Over Mexico* (33), *Our Town* (40), *Kontiki* (52), etc.

LESTER, BRUCE (1912–   ) (Bruce Lister). South African leading man who made some British and American films; now plays support roles. *Death at Broadcasting House* (34), *Crime over London* (37), *If I Were King* (39), *Pride and Prejudice* (40), *Above Suspicion* (43), *Golden Earrings* (47), *King Richard and the Crusaders* (54), etc.

†LESTER, DICK (1932–   ). American-born director, long in Britain; associated with radio and TV 'Goon' shows. *It's Trad, Dad* (61), *The Mouse on the Moon* (63), *A Hard Day's Night* (64), *The Knack* (65), *Help!* (65), *A Funny Thing Happened on the Way to the Forum* (66), *How I Won the War* (67), *Petulia* (67), *The Bed-Sitting Room* (69).

LESTER, MARK (1957–   ). British child actor: *Oliver* (title role) (68), *Run Wild Run Free* (69).

letters have provided a starting point or climax for several films. Undelivered ones for *Address Unknown*, *The Postman Didn't Ring*; misdelivered ones for *Dear Ruth*, *A Letter for Evie*; lost ones for *Cause for Alarm*, *Never Put It In Writing*; indiscreet ones for *A Letter To Three Wives*, *So Evil My Love*, *The Letter*; posthumous ones for *Letter from an Unknown Woman*, *The Lost Moment*, *Mister Roberts*.

LETTER FROM AN UNKNOWN WOMAN (US 1948). Out of Stefan Zweig's romantic novelette Max Ophuls fashioned a finely-decorated though studio-bound piece of middle-European nostalgia; elegant, tragic and luxurious. With Joan Fontaine, Louis Jourdan.

LEVANT, OSCAR (1906–   ). American actor-pianist who plays amiably grouchy neurotics in occasional films. *Dance of Life* (debut) (29), *Rhythm on the River* (40), *Kiss the Boys Goodbye* (41), *Rhapsody in Blue* (45), *Humoresque* (46), *Romance on the High Seas* (48), *You Were Meant for Me* (47), *The Barkleys of Broadway* (48), *An American in Paris* (51), *The Band Wagon* (53), *The Cobweb* (56), etc. Has published two autobiographical segments: *A Smattering of Ignorance* and *Memoirs of an Amnesiac.*

LEVEN, BORIS (c.1900–   ). Russian-born production designer, long in US. *Alexander's Ragtime Band* (38), *The Shanghai Gesture* (41), *Mr Peabody and the Mermaid* (48), *Sudden Fear* (52), *Giant* (56), *Anatomy of a Murder* (59), *West Side Story* (AA) (61), *The Sound of Music* (65), *The Sand Pebbles* (67), *Star!* (68), many others.

LEVENE, SAM (1906–   ). American stage actor, often in Runyon-esque film roles. *Three Men on a Horse* (debut) (36), *Golden Boy* (39),

Le Vien, Jack

The Purple Heart (43), *Crossfire* (47), *Boomerang* (47), *Act One* (63), etc.; more recently on Broadway.

LE VIEN, JACK (1918–   ). American documentarist responsible for several distinguished compilation films: *Black Fox* (62), *The Finest Hours* (64), *A King's Story* (67); also TV series on Churchill, *The Valiant Years* (60).

LEVIEN, SONYA (1888–1960). American writer, former lawyer. Story editor at various times for Fox, MGM, Paramount. Own scripts include *Cavalcade* (33), *State Fair* (33), *Berkeley Square* (33), *In Old Chicago* (38), *The Hunchback of Notre Dame* (40), *Ziegfeld Girl* (41), *Rhapsody in Blue* (45), *Cass Timberlane* (48), *Quo Vadis* (51), *Interrupted Melody* (AA) (55), *Jeanne Eagels* (58), etc.

LEVIN, HENRY (1909–   ). American director, in Hollywood from 1943 after stage experience. *Cry of the Werewolf* (44), *I Love a Mystery* (45), *The Guilt of Janet Ames* (47), *Jolson Sings Again* (49), *The Petty Girl* (50), *Convicted* (50), *Belles on Their Toes* (52), *The President's Lady* (52), *Mister Scoutmaster* (53), *Gambler from Natchez* (54), *The Mating of Millie* (55), *The Lonely Man* (57), *Bernardine* (57), *Let's Be Happy* (GB) (57), *The Remarkable Mr Pennypacker* (58), *Holiday for Lovers* (59), *Journey to the Centre of the Earth* (59), *Where the Boys Are* (60), *The Wonderful World of the Brothers Grimm* (62), *Come Fly with Me* (63), *Honeymoon Hotel* (64), *Genghis Khan* (65), *Kiss the Girls and Make Them Die* (66), *Murderers Row* (67), *The Desperados* (69), others.

LEVINE, JOSEPH E. (1905–   ). American production executive and showman, former theatre owner. Formed Embassy Pictures in late 50s, originally to exploit cheap European spectacles; also set up finance for films like *Eight and a Half*, *Divorce Italian Style*, *Boccaccio 70*. Personally produced *The Carpetbaggers* (63), *Where Love Has Gone* (64), *Harlow* (65). *The Oscar* (66), *The Spy With a Cold Nose* (67), etc.

LEVY, LOUIS (1893–   ). British musical director and composer, in films since 1916. Scored *Nanook of the North* (20). With Gaumont and Gainsborough 1928–47, supervising all musical productions; also *Pygmalion* (38), *The Citadel* (38), many others.

LEVY, RALPH (1919–   ). American director, in TV from 1947. *Bedtime Story* (64), *Do Not Disturb* (65).

LEVY, RAOUL (1922–67). French producer. *Les Orgueilleux* (53), *And God Created Woman* (also wrote) (56), *Heaven Fell That Night* (57), *En Cas de Malheur* (58), *Babette Goes to War* (also co-wrote) (59), *Moderato Cantabile* (60), *The Truth* (60), *The Defector* (also wrote and directed) (66), etc.

†LEWIN, ALBERT (1895–1968). American writer-producer-director with something of an Omar Khayyam fixation. Production executive 1931–41. *The Moon and Sixpence* (w, d) (42), *The Picture of Dorian Gray* (w, d) (44), *The Private Affairs of Bel Ami* (w, p, d) (47), *Pandora and the Flying Dutchman* (w, p, d) (51), *Saadia* (w, p, d) (54), *The Living Idol* (w, p, d) (57).

LEWIS, JAY (1914–1969). British producer, in films from 1933. *Morning Departure* (50), *The Gift Horse* (52), etc. Directed *The Baby and the Battleship* (55), *Invasion Quartet* (61), *Live Now Pay Later* (62), *A Home of Your Own* (65), etc.

LEWIS, JERRY (1926–   ) (Joseph Levitch). Goonish American comedian, formerly in partnership with DEAN MARTIN (qv). Their films together include *My Friend Irma* (49), *At War with the Army* (51), *Scared Stiff* (53), *Living It Up* (55), *Pardners* (57), *Hollywood or Bust* (57). On his own, Lewis has aroused both enthusiasm and antipathy for his mixture of sentimental mugging and knockabout farce. *The Bellboy* (59), *Cinderfella* (60), *Ladies' Man* (61), *The Nutty Professor* (63), *Who's Minding the Store* (64), *The Patsy* (65), *The Disorderly Orderly* (65), *The Family Jewels* (65), etc. Has also directed several of these. Recently trying new comedy styles: *Boeing Boeing* (66), *Three on a Couch* (66), *Way Way Out* (66), *The Big Mouth* (67), *Don't Raise the Bridge Lower the River* (68), *Hook Line and Sinker* (69). Director only of *One More Time* (70).

LEWIS, JOSEPH H. (1900–   ). American director, mainly of second features, some of them well above average. *Two-Fisted Rangers* (40), *The Mad Doctor of Market Street* (41), *Bombs over Burma* (42), *Minstrel Man* (44), *My Name Is Julia Ross* (45), *So Dark the Night* (46), *The Jolson Story* (musical numbers only) (46), *The Swordsman* (47), *The Undercover Man* (49), *A Lady without Passport* (50), *Gun Crazy* (50), *Retreat Hell* (52), *Cry of the Hunted* (53), *The Big Combo* (55), *A Lawless Street* (55), *The Halliday Brand* (56), *Terror in a Texas Town* (58), etc.

LEWIS, RONALD (1928–   ). British leading man, in films from 1953. *The Prisoner* (55), *Storm over the Nile* (55), *A Hill in Korea* (56), *Bachelor of Hearts* (59), *The Full Treatment* (61), *Twice Round the Daffodils* (62), *Mr Sardonicus* (63), *The Brigand of Kandahar* (65), etc.

LEWIS, SHELDON (1868–1958). American character actor of stage and screen. *The Exploits of Elaine* (15), *Dr Jekyll and Mr Hyde* (title role) (16), *Orphans of the Storm* (21), *The Red Kimono* (26), *Black Magic* (29), *The Monster Walks* (32), *The Cattle Thief* (last film) (36), many others.

LEWIS, SINCLAIR (1885–1951). American novelist. Works filmed include *Arrowsmith* (32), *Ann Vickers* (33), *Babbitt* (34), *Dodsworth* (36), *Untamed* (40), *Elmer Gantry* (60).

LEWIS, TED (1891–) (Theodore Friedman). American bandleader and entertainer ('Me and My Shadow') who appeared in a few movies: *Is Everybody Happy* (29), *Here Comes the Band* (35), *Hold that Ghost* (42), etc.

LEWTON, VAL (1904–1951). American producer, former writer, notable for a group of low-budget, high quality horror films made for RKO in the 40s. *Cat People* (42), *I Walked with a Zombie* (43), *The Seventh Victim* (43), *The Curse of the Cat People* (44), *The Body Snatcher* (45), *Isle of the Dead* (45), *Bedlam* (46), etc. Later films unremarkable.

LEXY, EDWARD (1897–) (Edward Gerald Little). British character actor in films from 1936, usually as sergeant-major, police inspector or irascible father. *Farewell Again* (37), *South Riding* (38), *Laugh It Off* (40), *Spare a Copper* (40), *Piccadilly Incident* (46), *It's Not Cricket* (48), *Miss Robin Hood* (52), *Orders Are Orders* (55), *The Man Who Wouldn't Talk* (58), many others.

LEYTON, JOHN (1939–). British pop singer who transferred to dramatic roles. *The Great Escape* (63), *Von Ryan's Express* (65), *Krakatoa* (68), etc. TV series: *Jericho* (67).

L'HERBIER, MARCEL (1890–). French director. *Rose France* (19), *Eldorado* (22), *The Late Mathias Pascal* (25), *L'Épervier* (33), *Nuits de Feu* (37), *La Nuit Fantastique* (42), *The Last Days of Pompeii* (49), *Le Père de Mademoiselle* (53), etc.

LIBERACE (1920–) (Wladziu Valentino Liberace). American pianist-showman of stage, night clubs and TV. Starred in his only major appearance, *Sincerely Yours* (55); also seen as a pianist in *East of Java* (49) and as a coffin salesman in *The Loved One* (65).

library shot. One hired to save the expense of shooting it; e.g. plane taking off, train in motion, etc., or historical newsreel shot.

LIEBELEI (Austria 1933). A sentimental love story culminating in a duel in which the hero is killed by the husband of an ex-mistress. All the film's merit is in the style of director Max Ophuls and cinematographer Franz Planer.

LICUDI, GABRIELLA (1943–). Italian leading lady in international films. *The Liquidators* (65), *The Jokers* (66), *Casino Royale* (66), *The Last Safari* (67), etc.

LIEVEN, ALBERT (1906–). German actor, in films from 1933, including many British productions. *Night Train to Munich* (40), *Jeannie* (40), *Yellow Canary* (43), *The Seventh Veil* (45), *Beware of Pity* (46), *Frieda* (47), *Sleeping Car to Trieste* (48), *Hotel Sahara* (50), *Conspiracy of Hearts* (60), *Foxhole in Cairo* (59), *The Victors* (63), *Traitor's Gate* (65), many others.

THE LIFE AND DEATH OF COLONEL BLIMP (GB 1943). This amiable and quite ambitiously-staged biography of a fictitious military man, whose career ranged from the Boer War to the London blitz, had delightful incidental detail even though it made no very obvious point and had the oddities one was coming to expect from films written, produced and directed by Michael Powell and Emeric Pressburger. Running three hours in its original form, in what then seemed exquisite colour, it had Roger Livesey in the title role, Deborah Kerr as the three women in his life, and Anton Walbrook as a sympathetic German friend.

THE LIFE OF EMILE ZOLA (US 1937: AA best film). This, the only Warner Brothers biographical film to win an award as the best film of its year, was probably the best of them. Stylishly directed by William Dieterle, it also gained Academy Awards for Joseph Schildkraut (as Dreyfus) and for the scenarists Norman Reilly Raine, Heinz Herald and Geza Herczeg. Paul Muni played Zola.

LIFE UPSIDE DOWN (LA VIE A L'ENVERS) (France 1964). A simple but curiously haunting little film in the introspective manner of the 60s, about a young man who withdraws from life into the simplicity and solitude of a small white room. Written and directed by Alain Jessua; with Charles Denner.

LIFEBOAT (US 1943). An Alfred Hitchcock movie notable for confining itself to the smallest acting space of any film ever made: a lifeboat on the open sea. John Steinbeck wrote the script and Tallulah Bankhead and Walter Slezak made the most of the acting chances.

lifts (or elevators) provided a convenient means of murder in *Garment Centre* and *The Lift of Adrian Messenger*, and of unwitting suicide in *Ivy*. People were trapped in lifts in *Cry Terror, A Night in Casablanca, Love Crazy* and *Lady in a Cage*, in which the lift was a domestic one, like the one in *Suddenly Last Summer*. Invalid chairlifts were sported by Ethel Barrymore in *The Farmer's Daughter* and Charles Laughton in *Witness for the Prosecution*.

light comedians, the lithe and dapper heroes who can be funny and romantic at the same time, have added a great deal to the mystique and nostalgia of the screen. Linder and Chaplin both partly belong to this debonair tradition, and indeed did much to mould it; but only sound could enable its full realization. Maurice Chevalier had the field pretty well to himself in Hollywood during the early 30s, with strong support from such stalwarts as Roland Young, Edward Everett Horton and Charles Butterworth. Soon Cary Grant entered the lists, along with David Niven, William Powell, Louis Hayward, Melvyn Douglas and Ronald Colman when he felt in lighter mood. Britain scored with Jack Buchanan, Jack

Hulbert, and the ineffable Aldwych team of Tom Walls and Ralph Lynn; while Leslie Howard scored a major hit in *Pygmalion* and Rex Harrison, who was to play the same role twenty-five years later in *My Fair Lady*, was already demonstrating his talent in less important comedies.

Back in Hollywood *The Philadelphia Story* was a milestone in light comedy and set Katharine Hepburn firmly on the road she later followed in her splendid series with Spencer Tracy. Bette Davis, too, had her moments in this field, and so did Rosalind Russell. Bob Hope and Danny Kaye both clowned around a good deal but still got the girl in the end . . . but Britishers Basil Radford and Naunton Wayne were bachelors bred and born. The more realistic approach of the 50s was stifling the genre, but Dennis Price managed a notable performance in *Kind Hearts and Coronets* before Ian Carmichael cornered the diminishing market. In more recent years actors have to turn comic or tragic at the drop of the hat: among those best able to manage the light touch are Jack Lemmon, Tony Curtis, Frank Sinatra and Peter O'Toole.

LIGHTNER, WINNIE (1901–) (Winifred Hanson). American vaudeville comedienne who appeared in several early talkies. *Gold Diggers of Broadway* (30), *Playgirl* (32), *Dancing Lady* (32), *I'll Fix It* (35), etc.

LIL ABNER. Al Capp's comic strip about the hillbilly inhabitants of Dogpatch was first filmed, unsuccessfully, in 1940 with Granville Owen; masks were rather oddly used for some characters. In 1957 Panama and Frank made a successful musical version with Peter Palmer, based on the Broadway show. Also, Paramount made a few Lil Abner cartoons in the late 40s.

LILIOM. Ferenc Molnar's play about the here and the hereafter was filmed in Hollywood in 1930 by Frank Borzage and in Germany in 1933 by Fritz Lang. In 1956 it turned up again, via a stage musical, as *Carousel*, directed by Henry King.

LILLIE, BEATRICE (1898–) (Lady Peel). British revue star, on stage from 1914. Very occasional films include *Exit Smiling* (debut) (1927), *Are you There?* (31), *Doctor Rhythm* (38), *On Approval* (43), *Around the World in Eighty Days* (56), *Thoroughly Modern Millie* (67).

LIMELIGHT (US 1952). Chaplin's last major film, a sentimental, old-fashioned back-stage story which succeeded by its sheer aplomb but overdid the pathos. His theme song, 'Eternally', made it a hit.

LINCOLN, ABRAHAM (1809–1865). Sixteenth American president, a familiar screen figure with his stovepipe hat, bushy whiskers, and his assassination during a performance of 'Our American Cousin'. More or less full length screen portraits include *Abraham Lincoln's*

Clemency (10); *Lincoln the Lover* (13); Joseph Henabery in *Birth of a Nation* (14); Frank McGlynnin in *The Life of Abraham Lincoln* (15); George A. Billings in *Abraham Lincoln* (25); Walter Huston in *Abraham Lincoln* (30); John Carradine in *Of Human Hearts* (38); Henry Fonda in *Young Mr Lincoln* (39); Raymond Massey in *Abe Lincoln in Illinois* (39).

LINCOLN, ELMO (1889–1952) (Otto Elmo Linkenhelter). American silent actor who became famous as the first *Tarzan of the Apes* (18). Also in *Birth of a Nation* (14), *Elmo the Mighty* (19), etc., and played small roles up to his death.

LINDER, MAX (1883–1925) (Gabriel Levielle). Dapper French silent comedian, a probable source for Chaplin. Scripted and directed most of his own films (1906–25), of which three were recently reissued by his daughter under the title *Laugh with Max Linder*.

LINDFORS, VIVECA (1920–   ). Swedish actress, in films from 1941, Hollywood from 1946. *To the Victor* (47), *Night Unto Night* (48), *The New Adventures of Don Juan* (48), *No Sad Songs for Me* (50), *Dark City* (50), *The Flying Missile* (51), *Four in a Jeep* (51), *The Raiders* (52), *Run for Cover* (55), *Moonfleet* (55), *I Accuse* (57), *Tempest* (58), *King of Kings* (61), *Sylvia* (65), *Brainstorm* (65), others.

LINDEN, ERIC (1909–   ). American juvenile lead of the 30s. *Are These Our Children* (32), *The Silver Cord* (33), *Girl of the Limberlost* (34), *The Voice of Bugle Ann* (36), *Gone With the Wind* (39), etc.

LINDO, OLGA (1898–1968). Anglo-Norwegian character actress, on British stage and screen. *The Shadow Between* (32), *The Last Journey* (35), *When We Are Married* (42), *Bedelia* (46), *Train of Events* (49), *An Inspector Calls* (54), *Woman in a Dressing Gown* (57), *Sapphire* (59), etc.

LINDON, LIONEL (* –   ). American cinematographer. *Going My Way* (44), *A Medal for Benny* (45), *Road to Utopia* (46), *Alias Nick Beal* (49), *Destination Moon* (50), *Conquest of Space* (55), *Around the World in Eighty Days* (AA) (56), *The Lonely Man* (57), *The Black Scorpion* (57), *Too Late Blues* (61), *The Manchurian Candidate* (62), *The Trouble with Angels* (66), *Boy Did I Get a Wrong Number* (66), *Grand Prix* (66), etc.

LINDGREN, LARS MAGNUS (1922–   ). Swedish director. *Do You Believe in Angels* (60), *Dear John* (64), *The Coffin* (*The Sadist*) (66).

LINDSAY, HOWARD (1889–1968). American actor-playwright-stage director. With Russell Crose wrote *Life with Father* and *State of the Union*, both filmed. Acted in and directed *Dulcy* (21), co-authored *She's My Weakness* (31).

595

LINDSAY, MARGARET (1910–   ) (Margaret Kies). American leading lady of the 30s, with stage experience; in Hollywood from 1931. *West of Singapore* (32), *Lady Killer* (34), *Bordertown* (35), *G-Men* (35), *The Green Light* (37), *Jezebel* (38), *The House of Seven Gables* (40), *There's Magic in Music* (41), *A Close Call for Ellery Queen* (42), *No Place for a Lady* (43), *Crime Doctor* (43), *Alaska* (44), *Club Havana* (45), *Scarlet Street* (45), *Her Sister's Secret* (47), *Cass Timberlane* (47), *Emergency Hospital* (56), *Jet over the Atlantic* (59), *Tammy and the Doctor* (63), many others, mostly routine.

LINDTBERG, LEOPOLD (1902–   ). Swiss director known chiefly for *Marie Louise* (44), *The Last Chance* (45), *Four Days Leave* (48), *The Village* (52).

THE LION IN WINTER (GB/US 1968). This curious treatment of the court of Henry II in the vein of *Who's Afraid of Virginia Woolf?* won Oscars for Katharine Hepburn, in her element as the wily Eleanor of Aquitaine, for John Barry's music and for James Goldman's screenplay from his off-Broadway original. Anthony Harvey's direction ensured good clear talk at the expense of cinema; Peter O'Toole was an amusingly rampant Henry.

LIPMAN, JERZY (1922–   ). Polish cinematographer. *A Generation* (54), *Kanal* (57), *The Eighth Day of the Week* (58), *Lotna* (59), *Knife in the Water* (62), *No More Divorces* (63), *Ashes* (65), etc.

LIPPERT, ROBERT L. (1909–   ). American exhibitor, latterly head of company making second features for 20th Century Fox, many of them produced by his son ROBERT L. LIPPERT JNR (1928–   ).

LIPSCOMB, W. P. (1887–1958). British screenwriter who spent some years in Hollywood. *French Leave* (27), *The Good Companions* (32), *I Was a Spy* (33), *Clive of India* (co-w) (34), *A Tale of Two Cities* (35), *The Garden of Allah* (36), *Pygmalion* (co-w) (38), *A Town Like Alice* (56), *Dunkirk* (co-w) (58), many others.

LISI, VIRNA (1937–   ) (Virna Pieralisi). Voluptuous Italian leading lady who after starring in innumerable local spectaculars came on to the international market. *The Black Tulip* (63), *Eva* (63), *How to Murder Your Wife* (US) (65), *Casanova 70* (65), *Signore e Signori* (65), *Assault on a Queen* (US) (66), *Not with My Wife You Don't* (US) (66), *The Girl and the General* (67), *The Twenty-fifth Hour* (67), *Arabella* (68), *The Secret of Santa Vittoria* (69), etc.

LISTEN TO BRITAIN (GB 1941). A classic impressionist documentary by Humphrey Jennings, blending the sights and sounds of a country at war.

LISTER, FRANCIS (1899–1951). Suave British character actor, mainly on stage. *Atlantic* (30), *Jack's the Boy* (32), *Clive of India* (35), *The*

Return of the Scarlet Pimpernel (38), *Henry V* (44), *The Wicked Lady* (45), *Home to Danger* (51), etc.

LISTER, MOIRA (1923–   ). South African leading lady and character actress, in British films. *My Ain Folk* (44), *Uneasy Terms* (48), *Another Shore* (48), *A Run for Your Money* (49), *Grand National Night* (53), *John and Julie* (55), *Seven Waves Away* (57), *The Yellow Rolls-Royce* (64), *Stranger in the House* (67), etc.

LITEL, JOHN (1892–1964). American character actor, in films since 1929; often seen as judge, lawyer or stern father. *Marked Woman* (37), *The Life of Emile Zola* (37), *Virginia City* (40), *They Died with Their Boots On* (41), *Kiss Tomorrow Goodbye* (50), *Houseboat* (58), *A Pocketful of Miracles* (61), *The Sons of Katie Elder* (65), many others. Occasionally played lead in second features: *Men Without Souls* (40), *Sealed Lips* (41), *Boss of Big Town* (43), etc.

LITTLE CAESAR (US 1930). The first talking gangster film glorifying the gang wars of the 20s, this powerful melodrama with its famous last line ('. . . is this the end of Rico?') caused a long-lasting controversy but sold a lot of tickets and produced a host of imitators. (The genre wore itself out in the 40s but was revived in the late 50s.) Edward G. Robinson was suddenly a star after his performance; Mervyn Le Roy directed.

LITTLEFIELD, LUCIEN (1895–1959). American character actor, in Hollywood from 1913 in supporting roles. Talkies include *Miss Pinkerton* (32), *Ruggles of Red Gap* (34), *Rose Marie* (36), *The Great American Broadcast* (40), *Scared Stiff* (44), *Susanna Pass* (51), *Pop Girl* (56), etc.

THE LITTLE FOXES (US 1941). This admirable adaptation of Lilian Hellman's play about a grasping family after the Civil War was an example of Hollywood at its best, with beautiful photography by Gregg Toland, subtle direction by William Wyler, and a gallery of first-rate performances: Bette Davis, Herbert Marshall, Ray Collins, Charles Dingle, Dan Duryea, Patricia Collinge and others. An unusual kind of sequel, *Another Part of the Forest*, was filmed in 1947: this showed the earlier lives of the Hubbard family.

LITTLE LORD FAUNTLEROY. The well-known children's novel by Frances Hodgson Burnett, about an American boy who becomes a British earl, was filmed in 1922 as a transvestite vehicle for Mary Pickford; direction appears to have been shared between Alfred E. Green, Jack Pickford and Alfred Werker. In 1936 it was remade by John Cromwell for Selznick, with Freddie Bartholemew in the title role.

LITTLE WOMEN. Louisa M. Alcott's cosy 19th-century saga of a nice widow's even nicer daughters was a major success when filmed in

1933 by George Cukor, with Katharine Hepburn and Paul Lukas. Remade in 1949 with June Allyson and Rossano Brazzi, it seemed calculated and coy. A sequel, *Little Men*, was filmed in 1940 as a vehicle for Kay Francis.

LITTLEWOOD, JOAN (1916–). British stage director whose only film to date is *Sparrows Can't Sing* (63). Created London's 'Theatre Workshop'.

LITVAK, ANATOLE (1902–). Russian-born director, in Germany and France from 1927, Hollywood from 1937. *Coeur de Lilas* (32), *Mayerling* (36), *The Amazing Dr Clitterhouse* (38), *Tovarich* (38), *The Sisters* (38), *Confessions of a Nazi Spy* (39), *All This and Heaven Too* (40), *Castle on the Hudson* (40), *City for Conquest* (40), *Out of the Fog* (41), *Blues in the Night* (41), *This Above All* (42); war service; *The Long Night* (47), *The Snake Pit* (48), *Sorry, Wrong Number* (48), *Decision before Dawn* (51), *Act of Love* (also produced) (54), *The Deep Blue Sea* (GB) (also produced) (55), *Anastasia* (56), *The Journey* (58), *Goodbye Again* (61), *Five Miles to Midnight* (63), *The Night of the Generals* (66), *The Lady in the Car* (70), etc.

LIVESEY, JACK (1901–). British actor, brother of Roger Livesey. *The Wandering Jew* (33), *The Passing of the Third Floor Back* (35), *Old Bill and Son* (40), *The First Gentleman* (47), *Paul Temple's Triumph* (51), etc.

LIVESEY, ROGER (1906–). Husky-voiced British leading man, later character actor, on stage from 1917. Films: *The Old Curiosity Shop* (debut) (20), *Lorna Doone* (35), *Rembrandt* (37), *The Drum* (38), *49th Parallel* (41), *The Life and Death of Colonel Blimp* (43), *I Know Where I'm Going* (45), *A Matter of Life and Death* (45), *Vice Versa* (48), *The Intimate Stranger* (56), *The Entertainer* (58), *The League of Gentlemen* (60), *Of Human Bondage* (64), *Moll Flanders* (65), *Oedipus the King* (67), *Hamlet* (69), many others; also on TV.

LIVESEY, SAM (1873–1936). British actor, father of Jack and Roger Livesey. *Young Woodley* (30), *The Flag Lieutenant* (32), *The Private Life of Henry VIII* (32), *Jew Suss* (34), *Turn of the Tide* (36), *Dark Journey* (37), etc.

LIVING (IKIRU) (Japan 1952). Edited, part-written, and directed by Akira Kurosawa, this step-by-step account of an elderly clerk dying of cancer could hardly have been made in the West at this time; certainly not with so fine and finally uplifting a touch.

THE LIVING DESERT (US 1953). The first of Walt Disney's feature-length 'True Life Adventures', an absorbing animal documentary despite the facetious Fitzpatrick-type monotone commentary and many suspect 'dramatic' sequences which must have been either staged or cleverly edited. (By reverse printing, Disney even made scorpions do a square dance.) Outraged scientific critics could not deny the charm and fascination of the piece, nor its popularity; and many of the shots were extremely rare. Disney followed it with *The Vanishing Prairie*, *The African Lion*, *Secrets of Life*, *The Jungle Cat*, and several two-reelers of the same kind: *Seal Island*, *Beaver Valley*, *Bear Country*, *Water Birds*, *Nature's Half Acre*, etc.

LIVINGSTON, JAY (1915–). American songwriter, usually of words and music; often worked with RAY EVANS. *To Each His Own* (47), *Golden Earrings* (48), *The Paleface* (AA for 'Buttons and Bows') (49), *Captain Carey USA* (AA for 'Mona Lisa') (50), *The Man Who Knew Too Much* (AA for 'Che Sera Sera') (56), *All Hands on Deck* (62), many others. Wrote TV themes for *Bonanza*, *Mister Ed*, etc.

LIZZANI, CARLO (1922–). Italian director. *Caccia Tragica* (co-w only) (47), *Bitter Rice* (co-w only) (48), *Achtung Banditi* (51), *Ai Margini Della Metropoli* (54), *The Great Wall* (58), *Hunchback of Rome* (60), etc.

LLOYD, DORIS (1899–1968). British actress with repertory experience; in Hollywood from the 20s. *Charley's Aunt* (as Donna Lucia) (30), *Disraeli* (30), *Tarzan the Ape Man* (32), *Oliver Twist* (33), *Clive of India* (35), *Vigil in the Night* (39), *Phantom Lady* (44), *The Secret Life of Walter Mitty* (47), *A Man Called Peter* (55), *The Time Machine* (60), *The Notorious Landlady* (62), *Rosie* (67), etc.

LLOYD, EUAN (1923–). British independent producer, former publicist. *Genghis Khan* (64), *Murderer's Row* (66), *Shalako* (68), etc.

LLOYD, FRANK (1888–1960). Scottish-born director, in Hollywood from 1913 after acting experience. *Les Misérables* (18), *Madame X* (20), *Oliver Twist* (22), *The Eternal Flame* (23), *The Sea Hawk* (24), *Dark Streets* (26), *The Divine Lady* (AA) (29), *East Lynne* (30), *Sin Flood* (31), *Passport to Hell* (32), *Cavalcade* (AA) (33), *Berkeley Square* (33), *Mutiny on the Bounty* (35), *Under Two Flags* (36), *Maid of Salem* (37), *Wells Fargo* (37), *If I Were King* (also produced) (39), *Rulers of the Sea* (39), *The Tree of Liberty* (also directed) (40), *The Lady from Cheyenne* (also produced) (41), *This Woman Is Mine* (41), *Blood on the Sun* (45), *The Shanghai Story* (also produced) (54), *The Last Command* (also produced) (55), many others.

LLOYD, HAROLD (1893–). American silent comedian, famous for his timid bespectacled 'nice boy' character and for thrill-comedy situations involving dangerous stunts. In hundreds of two-reelers from 1916. †Features: *A Sailor-Made Man* (21), *Grandma's Boy* (22), *Dr Jack* (22), *Safety Last* (23), *Why Worry?* (23), *Girl Shy* (24), *Hot Water* (24), *The Freshman* (25), *For Heaven's Sake* (26), *The Kid Brother* (27), *Speedy* (28), *Welcome Danger* (29), *Feet First* (30), *Movie*

Crazy (32), *The Catspaw* (34), *The Milky Way* (36), *Professor Beware* (38), *Mad Wednesday* (*The Sins of Harold Diddlebock*) (47). Recently produced two compilations of his comedy highlights: *World of Comedy* and *Funny Side of Life*. Special Academy Award 1952 as 'master comedian and good citizen'.

LLOYD, NORMAN (c. 1910–   ). British actor in Hollywood. Fell from the Statue of Liberty in Hitchcock's *Saboteur* (42); was later in *Spellbound* (45), *Scene of the Crime* (49), *M* (51), *Limelight* (52), etc. More recently has been executive producer of TV series *Alfred Hitchcock Presents*.

LLOYD-PACK, CHARLES (c. 1901–   ). British character actor of stage and screen, usually in self-effacing roles: butlers, etc. *High Treason* (51), *The Importance of Being Earnest* (52), *The Constant Husband* (55), *Night of the Demon* (57), *Dracula* (58), *Victim* (62), etc.

LOACH, KEN (1936–   ). British director from TV. *Poor Cow* (67), *A Kestrel for a Knave* (69).

location. A shooting site away from the studios.

LOCKHART, GENE (1891–1957). Canadian character actor at home in genial or shifty parts. Also writer: in films since 1922. Memorable in *Star of Midnight* (34), *Something to Sing About* (37), *Algiers* (38), *Blackmail* (39), *All That Money Can Buy* (41), *Meet John Doe* (41), *Hangmen Also Die* (43), *Going My Way* (44), *The House on 92nd Street* (45), *A Scandal in Paris* (46), *Miracle on 34th Street* (47), *The Inspector General* (49), *Rhubarb* (51), *Androcles and the Lion* (53), *Carousel* (56), many others.

LOCKHART, JUNE (1925–   ). American supporting actress, daughter of Gene. *All This and Heaven Too* (40), *Meet Me in St Louis* (44), *Keep Your Powder Dry* (45), *Bury Me Dead* (47), *Time Limit* (47), etc. From the mid-50s appeared in TV series *Lassie*.

LOCKWOOD, GARY (c. 1940–   ). American leading man. *Splendour in the Grass* (61), *Wild in the Country* (62), *2001: A Space Odyssey* (68), *The Model Shop* (69), etc. TV series: *The Lieutenant* (63).

LOCKWOOD, JULIA (1941–   ). British leading lady, daughter of Margaret Lockwood. *My Teenage Daughter* (56), *Please Turn Over* (59), *No Kidding* (60), etc. TV series: *The Flying Swan*.

LOCKWOOD, MARGARET (1916–   ) (Margaret Day). British leading lady, the most popular heroine of World War II escapist dramas. Also on stage and TV. *Lorna Doone* (debut) (35), *The Beloved Vagabond* (36), *Dr Syn* (37), *Bank Holiday* (38), *The Lady Vanishes* (38), *The Stars Look Down* (39), *Night Train to Munich* (40), *Quiet Wedding* (41), *Alibi* (42), *The Man in Grey* (43), *A Place of One's Own* (44), *Love Story* (44), *The Wicked Lady* (45), *Hungry Hill* (47), *Jassy*

(47), *Cardboard Cavalier* (48), *Highly Dangerous* (50), *Trent's Last Case* (52), *Laughing Anne* (53), *Cast a Dark Shadow* (55), etc. TV series: *The Flying Swan*. Published her autobiography 1955: *Lucky Star*.

LODER, JOHN (1898–) (John Lowe). Tall British leading man, in films from 1927 after varied experience. *The First Born* (29), *Java Head* (34), *Lorna Doone* (35), *Murder Will Out* (38), *Meet Maxwell Archer* (39), then to US: *How Green Was My Valley* (41), *Now Voyager* (42), *Old Acquaintance* (43), *The Hairy Ape* (44), *The Brighton Strangler* (45), *Wife of Monte Cristo* (46), *Dishonoured Lady* (47), *Woman and the Hunter* (57), etc., others; retired to Argentina.

LODGE, DAVID (c. 1922–). British character actor, with music-hall and stage experience. *Private's Progress* (56), *Two Way Stretch* (60), *The Dock Brief* (61), *Yesterday's Enemy* (61), *The Long Ships* (63), *Guns at Batasi* (64), *Catch Us If You Can* (65), *Press For Time* (66), etc.

LODGE, JOHN (1903–). American leading man of the 30s. *A Woman Accused* (debut) (32), *Little Women* (33), *The Scarlet Empress* (34), *Koenigsmark* (35), *Sensation* (36), *Bulldog Drummond at Bay* (37), *Bank Holiday* (38), *L'Esclave Blanche* (39). Retired to take up politics.

THE LODGER. Several versions have been made of Mrs Belloc Lowndes, Jack the Ripper story, notably by Hitchcock in 1926, by Maurice Elvey in 1932 and by John Brahm in 1944. Further slight variations were provided by *The Phantom Fiend* (35), *The Man in the Attic* (53) and *The Strangler* (64), while the long-standing puzzle was 'solved' in *Jack the Ripper* (58) and *A Study in Terror* (65).

LOESSER, FRANK (1910–1969). American songwriter, in films since 1930. 'Baby It's Cold Outside', 'Jingle Jangle', many others. Scores for *Hans Christian Andersen*, *Where's Charley*, *Guys and Dolls*, *How to Succeed in Business Without Really Trying*, etc.

LOEW, MARCUS (1870–1927). Austrian-American exhibitor and distributor, co-founder and controller of MGM, which is still run by 'Loew's Inc.'

LOFTUS, CECILIA (1876–1943). British character actress who went to Hollywood with a Shakespearean company in 1895, and stayed. *East Lynne* (31), *The Old Maid* (39), *The Bluebird* (40), *Lucky Partners* (40), *The Black Cat* (41), etc.

†LOGAN, JOSHUA (1908–). American stage producer who has directed films: *Picnic* (55), *Bus Stop* (56), *Sayonara* (57), *South Pacific* (58), *Fanny* (61), *Ensign Pulver* (64), *Camelot* (67), *Paint Your Wagon* (69).

LOGGIA, ROBERT (c. 1934–). American leading man. *Somebody Up There Likes Me* (56), *Cop Hater* (58), *The Nine Lives of Elfego Baca*

(59), *Guns of Wyoming (Cattle King)* (63), *Che* (69), etc. TV series: *T.H.E. Cat* (66).

LOHR, MARIE (1890–   ). Distinguished Australian stage actress, on London stage from 1901; since 1930 in dowager roles. *Aren't We All* (debut) (32), *Pygmalion* (38), *Major Barbara* (40), *The Winslow Boy* (48), *A Town Like Alice* (56), many others.

LOLA MONTES (France/Germany 1955). This last film by Max Ophuls, treating the life of the famous courtesan in a series of complex flashbacks from the circus act in which she later toured, was a bravura piece of cinema in typically tortuous but often stimulating style. Unfortunately it was generally shown in an atrocious dubbed and shortened version with the circus sequences removed and the remainder in roughly chronological order. Photographed in colour by Christian Matras; with Martine Carol, Anton Walbrook and Peter Ustinov.

LOLLOBRIGIDA, GINA (1927–   ). Italian glamour girl and international leading lady, in films since 1947. *Pagliacci* (47), *Fanfan la Tulipe* (51), *Belles de Nuit* (52), *The Wayward Wife* (52), *Bread, Love and Dreams* (53), *Beat the Devil* (54), *Le Grand Jeu* (54), *Trapeze* (56), *The Law (Where the Hot Wind Blows)* (58), *Solomon and Sheba* (59), *Come September* (61), *Woman of Straw* (64), *Strange Bedfellows* (65), *Four Kinds of Love (Bambole)* (65), *Hotel Paradiso* (66), *Buona Sera Mrs Campbell* (68), many others.

LOM, HERBERT (1917–   ) (Herbert Charles Angelo Kuchacevich ze Schluderpacheru). Czech actor whose personality adapts itself equally well to villainy or kindliness; in Britain from 1939. *Mein Kampf* (40), *The Young Mr Pitt* (as Napoleon) (41), *The Dark Tower* (43), *Hotel Reserve* (44), *The Seventh Veil* (45), *Night Boat to Dublin* (46), *Dual Alibi* (47), *Good Time Girl* (48), *The Golden Salamander* (49), *State Secret* (50), *The Black Rose* (50), *Hell Is Sold Out* (51), *The Ringer* (52), *The Net* (53), *The Love Lottery* (54), *The Ladykillers* (55), *War and Peace* (as Napoleon) (56), *Chase a Crooked Shadow* (57), *Roots of Heaven* (58), *Northwest Frontier* (59), *I Aim at the Stars* (US) (59), *Mysterious Island* (61), *El Cid* (61), *Phantom of the Opera* (title role) (62), *A Shot in the Dark* (64), *Return from the Ashes* (65), *Uncle Tom's Cabin* (Ger.) (65), *Gambit* (66), *Assignment to Kill* (67), *Villa Rides* (68), *Doppelganger* (69), others. TV series: *The Human Jungle.*

LOMAS, HERBERT (1887–1961). Gaunt, hollow-voiced British stage actor. Many cameo roles in films include *The Sign of Four* (32), *Lorna Doone* (35), *Rembrandt* (36), *Jamaica Inn* (39), *Ask a Policeman* (39), *The Ghost Train* (41), *I Know Where I'm Going* (45), *Bonnie Prince Charlie* (48), *The Net* (53), etc.

LOMBARD, CAROLE (1908–1942) (Jane Peters). American leading lady, a former child actress who developed into a highly individual comedienne. *A Perfect Crime* (21), *Marriage in Transit* (25), *Fast and Loose* (30), *Man of the World* (31), *Virtue* (32), *No Man of Her Own* (32), *Supernatural* (33), *White Woman* (33), *Rumba* (34), *Bolero* (34), *Twentieth Century* (34), *We're Not Dressing* (34), *Hands across the Table* (35), *My Man Godfrey* (36), *Nothing Sacred* (37), *Fools for Scandal* (38), *True Confession* (38), *In Name Only* (39), *Vigil in the Night* (39), *They Knew What They Wanted* (40), *Mr and Mrs Smith* (41), *To Be or Not To Be* (42), etc.

London has provided a background, usually highly inaccurate, for innumerable movies, but few have really explored it. *London Town* was a half-hearted musical; twenty years later *Three Hats for Lisa* captured the mood better but managed to seem old-fashioned *Indiscreet* prowled lovingly around the Embankment, and *A Run for Your Money* made good use of the Paddington area as well as suburban Twickenham. The City was the venue of part of *You Must Be Joking*, while *Morgan* used Hampstead to good advantage. The East End, especially the street markets and the railway sidings, were exploited in *Waterloo Road*, *A Kid for Two Farthings* and *It Always Rains on Sunday*. The docks had *Pool of London* to themselves. Hollywood's idea of London can be pretty weird, as in *Knock on Wood*, when Paramount went to the trouble of having special location material shot with Jon Pertwee doubling for Danny Kaye, but showed the star turning off Marble Arch into Fleet Street two miles away. Similarly in *Twenty-three Paces to Baker Street* the river frontage of the Savoy Hotel could be entered from Portman Square, in actuality another two-mile jaunt. London fog has been a useful cover for many a scrappy set, especially in films presenting the Victorian London associated with Sherlock Holmes. Going further back, *Henry V* presented in model form the London of 1600, and attempts at historical recreation were also made in *Tower of London*, *Fire over England*, *Elizabeth and Essex*, *Nell Gwyn*, *Forever Amber*, *Mrs Fitzherbert*, *The First Gentleman*, *Victoria the Great* and *The Mudlark*. It was probably Hitchcock who began the fashion of making London a stately background for thrillers, with his East End mission in *The Man Who Knew Too Much*, the music hall in *The Thirty-nine Steps*, the bus journey and the Lord Mayor's Show in *Sabotage*, and the fall from Westminster Cathedral in *Foreign Correspondent*. Latest follower is Stanley Donen, whose *Arabesque* has sequences on the Great West Road and in Regent's Park Zoo at night.
See also: *swinging London*.

LONDON, JACK (1876–1916). American adventure novelist, whose most-filmed stories include *The Sea Wolf*, *Adventures of Martin Eden*, *Call of the Wild* and *White Fang*.

LONDON, JULIE (1926–   ). American leading lady and singer. *Jungle Woman* (44), *The Red House* (47), *The Fat Man* (51), *The Great Man* (56), *Saddle the Wind* (58), *Man of the West* (58), *The Third Voice* (60), etc.

LONDON TOWN (GB 1947). An attempt by the Rank Organization to make a British musical, often quoted as proof that success in this genre is impossible outside Hollywood (a maxim not disproved till the 60s). Despite an imported American director, Wesley Ruggles, it's all lamentably dull except for Sid Field's sketches, here preserved intact.

THE LONE RANGER. This Western Robin Hood originally featured in a radio serial, later became a comic strip in 1935; twenty years later Clayton Moore played the hero in a successful TV series and a couple of feature films, with Jay Silverheels as Tonto.

THE LONE WOLF was a gentleman thief created by Louis Joseph Vance. On screen he was impersonated by Warren William in several films from 1939, and the role was later taken over by Gerald Mohr and Ron Randell. The Wolf's indispensable manservant was usually played by Eric Blore.

LONG, AUDREY (1924–   ). American leading lady of the 40s. *A Night of Adventure* (44), *Pan-Americana* (45), *Song of My Heart* (47), *The Petty Girl* (50), *Indian Uprising* (last to date) (52), etc.

LONG, RICHARD (1927–   ). American leading man, mainly in second features. *Tomorrow Is Forever* (44), *The Stranger* (45), *The Egg and I* (47), *Criss Cross* (49), *Saskatchewan* (54), *Cult of the Cobra* (55), *Home from the Hill* (59), *The Tenderfoot* (64), etc. TV series: *77 Sunset Strip*, *Bourbon Street Beat*, *The Big Valley*.

LONGDEN, JOHN (1900–   ). British leading man of the early 30s; later graduated to character roles. *Blackmail* (30), *Atlantic* (30), *The Ringer* (31), *Born Lucky* (33), *French Leave* (37), *The Gaunt Stranger* (38), *The Lion Has Wings* (39), *The Common Touch* (41), *The Silver Fleet* (43), *Bonnie Prince Charlie* (48), *The Man with the Twisted Lip* (as Sherlock Holmes) (51), *Quatermass II* (56), *An Honourable Murder* (60), many others.

LONGDEN, TERENCE (1922–   ). British actor, in secondary roles· *Never Look Back* (52), *Simon and Laura* (55), *Doctor at Large* (57), *Carry On Sergeant* (58), *Ben Hur* (59), *The Return of Mr Moto* (65), etc.

THE LONGEST DAY (US 1962). Darryl F. Zanuck master-minded this detailed reconstruction of D-Day 1944. Long and very noisy, it has some brilliantly-handled action sequences, and the all-star cast provided box-office insurance at the cost of verisimilitude.

long shot. One taken from a distance, usually to establish a scene or a situation but sometimes for dramatic effect. Opposite of *close-up.*

LONGSTREET, STEPHEN (1907–). American screenwriter, in Hollywood from 1942. *The Jolson Story* (46), *The Greatest Show on Earth* (co-w) (52), *The First Travelling Saleslady* (55), *The Helen Morgan Story* (57), etc.; n u t. TV.

LOO, RICHARD (c. 1903–). Hawaiian-Chinese actor who turned to films after business depression. Has played hundreds of oriental roles. *Dirigible* (31), *The Good Earth* (37), *The Keys of the Kingdom* (44), *Rogues' Regiment* (48), *Love Is a Many-Splendoured Thing* (54), *The Quiet American* (58), *The Sand Pebbles* (66), etc.

LOONEY TUNES and MERRIE MELODIES are the two umbrella titles under which Warners have long released their cartoon shorts featuring such characters as Bugs Bunny, Daffy Duck, Porky Pig, Pepe le Pew, Sylvester and Tweetie Pie. They have won Academy Awards for *Tweetie Pie* (47), *For Scentimental Reasons* (49), *Speedy Gonzales* (55), *Birds Anonymous* (57), *Knighty Knight Bugs* (58).

LOOS, ANITA (1893–). American humorous writer, best known for *Gentlemen Prefer Blondes* and *The Greeks Had a Word For It*, both filmed several times. Wrote over 200 scenarios for Fairbanks and Griffith (including the sub-titles for *Intolerance*). Published autobiography 1966: *A Girl Like I.*

LORD, JACK (1930–). American leading man with stage experience. *Cry Murder* (51), *The Court Martial of Billy Mitchell* (55), *God's Little Acre* (58), *Man of the West* (58), *Doctor No* (62), *The Name of the Game is Kill* (68), etc.; star of TV series *Stoney Burke* (62), *Hawaii Five-O* (68–69).

LORD JIM. Joseph Conrad's saga of a man in search of himself all over the Far East was filmed as a 1927 silent in Hollywood with Percy Marmont. In 1967 Richard Brooks wrote and directed a slap-up international version with Peter O'Toole, but it proved unintentionally dreary.

LORD, MARJORIE (c. 1921–). American leading lady of minor films in the 40s. *Forty Naughty Girls* (38), *Timber* (42), *Sherlock Holmes in Washington* (42), *Flesh and Fantasy* (44), *The Argyle Secrets* (48), *New Orleans* (49), *Port of Hell* (55), etc. Comeback in *Boy Did I Get a Wrong Number* (66).

LORD, PAULINE (1890–1950). American stage actress whose chief film role was as *Mrs Wiggs of the Cabbage Patch* (34).

LOREN, SOPHIA (1934–) (Sophia Scicoloni). Statuesque Italian leading lady, latterly an accomplished international actress. In films from 1950 (as extra). *Aida* (53), *The Sign of Venus* (53)

Lorenz, Pare

Tempi Nostri (54), *Attila* (54), *The Gold of Naples* (54), *Woman of the River* (55), *Too Bad She's Bad* (55), *The Miller's Wife* (55), *Scandal in Sorrento* (55), *Lucky To Be a Woman* (56), etc.; then to US: *The Pride and the Passion* (57), *Boy on a Dolphin* (57), *Legend of the Lost* (57), *Desire under the Elms* (58), *The Key* (58), *Houseboat* (58), *The Black Orchid* (59), *That Kind of Woman* (59), *Heller in Pink Tights* (60), *A Breath of Scandal* (61), *Two Women* (AA, BFA) (61), *The Millionairess* (GB) (61), *El Cid* (61), *Boccaccio 70* (61), *The Condemned of Altona* (62), *Madame Sans Gêne* (62), *Five Miles to Midnight* (62), *Yesterday, Today and Tomorrow* (63), *The Fall of the Roman Empire* (64), *Marriage Italian Style* (64), *Operation Crossbow* (65), *Judith* (65), *Arabesque* (66), *A Countess from Hong Kong* (66), *Once Upon a Time* (67), *Sunflower* (70), etc.

LORENZ, PARE (1905–). American documentarist, best known for *The Plow that Broke the Plains* (36), *The River* (37).

LORNE, MARION (1886–1968) (M. L. MacDougal). American character comedienne with long stage experience, latterly seen as eccentric old lady: *Strangers on a Train* (51), *The Girl Rush* (55), *The Graduate* (68), etc.; also as the dotty witch-aunt in TV series *Bewitched* (64–67).

LORRE, PETER (1904–1964) (Laszlo Löewenstein). Highly individual Hungarian character actor whose rolling eyes and timid manner could be either sympathetic or sinister. A weight problem restricted his later appearances. Made his first films in Germany, then after two in Britain settled mainly in Hollywood. *M* (31), *F.P.1 Antwortet Nicht* (32), *The Man who Knew Too Much* (GB) (34), *Mad Love* (*The Hands of Orlac*) (35), *Crime and Punishment* (36), *The Secret Agent* (GB) (36), *Lancer Spy* (37), *Think Fast Mr Moto* (and seven other Moto adventures 37–39), *Strange Cargo* (40), *Stranger on the Third Floor* (40), *The Face Behind the Mask* (41), *The Maltese Falcon* (41), *All Through the Night* (41), *Casablanca* (42), *The Constant Nymph* (43), *Background to Danger* (43), *Passage to Marseilles* (44), *The Mask of Dimitrios* (44), *Arsenic and Old Lace* (44), *The Conspirators* (44), *Confidential Agent* (45), *Hotel Berlin* (45), *Three Strangers* (46), *The Verdict* (46), *The Beast with Five Fingers* (46), *My Favourite Brunette* (47), *Casbah* (48), *Rope of Sand* (49), *Double Confession* (GB) (50), *Die Verlorene* (German; also directed) (51), *Beat the Devil* (53), *Twenty Thousand Leagues under the Sea* (54), *Congo Crossing* (56), *Silk Stockings* (57), *The Big Circus* (59), *Voyage to the Bottom of the Sea* (61), *Tales of Terror* (62), *Five Weeks in a Balloon* (62), *The Raven* (63), *A Comedy of Terrors* (63), *The Patsy* (64), many others.

LORRING, JOAN (1926–) (Magdalen Ellis). English-Russian actress, evacuated to US in 1939; played some nasty teenagers. *Girls under Twenty-one* (41), *Song of Russia* (44), *The Bridge of San*

606

Luis Rey (44), *The Corn Is Green* (45), *The Verdict* (46), *The Lost Moment* (47), *Good Sam* (49), *Stranger on the Prowl* (53), etc.

†LOSEY, JOSEPH (1909–   ). American director, in Britain since 1952 after McCarthy witch-hunt. *The Boy with Green Hair* (48), *The Lawless* (*The Dividing Line*) (50), *The Prowler* (50), '*M*' (51), *The Big Night* (51), *Stranger on the Prowl* (53), *The Sleeping Tiger* (54), *The Intimate Stranger* (56), *Time without Pity* (57), *The Gypsy and the Gentleman* (57), *Blind Date* (59), *The Criminal* (60), *The Damned* (61), *Eva* (62), *The Servant* (63), *King and Country* (64), *Modesty Blaise* (66), *Accident* (67), *Boom* (68), *Secret Ceremony* (68), *Figures in a Landscape* (70).

LOST HORIZON (US 1937). Frank Capra's uneven but attractive film from the James Hilton novel about a Tibetan Utopia made Shangri-La a household word. The actors were perfectly cast, with Ronald Colman as Conway, H. B. Warner as Chang and Sam Jaffe as the High Lama.

THE LOST PATROL (US 1934). An unconvincing but savage and relentless melodrama about a British desert patrol picked off one by one by Arabs until rescuers find the one survivor raving mad. Notable for photography by Harold Wendstrom, direction by John Ford (here on the brink of his best period), and heavily overacted but enjoyable performances from Victor McLaglen, Boris Karloff, Reginald Denny and Douglas Fairbanks Jnr. From a novel by Philip Macdonald which later inspired *Sahara* (43) and *The Sabre and the Arrow* (52).

THE LOST WEEKEND (US 1945; AA best picture). Three days in the life of a dipsomaniac, cunningly dramatized by its producer and director, Charles Brackett and Billy Wilder, from a novel by Charles Jackson. Ray Milland (AA) gave the performance of his life, and the film's success gave Hollywood realism a big stride forward.

THE LOST WORLD. The 1924 silent version of Arthur Conan Doyle's Edwardian adventure story was notable for the first efforts of Willis O'Brien in animating prehistoric dinosaurs. The 1961 remake was notable for nothing except doing everything wrong, including the hilarious miscasting of Claude Rains.

LOTINGA, ERNIE (1876–1951). British vaudeville comedian formerly known as Dan Roy. Made a few slapstick comedies which had their followers: *The Raw Recruit* (28), *PC Josser* (31), *Josser Joins the Navy* (32), *Josser in the Army* (33), *Love Up the Pole* (36), etc.

LOUISE, ANITA (1915–   ) (Anita Louise Fremault). American leading lady, usually in gentle roles. Played child parts from 1924; memorable in *A Midsummer Night's Dream* (35), *The Story of Louis*

Pasteur (35), *Anthony Adverse* (36), *The Green Light* (37), *Marie Antoinette* (38), *The Sisters* (39), *Phantom Submarine* (41), *The Fighting Guardsman* (45), *The Bandit of Sherwood Forest* (46), *Retreat, Hell!* (52). TV series: *My Friend Flicka* (56).

LOUISE, TINA (1935–). American leading lady: *God's Little Acre* (58), *Day of the Outlaw* (59), *The Wrecking Crew* (68), *The Good Guys and the Bad Guys* (69), etc. TV series: *Gilligan's Island* (64–66).

LOURIE, EUGENE (c. 1905–). French designer. *Les Bas Fonds* (36), *La Grande Illusion* (37), *La Règle du Jeu* (39), *This Land Is Mine* (US) (42), *The Southerner* (US) (44), *The River* (51), etc. Directed *The Beast from Twenty Thousand Fathoms* (53), *The Colossus of New York* (58), *Gorgo* (GB) (60), etc.

LOVE, BESSIE (1898–) (Juanita Horton). Vivacious, petite American leading lady of the 20s. In films from childhood; since the mid-30s resident in London, playing occasional cameo parts. *Intolerance* (15), *The Aryan* (16), *A Sister of Six* (17), *The Dawn of Understanding* (18), *The Purple Dawn* (20), *The Vermilion Pencil* (21), *Human Wreckage* (23), *Dynamite Smith* (24), *The Lost World* (25), *Lovey Mary* (26), *Sally of the Scandals* (27), *Broadway Melody* (28), *Chasing Rainbows* (30), *Morals for Women* (31), *Conspiracy* (32), *Atlantic Ferry* (42), *Journey Together* (45), *Touch and Go* (55), *The Wild Affair* (64), *Isadora* (68), many others.

LOVE ME TONIGHT (US 1932). An early sound musical with an apparent 'Lubitsch touch' which actually belongs to director Rouben Mamoulian, who also manages to provide a René Clair view of Paris as a place where everybody sings. Visual and aural experiments jostle the wit and good humour, and memorable songs like 'Mimi' and 'Isn't It Romantic' complete a masterpiece of light cinema. With Maurice Chevalier, Jeanette Macdonald, Myrna Loy, Charles Butterworth, Charles Ruggles. What plot there is concerns a tailor who makes it in high society.

LOVE, MONTAGU (1877–1943). British stage actor, formerly magazine illustrator, who went to America in 1913 and soon settled in Hollywood as character actor. *The Gilded Cage* (19), *Son of the Sheik* (26), *Out of Singapore* (32), *Clive of India* (35), *The Life of Emile Zola* (37), *Dr Ehrlich's Magic Bullet* (40), *Forever and a Day* (43), hundreds of others.

THE LOVED ONE (US 1965). Advertised as the film with something to offend everybody, this too-free adaptation of Evelyn Waugh's satirical account of the burial customs of Southern California got itself tangled up with a number of extraneous matters, including over-eating, film production and military bureaucracy. Despite central miscasting and some pretentious writing, a number of the bravura passages come off amusingly; but the film remains notable for effort rather than achievement. Directed by Tony Richardson, photographed by Haskell Wexler, with John Gielgud, Liberace, Rod Steiger, Milton Berle and others.

LOVEJOY, FRANK (1912–1962). American actor of tough roles, with stage and radio experience. *Home of the Brave* (debut) (49), *In a Lonely Place* (50), *The Sound of Fury* (51), *I Was a Communist for the FBI* (51), *Force of Arms* (51), *The Hitch Hiker* (52), *Retreat Hell* (52), *The System* (53), *House of Wax* (53), *The Charge at Feather River* (54), *Beachhead* (54), *The Americano* (55), *Top of the World* (55), *Strategic Air Command* (55), *The Crooked Web* (56), etc. TV series: *Meet McGraw* (57–58).

LOVELL, RAYMOND (1900–1953). Canadian stage actor long in Britain: often in pompous or sinister roles. *Warn London* (34), *Contraband* (40), *49th Parallel* (41), *Alibi* (42), *Warn That Man* (43), *The Way Ahead* (44), *Caesar and Cleopatra* (45), *The Three Weird Sisters* (48), *Time Gentlemen Please* (52), *The Steel Key* (53), etc.

THE LOVE PARADE (US 1929). An early sound comedy by Ernst Lubitsch which set his style, and that of other directors influenced by him, for many years to come. Brittle, sophisticated, finely mounted, with the story told in visual terms, it was written by Ernest Vajda and Guy Bolton, with sets designed by Hans Dreier and music by Victor Schertzinger; and it starred Maurice Chevalier, Jeanette Macdonald, Lupino Lane and Lilian Roth.

LOWE, EDMUND (1892–   ). Suave American leading man, in films from 1919, after academic experience. Was a big success as Quirt in *What Price Glory* (26), and subsequently played many similar roles; also *In Old Arizona* (32), *Chandu the Magician* (33), *Dinner at Eight* (33), *The Great Impersonation* (35), *The Wrecker* (GB) (36), *Seven Sinners* (GB) (36), *The Squeakers* (GB) (37), *Call Out the Marines* (41), later in detective second features; character comeback in *Dillinger* (46), *Good Sam* (48), *Heller in Pink Tights* (60), etc.

THE LOWER DEPTHS. Gorki's doss-house study has had two notable filmings. As *Les Bas Fonds*, it provided in 1936 memorable roles for Jean Gabin and Louis Jouvet, with direction by Jean Renoir. In 1958 in Japan, Akira Kurosawa directed Toshiro Mifune in a surprisingly faithful adaptation.

LOWERY, ROBERT (1916–   ) (R. L. Hanke). American leading man of the 40s, mainly in routine films. *Wake Up and Live* (37), *Young Mr Lincoln* (39), *Lure of the Islands* (42), *A Scream in the Dark* (44), *Prison Ship* (45), *The Mummy's Ghost* (46), *Death Valley* (48), *Batman and Robin* (serial) (as Batman) (50), *Crosswinds* (51), *Cow Country*

Loy, Myrna

(53), *The Rise and Fall of Legs Diamond* (60), *Johnny Reno* (66), many others.

LOY, MYRNA (1902–   ) (Myrna Williams). American leading lady, in films from 1922, associated for a time with oriental roles, later with sophisticated comedy. *Don Juan* (26), *Ben Hur* (27), *Show of Shows* (28), *The Desert Song* (29), *The Devil to Pay* (30), *A Connecticut Yankee* (31), *Transatlantic* (31), *Arrowsmith* (32), *Love Me Tonight* (32), *The Mask of Fu Manchu* (32), *Vanity Fair* (as Becky Sharp) (32), *When Ladies Meet* (33), *Men in White* (34), *Manhattan Melodrama* (34), *The Thin Man* (34) (and five sequels), *Wife Versus Secretary* (36), *Libelled Lady* (36), *The Great Ziegfeld* (36), *Parnell* (37), *Test Pilot* (38), *The Rains Came* (39), *I Love You Again* (40), *Love Crazy* (41), *A Genius in the Family* (45), *The Best Years of Our Lives* (46), *The Bachelor and the Bobbysoxer* (47), *Mr Blandings Builds His Dream House* (48), *Cheaper by the Dozen* (50), *Belles on Their Toes* (52), *The Ambassador's Daughter* (56), *Lonelyhearts* (59), *Midnight Lace* (60), *The April Fools* (69), many others.

LOY, NANNI (1925–   ). Italian director. *Parola di Ladra* (56), *The Four Days of Naples* (62), *Made in Italy* (68), etc.

LUBIN, ARTHUR (1901–   ). American director from 1935, mainly of light comedy. *Rookies* (*Buck Privates*) (39) (and other Abbott and Costello films), *Who Killed Aunt Maggie* (40), *Eagle Squadron* (42), *Phantom of the Opera* (43), *Ali Baba and the Forty Thieves* (44), *Delightfully Dangerous* (45), *New Orleans* (47), *Francis* (and several sequels) (50), *Rhubarb* (51), *It Grows on Trees* (52), *South Sea Woman* (53), *Lady Godiva* (55), *Escapade in Japan* (57), *The Thief of Baghdad* (61), *The Incredible Mr Limpet* (63), *Hold On* (66), many others. TV series: *Mr Ed* (producer-director).

LUBITSCH, ERNST (1892–1947). German director, once a comic actor, in a series of silent farces starring him as 'Meyer'. After a variety of subjects he settled for a kind of sophisticated sex comedy that became unmistakably his: the 'Lubitsch touch' was a form of visual innuendo, spicy without ever being vulgar. His greatest period came after 1922, when he settled in Hollywood and became Paramount's leading producer. Early films include many shorts; then *Carmen* (18), *Madame du Barry* (19), *Sumurun* (20), *Anne Boleyn* (20), *Pharaoh's Wife* (21), *The Flame* (21). †American films: *Rosita* (23), *The Marriage Circle* (24), *Three Women* (24), *Forbidden Paradise* (24), *Kiss Me Again* (25), *Lady Windermere's Fan* (25), *So This Is Paris* (26), *The Student Prince* (27), *The Patriot* (28), *Eternal Love* (29), *The Love Parade* (first sound film) (29), *Paramount on Parade* (Chevalier sequences) (30), *Monte Carlo* (30), *The Smiling Lieutenant* (31), *The Man I Killed* (32), *One Hour With You* (32), *Trouble in Paradise* (32), *If I Had a Million* (Laughton sequence) (32),

Design for Living (33), *The Merry Widow* (produced only) (36), *Angel* (37), *Bluebeard's Eighth Wife* (38), *Ninotchka* (39), *The Shop Around the Corner* (40), *That Uncertain Feeling* (41), *To Be or Not To Be* (42), *Heaven Can Wait* (43), *A Royal Scandal* (*Czarina*) (produced only) (45), *Cluny Brown* (46), *That Lady in Ermine* (finished by Otto Preminger) (48). Personally produced many of these. Awarded special Oscar 1946 'for his distinguished contributions to the art of the motion picture'. A splendid biographical book, *The Lubitsch Touch* (68) has been written by Herman G. Weinberg.

LUCAN, ARTHUR (1887–1954). British music-hall comedian famous as 'Old Mother Riley', in which guise he made over a dozen low comedies between 1937 and 1952, usually with his wife **Kitty** MacShane playing his daughter.

LUCAS, LEIGHTON (1903–   ). British composer and musical director; former ballet dancer. In films from 1934. *Target for Tonight* (41), *Stage Fright* (50), *A King in New York* (57), *Ice Cold in Alex* (58), *The Millionairess* (61), many others.

LUCAS, WILLIAM (1926–   ). British leading man of stage, TV and occasional films. *Timeslip* (55), *X the Unknown* (56), *Breakout* (59), *Sons and Lovers* (60), *The Devil's Daffodil* (61), *Calculated Risk* (63), etc.

LUCHAIRE, CORINNE (1921–50). French actress who was a big hit in *Prison Without Bars* (38). After World War II was convicted as a collaborationist and died in poverty.

LUDWIG, EDWARD (c. 1900–   ). American director, from 1932. *They Just Had To Get Married* (33), *Friends of Mr Sweeney* (34), *The Man Who Reclaimed His Head* (34), *Age of Indiscretion* (36), *That Certain Age* (38), *The Last Gangster* (39), *The Swiss Family Robinson* (40), *The Man Who Lost Himself* (41), *They Came To Blow Up America* (43), *The Fighting Seabees* (44), *Three's a Family* (45), *The Fabulous Texan* (47), *Wake of the Red Witch* (48), *Smuggler's Island* (51), *Big Jim McLain* (52), *Sangaree* (53), *Flame of the Islands* (56), *The Black Scorpion* (57), *The Gun Hawk* (63), etc.

LUDWIG, WILLIAM (1912–   ). American writer. The Hardy Family films (38–44), *Challenge to Lassie* (49), *Shadow on the Wall* (50), *The Great Caruso* (51), *Interrupted Melody* (AA) (55), *Back Street* (61), etc.

LUGOSI, BELA (1882–1956) (Bela Lugosi Blasko or Arisztid Olt). Hungarian stage actor of chilling presence; in Hollywood on and off from 1925, but became famous when he repeated his stage role as *Dracula* (30), and later became typecast in inferior horror roles. *The Silent Command* (24), *The Thirteenth Chair* (29), *The Murders in the Rue Morgue* (32), *Chandu the Magician* (32), *White Zombie* (32), *Island of Lost Souls* (33), *The Black Cat* (34), *The Mark of the Vampire* (35), *The Raven* (35), *The Invisible Ray* (36), *Son of Frankenstein* (39), *Dark Eyes of London* (GB) (39), *Ninotchka* (a rare non-horrific role) (39), *The Devil Bat* (40), *Spooks Run Wild* (41), *Return of the Vampire* (43), *Frankenstein Meets the Wolf Man* (as the monster) (43), *Zombies on Broadway* (45), *Abbott and Costello Meet Frankenstein* (48), *Mother Riley Meets the Vampire* (GB) (52), *The Black Sleep* (56), many others.

LUKAS, PAUL (1895–   ) (Pal Lukacs). Suave Hungarian actor with stage experience in Europe; in US from 1927. Film debut 1917. *Little Women* (33), *The Three Musketeers* (36), *Dodsworth* (36), *The Lady Vanishes* (GB) (38), *The Chinese Bungalow* (GB) (39), *A Window in London* (GB) (39), *Confessions of a Nazi Spy* (39), *Strange Cargo* (40), *The Monster and the Girl* (41), *They Dare Not Love* (41), *Watch on the Rhine* (AA) (43), *Hostages* (43), *Uncertain Glory* (44), *Address Unknown* (44), *Experiment Perilous* (44), *Deadline at Dawn* (46), *Temptation* (47), *Berlin Express* (48), *Kim* (50), *Twenty Thousand Leagues under the Sea* (54), *Roots of Heaven* (58), *Fifty-five Days at Peking* (62), *Lord Jim* (65), *Sol Madrid* (68), etc.

LUKE, KEYE (c. 1904–   ). Chinese actor, in Hollywood from 1934; popular for years as Charlie Chan's number two son. Other supporting roles in *The Painted Veil* (34), *The Hands of Orlac* (35), *Mr Moto's Gamble* (38), *Burma Convoy* (41), *Dr Gillespie's New Assistant* (42), *Sleep My Love* (48), *Hell's Half Acre* (54), *Yangtse Incident* (GB) (57), *Nobody's Perfect* (67), etc. Much TV work.

LULU (1948–   ) (Marie Lawrie). British pop singer whose film career began in *Gonks Go Beat* (65).

†LUMET, SIDNEY (1924–   ). American director, former child actor and TV producer. *Twelve Angry Men* (57), *Stage Struck* (58), *That Kind of Woman* (59), *The Fugitive Kind* (60), *A View from the Bridge* (61), *Long Day's Journey into Night* (62), *Fail-Safe* (64), *The Pawnbroker* (65), *The Hill* (65), *The Group* (65), *The Deadly Affair* (also produced) (66), *Bye Bye Braverman* (68), *The Seagull* (68), *The Appointment* (69), *Blood Kin* (69).

LUMIERE, LOUIS (1864–1948). Pioneer French cinematographer, with brother AUGUSTE LUMIERE (1862–1954). Gave first public demonstration 1895, including *Arrival of Train at Station* and other simple events; later made short comedies, e.g. *L'Arrosseur Arrossé* (1897).

LUNA, BARBARA (1937–   ). American actress who usually plays beautiful foreigners. *The Devil at Four O'Clock* (60), *Five Weeks in a Balloon* (62), *Synanon* (64), *Ship of Fools* (65), *Firecreek* (67), *Che!* (69,) etc.

LUND, JOHN (1913–). American leading man with Broadway experience; film roles mainly stodgy. *To Each His Own* (46), *The Perils of Pauline* (47), *A Foreign Affair* (47), *Night Has a Thousand Eyes* (48), *Miss Tatlock's Millions* (48), *My Friend Irma* (49), *Duchess of Idaho* (50), *Darling, How Could You?* (51), *Steel Town* (52), *Bronco Buster* (52), *The Woman They Almost Lynched* (53), *Chief Crazy Horse* (54), *White Feather* (55), *Battle Stations* (56), *High Society* (56), *The Wackiest Ship in the Army* (60), etc.; recently back on stage.

LUNDIGAN, WILLIAM (1914–). American leading man of routine features, formerly in radio. *Three Smart Girls Grow Up* (38), *The Old Maid* (39), *The Sea Hawk* (40), *Sunday Punch* (42), *What Next, Corporal Hargrove* (45), *Pinky* (49), *I'd Climb the Highest Mountain* (51), *Down among the Sheltering Palms* (52), *Inferno* (53), *Serpent of the Nile* (53), *The White Orchid* (54), *The Underwater City* (61), *The Way West* (67), etc. TV series: *Men into Space* (59).

LUNT, ALFRED (1893–). Distinguished American stage actor, husband of Lynn Fontanne. Film appearances include: *Backbone* (23), *Ragged Edge* (23), *Second Youth* (24), *Sally of the Sawdust* (26), *The Guardsman* (32).

LUPINO, IDA (1918–). British leading lady, daughter of stage comedian Stanley Lupino. Made a few British films in the early 30s: *Her First Affaire* (31), *I Lived with You* (34), etc. Then went to Hollywood and stayed: *The Search for Beauty* (34), *Peter Ibbetson* (35), *The Gay Desperado* (36), *One Rainy Afternoon* (36), *Artists and Models* (37), *The Adventures of Sherlock Holmes* (39), *The Light That Failed* (40), *They Drive by Night* (40), *The Sea Wolf* (41), *High Sierra* (41), *Ladies in Retirement* (41), *Moontide* (42), *The Light of Heart* (42), *The Hard Way* (42), *Devotion* (as Emily Bronte) (43), *Forever and a Day* (43), *In Our Time* (44), *Pillow to Post* (45), *The Man I Love* (46), *Escape Me Never* (46), *Deep Valley* (47), *Roadhouse* (48), *Woman in Hiding* (49), *On Dangerous Ground* (51), *Beware My Lovely* (52), *The Bigamist* (53), *Jennifer* (54), *The Big Knife* (55), *While the City Sleeps* (56), etc. Became Hollywood's only current woman director: *Outrage* (50), *Never Fear* (50), *Hard, Fast and Beautiful* (51), *The Bigamist* (53), *The Hitch-Hiker* (53), *The Trouble with Angels* (66), etc., many TV episodes. Starred in TV series *Mr Adams and Eve* (56–57).

LUPINO, STANLEY (1893–1942). British comedian on stage from 1900, especially in musical comedy. Films include *The Love Race* (32), *Sleepless Nights* (33), *Happy* (34), *Cheer Up* (36), *Sporting Love* (37), *Over She Goes* (38), *Lucky to Me* (39), etc.

LYDON, JIMMY (1923–). American actor, best known as the gangly teenager hero of the *Henry Aldrich* series in the early 40s. Also in *Back Door to Heaven* (debut) (39), *Tom Brown's Schooldays* (title role)

(39), *Naval Academy* (41), *The Town Went Wild* (45), *Strange Illusion* (45), *Life with Father* (47), *Island in the Sky* (53), *Battle Stations* (56), *Brainstorm* (65), etc.

LYE, LEN (1901–). New Zealander animator, associated from 1934 with GPO Film Unit propaganda shorts. *Colour Box* (34), *Rainbow Dance* (36), *Kaleidoscope* (36), *The Lambeth Walk* (41), etc. Later directed short documentaries.

LYEL, VIOLA (1900–) (Violet Watson). British character actress, mainly on stage in comedy roles. *Hobson's Choice* (leading role) (30), *Channel Crossing* (32), *Quiet Wedding* (40), *Wanted for Murder* (46), *No Place for Jennifer* (50), *Isn't Life Wonderful?* (53), *See How They Run* (56), etc.

LYLES, A. C. (1918–). American producer, former publicist; noted for his second-feature Westerns using veteran talent. *Short Cut to Hell* (57), *Raymie* (60), *The Young and the Brave* (61), *Law of the Lawless* (64), *Stagecoach to Hell* (64), *Young Fury* (65), *Black Spurs* (65), *Town Tamer* (65), *Apache Uprising* (66), *Johnny Reno* (66), *Waco* (66), *Red Tomahawk* (67), *Buckskin* (68), etc.

LYNCH, ALFRED (1936–). Raw-boned British actor who has played leads in *On the Fiddle* (61), *Two and Two Make Six* (61), *West Eleven* (63), *The Hill* (65), *The Taming of the Shrew* (67), *The Seagull* (68), etc; also on stage and TV.

lynch law has been condemned in many outstanding dramatic movies from Hollywood, including *Fury* (36), *They Won't Forget* (37), *Young Mr Lincoln* (39), *The Ox-Bow Incident* (43), *Storm Warning* (51), *The Sound of Fury* (51), *The Sun Shines Bright* (52) and *Rough Night in Jericho* (68). See also: *Ku Klux Klan*.

LYNDE, PAUL (1926–). American TV comedian who usually plays a flustered character with a funny voice. Film appearances include *New Faces* (54), *Send Me No Flowers* (64), *The Glass Bottom Boat* (66), *How Sweet It Is* (68).

LYNDON, BARRE (1896–). British playwright and screenwriter in Hollywood from 1941. *Sundown* (41), *The Lodger* (44), *Night Has a Thousand Eyes* (48), *Conquest of Space* (54), many others; also adapted his own plays, *The Amazing Dr Clitterhouse* (38), *The Man in Half Moon Street* (44).

LYNLEY, CAROL (1942–). American leading lady. *Holiday for Lovers* (59), *Blue Jeans* (59), *Return to Peyton Place* (61), *The Cardinal* (63), *Under the Yum Yum Tree* (64), *Harlow* (electronovision) (65), *Bunny Lake is Missing* (GB) (65), *The Shuttered Room* (GB) (66), *Danger Route* (GB) (68), *The Maltese Bippy* (69), *Norwood* (70), etc.

LYNN, ANN (c. 1939–   ). British actress, mainly on TV; grand-daughter of Ralph Lynn. *Piccadilly Third Stop* (60), *The Wind of Change* (61), *Strongroom* (61), *Flame in the Streets* (62), *Black Torment* (64), *Four in the Morning* (65), *Baby Love* (69), etc.

LYNN, DIANA (1924–   ) (Dolly Loehr). Former American child actress and pianist. *There's Magic in Music* (40), *The Major and the Minor* (42), *The Miracle of Morgan's Creek* (43), *Our Hearts Were Young and Gay* (44), *Out of This World* (44), *Our Hearts Were Growing Up* (45), *The Bride Wore Boots* (46), *Ruthless* (47), *Every Girl Should Be Married* (48), *Paid in Full* (49), *My Friend Irma* (49), *Bedtime for Bonzo* (50), *My Friend Irma Goes West* (50), *Peggy* (50), *The People Against O'Hara* (51), *Meet Me at the Fair* (53), *Plunder of the Sun* (54), *The Kentuckian* (55), *You're Never Too Young* (55), etc. Makes occasional TV appearances.

LYNN, JEFFREY (1909–   ) (Ragnar Lind). American leading man with varied experience, in films from 1938. *Four Daughters* (38), *Yes, My Darling Daughter* (39), *Espionage Agent* (39), *The Roaring Twenties* (40), *A Child Is Born* (40), *All This and Heaven Too* (40), *Four Mothers* (40), *Million Dollar Baby* (41), *The Body Disappears* (41); war service; *Whiplash* (47), *Black Bart* (48), *A Letter to Three Wives* (49), *Up Front* (51), *Captain China* (52), *Come Thursday* (64), *Tony Rome* (67), many others.

LYNN, LENI (1925–   ). American girl singer who after debut in *Babes in Arms* (39) came to England and starred in several low-budget musicals: *Heaven Is Round the Corner* (43), *Give Me the Stars* (44), *Spring Song* (46), etc.

LYNN, RALPH (1882–1964). British farceur, on stage from 1900; the incomparable silly ass hero of the Aldwych farces of the 20s, all later screened. *Rookery Nook* (30), *Turkey Time* (32), *Thark* (32), *A Cuckoo in the Nest* (33), *Fishing Stock* (35), *Foreign Affairs* (36), *For Valour* (37), *In the Soup* (37), etc.

LYNN, ROBERT (1918–   ). British director, in films from 1936 as camera assistant. Many TV films, also *Postman's Knock* (61), *Dr Crippen* (62), *Victim Five* (65), *Change Partners* (66), etc.

LYON, BEN (1901–   ). Former American leading man, latterly executive. In films since 1923: *Hell's Angels* (30), *I Cover the Water-front* (35), *I Killed the Count* (38), *Hi Gang* (40), *Life with the Lyons* (54), many others. Married to Bebe Daniels; they have lived in Britain since 1939 and were popular till recently on radio and TV.

LYON, FRANCIS D. (1905–   ). American director, former editor. *Crazylegs* (53), *Cult of the Cobra* (55), *The Great Locomotive Chase* (56), *Escort West* (58), *The Young and the Brave* (63), *Destination Inner Space* (66), *The Destructors* (66), etc.

LYON, SUE (1946–   ). American juvenile actress: *Lolita* (62), *Night of the Iguana* (64), *Seven Women* (65), *The Flim Flam Man* (67), *Tony Rome* (67).

LYTELL, BERT (1888–1954). American leading man of silent films. *To Have and to Hold* (17), *The Lone Wolf* (31), *A Message from Mars* (23), *Rupert of Hentzau* (23), *Lady Windermere's Fan* (25), *Steele of the Royal Mounted* (27), *Blood Brothers* (30), *The Single Sin* (31), etc. Retired apart from an appearance in *Stage Door Canteen* (43).

M

M. The shortest-ever film title. Fritz Lang was the first, in 1931, to film this story of a child-murderer who is finally hunted down by the city's organized criminal element, and Peter Lorre had his first great success as the psychopath. In 1950 Joseph Losey directed an almost scene-for-scene American remake starring David Wayne, but it generated no particular atmosphere.

MACARTHUR, CHARLES (1895–1956). American playwright and screenwriter, in Hollywood from 1932. *Rasputin and the Empress* (32), *Twentieth Century* (34), *Barbary Coast* (35), *Gunga Din* (39), *Wuthering Heights* (39), *His Girl Friday* (from his own play 'The Front Page') (40), etc. Most of these were written with Ben Hecht, and together they wrote, produced and directed *The Scoundrel* (34).

MACARTHUR, JAMES (1937–   ). American juvenile lead, son of Charles Macarthur and Helen Hayes. *The Young Stranger* (debut) (57), *The Light in the Forest* (58), *The Third Man on the Mountain* (59), *The Swiss Family Robinson* (60), *Spencer's Mountain* (63), *The Truth about Spring* (65), *The Bedford Incident* (65), etc.

MCAVOY, MAY (1901–   ). American leading lady of the 20s. *Sentimental Tommy* (21), *Clarence* (22), *Kick In* (23), *The Enchanted Cottage* (24), *West of the Water Tower* (24), *Ben Hur* (26), *Slightly Used* (27), *The Terror* (28), etc. The last-named caused her retirement, for talkies did not suit her.

MACBETH. Among many attempts to film Shakespeare's Scottish tragedy, none of them wholly successful, have been the following. 1. In 1915 John Emerson directed and D. W. Griffith produced a straightforward version starring Sir Herbert Beerbohm Tree and Constance Collier. 2. In 1948 Orson Welles directed and starred in his own adaptation, shot in 21 days for Republic; the would-be Scottish burr in which the cast was drilled completely obscured the poetry, but despite papier-maché sets there were some striking effects. 1956: Ken Hughes wrote and directed a modernized version, *Joe Macbeth*, in which the kings and princes became rival gangsters; Paul Douglas starred. 1957: Akira Kurosawa directed *Throne of Blood*, a stylized Japanese version. 1960: George Schaefer directed an honest G.C.E.-type rendering in colour with Maurice Evans and Judith Anderson; destined for American television, it was released theatrically in Britain.

MCBRIDE, DONALD (1894–1957). American character comedian adept at explosive editors, dumb policemen, etc. Made debut in his stage role as the harassed hotel manager in *Room Service* (38). Later: *The Story of Vernon and Irene Castle* (40), *Here Comes Mr Jordan* (41), *Topper Returns* (41), *Invisible Woman* (41), *They Got Me Covered* (42), *The Glass Key* (42), *Two Yanks in Trinidad* (42), *Abbott and Costello in Hollywood* (45), *Good News* (48), *Bowery Battalion* (51), *The Seven Year Itch* (55), many others.

MCCALLISTER, LON (1923–). American leading man, usually in callow roles. *Souls at Sea* (37), *Babes in Arms* (39), *Stage Door Canteen* (43), *Home in Indiana* (44), *Winged Victory* (44), *The Red House* (47), *The Big Cat* (50), *Letter from Korea* (50), *Combat Squad* (54), etc.

MCCALLUM, DAVID (1933–). Scottish-born actor, in films from 1953; lately settled in Hollywood. *The Secret Place* (56), *Robbery under Arms* (57), *Violent Playground* (58), *Billy Budd* (62), *Freud* (62), *The Great Escape* (63), *The Greatest Story Ever Told* (65), *Around the World Under the Sea* (66), *Three Bites of the Apple* (67), *Sol Madrid* (68), *Mosquito Squadron* (69), etc. Enormously popular in TV series *The Man from Uncle*, episodes of which have been expanded for play-off in cinemas: *To Trap a Spy*, *One Spy Too Many*, *The Spy with My Face*, *One of Our Spies is Missing*, etc.

MCCALLUM, JOHN (1917–). Australian leading man of stage and screen, in England 1945–55; married Googie Withers. *Joe Goes Back* (44), *The Root of All Evil* (47), *The Loves of Joanna Godden* (47), *The Woman in Question* (50), *Trent's Last Case* (52), *Trouble in the Glen* (53), *Port of Escape* (55), etc.

MCCAMBRIDGE, MERCEDES (c. 1918–). Intense American actress with stage experience, often in hard-bitten roles. *All the King's Men* (AA: debut) (50), *Lightning Strikes Twice* (51), *Johnny Guitar* (54), *Giant* (56), *A Farewell to Arms* (57), *Suddenly Last Summer* (60), *Cimarron* (61), *Angel Baby* (61), *99 Women* (69), etc. Published autobiography 1961: *The Two of Us*.

MCCAREY, LEO (1898–1969). American director with a sentimental streak. Directed many silent shorts, including several with Laurel and Hardy. From 1931 (†) made fewer films; usually wrote and produced as well as directing. *Indiscreet* (31), *The Kid from Spain* (32), *Duck Soup* (33), *Six of a Kind* (34), *Belle of the Nineties* (34), *Ruggles of Red Gap* (34), *The Milky Way* (36), *The Awful Truth* (AA direction) (37), *Make Way for Tomorrow* (37), *Love Affair* (AA screenplay) (39), *My Favourite Wife* (40), *Once Upon a Honeymoon* (42), *Going My Way* (AA writing and direction) (44), *The Bells of St Mary's* (45), *Good Sam* (48), *My Son John* (52), *An Affair to Remember* (remake of *Love Affair*) (57), *Rally Round the Flag Boys* (58), *Satan Never Sleeps* (62).

MCCAREY, RAY (1904–1948). American director of second features, formerly making Hal Roach shorts. *Pack Up Your Troubles* (32), *Millions in the Air* (36), *That Other Woman* (42), *Atlantic City* (44), *The Falcon's Alibi* (46), etc.

MCCARTHY, KEVIN (1914–   ). American leading man and latterly character actor, with stage experience. *Death of a Salesman* (debut) (52), *Stranger on Horseback* (55), *Invasion of the Body Snatchers* (56), *The Misfits* (61), *The Prize* (63), *The Best Man* (64), *Mirage* (65), *A Big Hand for the Little Lady* (66), *Hotel* (67), *If He Hollers Let Him Go* (68), etc. Much on TV: in series *The Survivors* (69).

MCCARTHY, MICHAEL (1917–59). British director, in films from 1934. *Assassin for Hire* (51), *Mystery Junction* (51), *Crow Hollow* (52), *Shadow of a Man* (54), *It's Never Too Late* (56), *Smoke Screen* (57), *The Traitor* (57), *Operation Amsterdam* (58), etc.

MCCLORY, KEVIN (1926–   ). Irish production executive, former sound technician. Wrote, produced and directed *The Boy and the Bridge* (59); produced *Thunderball* (65).

MCCLORY, SEAN (1923–   ). Irish actor with Abbey Theatre experience; long in Hollywood. *Beyond Glory* (49), *Rommel, Desert Fox* (51), *Les Misérables* (52), *Ring of Fear* (54), *Moonfleet* (55), *Diane* (57), *Bandolero* (68), etc.

MCCLURE, DOUGLAS (1935–   ). American leading man, from TV. *Because They're Young* (59), *The Unforgiven* (60), *Shenandoah* (65), *Beau Geste* (66), *The King's Pirate* (67). TV series: *Checkmate* (59–61), *Overland Trail* (60), *The Virginian* (64–69).

MCCLURE, GREG (1918–   ) (Dale Easton). American leading man who starred in his first film but did little thereafter. *The Great John L* (45), *Bury Me Dead* (47), *Lulu Belle* (48), *Joe Palooka in the Squared Circle* (50), *Stop That Cab* (51), etc.

MCCORD, TED (1912–   ). American cinematographer: *Treasure of Sierra Madre* (48), *Johnny Belinda* (48), *The Breaking Point* (50), *Young at Heart* (54), *East of Eden* (55), *The Proud Rebel* (58), *War Hunt* (61), *Two for the Seesaw* (63), *The Sound of Music* (AA) (65), *A Fine Madness* (66), etc.

MCCORMACK, JOHN (1884–1945). Irish tenor who appeared in *Song O' My Heart* (30), *Wings of the Morning* (37).

MCCORMACK, PATTY (1945–   ). American juvenile actress who went to Hollywood to repeat her stage role as the evil child of *The Bad Seed* (56). Later: *The Day They Gave Babies Away* (57), *Kathy 'O* (58), *The Adventures of Huckleberry Finn* (60), *The Explosive Generation* (61), *The Young Runaways* (68), etc.; much on TV.

MCCORMICK, F. J. (1891–1947) (Peter Judge). Irish character actor, long on the Abbey Theatre stage. Well remembered as Shell in *Odd Man Out* (46); also in *The Plough and the Stars* (37), *Hungry Hill* (46).

MCCORMICK, MYRON (1908–1962). American character actor, with stage experience. *Winterset* (37), *One-Third of a Nation* (39), *Jigsaw* (49), *Jolson Sings Again* (50), *No Time for Sergeants* (58), *The Hustler* (61), etc.

MCCOWEN, ALEC (1925–   ). Youthful-looking British stage actor, in occasional films: *Time without Pity* (57), *Town on Trial* (57), *The Loneliness of the Long Distance Runner* (62), *In the Cool of the Day* (63), *The Agony and the Ecstasy* (65), *The Witches* (*The Devil's Own*) (66), *The Hawaiians* (US) (70), etc.

MCCOY, TIM (1891–   ). American cowboy star, in films from 1923 when, an ex-army officer, he went to Hollywood as adviser on *The Covered Wagon*. *War Paint* (26), *The Indians Are Coming* (30), *The Fighting Fool* (31), *Texas Cyclone* (32), *Whirlwind* (33), *Hell Bent for Love* (34), *Square Shooter* (35), many others. Later played bit parts: *Around the World in Eighty Days* (56), *Run of the Arrow* (57), *Requiem for a Gunfighter* (65), etc.

MCCREA, JOEL (1905–   ). Amiable, dependable American leading man of the 30s and 40s, subsequently a Western star. Went to Hollywood from college and spent two years as an extra. *The Jazz Age* (first good role) (29), *Dynamite* (30), *Kept Husbands* (31), *Bird of Paradise* (32), *The Most Dangerous Game* (*The Hounds of Zaroff*) (32), *Our Betters* (33), *The Silver Cord* (33), *Private Worlds* (34), *Barbary Coast* (35), *These Three* (36), *Come and Get It* (36), *Banjo on My Knee* (37), *Interns Can't Take Money* (37), *Wells Fargo* (37), *Woman Chases Man* (37), *Dead End* (37), *Three Blind Mice* (38), *Union Pacific* (38), *They Shall Have Music* (39), *Espionage Agent* (39), *He Married His Wife* (40), *The Primrose Path* (40), *Foreign Correspondent* (40), *Sullivan's Travels* (41), *The Great Man's Lady* (41), *The Palm Beach Story* (42), *The More the Merrier* (43), *Buffalo Bill* (44), *The Great Moment* (44), *The Unseen* (45), *The Virginian* (46), *Ramrod* (47), *They Passed This Way* (48), *Colorado Territory* (49), *Stars in My Crown* (50), *Saddle Tramp* (51), *The San Francisco Story* (52), *Rough Shoot* (GB) (52), *Black Horse Canyon* (54), *The Oklahoman* (57), *Gunfight at Dodge City* (59), *Ride the High Country* (62), many others. TV series: *Wichita Town* (59).

MCCULLERS, CARSON (1916–1967). American novelist, usually on themes pertaining to her homeland, the deep south. Works filmed include *The Member of the Wedding*, *Reflections in a Golden Eye*, *The Heart is a Lonely Hunter*.

MCDANIEL, HATTIE (1895–1952). American Negro character actress of cheerful and immense presence; once a radio vocalist. *The Story of Temple Drake* (33), *Judge Priest* (35), *Nothing Sacred* (37), *Gone with the Wind* (AA) (39), *The Great Lie* (41), *Margie* (46), *Song of the South* (47), *Mr Blandings Builds His Dream House* (48), many others. TV series: *Beulah* (52).

MCDERMOTT, HUGH (1908–   ). Scottish-born character actor, in British films from mid-30s, specializing in hearty transatlantic types. *The Wife of General Ling* (38), *Pimpernel Smith* (41), *The Seventh Veil* (45), *No Orchids for Miss Blandish* (48), *Trent's Last Case* (52), *A King in New York* (57), *The First Men in the Moon* (64), many others.

MACDONALD, DAVID (1905–   ). Scottish-born film director, in films since 1929. Showed early promise with *Dead Men Tell No Tales* (38), *This Man Is News* (38), *This Man in Paris* (39), *This England* (41), *The Brothers* (47), etc.; *The Bad Lord Byron* (48) and *Christopher Columbus* (48) began a decline. Has more recently been directing routine TV films, his occasional features not rising above the level of *Diamond City* (49), *Cairo Road* (50), *The Adventurers* (50), *Tread Softly* (52), *Devil Girl from Mars* (54), *The Moonraker* (57), *Petticoat Pirates* (61), etc. Much TV work.

MCDONALD, FRANK (1899–   ). American director of second features; former stage actor and author. *The Murder of Dr Harrigan* (38), *Carolina Moon* (40), *One Body Too Many* (44), *My Pal Trigger* (46), *Father Takes the Air* (51), *The Treasure of Ruby Hills* (55), *The Underwater City* (61), etc.

MACDONALD, J. FARRELL (1875–1952). American minstrel singer who became a familiar Hollywood character actor. *The Maltese Falcon* (31), *The Thirteenth Guest* (32), *The Cat's Paw* (34), *The Irish in Us* (36), *Topper* (37), *Little Orphan Annie* (39), *Meet John Doe* (41), *My Darling Clementine* (46), *Mr Belvedere Rings the Bell* (51), etc.

MACDONALD, JEANETTE (1902–1965). American actress and singer fondly remembered for her co-starring appearances (after operatic training) with Nelson Eddy in a series of film operettas: *Naughty Marietta* (35), *Rose Marie* (36), *Maytime* (38), *The Girl of the Golden West* (38), *Sweethearts* (39), *New Moon* (40), *I Married an Angel* (42), etc. Film debut *The Love Parade* (30) opposite Maurice Chevalier, with whom she also appeared in *One Hour with You* (32), *Love Me Tonight* (32), *The Merry Widow* (34). Other films include *San Francisco* (36), *The Firefly* (37), *Bitter Sweet* (40), *Smilin' Through* (41), *Cairo* (42), *The Birds and the Bees* (48), *The Sun Comes Up* (49).

MACDONALD, JOSEPH (1906–1968). Distinguished American cinematographer. *Sunday Dinner for a Soldier* (44), *Yellow Sky* (48), *Panic in*

621

McDonald, Marie

the Streets (50), *Viva Zapata* (52), *Titanic* (53), *How to Marry a Millionaire* (53), *Broken Lance* (54), *A Hatful of Rain* (57), *Ten North Frederick* (57), *Pepe* (60), *Kings of the Sun* (63), *The Carpetbaggers* (63), *Rio Conchos* (64), *Invitation to a Gunfighter* (64), *Mirage* (65), *Blindfold* (65), *The Sand Pebbles* (66), *Mackenna's Gold* (68), many others.

MCDONALD, MARIE (1923–1965) (Marie Frye). American leading lady, publicized as 'The Body'; former model. *Pardon My Sarong* (42), *A Scream in the Dark* (44), *Getting Gertie's Garter* (46), *Living in a Big Way* (47), *Tell It to the Judge* (49), *Geisha Boy* (59), etc.

MACDONALD, RAY (1924–1959). American actor-dancer of lightweight 40s musicals. *Babes in Arms* (39), *Presenting Lily Mars* (43), *Good News* (47), *Till the Clouds Roll By* (48), etc.

MCDONELL, FERGUS (1910–1968). British director. *The Small Voice* (48), *Prelude to Fame* (50), *Private Information* (52), etc.

MACDOUGALL, RANALD (1915–   ). American writer (*Objective Burma* [45], *Mildred Pierce* [45], *Possessed* [47], *Mr Belvedere Rings the Bell* [51]) and writer-director (*Queen Bee* [55], *The World, the Flesh and the Devil* [59], *The Subterraneans* [60], *Go Naked in the World* [61], etc.).

MACDOUGALL, ROGER (1910–   ). Scottish playwright who in addition to having his theatrical work adapted for the screen (*The Man in the White Suit* [51], *To Dorothy a Son* [54], *Escapade* [55], etc.) has written directly for films: *This Man Is News* (38), *The Foreman Went to France* (42), *The Mouse that Roared* (59), *A Touch of Larceny* (60), etc.

MCDOWALL, RODDY (1928–   ). Former British child actor, evacuated to the US in 1940. *Murder in the Family* (debut) (36), *Just William* (37), *Hey Hey USA* (38), *This England* (40), *How Green Was My Valley* (41), *The Pied Piper* (42), *My Friend Flicka* (43), *Lassie Come Home* (43), *Macbeth* (48), *Killer Shark* (50), then after long absence on Broadway and TV, *Midnight Lace* (60), *Cleopatra* (62), *The Third Day* (65), *The Loved One* (65), *Inside Daisy Clover* (65), *That Darn Cat* (65), *Lord Love a Duck* (66), *Bullwhip Griffin* (66), *The Curse of the Golem* (*It*) (GB) (67), *Five Card Stud* (68), *Angel Angel Down You Go* (69), etc.

MCENERY, PETER (1940–   ). British leading man with TV experience. *Tunes of Glory* (60), *Victim* (62), *The Moonspinners* (64), *The Fighting Prince of Donegal* (66), *The Game Is Over* (66), *I Killed Rasputin* (68), *Negatives* (68), *Entertaining Mr Sloane* (70), etc.

MCEVEETY, BERNARD (* –   ). American director, from TV. *Broken Sabre* (65), *Ride Beyond Vengeance* (66), etc.

MCFARLAND, SPANKY (1928–   ). American child actor, the fat boy of 'Our Gang' in the 30s. Also: *Kidnapped* (34), *The Trail of the Lonesome Pine* (36), *Johnny Doughboy* (43), etc.

MCGANN, WILLIAM (1895–   *   ). American director of second features. *I Like Your Nerve* (31), *Illegal* (32), *The Case of the Black Cat* (36), *Penrod and Sam* (37), *Blackwell's Island* (39), *The Parson of Panamint* (41), *Frontier Badmen* (43), etc.

MCGAVIN, DARREN (1925–   ). American 'character lead' who can play unpleasant villains or tough heroes. *Fear* (46), *Summer Madness* (55), *The Court Martial of Billy Mitchell* (55), *The Man with the Golden Arm* (56), *The Delicate Delinquent* (57), *Beau James* (57), *The Case Against Brooklyn* (58), *Bullet for a Badman* (64), *The Great Sioux Massacre* (65), etc. TV series: *Mike Hammer* (58), *Riverboat* (60), *The Outsider* (68).

MACGINNIS, NIALL (1913–   ). Irish-born actor, in films since 1935. *Turn of the Tide* (35), *Edge of the World* (38), *49th Parallel* (41), *We Dive at Dawn* (43), *Henry V* (44), *No Highway* (51), *Martin Luther* (53), *The Battle of the River Plate* (55), *Night of the Demon* (57), *The Nun's Story* (58), *Billy Budd* (62), *A Face in the Rain* (62), *Becket* (64), *Island of Terror* (66), *Sinful Davey* (69), etc.; recently in TV films and plays.

MCGIVER, JOHN (c. 1915–   ). American character comedian with worried, owl-like features. Memorable in *Love in the Afternoon* (57), *Breakfast at Tiffany's* (61), *Mr Hobbs Takes a Vacation* (62), *Who's Minding the Store* (63), *Marriage on the Rocks* (65), *The Spirit is Willing* (67), *Fitzwilly* (67), *Midnight Cowboy* (69), etc. TV series: *Many Happy Returns* (64).

MCGOOHAN, PATRICK (1928–   ). American-born leading man with individual characteristics; in British films, after stage experience, from mid-50s. *Passage Home* (55), *High Tide at Noon* (56), *Hell Drivers* (57), *The Gypsy and the Gentleman* (57), *Nor the Moon by Night* (58), *All Night Long* (61), *The Quare Fellow* (62), *Life For Ruth* (62), *Dr Syn* (63), *Ice Station Zebra* (68), *The Moonshine War* (70), *Taipan* (70), etc. TV series: *Danger Man (Secret Agent)* (61–66), *The Prisoner* (67).

MACGOWAN, KENNETH (1888–1963). American film theorist and teacher (at UCLA) who was also a notable producer: *Little Women* (33), *Becky Sharp* (35), *Young Mr Lincoln* (39), *Man Hunt* (41), *Lifeboat* (43), *Jane Eyre* (44), etc. Author of several film textbooks.

MACGOWRAN, JACK (1916–   ). Irish character actor, usually of mean, sharp-featured fellows. *The Quiet Man* (52), *The Gentle Gunman* (52), *The Titfield Thunderbolt* (53), *The Rising of the Moon* (57),

McGrath, Frank

Darby O'Gill and the Little People (59), *Blind Date* (60), *Mix Me a Person* (61), *Lord Jim* (65), *Cul de Sac* (66), *The Fearless Vampire Killers* (67), *How I Won the War* (67), *Wonderwall* (68), etc. Also on stage and TV.

MCGRATH, FRANK (1903–1967). Grizzled American stunt man who appeared in countless westerns but achieved his greatest popularity as the trail cook in TV's *Wagon Train* series.

MCGRATH, JOE (1930–   ). Scottish TV director, at home with goonish comedy. Films: *Thirty Is a Dangerous Age, Cynthia* (68), *The Bliss of Mrs Blossom* (68).

MACGRAW, ALI (1938–   ). American leading lady who debuted in *Goodbye Columbus* (69).

MCGRAW, CHARLES (1914–   ). American actor, invariably in tough roles. *The Moon Is Down* (43), *The Killers* (46), *The Armoured Car Robbery* (50), *The Narrow Margin* (50), *His Kind of Woman* (51), *The Bridges at Toko-Ri* (54), *Away All Boats* (56), *Slaughter on Tenth Avenue* (58), *The Defiant Ones* (58), *The Wonderful Country* (59), *Spartacus* (60), *Cimarron* (61), *In Cold Blood* (67), *Pendulum* (69), etc. More recently on TV.

MCGUIRE, DON (1919–   ). American writer-director, former press agent. *Meet Danny Wilson* (w) (51), *Walking My Baby Back Home* (w) (52), *Three Ring Circus* (w) (54), *Bad Day at Black Rock* (co-w) (54), *Johnny Concho* (w, d) (56), *The Delicate Delinquent* (w, d) (57). Then to TV as producer-director of the *Hennessey* series.

†MCGUIRE, DOROTHY (1919–   ). American leading lady of the 40s, latterly playing mothers; always in gentle, sympathetic roles. Went to Hollywood in 1943 to repeat her Broadway success as the child-wife in *Claudia*. Then: *A Tree Grows in Brooklyn* (44), *The Enchanted Cottage* (44), *The Spiral Staircase* (45), *Claudia and David* (46), *Till the End of Time* (46), *Gentleman's Agreement* (47), *Mother Didn't Tell Me* (50), *Mister 880* (50), *Callaway Went Thataway* (50), *I Want You* (51), *Invitation* (52), *Make Haste to Live* (53), *Three Coins in the Fountain* (54), *Trial* (55), *Friendly Persuasion* (56), *Old Yeller* (57), *The Remarkable Mr Pennypacker* (59), *This Earth Is Mine* (59), *A Summer Place* (60), *The Dark at the Top of the Stairs* (60), *The Swiss Family Robinson* (60), *Susan Slade* (61), *Summer Magic* (63), *The Greatest Story Ever Told* (as the Virgin Mary) (65).

MACHATY, GUSTAV (1898–1963). Czech director best remembered for exposing Hedy Lamarr's naked charms in *Extase* (33). Also: *The Kreutzer Sonata* (26), *Erotikon* (29), *From Saturday to Sunday* (31), *Nocturno* (35), *Within the Law* (US) (39), *Jealousy* (US) (45), etc.

MCHUGH, FRANK (1899–   ). Amiable American character actor with surprised look, frequently in Irish-American roles. In Hollywood from late 20s; most popular in 30s. *If Men Played Cards as Women Do* (28), *Dawn Patrol* (30), *Footlight Parade* (33), *A Midsummer Night's Dream* (35), *Swing Your Lady* (38), *Going My Way* (44), *State Fair* (45), *Mighty Joe Young* (49), *My Son John* (51), *There's No Business Like Show Business* (54), *Career* (59), *A Tiger Walks* (64), *Easy Come Easy Go* (67), many others. TV series: *The Bing Crosby Show* (64).

MCHUGH, JIMMY (1895–   ). American song-writer: 'I Can't Give You Anything But Love, Baby', 'I Feel a Song Comin' On', 'On the Sunny Side of the Street', etc. Film scores include *You'll Find Out* (40), *Seven Days Ashore* (43), *Do You Love Me* (46), etc.

MCINTIRE, JOHN (1907–   ). Spare, laconic American character actor with radio and stage experience, in Hollywood from mid-40s, often as sheriff, editor, politician, cop. *The Asphalt Jungle* (50), *Lawless Breed* (52), *A Lion Is in the Streets* (53), *Apache* (54), *The Far Country* (54), *The Kentuckian* (55), *Backlash* (56), *The Phoenix City Story* (56), *The Tin Star* (57), *Flaming Star* (60), *Psycho* (60), *Summer and Smoke* (62), *Rough Night in Jericho* (67), etc. TV series: *Naked City* (59), *Wagon Train* (61–64).

MACK, HELEN (1913–   ). American leading lady of the 30s, former child actress. *Zaza* (24), *Grit* (28), *The Silent Witness* (31), *Son of Kong* (34), *She* (35), *The Milky Way* (36), *Last Train from Madrid* (37), *Gambling Ship* (39), *His Girl Friday* (40), *Divorce* (last to date) (45), etc.

MACKAIL, DOROTHY (1903–   ). British leading lady of the American silent screen, former Ziegfeld chorine. *The Face at the Window* (GB) (21), then to US; *Twenty-one* (26), *Dancer of Paris* (27), *Children of the Ritz* (29), *Once a Sinner* (30), *Kept Husbands* (31), *No Man of Her Own* (32), etc. Retired apart from an appearance in *Bulldog Drummond at Bay* (37).

MACKAY, BARRY (1906–   ). British stage leading man and singer. Occasional films include *Evergreen* (34), *Oh Daddy* (35), *Forever England* (35), *Glamorous Night* (37), *Gangway* (37), *Sailing Along* (38), *Smuggled Cargo* (40), *Pickwick Papers* (52), *Orders Are Orders* (55).

MCKELLEN, IAN (1935–   ). British stage actor, in occasional films. *Alfred the Great* (69), *A Touch of Love* (69), etc.

†MACKENDRICK, ALEXANDER (1912–   ). American-born director, long in Britain. Entered films via advertising, later joined Ealing as scriptwriter (*Saraband for Dead Lovers* [48], *The Blue Lamp* [50], etc.). Directed *Whisky Galore* (48), *The Man in the White Suit* (51), *Mandy* (52), *The Maggie* (53), *The Lady Killers* (55), *Sweet Smell*

of Success (US) (57), *Sammy Going South* (62), *A High Wind in Jamaica* (65), *Don't Make Waves* (67), *Mary Queen of Scots* (70).

MCKENNA, SIOBHAN (1923–   ). Fiery Irish actress, on stage from 1940, and in very occasional films. *Hungry Hill* (debut) (46), *Daughter of Darkness* (48), *The Last People* (49), *King of Kings* (61), *The Playboy of the Western World* (62), *Of Human Bondage* (64), *Doctor Zhivago* (65), etc.

MCKENNA, VIRGINIA (1931–   ). Demure-looking but spirited British leading lady with stage experience; married to Bill Travers. *The Second Mrs Tanqueray* (52), *Father's Doing Fine* (52), *The Cruel Sea* (54), *Simba* (55), *The Ship That Died of Shame* (55), *A Town Like Alice* (BFA) (56), *The Smallest Show on Earth* (57), *The Barretts of Wimpole Street* (57), *Carve Her Name with Pride* (58), *The Passionate Summer* (58), *The Wreck of the Mary Deare* (59), *Two Living One Dead* (62), *Born Free* (66), *Ring of Bright Water* (69), *Waterloo* (70), etc.

MCKERN, LEO (1925–   ). Australian character actor with wide stage experience and usually explosive personality. On stage from 1942, in England from 1946; in occasional films including *All for Mary* (55), *X the Unknown* (56), *Time without Pity* (57), *The Mouse That Roared* (59), *Mr Topaze* (61), *The Day the Earth Caught Fire* (62), *A Jolly Bad Fellow* (64), *King and Country* (64), *Moll Flanders* (65), *Help!* (65), *A Man for All Seasons* (66), *Decline and Fall* (68), etc.

MCKINNEY, NINA MAE (1909–1968). American Negro actress who appeared in *Hallelujah* (29), *Sanders of the River* (35), *Without Love* (45), *Pinky* (49), etc.

MCLAGLEN, ANDREW (1925–   ). American director, son of Victor McLaglen. Started with TV work and second features (*Gun the Man Down* [56], *The Man in the Vault* [57], etc.) before graduating to big-scale Westerns: *McLintock* (63), *Shenandoah* (65), *The Rare Breed* (66), *The Way West* (67), *The Devil's Brigade* (67), *The Undefeated* (69), etc.

MCLAGLEN, VICTOR (1883–1959). Burly, good-humoured star of British silent films; later became popular in Hollywood. *The Call of the Road* (20), *The Glorious Adventure* (21), *The Beloved Brute* (23), *Beau Geste* (26), *What Price Glory* (26), *Captain Lash* (27), *Mother Machree* (28), *The Cockeyed World* (29), *Dishonoured* (30), *Wicked* (31), *Rackety Rax* (32), *Hot Pepper* (33), *Dick Turpin* (33), *The Lost Patrol* (34), *The Informer* (AA) (35), *Under Two Flags* (36), *The Magnificent Brute* (37), *Gunga Din* (39), *Broadway Limited* (41), *Call Out the Marines* (42), *Powder Town* (42), *The Princess and the Pirate* (44), *The Michigan Kid* (47), *Fort Apache* (48), *She Wore a Yellow Ribbon* (49), *Rio Grande* (50), *The Quiet Man* (52), *Fair Wind to Java* (53), *Prince Valiant* (54),

Lady Godiva (55), *Many Rivers to Cross* (55), *Bengazi* (56), *The Abductors* (57), *Sea Fury* (58), many others.

†MACLAINE, SHIRLEY (1934–   ) (Shirley Maclean Beaty). Impish American leading lady, sister of Warren Beatty. Was signed for films while dancing in a Broadway chorus. *The Trouble with Harry* (debut) (55), *Artists and Models* (56), *Around the World in Eighty Days* (56), *Hot Spell* (57), *The Matchmaker* (58), *Some Came Running* (58), *Ask Any Girl* (BFA) (59), *Career* (59), *Can-Can* (59), *The Apartment* (BFA) (59), *All in a Night's Work* (61), *Two Loves* (*Spinster*) (61), *My Geisha* (62), *The Children's Hour* (*The Loudest Whisper*) (62), *Two for the Seesaw* (63), *Irma La Douce* (63), *What a Way To Go* (64), *The Yellow Rolls-Royce* (64), *John Goldfarb Please Come Home* (64), *Gambit* (66), *Woman Times Seven* (67), *Sweet Charity* (68), *The Bliss of Mrs Blossom* (GB) (68), *Two Mules for Sister Sara* (69).

MACLANE, BARTON (1900–1969). Tough-looking American character actor, often seen as crooked cop, sheriff or gangster. In hundreds of films since 1924 debut. *Tillie and Gus* (33), *Black Fury* (34), *Ceiling Zero* (36), *You Only Live Once* (37), *Gold Is Where You Find It* (38), *The Maltese Falcon* (41), *Bombardier* (43), *San Quentin* (46), *The Treasure of the Sierra Madre* (47), *Kiss Tomorrow Goodbye* (51), *Captain Scarface* (leading role) (53), *Backlash* (56), *Geisha Boy* (58), *Gunfighters of Abilene* (59), *Law of the Lawless* (63), *Town Tamer* (65), *Buckskin* (68), scores of others. TV series: *Outlaws* (60).

MCLAREN, NORMAN (1914–   ). British-born animator and director of short films. Long resident in Canada, where he has made many individual pieces for the National Film Board, sometimes with sound as well as picture drawn directly on to the celluloid, others using stop-motion techniques. Titles since 1940 include *Dots and Loops*, *Boogie Doodle*, *Fiddle-De-Dee*, *Hoppity Pop*, *Begone Dull Care*, *Around Is Around*, *Neighbours*, *Blinkety Blank*, *Rhythmetic*, *A Chairy Tale*, *Pas de Deux*, etc.

MCLAUGHLIN, GIBB (1884–   ). British character actor of stage and screen, once a stage monologuist and master of disguise. Uses his splendidly emaciated features to great advantage. *Carnival* (21), *Nell Gwyn* (24), *The Farmer's Wife* (27), *Kelly* (29), *Sally in Our Alley* (31), *The Private Life of Henry VIII* (32), *No Funny Business* (33), *The Scarlet Pimpernel* (34), *Where There's a Will* (36), *Mr Reeder in Room Thirteen* (title role) (40), *My Learned Friend* (43), *Caesar and Cleopatra* (45), *Oliver Twist* (48), *The Card* (52), *Hobson's Choice* (54), *Sea Wife* (57), many others.

MACLEAN, DOUGLAS (1890–1967). American silent screen comedian. *As Ye Sow* (19), *Captain Kidd Jnr* (19), *23½ Hours' Leave* (21), *The Hottentot* (22), *Never Say Die* (24), *Introduce Me* (25), *Seven Keys to Baldpate* (25), etc. Later became writer/producer. Retired 1938.

McLeod, Catherine

MCLEOD, CATHERINE (c. 1924–   ). American leading lady of the 40s. *Concerto* (46), *Will Tomorrow Ever Come?* (47), *So Young So Bad* (50), *The Fortune Hunter* (54), *Ride the Wild Surf* (64), etc.

MCLEOD, NORMAN Z. (1898–1964). American director, in Hollywood from the early 20s. Originally an animator; later wrote screenplays (e.g. *Skippy* [31]); then turned to direction. *Monkey Business* (31), *Horse Feathers* (32), *If I Had a Million* (part) (33), *Topper* (37), *Panama Hattie* (41), *The Kid from Brooklyn* (46), *The Secret Life of Walter Mitty* (48), *The Paleface* (48), *My Favourite Spy* (51), *Never Wave at a Wac* (53), *Casanova's Big Night* (54), etc.

MCLERIE, ALLYN (1926–   ). Canadian-born dancer and leading lady who made a few films amid stage work. *Words and Music* (48), *Where's Charley* (52), *The Desert Song* (53), *Phantom of the Rue Morgue* (54), *Battle Cry* (55), etc.

MACMAHON, ALINE (1899–   ). Gentle-mannered American stage and screen actress, in films occasionally since 1931. *Five Star Final* (31), *Gold Diggers of 1933*, *Ah Wilderness* (35), *A Woman in Her Thirties* (36), *Back Door to Heaven* (39), *The Search* (48), *The Eddie Cantor Story* (53), *The Man from Laramie* (55), *I Could Go On Singing* (63), *All the Way Home* (63), etc.

MACMAHON, HORACE (c. 1906–   ). American character actor, likely to be best remembered as the older cop in TV series *Naked City*. In films from 1937, often as cop or gangster. *Navy Blues* (37), *King of the Newsboys* (38), *Rose of Washington Square* (39), *Lady Scarface* (41), *Lady Gangster* (45), *Waterfront at Midnight* (48), *Detective Story* (51), *Man in the Dark* (53), *Susan Slept Here* (54), *My Sister Eileen* (55), *Beau James* (57), *The Swinger* (66), *The Detective* (68), many others.

MACMURRAY, FRED (1908–   ). American leading man, former band singer, saxophonist and Hollywood extra. *The Gilded Lily* (debut) (35), *Car 99* (35), *Alice Adams* (35), *Hands across the Table* (36), *The Trail of the Lonesome Pine* (36), *The Princess Comes Across* (36), *The Texas Rangers* (36), *Champagne Waltz* (37), *Maid of Salem* (37), *Swing High, Swing Low* (37), *True Confession* (38), *Men with Wings* (38), *Sing You Sinners* (38), *Café Society* (39), *Remember the Night* (39), *Little Old New York* (40), *Too Many Husbands* (40), *Virginia* (40), *One Night in Lisbon* (41), *Dive Bomber* (41), *New York Town* (41), *The Lady Is Willing* (42), *Take a Letter, Darling* (42), *The Forest Rangers* (42), *No Time for Love* (43), *Above Suspicion* (43), *And the Angels Sing* (43), *Standing Room Only* (43), *Double Indemnity* (44), *Practically Yours* (44), *Murder He Says* (44), *Pardon My Past* (45), *Where Do We Go from Here* (45), *Captain Eddie* (45), *Suddenly It's Spring* (46), *Smoky* (46), *The Egg and I* (47), *Singapore* (47), *The Miracle of the Bells* (48), *On Our Merry Way* (48), *Don't Trust Your Husband* (49), *Family Honeymoon* (50), *Never a Dull Moment* (51),

Callaway Went Thataway (52), *Fair Wind to Java* (53), *The Moon-lighter* (53), *The Caine Mutiny* (54), *Pushover* (54), *Woman's World* (54), *The Rains of Ranchipur* (55), *Gun for a Coward* (56), *Day of the Badman* (57), *Good Day for a Hanging* (58), *The Shaggy Dog* (59), *The Apartment* (60), *The Absent-minded Professor* (61), *Bon Voyage* (63), *Son of Flubber* (63), *Follow Me, Boys* (66), *The Happiest Millionaire* (67), many others. TV series: *My Three Sons* (60–69).

MCNALLY, STEPHEN (c. 1916–   ) (Horace McNally). American leading man and sometimes 'heavy', in films from 1942. Former lawyer. *The Man from Down Under* (43), *The Harvey Girls* (45), *Johnny Belinda* (48), *Rogues Regiment* (48), *No Way Out* (50), *Winchester 73* (50), *The Raging Tide* (51), *Devil's Canyon* (53), *Black Castle* (53), *Make Haste to Live* (54), *A Bullet Is Waiting* (54), *Tribute to a Bad Man* (56), *Hell's Five Hours* (58), *The Fiend Who Walked the West* (58), *Hell Bent for Leather* (59), *Requiem for a Gunfighter* (65), *Panic in the City* (68). TV series: *Target the Corruptors* (61).

MCNAMARA, MAGGIE (1928–   ). American leading lady, formerly fashion model, on stage from 1951. Occasional films include *The Moon Is Blue* (debut) (53), *Three Coins in the Fountain* (54), *Prince of Players* (55), *The Cardinal* (63).

MCNAUGHT, BOB (1915–   ). British director, *Grand National Night* (53), *Sea Wife* (57), *A Story of David* (61), etc. Also associate producer on many films.

MCNAUGHTON, GUS (1884–1969) (Augustus Howard). British comedy actor, once a Fred Karno singer. *Murder* (30), *The Thirty-nine Steps* (35), *Keep Your Seats Please* (37), *The Divorce of Lady X* (38), *Trouble Brewing* (39), *Jeannie* (41), *Much Too Shy* (42), *Here Comes the Sun* (last to date) (46), etc.

MACNEE, PATRICK (1922–   ). British leading man, famous as the immaculate John Steed in TV series *The Avengers*. Has played small film roles since 1942. *The Life and Death of Colonel Blimp* (43), *Hamlet* (48), *The Elusive Pimpernel* (50), *Three Cases of Murder* (54), *Les Girls* (57), etc. 1969: starring in *Doctors Wear Scarlet*.

MACOWAN, NORMAN (1877–1961). Scottish character actor. *Whisky Galore* (48), *Laxdale Hall* (53), *X the Unknown* (56), *Tread Softly Stranger* (58), *The Boy and the Bridge* (59), *Kidnapped* (60), etc.

MCQUEEN, BUTTERFLY (1911–   ) (Thelma McQueen). American Negro character actress best remembered as the weeping maid in *Gone With the Wind* (39). Later in *Cabin in the Sky* (43), *Since You Went Away* (44), *Duel in the Sun* (46), etc.

†MCQUEEN, STEVE (1932–   ). Offbeat American leading man, who came to films after starring in TV series *Wanted Dead or Alive* (58).

Never Love a Stranger (58), *The Blob* (58), *The Magnificent Seven* (60), *Hell Is for Heroes* (62), *The War Lover* (62), *The Great Escape* (63), *Love with the Proper Stranger* (64), *Soldier in the Rain* (64), *Baby, the Rain Must Fall* (65), *The Cincinnati Kid* (65), *Nevada Smith* (65), *The Sand Pebbles* (66), *Bullitt* (68), *The Thomas Crown Affair* (68), *The Reivers* (69), *Yucatan* (project) (70), *Le Mans* (project) (70).

MACQUITTY, WILLIAM (1905–   ). British producer who came to feature films via wartime MOI shorts. *The Happy Family* (52), *The Beachcomber* (54), *Above Us the Waves* (55), *A Night to Remember* (58), *The Informers* (64), etc.

MACRAE, DUNCAN (1905–1967). Scottish stage actor who only made occasional films after his impressive debut in *The Brothers* (47). *Whisky Galore* (48), *The Kidnappers* (53), *You're Only Young Twice* (53), *Rockets Galore* (56), *Tunes of Glory* (60), *The Best of Enemies* (61), *A Jolly Bad Fellow* (64), *Casino Royale* (67), etc. Also on TV.

MACRAE, GORDON (1921–   ). American actor-singer, a former child performer who broke into films from radio. *Look for the Silver Lining* (49), *Tea for Two* (50), *Fine and Dandy* (50), *By the Light of the Silvery Moon* (53), *Oklahoma* (55), *Carousel* (56), *The Best Things in Life Are Free* (56), etc.

MACREADY, GEORGE (1909–   ). American character actor, a descendant of Macready the tragedian. A splendid villain, neurotic or weakling, he ran an art gallery before coming to films in 1942. *The Commandos Strike at Dawn* (42), *The Seventh Cross* (44), *Wilson* (45), *I Love a Mystery* (45), *A Song to Remember* (46), *Gilda* (46), *Knock on Any Door* (49), *Alias Nick Beal* (*The Contact Man*) (49), *Detective Story* (51), *Julius Caesar* (53), *Vera Cruz* (54), *Paths of Glory* (58), *Seven Days in May* (64), *The Great Race* (65), etc. TV series: *Peyton Place* (66–68).

MCSHANE, IAN (1942–   ). British leading man with stage experience. *The Wild and the Willing* (62), *The Pleasure Girls* (65), *Sky West and Crooked* (*Gypsy Girl*) (66), etc.

MADAME DE (France/Italy 1952). Elegant adaptation by Max Ophuls of Louise de Vilmorin's novella about a pair of jewelled ear-rings which are passed back and forth between a husband, a wife and a lover. Photographed by Christian Matras, with music by Georges Van Parys and Oscar Straus; star performances from Danielle Darrieux, Charles Boyer and Vittorio de Sica.

MADAME DU BARRY. Lubitsch's German film of 1919, combining realism with spectacle, is probably still the best film made about the 18th-century French courtesan. Starring Pola Negri, it was the first post-war German film to find international favour. Other

Du Barrys have included Mrs Leslie Carter in *Du Barry* (15);
Theda Bara in *Du Barry* (17); Norma Talmadge in *Du Barry,
Woman of Passion* (30); Dolores del Rio in *Madame du Barry* (34);
Lucille Ball in *Du Barry Was a Lady* (43); and Martine Carol in
Mistress Du Barry (54).

MADAME X. This sentimental tearjerker about the woman whose son
grows up without knowing her, from the play by Alexander Bisson,
has been filmed four times. The lead was played by Pauline
Frederick in 1920, by Ruth Chatterton in 1929, by Gladys George
in 1937, and by Lana Turner in 1966.

MADDEN, PETER (c. 1910–). Gaunt British character actor of TV
and films. *Counterblast* (48), *Tom Brown's Schooldays* (51), *The Battle
of the V.1* (58), *Hell Is a City* (60), *Saturday Night and Sunday Morning*
(60), *The Loneliness of the Long Distance Runner* (62), *The Very Edge*
(63), *Doctor Zhivago* (66), etc.

MADDERN, VICTOR (1926–). Stocky Cockney character actor,
formerly on stage and radio. *Seven Days to Noon* (debut) (49),
Cockleshell Heroes (55), *Private's Progress* (56), *Blood of the Vampire*
(58), *I'm All Right, Jack* (59), *H.M.S. Defiant* (61), *Rotten to the Core*
(65), *Circus of Fear* (67), many others. TV series: *Fair Exchange*
(US) (62).

MADISON, GUY (1922–) (Robert Moseley). American leading man,
in films since 1944 after naval career. *Since You Went Away* (debut)
(44), *Till the End of Time* (46), *The Charge at Feather River* (53),
The Command (54), *Five Against the House* (55), *The Last Frontier* (56),
Hilda Crane (57), *Bullwhip* (58), *Gunmen of the Rio Grande* (65), *The
Mystery of Thug Island* (66), etc. TV series: *Wild Bill Hickock* (54–
57).

MADISON, NOEL (c. 1905–) (Noel Moscovitch). American actor
of sinister roles, especially gangsters. Formerly known as Nat
Madison; son of actor Maurice Moscovitch. *Sinners Holiday* (30),
Manhattan Melodrama (34), *G-Men* (35), *The Man Who Made
Diamonds* (37), *Crackerjack* (GB) (39), *Footsteps in the Dark* (41),
Jitterbugs (43), *Gentleman from Nowhere* (49), etc.

THE MAGIC BOX (GB 1951). The British film industry's ambitious but
uninspired contribution to the Festival of Britain: a sentimental
biography of film pioneer William Friese-Greene, played by Robert
Donat. An all-star cast appeared in cameo roles, including
Laurence Olivier as the startled policeman who saw the first
moving picture. Written by Eric Ambler, photographed by Jack
Cardiff, produced by Ronald Neame, directed by John Boulting.

MAGEE, PATRICK (1924–). British character actor of stage and
TV, often in sinister roles. Films include *The Criminal* (60), *The*

631

Servant (63), *Zulu* (64), *Masque of the Red Death* (64), *The Skull* (65), *The Marat/Sade* (67), etc.

MAGNANI, ANNA (1909–   ). Italian star actress (Egyptian-born) on screen since *The Blind Woman of Sorrento* (34). Known internationally after *Open City* (45). *The Miracle* (50), *Volcano* (53), *The Golden Coach* (54), *Bellissima* (54), *The Rose Tattoo* (AA) (55), *Wild is the Wind* (57), *The Fugitive Kind* (59), *Mamma Roma* (62), *The Secret of Santa Vittoria* (69), etc.

MAGNIFICENT OBSESSION. This tear-jerking novel by Lloyd C. Douglas, about an irresponsible playboy who becomes a surgeon and not only cures but falls in love with the woman he accidentally blinded, was filmed in 1935 by John M. Stahl, with Robert Taylor and Irene Dunne, and again in 1954 by Douglas Sirk, with Rock Hudson and Jane Wyman.

THE MAGNIFICENT AMBERSONS (US 1942). Orson Welles' fascinating but only partially successful follow-up to *Citizen Kane*. Besides directing, he adapted Booth Tarkington's novel about the decline of a mid-Western family in the early years of the century, and the eventual comeuppance of its arrogant son. The early scene-setting is brilliant, but the later reels and hurried happy ending seem unbalanced: Welles himself has said that his last three reels were cut by the RKO-Radio chiefs and a final scene tacked on by other hands. Photographed by Stanley Cortez, with impeccable performances from Joseph Cotten, Dolores Costello, Tim Holt, Agnes Moorehead, Anne Baxter and Ray Collins. Welles' end-credits are highly entertaining.

THE MAGNIFICENT SEVEN (US 1961). Lively Hollywood remake of the Japanese *Seven Samurai*, transferring the action to a standard Western setting but preserving the essential story of a group of mercenaries who defend a village from plundering by bandits. Yul Brynner leads the goodies, with Eli Wallach as a memorably murderous bandit. Directed by John Sturges, photographed by Charles Lang with music by Elmer Bernstein. A 1966 sequel, *Return of the Seven*, proved to be only a routine Western.

MAHARIS, GEORGE (1938–   ). American leading man of brooding mien. Won success in long-running TV series *Route 66*, and has since been in features: *Sylvia* (65), *Quick Before It Melts* (65), *The Satan Bug* (65), *Covenant with Death* (67), *The Happening* (67), *The Desperados* (68), *The Day of the Landgrabbers* (69), etc.

MAHONEY, JOCK (1919–   ) (Jacques O'Mahoney). Tall American actor, one-time stunt man who later won feature roles: *Away All Boats* (56), *Showdown at Abilene* (56), *The Land Unknown* (58), etc.

Has recently played Tarzan: *Tarzan Goes to India* (62), *Tarzan's Three Challenges* (64). TV series: *Yancey Derringer* (58).

MAIBAUM, RICHARD (1909–   ). American scriptwriter whose credits include *They Gave Him a Gun* (37), *Ten Gentlemen from West Point* (40), *O S.S.* (46), *The Great Gatsby* (49), *Cockleshell Heroes* (55), *Zarak* (57), *The Day They Robbed the Bank of England* (60), *Dr No* (62), *From Russia with Love* (63), *Goldfinger* (64), *Thunderball* (65), etc. Also produced several films for Paramount 1946–52.

MAILER, NORMAN (1923–   ). American sensational novelist. Works filmed include *The Naked and the Dead, An American Dream. The Deer Park* was an 'exposé' of Hollywood.

MAIN, MARJORIE (1890–   ) (Mary Tomlinson Krebs). American character actress, probably best remembered as Ma Kettle in the long-running hillbilly series which stemmed from *The Egg and I* (47). Many films include *Take a Chance* (33) (debut), *Dead End* (37), *Stella Dallas* (37), *Test Pilot* (38), *Angels Wash Their Faces* (39), *The Women* (39), *Turnabout* (40), *Bad Man of Wyoming* (40), *A Woman's Face* (41), *Honky Tonk* (41), *Jackass Mail* (42), *Tish* (42), *Heaven Can Wait* (43), *Rationing* (43), *Meet Me in St Louis* (44), *Murder He Says* (44), *The Harvey Girls* (45), *Bad Bascomb* (45), *Undercurrent* (46), *The Wistful Widow of Wagon Gap* (47), *Ma and Pa Kettle* (49), *Ma and Pa Kettle Go to Town* (50) (then one Kettle film a year till 1956), *Mrs O'Malley and Mr Malone* (50), *The Belle of New York* (52), *Rose Marie* (54), *Friendly Persuasion* (56), many others. Retired.

MAISIE. The hard-boiled (but soft-centred) heroine of ten MGM comedy-dramas between 1939 and 1947; played in all of them by Ann Sothern.

MAITLAND, MARNE (1920–   ). Anglo-Indian actor in British films; adept at sinister orientals. *Cairo Road* (50), *Father Brown* (54), *Bhowani Junction* (56), *The Camp on Blood Island* (58), *The Stranglers of Bombay* (59), *Sands of the Desert* (60), *Nine Hours to Rama* (62), *Lord Jim* (65), *The Reptile* (65), *Khartoum* (66), etc.

MAJOR BARBARA (GB 1940). Accomplished screen version of the Bernard Shaw play about a militant young Salvationist. Produced and directed by Gabriel Pascal, who even persuaded Shaw to write additional scenes. Cast includes Wendy Hiller, Rex Harrison, Robert Morley, Robert Newton, Marie Lohr, Emlyn Williams, Sybil Thorndike and Deborah Kerr.

MAJORS, LEE (c. 1940–   ). American leading man who became popular in TV series *The Big Valley* (65–68). Films: *Will Penny* (67), *The Liberation of Lord Byron Jones* (70).

MAKEHAM, ELIOT (1882–1956). British character actor of stage and screen, former accountant. For years played bespectacled little bank clerks who sometimes surprised by standing up for themselves. *Rome Express* (32), *Orders Is Orders* (32), *Lorna Doone* (35), *Dark Journey* (37), *Farewell Again* (37), *Saloon Bar* (40), *Night Train to Munich* (40), *The Common Touch* (42), *The Halfway House* (44), *Jassy* (47), *Trio* (50), *Scrooge* (51), *Doctor in the House* (53), *Sailor Beware* (56), etc.

MALDEN, KARL (1914–   ) (Malden Sekulovich). American stage actor who came into films after association with Elia Kazan. *They Knew What They Wanted* (40), *Winged Victory* (44), *Boomerang* (47), *Kiss of Death* (48), *The Gunfighter* (50), *Halls of Montezuma* (51), *A Streetcar Named Desire* (AA) (51), *Diplomatic Courier* (52), *Ruby Gentry* (52), *I Confess* (53), *Phantom of the Rue Morgue* (54), *On the Waterfront* (54), *Baby Doll* (56), *Fear Strikes Out* (57), *The Hanging Tree* (59), *One-Eyed Jacks* (59), *Parrish* (61), *Gypsy* (62), *Cheyenne Autumn* (64), *The Cincinnati Kid* (65), *Nevada Smith* (66), *Hotel* (66), *Murderers' Row* (66), *Billion Dollar Brain* (GB) (67), *Blue* (68), *Hot Millions* (68), *Patton—Blood and Guts* (69), others. Directed *Time Limit* (57).

MALLE, LOUIS (1932–   ). French 'new wave' director, former assistant to Robert Bresson. *World of Silence* (co-d) (56), *Lift to the Scaffold* (57), *The Lovers* (58), *Zazie dans le Metro* (61), *Le Feu Follet* (63), *Viva Maria* (65), *Le Voleur* (67), etc.

MALLESON, MILES (1888–1969). British playwright, screen writer and actor whose credits read like a potted history of the British cinema. As writer: *Nell Gwyn* (34), *Peg of Old Drury* (35), *Rhodes of Africa* (36), *Victoria the Great* (37), *The First of the Few* (42), *They Flew Alone* (43), *Mr Emmanuel* (44), etc. As actor: *Knight without Armour* (37), *Sixty Glorious Years* (38), *The Thief of Baghdad* (40), *Dead of Night* (45), *The Magic Box* (51), *The Importance of Being Earnest* (52), *The Man Who Never Was* (56), *Dracula* (58), *I'm All Right, Jack* (59), *Heavens Above* (63), *The Magnificent Showman* (64), many others.

MALO, GINA (1909–1963) (Janet Flynn). Irish-German-American leading lady of the 30s, usually in tempestuous roles. Filmed in Britain; married Romney Brent. *In a Monastery Garden* (32), *Good Night Vienna* (32), *Waltz Time* (33), *The Private Life of Don Juan* (34), *Jack of All Trades* (36), *Over She Goes* (38), *The Door with Seven Locks* (40), etc.

MALONE, DOROTHY (1925–   ) (Dorothy Maloney). American leading lady often seen in sultry roles: went to Hollywood straight from college. *The Big Sleep* (debut) (46), *Night and Day* (46), *One Sunday Afternoon* (48), *South of St Louis* (49), *Convicted* (50), *Slade* (53), *Pushover* (54), *Young at Heart* (54), *Battle Cry* (55), *Sincerely Yours*

(55), *Written on the Wind* (AA) (56), *Man of a Thousand Faces* (57), *Too Much Too Soon* (as Diana Barrymore) (58), *The Last Voyage* (60), *The Last Sunset* (61), *Fate Is the Hunter* (64), others. TV series: *Peyton Place* (64–69).

MALTBY, H. F. (1880–1963). British comedy playwright (*The Rotters, The Right Age to Marry*, etc.). Also screenwriter (*Over the Garden Wall* [44], etc.) and actor of choleric characters: *Jack of All Trades* (36), *Pygmalion* (38), *Under Your Hat* (40), *A Canterbury Tale* (44), *The Trojan Brothers* (45), etc.

THE MALTESE FALCON. Dashiell Hammett's brilliantly-written crime story was filmed three times by Warners. In 1931 it starred Bebe Daniels and Ricardo Cortez and was directed by Roy del Ruth; in 1936 it appeared as *Satan Met a Lady*, directed by William Dieterle, with Bette Davis and Warren William. The definitive version, however, did not come till 1941, when John Huston directed it (his first film) from his own script. Humphrey Bogart was the private eye, and the rogues' gallery included Mary Astor, Sidney Green-street, Peter Lorre, and Elisha Cook Jnr. It was highly influential on later crime films, and is often claimed as Huston's best film: he spoofed it unsuccessfully in his *Beat the Devil* (54).

MALTZ, ALBERT (1908–   ). American writer, blacklisted for a while during the McCarthy era. *This Gun for Hire* (43), *The Man in Half Moon Street* (44), *Cloak and Dagger* (46), *Naked City* (48), etc.

†MAMOULIAN, ROUBEN (1897–   ). American stage director of Armenian origin. Over the years he had made a number of films which vary in quality but at their best show a fluent command of the medium. *Applause* (29), *City Streets* (31), *Dr Jekyll and Mr Hyde* (32), *Love Me Tonight* (32), *Song of Songs* (33), *Queen Christina* (33), *We Live Again* (34), *Becky Sharp* (35), *The Gay Desperado* (36), *High, Wide and Handsome* (37), *Golden Boy* (39), *The Mark of Zorro* (40), *Blood and Sand* (41), *Rings on Her Fingers* (42), *Summer Holiday* (48), *Silk Stockings* (57). Began work on *Cleopatra* (62) but was replaced.

MANCINI, HENRY (c. 1922–   ). American composer. Was arranger on *The Glenn Miller Story* (53), *The Benny Goodman Story* (56), etc.; composed for *Touch of Evil* (58), *High Time* (60), *Breakfast at Tiffany's* (AA) (61), *Bachelor in Paradise* (61), *Hatari* (62), *The Pink Panther* (63), *Charade* (63), *A Shot in the Dark* (64), *Dear Heart* (65), *What Did You Do in the War, Daddy?* (66), *Two for the Road* (67), others. Academy Award songs: *Moon River, Days of Wine and Roses*.

m and e track. A sound track giving music and effects but not dialogue, necessary in dubbing stages.

MANDER, MILES (1888–1946) (Lionel Mander). British character actor, a former theatre manager with long experience of all kinds of stage work. *The Pleasure Garden* (26), *The First Born* (also wrote and directed) (28), *Loose Ends* (w, d only) (30), *The Missing Rembrandt* (w, d only) (31), *The Private Life of Henry VIII* (32), *Loyalties* (33), *The Morals of Marcus* (directed only) (35), etc.; then settled in Hollywood as actor. *The Three Musketeers* (as Richelieu) (36), *Lloyds of London* (37), *Slave Ship* (37), *Suez* (38), *The Three Musketeers* (musical version; as Richelieu again) (39), *Wuthering Heights* (39), *Tower of London* (39), *Lady Hamilton* (41), *Five Graves to Cairo* (43), *Farewell My Lovely* (44), *The Scarlet Claw* (44), *Pearl of Death* (45), *The Bandit of Sherwood Forest* (46), *The Walls Came Tumbling Down* (46), many others.

MANDY (GB 1952). A delicately handled mixture of fiction and documentary about the teaching of a congenitally deaf child. Directed by Alexander Mackendrick from a novel, 'The Day Is Ours', by Hilda Lewis; with Jack Hawkins, Phyllis Calvert and the child actress Mandy Miller.

MANGANO, SILVANA (1930–   ). Italian actress, wife of producer Dino de Laurentiis. Former model. Films include *L'Elisir d'Amore* (49), *Bitter Rice* (51), *Ulysses* (55), *The Sea Wall* (57), *Tempest* (59), *Fire Branded Women* (61), *Barabbas* (62), *Theorem* (68).

A MAN AND A WOMAN: see UN HOMME ET UNE FEMME.

A MAN FOR ALL SEASONS (AA) (GB 1966). A deceptively simple and straightforward piece of film-making by Fred Zinnemann (AA), based on Robert Bolt's play about Sir Thomas More but shedding its stylization in favour of a plain chronological treatment. The result was a triumph of sheer excellence in every department. Paul Scofield (AA) had the role of his life, with effective contributions from Wendy Hiller and Robert Shaw; the cinematography of Ted Moore (AA) was a constant delight. The film also marked an encouraging example of a sober, literate and thoughtful work gaining wide public acceptance.

MAN HUNT (US 1941). This then topical, though now dated, adventure melodrama from Geoffrey Household's 'Rogue Male' told of a big game hunter's 'stalk' of Hitler and the consequent espionage intrigues. Fritz Lang's directorial style was ponderous, the foggy London settings hilarious; Walter Pidgeon and George Sanders, however, had polish as hero and villain.

THE MAN IN GREY (GB 1943). Though fairly flat and unimaginative, this Regency melodrama from Lady Eleanor Smith's novel was so popular that it provoked a rash of similar costume pieces: *Madonna of the Seven Moons* (44), *The Wicked Lady* (45), *Caravan* (46),

Jassy (46), *Blanche Fury* (47), etc. It also did much for the careers of Margaret Lockwood, James Mason, Phyllis Calvert and Stewart Granger. Leslie Arliss directed.

THE MAN IN THE IRON MASK. No one knows what mixture of fact and fiction exists in the famous story of Louis XIV's mysterious prisoner who languished for years in the Bastille, his face always covered (actually with velvet). Some said it was Louis' bastard brother, others an Italian diplomat. Anyway, Dumas wrote an exciting novel on the subject, and it has been twice filmed: in 1929 (as *The Iron Mask*) with Douglas Fairbanks, and in 1939 (by James Whale) with Louis Hayward.

THE MAN IN THE WHITE SUIT (GB 1951). Bubbly Ealing satire, nimbly directed by Alexander Mackendrick, about a scientist who manages to antagonize both management and labour by inventing a fabric which never gets dirty and never wears out. Written by Mackendrick, Roger Macdougall and John Dighton; starring Alec Guinness, Joan Greenwood, Cecil Parker, Ernest Thesiger. A small classic.

MANKIEWICZ, DON (1922–). American scriptwriter and novelist, son of Herman Mankiewicz. Film credits include *Trial* (55), *House of Numbers* (57), *I Want to Live* (58).

MANKIEWICZ, HERMAN (1897–1953). American scriptwriter in Hollywood from 1926. Best known for his contribution to the script of *Citizen Kane* (41); some say he wrote virtually all of it. Also *The Road to Mandalay* (26), *Pride of the Yankees* (42), *Christmas Holiday* (43), *The Enchanted Cottage* (44), *The Spanish Main* (45), *A Woman's Secret* (48), etc.

MANKIEWICZ, JOSEPH L. (1909–). Multi-talented American executive and film creator. First in Hollywood as caption writer for silent films, including *The Mysterious Dr Fu Manchu* (29). Early sound writing credits: *Fast Company* (29), *Million Dollar Legs* (32), *Alice in Wonderland* (33), etc. Switched to producing: *Three Godfathers* (36), *Fury* (36), *The Bride Wore Red* (36), *Three Comrades* (38), *The Philadelphia Story* (40), *The Keys of the Kingdom* (43), etc. Became (†)writer-director: *Dragonwyck* (45), *Somewhere in the Night* (46), *The Late George Apley* (47), *The Ghost and Mrs Muir* (47), *Escape* (GB) (48), *A Letter to Three Wives* (AA script) (49), *House of Strangers* (50), *No Way Out* (50), *All About Eve* (AA script and direction) (50), *People Will Talk* (51), *Five Fingers* (52), *Julius Caesar* (53), *The Barefoot Contessa* (54), *Guys and Dolls* (55), *The Quiet American* (57), *Suddenly Last Summer* (directed only) (60), *Cleopatra* (62), *The Honey Pot* (67), *There Was a Crooked Man* (70), *Will* (project) (70).

MANKOWITZ, WOLF (1924–   ). British novelist and screenwriter. Film credits include *A Kid for Two Farthings* (56), *Expresso Bongo* (59), *Waltz of the Toreadors* (62), *The Day the Earth Caught Fire* (63), *Where the Spies Are* (65), *Casino Royale* (66), *Dr Faustus* (67), *The 25th Hour* (67).

MANN, ABBY (C.1922–   ). American TV writer who wrote the film of his own play *Judgment at Nuremberg* (61). Has since written *A Child Is Waiting* (63), *Ship of Fools* (65), etc.

†MANN, ANTHONY (1906–1967). American director, usually of outdoor films; his best work was concerned with the use of violence by thoughtful men. *Dr Broadway* (42), *Moonlight in Havana* (42), *Nobody's Darling* (43), *My Best Gal* (44), *Strangers in the Night* (44), *The Great Flamarion* (45), *Two O'Clock Courage* (45), *Sing Your Way Home* (45), *Strange Impersonation* (46), *The Bamboo Blonde* (46), *Desperate* (47), *Railroaded* (47), *T-Men* (47), *Raw Deal* (48), *The Black Book* (*Reign of Terror*) (49), *Border Incident* (49), *Side Street* (49), *Devil's Doorway* (50), *The Furies* (50), *Winchester 73* (50), *The Tall Target* (51), *Bend of the River* (51), *The Naked Spur* (52), *Thunder Bay* (53), *The Glenn Miller Story* (54), *The Far Country* (55), *Strategic Air Command* (55), *The Man from Laramie* (55), *The Last Frontier* (56), *Serenade* (56), *Men in War* (57), *The Tin Star* (57), *God's Little Acre* (58), *Man of the West* (58), *Cimarron* (60), *El Cid* (61), *The Fall of the Roman Empire* (64), *The Heroes of Telemark* (65), *A Dandy in Aspic* (completed by *Laurence Harvey*) (68).

MANN, DANIEL (1912–   ). American director, formerly musician and stage and TV director. *Come Back Little Sheba* (52), *About Mrs Leslie* (54), *The Rose Tattoo* (55), *The Teahouse of the August Moon* (56), *Hot Spell* (57), *The Last Angry Man* (59), *Butterfield 8* (60), *Ada* (61), *Five Finger Exercise* (62), *Who's Been Sleeping in My Bed* (63), *Our Man Flint* (65), *Judith* (65), etc.

MANN, DELBERT (1920–   ). American TV director who transferred to films. *Marty* (AA) (55), *The Bachelor Party* (57), *Separate Tables* (58), *Middle of the Night* (59), *The Dark at the Top of the Stairs* (60), *Lover Come Back* (61), *That Touch of Mink* (62), *A Gathering of Eagles* (63), *Quick Before It Melts* (65), *Mister Buddwing* (66), *Fitzwilly* (67), *David Copperfield* (69), etc.

MANN, NED (1893–1967). American special effects director, a one-time professional roller skater who entered films in 1920 as an actor. Best remembered for his long association with Alexander Korda, on such films as *The Man Who Could Work Miracles* (35), *The Ghost Goes West* (36), *Things to Come* (36), *The Thief of Bagdad* (40), *Anna Karenina* (47), *Bonnie Prince Charlie* (48). Later worked on *Around the World in 80 Days* (56).

MANNERS, DAVID (1902–   ) (Rauff de Ryther Duan Acklom). Canadian leading man of Hollywood films in the 30s; claimed to be descended from William the Conqueror. *Journey's End* (30), *Dracula* (30), *A Bill of Divorcement* (32), *The Mummy* (33), *Roman Scandals* (33), *The Mystery of Edwin Drood* (35), *A Woman Rebels* (37), etc. Returned to stage.

MANNHEIM, LUCIE (1905–   ). German-born character actress, married to Marius Goring. *The Thirty-nine Steps* (as the mysterious victim) (35), *The High Command* (37), *Yellow Canary* (43), *Hotel Reserve* (44), *So Little Time* (52), *Beyond the Curtain* (60), *Bunny Lake Is Missing* (65), etc.

MANNING, IRENE (1917–   ) (Inez Harvuot). American leading lady of the 40s, former café singer. *Two Wise Maids* (37), *The Big Shot* (42), *Yankee Doodle Dandy* (42), *The Desert Song* (44), *Shine On, Harvest Moon* (44), *Escape in the Desert* (45), *Bonnie Prince Charlie* (GB) (48), etc.

MAN OF ARAN (GB 1934). Influential documentarist Robert Flaherty came to Britain and took three years to film this sympathetic account of fisherfolk on a barren island off Ireland's west coast. It encouraged later films like *Edge of the World* (38) and generally opened the way for British film makers to look more closely at their natural surroundings.

MANSFIELD, JAYNE (1932–1967) (Jayne Palmer). Amply-proportioned American leading lady whose superstructure became the butt of many jokes. In films from 1955: *The Female Jungle* (55), *Illegal* (56), *Pete Kelly's Blues* (56), *The Burglar* (57), *The Girl Can't Help It* (57), *The Wayward Bus* (57), *The Sheriff of Fractured Jaw* (59), *Too Hot to Handle* (GB) (60), *The Challenge* (GB) (60), *It Happened in Athens* (62), *Panic Button* (64), *Country Music USA* (65), *The Fat Spy* (66), *A Guide for the Married Man* (67), etc.

MANVELL, ROGER (1909–   ). British film historian. Director of the British film academy since 1947 and author of many books on cinema, the most influential being the Penguin *Film* (44).

THE MAN WHO CAME TO DINNER (US 1941). George S. Kaufman and Moss Hart based their hilarious stage success on the real-life figure of Alexander Woolcott, who perfectly fitted the character of the cantankerous, megalomaniac broadcaster who is confined by a broken hip to a normal mid-western home which he turns into bedlam. Monty Woolley was just right in the film version, and had perfect support from Bette Davis, Reginald Gardiner, Jimmy Durante, Billie Burke and others. William Keighley directed.

THE MAN WHO KNEW TOO MUCH. Alfred Hitchcock twice filmed this thriller about a child held hostage by a gang planning to assassinate an international political figure: GB 1934, with Leslie Banks, Edna Best and Peter Lorre; and US 1956, with James Stewart, Doris Day and Bernard Miles. The first version, despite (or perhaps because of) its curious studio sets, made incomparably better entertainment.

THE MAN WITH THE GOLDEN ARM (US 1956). Otto Preminger produced and directed this film about drug addiction, from Nelson Algren's novel; at the time it not only flew in the face of the Hollywood production code, but also marked the first time the Rank circuit played an 'X' film since *Detective Story*, after the poor returns of which they had announced that 'X' films were for sensation-seekers and Rank theatres would henceforth play nothing but family entertainment. Frank Sinatra, Eleanor Parker and Kim Novak starred; Elmer Bernstein supplied the music. As a film it was rather a drag.

MARA, ADELE (1923–) (Adelaida Delgado). Spanish-American dancer who played leads in Hollywood co-features of the 40s. *Alias Boston Blackie* (42), *Bells of Rosarita* (45), *Tiger Woman* (46), *Diary of a Bride* (48), *The Sea Hornet* (51), *Back from Eternity* (56), *Curse of the Faceless Man* (58), *The Big Circus* (59), etc.

MARAIS, JEAN (1913–) (Jean Marais-Villain). French romantic actor well remembered in several Cocteau films: *L'Eternel Retour* (43), *La Belle et la Bête* (45), *L'Aigle a Deux Têtes* (47), *Les Parents Terribles* (48), *Orphée* (49), etc. Later films less notable; recently in cloak-and-sword epics, also playing 'The Saint', 'Fantomas' and various secret agents.

†MARCH, FREDRIC (1897–) (Frederick McIntyre Bickel). One of America's most respected stage and screen actors, who always projected intelligence and integrity and during the 30s and 40s was at time an agreeable light comedian. Long married to Florence Eldridge. *The Dummy* (29), *The Wild Party* (29), *The Studio Murder Mystery* (29), *Paris Bound* (29), *Jealousy* (29), *Footlights and Fools* (29), *The Marriage Playground* (29), *Sarah and Son* (30), *Ladies Love Brutes* (30), *Paramount on Parade* (30), *True to the Navy* (30), *Manslaughter* (30), *Laughter* (30), *The Royal Family of Broadway* (30), *Honour among Lovers* (30), *Night Angel* (31), *My Sin* (31), *Merrily We Go to Hell* (32), *Dr Jekyll and Mr Hyde* (AA) (32), *Smiling Through* (32), *Strangers in Love* (32), *The Sign of the Cross* (33), *The Eagle and the Hawk* (33), *The Affairs of Cellini* (34), *All of Me* (34), *Good Dame* (34), *Design for Living* (34), *Death Takes a Holiday* (34), *The Barretts of Wimpole Street* (as Robert Browning) (34), *We Live Again* (34), *Les Misérables* (35), *The Dark Angel* (35), *Anna Karenina* (35), *Mary of Scotland* (36), *Anthony Adverse* (36), *The Road to Glory* (36), *A Star Is Born* (37), *Nothing Sacred* (37), *The Buccaneer* (38), *There Goes*

My Heart (38), *Trade Winds* (39), *Susan and God* (40), *Victory* (40), *So Ends Our Night* (41), *One Foot in Heaven* (41), *Bedtime Story* (42), *I Married a Witch* (42), *Tomorrow the World* (44), *The Adventures of Mark Twain* (44), *The Best Years of Our Lives* (AA) (46), *Another Part of the Forest* (48), *An Act of Murder* (48), *Christopher Columbus* (GB) (49), *It's a Big Country* (51), *Death of a Salesman* (52), *Man on a Tightrope* (53), *Executive Suite* (54), *The Bridges at Toko Ri* (54), *The Desperate Hours* (55), *Alexander the Great* (55), *The Man in the Grey Flannel Suit* (56), *Middle of the Night* (59), *Inherit the Wind* (60), *The Young Doctors* (62), *Seven Days in May* (64), *Hombre* (67), *Tick Tick Tick* (70).

THE MARCH OF TIME. A highly influential series of two-reelers on current affairs, started and financed in 1934 by the founders of Time Magazine in association with film-maker Louis de Rochemont. The raucous American commentary marred it for European consumption, but its contents were a first-class in-depth examination of what was happening in the world. It ran with great success until the late 40s, when it was gradually replaced by TV series such as *NBC White Paper*, *CBS Reports*, Granada's *World in Action*, and the BBC's *Panorama*.

MARCUSE, THEODORE (1920–1967). Shaven-pated American character actor, usually in sinister roles. *The Glass Bottom Boat* (65), *The Cincinnati Kid* (65), *Last of the Secret Agents* (66), *The Wicked Dreams of Paula Schultz* (67), etc.

MARGETSON, ARTHUR (1897–1951). British stage actor, former stockbroker's clerk, who went to Hollywood in 1940 and played supporting roles. *Other People's Sins* (31), *His Grace Gives Notice* (33), *Little Friend* (34), *Broken Blossoms* (36), *Juggernaut* (37), *Action for Slander* (38), *Return to Yesterday* (40), *Random Harvest* (43), *Sherlock Holmes Faces Death* (44), etc.

MARGO (1918–   ) (Maria Marguerita Guadelupe Boldao y Castilla). Spanish-born actress, a one-time professional dancer who has been in occasional Hollywood films since 1933. Best remembered as the rapidly ageing refugee from Shangri-La in *Lost Horizon* (37). Other main films: *Crime without Passion* (34), *Winterset* (36), *The Leopard Man* (43), *Behind the Rising Sun* (63), *Gangway for Tomorrow* (44), *Viva Zapata* (52), *I'll Cry Tomorrow* (57), *Who's Got the Action* (63).

MARGOLIN, JANET (1943–   ). American leading lady. *David and Lisa* (62), *Bus Riley's Back in Town* (65), *The Greatest Story Ever Told* (65), *The Saboteur* (65), *Nevada Smith* (66), *Enter Laughing* (67), *Buona Sera Mrs Campbell* (68), etc.

Marin, Edwin L.

MARIN, EDWIN L. (1901–1951). American director. *A Study in Scarlet* (32), *The Casino Murder Case* (35), *I'd Give My Life* (36), *Florian* (40), *Maisie Was a Lady* (41), *Paris Calling* (41), *A Gentleman after Dark* (42), *Tall in the Saddle* (44), *Nocturne* (46), *Christmas Eve* (47), *Canadian Pacific* (49), *Sugarfoot* (51), etc.

MARION, FRANCES (1888–). American screenwriter. *Daughter of the Sea* (16), *Humoresque* (22), *Stella Dallas* (25), *The Winning of Barbara Worth* (26), *The Scarlet Letter* (27), *Love* (27), *The Wind* (28), *The Big House* (AA) (30), *The Champ* (AA) (32), *Dinner at Eight* (33), *Riff Raff* (36), *Knight without Armour* (37), *Green Hell* (40), etc.

MARION-CRAWFORD, HOWARD (1914–). British actor often seen in Watsonian roles or as jovial, beefy, sporting types. *Forever England* (32), *Freedom Radio* (40), *The Rake's Progress* (45), *The Hasty Heart* (49), *The Man in the White Suit* (51), *Where's Charley?* (52), *Reach for the Sky* (56), *Virgin Island* (58), *The Brides of Fu Manchu* (66), etc. Much on radio and TV.

MARIS, MONA (1903–) (Maria Capdevielle). Franco-Argentinian 'second lead' in Hollywood films. *Romance of the Rio Grande* (29), *Secrets* (33), *Law of the Tropics* (41), *Tampico* (44), *Heartbeat* (46), *The Avengers* (50), etc.

MARIUS (France 1931). The first of a trilogy (the others: *Fanny* [32], *César* [34]) written by Marcel Pagnol about characters of the Marseilles waterfront: saloon-owner César; his wayward son Marius; Fanny, the mother of Marius' child; Panisse, an ageing widower who marries Fanny. In 1938 James Whale directed *Port of Seven Seas*, a Hollywood remake with Wallace Beery in Raimu's role; in 1960 Joshua Logan directed another remake, *Fanny*, with Boyer and Chevalier but without the songs which had been used in a Broadway musical version shortly before.

MARKEN, JANE (1895–). French character actress with long stage experience. *Fioritures* (15), *Camille* (34), *Partie de Campagne* (37), *Hôtel du Nord* (38), *Lumière d'Été* (42), *Les Enfants du Paradis* (44), *L'Idiot* (46), *Clochemerle* (47), *Une Si Jolie Petite Plage* (48), *Manèges* (49), *Ma Pomme* (50), *Les Compagnes de la Nuit* (52), *Marie Antoinette* (55), *And God Created Woman* (56), *Pot Bouille* (57), *The Mirror Has Two Faces* (58), etc.

MARKER, CHRIS (1921–). French documentary director. *Olympia* (52), *Letter from Siberia* (58), *Description d'un Combat* (60), *Cuba Si* (61), *Le Joli Mai* (62), *La Jetée* (63), *If I Had Four Dromedaries* (66), etc. Leader of the modernist 'left bank' school.

MARKLE, FLETCHER (1921–). Canadian director, briefly in Hollywood. *Jigsaw* (49), *Night into Morning* (51), *The Man with a Cloak* (51); then into TV.

MARKS, ALFRED (1921–   ). British comedian, in films from 1950 but more usually seen on TV and stage. *Desert Mice* (59), *There Was a Crooked Man* (60), *Weekend with Lulu* (62), etc.

MARLEY, J. PEVERELL (1899–1964). American cinematographer who worked on de Mille's silent epics. *The Ten Commandments* (23), *The Volga Boatmen* (25), *King of Kings* (27), etc.; later worked on *Alexander's Ragtime Band* (38), *The Hound of the Baskervilles* (39), *Night and Day* (46), *Life with Father* (47), *House of Wax* (53), *Serenade* (56), *The Left-Handed Gun* (58), *A Fever in the Blood* (61), many others.

MARLOWE, HUGH (1920–   ) (Hugh Hipple). American actor, former radio announcer, in films from 1937. *Mrs Parkington* (44), *Meet Me in St Louis* (44), *Twelve o'Clock High* (50), *All about Eve* (50), *The Day the Earth Stood Still* (51), *Monkey Business* (52), *Garden of Evil* (54), *Earth Versus the Flying Saucers* (56), *Thirteen Frightened Girls* (64), *Castle of Evil* (66), *The Last Shot You Hear* (68), etc. Recently in TV.

MARLY, FLORENCE (c. 1915–   ) (Hana Smekalova). Franco-Czech leading lady, married to Pierre Chenal. Made a few films in Hollywood: *Sealed Verdict* (48), *Tokyo Joe* (49), *Cruising Casanovas (Gobs and Gals)* (52), *Undersea Girl* (58), *Games* (67), etc.

MARMONT, PERCY (1883–   ). Veteran British romantic actor of silent era, in films since 1913. Hollywood silents include *Lord Jim* (25), *Mantrap* (26); in England, *The Silver King* (24), *Rich and Strange* (27), etc. Became character actor during 30s: *The Silver Greyhound* (32), *Secret Agent* (36), *Action for Slander* (38), *I'll Walk Beside You* (41), *Loyal Heart* (45), *No Orchids for Miss Blandish* (48), *Lisbon* (56), many others.

MARQUAND, CHRISTIAN (1927–   ). French leading man, who turned director with *Candy* (68).

MARQUAND, JOHN P. (1893–1960). American novelist who wrote solid popular books about middle-aged men regretting their lost youth; also the Mr Moto series (filmed in the late 30s with Peter Lorre). Films of his books include *H. M. Pulham Esquire* (41), *The late George Apley* (47), *B.F.'s Daughter* (49), *Top Secret Affair (Melville Goodwin USA)* (56), *Stopover Tokyo* (57), etc.

THE MARRIAGE CIRCLE (US 1924). Ernst Lubitsch's famous silent comedy was adopted by Paul Bern from a play by Lothar Schmidt. Basically a very small comedy of adultery, it was impeccably done and gave new screen personas to Monte Blue, Marie Prevost and Adolphe Menjou, as well as bringing forth many imitators anxious to equal Lubitsch's flair for sophisticated sex. In 1932 Lubitsch

Marriott, Moore

remade it, equally delightfully, with dialogue, songs, recitative, and characters who frequently addressed the camera, as *One Hour With You*; with Maurice Chevalier, Genevieve Tobin, Jeanette Macdonald and Roland Young.

MARRIOTT, MOORE (1885–1949) (George Thomas Moore-Marriott). British character comedian specializing in hoary rustics, chiefly beloved as the ancient but resilient old Harbottle of the Will Hay comedies: *Convict 99* (36), *Oh Mr Porter* (38), *Ask a Policeman* (39), *Where's That Fire* (40), etc. Also notable with the Crazy Gang in *The Frozen Limits* (39) and *Gasbags* (40). Made over 300 films in all, including *Dick Turpin* (08), *Passion Island* (26), *The Lyons Mail* (31), *The Water Gypsies* (32), *As You Like It* (36), *Time Flies* (44), *Green for Danger* (46), *The History of Mr Polly* (49), *High Jinks in Society* (49).

LA MARSEILLAISE (France 1938). A revered but patchy and overlong account of the French Revolution, directed and co-written by Jean Renoir, with Pierre Renoir as Louis XVI.

MARSH, CAROL (1926–) (Norma Simpson). British leading lady whose career faltered when she outgrew ingénue roles. *Brighton Rock* (47), *Marry Me* (49), *Helter Skelter* (50), *Alice in Wonderland* (French puppet version) (50), *Salute the Toff* (51), *Dracula* (58), *Man Accused* (59), etc.

MARSH, GARRY (1902–) (Leslie March Geraghty). Robust, balding British character actor; in films since 1930, usually as harassed father, perplexed policeman or explosive officer. *Night Birds* (30), *Dreyfus* (30), *The Maid of the Mountains* (32), *Scrooge* (35), *When Knights Were Bold* (36), *Bank Holiday* (38), *It's in the Air* (38), *The Four Just Men* (39), *Hoots Mon* (40), etc.; war service; *I'll Be Your Sweetheart* (45), *The Rake's Progress* (45), *Dancing with Crime* (46), *Just William's Luck* (48), *Murder at the Windmill* (49), *Worm's Eye View* (51), *Mr Drake's Duck* (53), *Who Done It* (55), *Where the Bullets Fly* (66), many others.

MARSH, MAE (1895–1968) (Mary Warne Marsh). American leading lady of the silent screen; later played small character roles. *Man's Genesis* (12), *The Birth of a Nation* (14), *Intolerance* (15), *Polly of the Circus* (17), *Spotlight Sadie* (18), *The Little 'Fraid Lady* (20), *Flames of Passion* (22), *The White Rose* (23), *Daddies* (24), *The Rat* (GB) (25), *Tides of Passion* (26), *Over the Hill* (32), *Little Man What Now* (34), *Jane Eyre* (43), *A Tree Grows in Brooklyn* (44), *The Robe* (53), *Sergeant Rutledge* (60), many others.

MARSH, MARION (1913–) (Violet Krauth). American leading lady of English, German, French and Irish descent. Began in Hollywood as an extra; chosen by John Barrymore to play Trilby to his

Svengali (31). Later: *The Mad Genius* (32), *The Eleventh Commandment* (33), *Love at Second Sight* (GB) (34), *The Black Room* (35), *When's Your Birthday* (37), *Missing Daughters* (40), *House of Errors* (42), etc. Retired.

MARSHAL, ALAN (1909–1961). Australian-born actor of light romantic leads: came to films 1936 after New York stage experience. *The Garden of Allah* (36), *Night Must Fall* (38), *The Hunchback of Notre Dame* (40), *Tom, Dick and Harry* (40), *Lydia* (41), *The White Cliffs of Dover* (43), *The Barkeleys of Broadway* (48), *The House on Haunted Hill* (59), etc. Died while appearing on stage with Mae West in 'Sextet'.

MARSHALL, BRENDA (1915–   ) (Ardis Ankerson). American leading lady who married William Holden and retired. *Espionage Agent* (39), *The Sea Hawk* (40), *Footsteps in the Dark* (41), *Singapore Woman* (41), *Background to Danger* (43), *The Constant Nymph* (44), *Strange Impersonation* (45), *Whispering Smith* (49), *The Tomahawk Trail* (50), etc.

MARSHALL, E. G. (c. 1910–   ). American character actor with long Broadway experience. *The House on 92nd Street* (debut) (45), *The Caine Mutiny* (54), *Pushover* (55), *Twelve Angry Men* (57), *The Bachelor Party* (57), *Town without Pity* (61), *The Chase* (66), *The Bridge at Remagen* (69), etc. Known to millions as the elder lawyer in TV series *The Defenders* (61–65), also *The Bold Ones* (69).

MARSHALL, GEORGE (1891–   ). American director with over 400 features to his credit. Entered films 1912 as an extra; graduated to feature roles in early serials and comedies; began directing 1917 with a series of Harry Carey Westerns. Sound films have included *Pack Up Your Troubles* (32), *A Message to Garcia* (34), *The Crime of Dr Forbes* (37), *In Old Kentucky* (38), *The Goldwyn Follies* (38), *You Can't Cheat an Honest Man* (39), *Destry Rides Again* (39), *The Ghost Breakers* (40), *When the Daltons Rode* (40), *The Forest Rangers* (42), *Star Spangled Rhythm* (43), *And the Angels Sing* (43), *Incendiary Blonde* (44), *Hold That Blonde* (45), *The Blue Dahlia* (46), *The Perils of Pauline* (47), *Tap Roots* (48), *Fancy Pants* (50), *The Savage* (52), *Scared Stiff* (53), *Red Garters* (54), *The Second Greatest Sex* (55), *Beyond Mombasa* (GB) (56), *The Sad Sack* (57), *The Sheepman* (58), *Imitation General* (58), *The Gazebo* (59), *Cry for Happy* (61), *How the West Was Won* (part) (62), *Advance to the Rear* (64), *Boy, Did I Get a Wrong Number* (66), *Eight on the Lam* (67), *Hook Line and Sinker* (69).

MARSHALL, HERBERT (1890–1966). Urbane British actor, on stage since 1913, films since 1927, in Britain and America. He always played smooth roles despite loss of a leg in World War I. *Mumsie* (debut) (27), *Murder* (28), *Michael and Mary* (31), *Trouble in Paradise* (32), *I Was a Spy* (33), *Four Frightened People* (34), *The Dark Angel*

(36), *If You Could Only Cook* (37), *The Letter* (40), *The Little Foxes* (41), *The Moon and Sixpence* (as Somerset Maugham) (42), *Forever and a Day* (43), *The Enchanted Cottage* (44), *Duel in the Sun* (46), *The Razor's Edge* (46), *High Wall* (48), *Gog* (54), *The Black Shield of Falworth* (54), *The Virgin Queen* (55), *The Fly* (58), *The Third Day* (65), many others.

MARSHALL, HERBERT (1900–). British documentarist, married to Fredda Brilliant. Associate of John Grierson; worked on English dubbing of Russian films. Produced and directed feature, *Tinker* (49).

MARSHALL, TRUDY (1922–). American leading lady of minor films in the 40s. *Secret Agent of Japan* (42), *Girl Trouble* (44), *Sentimental Journey* (46), *Disaster* (48), *Mark of the Gorilla* (50), *The President's Lady* (53), etc.

MARSHALL, TULLY (1864–1943) (T. M. Phillips). American silent screen actor; stage experience from boyhood. *Intolerance* (15), *Oliver Twist* (as Fagin) (16), *Joan the Woman* (16), *The Slim Princess* (20), *The Hunchback of Notre Dame* (23), *The Merry Widow* (25), *The Red Mill* (27), *The Cat and the Canary* (28), *Trail of '98* (29), *Show of Shows* (29), *The Unholy Garden* (31), *Scarface* (32), *Grand Hotel* (33), *Diamond Jim* (35), *Souls at Sea* (37), *A Yank at Oxford* (38), *Brigham Young* (40), *Chad Hanna* (41), *This Gun for Hire* (42), many others.

MARSHALL, ZENA (1926–). British leading lady with French ancestry; stage experience. *Caesar and Cleopatra* (debut) (45), *Good Time Girl* (47), *Miranda* (48), *Sleeping Car to Trieste* (48), *Marry Me* (49), *Hell Is Sold Out* (51), *The Embezzler* (54), *My Wife's Family* (56), *The Story of David* (61), *Dr No* (62), etc.

MARTELLI, OTELLO (1903–). Italian cinematographer, especially associated with Fellini. *Paisa* (46), *Bitter Rice* (48), *I Vitelloni* (52), *La Strada* (54), *Il Bidone* (55), *La Dolce Vita* (59), *I Tre Volti* (63), etc.

MARTIN, CHRIS-PIN (1894–1953). Rotund Mexican actor who provided comic relief in many a Western. *Four Frightened People* (34), *The Gay Desperado* (36), *The Return of the Cisco Kid* (39) (and ensuing series), *The Mark of Zorro* (41), *Weekend in Havana* (42), *Mexican Hayride* (49), *Ride the Man Down* (53), etc.

MARTIN, DEAN (1917–) (Dino Crocetti). Heavy-lidded, husky-voiced, self-spoofing American actor-singer. Was prizefighter, mill-hand, petrol station attendant, etc., before joining Jerry Lewis in night club act. Appeared with him in many popular films: *My Friend Irma* (49), *At War with the Army* (51), *Scared Stiff* (53), *Three-Ring Circus* (55), *Living It Up* (56), *Hollywood or Bust* (56), etc.

Became best-selling crooner, went solo as actor, joined Sinatra 'clan'. *Ten Thousand Bedrooms* (57), *The Young Lions* (58), *Rio Bravo* (58), *Bells Are Ringing* (60), *Ocean's Eleven* (61), *Sergeants Three* (62), *Toys in the Attic* (63), *Robin and the Seven Hoods* (64), *Kiss Me Stupid* (65), *Marriage on the Rocks* (65), *The Sons of Katie Elder* (65), *The Silencers* (66), *Texas across the River* (66), *Murderers' Row* (66), *Rough Night in Jericho* (67), *How to Save a Marriage* (67), *The Ambushers* (67), *Bandolero* (68), *Five Card Stud* (68), *Wrecking Crew* (68), *Airport* (69), *The Ravagers* (70), etc.

MARTIN, DEWEY (1923–   ). American leading man. *Knock On Any Door* (debut) (49), *Kansas Raiders* (50), *The Thing* (52), *The Big Sky* (52), *Tennessee Champ* (54), *Prisoner of War* (54), *Land of the Pharaohs* (55), *The Desperate Hours* (55), *Ten Thousand Bedrooms* (57), etc.; more recently on TV.

MARTIN, EDIE (1880–1964). The frail, tiny old lady of scores of British films: *The History of Mr Polly* (49), *The Lavender Hill Mob* (51), *The Man in the White Suit* (52), *The Titfield Thunderbolt* (53), *The Ladykillers* (55), etc. On stage from 1886, films from 1932.

MARTIN, MARION (1916–   ). American leading lady of 'B' pictures, a statuesque blonde who graduated from the Ziegfeld chorus. *Boom Town* (40), *Mexican Spitfire at Sea* (41), *The Big Store* (41), *They Got Me Covered* (42), *Abbott and Costello in Hollywood* (45), *Queen of Burlesque* (47), *Oh You Beautiful Doll* (50), *Thunder in the Pines* (54), etc.

MARTIN, MARY (1913–   ). American musical comedy star, in occasional films from 1939. *The Great Victor Herbert* (39), *Birth of the Blues* (41), *Kiss the Boys Goodbye* (41), *True to Life* (42), *Happy Go Lucky* (43), *Night and Day* (46), etc.

MARTIN, MILLICENT (1934–   ). British songstress of stage and TV. Films include *The Horsemasters* (60), *The Girl on the Boat* (62), *Nothing But the Best* (64), *Those Magnificent Men in Their Flying Machines* (65), *Alfie* (66), *Stop the World I Want To Get Off* (66), etc.

MARTIN, ROSS (1920–   ) (Martin Rosenblatt). Polish-American actor with vaudeville experience; much on TV, especially in *The Wild West* series. *Conquest of Space* (55), *The Colossus of New York* (58), *Experiment in Terror* (as the killer) (62), *The Ceremony* (64), *The Great Race* (65).

MARTINS, ORLANDO (1899–   ). West African actor in British films. *Sanders of the River* (35), *Jericho* (37), *The Man from Morocco* (44), *Men of Two Worlds* (as the witch doctor) (46), *End of the River* (47), *Where No Vultures Fly* (52), *Simba* (55), *Sapphire* (59), etc.

MARTIN, TONY (1913–   ) (Alvin Morris). American cabaret singer and leading man, in Hollywood from 1936 after years of touring with dance bands. *Sing, Baby, Sing* (36), *Banjo on My Knee* (37), *Ali Baba Goes to Town* (38), *Music in My Heart* (40), *The Big Store* (41), *Ziegfeld Girl* (41), *Till the Clouds Roll By* (46), *Casbah* (48), *Two Tickets to Broadway* (51), *Here Come the Girls* (53), *Deep in My Heart* (54), *Hit the Deck* (55), *Let's Be Happy* (GB) (57), etc.

MARTINELLI, ELSA (1933–   ). Italian leading lady, in films from 1950. *The Indian Fighter* (US) (55), *Manuela* (GB) (57), *The Boatmen* (60), *Hatari* (US) (62), *The Trial* (63), *Marco the Magnificent* (65), *De l'Amour* (65), *The Tenth Victim* (65), *Candy* (68), etc.

MARTINI, NINO (1904–   ). Italian actor-singer, who made a few English-speaking films. *Here's to Romance* (US) (35), *The Gay Desperado* (US) (36), *One Night with You* (GB) (48), etc.

MARTINSON, LESLIE H. (* –   ). American director, from TV. *PT 109* (62), *For Those Who Think Young* (64), *Batman* (66), *Fathom* (67), *The Unexpected Mrs Pollifax* (70), etc.

MARTON, ANDREW (1904–   ). Hungarian-born director, in Hollywood from 1923; settled there after return visits to Europe. *SOS Iceberg* (32), *The Demon of the Himalayas* (34), *Wolf's Clothing* (GB) (37), *Secrets of Stamboul* (GB) (37), *Gentle Annie* (45), *The Wild North* (52), *Prisoner of War* (54), *Green Fire* (55), *The Thin Red Line* (64), *Crack in the World* (65), *Around the World under the Sea* (65), etc. Co-directed *King Solomon's Mines* (50). Also a notable second-unit director: *The Red Badge of Courage* (51), *A Farewell to Arms* (57), *Ben Hur* (59), *55 Days at Peking* (62), *The Longest Day* (62), *Cleopatra* (62), etc.

MARTY (US 1956) (AA). The film which started Hollywood's TV invasion. From Paddy Chayefsky's small-screen play about a shy butcher who courts an equally shy schoolteacher, its success started an influx of fresh talent from New York. Directed by Delbert Mann (AA), produced by Harold Hecht, with Ernest Borgnine (AA) and Betsy Blair. Chayefsky also won the best screenplay award.

MARVIN, LEE (1924–   ). Ruthless-looking American actor who lately switched from unpleasant villains to unsympathetic heroes. *You're in the Navy Now* (51), *Duel at Silver Creek* (52), *The Big Heat* (53), *The Wild One* (54), *Gorilla at Large* (54), *The Caine Mutiny* (54), *Bad Day at Black Rock* (54), *Violent Saturday* (55), *Not as a Stranger* (55), *Pete Kelly's Blues* (55), *Shack Out on 101* (55), *I Died a Thousand Times* (56), *Seven Men from Now* (57), *Attack* (57), *Raintree County* (57), *The Missouri Traveller* (58), *The Man Who Shot Liberty Vallance* (62), *Donovan's Reef* (63), *The Killers* (64), *Cat Ballou* (AA) (65), *Ship of Fools* (65), *The Professionals* (66), *The Dirty Dozen*

(67), *Point Blank* (67), *Hell on the Pacific* (68), *Paint Your Wagon* (69), *Monte Walsh* (70). TV series: *M Squad* (58–60).

†THE MARX BROTHERS. A family of American comedians whose zany humour convulsed minority audiences in its time and influenced later comedy writing to an enormous extent. CHICO (1891–1961) (Leonard Marx) played the piano eccentrically and spoke with an impossible Italian accent; HARPO (1893–1964) (Adolph Marx) was a child-like mute who also played the harp; GROUCHO (1895–) (Julius Marx) had a painted moustache, a cigar, a loping walk and the lion's share of the wisecracks. In vaudeville from childhood, they came to films after Broadway success. Originally there were two other brothers: GUMMO, who left the act early on, and ZEPPO, who didn't fit in with the craziness and left them after playing romantic relief in their first five films. These first five films contain much of their best work: later their concentrated anarchy was dissipated by musical and romantic relief. *The Coconuts* (29), *Animal Crackers* (30), *Monkey Business* (31), *Horse Feathers* (32), *Duck Soup* (33), *A Night at the Opera* (35), *A Day at the Races* (37), *Room Service* (38), *At the Circus* (39), *Go West* (40), *The Big Store* (41), *A Night in Casablanca* (46), *Love Happy* (a curious and unhappy failure) (50). They also made guest appearances in *The Story of Mankind* (57). Groucho alone has enlivened a few otherwise tedious comedies: *Copacabana* (47), *Mr Music* (50), *Double Dynamite* (51), *A Girl in Every Port* (52), *Skidoo* (68). Harpo published his autobiography 1961: *Harpo Speaks!* Among Groucho's semi-autobiographical works are *Groucho and Me* (59), *Memoirs of a Mangy Lover* (64) and *The Groucho Letters* (67).

MARY POPPINS (US 1964). Walt Disney's most successful film for years, a tricksy fantasy from the books by P. L. Travers about a magical nanny who descends on a family in Edwardian London. Overlong, but has pleasant songs and brilliant trick effects. With Julie Andrews (AA), Dick Van Dyke, David Tomlinson, etc.; directed by Robert Stevenson.

MASINA, GIULIETTA (1921–). Italian gamin-like actress, married to Federico Fellini. In films since 1941. *Senza Pieta* (47), *Lights of Variety* (48), *La Strada* (53), *Il Bidone* (55), *Nights of Cabiria* (57), *Juliet of the Spirits* (65), etc.

mask. A technical device for blocking out part of the image. *Masking* is the black cloth which surrounds the actual cinema screen: these days it has to be electrically adjustable to encompass the various screen sizes.

MASKELL, VIRGINIA (1936–1968). British leading lady seen in *Our Virgin Island* (58), *The Man Upstairs* (59), *Doctor in Love* (60), *The Wild and the Willing* (62), *Only Two Can Play* (62), *Interlude* (68), etc.

THE MASK OF DIMITRIOS (US 1944). Amusingly entangled and well-staged mystery film about a writer who sets out to uncover the truth about the career of an international crook. It boasted a splendid array of character actors in their best form : Sidney Greenstreet, Peter Lorre, Victor Francen, Steve Geray, Eduardo Cianelli, Kurt Katch, Florence Bates and John Abbott. It was stylishly directed by Jean Negulesco, who subsequently failed to live up to his promise, and introduced actor Zachary Scott, of whom likewise. Frank Gruber wrote the screenplay from Eric Ambler's novel.

MASON, ELLIOTT (c. 1897–1949). Scottish character actress with repertory experience. *The Ghost Goes West* (36), *Owd Bob* (38), *The Ghost of St Michael's* (41), *The Gentle Sex* (43), *The Captive Heart* (46), etc.

MASON, HERBERT (1891–). British director. *His Lordship* (36), *Strange Boarders* (38), *Back Room Boy* (41), *Flight from Folly* (45), etc. Moved into production.

MASON, JAMES (1909–). British leading man and latterly international star character actor, often in brooding or introspective roles. Trained as architect; stage debut 1931. *Late Extra* (debut) (35), *Prison Breakers* (36), *Fire over England* (36), *The Mill on the Floss* (36), *The High Command* (37), *Catch As Catch Can* (38), *The Return of the Scarlet Pimpernel* (38), *I Met a Murderer* (38), *This Man Is Dangerous* (39), *Hatter's Castle* (41), *Secret Mission* (42), *The Night Has Eyes* (42), *The Bells Go Down* (42), *Thunder Rock* (42), *The Man in Grey* (a key role as an 18th-century villain) (43), *Fanny by Gaslight* (43), *They Met in the Dark* (43), *Candlelight in Algeria* (44), *Hotel Reserve* (44), *A Place of One's Own* (44), *They Were Sisters* (45), *The Wicked Lady* (45), *The Seventh Veil* (45), *Odd Man Out* (46), *The Upturned Glass* (47), etc.; made some blunt remarks about British films and left for Hollywood, where at first he had a thin time. *Caught* (48), *Madame Bovary* (49), *East Side West Side* (49), *One-Way Street* (50), *A Lady Possessed* (51), *Pandora and the Flying Dutchman* (51), *Rommel, Desert Fox* (51), *Five Fingers* (52), *Botany Bay* (52), *The Prisoner of Zenda* (52), *Desert Rats* (53), *The Story of Three Loves* (53), *The Man Between* (53), *Charade* (also produced) (53), *Julius Caesar* (as Brutus) (53), *Prince Valiant* (54), *A Star Is Born* (54), *Twenty Thousand Leagues under the Sea* (as Captain Nemo) (54), *Forever Darling* (55), *Bigger than Life* (also produced) (56), *Island in the Sun* (56), *Cry Terror* (58), *North by Northwest* (59), *Journey to the Centre of the Earth* (59), *A Touch of Larceny* (60), *The Decks Ran Red* (60), *The Marriage Go Round* (61), *Lolita* (as Humbert Humbert) (62), *The Fall of the Roman Empire* (64), *The Pumpkin Eater* (64), *Lord Jim* (65), *Genghis Khan* (65), *The Blue Max* (66), *Georgy Girl* (66), *The Deadly Affair* (67), *Stranger in the House* (67), *Duffy* (68),

Mayerling (68), *The Seagull* (68), *Age of Consent* (69), *Spring and Port Wine* (69), others.

MASON, SHIRLEY (1900–) (Leona Flugrath). American leading lady of the silent screen, sister of Viola Dana. *Vanity Fair* (15), *Goodbye Bill* (18), *Treasure Island* (20), *Merely Mary Ann* (20), *Lights of the Desert* (22), *What Fools Men* (25), *Don Juan's Three Nights* (26), *Sally in Our Alley* (27), *Show of Stars* (29), etc.

MASSEN, OSA (1915–). Danish-born actress in Hollywood from late 30s. *Honeymoon in Bali* (39), *The Master Race* (44), *Tokyo Rose* (44), *Cry of the Werewolf* (44), *Deadline at Dawn* (47), *Rocketship XM* (50), etc.

MASSEY, DANIEL (1933–). British actor, son of Raymond Massey, usually seen on stage or TV. Films include *Girls at Sea* (57), *Upstairs and Downstairs* (59), *The Queen's Guard* (60), *Go to Blazes* (62), *Moll Flanders* (65), *The Jokers* (66), *Star!* (67), *Fragment of Fear* (69).

MASSEY, ILONA (1912–) (Ilona Hajmassy). Hungarian-born leading lady, in Hollywood from mid-30s. *Rosalie* (37), *Balalaika* (39), *International Lady* (41), *Invisible Agent* (42), *Frankenstein Meets the Wolf Man* (43), *End of the Rainbow* (47), *Love Happy* (50), *Jet over the Atlantic* (59), etc.

†MASSEY, RAYMOND (1896–). Canadian-born actor, on stage (in Britain) from 1922. In films, has played saturnine, benevolent or darkly villainous, with a penchant for impersonations of Abraham Lincoln; has lived in America for many years. *The Speckled Band* (as Sherlock Holmes) (31), *The Face at the Window* (31), *The Old Dark House* (32), *The Scarlet Pimpernel* (34), *Things to Come* (36), *Fire over England* (36), *Under the Red Robe* (37), *The Prisoner of Zenda* (37), *Dreaming Lips* (37), *The Hurricane* (38), *The Drum* (38), *Black Limelight* (39), *Abe Lincoln in Illinois* (39), *Santa Fe Trail* (as John Brown) (40), *49th Parallel* (41), *Dangerously They Live* (41), *Desperate Journey* (42), *Reap the Wild Wind* (42), *Action in the North Atlantic* (43), *Arsenic and Old Lace* (44), *The Woman in the Window* (44), *Hotel Berlin* (45), *God Is My Co-Pilot* (45), *A Matter of Life and Death* (46), *Possessed* (47), *Mourning Becomes Electra* (47), *The Fountainhead* (48), *Roseanna McCoy* (49) *Chain Lightning* (49), *Barricade* (50), *Dallas* (50), *Sugarfoot* (51), *Come Fill the Cup* (51), *David and Bathsheba* (51), *Carson City* (52), *The Desert Song* (53), *Prince of Players* (55), *Battle Cry* (55), *East of Eden* (55), *Seven Angry Men* (55), *Omar Khayyam* (57), *The Naked and the Dead* (58), *The Great Impostor* (60), *The Fiercest Heart* (61), *The Queen's Guard* (61), *How the West Was Won* (62), *Mackenna's Gold* (68), others. Star of long running TV series *Dr Kildare* (as Dr Gillespie) (61–65).

MASSIE, PAUL (1932–). Canadian-born actor, frequently on British stage and screen. *High Tide at Noon* (57), *Orders to Kill* (58), *Sapphire* (59), *Libel* (60), *The Two Faces of Dr Jekyll* (60), *The Pot Carriers* (62), etc.

MASSINGHAM, RICHARD (1898–1953). British actor-producer-director: a qualified doctor who abandoned his medical career to make numerous short propaganda films for government departments during World War II and after, infusing them with quiet wit and sympathy. Gratefully remembered as the stout party bewildered by government restrictions: bathing in five inches of water, collecting salvage, avoiding colds, preventing rumours, wearing a gas mask, etc.

MASTROIANNI, MARCELLO (1923–). Italian leading man, a former clerk who broke into films with a bit part in *I Miserabili* (47). Now Italy's most respected and sought-after lead. *Sunday in August* (49), *Girls of the Spanish Steps* (51), *The Bigamist* (55), *White Nights* (57), *I Soliti Ignoti* (58), *La Dolce Vita* (59), *Il Bell'Antonio* (60), *La Notte* (61), *Divorce Italian Style* (BFA) (62), *Yesterday, Today and Tomorrow* (BFA) (63), *Marriage Italian Style* (64), *Casanova 70* (65), *The Organizer* (65), *Shoot Loud, Louder, I Don't Understand* (66), *The Stranger* (67), *Diamonds for Breakfast* (GB) (68), *A Place for Lovers* (69), *Sunflower* (70), etc.

MATA HARI. Two films have been made about the famous spy of World War I: by George Fitzmaurice in 1932, with Greta Garbo, and by Jean-Louis Richard in 1964, with Jeanne Moreau.

MATE, RUDOLPH (1898–1964). Polish-born cameraman: *The Passion of Joan of Arc* (26), *Vampyr* (31), *Liliom* (33), *Dante's Inferno* (US) (35), *Dodsworth* (36), *Love Affair* (39), *Foreign Correspondent* (40), *To Be or Not To Be* (42), *Cover Girl* (44), etc. Later became director: *The Dark Past* (48), *D.O.A.* (50), *When Worlds Collide* (51), *The Siege of Red River* (53), *The Black Shield of Falworth* (54), *Three Violent People* (56), *For the First Time* (59), *The 300 Spartans* (62), etc.

MATHER, AUBREY (1885–1958). British character actor, on stage from 1905, films from 1931. Settled in Hollywood and became useful member of English contingent, playing butlers and beaming, bald-headed little men. *Young Woodley* (31), *As You Like It* (36), *When Knights Were Bold* (36), *Jane Eyre* (44), *The Keys of the Kingdom* (44), *The Forsyte Saga* (49), *The Importance of Being Earnest* (52), many others.

MATHIESON, MUIR (1911–). British musical director, in films from 1931. Has conducted the scores of hundreds of films, including *Things to Come* (36), *Dangerous Moonlight* (40), *In Which We Serve* (42), *Brief Encounter* (46), *The Sound Barrier* (52), *The Swiss Family Robinson* (60), *Becket* (64), etc.

MATHIS, JUNE (1892–1927). American screenwriter. *An Eye for an Eye* (18), *The Four Horsemen of the Apocalypse* (21), *Blood and Sand* (22), *Greed* (23), *Ben Hur* (27), etc.

MATRAS, CHRISTIAN (1903–   ). French cinematographer, in films from 1928. *La Grande Illusion* (37), *Boule de Suif* (45), *Les Jeux Sont Faits* (47), *La Ronde* (50), *Madame De* (53), *Lola Montes* (55), *Les Espions* (57), *Paris Blues* (61), *Les Fetes Galantes* (65), *The Milky Way* (68), many others.

matt or *matte*. A technique (sometimes known as *travelling matt*) for blending actors in the studio with location or trick scenes. The actor is photographed against a non-reflective background (e.g. black velvet) and a high-contrast negative of this image is combined with the desired background. Thus men can move among animated monsters, and ghosts can slowly disappear.

MATT HELM. The laconic hero of a number of self-spoofing private-eye dime novels by Donald Hamilton, personified on screen by a droopy-eyed Dean Martin. Over-sexed and witless, the series represents a rather miserable but commercial 60s blend of high camp, self-indulgence, comic strip and semi-pornography. *The Silencers* (66), *Murderers' Row* (66), *The Ambushers* (67) and *Wrecking Crew* (69) have appeared so far, and it seems to be a point of honour with the producer that the title shall have no relevance whatever to the movie.

A MATTER OF LIFE AND DEATH (GB 1946) (American title: *Stairway to Heaven*). The first film to be selected for the Royal Film Performance. Damned in some quarters and exalted in others, it was a typical product of the Archers (Michael Powell and Emeric Pressburger). A RAF pilot undergoes a brain operation and dreams the outcome as the result of a trial conducted in heaven: the theme seems curiously unthought through and full of irrelevances, but the production is full of enjoyable lapses of taste as well as flashes of sheer brilliance and incomparable imagination. Décor by Hein Heckroth; acting by David Niven, Roger Livesey, Marius Goring and Raymond Massey; colour and monochrome photography by Jack Cardiff.

MATTHAU, WALTER (1920–   ). American character actor with stage experience; equally adept at wry comedy or heavy villainy. *The Kentuckian* (debut) (55), *The Indian Fighter* (55), *A Face in the Crowd* (57), *Slaughter on Tenth Avenue* (58), *King Creole* (58), *Onionhead* (59), *Strangers When We Meet* (60), *Lonely Are the Brave* (62), *Charade* (63), *Fail Safe* (64), *Goodbye Charlie* (65), *Mirage* (65), *The Fortune Cookie The Secret Life of an American Wife* (68), *Candy* (68), *Hello Dolly* (69), *Cactus Flower* (69), *A New Leaf* (70), etc. TV series: *Tallahassee 7000* (59).

653

Matthews, A. E.

MATTHEWS, A. E. (1869–1960). British actor, on stage from 1886, films from mid-20s; in his youth a suave romantic lead, was later famous for the crotchety cheerfulness of his extreme longevity. *Quiet Wedding* (40), *The Life and Death of Colonel Blimp* (43), *Piccadilly Incident* (46), *Just William's Luck* (48), *The Chiltern Hundreds* (in his stage role as Lord Lister) (49), *The Galloping Major* (51), *Made in Heaven* (52), *The Million Pound Note* (54), *Three Men in a Boat* (56), *Inn for Trouble* (60), many others. Published his autobiography, *Matty*, in 1953.

MATTHEWS, FRANCIS (1927–). British leading man with TV and repertory experience. *Bhowani Junction* (56), *The Revenge of Frankenstein* (58), *The Lamp in Assassin Mews* (62), *Dracula, Prince of Darkness* (65), *That Riviera Touch* (66), *Just Like a Woman* (66), etc.

†MATTHEWS, JESSIE (1907–). Vivacious British singing and dancing star of light musicals in the 30s; on stage from 1917. *Out of the Blue* (31), *There Goes the Bride* (32), *The Midshipmaid* (32), *The Man from Toronto* (32), *The Good Companions* (32), *Friday the Thirteenth* (33), *Waltzes from Vienna* (33), *Evergreen* (34), *First a Girl* (35), *It's Love Again* (36), *Head over Heels* (37), *Gangway* (37), *Sailing Along* (38), *Climbing High* (39). Made only three further appearances: *Forever and a Day* (43), *Candles at Nine* (43), *Tom Thumb* (58).

MATTHEWS, KERWIN (1926–). American leading man, former teacher. *Five Against the House* (55), *The Seventh Voyage of Sindbad* (58), *The Three Worlds of Gulliver* (60), *Jack the Giant Killer* (61), *Maniac* (GB) (63), *Battle Beneath the Earth* (GB) (68), etc.

MATTHEWS, LESTER (1900–). British stage actor, in Hollywood from 1934. *Creeping Shadows* (31), *Facing the Music* (34), *Blossom Time* (34), *Werewolf of London* (35), *Thank You, Jeeves* (35), *The Prince and the Pauper* (37), *The Adventures of Robin Hood* (38), *Northwest Passage* (40), *Manhunt* (41), *Between Two Worlds* (44), *The Invisible Man's Revenge* (44), *Lorna Doone* (51), many others; recently in TV.

MATTSSON, ARNE (1919–). Swedish director, in films from 1942. *One Summer of Happiness* (51), *The Girl in Tails* (56), *Mannequin in Red* (59), *The Doll* (62), etc.

MATURE, VICTOR (1915–). American leading man, once known as 'The Hunk'. *The Housekeeper's Daughter* (debut) (39), *Man and His Mate* (40), *The Shanghai Gesture* (41), *Hot Spot* (42), *My Gal Sal* (42), *My Darling Clementine* (as Doc Holliday) (46), *Moss Rose* (47), *Kiss of Death* (47), *Cry of the City* (48), *Fury at Furnace Creek* (48), *Samson and Delilah* (49), *Wabash Avenue* (50), *Gambling House* (51), *The Las Vegas Story* (52), *Androcles and the Lion* (53), *Something for the Birds* (53), *Affair with a Stranger* (53), *The Robe* (53), *Demetrius and the Gladiators* (54), *Veils of Bagdad* (54), *The Egyptian* (55), *Chief Crazy*

Horse (55), *Violent Saturday* (55), *Safari* (GB) (56), *Zarak* (GB) (56), *Interpol* (GB) (57), *No Time To Die* (GB) (58), *The Bandit of Zhobe* (GB) (58), *The Big Circus* (59), *Timbuktu* (60), *Hannibal* (It.) (60), others; recent comeback, spoofing himself, in *After the Fox* (66).

mau mau. The terrorist activities in Kenya during the 50s were the subject of three very savage movies: *Simba* (55), *Safari* (56), *Something of Value* (56).

MAUCH, BILLY AND BOBBY (1925–   ). American twins, boy actors who appeared in several films in the mid-thirties, notably a 'Penrod' series and the Errol Flynn version of *The Prince and the Pauper* (37).

MAUGHAM, W. SOMERSET (1874–1965). Distinguished British novelist, short story writer and playwright whose works have often been filmed. *Smith* (17), *A Man of Honour* (19), *The Circle* (25 and 30)(as *Strictly Unconventional*), *Rain* (28) (as *Sadie Thompson*), (32), and (53) (as *Miss Sadie Thompson*), *Our Betters* (33), *The Painted Veil* (34 and 57) (as *The Seventh Sin*), *Of Human Bondage* (34, 46 and 64). *Ashenden* (as *Secret Agent*) (36), *Vessel of Wrath* (37 and 54) (as *The Beachcomber*), *The Letter* (40) (also very freely adapted as *The Unfaithful* [47]), *The Moon and Sixpence* (42), *Christmas Holiday* (44), *The Razor's Edge* (46), *Theatre* (as *Adorable Julia*) (63), etc. He also introduced three omnibus films of his stories: *Quartet* (48), *Trio* (50), *Encore* (51); and a film of his life is promised.

MAUREY, NICOLE (1925–   ). French leading lady. *Little Boy Lost* (US) (51), *The Secret of the Incas* (US) (54), *The Weapon* (GB) (56), *Me and the Colonel* (US) (58), *The House of the Seven Hawks* (GB) (59), *High Time* (US) (60), *The Day of the Triffids* (GB) (62), etc.

MAXWELL, JOHN (1875–1940). Scottish lawyer who turned distributor and became co-founder of Associated British productions and the ABC cinema chain.

MAXWELL, LOIS (1927–   ) (Lois Hooker). Canadian leading lady who had a brief Hollywood career (1946–48) before settling in England. *The Decision of Christopher Blake* (47), *Corridor of Mirrors* (48), *Women of Twilight* (49), *Domano E Troppo Tardi* (It.) (50), *The Woman's Angle* (52), *Aida* (It.) (53), *Passport to Treason* (55), *The High Terrace* (56), *Kill Me Tomorrow* (57), *Operation Kid Brother* (67), etc.; plays Miss Moneypenny in the James Bond films.

MAXWELL, MARILYN (1921–   ) (Marvel Maxwell). Blonde American radio singer and actress, formerly child dancer. *Cargo of Innocents* (debut) (42), *Swing Fever* (42), *Thousands Cheer* (43), *Lost in a Harem* (44), *Summer Holiday* (47), *The Lemon Drop Kid* (51), *Off Limits* (54), *New York Confidential* (55), *Rock-a-bye Baby* (58),

Critic's Choice (62), *Stagecoach to Hell* (64), etc. TV series: *Bus Stop* (61).

MAY, HANS (1891–1959). Viennese composer who settled in Britain in the early 30s. Scores include *The Stars Look Down* (39), *Thunder Rock* (42), *The Wicked Lady* (45), *Brighton Rock* (46), *The Gypsy and the Gentleman* (57), etc.

MAY, JOE (1880–1954) (Joseph Mandel). German director of early serials and thrillers: *Stuart Webb* (15), *Veritas Vincit* (16), *The Hindu Tomb* (21), etc. Best German film probably *Asphalt* (29); later went to Hollywood and directed mainly second features: *The Invisible Man Returns* (40), *The House of Seven Gables* (40), *Hit the Road* (41), *Johnny Doesn't Live Here Any More* (44), etc.

MAYEHOFF, EDDIE (1911–   ). American comic actor, former dance band leader. Chief film appearances: *That's My Boy* (51), *Off Limits* (52), *How to Murder Your Wife* (65).

MAYER, CARL (1894–1944). German writer whose script credits include *The Cabinet of Dr Caligari* (19), *The Last Laugh* (24), *Tartuffe* (26), *Berlin* (27), *Sunrise* (27), etc.

MAYER, GERALD (1919–   ). American director. *The Violent Hour* (50), *Inside Straight* (51), *The Sellout* (52), *Bright Road* (53), *The Marauders* (55), *Diamond Safari* (57), etc.; then to TV.

MAYER, LOUIS B. (1885–1957). American executive, former production head of MGM. Once a scrap merchant, he became a cinema manager and later switched to distribution. With Sam Goldwyn, formed Metro-Goldwyn-Mayer in 1924, and when Goldwyn bought himself out became one of Hollywood's most flamboyant and powerful tycoons until the 50s when he found himself less in touch and responsible to a board. A biography of him was published under the title *Hollywood Rajah*. Special Academy Award 1950 'for distinguished service to the motion picture industry'.

MAYERLING (France 1936). A well-remembered tragic-romantic movie about the love of Austrian Archduke Rudolph for Marie Vetsera. The pair were eventually found dead in a hunting lodge, but the suicide alleged by the film is not totally justified by historical facts: it derives from a novel by Claude Anet. The film made international stars of Charles Boyer and Danielle Darrieux, and led to a Hollywood career for director Anatole Litvak, who in 1956 remade it for TV with Mel Ferrer and Audrey Hepburn. Meanwhile in 1949 Jean Delannoy had made another French version under the title *The Secret of Mayerling*. In 1968 Terence Young concocted an expensive European rehash with Omar Sharif and Catherine Deneuve; despite its length and tedium, there are indications that public fashion is in its favour.

MAYNARD, KEN (1895–). American cowboy star, mainly seen in low-budget features. Once a rodeo rider; broke into films as a stunt man in *Janice Meredith* (24). Later: *Señor Daredevil* (26), *Texas Gunfighter* (32), *Come on, Tarzan* (32), *Wheels of Destiny* (34), *Heir to Trouble* (34), *Wild Horse Stampede* (45), many others.

MAYNARD, KERMIT (1902–). American action player, brother of Ken Maynard. Once doubled for George O'Brien, Victor McLaglen, Warner Baxter and Edmund Lowe. Later: *The Fighting Trooper* (34), *Sandy of the Mounted* (34), *Wild Bill Hickok* (38), many others.

MAYNE, FERDY (1917–). German-born actor, long in Britain; often seen as smooth villain. *Meet Sexton Blake* (debut) (44), *You Know What Sailors Are* (53), *Storm over the Nile* (55), *Ben Hur* (59), *Freud* (62), *Operation Crossbow* (65), *The Bobo* (67), *The Fearless Vampire Killers* (68), many others.

MAYO, ARCHIE (1891–1968). American director with stage experience; in Hollywood from 1916, but sound films were relatively few and far between. *The Sacred Flame* (29), *Svengali* (31), *Night after Night* (32), *Bordertown* (34), *The Petrified Forest* (36), *Black Legion* (36), *The Adventures of Marco Polo* (38), *The House Across the Bay* (40), *The Great American Broadcast* (41), *Moontide* (42), *Charley's American Aunt* (41), *Confirm or Deny* (42), *Crash Dive* (43), *A Night in Casablanca* (45), *Angel on My Shoulder* (46), etc. Inactive after 1946 apart from producing *The Beast of Budapest* (57).

MAYO, VIRGINIA (1922–) (Virginia Jones). American leading lady of the 40s, a former chorus girl who played a few bit parts before being cast as decoration in colour extravaganzas. *Salute to the Marines* (43), *Wonder Man* (45), *The Kid from Brooklyn* (46), *The Best Years of Our Lives* (46), *The Flame and the Arrow* (50), *She's Working Her Way Through College* (52), *King Richard and the Crusaders* (54), *The Big Land* (57), *Young Fury* (64), *Castle of Evil* (66), etc.

MAYSLES, DAVID (1931–) and ALBERT (1933–). American film-making brothers, semi-professional and semi-underground; apart from a number of shorts their main achievements are *Show-Man* (63), a study of Joe Levine, and *Salesman* (69).

MAZURKI, MIKE (1909–) (Mikhail Mazurwski). Immense American character actor of Ukrainian descent; former heavyweight wrestler. Began in Hollywood as an extra. *The Shanghai Gesture* (debut) (41), *Farewell My Lovely* (44), *The French Key* (46), *Unconquered* (47), *Rope of Sand* (49), *Ten Tall Men* (51), *My Favourite Spy* (52), *Blood Alley* (55), *Davy Crockett* (56), *Donovan's Reef* (63), *Cheyenne Autumn* (64), *Seven Women* (66), many others. TV series: *It's About Time* (66).

Mc

MC: see under MAC.

MEDINA, PATRICIA (1920–   ). British leading lady now married to Joseph Cotten and resident in the US. *Simply Terrific* (debut) (38), *The Day Will Dawn* (43), *Hotel Reserve* (43), *Kiss the Bride Goodbye* (44), *Don't Take It to Heart* (44), *The Secret Heart* (46), *The Foxes of Harrow* (47), *Sangaree* (53), *Uranium Boom* (56), *Stranger at My Door* (57), *The Killing of Sister George* (68), etc. Much on TV.

MEDWIN, MICHAEL (1923–   ). British light character comedian, usually seen as Cockney. Stage experience before film debut 1946, *Piccadilly Incident* (46), *Boys in Brown* (49), *Top Secret* (52), *Above Us the Waves* (55), *A Hill in Korea* (56), *I Only Arsked* (58), *Night Must Fall* (63), *Rattle of a Simple Man* (64), *I've Gotta Horse* (65), *The Sandwich Man* (66), many others. Became producer 1967: *Charlie Bubbles* (67), *If* (68), *Spring and Port Wine* (69).

MEEK, DONALD (1880–1946). Scottish-born character actor, long in Hollywood; a bald, worried and timidly respectable little man was his invariable role. *The Hole in the Wall* (debut) (28), *Mrs Wiggs of the Cabbage Patch* (34), *Barbary Coast* (35), *Captain Blood* (35), *Pennies from Heaven* (36), *The Adventures of Tom Sawyer* (38), *Stagecoach* (39), *Tortilla Flat* (42), *They Got Me Covered* (43), *State Fair* (45), *Magic Town* (46), many others.

MEEKER, RALPH (1920–   ) (Ralph Rathgeber). American leading man of the Brando type, with Broadway experience. *Teresa* (debut) (51), *Four in a Jeep* (51), *Shadow in the Sky* (51), *Glory Alley* (52), *The Naked Spur* (53), *Jeopardy* (53), *Code Two* (53), *Big House USA* (54), *Kiss Me Deadly* (as Mike Hammer) (55), *Desert Sands* (56), *Paths of Glory* (58), *Ada* (61), *Something Wild* (62), *The Dirty Dozen* (67), *The St Valentine's Day Massacre* (67), *Gentle Giant* (67), *The Detective* (68), etc.

MEERSON, LAZARE (1900–1938). Russian-born production designer. *An Italian Straw Hat* (28), *Sous les Toits de Paris* (29), *Le Million* (31), *A Nous la Liberté* (32), *La Kermesse Héroïque* (35), *As You Like It* (36), *The Citadel* (38), etc.

MEET JOHN DOE (US 1941). An interesting Frank Capra film in which pessimism almost won the upper hand: the one sane man nearly had to commit suicide in order to bring the grasping connivers to their senses. Otherwise a typically big, sprawling, superbly proficient Capra production with a newspaper setting, written by Robert Riskin with a cast headed by Barbara Stanwyck and Gary Cooper.

MEET ME IN ST LOUIS (US 1944). A somewhat overrated but enjoyable period musical which purveyed charm at a time when it was most needed and can now be seen to have contained much of the best Hollywood talent of the 40s. Simply concerned with the ups-and-downs of a middle-class family at the turn of the century, it was directed by Vincente Minnelli from a script by Irving Brecher and Fred Finklehoffe; the songs were by Hugh Martin and Ralph Blane, and included 'The Trolley Song', 'Have Yourself a Merry Little Christmas', and 'The Boy Next Door'. The cast included Judy Garland, Margaret O'Brien, Leon Ames, Mary Astor and Harry Davenport; and the colour at the time seemed rich and luscious.

MEHBOOB (1907–   ) (Ramjankhan Mehboobkhan). Prolific Indian director, few of whose films have been seen in the West. *Aan* (49), *Mother India* (56), etc.

MEIGHAN, THOMAS (1879–1936). American leading man of the silent screen. *The Trail of the Lonesome Pine* (16), *Male and Female* (19), *The Miracle Man* (19), *The New Klondyke* (21), *Conrad in Quest of His Youth* (22), *Manslaughter* (23), *The Alaskan* (24), *Tin Gods* (26), *The Racket* (27), *Young Sinners* (31), *Peck's Bad Boy* (34), etc.

MEILLON, JOHN (1933–   ). Australian character actor, in Britain from 1960. *On the Beach* (59), *The Sundowners* (59), *Offbeat* (60), *The Valiant* (61), *Billy Budd* (62), *The Running Man* (63), *They're a Weird Mob* (66), etc.

MEKAS, JONAS (1922–   ). American 'underground' film maker, of Lithuanian origin. *The Secret Passions of Salvador Dali* (61), *The Brig* (64), *Hare Krishna* (66), etc. Founder of magazine *Film Culture*. His brother ADOLFAS MEKAS (1925–   ) made the Surrealist comedy *Hallelujah the Hills* (63).

MELCHER, MARTIN (1915–1968). American producer, married to Doris Day and from 1952 the co-producer of all her films: *Calamity Jane* (53), *Julie* (56), *Pillow Talk* (59), *Jumbo* (62), *Move Over, Darling* (63), *Send Me No Flowers* (64), *Where Were You When the Lights Went Out?* (68), etc.

MELCHIOR, IB (1917–   ). Danish-born writer-director, long in US; former actor and set designer. *Angry Red Planet* (w, d) (59), *Reptilicus* (w, d) (61), *The Time Travellers* (w, d) (64), *Robinson Crusoe on Mars* (w) (65), etc. Son of Lauritz Melchior.

MELCHIOR, LAURITZ (1890–   ). Danish operatic tenor, in a few Hollywood films. *Thrill of a Romance* (45), *Two Sisters from Boston* (46), *This Time for Keeps* (47), *Luxury Liner* (48), *The Stars Are Singing* (53), etc.

MELIES, GEORGES (1861–1938). French film pioneer, an ex-conjuror who produced the cinema's first trick films, most of them ambitious and still effective. Credited with being the first to use the dissolve, double exposure, and fades. *Une Partie de Cartes* (debut) (96), *The Artist's Dream* (98), *The Dreyfus Affair* (99), *Cinderella* (1900), *Indiarubber Head* (01), *Voyage to the Moon* (02), *The Kingdom of the Fairies* (03), *The Impossible Voyage* (04), *Twenty Thousand Leagues under the Sea* (07), *Baron Munchausen* (11), *The Conquest of the Pole* (12), many others. After World War I he found his films out of date and his talents unwanted.

MELLOR, WILLIAM C. (1904–1963). American cinematographer. *A Place in the Sun* (AA) (51), *The Naked Spur* (52), *Give a Girl a Break* (53), *Bad Day at Black Rock* (54), *Giant* (56), *The Diary of Anne Frank* (59), *State Fair* (62), etc.

MELTON, JAMES (1904–1961). American operatic tenor, in a few Hollywood films. *Stars over Broadway* (35), *Sing Me a Love Song* (36), *Melody for Two* (37), *Ziegfeld Follies* (45).

MELVILLE, JEAN-PIERRE (1917–). French director, with stage experience. *Le Silence de la Mer* (47), *Les Enfants Terribles* (48), *Quand Tu Liras Cette Lettre* (52), *Bob le Flambeur* (55), *Leon Morin Priest* (61), *Second Wind* (66), etc.

MELVIN, MURRAY (1932–). British light character actor with stage experience in Theatre Workshop. Films include *The Criminal* (debut) (60), *A Taste of Honey* (61), *HMS Defiant* (62), *Sparrows Can't Sing* (63), *The Ceremony* (64), *Alfie* (66).

THE MEN (US 1950). A typical early Stanley Kramer production, making drama out of an urgent real-life problem, in this case that of paraplegics—war veterans paralysed below the waist. Directed by Fred Zinnemann from a script by Carl Foreman, with Marlon Brando, Teresa Wright, Jack Webb and Everett Sloane.

MENDES, LOTHAR (1894–). Hungarian director, mainly in US. *A Night of Mystery* (27), *The Four Feathers* (29), *Payment Deferred* (32), *Jew Suss* (GB) (34), *The Man Who Could Work Miracles* (GB) (36), *Moonlight Sonata* (GB) (38), *International Squadron* (41), *Flight for Freedom* (43), *The Walls Came Tumbling Down* (46), etc.

MENJOU, ADOLPHE (1890–1963). Dapper American leading man and later character actor, once known as the screen's best-dressed man. Stage experience before arriving in Hollywood c. 1919; after roles in *The Sheik* and *The Three Musketeers* he established himself as star of Chaplin's *A Woman of Paris* (23). Also played in French silents. Later: *The Marriage Circle* (23), *The Grand Duchess and the Waiter* (25), *Are Parents People* (25), *The Kiss* (29), *The Front Page* (30), *Morning Glory* (32), *A Farewell to Arms* (32), *The Mighty Barnum* (34), *Little Miss Marker* (34), *Gold Diggers of 1935*, *The Milky Way*

(35), *Wives Never Know* (36), *Sing, Baby, Sing* (36), *One Hundred Men and a Girl* (37), *Stage Door* (37), *The Goldwyn Follies* (38), *Letter of Introduction* (39), *King of the Turf* (39), *The Housekeeper's Daughter* (39), *A Bill of Divorcement* (40), *Turnabout* (40), *Road Show* (41), *Father Takes a Wife* (41), *Roxie Hart* (42), *Syncopation* (42), *You Were Never Lovelier* (42), *Sweet Rosie O'Grady* (43), *Hi Diddle Diddle* (43), *Step Lively* (44), *Man Alive* (45), *Heartbeat* (46), *Bachelor Girls* (47), *The Hucksters* (47), *State of the Union* (48), *Dancing in the Dark* (49), *To Please a Lady* (50), *The Tall Target* (51), *Across the Wide Missouri* (51), *The Sniper* (52), *Man on a Tightrope* (53), *Timberjack* (54), *The Ambassador's Daughter* (56), *Paths of Glory* (58), *Pollyanna* (60), many others. Published autobiography 1952: *It Took Nine Tailors*.

MENZEL, JIRI (1938–   ). Czech director of *Closely Observed Trains* (AA) (66), *Capricious Summer* (68).

MENZIES, WILLIAM CAMERON (1896–1957). American art director, in films from the early twenties. Did memorable work on *The Thief of Bagdad* (24), *The Dove* (AA) (28), *Things to Come* (which he co-directed) (36), *The Adventures of Tom Sawyer* (38), *Gone with the Wind* (AA) (39), *Foreign Correspondent* (40), *Arch of Triumph* (48), *Around the World in Eighty Days* (56). Also directed: *Chandu the Magician* (32), *The Green Cockatoo* (GB) (40), *Address Unknown* (44), *Drums in the Deep South* (51), *Invaders from Mars* (53), etc.

MERCER, BERYL (1882–1939). British character actress, of small stature, in Hollywood from 1923; played mothers, maids, land-ladies. *The Christian* (23), *Seven Days' Leave* (29), *Outward Bound* (30), *Merely Mary Ann* (31), *Supernatural* (32), *Cavalcade* (33), *Berkeley Square* (33), *The Little Minister* (34), *Night Must Fall* (37), *The Hound of the Baskervilles* (39), etc.

MERCER, JOHNNY (1909–   ). American lyricist and composer, active in Hollywood from the early 30s. Songs include 'Blues in the Night', 'Black Magic', 'Something's Got to Give', 'Accentuate the Positive', etc. Film scores include *The Harvey Girls* (AA) (46), *Here Comes the Groom* (AA) (51), *Seven Brides for Seven Brothers* (AA) (54), *Lil Abner* (59), etc.

MERCHANT, VIVIEN (1929–   ) (Ada Thompson). British leading actress, mainly on TV: wife of Harold Pinter. *Alfie* (66), *Accident* (67), etc.

MERCIER, MICHELE (1942–   ). French leading lady, seen abroad in *Retour de Manivelle* (61), *A Global Affair* (US) (63), more recently in a series about the amorous historical adventures of *Angelique*.

MERCOURI, MELINA (1923–   ). Volatile Greek star actress with wide stage experience before film debut in *Stella* (54). Later in international films: *He Who Must Die* (56), *The Gypsy and the Gentleman* (58), *Never on Sunday* (60), *Phaedra* (61), *The Victors* (63), *Topkapi* (64), *A Man Could Get Killed* (65), *10.30 p.m. Summer* (66), etc.

MEREDITH, BURGESS (1909–). American character actor with wide and varied stage experience from 1929. *Winterset* (film debut) (36), *Idiot's Delight* (38), *Of Mice and Men* (39), *That Uncertain Feeling* (41), *Tom, Dick and Harry* (41), *The Story of G.I. Joe* (45), *Diary of a Chambermaid* (45), *Magnificent Doll* (46), *Mine Own Executioner* (GB) (47), *On Our Merry Way* (48), *The Man on the Eiffel Tower* (also directed) (50), *Joe Butterfly* (57), *Advise and Consent* (62), *The Cardinal* (63), *In Harm's Way* (65), *Madame X* (65), *A Big Hand for the Little Lady* (66), *Hurry Sundown* (67), *The Torture Garden* (GB) (67), *Stay Away Joe* (68), *There Was a Crooked Man* (69), etc. TV series: *Mr Novak* (65), and many guest appearances. Still directs stage plays.

MERIVALE, PHILIP (1886–1946). British stage actor who moved to Hollywood in the late 30s. *The Passing of the Third Floor Back* (35), *Rage in Heaven* (40), *This Land Is Mine* (42), *This Above All* (42), *Lost Angel* (44), *The Stranger* (45), etc.

MERKEL, UNA (1903–). American character actress who started in 30s as heroine's girl friend type, now plays mothers and aunts. Stage experience, then became Lilian Gish's double. *Abraham Lincoln* (30), *The Merry Widow* (34), *Saratoga* (37), *Destry Rides Again* (39), *Road to Zanzibar* (41), *This Is the Army* (43), *Twin Beds* (44), *With a Song in My Heart* (52), *The Kentuckian* (55), *The Mating Game* (59), *Summer and Smoke* (62), *A Tiger Walks* (63), *Spinout* (*California Holiday*) (66), many others.

MERMAN, ETHEL (1908–) (Ethel Zimmerman). Vibrant-voiced American musical comedy star, a great song-belter. In occasional films from mid-30s. *We're Not Dressing* (34), *The Big Broadcast of 1936*, *Anything Goes* (36), *Alexander's Ragtime Band* (38), *Call Me Madam* (53), *There's No Business Like Show Business* (54), *It's a Mad Mad Mad Mad World* (63), *The Art of Love* (65), etc. Published biography 1956: *Who Could Ask For Anything More?* (UK title: *Don't Call Me Madam*).

MERRALL, MARY (1890–) (Mary Lloyd). British character actress, on stage from 1907. Films, often in fey or absent-minded roles, include *The Duke's Son* (20), *You Will Remember* (39), *Love on the Dole* (41), *Squadron Leader X* (42), *Dead of Night* (45), *Nicholas Nickleby* (47), *Badger's Green* (48), *The Late Edwina Black* (51), *The Pickwick Papers* (52), *The Belles of St Trinian's* (54), *It's Great To Be Young* (56), *The Camp on Blood Island* (58), *Spare the Rod* (61), *Who Killed the Cat?* (66), many others.

merrie melodies : see *looney tunes.*

MERRILL, DINA (1928–) (Nadina Hutton). American leading lady, and leading socialite. In films from mid-50s. *The Desk Set* (57), *The Sundowners* (59), *The Courtship of Eddie's Father* (63), *The Pleasure Seekers* (64), *I'll Take Sweden* (65), etc. Makes TV appearances.

MERRILL, GARY (1914–). Tough-looking American actor, in films from the mid-40s. *Slattery's Hurricane* (48), *Twelve o'Clock High* (49), *All About Eve* (50), *Decision Before Dawn* (51), *Another Man's Poison* (GB) (51), *Phone Call from a Stranger* (53), *Night Without Sleep* (52), *Blueprint for Murder* (53), *The Human Jungle* (54), *The Black Dakotas* (54), *Bermuda Affair* (56), *The Pleasure of His Company* (61), *The Woman Who Wouldn't Die* (65), *Around the World under the Sea* (66), *Destination Inner Space* (66), *Catacombs* (GB) (66), others. Many TV appearances.

MERRITT, GEORGE (1890–). British character actor of solid presence, usually seen as trades unionist, policeman, or gruff north-country type. Many years on stage. *Dreyfus* (30), *The Lodger* (32), *I Was a Spy* (33), *Dr Syn* (37), *Q Planes* (39), *He Found a Star* (41), *Hatter's Castle* (41), *Waterloo Road* (45), *I'll Be Your Sweetheart* (45), *I'll Turn to You* (46), *Nicholas Nickleby* (47), *Marry Me* (49), *The Green Scarf* (54), *Quatermass II* (57), *Tread Softly Stranger* (58), etc.

MERROW, JANE (1941–). British leading lady. *The Wild and the Willing* (62), *The System* (63), *The Lion in Winter* (68), etc.

THE MERRY WIDOW. Franz Lehar's operetta has been filmed at least three times. 1. US 1925: as a silent, by Erich Von Stroheim, with John Gilbert, Mae Murray and Roy d'Arcy. 2. US 1934: by Ernst Lubitsch, with Maurice Chevalier and Jeanette Macdonald; added lyrics by Gus Kahn and Lorenz Hart. 3. US 1952, by Curtis Bernhardt, with Fernando Lamas, Lana Turner and Richard Haydn; added lyrics by Paul Francis Webster.

MESCALL, JOHN (1899–). American cinematographer. *So This Is Paris* (26), *The Black Cat* (34), *Bride of Frankenstein* (35), *Showboat* (36), *Josette* (38), *Kit Carson* (40), *Dark Waters* (44), *Bedside Manner* (45), *The Desperadoes Are In Town* (56), *Not of This Earth* (57), many others.

MESSEL, OLIVER (1904–). British stage designer who has occasionally worked in films. *The Scarlet Pimpernel* (34), *Romeo and Juliet* (36), *The Thief of Bagdad* (40), *Caesar and Cleopatra* (45), *The Queen of Spades* (48), etc.

Metro-Goldwyn-Mayer. For many years the undoubted leader of the industry, this famous American production company has lately suffered most from the lack of 'front office' control and the proliferation of independent productions: now that it doesn't own the racecourse, it can't seem to pick the winners. The company stems from Loew's Inc, an exhibiting concern which in 1920 bought into Metro Pictures, which then produced two enormous money-spinners, *The Four Horsemen of the Apocalypse* and *The Prisoner of Zenda*. In 1924 Metro was merged with the Goldwyn production company (though Samuel Goldwyn himself promptly opted out and set up independently); and the next year Louis B. Mayer Pictures joined the flourishing group to add further power. Mayer himself became studio head and remained the dominant production force for over twenty-five years. Ideas man and executive producer in the early years was young Irving Thalberg, whose artistic flair provided a necessary corrective to Mayer's proletarian tastes, and who, before his death in 1936, had established a lofty pattern with such successes as *Ben Hur*, *The Big Parade*, *Anna Christie*, *Grand Hotel*, *The Thin Man*, *David Copperfield* and *Mutiny on the Bounty*, and stars like Garbo, Gable, Beery, Lionel Barrymore, Joan Crawford, John Gilbert, Lon Chaney, William Powell, Jean Harlow, Spencer Tracy, Lewis Stone, Nelson Eddy, Jeanette Macdonald, Laurel and Hardy and the Marx Brothers. (MGM's motto was in fact 'more stars than there are in heaven . . .'). The success story continued through the 40s with *Goodbye Mr Chips*, Greer Garson, *The Wizard of Oz*, Judy Garland, the Hardy Family, Gene Kelly and Esther Williams. Such continuity of product is a thing of the past, but MGM keeps its end up with occasional big guns like *Doctor Zhivago*, remakes of *Ben Hur* and *Mutiny on the Bounty*, and a flourishing TV subsidiary.

METROPOLIS (Germany 1926). Fritz Lang's futuristic fantasy, from a script by himself and Thea Von Harbou, details the horrors of a mechanized Utopia. The actual story is a dull revamping of the struggle between capital and labour; but the great geometric sets are imaginatively handled. With Brigitte Helm (as a robot) and Rudolf Klein-Rogge; photographed by Karl Freund.

METTY, RUSSEL (c. 1900–   ). American cinematographer: *Sylvia Scarlett* (35), *Bringing Up Baby* (38), *Music in Manhattan* (44), *The Story of G.I. Joe* (45), *The Stranger* (45), *Ivy* (47), *All My Sons* (48), *We Were Strangers* (49), *Magnificent Obsession* (54), *Man without a Star* (55), *Miracle in the Rain* (56), *Written on the Wind* (56), *Man with a Thousand Faces* (57), *A Time to Love and a Time to Die* (58), *The Misfits* (60), *Spartacus* (AA) (61), *The Art of Love* (65), *The War Lord* (65), *Madame X* (66), *The Appaloosa (Southwest to Sonora)* (66), *The Secret War of Harry Frigg* (67), *Madigan* (68), many others.

MEURISSE, PAUL (1912–   ). French general purpose actor. *Montemartre sur Seine* (41), *Marie la Misère* (45), *Diabolique* (54), *La Tétcontre les Murs* (58), *Lunch on the Grass* (59), *La Vérité* (60), etc.

MEXICAN SPITFIRE. This was the first (1939) of a series of American second-feature comedies which ran till 1943 with such titles as *Mexican Spitfire Sees a Ghost, Mexican Spitfire at Sea*. Donald Woods was a young businessman with a temperamental wife (Lupe Velez), a scheming Uncle Matt (Leon Errol) and a drunken English client, Lord Epping (also played by Leon Errol). The films were only tolerably well made, but always managed a hectic finale of impersonation and mistaken identity which allowed full play to Mr Errol's jerky convulsions.

MEYER, EMILE (C. 1903–   ). American character actor typically cast as crooked cop or prizefight manager; but sometimes an honest Joe. *The People against O'Hara* (51), *Shane* (53), *The Blackboard Jungle* (55), *The Man with the Golden Arm* (56), *Sweet Smell of Success* (57), *Baby Face Nelson* (57), *Paths of Glory* (58), *The Fiend Who Walked the West* (59), *Young Jesse James* (60), *Taggart* (64), *Young Dillinger* (65), *Hostile Guns* (67), etc.

MICHAEL, GERTRUDE (1911–1964). American actress usually seen in secondary roles. *I'm No Angel* (33), *The Notorious Sophie Lang* (lead) (37), *Women in Bondage* (44), *Caged* (50), *Women's Prison* (55), *Twist All Night* (62), etc.

MICHAEL, RALPH (1907–   ) (Ralph Champion Shotter). British character actor of stage and screen, often in stiff-upper-lip roles. *John Halifax Gentleman* (38), *San Demetrio, London* (43), *For Those in Peril* (44), *Dead of Night* (45), *Johnny Frenchman* (45), *The Captive Heart* (46), *Eureka Stockade* (48), *The Astonished Heart* (49), *The Sound Barrier* (52), *King's Rhapsody* (56), *Seven Waves Away* (57), *A Night To Remember* (58), *A Jolly Bad Fellow* (64), *House of Cards* (68), others.

MICHAEL STROGOFF. Jules Verne's historical adventure novel, about espionage in war-torn Russia of 1870, has been a favourite with film makers. Tourjansky made a version with Mosjoukine in 1926. George Nicholls Jnr directed a Hollywood version with Anton Walbrook in 1937. Carmine Gallone made the story again in colour in 1956, with an international cast headed by Curt Jurgens.

MICHELL, KEITH (1926–   ). Australian leading man, on British stage and screen from mid-50s. *True as a Turtle* (57), *Dangerous Exile* (57), *The Gypsy and the Gentleman* (58), *The Hellfire Club* (61), *Seven Seas to Calais* (63), *Prudence and the Pill* (68), *House of Cards* (68), etc.

MICHENER, JAMES A. (1907–   ). American adventure-epic novelist. Works filmed include *South Pacific, Return to Paradise, The Bridges at Toko Ri, Sayonara, Hawaii.*

MIDDLETON, CHARLES (1879–1949). American character actor usually in villainous roles; especially remembered as Ming the Merciless in the Flash Gordon serials. *Mystery Ranch* (32), *Mrs Wiggs of the Cabbage Patch* (34), *Kentucky* (39), *The Grapes of Wrath* (40), *Our Vines Have Tender Grapes* (45), *The Black Arrow* (49), many others.

MIDDLETON, GUY (1906–). Hearty-type British light character actor, in films as amiable idiot or other man since the early 30s after Stock Exchange career. *A Woman Alone* (32), *Fame* (34), *Keep Fit* (37), *French Without Tears* (39), *Dangerous Moonlight* (40), *The Demi-Paradise* (43), *Champagne Charlie* (44), *The Rake's Progress* (45), *The Captive Heart* (46), *One Night with You* (48), *The Happiest Days of Your Life* (49), *Never Look Back* (52), *Albert RN* (53), *The Belles of St Trinian's* (54), *The Passionate Summer* (58), *The Waltz of the Toreadors* (62), etc.

MIDDLETON, ROBERT (1911–) (Samuel G. Messer). Weighty American character actor usually cast as villain. Radio and TV experience before film debut in *The Silver Chalice* (55). Later: *The Big Combo* (55), *The Desperate Hours* (55), *The Court Jester* (55), *The Friendly Persuasion* (56), *The Tarnished Angels* (58), *Career* (59), *Gold of the Seven Saints* (61), *For Those who Think Young* (64), *Big Hand for a Little Lady* (66), many others.

A MIDSUMMER NIGHT'S DREAM. Shakespeare's fairy play was filmed in America in 1929 by J. Stuart Blackton, starring Maurice Costello; and there is a Czechoslovakian puppet version by Jiri Trnka. But the best-known version is Max Reinhardt's lavish production for Warners in 1935, directed by Reinhardt and William Dieterle, with a surprising cast including James Cagney as Bottom, Mickey Rooney as Puck, Hugh Herbert, Arthur Treacher, Dick Powell, Anita Louise, Victor Jory and Olivia de Havilland. Peter Hall's 'realistic' version of 1968, aimed primarily at American TV, was generally thought unsuccessful.

MIFUNE, TOSHIRO (1920–). Versatile Japanese actor seen in many films by Kurosawa and others: *The Drunken Angel* (48), *The Stray Dog* (49), *Rashomon* (50), *Seven Samurai* (54), *The Lower Depths* (57), *Throne of Blood* (57), *The Hidden Fortress* (58), *The Bad Sleep Well* (59), *Yojimbo* (61), *Red Beard* (64), *The Lost World of Sinbad* (64), *Grand Prix* (US) (66), *Rebellion* (67), *Hell in the Pacific* (US) (68), *Tora! Tora! Tora!* (US) (69), etc. Also directed one feature: *Legacy of the Five Hundred Thousand* (63).

MIKE HAMMER. The tough, immoral private eye created by Mickey Spillane (qv for list of films).

MILES, BERNARD (1907–). British actor specializing in slow speaking countryfolk and other ruminating types. An ex-school

master on stage since 1930, films from *Channel Crossing* (32). Later:
Quiet Wedding (40), *In Which We Serve* (42), *Tawny Pipit* (co-author
and director) (44), *Carnival* (46), *Great Expectations* (46), *Nicholas
Nickleby* (47), *The Guinea Pig* (48), *Chance of a Lifetime* (also wrote,
produced and directed) (49), *Never Let Me Go* (53), *The Man Who
Knew Too Much* (56), *Moby Dick* (56), *The Smallest Show on Earth* (57),
Tom Thumb (58), *Sapphire* (59), *Heavens Above* (63), *Run Wild Run
Free* (69), etc. Founder of London's Mermaid Theatre (1959) with
which he is nowadays mainly concerned.

MILES, CHRISTOPHER (1939–   ). British director, brother of Sarah
Miles, *Six-Sided Triangle* (64), *Up Jumped A Swagman* (65), *The
Virgin and the Gypsy* (70).

MILES, PETER (1938–   ) (Gerald Perreau). American child actor
of the 40s, brother of Gigi Perreau. *Passage to Marseilles* (44), *The
Red Pony* (48), *Roseanna McCoy* (50), *Quo Vadis* (51), etc.

MILES, SARAH (1941–   ). British leading lady who came straight to
films from RADA. *Term of Trial* (62), *The Servant* (63), *The
Ceremony* (64), *Those Magnificent Men in Their Flying Machines* (65),
I Was Happy Here (66), *Blow-Up* (66), etc.

MILES, VERA (1929–   ) (Vera Ralston). American leading lady
who came from TV to films. *For Men Only* (debut) (52), *Charge at
Feather River* (54), *23 Paces to Baker Street* (55), *The Searchers* (56),
The Wrong Man (57), *Psycho* (60), *A Tiger Walks* (63), *Those Calloways*
(65), *Follow Me, Boys* (66), *The Spirit is Willing* (66), *Hellfighters* (68),
many others. Innumerable TV guest appearances.

†MILESTONE, LEWIS (1895–   ). Veteran American director whose
later films have never quite matched up to his early achievements.
Former editor, in Hollywood from 1918. *Seven Sinners* (25), *The
Cave Man* (26), *The New Klondike* (26), *Two Arabian Knights* (AA)
(27), *The Garden of Eden* (28), *The Racket* (28), *Betrayal* (29), *New
York Nights* (29), *All Quiet on the Western Front* (AA) (30), *The Front
Page* (31), *Rain* (32), *Hallelujah I'm a Bum* (33), *The Captain Hates
the Sea* (34), *Paris in Spring* (35), *Anything Goes* (36), *The General
Died at Dawn* (36), *Of Mice and Men* (39), *Night of Nights* (40), *Lucky
Partners* (40), *My Life with Caroline* (also produced) (41), *Edge of
Darkness* (43), *North Star* (43), *The Purple Heart* (44), *The Strange
Love of Martha Ivers* (46), *A Walk in the Sun* (46), *No Minor Vices*
(47), *Arch of Triumph* (48), *The Red Pony* (48), *Halls of Montezuma*
(51), *Kangaroo* (52), *Les Misérables* (52), *Melba* (53), *They Who
Dare* (GB) (54), *Pork Chop Hill* (59), *Ocean's Eleven* (61), *Mutiny
on the Bounty* (62).

MILHOLLIN, JAMES (1920–   ). Crumple-faced American character
comedian, mostly on TV. *No Time For Sergeants* (58), *Bon Voyage*
(62), etc.

MILJAN, JOHN (1893–1960), American character actor with stage experience; often played the suave villain. *Love Letters* (23), *The Amateur Gentleman* (26), *The Painted Lady* (29), *The Ghost Walks* (35), *Double Cross* (41), *The Merry Monahans* (44), *The Killers* (46), *Samson and Delilah* (50), *Pirates of Tripoli* (55), etc.

MILLAND, RAY (1905–   ) (Reginald Truscott-Jones). Welsh-born light leading man with ready smile and cheerful disposition; later surprised many by becoming a serious actor and a competent director. *The Plaything* (GB) (29), *The Flying Scotsman* (GB) (31), *Polly of the Circus* (32), *Payment Deferred* (32), *Orders Is Orders* (33), *Bolero* (34), *We're Not Dressing* (34), *The Glass Key* (35), *The Gilded Lily* (35), *The Jungle Princess* (36), *The Return of Sophie Lang* (37), *Easy Living* (37), *Ebb Tide* (37), *Three Smart Girls* (37), *Her Jungle Love* (38), *Men with Wings* (38), *Tropic Holiday* (39), *Beau Geste* (39), *French Without Tears* (GB) (39), *Irene* (40), *Arise My Love* (40), *Untamed* (40), *The Doctor Takes a Wife* (40), *I Wanted Wings* (41), *Skylark* (41), *The Lady Has Plans* (42), *The Major and the Minor* (42), *Reap the Wild Wind* (42), *The Crystal Ball* (43), *Lady in the Dark* (43), *Ministry of Fear* (43), *The Uninvited* (44), *Till We Meet Again* (44), *The Lost Weekend* (as a dipsomaniac) (AA) (45), *Kitty* (45), *The Well-Groomed Bride* (46), *California* (46), *Golden Earrings* (47), *So Evil, My Love* (48), *The Big Clock* (48), *Sealed Verdict* (48), *Alias Nick Beal* (as Satan) (49), *Circle of Danger* (50), *Night into Morning* (51), *Rhubarb* (51), *Something to Live For* (52), *The Thief* (52), *Let's Do It Again* (53), *Dial M for Murder* (54), *A Man Alone* (also directed) (54), *The Girl in the Red Velvet Swing* (55), *Lisbon* (also directed) (56), *Three Brave Men* (57), *The River's Edge* (57), *The Premature Burial* (61), *Panic in Year Zero* (also directed) (62), *The Man with X-Ray Eyes* (63), *The Confession* (65), *Hostile Witness* (GB) (68), others. TV series: *Markham* (59–60).

MILLAR, STUART (1929–   ). American producer. Was Wyler's assistant on *The Desperate Hours* (55) and *The Friendly Persuasion* (56). Solo: *The Young Stranger* (57). *The Young Doctors* (61), *I Could Go On Singing* (63), *The Best Man* (64), etc.

MILLER, ANN (1919–   ) (Lucy Ann Collier). Long-legged American dancer, in films from mid-30s. *New Faces of 1937*, *You Can't Take It With You* (38), *Go West, Young Lady* (41), *Reveille with Beverly* (43), *Jam Session* (44), *Eve Knew Her Apples* (45), *Easter Parade* (48), *On the Town* (49), *Two Tickets to Broadway* (51), *Kiss Me Kate* (53), *The Opposite Sex* (56), etc.

MILLER, ARTHUR (1915–   ). American playwright whose work has frequently been adapted for the cinema: *All My Sons* (48), *Death of a Salesman* (52), *The Witches of Salem* (56), etc. Wrote scenes for

Let's Make Love (60), starring his then wife Marilyn Monroe; also complete screenplay *The Misfits* (61).

MILLER, ARTHUR (c. 1895–   ). Distinguished American cinematographer. *Forever* (21), *The Bluebird* (40), *How Green Was My Valley* (AA) (41), *The Ox Bow Incident* (42), *The Song of Bernadette* (AA) (43), *The Razor's Edge* (46), *Anna and the King of Siam* (AA) (46), *A Letter to Three Wives* (48), *The Gunfighter* (50), many others.

MILLER, COLLEEN (1932–   ). American leading lady. *The Las Vegas Story* (52), *The Purple Mask* (55), *Pay the Devil* (57), *Step Down to Terror* (59), etc.

MILLER, DAVID (1909–   ). American director, formerly editor, in Hollywood from 1930. *Billy the Kid* (41), *Sunday Punch* (42), *Flying Tigers* (43), *Top o' the Morning* (49), *Love Happy* (50), *Our Very Own* (51), *Saturday's Hero* (52), *Sudden Fear* (53), *Diane* (55), *The Opposite Sex* (56), *The Story of Esther Costello* (57), *Midnight Lace* (60), *Back Street* (61), *Lonely Are the Brave* (62), *Captain Newman* (63), *Hammerhead* (GB) (68), etc.

MILLER, GLENN (1904–1944). American bandleader and composer, whose 'new sound' was immensely popular during World War II. Appeared in *Orchestra Wives* (42), *Sun Valley Serenade* (42). Was impersonated by James Stewart in *The Glenn Miller Story* (53).

MILLER, MANDY (1944–   ). British child star of *Mandy* (52); later in *Dance Little Lady* (54), *A Child in the House* (56), *The Snorkel* (61), etc.; also on TV.

MILLER, MARILYN (1898–1936). American dancing and singing star of Broadway musicals in the 20s. Films include *Sally* (30), *Sunny* (31), *Her Majesty Love* (32). She was impersonated by June Haver in a biopic, *Look for the Silver Lining* (49).

MILLER, MARTIN (1899–   ) (Rudolph Muller). Czechoslovakian character actor active in Britain from late 30s. *Squadron Leader X* (40), *The Huggetts Abroad* (51), *Front Page Story* (53), *Libel* (60), *55 Days at Peking* (62), *Children of the Damned* (64), *Up Jumped a Swagman* (65), scores of others; also much on TV.

MILLER, MARVIN (1913–   ) (M. Mueller). American 'tough guy' supporting actor who has represented menaces of various nations. *Johnny Angel* (45), *Intrigue* (47), *The High Window* (47), *Off Limits* (53), *The Shanghai Story* (54), etc.; also does much radio narration, Disney voices, etc.

MILLER. MAX (1895–1963). Ribald British music-hall comedian ('the cheeky chappie'). Starred in several vehicles during 20s but his style had to be considerably toned down for the screen. *The Good Companions* (32), *Friday the Thirteenth* (33), *Princess Charming* (34), *Educated Evans* (36), *Hoots Mon* (40), *Asking for Trouble* (43), etc.

MILLER, PATSY RUTH (1905–   ). American leading lady of the silent screen, former juvenile player. *Camille* (15), *Judgment* (18), *The Hunchback of Notre Dame* (23), *Lorraine of the Lions* (24), *Why Girls Go Back Home* (27), *The Hottentot* (28), *Lonely Wives* (31), etc., then nothing till a small part in *Quebec* (51).

†MILLER, ROBERT ELLIS (1927–   ). American director, from TV. *Any Wednesday* (66), *Sweet November* (68), *The Heart is a Lonely Hunter* (68), *The Buttercup Chain* (69).

MILLER, SETON I. (1902–   ). American silent actor (*Brown of Harvard* [26], etc.) who turned into one of Hollywood's most prolific screenwriters. *Dawn Patrol* (30), *The Criminal Code* (32), *Scarface* (32), *The Adventures of Robin Hood* (38), *Here Comes Mr Jordan* (AA) (41), *The Ministry of Fear* (43), *Two Years Before the Mast* (also produced) (46), *Istanbul* (57), etc.

MILLHAUSER, BERTRAM (1892–1958). American screenwriter mainly engaged on second features, some of them better than average: *The Garden Murder Case* (36), *Sherlock Holmes in Washington* (42) (and others in this series including *Pearl of Death* [44]), *The Invisible Man's Revenge* (44), *Patrick the Great* (45), *Walk a Crooked Mile* (48), *Tokyo Joe* (48), etc.

MILLICAN, JAMES (1910–1955). American general purpose actor, often in low budget westerns. *The Remarkable Andrew* (42), *Bring on the Girls* (44), *Hazard* (47), *Rogues Regiment* (48), etc.

MILLICHIP, ROY (1930–   ). British independent producer. *Girl with Green Eyes* (64), *The Uncle* (65), *I Was Happy Here* (66), *A Nice Girl Like Me* (69), etc.

MILLIGAN, SPIKE (1918–   ) (Terence Alan Milligan), Irish comedian and arch-goon of stage, TV and radio. Occasional films include *The Case of the Mukkinese Battlehorn* (56), *Watch Your Stern* (60), *Suspect* (60), *Invasion Quartet* (61), *Postman's Knock* (62), etc.

LE MILLION (France 1930). Brilliant early sound comedy with music, ranging from slapstick to satire in a zany tale about a search for a lost lottery ticket. Written and directed by René Clair: probably his best film and certainly his most engaging. With René Lefebre, Annabella; photography by Georges Perinal; music by Georges Van Parys, Armand Bernard, Phillipe Pares.

MILLS, HAYLEY (1946–   ). Tomboy British juvenile actress, daughter of John Mills. *Tiger Bay* (59), *Pollyanna* (US) (special AA) (60),

The Parent Trap (US) (61), *Whistle Down the Wind* (61), *Summer Magic* (US) (62), *In Search of the Castaways* (63), *The Chalk Garden* (64), *The Moonspinners* (65), *The Truth about Spring* (65), *Sky West and Crooked* (66), *The Trouble with Angels* (66), *The Family Way* (66), *Pretty Polly* (67), *Twisted Nerve* (68), *Take A Girl Like You* (69), etc.

MILLS, HUGH (c. 1913–   ). British writer. *Blanche Fury* (47), *Blackmailed* (co-w) (50), *Knave of Hearts* (52), *The House by the Lake* (54), *Prudence and the Pill* (68), etc.

MILLS, JOHN (1908–   ). Popular British leading actor, in films from 1933 after musical comedy experience. After many years as a genial stiff-upper-lip type, he became in the 50s a character actor of some versatility. *The Midshipmaid* (32), *Those Were the Days* (34), *Britannia of Billingsgate* (35), *Tudor Rose* (36), *OHMS* (37), *Goodbye Mr Chips* (39), *The Green Cockatoo* (40), *Old Bill and Son* (40), *Cottage To Let* (41), *The Black Sheep of Whitehall* (42), *The Big Blockade* (42), *The Young Mr Pitt* (42), *In Which We Serve* (42), *We Dive at Dawn* (43), *This Happy Breed* (44), *Waterloo Road* (44), *The Way to the Stars* (45), *Great Expectations* (46), *The October Man* (47), *So Well Remembered* (47), *Scott of the Antarctic* (48), *The History of Mr Polly* (also produced) (49), *The Rocking Horse Winner* (also produced) (49), *Morning Departure* (50), *Mr Denning Drives North* (41), *The Long Memory* (52), *The Colditz Story* (53), *Above Us the Waves* (54), *Escapade* (55), *It's Great To Be Young* (56), *The Baby and the Battleship* (56), *War and Peace* (56), *Town on Trial* (57), *The Vicious Circle* (57), *Ice Cold in Alex* (58), *I Was Monty's Double* (58), *Dunkirk* (58), *Tiger Bay* (59), *Summer of the Seventeenth Doll* (59), *The Swiss Family Robinson* (US) (60), *Tunes of Glory* (60), *The Singer Not the Song* (61), *Flame in the Streets* (61), *Tiara Tahiti* (62), *The Chalk Garden* (64), *The Truth about Spring* (65), *Operation Crossbow* (65), *King Rat* (65), *Sky West and Crooked* (directed only) (66), *The Wrong Box* (66), *The Family Way* (66), *Africa Texas Style* (67), *Chuka* (US) (67), *Lady Hamilton* (Ger.) (68), *Oh What a Lovely War* (69), *Run Wild, Run Free* (69), *Return of the Boomerang* (70), etc. TV series: *Dundee and the Culhane* (67).

MILLS, JULIET (1941–   ). British leading lady, daughter of John Mills and sister of Hayley. *No My Darling Daughter* (debut) (61), *Twice Round the Daffodils* (62), *Nurse on Wheels* (63), *Carry on, Jack* (64), *The Rare Breed* (US) (66), etc.

MILNER, MARTIN (1927–   ). Youthful-looking American actor, best known as a co-star of the *Route 66* TV series. Films include *Life with Father* (debut) (47), *Our Very Own* (50), *I Want You* (52), *Pete Kelly's Blues* (55), *The Sweet Smell of Success* (57), *Marjorie Morningstar* (58), *Thirteen Ghosts* (60), *Sullivan's County* (67), *Valley*

671

of the Dolls (67), etc. TV series: *The Trouble With Father* (53–55), *The Life of Riley* (56–57), *Adam 12* (68–69).

MILTON, BILLY (1905–   ). British light actor of the 30s, now in small parts. *Young Woodley* (30), *Three Men in a Boat* (33), *Someone at the Door* (36), *Aren't Men Beasts* (37), *Yes Madam* (39), etc. Also singer, pianist and composer.

MILTON, ERNEST (1890–   ). American-born Shakespearean actor with long theatrical history on both sides of the Atlantic. Few film appearances, in small parts, include *A Wisp in the Woods* (17), *The Scarlet Pimpernel* (34), *Fiddlers Three* (44).

MIMIEUX, YVETTE (1939–   ). American leading lady signed up for films almost straight from college. *The Time Machine* (debut) (60), *Where the Boys Are* (61), *The Four Horsemen of the Apocalypse* (62), *The Light in the Piazza* (62), *The Wonderful World of the Brothers Grimm* (63), *Diamondhead* (63), *Joy in the Morning* (65), *Monkeys Go Home* (66), *The Caper of the Golden Bulls* (67), *Dark of the Sun* (67), *Three in an Attic* (68), etc.

MINE OWN EXECUTIONER (GB 1947). Hailed as the first 'adult' film to come out of post-war Britain, this interesting melodrama from Nigel Balchin's novel had Burgess Meredith as a lay psychiatrist unsure how to handle a homicidal patient. Directed by Anthony Kimmins.

MINEO, SAL (1939–   ). Diminutive American actor, on Broadway as a child before going to Hollywood. *Six Bridges to Cross* (debut) (55), *Rebel without a Cause* (55), *Somebody Up There Likes Me* (57), *Tonka* (58), *Exodus* (60), *Escape from Zahrain* (62), *Cheyenne Autumn* (64), *The Greatest Story Ever Told* (65), *Who Killed Teddy Bear?* (66), *Krakatoa* (68), etc.

MINER, ALLEN H. (* –   ). American director. *Ghost Town* (55), *The Ride Back* (57), *Black Patch* (also produced) (57), *Chubasco* (67), etc.

MINNELLI, LIZA (1946–   ). American singer-actress, daughter of Judy Garland and Vincente Minnelli. Film debut: *Charlie Bubbles* (67); then *The Sterile Cuckoo* (69), *Tell Me That You Love Me* (70).

†MINNELLI, VINCENTE (1913–   ). American director who earned a reputation as a stylist with MGM musicals but whose other output has been very variable. Stage experience as art director and producer. *Cabin in the Sky* (43), *I Dood It* (43), *Ziegfeld Follies* (44), *Meet Me in St Louis* (44), *Under the Clock* (44), *Yolanda and the Thief* (45), *Undercurrent* (46), *The Pirate* (47), *Madame Bovary* (49), *Father of the Bride* (50), *Father's Little Dividend* (51), *An American in Paris* (51), *The Bad and the Beautiful* (52), *The Story of Three Loves* (part) (52),

The Band Wagon (53), *The Long, Long Trailer* (54), *Brigadoon* (54), *Kismet* (55), *The Cobweb* (55), *Lust for Life* (56), *Tea and Sympathy* (56), *Designing Woman* (57), *Gigi* (AA) (58), *The Reluctant Debutante* (58), *Some Came Running* (58), *Home from the Hill* (59), *Bells Are Ringing* (60), *The Four Horsemen of the Apocalypse* (62), *Two Weeks in Another Town* (62), *The Courtship of Eddie's Father* (63), *Goodbye Charlie* (65), *The Sandpiper* (65), *On A Clear Day You Can See Forever* (69).

MINNEY, R. J. (1895–   ). British producer and screenwriter, former journalist, in films since 1934. Wrote *Clive of India* (35), *Dear Octopus* (42), *Carve Her Name with Pride* (58), many others; produced *Madonna of the Seven Moons* (44), *The Wicked Lady* (45), *The Final Test* (53), *Carve Her Name with Pride* (58), etc.

MINTER, GEORGE (1911–1966). British producer-distributor, in films from 1938. For his company, Renown, made such films as *The Glass Mountain* (48), *Tom Brown's Schooldays* (50), *Pickwick Papers* (52), *The Rough and the Smooth* (58), scores of others.

MINTER, MARY MILES (1902–   ) (Juliet Shelby). American silent screen heroine, in films from 1915. *Barbara Frietchie* (15), *Anne of Green Gables* (18), *Moonlight and Honeysuckle* (21), *Trail of the Lonesome Pine* (23), *The Drums of Fate* (24), many others.

MIRACLE IN MILAN (Italy 1951). Beguiling fantasy about a colony of shantytown poor led by a young idealist whose fervency gives him the power to work miracles and finally flies them all on broomsticks to another, better place. Directed by Vittorio de Sica with a strong element of René Clair; written by Cesare Zavattini and others; with special effects by Ned Mann. By its indirect methods the film managed to make as much protest about post-war conditions as its predecessor *Bicycle Thieves*.

THE MIRACLE OF MORGAN'S CREEK (US 1943). An outrageous satirical farce, written and directed in whirlwind style by Preston Sturges, about a small-town girl who gets drunk at an army party, marries a soldier whose name she thinks is Ratskywatsky, can't find him, and has terrible trouble getting someone else to marry her without admitting she's pregnant; finally becomes a heroine by presenting the nation with sextuplets. Funny? Oddly enough, very, and fast enough to stop tastelessness from creeping in. Apart from the usual Sturges repertory company, the film is well served by Betty Hutton and Eddie Bracken, by Diana Lynn as the heroine's sharp young sister, and especially by William Demarest as her father, the outraged Officer Kockenlocker. Prudes could console themselves with the thought that the film made quite a comment on the morals of the nation in time of war.

Miracle on 34th Street

MIRACLE ON 34TH STREET (US 1946) (British title: *The Big Heart*). A charming, endearing piece of whimsy in Hollywood's best style, with Edmund Gwenn as a benevolent old fellow who may or may not be Santa Claus. Never nauseating in its abundance of goodwill towards men, the film moves smoothly to a hilarious courtroom climax in the Capra manner. Written and directed by George Seaton against pleasantly-observed New York backgrounds.

MIRANDA (GB 1948). A mild British comedy about a mermaid (played by Glynis Johns) which had sufficient moments of hilarity to call for a sequel (*Mad about Men*) and a Hollywood imitation (*Mr Peabody and the Mermaid*).

MIRANDA, CARMEN (1904–1955) (Maria de Carmo Miranda de Cunha). American singer, the 'Brazilian Bombshell'; always fantastically over-dressed and harshly made-up, yet emitting a force of personality which was hard to resist. *Down Argentine Way* (debut) (40), *That Night in Rio* (41), *Weekend in Havana* (41), *Four Jills in a Jeep* (44), *Greenwich Village* (44), *Copacabana* (47), *A Date with Judy* (48), *Nancy Goes to Rio* (50), *Scared Stiff* (53), etc.

MIRANDA, ISA (1909–   ) (Ines Isabella Sanpietro). Italian star actress. Occasional films include *Hotel Imperial* (US) (40), *Adventure in Diamonds* (US) (41), *La Ronde* (Fr.) (50), *Summertime* (GB) (55), *The Yellow Rolls-Royce* (GB) (64).

THE MIRISCH BROTHERS: Harold (1907–1968), Marvin (1918–   ), Walter (1921–   ). American producers, founders in 1957 of the Mirisch company, one of the most successful independent production groups since the decline of the big studios. Formerly the two elder brothers had been exhibitors, the youngest a producer of cheap second features: the 'Bomba' series, etc. *Man of the West* (58), *The Magnificent Seven* (60), *West Side Story* (61), *Two for the See-Saw* (62), *The Great Escape* (63), *Toys in the Attic* (63), *The Satan Bug* (65), *The Russians Are Coming, The Russians Are Coming* (66), *What Did You Do in the War, Daddy?* (66), *Hawaii* (66), *The Fortune Cookie* (66), *In the Heat of the Night* (68), etc. Now making TV series: *The Rat Patrol*, etc.

MIROSLAVA (1930–1955) (Miroslava Stern). Greek-American actress who appeared in *The Brave Bulls* (51), *Stranger on Horseback* (55).

mirrors have a clear psychological fascination, and cameramen have frequently derived dramatic compositions from the use of them. Innumerable characters have talked to their reflections, and *The Man in the Mirror* changed places with his. *Dracula* and his kind cast no reflection; a switch on this was provided in *The Gorgon*, where looking at the monster turned one to stone, but looking at her through a mirror was OK. In *The Lady in the Lake* Robert

674

Montgomery played the lead from the position of the camera lens, so the only time we saw him was when he looked in a mirror. Then there was the magic mirror in *Snow White and the Seven Dwarfs*, which told the queen all she wanted to hear; and the more evil magic mirror in *Dead of Night*, which had belonged to a murderer and caused Ralph Michael when he looked in it to strangle his wife. Two-way mirrors are now familiar, especially since *From Russia With Love*; but they were used as long ago as 1946 in *The House on 92nd Street*. In *Orphée* a full-length mirror proved liquid to the touch and was the doorway to the other world. *The Lady from Shanghai* had a splendidly confusing finale in a mirror maze which was gradually shot to pieces; *Up Tight* made dramatic use of a distorting mirror arcade. The most-used mirror joke is that in which the glass is broken and a 'double' tries to take the place of the reflection: Max Linder performed it in 1919 in *Seven Years Bad Luck*, and it was superbly reprised by the Marx Brothers in *Duck Soup* (33), and by Abbott and Costello in *The Naughty Nineties* (45).

THE MISFITS (US 1961). A sad film, over-loaded with talent, notable chiefly for the last appearance of both Clark Gable and Marilyn Monroe, whose then husband Arthur Miller wrote the heavy-going script about cowboys on a savage hunt for wild mustangs. John Huston's direction was lethargic. This kind of pseudo-highbrow non-money-maker would in the old days have been vetoed at script stage by the studio's front office; failures like this are the price of independence.

MISRAKI, PAUL (1908–). French composer. *Retour à l'Aube* (38), *Battement de Cœur* (39), *Manon* (48), *Confidential Report* (55), *Les Cousins* (59), *Alphaville* (65), etc.

MISS JULIE. Strindberg's play about a nobleman's daughter who commits suicide because she loves a valet was filmed in 1912 (Sweden), 1921 (Germany) and 1947 (Argentina), but the best-known version was written and directed by Alf Sjoberg in Sweden (1951) with Anita Bjork and Ulf Palme.

MISSION TO MOSCOW (US 1942). A remarkable semi-documentary made by Warners as a modern addendum to their biographical series. Based on U.S. Ambassador Joseph Davies's account of his dealings with the Russians between 1936 and 1941, it was notable for its impersonations of living politicians: Churchill, Stalin, Roosevelt, etc. Walter Huston was ideally cast as Davies, and Michael Curtiz directed with his usual expertise.

MR BLANDINGS BUILDS HIS DREAM HOUSE (US 1948). A highly civilized and likeable American domestic comedy from the delightful book by Eric Hodgins; it shows Hollywood in the late 40s getting its

675

humour a little nearer to life and away from the studio. H. C. Potter directs with quiet aplomb, and no one would wish for a better husband, wife and friend of the family than Cary Grant, Myrna Loy and Melvyn Douglas as they doggedly build a house in Connecticut.

MR DEEDS GOES TO TOWN (US 1936). The first of the big social comedies of the 30s, directed by Frank Capra (AA), demonstrating the victory of small-town innocence and good intentions over big city sophistication. Gary Cooper was perfectly cast as the naïve hero who refuses to be swindled out of a huge legacy even though he may be a little 'pixillated'. Robert Riskin wrote the script, which today seems slow-moving. In 1969 a TV series starring Monte Markham was based on the original script.

MR MAGOO. Myopic, bumbling cartoon character created by UPA in the early 50s and voiced by Jim Backus. He quickly became a bore, but some of the early shorts were outstandingly funny: *Barefaced Flatfoot*, *Fuddy Duddy Buddy*, *Spellbound Hound*, etc.

MR MOTO. A Japanese detective created by novelist John P. Marquand and played in nearly a dozen films by Peter Lorre: from *Think Fast Mr Moto* in 1937 to *Mr Moto Takes a Vacation* in 1939. In 1965 Henry Silva played the role in an unsuccessful second feature.

MR SMITH GOES TO WASHINGTON (US 1939). Another of Frank Capra's 30s social comedies, a kind of 'Mr Deeds in Politics' with James Stewart as the idealistic young senator from Wisconsin who uproots the evil of Claude Rains. This is a beautifully-made picture which judges all its effects exactly and remains consistently entertaining for over two hours. It was the last of its type: World War II made America's country cousins more sophisticated than Capra could have imagined. Among a superb cast were Jean Arthur, Guy Kibbee, Thomas Mitchell, H. B. Warner, Edward Arnold, Harry Carey, Eugene Pallette and William Demarest. The script is by Sidney Buchman.

MRS MINIVER (US 1942). Hollywood's emotional tribute to England's women in wartime was never a good film, but its sentimentality and its never-never picture of the English middle-class scene made it an enormous box-office hit even though most people privately jibed at it afterwards and it had absolutely no reissue value. It now seems a quaint curiosity, with Greer Garson tending the roses while Walter Pidgeon dashes off to rescue some chaps from Dunkirk. William Wyler directed fluently in the circumstances; among the many contributors to the script were Arthur Wimperis and James Hilton, who should have known better. However, the film won Academy Awards for Garson, Wyler, the scriptwriters, and the photographer Joe Ruttenberg; it was also named best film. In

1950 a sequel was made showing Mrs Miniver dying of cancer, but not surprisingly *The Miniver Story* flopped.

MITCHELL, CAMERON (1918–   ). American actor, ex-radio commentator and Broadway player. *They Were Expendable* (45), *Command Decision* (48), *Death of a Salesman* (52), *Love Me or Leave Me* (55), *Monkey on My Back* (57), *The Last of the Vikings* (61), *Blood and Black Lace* (65), *Minnesota Clay* (It.) (66), *Hombre* (67), *Monster of the Wax Museum* (67), many others. TV series: *High Chaparral*.

MITCHELL, GRANT (1874–1957). American character actor, often seen as a worried father, lawyer or small-town politician. *Man to Man* (31), *Dinner at Eight* (33), *The Life of Émile Zola* (37), *New Moon* (40), *Tobacco Road* (41), *The Man Who Came to Dinner* (41), *Orchestra Wives* (42), *Father is a Prince* (43), *Arsenic and Old Lace* (44), *Blondie's Anniversary* (48), many others.

MITCHELL, GUY (1927–   ). Boyish, stocky American singer with a brief career in films: *Those Redheads from Seattle* (53), *Red Garters* (54), etc. TV series: *Whispering Smith*. Real name: Al Cernick.

MITCHELL, JULIEN (1888–1954). British stage character actor who made film debut as a crazed train driver in *The Last Journey* (36). Later: *It's in the Air* (37), *The Drum* (38), *The Sea Hawk* (US) (40), *Hotel Reserve* (44), *Bedelia* (46), *Bonnie Prince Charlie* (48), *The Galloping Major* (51), *Hobson's Choice* (54), etc.

MITCHELL, LESLIE (1905–   ). British commentator and broadcaster; the voice of British Movietone News from 1938; co-author of a 1946 book 'The March of the Movies'.

MITCHELL, MARGARET (1900–49). American author of the novel on which Hollywood's most famous film, *Gone with the Wind*, was based.

MITCHELL, MILLARD (1900–1953). Nasal-voiced, rangy American character actor, in films from 1940. *Mr and Mrs Smith* (40), *Grand Central Murder* (42), *A Double Life* (47), *A Foreign Affair* (48), *Twelve o'Clock High* (49), *The Gunfighter* (50), *My Six Convicts* (52), *Singin' in the Rain* (52), *The Naked Spur* (52), *Here Come the Girls* (53), etc.

MITCHELL, OSWALD (c. 1890–1949). British director. *Old Mother Riley* (37), *Danny Boy* (41), *The Dummy Talks* (43), *Loyal Heart* (46), *Black Memory* (47), *The Greed of William Hart* (47), *The Man from Yesterday* (49), etc.

MITCHELL, THOMAS (1892–1962). Irish-American character actor of great versatility; could be tragic or comic, evil or humane. Former reporter, Broadway star and playwright; in Hollywood from mid-30s. *Craig's Wife* (debut) (36), *Theodora Goes Wild* (36), *Lost Horizon* (37), *Make Way for Tomorrow* (37), *The Hurricane* (38), *Mr Smith*

Goes to Washington (39), *Stagecoach* (AA) (39), *Gone with the Wind* (39), *Only Angels Have Wings* (39), *The Hunchback of Notre Dame* (40), *Three Cheers for the Irish* (40), *Our Town* (40), *The Long Voyage Home* (40), *Angels over Broadway* (40), *Out of the Fog* (41), *Song of the Islands* (42), *This Above All* (42), *Moontide* (42), *The Black Swan* (42), *The Immortal Sergeant* (43), *The Outlaw* (43), *Bataan* (43), *The Sullivans* (44), *Wilson* (44), *Buffalo Bill* (44), *Dark Waters* (44), *The Keys of the Kingdom* (44), *The Dark Mirror* (45), *It's a Wonderful Life* (45), *Adventure* (46), *High Barbaree* (47), *Silver River* (47), *Alias Nick Beal* (49), *The Big Wheel* (50), *High Noon* (52), *The Secret of the Incas* (54), *Destry* (55), *While the City Sleeps* (56), *Too Young for Love* (GB) (59), *A Pocketful of Miracles* (61), others. TV series: *O. Henry Playhouse* (56), *Glencannon* (58).

MITCHELL, WARREN (1926–   ). British comedy character actor, mainly on TV, especially in series *Till Death Us Do Part*. Films include *Tommy the Toreador* (60), *Postman's Knock* (62), *Where Has Poor Mickey Gone?* (63), *The Intelligence Men* (65), *Arrivederci Baby* (66), *Till Death Us Do Part* (68), *The Assassination Bureau* (68), *The Best House in London* (69), *All the Way Up* (70), many others.

MITCHELL, YVONNE (1925–   ). British actress and playwright, on stage from 1940. *The Queen of Spades* (film debut) (48), *Turn the Key Softly* (53), *The Divided Heart* (54), *Yield to the Night* (56), *Woman in a Dressing Gown* (57), *The Passionate Summer* (58), *Tiger Bay* (59), *Sapphire* (59), *The Trials of Oscar Wilde* (61), *The Main Attraction* (63), *Genghis Khan* (65), etc. Published autobiography 1957: *Actress*.

MITCHUM, JAMES (1938–   ). American actor, son of Robert Mitchum. Infrequent films include *Thunder Road* (debut) (58), *The Young Guns of Texas* (62), *The Victors* (63), *The Tramplers* (66).

MITCHUM, ROBERT (1917–   ). Sleepy-eyed American leading man who sometimes hides his talent behind an excess of mannerisms. Entered films by playing bit parts in Hopalong Cassidy Westerns, but quickly established himself after World War II. *We've Never Been Licked* (43), *Hoppy Serves a Writ* (43), *Gung Ho* (43), *When Strangers Marry* (44), *Nevada* (44), *Thirty Seconds over Tokyo* (44), *The Story of G.I. Joe* (first notable role) (45), *Undercurrent* (46), *Till the End of Time* (46), *The Locket* (46), *Pursued* (47), *Out of the Past* (*Build My Gallows High*) (47), *Desire Me* (47), *Crossfire* (47), *Rachel and the Stranger* (48), *Blood on the Moon* (48), *The Red Pony* (48), *The Big Steal* (49), *Where Danger Lives* (50), *My Forbidden Past* (51), *His Kind of Woman* (51), *Macao* (52), *One Minute to Zero* (52), *The Racket* (52), *The Lusty Men* (52), *Angel Face* (52), *White Witch Doctor* (53), *River of No Return* (54), *Track of the Cat* (54), *Not as a Stranger* (55), *Foreign Intrigue* (56), *Bandido* (56), *Heaven Knows Mr Alison* (57), *Fire Down Below* (GB) (57), *The Wonderful Country* (58), *Thunder*

Road (58), *The Angry Hills* (GB) (59), *Home from the Hill* (59), *The Sundowners* (60), *A Terrible Beauty* (GB) (60), *The Grass Is Greener* (GB) (60), *The Last Time I Saw Archie* (62), *Cape Fear* (62), *Two for the Seesaw* (63), *What a Way To Go* (64), *Mister Moses* (65), *El Dorado* (66), *The Way West* (67), *Villa Rides* (68), *Anzio* (68), *Five Card Stud* (68), *Secret Ceremony* (68), *Young Billy Young* (69), etc.

MIX, TOM (1880–1940). A US Marshal who turned actor and starred in over 400 low-budget Westerns. *The Ranch Life in the Great Southwest* (10), *Child of the Prairie* (13), *Cupid's Round-Up* (18), *Tom Mix in Arabia* (22), *North of Hudson Bay* (24), *The Last Trail* (27), *Destry Rides Again* (27), *My Pal the King* (32), *The Terror Trail* (33), etc.

MIZOGUCHI, KENJI (1898–1956). Japanese director, former actor. Directed from 1923, though few of his films were seen in the West. *A Paper Doll's Whisper of Spring* (25), *The Gorge between Love and Hate* (32), *The Story of the Last Chrysanthemums* (39), *Woman of Osaka* (40), *The Forty-nine Ronin* (42), *The Life of O'Haru* (52), *Ugetsu Monogatari* (52), *Street of Shame* (56), many others.

MOBLEY, MARY ANN (1939–). American leading lady, former 'Miss America'. *Girl Happy* (65), *Three on a Couch* (66), etc.

MOBY DICK. Herman Melville's allegorical novel about the pursuit by an obsessed sea captain of a white whale, has been seen on the screen in at least three versions, all American. 1. *The Sea Beast* (26), directed by Millard Webb, with John Barrymore, Dolores Costello and George O'Hara. 2. *Moby Dick* (30), directed by Lloyd Bacon, with John Barrymore, Joan Bennett and Lloyd Hughes. 3. *Moby Dick* (56), directed by John Huston, with Gregory Peck, Richard Basehart and no feminine lead.

MOCKRIDGE, CYRIL (1896–). British-born composer in America from 1921, films from 1932. Scores include *The Sullivans* (44), *My Darling Clementine* (46), *How to Marry a Millionaire* (53), *Many Rivers to Cross* (55), *Flaming Star* (60), many others.

MOCKY, JEAN-PIERRE (1929–) (Jean Mokiejeswki). French director. *Un Couple* (60), *Snobs* (62), *Les Vierges* (63), *La Bourse et la Vie* (65), *Les Compagnons de la Marguerite* (67), etc.

MODERN TIMES (US 1936). The film in which Chaplin's voice was first heard—though only in a gibberish song. Basically this is a dated—almost period—sociological comedy about how to be happy though poor in the machine age. Best to forget the propaganda and see it as a wonderful series of hilarious gags, impeccably timed and edited; in fact, one of Chaplin's most consistently funny films. As usual, he wrote (words and music), directed, produced and starred; Paulette Goddard played the waif.

MOFFATT, GRAHAM (1919–1965). British actor, fondly remembered as the impertinent fat boy of the Will Hay comedies: *Oh Mr Porter* (38), *Ask a Policeman* (39), *Where's That Fire* (40), etc. Other films include *A Cup of Kindness* (debut) (34), *Dr Syn* (38), *I Thank You* (41), *I Know Where I'm Going* (45), many others. Retired to keep a pub, but made very occasional appearances: *The Second Mate* (50), *Inn for Trouble* (59), *Eighty Thousand Suspects* (63).

MOFFETT, SHARYN (1936–). American child actress of the 40s. *My Pal Wolf* (44), *The Body Snatcher* (45), *Child of Divorce* (47), *The Judge Steps Out* (47), *Mr Blandings Builds His Dream House* (48), *Girls Never Tell* (51), etc.

MOGUY, LEONIDE (1899–) (L. Maguilevsky). Russian newsreel producer, later in France and US as director. *Prison Without Bars* (38), *The Night Is Ending* (43), *Action in Arabia* (44), *Whistle Stop* (46), *Tomorrow Is Too Late* (50), etc.

MOHNER, CARL (1921–). Austrian actor in films from 1949. *Rififi* (55), *He Who Must Die* (56), *The Key* (58), *Camp on Blood Island* (58), *The Kitchen* (61), etc.

MOHR, GERALD (1914–1968). Suave American actor, in films from 1941; played the 'Lone Wolf', a gentleman crook, in a mid-40s series. Also in *The Monster and the Girl* (41), *Ten Tall Men* (51), *Detective Story* (53), *The Eddie Cantor Story* (53), *Angry Red Planet* (59), *Funny Girl* (68), innumerable others; and on TV.

MOHR, HAL (1894–). American cinematographer, in Hollywood from 1915. *Little Annie Rooney* (25), *The Jazz Singer* (27), *Noah's Ark* (28), *King of Jazz* (30), *A Midsummer Night's Dream* (co-ph) (AA) (35), *Green Pastures* (36), *Rio* (39), *Phantom of the Opera* (43), *The Climax* (44), *The Lost Moment* (48), *The Big Night* (51), *The Wild One* (54), *The Gun Runners* (58), *The Last Voyage* (60), *The Man from the Diners' Club* (64), many others.

MOLANDER, GUSTAF (1888–). Veteran Swedish director, former actor and writer (including *Sir Arne's Treasure* [19]). Directing since 1922, but few of his films have been seen abroad: *Sin* (28), *Intermezzo* (36), *A Woman's Face* (38), *Woman without a Face* (47), *Sir Arne's Treasure* (remake) (55), many others.

MOLINARO, EDOUARD (1928–). French director. *Evidence in Concrete* (*Le Dos au Mur*) (57), *Girls for the Summer* (60), *A Ravishing Idiot* (63), *The Gentle Art of Seduction* (64), etc.

MONDO CANE (Italy 1961). The first of many so-called documentaries consisting of a ramshackle collection of true incidents showing humanity at its most ignorant and depraved, mostly involving sex, sadism or paranoia. Director Jacopetti meanwhile found the business very profitable, and after watching his many imitators, produced in 1965 his *Mondo Cane 2*, showing that the field of degradation is far from exhausted.

MONDY, PIERRE (1925–   ) (Pierre Cuq). French actor. *Rendezvous de Juillet* (49), *Sans Laisser d'Adresse* (50), *Les Louves* (57), *Austerlitz* (as Napoleon) (60), *Bebert et l'Omnibus* (63), etc.

MONICELLI, MARIO (1915–   ). Italian director. *Cops and Robbers* (co-d) (51), *Persons Unknown* (58), *Boccacio 70* (part) (61), *The Organizer* (63), *Casanova 70* (66), etc.

THE MONKEES sprang to fame in an American TV series of that title (66–67). They are a pop quartet deliberately recruited by Screen Gems to emulate the Beatles in crazy comedy with music; their ensuing popularity surprised not only themselves but their sponsors, and in 1969 they made a movie called *Head*. Individually they are: PETER TORK (1942–   ) (Peter Torkelson); MIKE NESMITH (1943–   ); MICKY DOLENZ (1945–   ), who is the son of George Dolenz and previously starred in the TV series *Circus Boy* (56–57); DAVY JONES (1944–   ), the only Britisher in the group.

MONKHOUSE, BOB (1928–   ). British comedian of TV, radio and occasional films (from 1949). *Carry On, Sergeant* (58), *Dentist in the Chair* (59), *Weekend with Lulu* (61), *She'll Have to Go* (61), *The Bliss of Mrs Blossom* (68), etc. TV series: *Mad Movies*.

monks in films have usually been caricatures of the Friar Tuck type; Tuck himself turned up, personified by Eugene Pallette or Alexander Gauge, in most of the versions of Robin Hood (qv). The funny side of monastery life was presented in *Crooks in Cloisters*, while milder humour came from Edward G. Robinson's conversion to the simple life in *Brother Orchid*. Serious crises of the monastic spirit have been treated in two American films, *The Garden of Allah* and *The First Legion*; but on the whole monks have appealed less than priests to film-makers in search of an emotional subject. See also: *Nuns; Priests; Churches*.

Monogram Pictures: see *Allied Artists*

†MONROE, MARILYN (1926–1962) (Norma Jane Baker or Mortenson). American leading lady, a former model whose classic rags-to-riches story was built on a super-sexy image which quickly tarnished, leaving her a frustrated, neurotic and tragic victim of the Hollywood which created her. The pity was that she had real talent as well as sex appeal. *Dangerous Years* (48), *Ladies of the Chorus* (48), *Love Happy* (50), *A Ticket to Tomahawk* (50), *The Asphalt Jungle* (50), *All About Eve* (50), *The Fireball* (50), *Right Cross* (50), *Home Town Story* (51), *As Young as You Feel* (51), *Love Nest* (51), *Let's Make It*

x*   681

Legal (51), *We're Not Married* (52), *Clash by Night* (52), *Full House* (52), *Monkey Business* (52), *Don't Bother to Knock* (52), *Niagara* (here the build-up really started) (52), *Gentlemen Prefer Blondes* (53), *How to Marry a Millionaire* (53), *River of No Return* (54), *There's No Business Like Show Business* (54), *The Seven-Year Itch* (55), *Bus Stop* (56), *The Prince and the Showgirl* (GB) (57), *Some Like It Hot* (59), *Let's Make Love* (60), *The Misfits* (60). *Marilyn*, a compilation feature, was released after her death. Several biographies have been published.

MONROE, VAUGHAN (1911–   ). American bandleader who unexpectedly appeared as hero of a few westerns. *Meet the People* (44), *Carnegie Hall* (47), *Singing Guns* (50), *The Toughest Man in Arizona* (52), etc.

MONSIEUR BEAUCAIRE. Booth Tarkington's light novel about a barber who impersonates the King of France was filmed as a straight romantic vehicle for Rudolph Valentino and Bebe Daniels in 1924, directed by Sidney Olcott. In 1946 Bob Hope had his way with it in a version directed by George Marshall.

MONSIEUR HULOT'S HOLIDAY (France 1952). Written and directed by Jacques Tati, this comedy in which he also stars as an accident-prone do-gooder on a seaside holiday will probably be remembered as his best. It has no story, just a collection of tiny incidents: many are hilarious, but some so untidily executed as to make one suspect that Tati would be even more marvellous under someone else's direction.

monster animals. The 1924 version of *The Lost World* set a persisting fashion for giant animals operated by technical ingenuity. The supreme achievement in the genre was of course *King Kong*, who carried on in *Son of Kong* and (more or less) in *Mighty Joe Young*. Dinosaurs and other creatures which once did exist were featured in such films as *Man and His Mate* (in which what we saw were actually magnified lizards), *The Land Unknown*, *Dinosaurus*, *The Lost Continent*, *Gorgo*, *The Beast from Twenty Thousand Fathoms*, *Godzilla*, *Rodan*, *One Million Years B.C.* and *When Dinosaurs Ruled the Earth*. Other films concentrated on normal species which had been giantized by radiation or some other accident of science: *The Black Scorpion*, *Them*, *The Deadly Mantis*, *The Giant Claw*, *Tarantula*, *Mysterious Island*. More fanciful giant animals were created for *Jason and the Argonauts*, *Jack the Giant Killer* and *The Seventh Voyage of Sindbad*.

montage. In the most general sense, the whole art of editing or assembling scenes into the finished film. Specifically, 'a montage' is understood as an impressionistic sequence of short dissolve-shot-either bridging a time gap, setting a situation or showing the background to the main story. Classic montages which come to mind are in *The Battleship Potemkin, The Roaring Twenties*, and *Citizen Kane*.

MONTAGU, IVOR (1904–   ). British producer, director and film theorist. In films from 1925; was associate of Hitchcock on several of his mid-30s thrillers; produced *Behind the Spanish Lines* (38), *Spanish ABC* (38), etc.; co-authored many screenplays including *Scott of the Antarctic* (48). Latest publication 'Film World' (64).

MONTAGUE, LEE (1927–   ). British actor, mainly seen on stage and TV. Films include *Savage Innocents* (59), *The Secret Partner* (60), *Billy Budd* (61), *The Horse without a Head* (62), *You Must Be Joking* (65), etc.

MONTALBAN, RICARDO (1920–   ). Mexican leading man whose Hollywood pictures include *Fiesta* (47), *The Kissing Bandit* (49), *Border Incident* (49), *Battleground* (50), *Right Cross* (50), *Across the Wide Missouri* (51), *My Man and I* (52), *Sombrero* (53), *Latin Lovers* (54), *A Life in the Balance* (55), *Sayonara* (57), *Adventures of a Young Man* (62), *Love Is a Ball* (63), *The Money Trap* (65), *Madame X* (66), *Sol Madrid* (68), *Blue* (68), *Sweet Charity* (68), others.

MONTAND, YVES (1921–   ) (Ivo Levi). French actor-singer in films from the mid-40s; married to Simone Signoret. *Les Portes de la Nuit* (46), *Lost Property* (50), *The Wages of Fear* (53), *The Heroes Are Tired* (55), *The Witches of Salem* (56), *Let's Make Love* (US) (60), *Sanctuary* (US) (61), *My Geisha* (US) (62), *The Sleeping Car Murders* (65), *The War Is Over* (66), *Is Paris Burning?* (66), *Grand Prix* (67), *Vivre Pour Vivre* (67), *On A Clear Day You Can See Forever* (69), etc.

MONTES, LOLA (1818–1861) (Eliza Gilbert). Irish dancer who became world-famous as the mistress of King Ludwig I of Bavaria. Max Ophuls made a film about her in 1955, with Martine Carol, and Yvonne de Carlo played her in *Black Bart* (48).

MONTEZ, MARIA (1918–1951) (Maria de Santo Silas). Exotic Hollywood leading lady mainly seen in hokum adventures. Born in West Indies. *The Invisible Woman* (debut) (41), *South of Tahiti* (41), *The Mystery of Marie Roget* (42), *Arabian Nights* (42), *White Savage* (43), *Cobra Woman* (44), *Ali Baba and the Forty Thieves* (44), *Gypsy Wildcat* (44), *Sudan* (45), *Tangier* (46), *Pirates of Monterey* (47), *The Exile* (47), *Siren of Atlantis* (48), *The Thief of Venice* (51), etc.

MONTGOMERY, DOUGLASS (1908–1966) (Robert Douglass Montgomery). Canadian leading man with stage experience; once known as KENT DOUGLASS. Comparatively few films include *Paid* (debut) (31), *Waterloo Bridge* (31), *Little Women* (33), *A House Divided* (33), *Little Man, What Now?* (34), *The Mystery of Edwin Drood* (35), *Counsel for*

Montgomery, Elizabeth

Crime (37), *The Cat and the Canary* (39), *The Way to the Stars* (GB) (45), *Woman to Woman* (GB) (47), *Forbidden* (GB) (48), etc.

MONTGOMERY, ELIZABETH (1933–   ). Pert American leading lady, daughter of Robert Montgomery; most familiar as the witch-wife of TV series *Bewitched* (64–69). Films include *The Court Martial of Billy Mitchell* (55), *Who's Been Sleeping in My Bed* (63), *Johnny Cool* (63).

MONTGOMERY, GEORGE (1916–   ) (George Montgomery Letz). American leading man, mostly in low-budget Westerns; married to Dinah Shore. Former boxer; started in films as stuntman. *The Cisco Kid and the Lady* (39), *Stardust* (40), *Roxie Hart* (42), *Coney Island* (44), *Three Little Girls in Blue* (46), *The High Window* (*The Brasher Doubloon*) (47), *Sword of Monte Cristo* (51), *Cripple Creek* (52), *Jack McCall, Desperado* (53), *Robbers' Roost* (55), *The Steel Claw* (also directed) (61), *Samar* (also directed) (62), *The Battle of the Bulge* (65), *Huntsville* (67), many others. TV series: *Cimarron City* (58).

MONTGOMERY, ROBERT (1904–   ). American leading man with stage experience; has recently forsaken entertainment for politics. *So This Is College* (debut) (29), *Three Live Ghosts* (29), *Our Blushing Brides* (30), *The Big House* (30), *Inspiration* (31), *The Ma in Possession* (31), *Private Lives* (32), *Letty Lynton* (32), *Hell Below* (33), *When Ladies Meet* (33), *Night Flight* (33), *Vanessa* (34), *No More Ladies* (34), *Biography of a Bachelor Girl* (34), *Petticoat Fever* (35), *The Suicide Club* (36), *Piccadilly Jim* (36), *The Last of Mrs Cheyney* (37), *Night Must Fall* (37), *Live, Love and Learn* (38), *Yellow Jack* (39), *Three Loves Has Nancy* (38), *Fast and Loose* (39), *The Earl of Chicago* (39), *Busman's Honeymoon* (GB) (40), *Mr and Mrs Smith* (40), *Rage in Heaven* (41), *Here Comes Mr Jordan* (41), *Unfinished Business* (41), etc.; war service; *They Were Expendable* (45), *The Lady in the Lake* (also directed) (46), *Ride the Pink Horse* (also directed) (47), *June Bride* (48), *The Saxon Charm* (49), *Once More My Darling* (also directed) (50), *The Gallant Hours* (directed only) (60), others.

MOODY, RON (1924–   ) (Ronald Moodnick). British character comedian of stage and TV. Films include *Summer Holiday* (63), *The Mouse on the Moon* (63), *Murder Most Foul* (64), *Every Day's a Holiday* (64), *Oliver* (as Fagin) (68), *David Copperfield* (69), *The Twelve Chairs* (70).

THE MOON AND SIXPENCE (US 1942). A remarkable first film written and directed by Albert Lewin, whose exotic literary talent later got out of control. From the novel by Somerset Maugham based on the life of Gauguin, it was remarkable in remaining more faithful to its original than most Hollywood films of the period, while still managing to do well at the box-office. Herbert Marshall appeared (not for the last time) as Maugham, George Sanders made the most of his meaty role as Strickland, and Steve Geray had his best part as Dirk Stroeve.

THE MOON IS BLUE (US 1953). This straightforward version by Otto Preminger of F. Hugh Herbert's frothy Broadway comedy marked the first breaking-down of the Hollywood Production Code and the Legion of Decency, which Preminger defied by retaining the words 'virgin', 'mistress' and 'seduction' and treating these matters as a great joke. After the film's enormous box-office success, Hollywood's mind quickly broadened. The actors involved were David Niven, William Holden and Maggie McNamara.

MOORE, CLEO (1928–   ). American leading lady who appeared chiefly in Hugo Haas's low-budget emotional melodramas. *This Side of the Law* (50), *On Dangerous Ground* (50), *One Girl's Confession* (53), *Bait* (54), *Women's Prison* (55), *Over-Exposed* (56), etc.

MOORE, COLLEEN (1900–   ) (Kathleen Morrison). American leading lady of the silent screen. *Intolerance* (16), *The Bad Boy* (17), *Little Orphan Annie* (18), *So Long Letty* (20), *Come On Over* (22), *Flaming Youth* (23), *So Big* (25), *Synthetic Sin* (28), *Lilac Time* (28), *Why Be Good?* (29), etc. Sound finished her career apart from appearances in *The Power and the Glory* (33), *The Scarlet Letter* (34). Published autobiography 1968: *Silent Star*.

MOORE, CONSTANCE (1919–   ). American leading lady and singer, mildly popular in the 40s; usually in 'sensible' roles. *Prison Break* (38), *You Can't Cheat an Honest Man* (39), *La Conga Nights* (40), *Ma, He's Making Eyes at Me* (40), *I Wanted Wings* (41), *Take a Letter, Darling* (42), *Show Business* (43), *Atlantic City* (44), *Delightfully Dangerous* (45), *Earl Carroll's Vanities* (45), *In Old Sacramento* (46), *Hit Parade of 1947*, *Hats Off to Rhythm* (47), etc. Latterly touring night clubs.

MOORE, DICKIE (1925–   ). American child actor of the 30s, first on screen when one year old. *The Beloved Rogue* (26), *Oliver Twist* (33), *Peter Ibbetson* (34), *Sergeant York* (41), *Miss Annie Rooney* (42), *Dangerous Years* (47), *Out of the Past (Build My Gallows High)* (48), *Killer Shark* (50), *The Member of the Wedding* (last to date) (52), etc.

MOORE, DUDLEY (1935–   ). British cabaret pianist and comedian, often teamed with Peter Cook. *The Wrong Box* (66), *Thirty is a Dangerous Age Cynthia* (67).

MOORE, EVA (1870–1955). British stage actress who made a few films in the 30s. *Brown Sugar* (31), *The Old Dark House* (splendid in her cries of 'No beds! They can't have beds!') (US) (32), *I Was a Spy* (33), *A Cup of Kindness* (34), *Vintage Wine* (35), *Old Iron* (39), *The Bandit of Sherwood Forest* (US) (46), etc.

MOORE, GRACE (1902–1947). American operatic singer in occasional films: *A Lady's Morals* (31), *New Moon* (32), *One Night of Love* (34), *Love Me Forever* (35), *The King Steps Out* (36), *I'll Take Romance* (37), etc. Kathryn Grayson played her in a biopic, *The Grace Moore Story* (*So This Is Love*) (53).

MOORE, KIERON (1925–   ) (Kieron O'Hanrahan). Irish leading man with stage experience before film debut in *The Voice Within* (44). Later in *A Man about the House* (46), *Mine Own Executioner* (47), *Anna Karenina* (48), *Ten Tall Men* (51), *The Key* (58), *The Day They Robbed the Bank of England* (60), *The Thin Red Line* (64), *Crack in the World* (65), *Arabesque* (66), *Custer of the West* (67), etc.

MOORE, MARY TYLER (1936–   ). American leading lady with long TV experience: *Steve Canyon* (58), *The Dick Van Dyke Show* (61–66). Films include *X-15* (61), *Thoroughly Modern Millie* (67), *Don't Just Stand There* (68), *What's So Bad about Feeling Good* (68), *Change of Habit* (69).

MOORE, ROGER (1928–   ). British leading man who after stage experience made film debut in Hollywood. *The Last Time I Saw Paris* (55), *Interrupted Melody* (55), *The King's Thief* (56), *Diane* (57), *The Miracle* (59), *Gold of the Seven Saints* (61), *The Sins of Rachel Cade* (61), *Crossplot* (69), etc. TV series: *Ivanhoe* (57), *The Alaskans* (59), *Maverick* (61), *The Saint* (63–68).

MOORE, TED (1914–   ). South African cinematographer, in British films. *The African Queen* (51), *Genevieve* (53), *The Black Knight* (54), *Cockleshell Heroes* (56), *A Man for All Seasons* (AA) (66), *Shalako* (68), *The Prime of Miss Jean Brodie* (69), *The Most Dangerous Man in the World* (69), *Country Dance* (70), etc.

MOORE, TERRY (1932–   ) (Helen Koford). American leading lady, former child model, in films from infancy. *The Murder in Thornton Square* (43), *Mighty Joe Young* (50), *The Sunny Side of the Street* (53), *King of the Khyber Rifles* (54), *Bernardine* (57), *A Private's Affair* (59), *Why Must I Die?* (60), *Town Tamer* (65), etc. TV series: *Empire*.

MOORE, VICTOR (1876–1962). Veteran American vaudeville comedian with hesitant, bumbling manner, in films occasionally from 1915. *Snobs* (15), *The Clown* (16), many one-reelers through 20s, *Romance in the Rain* (34), *Swing Time* (36), *Gold Diggers of 1937*, *Louisiana Purchase* (41), *Duffy's Tavern* (45), *The Fifth Chair* (*It's in the Bag*) (45), *It Happened on Fifth Avenue* (47), *We're Not Married* (52), *The Seven-Year Itch* (55), etc.

MOOREHEAD, AGNES (1906–   ) American character actress often seen in waspish or neurotic roles; brought to Hollywood from Broadway by Orson Welles. *Citizen Kane* (debut) (41), *The Magnifi-*

cent Ambersons (42), *The Big Street* (42), *Journey into Fear* (43), *Jane Eyre* (43), *The Seventh Cross* (44), *Dragon Seed* (44), *Since You Went Away* (44), *Mrs Parkington* (44), *Tomorrow the World* (44), *Our Vines Have Tender Grapes* (45), *Dark Passage* (47), *The Lost Moment* (as a centenarian) (48), *Johnny Belinda* (48), *The Stratton Story* (49), *The Great Sinner* (49), *Caged* (50), *Fourteen Hours* (51), *The Blue Veil* (51), *Scandal at Scourie* (52), *Magnificent Obsession* (54), *All That Heaven Allows* (55), *The Conqueror* (55), *The Swan* (56), *The Opposite Sex* (56), *Pardners* (56), *Raintree County* (57), *Jeanne Eagels* (57), *The Bat* (59), *Pollyanna* (60), *Bachelor in Paradise* (61), *How the West Was Won* (62), *Jessica* (63), *Who's Minding the Store* (64), *Hush Hush Sweet Charlotte* (64), *The Singing Nun* (66), others. TV series: *Bewitched* (64–69).

MORAHAN, CHRISTOPHER (c. 1930–   ). British director with stage and TV experience. *Diamonds for Breakfast* (68), *All Neat in Black Stockings* (69).

MORAN, PEGGY (1918–   ). American leading lady of the 40s, with radio experience; married Henry Koster and retired. *Girls' School* (39), *The Mummy's Hand* (40), *Horror Island* (41), *Drums of the Congo* (42), *Seven Sweethearts* (42), etc.

MORAN, POLLY (1885–1952). American vaudeville comedienne who made some early sound films, notably in partnership with Marie Dressler. *Hollywood Revue* (29), *Caught Short* (29), *Reducing* (30), *Politics* (31), *The Passionate Plumber* (32), *Alice in Wonderland* (33); later played smaller roles in *Two Wise Maids* (37), *Tom Brown's Schooldays* (39), *Petticoat Politics* (41), *Adam's Rib* (49), etc.

MORE O'FERRALL, GEORGE (c. 1906–   ). British director who has been mainly successful in TV. Was assistant director from *Midshipman Easy* (34) to *No Highway* (50); his solo films include *Angels One Five* (52), *The Holly and the Ivy* (53), *The Heart of the Matter* (53), *The Green Scarf* (53), *A Woman for Joe* (55), *The March Hare* (56).

MORE, KENNETH (1914–   ). British leading man with a tendency to breezy roles. Considerable stage experience before film debut in *Scott of the Antarctic* (48). Later: *Chance of a Lifetime* (49), *No Highway* (50), *Appointment with Venus* (51), *Brandy for the Parson* (51), *The Yellow Balloon* (52), *Never Let Me Go* (53), *Genevieve* (great personal success) (53), *Our Girl Friday* (53), *Doctor in the House* (BFA) (54), *Raising a Riot* (54), *The Deep Blue Sea* (55), *Reach for the Sky* (as Douglas Bader) (56), *Next to No Time* (57), *The Admirable Crichton* (57), *The Sheriff of Fractured Jaw* (58), *A Night to Remember* (58), *The Thirty-nine Steps* (59), *Northwest Frontier* (59), *Sink the Bismarck* (60), *The Man in the Moon* (61), *The Greengage Summer* (61), *Some People* (62), *We Joined the Navy* (62), *The Comedy Man* (64), *Dark*

Moreau, Jeanne

of the Sun (68), *The Betrayal* (69), *Battle of Britain* (69), etc. Recently on stage. Published autobiography 1959: *Happy Go Lucky*.

MOREAU, JEANNE (1928–   ). French actress of stage and screen; the Bette Davis of her time. *The She-Wolves* (55), *Lift to the Scaffold* (57), *The Lovers* (59), *Le Dialogue des Carmelites* (59), *Les Liaisons Dangereuses* (60), *Moderato Cantabile* (60), *La Notte* (61), *Jules et Jim* (61), *Eva* (62), *The Trial* (63), *The Victors* (63), *Le Feu Follet* (64), *Diary of a Chambermaid* (64), *The Yellow Rolls-Royce* (64), *The Train* (64), *Mata Hari* (65), *Viva Maria* (65), *Mademoiselle* (65), *Chimes at Midnight* (66), *Sailor from Gibraltar* (66), *The Bride Wore Black* (67), *Great Catherine* (68), *Le Corps de Diane* (68), *Monte Walsh* (70), etc.

MORECAMBE, ERIC (1926–   ) (Eric Bartholomew) and WISE, ERNIE (1925–   ) (Ernest Wiseman). British comedy team with music-hall experience since 1943. In the 60s they became immensely popular on TV, but their films have been rather less than satisfactory: *The Intelligence Men* (64), *That Riviera Touch* (66), *The Magnificent Two* (67).

MORELAND, MANTAN (* –   ). American Negro actor, long cast as frightened valet. *Frontier Scout* (38), *Laughing at Danger* (40), *King of the Zombies* (41), *The Strange Case of Doctor RX* (41), *Charlie Chan in the Secret Service* (and many others in this series) (44), *Murder at Malibu Beach* (47), *The Feathered Serpent* (49), *Enter Laughing* (68), etc.

MORELL, ANDRE (1909–   ) (André Mesritz). British character actor, on stage from 1938, films from 1938. *Thirteen Men and a Gun* (debut) (38), *No Place for Jennifer* (49), *Seven Days to Noon* (50), *High Treason* (51), *Summer Madness* (55), *The Bridge on the River Kwai* (57), *Ben Hur* (59), *The Hound of the Baskervilles* (59), *Cone of Silence* (60), *Mysterious Island* (61), *Shadow of the Cat* (62), *Cash on Demand* (64), *She* (65), *Plague of the Zombies* (65), *The Mummy's Shroud* (67), etc. Many TV appearances.

MORENO, ANTONIO (1886–1967). Romantic Spanish star of Hollywood silent films: *Voice of the Million* (12), *House of Hate* (18), *The Trail of the Lonesome Pine* (23), *The Spanish Dancer* (24), *Mare Nostrum* (25), *Beverly of Graustark* (26), *The Temptress* (26), *It* (27), *Synthetic Sin* (28), etc. His accent forced him from the top when sound came, but he continued in character parts: *One Mad Kiss* (30), *Storm over the Andes* (35), *Rose of the Rio Grande* (38), *Valley of the Giants* (42), *The Spanish Main* (45), *Captain from Castile* (47), *Thunder Bay* (53), *The Creature from the Black Lagoon* (54), *The Searchers* (56), many others.

MORENO, RITA (1931–   ). Puerto Rican actress-dancer, in films sporadically since 1950, between stage appearances. *Pagan Love*

Song (50), *Singing in the Rain* (52), *Garden of Evil* (54), *The Vagabond King* (55), *The King and I* (56), *The Deerslayer* (57), *West Side Story* (AA) (61), *The Night of the Following Day* (68), *Popi* (69), etc.

THE MORE THE MERRIER (US) (1943). Perhaps the best of the several farces about overcrowding in Washington hotels during World War II, this amiable movie starred Charles Coburn, Jean Arthur and Joel McCrea, was written by Robert Russell and Frank Ross, and directed by George Stevens. In 1966 it was lethargically remade by Charles Walters, its setting changed to the Tokyo Olympics, as *Walk Don't Run*; Cary Grant took over as ageing Cupid to Samantha Eggar and Jim Hutton.

MORGAN: A SUITABLE CASE FOR TREATMENT (GB 1966). A serio-comedy which takes the *Lucky Jim/Look Back in Anger* type of 50s hero to the logical conclusion of madness, wretched by his own selfishness nihilism and fantasy. David Mercer's script, extended from his own TV play, had very little to say, but there are intermittent enjoyments coupled with uneasy moments of flashy editing and slapstick. (The actual ending is borrowed from Bunuel.) David Warner enjoys himself in the title role; Karel Raisz directs rather uncertainly.

MORGAN, DENNIS (1910–) (Stanley Morner). American leading man, former opera singer. *Suzy* (debut) (36), *The Great Ziegfeld* (36), *Kitty Foyle* (40), *Captains of the Clouds* (42), *Thank Your Lucky Stars* (43), *The Time, the Place and the Girl* (46), *My Wild Irish Rose* (47), *Painting the Clouds with Sunshine* (51), *The Gun That Won the West* (55), *Uranium Boom* (56), *Rogues' Gallery* (68), etc. TV series: *21 Beacon Street* (58).

MORGAN, FRANK (1890–1949) (Francis Wupperman). American character actor. In films from 1916, usually playing his endearing if slightly fuddled self, but his real popularity came with sound, when he was an MGM contract player for over twenty years. *A Modern Cinderella* (17), *Queen High* (26), *Dangerous Dan McGrew* (30), *Reunion in Vienna* (33), *Hallelujah I'm a Bum* (33), *Naughty Marietta* (35), *The Great Ziegfeld* (35), *The Last of Mrs Cheyney* (37), *The Crowd Roars* (38), *Sweethearts* (38), *Serenade* (39), *Balalaika* (39), *The Wizard of Oz* (title role) (39), *The Shop Around the Corner* (40), *Boom Town* (40), *Washington Melodrama* (leading role) (41), *Honky Tonk* (41), *Tortilla Flat* (42), *White Cargo* (42), *The Human Comedy* (43), *The White Cliffs of Dover* (43), *Yolanda and the Thief* (45), *Courage of Lassie* (45), *The Great Morgan* (leading role) (46), *Mr Griggs Returns* (leading role) (46), *Summer Holiday* (47), *The Stratton Story* (49), *The Great Sinner* (49), *Any Number Can Play* (49), many others.

MORGAN, HARRY (1915–   ) (Harry Bratsburg). Mild-looking American character actor with stage experience. *To the Shores of Tripoli* (debut) (42), *From This Day Forward* (45), *The Saxon Charm* (49), *Moonrise* (50), *The Well* (51), *High Noon* (52), *The Glenn Miller Story* (54), *Not as a Stranger* (55), *The Teahouse of the August Moon* (56), *Inherit the Wind* (60), *John Goldfarb Please Come Home* (64), *What Did You Do in the War, Daddy?* (66), *Support Your Local Sheriff* (69), many others. TV series: *December Bride* (54–59), *Pete and Gladys* (60–61), *The Richard Boone Show* (64), *Kentucky Jones* (65).

MORGAN, HELEN (1900–1941). American café singer of the 20s. Film appearances include *Applause* (29), *Roadhouse Nights* (30), *Marie Galante* (35), *Go into Your Dance* (36), *Showboat* (36), etc. A biopic was made in 1957: *The Helen Morgan Story* (*Both Ends of the Candle*).

MORGAN, MICHELE (1920–   ) (Simone Roussel). French leading lady, in films from mid-30s. *Orage* (36), *Quai des Brumes* (38), *La Symphonie Pastorale* (40), *Joan of Paris* (US) (41), *Higher and Higher* (US) (43), *Passage to Marseilles* (US) (44), *The Fallen Idol* (GB) (48), *Les Orgeuilleux* (50), *The Seven Deadly Sins* (51), *Les Grandes Manoeuvres* (55), *Marguerite de la Nuit* (56), *The Mirror Has Two Faces* (60), *Landru* (63), *Benjamin* (68), etc.

MORGAN, RALPH (1882–1956) (Ralph Wupperman). American character actor, brother of Frank Morgan. Former lawyer; went on stage, then to films in 20s. *Charlie Chan's Chance* (31), *Rasputin and the Empress* (32), *Strange Interlude* (32), *Anthony Adverse* (36), *The Life of Emile Zola* (37), *Forty Little Mothers* (40), *Black Market Babies* (45), *The Monster Maker* (45), *Sleep My Love* (48), *Gold Fever* (52), many others.

MORGAN, TERENCE (1921–   ). British leading man. *Hamlet* (debut) (48), *Mandy* (52), *Turn the Key Softly* (53), *They Can't Hang Me* (55), *The Scamp* (56), *Shakedown* (58), *Piccadilly Third Stop* (61), *The Curse of the Mummy's Tomb* (64), others. TV series: *Sir Francis Drake* (62).

MORISON, PATRICIA (1915–   ) (Eileen Morrison). American leading lady. *Persons in Hiding* (38), *Untamed* (40), *The Round-Up* (41), *Calling Dr Death* (44), *The Secret Code* (45), *Queen of the Amazons* (46), *Sofia* (48), *Brave Stallion* (50), *Song Without End* (60), etc.

MORLAY, GABY (1897–1964) (Blanche Fumoleau). French character actress. *La Sandale Rouge* (13), *Les Nouveaux Messieurs* (28), *Derrière la Façade* (38), *Le Voile Bleu* (42), *Gigi* (48), *Le Plaisir* (51), *Mitsou* (55), *Ramuntcho* (58), many others.

MORLEY, KAREN (1905–   ) (Mildred Linton). American leading lady of the 30s. *Inspiration* (31), *Scarface* (32), *Dinner at Eight* (33),

Morris, Lana

Beloved Enemy (36), *Kentucky* (39), *Pride and Prejudice* (as Charlotte Lucas) (40), *Jealousy* (45), *The Unknown* (46), *M* (51), others.

MORNING GLORY (US 1933). Zoe Akins' play about a maddening but talented young actress in New York was filmed by Lowell Sherman with Katharine Hepburn (who won an Academy Award) and Adolphe Menjou. In 1957 Sidney Lumet remade it as *Stage Struck*, with Susan Strasberg and Henry Fonda.

MORLEY, ROBERT (1908–   ). Portly British character actor (and playwright), on stage from 1929, films from 1938. *Marie Antoinette* (US) (38), *Major Barbara* (40), *The Young Mr Pitt* (42), *I Live in Grosvenor Square* (45), *An Outcast of the Islands* (51), *Gilbert and Sullivan* (53), *Beat the Devil* (53), *Around the World in Eighty Days* (56), *The Doctor's Dilemma* (59), *Oscar Wilde* (60), *The Young Ones* (61), *Murder at the Gallop* (63), *Those Magnificent Men in Their Flying Machines* (65), *Amanda* (*The Alphabet Murders*) (65), *Genghis Khan* (65), *A Study in Terror* (65), *Hotel Paradiso* (66), *Way Way Out* (US) (66), *The Trygon Factor* (67), *Sinful Davey* (69). Published autobiography 1966: *Robert Morley, Responsible Gentleman*.

MOROCCO (US 1930). The film in which Marlene Dietrich made her American debut, directed by Josef Von Sternberg. Remembered chiefly for the impudence of the scenes in which Marlene (*a*) dressed in a tuxedo, kisses a young woman on the lips, and (*b*) strides into the Sahara in high heels to follow her departed lover.

MORRIS, CHESTER (1901–   ). Jut-jawed American leading man in films from *Alibi* (28) after stage experience. *The Big House* (32), *Five Came Back* (36), *Blind Alley* (38), *Meet Boston Blackie* (41), *Boston Blackie's Chinese Venture* (49) (and several other episodes of this crime series in between), *Unchained* (55), many others. Latterly on TV.

MORRIS, ERNEST (1915–   ). British director, mainly of second features for the Danzigers, the best of them being *The Tell-Tale Heart* (60). Recently: *Echo of Diana* (64), *The Return of Mr Moto* (65). Directed many TV episodes.

MORRIS, HOWARD (1919–   ). American TV comedian and writer; he appeared in a few movies including *Boys Night Out* (62), and directed *With Six You Get Egg Roll* (68).

MORRIS, LANA (1930–   ). British leading lady, in films from 1946. *Spring in Park Lane* (47), *The Weaker Sex* (48), *Trottie True* (49), *The Chiltern Hundreds* (49), *The Woman in Question* (50), *Trouble in Store* (53), *Man of the Moment* (55), *Home and Away* (56), others; in recent years has worked almost entirely in TV.

Morris, Mary

MORRIS, MARY (1915–). British character actress with dominant personality, on stage from 1925. *Prison without Bars* (film debut) (38), *The Spy in Black* (39), *The Thief of Bagdad* (40), *Pimpernel Smith* (41), *Undercover* (43), *The Man from Morocco* (45), *Train of Events* (49), *High Treason* (51), others. Lately on TV.

MORRIS, OSWALD (1915–). British cinematographer, in films from 1932. *Green for Danger* (46), *Moulin Rouge* (53), *Knave of Hearts* (53), *Beat the Devil* (53), *Beau Brummell* (54), *Moby Dick* (56), *A Farewell to Arms* (57), *The Key* (58), *Roots of Heaven* (59), *Look Back in Anger* (59), *Our Man in Havana* (59), *The Entertainer* (60), *Lolita* (62), *Of Human Bondage* (64), *The Pumpkin Eater* (BFA) (64), *The Hill* (BFA) (65), *Life at the Top* (65), *The Spy Who Came In from the Cold* (65), *Stop the World I Want To Get Off* (66), *The Taming of the Shrew* (67), *Reflections in a Golden Eye* (67), *Oliver!* (68), *Goodbye Mr Chips* (69), many others.

MORRIS, WAYNE (1914–1959) (Bert de Wayne Morris). Brawny American leading man with stage experience. *China Clipper* (debut) (36), *Kid Galahad* (37), *Brother Rat and a Baby* (39), *Bad Men of Missouri* (40), *The Smiling Ghost* (41), *Deep Valley* (47), *The Time of Your Life* (47), *The Tougher They Come* (50), *The Master Plan* (55), *The Crooked Sky* (57), *Paths of Glory* (58), etc.

MORROS, BORIS (1895–1963) (Boris Milhailovitch). Russian-born independent producer in America from late 30s. *The Flying Deuces* (39), *Second Chorus* (41), *Tales of Manhattan* (42), *Carnegie Hall* (48), others. Later revealed as an American agent via his 1957 book 'Ten Years a Counterspy', filmed in 1960 as *Man on a String*, with Ernest Borgnine as Morros.

MORROW, JEFF (c. 1916–). Mature American leading man, former Broadway and TV actor, in Hollywood from 1953. *The Robe* (53), *Siege of Red River* (54), *This Island Earth* (55), *The Creature Walks Among Us* (56), *The Giant Claw* (57), *The Story of Ruth* (60), *Harbour Lights* (63). TV series: *Union Pacific* (58).

MORROW, VIC (1932–). American actor usually cast as a muttering juvenile delinquent. Stage experience. *The Blackboard Jungle* (film debut) (55), *Tribute to a Bad Man* (56), *Men in War* (57), *God's Little Acre* (58), *Cimarron* (61), *Portrait of a Mobster* (61), etc. TV series: *Combat* (62–66).

MORSE, BARRY (1919–). British leading man who moved to Canada and became star of stage and TV there. *The Goose Steps Out* (42), *When We Are Married* (42), *There's a Future in It* (43), *Late at Night* (46), *Daughter of Darkness* (48), *No Trace* (50), then long gap before *Kings of the Sun* (63), *Justine* (69). Played Lieut. Gerard in TV series *The Fugitive* (63–67).

MORSE, ROBERT (1931–   ). American comedy actor who usually plays the befuddled innocent. Broadway stage experience. *The Matchmaker* (58), *Honeymoon Hotel* (64), *Quick Before It Melts* (65), *The Loved One* (65), *Oh Dad, Poor Dad* (66), *How to Succeed in Business without Really Trying* (67), *Where Were You When the Lights Went Out?* (68), etc. TV series: *That's Life* (68).

morticians : see *undertakers.*

MORTIMER, JOHN (1923–   ). British playwright who has worked in films. Originally scriptwriter for Crown Film Unit; later *The Innocents* (61), *Guns of Darkness* (63), *The Dock Brief* (63), *The Running Man* (63), *Bunny Lake Is Missing* (65), etc.

MORTON, CLIVE (1904–   ). Straight-faced British character actor on stage from 1926, films from 1932, usually in slightly pompous roles. *The Blarney Stone* (32), *Dead Men Tell No Tales* (39), *While the Sun Shines* (46), *Scott of the Antarctic* (48), *The Blue Lamp* (49), *His Excellency* (51), *Carrington VC* (54), *Richard III* (56), *Shake Hands with the Devil* (59), *Lawrence of Arabia* (62), *Stranger in the House* (67), many others.

MOSJOUKINE, IVAN (1889–1939). Russian actor of the old school, who appeared in many international films including *The Defence of Sevastopol* (11), *Satan Triumphant* (22), *Tempest* (Fr.) (22), *Shadows That Mass* (Fr.) (23), *Casanova* (Fr./It.) (27), *Sergeant X* (Fr.) *Nitchevo* (Fr.) (36).

MOSS, ARNOLD (c. 1905–   ). American character actor often seen in sly or sinister roles. *Temptation* (47), *The Black Book* (as Napoleon) (49), *Kim* (51), *Viva Zapata* (52), *Casanova's Big Night* (54), *The Twenty-seventh Day* (57), *The Fool Killer* (64), *Gambit* (66), *Caper of the Golden Bulls* (67), many others.

THE MOST DANGEROUS GAME : see THE HOUNDS OF ZAROFF.

MOSTEL, ZERO (1915–   ). Heavyweight American comedian principally seen on Broadway stage. Occasional films include *Panic in the Streets* (50), *Murder Inc.* (*The Enforcer*) (51), *A Funny Thing Happened on the Way to the Forum* (66), *Great Catherine* (68), *The Producers* (68), *The Great Bank Robbery* (69), *The Angel Levine* (69).

mother love has been the driving force of many of the screen's most popular, and therefore most remade, melodramas, such as *Imitation of Life, Madame X, Stella Dallas, Mrs Wiggs of the Cabbage Patch* and *To Each His Own.* Britain chipped in with *The Woman in the Hall, The White Unicorn,* and *When the Bough Breaks.* Some say that Hitchcock made *Psycho* as the ultimate riposte to this sentimental tendency; but *The Anniversary* came a close second.

motor-cycles, hideous and unbearably noisy machines, have become a badge of aggressive youth, and since *The Wild Angels* in 1966 American drive-in screens have been filled with a host of cheap movies extolling the pleasures of leather-jacketed speed with a bird on the back. All of these appear to have been banned in Britain, as was *The Wild One*, an early example of the genre, in 1954. But we did let through Elvis Presley in *Roustabout*, and Steve McQueen doing his own stunt sequence in *The Great Escape*, and we even made *The Leather Boys*, about our own ton-up teenagers. As for *Girl on a Motorcycle*, in which the bike becomes the ultimate sex symbol, words fail one. There was a good British film about speedway racing, *Once a Jolly Swagman*, and one about the fairground called *Wall of Death*. Comedian George Formby went in for the TT races in *No Limit*, and rode a motor-bike also in *It's In the Air*. In American films, the motor-cycle cops are too familiar to warrant individual attention.

motor racing has been the subject of many a routine melodrama, and always seems to reduce the writer to banalities, even in a spectacular like *Grand Prix*. Some other examples of the genre include *The Crowd Roars*, *Indianapolis Speedway*, *Checkpoint*, *The Green Helmet*, *The Devil's Hairpin*, *Red Line 7000* and *Winning*. The funniest comedy use of the sport was probably in *Ask a Policeman*, when Will Hay accidentally drove a bus onto Brooklands racetrack in the middle of a race.

MOULIN ROUGE. The three films made under this title are unconnected with each other. 1. US 1928; a drama directed by E. A. Dupont, with Eve Grey. 2. US 1933: a romantic comedy directed by Sidney Lanfield, with Constance Bennett and Franchot Tone. 3. GB 1952: a life of Toulouse Lautrec, from Pierre la Mure's novel, directed by John Huston and starring Jose Ferrer; mainly notable for its period atmosphere and Oswald Morris's colour photography.

MOUNT, PEGGY (1916–). British character comedienne with long experience in repertory before starring as the termagant mother-in-law in *Sailor Beware*, filmed in 1956. *Dry Rot* (57), *The Naked Truth* (58), *Inn for Trouble* (60), *Ladies Who Do* (63), *One Way Pendulum* (65), *Hotel Paradiso* (66), *Finders Keepers* (66), *Oliver!* (68), etc. TV series: *The Larkins, George and the Dragon*.

MOWBRAY, ALAN (1896–1969). Imperious-mannered British character actor, in America since early 1920s; appeared later in nearly 400 films, often as butler or pompous emissary. *Alexander Hamilton* (31), *Sherlock Holmes* (32), *Roman Scandals* (33), *Becky Sharp* (35), *Desire* (36), *My Man Godfrey* (36), *Topper* (37), *Stand In* (37), *The Villain Still Pursued Her* (40), *Lady Hamilton* (41), *That Uncertain Feeling* (41), *A Yank at Eton* (42), *His Butler's Sister* (43), *Holy Matrimony* (43),

Where Do We Go from Here? (45), *Terror by Night* (45), *Merton of the Movies* (46), *My Darling Clementine* (46), *Prince of Thieves* (47), *The Jackpot* (50), *Wagonmaster* (50), *Dick Turpin's Ride* (51), *Androcles and the Lion* (53), *The King's Thief* (55), *The King and I* (56), many others. TV series: *Colonel Flack* (57–58).

MOXEY, JOHN (c. 1920–   ). British TV director who has made occasional films: *City of the Dead* (59), *The £20,000 Kiss* (63), *Ricochet* (63), *Strangler's Web* (65), *Circus of Fear* (67), etc.

MUELLER, ELIZABETH (1926–   ). German leading lady who made some Hollywood films. *The Power and the Prize* (56), *El Hakim* (58), *Confess Dr Corda* (58), *The Angry Hills* (59), etc.

MUHL, EDWARD E. (1907–   ). American executive, an ex-accountant who has been in charge of Universal production since 1953.

MUIR, ESTHER (1895–   ). American character actress, the statuesque blonde who suffered at the hands of the Marx Brothers in *A Day at the Races* (37). Also: *A Dangerous Affair* (31), *The Bowery* (33), *Stolen Paradise* (41), *X Marks the Spot* (last to date) (42), etc.

MUIR, GAVIN (1907–   ). Quiet-spoken British actor who went to Hollywood in 1936 but did not get the parts he seemed to deserve. *Lloyds of London* (37), *Eagle Squadron* (41), *Nightmare* (best role) (41), *O.S.S.* (46), *Unconquered* (47), *Prince of Thieves* (48), *King of the Khyber Rifles* (54), *The Abductors* (57), *Johnny Trouble* (59), etc. TV series: *Goldie*.

MUIR, JEAN (1911–   ) (J. M. Fullerton). American leading lady of the 30s. *Female* (34), *A Midsummer Night's Dream* (35), *Jane Steps Out* (GB) (37), *And One Was Beautiful* (40), *The Lone Wolf Meets a Lady* (40), *The Constant Nymph* (last to date) (44), etc.

MULHALL, JACK (1891–   ). American silent-screen leading man. *Sirens of the Sea* (17), *Mickey* (18), *All of a Sudden Peggy* (20), *Molly'O* (21), *The Bad Man* (23), *The Goldfish* (24), *Friendly Enemies* (25), *The Poor Nut* (27), *Just Another Blonde* (28), *Dark Streets* (29), many others; appeared as an 'old-timer' in *Hollywood Boulevard* (36).

MULHARE, EDWARD (1923–   ). British leading man who has been on American stage. Films include *Hill 24 Does Not Answer* (55), *Signpost to Murder* (64), *Von Ryan's Express* (65), *Our Man Flint* (65), *Eye of the Devil* (67), *Caprice* (67). TV series: *The Ghost and Mrs Muir* (68).

MULLEN, BARBARA (1914–   ). Irish actress, former dancer, who came to films as star of *Jeannie* (42). Since seen in *Thunder Rock* (42), *A Place of One's Own* (44), *The Trojan Brothers* (45), *Corridor of Mirrors* (48), *So Little Time* (52), *The Challenge* (60), etc.; latterly on TV, especially in series *Dr Finlay's Casebook*. 1967 film: *Miss MacTaggart Won't Lie Down*.

MULLER, RENATE (1907–1937). German leading lady best known abroad for *Sunshine Susie* (31). Also: *Liebling der Götter* (30), *Viktor und Viktoria* (34), *Allotria* (36).

MULLIGAN, RICHARD (1932–   ). Lanky American leading man seen in *The Group* (66) and in TV series *The Hero* (66).

†MULLIGAN, ROBERT (1925–   ). American director, from television. *Fear Strikes Out* (57), *The Rat Race* (60), *Come September* (61), *The Great Impostor* (61), *The Spiral Road* (62), *To Lill a Mockingbird* (62), *Love with the Proper Stranger* (64), *Baby the Rain Must Fall* (65), *Inside Daisy Clover* (65), *Up the Down Staircase* (67), *The Stalking Moon* (68), *The Pursuit of Happiness* (70).

multiplane. A word introduced by Walt Disney to explain his new animation process for *Fantasia* (40). Instead of building up a drawing by laying 'cells' directly on top of each other, a slight illusion of depth was obtained by leaving space between the celluloid images of foreground, background, principal figure, etc.

multiple roles. The record for the number of characters played by one actor in a film is held not by Alec Guinness in *Kind Hearts and Coronets* but (probably) by Lupino Lane, who played twenty-four parts in a 1929 comedy called *Only Me*. Others with high scores, apart from Guinness's eight, include Robert Hirsch's dozen in *No Questions on Saturday*, Paul Muni's seven in *Seven Faces*, Tony Randall's seven in *The Seven Faces of Dr Lao*, Hugh Herbert's six in *La Conga Nights*, Fernandel's six in *The Sheep Has Five Legs*, Anna Neagle's four in *Lilacs in the Spring*, Françoise Rosay's four in *Une Femme Disparait*, Louis Jourdan's and Joan Fontaine's four each in *Decameron Nights*, Alan Young's four in *Gentlemen Prefer Brunettes*, Terry Kilburn's four generations of boy in *Goodbye Mr Chips*, Moira Shearer's three in *The Man Who Loved Redheads*, Deborah Kerr's three in *The Life and Death of Colonel Blimp*, Peter Sellers' three in *The Mouse That Roared*, Leon Errol's three in some episodes of the *Mexican Spitfire* series, Joanne Woodward's three in *The Three Faces of Eve* and Eleanor Parker's three in *Lizzie*. One should perhaps also count Danny Kaye's various dream selves in *The Secret Life of Walter Mitty*.

Dual roles have frequently been of the schizophrenic type of which *Dr Jekyll and Mr Hyde* (qv) is the most obvious example. This category includes Henry Hull in *Werewolf of London* and Lon Chaney Jnr in *The Wolf Man*, Phyllis Calvert in *Madonna of the Seven Moons*, Phyllis Thaxter in *Bewitched*, and Alec Guinness in *The Captain's Paradise*. Two-character dual roles include Ronald Colman in *The Masquerader*, *The Prisoner of Zenda* and *A Tale of*

Two Cities (also several other actors in other versions of the latter two), Lon Chaney in *London After Midnight*, Edward G. Robinson in *The Man with Two Faces*, Laurel and Hardy in *Our Relations*, Allan Jones and Joe Penner in *The Boys from Syracuse*, Chaplin in *The Great Dictator*, Louis Hayward in *The Man in the Iron Mask*, Olivia de Havilland in *The Dark Mirror*, Boris Karloff in *The Black Room*, Herbert Lom in *Dual Alibi*, George M. Cohan in *The Phantom President*, Jack Palance in *House of Numbers*, Peter Whitney in *Murder He Says*, Elizabeth Bergner (and later Bette Davis) in *Stolen Life*, Bette Davis in *Dead Ringer*, Yul Brynner in *The Double Man*, Stanley Baxter in *Very Important Person*, Alain Delon in *The Black Tulip*, John McInture in *The Lawless Breed*, Valentino in *Son of the Sheik*, Jack Mulhall in *Dark Streets* (allegedly the first to use the split-image technique) and Larry Parks (playing Jolson *and* himself) in *Jolson Sings Again*.

THE MUMMY. Interest in avenging mummies was aroused during the 20s by the widespread stories of the curse of Tutankhamen whose tomb had recently been discovered and opened. In 1932 Karl Freund directed a rather tedious and silly film on the subject with Boris Karloff as a desiccated but active three-thousand-year-old still on the track of his lost love. Despite good box-office it was not reprised until 1940, when *The Mummy's Hand* appeared with Tom Tyler in the role. Between 1942 and 1944 there were three increasingly foolish sequels starring (if it really *was* him under the bandages) Lon Chaney Jnr: they were *The Mummy's Tomb*, *The Mummy's Ghost* and *The Mummy's Curse*. In 1959 Hammer took over the character and remade *The Mummy* with an English Victorian setting: Christopher Lee was the monster. There have been two poor sequels, *The Curse of the Mummy's Tomb* (64) and *The Mummy's Shroud* (66). The lighter side of the subject was viewed by Wheeler and Wolsey in *Mummy's Boys* (35), the Three Stooges in *Mummie's Dummies* (38), and Abbott and Costello in *Meet the Mummy* (54).

MUNDIN, HERBERT (1898–1939). British character actor with stage experience, in British films in 20s, Hollywood from 1930. Remembered warmly as Barkis in *David Copperfield* (34) and Much the Miller in *The Adventures of Robin Hood* (38); also in *The Devil's Lottery* (31), *Sherlock Holmes* (32), *Cavalcade* (33), *Mutiny on the Bounty* (35), *Another Dawn* (37), *Society Lawyer* (39), etc.

†MUNI, PAUL (1896–1967) (Muni Weisenfreund). Distinguished American actor of middle-European parentage. Long stage experience. *The Valiant* (film debut) (28), *Seven Faces* (29), *Scarface* (32), *I Am a Fugitive from a Chain Gang* (32), *The World Changes* (33), *Hi Nellie* (33), *Bordertown* (34), *Black Fury* (35), *Dr Socrates* (35), *The Story of Louis Pasteur* (AA) (36), *The Good Earth* (37), *The Life*

of Emile Zola (37), *The Woman I Love* (38), *Juarez* (39), *We Are Not Alone* (39), *Hudson's Bay* (40), *The Commandos Strike at Dawn* (42), *A Song to Remember* (44), *Counter Attack* (45), *Angel on My Shoulder* (46), *Stranger on the Prowl* (51), *The Last Angry Man* (59).

MUNK, ANDRZEJ (1921–1961). Polish director. *Men of the Blue Cross* (55), *Eroica* (57), *Bad Luck* (60), *The Passenger* (incomplete) (61), etc.

MUNRO, JANET (1934–   ). Scottish leading lady with brief stage experience before films in both GB and US. *The Trollenberg Terror* (57), *The Young and the Guilty* (57), *Darby O'Gill and the Little People* (58), *Third Man on the Mountain* (59), *The Swiss Family Robinson* (60), *The Day the Earth Caught Fire* (62), *Life for Ruth* (62), *Bitter Harvest* (63), *A Jolly Bad Fellow* (64), *Sebastian* (67), etc.

MUNSEL, PATRICE (1925–   ). American operatic soprano who played the title role in *Melba* (53).

MUNSHIN, JULES (1915–   ). Rubber-limbed American comedian, in occasional films from the mid-40s. *Easter Parade* (48), *Everybody's Cheering* (*Take Me Out to the Ball Game*) (48), *On the Town* (49), *Ten Thousand Bedrooms* (56), *Silk Stockings* (57), *Wild and Wonderful* (64), etc.

MUNSON, ONA (1906–1955) (Ona Wolcott). American character actress, former dancer. *Going Wild* (30), *Five Star Final* (32), *Gone with the Wind* (39), *Drums of the Congo* (40), *The Shanghai Gesture* (as Mother Gin Sling) (41), *The Cheaters* (45), *The Red House* (47), etc.

MURDER INC. (THE ENFORCER) (US 1951). A cleverly constructed police thriller, plainly but well done in all departments, based on the discovery of America's murder-for-payment organization. Filled with shock force but playing down the on-screen violence, it gave Humphrey Bogart a strong but unobtrusive part as the police chief, with clever cameos from Everett Sloane, Zero Mostel, Laurence Tolan and Ted de Corsia as the chief thugs. Written by Martin Rackin, photographed by Robert Burks, directed by Bretaigne Windust.

MURDOCH, RICHARD (1907–   ). British radio entertainer, long partnered with Arthur Askey; film appearances include *Band Wagon* (39), *The Ghost Train* (41), *It Happened in Soho* (48), *Golden Arrow* (52), *Not a Hope in Hell* (59), *Strictly Confidential* (61), etc.

MURNAU, F. W. (or FRIEDRICH) (1889–1931) (F. W. Plumpe). German director in films from 1919; Hollywood from 1927. *Satanas* (19), *Dr Jekyll and Mr Hyde* (20), *Nosferatu* (*Dracula*) (22), *The Last Laugh* (24), *Tartuffe* (24), *Faust* (26), *Sunrise* (27), *Four Devils* (28), *Our Daily Bread* (*City Girl*) (30), *Tabu* (co-d) (31), etc.

MURPHY, AUDIE (1924–   ). Boyish American leading man who came to films on the strength of his record as World War II's most decorated soldier. Has made innumerable low-budget Westerns. *Beyond Glory* (debut) (48), *The Kid from Texas* (50), *The Red Badge of Courage* (51), *Ride Clear of Diablo* (54), *Destry* (55), *To Hell and Back* (his autobiography) (55), *Night Passage* (57), *No Name on the Bullet* (58), *The Quiet American* (58), *The Unforgiven* (59), *Six Black Horses* (62), *Gunpoint* (65), *Arizona Raiders* (65), *A Time For Dying* (69), etc. TV series: *Whispering Smith* (61).

MURPHY, GEORGE (1904–   ). Irish-American actor-dancer, in films from 1934 after stage experience. *Kid Millions* (34), *You're a Sweetheart* (37), *Broadway Melody of 1938*, *Little Nellie Kelly* (40), *Tom, Dick and Harry* (41), *For Me and My Girl* (42), *This Is the Army* (43), *Show Business* (43), *Step Lively* (44), *The Arnelo Affair* (47), *Big City* (48), *It's a Big Country* (52), *Walk East on Beacon* (52), etc. Retired from acting in favour of business, public relations and politics (now senator for California). Special AA 1950 'for interpreting the film industry to the nation at large'.

MURPHY, MARY (c. 1931–   ). American leading lady. *The Lemon Drop Kid* (debut) (51), *The Wild One* (54), *The Desperate Hours* (55), *The Intimate Stranger* (GB) (56), *Crime and Punishment U.S.A.* (59), *Forty Pounds of Trouble* (63), etc.

MURPHY, RALPH (1895–1967). American director, in Hollywood from silent days. *The Gay City* (41), *Hearts in Springtime* (41), *Mrs Wiggs of the Cabbage Patch* (42), *Rainbow Island* (44), *The Man in Half Moon Street* (44), *Red Stallion in the Rockies* (49), *Dick Turpin's Ride* (51), *Captain Blood, Fugitive* (52), *Desert Rats* (53), *The Lady in the Iron Mask* (53), *Three Stripes in the Sun* (also wrote) (55), etc.

MURPHY, RICHARD (1912–   ). American writer, in Hollywood from 1937. *Boomerang* (47), *Cry of the City* (48), *Panic in the Streets* (50), *Les Misérables* (52), *Broken Lance* (54), *Compulsion* (58), *The Wackiest Ship in the Army* (also directed) (60), etc.

MURPHY, ROSEMARY (1927–   ). German-born American stage actress. Film debut: *Any Wednesday* (66).

MURRAY, BARBARA (1929–   ). British leading lady with stage experience. *Anna Karenina* (film debut) (48), *Passport to Pimlico* (48), *Doctor at Large* (56), *Campbell's Kingdom* (58), *A Cry from the Streets* (58), *Girls in Arms* (60), many others; also much on TV.

MURRAY, CHARLIE (1872–1941). American vaudeville comedian long with Mack Sennett. In *Tillie's Punctured Romance* (15), and later played with George Sidney in a long series about the Cohens and Kellys.

MURRAY, DON (1929–   ). American leading man with stage experience. *Bus Stop* (film debut) (56), *The Bachelor Party* (57), *A Hatful of Rain* (57), *The Hoodlum Priest* (also co-produced) (61), *Tunnel Six* (also co-produced) (62), *Advise and Consent* (62), *Baby the Rain Must Fall* (65), *Kid Rodelo* (65), *The Viking Queen* (GB) (67), *Childish Things* (also wrote and produced) (69), etc. TV series: *The Outcasts* (68–69).

MURRAY, JAMES (1901–1936). American leading man, a former extra who was chosen by King Vidor to play the hero of *The Crowd* (28), but subsequently took to drink and died in obscurity. *The Big City* (28), *Thunder* (29), *Bright Lights* (30), *The Reckoning* (32), *Heroes for Sale* (32), *Skull and Crown* (35), etc.

MURRAY, KEN (c. 1907–   ) (Don Court). American comedy actor, radio and TV entertainer, especially as collector of old 'home movies' of the stars. Film appearances include *Half Marriage* (29), *A Night at Earl Carroll's* (41), *Follow Me Boys* (66). Collected special Oscar for his 1947 bird fantasy *Bill and Coo*.

MURRAY, MAE (1889–1965) (Marie Adrienne Koenig). American leading lady of the silent screen; former dancer; usually in flashy roles. *Sweet Kitty Bellairs* (17), *Her Body in Bond* (18), *The Mormon Maid* (20), *Jazz Mania* (21), *Fashion Row* (23), *The Merry Widow* (25), *Circe the Enchantress* (27), *Peacock Alley* (31), etc. Retired to marry.

MURRAY, STEPHEN (1912–   ). British character actor, on stage from 1933. Film debut: as Gladstone in *The Prime Minister* (41). Later: *Next of Kin* (42), *Undercover* (43), *Master of Bankdam* (46), *London Belongs to Me* (48), *The Magnet* (50), *Four-Sided Triangle* (53), *Guilty* (55), *A Tale of Two Cities* (57), *The Nun's Story* (59), etc.; also many TV appearances.

MURRAY-HILL, PETER (1908–1957). British leading man of stage and screen; was married to Phyllis Calvert. *A Yank at Oxford* (38), *The Outsider* (39), *Jane Steps Out* (40), *The Ghost Train* (41), *Madonna of the Seven Moons* (44), *They Were Sisters* (last film) (45), etc.

MURTON, LIONEL (1915–   ). Canadian character actor resident in Britain. *Meet the Navy* (46), *The Long Dark Hall* (51), *The Runaway Bus* (54), *The Battle of the River Plate* (55), *Up the Creek* (58), *Northwest Frontier* (59), many others. TV series: *The Dickie Henderson Show*.

MUSE, CLARENCE (1889–   ). American Negro character actor. *Hearts in Dixie* (28), *Cabin in the Cotton* (32), *Showboat* (36), *Tales of Manhattan* (42), *An Act of Murder* (48), *So Bright the Flame* (52), many others.

musical remakes are becoming thicker on the ground than musical originals. All the following had been filmed at least once before, as straight dramas or comedies without music:

Where's Charley	as *Charley's Aunt*
Three for the Show	as *My Two Husbands*
Annie Get Your Gun	as *Annie Oakley*
Kismet	as *Kismet*
The King and I	as *Anna and the King of Siam*
Carousel	as *Liliom*
High Society	as *The Philadelphia Story*
Silk Stockings	as *Ninotchka*
Gigi	as *Gigi*
My Fair Lady	as *Pygmalion*
The Sound of Music	as *The Trapp Family*
Funny Girl	as *Rose of Washington Square*
Sweet Charity	as *Nights of Cabiria*
Camelot	as *Lancelot and Guinevere*
Oliver!	as *Oliver Twist*
Hello Dolly	as *The Matchmaker*
Cabaret	as *I Am a Camera*
Fiddler on the Roof	as *Tevye the Milkman*

musicals obviously could not exist before Al Jolson sang 'Mammy, in 1927. During the first two or three years of talkies, however' Hollywood produced so many gaudy back-stage stories and all-star spectacles that the genre quickly wore out its welcome: *Broadway Melody, The Singing Fool, The Desert Song, Showboat, Chasing Rainbows, Show of Shows, Hollywood Revue, Lights of New York, On with the Show, King of Jazz, Gold Diggers of Broadway, Sunny Side Up* . . . all these before the end of 1930, and there were many poorer imitations. Discipline was needed, and the disciplinarian who emerged was Broadway dance director, Busby Berkeley. His kaleidoscopic ensembles first dazzled the eye in Goldwyn/Cantor extravaganzas like *Whoopee* and *Palmy Days*, and came to full flower in the Warner musicals which brought to the fore stars like Joan Blondell, Ruby Keeler and Dick Powell, filling the years from 1933 to 1937 with such shows as *Footlight Parade, Forty-second Street, Dames, Wonder Bar, Flirtation Walk* and the annual *Gold-Digger* comedies. Meanwhile at Paramount Lubitsch had been quietly establishing a quieter style, using recitative, with *The Love Parade* and *One Hour with You*; Mamoulian was equally successful with *Love Me Tonight*; and the Marx Brothers contributed their own brand of musical anarchy. From 1933 to 1940 at RKO Fred Astaire and Ginger Rogers were teamed in an affectionately-remembered series of light comedy-musicals. MGM made sporadic efforts with creaky vehicles like *Cuban Love Song* but did not come into their own until 1935, when they started the Jeanette Macdonald/Nelson Eddy series of operettas; these were followed by a dramatic musical, *The Great Ziegfeld*, by the Eleanor Powell spectaculars like *Rosalie*, by a revived *Broadway Melody* series, and by *The Wizard of Oz* and the early Judy Garland/Mickey Rooney teenage extravaganzas, *Babes in Arms* and *Strike Up the Band*. Fox had Shirley Temple, Sonja Henie and Alice Faye; Goldwyn contributed Cantor and *The Goldwyn Follies*.

The popularity of musicals continued into the war-torn 40s, when escapism was *de rigueur*. Universal, whose only major musical pre-war was *Showboat*, continued to build up Deanna Durbin and threw in Donald O'Connor and Gloria Jean for good measure. Warners had *This Is the Army* and several musical biopics: *Yankee Doodle Dandy*, *Night and Day*, *Rhapsody in Blue*. RKO had a young man named Sinatra. Fox found goldmines in Carmen Miranda and Betty Grable, but their vehicles were routine; Columbia did slightly better by Rita Hayworth, and then surprised everyone with *The Jolson Story*, which set the musical back on top just when it was flagging. Paramount was doing very nicely with Bing Crosby and Bob Hope. Everybody did at least one big morale-building musical with all the stars on the payroll blowing kisses to the boys out there: *Star-Spangled Rhythm*, *Thank Your Lucky Stars*, *Hollywood Canteen*, *Thousands Cheer* and so on.

Top dog in the 40s—and 50s—was undoubtedly MGM. Specialities like *Ziegfeld Follies*, *Till the Clouds Roll By* and *Words and Music* came side by side with more routine productions starring Gene Kelly, Judy Garland, and Esther Williams (in aqua-musicals, of course). The decade ended in a blaze of glory with *On the Town*, which led to the even more spectacular heights of *An American in Paris* and *Singin' in the Rain*. By this time Mario Lanza and Howard Keel were needing new vehicles to themselves, *The Great Caruso* and *Seven Brides for Seven Brothers* being outstanding productions in their own right. But by the mid-50s the demand, or the fashion, for musicals, was dying. It lasted longest at Metro, who doggedly remade pictures like *The Belle of New York* and *Rose Marie*, added music to *Ninotchka* and *The Philadelphia Story* and *Gigi*. Warners plugged on until their bright star of 1948, Doris Day, signed with another studio and turned dramatic; Fox had two mammoth tries in *Call Me Madam* and *There's No Business Like Show Business*; Paramount came up with *White Christmas*, the enterprising *Red Garters* and *Funny Face*, and even *Lil' Abner*. But the risk was becoming too great in a chancy market, with expenses growing by the minute; and for the last few years no original musicals have been written in Hollywood, with the exception of the family-aimed *Mary Poppins*, *Thoroughly Modern Millie* and the twenty-odd look-alike vehicles of Elvis Presley. Copper-bottomed Broadway hits like *Pal Joey*, *Oklahoma*, *Carousel*, *The Pajama Game*, *South Pacific*, *The King and I*, *West Side Story*, *Guys and Dolls*, *The Sound of Music* and

My Fair Lady are still filmed, at gargantuan cost, but as cinema they all too often disappoint filmgoers with memories of Berkeley and Kelly and Donen. The most inventive screen musical has been Bob Fosse's *Sweet Charity*.

In Britain, the 30s were a highpoint of the light musical starring such talents as Jack Buchanan, Jessie Matthews, Gracie Fields, George Formby and Anna Neagle; Miss Neagle indeed carried on, dauntless, into the less favourable climate of the 50s. The 40s were pretty barren apart from the Rank spectacular *London Town*, which flopped; and it wasn't until the 60s that Elstree struck something like the right note with its energetic though derivative series starring Cliff Richard. In 1968 the old-fashioned though energetic *Oliver!* proved that Britain can handle a really big musical.

THE MUSKETEERS OF PIG ALLEY (US 1912). A D. W. Griffith melodrama starring Mary Pickford, often quoted as the screen's first step towards social realism; set in the teeming slums of New York.

MUSURACA, NICHOLAS (c. 1908–   ). American cinematographer. *Curse of the Cat People* (44), *The Spiral Staircase* (45), *The Locket* (46), *Build My Gallows High* (*Out of the Past*) (48), *I Remember Mama* (48), *Split Second* (52), *The Story of Mankind* (57), *Too Much Too Soon* (58), etc.

mute print. One with only the picture, no sound tracks.

MUTINY ON THE BOUNTY. Two films have been made of this semi-historical account of how Captain Bligh was cast adrift in an open boat in 1781. 1. US 1935; directed by Frank Lloyd, with Clark Gable and Charles Laughton. 2. US 1962: directed by Carol Reed (who resigned) and Lewis Milestone, with Marlon Brando and Trevor Howard. The first remains the most impressive despite its technical limitations.

MUYBRIDGE, EDWARD or EADWEARD (1830–1904). British photographer who in 1877, in America, succeeded in analysing motion with a camera by taking a series of pictures of a horse in motion. (He used twenty-four cameras each attached to a trip wire.) Later he invented a form of projector which reassembled his pictures into the appearance of moving actuality.

MYCROFT, WALTER (1891–1959). British director. *Spring Meeting* (40), *My Wife's Family* (41), *Banana Ridge* (41), *The Woman's Angle* (producer only) (52), etc. Chief scriptwriter and director of productions at Elstree in the 30s.

MY DARLING CLEMENTINE (US 1946). A highly atmospheric, semi-literary Western based on Stuart N. Lake's book 'Wyatt Earp

Frontier Marshal' which had been previously filmed as *Frontier Marshal* with Randolph Scott in 1939. Excellent performances by Henry Fonda as Earp, Victor Mature as Doc Holliday, and Walter Brennan as the head of the Clantons who get shot up in the OK corral. John Ford directs affectionately. *Gunfight at the OK Corral* (57), with Burt Lancaster and Kirk Douglas, is a partial remake.

MY FAIR LADY (US 1964) (AA, BFA). A professional but uninspired celluloid version of the fabulous Lerner-Loewe musical play from Shaw's 'Pygmalion' (qv). A prodigious expenditure of talent, and to a lesser degree money, is evident, and there is plenty to enjoy; but more might have been packed into the most eagerly anticipated film of the decade. With Audrey Hepburn, Rex Harrison (AA), Stanley Holloway; directed by George Cukor (AA); designed by Cecil Beaton (AA); photographed by Harry Stradling (AA). A special word is surely due for Marni Nixon, whose singing voice Audrey Hepburn mimes.

MY GIRL TISA (US 1947). A charming, neglected, period romance set in New York's immigrant quarter at the turn of the century, with special reference to the political scene and an amusing if unlikely ending with Teddy Roosevelt as *deus ex machina*. Delightfully played by Lilli Palmer, Sam Wanamaker, Alan Hale, Stella Adler and a large cast; written by Allen Boretz, photographed by Ernest Haller, directed by Elliott Nugent. On the film's original British release the last reel was oddly butchered to give an unhappy ending (Tisa being deported) instead of the actual one.

MY LITTLE CHICKADEE (US 1940). An outlandish comedy-Western starring, and written by, W. C. Fields and Mae West, the former as Cuthbert J. Twillie, the latter as Flower Belle Lee. Edward Cline was faced with the task of directing these strange personalities, and didn't quite manage it; the result is one of those engaging Hollywood freaks which no one can afford to have happen any more.

MY MAN GODFREY. Twice-filmed crazy comedy about a family of bored millionaires brought to heel by a butler they pick up in the gutter. 1936: directed by Gregory La Cava, with William Powell and Carole Lombard. 1957: directed by Henry Koster, with David Niven and June Allyson.

MY SISTER EILEEN. Another twice-filmed comedy, from the book by Ruth McKinley about two sisters on the hunt for fame and men in New York. 1942: directed by Alexander Hall, with Rosalind Russell and Janet Blair. 1955: a semi-musical directed by Richard Quine, with Betty Garrett and Janet Leigh. There has also been a TV series with Elaine Stritch and Shirley Bonne. The men in the case were (1) Brian Aherne, (2) Jack Lemmon, (3) Jack Weston (later replaced by Stubby Kaye).

mystery has always been a popular element of motion picture entertainment. Always providing scope for sinister goings-on and sudden revelations, mystery films divide themselves into two basic genres: who done it, and how will the hero get out of it? Silent melodramas like *The Perils of Pauline* were full of clutching hands and villainous masterminds, devices adopted by the German post-war cinema for its own purposes: *The Cabinet of Dr Caligari*, *Dr Mabuse* and *Warning Shadows* are all mysteries, peopled by eccentrics and madmen. American silent who-done-its like *The Cat and the Canary*, *The Thirteenth Chair* and *One Exciting Night* set a pattern for thrillers which could not come fully into their own until music and sound were added. In the 30s the 'thunderstorm mystery', with its spooky house and mysterious servants (the butler usually did it) quickly became a cliché; but this is not to denigrate the entertainment value of such movies as *The Bat*, *The Terror*, *Murder by the Clock*, *The Gorilla*, *Seven Keys to Baldpate*, *Double Door*, *You'll Find Out*, *Topper Returns*, *The House on Haunted Hill*, and the Bob Hope remakes of *The Cat and the Canary* and *The Ghost Breakers*.

The 30s also saw a movement to relegate the puzzle film to the detective series, a genre later taken over eagerly by TV. These films were built around such protagonists as Charlie Chan, Sherlock Holmes, Hercule Poirot, Inspector Hanaud, Ellery Queen, Perry Mason, Inspector Hornleigh, Nero Wolfe, Philo Vance, Nick Carter, The Crime Doctor, The Saint, The Falcon, Bulldog Drummond, Mrs Pym, the 'Thin Man' (the thin man was actually the victim of the first story, but the tag stuck to William Powell), Mr Moto, Michael Shayne, Hildegarde Withers, Mr Wong, Arsène Lupin, Dick Barton, The Baron, The Toff, Gideon, Slim Callaghan, Lemmy Caution and Maigret . . . all soundly spoofed by Groucho Marx as Wolf J. Flywheel in *The Big Store*. The best of these fictional detectives were the creations of Dashiell Hammett (Sam Spade in *The Maltese Falcon*) and Raymond Chandler (Philip Marlowe in *The Big Sleep*, *Farewell My Lovely* and *The High Window*); and after a twenty-year hiatus the threads are being picked up in what promises to be a series built around John Ross Macdonald's *Harper*. Single who-done-its of great merit were *Gaslight*, *Laura*, *Green for Danger* (one ached for a whole series starring Alastair Sim as Inspector Cockrill), *The Spiral Staircase*, *Crossfire*, *Boomerang*, *Bad Day at Black Rock*, *Les Diaboliques*, *Charade*, *Mirage*, *Taste of Fear*, *The List of Adrian Messenger*, and the two versions of *Ten Little Niggers*. Two gentler detectives were provided by Alec Guinness's *Father Brown* and Margaret Rutherford's Miss Marple.

The other type of mystery, with a hero on the run, usually suspected of murder, finally uncovering the real villain after many narrow escapes from death, was developed mainly by Alfred Hitchcock in such films as *The Thirty-nine Steps*, *The Lady Vanishes*, *Saboteur*, *Spellbound*, *Strangers on a Train*, *North by Northwest* and

Torn Curtain. But stars as various as Alan Ladd, Bob Hope, Danny Kaye, Robert Mitchum, and Paul Newman have also found the device useful.

The recent vogue for tongue-in-cheek spy thrillers is to all intents and purposes a reversion to the Pearl White school, with the hero menaced at every turn but, of course, finally triumphant.

See also: *spies*; *private eyes*.

N

NADER, GEORGE (1921–   ). American leading man who after TV experience starred in many Universal action films of the 50s but has lately been less active. *Monsoon* (debut) (52), *Four Guns to the Border* (54), *The Second Greatest Sex* (55), *Away All Boats* (56), *Congo Crossing* (56), *Four Girls in Town* (57), *Joe Butterfly* (57), *Nowhere to Go* (GB) (58), *The Human Duplicators* (65), *The Million Eyes of Su-Muru* (66), etc. TV series: *Ellery Queen* (56), *The Man and the Challenge* (59), *Shannon* (61).

NAGEL, ANNE (1912–1966). American supporting actress, the heroine's friend in countless movies of the 40s.

NAGEL, CONRAD (1896–1970). American leading man of the 20s who came to Hollywood after stage experience; latterly ran acting school. *Little Women* (19), *Fighting Chance* (20), *Three Weeks* (24), *The Exquisite Sinner* (26), *Slightly Used* (27), *Quality Street* (27), *East Lynne* (31), *Dangerous Corner* (34), *Navy Spy* (37), *I Want a Divorce* (40), *The Woman in Brown* (48), *All That Heaven Allows* (55), *Stranger in My Arms* (58), *The Man Who Understood Women* (59), many others.

NAISH, J. CARROL (1900–   ). American character actor with stage experience, in films from 1930. *The Hatchet Man* (32), *Lives of a Bengal Lancer* (35), *Anthony Adverse* (36), *Beau Geste* (39), *Birth of the Blues* (41), *Blood and Sand* (41), *The Corsican Brothers* (41), *The Pied Piper* (42), *Dr Renault's Secret* (42), *Batman* (serial) (43), *Behind the Rising Sun* (43), *Gung Ho!* (44), *A Medal for Benny* (45), *House of Frankenstein* (45), *The Southerner* (45), *Enter Arsène Lupin* (45), *The Beast with Five Fingers* (46), *Joan of Arc* (48), *Black Hand* (49), *Annie Get Your Gun* (50), *Across the Wide Missouri* (51), *Sitting Bull* (54), *Violent Saturday* (54), *New York Confidential* (54), *The Young Don't Cry* (57), *The Hanged Man* (64), many others. Many TV appearances including series: *Life With Luigi* (54), *The New Adventures of Charlie Chan* (57), *Guestward Ho!* (60).

NAISMITH, LAURENCE (1908–   ) (Lawrence Johnson). British character actor with wide stage experience. *Trouble in the Air* (47), *A Piece of Cake* (48), *I Believe in You* (51), *The Beggar's Opera* (52), *Mogambo* (53), *Carrington VC* (55), *Richard III* (56), *Boy on a Dolphin* (57), *Tempest* (58), *A Night to Remember* (58), *Sink the Bismarck* (60), *The Singer Not the Song* (61), *Jason and the Argonauts* (63), *The Three Lives of Thomasina* (63), *Sky West and Crooked* (65), *The Scorpio*

Letters (67), *The Long Duel* (67), *A Garden of Cucumbers* (US) (67), *Camelot* (US) (67), many others.

NAKED CITY (US 1948). Mark Hellinger's last production was a highly influential police thriller shot on location in New York and using a development of the semi-documentary approach first seen in such films as *The House on 92nd Street* two years earlier. It ended with the famous tag used in all 99 episodes of the TV series which followed twelve years later: 'There are eight million stories in the naked city: this has been one of them.' Barry Fitzgerald played the leading cop and Don Taylor his aide; Jules Dassin directed, enlivening a basically routine story with striking detail; the script was by Albert Maltz and Marvin Wald with photography by William Daniels (AA). Despite hundreds of imitations the 'authentic' crime thriller is still popular.

NALDI, NITA (1899–1961) (Anita Donna Dooley). Italian-American leading lady of the 20s, formerly in the Ziegfeld Follies. *Dr Jekyll and Mr Hyde* (20), *The Unfair Sex* (22), *Blood and Sand* (22), *The Ten Commandments* (23), *A Sainted Devil* (25), *The Marriage Whirl* (26), *The Lady Who Lied* (27), etc. Sound ended her career.

NANA. Zola's novel of the Paris demi-monde in the 80s has been seen in three major film versions. 1. Jean Renoir directed a silent French version in 1926, with Catherine Hessling and Werner Krauss. 2. Dorothy Arzner directed an American version, sometimes known as *Lady of the Boulevards*, in 1934 with Anna Sten, Lionel Atwill and Phillips Holmes. 3. Christian-Jaque directed a second French version in 1955, this time in colour, with Martine Carol and Charles Boyer. None was faultless.

NANCY DREW. The teenage heroine of a number of American second features made in 1938–39; all were directed by William Clemens and starred Bonita Granville. The titles included *Nancy Drew Detective*, *Nancy Drew Reporter*, *Nancy Drew and the Hidden Staircase*, *Nancy Drew Trouble Shooter*.

NANOOK OF THE NORTH (US 1921). This classic documentary was made by explorer-director Robert Flaherty, who was commissioned by Revillion Frères, a fur company, and spent years in the Arctic among the Eskimos while amassing his material. It is virtually the first significant documentary in the history of the cinema, and even today remains watchable.

NAPIER, ALAN (1903–   ) (Alan Napier-Clavering). Dignified British character actor, in Hollywood since 1940; usually plays butlers or noble lords. *In a Monastery Garden* (31), *Loyalties* (32), *For Valour* (37), *The Four Just Men* (39), *The Invisible Man Returns* (40), *Random Harvest* (42), *Ministry of Fear* (43), *Lost Angel* (44),

Forever Amber (47), *Tarzan's Magic Fountain* (50), *Julius Caesar* (53), *The Court Jester* (55), *Journey to the Centre of the Earth* (59), *Marnie* (64), scores of others. TV series: *Batman*.

NAPIER, DIANA (1908–   ) (Molly Ellis). British leading lady of the 30s; married Richard Tauber. *Wedding Rehearsal* (33), *Catherine the Great* (34), *The Private Life of Don Juan* (34), *Mimi* (35), *Land Without Music* (36), *Pagliacci* (37), then retired until *I Was a Dancer* (48).

NAPIER, RUSSELL (1910–   ). Australian-born actor, long in Britain. Has been in numerous small parts, usually as officials; also played the chief inspector in many of the 3-reel 'Scotland Yard' series.

NAPOLEON, ART (* –   ). American director. *Man on the Prowl* (also wrote) (57), *Too Much Too Soon* (58), *Ride the Wild Surf* (wrote only) (64).

NAPOLEON BONAPARTE has been impersonated on screen by Charles Boyer in *Marie Walewska* (*Conquest*), Esme Percy in *Invitation to the Waltz*, Emile Drain in *Madame sans Gene* and *Les Perles de la Couronne*, Rollo Lloyd in *Anthony Adverse*, Julien Berthau in *Madame*, Marlon Brando in *Desirée*, Arnold Moss in *The Black Book*, Pierre Mondy in *Austerlitz*, Herbert Lom in several films including *The Young Mr Pitt* and *War and Peace*, and Rod Steiger in *Waterloo*.

Abel Gance's 1925 film *Napoleon* (with Albert Dieudonne) is noted for the first use of a triptych screen corresponding very closely to Cinerama.

NARDINI, TOM (1945–   ). American juvenile: *Cat Ballou* (65), *Africa Texas Style* (67), *The Young Animals* (68), etc. TV series: *Cowboy in Africa*.

NARES, OWEN (1888–1943) (O. N. Ramsay). British matinée idol and silent screen star. *Dandy Donovan* (14), *God Bless the Red, White and Blue* (18), *Indian Love Lyrics* (23), *Young Lochinvar* (23), *The Sorrows of Satan* (27), *Milestones* (28), *The Middle Watch* (30), *Sunshine Susie* (31), *The Impassive Footman* (32), *The Private Life of Don Juan* (34), *The Show Goes On* (37), *The Prime Minister* (41), etc.

NARIZZANO, SILVIO (c. 1927–   ). Canadian director in Britain, from TV. *Under Ten Flags* (co-d) (60), *Fanatic* (65), *Georgy Girl* (66), *Blue* (US) (67), *The Man Who Had Power Over Women* (69), *Loot* (70).

narrators are heard at the beginning of, or even throughout, many important movies, and although a few have been credited, very often a nagging doubt persists about the owner of the voice. Here then are a few for the record:

The War of the Worlds	Cedric Hardwicke
Mother Wore Tights	Anne Baxter

A Letter to Three Wives	Celeste Holm
The Unseen	Ray Collins
The Picture of Dorian Gray	Cedric Hardwicke
To Kill a Mockingbird	Kim Stanley
How the West was Won	Spencer Tracy
The Night they Raided Minsky's	Rudy Vallee
Mackenna's Gold	Victor Jory
The Hallelujah Trail	John Dehner
The Red Badge of Courage	James Whitmore
It's a Big Country	Louis Calhern
Duel in the Sun	Orson Welles
The Vikings	Orson Welles
Zulu	Richard Burton
The Solid Gold Cadillac	George Burns

NASH, MARY (1885–1966). American stage actress whose best film role was as Mrs Lord in *The Philadelphia Story* (40).

National Film Archive. The government-financed museum of films of artistic and historical value. Operated by the British Film Institute.

National Film Finance Corporation. A government body which lends a proportion of capital to British independent producers.

NATWICK, MILDRED (1908–   ). American character actress, at her best in slightly macabre or fey roles. Wide stage experience since 1932. Films include *The Long Voyage Home* (40), *The Enchanted Cottage* (44), *She Wore a Yellow Ribbon* (49), *The Quiet Man* (52), *The Trouble with Harry* (55), *The Court Jester* (56), *Tammy and the Bachelor* (57), *Barefoot in the Park* (67), *If It's Tuesday This Must Be Belgium* (69), *The Maltese Bippy* (69), etc.

NAUGHTON, CHARLES: see THE CRAZY GANG.

naval comedy in British movies usually has a 30s look about it, may well be written by Ian Hay, and almost always concerns the officers; as in *The Middle Watch, Carry on Admiral, The Midshipmaid, The Flag Lieutenant* and *Up the Creek* (though the other ranks had their look in with *The Bulldog Breed, The Baby and the Battleship* and *Jack Ahoy*). In Hollywood movies the focus of interest is set firmly among the other ranks: *Follow the Fleet, Abbott and Costello in the Navy, Anchors Aweigh, On the Town, You're in the Navy Now, The Fleet's In, Onion-head, Don't Go Near the Water, Don't Give Up the Ship*.

THE NAVIGATOR (US 1924). One of Buster Keaton's classic silent comedies, a succession of brilliant sight gags showing the comedian marooned with a girl at sea on an otherwise empty luxury liner. Written by Clyde Bruckman and Joseph Mitchell; directed by Keaton and Donald Crisp.

NAZARIN (Mexico 1959). An arresting and imaginative fantasy about the misadventures of a Roman Catholic priest hounded by the sins of the world. Directed and co-written by Luis Bunuel; with Francisco Rabal.

NAZARRO, RAY (* –). American director of second features. *The Tougher They Come* (50), *The Return of the Corsican Brothers* (53), *Top Gun* (55), *The Hired Gun* (57), etc.; then into TV.

NAZIMOVA, ALLA (1879–1945). Russian-born stage actress who made a number of films in America: *War Brides* (16), *Camille* (21), *A Doll's House* (22), *Salome* (23), *Escape (When the Door Opened)* (40), *The Bridge of San Luis Rey* (44), etc.

NAZZARI, AMEDEO (1907–). Virile Italian leading man, in films since 1935 although few have travelled. *The Wolf of Sila* (47), *The Brigand* (51), *Nights of Cabiria* (57), *Labyrinth* (59), *The Best of Enemies* (61), etc.

†NEAGLE, ANNA (1904–) (Marjorie Robertson). British leading lady, a former chorus dancer who after her marriage in the 30s to producer Herbert Wilcox built up a formidable film gallery of historical heroines. *Should a Doctor Tell* (30), *The Chinese Bungalow* (31), *Goodnight Vienna* (32), *The Flight Lieutenant* (33), *The Little Damozel* (33), *Bitter Sweet* (33), *The Queen's Affair* (33), *Nell Gwyn* (34), *Peg of Old Drury* (35), *Limelight* (36), *The Three Maxims* (36), *London Melody* (37), *Victoria the Great* (37), *Sixty Glorious Years* (38), *Nurse Edith Cavell* (39), *Irene* (US) (40), *No No Nanette* (US) (40), *Sunny* (US) (41), *They Flew Alone* (as Amy Johnson) (42), *Forever and a Day* (43), *Yellow Canary* (43), *I Live in Grosvenor Square* (45), *Piccadilly Incident* (46), *The Courtneys of Curzon Street* (47), *Spring in Park Lane* (48), *Elizabeth of Ladymead* (49), *Maytime in Mayfair* (49), *Odette* (50), *The Lady with a Lamp* (51), *Derby Day* (52), *Lilacs in the Spring* (55), *King's Rhapsody* (56), *My Teenage Daughter* (56), *No Time for Tears* (57), *The Man Who Wouldn't Talk* (58), *The Lady Is a Square* (58). In 1958–61 produced three Frankie Vaughan films; returned to stage.

NEAL, PATRICIA (1926–). American leading actress with Broadway experience. *John Loves Mary* (film debut) (48), *The Fountainhead* (49), *The Hasty Heart* (GB) (49), *Bright Leaf* (50), *Three Secrets* (50), *The Breaking Point* (51), *Canyon Pass* (51), *The Day the Earth Stood Still* (51), *Diplomatic Courier* (52), *Stranger from Venus* (GB) (54), *A Face in the Crowd* (57), *Breakfast at Tiffany's* (61), *Hud* (AA, BFA) (63), *Psyche 59* (GB) (64), *In Harm's Way* (BFA) (65), *The Subject was Roses* (68), others.

NEAL, TOM (1915–). American leading man, mainly in second features; former athlete. *Out West with the Hardys* (39), *One Thrilling*

Night (42), *The Racket Man* (45), *Detour* (47), *Navy Bound* (51), *Red Desert* (54), etc.

NEAME, RONALD (1911–   ). British cinematographer, in films from 1928: *Blackmail* (29), *The Gaunt Stranger* (37), *Major Barbara* (40); *In Which We Serve* (42), *Blithe Spirit* (45), etc. Turned producer, *Great Expectations* (46), *Oliver Twist* (48), *The Passionate Friends* (49), etc. Since then has been director: *Take My Life* (48), *The Golden Salamander* (50), *The Card* (52), *The Man Who Never Was* (56), *The Horse's Mouth* (59), *Tunes of Glory* (60), *I Could Go On Singing* (63), *The Chalk Garden* (64), *Mister Moses* (65), *A Man Could Get Killed* (co-d) (66), *Gambit* (66), *The Prime of Miss Jean Brodie* (69), etc.

NEBENZAL, SEYMOUR (1899–1961). Distinguished German producer who had a disappointing career after going to Hollywood in the late 30s. *Westfront* (30,) *M* (32), *Kameradschaft* (32), *The Testament of Dr Mabuse* (33), *Mayerling* (36), *We Who Are Young* (40), *Summer Storm* (44), *Whistle Stop* (46), *Heaven Only Knows* (47), *Siren of Atlantis* (48), *M* (remake) (51), etc.

NEFF, HILDEGARDE (1925–   ) (Hildegarde Knef). German leading lady, former artist and film cartoonist. Briefly on German stage, then to films, and for a time in Hollywood. *The Murderers Are Amongst Us* (46), *Film without Title* (47), *The Sinner* (50), *Decision before Dawn* (51), *The Snows of Kilimanjaro* (52), *Diplomatic Courier* (52), *Henriette* (52), *The Man Between* (53), *The Girl from Hamburg* (57), *And So To Bed* (63), *Landru* (63), *Mozambique* (65) *The Lost Continent* (GB) (68), etc.

NEGRI, POLA (1897–   ) (Appolonia Chalupek). Polish-born leading lady with experience on German stage and screen; went to Hollywood in 20s and was popular until sound came in. *Die Bestie* (15), *Madame du Barry* (18), *The Flame* (20), *Bella Donna* (US) (23), *Forbidden Paradise* (24), *Hotel Imperial* (26), *Three Sinners* (28), *A Woman Commands* (31), *Madame Bovary* (35), *Hi Diddle Diddle* (43), *The Moonspinners* (64), etc.

Negroes in films have only slowly attained equal status with whites· In early silents they were invariably depicted as slaves, a fact encouraged by the several popular versions of *Uncle Tom's Cabin*. If a film had a Negro role of consequence, it was usually played by a white man in blackface. But Negroes began to make their own films for their own audiences, and still do, though these seldom get a general showing. The first all-Negro film was *Darktown Jubilee* in 1914 . . . the year that Griffith made *The Birth of a Nation*, with its strong anti-Negro bias. Griffith atoned for this in *The Greatest Thing in Life* (18), in which a white soldier and a Negro embraced, but in 1922 he again incurred the wrath of colour-sensitive critics by making *One Exciting Night*, the first film to boast the quickly stereotyped figure of the terrified Negro manservant. Early talkies included such all-Negro films as *Hearts in Dixie* and Vidor's *Hallelujah*, and in 1933 Paul Robeson appeared in a version of Eugene O'Neill's *The Emperor Jones*. Much of the interest of *Imitation of Life* (34) centred on the problems of Negro servant Louise Beavers and her half-white daughter. In 1936 the screen version of *Green Pastures*, depicting the simple Negro's idea of the Bible, was widely acclaimed but tended to perpetuate a patronizing attitude. The feeling of the South for its Negroes was strongly outlined in *They Won't Forget* (37) and *Gone with the Wind* (39). *Stormy Weather* (42) and *Cabin in the Sky* (43) were all-Negro musicals in Hollywood's best manner, but *Tales of Manhattan* (42) was retrogressive in showing Negroes as inhabitants of a vast shanty town. In *Casablanca* (42), however, Dooley Wilson was accepted on equal terms by Humphrey Bogart. Disney's *Song of the South* (46), despite an engaging performance by James Baskett, brought back the old Uncle Remus image. The post-war period generally permitted the emergence of serious Negro actors like James Edwards and Sidney Poitier, and films on racial themes such as *Intruder in the Dust* and *Pinky*. At last, in 1965, came films in which a Negro could play a straight part utterly unrelated to his colour.

Britain, less affected by Negro problems, moved in parallel fashion. In the early 30s, films of *The Kentucky Minstrels*; then Paul Robeson dominating somewhat insulting material in *Sanders of the River* and subsequently earning three or four serious film vehicles of his own; the post-war attempt to understand in *Men of Two Worlds*; and problem pictures like *Simba*, about the Mau-Mau, and *Flame in the Streets*, about the prospect of a Negro in an East End family.

†NEGULESCO, JEAN (1900–). Rumanian-born director, in US from 1927. *Kiss and Make Up* (34), *Singapore Woman* (41), *The Mask of Dimitrios* (44), *The Conspirators* (44), *Three Strangers* (46), *Nobody Lives Forever* (46), *Humoresque* (46), *Deep Valley* (47), *Roadhouse* (48), *Johnny Belinda* (48), *Britannia Mews* (49), *Under My Skin* (50), *Three Came Home* (50), *The Mudlark* (51), *Take Care of My Little Girl* (51), *Phone Call from a Stranger* (52), *Lydia Bailey* (52), *Lure of the Wilderness* (52), *Full House* (part) (52), *Titanic* (53), *How to Marry a Millionaire* (53), *Three Coins in the Fountain* (54), *Woman's World* (54), *Daddy Longlegs* (55), *The Rains of Ranchipur* (55), *Boy on a Dolphin* (57), *A Certain Smile* (58), *Count Your Blessings* (59), *The Best of Everything* (59), *Jessica* (62), *The Pleasure Seekers* (65), *Hello and Goodbye* (70), many others.

NEILAN, MARSHAL (1891–1958). American director who had meteoric success in the 20s and just as suddenly failed in the mid-30s. *The*

Cycle of Fate (16), *Freckles* (17), *Rebecca of Sunnybrook Farm* (17), *M'Liss* (18), *Daddy Longlegs* (19), *The Lotus Eater* (21), *Tess of the D'Urbervilles* (25), *Her Wild Oat* (27), *Three Ring Marriage* (28), *The Awful Truth* (29), *Sweethearts on Parade* (30), *The Lemon Drop Kid* (34), *Swing It, Professor* (37), many others. Also acted from 1912; last role *A Face in the Crowd* (57).

NEILL, ROY WILLIAM (1890–1946) (Roland de Gostrie). Irish-born director, long in Hollywood; never rose above low-budget thrillers but often did them well. *Love Letters* (17), *Toilers of the Sea* (23), *The Good Bad Girl* (31), *The Black Room* (34), *The Good Old Days* (GB) (35), *Eyes of the Underworld* (41), *Frankenstein Meets the Wolf Man* (43), *Gypsy Wildcat* (44), *Black Angel* (46), etc.; also produced and directed most of the Sherlock Holmes series starring Basil Rathbone (42–46).

NEILSON, JAMES (1918–   ). American director, former war photographer, who has worked almost entirely for Walt Disney. *Night Passage* (57), *The Country Husband* (58), *Moon Pilot* (61), *Summer Magic* (62), *Bon Voyage* (62), *Dr Syn* (63), *The Moonspinners* (64), *Bullwhip Griffin* (66), *Where Angels Go Trouble Follows* (68), *The First Time* (69), etc.

NELL GWYN. Charles II's orange-seller has appeared briefly in many films, but the two devoted to her story were both made in Britain by Herbert Wilcox: in 1927 with Dorothy Gish and in 1934 with Anna Neagle.

NELSON, BARRY (1920–   ). Stocky American leading man who makes films between stage shows. *China Caravan* (42), *A Guy Named Joe* (43), *Winged Victory* (44), *The Beginning of the End* (45), *The Man with My Face* (51), *The First Travelling Saleslady* (56), *Mary Mary* (63), others. TV series: *My Favourite Husband, Hudson's Bay*.

NELSON, ED (1928–   ). American actor who played gangsters, brothers-in-law and boy friends in innumerable 50s second features, then went into TV and found himself a secure niche as Dr Rossi in *Peyton Place* (63–68).

NELSON, GENE (1920–   ) (Gene Berg). American actor-dancer, on stage from 1938, films from 1950. *The Daughter of Rosie O'Grady* (debut) (50), *Tea for Two* (51), *Lullaby of Broadway* (52), *She's Working Her Way through College* (52), *So This Is Paris* (55), *Oklahoma* (55), etc. More recently has directed: *Kissin' Cousins* (64), *Harem Scarem* (65), *The Perils of Pauline* (67), etc.; also TV films.

NELSON, LORD HORATIO (1758–1805), the hero of Trafalgar, was portrayed in *Nelson* (19) by Donald Calthrop; in *Nelson* (26) by Cedric Hardwicke; in *Lady Hamilton* (42), by Laurence Olivier; in *Lady Hamilton* (Ger.) (68) by Richard Johnson.

NELSON, LORI (1933–). American light leading lady. *Ma and Pa Kettle at the Fair* (52), *Bend of the River* (52), *Walking My Baby Back Home* (53), *Destry* (55), *Mohawk* (56), *Hot Rod Girl* (56), etc.

†NELSON, RALPH (1916–). American actor-producer-director-playwright. Actor 1933–41, then Broadway and TV writer-producer. To Hollywood 1962 to direct *Blood Money (Requiem for a Heavyweight)*; subsequently *Lilies of the Field* (p, d) (63), *Soldier in the Rain* (64), *Fate Is the Hunter* (64), *Father Goose* (64), *Once a Thief* (65), *Duel at Diablo* (66), *Counterpoint* (67), *Charly* (68), *Tick Tick Tick* (70).

NELSON, RICK (1940–). American singer and light actor, son of bandleader Ozzie Nelson and his wife Harriet (formerly Harriet Hilliard: qv) with whom he appeared in the long-running TV series *The Adventures of Ozzie and Harriet* (52–66). Films on his own include *Here Come the Nelsons* (52), *Rio Bravo* (59), *The Wackiest Ship in the Army* (60), *Love and Kisses* (65).

NEMEC, JAN (1936–). Czech director. *Diamonds of the Night* (64), *The Party and the Guests* (66), *The Martyrs of Love* (67), etc.

NERO, FRANCO (1942–). Italian leading man who after starring in many home-produced adventures came to Hollywood for *Camelot* (67). 1968: *Day of the Owl (Mafia)* (It.). 1970: *The Virgin and the Gypsy*, *The Battle of Neretva*.

NERVO, JIMMY: see THE CRAZY GANG.

NESBITT, CATHLEEN (1889–). British character actress, on stage from 1910; very occasional films include *The Case of the Frightened Lady* (32), *Fanny by Gaslight* (43), *Nicholas Nickleby* (47), *Three Coins in the Fountain* (54), *Desiree* (54), *An Affair to Remember* (57), *Promise Her Anything* (66), *The Trygon Factor* (67), *Staircase* (69), etc.

NESBITT, DERREN (c. 1932–). British character actor, usually a smiling villain. *The Man in the Back Seat* (60), *Victim* (62), *Strongroom* (62), *The Naked Runner* (67), *Nobody Runs Forever* (68), *Where Eagles Dare* (68), etc.

NETTLETON, LOIS (c. 1929–). American character actress. *Period of Adjustment* (62), *Come Fly With Me* (63), *Mail Order Bride* (64), etc.

NEUMANN, KURT (1908–1958). German director, in Hollywood from 1925. Directed short comedies, then *My Pal the King* (32), *The Big Cage* (33), *Rainbow on the River* (36), *Island of Lost Men* (39), *Ellery Queen Master Detective* (40), *Tarzan and the Leopard Woman* (46), *Bad Boy* (49), *Rocketship XM* (also wrote and produced) (50),

715

Son of Ali Baba (53), *Carnival Story* (54), *Mohawk* (56), *Kronos* (57), *The Fly* (58), *Watusi* (58), etc.

NEVER GIVE A SUCKER AN EVEN BREAK (US 1941). The wildest of W. C. Fields' comedies, known in GB as *What a Man!*; Fields himself suggested that the billing should be shortened to '*Fields: Sucker*'. The ridiculous plot, reputedly written by Fields on the back of an envelope and sold to Universal for 25,000 dollars, concerns his experiences when, after dropping a bottle of whisky from a plane and diving out after it, he lands on a mountain top where there lives a girl who has never seen a man and promptly falls in love with him, despite the disapproval of her guardian Mrs Haemoglobin. . . . As with all Fields, the humour is a matter of taste.

NEVER ON SUNDAY (Greece 1960). An inexpensive but highly commercial location comedy made by Jules Dassin, who also played the shy American tourist who 'improves' a vivacious Greek prostitute. The music score by Manos Hadjidakis was as great an asset as Melina Mercouri's performance, and the film as a whole was another significant nail in the coffin of the Hays code, as vice remained triumphant.

NEVILLE, JOHN (1925–   ). British leading man, primarily on stage. Films: *Oscar Wilde* (60), *Billy Budd* (62), *Unearthly Stranger* (63), *A Study in Terror* (as Sherlock Holmes) (65).

NEWALL, GUY (1885–1937). British stage actor who became a popular leading man in silent sentimental dramas, especially with his wife Ivy Duke. Also directed most of his films. *Comradeship* (18), *The Garden of Resurrection* (19), *The Lure of Crooning Water* (20), *The Duke's Son* (20), *Beauty and the Beast* (22), *Boy Woodburn* (22), *The Starlit Garden* (23), *The Ghost Train* (27), *The Eternal Feminine* (30), *The Marriage Bond* (30), *Grand Finale* (37), etc.

NEWBROOK, PETER (1916–   ). British producer, former cinematographer. *The Yellow Teddy Bears* (63), *Black Torment* (64), *Gonks Go Beat* (65), *The Sandwich Man* (66), *Press for Time* (66), *Corruption* (68), etc.

NEWFELD, SAM (1900–1964). American director of second features. *The Black Raven* (43), *Dead Men Walk* (43), *I Accuse My Parents* (44), *Queen of Burlesque* (46), *Lost Continent* (51), *Lady in the Fog* (GB) (52), many others.

NEWHART, BOB (c. 1929–   ). American TV and record comedian who has appeared in a few movies: *Hell is for Heroes* (62), *Hot Millions* (68), *On a Clear Day You Can See Forever* (69), *Catch 22* (70)·

NEWLAND, JOHN (c. 1916–). American TV actor (the host of *One Step Beyond*) who also directed a few films: *That Night* (57), *The Violators* (57), *The Spy with My Face* (65), *Hush-a-Bye Murder* (70). Played Algy in the Tom Conway Bulldog Drummond films 1948–49.

NEWLANDS, ANTHONY (1926–). British character actor, mainly on TV; usually plays schemers. *Beyond This Place* (59), *The Trials of Oscar Wilde* (60), *Hysteria* (64), etc.

NEWLEY, ANTHONY (1931–). British actor, composer, singer, comedian. Former child star: notable in *Oliver Twist* (48), *Vice Versa* (48), *Those People Next Door* (53), *Cockleshell Heroes* (56), *X the Unknown* (57), *High Flight* (57), *No Time to Die* (58), *Idle on Parade* (60), *In the Nick* (61), *The Small World of Sammy Lee* (63), *Dr Doolittle* (US) (67), *Sweet November* (US) (68), *Can Heironymus Merkin Ever Forget Mercy Humpe and Find True Happiness?* (also wrote and directed) (69).

NEWMAN, ALFRED (1901–1970). American composer, former child pianist; an eminent Hollywood musical director since early sound days, and has composed over 250 film scores. *The Devil To Pay* (30), *Whoopee* (31), *Arrowsmith* (31), *Cynara* (32), *The Bowery* (33), *Nana* (34), *Dodsworth* (36), *Dead End* (37), *Alexander's Ragtime Band* (AA) (38), *Gunga Din* (39), *Tin Pan Alley* (AA) (40), *The Grapes of Wrath* (40), *Son of Fury* (42), *The Song of Bernadette* (43), *The Razor's Edge* (46), *Mother Wore Tights* (AA) (47), *Unfaithfully Yours* (48), *With a Song in My Heart* (AA) (52), *Call Me Madam* (AA) (53), *Love Is a Many Splendoured Thing* (AA) (55), *The King and I* (AA) (56), *Flower Drum Song* (61), *The Counterfeit Traitor* (62), *How the West Was Won* (62), *Nevada Smith* (66), many others.

NEWMAN, JOSEPH M. (1909–). American director, in films from 1931. *Jungle Patrol* (48), *711 Ocean Drive* (50), *The Outcasts of Poker Flats* (52), *Red Skies of Montana* (52), *Pony Soldier* (*Macdonald of the Canadian Mounties*) (53), *The Human Jungle* (54), *Dangerous Crossing* (54), *Kiss of Fire* (55), *This Island Earth* (55), *Flight to Hong Kong* (also produced) (56), *Gunfight at Dodge City* (58), *The Big Circus* (59), *Tarzan the Ape Man* (59), *King of the Roaring Twenties* (61), *A Thunder of Drums* (61), *The George Raft Story* (*Spin of a Coin*) (61), etc.

NEWMAN, NANETTE (c. 1934–). British leading lady, married to Bryan Forbes. *Personal Affair* (33), *Faces in the Dark* (59), *The League of Gentlemen* (59), *Twice Round the Daffodils* (62), *Of Human Bondage* (64), *Seance on a Wet Afternoon* (64), *The Wrong Box* (66), *The Whisperers* (66), *The Madwoman of Chaillot* (69), etc.

†NEWMAN, PAUL (1925–   ). American leading actor who suffered somewhat from being too similar to Marlon Brando. Stage and TV experience; married to Joanne Woodward. *The Silver Chalice* (debut) (55), *The Rack* (56), *Somebody Up There Likes Me* (57), *The Long Hot Summer* (58), *Rally Round the Flag Boys* (58), *The Left-Handed Gun* (58), *Cat on a Hot Tin Roof* (59), *The Young Philadelphians* (*The City Jungle*) (59), *Exodus* (61), *The Hustler* (BFA) (62), *Sweet Bird of Youth* (62), *Adventures of a Young Man* (62), *Hud* (63), *A New Kind of Love* (63), *The Prize* (64), *What a Way to Go* (64), *The Outrage* (64), *Lady L* (65), *Harper* (*The Moving Target*) (66), *Torn Curtain* (66), *Hombre* (66), *The Secret War of Harry Frigg* (67), *Cool Hand Luke* (67), *Rachel Rachel* (directed only) (68), *Winning* (69), *Butch Cassidy and the Sundance Kid* (69), *Hall of Mirrors* (69).

NEWMAR, JULIE (1933–   ). Tall Swedish blonde in Hollywood movies. *The Marriage Go Round* (60), then lead as girl robot in TV series *My Living Doll*. 1968: *Mackenna's Gold*, 1969: *The Maltese Bippy*.

NEWTON, ROBERT (1905–56). British character actor with a rich rolling voice and eyes to match. On stage from 14 years old. *Fire over England* (film debut) (36), *Farewell Again* (37), *Vessel of Wrath* (38), *Jamaica Inn* (39), *Major Barbara* (40), *Hatter's Castle* (41), *They Flew Alone* (42), *This Happy Breed* (44), *Henry V* (44), *Odd Man Out* (47), *Oliver Twist* (48), *Treasure Island* (50), *Les Misérables* (52), *Androcles and the Lion* (53), *The Beachcomber* (55), *Around the World in Eighty Days* (56), etc. TV series: *Long John Silver* (55).

'*new wave*' or '*nouvelle vague*'. Term given (by themselves?) to a group of new, exploring young French directors towards the end of the 50s: François Truffaut, Jean-Luc Godard, Louis Malle, Alain Resnais, etc. As their talents were widely divergent, the term meant very little. It was coined by Françoise Giroud.

New York has provided a vivid backcloth for films of many types. Studio re-creations provided the period flavour of *Little Old New York*, *New York Town*, *A Tree Grows in Brooklyn*, *Incendiary Blonde*, *My Girl Tisa* and *The Bowery*; and it was a studio city which was wrecked by *King Kong*. But in recent years the camera has explored the real article, notably in thrillers like *Saboteur*, *Naked City*, *Union Station*, *The FBI Story* and *North by Northwest*; in realistic comedy dramas like *Lovers and Lollipops*, *Marty*, *It Should Happen to You*, *Sunday in New York*, *Breakfast at Tiffany's*, *The Lost Weekend*, *The Bachelor Party*, *A Man Ten Feet Tall*, *A Fine Madness*, *Love with the Proper Stranger* and *Any Wednesday*; in hard-hitting social melodramas like *On the Waterfront*, *Sweet Smell of Success*, and *The Young Savages*; and in musicals like *On the Town* and *West Side Story*. Other films which concern the effect of New York without showing much of the actuality include *Mr Deeds Goes to Town, Bachelor Mother, Lady on a Train, Bell, Book and Candle, Kid Millions, Dead End, The Apartment, Patterns of Power, The Garment Jungle, Mr Blandings Builds His Dream House* and *America, America.* Finally Manhattan Island was bought from the Indians by Groucho Marx in *The Story of Mankind,* and *Knickerbocker Holiday* pictured the city in its Dutch colonial days as New Amsterdam.

NEXT OF KIN (GB 1942). An official wartime film on the dangers of careless talk, treated as a documentary thriller but intended for military audiences, this was successful enough to be sent on general release and proved very popular. It still makes good cinema. Directed by Thorold Dickinson, with Mervyn Johns and Stephen Murray.

NEY, RICHARD (c. 1916–   ). American financier who almost accidentally went into acting but appears only occasionally. *Mrs Miniver* (42), *The Late George Apley* (46), *Joan of Arc* (48), *Babes in Bagdad* (52), *The Premature Burial* (61), etc.; recently on TV. Was married to Greer Garson.

NIBLO, FRED (1874–1948) (Federico Nobile). American director of silent films; had stage experience. *The Marriage Ring* (18), *Sex* (20), *The Mark of Zorro* (20), *The Three Musketeers* (21), *Blood and Sand* (23), *Thy Name Is Woman* (24), *The Temptress* (26), *Ben Hur* (27), *Camille* (27), *Redemption* (29), *The Big Gamble* (33). Returned to stage apart from second feature, *Three Sons o' Guns* (41).

NICHOLLS, ANTHONY (1902–   ). Distinguished-looking British stage actor, in occasional films. *The Laughing Lady* (47), *The Guinea Pig* (49), *The Hasty Heart* (49), *The Dancing Years* (50), *The Franchise Affair* (50), *The Weak and the Wicked* (54), *Make Me an Offer* (55), *The Safecracker* (58), *Victim* (62), *Mister Ten Per Cent* (66), etc.

NICHOLS, BARBARA (1932–   ). American comedy actress, former model; adept at portraying not-so-dumb blondes. *Miracle in the Rain* (56), *The King and Four Queens* (57), *The Scarface Mob* (60), *The George Raft Story* (61), *Where the Boys Are* (63), *The Disorderly Orderly* (64), *Dear Heart* (65), *The Loved One* (65), etc.; also much on TV.

NICHOLS, DANDY (1907–   ). British character comedienne, often seen as nervous maid or cockney char. *Hue and Cry* (46), *Here Come the Huggetts* (49), *Street Corner* (52), *The Deep Blue Sea* (55), many others. Became famous on TV as the long-suffering Else in *Till Death Do Us Part* (66–68); appeared in the film version (68).

NICHOLS, DUDLEY (1895–1960). American screenwriter, in Hollywood from 1929. *Born Reckless* (30), *The Lost Patrol* (34), *The*

Nichols, Mike

Informer (AA) (35), *Mary of Scotland* (36), *The Hurricane* (37), *Stagecoach* (39), *The Long Voyage Home* (40), *It Happened Tomorrow* (44), *Ten Little Niggers* (45), *Scarlet Street* (45), *Sister Kenny* (also directed) (46), *Mourning Becomes Electra* (also produced and directed) (47), *Pinky* (49), *Prince Valiant* (54), *The Tin Star* (57), *The Hangman* (59), many others.

†NICHOLS, MIKE (1931–   ) (Michael Igor Peschkowsky). German-born American cabaret entertainer and latterly film director: *Who's Afraid of Virginia Woolf?* (66), *The Graduate* (AA) (67), *Catch 22* (69).

NICHOLSON, JAMES H. (1916–   ). American executive, former theatre owner and distributor, now president of American International Pictures which has been successful with Roger Corman's Poe adaptations, etc.

NICHOLSON, NORA (1892–   ). British stage character actress whose film roles have usually been fey or eccentric. *The Blue Lagoon* (48), *Tread Softly* (48), *Crow Hollow* (52), *Raising a Riot* (54), *A Town Like Alice* (56), *The Captain's Table* (59), etc.

nickelodeon. A humorous term applied to early American cinemas once they had become slightly grander than the converted stores which were used for the purpose at the turn of the century.

NICOL, ALEX (1919–   ). American leading man with stage experience, mainly in Universal action pictures since 1950. *The Sleeping City* (50), *Because of You* (52), *Law and Order* (54), *The Man from Laramie* (55), *Sincerely Yours* (55), *Under Ten Flags* (60), *Three Came Back* (also produced and directed) (60), *Look in Any Window* (61), *The Savage Guns* (62), *Ride and Kill* (63), *Gunfighters of Casa Grande* (65), etc.

NIELSEN, ASTA (1883–   ). Danish stage actress whose most famous film was *Hamlet* (20), in which she played the lead. Also: *Der Abgrund* (10), *Engelein* (13), *Hedda Gabler* (24), *Pandora's Box* (28), etc.

NIELSEN, LESLIE (1925–   ). Canadian leading man, former radio disc jockey; much TV work. Hollywood films include *The Vagabond King* (55), *Forbidden Planet* (56), *Ransom* (56), *Tammy and the Bachelor* (57), *Harlow* (65), *Beau Geste* (66), etc. TV series: *The Bold Ones* (69).

NIGH, WILLIAM (* –   ). American director of second features in the 40s. *Corregidor* (42), *The Right to Live* (45), *Divorce* (45), etc.

A NIGHT AT THE OPERA (US 1935). The Marx Brothers' first film for MGM. Given a big budget, they also had to suffer romantic and musical interludes which made their fans impatient; but the film contained some of their best routines, including the cabin scene, and the final sabotaging of *Il Trovatore* is brilliantly timed. As usual, Margaret Dumont stood the brunt of the insults.

NIGHTINGALE, FLORENCE (1820–1910). English nurse who organized hospitals at the front during the Crimean War, with little official help and under appalling conditions. There have been two biopics of her: *The White Angel* (US) (35), with Kay Francis, and *The Lady with a Lamp* (GB) (51), with Anna Neagle.

NIGHT MAIL (GB 1936). A highly influential two-reel documentary made by Harry Watt and Basil Wright for the GPO Film Unit, building up an exciting pattern of images and sounds as the night mail train steams from London to Scotland. The verse which largely replaces commentary was written by W. H. Auden.

NIGHT MUST FALL. Emlyn Williams' macabre play about the homicidal Welsh pageboy who keeps his victim's head in a hatbox was filmed in 1938 by Richard Thorpe for MGM, with Robert Montgomery. When Karel Reisz produced a somewhat modernized version in 1963 with Albert Finney, the critics all yearned for the 1938 film, which they hadn't seen for twenty years. One doubts whether either version really pleased the author.

THE NIGHT OF THE DEMON (GB 1957) (US title: *Curse of the Demon*). Charles Bennett adapted M. R. James' story 'Casting the Runes' for this unassuming little thriller which was directed by Jacques Tourneur with a strong Hitchcock flavour. It remains one of the screen's best ventures into the supernatural, though not helped by the colourless playing of the romantic leads. Niall MacGinnis, however, gives a roistering performance as the evil Karswell, and the final train sequence is genuinely exciting.

THE NIGHT OF THE HUNTER (US 1955). One of the strangest films to come out of Hollywood, an allegory of good and evil from Davis Grubb's novel about the escape of two children from a psycho-pathic preacher (Robert Mitchum). Impeccably directed by Charles Laughton so that, although the film does not satisfy as a whole, fragments of it linger in the memory; enhanced by Stanley Cortez' splendid photography.

NIGHTS OF CABIRIA: see under CABIRIA.

NILSSON, ANNA Q. (1894–   ). Swedish-born actress, long in America and popular in silent films from 1911. *The Isle of Lost Ships*, *The Masked Woman*, *The Greater Glory*, *Sorrell and Son*, etc. Little seen in talkies apart from her appearance as one of Swanson's friends in *Sunset Boulevard* (50): *The World Changes* (34), *Prison Farm* (38), *Girls' Town* (42), *The Farmer's Daughter* (47), etc.

NILSSON, LEOPOLD TORRE: see TORRE-NILSSON, LEOPOLD.

Nimmo, Derek

NIMMO, DEREK (1931–). British character comedian who gets laughs from toe-twiddling and funny voices (especially of the comedy curate kind). *The Millionairess* (61), *The Amorous Prawn* (62), *The Bargee* (64), *Joey Boy* (65), *The Liquidator* (65), *Casino Royale* (66), *Mister Ten Per Cent* (66), *A Talent for Loving* (69), etc. TV series include *All Gas and Gaiters*, *The World of Wooster*, *Oh Brother*.

NINOTCHKA (US 1939). A blithe satire about communism meeting capitalism in Paris, in the shapes of Greta Garbo and Melvyn Douglas. For the most part a felicitous though over-long comedy, with engaging performances from the principals and from Sig Ruman, Alexander Granach and Felix Bressart as the incompetent Russian emissaries. Directed by Ernst Lubitsch from a script by Charles Brackett, Billy Wilder and Walter Reisch. The film in which 'Garbo laughs!'. Remade in 1957 as a musical, *Silk Stockings* with Cyd Charisse and Fred Astaire.

NIVEN, DAVID (1909–). Debonair British leading man with a highly varied background—army, waiter, lumberjack, barman, reporter—before he found himself in Hollywood as an extra and was signed by Samuel Goldwyn. *Barbary Coast* (35), *Thank You, Jeeves* (35), *Dodsworth* (36), *Beloved Enemy* (36), *The Charge of the Light Brigade* (36), *The Prisoner of Zenda* (37), *Dinner at the Ritz* (GB) (37), *Four Men and a Prayer* (38), *The Dawn Patrol* (38), *Three Blind Mice* (38), *Bluebeard's Eighth Wife* (38), *Wuthering Heights* (39), *The Real Glory* (39), *Raffles* (39), *Bachelor Mother* (39), *Eternally Yours* (39); war service; *The First of the Few* (GB) (42), *The Way Ahead* (GB) (44), *A Matter of Life and Death* (GB) (46), *The Perfect Marriage* (46), *Magnificent Doll* (47), *The Bishop's Wife* (47), *Enchantment* (47), *Bonnie Prince Charlie* (GB) (48), *A Kiss in the Dark* (49), *The Elusive Pimpernel* (GB) (50), *A Kiss for Corliss* (50), *Happy Go Lovely* (GB) (51), *Appointment with Venus* (GB) (51), *The Love Lottery* (GB) (53), *The Moon Is Blue* (53), *Happy Ever After* (GB) (54), *Carrington VC* (GB) (55), *The King's Thief* (55), *Around the World in Eighty Days* (as Phileas Fogg) (56), *The Birds and the Bees* (56), *My Man Godfrey* (57), *Separate Tables* (AA) (58), *Ask Any Girl* (59), *Happy Anniversary* (60), *Please Don't Eat the Daisies* (61), *The Guns of Navarone* (61), *Guns of Darkness* (62), *The Best of Enemies* (62), *Fifty-five Days at Peking* (62), *The Pink Panther* (63), *Bedtime Story* (64), *Lady L* (65), *Where the Spies Are* (66), *Eye of the Devil* ('*13*') (66), *Casino Royale* (67), *Prudence and the Pill* (GB) (68), *The Extraordinary Seaman* (68), *The Impossible Years* (68), *Before Winter Comes* (69), *The Brain* (69), etc. TV series: *The David Niven Show* (59), *The Rogues* (64).

NIXON, MARNI (c. 1929–). American singer, former MGM messenger, who has dubbed in high notes for many stars including Margaret O'Brien in *Big City*, Deborah Kerr in *The King and I*,

Natalie Wood in *West Side Story* and Audrey Hepburn in *My Fair Lady*. Has made no film appearances as herself.

NOEL, MAGALI (1932–   ). French leading lady. *Seul dans Paris* (51), *Razzia sur la Chnouf* (55), *Rififi* (55), *Elena et les Hommes* (56), *Desire Takes the Men* (58), *La Dolce Vita* (59), etc.

NOEL-NOEL (1897–   ) (Lucien Noel). Dapper French character comedian. *Octave* (32), *A Cage of Nightingales* (43), *Le Père Tranquille* (46), *The Seven Deadly Sins* (51), *The Diary of Major Thompson* (55), *Jessica* (62), etc.

NOLAN, DORIS (1916–   ). American leading lady who married Alexander Knox and retired. *The Man I Married* (37), *Holiday* (38), *Irene* (40), *Moon over Burma* (41), *Follies Girl* (44), etc.

NOLAN, JEANETTE (c. 1911–   ). American character actress, much on TV. Films include *Macbeth* (as Lady Macbeth) (48), *The Secret of Convict Lake* (51), *The Happy Time* (52), *The Big Heat* (53), *The Guns of Fort Petticoat* (57), *The Rabbit Trap* (58). TV series: *The Richard Boone Show* (64).

NOLAN, LLOYD (1903–   ). American character actor, with stage experience from 1927. *Stolen Harmony* (film debut) (34), *G Men* (35), *Ebb Tide* (37), *Gangs of Chicago* (40), *Michael Shayne, Private Detective* (40), *Blues in the Night* (41), *Bataan* (43), *A Tree Grows in Brooklyn* (44), *The House on 92nd Street* (45), *The Lady in the Lake* (46), *The Street with No Name* (48), *The Last Hunt* (56), *Peyton Place* (58), *The Magnificent Showman* (*Circus World*) (64), *Never Too Late* (65), *An American Dream* (*See You in Hell, Darling*) (66), *The Double Man* (GB) (67), *Ice Station Zebra* (68), *Airport* (69), many others. TV series: *Julia* (68–69).

NOLBANDOV, SERGEI (c. 1902–   ). Russian-born writer-producer, in Britain from 1926. *City of Song* (w) (30), *Fire over England* (w) (36), *Ships with Wings* (w, d) (42), *This Modern Age* series (p) from 1946, *The Kidnappers* (p) (53), *Mix Me a Person* (p) (62), many others.

non-theatrical. A descriptive adjective usually applied to film showings at which there is no paid admission on entrance, e.g. schools, clubs, etc. Some distributors apply the term to all 16mm showings.

NOONAN, TOMMY (1921–1968) (Thomas Noon). Ebullient American comedian and writer. Appearances include *Starlift* (51), *Gentlemen Prefer Blondes* (53), *A Star Is Born* (54), *How to Be Very Very Popular* (55), *Bundle of Joy* (56), *The Ambassador's Daughter* (56), *The Rookie* (also produced) (60), etc.

NORDEN, CHRISTINE (1923–   ). British leading lady, a sex symbol of the late 40s. Came to films after ENSA experience. *Night Beat*

Norman, Leslie

(47), *Mine Own Executioner* (48), *Idol of Paris* (48), *A Case for PC 49* (51), *Reluctant Heroes* (51), etc.

NORMAN, LESLIE (1911–   ). British producer-director, former editor, in films from late 20s. *Where No Vultures Fly* (p) (51), *The Cruel Sea* (p) (54), *The Night My Number Came Up* (d) (56), *X the Unknown* (d) (57), *The Shiralee* (d) (58), *Dunkirk* (d) (58), *The Long, the Short and the Tall* (d) (60), *Mix Me a Person* (d) (61), *Summer of the 17th Doll* (61), etc.

NORMAND, MABEL (1894–1930) (Mabel Fortescue). American comedienne, a leading player of Vitagraph and Keystone comedies from 1911, and a Chaplin co-star. *Barney Oldfield's Race for Life* (12), *Fatty and Mabel Adrift* (15), *Mickey* (17), *Sis Hopkins* (18), *Molly O* (21), *Suzanna* (22), many others.

NORRIS, EDWARD (1910–   ). American leading man of second features; former reporter. *Queen Christina* (33), *The Man with Two Lives* (41), *End of the Road* (44), *Decoy* (47), *Forbidden Women* (49), *Inside the Walls of Folsom Prison* (51), *The Man from the Alamo* (53), *The Kentuckian* (last to date) (55), many others.

NORTH, ALEX (1910–   ). American composer. Scores include *A Streetcar Named Desire* (51), *Death of a Salesman* (52), *Desirée* (54), *The Rose Tattoo* (55), *I'll Cry Tomorrow* (57), *Cleopatra* (62), *Cheyenne Autumn* (64), *The Agony and the Ecstasy* (65).

NORTH BY NORTHWEST (US 1959). A gay comedy-thriller, possibly Hitchcock's most likeable film if only because it is an over-size bag of his best old tricks. Cary Grant is irresistibly debonair as the innocent hero chased by spies over the great stone faces of Mount Rushmore and savaged by an aeroplane in a cornfield; Leo G. Carroll and James Mason smoothly represent law and disorder respectively. Written by Ernest Lehman, photographed by Robert Burks, with music by Bernard Herrmann.

NORTH, JAY (1951–   ). American juvenile actor, popular as a child on TV in *Dennis the Menace* (59–63) and later *Maya* (67). Film appearance: *Zebra in the Kitchen* (65).

NORTH, SHEREE (1933–   ) (Dawn Bethel). Blonde American leading lady, former dancer. *Excuse My Dust* (51), *How to Be Very Very Popular* (55), *The Best Things in Life Are Free* (56), *The Way to the Gold* (57), *No Down Payment* (57), *Mardi Gras* (58), *Destination Inner Space* (66), *Madigan* (68), etc. Makes TV guest appearances.

NORTHWEST PASSAGE (US 1940). Actually this was only part one of Kenneth Roberts' novel, and bore the subtitle 'Rogers' Rangers'; part two unfortunately was never made, and in the film as it stands the northwest passage is never seen and barely talked about.

Spencer Tracy gives a splendid performance as the indomitable major exacting retribution from the Indians and nearly killing off his own men in the process. Directed by King Vidor, and beautifully photographed in fairly early Technicolor, it remains one of the screen's most invigorating Westerns.

NORTON, JACK (1889–1958). One of the screen's two most delightful bit-part drunks, the other being ARTHUR HOUSMAN (c. 1883– *). Both American, with stage backgrounds, it was rare for either to have a coherent speaking part in movies. Housman is best remembered in the Laurel and Hardy comedies of the early 30s; Norton's peak was a little later, with memorable appearances in *The Fleet's In* (in which he was sober) (41) and *Hold that Blonde* (45).

NOSSECK, MAX (1902–   ) (Alexander Norris). Polish director in Hollywood from 1939; former stage and film actor/director in Europe. *The Brighton Strangler* (also wrote) (45), *Dillinger* (45), *Black Beauty* (46), *The Return of Rin Tin Tin* (47), *Kill or Be Killed* (50), *The Hoodlum* (51), *Overture to Glory* (53), *Miss Body Beautiful* (also produced) (57), etc. Returned to Europe.

NOTHING BUT THE TRUTH. James Montgomery's Broadway comedy about a man who takes a bet to tell the absolute truth for twenty-four hours was filmed in 1920, with Taylor Holmes; in 1929, with Richard Dix; and in 1941, with Bob Hope.

NOTHING SACRED (US 1937). One of Hollywood's most successful satirical comedies, perhaps because the bitterness was mixed with slapstick. Carole Lombard plays the girl who thinks she is dying of a rare disease and is propelled by reporter Fredric March to the status of a national heroine; Walter Connolly is a magnificently wrathful editor. Most memorable moment: March finds himself in an unfriendly small town, where the natives are all surly and mutter at him in monosyllables; suddenly a small boy darts out from behind a picket fence and bites him in the leg. Written by Ben Hecht; directed by William Wellman; in Technicolor. Remade 1954, with Jerry Lewis(!) in the Lombard part, as *Living It Up*.

NOVAK, KIM (1933–   ) (Marilyn Novak). American leading lady carefully moulded as a sex symbol; has lately forsaken vacuous blonde roles for acting parts somewhat beyond her range. *Pushover* (debut) (54), *Phffft* (54), *Five Against the House* (55), *The Man with the Golden Arm* (56), *Picnic* (56), *Jeanne Eagels* (57), *Pal Joey* (57), *Bell, Book and Candle* (57), *Vertigo* (58), *Middle of the Night* (59), *Strangers When We Meet* (61), *The Notorious Landlady* (63), *Boys' Night Out* (63), *Of Human Bondage* (64), *Kiss Me Stupid* (64), *Moll Flanders* (65), *The Legend of Lylah Clare* (68), *The Great Bank Robbery* (69), etc.

NOVARRO, RAMON (1899–1968) (Ramon Samaniegoes). Mexican leading man popular in Hollywood's silent days; later made comeback as character actor. *The Prisoner of Zenda* (22), *Scaramouche* (22), *The Midshipman* (25), *Ben Hur* (27), *The Student Prince* (27), *Mata Hari* (32), *The Barbarian* (33), *The Sheik Steps Out* (37), *We Were Strangers* (48), *The Big Steal* (49), *Crisis* (50), *Heller in Pink Tights* (60), etc.

NOVELLO, IVOR (1893–1951) (Ivor Davies). Welsh matinée idol with an incredibly successful career in stage musical comedy; also prolific playwright and composer. Films include *Carnival* (22), *The Bohemian Girl* (22), *The White Rose* (23), *The Man Without Desire* (23), *The Rat* (25), *The Lodger* (26), *The Triumph of the Rat* (27), *The Constant Nymph* (27), *Downhill* (27), *The Vortex* (28), *The Lodger* (remake) (32), *Sleeping Car* (33), *I Lived with You* (34), *Autumn Crocus* (34), etc.; proved somewhat unsuited to talkies and returned to the stage.

NUGENT, ELLIOTT (1900–   ). American stage actor, producer and playwright who acted in a few early talkies: *So This Is College* (29), *Not So Dusty* (29), *Wise Girls* (30), etc. Returned sporadically to Hollywood as a director, mainly of comedies: *Life Begins* (32), *The Mouthpiece* (32), *Whistling in the Dark* (33), *Three-Cornered Moon* (33), *Professor Beware* (38), *The Cat and the Canary* (39), *Nothing But the Truth* (41), *The Male Animal* (42), *Up In Arms* (44), *My Favourite Brunette* (47), *My Girl Tisa* (47), *The Great Gatsby* (49), *The Skipper Surprised His Wife* (50), *My Outlaw Brother* (51), *Just for You* (52), etc. Wrote autobiography 1965: *Events Leading Up to the Comedy*.

NUGENT, FRANK (1908–1966). American screenwriter, former reporter and critic. *Fort Apache* (48), *She Wore a Yellow Ribbon* (49), *The Quiet Man* (52), *Trouble in the Glen* (53), *The Searchers* (56), *The Last Hurrah* (58), *Donovan's Reef* (63), etc.

nuns have been popular figures on the screen, though only in *The Nun's Story* and the Polish *The Devil and the Nun* has any real sense of dedication been achieved; the French *Dialogue des Carmélites* tried hard but failed. Sentimentalized nuns were seen in *The Cradle Song, Bonaventure, The White Sister, Conspiracy of Hearts, The Bells of St Mary, Come to the Stable, Portrait of Jennie, Heaven Knows Mr Allison, Black Narcissus, Lilies of the Field, The Miracle, The Song of Bernadette* and *The Sound of Music*; while nuns who combined modern sophistication with sweetness and light afflicted us in *The Singing Nun* and *The Trouble with Angels*, and in *Two Mules for Sister Sara* Shirley Maclaine played a prostitute disguised as a nun. The most sinister nun was perhaps Catherine Lacey, with her high heels, in *The Lady Vanishes*.

THE NUN'S STORY (US 1959). Written by Robert Anderson from Kathryn Hulme's book, and directed by Fred Zinnemann, this long and sincere film lapsed into conventional melodrama after a brilliant first half showing the training of a novice. But at least it marked an advance in the kind of subject that can be tackled by a big, expensive movie. Photographed by Franz Planer, with music by Franz Waxman; with Audrey Hepburn in the leading role.

nurses have inspired biopics (*Sister Kenny, The Lady with a Lamp, Nurse Edith Cavell*); sentimental low-key studies of the profession (*The Lamp Still Burns, The Feminine Touch, No Time for Tears, White Corridors, Prison Nurse, Private Nurse, Night Nurse*); even comedies (*Carry On Nurse, Twice Round the Daffodils, Nurse on Wheels*). *Green For Danger* is probably still the only thriller in which both victim and murderer were nurses. There was a popular TV series called *Janet Dean Registered Nurse* (53), and later *The Nurses* (62–64). See also *hospitals; doctors*.

NUYEN, FRANCE (1939–). Franco-Chinese leading lady, former model, who made some Hollywood films. *In Love and War* (57), *South Pacific* (58), *Satan Never Sleeps* (61), *The Last Time I Saw Archie* (62), *A Girl Named Tamiko* (63), *Diamondhead* (63), *The Man in the Middle* (64), *Dimension Five* (66), etc.

NYBY, CHRISTIAN (* –). American director. *The Thing* (52), *Hell on Devil's Island* (57), *Six-Gun Law* (62), *Young Fury* (64), *Operation CIA* (65), *First to Fight* (66), etc.

NYKVIST, SVEN (1922–). Swedish cinematographer. *Sawdust and Tinsel* (53), *Karin Mansdotter* (53), *The Silence* (64), *Loving Couples* (65), *Persona* (66), *Hour of the Wolf* (67), etc.

nymphomaniacs are still fairly rare on the screen. Since the early fifties there have been Françoise Arnoul in *La Rage au Corps*; Clare Bloom in *The Chapman Report*; Elizabeth Taylor in *Butterfield 8*; Suzanne Pleshette in *A Rage to Live*; Sue Lyon in *Lolita*; Merle Oberon in *Of Love and Desire*; and Sue Lyon again in *Night of the Iguana*. A small but choice collection which excludes all the numerous Scandinavian varieties.

O

OAKIE, JACK (1903–   ) (Lewis D. Offield). Cheerful American comic actor well-known for a startled 'double take'; formerly in vaudeville. *Finders Keepers* (debut) (27), *Paramount on Parade* (30), *Million Dollar Legs* (32), *College Humour* (33), *If I Had a Million* (33), *Call of the Wild* (35), *The Texas Rangers* (36), *The Toast of New York* (37), *Rise and Shine* (39), *The Great Dictator* (as caricature of Mussolini) (40), *Tin Pan Alley* (40), *Footlight Serenade* (42), *Song of the Islands* (42), *Something to Shout About* (43), *It Happened Tomorrow* (44), *That's the Spirit* (44), *The Merry Monahans* (44), *On Stage Everybody* (45), *When My Baby Smiles at Me* (48), *Thieves' Highway* (49), *Last of the Buccaneers* (50), *The Battle of Powder River* (52), *Around the World in Eighty Days* (56), *The Wonderful Country* (59), *The Rat Race* (60), *Lover Come Back* (62), many others.

OAKLAND, SIMON (1922–   ). American general purpose actor with stage experience. *The Brothers Karamazov* (58), *I Want to Live* (58), *Psycho* (60), *West Side Story* (61), *Follow That Dream* (62), *Wall of Noise* (63), *The Satan Bug* (65), *The Plainsman* (66), *The Sand Pebbles* (67), *Tony Rome* (67), *Chubasco* (68), etc.

OAKLAND, VIVIAN (1895–1958) (V. Anderson). American child star and vaudeville artiste, who later became familiar as wife to either Laurel or Hardy in many a two-reeler. *Gold Dust Gertie* (31), *Only Yesterday* (32), *The Bride Walks Out* (36), *Way Out West* (37), *The Man in the Trunk* (42), *Bunco Squad* (51), many others.

OAKLEY, ANNIE (1859–1926) (Phoebe Annie Oakley Mozee). American sharpshooter who gained fame in her teens as star of Buffalo Bill's Wild West show. Played on screen by Barbara Stanwyck in *Annie Oakley* (35), and by Betty Hutton in *Annie Get Your Gun* (50).

OATES, WARREN (c. 1932–   ). American supporting actor who has tended towards psychopathic heavies. *Yellowstone Kelly* (59), *Private Property* (60), *Hero's Island* (61), *Mail Order Bride* (64), *Major Dundee* (65), *Return of the Seven* (67), *In the Heat of the Night* (67), *The Split* (68), *Crooks and Coronets* (GB) (69), *The Wild Bunch* (69) etc.

OBER, PHILIP (1902–   ). American general purpose character actor. *The Secret Fury* (50), *From Here to Eternity* (53), *Tammy* (56), *North by Northwest* (59), *Let No Man Write My Epitaph* (60), etc.

OBERON, MERLE (1911–   ) (Estelle O'Brien Merle Thompson). British leading lady. Educated in India; came to Britain 1928, worked as dance hostess until signed up by Korda. *Service for Ladies* (debut) (31), *The Private Life of Henry VIII* (32), *The Private Life of Don Juan* (34), *The Scarlet Pimpernel* (35), *The Dark Angel* (US) (36), *These Three* (36), *Beloved Enemy* (36), *The Divorce of Lady X* (38), *Over the Moon* (39), *Wuthering Heights* (39), *The Lion Has Wings* (39), *Affectionately Yours* (41), *The Lodger* (44), *A Song to Remember* (as George Sand) (44), *This Love of Ours* (45), *Berlin Express* (46), *Temptation* (46), *Night Song* (48), *The Lady from Boston* (51), *Twenty-four Hours of a Woman's Life* (52), *Deep in My Heart* (54), *Désirée* (54), *The Price of Fear* (56), *Of Love and Desire* (63), *Hotel* (67), etc. TV series: *Assignment Foreign Legion* (56).

OBJECTIVE BURMA (US 1945). The film which brought to a head British resentment about America appearing to have won the war single-handed; in this case it was Errol Flynn who took Burma without any British help. The outcry was so great that the film was withdrawn in Britain. In fact it tells a good yarn efficiently if at too great length, with photography by James Wong Howe and direction by Raoul Walsh. Ranald Macdougall and Lester Cole wrote the script.

OBOLER, ARCH (1909–). American writer-producer-director with a long career in radio. Has made mainly stunt films. *Bewitched* (w, d) (46), *The Arnelo Affair* (w, d) (46), *Five* (w, p, d) (51), *Bwana Devil* (w, p, d) (53), *The Kinsey Report* (w, p, d) (61), *The Bubble* (w, p, d) (67), etc.

O'BRIAN, HUGH (1925–) (Hugh Krampke). Leathery American leading man, former athlete; best known as TV's *Wyatt Earp*. Films include *Never Fear* (50), *On the Loose* (51), *Red Ball Express* (52), *Seminole* (54), *There's No Business Like Show Business* (54), *White Feather* (55), *The Brass Legend* (56), *The Fiend Who Walked the West* (58), *Come Fly With Me* (62), *In Harm's Way* (65), *Love Has Many Faces* (65), *Ten Little Indians* (65), *Ambush Bay* (66), *Africa Texas Style* (67), etc.

O'BRIEN, DAVE (1912–1969) (David Barclay). American light character actor, in Hollywood from the early 30s. Played supporting roles in innumerable films; most familiar as the hero/victim of the Pete Smith comedy shorts of the 40s. *Jennie Gerhardt* (33), *East Side Kids* (39), *Son of the Navy* (40), *'Neath Brooklyn Bridge* (43), *Tahiti Nights* (44), *Phantom of 42nd Street* (45), *The Desperadoes Are in Town* (56), etc.

O'BRIEN, EDMOND (1915–). Anglo-Irish leading man of the 40s, latterly character actor; long in Hollywood. *The Hunchback of Notre Dame* (40), *Parachute Battalion* (41), *Powder Town* (42), etc.; war service; *The Killers* (46), *The Web* (47), *A Double Life* (47), *Another Part of the Forest* (48), *An Act of Murder* (48), *White Heat* (49), *D.O.A.*

(49), *Between Midnight and Dawn* (50), *Two of a Kind* (51), *Denver and Rio Grande* (52), *Julius Caesar* (53), *The Hitch Hiker* (53), *Man in the Dark* (53), *The Bigamist* (53), *Cow Country* (53), *The Barefoot Contessa* (AA) (54), *Shield for Murder* (also co-directed) (54), *1984* (GB) (55), *The Girl Can't Help It* (57), *The Third Voice* (59), *The Last Voyage* (60), *The Great Impostor* (61), *The Man Who Shot Liberty Valance* (62), *Birdman of Alcatraz* (62), *Seven Days in May* (64), *Sylvia* (65), *Fantastic Voyage* (66), *The Viscount* (Fr.) (67), *The Wild Bunch* (69), *The Love God* (69), etc. Produced and directed but did not act in *Mantrap* (61). TV series: *Sam Benedict, The Long Hot Summer.*

O'BRIEN, GEORGE (1900–). American cowboy star, who entered films as stunt man. *The Iron Horse* (first starring role) (24), *Sunrise* (27), *Noah's Ark* (28), *Lone Star Ranger* (30), *Riders of the Purple Sage* (31), *The Last Trail* (33), *O'Malley of the Mounted* (36), *Daniel Boone* (36), *The Painted Desert* (38), *Stage to Chino* (40), *Legion of the Lawless* (42), etc. Still plays small parts: *She Wore a Yellow Ribbon* (49), *Cheyenne Autumn* (64), others.

O'BRIEN, MARGARET (1937–). American child star of the 40s: *Babes on Broadway* (41), *Journey for Margaret* (42), *Madame Curie* (43), *Lost Angel* (43), *Jane Eyre* (44), *The Canterville Ghost* (44), *Meet Me in St Louis* (44), *Music for Millions* (44), *Our Vines Have Tender Grapes* (45), *Three Wise Fools* (46), *Tenth Avenue Angel* (47), *The Unfinished Dance* (47), *Big City* (48), *Little Women* (50), etc. Does not seem to have managed adult comeback: *Glory* (56), *Heller in Pink Tights* (60), etc. Special Academy Award 1944 as 'outstanding child actress'.

O'BRIEN, PAT (1899–). Irish-American leading man and later character actor, former lawyer and song-and-dance man. Came to films by repeating his stage role of Hildy Johnson in *The Front Page* (30). Later: *Final Edition* (31), *Hell's House* (32), *Blonde Bombshell* (33), *Oil for the Lamps of China* (33), *Devil Dogs of the Air* (34), *Here Comes the Navy* (35), *Flirtation Walk* (35), *The Irish In Us* (36), *The Great O'Malley* (37), *Angels with Dirty Faces* (38), *Boy Meets Girl* (39), *The Fighting 69th* (40), *Escape to Glory* (41), *Broadway* (42), *His Butler's Sister* (43), *Having Wonderful Crime* (45), *Man Alive* (45), *Crack Up* (46), *Riff Raff* (47), *Fighting Father Dunne* (47), *The Boy with Green Hair* (48), *Johnny One-Eye* (50), *The People against O'Hara* (51), *Okinawa* (52), *Jubilee Trail* (54), *Ring of Fear* (54), *Inside Detroit* (56), *The Last Hurrah* (58), *Town Tamer* (65), many others. TV series: *Harrigan and Son* (60). Published autobiography, *Wind on My Back* (63).

O'BRIEN, VIRGINIA (c. 1923–). American comedienne, the 'dead pan' singer of the 40s. *Hullaballoo* (40), *The Big Store* (41), *Ship Ahoy*

(42), *Thousands Cheer* (43), *Dubarry Was a Lady* (44), *The Harvey Girls* (45), *Till the Clouds Roll By* (46), *Merton of the Movies* (47), etc. Retired.

O'CASEY, SEAN (1884–1964). Irish playwright, much preoccupied by 'the troubles'. Works filmed include *Juno and the Paycock* and *The Plough and the Stars*; an alleged biopic, *Young Cassidy*, was made in 1964 with Rod Taylor.

OCCUPE-TOI D'AMELIE (France 1949). High-speed film version of a Feydeau farce, flawlessly and wittily put together by Claude Autant-Lara. Like *Henry V*, it begins and ends with a stage performance of the play, but every minute is highly cinematic. Scripted by Jean Aurenche and Pierre Bost, photographed by André Bac; with Danielle Darrieux, Jean Desailly and a nimble cast.

O'CONNELL, ARTHUR (1908–   ). American character actor with long Broadway experience; usually in mildly bewildered roles. *Law of the Jungle* (42), *Countess of Monte Cristo* (49), *The Whistle at Eaton Falls* (51), *Picnic* (55), *The Solid Gold Cadillac* (56), *The Man in the Grey Flannel Suit* (56), *Bus Stop* (56), *Operation Mad Ball* (57), *Follow That Dream* (61), *Kissin' Cousins* (64), *The Monkey's Uncle* (65), *Your Cheating Heart* (65), *The Great Race* (65), *The Silencers* (66), *Fantastic Voyage* (66), etc.

O'CONNOLLY, JIM (1926–   ). British director. *The Traitors* (62), *The Little Ones* (64), *Berserk* (67), *Crooks and Coronets* (69).

O'CONNOR, CARROLL (c. 1923–   ). American character actor† usually in blustery roles. *Lonely are the Brave* (62), *What Did You Do in the War Daddy?* (65), *Waterhole Three* (67), *Point Blank* (68), etc.

O'CONNOR, DONALD (1925–   ). American singer, dancer, ligh comedian, former child star. *Sing You Sinners* (debut) (38), *Beau Geste* (39), *When Johnny Comes Marching Home* (42), *Mr Big* (43), *Top Man* (43), *Chip Off the Old Block* (44), *The Merry Monahans* (44), *Bowery to Broadway* (44), *Patrick the Great* (45), *Something in the Wind* (47), *Are You With It?* (48), *Yes, Sir, That's My Baby* (49), *Francis* (50) (and five subsequent films in this series), *Curtain Call at Cactus Creek (Take the Stage)* (50), *The Milkman* (51), *Singin' in the Rain* (52), *Call Me Madam* (53), *There's No Business Like Show Business* (54), *Anything Goes* (56), *The Buster Keaton Story* (57), *Cry for Happy* (61), *The Wonders of Aladdin* (61), *That Funny Feeling* (65), etc.

O'CONNOR, ROBERT EMMETT (1885–   ). American small part player, often as snoop or policeman, on screen from 1909 after circus and vaudeville experience. *Public Enemy* (31), *A Night at the Opera* (35), *Tight Shoes* (41), *Whistling in Brooklyn* (44), *Boys' Ranch* (46), many others.

731

O'CONNOR, UNA (1893-1959). Sharp-featured Irish character actress with stage experience before film debut in 1929; in Hollywood from 1932. *Cavalcade* (33), *The Invisible Man* (33), *The Barretts of Wimpole Street* (34), *Bride of Frankenstein* (35), *The Informer* (35), *The Plough and the Stars* (36), *The Adventures of Robin Hood* (38), *The Sea Hawk* (40), *Random Harvest* (42), *Holy Matrimony* (43), *Cluny Brown* (46), *The Corpse Came C.O.D.* (48), *Witness for the Prosecution* (57), many others.

O'CONOR, JOSEPH (c. 1910–   ). British character actor, mainly on stage and TV. *Crooks in Cloisters* (63), *Oliver!* (68). Notable TV series: *The Forsyte Saga* (as Old Jolyon), (66).

OCTOBER (TEN DAYS THAT SHOOK THE WORLD) (USSR 1928). Eisenstein's spectacular and exciting reconstruction of the Russian revolution, brilliantly photographed by Tisse. The screen's most persuasive re-creation of fact, and one of its most powerful pieces of propaganda.

ODD MAN OUT (GB 1947). The film which established Carol Reed as a major director; with considerable help from the Abbey Theatre players he created a moving and cinematic impression of the last hours of an IRA gunman on the run. The more theatrical aspects of the picture have not worn well, but it has enough brilliant moments to preserve its reputation. R. C. Sherriff and F. L. Green wrote the script from the latter's novel; photography by Robert Krasker. James Mason played the pathetic central figure, with notable contributions from F. J. McCormick, Robert Newton and many others. BFA: best British film.

O'DEA, DENIS (1905–   ). Irish stage actor who has been in occasional films. *The Informer* (35), *The Plough and the Stars* (47), *Odd Man Out* (47), *The Fallen Idol* (48), *Under Capricorn* (49), *Treasure Island* (50), *Niagara* (52), *Mogambo* (53), *The Rising of the Moon* (57), *The Story of Esther Costello* (58), etc.

ODETS, CLIFFORD (1903-1963). American playwright who also wrote a number of film scripts: *The General Died at Dawn* (36), *Golden Boy* (from his play) (39), *None But the Lonely Heart* (44), *Deadline at Dawn* (46), *The Country Girl* (from his play) (54), *The Big Knife* (from his play) (55), *The Story on Page One* (also directed) (60).

ODETTE, MARY (1901–   ) (Odette Goimbault). French actress in many British silent films from 1915, at first as juvenile. *Dombey and Son, A Spinner of Dreams, With All Her Heart, Mr Gilfil's Love Story*, etc.

O'DONNELL, CATHY (1924–   ) (Ann Steely). American leading lady with brief stage experience. *The Best Years of Our Lives* (debut) (46), *They Live by Night* (48), *Detective Story* (51), *Never Trust a Gambler*

(52), *The Woman's Angle* (GB) (52), *Eight O'clock Walk* (GB) (54), *The Man from Laramie* (55), *Ben Hur* (59), etc.

O'DRISCOLL, MARTHA (1922–   ). American leading lady of the 40s, mainly in second features. *The Secret of Dr Kildare* (40), *The Lady Eve* (41), *My Heart Belongs to Daddy* (42), *Follow the Boys* (44), *Ghost Catchers* (44), *House of Dracula* (45), *Criminal Court* (last to date) (47), etc.

O'FARRELL, BERNADETTE (1926–   ). British leading lady who married her director, Frank Launder. *Captain Boycott* (48), *The Happiest Days of Your Life* (49), *Lady Godiva Rides Again* (51), *The Story of Gilbert and Sullivan* (53), etc.

offices have provided the setting for many a film. *The Crowd* in 1926 and *The Rebel* in 1961 chose pretty much the same way of stressing the dreariness of daily routine; but *Sunshine Susie* in 1931 and *How to Succeed in Business without Really Trying* in 1967 both saw the office as a gay place full of laughter and song. Billy Wilder took a jaundiced view of it in *The Apartment*, as did the makers of *Patterns of Power*, *Executive Suite* and *The Power and the Prize*. Romantic comedies of the 30s like *Wife versus Secretary*, *After Office Hours* and *Take a Letter Darling* saw it as ideal for amorous intrigue, and in 1964 *The Wild Affair* took pretty much the same attitude. Orson Welles in *The Trial* made it nightmarish; Preston Sturges in *Christmas in July* made it friendly; Delbert Mann in *The Bachelor Party* made it frustrating. Perhaps the best film office is that of Philip Marlowe in the Raymond Chandler films: there's seldom anyone in it but himself.

OF HUMAN BONDAGE. Somerset Maugham's novel has been filmed three times. 1. US 1934, directed by John Cromwell, with Leslie Howard and Bette Davis. 2. US 1946, directed by Edmund Goulding, with Paul Henreid and Eleanor Parker. 3. GB 1964, directed by Ken Hughes and Henry Hathaway, with Laurence Harvey and Kim Novak. None could prevent the hero's tribulations with a tart from seeming mawkishly unlikely, but the first version was the best acted.

OF MICE AND MEN (US 1940). A curious film to come from comedy producer Hal Roach, this spare little morality about a gentle but homicidal giant who has to be killed by his best friend seemed striking at the time but has dated badly. From John Steinbeck's novel; directed by Lewis Milestone; with Lon Chaney Jnr, Burgess Meredith and Betty Field.

OGILVY, IAN (1943–   ). Slightly-built British leading man. *Stranger in the House* (67), *The Sorcerers* (67), *Witchfinder General* (68), etc.

O'HANLON, GEORGE (1917–) (George Rice). American comedy actor with stage experience; plays Joe McDoakes in the one-reeler 'Behind the Eight Ball' series. Also: *The Great Awakening* (41), *The Hucksters* (47), *The Tanks Are Coming* (51), *Battle Stations* (55), *Bop Girl* (57), *The Rookie* (59), etc.

O'HARA, GERRY (c.1925–). British director. *That Kind of Girl* (61), *The Pleasure Girls* (64), *Maroc 7* (67), *Amsterdam Affair* (68), *All the Right Noises* (69), etc.

O'HARA, JOHN (1905–). American best-selling novelist who wrote chiefly about sex in suburbia. Works filmed include *Pal Joey*, *From the Terrace*, *A Rage to Live*, *Butterfield 8*. Also co-wrote screenplays: *I Was an Adventuress* (40), *Moontide* (42), *Strange Journey* (46), *On Our Merry Way* (48), *The Best Things in Life Are Free* (56), etc.

O'HARA, MAUREEN (1920–) (Maureen Fitzsimmons). Red-haired Irish leading lady who came to films straight from drama school. *Jamaica Inn* (debut) (39), *The Hunchback of Notre Dame* (40), *A Bill of Divorcement* (40), *How Green Was My Valley* (41), *The Black Swan* (42), *The Fallen Sparrow* (43), *The Spanish Main* (45), *Sentimental Journey* (46), *The Foxes of Harrow* (47), *Rio Grande* (50), *The Quiet Man* (52), *Kangaroo* (52), *Redhead from Wyoming* (53), *Malaga* (GB) (54), *The Long Gray Line* (55), *Lady Godiva* (55), *The Magnificent Matador* (56), *Everything But the Truth* (56), *The Wings of Eagles* (57), *Our Man in Havana* (59), *The Deadly Companions* (61), *Mr Hobbs Takes a Vacation* (62), *McLintock* (63), *The Battle of the Villa Fiorita* (65), *The Rare Breed* (66), many others.

O'HERLIHY, DAN (1919–). Irish character actor and occasional off-beat leading man, with Abbey Theatre and radio experience. Long in US. *Odd Man Out* (GB) (46), *Hungry Hill* (GB) (46), *Kidnapped* (48), *Macbeth* (48), *Actors and Sin* (50), *Rommel, Desert Fox* (51), *The Blue Veil* (51), *The Highwayman* (52), *The Adventures of Robinson Crusoe* (52), *Bengal Brigade* (53), *The Black Shield of Falworth* (54), *The Purple Mask* (55), *The Virgin Queen* (55), *That Woman Opposite* (GB) (57), *Home Before Dark* (58), *Imitation of Life* (59), *The Cabinet of Dr Caligari* (61), *Fail Safe* (64), *100 Rifles* (69), *Waterloo* (69), others. TV series: *The Travels of Jaimie McPheeters*.

O'HERLIHY, MICHAEL (1929–). Irish director in Hollywood, with TV experience. *The Fighting Prince of Donegal* (66), *The One and Only Genuine Original Family Band* (68), *Smith!* (69).

OHMART, CAROL (c. 1931–). American leading lady with stage experience, whose career in films did not develop. *The Scarlet Hour* (debut) (55), *The Wild Party* (56), *The House on Haunted Hill* (60), *One Man's Way* (64), etc.

OH MR PORTER (GB 1938). One of the funniest British comedies in the music-hall tradition of the 30s. About an incompetent station-master who clears an Irish branch line of gun-runners posing as ghosts, it is superbly written around the talents of Will Hay, with Graham Moffatt (the fat boy) and Moore Marriott (old Harbottle) as foils. Written by Val Guest, Marriott Edgar and J. O. C. Orton, directed by Marcel Varnel.

O'KEEFE, DENNIS (1908–1968) (Edward 'Bud' Flanagan). Cheerful American leading man of the 40s; began as an extra after vaudeville experience with his parents. *Bad Man of Brimstone* (38), *That's Right, You're Wrong* (39), *La Conga Nights* (40), *You'll Find Out* (40), *Lady Scarface* (41), *Topper Returns* (41), *Broadway Limited* (41), *The Affairs of Jimmy Valentine* (42), *Good Morning Judge* (42), *The Leopard Man* (43), *The Fighting Seabees* (43), *Up in Mabel's Room* (44), *Abroad with Two Yanks* (44), *The Affairs of Susan* (45), *Brewster's Millions* (45), *Come Back to Me* (46), *Dishonoured Lady* (47), *Mr District Attorney* (47), *Raw Deal* (48), *Walk a Crooked Mile* (49), *The Company She Keeps* (51), *Follow the Sun* (52), *The Fake* (GB) (53), *The Diamond Wizard* (GB) (also directed) (54), *Angela* (also directed) (55), *Inside Detroit* (56), *Dragoon Wells Massacre* (57), *Graft and Corruption* (58), *All Hands on Deck* (61), many others. TV series: *The Dennis O'Keefe Show* (59).

OLAND, WARNER (1880–1938). Swedish actor in America from child-hood, films from 1917. *The Jazz Singer* (27), *The Mysterious Dr Fu Manchu* (28), *Charlie Chan Carries On* (31) (and 16 other Chan films before 1938), *Shanghai Express* (32), *Werewolf of London* (34), etc.

OLCOTT, SIDNEY (1873–1949) (John S. Alcott). Irish-Canadian director, in Holywood from the beginning. *Ben Hur* (one reel) (07). *Florida Crackers* (08), *Judgment* (09), *The Miser's Child* (10), *The O'Neil* (Irish) (11), *From the Manger to the Cross* (12), *Madame Butterfly* (15), *The Innocent Lie* (17), *Scratch My Back* (20), *Little Old New York* (21), *The Humming Bird* (23), *The Green Goddess* (23), *Monsieur Beaucaire* (24), *The Amateur Gentleman* (26), *The Claw* (27), etc.

old age on the screen has seldom been explored, and the commercial reasons for this are obvious. Among the serious studies are *The Whisperers*, with Edith Evans; *Umberto D*, with Carlo Battisti; *The Shameless Old Lady*, with Sylvie; *Ikru*, with Takashi Shimura; *The End of the Road*, with Finlay Currie; and *Alive and Kicking*, with Sybil Thorndike and Estelle Winwood. Sentimentality crept in in *Mr Belvedere Rings the Bell*; and *The Old Man and the Sea* was merely pretentious.

There was an element of black comedy in the attitudes expressed towards the old people in *Grapes of Wrath*, *Tobacco Road* and *Night of the Iguana*; and more melodramatic caricatures were presented in *The Lost Moment* (Agnes Moorehead), *The Queen of Spades* (Edith Evans), and *The Old Dark House* (John Dudgeon). Fantasy crept in with *Lost Horizon*, in which the lamas grew incredibly old by natural processes, and *The Man in Half Moon Street*, in which Nils Asther was assisted by science. Other actors who have specialized in geriatric portraits include A. E. Matthews, Edie Martin, Clem Bevans, Andy Clyde, Maria Ouspenskaya, Jessie Ralph, Nancy Price and Adeline de Walt Reynolds, who did not become an actress until she was eighty. Perhaps the screen's most delightful senior citizens were the capering Harbottle, played by Moore Marriott in the Will Hay comedies, and Barry Fitzgerald in *Broth of a Boy*; the most horrific has been Cathleen Nesbit in *Staircase*.

THE OLD DARK HOUSE (US 1932). A connoisseur's horror film, from J. B. Priestley's novel about an assorted group of people marooned in an inhospitable old mansion on a stormy night. Directed by James Whale with a rare sense of the eccentric and bizarre; acted by a splendid cast including Ernest Thesiger ('Have some gin: it's my only weakness'), Eva Moore ('No beds—they can't have beds'), Melvyn Douglas, Charles Laughton, Raymond Massey, Boris Karloff and Brember Wills. The Hammer remake (GB 1963) proved completely unsatisfactory.

OLDLAND, LILIAN (1905–   ). British leading lady of the silents, who later changed her name to Mary Newland. *The Secret Kingdom* (25), *The Flag Lieutenant* (26), *Troublesome Wives* (27), *Jealousy* (31), *Ask Beccles* (34), *Death at Broadcasting House* (34), *The Silent Passenger* (last to date) (35), etc.

OLD MOTHER RILEY. The vociferous Irish washerwoman was impersonated by Arthur Lucan for years on the music halls and in a dozen or more films between 1937 and 1952, the last one being *Mother Riley Meets the Vampire*. Daughter Kitty was played by the resistible Kitty Macshane. Most of the films were atrociously made but all of them made a sizeable profit from British provincial showings.

OLIVER!: see OLIVER TWIST.

OLIVER, ANTHONY (1923–   ). Welsh general purpose actor, in British films and TV. *Once a Jolly Swagman* (48), *The Clouded Yellow* (50), *The Runaway Bus* (54), *Lost* (56), others.

OLIVER, EDNA MAY (1883–1942) (Edna May Cox-Oliver). American character actress, usually of acidulous but often warm-hearted spinsters; on stage from 1912. *Icebound* (23), *The American Venus* (26), *Saturday Night Kid* (29), *Half Shot at Sunrise* (31), *Cimarron* (31), *Fanny Foley Herself* (31), *The Penguin Pool Murder* (32), *Little Women*

(33), *Alice in Wonderland* (33), *David Copperfield* (as Aunt Betsy) (34), *A Tale of Two Cities* (35), *Romeo and Juliet* (as the Nurse) (36), *Parnell* (37), *Rosalie* (38), *Second Fiddle* (38), *The Story of Vernon and Irene Castle* (39), *Nurse Edith Cavell* (39), *Pride and Prejudice* (as Lady Catherine de Bourgh) (40), *Lydia* (41), etc.

OLIVER, SUSAN (1937–). American leading TV actress whose film roles have been few. *Green-Eyed Blonde* (57), *The Gene Krupa Story* (60), *Looking for Love* (64), *The Disorderly Orderly* (65), *Your Cheating Heart* (66), *A Man Called Gannon* (68), etc.

OLIVER TWIST. Dickens' novel was filmed many times in the early silent period: in 1909 by Pathé, in 1910 by Vitagraph, in 1912 by an independent company with Nat C. Goodwin as Fagin. A famous American version of 1916 had Tully Marshall as Fagin and Marie Doro as Oliver; in 1922 the roles were played by Lon Chaney and Jackie Coogan, and in 1933 by Irving Pichel and Dickie Moore. The definitive version to date, however, is the British one directed by David Lean in 1948, with John Howard Davies in the title role. Alec Guinness' brilliant performance as Fagin caused a hold-up in American distribution as it was accused of anti-semitism. Technically a remarkable evocation of the book's melodramatic realism, the film was photographed by Guy Green, designed by John Bryan, with music by Arnold Bax. *Oliver!*, a 1968 musical version, won six Oscars: best film, best director (Carol Reed), best art directions (John Box and Terence Marsh), best score (John Green), best sound (Shepperton Studios), best choreography (Onna White).

OLIVER, VIC (1898–1964) (Victor von Samek). Austrian-born comedian, pianist, violinist and conductor, long in Britain. Occasional films include *Rhythm in the Air* (37), *Room for Two* (40), *He Found a Star* (41), *Hi Gang* (41), *Give Us the Moon* (44), *I'll Be Your Sweetheart* (45), etc.

†OLIVIER, SIR LAURENCE (1907–). Distinguished British stage actor whose film appearances have been reasonably frequent. *Too Many Crooks* (30), *The Temporary Widow* (30), *Potiphar's Wife* (30), *The Yellow Ticket* (31), *Friends and Lovers* (31), *Westward Passage* (31), *No Funny Business* (32), *Perfect Understanding* (US) (32), *Conquest of the Air* (35), *Moscow Nights* (35), *As You Like It* (as Orlando) (36), *Fire over England* (36), *The Divorce of Lady X* (38), *Twenty-one Days* (39), *Q Planes* (39), *Wuthering Heights* (US) (39), *Rebecca* (US) (40), *Pride and Prejudice* (US) (40), *Lady Hamilton* (US) (as Nelson) (41), *49th Parallel* (42), *The Demi-Paradise* (43), *Henry V* (also produced and co-directed) (special AA) (44), *Hamlet* (also produced and directed) (AA) (48), *The Magic Box* (cameo role) (51), *Carrie* (US)

(52), *The Beggar's Opera* (as Macheath) (52), *Richard III* (also produced and directed) (56), *The Prince and the Showgirl* (also directed) (58), *The Devil's Disciple* (59), *Spartacus* (US) (60), *The Entertainer* (60), *Term of Trial* (62), *Bunny Lake Is Missing* (65), *Othello* (65), *Khartoum* (66), *The Shoes of the Fisherman* (68), *Oh What a Lovely War* (69), *The Dance of Death* (69), *The Battle of Britain* (69), *David Copperfield* (69), *Three Sisters* (also directed) (70).

OLMI, ERMANNO (1931–   ). Italian director, best known abroad for *Il Posto* (*The Job*) (61), *I Fidanzati* (62), *And There Came a Man* (65).

OLSEN, OLE (1892–1965) (John Sigurd Olsen). Norwegian-American comedian, in vaudeville from 1914, almost always with partner Chic Johnson. *Gold Dust Gertie* (31), *Fifty Million Frenchmen* (31), *The Country Gentleman* (37), *Hellzapoppin* (42), *Crazy House* (44), *Ghost Catchers* (44), *See My Lawyer* (45), etc.

OLSON, MORONI (1889–1954). Heavily-built American character actor, with stage experience. *The Three Musketeers* (as Porthos) (36), *The Witness Chair* (38), *The Three Musketeers* (as bailiff) (39), *Kentucky* (39), *The Glass Key* (42), *Call Northside 777* (48), *Father of the Bride* (50), *The Long, Long Trailer* (54), many others.

OLSON, NANCY (1928–   ). American leading lady who came to films from college, retired after a few years and recently reappeared in more mature roles. *Union Station* (50), *Sunset Boulevard* (50), *Submarine Command* (51), *So Big* (52), *Battle Cry* (55), *Pollyanna* (60), *The Absent-minded Professor* (61), *Son of Flubber* (63), *Smith!* (69), etc.

LOS OLVIDADOS (Mexico 1950). Luis Bunuel's study of depraved and deprived adolescents in Mexico: the young anti-hero ends up dead on a dung heap. Photographed by Figueroa, it is a comfortless film, but important in the history of social realism.

OLYMPISCHE SPIELE (Germany 1936). Leni Riefenstahl's brilliantly-photographed account of the Olympic Games of 1936 is a hymn to the human body and a superb example of film reporting.

O'MALLEY, J. PAT (1904–   ). Irish character actor long in Hollywood. *Paris Calling* (41), *Lassie Come Home* (43), *The Long Hot Summer* (57), *Blueprint for Robbery* (60), *A House is not a Home* (64), many others.

O'MARA, KATE (1939–   ). British leading lady. *Great Catherine* (68), *The Limbo Line* (68), *The Desperados* (69).

ON APPROVAL (GB 1944). A curious but very successful one-shot at directing by Clive Brook, who with Googie Withers, Beatrice Lillie and Roland Culver made up the romantic quartet involved in this unexpected version of Frederick Lonsdale's Edwardian comedy. There was a touch of the Marx Brothers about the semi-mocking treatment of the faded material, but it certainly came off even though it had no imitators at the time.

ONDRA, ANNY (1903–   ) (A. Ondrakova). Polish leading lady of British silent films; her accent killed her career when sound came. *Chorus Girls* (28), *The Manxman* (29), *Blackmail* (30), *Glorious Youth* (31), etc. Returned to Europe and appeared in a few German films, e.g. *Schön Muss Man Sein* (50).

O'NEAL, FREDERICK (1905–   ). Powerful American Negro character actor, mainly on stage. *Pinky* (49), *No Way Out* (50), *Something of Value* (56), *Anna Lucasta* (58), *Take a Giant Step* (59), etc. TV series: *Car 54 Where Are You?* (61–62).

O'NEAL, PATRICK (1927–   ). American general purpose actor with stage and TV experience. *The Mad Magician* (54), *From the Terrace* (60), *The Cardinal* (63), *In Harm's Way* (65), *King Rat* (65), *A Fine Madness* (66), *Chamber of Horrors* (66), *Alvarez Kelly* (66), *Assignment to Kill* (67), *Where Were You When the Lights Went Out?* (68), *The Secret Life of an American Wife* (68), *Castle Keep* (69), *Stiletto* (69), etc. TV series: *Dick and the Duchess* (58).

ONE HOUR WITH YOU: see THE MARRIAGE CIRCLE.

ONE HUNDRED AND ONE DALMATIANS (US 1960). Disney's most pleasing post-war full-length cartoon, with a strength but delicacy of line which he has not been able to maintain. Based on an amusing story by Dodie Smith, it makes play with a well-observed London background.

O'NEIL, BARBARA (c. 1903–   ). American character actress who made a corner in mad wives and other neurotic roles. *Stella Dallas* (37), *When Tomorrow Comes* (39), *Tower of London* (39), *Gone with the Wind* (39), *All This and Heaven Too* (40), *Shining Victory* (41), *I Remember Mama* (47), *Whirlpool* (49), *Angel Face* (52), *Flame of the Islands* (55), *The Nun's Story* (58), others.

O'NEILL, EUGENE (1888–1953). Irish-American playwright of self-pitying disposition and a tendency in his plays to tragic despair. His gloominess led Hollywood to regard his works as art, which killed many of the film versions stone dead. *Anna Christie* (23 with Blanche Sweet, 30 with Garbo), *Strange Interlude* (32), *The Emperor Jones* (33), *Ah Wilderness* (35), *The Long Voyage Home* (40), *The Hairy Ape* (44), *Summer Holiday* (47), *Mourning Becomes Electra* (48), *Desire under the Elms* (57), *Long Day's Journey into Night* (62), etc.

O'NEILL, HENRY (1891–1964). American character actor with stage experience, in Hollywood from early 30s. Played scores of judges, guardians, fathers, lawyers, etc., from *Strong Arm* (34) to *Untamed* (55).

o'NEILL, MAIRE (1885–1952) (Maire Allgood). Irish character actress, an Abbey player; sister of Sara Allgood. Films include *Juno and the Paycock* (30), *Sing As We Go* (34), *Farewell Again* (37), *Love on the Dole* (41), *Gaiety George* (46), *Someone at the Door* (50), *Treasure Hunt* (52), etc.

ONE MILLION YEARS B.C. (US 1939). This curious film, also known as *The Cave Dwellers* and *Man and His Mate*, was produced and directed in 1939 by Hal Roach with assistance from D. W. Griffith, upon whose 1912 *Man's Genesis* it was based. A highly unscientific account of the tribulations of primitive man, it featured Carole Landis and Victor Mature, whose dialogue consisted largely of grunts, and who came up against a remarkable variety of prehistoric monsters which were rather obviously normal reptiles crudely decorated and magnified. In 1966 Hammer remade it in a rather pedestrian colour version with Raquel Welch and John Richardson, directed by Don Chaffey; this time the monsters were plastic animations. 1969 brought a kind of sequel, *When Dinosaurs Ruled the Earth*, directed by Val Guest.

ONE SUNDAY AFTERNOON (US 1933). This pleasant romantic comedy-drama, set in Brooklyn in the 90s, was made three times within fifteen years by the same company, Warners. The first version, directed by Stephen Roberts, had Gary Cooper, Neil Hamilton, Fay Wray and Frances Fuller. The second version, made in 1941 under the title *Strawberry Blonde*, was directed by Raoul Walsh and starred James Cagney, Jack Carson, Olivia de Havilland and Rita Hayworth. In 1948 Raoul Walsh again directed, under the original title, this time with songs added; the stars were Dennis Morgan, Don Defore, Dorothy Malone and Janis Paige. The scripts stemmed from a play by James Hagan, about a dentist who fell for a glamorous girl but eventually returned to his artless sweetheart.

ONE, TWO, THREE (US 1961). Billy Wilder has always liked to take his stories from the newspaper headlines, but this frantic comedy was his most daring, being all about the Berlin Wall at a time when it seemed we were in for a Third World War over it. Based on a Molnar play, brought up to date by Wilder and I. A. L. Diamond, it scuttles along with tremendous zip until round about the third act, when the pace flags. James Cagney as an exuberant Coca-Cola salesman makes it practically a one-man show. Photographed by Daniel Fapp.

ONE WAY PASSAGE (US 1932). A popular tear-jerker of its time, about a dying beauty (Kay Francis) and a convicted murderer (William

Powell) who meet on an ocean liner and fall in love while keeping their secrets; written and directed by Tay Garnett. In 1940 it was remade by Edmund Goulding as *Till We Meet Again*, with Merle Oberon and George Brent.

ONIBABA (Japan 1964). A stylish medieval horror comic set entirely within a forest of tall reeds by a river, where two penniless women murder strangers for their clothing, finally coming to grief through lust and jealousy. Its remarkable holding power is attributable to Kaneto Shindo's direction and Kyomi Kuroda's photography.

ON THE BEACH (US 1959). Stanley Kramer's bleak film about the end of the world, from Nevil Shute's novel, was about the most downbeat product ever to come from Hollywood. Although interesting it seemed in the long run over-slow and rather pointless, but the last rites of mankind were glossily photographed by Sam Leavitt.

ON THE TOWN (US 1949). One of Hollywood's most exhilarating and influential musicals. The simple tale of three sailors on a day's leave in New York, it had a sextet of principals who lit up the screen with their sheer vivacity and well-nigh perpetual motion: Gene Kelly, Frank Sinatra, Jules Munshin, Betty Garrett, Ann Miller and Vera-Ellen. No one talks in this film when song or dance will do. Direction by Kelly and Stanley Donen; music by Leonard Bernstein; words by Adolph Green and Betty Comden; photography by Harold Rossen.

ON THE WATERFRONT (US 1954). Basically a good location thriller about the docks protection rackets, this film from Budd Schulberg's novel had enough pretensions to win it several Academy Awards: best actor (Marlon Brando), best supporting actress (Eva Marie Saint), best art direction (Richard Day), best picture, best cinematography (Boris Kaufman), best direction (Elia Kazan), best editing (Gene Milford). It wasn't really all that good; but it did bring the Method to the masses, mumblings and all.

OPATOSHU, DAVID (1919–   ). American general purpose actor, often seen as villain. *Exodus* (60), *Guns of Darkness* (63), *Torn Curtain* (66), *The Defector* (67), *Enter Laughing* (67), *Death of a Gunfighter* (69), etc.

OPEN CITY (Italy 1945). A semi-documentary record, shot under the noses of the retreating German army by Italian patriots, of what Italy had suffered under the occupation. Occasionally melodramatic but always moving, with a rawness fresh to the western cinema at the time. Also the film which introduced Anna Magnani to a wider audience. Directed by Roberto Rossellini from a script by

Sergei Amidei and Federico Fellini; photographed by Uberto Arato.

†OPHULS, MAX (1902–1957) (Max Oppenheimer). German director of international, highly decorated, romantic films. *Dann Schön Lieber Lebertran* (30), *Der Verkaufte Braut* (32), *Liebelei* (32), *On a Volé un Homme* (34), *La Signora di Tutti* (34), *Trouble With Money* (34), *La Tendre Ennemie* (36), *Yoshimara* (37), *Werther* (38), *Sans Lendemain* (39), *De Mayerling à Sarajevo* (40), *The Exile* (47), *Letter from an Unknown Woman* (48), *Caught* (48), *The Reckless Moment* (49), *La Ronde* (50), *Le Plaisir* (51), *Madame De* (53), *Lola Montes* (55).

opticals. A general term indicating all the visual tricks such as wipes, dissolves, invisibility, mattes, etc., which involve laboratory work.

ORCHARD, JULIAN (1930–). Lugubrious British revue comedian who has enlivened a number of bit parts. *Crooks Anonymous* (58), *On the Beat* (60), *Kill or Cure* (62), *The Spy with a Cold Nose* (66), *Carry On Doctor* (68), *Heironymus Merkin* (69), others.

ORESTE: see KIRKOP, ORESTE.

orchestral conductors have figured as leading men in *Intermezzo, Interlude, Once More With Feeling, Song of Russia, Break of Hearts, Prelude to Fame, Counterpoint*; Charles Laughton cut a tragi-comic figure in *Tales of Manhattan*. Real conductors who have played dramatic roles in movies include Leopold Stokowski, Jose Iturbi and many swing or jazz figures such as Paul Whiteman, Tommy Dorsey, Henry Hall, Glenn Miller, Benny Goodman, Xavier Cugat.

original version. In European countries, this indicates a foreign language film which is sub-titled and not dubbed.

O'ROURKE, BREFNI (1889–1945). Irish stage actor, an Abbey player, who made some British films, usually as testy types. *The Ghost of St Michael's* (41), *Hatter's Castle* (41), *The Lamp Still Burns* (43), *Don't Take It to Heart* (44), *I See a Dark Stranger* (45), etc.

ORPHEE (France 1949). A strange poetic fantasy written and directed by Jean Cocteau, based on the myth of Orpheus and Eurydice but with twists of his own. Its real meaning is almost as obscure as that of his 1930 surrealist film *Le Sang d'un Poète*, but there is much pleasure to be gained from watching it purely as a piece of instinctively successful cinema using all the devices of the medium. Photographed by Nicolas Hayer, music by Georges Auric, with Jean Marais as Orpheus and Maria Casares as Death. Cocteau in 1960 made an even stranger sequel, *Le Testament D'Orphée*.

ORRY-KELLY (1897–1964). Australian designer, in Hollywood from 1923 after Broadway experience. For many years with Warner, then with Fox. Won Academy Award for costumes of *An American in Paris* (51).

ORTH, FRANK (1880–1962). American small part actor who must have played more bartenders than he could count. *Hot Money* (36), *Serenade* (39), *The Lost Weekend* (45), *Father of the Bride* (50), *Here Come the Girls* (54), many others.

OSBORN, ANDREW (1912–   ). British stage and film actor: *Who Goes Next* (38), *Idol of Paris* (48), *Dark Interval* (50), *Angels One Five* (51), *The Second Mrs Tanqueray* (53), etc. More recently BBC TV producer: *Maigret* series, etc.

OSBORNE, JOHN (1929–   ). British dramatist. Plays filmed: *Look Back in Anger* (59), *The Entertainer* (60), *Inadmissible Evidence* (68). Also wrote screenplay for *Tom Jones* (63).

'*Oscar*'. An affectionate name given to the Academy Award statuette; reputedly because when the figure was first struck in 1927 a secretary said: 'It reminds me of my Uncle Oscar'.

OSCAR, HENRY (1891–   ) (Henry Wale). British character actor, on stage from 1911, films from 1932, usually as meek or scheming fellows. *After Dark* (debut) (32), *I Was a Spy* (33), *The Man Who Knew Too Much* (34), *Fire over England* (37), *The Return of the Scarlet Pimpernel* (as Robespierre) (39), *Hatter's Castle* (41), *They Made Me a Fugitive* (47), *The Greed of William Hart* (48), *The Black Rose* (50), *Private's Progress* (55), *Foxhole in Cairo* (60), etc.

O'SHEA, MICHAEL (1906–   ). American actor with a 'good guy' personality, who, after circus and vaudeville experience, made several films in the 40s and 50s. *Striptease Lady* (*The G String Murders*) (43), *The Eve of St Mark* (44), *It's a Pleasure* (45), *Circumstantial Evidence* (45), *The Big Wheel* (49), *The Model and the Marriage Broker* (52), *It Should Happen To You* (54), etc.

O'SHEA, MILO (c. 1923–   ). Irish character comedian, an Abbey player; recently in *Never Put It in Writing* (64), *Ulysses* (as Bloom) (67), *Romeo and Juliet* (68), *Barbarella* (68), *The Adding Machine* (69).

O'SULLIVAN, MAUREEN (1911–   ). Irish leading lady, spotted by talent scout and taken to Hollywood with no dramatic training. *The Big Shot* (debut) (31), *Tarzan and His Mate* (32) (she played Jane also in several later episodes of the series), *Tugboat Annie* (33), *The Barretts of Wimpole Street* (34), *The Thin Man* (34), *David Copperfield* (34). *Anna Karenina* (35), *A Day at the Races* (37), *Pride and Prejudice* (40), *Maisie Was a Lady* (41), etc.; then retired apart from occasional appearances. *The Big Clock* (48), *Where Danger Lives* (50), *Bonzo Goes to College* (52), *All I Desire* (53), *The Steel*

Cage (54), *Never Too Late* (65), etc. Widow of John Farrow, mother of Mia.

o'sullivan, richard (1943–   ). British juvenile, formerly child actor. *The Stranger's Hand* (53), *Dangerous Exile* (56), *A Story of David* (60), *The Young Ones* (61), *Wonderful Life* (64), etc.

†oswald, gerd (1916–   ). German-American director, son of Richard Oswald. *A Kiss Before Dying* (56), *The Brass Legend* (57), *Fury at Sundown* (57), *Valerie* (57), *Crime of Passion* (57), *Paris Holiday* (57), *Screaming Mimi* (58), *Brainwashed* (61), *Agent for H.A.R.M.* (66). Also directed many episodes of TV series.

oswald, richard (1880–1963) (R. Ornstein). German director, father of Gerd Oswald. *Pagu* (16), *Round the World in Eighty Days* (19), *Victoria and Her Hussar* (31), *Der Hauptmann von Kopenick* (32), *I Was a Criminal* (US) (41), *Isle of Missing Men* (US) (42), *The Lovable Cheat* (US) (49), etc.

†o'toole, peter (1932–   ). British leading man who after stage and TV experience had fairly meteoric rise to stardom in films. *Kidnapped* (debut) (59), *Savage Innocents* (59), *The Day They Robbed the Bank of England* (60), *Lawrence of Arabia* (62), *Becket* (64), *Lord Jim* (65), *What's New, Pussycat?* (65), *How to Steal a Million* (66), *The Night of the Generals* (66), *The Bible* (66), *Great Catherine* (67), *The Lion in Winter* (68), *Goodbye Mr Chips* (69), *Country Dance* (70).

ottiano, rafaela (1894–1942). Italian-born stage actress who went to Hollywood and played sinister housekeepers, etc. *As You Desire Me* (32), *Grand Hotel* (32), *She Done Him Wrong* (33), *Great Expectations* (34), *Maytime* (37), *Topper Returns* (41), etc.

oulton, brian (1908–   ). British stage and film comedy actor, usually in unctuous or prim roles. *Too Many Husbands* (39), *Miranda* (48), *Last Holiday* (50), *Castle in the Air* (52), *The Million Pound Note* (54), *Private's Progress* (55), *Happy Is the Bride* (57), *The Thirty-nine Steps* (59), *A French Mistress* (60), *Kiss of the Vampire* (62), *Carry On Cleo* (64), *The Intelligence Men* (64), etc.

our daily bread (US 1933). King Vidor wrote and directed this sequel to his 1928 urban movie *The Crowd*; he now showed his downtrodden hero making good during the depression years by taking to collective farming. Photographed by Robert Planck; with Tom Keene and Karen Morley.

'*Our Gang*'. A collection of child actors first gathered together in short slapstick comedies by producer Hal Roach in the mid-20s. They remained popular through the 30s and 40s, though the personnel of the team naturally changed. The originals included Mary Kornman, Farina, Joe Cobb, Mickey Daniels and Jackie Condon;

a later generation included Spanky Macfarland, Darla Hood and Buckwheat Thomas. Robert McGowan directed most of the films, many of which have been revived on TV.

OURY, GERARD (1919–   ) (Max-Gerard Tannenbaum). Dapper French character actor: *Antoine et Antonette* (46), *La Belle Que Voilà* (49), *Sea Devils* (GB) (52), *Father Brown* (GB) (54), *House of Secrets* (GB) (56), *The Journey* (US) (58), *The Mirror Has Two Faces* (59), etc. Now director: *La Main Chaude* (60), *The Sucker* (*Le Corniaud*) (64), *The Big Spree* (66), *The Brain* (69), etc.

†OUSPENSKAYA, MARIA (1876–1949). Distinguished, diminutive European character actress who enlivened some Hollywood films after the mid-30s. *Dodsworth* (36), *Conquest* (*Marie Walewska*) (37), *Love Affair* (39), *The Rains Came* (39), *Judge Hardy and Son* (39), *Dr Ehrlich's Magic Bullet* (40), *Waterloo Bridge* (40), *The Mortal Storm* (40), *The Man I Married* (40), *Dance Girl Dance* (40), *Beyond Tomorrow* (40), *The Wolf Man* (41), *The Shanghai Gesture* (41), *King's Row* (42), *The Mystery of Marie Roget* (42), *Frankenstein Meets the Wolf Man* (43), *Tarzan and the Amazons* (45), *I've Always Loved You* (*Concerto*) (46), *Wyoming* (47), *A Kiss in the Dark* (49).

THE OUTLAW (1941–1945). This notorious censor-baiting western, with its advertising campaign based on Jane Russell's cleavage, has historical interest as an example of how producer-director Howard Hughes managed to fool all of the people all of the time. The movie is neither sensational nor very entertaining, but by withholding it from release for three years and getting into a lot of argument with censor boards, Hughes made the world's press believe it was. Basically a fanciful tale of an encounter between Billy the Kid and Doc Holliday, it needed firmer handling than Hughes was able to supply. The full story of the film's making can be found in the recent biographies of Hughes (qv).

OUT OF THE INKWELL (US 1920–1924). An influential series of silent cartoons by Max Fleischer, in which the artist's hands and drawing pad were in normal photography and the cartoon characters, superimposed, appeared to animate themselves.

OUTWARD BOUND. Sutton Vane's 20s play concerns a group of people who find themselves travelling on a luxurious but mysterious ship and slowly realize they are dead. It was filmed in 1930 by Robert Milton, with Leslie Howard and Douglas Fairbanks Jnr, and ran into considerable censor trouble. In 1944 an updated and extremely dreary version was directed by Edward A. Blatt under the title *Between Two Worlds*: Paul Henried and John Garfield had the leads, and Sidney Greenstreet livened up the last half as the heavenly examiner.

z*

THE OVERLANDERS (GB 1946). Made on location in Australia, this story of an arduous cattle drive seemed to open new horizons for colonial film-making, but they did not develop significantly and the later Australian productions proved disappointing. Even star Chips Rafferty waned in appeal. But this was a good Western in a fresh locale, written and directed by Harry Watt and photographed by Osmond Borrodaile.

OVERMAN, LYNNE (1887–1943). American character actor with stage experience. Memorable in cynical comedy roles for his relaxed manner and sing-song voice. *Rumba* (35), *The Jungle Princess* (36), *Spawn of the North* (38), *Typhoon* (40), *Aloma of the South Seas* (40), *Caught in the Draft* (41), *Roxie Hart* (42), *Reap the Wild Wind* (42), *Dixie* (43), etc.

OWEN, BILL (1914–) (Bill Rowbotham). British character comedian, former dance band musician and singer. *The Way to the Stars* (debut) (45), *When the Bough Breaks* (47), *The Girl Who Couldn't Quite* (49), *Trottie True* (49), *Hotel Sahara* (51), *The Square Ring* (53), *The Rainbow Jacket* (54), *Davy* (57), *Carve Her Name with Pride* (58), *The Hellfire Club* (61), *The Secret of Blood Island* (65) *Georgy Girl* (66), etc.

OWEN, CLIFF (1919–). British director, in films from 1937. *Offbeat* (60), *A Prize of Arms* (62), *The Wrong Arm of the Law* (63), *A Man Could Get Killed* (66), *That Riviera Touch* (66), *The Magnificent Two* (67), etc. Also TV work.

OWEN, REGINALD (1887–). British character actor, on stage from 1905, films (in Hollywood) from 1929. *The Letter* (debut) (29), *Platinum Blonde* (32), *Queen Christina* (33), *Call of the Wild* (35), *Anna Karenina* (35), *The Great Ziegfeld* (36), *A Tale of Two Cities* (36), *The Suicide Club* (36), *Conquest (Marie Walewska)* (37), *The Earl of Chicago* (39), *Florian* (40), *Charley's Aunt* (41), *Tarzan's Secret Treasure* (41), *Mrs Miniver* (42), *Random Harvest* (42), *White Cargo* (44), *Madame Curie* (43), *Lassie Come Home* (43), *The Canterville Ghost* (44), *Kitty* (45), *The Diary of a Chambermaid* (45), *Cluny Brown* (46), *If Winter Comes* (47), *The Three Musketeers* (48), *The Miniver Story* (50), *Kim* (51), *Red Garters* (54), *The Young Invaders* (58), *Voice of the Hurricane* (MRA film) (63), *Mary Poppins* (64), hundreds of others.

OWEN, SEENA (1894–1966) (Signe Auen). American silent screen lady. *Intolerance* (15), *Victory* (19), *Shipwrecked* (23), *Flame of the Yukon* (25), *The Rush Hour* (28), others.

OWENS, PATRICIA (1925–). Canadian leading lady who made films in Britain and America. *Miss London Ltd* (43), *While the Sun Shines* (46), *The Happiest Days of Your Life* (49), *Mystery Junction* (52), *The Good Die Young* (53), *Windfall* (55), *Island in the Sun* (56),

Sayonara (US) (57), *No Down Payment* (US) (57), *The Fly* (US) (58), *Five Gates to Hell* (US) (59), *Hell to Eternity* (US) (60), etc. Retired.

THE OX-BOW INCIDENT (US 1943). A striking Western indictment of lynch law, from the novel by Walter Van Tilburg Clark. A remarkably sombre and atmospheric film to come out of Hollywood in the middle of World War II, it had no popular success. Henry Fonda led an excellent cast; William Wellman directed from a script by Lamar Trotti. Released in Britain as *Strange Incident*.

OXLEY, DAVID (c. 1929–   ). British actor. *Ill Met by Moonlight* (57), *Saint Joan* (58), *The Hound of the Baskervilles* (59), etc.

OZEP, FEDOR (1895–1949). Russian director: *The Crime of Dmitri Karamazov* (31), *The Living Dead* (33), *Amok* (34), *Gibraltar* (38), *She Who Dares* (US) (44), *Whispering City* (Can.) (48), etc.

OZU, YASUJIRO (1903–1963). Japanese director, since 1927. *A Story of Floating Weeds* (34), *Late Spring* (49), *Early Summer* (51), *Tokyo Story* (53), *Early Spring* (56), *Late Autumn* (61), *Early Autumn* (62), etc.

P

ABST, G. W. (Georg Wilhelm) (1885–1967). Distinguished German director, with theatrical training. *Joyless Street* (25), *The Love of Jeanne Ney* (27), *Secrets of the Soul* (27), *Pandora's Box* (28), *Diary of a Lost Girl* (29), *The White Hell of Pitz Palu* (29), *Westfront 1918* (30), *Die Dreigroschenoper* (31), *Kameradschaft* (31), *L'Atlantide* (32), *Don Quixote* (33), *A Modern Hero* (US) (34), *Mademoiselle Docteur* (37), *Paracelsus* (43), *The Trial* (48), *The Last Act* (54), *Der 20 Juli* (*Jackboot Mutiny*) (55), etc.

PADEREWSKI, IGNACE (1860–1941). Polish prime minister and classical pianist. Appeared in a few films including the British *Moonlight Sonata* (37).

PADOVANI, LEA (1920–). Italian leading actress, in films from 1945. *Give Us This Day* (GB) (49), *Three Steps North* (US) (51), *Tempi Nostri* (53), *Montparnasse 19* (57), *The Naked Maja* (US) (58), etc.

PAGE, GALE (c. 1918–) (Sally Rutter). American leading lady. *Four Daughters* (38), *Crime School* (38), *They Drive by Night* (40), *Four Wives* (40), *Four Mothers* (41), *The Time of Your Life* (48), *About Mrs Leslie* (54), etc.

PAGE, GENEVIEVE (c. 1930–). French leading lady who has made American films. *Foreign Intrigue* (56), *Trapped in Tangiers* (60), *Song Without End* (60), *El Cid* (61), *L'Honorable Stanislas* (63), *Youngblood Hawke* (64), *Les Corsaires* (65), *Belle De Jour* (67), *Decline and Fall* (68), etc.

PAGE, GERALDINE (1924–). American leading actress, on stage from 1940; occasional films include *Hondo* (54), *Summer and Smoke* (61), *Sweet Bird of Youth* (62), *Toys in the Attic* (63), *Dear Heart* (65), *The Happiest Millionaire* (67), *You're a Big Boy Now* (67), *Whatever Happened to Aunt Alice?* (69), etc.

PAGE, PATTI (1927–) (Clara Ann Fowler). American TV singer. Film appearances include *Elmer Gantry* (60), *Dondi* (61), *Boys' Night Out* (63).

PAGET, DEBRA (1933–) (Debralee Griffin). American leading lady with brief stage experience. *Cry of the City* (film debut) (48), *House of Strangers* (49), *Broken Arrow* (50), *Les Misérables* (52), *Love Me Tender* (56), *Tales of Terror* (62), *The Haunted Palace* (64), others.

PAGNOL, MARCEL (1895–   ). French writer-director noted for sprawling comedy dramas which strongly evoke country life without being very cinematic. *Marius* (script only) (31), *Fanny* (script only) (32), *César* (34), *Joffroi* (34), *Regain (Harvest)* (37), *La Femme du Boulanger* (38), *La Fille du Puisatier* (40), *La Belle Meunière* (48), *Manon des Sources* (53), *Lettres de Mon Moulin* (55), etc. 1970 project: *Le Chateau de Ma Mere.*

PAIGE, JANIS (1922–   ) (Donna Mae Jaden). American leading lady with operatic training. *Hollywood Canteen* (debut) (44), *Cheyenne* (46), *Romance on the High Seas (It's Magic)* (48), *Mr Universe* (51), *Remains To Be Seen* (53), *Please Don't Eat the Daisies* (61), *The Caretakers (Borderlines)* (63), *Welcome to Hard Times* (67). In recent years mostly on stage.

PAIGE, MABEL (c. 1880–c. 1953). American character actress. *My Heart Belongs to Daddy* (42), *Lucky Jordan* (43), *The Good Fellows* (43), *Someone to Remember* (lead role) (43), *If You Knew Susie* (48), *The Sniper* (52), etc.

PAIGE, ROBERT (1910–   ) (John Arthur Page). American leading man, former radio announcer, in many films of the 40s, little since. *Cain and Mabel* (37), *Hellzapoppin* (42), *Shady Lady* (42), *Son of Dracula* (43), *Can't Help Singing* (44), *Red Stallion* (47), *The Flame* (48), *Raging Waters* (51), *Abbott and Costello Go to Mars* (53), *The Big Payoff* (58), *The Marriage Go Round* (61), *Bye Bye Birdie* (63), etc.

PAINLEVE, JEAN (1902–   ). French documentarist, famous for short scientific naturalist studies of sea horses, sea urchins, shrimps, etc.

painters have frequently had their lives glamorized to provide film. makers with drama to counterpoint art. Among the most notable are Charles Laughton as *Rembrandt*, George Sanders as Gauguin in *The Moon and Sixpence*, Jose Ferrer as Toulouse Lautrec in *Moulin Rouge*, Anthony Franciosa as Goya in *The Naked Maja*, Kirk Douglas as Van Gogh and Anthony Quinn as Gauguin in *Lust for Life*, Gerard Philipe as Modigliani in *Montparnasse 19*, Cecil Kellaway as Gainsborough in *Kitty*, Charlton Heston as Michelangelo in *The Agony and the Ecstasy*, and Mel Ferrer as *El Greco*.

PAISA (Italy 1946). Episodic story film, a kind of sequel to *Open City*, dramatizing incidents in the German retreat through Italy, Directed by Roberto Rossellini from a script by himself, Fellini, and others. Its success encouraged later short story compendiums such as *Quartet* (48).

PAIVA, NESTOR (1905–1966). American character actor of assorted foreign peasant types. *Ride a Crooked Mile* (38), *The Marines Fly High* (40), *The Falcon in Mexico* (44), *Fear* (46), *Road to Rio* (46),

749

Five Fingers (52), *The Creature from the Black Lagoon* (55), *The Deep Six* (57), *The Nine Lives of Elfego Baca* (59), *The Spirit is Willing* (66), many others.

THE PAJAMA GAME (US 1957). A wholly successful—and cinematic—version of the stage musical with the unlikely subject of labour unrest in a pajama factory. Stanley Donen's lively direction and Bob Fosse's choreography survive disagreeable colour, and the songs by Richard Adler and Jerry Ross are among the brightest ever written for one show. Book by Richard Bissell and George Abbott. Doris Day and Eddie Foy Jnr head the cast.

PAKULA, ALAN (1928–). American producer with stage experience; works with director Robert Mulligan. *Fear Strikes Out* (57), *To Kill a Mockingbird* (62), *Love with the Proper Stranger* (64), *Baby the Rain Must Fall* (65), *Inside Daisy Clover* (65), *The Stalking Moon* (68), etc. 1969: produced and directed *The Sterile Cuckoo*.

PAL, GEORGE (1908–). Hungarian puppeteer whose short advertising films enlivened programmes in the late 30s; went to Hollywood 1940 and produced series of 'Puppetoons'; later produced many adventure films involving trick photography, e.g. *Destination Moon* (AA) (50), *When Worlds Collide* (AA) (51), *The War of the Worlds* (AA) (53), *The Naked Jungle* (55), *Tom Thumb* (AA) (58), *The Time Machine* (AA) (61), *The Wonderful World of the Brothers Grimm* (63). Special Academy Award 1943 'for the development of novel methods and techniques'. 1967: *The Power*.

PALANCE, JACK (1920–) (Walter Palanuik). Gaunt American leading man with stage experience; started in films playing villains. *Panic in the Streets* (50), *Halls of Montezuma* (51), *Shane* (53), *Sign of the Pagan* (54), *The Big Knife* (55), *I Died a Thousand Times* (56), *Attack* (56), *The Man Inside* (57), *The Lonely Man* (57), *House of Numbers* (57), *Ten Seconds to Hell* (58), *The Mongols* (60), *Barabbas* (62), *Le Mépris* (63), *Once a Thief* (65), *The Professionals* (66), *The Torture Garden* (GB) (67), *Ché!* (69), *The Desperados* (69), etc. TV series. *The Greatest Show on Earth* (63).

THE PALEFACE (US 1948). A western romp written by Edmund Hartman and Frank Tashlin, directed by Norman Z. McLeod, this had Bob Hope as a cowardly dentist and Jane Russell as Calamity Jane. In 1952 these stars were joined by Roy Rogers for an even crazier extravaganza called *Son of Paleface*. In 1968 the original was revamped for Don Knotts under the title *The Shakiest Gun in the West*.

PALLETTE, EUGENE (1889–1954). Rotund American actor, in films from 1913: *Intolerance* and many other silents; his gravel voice proved an asset with the coming of sound. *Shanghai Express* (32),

Bordertown (35), *My Man Godfrey* (36), *The Ghost Goes West* (GB) (36), *Topper* (37), *The Adventures of Robin Hood* (as Friar Tuck) (38), *The Mark of Zorro* (40), *He Stayed for Breakfast* (40), *Unfinished Business* (41), *Tales of Manhattan* (42), *Heaven Can Wait* (43), *Step Lively* (44), *The Cheaters* (45), *Suspense* (47), *Silver River* (48), many others.

PALLOS, STEPHEN (1902–   ). Hungarian producer who worked with Korda in England from 1942. Later, as independent: *Call of the Blood* (46), *The Golden Madonna* (48), *Jet Storm* (59), *Foxhole in Cairo* (60), *A Jolly Bad Fellow* (64), *Where the Spies Are* (65), others.

PALMER, GREGG (1927–   ) (Palmer Lee). American 'second lead', former disc jockey. *Son of Ali Baba* (51), *Veils of Baghdad* (53), *Magnificent Obsession* (54), *The Creature Walks Among Us* (56), *Forty Pounds of Trouble* (62), etc.

PALMER, LILLI (1914–   ) (Lilli Peiser). Austrian leading actress, on stage from childhood, in films from teenage. *Crime Unlimited* (GB) (34), *Good Morning, Boys* (GB) (36), *Secret Agent* (GB) (36), *A Girl Must Live* (GB) (38), *The Door with Seven Locks* (GB) (40), *Thunder Rock* (GB) (42), *The Gentle Sex* (GB) (43), *English Without Tears* (GB) (44), *The Rake's Progress* (GB) (45), *Beware of Pity* (GB) (46), *Cloak and Dagger* (US) (46), *My Girl Tisa* (US) (47), *Body and Soul* (US) (48), *No Minor Vices* (US) (48), *The Long Dark Hall* (GB) (51), *The Fourposter* (US) (52), *Is Anna Anderson Anastasia* (Ger.) (56), *La Vie à Deux* (Fr.) (58), *But Not For Me* (US) (58), *Conspiracy of Hearts* (GB) (60), *Rendezvous at Midnight* (Fr.) (60), *The Pleasure of His Company* (US) (61), *The Counterfeit Traitor* (US) (62), *Adorable Julia* (Ger.) (63), *The Flight of the White Stallions* (US) (64), *Operation Crossbow* (GB) (65), *Moll Flanders* (GB) (65), *Sebastian* (GB) (67), *Oedipus the King* (67), *Nobody Runs Forever* (GB) (68), *The Dance of Death* (Sw.) (68), *De Sade* (69), others.

PALMER, MARIA (1924–   ). Austrian leading lady, sister of Lilli Palmer. Wide stage experience at home, TV and films in America. *Mission to Moscow* (42), *Lady on a Train* (44), *Rendezvous 24* (46), *Slightly Dishonourable* (51), *Three for Jamie Dawn* (56), others.

PALMER, PETER (1931–   ). American actor-singer who repeated his stage role as *Lil Abner* (59). TV series: *Custer* (67).

PALUZZI, LUCIANA (1939–   ). Italian leading lady in international films. *Three Coins in the Fountain* (54), *Sea Fury* (58), *Thunderball* (65), *The Venetian Affair* (66), *Chuka* (67), *99 Women* (69), etc. TV series: *Five Fingers* (59).

pan. A shot in which the camera rotates horizontally. Also used as a verb.

Pan, Hermes

PAN, HERMES (* –). American dance director: *Top Hat* (35), *Swing Time* (36), *Damsel in Distress* (AA) (37), *Let's Dance* (50), *Lovely to Look At* (52), *Silk Stockings* (57), *Can Can* (59), *My Fair Lady* (64), many others.

PANAMA, NORMAN (1914–). Writer-producer-director who has long worked in collaboration with Melvin Frank, qv for note on films. Now working solo: *Not with My Wife You Don't* (w, p, d) (66), *How to Commit Marriage* (directed only) (69), *The Maltese Bippy* (w, d) (69).

PANGBORN, FRANKLIN (1894–1958). American character comedian with long stage experience; in scores of films from the 20s, typically as flustered hotel clerk or organizer. *My Friend from India* (27), *My Man* (30), *International House* (33), *My Man Godfrey* (36), *Stage Door* (37), *Christmas in July* (41), *The Bank Dick* (41), *The Palm Beach Story* (42), *The Carter Case* (42), *Now Voyager* (42), *Hail the Conquering Hero* (43), *Mad Wednesday* (47), *Romance on the High Seas* (48), *The Story of Mankind* (57), etc.

PAPAS, IRENE (1926–). Greek stage actress who has made films at home and abroad. *Necripolitia* (debut) (51), *Theodora Slave Empress* (54), *Attila the Hun* (54), *Tribute to a Bad Man* (US) (55), *The Power and the Prize* (US) (56), *The Guns of Navarone* (61), *Electra* (62), *Zorba the Greek* (64), *Beyond the Mountains* (66), *The Brotherhood* (68), etc.

Paramount Pictures Corporation was basically the creation of Adolph Zukor (qv), a nickelodeon showman who in 1912 founded Famous Players, with the intention of presenting photographed versions of stage successes. In 1914 W. W. Hodkinson's Paramount Pictures took over distribution of Famous Players and Lasky product; and in the complex mergers which resulted, Zukor came out top man. Through the years his studio more than any other gave a family atmosphere, seldom producing films of depth but providing agreeable light entertainment with stars like Valentino, Maurice Chevalier, the Marx Brothers, Mary Pickford, Claudette Colbert, Bob Hope, Bing Crosby, Dorothy Lamour, Alan Ladd, and directors like Lubitsch, De Mille and Wilder. Notable films include *The Sheik, The Covered Wagon, The Ten Commandments* (both versions), *Trouble in Paradise, The Crusades, Union Pacific*, the Road films, *Going My Way, The Greatest Show On Earth*, etc. In recent years, since Zukor's virtual retirement, the company has had many difficulties, but now seems assured of continuity of product through associations with Hal Wallis (*Gunfight at the OK Corral, Becket*, etc.); Joseph E. Levine, who has contributed *The Carpetbaggers, Harlow, Where Love Has Gone*; and a takeover by Gulf and Western Industries which has spurred the commercial instinct.

LES PARAPLUIES DE CHERBOURG: see THE UMBRELLAS OF CHERBOURG.

LES PARENTS TERRIBLES (France 1948). A straight film version by Jean Cocteau of his own claustrophobic play about a family always on the verge of hysteria who come to an emotional crisis when the son announces his intention to marry. With Yvonne de Bray, Jean Marais, Gabrielle Dorziat. Disastrously remade in English by Charles Frank as *Intimate Relations* (53), with Marian Spencer, Russell Enoch and Ruth Dunning.

Paris has usually figured in films as the centre of sophistication, romance and luxury: thus *Ninotchka, I Met Him in Paris, The Last Time I Saw Paris, Innocents in Paris, April in Paris, How to Steal a Million, To Paris With Love, Paris When it Sizzles, A Certain Smile, Funny Face, Paris Holiday, Can Can, Parisienne, Paris Palace Hotel, Two for the Road* and innumerable others. The bohemian aspect is another favourite, as depicted in *An American in Paris, Latin Quarter, Paris Blues, What's New Pussycat, Svengali, French Can Can, Moulin Rouge, What a Way to Go, The Moon and Sixpence*, etc. The tourists' Paris has provided a splendid backcloth for films as diverse as *The Great Race, The Man on the Eiffel Tower, Charade, Those Magnificent Men in their Flying Machines, Zazie dans le Metro, Pig Across Paris, The Red Balloon, Father Brown, Charade, Take Her She's Mine, Dear Brigitte, Bon Voyage*, and *Paris Nous Appartient*. French film-makers seem particularly fond of showing the city's seamy side in thrillers about vice, murder and prostitution: *Quai de Grenelle, Quai des Orfevres, Les Compagnes de la Nuit, Le Long des Trottoirs, Rififi*, etc. Rene Clair has always had his own slightly fantastic view of Paris, from *Paris Qui Dort* through *Sous les Toits de Paris, A Nous la Liberté, Le Million, Le Quatorze Juillet*, and *Porte des Lilas*. Historical Paris has been re-created for *The Hunchback of Notre Dame, The Scarlet Pimpernel, The Three Musketeers, Camille, A Tale of Two Cities, Marie Antoinette, So Long at the Fair* and *Les Enfants du Paradis*; while Paris under fire in World War II was depicted in *Is Paris Burning?*

PARIS, JERRY (c. 1926–   ). American supporting actor: *The Caine Mutiny* (54), *Marty* (55), *Unchained* (55), many others; also played the neighbour in *The Dick Van Dyke Show* (61–66). Turned director: *Never a Dull Moment* (68), *Don't Raise the Bridge Lower the River* (68).

PARIS QUI DORT (France 1924). Also known as *The Crazy Ray*, this first film to be written and directed by René Clair is an amusing trifle mostly shot on the Eiffel Tower, about a mad professor whose new invention reduces Paris to silence and sleep.

PARKER, CECIL (1897–   ) (Cecil Schwabe). British character actor with upper-class personality which can be amiable or chill. On stage from 1922. *The Silver Spoon* (film debut) (33), *A Cuckoo in the Nest* (33), *Storm in a Teacup* (37), *Dark Journey* (37), *The Lady*

Vanishes (38), *The Citadel* (38), *Caesar and Cleopatra* (45), *Hungry Hill* (46), *Captain Boycott* (47), *The First Gentleman* (as the Prince Regent) (47), *Quartet* (48), *Dear Mr Prohack* (49), *The Chiltern Hundreds* (49), *Tony Draws a Horse* (51), *The Man in the White Suit* (52), *His Excellency* (52), *I Believe in You* (52), *Isn't Life Wonderful* (54), *Father Brown* (54), *The Constant Husband* (55), *The Ladykillers* (55), *The Court Jester* (US) (55), *It's Great To Be Young* (56), *The Admirable Crichton* (57), *Indiscreet* (58), *I Was Monty's Double* (58), *Happy Is the Bride* (58), *A Tale of Two Cities* (58), *The Navy Lark* (59), *A French Mistress* (60), *On the Fiddle* (US) (61), *Petticoat Pirates* (62), *Heavens Above* (63), *The Comedy Man* (64), *Guns at Batasi* (64), *Moll Flanders* (65), *A Study in Terror* (65), *Circus of Fear* (67), *Oh What a Lovely War* (69), others.

PARKER, CECILIA (1905–). Canadian leading lady who played many Hollywood roles but is best remembered as Andy's sister in the *Hardy Family* series (37–44). Also: *Young As You Feel* (31), *The Painted Veil* (34), *Naughty Marietta* (35), *A Family Affair* (first of the Hardy films) (37), *Seven Sweethearts* (42). Came out of retirement for *Andy Hardy Comes Home* (58).

PARKER, CLIFTON (1905–). British composer. *Yellow Canary* (43), *Johnny Frenchman* (46), *Blanche Fury* (47), *Treasure Island* (50), *The Gift Horse* (52), *Hell Below Zero* (54), *Night of the Demon* (57), *Sea of Sand* (59), *Sink the Bismarck* (60), *Taste of Fear* (62), *The Informers* (64), etc.

†PARKER, ELEANOR (1922–). American leading lady with brief stage experience before a Hollywood contract; her career followed a typical pattern, with increasingly good leading roles followed by a decline, with a later comeback in character roles. *They Died with Their Boots On* (debut as extra) (41), *Busses Roar* (42), *Mysterious Doctor* (43), *Mission to Moscow* (43), *The Very Thought of You* (44), *Crime by Night* (44), *The Last Ride* (44), *Pride of the Marines* (45), *Of Human Bondage* (as Mildred) (46), *Never Say Goodbye* (46), *Escape Me Never* (47), *The Voice of the Turtle* (47), *The Woman in White* (48), *Chain Lightning* (49), *Three Secrets* (50), *Caged* (50), *Valentino* (51), *A Millionaire for Christy* (51), *Detective Story* (51), *Scaramouche* (52), *Above and Beyond* (52), *Escape from Fort Bravo* (53), *The Naked Jungle* (54), *Valley of the Kings* (54), *Many Rivers to Cross* (54), *Interrupted Melody* (55), *The Man with the Golden Arm* (56), *The King and Four Queens* (56), *Lizzie* (57), *The Seventh Sin* (57), *A Hole in the Head* (59), *Home from the Hill* (60), *Return to Peyton Place* (61), *Madison Avenue* (62), *The Sound of Music* (65), *The Oscar* (66), *An American Dream* (66), *Warning Shot* (66), *Eye of the Cat* (69). TV series: *Bracken's World* (69).

PARKER, FESS (1926–). American leading man with some stage experience. Film debut *Untamed Frontier* (52); several subsequent appearances before being signed up by Walt Disney. *Davy Crockett* (55) (and two sequels), *The Great Locomotive Chase* (56), *Westward Ho the Wagons* (56), *Old Yeller* (57), *The Hangman* (59), *Hell Is for Heroes* (62), *Smoky* (66), etc. TV series: *Mr Smith Goes to Washington* (62).

PARKER, JEAN (1915–) (Mae Green). Once-demure American leading lady, popular in the 30s; latterly playing hard-boiled roles. *Rasputin and the Empress* (32), *Little Women* (33), *Sequoia* (34), *The Ghost Goes West* (GB) (36), *Princess O'Hara* (37), *The Flying Deuces* (39), *Beyond Tomorrow* (40), *No Hands on the Clock* (42), *One Body Too Many* (42), *Minesweeper* (43), *Bluebeard* (44), *Detective Kitty O'Day* (44), *Lady in the Death House* (44), *The Gunfighter* (50), *Those Redheads from Seattle* (53), *Black Tuesday* (54), *A Lawless Street* (55), *Apache Uprising* (65), others.

PARKER, SUZY (1932–) (Cecelia Parker). Statuesque American leading lady, former model. *Kiss Them for Me* (debut) (57), *Ten North Frederick* (58), *The Best of Everything* (59), *Circle of Deception* (61), *The Interns* (62), *Chamber of Horrors* (66), etc. Also on TV.

PARKER, WILLARD (1912–) (Worster van Eps). Tall American 'second lead', in films from 1938 after stage experience. *A Slight Case of Murder* (debut) (38), *The Fighting Guardsman* (43), *You Gotta Stay Happy* (48), *Sangaree* (53), *The Great Jesse James Raid* (53), *The Earth Dies Screaming* (64), etc. TV series: *Tales of the Texas Rangers* (55–57).

PARKINS, BARBARA (1946–). American leading lady, groomed after success in TV series *Peyton Place* (63–67). *Valley of the Dolls* (67), *The Kremlin Letter* (69).

PARKS, LARRY (1914–). American leading man with varied experience before being signed for Hollywood 'B' pictures: *Mystery Ship* (debut) (41), *Blondie Goes to College* (42), *The Boogie Man Will Get You* (42), *Destroyer* (43), *Counter Attack* (45), etc.; then sensational success in *The Jolson Story* (46). Later: *Down to Earth* (47), *The Swordsman* (47), *The Gallant Blade* (48), *Jolson Sings Again* (49), *Jealousy* (50), *The Light Fantastic* (51), *Tiger by the Tail* (GB) (55), *Freud* (63). Career marred by McCarthy blacklisting. Married to Betty Garrett.

PARKS, MICHAEL (1938–). Brooding American leading man. *Fargo (Wild Seed)* (64), *Bus Riley's Back in Town* (65), *The Bible* (as Adam) (66), *The Idol* (GB) (66), *The Happening* (67), etc. TV series: *Bronson* (69).

PARKYAKARKUS (1904–1958) (Harry Einstein). American radio comedian formerly known as Harry Parke. Film appearances include *Strike Me Pink* (36), *Night Spot* (38), *Glamour Boy* (40), *Earl Carroll's Vanities* (45).

PARKYN, LESLIE (* –). British executive producer, associated with Sergei Nolbandov 1951–57, subsequently with Julian Wintle. *The Kidnappers* (53), *Tiger Bay* (59), *The Waltz of the Toreadors* (62), *Father Came Too* (64), many others. TV series: *The Human Jungle*.

PARLO, DITA (1907–) (Greta Kornwald). German actress active in 30s, later as character player: *L'Atalante* (33), *Mademoiselle Docteur* (37), *La Grande Illusion* (37), *Justice Est Faite* (50), *Quand le Soleil Montera* (56), etc.

PARNELL, EMORY (c. 1900–). American general purpose character actor: can be villain, prison warden, weakling or kindly father. *King of Alcatraz* (39), *I Married a Witch* (42), *Mama Loves Papa* (46), *Words and Music* (48), *Call Me Madam* (53), *Man of the West* (58), many others.

PARRISH, HELEN (1922–1959). American leading lady, former baby model and child actress. *The Big Trail* (31), *A Dog of Flanders* (34), *Mad about Music* (38), *You'll Find Out* (40), *They All Kissed the Bride* (42), *The Mystery of the Thirteenth Guest* (44), *The Wolf Hunters* (50), etc.

PARRISH, ROBERT (1916–). American producer-director, former actor and editor. *Cry Danger* (d) (51), *Assignment Paris* (d) (52), *The San Francisco Story* (d) (52), *Rough Shoot* (d) (GB) (52), *The Purple Plain* (p, d) (GB) (54), *Lucy Gallant* (d) (54), *Fire Down Below* (d) (GB) (57), *Saddle the Wind* (d) (58), *The Wonderful Country* (d) (59), *In the French Style* (p, d) (GB) (63), *Up from the Beach* (d) (65), *The Bobo* (d) (67), *Doppelganger* (d) (69), etc.

PARROTT, JAMES (1892–1939). American director, mainly of two-reelers featuring Laurel and Hardy (*Blotto*, *The Music Box*, *County Hospital*, etc.), Charley Chase and Max Davidson. Features include *Jailbirds* (31), *Sing, Sister, Sing* (35).

PARRY, GORDON (1908–). British director of mainly secondary films: former actor, production manager, etc. *Bond Street* (48), *Third Time Lucky* (48), *Now Barabbas* (49), *Midnight Episode* (50), *Innocents in Paris* (52), *Women of Twilight* (52), *A Yank in Ermine* (55), *Sailor Beware* (56), *Tread Softly Stranger* (58), *The Navy Lark* (60), etc.

PARRY, NATASHA (1930–). British leading lady, married to Peter Brook. Appears occasionally on stage and screen. *Dance Hall* (49), *The Dark Man* (50), *Crow Hollow* (52), *Knave of Hearts* (53), *Windom's Way* (57), *The Rough and the Smooth* (59), *Midnight Lace* (60), *The Fourth Square* (62), *Romeo and Juliet* (68), etc.

PARSONS, ESTELLE (1927–   ). American character actress with stage background. *Bonnie and Clyde* (AA) (67), *Rachel Rachel* (68), *Don't Drink the Water* (69).

PARSONS, LOUELLA (1890–   ) (L. Oettinger). Hollywood columnist whose gossip rivalled in readership that of Hedda Hopper. In occasional films as herself, e.g. *Hollywood Hotel* (37), *Starlift* (51). Published autobiographical books: *The Gay Illiterate* (44), *Tell It To Louella* (62).

UNE PARTIE DE CAMPAGNE (France 1936). A rare instance of a film which is unfinished and all the better for it. Based on a Maupassant story, it describes a romantic idyll in the countryside; the spot is revisited fourteen years later by the protagonists, who are of course unable to recapture their original feeling. The film's first and last sequences were filmed by Renoir before production was halted for various reasons. It proved impossible to get the actors together again to film the middle sequence showing how the lives of the characters diverge, and the incomplete film was issued in 1946 to general acclaim. The cast included Sylvia Bataille, Georges Saint-Saens and Jeanne Marken.

parties in movies have often been wild, as for instance in *The Wild Party*, also *The Party's Over*, *I'll Never Forget Whatshisname*, *Breakfast at Tiffany's*, *I Love You Alice B. Toklas*, *The Impossible Years*, *Skidoo*, *The Party Crashers*, and *The Party* itself, which started out sedately but finished with an elephant in the swimming pool. Some of the more amusing film parties however were better behaved, as in *The Apartment*, *Only Two Can Play*, *All About Eve* and *Citizen Kane*.

PASCAL, GABRIEL (1894–1954). Hungarian producer-director who came to Britain in the thirties, won the esteem of Bernard Shaw, and was entrusted with the filming of several of his plays. *Pygmalion* (p) (38), *Major Barbara* (p, d) (40), *Caesar and Cleopatra* (p, d; a notoriously extravagant production) (45), *Androcles and the Lion* (p) (US) (53).

PASCO, RICHARD (1926–   ). British character actor, mainly on stage and TV. *Room at the Top* (59), *Yesterday's Enemy* (60), *The Gorgon* (64), etc.

PASOLINI, PIER PAOLO (1922–   ). Italian director: *Accattone* (61,) *Mamma Roma* (62), *The Gospel According to St Matthew* (64), *Oedipus Rex* (67), *Theorem* (68), *Medea* (70), etc.

THE PASSING OF THE THIRD FLOOR BACK. Jerome K. Jerome's popular novel and play, about a Christ-like stranger who has a benign influence on the down-at-heel inhabitants of a boarding house, was filmed in 1918 with Johnston Forbes-Robertson and in 1935 with Conrad Veidt.

LA PASSION DE JEANNE D'ARC (France 1928). A notable silent film directed by Carl Dreyer and photographed by Rudolph Mate. It tells the familiar story as a series of Rembrandtesque tableaux, with stark white décor by Hermann Warm. Falconetti gives a remarkable performance in this her only film.

PASSPORT TO PIMLICO (GB 1948). The first of the Ealing comedies, whose special quality was to find humour and wit in the lives of ordinary people who are not music-hall caricatures. This one concerns the discovery that part of London belongs to France, and is acted by a notable gallery of character players. Directed by Henry Cornelius from a script by T. E. B. Clarke.

PASTERNAK, JOE (1901–   ). Hungarian producer, in Hollywood from the mid-20s, who had special success with light musical films. *Three Smart Girls* (36) (and most of the later Deanna Durbin films), *Destry Rides Again* (39), *Two Girls and a Sailor* (44), *Anchors Aweigh* (45), *In the Good Old Summertime* (48), *The Great Caruso* (51), *The Opposite Sex* (56), *Jumbo* (62), *Girl Happy* (65), *Made in Paris* (65), *Penelope* (66), many others. Published autobiography 1956: *Easy the Hard Way.*

PATCH, WALLY (1888–   ) (Walter Vinicombe). Burly British Cockney character actor, in films since 1920 after varied show business experience. *Shadows* (31), *The Good Companions* (32), *Get Off My Foot* (35), *Not So Dusty* (36), *Bank Holiday* (38), *Quiet Wedding* (40), *Gasbags* (40), *The Common Touch* (41), *Old Mother Riley at Home* (45), *The Ghosts of Berkeley Square* (47), *The Guinea Pig* (49), *Will Any Gentleman?* (53), *Private's Progress* (55), *I'm All Right, Jack* (59), *Sparrows Can't Sing* (63), scores of others.

PATE, MICHAEL (1920–   ). Australian actor in Hollywood from c. 1950, usually in villainous or Red Indian roles. *The Strange Door* (51), *Julius Caesar* (53), *Hondo* (54), *The Court Jester* (56), *Congo Crossing* (57), *Major Dundee* (65), many others. Also writer: *Escape from Fort Bravo* (53), etc.

PATERSON, NEIL (1916–   ). British screenwriter (and novelist). Films include *The Kidnappers* (53), *High Tide at Noon* (57), *Room at the Top* (AA) (59), *The Spiral Road* (62), *Mister Moses* (65).

PATHE, CHARLES (1863–1957). Pioneer French executive and producer, founder of Pathé Frères and later Pathé Gazette. Also credited with making the first 'long' film: *Les Misérables.* (Made in 1909, it ran four whole reels.)

PATHER PANCHALI (India 1954). The first of a trilogy written and directed by Satyajit Ray (the other titles are *The Unvanquished* [56] and *The World of Apu* [59]) showing the hero's development from childhood to manhood against a background of the poverty of modern India. The three films provide the best documentation available on a country whose films have normally been too traditional to interest Western audiences.

PATHS OF GLORY (US 1957). A harsh attack on the futility of war in general and in particular the cynical manœuvrings of World War I. Full of brilliant dialogue and action sequences. Directed by Stanley Kubrick from a script by Calder Willingham and Jim Thompson and a novel by Humphrey Cobb; photographed by George Krause; with Kirk Douglas, Adolphe Menjou and George Macready.

PATRICK, GAIL (1915–) (Margaret Fitzpatrick). American leading lady in Hollywood from early 30s, usually in routine smart woman roles. *The Phantom Broadcast* (32), *Cradle Song* (33), *No More Ladies* (35), *Artists and Models* (37), *Reno* (40), *Quiet, Please, Murder* (43), *Women in Bondage* (44), *Twice Blessed* (45), *The Plainsman and the Lady* (46), *Calendar Girl* (47), many others. Retired from acting and became a TV producer, notably of the successful *Perry Mason* series.

PATRICK, LEE (c. 1911–). American character actress with stage experience, in Hollywood from 1937, usually as hard-bitten blondes. *Strange Cargo* (debut) (40), *The Maltese Falcon* (41), *Now Voyager* (42), *Mother Wore Tights* (47), *Caged* (50), *There's No Business Like Show Business* (54), *Summer and Smoke* (61), *The New Interns* (64), many others. TV series: *Topper* (53–55), *Mr Adams and Eve* (56–57).

PATRICK, NIGEL (1913–). British leading man, on stage from 1932. *Mrs Pym of Scotland Yard* (film debut) (39), *Spring in Park Lane* (47), *Noose* (47), *The Perfect Woman* (49), *Trio* (50), *The Browning Version* (51), *The Sound Barrier* (52), *The Pickwick Papers* (53), *The Sea Shall Not Have Them* (55), *All for Mary* (56), *Raintree County* (US) (57), *How to Murder a Rich Uncle* (also directed) (57), *Sapphire* (59), *The League of Gentlemen* (60), *The Trials of Oscar Wilde* (60), *Johnny Nobody* (also directed) (61), *The Informers* (63), *The Executioner* (69), etc. TV series: *Zero One* (62).

PATTERSON, ELIZABETH (1876–1966). American character actress with stage experience; in Hollywood from the late 20s, usually as kindly or shrewish elderly ladies. *Daddy Longlegs* (30), *A Bill of Divorcement* (32), *Miss Pinkerton* (32), *Dinner at Eight* (33), *So Red the Rose* (36), *Sing You Sinners* (38), *The Cat and the Canary* (39), *Tobacco Road* (41),

759

Hail the Conquering Hero (43), *Lady on a Train* (45), *Intruder in the Dust* (48), *Little Women* (49), *Bright Leaf* (50), *Pal Joey* (57), *The Oregon Trail* (59), many others.

PATTERSON, LEE (1929–). Canadian leading man in Britain from c. 1950. *Thirty-six Hours* (51), *Above Us the Waves* (55), *Soho Incident* (56), *Cat and Mouse* (58), *Jack the Ripper* (60), etc. Also stage and TV, especially in series *Surfside Six* (60–61).

PAUL, ROBERT (1870–1943). Pioneer British movie camera inventor (1895). The following year he invented a projector, which he called a theatrograph. Later turned showman.

PAVAN, MARISA (1932–) (Marisa Pierangeli). Italian leading lady, sister of Pier Angeli. In Hollywood from 1950. *What Price Glory* (debut) (52), *The Rose Tattoo* (55), *The Man in the Grey Flannel Suit* (56), *Solomon and Sheba* (59), *John Paul Jones* (59), etc.

PAVLOW, MURIEL (1921–). British leading lady, on stage and screen from 1936; her youthful appearance enabled her to continue in juvenile roles for many years. *A Romance in Flanders* (debut) (36), *Quiet Wedding* (40), *Night Boat to Dublin* (45), *The Shop at Sly Corner* (47), *Malta Story* (53), *Doctor in the House* (54), *Reach for the Sky* (56), *Tiger in the Smoke* (57), *Rooney* (58), *Murder She Said* (62), etc. Married to Derek Farr.

THE PAWNBROKER (US 1964). A somewhat overheated but impressive modern morality with Rod Steiger (BFA) as a Jewish pawnbroker in New York, drained of humanity by his experiences in a Nazi concentration camp. Striking scenes and moments somehow fail to add up to more than a well-meaning melodrama. Photographed by Boris Kaufman; directed by Sidney Lumet from a script by David Friedkin and Morton Fine.

PAWLE, LENNOX (1872–1936). British character actor, mainly on stage. *The Admirable Crichton* (GB) (18), *The Great Adventure* (GB) (21), *Married in Hollywood* (US) (29), *The Sin of Madeleine Claudet* (US) (32), *David Copperfield* (as Mr Dick) (34), *Sylvia Scarlett* (US) (35), etc.

PAXINOU, KATINA (1900–). Greek actress with international experience; played in some Hollywood films. *For Whom the Bell Tolls* (AA) (42), *Confidential Agent* (44), *Uncle Silas* (GB) (47), *Mourning Becomes Electra* (47), *Confidential Report* (55), *Rocco and his Brothers* (60), *Zita* (68), etc.

PAXTON, JOHN (1911–). American screenwriter. *Farewell My Lovely* (43), *So Well Remembered* (47), *Crossfire* (47), *Fourteen Hours* (51), *The Wild One* (54), *On the Beach* (59), others.

PAYNE, JOHN (1912–   ). American leading man, formerly on radio. *Dodsworth* (debut) (36), *Kid Nightingale* (39), *Tin Pan Alley* (40), *Sun Valley Serenade* (42), *Hello, Frisco, Hello* (43), *The Dolly Sisters* (45), *Sentimental Journey* (46), *The Razor's Edge* (46), *Miracle on 34th Street* (*The Big Heart*) (47), *Captain China* (49), *Caribbean Gold* (52), *Hell's Island* (55), *The Boss* (56), *Hidden Fear* (57), many others. TV series: *The Restless Gun* (58–59). Recently in TV guest appearances.

PAYNE, LAURENCE (1919–   ). British leading man, on stage and (occasionally) screen from 1945. *Train of Events* (49), *Ill Met By Moonlight* (57), *The Tell Tale Heart* (61), *The Court Martial of Major Keller* (61), etc.

PAYTON, BARBARA (1927–1967). American leading lady. *Once More My Darling* (49), *Dallas* (50), *Kiss Tomorrow Goodbye* (51), *Drums in the Deep South* (51), *Bride of the Gorilla* (52), *The Great Jesse James Raid* (53), *Four-Sided Triangle* (GB) (54), *The Flanagan Boy* (GB) (55), etc.

PEACH, MARY (1934–   ). British leading lady, in films from 1957. Main roles: *Follow That Horse* (59), *Room at the Top* (59), *No Love for Johnnie* (61), *A Pair of Briefs* (62), *A Gathering of Eagles* (US) (63), *Ballad in Blue* (65), *The Projected Man* (66).

PEARCE, ALICE (1913–1966). American character comedienne, usually in adenoidal roles. *On the Town* (49), *The Opposite Sex* (56), *The Disorderly Orderly* (64), *Dear Brigitte* (65), *The Glass Bottom Boat* (66), etc. TV series: *Bewitched*.

PEARSON, BEATRICE (1920–   ). American leading lady with a brief career: *Force of Evil* (49), *Lost Boundaries* (49).

PEARSON, GEORGE (1875–   ). British writer-producer-director who came to films at the age of 37 after being a schoolmaster. Has hundreds of films to his credit. *The Fool* (12), *A Study in Scarlet* (14), *Ultus the Man from the Dead* (15), *The Better Ole* (18), *The Old Curiosity Shop* (20), *Squibs* (21), *Squibs Wins the Calcutta Sweep* (22), *Satan's Sister* (25), *Huntingtower* (27), *The Silver King* (38), *Journey's End* (produced) (30), *The Good Companions* (produced) (32), *Four Marked Men* (34), *The Pointing Finger* (38), etc.; later with Colonial Film Unit. Published autobiography 1957: *Flashback*.

PEARSON, LLOYD (1897–1966). Portly British character actor, usually of bluff Yorkshire types. *The Challenge* (38), *Tilly of Bloomsbury* (40), *Kipps* (41), *When We Are Married* (42), *Schweik's New Adventures* (leading role) (43), *My Learned Friend* (44), *Mr Perrin and Mr Traill* (49), *Hindle Wakes* (52), *The Good Companions* (57), *The Angry Silence* (59), etc.

Peck, Gregory

†PECK, GREGORY (1916–   ). Durable and likeable American leading actor, with stage experience before sudden success in Hollywood. *Days of Glory* (43), *The Keys of the Kingdom* (44), *The Valley of Decision* (44), *Spellbound* (45), *The Yearling* (46), *Duel in the Sun* (46), *The Macomber Affair* (47), *Gentleman's Agreement* (47), *The Paradine Case* (47), *Yellow Sky* (48), *The Great Sinner* (49), *Twelve O'clock High* (49), *The Gunfighter* (50), *David and Bathsheba* (51), *Captain Horatio Hornblower* (GB) (51), *Only the Valiant* (52), *The World in His Arms* (52), *The Snows of Kilimanjaro* (52), *Roman Holiday* (53), *Night People* (54), *The Million Pound Note* (GB) (54), *The Purple Plain* (GB) (55), *The Man in the Grey Flannel Suit* (56), *Moby Dick* (56), *Designing Woman* (57), *The Bravados* (58), *The Big Country* (58), *Pork Chop Hill* (59), *Beloved Infidel* (as Scott Fitzgerald) (59), *On the Beach* (59), *The Guns of Navarone* (GB) (61), *Cape Fear* (62), *How the West Was Won* (62), *To Kill a Mockingbird* (AA) (63), *Captain Newman* (63), *Behold a Pale Horse* (64), *Mirage* (65), *Arabesque* (66), *Mackenna's Gold* (68), *The Stalking Moon* (68), *The Most Dangerous Man in the World* (69), *Marooned* (69), *An Exile* (70).

†PECKINPAH, SAM (1926–   ). American director of tough Westerns: *Guns in the Afternoon* (*Ride the High Country*) (61), *The Deadly Companions* (62), *Major Dundee* (65), *The Wild Bunch* (69), *The Ballad of Cable Hogue* (69), *The Chill* (project) (70).

PEG O' MY HEART. This sentimental play by J. Hartley Manners, about an Irish servant girl who stays with her English relatives, was filmed in 1922 by King Vidor with Laurette Taylor, and in 1932 by Robert Z. Leonard, with Marion Davies.

PELISSIER, ANTHONY (1912–   ). British director with stage experience; son of Fay Compton. *The History of Mr Polly* (49), *The Rocking Horse Winner* (50), *Night Without Stars* (50), *Meet Me Tonight* (52), *Meet Mr Lucifer* (54), etc. Wrote script of *Tiger in the Smoke* (56); recently inactive.

PENDLETON, NAT (1895–1967). American character actor, formerly professional wrestler, usually seen in 'dumb ox' roles. In films from c. 1930. *You Said a Mouthful* (32), *The Sign of the Cross* (32), *Manhattan Melodrama* (34), *The Great Ziegfeld* (36), *The Marx Brothers at the Circus* (39), *Young Dr Kildare* (and series) (39), *On Borrowed Time* (39), *Northwest Passage* (40), *Top Sergeant Mulligan* (42), *Rookies Come Home* (45), *Scared to Death* (47), *Death Valley* (49), many others.

†PENN, ARTHUR (1922–   ). American director, from TV. *The Left Handed Gun* (58), *The Miracle Worker* (62), *Mickey One* (65,) *The Chase* (66), *Bonnie and Clyde* (67), *Alice's Restaurant* (69), etc.

PENNER, JOE (1904–1941) (J. Pinter). Hungarian-American radio comedian who made a few films: *College Rhythm* (33), *Go Chase Yourself* (38), *Glamour Boy* (40), *The Boys from Syracuse* (40), etc.

PENNINGTON-RICHARDS, C. M. (c. 1910–   ). British director, former photographer. *The Oracle* (54), *Inn for Trouble* (60), *Double Bunk* (62), *Ladies Who Do* (63), *A Challenge for Robin Hood* (67), etc. Also produced and directed many TV films.

PENROD. Booth Tarkington's American boy character, in his midwest small town setting, was for many years a favourite Hollywood subject. Marshall Neilan directed Gordon Griffith in a 1922 version. In 1923 William Beaudine directed Ben Alexander in the role in *Penrod and Sam*, which was remade by Beaudine in 1931 with Leon Janney, and again by William McGann in 1937 with Billy Mauch. Mauch and his twin brother Bobby appeared in two sequels: *Penrod's Double Trouble* (38) directed by Lewis Seiler, and *Penrod and His Twin Brother* (38) directed by McGann. Two Doris Day musicals, *On Moonlight Bay* (51) and *By the Light of the Silvery Moon* (53), were also lightly based on the Tarkington stories: Penrod, unaccountably disguised as 'Wesley', was played by Billy Gray.

PEOPLE ON SUNDAY (MENNSCHEN AM SONNTAG) (Germany 1929). A rare combination of talents made this attractive comedy-drama showing how Berliners spent their week-ends in pre-Hitler days. Written by Robert Siodmak and Billy Wilder, it was directed by Siodmak with assistance from Fred Zinnemann and Edgar G. Ulmer, photographed by Eugene Schuftan.

PEPE LE MOKO: see ALGIERS.

PEPPARD, GEORGE (1929–   ). American leading man with widely varied experience including Broadway stage. *End as a Man* (*The Strange One*) (57), *Pork Chop Hill* (59), *Home from the Hill* (59), *Breakfast at Tiffany's* (61), *How the West Was Won* (62), *The Victors* (63), *The Carpetbaggers* (64), *Operation Crossbow* (65), *The Third Day* (65), *The Blue Max* (66), *Tobruk* (*The Cliffs at Mersa*) (66), *Rough Night in Jericho* (67), *P.J.* (*New Face in Hell*) (67), *What's So Bad About Feeling Good?* (68), *House of Cards* (68), *Pendulum* (68), *The Executioner* (69), etc.

PERCIVAL, LANCE (1933–   ). British light comedian. *Twice Round the Daffodils* (62), *The VIPs* (63), *Carry On Cruising* (63), *The Yellow Rolls-Royce* (64), *The Big Job* (65), etc. A familiar face on TV.

PERCY, ESME (1887–1957). Distinguished British stage actor, especially of Shavian parts. On stage from 1904; occasional films from 20s. *The Frog* (36), *Pygmalion* (38), *Caesar and Cleopatra* (45), *The Ghosts of Berkeley Square* (46), *Death in the Hand* (48), etc.

PERIER, FRANÇOIS (1919–   ) (François Pilu). Sturdy French actor, in films from mid-30s. *Hotel du Nord* (38), *Un Revenant* (46), *Le*

Silence Est d'Or (48), *Orphée* (49), *The Bed* (53), *Gervaise* (55), *Nights of Cabiria* (56), *Charmants Garçons* (57), *Weekend at Dunkirk* (65), many others.

THE PERILS OF PAULINE. Pearl White's famous 1914 serial was directed by Donald Mackenzie, co-starred Crane Wilbur, and concerned the heroine's evasion of attempts on her life by her dastardly guardian. The 1947 film of the same name was a lightly fictionalized biography of Pearl White, with Betty Hutton in the role; George Marshall directed. The 1967 film was vaguely based on the original serial, with Pamela Austin as the heroine, now involved in goings-on zanier than anything Pearl White dreamed of. Direction was by Herbert Leonard and Joshua Shelley.

PERINAL, GEORGES (1897–1965). French cinematographer, in films from 1913. *Les Nouveaux Messieurs* (28), *Sous Les Toits de Paris* (30), *Le Sang d'un Poète* (30), *Le Million* (31), *A Nous la Liberté* (32), *The Private Life of Henry VIII* (32), *Rembrandt* (36), *The Thief of Bagdad* (AA) (40), *The Life and Death of Colonel Blimp* (43), *Nicholas Nickleby* (47), *An Ideal Husband* (47), *The Fallen Idol* (48), *Lady Chatterley's Lover* (55), *A King in New York* (57), *Saint Joan* (57), *Bonjour Tristesse* (58), *Oscar Wilde* (60), many others.

PERKINS, ANTHONY (1932–   ). American leading man specializing in neurotics. Some TV and stage experience. *The Actress* (debut) (53), *The Friendly Persuasion* (56), *Fear Strikes Out* (57), *Desire under the Elms* (57), *The Matchmaker* (58), *On the Beach* (59), *Psycho* (60), *Goodbye Again* (61), *Phaedra* (62), *The Trial* (63), *Two Are Guilty* (64), *The Fool Killer* (65), *Is Paris Burning?* (66), *La Scandale* (*The Champagne Murders*) (66), *Pretty Poison* (68), *Catch 22* (69), *Hall of Mirrors* (69), etc.

PERKINS, MILLIE (1939–   ). American leading lady who went to Hollywood from dramatic school. *The Diary of Anne Frank* (59), *Wild in the Country* (61), *Wild in the Streets* (68), etc.

PERKINS, OSGOOD (1893–1937). American stage actor, father of Anthony Perkins. Films include *Scarface* (32), *Kansas City Princess* (35).

PERLBERG, WILLIAM (1899–1969). American producer, often in conjunction with George Seaton; came from agency business, in Hollywood from mid-30s. *Golden Boy* (39), *The Song of Bernadette* (43), *Forever Amber* (47), *The Country Girl* (54), *Teacher's Pet* (58), *The Counterfeit Traitor* (62), *Thirty-six Hours* (64), many others.

PERREAU, GIGI (1941–   ) (Ghislaine Perreau-Saussine). American child actress of the 40s who seems not quite to have managed the transition to adult stardom. *Madame Curie* (43), *Song of Love* (47),

My Foolish Heart (49), *Has Anybody Seen My Gal* (51), *The Man in the Grey Flannel Suit* (56), *Wild Heritage* (58), *Look in Any Window* (61), others.

PERRINS, LESLIE (1902–1962). British character actor, often seen as a smooth crook. *The Sleeping Cardinal* (31), *The Pointing Finger* (34), *Tudor Rose* (36), *Old Iron* (39), *The Woman's Angle* (43), *A Run for Your Money* (49), *Guilty* (56), many others.

†PERRY, FRANK (1930–   ). American director. *David and Lisa* (63), *Ladybug, Ladybug* (64), *The Swimmer* (68), *Trilogy* (68). Usually writes his own scripts with his wife Eleanor.

PERRY, PAUL P. (1891–1963). Pioneer American cinematographer who experimented with colour. *Rose of the Rancho* (14), *The Cheat* (15), *Hidden Pearls* (17), *The Sea Wolf* (21), *Rosita* (23), *Souls for Sables* (26), many others.

persistence of vision. The medical explanation for our being able to see moving pictures. Twenty-four ordered still pictures are shown to us successively each second, and our sense of sight is slow enough to merge them into one continuous action. The retina of the eye retains each still picture just long enough for it to be replaced by another only slightly different.

PERSOFF, NEHEMIAH (1920–   ). Israeli actor, long in America; trained at Actors Studio. *On the Waterfront* (54), *The Harder They Fall* (56), *The Sea Wall* (*This Angry Age*) (57), *The Badlanders* (58), *Never Steal Anything Small* (58), *Al Capone* (59), *Some Like It Hot* (59), *The Big Show* (61), *The Comancheros* (62), *The Hook* (63), *Fate is the Hunter* (64), *The Greatest Story Ever Told* (65), *Panic in the City* (68), etc. Much on TV.

PERTWEE, JON (1919–   ). British comic actor, brother of Michael Pertwee, son of Roland. *Murder at the Windmill* (48), *Mr Drake's Duck* (51), *Will Any Gentleman* (53), *A Yank in Ermine* (56), *Carry On Cleo* (64), *Carry On Screaming* (66), etc. Also on stage and radio.

PERTWEE, MICHAEL (1916–   ). British playwright who has been involved in many screenplays: *Silent Dust* (48) (from his play), *The Interrupted Journey* (49), *Laughter in Paradise* (51), *Top Secret* (52), *Now and Forever* (54), *The Naked Truth* (58), *In the Doghouse* (62), *The Mouse on the Moon* (62), *Ladies Who Do* (63), *A Funny Thing Happened on the Way to the Forum* (66), *Finders Keepers* (66), *The Magnificent Two* (67), etc.

PETERS, BROCK (c. 1928–   ). American Negro actor. *To Kill a Mockingbird* (62), *Heavens Above* (GB) (63), *The Pawnbroker* (64), *Major Dundee* (65), *P.J.* (*New Face in Hell*) (67), etc.

PETERS, HOUSE (1880–1967). American silent screen leading man. *Leah Kleschna* (12), *The Pride of Jennico* (14), *The Great Divide* (15), *Mignon* (15), *The Storm* (22), *Held to Answer* (23), *Raffles* (25), *Head Winds* (25), many others.

PETERS, JEAN (1926–   ). American leading lady who went straight to Hollywood from college. *Captain from Castile* (debut) (47), *Anne of the Indies* (51), *Viva Zapata* (52), *Niagara* (53), *Three Coins in the Fountain* (54), *Broken Lance* (54), *A Man Called Peter* (55), etc. Retired to marry Howard Hughes.

PETERS, SUSAN (1921–1952) (Suzanne Carnahan). American leading lady of the 40s; badly injured in an accident, she continued her career from a wheelchair. *Santa Fe Trail* (40), *Random Harvest* (42), *Adventure in Brittany* (43), *Song of Russia* (44), *Keep Your Powder Dry* (45), *The Sign of the Ram* (48), etc.

PETIT, PASCALE (1938–   ) (Anne-Marie Petit). French leading lady. *The Witches of Salem* (57), *Les Tricheurs* (58), *Girls for the Summer* (59), *L'Affaire d'Une Nuit* (60), *Demons at Midnight* (62), etc.

†PETRIE, DANIEL (1920–   ). American director with academic background; stage and TV experience. *The Bramble Bush* (59), *A Raisin in the Sun* (61), *The Main Attraction* (62), *Stolen Hours* (63), *The Idol* (66), *The Spy with a Cold Nose* (67).

PETRIE, HAY (1895–1948). British character actor of stage and screen, specializing in eccentrics. *Suspense* (30), *The Private Life of Henry VIII* (32), *Nell Gwyn* (34), *The Old Curiosity Shop* (as Quilp) (34), *The Ghost Goes West* (36), *Twenty-One Days* (38), *The Spy in Black* (39), *Q Planes* (39), *Jamaica Inn* (39), *Crimes at the Dark House* (40), *The Thief of Bagdad* (40), *One of Our Aircraft is Missing* (42), *A Canterbury Tale* (44), *Great Expectations* (46), *The Red Shoes* (48), *The Guinea Pig* (49), etc.

THE PETRIFIED FOREST (US 1936). A simple photographed version o Robert Sherwood's talkative play about an idealist, held captive by a gangster in a remote inn, who finally gives his life to save the other hostages. Remarkable chiefly for the opportunities it gave to three talents: Leslie Howard, Humphrey Bogart and Bette Davis. Directed by Archie Mayo.

PETROV, VLADIMIR (1896–1966). Russian director. *The Overcoat* (26), *Thunderstorm* (34), *Peter the Great* (38), etc.

PETROVA, OLGA (1886–   ) (Muriel Harding). British born leading lady of Hollywood silents in which she played femmes fatales. *The Tigress* (14), *The Soul Market* (16), *The Undying Flame* (17), *Daughter of Destiny* (18), *The Panther Woman* (18), etc.

PETTET, JOANNA (1945–   ). Anglo-American leading lady. *The Group* (65), *Night of the Generals* (66), *Robbery* (67), *Blue* (68).

PETTINGELL, FRANK (1891–1966). British (north-country) character actor who dispensed rough good humour on stage from 1910, films from 1931. *Hobson's Choice* (as Mossop), (31), *Jealousy* (31), *The Good Companions* (32), *Sing As We Go* (34), *The Last Journey* (36), *Fame* (36), *Millions* (36), *Sailing Along* (38), *Gaslight* (39), *Busman's Honeymoon* (40), *The Seventh Survivor* (41), *This England* (41), *Kipps* (41), *Once a Crook* (41), *When We Are Married* (42), *The Young Mr Pitt* (42), *Get Cracking* (44), *Gaiety George* (46), *The Magic Box* (51), *Value for Money* (57), *Becket* (64), many others.

PEVNEY, JOSEPH (1920–   ). American director, former stage actor. *Shakedown* (50), *Undercover Girl* (50), *The Iron Man* (51), *The Strange Door* (51), *Meet Danny Wilson* (51), *Just across the Street* (52), *Because of You* (54), *Desert Legion* (54), *The Female on the Beach* (55), *Three Ring Circus* (55), *Away All Boats* (56), *Congo Crossing* (56), *Tammy* (57), *Man of a Thousand Faces* (57), *Twilight for the Gods* (58), *Cash McCall* (60), *Night of the Grizzly* (66), etc.

PEYTON PLACE (US 1957). The film version of Grace Metalious' novel started a fashion for small-town sex exposés on the screen. A well-made film with particularly good colour photography by William Mellor, it was carefully produced by Jerry Wald, directed by Mark Robson and scripted by John Michael Hayes. A sequel, *Return to Peyton Place*, followed in 1961, and in 1964 came a TV serial of two half-hours a week; it proved so popular that from 1965 it was given three half-hours.

THE PHANTOM OF THE OPERA. The melodramatic tale of the embittered disfigured composer who haunts the sewers beneath the Paris Opera House and takes a pretty young singer as his protégée has been filmed three times. 1. US 1925; directed by Rupert Julian; with Lon Chaney and Mary Philbin. 2. US 1943; directed by Arthur Lubin; with Claude Rains and Susanna Foster. 3. GB 1962; directed by Terence Fisher; with Herbert Lom and Heather Sears. The first version is without doubt the most interesting.

THE PHILADELPHIA STORY (US 1940). This glossy cocktail comedy, not without its serious points, stands out as by far the most adult and successful film of its type. Adapted by Donald Ogden Stewart from the play by Philip Barry, it stars Katharine Hepburn in her stage role as Tracy Lord the idle rich heiress with the wrong kind of standards; Cary Grant as C. K. Dexter Haven, her ex-husband; James Stewart (AA) as Macaulay Connor, her would-be next; and in sterling support, Ruth Hussey, Roland Young, John Halliday, Mary Nash, Virginia Weidler and Henry Daniell. George Cukor directed with his accustomed dexterity. In 1956 the script was

shortened and devitalized to permit the inclusion of some poor
Cole Porter numbers under the title *High Society*. Grace Kelly filled
Hepburn's shoes comfortably but Bing Crosby and Frank Sinatra
were miscast and the whole thing was a fairly complete disaster;
at least for anyone who remembered the original.

PHILBIN, MARY (1903–). American leading lady of the silent
screen. *The Blazing Trail* (21), *Merry Go Round* (23), *Phantom of the
Opera* (26), *The Man Who Laughs* (28), *After the Fog* (30), etc.

PHILIPE, GERARD (1922–1959). France's leading young actor of the
50s, who alternated stage and screen activities. *Le Diable au Corps*
(46), *L'Idiot* (47), *Une Si Jolie Petite Plage* (48), *La Beauté du Diable*
(49), *La Ronde* (50), *Fanfan La Tulipe* (52), *Belles de Nuit* (52), *Les
Orgeuilleux* (53), *Knave of Hearts* (*Monsieur Ripois*) (GB) (53), *Le
Rouge et le Noir* (54), *Les Grandes Manoeuvres* (55), *Till Eulenspiegel*
(also co-directed) (56), *Pot-Bouille* (58), *Les Liaisons Dangereuses* (59),
etc.

PHILIPS, ROBIN (1941–). British juvenile lead. *Decline and Fall*
(68), *David Copperfield* (69).

PHILLIPS, LESLIE (1924–). British light comedian, former child
actor, on stage from 1935, occasional films from 1936. *The Citadel*
(38), *Train of Events* (49), *The Sound Barrier* (52), *Value for Money*
(57), *Carry On Nurse* (59), *Very Important Person* (59), *Carry On
Constable* (60), *Doctor in Love* (60), *Watch Your Stern Go* (60), *Very
Important Person* (61), *Raising the Wind* (61), *In the Doghouse* (62),
Crooks Anonymous (62), *The Fast Lady* (62), *And Father Came Too* (64),
Doctor in Clover (66), *Maroc 7* (also produced) (66), others. TV
series: *Our Man at St Mark's, Foreign Affairs*.

PHILO VANCE: see VAN DINE, S. S.

PHILPOTTS, AMBROSINE (1912–). British character actress, mainly
on stage. *This Man Is Mine* (46), *The Franchise Affair* (51), *The
Captain's Paradise* (53), *Up in the World* (56), *Room at the Top* (59),
Doctor in Love (60), *Life at the Top* (65), etc.

PHIPPS, NICHOLAS (1913–). British light comedian often seen in
cameo roles. On stage from 1932. Has also scripted or co-scripted
many films including *Piccadilly Incident* (36), *Spring in Park Lane* (48),
Doctor in the House (53), *Doctor in Love* (60), *The Wild and the Willing*
(62), many others. Has appeared in most of these.

PIAZZA, BEN (1934–). Canadian actor who went to Hollywood,
but was little heard from. *A Dangerous Age* (Can.) (58), *The Hanging
Tree* (59), etc.

PICCOLI, MICHEL (1925–). Franco-Italian leading man. *French
Can Can* (55), *The Witches of Salem* (56), *Dairy of a Chambermaid* (64),

De L'Amour (65), *La Curee* (66), *The Young Girls of Rochefort* (67), *Un Homme de Trop* (67), *Dillinger is Dead* (68), others.

PICERNI, PAUL (1922–). American leading man, usually in second features. *Saddle Tramp* (debut) (50), *Mara Maru* (52), *House of Wax* (53), *Drive a Crooked Road* (54), *Hell's Island* (55), *Omar Khayyam* (57), *Strangers When We Meet* (60), *The Scalphunters* (68), etc. TV series: *The Untouchables*.

PICHEL, IRVING (1891–1954). American actor-director, in Hollywood from 1930. As actor: *The Right to Love* (30), *The Miracle Man* (31), *Oliver Twist* (as Fagin) (33), *Cleopatra* (34), *Jezebel* (38), *Juarez* (40), *Sante Fe* (51), many others. As director: *The Hounds of Zaroff* (co-d) (32), *She* (co-d) (35), *The Sheik Steps Out* (37), *Hudson's Bay* (40), *The Light of Heart* (42), *The Pied Piper* (42), *The Moon is Down* (43), *And Now Tomorrow* (44), *A Medal for Benny* (45), *Tomorrow is Forever* (45), *O.S.S.* (46), *They Won't Believe Me* (47), *Mr Peabody and the Mermaid* (48), *Destination Moon* (50), *Quicksand* (51), *Martin Luther* (53), etc.

PICKENS, SLIM (1919–) (Louis Bert Lindley). Slow-talking American character actor, in scores of low-budget Westerns from mid-40s, more recently in bigger films: *The Sun Shines Bright* (53), *The Great Locomotive Chase* (56), *One-Eyed Jacks* (59), *Dr Strangelove* (64), *Major Dundee* (65), *Rough Night in Jericho* (67), etc. TV series: *Custer* (67).

PICKFORD, MARY (1893–) (Gladys Smith). Canadian actress who in the heyday of silent films was known as 'the world's sweetheart'; became a co-founder of United Artists Films and one of America's richest women. Acting on stage from five years old; was brought into films by D. W. Griffith. *Her First Biscuits* (09), *The Violin Maker of Cremona* (10), *The Paris Hat* (13), *Madame Butterfly* (15), *Less Than the Dust* (16), *The Little Princess* (17), *Stella Maris* (18), *Pollyanna* (19), *Suds* (20), *Little Lord Fauntleroy* (21), *The Love Light* (21), *Tess of the Storm Country* (22), *Rosita* (23), *Dorothy Vernon of Haddon Hall* (24), *Little Annie Rooney* (25), *My Best Girl* (27), *The Taming of the Shrew* (29), *Secrets* (29), *Coquette* (AA) (29), many others. Retired; widow of Douglas Fairbanks. Published autobiography 1955: *Sunshine and Shadow*.

PICKLES, WILFRED (1904–). British radio personality and latterly character actor; plays Yorkshiremen. *The Gay Dog* (53), *Billy Liar* (63), *The Family Way* (66), etc.

PICNIC (US 1955). Based on the play by William Inge, this over-heated melodrama of small town American sex life—or rather the lack of it—seemed at the time to be starting an American 'new wave'. It had the new sex symbol Kim Novak; the popular William

Holden as the virile young stranger; Rosalind Russell as the repressed schoolmistress; and an insistent theme tune called 'Moonglow' by George Duning. Joshua Logan's direction was generally lethargic, but James Wong Howe's colour photography did a lot to compensate. The success of the movie led to a long spate of imitations: *The Long Hot Summer, Peyton Place, The Bramble Bush, A Summer Place*, etc.

THE PICTURE OF DORIAN GRAY (US 1944). Albert Lewin adapted and directed Oscar Wilde's macabre fantasy about a man who stays young while his portrait shows his debauchery, and a remarkably successful film it was, like an exotic Victorian hothouse, with Hurd Hatfield suitably impassive in the lead and George Sanders uttering epigrams in the background. The director's obvious passion for Egyptian cats and Omar Khayyam, however, was a signpost to the absurdity of his later films. Photographed by Harry Stradling.

PIDGEON, WALTER (1897–   ). Canadian leading man with stage experience before coming to Hollywood in mid-20s. *Mannequin* (debut) (26), *A Most Immoral Lady* (30), *The Kiss Before the Mirror* (33), *Fatal Lady* (36), *Saratoga* (37), *Girl of the Golden West* (38), *Nick Carter, Master Detective* (39), *The House Across the Bay* (40), *Blossoms in the Dust* (41), *Manhunt* (41), *How Green Was My Valley* (41), *Mrs Miniver* (42), *White Cargo* (42), *Madame Curie* (43), *Weekend at the Waldorf* (45), *If Winter Comes* (47), *The Forsyte Saga* (49), *Calling Bulldog Drummond* (51), *The Bad and the Beautiful* (52), *Hit the Deck* (55), *Forbidden Planet* (56), *Big Red* (60), *Advise and Consent* (62), *Warning Shot* (66), *Funny Girl* (as Florenz Ziegfeld) (68), many others.

PIERCE, JACK (1889–1968). American make-up artist who worked at Universal for many years and created the familiar images of Dracula, the Mummy and the Frankenstein monster.

PILBEAM, NOVA (1919–   ). British teenage star of the 30s. *Little Friend* (34), *The Man Who Knew Too Much* (34), *Tudor Rose* (35), *Young and Innocent* (37), *Spring Meeting* (40), *Banana Ridge* (41), *Next of Kin* (42), *This Man is Mine* (46), *Counterblast* (47), *The Three Weird Sisters* (48), etc. Retired.

PINE, WILLIAM H. (1896–   ) and THOMAS, WILLIAM C. (1892–   ). An American production executive and an exhibitor-writer who banded together in the early 40s to make scores of second features for Paramount. *Power Dive, Wildcat, Midnight Manhunt, They Made Me a Killer, Wrecking Crew, Torpedo Boat, I Cover Big Town*, etc. Continued into the 50s with larger-scale adventures: *Sangaree, Jamaica Run, The Far Horizons*, etc., but never managed a top-notcher.

THE PINK PANTHER (US 1963). An amiable star-studded romp about jewel robbers, this rather patchy comedy by Blake Edwards surprisingly triggered off a cartoon series featuring the Pink Panther (who does not appear in the film: the title refers to a jewel) as well as two sequels about the accident-prone detective created by Peter Sellers: *A Shot in the Dark* (64) (with Sellers) and *Inspector Clouseau* (68) (with Alan Arkin).

PINKY (US 1949). A moderately pioneering Hollywood contribution to race relations, this quiet tale of a negress who 'passed for white' but felt bound to tell the truth about herself was somewhat compromised by the casting of white Jeanne Crain in the role. But the script by Philip Dunne and Dudley Nichols was generally intelligent and thoughtful, and both the photography by Joe Macdonald and the direction by Elia Kazan were more than competent.

PINTER, HAROLD (1930–   ). British playwright, usually juggling with obscure plot and clever dialogue. *The Caretaker* (64) is his only play filmed, but he has written scripts for *The Servant* (63), *The Pumpkin Eater* (BFA) (64), *The Quiller Memorandum* (66), *Accident* (66), etc.

PINTOFF, ERNEST (1931–   ). Modernist American cartoon maker: *Flebus* (57), *The Violinist* (59), *The Interview* (60), *The Critic* (63), etc. Also wrote and directed one live-action feature, *Harvey Middlemann, Fireman* (64).

PINZA, EZIO (1893–1957) (Fortunato Pinza). Italian opera singer whose films include *Carnegie Hall* (47), *Mr Imperium* (51), *Slightly Dishonourable* (51), *Tonight We Sing* (53), etc.

PIPER, FREDERICK (1902–   ). British character actor, mostly on stage: usually plays the average man or police inspector. *The Good Companions* (32), *Jamaica Inn* (39), *Hue and Cry* (46), *Passport to Pimlico* (49), *The Blue Lamp* (50), *Doctor at Sea* (55), *Very Important Person* (61), *One Way Pendulum* (64), *He Who Rides a Tiger* (65), etc.

THE PIRATE (US 1948). One of the first signs of the new trend in musicals which was to come with *On the Town* and *An American in Paris*, this stage-bound operetta didn't manage as a whole to rise above its conventions, but it did have splendid moments. Judy Garland, Gene Kelly and the Nicholas Brothers were involved, and although Cole Porter's songs were below his best, they were put over with vigour. Directed by Vincente Minnelli, photographed by Harry Stradling, book by Albert Hackett and Frances Goodrich.

pirates have regularly appeared on the screen. Stories with some claim to historical authenticity, or at least based on the exploits of a pirate who once lived, include *Captain Blood* (and its various sequels), *The Black Swan, Morgan the Pirate, Seven Seas to Calais, Blackbeard the Pirate, Captain Kidd, The Buccaneer,* and *Anne of the Indies* (a rare female pirate: one other was depicted in *The Pirate Queen*). Totally fictitious stories are of course headed by *Treasure Island* (qv) in its various versions; other swashbuckling yarns included *The Sea Hawk, The Black Pirate, The Crimson Pirate, The Golden Hawk, A High Wind in Jamaica, Pirates of Tortuga, Yankee Buccaneer, The Spanish Main, Pirates of Tripoli, Devil Ship Pirates, Pirates of Blood River, Prince of Pirates,* and *Raiders of the Seven Seas.* The only notable musical pirate was Gene Kelly in *The Pirate*; comic pirates are also rare, but they do include *The Princess and the Pirate, Blackbeard's Ghost, The Dancing Pirate* and *Old Mother Riley's Jungle Treasure.*

PIROSH, ROBERT (1910–   ). American writer-director. As writer: *The Winning Ticket* (35), *A Day at the Races* (co-w) (37), *I Married a Witch* (42), *Up In Arms* (44), *Battleground* (AA) (49), *A Gathering of Eagles* (63), etc. As director: *Go For Broke* (51), *The Girl Rush* (55), *Spring Reunion* (57), etc.

PITTS, ZASU (1898–1963). American actress, a heroine of the 20s and a tearful comedienne of the 30s. *The Little Princess* (17), *Early to Wed* (21), *Greed* (23), *Twin Beds* (27), *The Wedding March* (28), *Seed* (30), *Bad Sister* (31), *The Guardsman* (32), *Back Street* (32), *Walking Down Broadway* (32), many two-reeler comedies with Thelma Todd (32–34), *Dames* (34), *Mrs Wiggs of the Cabbage Patch* (34), *So's Your Aunt Emma* (38), *Buck Privates* (39), *Nurse Edith Cavell* (40), *Niagara Falls* (41), *Let's Face It* (43), *Life with Father* (47), *Francis* (50), *Francis Joins the Wacs* (55), *This Could Be the Night* (57), *It's a Mad Mad Mad Mad World* (63), many others. TV series: *Oh Susanna* (56–59).

A PLACE IN THE SUN (US 1951). Now almost forgotten, this version of Theodore Dreiser's 'An American Tragedy' (previously filmed in 1931 with Philips Holmes) was hailed by some critics at the time of its release as one of the greatest films of all time. It is now difficult to see why. Slowly and pretentiously directed by George Stevens, its story of a young man's efforts to get into high society at any cost even then seemed dated and empty. Montgomery Clift did what he could with an unsympathetic role, and William C. Mellor's photography was luxurious.

THE PLAINSMAN (US 1937). Cecil B. de Mille's well-remembered western starred Gary Cooper as Wild Bill Hickok, James Ellison as Buffalo Bill, and Jean Arthur as Calamity Jane. It was poorly remade in 1966 with Don Murray, Guy Stockwell and Abby Dalton.

PLANCK, ROBERT (* –). American cinematographer. *Our Daily Bread* (33), *Jane Eyre* (43), *Cass Timberlane* (47), *The Three Musketeers* (48), *Little Women* (50), *Rhapsody* (54), *Moonfleet* (55), etc.

PLANER, FRANZ (1894–1963). German cinematographer, in Hollywood from 1937. *Drei von Der Tankstelle* (30), *Liebelei* (33), *Maskerade* (34), *The Beloved Vagabond* (GB) (36), *Holiday* (38), *The Face Behind the Mask* (41), *The Adventures of Martin Eden* (42), *Once Upon a Time* (44), *The Chase* (47), *Letter from an Unknown Woman* (48), *Criss Cross* (48), *The Scarf* (51), *The Blue Veil* (51), *Death of a Salesman* (52), *Twenty Thousand Leagues under the Sea* (54), *Not as a Stranger* (55), *The Pride and the Passion* (57), *The Big Country* (58), *The Nun's Story* (59), *The Unforgiven* (60), etc.

PLATT, EDWARD (1916–). American character actor. Many films include *The Shrike* (debut) (48), *Rebel Without a Cause* (55), *Pollyanna* (61). TV series: *Get Smart* (66–69).

PLATT, LOUISE (1914–). American leading lady who retired after a brief career. *Spawn of the North* (38), *Stagecoach* (39), *Forgotten Girls* (40), *Captain Caution* (40), *Street of Chance* (41), etc.

PLATT, MARC (1913–). American dancer and lightweight actor: few appearances. *Tonight and Every Night* (44), *Tars and Spars* (45), *Down to Earth* (47), *Seven Brides for Seven Brothers* (54), *Oklahoma* (55), etc.

PLEASENCE, DONALD (1919–). British character actor on stage since World War II. Films include *Manuela* (57), *The Flesh and the Fiends* (59), *Hell Is a City* (60), *No Love for Johnnie* (61), *The Caretaker* (*The Guest*) (63), *The Great Escape* (63), *The Greatest Story Ever Told* (65), *The Hallelujah Trail* (65), *Cul de Sac* (66), *Fantastic Voyage* (66), *The Night of the Generals* (67), *You Only Live Twice* (67), *Eye of the Devil* (67), *Will Penny* (67), *Mr Freedom* (68), others.

PLESCHKES, OTTO (1931–). Austrian producer, in Britain. *Georgy Girl* (66), *The Bofors Gun* (68).

PLESHETTE, SUZANNE (c. 1940–). American leading lady with stage and TV experience. *Geisha Boy* (debut) (58), *Forty Pounds of Trouble* (62), *The Birds* (63), *Wall of Noise* (63), *Youngblood Hawke* (64), *A Rage to Live* (65), *The Ugly Duckling* (66), *Bullwhip Griffin* (66), *Mister Buddwing* (66), *Blackbeard's Ghost* (67), *The Power* (67), *If It's Tuesday This Must be Belgium* (69), etc.

PLUMMER, CHRISTOPHER (1927–). Canadian leading man with stage experience including Shakespeare. *Stage Struck* (film debut) (58), *Wind Across the Everglades* (58), *The Fall of the Roman Empire*

(64), *The Sound of Music* (65), *Inside Daisy Clover* (65), *The Night of the Generals* (67), *Triple Cross* (67), *Oedipus the King* (67), *Nobody Runs Forever* (68), *Lock Up Your Daughters* (69), *The Royal Hunt of the Sun* (69), *The Battle of Britain* (69), *Waterloo* (as the Duke of Wellington) (69), etc.

PODESTA, ROSANNA (1934–   ). Italian leading lady who has been in international films. *Cops and Robbers* (51), *Ulysses* (54), *Helen of Troy* (56), *Santiago* (58), *The Golden Arrow* (65), many others.

POE, EDGAR ALLAN (1809–1849). American poet, story-writer and manic depressive, whose tortured life as well as his strange tales have been eagerly seized upon by film-makers. Griffith made *The Life of Edgar Allan Poe* in 1909, and in 1912 another version was disguised as *The Raven*. In 1915 Herbert Brabin made another film called *The Raven* with H. B. Warner as Poe; a few months earlier Griffith had released his own alternative version under the title *The Avenging Conscience*. The next film called *The Raven*, in 1935, starred Karloff and Lugosi and had nothing to do with Poe's life, being merely an amalgam of his stories; but in 1942 Fox brought out *The Loves of Edgar Allan Poe* starring Shepperd Strudwick; and in 1951 MGM made a curious melodrama called *Man with a Cloak*, in which the dark stranger who solved the mystery signed himself 'Dupin' and was played by Joseph Cotten in the Poe manner.

Of the stories, *The Mystery of Marie Roget* was filmed by Universal in 1931 and 1942; *The Tell-Tale Heart* was told as an MGM short directed by Jules Dassin in 1942, by a British company with Stanley Baker in 1950, by UPA as a cartoon narrated by James Mason in 1954, by an independent American company in a film known as both *Manfish* and *Calypso* in 1956 (the film also claimed to be partly based on 'The Gold Bug') and by the Danzigers in Britain in 1960. *The Fall of the House of Usher* was filmed in France by Jean Epstein in 1929, in Britain by semi-professionals in 1950, and in Hollywood by Roger Corman in 1960. Universal released films called *The Black Cat* in 1934 and 1941, both claiming to be 'suggested' by Poe's tale; in fact, neither had anything at all to do with it, but the genuine story was told in a German film called *The Living Dead* in 1933, and in Corman's 1962 *Tales of Terror*. *The Pit and the Pendulum* was filmed in 1913 and 1961, and the central idea has been borrowed by many film-makers without credit, mostly recently by the 'Uncle' boys in *One Spy Too Many*. *The Premature Burial* was filmed straight in 1962, and around the same time TV's *Thriller* series presented a fairly faithful adaptation; the idea was also used in 1934 in *The Crime of Dr Crespi*, a low-budgeter starring Erich Von Stroheim. *The Murders in the Rue Morgue* was filmed in 1914 and 1932, and turned up again in 3-D in 1954 under the title *Phantom of the Rue Morgue*. Other Poe stories filmed once include *The Bells* (13), *The Facts in the Case of M. Valdemar* (in *Tales of Terror* [62]), *The Haunted Palace* (63), *The Masque of the Red Death* (64), and *The Tomb of Ligeia* (64).

POE, JAMES (c. 1923–   ). American writer, from radio and TV. *Around the World in Eighty Days* (co-w) (56), *Attack* (57), *Cat on a Hot Tin Roof* (58), *Summer and Smoke* (61), *Toys in the Attic* (63), *Lilies of the Field* (64), *The Bedford Incident* (65), etc.

POHLMANN, ERIC (1913–   ). Viennese character actor, on British stage and radio from 1948; also a familiar bald, portly villain on screen. *The Constant Husband* (55), *House of Secrets* (56), *Expresso Bongo* (59), *The Kitchen* (62), *Carry On Spying* (64), *The Million Dollar Collar* (US) (67), many others.

POIL DE CAROTTE (France 1932). Julien Duvivier, who had also directed a silent version of the same story in 1925, made his international reputation with this sensitive, grim story of an unwanted boy being driven to the brink of suicide. It shows a French countryside quite different from Pagnol's: sunlit but bleak and inhospitable. Jules Renard's screenplay and Thirard Monniot's photography enhanced the performances of Harry Baur as the father and Robert Lynen (who was later killed in the Maquis) as the boy.

POITIER, SIDNEY (1924–   ). American Negro leading man, with stage experience. *No Way Out* (film debut) (50), *Cry the Beloved Country* (52), *The Blackboard Jungle* (55), *A Man Ten Feet Tall* (*Edge of the City*) (57), *Something of Value* (57), *The Defiant Ones* (58), *Porgy and Bess* (59), *A Raisin in the Sun* (60), *Lilies of the Field* (AA) (63), *The Long Ships* (64), *The Bedford Incident* (65), *The Slender Thread* (66), *A Patch of Blue* (66), *Duel at Diablo* (66), *To Sir with Love* (67), *Guess Who's Coming to Dinner* (67), *In the Heat of the Night* (67), *For Love of Ivy* (68), *The Lost One* (69), etc.

†POLANSKI, ROMAN (1933–   ). Polish director, former actor. Gained a reputation with shorts such as *Two Men and a Wardrobe* (58). Features: *Knife in the Water* (61), *Repulsion* (GB) (65), *Cul de Sac* (GB) (66), *The Fearless Vampire Killers* (GB) (67), *Rosemary's Baby* (US) (68).

POLGASE, VAN NEST (1898–   ). American art director, in films from 1919. With RKO 1932-43, since then with Columbia.

police in the 40s and earlier were offered in British films only for our admiration; in the 50s they began to have human frailties; and in the 60s many of them were shown, truthfully or not, to be corrupt. *The Blue Lamp*, *The Long Arm*, and *Gideon of Scotland Yard* are only three of many of the first kind, *Violent Playground* one of the second, and *The Strange Affair* a corking example of the last. But the *Z Cars* series on British TV will long uphold the best traditions of the force . . . as will *Maigret* for France.

American cops have always been tougher, but even so a gradual change can be traced through *Naked City*, *The Big Heat*, *Detective Story*, *Shield for Murder*, *Experiment in Terror*, *Madigan* and *The Detective*. TV series which have been influential include *Dragnet* (52–59 and 67–69), *Naked City* (58–62), *87th Precinct* (61), *M Squad* (57–60), *The Detectives* (60–61), *The Line Up* (54–59), *Hawk* (66), *The New Breed* (61), *Adam 12* (68).

Comic policemen go right back to the Keystone Kops. More recent examples: Will Hay in *Ask a Policeman*, George Formby in *Spare a Copper*, Norman Wisdom in *On the Beat*, Alastair Sim in *Green for Danger*, Peter Sellers in *The Pink Panther*, Lionel Jeffries in *The Wrong Arm of the Law*, Sidney James and crew in *Carry On Constable*, Laurel and Hardy in *Midnight Patrol*, Buster Keaton in *Cops*, Charles Chaplin in *Easy Street* . . . and on TV, *Car 54 Where Are You?*

politics, as any exhibitor will tell you, is the kiss of death to a film as far as box-office is concerned. Nevertheless many films with serious political themes have been made. Among those presenting biographies of actual political figures, the American ones include *Young Mr Lincoln*, *Abe Lincoln in Illinois*, *Tennessee Johnson*, *The Man with Thirty Sons* (Oliver Wendell Holmes), *Magnificent Doll* (Dolly Madison and Aaron Burr), *The President's Lady* (Andrew Jackson), *Wilson*, Teddy Roosevelt (in *My Girl Tisa* and others), Franklin Roosevelt (in *Sunrise at Campobello*), *Beau James* (Jimmy Walker) and John Kennedy (*PT 109*), while *All the King's Men* and *A Lion Is in the Streets* are clearly based on Huey Long, and there was a real-life original for the idealistic young senator from Wisconsin in *Mr Smith Goes to Washington*. Fictional presidencies have been involved in *Gabriel over the White House*, *First Lady*, *The Tree of Liberty* (*The Howards of Virginia*), *Advise and Consent*, *The Manchurian Candidate*, *Seven Days in May*, *Dr Strangelove*, *Kisses for My President*, and *Fail Safe*. Among the many films alleging political graft and corruption in the US are *Mr Smith Goes to Washington*, *Confessions of a Nazi Spy*, *Louisiana Purchase*, *Alias Nick Beal*, *State of the Union*, *Lil' Abner*, *The Great McGinty*, *The Glass Key*, *Citizen Kane*, *All the King's Men*, *Bullets or Ballots*, *A Lion Is in the Streets*, *The Last Hurrah* and *The Best Man*. The witch-hunts of 1948 produced a series of right-wing melodramas like *I Was a Communist for the FBI*, *I Married a Communist* and *My Son John* . . . a striking contrast to 1942, when *Mission to Moscow* could be made.

The British House of Commons and its characters have been involved in many a film with Disraeli (qv) coming out as favourite. Pitt the Younger was impersonated by Robert Donat, and Charles James Fox by Robert Morley, in *The Young Mr Pitt*; Gladstone was played by Ralph Richardson in *Khartoum*, Malcolm Keen in *Sixty Glorious Years* and Stephen Murray in *The Prime Minister*;

while Ramsay MacDonald was allegedly pictured in *Fame Is the Spur*. MPs were also the leading figures of the fictional *No Love for Johnnie*.

Political films from other countries abound; one might almost say that every Soviet film is political. But politics do not export well, so that for the life of Villa, Zapata and Juarez we have to turn to glamorized Hollywood versions of the truth; ditto for Parnell, Richelieu and even Hitler.

That politics is not entirely a serious matter can be seen from the number of comedies about it. The best of them is the already mentioned *State of the Union*, but one can also instance the *Don Camillo* series, *Old Mother Riley MP*, *Angelina MP*, *Dad Rudd MP*, *Louisiana Purchase*, *Kisses for My President*, *The Great Man Votes*, *Left Right and Centre* and *Vote for Huggett*.

POLITO, SOL (1892–1960). American cinematographer. *Treason* (18), *Hard-Boiled Haggerty* (27), *Five Star Final* (31), *I Am a Fugitive from a Chain Gang* (32), *Forty-second Street* (33), *G Men* (35), *The Petrified Forest* (36), *The Charge of the Light Brigade* (36), *The Adventures of Robin Hood* (38), *Confessions of a Nazi Spy* (39), *The Sea Hawk* (40), *The Sea Wolf* (41), *Now Voyager* (42), *Arsenic and Old Lace* (44), *Rhapsody in Blue* (45), *The Long Night* (47), *Anna Lucasta* (48), many others.

POLL, MARTIN H. (1922–   ). American producer. *Love is a Ball* (62), *Sylvia* (65), *The Lion in Winter* (68), etc.

POLLACK, SYDNEY (* –   ). American director, from TV. *The Slender Thread* (65), *This Property Is Condemned* (66), *Castle Keep* (69), *They Shoot Horses Don't They* (69).

POLLARD, HARRY (1883–1934). American silent-screen director. *Motherhood* (14), *The Leather Pushers* (22), *Oh Doctor* (24), *California Straight Ahead* (25), *Uncle Tom's Cabin* (27), *Showboat* (first talkie) (29), *The Prodigal* (31), *Fast Life* (32), etc.

POLLARD, MICHAEL J. (1939–   ) (M. J. Pollack). Pint-sized American character actor, in countless small roles before instant popularity in *Bonnie and Clyde* (67). Other films include *Adventures of a Young Man* (62), *Summer Magic* (62), *The Stripper* (64), *Hannibal Brooks* (69).

POLLARD, SNUB (1886–1962) (Harold Fraser). Australian comedian, in America from early silent film days. In many silent slapstick shorts, and later continued to play bit parts, the last being in *A Pocketful of Miracles* (61).

POLLOCK, GEORGE (1907–   ). British director, former assistant, in films since 1933. *A Stranger in Town* (56), *Rooney* (58), *Don't Panic Chaps* (60), *Murder She Said* (63), *Murder at the Gallop* (63), *Murder Most Foul* (64), *Ten Little Indians* (65), etc.

POLONSKY, ABRAHAM (c. 1910–   ). American writer who fell foul of the McCarthy witch-hunt. *Body and Soul* (47), *Force of Evil* (also directed) (49), *I Can Get It for You Wholesale* (50), *Willie Boy* (also directed) (69), etc.

POMMER, ERICH (1889–1966). German producer since 1915. During the 30s worked briefly in the US and also, with Charles Laughton, formed Mayflower Films in Britain. *The Cabinet of Dr Caligari* (19), *Dr Mabuse* (22), *Die Nibelungen* (24), *Variety* (25), *Metropolis* (26), *The Blue Angel* (30), *Congress Dances* (31), *Liliom* (34), *Fire over England* (36), *Vessel of Wrath* (38), *Jamaica Inn* (39), *They Knew What They Wanted* (40), *Illusion in Moll* (52), *Kinder Mutter und Ein General* (55), etc.

PONS, LILY (1898–   ). French-born operatic singer who starred in some Hollywood films. *I Dream Too much* (35), *That Girl from Paris* (36), *Carnegie Hall* (47), etc.

PONTI, CARLO (1913–   ). Italian producer, now involved in international productions. *I Miserabili* (47), *Attila the Hun* (52), *Ulysses* (54), *War and Peace* (56), *Black Orchid* (58), *That Kind of Woman* (59), *Marriage, Italian Style* (65), *Operation Crossbow* (65), *Smashing Time* (67), *Sunflower* (70), etc. Married to Sophia Loren.

POPEYE. Tough sailorman hero of over 250 cartoon shorts produced by Max Fleischer c. 1933–50. Other characters involved were girl-friend Olive Oyl and tough villain Bluto, against whose wiles Popeye fortified himself with tins of spinach. The films were so popular on TV that a newly-drawn series was produced c. 1959 by King Features—but the old vulgar panache was missing.

POPKIN, HARRY M. (* –   ). American independent producer. *Ten Little Niggers* (45), *Impact* (48), *D.O.A.* (49), *Champagne for Caesar* (49), *The Well* (51), *The Thief* (52), etc.

PORCASI, PAUL (1880– *). Sicilian character actor in Hollywood films; former opera singer. *The Devil and the Deep* (32), *Maytime* (37), *Torrid Zone* (40), *Quiet Please Murder* (43), *I'll Remember April* (45), etc.

PORTER, COLE (1893–1964). American songwriter and composer whose lyrics were probably the wittiest ever appended to popular songs. Cary Grant played Porter in a biopic, *Night and Day* (46); other films using Porter scores are: *Anything Goes* (36 and 56), *Rosalie* (38), *Broadway Melody of 1940*, *Something to Shout About* (42), *The Pirate* (48), *Kiss Me Kate* (53), *High Society* (56), *Can Can* (59), etc.

PORTER, DON (1912–   ). American leading man of second features, *Top Sergeant* (42), *Night Monster* (43), *The Curse of the Allenbys* (48),

711 Ocean Drive (50), *Because You're Mine* (52), *The Racket* (52), *Our Miss Brooks* (56), *Bachelor in Paradise* (61), *Youngblood Hawke* (64), etc. TV series: *Private Secretary*, *Our Miss Brooks*, *The Ann Sothern Show*.

PORTER, EDWIN S. (1869–1941). America's first notable director, who later found himself in D. W. Griffith's shadow and left the industry. *The Life of an American Fireman* (02), *The Great Train Robbery* (03), *The Ex-Convict* (05), *Rescued from an Eagle's Nest* (07), *Alice's Adventures in Wonderland* (10), *The Count of Monte Cristo* (12), *The Eternal City* (15), etc.

PORTER, ERIC (1928–   ). British stage actor who became nationally known as Soames in the TV version of *The Forsyte Saga*. Films include *The Heroes of Telemark* (65), *Kaleidoscope* (66), *The Lost Continent* (68).

PORTMAN, ERIC (1903–1969). Distinguished British stage actor who has appeared sporadically in films. *The Murder in the Red Barn* (debut) (34), *Hyde Park Corner* (35), *The Prince and the Pauper* (US) (37), *Moonlight Sonata* (37), *49th Parallel* (41), *One of Our Aircraft Is Missing* (42), *Uncensored* (42), *Squadron Leader X* (43), *We Dive at Dawn* (43), *Millions Like Us* (43), *A Canterbury Tale* (44), *Great Day* (45), *Men of Two Worlds* (46), *Wanted for Murder* (46), *Dear Murderer* (47), *Daybreak* (48), *The Mark of Cain* (48), *Corridor of Mirrors* (48), *The Blind Goddess* (48), *The Spider and the Fly* (50), *His Excellency* (51), *The Deep Blue Sea* (55), *Child in the House* (56), *The Good Companions* (57), *The Naked Edge* (61), *West Eleven* (63), *The Bedford Incident* (65), *The Whisperers* (66), *The Spy with a Cold Nose* (67), *Assignment to Kill* (67), *Deadfall* (68), etc.

PORTRAIT OF JENNIE (US 1948). A pretentious but enjoyable fantasy in Hollywood's lushest manner, about a penniless artist who meets a fey young girl in Central Park and discovers not only that she grows much older every time he sees her but that she actually died many years ago. She finally dies again in a storm off Cape Cod. Not even the author could possibly understand this plot, and even the light relief is of a whimsical nature; but the acting (Joseph Cotten, Jennifer Jones, Ethel Barrymore, David Wayne, Lilian Gish) is so good, the direction (William Dieterle) so accomplished and the photography (Joseph August) so striking that the thing comes off.

POST, TED (1925–   ). American director, from TV. *The Legend of Tom Dooley* (59), *Hang 'Em High* (68), *Beneath the Planet of the Apes* (69).

POSTA, ADRIENNE (1948–   ). British juvenile actress specializing in cheeky teenagers. *To Sir With Love* (67), *Here We Go Round the Mulberry Bush* (67), *Up the Junction* (68), *Some Girls Do* (69), etc.

779

Poston, Tom

POSTON, TOM (1927–   ). American light comedian. *City That Never Sleeps* (53), *Zotz!* (62), *The Old Dark House* (63).

post-synchronization. Adding sound, by dubbing, to visuals already shot. Sound can only rarely be recorded at the time of shooting because of extraneous noise and requirements of volume, pitch, etc.; actors must usually repeat their lines in accordance with their image on screen.

POTTER, H. C. (1904–   ). American director with stage experience, in Hollywood from 1935; an expert at comedy. *Beloved Enemy* (36), *Adventures of Tom Sawyer* (38), *The Cowboy and the Lady* (39), *The Story of Vernon and Irene Castle* (39), *Hellzapoppin* (42), *Mr Lucky* (44), *You Gotta Stay Happy* (47), *The Farmer's Daughter* (47), *Mr Blandings Builds His Dream House* (48), *The Time of Your Life* (48), *The Miniver Story* (50), *Three for the Show* (55), *Top Secret Affair* (57), etc. Recently directing Broadway plays.

POUJOULY, GEORGES (1940–   ). French boy actor of the early 50s. *Jeux Interdits* (52), *Nous Sommes Tous Des Assassins* (52), *Les Diaboliques* (54), *Lift to the Scaffold* (57), *Girls for the Summer* (59), etc.

POWELL, DICK (1904–1963). American actor with limited stage experience before Hollywood contract 1932; played romantic singing leads in 30s, later changed to tough roles and smart comedy; founded Four Star Television and produced many top-rated series including *The Dick Powell Theatre*. Films include *Blessed Event* (debut) (32), *Forty-second Street* (33), *Dames* (34), *Wonder Bar* (34), *Flirtation Walk* (34), *A Midsummer Night's Dream* (35), *Page Miss Glory* (35), *Shipmates Forever* (35), *On the Avenue* (37), *Cowboy from Brooklyn* (38), *Christmas in July* (40), *Model Wife* (41), *Happy Go Lucky* (42), *True to Life* (43), *It Happened Tomorrow* (44), *Farewell My Lovely* (*Murder My Sweet*) (44), *Cornered* (45), *Johnny o'Clock* (46), *To the Ends of the Earth* (48), *The Reformer and the Redhead* (50), *The Tall Target* (51), *The Bad and the Beautiful* (52), *Split Second* (director only) (53), *Susan Slept Here* (54), *The Conqueror* (producer/director only) (55), *You Can't Run Away From It* (producer/director only) (56), *The Enemy Below* (producer/director only) (57). *The Hunters* (director only) (58), etc.

POWELL, ELEANOR (1912–   ). American dancing star of the 30s and 40s; was married to Glenn Ford. *George White's Scandals* (35), *Broadway Melody* (36), *Rosalie* (37), *Honolulu* (38), *Broadway Melody of 1940*, *I Dood It* (40), *Lady Be Good* (41), *Born to Dance* (42), *Ship Ahoy* (42), *Thousands Cheer* (43), *Sensations of 1945*, *Duchess of Idaho* (50), etc.

POWELL, JANE (1929–   ) (Suzanne Burce). Diminutive American leading lady and singer; sang on radio as a child. *Song of the Open*

Road (debut) (44), *Holiday in Mexico* (46), *Luxury Liner* (48), *A Date with Judy* (48), *Rich, Young and Pretty* (51), *Seven Brides for Seven Brothers* (54), *Hit the Deck* (55), *Deep in My Heart* (55), *The Girl Most Likely* (58), *Enchanted Island* (58), others.

POWELL, MICHAEL (1905–   ). British writer-producer-director whose imaginative work has often been marred by a streak of tastelessness. In films from 1925. Directed *The Phantom Light* (34), *Her Last Affair* (35), *The Edge of the World* (38), etc. Then formed partnership with EMERIC PRESSBURGER ('The Archers') and created a long series of major films: *The Spy in Black* (39), *Contraband* (40), *49th Parallel* (41), *One of Our Aircraft Is Missing* (42), *The Life and Death of Colonel Blimp* (43), *I Know Where I'm Going* (45), *A Matter of Life and Death (Stairway to Heaven)* (46), *Black Narcissus* (46), *The Red Shoes* (48), *The Small Back Room* (49), *The Elusive Pimpernel* (50), *Tales of Hoffman* (51), *Oh Rosalinda* (55), *The Battle of the River Plate* (55), *Ill Met by Moonlight* (57), etc. Powell alone directed *Peeping Tom* (59), *The Queen's Guards* (60), *Honeymoon* (61), *They're a Weird Mob* (66); and he co-directed *The Thief of Baghdad* (40) and co-produced *Mr Sebastian* (67). 1969: *Age of Consent*.

POWELL, SANDY (1898–   ). British music-hall comedian who made some knockabout films using his radio catch-phrase 'Can you hear me, mother?' *The Third String* (32), *Leave It to Me* (36), *I've Got a Horse* (38), *Cup Tie Honeymoon* (48), etc. Recently touring in clubs.

POWELL, WILLIAM (1892–   ). Debonair, mature American leading man of the 30s; started in Hollywood as cowboy villain after stage experience. *Sherlock Holmes* (21), *Under the Red Robe* (23), *Beau Geste* (26), *The Last Command* (28), *The Four Feathers* (29), *Street of Chance* (30), *The Road to Singapore* (32), *Ladies Man* (33), *Fashions of 1934*, *Manhattan Melodrama* (34), *The Thin Man* (34), *Reckless* (35), *The Great Ziegfeld* (36), *Libelled Lady* (36), *After the Thin Man* (37), *The Emperor's Candlesticks* (38), *Another Thin Man* (39), *Love Crazy* (41), *Shadow of the Thin Man* (42), *The Heavenly Body* (43), *The Thin Man Goes Home* (44), *Ziegfeld Follies* (46), *Life with Father* (47), *Song of the Thin Man* (47), *Mr Ashton Was Indiscreet* (48), *Mr Peabody and the Mermaid* (48), *Dancing in the Dark* (50), *It's a Big Country* (52), *How To Marry a Millionaire* (53), *Mister Roberts* (55), many others.

POWER, HARTLEY (1894–1966). American character actor who settled in Britain; usually seen as hard-headed agent, general or con man.

†POWER, TYRONE (1913–1958). American leading man, of theatrical family; in films from 1932, usually deploying gentle personality. *Tom Brown of Culver* (32), *Girls' Dormitory* (36), *Ladies in Love* (36), *Lloyds of London* (37), *Love is News* (37), *Café Metropole* (37), *This Ice* (37), *Second Honeymoon* (37), *In Old Chicago* (38), *Alexander's*

Powers, Mala

Ragtime Band (38), *Marie Antoinette* (38), *Suez* (38), *Rose of Washington Square* (39), *Jesse James* (39), *Second Fiddle* (39), *The Rains Came* (39), *Daytime Wife* (39), *Johnny Apollo* (40), *Brigham Young* (40), *The Mark of Zorro* (40), *A Yank in the R.A.F.* (41), *Blood and Sand* (41), *This Above All* (42), *Son of Fury* (42), *The Black Swan* (42), *Crash Dive* (42); war service; *The Razor's Edge* (46), *Captain from Castile* (47), *Nightmare Alley* (47), *The Luck of the Irish* (48), *That Wonderful Urge* (48), *Prince of Foxes* (49), *The Black Rose* (50), *An American Guerilla in the Philippines* (51), *Rawhide* (51), *I'll Never Forget You* (51), *Diplomatic Courier* (52), *Pony Soldier* (52), *Mississippi Gambler* (53), *King of the Khyber Rifles* (53), *The Long Gray Line* (54), *Untamed* (55), *The Eddy Duchin Story* (56), *Seven Waves Away* (57), *The Rising of the Moon* (narrated only) (57), *The Sun Also Rises* (57), *Witness for the Prosecution* (57). Died during filming of *Solomon and Sheba*: Yul Brynner took over his role.

POWERS, MALA (1931–) (Mary Ellen Powers). American leading lady, former child actress. *Tough As They Come* (41), *Outrage* (47), *Cyrano de Bergerac* (50), *Rose of Cimarron* (52), *Rage at Dawn* (55), *Benghazi* (55), *The Storm Rider* (57), *Daddy's Gone A-Hunting* (69), etc.

POWERS, STEFANIE (1942–) (Taffy Paul). American leading lady. *Experiment in Terror* (62), *Fanatic* (GB) (64), *Stagecoach* (66), *Warning Shot* (67), etc. TV series: *The Girl from Uncle* (66).

pre-credits sequence. It has recently become fashionable to start films with an explosive opening scene, sometimes running seven or eight minutes, before the titles appear. This now over-worked device, used by almost all American TV series, is generally traced back to *Rommel, Desert Fox* (51), which had a long pre-credits sequence showing a commando raid; but the titles come quite late in *The Egg and I* (47), and even in *Destry Rides Again* there is nearly a minute of shooting before they appear; while in *The Magnificent Ambersons* (42) they are not seen at all, only spoken at the end of the picture.

PREJEAN, ALBERT (1898–). French light character actor who was in most of René Clair's early successes. *Le Voyage Imaginaire* (25), *An Italian Straw Hat* (27), *Sous les Toits de Paris* (30), *Die Dreigroschenoper* (*L'Opéra de Quat'Sous*) (31), *Jenny* (36), *Métropolitain* (40), *L'Etrange Suzy* (43), *Les Nouveaux Maîtres* (49), *Les Amants du Tage* (54), etc.

†PREMINGER, OTTO (1906–). Austrian director with theatrical background. Always a good craftsman, he has latterly applied heavy-handed treatment to potentially interesting subjects. *Die Grosse Liebe* (Austrian) (32), then to US: *Under Your Spell* (36), *Danger, Love at Work* (37), *They Got Me Covered* (acted only) (42),

Margin for Error (also acted) (43), *In the Meantime, Darling* (44), *Laura* (44), *Royal Scandal* (45), *Centennial Summer* (46), *Fallen Angel* (46), *Forever Amber* (47), *Daisy Kenyon* (47), *The Fan* (49), *Whirlpool* (50), *Where the Sidewalk Ends* (50), *The Thirteenth Letter* (51), *Angel Face* (53), *The Moon Is Blue* (53), *Stalag 17* (acted only) (53), *River of No Return* (54), *Carmen Jones* (54), *The Court Martial of Billy Mitchell* (55), *The Man with the Golden Arm* (56), *Bonjour Tristesse* (57), *Saint Joan* (GB) (57), *Porgy and Bess* (59), *Anatomy of a Murder* (59), *Exodus* (60), *Advise and Consent* (61), *The Cardinal* (63), *In Harm's Way* (65), *Bunny Lake Is Missing* (GB) (65), *Hurry Sundown* (67), *Skidoo* (68), *Tell Me That You Love Me, June Moon* (70).

PRENTISS, PAULA (1939–) (Paula Ragusa). Tall American leading lady who came almost straight from college to Hollywood. *Where the Boys Are* (61), *The Honeymoon Machine* (62), *Bachelor in Paradise* (62), *The Horizontal Lieutenant* (63), *Man's Favourite Sport* (64), *The World of Henry Orient* (64), *In Harm's Way* (65), *Catch 22* (69). TV series: *He and She* (67).

PRESLE, MICHELINE (1922–) (Micheline Chassagne). French leading actress with stage experience. *Jeunes Filles en Détresse* (38), *La Nuit Fantastique* (41), *Boule de Suif* (45), *Le Diable au Corps* (46), *Les Jeux Sont Faits* (47), *Under My Skin* (US) (50), *The Adventures of Captain Fabian* (US) (51), *La Dame aux Camélias* (52), *Villa Borghese* (54), *The She Wolves* (57), *Blind Date* (GB) (59), *The Prize* (63), *La Religieuse* (65), *King of Hearts* (67), etc.

PRESLEY, ELVIS (1935–). Heavy-lidded American pop singer and guitarist, known as 'the Pelvis' from his swivel-hipped style. *Love Me Tender* (56), *Loving You* (57), *Jailhouse Rock* (58), *King Creole* (58), *Follow That Dream* (62), *Viva Las Vegas* (63), *Kissin' Cousins* (64), *Harem Scarem* (65), *Tickle Me* (65), *Frankie and Johnny* (65), *Paradise Hawaiian Style* (66), *Spinout* (*California Holiday*) (66), *Double Trouble* (67), *Stay Away Joe* (68), *Charro* (69), *Change of Habit* (69), etc.

PRESNELL, HARVE (1933–). American light opera singer, now in occasional films. *The Unsinkable Molly Brown* (64), *The Glory Guys* (65), *Girl Crazy* (66), *Paint Your Wagon* (69).

PRESNELL, ROBERT, SNR (c. 1892–). American writer, usually in collaboration. *Hi Nellie* (32), *My Man Godfrey* (36), *The Real Glory* (39), *Meet John Doe* (41), *Second Chance* (53), etc.; then to TV.

PRESNELL, ROBERT, JNR (1914–). American writer. *The Man in the Attic* (53), *Legend of the Lost* (57), *Conspiracy of Hearts* (GB) (59), *Let No Man Write My Epitaph* (60), *The Third Day* (65), etc.

PRESSBURGER, ARNOLD (1885–1951). Hungarian producer who worked in Germany, Britain and Hollywood. *City of Song* (30), *Tell Me*

Tonight (32), *The Return of the Scarlet Pimpernel* (38), *The Shanghai Gesture* (41), *Hangmen Also Die* (43), *It Happened Tomorrow* (44), *A Scandal in Paris* (46), etc.

PRESSBURGER, EMERIC (1902–   ). Hungarian journalist and script-writer, in Britain from 1935. Worked on script of *The Challenge* (37) and met Michael Powell, qv for list of their joint films as 'The Archers'. Solo: *Twice upon a Time* (w, p, d) (52), *Miracle in Soho* (w, p) (56), *Behold a Pale Horse* (from his novel) (64).

†PRESTON, ROBERT (1917–   ) (Robert Preston Messervey). Ameri-can leading man who made routine films from 1938, became a theatre star in the 50s. *King of Alcatraz* (38), *Illegal Traffic* (38), *Disbarred* (38), *Union Pacific* (39), *Beau Geste* (39), *Typhoon* (39), *Moon over Burma* (39), *Northwest Mounted Police* (40), *New York Town* (40), *The Lady from Cheyenne* (40), *The Night of January 16th* (41), *Parachute Battalion* (41), *Pacific Blackout* (41), *Reap the Wild Wind* (42), *This Gun for Hire* (42), *Wake Island* (42), *Night Plane to Chungking* (42); war service; *Wild Harvest* (47), *The Macomber Affair* (47), *Variety Girl* (47), *Whispering Smith* (47), *Blood on the Moon* (48), *Big City* (48), *The Lady Gambles* (48), *Tulsa* (49), *The Sundowners* (49), *Best of the Badmen* (51), *When I Grow Up* (51), *Face to Face* (52), *Cloudburst* (GB) (53), *The Last Frontier* (56), *The Dark at the Top of the Stairs* (60), *The Music Man* (his stage role) (61), *Island of Love* (63), *All the Way Home* (63).

PREVERT, JACQUES (1900–   ). French screenwriter whose most memorable work has been in conjunction with Marcel Carné: *Drôle de Drame* (37), *Quai des Brumes* (38), *Le Jour Se Lève* (39), *Les Visiteurs du Soir* (42), *Les Enfants du Paradis* (44), *Les Portes de la Nuit* (46), *Les Amants de Verone* (48). Other scripts include *L'Affaire Est dans le Sac* (also acted) (32), *Le Crime de Monsieur Lange* (35), *Une Partie de Campagne* (36), *Lumière d'Eté* (42), *Notre Dame de Paris* (56), etc.

PREVIN, ANDRE (1929–   ). German composer and arranger, long in Hollywood. Film scores include *Scene of the Crime* (49), *Three Little Words* (51), *Bad Day at Black Rock* (54), *The Fastest Gun Alive* (56), *Designing Woman* (57), *Gigi* (AA) (58), *Porgy and Bess* (AA) (59), *Elmer Gantry* (60), *One, Two, Three* (62), *Irma La Douce* (AA) (63), *My Fair Lady* (AA) (64), *Goodbye Mr Chips* (project) (67).

PREVOST, MARIE (1898–1937) (Marie Bickford Dunn). Anglo-French leading lady of American silent films. *East Lynne with Variations* (20), *Her Night of Nights* (22), *The Marriage Circle* (24), *Red Lights* (24), *The Loves of Camille* (25), *Up in Mabel's Room* (26), *Getting Gertie's Garter* (27), *Lady of Leisure* (28), *Side Show* (30), *Sporting Blood* (31), *Parole Girl* (33), *Tango* (last film) (36), etc.

PRICE, DENNIS (1915–   ) (Dennistoun Franklyn John Rose-Price). British light leading man and latterly equally light character actor; on stage from 1937. *A Canterbury Tale* (debut) (44), *A Place of One's Own* (44), *The Magic Bow* (46), *Hungry Hill* (46), *Dear Murderer* (47), *Jassy* (47), *Holiday Camp* (47), *Master of Bankdam* (47), *The White Unicorn* (47), *Good Time Girl* (48), *The Bad Lord Byron* (48), *Kind Hearts and Coronets* (his best role) (49), *The Dancing Years* (49), *The Adventurers* (50), *Lady Godiva Rides Again* (51), *The House in the Square* (52), *Song of Paris* (52), *The Intruder* (53), *That Lady* (54), *Oh Rosalinda* (55), *Private's Progress* (55), *Charley Moon* (56), *The Naked Truth* (58), *I'm All Right, Jack* (59), *Tunes of Glory* (60), *Victim* (61), *Play It Cool* (62), *Tamahine* (63), *A High Wind in Jamaica* (65), *Ten Little Indians* (65), many others. TV series: *The World of Wooster* (as Jeeves).

PRICE, NANCY (1880–   ). Dominant British character actress with long stage experience, especially remembered as Grandma in 'Whiteoaks'. Also an indefatigable traveller, naturalist and semi-mystic. Films include *The Stars Look Down* (39), *Madonna of the Seven Moons* (44), *I Live in Grosvenor Square* (45), *The Three Weird Sisters* (48), *Mandy* (52), etc.

PRICE, VINCENT (1911–   ). Tall, gentle-voiced American character actor, lately typed in horror films. On stage since 1934; also a well-known art expert. *Service de Luxe* (debut) (38), *Elizabeth and Essex* (39), *Green Hell* (40), *Tower of London* (40), *Brigham Young* (40), *The Song of Bernadette* (43), *The Keys of the Kingdom* (44), *Laura* (44), *Czarina* (45), *Dragonwyck* (46), *Shock* (46), *The Long Night* (47), *The Three Musketeers* (49), *Champagne for Caesar* (49), *His Kind of Woman* (51), *House of Wax* (53), *The Mad Magician* (54), *The Ten Commandments* (56), *The Story of Mankind* (57), *The Fly* (58), *The Bat* (59), *The House on Haunted Hill* (60), *The Fall of the House of Usher* (61), *The Pit and the Pendulum* (61), *Tales of Terror* (62), *The Raven* (63), *A Comedy of Terrors* (63), *The Tomb of Ligeia* (64), *City in the Sea (War Gods of the Deep)* (65), *Dr Goldfoot and the Sex Machine* (65), *House of a Thousand Dolls* (67), *The Oblong Box* (69), *Scream and Scream Again* (69), *Cry of the Banshee* (70), etc.

PRIDE AND PREJUDICE (US 1940). A delightful example of Hollywood 'Englishness'. Though Aldous Huxley's script was a simplification of Jane Austen and advanced the period forty years to take advantage of the fuller fashions, this remains a splendid romantic comedy of a more polite age, full of richly satisfying performances: Greer Garson as Elizabeth, Laurence Olivier as Darcy, Edmund Gwenn as Mr Bennet, Edna May Oliver as Lady Catherine, Melville Cooper as Mr Collins. Directed by Robert Z. Leonard in just the right unhurried style.

Priestley, J. B.

PRIESTLEY, J. B. (1894–   ). British author whose best novel, *The Good Companions*, was filmed in 1932 and 1957. Also his plays: *Dangerous Corner* (34), *When We Are Married* (43), *They Came to a City* (45), *An Inspector Calls* (54), etc. His early thriller novel, 'Benighted', was filmed as *The Old Dark House* (32). Original film scripts: *The Foreman Went to France* (42), *Last Holiday* (50), etc.

priests have been a godsend to film-makers, and most male stars have played one at some time or other: the combination of attraction and non-availability is apparently a box-office certainty. Thus Frank Sinatra in *The Miracle of the Bells*; William Holden and Clifton Webb in *Satan Never Sleeps*; Bing Crosby in *Going My Way*, *The Bells of St Mary* and *Say One for Me*; David Niven in *The Bishop's Wife*; Richard Dix in *The Christian*; Pat O'Brien in more films than one can count, notably *Angels with Dirty Faces* and *Fighting Father Dunne*; ditto Spencer Tracy, in *Boys' Town*, *San Francisco* and others; Don Murray in *The Hoodlum Priest*; Karl Malden in *On the Waterfront*; Richard Todd in *A Man Called Peter*; Pierre Fresnay in *Monsieur Vincent*; Claude Laydu in *Diary of a Country Priest*; Jean-Paul Belmondo in *Leon Morin Priest*; John Mills in *The Singer Not the Song*; Tom Tryon in *The Cardinal*; Robert Donat in *Lease of Life*; Gregory Peck in *The Keys of the Kingdom*; Anthony Quayle in *Serious Charge*; Humphrey Bogart in *The Left Hand of God*; and Geoffrey Bayldon in *Sky West and Crooked*. Most of these were doing a good job despite occasional doubts and lapses; but the same could hardly be said of Robert Mitchum in *Night of the Hunter*, Henry Fonda in *The Fugitive*, Richard Burton in *Night of the Iguana*, Pierre Fresnay in *Le Défroque* or *Dieu A Besoin des Hommes*, Peter Sellers and Ian Carmichael in *Heavens Above*, Keenan Wynn in *Johnny Concho*, or Max von Sydow in *Hawaii*.

PRIGGEN, NORMAN (1924–   ). British producer, with Ealing Studios from 1939, later independent. *The Professionals* (61), *Payroll* (61), *The Servant* (64), *Secret Ceremony* (co-p) (68), etc.

THE PRINCE AND THE PAUPER. Mark Twain's medieval story, about a prince and a commoner who change places, was filmed in 1909; in 1915 with Marguerite Clark; in 1923 with Tibi Lubin; in 1937 with the Mauch twins (and Errol Flynn); and in 1962 with Sean Scully.

PRINCE, WILLIAM (1913–   ). American stage leading man who has been less successful in films. *Destination Tokyo* (44), *Pillow to Post* (46), *Dead Reckoning* (47), *Carnegie Hall* (48), *Cyrano de Bergerac* (51), *The Vagabond King* (55), *Macabre* (58), etc.

PRINE, ANDREW (1936–   ). American leading man. *The Miracle Worker* (62), *Company of Cowards* (64), *The Devil's Brigade* (68), etc.

PRINGLE, AILEEN (1895–   ) (Aileen Bisbee). American actress of the silent screen, best remembered for her performance in Elinor Glyn's *Three Weeks* (24). Also: *Redhead* (19), *The Christian* (23), *Wife of a Centaur* (24), *Dance Madness* (24), *Adam and Evil* (27), *Soldiers and Women* (30), *Convicted* (32), *Jane Eyre* (33), *Piccadilly Jim* (36), *Nothing Sacred* (37), *The Girl from Nowhere* (last film) (39), etc.

PRINZ, LE ROY (1895–   ). American choreographer who after adventurous early life came to Hollywood and worked on many Paramount and Warner films: *The Sign of the Cross* (32), the '*Road*' films (39–42), *Yankee Doodle Dandy* (42), *Night and Day* (46), *The Ten Commandments* (56), *South Pacific* (58), many others. Directed short subject *A Boy and His Dog* (AA) (48).

prison films have always had an audience, but did not reach their full potential until sound. Then and through the 30s, film-makers took us on a conducted tour of American prisons. *The Big House, The Last Mile, I Was a Fugitive from a Chain Gang, Twenty Thousand Years in Sing Sing, Front Page Woman* (with its gas chamber scene), *Angels with Dirty Faces, San Quentin, Blackwell's Island, Each Dawn I Die, Invisible Stripes, King of Alcatraz, Prison Ship, Prison Doctor, Mutiny in the Big House* and many others. During the war prison films were surpassed in excitement, but they came back with a bang in *Brute Force*, the toughest of them all, and *White Heat*. The 50s brought *Behind the High Wall, Duffy of San Quentin, Riot in Cell Block Eleven, Inside the Walls of Folsom Prison, Black Tuesday, I Want to Live, Cell 2455 Death Row*, and a remake of *The Last Mile*. More recently Burt Lancaster appeared in the factual *Bird Man of Alcatraz*; and in she second half of the 60s the subject became popular again with *The Brig, The Ceremony, Reprieve, Point Blank, The Dirty Dozen, Triple Cross, Riot*.

British studios have produced few prison films until the recent realist wave, which brought with it *The Criminal, The Pot Carriers*, and the army prison film *The Hill*.

Unusual prisons were shown in *Sullivan's Travels, Devil's Canyon*, and *Nevada Smith*; while among the films poking fun at prison life are *Up the River, Jailbirds* (Laurel and Hardy), *Convict 99* (Will Hay), *Jailhouse Rock* and *Two-Way Stretch*.

Prisons for women crop up quite regularly in such films as *Prison Without Bars, Caged* (American), *Caged* (Italian), *Au Royaume des Cieux, Women's Prison, Girls Behind Bars, So Evil So Young, The Weak and the Wicked, Yield to the Night* and *The Smashing Bird I Used to Know*.

THE PRISONER OF ZENDA. At least three versions have been made of Anthony Hope's classic Ruritanian romance about a great impersonation, all in Hollywood. 1. 1927: directed by Rex Ingram, with Lewis Stone and Ramon Novarro. 2. 1937: directed by John

Cromwell, with Ronald Colman and Douglas Fairbanks Jnr. 3. 1952: directed by Richard Thorpe, with Stewart Granger and James Mason. The 1937 version remains a model of its kind, with a fine cast including C. Aubrey Smith, David Niven, Raymond Massey and Madeleine Carroll; the 1952 version is a mechanical scene-for-scene remake.

prisoners of war were featured in many films after World War II. The British examples often made the camps seem almost too comfortable, despite the possibility of being shot while attempting escape; this was perhaps because they were all filled with the same familiar faces. *Albert RN, The Captive Heart, The Colditz Story, The Betrayal, Danger Within, Reach for the Sky* all found humour in the situation at any rate; whereas the American counterparts, *The Purple Heart, Prisoner of War, Stalag 17*, saw the harsher side which doubtless existed. The co-production, *The Bridge on the River Kwai*, gave a mixed picture of a Japanese camp; Britain's Hammer horror studio then produced *The Camp on Blood Island*, a fictitious record of atrocity, followed some years later by *The Secret of Blood Island*. Meanwhile the British in *The One That Got Away* paid tribute to the one German to escape from a British camp; and more recently *The Great Escape* showed the Americans coming some way towards the British idea of how jolly life in a camp can be. The ultimate absurdity was reached by an American TV series, *Hogan's Heroes*, which has a camp almost entirely controlled by the prisoners. The best serious film about prisoners of war remains undoubtedly Renoir's *La Grande Illusion*, made in 1937; though *King Rat* in 1965 made a fair bid to reveal the squalor and futility of the life. Recently comic adventure stories about the escape of POWs have included *Very Important Person, The Secret War of Harry Frigg, Where Eagles Dare* and *Hannibal Brooks*.

Women's camps were shown in *Two Thousand Women* (GB 1944), *Three Came Home* (US 1950) and *A Town Like Alice* (GB 1956).

private eyes : see *mystery.*

THE PRIVATE LIFE OF HENRY VIII (GB 1932). Credited with being the first British film to win success in the American market, this enjoyable historical romp was directed by Alexander Korda from a script by Lajos Biro and Arthur Wimperis. Charles Laughton (AA) gave one of his richest performances, with memorable assistance from Robert Donat, Elsa Lanchester and Binnie Barnes. Design by Vincent Korda, photography by Georges Perinal.

PRIVATE'S PROGRESS (GB 1956). The first of the Boulting Brothers' anti-establishment comedies, this took a sound swipe at the army, with Ian Carmichael as the innocent involved in red tape and regulations. Directed by John Boulting, written by himself and Frank Harvey from Alan Hackney's novel. Subsequent Boulting films attacked the unions (*I'm All Right, Jack* [59]) and the Church (*Heavens Above* [63]).

prizefighting: see *boxing*.

producer. On the stage this term may be equivalent to 'director', i.e. the man who actually marshals the actors and whose conception of the show is supreme. In the film world it almost always indicates the man in control of the budget, whether an independent or working for a big studio. He controls all personnel including the director, and though the film may originally be his overall conception, he normally delegates his artistic responsibilities, remaining responsible chiefly for the film's ultimate commercial success or failure.

production manager. The person responsible for administrative details of a production, e.g. salaries, transport, departmental expenditure.

programmer. Trade term for a routine feature of only moderate appeal, likely to form half a bill; similar to 'co-feature'.

PROKOVIEV, SERGEI (1891–1953). Russian composer whose main film scores were *Alexander Nevsky* (39), *Lermontov* (43) and *Ivan the Terrible* (42 and 46).

prophecy has interested film-makers only occasionally, but at least two outstanding films have resulted: *Metropolis* and *Things To Come*. *Just Imagine* painted a light-hearted picture, and *Seven Days in May* was not too frightening about what might be happening politically a few years from now; but one hopes not to take too seriously the predictions in *1984*, *The Time Machine*, *Fahrenheit 451*, *Alphaville*, *When Worlds Collide*, and *The World, the Flesh and the Devil*.

prostitutes for many years could not be so labelled in Hollywood films, which featured a surprising number of 'café hostesses'. It was however fairly easy to spot the real profession of the various ladies who played Sadie Thompson in *Rain*, of Marlene Dietrich in *Dishonoured* and *Shanghai Express*, of Bette Davis in *Of Human Bondage*, of Vivien Leigh in *Waterloo Bridge*, and of Joan Bennett in *Man Hunt*, to name but a few. The French, who have always called a spade a spade, flaunted the calling in hundreds of films including *Dedee D'Anvers*, *La Ronde*, *Le Plaisir*, *Boule de Suif*, *Le Long des Trottoirs*, *La Bonne Soupe*, *Adua et sa Compagnie* and *Les Compagnons de la Nuit*; Italy chipped in with *Mamma Roma* and Japan with *Street of Shame*. In the 50s Britain moved into the field with surprising eagerness—every other movie seemed to feature Dora Bryan in a plastic mac—and there were several alleged exposés of Soho corruption under such titles as *The Flesh is Weak*, *Passport to Shame* and *The World Ten Times Over*. Hollywood half-heartedly followed with some double-talking second features about call girls—*Why Girls Leave Home, Call Girl, Girls in the Night*—and some 'medical case histories' such as *The Three Faces of Eve, Girl of the Night*. Around 1960 the floodgates opened, eased by the sensationally successful Greek comedy *Never on Sunday* (and some continental imitators like *Always on Saturday* and *Every Night of the Week*). Among English-speaking stars who have since played prostitutes are Shirley Maclaine in *Irma La Douce*, Sophia Loren in *Lady L*, Carroll Baker in *Sylvia*, Shirley Jones in *Elmer Gantry*, Nancy Kwan in *The World of Suzie Wong*, Elizabeth Taylor in *Butterfield 8*, Diane Cilento in *Rattle of a Simple Man*, Carol White in *Poor Cow*, Inger Stevens in *Five Card Stud*. Brothels have been shown in *Lady L, A Walk on the Wild Side, The Revolt of Mamie Stover, A House is not a Home, Ulysses, The Balcony, A Funny Thing Happened on the Way to the Forum, The Assassination Bureau, The Best House in London*, and an increasing number of westerns. In *Our Man Flint*, girls were described as 'pleasure units' . . .

See also: *courtesans*.

PROUTY, JED (1879–1956). American character actor with stage experience, in films from the mid-20s. Best remembered as father of *The Jones Family*; he appeared in over a dozen episodes of this domestic comedy series between 1935 and 1940. Also: *Broadway Melody* (28), *George White's Scandals* (35), *The Texas Rangers* (36), *Roar of the Press* (41), *Mug Town* (43), *Guilty Bystander* (49), many others.

PROVINE, DOROTHY (1937–). American leading lady who became well known as night club entertainer in TV series *The Roaring Twenties*. Films include *Wall of Noise* (63), *It's a Mad Mad Mad Mad World* (63), *Good Neighbour Sam* (64), *That Darn Cat* (65), *The Great Race* (65), *One Spy Too Many* (66), *Kiss the Girls and Make Them Die* (66), *Who's Minding the Mint* (67), etc.

PROWSE, JULIET (1937–). South African leading lady, in Hollywood from 1958, at first as dancer. *Can Can* (59), *G.I. Blues* (60), *The Fiercest Heart* (61), *The Right Approach* (61), *The Second Time Around* (61), *Run For Your Wife* (66), etc. TV series: *Meet Mona McCluskey* (65).

PSYCHO (US 1960). Alfred Hitchcock's horror comic, which he appears to have made as a joke, in the spirit of seeing whether he could get away with its nastiness. The critics found it revolting at first, but some later came round and admitted that once you were used to the idea of vivid bathtub murders, etc., it was done in Hitchcock's usual accomplished manner. Unfortunately it enabled less talented producers subsequently to indulge in similar shock tactics and is partly responsible for the low ebb of the thriller today with its emphasis on gore. Written by Joseph Stefano from a novel by

Robert Bloch which is rather more subtle than the film; photographed by John L. Russell; with Anthony Perkins.

psychology is featured most prominently in American films—quite
naturally since the United States is the home of the psychiatrist.
However, one of the best serious psychological films, *Mine Own
Executioner*, did come from Britain and showed the doctor to be
more in need of help than the patient; while two other notable
British films, *Thunder Rock* and *Dead of Night*, centred on the
depiction of psychological states.

   Although films about psychology can be firmly traced back to
The Cabinet of Dr Caligari and *Secrets of a Soul*, the subject took its
firmest hold in the middle of World War II, when so many people
needed reassurance; the recounting of dreams to an analyst could
even take the place of musical numbers in a romantic trifle like
Lady in the Dark. Soon we were inundated with melodramas like
Spellbound, *The Dark Mirror* and *Possessed*, in which the question
to be answered was not so much who or how but why; and it
wasn't until about 1950, with *Harvey*, that analysts could be
laughed at. In the 50s the schizophrenic drama took on a new
lease of life (*The Three Faces of Eve*, *Lizzie*, *Vertigo*), as did the
tendency to guy individual psychiatrists while still claiming to
respect the profession (*Oh Men Oh Women*, *Mirage*, *A Fine Madness*,
The Group, *What a Way To Go*). Of course, films were still made
which took the whole matter with deadly seriousness, as in *The
Cobweb*, *The Mark*, *The Third Secret* and *Pressure Point*. John Huston's
under-rated film on the life of *Freud* may have been unlucky to
arrive at a time of change: the fashion is now for case histories
in which no solution is offered (*Repulsion*, *Morgan*, *Cul-de-Sac*) or
psychological horror comics such as *Psycho*, *Homicidal*, and *The
Night Walker*; while in *Promise Her Anything* we are finally shown a
psychiatrist (Robert Cummings) who doesn't believe in psychiatry.
   See also *dreams*; *fantasy*; *amnesia*; *case histories*.

PUBLIC ENEMY (US 1931). One of the most violent of the early sound
   gangster films; it helped to swell official opinion against them, and
   James Cagney, who dispensed a lot of sudden death in this one, had
   to reform in *G-Men* (35), in which he stays on the right side of the
   law. Directed by William Wellman from a script by Harvey Thew;
   photographed by Dev Jennings. It still has powerful sequences
   despite its undeniably dated air.

PUDOVKIN, V. (VSEVOLOD) (1893–1953). Russian film theorist, writer
   and actor. Best remembered as director: *Mother* (26), *The End of St
   Petersburg* (27), *Storm over Asia* (28), *The Deserter* (33), *General
   Suvorov* (41), many others which have not travelled.

PUGLIA, FRANK (c. 1894–   ). American character actor with
   vaudeville experience. *Viva Villa* (34), *Maisie* (39), *The Mark of*

Zorro (40), *Jungle Book* (42), *Phantom of the Opera* (43), *Blood on the Sun* (45), *The Desert Hawk* (50), *The Burning Hills* (56), *Cry Tough* (59), many others.

PULVER, LILO or LISELOTTE (1929–   ). Swiss/German leading lady. Films include *A Time to Live and a Time to Die* (US) (59), *One, Two, Three* (US) (61), *A Global Affair* (US) (63), *La Religieuse* (Fr.) (65), *Le Jardinier d'Argentueil* (Fr.) (66).

THE PUMPKIN EATER (GB 1964). A flashily-made, kaleidoscopic film by Jack Clayton about an unhappily married well-to-do woman in London; from Penelope Mortimer's novel. Despite the tiresomeness of the character, there are many brilliantly-handled sequences and Anne Bancroft gives a superb performance. The whole film, indeed, has the feel of life about it. With Peter Finch, James Mason; scripted by Harold Pinter; photographed by Oswald Morris; music by Georges Delerue.

PURCELL, DICK (1908–1944). American leading man of second features. *Man Hunt* (36), *Navy Blues* (37), *Air Devils* (38), *Nancy Drew, Detective* (39), *King of the Zombies* (41), *Phantom Killer* (42), *The Mystery of the Thirteenth Guest* (43), *Timber Queen* (44), etc.

PURCELL, NOEL (1900–   ). Tall, usually bearded, Irish character actor and comedian. Films include *Captain Boycott* (47), *The Blue Lagoon* (48), *Doctor in the House* (53), *Moby Dick* (56), *Watch Your Stern* (60), *Mutiny on the Bounty* (62), *Lord Jim* (65), *Arrivederci Baby* (66), many others.

PURDELL, REGINALD (1896–1953) (R. Grasdorf). British light character actor, mostly on stage and music hall. *Congress Dances* (31), *Q Planes* (38), *Many Tanks Mr Atkins* (40), *Pack Up Your Troubles* (40), *Variety Jubilee* (43), *We Dive at Dawn* (43), *2000 Women* (44), *Holiday Camp* (47), *Captain Boycott* (48), etc.

PURDOM, EDMUND (c. 1926–   ). British light leading man with stage experience. *Titanic* (52), *Julius Caesar* (53), *The Student Prince* (54), *The Egyptian* (54), *The King's Thief* (56), *Nights of Rasputin* (61), *The Comedy Man* (63), *The Beauty Jungle* (64), etc.

PURVIANCE, EDNA (1894-1958). American leading lady of silent days. *A Night Out* (15) (and other early Chaplin films including *Easy Street, The Count, The Cure, The Adventurer, Shoulder Arms*), *Sunnyside* (19), *The Kid* (21), *The Pilgrim* (23), *A Woman of Paris* (23), *The Seagull* (26), *Limelight* (52), many others.

PYGMALION (GB 1938). Despite 1964's *My Fair Lady*, this straight version of Shaw's play, directed by Anthony Asquith and Leslie Howard, remains the most satisfying and perfectly cast: Howard as Higgins, Wendy Hiller as Eliza, Scott Sunderland as Pickering and

Wilfrid Lawson as Doolittle. Produced by Gabriel Pascal, photographed by Harry Stradling, with music by Arthur Honegger, it remains one of the cinema's most civilized comedies.

PYLE, DENVER (1921–   ). American character actor, mostly in TV and big-screen westerns. Played the sheriff who shot *Bonnie and Clyde* (67). TV series: *The Doris Day Show* (68–69).

Q

QUAI DES BRUMES (France 1938). A highly influential study in poetic pessimism, directed by Marcel Carne from Jacques Prevert's script. Romance of the highest order is distilled from a squalid situation in foggy Le Havre, with Jean Gabin as a victim of circumstances on the run from the police, and Michele Morgan on hand to comfort him briefly before the inevitable tragic finale. Music by Maurice Jaubert.

QUALEN, JOHN (1899–   ) (John Oleson). Canadian-born Norwegian character actor, in Hollywood from the 30s playing amiably ineffectual foreign types. *Arrowsmith* (debut) (32), *Black Fury* (35), *Seventh Heaven* (37), *The Grapes of Wrath* (40), *Out of the Fog* (41), *All That Money Can Buy* (41), *Jungle Book* (42), *Casablanca* (42), *Fairy Tale Murder* (45), *Adventure* (46), *The Fugitive* (48), *The Big Steal* (49), *Hans Christian Andersen* (52), *The High and the Mighty* (54), *The Searchers* (56), *Two Rode Together* (60), *The Man Who Shot Liberty Valance* (62), *The Prize* (63), *The Seven Faces of Dr Lao* (64), *Cheyenne Autumn* (64), *The Sons of Katie Elder* (65), *A Big Hand for the Little Lady* (66), *Firecreek* (67), many others.

QUAYLE, ANNA (1937–   ). British comedienne. *Drop Dead Darling* (67), *Smashing Time* (67), *Chitty Chitty Bang Bang* (68), etc.

QUAYLE, ANTHONY (1913–   ). Distinguished British stage actor and director, in occasional films as actor. *Hamlet* (48), *Saraband for Dead Lovers* (48), *Oh Rosalinda* (55), *The Battle of the River Plate* (56), *The Wrong Man* (US) (57), *Woman in a Dressing-Gown* (57), *Ice Cold in Alex* (58), *Serious Charge* (59), *The Challenge* (60), *The Guns of Navarone* (61), *Lawrence of Arabia* (62), *HMS Defiant* (62), *The Fall of the Roman Empire* (64), *East of Sudan* (64), *Operation Crossbow* (64), *A Study in Terror* (65), *Before Winter Comes* (69), *Anne of the Thousand Days* (70), etc. TV series: *Strange Report* (69).

QUEEN CHRISTINA (US 1933). This historical romance seemed less a calculated box-office film than an act of homage by its production company (MGM) towards its star (Greta Garbo). Expensively presented, directed with care and craft by Rouben Mamoulian, it makes a flawless example of bespoke tailoring from Hollywood's golden age. The plot, concerning a royal love affair in 16th-century Sweden, is fictitious. John Gilbert co-starred at Garbo's own request, but it was his last major role.

794

QUEEN KELLY (US 1928). A typical unfinished extravagance written and directed by Erich Von Stroheim, about an ill-fated romance between a young convent girl and the consort of the mad queen of a petty European principality. Further fragments keep on turning up, taking the story into a brothel and to Africa. Gloria Swanson starred, with Walter Byron and Seena Owen.

THE QUEEN OF SPADES (GB 1949). The Pushkin story has been filmed several times in Russia. This atmospheric version by Rodney Ackland and Arthur Boys, directed by Thorold Dickinson, goes all out to surpass Eisenstein in imagery but despite brilliant moments is finally too slow to have the necessary grip. Edith Evans plays the aged countess who has reputedly sold her soul to the devil in exchange for the secret of winning at faro, Anton Walbrook the soldier desperate to learn the trick.

QUE VIVA MEXICO (Mexico 1932). Eisenstein's famous epic of Mexican history, based on funds supplied and later withdrawn by Upton Sinclair, was to have been an episodic semi-documentary. It was never completed, but fragments have been bought up and shown as *Thunder over Mexico* (by Sol Lesser), *Death Day* (by Upton Sinclair) and *Time in the Sun* (by Marie Seton).

THE QUIET MAN (US 1952). Typically easy-going romantic comedy of John Ford's later period, enjoyably set in a never-never Ireland and concerning an ex-boxer's Petruchio-like courtship of a fiery colleen. John Wayne, Maureen O'Hara, Victor McLaglen and Barry Fitzgerald head a hand-picked cast; music by Victor Young; original story by Maurice Walsh.

QUILLAN, EDDIE (1907–). Bouncy, beaming American comic actor, in Hollywood from 1930. Many films include *Big Money* (30), *Mutiny on the Bounty* (35), *Young Mr Lincoln* (39), *The Grapes of Wrath* (40), *Dark Streets of Cairo* (40), *Flying Blind* (41), *Sideshow* (50), *Brigadoon* (54), *The Ghost and Mr Chicken* (66); latterly on TV.

QUIMBY, FRED (1886–1965). American producer, head of MGM's short subjects department 1926–56. Specially known for development of Tom and Jerry cartoons.

QUINE, RICHARD (1920–). American director, former leading man (*The World Changes* [32] as juvenile, *Babes on Broadway* [40], *My Sister Eileen* [41], *For Me and My Gal* [42], etc.). Directed *The Sunny Side of the Street* (51), *Drive a Crooked Road* (54), *Pushover* (54), *My Sister Eileen* (55), *The Solid Gold Cadillac* (56), *Operation Mad Ball* (58), *Bell, Book and Candle* (58), *The World of Suzie Wong* (60), *The Notorious Landlady* (62), *Paris When It Sizzles* (64), *How to Murder Your Wife* (65), *Oh Dad, Poor Dad* (66), *Hotel* (67), *A Talent for Loving* (69), *The Moonshine War* (70), etc.

Quinn, Anthony

QUINN, ANTHONY (1915–   ). Mexican-born leading actor, in films since 1936, latterly noted for full-blooded performances. *Parole* (36), *The Plainsman* (36), *Union Pacific* (39), *Blood and Sand* (41), *Ghost Breakers* (41), *The Black Swan* (42), *The Ox-Bow Incident* (43), *Buffalo Bill* (44), *China Sky* (45), *Tycoon* (48), *The Brave Bulls* (51), *Viva Zapata* (AA) (52), *The World in His Arms* (52), *Ride Vaquero* (53), *Blowing Wild* (54), *The Long Wait* (54), *La Strada* (It.) (54), *Attila the Hun* (It.) (54), *Ulysses* (55), *Lust for Life* (AA) (56), *The Man from Del Rio* (56), *The Hunchback of Notre Dame* (56), *The River's Edge* (57), *Hot Spell* (58), *Black Orchid* (58), *Last Train from Gun Hill* (58), *Warlock* (59), *Heller in Pink Tights* (60), *Savage Innocents* (60), *The Guns of Navarone* (61), *Barabbas* (62), *Blood Money (Requiem for a Heavyweight)* (63), *The Visit* (63), *Zorba the Greek* (64), *A High Wind in Jamaica* (65), *Lost Command* (66), *The Happening* (67), *The Twenty-fifth Hour* (67), *The Rover* (67), *The Shoes of the Fisherman* (68), *The Magus* (68), *The Secret of Santa Vittoria* (69), *A Walk in the Spring Rain* (69), *Nobody Loves Flapping Eagle* (70), others. Directed one film: *The Buccaneer* (59).

quota. By Act of Parliament renters are obliged to sell, and exhibitors to show, a varying proportion of British-made films. There has not always been enough British talent to fill the necessary number of releases: hence the notorious 'quota quickies' of the 20s and 30s, and much second-feature material more recently, which however bad can invariably get a circuit booking providing it has a British quota ticket. The normal quota which an exhibitor has to fill is 30% for features, 25% for supporting programme. This contrasts markedly with independent television contractors, whose programmes must be 86% British.

QUO VADIS? The Biblical epic by Henryk Sienkiewicz has been filmed three times: in Italy in 1912 and 1924, and in the US in 1951. The third version, though less impressive as a product of its period than the others, was certainly the most spectacular, with the appropriate cast of thousands and a well-drilled squad of Christian-gorging lions. Robert Taylor and Deborah Kerr suffered under Peter Ustinov's Nero; Mervyn Le Roy directed.

R

RABIER, JEAN (1927–   ). French cinematographer. *Cleo de 5 à 7* (61), *Ophelia* (62), *Landru* (62), *La Baie des Anges* (63), *Les Parapluies de Cherbourg* (64), *Le Bonheur* (65), *The Champagne Murders* (66), *Les Biches* (68), etc.

RACKIN, MARTIN LEE (1918–   ). American screenwriter (*Air Raid Wardens* [42], *Murder Inc. (The Enforcer)* [51], *Long John Silver* [55], *North to Alaska* [59], many others). Also producer: *Santiago* (56), *Top Secret Affair* (57), *The Horse Soldiers* (also co-wrote) (59), *Stagecoach* (66), *Rough Night in Jericho* (67), others.

RADD, RONALD (c. 1926–   ). British character actor, usually in heavy roles. *The Camp on Blood Island* (58), *The Small World of Sammy Lee* (63), *Up Jumped a Swagman* (65), *Where the Spies Are* (65), *Mr Ten Per Cent* (66), etc. Much on TV.

RADEMAKERS, FONS (1921–   ). Dutch director, with stage experience. *Doctor in the Village* (58), *The Knife* (61), etc.

RADFORD, BASIL (1897–1952). British light character comedian, on stage from 1922, films from 1929 (*Barnum Was Right*). Became popular when he and Naunton Wayne played two imperturbable Englishmen abroad in *The Lady Vanishes* (38). Later: *Just William* (38), *Night Train to Munich* (40), *Crooks Tour* (40), *Next of Kin* (42), *Millions Like Us* (43), *The Way to the Stars* (45), *Dead of Night* (45), *The Captive Heart* (46), *Girl in a Million* (46), *It's Not Cricket* (48), *Passport to Pimlico* (48), *The Winslow Boy* (48), *Quartet* (48), *Whisky Galore* (48), *Chance of a Lifetime* (50), *The Galloping Major* (51), etc.

RADNITZ, ROBERT B. (1925–   ). American producer of 'family' films. *A Dog of Flanders* (60), *Misty* (62), *Island of the Blue Dolphins* (64), *And Now Miguel* (66), *My Side of the Mountain* (68), etc.

RAFFERTY, CHIPS (1909–   ) (John Goffage). Rangy Australian character actor with varied experience before coming to films. *Dad Rudd, M.P.* (39), *Forty Thousand Horsemen* (40), *The Rats of Tobruk* (42), *The Overlanders* (46), *The Loves of Joanna Godden* (GB) (46), *Eureka Stockade* (47), *Bitter Springs* (51), *Kangaroo* (52), *King of the Coral Sea* (54), *Walk into Paradise* (56), *The Sundowners* (60), *Mutiny on the Bounty* (62), *They're a Weird Mob* (66), *Kona Coast* (68), etc.

Rafferty, Frances

RAFFERTY, FRANCES (1922–). American leading lady. *Seven Sweethearts* (42), *Dragon Seed* (44), *Abbott and Costello in Hollywood* (45), *Lady at Midnight* (48), *Rodeo* (52), *The Shanghai Story* (54), etc. TV series: *December Bride*.

RAFT, GEORGE (1895–). Smooth American leading man of the 30s and 40s; former professional athlete, gambler, etc. (His biopic, *Spin of a Coin* [61], starred Ray Danton.) Also a night club dancer. Films include: *Quick Millions* (31), *Scarface* (32), *Night After Night* (33), *If I Had a Million* (33), *The Bowery* (33), *Bolero* (34), *Limehouse Blues* (35), *Rumba* (36), *The Glass Key* (36), *Souls at Sea* (37), *You and Me* (38), *Spawn of the North* (39), *Each Dawn I Die* (39), *Invisible Stripes* (40), *The House Across the Bay* (40), *They Drive By Night* (40), *Manpower* (41), *Broadway* (42), *Background to Danger* (43), *Nob Hill* (45), *Mr Ace* (46), *Christmas Eve* (47), *Hounded* (*Johnny Allegro*) (49), *Rogue Cop* (53), *The Black Widow* (54), *A Bullet for Joey* (55), *Some Like It Hot* (59), *Jet Over the Atlantic* (59), *Rififi in Panama* (Fr.) (66), *Skidoo* (68), many others.

RAGLAND, RAGS (1905–1946). American character comedian, former boxer. *Whistling in the Dark* (41), *The War Against Mrs Hadley* (42), *Panama Hattie* (42), *Girl Crazy* (43), *Her Highness and the Bellboy* (45), *Anchors Aweigh* (45), etc.

railway stations have provided a major setting for some memorable films including *The Ghost Train, Doctor Zhivago, Knight Without Armour, I'll Never Forget Whatshisname* (with its white 'dream' station), *Union Station, Waterloo Road, Anna Karenina, Grand Central Station, Under the Clock, Brief Encounter, Oh Mr Porter, The Titfield Thunderbolt, High Noon, In the Heat of the Night* and *The Train* . . . while Orson Welles made *The Trial* entirely within a deserted station, and de Sica made *Indiscretion* among the crowds of Rome's Stazione Termini.

See also: *trains*.

RAIMU (1883–1946) (Jules Muraire). French character actor and comedian with music-hall background. *Marius* (31), *Fanny* (32), *César* (34), *Un Carnet de Bal* (37), *La Femme du Boulanger* (39), *La Fille du Puisatier* (40), *Heart of a Nation* (40), *Les Inconnus dans la Maison* (42), *Colonel Chabert* (44), *L'Homme au Chapeau Rond* (46), etc.

RAIN. Somerset Maugham's story of the conflict between a missionary and a woman of highly doubtful character has been filmed three times in Hollywood: in 1928 with Gloria Swanson and Lionel Barrymore, in 1932 with Joan Crawford and Walter Huston, and in 1956 (as *Miss Sadie Thompson*) with Rita Hayworth and Jose Ferrer. In each case the production code made you guess what the lady's actual profession was.

rain has been put to many uses by film scenarists. It was the direct
cause of dramatic situations in *Rebecca* (a shower flattened Joan
Fontaine's hair-do just as she arrived at Manderley); in *The
Loneliness of the Long Distance Runner* (it revealed evidence which
the hero was trying to conceal); in *Floods of Fear* (it permitted the
escape of three convicts, one of whom then rescued the heroine);
in *The African Queen* (it raised the water level and so released the
boat from the reeds which held it captive); in *Desk Set* (it persuaded
Spencer Tracy to accept Katharine Hepburn's offer of hospitality);
in *Pygmalion* (it caused the meeting of Higgins and Eliza); in *Sands
of the Kalahari* (it flooded a pit in which Stuart Whitman was
imprisoned, and permitted his escape); in *When Tomorrow Comes*
(it stranded Charles Boyer and Irene Dunne in a remote church
for the night); and in many others. Two splendid symbolic uses
were in *Saraband for Dead Lovers* (a raindrop made a stained glass
madonna appear to weep at the ill-fated wedding) and *The Stars
Look Down* (as the hero and heroine make love, two raindrops
intertwine on the window pane).

   Rain has often been used symbolically as a relief from tension
and heat, in films as diverse as *Night of the Iguana*, *Passport to Pimlico*,
The Long Hot Summer, *Key Largo*, *Twelve Angry Men*, *Black Narcissus*,
The Good Earth and *Rain* itself. It has provided a solemn or ominous
background in *Psycho*, *Term of Trial*, *Rashomon*, *It Always Rains on
Sunday*, *Room at the Top*, *Julius Caesar*, *The Robe*, *Fires on the Plain*,
The Collector and many others. It has a particularly depressing
effect at a funeral, as was shown in *The Glass Key* and *Our Town*;
or at an assassination (*Foreign Correspondent*). But it can also be used
for farcical purposes: in *Three Men in a Boat*, *The Silencers*, *Fraternally
Yours*, *Oh Mr Porter*, etc. And it can provide a comedy twist, as at
the end of *The Lady Vanishes*, when the English travellers so eager
to get back to the test match find that rain has stopped play.

   It can produce a decorative effect (*Les Parapluies de Cherbourg*,
Miracle in the Rain, *Breakfast at Tiffany's*). It can be spectacular
(the climax of *Journey into Fear*, the glistening streets in *The Third
Man*, the downpour in *The Rains Came*, the battle in the rain in
Tower of London). And it can provide a cue for song: 'Isn't it a
Lovely Day to Be Caught in the Rain' in *Top Hat*, the title songs
of *Singing in the Rain* and *Stormy Weather*, 'The Rain in Spain' in
My Fair Lady, 'April Showers' in *The Jolson Story*, 'Little April
Shower' in *Bambi*. In fact, it seems to be by far the most versatile
of all the film-maker's effects.

†RAINER, LUISE (1910–   ). Austrian actress on stage from 1930;
later in Hollywood films. *Escapade* (35), *The Great Ziegfeld* (AA)
(36), *The Good Earth* (AA) (37), *The Emperor's Candlesticks* (37),
The Big City (37), *The Great Waltz* (38), *The Toy Wife* (38), *Dramatic
School* (38), *Hostages* (43). Retired.

RAINES, ELLA (1921–   ). American leading lady of the 40s, with brief stage experience. *Phantom Lady* (43), *Hail the Conquering Hero* (43), *Enter Arsène Lupin* (44), *The Suspect* (45), *The Runaround* (46), *Time Out of Mind* (47), *Brute Force* (47), *Mr Ashton Was Indiscreet* (48), *Ride the Man Down* (52), *Man in the Road* (GB) (54), etc. Retired. TV series: *Janet Dean Registered Nurse.*

THE RAINS CAME. Louis Bromfield's novel of the high days of British India was filmed in 1939 with Myrna Loy and Tyrone Power, and in 1955 with Lana Turner and Richard Burton. (The title was changed to *The Rains of Ranchipur.*)

†RAINS, CLAUDE (1889–1967). Suave, incisive British character actor, long resident in America. Wide stage experience. *The Invisible Man* (33), *Crime without Passion* (34), *The Man Who Reclaimed His Head* (34), *The Mystery of Edwin Drood* (35), *The Clairvoyant* (GB) (35), *The Last Outpost* (35), *Anthony Adverse* (36), *Hearts Divided* (36), *Stolen Holiday* (36), *The Prince and the Pauper* (37), *They Won't Forget* (37), *Gold Is Where You Find It* (38), *The Adventures of Robin Hood* (38), *White Banners* (38), *Four Daughters* (38), *They Made Me a Criminal* (39), *Juarez* (39), *Mr Smith Goes to Washington* (39), *Four Wives* (39), *Daughters Courageous* (39), *Saturday's Children* (39), *The Sea Hawk* (40), *Lady with Red Hair* (as David Belasco) (40), *Four Mothers* (40), *Here Comes Mr Jordan* (41), *The Wolf Man* (41), *King's Row* (41), *Moontide* (42), *Now Voyager* (42), *Casablanca* (42), *Forever and a Day* (43), *Phantom of the Opera* (title role) (43), *Passage to Marseilles* (44), *Mr Skeffington* (44), *This Love of Ours* (45), *Caesar and Cleopatra* (GB) (45), *Angel on My Shoulder* (46), *Deception* (46), *Notorious* (46), *The Unsuspected* (47), *Strange Holiday* (47), *The Passionate Friends* (GB) (47), *Rope of Sand* (49), *Song of Surrender* (49), *The White Tower* (50), *Where Danger Lives* (50), *Sealed Cargo* (51), *The Man Who Watched Trains Go By* (GB) (52), *Lisbon* (56), *This Earth Is Mine* (59), *The Lost World* (60), *Lawrence of Arabia* (62), *Twilight of Honour* (63). Made several TV guest appearances.

RAKOFF, ALVIN (1927–   ). Canadian TV director resident in Britain. Films include *Passport to Shame* (58), *Treasure of San Teresa* (59), *On Friday at Eleven* (61), *The Comedy Man* (64), *Hoffman* (70), etc.

RAKSIN, DAVID (1912–   ). American composer, in Hollywood from mid-30s. Arranged Chaplin's score for *Modern Times* (36); own scores include *Laura* (44), *The Secret Life of Walter Mitty* (47), *The Bad and the Beautiful* (52), *Separate Tables* (58), *Too Late Blues* (62), *Two Weeks in Another Town* (62), *Invitation to a Gunfighter* (65), *A Big Hand for the Little Lady* (66), etc.

RALLI, GIOVANNI (1935–   ). Italian leading lady. *The Children are Watching Us* (43), *Lights of Variety* (49), *La Lupa* (53), *The Bigamist* (56), *Il Generale Della Rovere* (59), *Deadfall* (68), *Cannon For Cordoba* (70), many others.

RALPH, JESSIE (1864–1944) (Jessie Ralph Chambers). American character actress who came to Hollywood late in life and played many endearing granny roles. *Child of Manhattan* (33), *David Copperfield* (as Peggotty) (34), *Captain Blood* (35), *Camille* (36), *San Francisco* (36), *Café Society* (39), *The Bluebird* (40), *They Met in Bombay* (last film) (41), etc.

RALSTON, ESTHER (1902–). American leading lady of the 20s and 30s. *The Phantom Fortune* (serial) (23), *Peter Pan* (24), *A Kiss for Cinderella* (25), *Lucky Devil* (26), *Old Ironsides* (26), *Figures Don't Lie* (27), *The Sawdust Parade* (28), *The Prodigal* (31), *Sadie McKee* (33), *Hollywood Boulevard* (36), *Tin Pan Alley* (last to date) (40), etc.

RALSTON, JOBYNA (1901–). American leading lady of the 20s, especially with Harold Lloyd. *Why Worry* (23), *Girl Shy* (24), *The Freshman* (24), *For Heaven's Sake* (26), *Wings* (27), many others.

RALSTON, VERA HRUBA (1921–). Czech actress, former skating champion. In US from late 30s, films from 1942. Married Herbert Yates, boss of Republic Studios, and appeared exclusively in his pictures. *Ice Capades* (42), *Storm over Lisbon* (44), *Dakota* (45), *Murder in the Music Hall* (46), *The Plainsman and the Lady* (47), *Fair Wind to Java* (53), *Jubilee Trail* (54), *Accused of Murder* (57), etc. Retired.

RAMBEAU, MARJORIE (1889–). American character actress. *Her Man* (30), *Man's Castle* (34), *The Rains Came* (39), *Tugboat Annie Sails Again* (title role) (41), *So Ends Our Night* (41), *Tobacco Road* (41), *Broadway* (42), *Army Wives* (45), *Abandoned* (49), *Torch Song* (53), *The View from Pompey's Head* (56), *Man of a Thousand Faces* (57), others.

RAMONA. Helen Hunt Jackson's novel about an Indian girl was filmed four times: by Griffith in 1910, with Mary Pickford and Henry B. Walthall; by Donald Crisp in 1916, with Adda Gleason and Monroe Salisbury; by Edwin Carewe in 1928, with Dolores del Rio and Warner Baxter; and by Henry King in 1936, with Loretta Young and Don Ameche.

RAMPLING, CHARLOTTE (c. 1944–). British leading lady. *Rotten to the Core* (65), *Georgy Girl* (66), *The Long Duel* (67), *The Damned* (69).

RANDALL, TONY (1920–). American comedy actor adept at light drunks, depressives and friends of the hero. Stage and radio experience. *Oh Men, Oh Women* (57), *No Down Payment* (58), *Pillow Talk* (59), *Huckleberry Finn* (60), *Let's Make Love* (61), *Boys' Night Out* (62), *The Brass Bottle* (63), *The Seven Faces of Dr Lao* (64), *Send Me No Flowers* (64), *Amanda* (*The ABC Murders*) (65), *Fluffy* (65), *Our Man in Marrakesh* (*Bang! Bang! You're Dead*) (66), *Hello Down There* (68), etc. TV series: *Mr Peepers* (52–55).

RANDELL, RON (1918–   ). Australian leading man with radio experience; has appeared in films and TV episodes all over the world. *It Had To Be You* (47), *Lorna Doone* (50), *Kiss Me Kate* (53), *Bulldog Drummond at Bay* (54), *I Am a Camera* (55), *Beyond Mombasa* (56), *The Story of Esther Costello* (58), *King of Kings* (61), *The Longest Day* (62), *Gold for the Caesars* (63), scores of others.

RANDLE, FRANK (1901–1957) (Arthur McEvoy). Lancashire music-hall comedian of immense vulgarity; made his own slapdash but highly popular films in the 40s. *Somewhere in England* (40), *Somewhere in Camp* (42), *Somewhere in Civvies* (43), *School for Randle* (47), *Home Sweet Home* (47), *Holidays with Pay* (48), *It's a Grand Life* (53), etc.

RANDOLPH, ELSIE (1904–   ). British revue artiste, often teamed in the 30s with Jack Buchanan. Films include *Rise and Shine* (32), *Yes, Mr Brown* (33), *That's a Good Girl* (33), *This'll Make You Whistle* (35), *Smash and Grab* (38), *Cheer the Brave* (50), etc.

RANDOLPH, JANE (1919–   ). American leading lady of the 40s. *Highways by Night* (42), *Cat People* (42), *In the Meantime, Darling* (44), *Jealousy* (46), *T Men* (48), *Abbott and Costello Meet Frankenstein* (last to date) (49), etc.

RANDOM HARVEST (US 1942). Immensely popular in the drab wartime days of its release, this romantic film was taken from a James Hilton novel about a man who marries while suffering from amnesia; he gets his memory back, is restored to his former position in life, and fails to recognize his wife when she comes to work as his secretary. Sheer hokum complete with roses round the door, but persuasively produced in MGM's best manner, carefully directed by Mervyn le Roy, and with irresistible star performances from Ronald Colman and Greer Garson.

RANK, J. ARTHUR (LORD RANK) (1888–   ). British flour magnate who entered films in the mid-30s in the hope of promoting interest in religion. Formed or took over so many companies including production, distribution and exhibition that by the mid-40s he was accused of monopolistic tendencies. His influence was generally excellent, and he encouraged independent producers (sometimes unwisely) but his organization generally suffered from a preponderance of accountants unable to understand the ingredients of a good film. Without their financial advice, however, the empire might well have perished altogether. At its height it fostered such production companies as the Archers, Cineguild, Wessex, Individual and Two Cities. In recent years the film side of the organization has proved less important than its hotels, bowling alleys and such developments as Xerox-copying; but it includes Odeon and Gaumont Theatres, Rank Film Distributors, Pinewood Studios,

Denham Laboratories, etc. A biography, *Mr Rank*, by Alan Wood, was published in 1952.

RANSOHOFF, MARTIN (1927–   ). American writer and executive. Chairman of Filmways, producers of such TV series as *The Beverly Hillbillies* and *The Addams Family*. Has also produced films: *Boys' Night Out* (62), *The Wheeler Dealers* (63), *The Americanization of Emily* (64), *Topkapi* (64), *The Sandpiper* (65), *The Loved One* (65), *The Cincinnati Kid* (65), *Don't Make Waves* (67), *Ice Station Zebra* (68), *The Moonshine War* (70), etc.

rape was virtually unmentionable in English-speaking films until Warners got away with it in *Johnny Belinda* in 1947. Then it became the centre of attention in *Outrage, Peyton Place, Wicked As They Come, A Streetcar Named Desire, Last Train from Gun Hill, Trial, Five Gates to Hell* (in which the victim was a nun), *The Chapman Report, The Mark, Anatomy of a Murder, Town Without Pity, The Party's Over* (in which the victim proved to be dead), and *The Penthouse*. In *Waterhole Three* James Coburn, accused of the crime, shrugged it off as 'assault with a friendly weapon'. There was much talk of rape in *The Knack* and *Lock Up Your Daughters*, threat of rape in *Experiment in Terror* and *Cape Fear*, and an accusation of rape in *Term of Trial*. Foreign language films on the subject have included *Rashomon, The Virgin Spring, Two Women, Viridiana* and the Greek *Amok*.

RAPHAEL, FREDERIC (1931–   ). British writer. *Nothing But the Best* (64), *Darling* (AA, BFA) (65), *Two for the Road* (67), *Far From the Madding Crowd* (67), etc.

RAPHAELSON, SAMSON (c. 1896–   ). American writer of plays (including *The Jazz Singer*, filmed 1927) and screenplays, mainly sophisticated comedies for Lubitsch: *The Smiling Lieutenant* (30), *One Hour With You* (32), *Trouble in Paradise* (32), *The Merry Widow* (34), *Angel* (37), *The Shop around the Corner* (39), *Heaven Can Wait* (43), *The Harvey Girls* (45), *Mr Music* (50), *Hilda Crane* (56), *But Not for Me* (58), etc.

RAPPER, IRVING (c. 1898–   ). American director with stage experience, long associated with Warner films. *Shining Victory* (41), *One Foot in Heaven* (41), *The Gay Sisters* (42), *Now Voyager* (42), *The Adventures of Mark Twain* (44), *Rhapsody in Blue* (45), *The Corn Is Green* (46), *Deception* (46), *The Voice of the Turtle* (48), *The Glass Menagerie* (50), *Another Man's Poison* (GB) (51), *Forever Female* (52), *The Brave One* (56), *Strange Intruder* (57), *Marjorie Morningstar* (58), *The Miracle* (59), others.

RASHOMON (IN THE WOODS) (Japan 1951). The film which after many years opened Western cinemas to Japanese films; America has even paid it the compliment of remaking it (1964) as *The Outrage*. Concerning the different views of the four people concerned about a moment of violence, it was a stylistic revelation and established Akira Kurosawa as an O.K. name even though his subsequent films seldom got beyond the very specialized halls.

RASPUTIN, the mysterious monk who dominated members of the Tsar's family just before the Russian revolution, has been a popular film subject. Conrad Veidt played him in *Rasputin* (Germany 1930); Lionel Barrymore in *Rasputin and the Empress* (US 1932); Harry Baur in *Rasputin* (France 1938); Edmund Purdom in *Nights of Rasputin* (Italy 1960) and Christopher Lee in *Rasputin the Mad Monk* (Britain 1966); while 1968 brought Gert Frobe in the role in *I Killed Rasputin*.

RASUMNY, MIKHAIL (1890–1956). Russian character actor with stage experience, long in Hollywood. *Comrade X* (40), *This Gun for Hire* (42), *For Whom the Bell Tolls* (43), *Saigon* (47), *The Kissing Bandit* (49), *Hot Blood* (55), many others.

RATHBONE, BASIL (1892–1967). Incisive British actor, on stage since 1911, in America from the mid-20s. An excellent villain and a fine Sherlock Holmes. *The Fruitful Vine* (GB) (21), *The Masked Bride* (25), *The Last of Mrs Cheyney* (30), *After the Ball* (GB) (32), *Loyalties* (GB) (33), *David Copperfield* (34), *Anna Karenina* (35), *The Last Days of Pompeii* (35), *Captain Blood* (35), *A Tale of Two Cities* (36), *Romeo and Juliet* (36), *The Garden of Allah* (37), *Love from a Stranger*) (BG (37), *The Adventures of Marco Polo* (37), *Dawn Patrol* (38), *If I Were King* (38), *The Adventures of Robin Hood* (38), *The Hound of the Baskervilles* (39), *Sherlock Holmes* (39), *Son of Frankenstein* (39), *Tower of London* (40), *Rio* (40), *A Date With Destiny* (40), *The Mark of Zorro* (40), *International Lady* (41), *Fingers at the Window* (42), *Sherlock Holmes and the Voice of Terror* (42) (and a dozen other 'modernized' adventures before 1946 including *House of Fear* [43], *The Scarlet Claw* [44], *Pearl of Death* [44]), *Crossroads* (42), *Above Suspicion* (43), *Frenchman's Creek* (44), *Heartbeat* (46), *Casanova's Big Night* (54) (after years on Broadway), *We're No Angels* (55), *The Court Jester* (56), *The Black Sleep* (57), *Tales of Terror* (62), *A Comedy of Terrors* (63), *Prehistoric Planet Women* (66), *The Ghost in the Invisible Bikini* (66), etc.

RATOFF, GREGORY (1897–1961). Russian actor and impresario, in Hollywood and Britain from mid-30s as actor or director. *I'm No Angel* (a) (33), *Under Two Flags* (a) (36), *Lancer Spy* (d) (37), *Rose of Washington Square* (d) (39), *Intermezzo (Escape to Happiness)* (d) (39), *I Was an Adventuress* (d) (40), *Adam Had Four Sons* (d) (41), *The Corsican Brothers* (a) (41), *The Men in Her Life* (d) (42), *Song of Russia* (d) (44), *Where Do We Go from Here* (d) (45), *Moss Rose* (d)

(47), *All about Eve* (a) (50), *Abdullah the Great* (a, d) (57), *Oscar Wilde* (d) (60), *The Big Gamble* (a) (61), many others.

RATTIGAN, TERENCE (1912–   ). Distinguished British playwright, many of whose successes have been filmed: *French Without Tears* (39), *While the Sun Shines* (46), *The Winslow Boy* (48), *The Browning Version* (51), *The Deep Blue Sea* (55), *Separate Tables* (58), etc. Has also written screen originals: *English without Tears* (43), *The Way to the Stars* (45), *The Sound Barrier* (52), *The VIPs* (63), *The Yellow Rolls-Royce* (64), *Goodbye Mr Chips* (project) (67), *The Battle of Britain* (project) (67), others.

RAVETCH, IRVING (c. 1915–   ). American writer who with his wife HARRIET FRANK has frequently worked with director Martin Ritt on scripts that include *Hud* (63), and *Hombre* (67). Turned writer-producer with *The Reivers* (69).

RAWLINS, JOHN (1902–   ). American director, mainly of second features. *State Police* (38), *Six Lessons from Madame La Zonga* (41), *Halfway to Shanghai* (42), *Sherlock Holmes and the Voice of Terror* (42), *The Great Impersonation* (42), *Ladies Courageous* (44), *Sudan* (45), *Dick Tracy Meets Gruesome* (47), *Fort Defiance* (51), *Shark River* (53), *The Lost Legion* (57), etc. Recently inactive.

RAWNSLEY, DAVID (1909–   ). British art director (*49th Parallel, In Which We Serve, The Rake's Progress, I See a Dark Stranger*, etc.). Inventor of the Independent Frame system, intended as a production economy; it caused constriction in practice and was quickly abandoned.

RAWSTHORNE, ALAN (1905–   ). British composer. *Burma Victory* (45), *The Captive Heart* (46), *Uncle Silas* (47), *Saraband for Dead Lovers* (48), etc.

RAY, ALDO (1926–   ) (Aldo daRe). Beefy American actor, in local politics before film career. *Idols in the Dust* (51), *The Marrying Kind* (51), *Pat and Mike* (52), *Let's Do It Again* (53), *Miss Sadie Thompson* (54), *We're No Angels* (55), *The Gentle Sergeant* (56), *Men in War* (57), *God's Little Acre* (58), *The Naked and the Dead* (58), *The Siege of Pinchgut* (GB) (58), *The Day They Robbed the Bank of England* (GB) (60), *Johnny Nobody* (GB) (61), *Nightmare in the Sun* (64), *Sylvia* (65), *What Did You Do in the War, Daddy?* (66), *Dead Heat on a Merry-Go-Round* (66), *Welcome to Hard Times* (67), *Riot on Sunset Strip* (67), *The Power* (67), *The Green Berets* (68), *Man Without Mercy* (69), etc.

RAY, ANDREW (1939–   ). British juvenile lead, son of Ted Ray. *The Mudlark* (debut) (50), *The Yellow Balloon* (52), *Escapade* (55), *Woman in a Dressing-Gown* (57), *Serious Charge* (59), *Twice Round the Daffodils* (62), *The System* (64), *The Blow-Up* (66), etc.

RAY, CHARLES (1891–1943). American leading man of the silent. screen, often in country boy roles. *Bill Henry* (19), *The Old Swimming Hole* (20), *The Barnstormer* (22), *The Girl I Love* (23), *Sweet Adeline* (23), *The Courtship of Miles Standish* (also produced) (23), *Vanity* (25), *Getting Gertie's Garter* (27), *The Garden of Eden* (28), etc. Few sound films include *Ladies Should Listen* (34), *By Your Leave* (35), *Just My Luck* (37).

RAY, JOHNNIE (1927–   ). American 'crying' singer of the 50s who played a leading role in *There's No Business Like Show Business* (54)

†RAY, NICHOLAS (1911–   ) (Raymond N. Kienzle). American director, former writer and stage director. Acclaimed for his first film, he later seemed to lack a particular style. *They Live by Night* (47), *A Woman's Secret* (49), *Knock On Any Door* (49), *Born To Be Bad* (50), *In a Lonely Place* (50), *Flying Leathernecks* (51), *On Dangerous Ground* (51), *The Lusty Men* (52), *Johnny Guitar* (54), *Run for Cover* (55), *Rebel without a Cause* (55), *Hot Blood* (56), *Bigger Than Life* (56), *The True Story of Jesse James* (57), *Bitter Victory* (57), *Wind Across the Everglades* (58), *Party Girl* (58), *Savage Innocents* (59), *King of Kings* (61), *55 Days at Peking* (62).

RAY, RENE (1912–   ) (Irene Creese). British actress, on stage from childhood; has often played downtrodden waifs. *Young Woodley* (30), *The Passing of the Third Floor Back* (35), *Crime over London* (36), *Farewell Again* (37), *The Rat* (38), *Bank Holiday* (38), *The Return of the Frog* (39), *They Made Me a Fugitive* (47), *If Winter Comes* (US) (47), *Women of Twilight* (52), *The Good Die Young* (53), etc. Has also written novels.

RAY, SATYAJIT (1921–   ). Indian director, famous for the 'Apu' trilogy of a child growing up in modern India: *Pather Panchali* (54), *The Unvanquished (Aparajito)* (56), *The World of Apu* (59). Other films: *The Music Room* (58), *The Goddess* (60), *Kanchenjunga* (62), etc.

RAY, TED (c. 1909–   ) (Charles Olden). British music-hall comedian and violinist who has been in occasional films. *Elstree Calling* (30), *Radio Parade of 1935*, *A Ray of Sunshine* (47), *Meet Me Tonight* (50), *Escape by Night* (52), *My Wife's Family* (54), *Carry On, Teacher* (59), *Please Turn Over* (60), etc.

RAYE, CAROL (1923–   ) (Kathleen Corkrey). British leading lady of the 40s. *Strawberry Roan* (45), *Spring Song* (46), *While I Live* (48), etc.

RAYE, MARTHA (1916–   ) (Martha Reed). Wide-mouthed American comedienne and vocalist, popular on radio and TV. *Rhythm on the Range* (debut) (36), *Waikiki Wedding* (37), *Artists and Models* (38), *The Boys from Syracuse* (40), *Keep 'Em Flying* (41), *Hellzapoppin* (42), *Pin-Up Girl* (43), *Four Jills in a Jeep* (44), *Monsieur Verdoux* (47), *Jumbo* (62), etc. Recently in cabaret.

RAYMOND, CYRIL (c. 1897–   ). British stage and screen actor often seen as the dull husband or professional man. *The Shadow* (32), *Mixed Doubles* (33), *The Tunnel* (35), *Dreaming Lips* (37), *Come On George* (39), *Brief Encounter* (46), *This Was a Woman* (47), *Jack of Diamonds* (48), *Angels One Five* (51), *Lease of Life* (53), *Charley Moon* (56), etc.

RAYMOND, GARY (1935–   ). British leading man. *The Moonraker* (58), *Look Back in Anger* (59), *Suddenly Last Summer* (59), *The Millionairess* (61), *El Cid* (61), *Jason and the Argonauts* (63), *The Greatest Story Ever Told* (65), *Traitor's Gate* (65), etc. TV series: *The Rat Patrol*.

RAYMOND, GENE (1908–   ) (Raymond Guion). American leading man of the 30s, recently character actor; was married to Jeanette Macdonald. On stage from childhood. *Personal Maid* (debut) (31), *Zoo in Budapest* (33), *Flying Down to Rio* (33), *Seven Keys to Baldpate* (34), *That Girl from Paris* (37), *Mr and Mrs Smith* (41), *Smilin' Through* (41), *The Locket* (46), *Assigned to Danger* (49), *Hit the Deck* (55), *The Best Man* (64), etc. Directed one film, *Million Dollar Weekend* (also acted) (48).

RAYMOND, JACK (1892–1953). British producer, mainly of lightweight comedy films. *The Frog* (36), *Splinters* (37), *The Rat* (38), *The Mind of Mr Reeder* (also directed) (39), *You Will Remember* (41), *Up for the Cup* (50), *Worm's Eye View* (51), *Reluctant Heroes* (52), many others.

RAYMOND, PAULA (c. 1928–   ) (Paula Ramona Wright). American leading lady, former model. *Devil's Doorway* (49), *Crisis* (50), *The Tall Target* (51), *The Beast from Twenty Thousand Fathoms* (53), *The Human Jungle* (last to date) (54), etc.

REAGAN, RONALD (1911–   ). American leading man of the 40s, former sports reporter. *Love Is on the Air* (37), *Accidents Will Happen* (38), *Dark Victory* (39), *Hell's Kitchen* (39), *Brother Rat and a Baby* (40), *Santa Fe Trail* (40), *International Squadron* (41), *Nine Lives Are Not Enough* (41), *King's Row* (41), *Juke Girl* (42), *This Is the Army* (43), etc.; war service; *Stallion Road* (47), *That Hagen Girl* (47), *The Voice of the Turtle* (47), *Night Unto Night* (48), *John Loves Mary* (49), *The Hasty Heart* (GB) (49), *Louisa* (50), *Storm Warning* (51), *Hong Kong* (52), *Prisoner of War* (54), *Law and Order* (54), *Tennessee's Partner* (55), *Hellcats of the Navy* (57), *The Killers* (64), etc. Went into politics and in 1966 was elected Governor of California. Published autobiography 1965: *Where's the Rest of Me?*

REAR WINDOW (US 1954). Alfred Hitchcock here set himself the task of making a thriller in which the action is all confined to one room —and the block of flats opposite at whose inhabitants the peeping-tom hero peers through his binoculars and uncovers a murder. Successful less because of Cornell Woolrich's story than because of John Michael Hayes' witty dialogue; Hitchcock's own talent seemed cramped. Photographed by Robert Burks, with music by Franz Waxman; with James Stewart, Grace Kelly.

REASON, REX (1928–   ). American leading man, mainly in routine films. *Storm Over Tibet* (52), *Salome* (53), *This Island Earth* (55), *Raw Edge* (56), *The Rawhide Trail* (60), etc. TV series: *The Roaring Twenties*.

REASON, RHODES (1930–   ). American leading man, mainly in second features. *Crime Against Joe* (56), *Jungle Heat* (57), *Yellowstone Kelly* (59), *King Kong Escapes* (Jap.) (68), etc. TV series: *White Hunter*.

REBECCA (US 1940). A splendid example of the cinema as a popular storyteller. From Daphne du Maurier's smash-hit novel of passion and mystery in a Cornish stately home, Hitchcock fashioned an impeccable film, with the help of a clever screenplay by Robert E. Sherwood and Joan Harrison, and a cast including Laurence Olivier, Joan Fontaine, Judith Anderson, Reginald Denny, George Sanders, Florence Bates, Gladys Cooper, C. Aubrey Smith and Nigel Bruce. Commercial film-making at its best. AA best film, best photography (George Barnes).

REBECCA OF SUNNYBROOK FARM. The American children's classic by Kate Douglas Wiggin was filmed in 1917 by Marshall Neilan, with Mary Pickford; in 1932 by Alfred Santell, with Marian Nixon; and in 1938 (much changed) by Allan Dwan, with Shirley Temple.

REBEL WITHOUT A CAUSE (US 1955). This story of teenage restlessness directed by Nicholas Ray and starring James Dean was felt to be of some significance because for the first time the hoodlums were shown as coming from rich, comfortable homes. Otherwise it was a straightforward star vehicle.

THE RED BADGE OF COURAGE (US 1951). The story of the making of this film is told in hilarious detail by Lilian Ross in her book 'Picture', and it is a classic example of what happens to artistic intentions when the commercial element of film-making gets its teeth into them. The film as released did not do justice to Stephen Crane's civil war history, or to the box-office; director John Huston had tired of the unhappy compromise, and all the viewer could salvage were some stirring battle scenes directed by Andrew Marton, with accomplished photography by Harold Rossen and music by Bronislau Kaper.

THE RED BALLOON (France 1956). A thirty-six-minute fantasy written and directed by Albert Lamorisse, about a boy's pursuit of a balloon through the streets of Paris. A uniquely charming and happy film which succeeds in a field the cinema should tackle more often.

RED DUST (US 1932). This Malayan jungle adventure is remembered for the teaming of Clark Gable and Jean Harlow, and for the scene in which Harlow takes a primitive shower. It was remade in 1939 as *Congo Maisie*, with Ann Sothern and John Carroll; and in 1954 Gable himself appeared opposite Ava Gardner in a lavish restyling under the title *Mogambo*.

THE RED INN (France 1951). A direction-pointing black comedy which came somewhat ahead of its time. The script by Aurenche and Bost satirizes society, religion and everything else within sight in its nineteenth-century fable of two innkeepers (Carette and Françoise Rosay) who murder travellers for money. A monk (Fernandel) gets one batch safely away, only to see their carriage topple over a precipice. Claude Autant-Lara directed.

REDFIELD, WILLIAM (1928–   ). American general purpose actor with long stage experience: former boy actor. *I Married a Woman* (58), *Fantastic Voyage* (66), *Duel at Diablo* (66), *A New Leaf* (70), etc.

REDFORD, ROBERT (1936–   ). American leading man. *Inside Daisy Clover* (65), *The Chase* (66), *This Property Is Condemned* (66), *Barefoot in the Park* (67), *Blue* (67), *Willie Boy* (69), *Butch Cassidy and the Sundance Kid* (69), *Downhill Racer* (69), etc.

RED GARTERS (US 1954). Only a minor musical, but it set out with fair success to stylize the Western form, and if the pretty Technicolor sets hadn't got so monotonous it might have had more recognition. Michael Fessier's script was lively and pleasant, George Marshall's direction smooth, and the songs by Jay Livingston and Ray Evans very hummable. With Rosemary Clooney, Gene Barry, Jack Carson, Guy Mitchell.

†REDGRAVE, LYNN (1944–   ). British actress, mainly on stage: daughter of Michael Redgrave and sister of Vanessa. Usually plays gauche roles. *Girl with Green Eyes* (64), *Georgy Girl* (66), *Smashing Time* (67), *The Virgin Soldiers* (69), *Blood Kin* (US) (69).

REDGRAVE, SIR MICHAEL (1908–   ). Tall, distinguished British actor, former schoolmaster, on stage from 1934. *The Lady Vanishes* (film debut) (38), *Climbing High* (38), *A Stolen Life* (39), *The Stars Look Down* (39), *Kipps* (41), *Jeannie* (41), *Thunder Rock* (42), *The Way to the Stars* (45), *Dead of Night* (45), *The Captive Heart* (46), *The Man Within* (47), *Fame Is the Spur* (47), *Mourning Becomes Electra* (US) (47), *The Secret Beyond the Door* (US) (48), *The Browning Version* (51), *The Importance of Being Earnest* (52), *Oh Rosalinda* (55), *Confidential Report* (55), *The Dam Busters* (55), *Nineteen Eighty-four* (56), *Time without Pity* (57), *The Quiet American* (58), *Law and Disorder* (58), *The Innocents* (61), *The Loneliness of the Long Distance Runner* (63), *Young Cassidy* (64), *The Hill* (65), *The Heroes of Telemark* (65), *Department K* (67), *Oh What a Lovely War* (69), *Goodbye Mr Chips* (69), *The Battle of Britain* (69), *David Copperfield* (69), etc.

†REDGRAVE, VANESSA (1937–   ). British leading actress, daughter of Michael Redgrave and sister of Lynn. Was on stage for years before film debut. *Morgan* (66), *Red and Blue* (66), *Sailor from Gibraltar* (66), *Blow-Up* (67), *Camelot* (67), *The Charge of the Light Brigade* (68), *Isadora* (68), *The Seagull* (68), *Oh What a Lovely War* (69).

Red Indians, it is generally thought, were always portrayed as villains on screen until *Broken Arrow* in 1950, when Jeff Chandler played Cochise. But in fact there were many silent films in which Indians were not only on the side of right but the leading figures in the story. In 1911 one finds titles like *An Indian Wife's Devotion, A Squaw's Love, Red Wing's Gratitude*; *Ramona* (qv) had already been made once and was to survive three remakes; 1913 brought *Heart of an Indian* and *The Squaw Man*. Later there were versions of *In the Days of Buffalo Bill* (21), *The Vanishing American* (25), and *Redskin* (28). It seems to have been sound that made the Indians villainous, and kept them that way for twenty-two years.

After *Broken Arrow* there was a deluge of pro-Indian films. *Devil's Doorway, Across the Wide Missouri, The Savage, Arrowhead, The Big Sky, Apache, Taza—Son of Cochise, Chief Crazy Horse, Sitting Bull, White Feather, Navajo, Hiawatha*, all came within four years. There were even biopics of modern Indians: *The Outsider* (Ira Hayes) and *Jim Thorpe, All American*. In recent years the Indians have been slipping back into villainy: but TV in 1966 boasted a series based on a Red Indian cop in New York (the name is *Hawk*), and Elvis Presley played a Red Indian hero in *Stay Away Joe*.

REDMAN, JOYCE (1918–   ). Irish stage actress whose most memorable film role was in the eating scene in *Tom Jones* (63).

REDMOND, LIAM (1913–   ). Irish character actor, an Abbey player. *I See a Dark Stranger* (45), *Captain Boycott* (48), *High Treason* (51), *The Gentle Gunman* (52), *The Divided Heart* (54), *Jacqueline* (56), *Night of the Demon* (57), *The Boy and the Bridge* (59), *The Ghost and*

Mr Chicken (US) (65), *Tobruk* (US) (66), *The Twenty-fifth Hour* (66), *The Last Safari* (67), etc. Also on TV.

THE RED SHOES (GB 1948). Michael Powell and Emeric Pressburger always aimed high in their choice of subject, and here their aim was to give us the feel of the world of ballet: the backstage and private lives of those concerned in it. The detail remains fascinating, the colour evocative, the dancing superb; only the story is rather trite and lumpy. Moira Shearer made a hit as the tragic heroine, Anton Walbrook spat superbly as the impresario; Jack Cardiff's photography was near his best.

†REED, SIR CAROL (1906–   ). Distinguished British director who after a peak in the late 40s seemed to lose his way; his infrequent later films, though always civilized, have been generally disappointing. *Midshipman Easy* (34), *Laburnum Grove* (36), *Talk of the Devil* (36), *Who's Your Lady Friend* (37), *Bank Holiday* (38), *Penny Paradise* (38), *Climbing High* (38), *A Girl Must Live* (39), *The Stars Look Down* (39), *Night Train to Munich* (40), *The Girl in the News* (40), *Kipps* (41), *The Young Mr Pitt* (41), *The Way Ahead* (44), *The True Glory* (co-directed) (45), *Odd Man Out* (46), *The Fallen Idol* (48), *The Third Man* (49), *An Outcast of the Islands* (51), *The Man Between* (53), *A Kid for Two Farthings* (55), *Trapeze* (56), *The Key* (58), *Our Man in Havana* (59), *The Running Man* (63), *The Agony and the Ecstasy* (65), *Oliver!* (AA) (68), *Nobody Loves a Flapping Eagle* (project) (70).

REED, DONNA (1921–   ) (Donna Mullenger). American leading lady of the 40s, recently starring in long-running TV series *The Donna Reed Show*. Won screen test after a beauty contest while still at college. *The Getaway* (debut) (41), *Shadow of the Thin Man* (42), *The Courtship of Andy Hardy* (42), *Calling Dr Gillespie* (42), *The Human Comedy* (43), *See Here, Private Hargrove* (44), *The Picture of Dorian Gray* (44), *It's a Wonderful Life* (46), *Green Dolphin Street* (47), *Chicago Deadline* (49), *From Here to Eternity* (AA) (53), *The Last Time I Saw Paris* (55), *Ransom* (56), *Backlash* (56), *Beyond Mombasa* (57), etc.

REED, MAXWELL (1920–   ). Brooding Irish leading man in British films from 1946, after repertory experience. *The Years Between* (46), *Daybreak* (47), *The Brothers* (48), *Holiday Camp* (48), *The Dark Man* (49), *The Square Ring* (53), *Before I Wake* (56), etc.

REED, OLIVER (1938–   ). Burly British leading man, usually in sullen roles. *The Rebel* (60), *No Love for Johnnie* (61), *Curse of the Werewolf* (62), *Pirates of Blood River* (62), *The Damned* (62), *Paranoiac* (63), *The System* (64), *The Party's Over* (64), *The Brigand of Kandahar* (65), *The Trap* (66), *The Shuttered Room* (66), *The Jokers* (66), *I'll Never Forget Whatshisname* (67), *The Assassination Bureau* (68),

Reed, Philip

Oliver! (68), *Hannibal Brooks* (68), *Women in Love* (69), *Take A Girl Like You* (69), etc.

REED, PHILIP (1908–   ). American leading man with long stage experience. *Female* (34), *Last of the Mohicans* (36), *Aloma of the South Seas* (41), *Old Acquaintance* (44), *I Cover Big Town* (47), *Unknown Island* (50), *The Tattered Dress* (57), *Harem Scarem* (67), etc.

reel. A loose term generally taken to mean 1,000 feet of 35mm film, i.e. the amount which would fit on to a reel of the old-fashioned kind, running about ten minutes. Thus short films were spoken of as two-reelers, three-reelers, etc., and charged accordingly. But modern 35mm projector spools will take 2,000 feet and sometimes 3,000 feet, so the term is slowly falling into disuse . . . especially as 16mm projectors have always taken spools of either 400, 800 or 1,600 feet.

REESE, TOM (1930–   ). American character actor, a notable 'heavy'. *Flaming Star* (60), *Marines Let's Go* (61), *Forty Pounds of Trouble* (62), *Murderers' Row* (66), etc.

REEVE, ADA (1874–1966). British character actress with long stage career. Film appearances include *They Came to a City* (44), *When the Bough Breaks* (47), *Night and the City* (50), *Eye Witness* (56), etc. Published autobiography, *Take It for a Fact*.

REEVES, GEORGE (1914–1959) (George Besselo). American leading man. *Gone with the Wind* (debut) (39), *Strawberry Blonde* (41), *Blood and Sand* (42), *Bar 20* (44), *Jungle Jim* (49), *Samson and Delilah* (50), *Sir Galahad* (serial) (50), *Superman* (serial) (51), *From Here to Eternity* (53), also *Superman* TV series.

REEVES, KYNASTON (1893–   ). British character actor of stage and screen, often seen as academic. *The Lodger* (32), *The Housemaster* (38), *The Prime Minister* (40), *Vice Versa* (48), *The Guinea Pig* (49), *The Mudlark* (50), *Top of the Form* (53), *Brothers in Law* (57), *School for Scoundrels* (60), many others.

†REEVES, MICHAEL (1944–1969). British director whose promising career barely got started. *Sister of Satan* (It.) (65), *The Sorcerers* (67), *Witchfinder General* (68).

REEVES, STEVE (1926–   ). American actor, formerly 'Mr World' and 'Mr Universe'; has found stardom since 1953 in Italian muscle-man spectacles, e.g. *Goliath and the Barbarians*, *The Giant of Marathon*, *Hercules Unchained*, *The Thief of Bagdad*.

REGGIANI, SERGE (1922–   ). Slightly-built French-Italian actor with stage experience. *Les Portes de la Nuit* (46), *Manon* (48), *Les Amants de Vérone* (48), *La Ronde* (50), *Secret People* (GB) (51), *Casque*

d'Or (51), *The Wicked Go to Hell* (55), *Les Misérables* (57), *Marie
Octobre* (58), *Paris Blues* (60), *The Leopard* (63), *The 25th Hour* (67),
Les Aventuriers (67), *Day of the Owl* (It.) (68), etc.

LA RÈGLE DU JEU (France 1939). A satire on the decadence of the
pre-1939 French aristocracy, directed by Jean Renoir from a script
by himself and Carl Koch. Only a butchered version was released
after his flight to America, and not until 1958 was the original
version pieced together. Not an easy film for any but Frenchmen
to understand fully; but well worth the effort if only to appreciate
its curious mixture of comedy and farce. Photographed by Claude
Renoir; with Marcel Dalio, Nora Gregor and Jean Renoir himself.

REICHENBACH, FRANÇOIS (1922–). French documentarist with an
ironic viewpoint. Best known for *L'Americque Insolite* (59), *Un
Coeur Gros Comme Ca* (61), *Les Amoureux du France* (64), *Hollywood
Through a Keyhole* (66).

REICHER, FRANK (1875–1965). German-born character actor, long in
Hollywood. *Mata Hari* (32), *King Kong* (33), *Kind Lady* (36),
Anthony Adverse (36), *Lancer Spy* (38), *They Dare Not Love* (41),
House of Frankenstein (45), *The Mummy's Ghost* (46), *The Secret Life
of Walter Mitty* (47), *Samson and Delilah* (50), many others.

REID, BERYL (1918–). British revue comedienne who has latterly
weathered a transition to character acting. *The Belles of St Trinian's*
(54), *The Extra Day* (56), *The Dock Brief* (62), *Star* (68), *Inspector
Clouseau* (68), *The Assassination Bureau* (68), *The Killing of Sister
George* (her stage rôle) (US) (68), *Entertaining Mr Sloane* (70), etc.

REID, CARL BENTON (1895–). American character actor with
stage career before settling in Hollywood. *The Little Foxes* (41),
In a Lonely Place (50), *Convicted* (50), *The Great Caruso* (51), *Lorna
Doone* (51), *Carbine Williams* (52), *The Egyptian* (54), *The Left Hand
of God* (55), *The Gallant Hours* (59), etc. TV series: *Amos Burke—
Secret Agent* (65).

REID, WALLACE (1890–1923). American leading man of the silent
screen. *The Deerslayer* (11), *The Birth of a Nation* (14), *The Love Mask*
(16), *House of Silence* (18), *The Dancing Fool* (20), *The Affairs of
Anatol* (21), *The Ghost Breaker* (22), *Adam's Rib* (23), many others.

reincarnation has seldom been seriously tackled in the cinema: *The
Search for Bridey Murphy* (56) is almost the only example. Many
characters of farce and melodrama have *thought* they were reincarnated, including the hero of *She* and the heroine of *The Vengeance
of She*. The real thing happened to Oliver Hardy in *The Flying
Deuces* (he came back as a horse); to a dog in *You Never Can Tell*
(he came back as Dick Powell); and to the luckless heroine of *The*

Bride and the Beast, who found that in a former existence she had been a gorilla. Reincarnation was also the basis of *Here Comes Mr Jordan*, and of *The Mummy*. In 1968 a version was made of Elmer Rice's *The Adding Machine*, with its celestial laundry for souls; and in 1969 there was even a musical on the subject, *On a Clear Day You Can See Forever*.

REINER, CARL (1923–). American comedy writer, primarily active on TV (e.g. *The Dick Van Dyke Show*) but now writing for films: *The Thrill of It All* (63), *The Art of Love* (65), etc. Usually plays a cameo role himself, and has lately developed his acting career: *The Gazebo* (59), *The Russians Are Coming, The Russians Are Coming* (66), *Enter Laughing* (also produced and directed) (67), *Billy Bright* (69).

REINHARDT, GOTTFRIED (1911–). Austrian producer, son of theatrical producer Max Reinhardt. Went to US with his father and became assistant to Walter Wanger. Has since produced and occasionally directed. *The Great Waltz* (script) (37), *Comrade X* (p) (40), *Two-Faced Woman* (p) (41), *Command Decision* (p) (48), *The Red Badge of Courage* (p) (51), *The Story of Three Loves* (d) (53), *Betrayed* (d) (54), *The Good Soldier Schweik* (p) (59), *Town without Pity* (p, d) (61), *Situation Hopeless But Not Serious* (p, d) (65), etc.

REINHARDT, MAX (1873–1943). Austrian theatrical producer of great pageants. His only screen direction (with William Dieterle) was *A Midsummer Night's Dream* (35), from his stage production.

REINIGER, LOTTE (1899–). German animator, well-known for her silhouette cartoons. *The Adventures of Prince Achmed* (26), *Dr Doolittle* (series) (28), *Carmen* (33), *Papageno* (35), *The Brave Little Tailor* (55), etc.

REIS, IRVING (1906–1953). American director, with radio experience. *One Crowded Night* (40), *The Gay Falcon* (41), *The Big Street* (43), *Hitler's Children* (43), *Crack Up* (46), *The Bachelor and the Bobby-soxer* (47), *All My Sons* (48), *Roseanna McCoy* (49), *Three Husbands* (50), *New Mexico* (53), *The Fourposter* (53), etc.

REISCH, WALTER (1900–). Austrian writer who in the 30s came to Britain, then Hollywood. *Men Are Not Gods* (also directed) (36), *Ninotchka* (39), *Comrade X* (40), *The Heavenly Body* (43), *Song of Scheherezade* (also directed) (46), *Titanic* (52), *The Girl in the Red Velvet Swing* (55), *Journey to the Centre of the Earth* (59), etc.

REISNER, ALLEN (* –). American director, from TV. *The Day They Gave Babies Away* (56), *St Louis Blues* (58), etc.

REISNER, CHARLES (1887–1962). American director. *The Man in the Box* (25), *Reducing* (32), *Sophie Lang Goes West* (37), *The Big Store*

(41), *Meet the People* (44), *Lost in a Harem* (44), *The Cobra Strikes* (48), *The Travelling Saleswoman* (50), many others, mainly second features.

†REISZ, KAREL (1926–   ). Czech director, in Britain from childhood. Former film critic. *We Are the Lambeth Boys* (58), *Saturday Night and Sunday Morning* (60), *Night Must Fall* (63), *This Sporting Life* (produced only) (63), *Morgan: A Suitable Case for Treatment* (66), *Isadora* (68).

religion has inspired film-makers from the beginning—as a commercial trump card. In the early years of the century it was the Italians who produced vast semi-biblical spectacles like *Quo Vadis* and *Cabiria*, but Hollywood was not slow to catch on, and producers soon found that religious shorts gave them extra prestige. There were several versions of *From the Manger to the Cross*; Griffith, in *Judith of Bethulia* and *Intolerance*, contributed his share; but it was C. B. De Mille in the 20s who brought the Bible to full commercial flower with *The Ten Commandments* and *King of Kings*. (His 1932 *The Sign of the Cross*, 1950 *Samson and Delilah* and 1956 remake of *The Ten Commandments* show that for him at least time continued to stand still.) In 1929, though *Noah's Ark* was spectacle pure and simple, Vidor's *Hallelujah* at least partially transmitted Negro religious fervour. In the 30s Hollywood was seeking fresh ways to combine religion with sentiment or spectacle, in *The Cradle Song*, *Dante's Inferno*, *The Garden of Allah*, *The Green Light* and *Boys' Town*. One result was a new characterization of priests (qv) as jolly good fellows: stars like Spencer Tracy and Pat O'Brien were eager to play them. Yet none had the quiet dignity of Rex Ingram as De Lawd in *Green Pastures*, a Negro version of the Scriptures.

The war naturally brought a religious revival. Every film set in England seemed to end with a service in a bombed church, and religious figures became big time in films like *The Song of Bernadette*, *Going My Way*, *The Keys of the Kingdom* and *The Bells of St Mary*. Savage war films masqueraded under such titles as *God Is My Co-Pilot* and *A Wing and a Prayer*. And heaven was used as a background for light-hearted fantasy films about death and judgment day, such as *Here Comes Mr Jordan*, *Heaven Can Wait*, and *The Horn Blows at Midnight*. The only film of this period to question religion at all was the British *Major Barbara*.

In the cynical post-war years religion was at a low ebb. An expensive *Joan of Arc* in 1948 failed disastrously, and an attempt to bring God into our everyday life, *The Next Voice You Hear*, fared no better. A sincere performance by Robert Donat could not bring people to see *Lease of Life*. Indeed, the only religious films to break even at the box office were those with a direct Roman Catholic appeal, such as *Monsieur Vincent* and *The Miracle of Fatima*. True religion, to Hollywood, was out, and the Bible became once more a source book for a string of tawdry commercial epics: *Quo Vadis*, *Salome*, *The Prodigal*, *The Robe*, *Ben Hur*, *Sodom and Gomorrah* and many cut-rate dubbed Italian spectacles of a similar kind (many with Hollywood stars). Occasionally a spark of sincerity would flash through, as in the otherwise dull *David and Bathsheba*; while small independent companies could produce interesting films like *The First Legion*. Towards the end of the 50s there were occasional attempts to see religion afresh: *A Man Called Peter*, *The Nun's Story*, *Inn of the Sixth Happiness*, *Whistle Down the Wind*. Otto Preminger, despite a 1957 failure with *Saint Joan*, tried again in 1963 with *The Cardinal*. In 1965 George Stevens unveiled *The Greatest Story Ever Told*, a tepid life of Jesus which found little box-office favour, being overtaken in some quarters by Pasolini's *The Gospel According to St Matthew*. 1966 brought the long-promised Italian-American epic known as *The Bible*: in fact it dealt only with the Book of Genesis, and that at such a dull pace and inordinate length that it is doubtful whether sequels will be called for.

RELPH, GEORGE (1888–1960). British character actor mainly seen on stage. Films include *Nicholas Nickleby* (47), *I Believe in You* (52), *The Titfield Thunderbolt* (leading role as the vicar) (53), *Doctor at Large* (57), *Davy* (57), etc.

RELPH, MICHAEL (1915–). British producer-director, son of George Relph. Former art director and production designer; since 1947 has worked almost exclusively with Basil Dearden, usually producing while Dearden directs. *The Captive Heart* (46), *Frieda* (47), *Saraband for Dead Lovers* (48), *The Blue Lamp* (50), *I Believe in You* (also co-wrote) (52), *The Rainbow Jacket* (54), *Davy* (d) (57), *Rockets Galore* (d) (57), *Violent Playground* (58), *Sapphire* (59), *The League of Gentlemen* (59), *Victim* (61), *Life for Ruth* (62), *The Mind Benders* (63), *Woman of Straw* (63), *Masquerade* (65), *The Assassination Bureau* (68), etc.

REMARQUE, ERICH MARIA (1898–). German novelist. Works filmed include *All Quiet on the Western Front* (30), *The Road Back* (37), *Three Comrades* (38), *So Ends Our Night* (41), *Arch of Triumph* (48), *A Time to Love and a Time to Die* (57), etc.

REMBRANDT (US 1937). Perhaps the most satisfying film ever produced about a painter, its hypnotic effect stemming from Charles Laughton's brilliant performance. Script by Carl Zuckmayer, direction by Alexander Korda, design by Vincent Korda, photography by Georges Perinal.

REMICK, LEE (1937–). American leading lady with stage and TV experience. *A Face in the Crowd* (film debut) (57), *The Long Hot Summer* (58), *Anatomy of a Murder* (59), *Sanctuary* (61), *The Grip of*

Fear (Experiment in Terror) (62), *Days of Wine and Roses* (63), *The Wheeler Dealers* (64), *Baby the Rain Must Fall* (65), *The Hallelujah Trail* (65), *No Way to Treat a Lady* (68), *A Severed Head* (69), etc.

RENALDO, DUNCAN (1904–   ) (Renault Renaldo Duncan). American actor and painter with varied experience. In many films from *Trader Horn* (30) to *For Whom the Bell Tolls* (42); later more famous as The Cisco Kid in a series of second-feature Westerns (1945–50). Directed some films in the 20s.

RENNAHAN, RAY (1898–   ). American cinematographer, in Hollywood from 1917. Films include *Gone with the Wind* (co-ph) (AA) (39), *The Blue Bird* (40), *Down Argentine Way* (40), *Blood and Sand* (co-ph) (AA) (42), *For Whom the Bell Tolls* (43), *Belle of the Yukon* (44), *The Perils of Pauline* (47), *The Paleface* (48), *A Yankee at King Arthur's Court* (49), *Arrowhead* (53), *Terror in a Texas Town* (58), many others.

RENNIE, MICHAEL (1909–   ). Tall, good-looking British leading man best known as TV's *The Third Man*. Varied experience before going into repertory and film stand-in work. *The Divorce of Lady X* (38), *Dangerous Moonlight* (40), *Ships with Wings* (41), *I'll Be Your Sweetheart* (45), *The Wicked Lady* (45), *The Root of All Evil* (47), *Idol of Paris* (48), *The Black Rose* (50), then to US: *Five Fingers* (52), *Les Misérables* (52), *The Day the Earth Stood Still* (52), *The Robe* (53), *Désirée* (54), *The Rains of Ranchipur* (55), *Island in the Sun* (56), *Omar Khayyam* (57), *Third Man on the Mountain* (59), *The Lost World* (60), *Mary, Mary* (63), *Ride Beyond Vengeance* (65), *Hotel* (67), *The Power* (67), *Subterfuge* (69), etc.

RENOIR, CLAUDE (1914–   ). French cinematographer. *Toni* (34), *Une Partie de Campagne* (36), *La Règle du Jeu* (39), *Monsieur Vincent* (47), *The River* (51), *The Green Glove* (52), *The Golden Coach* (53), *Elena et les Hommes* (55), *Crime and Punishment* (56), *The Witches of Salem* (56), *Les Tricheurs* (58), *Blood and Roses* (60), *Lafayette* (61), *Circus World (The Magnificent Showman)* (64), *The Game is Over* (66), *Barbarella* (68), *The Madwoman of Chaillot* (co-ph) (69), many others.

RENOIR, JEAN (1894–   ). Distinguished French director, son of the painter Auguste Renoir, brother of Pierre Renoir. Stage experience including production of his own plays. *La Fille de l'Eau* (24), *Nana* (26), *Charleston* (27), *The Little Match-Seller* (28), *La Chienne* (31), *Bondu Sauve des Eaux* (32), *Toni* (34), *Madame Bovary* (34), *Le Crime de Monsieur Lange* (35), *Les Bas Fonds* (36), *Une Partie de Campagne* (36), *La Grande Illusion* (37), *La Marseillaise* (38), *La Bête Humaine* (38), *La Règle du Jeu* (also acted) (39); to US: *Swamp Water* (41), *This Land Is Mine* (43), *The Southerner* (44), *Diary of a Chambermaid* (45), *The Woman on the Beach* (47); back to Europe: *The River* (51), *The Golden Coach* (53), *French Cancan* (55), *Elena et les Hommes* (56),

Renoir, Pierre

Lunch on the Grass (59), *The Vanishing Corporal* (61), *C'est la Revolution* (67), etc.

RENOIR, PIERRE (1885–1952). French character actor, brother of Jean Renoir. *Madame Bovary* (34), *La Marseillaise* (38), *Les Enfants du Paradis* (44), *Doctor Knock* (50), many others.

reporters in American films have since the beginning of the sound era been pictured as trench-coated, trilby-hatted, good-looking guys with a smart line in wisecracks. Among the outstanding examples of this tradition are Pat O'Brien in *The Front Page*, Robert Williams in *Platinum Blonde*, Clark Gable in *It Happened One Night*, Fredric March in *Nothing Sacred*, James Stewart in *The Philadelphia Story*, Lynne Overman in *Roxie Hart*, Gene Kelly in *Inherit the Wind*; while on the distaff side one can't overlook Bette Davis in *Front Page Woman*, Jean Arthur in *Mr Deeds Goes to Town*, Rosalind Russell in *His Girl Friday* or Barbara Stanwyck in *Meet John Doe*. Presented somewhat more realistically were William Alland in *Citizen Kane*, James Stewart in *Call Northside 777*, Kirk Douglas in *Ace in the Hole*, and Arthur Kennedy in *Lawrence of Arabia*. British films have used their newshawks more flippantly, especially in the case of *This Man Is News* with Barry K. Barnes and *A Run for Your Money* with Alec Guinness. Just as well; for Edward Judd in *The Day the Earth Caught Fire*, Jack Hawkins in *Front Page Story*, Sidney James in *Quatermass II* and Norman Wooland in *All Over the Town* were a pretty dull lot, and Colin Gordon's imitation of the American model in *Escapade* was hardly convincing. Television series, of course, have found the reporter a convenient peg, as in the British *Deadline Midnight* and the American *Saints and Sinners* and *The Reporter*.

Republic Pictures Corporation. A small Hollywood production and distribution company founded in 1935 by a former tobacco executive named Herbert J. Yates (qv) who had spent some years building up a film laboratory. Republic continued as a one-man concern, producing innumerable competently-made second-feature Westerns and melodramas with such stars as Roy Rogers, Vera Hruba Ralston (Yates' wife), John Carroll, Constance Moore. Very occasionally there would be a major production such as *Rio Grande* or *The Quiet Man*. Production stopped in the mid-50s, when 'bread and butter' pictures were no longer needed, and the company's interests moved into TV.

REPULSION (GB 1965). A curious film setting down in detail the horrifying case history of a homicidal girl repelled by sex. Shot by Roman Polanski almost entirely in a London flat, the film has clever cinematic shock effects but little ear for dialogue. With Catherine Deneuve.

RESNAIS, ALAIN (1922–   ). Controversial French director, former editor. *Nuit et Brouillard* (short) (55), *Hiroshima Mon Amour* (59), *Last Year at Marienbad* (61), *Muriel* (62), *The War is Over* (66), *Je t'Aime* (69), etc.

RETTIG, TOMMY (1941–   ). American boy actor. *Panic in the Streets* (50), *The Five Thousand Fingers of Dr T* (53), *The Egyptian* (54), *The Last Wagon* (56), *At Gunpoint* (57), etc. TV series: *Lassie*.

REVERE, ANNE (1903–   ). American character actress, mainly on stage. *Double Door* (34), *The Devil Commands* (41), *The Gay Sisters* (42), *The Keys of the Kingdom* (44), *National Velvet* (45), *Dragonwyck* (46), *Body and Soul* (47), *Gentlemen's Agreement* (48), *A Place in the Sun* (51), etc.

REVILL, CLIVE (1930–   ). New Zealander in Britain playing mainly comic character roles. *Bunny Lake Is Missing* (65), *Modesty Blaise* (66), *A Fine Madness* (US) (66), *The Double Man* (66), *Fathom* (67), *Nobody Runs Forever* (68).

REVILLE, ALMA (1900–   ). British screenwriter, married to Alfred Hitchcock; worked on many of his films. *The Ring* (27), *Rich and Strange* (32), *The Thirty-nine Steps* (35), *Secret Agent* (36), *Sabotage* (37), *Young and Innocent* (37), *The Lady Vanishes* (38), *Suspicion* (41), *Shadow of a Doubt* (43), *The Paradine Case* (47), *Stage Fright* (50), etc.

REYNOLDS, ADELINE DE WALT (1862–1961). American character actress with long stage experience; for many years Hollywood's oldest bit player. *Come Live With Me* (film debut) (41), *The Human Comedy* (43), *Going My Way* (44), *A Tree Grows in Brooklyn* (45), *The Girl from Manhattan* (48), *Lydia Bailey* (52), *Witness to Murder* (54), etc.

REYNOLDS, BURT (1936–   ). Tough-guy American leading man best known for TV series *Riverboat* and *Hawk*. Films include *Angel Baby* (60), *Operation CIA* (65), *100 Rifles* (69), *Sam Whiskey* (69), *Skullduggery* (69).

REYNOLDS, DEBBIE (1932–   ) (Mary Frances Reynolds). Small, vivacious American leading lady, winner of a beauty contest and hence a screen test. *The Daughter of Rosie O'Grady* (50), *Singin' in the Rain* (52), *Susan Slept Here* (54), *Hit the Deck* (55), *The Catered Affair* (56), *Bundle of Joy* (56), *Tammy* (57), *It Started with a Kiss* (58), *The Rat Race* (60), *The Pleasure of His Company* (61), *How the West Was Won* (62), *My Six Loves* (63), *The Unsinkable Molly Brown* (64), *Goodbye Charlie* (65), *The Singing Nun* (66), *Divorce American Style* (67), *How Sweet It Is* (68), etc. TV series: *Debbie* (69).

REYNOLDS, JOYCE (1924–   ). Vivacious American leading lady of the 40s, usually in teenage roles. *George Washington Slept Here* (42), *Janie* (44), *Always Together* (48), *Dangerous Inheritance* (50), etc.

REYNOLDS, MARJORIE (1921–   ) (Marjorie Goodspeed). American leading lady of the 40s, now character actress on TV. Former child actress. *Up in the Air* (40), *Holiday Inn* (42), *Star Spangled Rhythm* (43), *Ministry of Fear* (43), *Dixie* (43), *Three is a Family* (44), *Bring on the Girls* (45), *Meet Me on Broadway* (46), *Heaven Only Knows* (47), *Home Town Story* (51), *The Great Jewel Robber* (51), *The Silent Witness* (54), etc. TV series: *The Life of Riley* (52–57), *Our Man Higgins* (62).

REYNOLDS, PETER (1926–   ) (Peter Horrocks). British light character actor, given to shifty roles. *The Captive Heart* (46), *Guilt Is My Shadow* (49), *Smart Alec* (50), *Four Days* (51), *The Last Page* (52), *Devil Girl from Mars* (54), *You Can't Escape* (55), *The Delavine Affair* (56), *Shake Hands with the Devil* (59), *West Eleven* (63), etc.

REYNOLDS, SHELDON (1923–   ). American radio and TV writer who wrote, produced and directed two films: *Foreign Intrigue* (56), *Assignment to Kill* (68).

RHODES, ERIK (1906–   ). American comic actor from the musical comedy stage, best remembered as the excitable Italian in two Astaire-Rogers films, *The Gay Divorce* (34) and *Top Hat* (35). ('Your wife is safe with Tonetti—he prefers spaghetti.') Also in *One Rainy Afternoon* (36), *Criminal Lawyer* (37), *Woman Chases Man* (37), *Dramatic School* (38), *On Your Toes* (39), etc., then back to stage. Recently on TV.

RHODES, MARJORIE (1902–   ). British character actress, on stage from 1920; usually plays warm-hearted mums, nosey neighbours, etc. *Poison Pen* (debut) (39), *Love on the Dole* (40), *World of Plenty* (41), *When We Are Married* (43), *Uncle Silas* (47), *The Cure for Love* (50), *Those People Next Door* (53), *Hell Drivers* (58), *Watch It, Sailor* (62), *The Family Way* (66), many others.

RICE, ELMER (1892–1967) (Elmer Reizenstern). American playwright. Works filmed include *Street Scene*, *The Adding Machine*, *Dream Girl* and *Counsellor at Law*.

RICE, FLORENCE (1911–   ). American leading lady of the late 30s, always in sweet-tempered roles. *The Best Man Wins* (35), *Sweethearts* (39), *Miracles for Sale* (39), *At the Circus* (39), *Fighting Marshal* (41), *The Ghost and the Guest* (43), etc. Retired.

RICE, JOAN (1930–   ). British leading lady, former waitress, briefly popular in the 50s. *The Story of Robin Hood and His Merrie Men* (52), *A Day to Remember* (54), *His Majesty O'Keefe* (US) (55), *One Good Turn* (56), etc.

RICH, DAVID LOWELL (c. 1923–   ). American director, from TV. *Senior Prom* (58), *Hey Boy, Hey Girl* (59), *Have Rocket Will Travel*

(59), *Madame X* (66), *The Plainsman* (66), *Rosie* (67), *A Lovely Way to Die* (68), *Eye of the Cat* (69), etc.

RICH, IRENE (1894–   ) (Irene Luther). American silent screen heroine, little seen since sound. *Stella Maris* (18), *Beau Brummell* (24), *So This is Paris* (26), *Craig's Wife* (28), *Shanghai Rose* (29), *That Certain Age* (38), *The Lady in Question* (41), *New Orleans* (47), etc.

RICH, JOHN (1925–   ). American director, from TV. *Wives and Lovers* (63), *The New Interns* (64), *Boeing Boeing* (65), *Easy Come Easy Go* (67), etc.

RICH, ROY (1909–   ). British producer, director and executive, with widely varied experience including radio and TV. Married to Brenda Bruce. Directed *My Brother's Keeper* (47), *It's Not Cricket* (48), *Double Profile* (54), *Phantom Caravan* (54), etc.

RICHARD III (GB 1956). Laurence Olivier's third Shakespearean production has a more direct popular appeal than either *Henry V* or *Hamlet*, perhaps because it centres firmly on Olivier's rich caricature of Crookback. It tells its story in a leisurely fashion, production values are economical, and the battle skimped, but Shakespeare and the acting win the day, with an especially fascinating performance from Ralph Richardson as Buckingham. The only other talking version of the story, oddly enough, is Rowland V. Lee's outrageous but amusing *Tower of London* (39), with Basil Rathbone as Richard and Boris Karloff as Mord the executioner: this was remade in 1963 by Roger Corman, with Vincent Price as Richard.

RICHARD, CLIFF (1940–   ) (Harold Webb). Boyish British pop singer who has succeeded by restricting his film appearances. *Serious Charge* (59), *Expresso Bongo* (60), *The Young Ones* (61), *Summer Holiday* (62), *Wonderful Life* (64), *Finders Keepers* (66), *Two a Penny* (68).

RICHARDS, ADDISON (c. 1887–1964). American character actor with long stage experience; in Hollywood from early 30s, usually as professional man. *Riot Squad* (34), *Coleen* (36), *Black Legion* (37), *Boom Town* (40), *My Favourite Blonde* (42), *Since You Went Away* (44), *The Mummy's Curse* (46), *Indian Scout* (50), *Illegal* (56), *The Oregon Trail* (59), hundreds of others; later in TV series.

RICHARDS, ANN (1918–   ). Australian leading lady. *Tall Timbers* (38), *The Rudd Family* (39), etc.; then to Hollywood. *Random Harvest* (42), *Dr Gillespie's New Assistant* (43), *An American Romance* (44), *Love Letters* (45), *The Searching Wind* (46), *Sorry, Wrong Number* (48), *Breakdown* (52), etc. Retired.

RICHARDSON, JOHN (1936–   ). British leading man, mainly in fancy dress. *Bachelor of Hearts* (58), *She* (65), *One Million Years BC* (66), *The Vengeance of She* (68), *The Chastity Belt* (68), etc.

RICHARDSON, SIR RALPH (1902–   ). Distinguished British actor, on stage from 1921. Occasional films include *The Ghoul* (debut) (33), *Friday the Thirteenth* (33), *The Return of Bulldog Drummond* (34), *Bulldog Jack* (35), *The Man Who Could Work Miracles* (35), *Things to Come* (36), *The Divorce of Lady X* (38), *South Riding* (38), *The Citadel* (38), *Q Planes* (39), *The Four Feathers* (39), *The Lion Has Wings* (39), *The Silver Fleet* (43), *School for Secrets* (46), *Anna Karenina* (48), *The Fallen Idol* (48), *The Heiress* (49), *An Outcast of the Islands* (51), *The Sound Barrier* (52), *Home at Seven* (also directed) (52), *The Holly and the Ivy* (53), *Richard III* (56), *Our Man in Havana* (59), *Exodus* (60), *The 300 Spartans* (62), *Long Day's Journey into Night* (62), *Woman of Straw* (64), *Dr Zhivago* (66), *Khartoum* (66), *The Wrong Box* (66), *Oh What a Lovely War* (69), *The Midas Run* (69), *The Bed Sitting Room* (69), *The Battle of Britain* (69), *The Looking Glass War* (69), *David Copperfield* (69), etc.

RICHARDSON, TONY (1928–   ). British director of stage and screen. *Momma Don't Allow* (short: co-d) (55), *Look Back in Anger* (58), *The Entertainer* (60), *Sanctuary* (US) (61), *A Taste of Honey* (61), *The Loneliness of the Long-Distance Runner* (63), *Tom Jones* (63), *The Loved One* (US) (65), *Sailor from Gibraltar* (66), *Mademoiselle* (66), *Red and Blue* (67), *The Charge of the Light Brigade* (68), *Laughter in the Dark* (69), *Hamlet* (69), etc.

RICHMAN, MARK (1927–   ). American general purpose actor, much on TV. *Friendly Persuasion* (56), *The Strange One* (57), *The Black Orchid* (58), *The Crime Busters* (61), etc. TV series: *Cain's Hundred* (61).

RICHMOND, KANE (1906–   ) (Frederick W. Bowditch). American leading man of second features. *The Leather Pushers* (serial) (30), *Nancy Steele Is Missing* (36), *Hard Guy* (41), *Action in the North Atlantic* (43), *Tiger Woman* (45), *Black Gold* (47), many others. Recently inactive.

RICHMOND, TED (1912–   ). American producer, former writer. *So Dark the Night* (46), *The Milkman* (50), *The Strange Door* (51), *Desert Legion* (53), *Forbidden* (54), *Count Three and Pray* (55), *Seven Waves Away* (57), *Solomon and Sheba* (59), *Company of Cowards* (*Advance to the Rear*) (64), *Return of the Seven* (66), *Villa Rides* (68), others.

RICHTER, HANS (1888–   ). German director of animated and surrealist films, most active in 20s. *Prelude and Fugue* (20), *Rhythm*

(22), *Vormittagspuk* (28), *New Life* (30), *Dreams That Money Can Buy* (44), etc.

RIDGELEY, JOHN (1909–1968) (John Huntingdon Rea). American supporting actor generally cast as gangster. *Invisible Menace* (38), *They Made Me a Fugitive* (39), *Brother Orchid* (40), *The Big Shot* (42), *Destination Tokyo* (44), *My Reputation* (46), *The Big Sleep* (46), *Possessed* (47), *Command Decision* (48), *The Blue Veil* (52), many others.

RIDGES, STANLEY (1892–1951). Incisive, heavy-featured British character actor who appeared in many Hollywood films. *The Scoundrel* (34), *Yellow Jack* (38), *If I Were King* (39), *Black Friday* (40), *Sergeant York* (41), *To Be Or Not To Be* (42), *The Big Shot* (42), *The Master Race* (45), *Possessed* (47), *No Way Out* (50), *The Groom Wore Spurs* (51), others.

RIEFENSTAHL, LENI (1902–). German woman director, former dancer, who made brilliant propaganda films for Hitler. *The White Hell of Pitz Palu* (acted) (29), *The Blue Light* (a, d) (32), *S.O.S. Iceberg* (a) (33), *Triumph of the Will* (the Nuremberg Rally) (wrote, d) (34), *Olympische Spiele* 1936, *Tiefland* (45), etc.

RIFIFI (France 1955). The film which re-established Jules Dassin as an international director after years of inactivity following his black-listing by the Un-American Activities tribunals; also the film which triggered off an unending series of stories about big-c ale robberies which come unstuck. Its particular selling-point was that the entire twenty-minute robbery sequence took place in complete silence. Written by René Wheeler and Dassin from a novel by Auguste le Breton; photographed by Philippe Agostini; music by Georges Auric; with Jean Servais, Carl Mohner, Dassin.

RIGBY, EDWARD (1879–1951). British stage character actor in films since 1934; became a familiar figure in endearingly doddery roles. *Lorna Doone* (35), *Mr Smith Carries On* (37), *The Proud Valley* (39), *Kipps* (41), *The Common Touch* (41), *Let the People Sing* (42), *Salute John Citizen* (42), *Get Cracking* (43), *Don't Take It to Heart* (44), *Quiet Weekend* (47), *Easy Money* (48), *It's Hard To Be Good* (49), *The Happiest Days of Your Life* (49), *The Mudlark* (50), many others.

RIGG, DIANA (1938–). British leading actress who came to fame in *The Avengers* TV series (65–67). *The Assassination Bureau* (68), *A Midsummer Night's Dream* (68), *On Her Majesty's Secret Service* (69), etc.

RILLA, WALTER (1895–). German actor on stage from 1921; in Britain from mid-30s. *Der Geiger von Florenz* (26), *The Scarlet Pimpernel* (35), *Victoria the Great* (37), *At the Villa Rose* (39), *The*

Rilla, Wolf

Adventures of Tartu (43), *The Lisbon Story* (46), *State Secret* (50), *Cairo* (61), *The Thousand Eyes of D Mabuse* (63), etc. Produced and directed religious film, *Behold the Man* (51).

RILLA, WOLF (1920–). British director, son of Walter Rilla. *Noose for a Lady* (53), *The End of the Road* (54), *Pacific Destiny* (56), *The Scamp* (57), *Bachelor of Hearts* (58), *Witness in the Dark* (50), *Piccadilly Third Stop* (60), *Village of the Damned* (62), *Cairo* (63), *The World Ten Times Over* (also wrote) (63), etc.

RIN TIN TIN (1916–32). An ex-German Army dog which became one of the biggest box office draws of the American silent screen. *Where the North Begins* (23), *The Night Cry* (25), *The Clash of the Wolves* (24), *Jaws of Steel* (27), *The Frozen River* (29), *A Dog of the Regiment* (30), etc.; also in serials.

RIPLEY, ARTHUR (1895–1961). American director whose films are oddly sparse. Former writer. *I Met My Love Again* (38), *A Voice in the Wind* (44), *The Chase* (47), *Thunder Road* (58), etc.

RIPPER, MICHAEL (c. 1925–). British character actor, often in comic roles. *Captain Boycott* (48), *Treasure Hunt* (52), *The Belles of St Trinian's* (54), *Richard III* (56), *Quatermass II* (57), *The Revenge of Frankenstein* (58), *Brides of Dracula* (60), *Captain Clegg* (62), *The Secret of Blood Island* (65), *The Reptile* (66), *The Plague of the Zombies* (66), *Where the Bullets Fly* (66), etc.

RISCOE, ARTHUR (1896–1954). British stage comedian. Rare film appearances include *Going Gay* (34), *Paradise for Two* (38), *Kipps* (as Chitterlow) (41), etc.

RISDON, ELIZABETH (1887–1958) (E. Evans). British stage actress who in later life went to Hollywood and played many character roles. *Guard That Girl* (35), *Crime and Punishment* (36), *The Great Man Votes* (39), *Lost Angel* (44), *Grissly's Millions* (44), *Mama Loves Papa* (45), *Life with Father* (47), *Bannerline* (51), *Scaramouche* (52), many others.

RISI, DINO (1916–). Italian director: *The Sign of Venus* (55), *Poveri ma Belli* (56), *Il Sorpasso* (62), etc.

RISKIN, ROBERT (1897–1955). Distinguished American screenwriter. *Illicit* (31), *The Miracle Woman* (31), *Lady for a Day* (33), *It Happened One Night* (34), *The Whole Town's Talking* (35), *Mr Deeds Goes To Town* (36), *Lost Horizon* (37), *You can't Take It With You* (38), *The Real Glory* (39), *Meet John Doe* (41), *The Thin Man Goes Home* (44), *Magic Town* (46), *Riding High* (50), *Mister 880* (50), *The Groom Wore Spurs* (51), etc.

RITCHARD, CYRIL (1896–). British dancer and light comedian, mainly on stage. Few films include *Piccadilly* (29), *Blackmail* (30), *I See Ice* (38), *Half a Sixpence* (67).

824

RITCHIE, JUNE (c. 1938–   ). British leading lady, mainly in 'realist' films. *A Kind of Loving* (61), *Live Now Pay Later* (63), *The Mouse on the Moon* (63), *The World Ten Times Over* (63), *This Is My Street* (64), *The Syndicate* (GB) (67), etc.

†RITT, MARTIN (1919–   ). American director with stage and TV experience. *Edge of the City* (56), *No Down Payment* (57), *The Long Hot Summer* (58), *The Sound and the Fury* (59), *The Black Orchid* (59), *Five Branded Women* (60), *Paris Blues* (61), *Hemingway's Adventures of a Young Man* (62), *Hud* (63), *The Outrage* (64), *The Spy Who Came in from the Cold* (65), *Hombre* (67), *The Brotherhood* (68), *The Molly Maguires* (69).

RITTER, TEX (1907–   ) (Woodward Ritter). American singing cowboy star of innumerable second features. *Song of the Gringo* (36), *Sing, Cowboy, Sing* (38), *The Old Chisholm Trail* (43), *Marshal of Gunsmoke* (46), etc.; sang ballad in *High Noon* (52).

RITTER, THELMA (1905–1969). Wry-faced American character actress with long stage experience before coming to Hollywood. *The Big Heart* (*Miracle on 34th Street*) (debut) (47), *A Letter to Three Wives* (49), *All about Eve* (50), *The Mating Season* (50), *As Young as You Feel* (51), *The Model and the Marriage Broker* (51), *With a Song in My Heart* (52), *Titanic* (53), *Rear Window* (54), *Daddy Longlegs* (55), *The Proud and Profane* (56), *Pillow Talk* (59), *The Misfits* (60), *A New Kind of Love* (63), *Move Over, Darling* (63), *Boeing Boeing* (66), etc.

THE RITZ BROTHERS: AL (1901–65), JIM (1903–   ) and HARRY (1906–   ). Zany American night-club comedians who made many enjoyable appearances in films of the 30s; recently (1964) made cabaret comeback. *Sing Baby Sing* (36), *One in a Million* (37), *You Can't Have Everything* (38), *The Goldwyn Follies* (38), *The Three Musketeers* (39), *The Gorilla* (39), *Pack Up Your Troubles* (*We're in the Army Now*) (39), *Argentine Nights* (40), *Everything Happens to Us* (45), etc.

RIVA, EMMANUELE (1932–   ). French leading actress. *Hiroshima Mon Amour* (58), *Adua et sa Compagnie* (*Hungry for Love*) (58), *Kapo* (59), *Leon Morin Priest* (60), *Climats* (61), *Therese Desqueyroux* (63), *Soledad* (66), etc.

THE RIVER. There are two famous films of this title. 1. US 1938: a documentary by Pare Lorenz, with free-verse commentary, about the Tennessee Valley Authority and its effect on the dwellers in the Mississippi Basin. Words by Thomas Chalmers, music by Virgil Thompson. 2. India 1951: Jean Renoir's colour romance in which the story serves as a slender thread on which to hold the decoration; with Adrienne Corri, Esmond Knight.

825

RIVETTE, JACQUES (1928–). French director, former critic. *Le Coup du Berger* (56), *Paris Nous Appartient* (60), *La Religieuse* (also wrote) (65), *L'Amour Fou* (also wrote) (68).

RIX, BRIAN (1924–). British actor-manager associated with the Whitehall farces. Occasional films include *Reluctant Heroes* (51), *What Every Woman Wants* (54), *Up to His Neck* (54), *Dry Rot* (55), *The Night We Dropped a Clanger* (59), *And the Same to You* (60), *Nothing Barred* (61), etc.

RKO Radio Pictures Inc was for many years one of Hollywood's 'big five' production companies, with its own distribution arm. It started in 1921 as a joint enterprise of the Radio Corporation of America and the Keith-Orpheum cinema circuit. Despite severe financial vicissitudes, it struggled on for twenty-seven years, buoyed by a generally decent production standard; stars like Cary Grant, Katharine Hepburn, Wheeler and Wolsey, Leon Errol; individual films such as *Cimarron, King Kong, The Informer, Suspicion, Mr Blandings Builds His Dream House* and *Fort Apache*; and the participation of Goldwyn, Disney and Selznick, who all released through RKO at its peak. In 1948 Howard Hughes (qv) acquired a large share of the stock; but after a period of uncertainty RKO ceased production in 1953 and the studio was sold to Desilu TV.

ROACH, HAL (1892–). American producer chiefly associated with gag comedies. Varied early experience before he teamed with Harold Lloyd 1916; later made films with Our Gang, Laurel and Hardy, etc. Sound films: *Fraternally Yours* (32), *Way Out West* (36), *Topper* (37), *Of Mice and Men* (40), *Turnabout* (40), *One Million B.C.* (*Man and His Mate*) (40), *Topper Returns* (41), scores of others.

road show. A term which used to mean a travelling show; latterly in cinema terms it indicates the special, prolonged pre-release at advanced prices of a big-screen attraction, e.g. *My Fair Lady* or *The Sound of Music*, which may in this way run for years in a big city before being released to local theatres.

ROAD TO SINGAPORE (US 1940). This modest studio-made romantic comedy happened to star three Paramount contract players: Bing Crosby, Bob Hope and Dorothy Lamour. They worked so well together, with successful ad-libbing and an easy style, that several other 'Road' comedies were made, getting crazier each time and using every kind of gag the writers could think of. The only thing you were sure of in these pictures was that Bob wouldn't get the girl; otherwise anything could happen, from inside gags about Paramount to talking camels. They all date badly. *Road to Zanzibar* (41), *Road to Morocco* (42), *Road to Utopia* (46), *Road to Rio* (47), *Road to Bali* (52), *Road to Hong Kong* (62).

ROBARDS, JASON (1893–1963). American stage actor. Few film appearances include *On Trial* (28), *Abraham Lincoln* (30), *The Crusades* (35), *I Stole a Million* (39), *Riff Raff* (47).

ROBARDS, JASON JNR (1920–   ). American stage actor, of theatrical family. Films include *The Journey* (58), *By Love Possessed* (59), *Tender Is the Night* (61), *Long Day's Journey into Night* (62), *A Big Hand for the Little Lady* (66), *A Thousand Clowns* (66), *Any Wednesday* (66), *Divorce American Style* (67), *The Law and Tombstone* (67), *The St Valentine's Day Massacre* (67), *The Night They Raided Minsky's* (68), *Isadora* (68), *Once Upon a Time in the West* (69), *Tora! Tora! Tora!* (69), *Julius Caesar* (70), etc.

ROBBE-GRILLET, ALAIN (c. 1917–   ). French writer, associated with Resnais in *Last Year at Marienbad* (60). Also wrote and directed *L'Immortelle* (62), *Trans-Europe Express* (66).

robberies have been a commonplace of film action fare since *The Great Train Robbery* itself; but of late there has been a fashion for showing the planning and execution of robberies through the eyes of the participants. Perhaps this started in 1950 with *The Asphalt Jungle* (and its two remakes *The Badlanders* and *Cairo*); anyway, some of the films built on this mould are *Rififi*, *Five Against the House*, *Seven Thieves*, *The Killing*, *Payroll*, *Piccadilly Third Stop*, *The Day They Robbed the Bank of England*, *A Prize of Gold*, *On Friday at Eleven*, *Once a Thief*, *He Who Rides a Tiger* and *Robbery*; while films treating the same subject less seriously included *The Lavender Hill Mob*, *The Lady Killers*, *Ocean's Eleven*, *Persons Unknown*, *The League of Gentlemen*, *Topkapi*, *The Big Job*, *Assault on a Queen*, *The Biggest Bundle of Them All*, *Grand Slam*, *They Came to Rob Las Vegas*, *The Italian Job*. The biggest attempted robbery of all was probably the raid on Fort Knox in *Goldfinger*. Sometimes one longs for a return to the days of the dapper jewel thieves: Ronald Colman or David Niven in *Raffles*, Herbert Marshall in *Trouble in Paradise*, Charles Korvin as Arsène Lupin. The closest we have come to this style for many years is William Wyler's *How to Steal a Million*.

ROBBINS, HAROLD (1916–   ). American best-selling novelist whose over-sexed tales have been readily translated to the screen. *The Carpetbaggers* (63), *Where Love Has Gone* (64), *Nevada Smith* (66), *Stiletto* (69), *The Adventurers* (69), etc. TV series: *The Survivors* (69).

ROBBINS, JEROME (1918–   ). American dancer and ballet-master who has choreographed several films: *The King and I* (56), *West Side Story* (AA) (also co-directed) (61), etc.

THE ROBE (US 1953). This solemn epic from Lloyd C. Douglas' novel about the aftermath of the Crucifixion is unremarkable except as the first film in CinemaScope (qv). Photographer Leon Shamroy

operated under difficulties with a lens as yet imperfect. Victor
Mature, who gave the best performance, appeared two years later
in a sequel, *Demetrius and the Gladiators.*

ROBER, RICHARD (1906–1952). American general purpose actor with
stage experience. *Smart Girls Don't Talk* (48), *Deported* (50), *The
Well* (52), *The Devil Makes Three* (52), etc. Killed in car accident.

ROBERT, YVES (1920–   ). French director, former actor. Gained
fame with *The War of the Buttons* (61); then *Bebert et l'Omnibus* (63),
Copains (64).

ROBERTI, LYDA (c. 1909–1938). German-Polish leading lady, former
child café singer, in several Hollywood films of the 30s. *Million
Dollar Legs* (32), *The Kid from Spain* (32), *Three-Cornered Moon* (33),
George White's Scandals (35), *Pick a Star* (37), *Wide Open Faces* (37),
etc.

ROBERTS, FLORENCE (1860–1940). American character actress best
remembered as Granny in the Jones Family series 1936–40.

ROBERTS, RACHEL (1927–   ). British stage actress, married to Rex
Harrison. Films include *Valley of Song* (52), *The Good Companions*
(57), *Our Man in Havana* (59), *Saturday Night and Sunday Morning*
(BFA) (69), *This Sporting Life* (BFA) (63), *A Flea in Her Ear* (68),
etc.

ROBERTS, ROY (1900–   ). American character actor who once
played cops but has graduated to senior executives. *Guadalcanal
Diary* (43), *My Darling Clementine* (46), *Flaming Fury* (49), *The Big
Trees* (52), *The Glory Brigade* (53), *The Boss* (56), many others. TV
series: *Petticoat Junction.*

ROBERTSHAW, JERROLD (1866–1941). Gaunt British stage actor who
made several film appearances. *Dombey and Son* (18), *She* (25),
Downhill (27), *Kitty* (29), *Don Quixote* (title role) (33), etc.

†ROBERTSON, CLIFF (1925–   ). American leading man with long
stage experience before being spotted for films. *Picnic* (debut) (55),
Autumn Leaves (56), *The Girl Most Likely* (57), *The Naked and the
Dead* (58), *Gidget* (59), *Battle of the Coral Sea* (59), *As the Sea Rages*
(60), *All in a Night's Work* (61), *The Big Show* (61), *Underworld USA*
(61), *The Interns* (62), *My Six Loves* (63), *PT 109* (as President
Kennedy) (63), *Sunday in New York* (64), *The Best Man* (64),
633 Squadron (64), *Love Has Many Faces* (65), *Masquerade* (GB) (65),
Up from the Beach (65), *The Honey Pot* (67), *The Devil's Brigade* (68),
Charly (AA) (68), *Too Late the Hero* (69). TV series: *Rod Brown of the
Rocket Rangers* (53).

ROBERTSON, DALE (1923–   ). American Western star, former
schoolteacher. *Fighting Man of the Plains* (debut) (49), *Two Flags*

West (50), *Lydia Bailey* (52), *The Silver Whip* (53), *Sitting Bull* (54), *A Day of Fury* (56), *Law of the Lawless* (63), *Blood on the Arrow* (65), *Coast of Skeletons* (65), etc. TV series: *Tales of Wells Fargo* (57–61), *The Iron Horse* (66).

†ROBESON, PAUL (1898–   ). American Negro actor and singer, on stage, including concerts, from mid-20s. *The Emperor Jones* (33), *Sanders of the River* (35), *Showboat* (36), *Song of Freedom* (37), *Jericho* (38), *King Solomon's Mines* (38), *The Proud Valley* (39), *Tales of Manhattan* (42).

ROBEY, GEORGE (1869–1954) (George Edward Wade). British music-hall comedian, 'the prime minister of mirth'. Appeared in silent farcical comedies, later in character roles. *The Rest Cure* (23), *Don Quixote* (as Sancho Panza) (23 and 33), *Her Prehistoric Man* (24), *Chu Chin Chow* (33), *Marry Me* (33), *Birds of a Feather* (36), *A Girl Must Live* (39), *Variety Jubilee* (40), *Salute John Citizen* (42), *Henry V* (44), *The Trojan Brothers* (45), *The Pickwick Papers* (52), etc.

ROBIN, DANY (1927–   ). French leading lady. *Le Silence est D'Or* (46), *Histoire D'Amour* (52), *Act of Love* (54), *In Six Easy Lessons* (60), *The Waltz of the Toreadors* (62), etc.

ROBIN HOOD. The legendary outlaw leader of Plantagenet England is one of literature's most oft-filmed characters. There were film versions in 1909 (GB), 1912 (GB), 1912 (US), 1913 (US), and 1913 (GB). Douglas Fairbanks made his big-scale *Robin Hood* in 1922, with Wallace Beery as King Richard. In 1938 came *The Adventures of Robin Hood*, one of Hollywood's most satisfying action adventures, with Errol Flynn as Robin, Claude Rains as Prince John and Basil Rathbone as Guy of Gisbourne; directed by William Keighley and Michael Curtiz, from a script by Norman Reilly Raine and Seton I. Miller. Its exhilaration has not diminished with time. In 1946 (US) Cornel Wilde played Robin's son in *Bandit of Sherwood Forest*; in 1948 (US) Jon Hall was Robin in *Prince of Thieves*; in 1950 (US) John Derek was Robin's son in *Rogues of Sherwood Forest*; Robert Clarke played Robin in an odd concoction called *Tales of Robin Hood* (US 1952). Also in 1952, in Britain, Disney filmed Richard Todd in *The Story of Robin Hood and His Merrie Men*, with only fair success, though the real Sherwood Forest was used for the first time. Robin also appeared briefly (played by Harold Warrender) in *Ivanhoe* (52). *Men of Sherwood Forest* (GB 1956) had Don Taylor as Robin; *Son of Robin Hood* (GB 1959) turned out to be a daughter, played by June Laverick. Most durable Robin is Richard Greene, who played the role not only in 165 half-hour TV films but in a feature, *Sword of Sherwood Forest* (GB 1961). In 1967 Barrie Inghain took over in *A Challenge for Robin Hood*.

Robin, Leo

ROBIN, LEO (1899–   ). American lyricist. *Innocents of Paris* (29), *Monte Carlo* (30), *One Hour with You* (32), *Little Miss Marker* (34), *The Big Broadcast of* 1938 (AA for 'Thanks for the Memory'), *Gulliver's Travels* (39), *My Gal Sal* (43), *Meet Me after the Show* (50), *My Sister Eileen* (55), etc. Songs include 'Louise', 'Beyond the Blue Horizon', 'June in January', 'No Love No Nothing'.

ROBINSON, BILL (1878–1949). American Negro tap-dancer and entertainer, famous for his stairway dance. Films include *The Little Colonel* (35), *In Old Kentucky* (36), *Rebecca of Sunnybrook Farm* (38), *Stormy Weather* (43).

ROBINSON, CASEY (1903–   ). American screenwriter, in Hollywood from 1921. *I Love That Man* (33), *Captain Blood* (35), *Call it a Day* (37), *It's Love I'm After* (37), *Four's a Crowd* (39), *King's Row* (42), *Passage to Marseilles* (44), *Days of Glory* (44), *The Macomber Affair* (47), *Under My Skin* (also produced) (50), *Two Flags West* (also produced) (50), *Diplomatic Courier* (also produced) (52), *The Snows of Kilimanjaro* (52), *While the City Sleeps* (56), *This Earth Is Mine* (also produced) (59), etc.

ROBINSON CRUSOE. There have been many film variations on Defoe's novel. The closest to the original have been Luis Bunuel's *The Adventures of Robinson Crusoe* (Mexico 1953) with Dan O'Herlihy, and, oddly enough, Byron Haskin's *Robinson Crusoe on Mars* (US 1964) with Paul Mantee.

†ROBINSON, EDWARD G. (1893–   ) (Emanuel Goldenberg). American star actor of Rumanian origin. On stage from 1913; later settled in Hollywood. *The Bright Shawl* (23), *The Hole in the Wall* (29), *Night Ride* (30), *A Lady to Love* (30), *Outside the Law* (30), *East Is West* (30), *Widow from Chicago* (30), *Little Caesar* (which made him a star) (30), *Five Star Final* (31), *Smart Money* (31), *The Hatchet Man* (31), *Two Seconds* (32), *Tiger Shark* (32), *Silver Dollar* (32), *The Little Giant* (33), *I Loved a Woman* (33), *Dark Hazard* (34), *The Man with Two Faces* (34), *The Whole Town's Talking* (34), *Barbary Coast* (35), *Bullets or Ballots* (36), *Thunder in the City* (GB) (37), *Kid Galahad* (37), *The Last Gangster* (38), *A Slight Case of Murder* (38), *The Amazing Dr Clitterhouse* (38), *I Am the Law* (38), *Confessions of a Nazi Spy* (39), *Blackmail* (39), *Dr Ehrlich's Magic Bullet* (40), *Brother Orchid* (40), *A Dispatch from Reuters* (41), *The Sea Wolf* (41), *Manpower* (41), *Unholy Partners* (41), *Larceny Inc.* (42), *Tales of Manhattan* (42), *Destroyer* (43), *Tampico* (44), *Double Indemnity* (44), *Mr Winkle Goes to War* (44), *The Woman in the Window* (44), *Our Vines Have Tender Grapes* (45), *Scarlet Street* (45), *Journey Together* (GB) (45), *The Stranger* (46), *The Red House* (47), *All My Sons* (48), *Key Largo* (48), *Night Has a Thousand Eyes* (48), *House of Strangers* (49), *My Daughter Joy* (GB) (50), *Actors and Sin* (52), *Vice Squad* (53), *Big*

Leaguer (53), *The Glass Web* (53), *Black Tuesday* (54), *The Violent Men* (55), *Tight Spot* (55), *A Bullet for Joey* (55), *Illegal* (55), *Hell on Frisco Bay* (56), *Nightmare* (56), *The Ten Commandments* (56), *A Hole in the Head* (59), *Seven Thieves* (59), *Pepe* (60), *My Geisha* (62), *Two Weeks in Another Town* (62), *Sammy Going South* (GB) (62), *The Prize* (63), *Good Neighbour Sam* (64), *Robin and the Seven Hoods* (64), *Cheyenne Autumn* (64), *The Outrage* (64), *The Cincinnati Kid* (65), *The Biggest Bundle of Them All* (66), *Grand Slam* (67), *Mackenna's Gold* (68), *Song of Norway* (69).

ROBINSON, JAY (1930–). American stage actor of eccentric roles. Films include *The Robe* (53), *Demetrius and the Gladiators* (54), *The Virgin Queen* (55), *My Man Godfrey* (57).

ROBINSON, JOHN (1908–). British stage actor, familiar in heavy father or tough executive roles. *The Scarab Murder Case* (36), *The Lion Has Wings* (40), *Uneasy Terms* (49), *Hammer the Toff* (51), *The Constant Husband* (55), *Fortune Is a Woman* (58), *And the Same to You* (61), etc.

ROBINSON, MADELEINE (1916–) (Madeleine Svoboda). French stage and film actress. *Soldats Sans Uniformes* (34), *Douce* (43), *Une Si Jolie Petite Plage* (48), *Dieu a Besoin des Hommes* (50), *Le Garçon Sauvage* (51), *The She Wolves* (57), *A Double Tour* (59), *The Trial* (64), *A Trap for Cinderella* (65), *A New World* (66), *Le Voyage du Père* (66), etc.

ROBISON, ARTHUR (1888–). Chicago-born director of German films, remembered for *Warning Shadows* (24), *The Informer* (GB) (29), *The Student of Prague* (35).

ROBSON, FLORA (1902–). Distinguished British stage actress. *Dance Pretty Lady* (film debut) (31), *Catherine the Great* (34), *Fire over England* (36), *Wuthering Heights* (US) (39), *Poison Pen* (39), *The Sea Hawk* (US) (40), *Saratoga Trunk* (US) (42), *2000 Women* (44), *Great Day* (45), *Caesar and Cleopatra* (45), *Black Narcissus* (47), *Holiday Camp* (47), *Saraband for Dead Lovers* (48), *The Malta Story* (52), *Romeo and Juliet* (54), *Innocent Sinners* (57), *55 Days at Peking* (62), *Murder at the Gallop* (63), *Guns at Batasi* (64), *Young Cassidy* (65), *Seven Women* (65), *The Shuttered Room* (66), *A Cry in the Wind* (Gk.) (66), etc.

†ROBSON, MARK (1913–). American director, former editor: began with Lewton and Kramer but progressed to more solidly commercial subjects. *The Seventh Victim* (43), *The Ghost Ship* (43), *Youth Runs Wild* (44), *Isle of the Dead* (45), *Bedlam* (46), *Champion* (49), *Home of the Brave* (49), *Roughshod* (49), *My Foolish Heart* (50), *Edge of Doom* (50), *Bright Victory* (51), *I Want You* (51), *Return to Paradise* (53), *Hell below Zero* (GB) (54), *The Bridges at Toko-Ri* (54),

Phffft (54), *A Prize of Gold* (55), *Trial* (55), *The Harder They Fall* (56), *The Little Hut* (also produced) (57), *Peyton Place* (58), *The Inn of the Sixth Happiness* (GB) (58), *From the Terrace* (also produced) (59), *Lisa* (*The Inspector*) (produced only) (62), *Nine Hours to Rama* (GB) (also produced) (63), *The Prize* (63), *Von Ryan's Express* (also produced) (65), *Lost Command* (also produced) (66), *Valley of the Dolls* (also produced) (67), *Daddy's Gone a-Hunting* (also produced) (69).

ROBSON, MAY (1865–1942). Australian actress, in America from childhood. Long experience on stage tours before coming to Hollywood, where she played domineering but kindly old ladies. *The Rejuvenation of Aunt Mary* (27), *Mother's Millions* (29), *Strange Interlude* (32), *Letty Lynton* (32), *Lady for a Day* (33), *Alice in Wonderland* (33), *Dinner at Eight* (33), *Grand Old Girl* (35), *The Baxter Millions* (36), *Rhythm of the River* (37), *A Star Is Born* (37), *Four Daughters* (38), *Bringing Up Baby* (38), *The Adventures of Tom Sawyer* (38), *Nurse Edith Cavell* (39), *Irene* (40), *Granny Get Your Gun* (40), *Million Dollar Baby* (41), *Playmates* (42), many others.

ROC, PATRICIA (1918–   ) (Felicia Riese). British leading lady of the 40s, signed for films after brief stage experience. *The Rebel Son* (*Taras Bulba*) (38), *The Gaunt Stranger* (39), *The Mind of Mr Reeder* (39), *Three Silent Men* (40), *Let the People Sing* (42), *Millions Like Us* (43), *2000 Women* (44), *Love Story* (44), *Madonna of the Seven Moons* (44), *The Wicked Lady* (45), *Canyon Passage* (US) (46), *The Brothers* (47), *Jassy* (47), *When the Bough Breaks* (48), *One Night with You* (48), *The Perfect Woman* (49), *The Man on the Eiffel Tower* (51), *The Hypnotist* (55), *Bluebeard's Ten Honeymoons* (60), etc.

ROCCO AND HIS BROTHERS (Italy 1960). A super-realistic story of a peasant family in the big city, this film by Luchino Visconti was highly acclaimed on its first appearance but seems to have left little mark. Written by Suso Cecchi d'Amico, Vasco Pratolini and Visconti; photographed by Giuseppe Rotunno.

RODGERS, RICHARD (1901–   ). American composer who has worked variously with lyricists Lorenz Hart and Oscar Hammerstein II. *Love Me Tonight* (32), *Hallelujah I'm a Bum* (33), *On Your Toes* (38), *Babes in Arms* (39), *The Boys from Syracuse* (40), *State Fair* (45), *Oklahoma* (55), *The King and I* (56), *Pal Joey* (57), *South Pacific* (58), *The Sound of Music* (65), many other complete scores and single songs.

ROEG, NICOLAS (* –   ). British cinematographer. *Far From the Madding Crowd* (67), *Petulia* (68), etc.

ROGELL, ALBERT S. (1901–   ). American director of second features, former cameraman. *Riders of Death Valley* (32), *Argentine Nights*

(40), *Trouble Chaser* (*Lil Abner*) (40), *The Black Cat* (41), *Tight Shoes* (41), *In Old Oklahoma* (43), *Heaven Only Knows* (47), *Northwest Stampede* (48), *The Admiral Was a Lady* (also produced) (50), *Men Against Speed* (58), etc.; moved into TV.

ROGERS, CHARLES 'BUDDY' (1904–   ). American light leading man of the 20s and 30s; married to Mary Pickford. *Fascinating Youth* (26), *Wings* (27), *Abie's Irish Rose* (29), *Paramount on Parade* (30), *Varsity* (30), *Young Eagles* (31), *This Reckless Age* (32), *Old Man Rhythm* (35), *Once in a Million* (36), *This Way Please* (38), *Golden Hooves* (41), *Mexican Spitfire's Baby* (43), *Don't Trust Your Husband* (48), many others.

ROGERS, GINGER (1911–   ) (Virginia McMath). American leading actress, comedienne and dancer, affectionately remembered for her 30s musicals with Fred Astaire. Former band singer; then brief Broadway experience before being taken to Hollywood. *Young Man of Manhattan* (30), *Gold Diggers of 1933*, *Forty-second Street* (33), *Flying Down to Rio* (33), *The Gay Divorce* (34), *Roberta* (34), *Top Hat* (35), *In Person* (36), *Follow the Fleet* (36), *Shall We Dance* (37), *Having Wonderful Time* (38), *Stage Door* (38), *Carefree* (38), *The Story of Vernon and Irene Castle* (39), *Bachelor Mother* (39), *Fifth Avenue Girl* (39), *The Primrose Path* (40), *Lucky Partners* (40), *Kitty Foyle* (AA) (40), *Tom, Dick and Harry* (41), *Roxie Hart* (42), *Once upon a Honeymoon* (42), *The Major and the Minor* (43), *Lady in the Dark* (43), *I'll Be Seeing You* (44), *Weekend at the Waldorf* (45), *Magnificent Doll* (47), *It Had To Be You* (48), *The Barkeleys of Broadway* (48), *Storm Warning* (51), *We're Not Married* (52), *Monkey Business* (53), *Black Widow* (54), *Tight Spot* (55), *Oh Men, Oh Women* (57), *Harlow* (electronovision version) (65), *The Confession* (65), etc.

ROGERS, MACLEAN (1899–   ). British director, mainly of low-budget features for which he has often written his own unambitious scripts. *The Third Eye* (29), *Busman's Holiday* (36), *Old Mother Riley Joins Up* (39), *Gert and Daisy's Weekend* (42), *Variety Jubilee* (43), *The Trojan Brothers* (45), *Calling Paul Temple* (48), *The Story of Shirley Yorke* (49), *Johnny on the Spot* (54), *Not so Dusty* (56), *Not Wanted on Voyage* (57), *Not A Hope in Hell* (60), many others.

ROGERS, PAUL (1917–   ). British character actor, on stage from 1938, occasional films from 1932. *Beau Brummell* (53), *Our Man in Havana* (59), *The Trials of Oscar Wilde* (60), *No Love for Johnnie* (61), *Billy Budd* (62), *The Wild and the Willing* (63), *The Third Secret* (64), *He Who Rides a Tiger* (65), *A Midsummer Night's Dream* (68), *The Looking Glass War* (69), etc.

ROGERS, PETER (1916–   ). British producer, in films from 1942; wrote and co-produced many comedies during 40s and early 50s; conceived and produced the 'Carry On' series (qv) (58–69).

ROGERS, ROY (1912–   ) (Leonard Slye). American singing cowboy star, usually seen with horse 'Trigger'. Varied early experience; formed 'Sons of the Pioneers' singing group; in small film roles from 1935, a star from 1938 till 1953. *Under Western Skies* (38), *The Carson City Kid* (40), *Robin Hood of the Pecos* (42), *The Man from Music Mountain* (44), *Along the Navajo Trail* (46), *Roll on Texas Moon* (47), *Night Time in Nevada* (49), *Trail of Robin Hood* (51), *Pals of the Golden West* (53), etc. TV series: *The Roy Rogers Show* (52–54). Now tours in rodeos, etc.

ROGERS, WILL (1879–1935). American comedian whose cracker-barrel philosophy almost moved nations. In Ziegfeld Follies before film debut in 1918 (*Laughing Bill Hyde*). Talkies include *Lightnin'* (30), *A Connecticut Yankee at the Court of King Arthur* (30), *Down to Earth* (32), *Too Busy to Work* (32), *State Fair* (33), *David Harum* (34), *Handy Andy* (34), *Judge Priest* (34), *In Old Kentucky* (35), etc. His son WILL ROGERS JNR, (1911–   ) played him in *The Story of Will Rogers* (52). A biography, *Our Will Rogers*, by Homer Croy, was published in 1953.

ROLAND, GILBERT (1905–   ) (Luis Antonio Damaso De Alonso). Mexican leading man, trained as bullfighter, who gate-crashed Hollywood in the mid-20s and became immediately popular. *The Plastic Age* (debut) (25), *Camille* (27), *Monsieur La Fox* (29), *Call Her Savage* (32), *She Done Him Wrong* (33), *Last Train from Madrid* (37), *Juarez* (39), *The Sea Hawk* (40), *My Life with Caroline* (41), *Isle of Missing Men* (42), *Captain Kidd* (45), *Pirates of Monterey* (47), *Riding the California Trail* (48), *We Were Strangers* (49), *The Furies* (50), *The Bullfighter and the Lady* (51), *The Bad and the Beautiful* (52), *The Racers* (54), *Treasure of Pancho Villa* (56), *Guns of the Timberland* (58), *The Big Circus* (59), *Cheyenne Autumn* (64), *The Reward* (65), *The Poppy is Also a Flower* (*Danger Grows Wild*) (66), many others.

ROLAND, RUTH (1896–1937). American leading lady, a silent serial queen: *The Red Circle* (15), *The Neglected Wife* (17), *Hands Up* (18), *Tiger's Trail* (19), etc. Also in features: *While Father Telephoned* (13), *The Masked Woman* (26), *Reno* (30), *From Nine to Nine* (36), many others.

ROLFE, GUY (1915–   ). Lean British leading man and character actor, former racing driver and boxer. *Hungry Hill* (debut) (46), *Nicholas Nickleby* (47), *Uncle Silas* (47), *Broken Journey* (47), *Portrait from Life* (49), *The Spider and the Fly* (50), *Prelude to Fame* (51), *Ivanhoe* (52), *King of the Khyber Rifles* (54), *It's Never Too Late* (56), *Snow White and the Three Stooges* (62), *Taras Bulba* (62), *Mr Sardonicus* (63), *The Fall of the Roman Empire* (64), *The Alphabet Murders* (65), etc.

ROMAN, RUTH (1924–   ). American leading lady with stage experience, in small film roles from 1946. *The Window* (48), *Champion* (49), *Always Leave Them Laughing* (50), *Three Secrets* (50), *Strangers on a Train* (51), *Mara Maru* (53), *Blowing Wild* (54), *Down Three Dark Streets* (55), *Joe Macbeth* (55), *Bitter Victory* (57), *Love Has Many Faces* (65), many others, mostly routine. Also on TV, especially in series *The Long Hot Summer* (64).

romantic teams who have been popular enough to make several films together are headed by William Powell and Myrna Loy, who made 12 joint appearances. Runners-up include Janet Gaynor and Charles Farrell (11 appearances); Fred Astaire and Ginger Rogers (10); Spencer Tracy and Katherine Hepburn (9); Judy Garland and Mickey Rooney (8); Clark Gable and Joan Crawford (8); Nelson Eddy and Jeanette Macdonald (8); Greer Garson and Walter Pidgeon (8); Errol Flynn and Olivia de Havilland (8); Bette Davis and George Brent (7); James Cagney and Joan Blondell (6). Even though most of these teamings began because both stars happened to be under contract to the same studio, they would not have continued had they not been felicitous. Other teams who struck notable sparks off each other but have fewer films to their credit include Humphrey Bogart and Lauren Bacall; Ronald Colman and Greer Garson; Cary Grant and Irene Dunn; Greta Garbo and John Gilbert; Greta Garbo and Melvyn Douglas; Bob Hope and Paulette Goddard; Danny Kaye and Virginia Mayo; Alan Ladd and Veronica Lake; Donald O'Connor and Peggy Ryan; Marie Dressler and Wallace Beery; Rita Hayworth and Glenn Ford; John Barrymore and Carole Lombard; Charlie Ruggles and Mary Boland; Rock Hudson and Doris Day; Jack Hulbert and Cicely Courtneidge; Richard Burton and Elizabeth Taylor.

ROMBERG, SIGMUND (1887–1951). Hungarian composer of light music. Scores include *The Desert Song* (29 and 43), *New Moon* (31 and 40), *Blossom Time* (34), *Maytime* (37), *Balalaika* (39), *The Student Prince* (54). (Most of these began as stage operettas.)

Rome in its ancient days was reconstructed for *Quo Vadis*, *The Sign of the Cross*, *Androcles and the Lion*, *The Fall of the Roman Empire*, *The Robe*, *I Claudius*, *Julius Caesar*, *Cleopatra* and *Spartacus*. The funny side of its life was depicted in *Roman Scandals*, *Fiddlers Three*, *Carry On Cleo*, *Scandal in the Roman Bath* and *A Funny Thing Happened on the Way to the Forum*. Modern Rome has been seen hundreds of times in Italian movies, notably *Bicycle Thieves*, *Paisa*, *The Girls of the Spanish Steps*, *Sunday in August*, *Rome Eleven o'Clock* and the American co-production *Indiscretion* which was shot entirely within Rome's railway station. American views of Rome include *Three Coins in the Fountain*, *Seven Hills of Rome* and *Roman Holiday*, while the Colosseum was used for the finale of films as various as *House of Cards* and *Twenty Million Miles to Earth*. The Vatican was well shown in *Never Take No for an Answer*, about the small boy who persists in getting an audience with the Pope.

ROME EXPRESS. A British train thriller directed by Walter Forde in 1933, starring Conrad Veidt; John Paddy Carstairs remade it in 1948, almost word for word and scene for scene, starring Albert Lieven, as *Sleeping Car to Trieste*. Finlay Currie played the same supporting role in both versions.

ROME, STEWART (1886–1965) (Septimus William Ryott). British stage matinée idol who made several romantic films in the 20s and later appeared in character roles. *The Prodigal Son* (25), *Sweet Lavender* (26), *The Gentleman Rider* (27), *Thou Fool* (28), *Dark Red Roses* (29), *The Man Who Changed His Name* (30), *Designing Women* (33), *Men of Yesterday* (34), *Wings of the Morning* (37), *Dinner at the Ritz* (37), *Banana Ridge* (41), *The White Unicorn* (47), *Woman Hater* (48), etc.

ROMEO AND JULIET. Apart from the numerous silent versions of Shakespeare's play, and the ballet adaptations, there have been two major straight versions since sound. In 1936 George Cukor directed Leslie Howard and Norma Shearer in a lavish studio-bound semi-pop version for MGM; in 1953 Renato Castellani came to Britain and made for Rank a more sober, but duller film in colour, with Laurence Harvey and Susan Shentall; and in 1968 came Franco Zeffirelli's version with Leonard Whiting and Olivia Hussey. (This won Oscars for Pasqualino de Santis' cinematography, and Danilo Donati's costumes). The musical *West Side Story* (61) is a violent modernization of Shakespeare's tale.

ROMERO, CESAR (1907–   ). Handsome Latin-American leading man, former dancer and Broadway actor. *Metropolitan* (film debut) (35), *Wee Willie Winkie* (37), *The Return of the Cisco Kid* (and others in this series) (39), *The Gay Caballero* (40), *Weekend in Havana* (41), *Tales of Manhattan* (42), *Orchestra Wives* (42), *Coney Island* (43), war service, *Carnival in Costa Rica* (47), *That Lady in Ermine* (48), *Happy Go Lovely* (51), *Prisoners of the Casbah* (53), *Vera Cruz* (54), *The Racers (Such Men Are Dangerous)* (55), *The Leather Saint* (56), *Villa* (58), *Two on a Guillotine* (64), *Marriage on the Rocks* (65), *Batman* (66), *Hot Millions* (68), *Crooks and Coronets* (GB) (69), *The Midas Run* (GB) (69), *A Talent for Loving* (69), many others. Also on TV.

ROMM, MIKHAIL (1901–   ). Russian director. *Boule de Suif* (34), *Lenin in October* (37), *Lenin in 1918* (39), *The Russian Question* (48), *Nine Days of One Year* (62), *Ordinary Fascism* (64), *Tschaikowsky* (project) (67).

ROMNEY, EDANA (1919–   ) (E. Rubenstein). South African-born leading lady, in three British films of the 40s: *East of Piccadilly* (41),

Alibi (42), *Corridor of Mirrors* (48). Later became TV personality and columnist.

LA RONDE. There had been earlier continental films of Arthur Schnitzler's 'Reigen', a light play about love's merry-go-round; but Max Ophuls' 1950 French version was so piquantly presented by a highly sophisticated cast that it seemed to expand suddenly the possibilities of sex comedy on British and American screens. Previously this sort of thing had always been left to the French, but 'La Ronde' was so internationally popular that everyone wanted to get in on the act. Jacques Natanson and Ophuls wrote the screenplay, Christian Matras was photographer, Oscar Straus wrote the music, and the top-flight cast included Anton Walbrook, Jean-Louis Barrault, Danielle Darrieux, Simone Signoret, Daniel Gelin, Simone Simon, Fernand Gravet and Gerard Philipe. Roger Vadim's 1963 remake, with colour but less interesting performers, substituted sensation for subtlety.

RONET, MAURICE (1927–   ). French leading man. *Rendezvous de Juillet* (49), *La Sorcière* (56), *He Who Must Die* (56), *Lift to the Scaffold* (57), *Carve Her Name With Pride* (GB) (58), *Plein Soleil* (59), *Rendezvous de Minuit* (61), *Le Feu Follet* (*A Time to Live and a Time to Die*) (63), *Enough Rope* (63), *The Victors* (63), *La Ronde* (64), *Three Weeks in Manhattan* (65), *Lost Command* (66), *The Champagne Murders* (*La Scandale*) (67), *The Road to Corinth* (68), *How Sweet It Is* (US) (68), etc.

ROOKERY NOOK (GB 1930). Although this early talkie was a straight transference of the popular Aldwych farce, directed by Tom Walls as though the camera were in the front row of the stalls, it admirably preserves Ben Travers' very clever dialogue and stage business along with the best performances of a classic team of farceurs: Walls with a perpetually roving eye, Ralph Lynn dropping his monocle at every untoward event, Robertson Hare moaning calamitously and losing his trousers, Mary Brough sniffing suspiciously, and whoever played Poppy Dickey selling flags for the lifeboat in her cami-knickers. No later farce was ever quite so hilariously well-judged.

ROOM, ABRAM (1894–   ). Russian director, former journalist, with stage experience. *In Pursuit of Moonshine* (24), *The Haven of Death* (26), *Bed and Sofa* (27), *The Five Year Plan* (30), *Invasion* (44), *Silver Dust* (53), etc.

ROOM AT THE TOP (GB 1959). This raw version of John Braine's novel about a young man's burning ambition to get to the top in a northern town was significant on several counts. It was franker about sex than any previous British movie. It introduced a new directorial talent in Jack Clayton. And it was the spearhead of a new and successful drive to get British films a wider showing in the US. Simone Signoret was imported from France to put the sex over, and won an Academy Award; so did Neil Paterson who wrote the screenplay. *Room at the Top* was logically followed by an over-dose of equally raw films about British provincial life: *Saturday Night and Sunday Morning* (60), *A Taste of Honey* (62), *The Leather Boys* (63), etc.; also by its own sequel *Life at the Top* (65), showing what happened to the same characters ten years after.

ROOM SERVICE (US 1938). This George Abbott farce about a theatrical troupe stranded without cash in a smart hotel made too restricted a vehicle for the Marx Brothers but permitted a splendid comedy performance from Donald McBride as the frantic manager. William Seiter directed. It was remade in 1944 by Tim Whelan as a musical, with Frank Sinatra and George Murphy.

ROONEY, MICKEY (1922–) (Joe Yule). Diminutive, aggressively talented American performer, on stage from the age of two (in parents' vaudeville act). In films from 1926 (short comedies) as Mickey McGuire, then returned to vaudeville; came back as Mickey Rooney in 1932. *My Pal the King* (32), *The Hide-Out* (34), *A Midsummer Night's Dream* (as Puck) (35), *Ah Wilderness* (35), *Little Lord Fauntleroy* (not in title role) (36), *Captains Courageous* (37), *A Family Affair* (as Andy Hardy) (37), *Judge Hardy's Children* (38), *Love Finds Andy Hardy* (38), *Boys' Town* (special AA) (38), *The Adventures of Huckleberry Finn* (39), *Babes in Arms* (39), *Young Tom Edison* (40), *Strike Up the Band* (40), *Men of Boys' Town* (41), *Babes on Broadway* (41), *A Yank at Eton* (42), *Andy Hardy's Double Life* (42), *The Human Comedy* (43), *Girl Crazy* (43), *Andy Hardy's Blonde Trouble* (44), *National Velvet* (44), war service, *Love Laughs at Andy Hardy* (46), *Summer Holiday* (47), *The Fireball* (50), *The Strip* (51), *A Slight Case of Larceny* (53), *The Bold and the Brave* (56), *Baby Face Nelson* (58), *Andy Hardy Comes Home* (58), *The Big Operator* (59), *Breakfast at Tiffany's* (61), *It's a Mad Mad Mad Mad World* (63), *Twenty-four Hours to Kill* (65), *Ambush Bay* (66), *The Extraordinary Seaman* (68), *Skidoo* (68), *Billy Bright* (69), others. Also directed: *My True Story* (51). TV series: *The Mickey Rooney Show, Mickey*, etc. Special Academy Award 1938. Published autobiography 1965: *I.E.*

ROOSEVELT, FRANKLIN DELANO (1882–1945). American president 1933–45, exponent of the 'new deal'. He was played by Ralph Bellamy in Dore Schary's play and film of his life, *Sunrise at Campbello* (60).

ROOSEVELT, THEODORE (TEDDY) (1858–1919). American president 1901–09. His extrovert personality and cheerful bullish manners have been captured several times on screen, notably by John

Alexander in *Arsenic and Old Lace* (a parody) and *Fancy Pants*, and by Sidney Blackmer in *My Girl Tisa*.

ROPE (US 1948). The first film from Transatlantic Pictures, the Alfred Hitchcock/Sidney Bernstein company, showed Hitch trying out a new trick: confining the action to one continuous take by using a constantly roving camera and passing something black at reel changes. Patrick Hamilton's suspenseful one-room play about a body in a chest was as suitable for the method as anything ever would be, but the 'ten-minute take' was in fact the negation of cinema and even took away the play's theatrical impact by incessant bewildering movement. It was never tried again. The photographers were Joseph Valentine and William V. Skall.

ROSAY, FRANÇOISE (1891–). Distinguished French actress in films from the mid-20s. *Gribiche* (25), *Le Grand Jeu* (33), *La Kermesse Heroïque* (35), *Jenny* (36), *Un Carnet de Bal* (37), *Les Gens du Voyage* (38), *Une Femme Disparait* (41), *Johnny Frenchman* (GB) (45), *Macadam* (46), *Quartet* (GB) (48), *September Affair* (US) (49), *The Red Inn* (51), *The Thirteenth Letter* (US) (51), *That Lady* (GB) (54), *The Seventh Sin* (US) (57), *Le Joueur* (58), *The Sound and the Fury* (US) (58), *The Full Treatment* (GB) (60), *Up from the Beach* (US) (65), etc. Widow of Jacques Feyder.

ROSE, DAVID (1910–). British-born composer, long in US. *Winged Victory* (44), *Texas Carnival* (51), *Jupiter's Darling* (54), many others.

ROSE, DAVID E. (1895–). American producer, in films from 1930, long in charge of United Artists productions. More recently, in Britain, *The End of the Affair* (55), *The Safecracker* (58), *The House of the Seven Hawks* (59), etc.

ROSE, GEORGE (1920–). British stage and screen character actor. *Pickwick Papers* (52), *Grand National Night* (53), *The Sea Shall Not Have Them* (54), *The Night My Number Came Up* (56), *Brothers in Law* (57), *A Night to Remember* (58), *Jack the Ripper* (59), *The Flesh and the Fiends* (60), *Hawaii* (US) (66), etc.

ROSE, JACK; see SHAVELSON, MELVILLE.

ROSE MARIE. The Rudolph Friml/Oscar Hammerstein operetta about the mounties getting their man was first filmed in 1928 by Lucien Hubbard as a silent: Joan Crawford had the title role. In 1936 W. S. Van Dyke made the well-remembered version with Jeanette Macdonald and Nelson Eddy, and in 1954 Mervyn le Roy directed a remake with Ann Blyth and Howard Keel.

ROSE, REGINALD (1921–). American writer who has created numerous TV plays, also a series, *The Defenders*; films include *Crime in the Streets* (56), *Twelve Angry Men* (57), *The Man in the Net* (59), etc.

ROSE, WILLIAM (1918–). American screenwriter who spent some years in Britain. *Once a Jolly Swagman* (co-w) (48), *The Gift Horse* (51), *Genevieve* (53), *The Maggie* (54), *The Lady Killers* (55), *The Smallest Show on Earth* (57), *It's a Mad Mad Mad Mad World* (63), *The Russians Are Coming* (66), *The Flim Flan Man* (67), *Guess Who's Coming to Dinner* (AA) (67), *The Secret of Santa Vittoria* (69), etc.

ROSEN, PHIL (1888–1951). Russian-born American director of second features. *The Single Sin* (21), *The Young Rajah* (22), *Abraham Lincoln* (25), *Burning Up Broadway* (28), *Two-Gun Man* (31), *Beggars in Ermine* (34), *Two Wise Maids* (37), *Double Alibi* (40), *Forgotten Girls* (40), *Spooks Run Wild* (41), *Prison Mutiny* (43), *Step by Step* (46), *The Secret of St Ives* (49), many others.

ROSENBERG, AARON (1912–). American producer, in Hollywood from 1934; working for Universal from 1946. Films include *Johnny Stool Pigeon* (47), *Winchester 73* (50), *The Glenn Miller Story* (54), *To Hell and Back* (55), *The Great Man* (57), *Morituri* (65), *The Reward* (65), *Tony Rome* (67), many others.

ROSENBERG, STUART (1925–). American director with long TV experience. *Murder Inc.* (60), *Cool Hand Luke* (67), *The April Fools* (69), *Hall of Mirrors* (69).

ROSENBLOOM, 'SLAPSIE' MAXIE (c. 1903–). American 'roughneck' comedian, ex-boxer, in occasional comedy films as gangster or punch-drunk type. *Mr Broadway* (33), *Nothing Sacred* (37), *Louisiana Purchase* (41), *Hazard* (48), *Mr Universe* (51), *Abbott and Costello Meet the Keystone Kops* (55), *The Beat Generation* (59), etc.

ROSHER, CHARLES (1885–). Distinguished American cinematographer. *The Love Night* (20), *Sunrise* (AA) (27), *Tempest* (28), *The Yearling* (co-ph) (AA) (46), *Show Boat* (51), *Kiss Me Kate* (53), *Young Bess* (54), many others.

ROSI, FRANCESCO (1922–). Italian director. *La Sfida* (57), *Salvatore Giuliano* (also wrote) (61), *Hands over the City* (63), *The Moment of Truth* (64), *More than a Miracle* (68), etc.

ROSMER, MILTON (1881–) (Arthur Milton Lunt). British stage actor, in many films from 1913. *General John Regan* (21), *The Passionate Friends* (22), *The Phantom Light* (35), *South Riding* (38), *Goodbye Mr Chips* (39), *Atlantic Ferry* (41), *Fame Is the Spur* (47), *The Monkey's Paw* (48), *The Small Back Room* (49), etc. Also directed many films including *Dreyfus* (31), *Channel Crossing* (32), *The Guvnor* (36), *The Challenge* (37).

ROSS, FRANK (1904–   ). American producer, in Hollywood from early 30s. *Of Mice and Men* (associate) (39), *The Devil and Miss Jones* (41), *The Robe* (53), *The Rains of Ranchipur* (55), *Kings Go Forth* (58), *Mister Moses* (65), others.

ROSS, HERBERT (1927–   ). American choreographer (*Doctor Dolittle, Funny Girl*, etc.) who became director with *Goodbye Mr Chips* (69).

ROSS, KATHARINE (1942–   ). American leading lady. *Mr Buddwing* (66), *The Graduate* (67), *Hellfighters* (68), *Willie Boy* (69), *Butch Cassidy and the Sundance Kid* (69), etc.

ROSS, SHIRLEY (1909–   ) (Bernice Gaunt). American pianist and singer who appeared as leading lady in a few films. *The Age of Indiscretion* (35), *Thanks for the Memory* (38), *Paris Honeymoon* (39), *Kisses for Breakfast* (41), *A Song for Miss Julie* (45), etc.

ROSSELLINI, ROBERTO (1906–   ). Italian director, in films from 1938. Started as writer; co-scripts his own films. *Open City* (45), *Paisa* (46), *Germany Year Zero* (48), *Stromboli* (49), *Europa 51* (51), *General Della Rovere* (59), *Louis XIV seizes Power* (66), others.

†ROSSEN, ROBERT (1908–1966). American writer-producer-director, in Hollywood from 1936 after stage experience. *Marked Woman* (w) (37), *They Won't Forget* (w) (37), *Racket Busters* (w) (38), *Dust Be My Destiny* (w) (39), *The Roaring Twenties* (w) (39), *A Child Is Born* (w) (39), *The Sea Wolf* (w) (41), *Blues in the Night* (w) (41), *Edge of Darkness* (w) (42), *A Walk in the Sun* (w) (45), *The Strange Love of Martha Ivers* (w) (46), *Desert Fury* (w) (47), *Johnny O'clock* (w, d) (47), *Body and Soul* (d) (47), *All the King's Men* (w, p, d) (AA) (49), *The Brave Bulls* (p, d) (50), *Mambo* (w, d) (54), *Alexander the Great* (w, p, d) (56), *Island in the Sun* (w, d) (57), *They Came to Cordura* (w, d) (59), *The Hustler* (w, p, d) (61), *Lilith* (w, p, d) (64).

ROSSI, FRANCO (1919–   ). Italian writer-director. *I Falsari* (52), *Il Seduttore* (54), *Amici per la Pelle* (Friends for Life) (55), *Morte di un Amico* (60), *Smog* (62), etc.

ROSSI-DRAGO, ELEONORA (1925–   ) (Palmina Omiccioli). Italian leading lady. *Pirates of Capri* (48), *Persiane Chiuse* (50), *Three Forbidden Stories* (51), *The White Slave* (53), *Le Amiche* (55), *Maledetto Imbroglio* (59), *David and Goliath* (59), *Under Ten Flags* (60), *Uncle Tom's Cabin* (Ger.) (65), etc.

ROSSIF, FREDERIC (1922–   ). French documentarist. *Les Temps du Ghetto* (61), *Mourir a Madrid* (62), *The Fall of Berlin* (65), etc.

ROSSINGTON, NORMAN (1928–   ). British character actor of stage, TV and films. *A Night to Remember* (58), *Carry On Sergeant* (58),

Saturday Night and Sunday Morning (60), *Go to Blazes* (62), *The Comedy Man* (63), *Tobruk* (US) (66), many others.

ROSSON, HAL or HAROLD (1895–   ). American cinematographer. *The Cinema Murder* (19), *Manhandled* (24), *Gentlemen Prefer Blondes* (28), *Tarzan of the Apes* (32), *The Scarlet Pimpernel* (35), *The Ghost Goes West* (36), *The Wizard of Oz* (39), *Johnny Eager* (42), *The Hucksters* (47), *On the Town* (49), *The Red Badge of Courage* (51), *Singing in the Rain* (52), *The Bad Seed* (56), *No Time for Sergeants* (58), many others.

ROTA, NINO (1911–   ). Italian composer. *My Son the Professor* (46), *Flight into France* (48), *E Primavera* (49), *Anna* (52), *I Vitelloni* (53), *La Strada* (54), *Amici per la Pelle* (56), *Il Bidone* (56), *Cabiria* (58), *La Dolce Vita* (59), *Plein Soleil* (60), *Rocco and His Brothers* (60), *Boccaccio 70* (62), *Eight and a Half* (63), *Juliet of the Spirits* (65), *Shoot Loud, Louder, I Don't Understand* (66), etc.

ROTH, LILLIAN (1911–   ). American leading lady in films (as a child) from 1916. Popular in early sound films, but personal problems caused her retirement. Later wrote her autobiography, *I'll Cry Tomorrow*, which was filmed with Susan Hayward. *The Love Parade* (30), *Madame Satan* (30), *Animal Crackers* (31), *Sea Legs* (31), *Ladies They Talk About* (33), *Take a Chance* (34).

ROTHA, PAUL (1907–   ). British documentarist and film theorist. With GPO Film Unit in 30s, later independent. *Shipyard* (30), *Contact* (33), *The Rising Tide* (33), *The Face of Britain* (34), *The Fourth Estate* (40), *World of Plenty* (42), *Land of Promise* (46), *The World Is Rich* (48), *No Resting Place* (50), *World Without End* (co-d) (52), *Cat and Mouse* (57), *The Life of Adolf Hitler* (62), *The Silent Raid* (62), etc. Author of 'The Film Till Now', 'Documentary Film', etc.

ROTUNNO, GIUSEPPE (* –   ). Italian cinematographer. *Scandal in Sorrento* (55), *White Nights* (57), *Anna of Brooklyn* (58), *The Naked Maja* (59), *The Angel Wore Red* (60), *Rocco and His Brothers* (60), *The Best of Enemies* (61), *The Leopard* (62), *Yesterday, Today and Tomorrow* (63), *Anzio* (68), *The Secret of Santa Vittoria* (69), etc.

rough cut. The first assembly of shots in the order in which they will be seen in the finished film, used to show those involved what work still needs to be done.

ROUQUIER, GEORGES (1909–   ). French documentarist. *Le Tonnelier* (42), *Farrébique* (46), *Salt of the Earth* (50), *Lourdes and Its Miracles* (56), etc.

ROUSE, RUSSELL (c. 1916–   ). American director and co-writer, usually in partnership with Clarence Greene (qv). *D.O.A.* (50),

The Well (51), *The Thief* (52), *New York Confidential* (55), *The Fastest Gun Alive* (56), *Thunder in the Sun* (59), *A House Is Not a Home* (64), *The Oscar* (66), *Caper of the Golden Bulls* (67), etc.

ROWLAND, ROY (c. 1910–). American director, mainly of routine features, in Hollywood from mid-30s. Many shorts, including Benchley, Pete Smith, Crime Does Not Pay. *Scene of the Crime* (42), *Lost Angel* (44), *Our Vines Have Tender Grapes* (45), *Killer McCoy* (48), *Tenth Avenue Angel* (48), *Scene of the Crime* (49), *Two Weeks with Love* (50), *Bugles in the Afternoon* (53), *The Moonlighter* (53), *Rogue Cop* (53), *The Five Thousand Fingers of Doctor T* (53), *Affair with a Stranger* (53), *Many Rivers To Cross* (55), *Hit the Deck* (55), *Meet Me in Las Vegas* (56), *These Wilder Years* (56), *Gun Glory* (57), *Seven Hills of Rome* (58), *The Girl Hunters* (64), *Gunfighters of Casa Grande* (66), others.

ROWLANDS, GENA (c. 1932–). American leading actress, mostly on stage. *The High Cost of Loving* (58), *Tony Rome* (67), *Faces* (68), *The Happy Ending* (69), etc. TV series: *87th Precinct* (61).

ROXIE HART (US 1942). Brilliantly scathing, zippy and entertaining satire, now unjustly forgotten, of Chicago in the 20s, with Ginger Rogers as a chorus girl who confesses to a murder for the sake of the publicity. She is splendidly abetted by Adolphe Menjou, Lynne Overman and George Montgomery; script and production are by Nunnally Johnson, music by Alfred Newman, direction by William Wellman.

ROZSA, MIKLOS (1907–). Hungarian composer, in Hollywood from 1940. *Knight without Armour* (37), *The Four Feathers* (39), *The Thief of Bagdad* (40), *Lady Hamilton* (41), *Five Graves to Cairo* (43), *Double Indemnity* (44), *A Song To Remember* (44), *The Lost Weekend* (45), *Spellbound* (AA) (45), *The Killers* (46), *Brute Force* (47), *A Double Life* (AA) (47), *Naked City* (48), *Adam's Rib* (49), *The Asphalt Jungle* (50), *Quo Vadis* (51), *Ivanhoe* (52), *Julius Caesar* (53), *Moonfleet* (55), *Lust for Life* (56), *Ben Hur* (AA) (59), *King of Kings* (61), *El Cid* (61), *Sodom and Gomorrah* (62), *The VIPs* (63), many others.

RUB, CHRISTIAN (1887–1956). Austrian character actor, long in Hollywood. *The Trial of Vivienne Ware* (32), *The Kiss behind the Mirror* (33), *A Dog of Flanders* (35), *Dracula's Daughter* (36), *Heidi* (37), *Mad about Music* (38), *The Great Waltz* (38), *The Swiss Family Robinson* (40), *Tales of Manhattan* (42), *Fall Guy* (48), *Something for the Birds* (52), many others. Was the model and voice for Gepetto the woodcarver in Disney's *Pinocchio*.

RUBENS, ALMA (1897–1931) (Alma Smith). American leading lady of the silent screen: her career was prematurely ended by drug addiction. *Intolerance* (15), *The Firefly of Tough Luck* (17), *Humoresque*

Rudley, Herbert

(20), *Cytherea* (24), *Fine Clothes* (25), *Siberia* (26), *Masks of the Devil* (28), *Showboat* (29), etc.

RUDLEY, HERBERT (1911–). American supporting actor. *Abe Lincoln in Illinois* (39), *The Seventh Cross* (44), *Rhapsody in Blue* (as Ira Gershwin) (45), *A Walk in the Sun* (46), *Joan of Arc* (48), *The Silver Chalice* (55), *Beloved Infidel* (59), etc.

RUGGLES, CHARLES (1890–). American character comedian, brother of Wesley Ruggles. In films from 1928 after stage experience; quickly became popular for his inimitably diffident manner, *Gentlemen of the Press* (28), *Her Wedding Night* (29), *Charley's Aunt* (leading role) (30), *Trouble in Paradise* (32), *Love Me Tonight* (32), *The Smiling Lieutenant* (32), *One Hour with You* (32), *Alice in Wonderland* (33), *Mama Loves Papa* (34), *Ruggles of Red Gap* (34), *Friends of Mr Sweeney* (35), *Anything Goes* (36), *Wives Never Know* (37), *Early to Bed* (37), *Bringing Up Baby* (38), *No Time for Comedy* (40), *Invisible Woman* (41), *Friendly Enemies* (42), *Dixie Dugan* (43), *Our Hearts Were Young and Gay* (43), *Three Is a Family* (44), *Incendiary Blonde* (44), *Bedside Manner* (45), *The Perfect Marriage* (46), *It Happened on Fifth Avenue* (47), *Ramrod* (47), *Give My Regards to Broadway* (48), *Look for the Silver Lining* (49), *The Loveable Cheat* (49), etc.; then long absence from screen during which he played many guest roles on TV; *The Pleasure of His Company* (61), *All in a Night's Work* (61), *I'd Rather Be Rich* (64), *The Ugly Duckling* (66), *Follow Me, Boys* (66), etc. TV series: *The World of Mr Sweeney* (53).

RUGGLES OF RED GAP. This well-known story by Harry Leon Wilson, about a British butler exported to the American mid-west, was filmed with Edward Everett Horton in 1923 and with Charles Laughton in 1934. Bob Hope's *Fancy Pants* in 1950 bore more than a passing resemblance to it. In 1969 came the inevitable musical remake.

RUGGLES, WESLEY (1889–). American director, in Hollywood from 1914. One of the original Keystone Kops. Films since sound include *Are These Our Children?* (30), *Cimarron* (31), *No Man of Her Own* (32), *College Humour* (33), *I'm No Angel* (33), *Bolero* (34), *The Gilded Lily* (35), *Valiant Is the Word for Carrie* (36), *I Met Him in Paris* (37), *True Confession* (37), *Sing You Sinners* (also produced) (38), *Invitation to Happiness* (39), *My Two Husbands* (40), *Arizona* (also produced) (40), *Good Morning Doctor* (41), *Somewhere I'll Find You* (42), *See Here Private Hargrove* (44), *London Town* (GB) (46), many others. Brother of Charles Ruggles.

RUHMANN, HEINZ (c. 1908–). German actor whose films have been little seen abroad. *Drei von der Tankstelle* (30), *Ship of Fools* (US) (65).

RULE, JANICE (1931–   ). American leading lady with stage and TV experience. *Goodbye My Fancy* (51), *Rouges' March* (53), *Gun for a Coward* (57), *Bell, Book and Candle* (58), *The Subterraneans* (60), *Invitation to a Gunfighter* (64), *The Chase* (66), *Alvarez Kelly* (66), *The Ambushers* (67), *The Swimmer* (68), etc.

RUMAN, SIG (or RUMANN, SIEGFRIED) (c. 1884–1967). German character actor, usually of explosive roles, in Hollywood from 1934. *The Wedding Night* (35), *A Night at the Opera* (35), *A Day at the Races* (37), *Ninotchka* (39), *Bitter Sweet* (41), *To Be or Not To Be* (42), *The Hitler Gang* (44), *A Night in Casablanca* (45), *On the Riviera* (49), *Stalag 17* (53), *The Glenn Miller Story* (54), *Three-Ring Circus* (56), *The Wings of Eagles* (57), *Robin and the Seven Hoods* (64), *Last of the Secret Agents* (66), scores of others.

running shot. One in which the camera, mounted on wheels, keeps pace with its subject, a moving actor or vehicle.

running speed. In silent days, 35 mm. ran through the projector at 16 frames per second or 60 feet per minute. When sound came, this was amended for technical reasons to 24 frames per second or 90 feet per minute. No normal 35 mm. projector can now operate at silent speed, which is why silent films look jerky when you see them (unless a special and very expensive laboratory process is adopted). It is said that many films made in the later silent period were in fact intended for showing at about 20 frames per second, and as machines were variable this was easily accomplished: such films now seem unduly slow when projected at 16 frames per second.

See: *slow motion, accelerated motion.*

RUNYON, DAMON (1884–1946). Inimitable American chronicler of the ways of a never-never New York inhabited by good-hearted and weirdly-named guys and dolls who speak a highly imaginative brand of English. Among the films based on his stories are *Lady for a Day* (33) (and its remake *Pocketful of Miracles* [61]), *The Lemon Drop Kid* (34 and 51), *A Slight Case of Murder* (38) (and *Stop You're Killing Me* [52]), *The Big Street* (42), and *Guys and Dolls* (55).

RUSH, BARBARA (1929–   ). American leading lady who came to Hollywood from college. *The First Legion* (51), *When Worlds Collide* (51), *Flaming Feather* (52), *It Came from Outer Space* (53), *Magnificent Obsession* (54), *The Black Shield of Falworth* (54), *Captain Lightfoot* (55), *The World in My Corner* (56), *Bigger Than Life* (57), *Oh Men! Oh Women!* (58), *Harry Black* (58), *The Young Philadelphians* (*The City Jungle*) (59), *The Bramble Bush* (60), *Strangers When We Meet* (60), *Come Blow Your Horn* (63), *Robin and the Seven Hoods* (64), *Hombre* (67), others.

rushes. A day's shooting on film when it comes back from the laboratories and is ready for viewing by those involved.

RUSSELL, GAIL (1924–61). American leading lady of the 40s; came to Hollywood straight from dramatic training. *Henry Aldrich Gets Glamour* (debut) (43), *Lady in the Dark* (43), *The Uninvited* (44), *Our Hearts Were Young and Gay* (44), *Salty O'Rourke* (45), *Night Has a Thousand Eyes* (47), *Moonrise* (48), *Wake of the Red Witch* (49), *Air Cadet* (51), *The Tattered Dress* (57), *The Silent Call* (61), etc.

RUSSELL, HAROLD (1914–). American paratroop sergeant who lost both hands in an explosion during World War II and demonstrated his ability not only to use hooks in their place but to act as well in *The Best Years of Our Lives* (45), for which he won two Oscars. Published autobiography 1949: *Victory in my Hands*. Became a public relations executive.

RUSSELL, JANE (1921–). American leading lady who came to Hollywood when an agent sent her photo to producer Howard Hughes; he starred her in *The Outlaw* (43) but it was held up for three years by censor trouble and the publicity campaign emphasized the star's physical attributes. Later: *The Young Widow* (47), *The Paleface* (48), *Double Dynamite* (50), *Macao* (51), *Montana Belle* (51), *His Kind of Woman* (51), *Son of Paleface* (52), *The Las Vegas Story* (52), *Gentlemen Prefer Blondes* (53), *The French Line* (54), *Underwater* (55), *Gentlemen Marry Brunettes* (55), *Foxfire* (55), *Hot Blood* (56), *The Tall Men* (56), *The Revolt of Mamie Stover* (57), *The Fuzzy Pink Nightgown* (57), *Fate Is the Hunter* (guest appearance) (64), *Waco* (66).

RUSSELL, JOHN (1921–). American 'second lead'. *Jesse James* (39), *The Bluebird* (40), *A Bell for Adano* (45), *The Fat Man* (51), *The Sun Shines Bright* (53), *The Last Command* (55), *Rio Bravo* (59), *Fort Utah* (66), many others. TV series: *Soldiers of Fortune* (55), *Lawman* (58–60).

RUSSELL, KEN (1927–). British director with high TV reputation. *French Dressing* (64), *Billion Dollar Brain* (67), *Women in Love* (69), *The Lonely Heart* (70).

RUSSELL, LILIAN (1861–1922) (Helen Louise Leonard). Statuesque American singer-entertainer, highly popular around the turn of the century. Made no films, but was played by Alice Faye in a 1940 biopic.

RUSSELL, ROSALIND (1911–). American leading lady of the 30s and 40s, with stage experience; usually plays career women. *Evelyn Prentice* (debut) (34), *China Seas* (35), *Under Two Flags* (36), *Craig's Wife* (37), *Night Must Fall* (38), *The Citadel* (GB) (38), *The Women* (39), *His Girl Friday* (40), *No Time for Comedy* (40),

They Met in Bombay (41), *Take a Letter, Darling* (42), *My Sister Eileen* (42), *Flight for Freedom* (43), *Roughly Speaking* (45), *Sister Kenny* (46), *Mourning Becomes Electra* (47), *The Velvet Touch* (48), *A Woman of Distinction* (50), *Never Wave at a WAC* (53), *Picnic* (55), *Auntie Mame* (57), *Five-Finger Exercise* (62), *Gypsy* (62), *A Majority of One* (63), *Oh Dad, Poor Dad* (66), *The Trouble with Angels* (66), *Rosie* (67), *Where Angels Go Trouble Follows* (68), *The Amazing Mrs Pollifex* (70), etc.

RUSSELL, WILLIAM D. (1908–1968). American director. *Our Hearts Were Growing Up* (45), *Dear Ruth* (47), *Bride for Sale* (49), *Best of the Badmen* (51), others; went into TV and directed hundreds of episodes, especially of *Dennis the Menace*.

the Russian Cinema has been one of the most influential in the world, chiefly owing to a small group of highly talented men. Before the revolution Russian films were old-fashioned and literary; but the Bolsheviks saw the great potential of the film as propaganda and actively encouraged the maturing talents of such men as Eisenstein (*Battleship Potemkin, October, The General Line, Alexander Nevsky, Ivan the Terrible*), Pudovkin (*Mother, The End of St Petersburg, The Deserter, General Suvorov*), Dovzhenko (*Arsenal, Earth*), Turin (*Turksib*) and Petrov (*Peter the Great*). Donskoi in *The Childhood of Maxim Gorki* and its two sequels was allowed to be nostalgic, but this vein only occasionally comes to the surface, most recently in *The Lady with a Little Dog*. The light touch comes hard to Russian film-makers, but Alexandrov achieved it in *Volga Volga*, and recently there have been signs of greater effort in this direction, at least for home consumption. The stolidity of most Russian films since World War II should not blind anyone to the enormous influence which the best Soviet work has had on film-makers the world over, especially in its exploration of the potentialities of camera movement, editing and sound.

RUTHERFORD, ANN (1920–). American leading lady of the 40s, former child stage star. *Love Finds Andy Hardy* (38), *The Hardys Ride High* (39), *Gone with the Wind* (39), *Pride and Prejudice* (40), *Happy Land* (43), *Two o'Clock Courage* (45), *The Secret Life of Walter Mitty* (47), *The Adventures of Don Juan* (48), others. Retired.

RUTHERFORD, MARGARET (1892–). Inimitable British character comedienne, on stage from 1925, films from 1936. *Talk of the Devil* (debut) (36), *Dusty Ermine* (38), *Yellow Canary* (43), *English without Tears* (44), *Blithe Spirit* (45), *While the Sun Shines* (46), *Miranda* (47), *Passport to Pimlico* (48), *The Happiest Days of Your Life* (50), *The Importance of Being Earnest* (52), *Trouble in Store* (53), *The Runaway Bus* (54), *Aunt Clara* (54), *The Smallest Show on Earth* (57), *I'm All Right, Jack* (59), *Murder, She Said* (62), *Murder at the Gallop* (63),

The VIPs (AA) (63), *Murder Most Foul* (64), *Murder Ahoy* (65), *Chimes at Midnight* (66), *A Countess from Hong Kong* (67), *Arabella* (68), *The Virgin and the Gypsy* (70), etc.

RUTTENBERG, JOSEPH (1889–). Russian cinematographer, in Hollywood from 1915. Films include *Over the Hill* (28), *Fury* (36), *The Great Waltz* (AA) (38), *Mrs Miniver* (AA) (42), *Madame Curie* (43), *Adventure* (46), *BF's Daughter* (48), *Side Street* (49), *The Forsyte Saga* (49), *The Great Caruso* (51), *Julius Caesar* (53), *The Last Time I Saw Paris* (54), *The Swan* (56), *Somebody Up There Likes Me* (AA) (56), *Gigi* (AA) (58), *The Reluctant Debutante* (AA) (58), *Butterfield 8* (60), *Bachelor in Paradise* (61), *Who's Been Sleeping in My Bed* (63), *Sylvia* (63), *Harlow* (65), *Love Has Many Faces* (65), *The Oscar* (66), many others.

RUTTMAN, WALTER (1887–1941). German director most famous for his experimental film *Berlin* (27). Later: *Weekend* (30), *Mannesmann* (37), *Deutsche Panzer* (40), etc.

RUYSDAEL, BASIL (1888–1960). Russian-American character actor, former opera singer; in authoritative roles in the 30s and 40s.

RYAN, FRANK (1907–1947). American director. *Hers to Hold* (43), *Can't Help Singing* (44), *Patrick the Great* (45), *A Genius in the Family* (46), etc.

RYAN, IRENE (c. 1906–) (Irene Riordan). Wiry American comedienne now famous as Granny in TV's *The Beverly Hillbillies*. Films include *Melody for Three* (41), *San Diego I Love You* (44), *Diary of a Chambermaid* (45), *Meet Me After the Show* (51), *Blackbeard the Pirate* (52), *Spring Reunion* (57).

RYAN, KATHLEEN (1922–). Irish leading lady with stage experience. *Odd Man Out* (debut) (47), *Captain Boycott* (47), *Esther Waters* (48), *Give Us This Day* (50), *The Yellow Balloon* (52), *Captain Lightfoot* (53), *Laxdale Hall* (53), *Jacqueline* (56), *Sail into Danger* (58), etc.

RYAN PEGGY (1924–). American teenage comedienne of the early 40s, often teamed with Donald O'Conner. In vaudeville from childhood. *Top of the Town* (37), *Give Out Sisters* (42), *Top Man* (43), *The Merry Monahans* (44), *Bowery to Broadway* (44), *That's the Spirit* (45), *On Stage Everybody* (45), *All Ashore* (52), etc.

†RYAN, ROBERT (1909–). American leading actor who never seemed to get the roles he deserved. *Golden Gloves* (40), *Queen of the Mob* (40), *Northwest Mounted Police* (40), *Bombardier* (43), *Gangway for Tomorrow* (43), *The Sky's the Limit* (43), *Behind the Rising Sun* (43), *The Iron Major* (43), *Tender Comrade* (43), *Marine Raiders* (44), *Trail Street* (47), *The Woman on the Beach* (47), *Crossfire* (47), *Berlin Express* (48), *Return of the Badmen* (48), *The Boy with Green Hair* (48),

Act of Violence (49), *Caught* (49), *The Set-Up* (49), *The Woman on Pier 13* (49), *The Secret Fury* (50), *Born To Be Bad* (50), *Best of the Badmen* (51), *Flying Leathernecks* (51), *The Racket* (51), *On Dangerous Ground* (51), *Clash by Night* (52), *Beware My Lovely* (52), *Horizons West* (52), *City Beneath the Sea* (53), *The Naked Spur* (53), *Inferno* (53), *Alaska Seas* (54), *About Mrs Leslie* (54), *Her Twelve Men* (54), *Bad Day at Black Rock* (55), *Escape to Burma* (55), *House of Bamboo* (55), *The Tall Men* (55), *The Proud Ones* (56), *Back from Eternity* (56), *Men in War* (57), *God's Little Acre* (58), *Lonely Hearts* (59), *Day of the Outlaw* (59), *Odds Against Tomorrow* (59), *Ice Palace* (60), *The Canadians* (61), *King of Kings* (61), *The Longest Day* (62), *Billy Budd* (62), *The Crooked Road* (65), *Battle of the Bulge* (65), *The Dirty Game* (66), *The Professionals* (66), *The Busy Body* (67), *The Dirty Dozen* (67), *Hour of the Gun* (67), *Custer of the West* (67), *Dead or Alive* (67), *Anzio* (68), *The Wild Bunch* (69).

RYAN, SHEILA (1921–). American light leading lady of the 40s. *Something for the Boys* (44), *The Lone Wolf in London* (46), *Caged Fury* (47), *Mask of the Dragon* (51), *Pack Train* (53), etc.

RYAN, TIM (* –1956). American comedy supporting actor, adept at drunks, wisecracking reporters, dumb cops, etc. *Brother Orchid* (40), *The Mystery of the Thirteenth Guest* (43), *Crazy Knights* (45), *The Shanghai Chest* (48), *Sky Dragon* (49), *Cuban Fireball* (51), *From Here to Eternity* (53), *Fighting Trouble* (56), etc.

RYDELL, MARK (c. 1934–). American director, from TV. Former actor: *Crime in the Streets* (56), etc. As director: *The Fox* (68), *The Reivers* (69).

RYSKIND, MORRIS (1895–1899). American writer who worked on *Animal Crackers* (31), *A Night at the Opera* (35), *My Man Godfrey* (36), *Room Service* (39), *Claudia* (41), *Where Do We Go from Here* (45), etc.

S

SABATINI, RAFAEL (1875–1950). Anglo-Italian author of swashbuckling historical novels, several of which have been filmed more than once: *The Sea Hawk, Scaramouche, Captain Blood, The Black Swan, Bardelys the Magnificent,* etc.

SABU (1924–1963) (Sabu Dastagir). Boyish Indian actor, a stable lad in Mysore when he was noticed by director Robert Flaherty and appeared in *Elephant Boy* (37). Came to England, later America. *The Drum* (38), *The Thief of Bagdad* (40), *The Jungle Book* (42), *White Savage* (43), *Cobra Woman* (44), *Tangier* (46), *Black Narcissus* (46), *The End of the River* (47), *Maneater of Kumaon* (48), *Song of India* (49), *Hello, Elephant* (52), *Jaguar* (56), *A Tiger Walks* (63), others.

SACKHEIM, WILLIAM (1919–   ). American writer. *Smart Girls Don't Talk* (48), *A Yank in Korea* (51), *Column South* (53), *Border River* (54), *The Human Jungle* (55), etc.

SAFETY LAST (US 1923). One of Harold Lloyd's classic gag-and-thrill comedies, probably the best of them, culminating with his climb up a building and many predictable but hilarious mishaps. Directed by Sam Taylor and Fred Newmeyer.

SAGAL, BORIS (1923–   ). American director, from TV. *Dime with a Halo* (62), *The Charge is Murder* (*Twilight of Honour*) (63), *Girl Happy* (64), *Made in Paris* (65), *Mosquito Squadron* (69), etc. TV series as executive producer: *T.H.E. Cat* (67).

SAGAN, FRANÇOISE (1935–   ) (F. Quoirez). French novelist very popular in the late 50s. Works filmed include *Bonjour Tristesse, A Certain Smile, Aimez-Vous Brahms?* (*Goodbye Again*).

SAHL, MORT (1926–   ). American night club comedian popular among intellectuals in early 60s. Made only one film, *In Love and War* (58).

sailors of whom screen accounts have been given include Christopher Columbus (1446–1506), by Frederic March in *Christopher Columbus* (49); Horatio Nelson (qv); John Paul Jones (1747–1792), by Robert Stack in *John Paul Jones* (59); Francis Drake (1540–1596), by Matheson Lang in *Drake of England* (35) and by Rod Taylor in *Seven Seas to Calais* (62).

THE SAINT. Among the actors who have played Leslie Charteris' 'Robin Hood of crime' in both British and American films since

1937 are Louis Hayward, Hugh Sinclair and George Sanders. One feels that 'the Falcon', a series character played in the 40s by George Sanders and later Tom Conway, was heavily indebted to the Saint, who has recently made a strong comeback on television in the person of Roger Moore. In France, a barely recognizable 'Saint' has been played in several films by Jean Marais.

SAINT, EVA MARIE (c. 1930–   ). American leading actress with Broadway experience. *On the Waterfront* (debut: AA) (54), *That Certain Feeling* (56), *Raintree County* (57), *A Hatful of Rain* (57), *North by Northwest* (59), *Exodus* (60), *All Fall Down* (62), *Thirty-six Hours* (64), *The Sandpiper* (65), *The Russians Are Coming, The Russians Are Coming* (66), *Grand Prix* (67), *The Stalking Moon* (68), *A Talent for Loving* (69), etc.

ST CLAIR, MALCOLM (1897–1952). American director (from 1915). *Are Parents People?* (25), *The Grand Duchess and the Waiter* (26), *Gentlemen Prefer Blondes* (28), *The Canary Murder Case* (29), *Dangerous Nan McGrew* (30), *Olsen's Big Moment* (33), *The Jones Family* (several in series (36–40), *The Man in the Trunk* (42), *The Big Noise* (44), many others.

ST JACQUES, RAYMOND (1930–   ). American Negro leading man. *Mister Buddwing* (66), *The Comedians* (68), *If He Hollers Let Him Go* (68), *Uptight* (68), etc.

SAINT JAMES, SUSAN (1946–   ) (Susan Miller). American leading lady of a somewhat kooky kind, in TV series *The Name of the Game* (68). Films include *P.J.* (68), *Where Angels Go Trouble Follows* (68).

ST JOHN, AL ('FUZZY') (1893–1963). American character actor, in films from 1913; latterly played comic side-kick in numerous second-feature Westerns. *Mabel's Strange Predicament* (13), many Fatty Arbuckle comedies, *Special Delivery* (27), *Dance of Life* (29), *Wanderer of the Wasteland* (35), *Call of the Yukon* (37), *Arizona Terrors* (42), *Frontier Revenge* (49), hundreds of others.

ST JOHN, BETTA (1930–   ) (Betty Streidler). American leading lady with stage experience. *Dream Wife* (debut) (53), *The Robe* (53), *The Student Prince* (54), *The Naked Dawn* (55), *High Tide at Noon* (GB) (57), *City of the Dead* (GB) (61), etc.

ST JOHN, HOWARD (1905–   ). American character actor on stage from 1925, films from 1948, usually as father, executive or military commander. *Born Yesterday* (50), *David Harding, Counterspy* (50), *Counterspy Meets Scotland Yard* (51), *The Tender Trap* (55), *Lil Abner* (59), *Straitjacket* (63), *Sex and the Single Girl* (64), *Strange Bedfellows* (65), many others.

St John, Jill

ST JOHN, JILL (1940–) (J. Oppenheim). American leading lady. *Summer Love* (57), *The Lost World* (60), *Come Blow Your Horn* (62), *Who's Been Sleeping in My Bed?* (63), *The Liquidator* (GB) (65), *The Oscar* (66), *Eight on the Lam* (67), *Banning* (67), *Tony Rome* (67), etc.

ST TRINIAN'S. This school full of little female horrors was originally conceived by cartoonist Ronald Searle. From his formula Frank Launder and Sidney Gilliat have made four commercially success-ful if disappointing farces: *The Belles of St Trinian's* (54), *Blue Murder at St Trinian's* (57), *The Pure Hell of St Trinian's* (60), *The Great St Trinian's Train Robbery* (66).

SAKALL, S. Z. (1884–1955) (Eugene Gero Szakall). Hungarian character actor with vaudeville and stage experience. In films from 1916, Hollywood from 1939; became popular comic support and was nicknamed 'Cuddles'. *It's a Date* (40), *Ball of Fire* (41), *Casablanca* (42), *Thank Your Lucky Stars* (43), *Wonder Man* (45), *Cinderella Jones* (46), *Whiplash* (48), *Tea for Two* (50), *The Student Prince* (54), many others. Published autobiography 1953: *The Story of Cuddles.*

SAKS, GENE (1921–). American director, from Broadway. *Barefoot in the Park* (67), *The Odd Couple* (67).

SALE, RICHARD (1911–). Prolific American writer of stories and screenplays, none very memorable: *Rendezvous With Annie* (46), *Spoilers of the North* (directed only) (47), *A Ticket to Tomahawk* (49), *Meet Me After the Show* (51), *Half Angel* (directed only) (51), *Let's Make It Legal* (directed only) (51), *My Wife's Best Friend* (directed only) (52), *Suddenly* (54), *Woman's World* (54), *Gentlemen Marry Brunettes* (also wrote words and music and co-produced) (55), *Seven Waves Away* (also directed) (56), etc. Author of novel, *The Oscar* (64), now filmed.

SALES, SOUPY (c. 1927–) (Milton Hines). American entertainer, popular on children's TV. Film debut in *Birds Do It* (66).

SALKOW, SIDNEY (1909–). American director of second features from mid-30s. *Woman Doctor* (39), *Café Hostess* (40), *The Lone Wolf Strikes* (40) (and others in this series), *The Adventures of Martin Eden* (42), *Millie's Daughter* (46), *Bulldog Drummond at Bay* (47), *Shadow of the Eagle* (GB) (50), *Sitting Bull* (52), *The Golden Hawk* (52), *Jack McCall, Desperado* (53), *Raiders of the Seven Seas* (53), *College Confidential* (57), *Twice Told Tales* (63), *The Great Sioux Massacre* (65), many others.

SALLIS, PETER (1921–). Bemused-looking British character actor, often in 'little man' roles. *Anastasia* (56), *The Doctor's Dilemma* (58),

Saturday Night and Sunday Morning (60), *Charlie Bubbles* (67), *Inadmissible Evidence* (68), many others.

SALMI, ALBERT (1928–). Chubby American character actor, mainly on stage. *The Brothers Karamazov* (58), *The Unforgiven* (59), *Wild River* (60), *The Ambushers* (67) etc.

SALTZMAN, HARRY (1915–). Canadian-born independent producer with TV experience. Recently very successful in Britain with *Look Back in Anger*, the James Bond films, *The Ipcress File*, *The Battle of Britain*, etc.

SAMUELSON, G. B. (1887–1945). British producer and distributor of silent films. *A Study in Scarlet* (14), *Little Women* (17), *Hindle Wakes* (18), *Quinneys* (19), *The Last Rose of Summer* (21), *Should a Doctor Tell?* (23), *She* (25), many others.

SANDERS, DENIS (1929–) and TERRY (1931–). American brothers who for ten years have been promising great things but never quite fulfilling them. *A Time Out of War* (short) (54), *Crime and Punishment USA* (58), *War Hunt* (61), *Shock Treatment* (63), etc.

SANDERS, GEORGE (1906–). Suave British actor who has been playing cads and crooks for thirty years. Varied early experience including London revue. *Strange Cargo* (film debut) (29), *The Man Who Could Work Miracles* (35), *Dishonour Bright* (37), *The Outsider* (39), etc., in Britain; but in 1939 settled firmly in Hollywood and quickly became a star. *Lloyds of London* (37), *Lancer Spy* (37), *Four Men and a Prayer* (38), *Nurse Edith Cavell* (39), *Confessions of a Nazi Spy* (39), *The House of Seven Gables* (40), *Rebecca* (40), *Foreign Correspondent* (40), *The Saint* (series) (40–42), *The Falcon* (series) (41–43), *Rage in Heaven* (41), *The Moon and Sixpence* (42), *Quiet, Please, Murder* (43), *The Lodger* (44), *Action in Arabia* (44), *Summer Storm* (44), *The Picture of Dorian Gray* (44), *Hangover Square* (44), *Uncle Harry* (45), *A Scandal in Paris* (46), *The Strange Woman* (47), *The Ghost and Mrs Muir* (47), *Forever Amber* (47), *Bel Ami* (48), *Personal Column* (48), *Lady Windermere's Fan* (49), *Samson and Delilah* (49), *All about Eve* (AA) (50), *I Can Get It for You Wholesale* (51), *Ivanhoe* (52), *Call Me Madam* (53), *Witness to Murder* (54), *King Richard and the Crusaders* (54), *Jupiter's Darling* (54), *Moonfleet* (55), *The King's Thief* (55), *Never Say Goodbye* (56), *While the City Sleeps* (56), *Death of a Scoundrel* (56), *The Whole Truth* (GB) (57), *From the Earth to the Moon* (58), *Solomon and Sheba* (59), *That Kind of Woman* (59), *A Touch of Larceny* (GB) (60), *Bluebeard's Ten Honeymoons* (60), *Village of the Damned* (GB) (62), *A Shot in the Dark* (64), *The Golden Head* (64), *Moll Flanders* (65), *The Quiller Memorandum* (66), *The Kremlin Letter* (69), many others. TV series: *George Sanders Mystery*

Theatre (58). Published autobiography 1960: *Memoirs of a Professional Cad.*

SANDRICH, MARK (1900–1945). American director who came to Hollywood in 1927 as director of Lupino Lane two-reelers; later associated with musicals. *Melody Cruise* (33), *The Gay Divorce* (34), *Top Hat* (35), *Follow the Fleet* (36), *Shall We Dance?* (37), *Carefree* (38), *Buck Benny Rides Again* (40), *Skylark* (41), *Holiday Inn* (42), *So Proudly We Hail* (43), *Here Come the Waves* (44), *I Love a Soldier* (44), etc.

SANDS, TOMMY (1937–). American 'teenage rave' singer. *Sing Boy Sing* (57), *Love in a Goldfish Bowl* (59), *Babes in Toyland* (60), *The Longest Day* (62), etc.

SANFORD, RALPH (1899–1963). American supporting player, usually in burly 'good guy' roles. *Thunderhead, Son of Flicka* (45), *Champion* (49), *Blackjack Ketchum Desperado* (56), *The Purple Gang* (59), many others.

San Francisco, because of its distinctive hills and Alcatraz out there in the bay, is a city we feel we know from the movies . . . so many movies. It was particularly well captured in *The Well-Groomed Bride, The Glenn Miller Story, D.O.A., Guess Who's Coming to Dinner, Point Blank, Yours Mine and Ours, Petulia* and *Bullitt.* The Barbary Coast days, all done with sets of course, were best caught in *Flame of the Barbara Coast, Barbary Coast,* and *San Francisco* itself.

SAN FRANCISCO (US 1936). A large-scale Hollywood entertainment of the 30s, its melodramatic story built round a reconstruction of the 1906 earthquake. Typically good performances from Clark Gable, Jeanette Macdonald, Spencer Tracy and Jack Holt; direction by W. S. Van Dyke; special effects, including a still-unsurpassed earthquake sequence, by John Hoffman and others; script by Anita Loos; lavish production values by MGM.

LE SANG D'UN POÈTE (France 1930). Jean Cocteau's first film was short and surrealist, full of nightmare images with a tendency to the erotic, all sandwiched between shots of a chimney falling. Full of interesting pointers to his later work.

SANGSTER, JIMMY (c. 1925–). British screenwriter, former production manager; associated with Hammer horror films. *Dracula* (57), *The Mummy* (58), *Brides of Dracula* (60), *The Criminal* (60), *The Hellfire Club* (61), *Taste of Fear* (also produced) (61), *Maniac* (also produced) (63), *Hysteria* (65), *The Nanny* (also produced) (65), many others.

SAN JUAN, OLGA (1927–). Vivacious American dancer and comedienne, with radio experience. Married to Edmond O'Brien

Rainbow Island (44), *Blue Skies* (46), *The Beautiful Blonde from Bashful Bend* (49), *Countess of Monte Cristo* (49), then stage work. Only recent film: *The Third Voice* (60).

SANTELL, ALFRED (1895–   ). American director, former architect. With Mack Sennett as writer and director in 20s. Films mainly routine. *Wildcat Jordan* (22), *Subway Sadie* (26), *The Patent Leather Kid* (27), *The Little Shepherd of Kingdom Come* (28), *Daddy Longlegs* (30), *The Sea Wolf* (30), *Tess of the Storm Country* (33), *Winterset* (36), *Having Wonderful Time* (38), *Aloma of the South Seas* (41), *Beyond the Blue Horizon* (42), *Jack London* (44), *The Hairy Ape* (44), *That Brennan Girl* (46), others.

SANTSCHI, TOM (1879–1931). American leading man of the silents. *The Sultan's Power* (09), *The Spoilers* (14), *The Garden of Allah* (16), *Little Orphan Annie* (19), *Three Bad Men* (26), *In Old Arizona* (29), *Ten Nights in a Bar-Room* (31), etc.

SANTLEY, JOSEPH (1889–   ). American director, former child actor and vaudevillian. *The Smartest Girl in Town* (32), *Spirit of Culver* (37), *Swing, Sister, Swing* (41), *Hitting the Headlines* (42), *Brazil* (44), *Shadow of a Woman* (47), *Make Believe Ballroom* (49), etc.

SANTONI, RENI (1939–   ). American actor, of French/Spanish ancestry; former TV writer. *Enter Laughing* (67), *Anzio* (68), etc.

SARAFIAN, RICHARD C. (c. 1927–   ). American director, of Armenian descent; much TV experience. *Andy* (65), *Run Wild Run Free* (69), *Fragment of Fear* (69).

SAROYAN, WILLIAM (1908–   ). American writer, mainly of fantasies about gentle people. Chief films of his work: *The Human Comedy* (43), *The Time of your Life* (48).

SARRAZIN, MICHAEL (c. 1942–   ). American leading man, usually as the young innocent. *The Flim Flam Man* (67), *Journey to Shiloh* (67), *The Sweet Ride* (68), *A Man Called Gannon* (68), *Eye of the Cat* (69), *They Shoot Horses Don't They* (69).

SARTRE, JEAN-PAUL (1905–   ). French existentialist writer. Works filmed include *Huis Clos* (*No Exit*), *Crime Passionel*, *La Putain Respectueuse*, *Les Jeux Sont Faits*, *The Condemned of Altona*.

SASSARD, JACQUELINE (1940–   ). French leading lady seen abroad in *Accident* (66), *Les Biches* (68).

satire, being defined in theatrical circles as 'what closes Saturday night', has seldom been encouraged by Hollywood, and the few genuinely satirical films have not been commercially successful, from *A Nous La Liberté* through *American Madness*, *Nothing Sacred* and *Roxie Hart* to *The Loved One*. However, the odd lampoon in the middle of an otherwise straightforward comedy has often brought critical enthusiasm for films as diverse as *Modern Times*, *Boy Meets Girl*, *I'm All Right, Jack* and *The President's Analyst*; and in future it looks as though one can at least expect that the range of permissible targets will become even wider.

SATURDAY NIGHT AND SUNDAY MORNING (GB 1960). Alan Sillitoe's raw, humorous wallow in the sub-life of Nottingham was filmed by Karel Reisz, whose directorial talent has oddly found no satisfactory expression since. The film broadened still further the British attitude to illicit sex and taught us that the subject needn't be treated very seriously. It also introduced a new star in Albert Finney. Photographed by Freddie Francis. BFA: best British film.

SAUNDERS, CHARLES (1904–). British director, former editor. *Tawny Pipit* (co-d) (44), *Fly Away Peter* (47), *One Wild Oat* (51), *Meet Mr Callaghan* (54), *Kill Her Gently* (57), *Womaneater* (58), *Danger by My Side* (62), etc.

SAUNDERS, JOHN MONK (1895–1940). American screenwriter with a special interest in aviation. *Wings* (28), *Dawn Patrol* (30), *The Last Flight* (31), etc.

THE SAVAGE EYE (US 1959). One of the first of the exposé pictures which have since flooded the market, this semi-professional job with flashes of brilliance attempts to take the lid off a big American city, with scenes of faith healing, strip-tease and wrestling to show its decadence. The connecting narration by a neurotic woman is unfortunate. Produced and directed by Ben Maddow and Joseph Strick.

SAVALAS, TELLY (1924–). Greek-American character actor with TV experience; former academic. *The Young Savages* (59), *Birdman of Alcatraz* (62), *The Interns* (63), *Cape Fear* (63), *The Man from the Diners' Club* (63), *The New Interns* (64), *Genghis Khan* (65), *The Battle of the Bulge* (65), *The Slender Thread* (66), *Beau Geste* (66), *The Dirty Dozen* (67), *The Scalphunters* (68), *Buona Sera Mrs Campbell* (68), *The Assassination Bureau* (GB) (68), *Crooks and Coronets* (GB) (69), *Day of the Landgrabbers* (69), *The Warriors* (70), etc.

SAVILLE, VICTOR (1897–). British director who after making some outstanding films in the thirties went to Hollywood with very meagre results. Former film salesman and exhibitor. *The Arcadians* (27), *Roses of Picardy* (28), *Woman to Woman* (US) (29), *Hindle Wakes* (31), *Sunshine Susie* (31), *The Good Companions* (32), *I Was a Spy* (33), *Friday the Thirteenth* (33), *Evergreen* (34), *The Iron Duke* (36), *Dark Journey* (37), *Storm in a Teacup* (37), *South Riding* (38), *The Citadel* (produced only) (38), *Goodbye Mr Chips* (produced only) (39), then to MGM Hollywood as producer, *Bitter Sweet* (p) (40), *Dr*

Jekyll and Mr Hyde (p) (41), *White Cargo* (p) (42), *Tonight and Every Night* (p, d) (44), *The Green Years* (p, d) (46), *If Winter Comes* (d) (47), *The Conspirator* (d) (47), *Kim* (p) (51), *I the Jury* (p) (53), *The Long Wait* (p, d) (54), *The Silver Chalice* (p, d) (55), *Kiss Me Deadly* (p) (55), *The Greengage Summer* (p) (61).

SAWDUST AND TINSEL (Sweden 1953). The first of writer-director Ingmar Bergman's films to be internationally noticed, this deftly handled melodrama has Ake Gromberg as the foolish owner of a travelling circus and Harriet Andersson as his repressed wife.

SAWYER, JOSEPH (c. 1908–) (Joseph Sauer). American comedy actor usually seen as tough cop or army sergeant. *College Humour* (33), *The Marines Have Landed* (36), *About Face* (42), *The McGuerins from Brooklyn* (42), *Fall In* (44), *Joe Palooka, Champ* (46), *Fighting Father Dunne* (49), *It Came from Outer Space* (53), *The Killing* (56), many others.

SAXON, JOHN (1935–) (Carmen Orrico). American leading man, former model. *Running Wild* (debut) (55), *The Unguarded Moment* (56), *The Reluctant Debutante* (58), *Portrait in Black* (59), *The Unforgiven* (59), *The Plunderers* (60), *Posse from Hell* (61), *War Hunt* (62), *The Cardinal* (63), *The Evil Eye* (It.) (63), *The Appaloosa* (*Southwest to Sonora*) (66), *The Night Caller* (GB) (67), *Death of a Gunfighter* (69). TV series: *The Bold Ones* (69).

SAYONARA (US 1957). A solemn burying of the hatchet between two countries in the form of a romantic idyll between an American air force officer and a Japanese girl after World War II. Immensely good to look at but extremely long drawn out by director Joshua Logan, with little meat to be had from Paul Osborn's script or James Michener's original novel, and a mumbling Southern-accented performance from Marlon Brando. The armchair travelogue elements come off best, via Ellsworth Fredericks' cinematography. AA best art direction, sound recording, supporting actors Red Buttons and Miyoshi Umeki.

SCAIFE, TED (1912–). British cinematographer. *The Life and Death of Colonel Blimp* (43), *Caesar and Cleopatra* (45), *Bonnie Prince Charlie* (48), *An Inspector Calls* (54), *Sea Wife* (57), *Night of the Demon* (57), *633 Squadron* (64), *Khartoum* (66), *The Dirty Dozen* (67), *Play Dirty* (68), *Sinful Davey* (69), many others.

SCALA, GIA (1936–) (Giovanna Scoglio). Italian leading lady who made a few American films. *The Price of Fear* (56), *Four Girls in Town* (56), *The Garment Jungle* (57), *The Two-Headed Spy* (GB) (58), *I Aim at the Stars* (59), *The Guns of Navarone* (61), etc.

SCARAMOUCHE. Rafael Sabatini's tongue-in-cheek French Revolutionary romance, about a nobleman who, to outwit his enemies,

857

disguises himself as a clown in a travelling theatre, was filmed in 1922 by Rex Ingram, with Ramon Novarro, and in 1952 by George Sidney, with Stewart Granger.

SCARFACE (US 1932). A highly professional and exciting gangster film based on the career of Al Capone. Written by Seton I. Miller, John Lee Mahin, W. R. Burnett and Ben Hecht, directed by Howard Hawks, it made crime so attractive that the moralists were subsequently able to curb Hollywood's freedom by means of a tougher code. Photography by Lee Garmes and L. W. O'Connell, production by Howard Hughes; cast headed by Paul Muni and George Raft, who have been associated with these roles ever since.

THE SCARLET EMPRESS (US 1934). For its superb visual flair rather than its dramatic sense, this highly romanticized biography of Catherine the Great remains a cinema classic. Fantastically baroque décor, a hypnotic performance from Sam Jaffe as the mad prince, and the mysterious depths of Marlene Dietrich's personality (here suggested but not plumbed) are brought together by Joseph Von Sternberg into a fantasy he relishes to the last hysterical note. See also: *Catherine the Great.*

THE SCARLET LETTER. Nathaniel Hawthorne's story of puritanical eighteenth-century New England was filmed in 1917 with Mary Martin as the adulteress and Stuart Holmes as her priest-lover forced to accuse her. In 1926 came Victor Sjostrom's more famous version with Lillian Gish and Lars Hanson. 1934 brought a talkie remake with Cora Sue Collins and Hardie Albright.

THE SCARLET PIMPERNEL. Baroness Orczy's foppish hero of the French Revolution has been filmed three times since sound. GB 1935: by Harold Young, with Leslie Howard, opposing Raymond Massey as Chauvelin. GB 1938: by Hans Schwarz, with Barry K. Barnes winning out over Francis Lister. GB 1950: by Michael Powell and Emeric Pressburger, with David Niven as Sir Percy. There has also been a TV series starring Marius Goring. Silent versions included one in 1917 starring Dustin Farnum and one in 1929 starring Matheson Lang. The idea was modernized in Leslie Howard's *Pimpernel Smith* (41).

SCARLET STREET (US 1945). This sombre drama directed by Fritz Lang concerns a professor (Edward G. Robinson) who is taken in by a tart, finally murders her, and allows her gigolo friend to be executed for the crime. A remake of Renoir's 1931 French film *La Chienne*, it was notable as the first American film in which a character is allowed to commit murder and get away with it— though he is shown to be still tortured by remorse many years later.

Scattergood Baines, an amiable small-town busybody created by Booth Tarkington, was personified by Guy Kibbee in five second features (41–42), all directed by Christy Cabanne.

scenario : see *shooting script.*

SCHAEFER, GEORGE (1920–   ). American director with TV experience. *Macbeth* (61), *Pendulum* (68).

SCHAEFER, NATALIE (1912–   ). American comedienne usually seen as a dizzy rich woman. *Marriage is a Private Affair* (43), *Wonder Man* (45), *The Snake Pit* (48), *Caught* (49), *Anastasia* (56), *Oh Men Oh Women* (57), etc. TV series: *Gilligan's Island* (64–67).

†SCHAFFNER, FRANKLIN (1920–   ). American director, from TV. *The Stripper* (*Woman of Summer*) (63), *The Best Man* (64), *The War Lord* (65), *The Double Man* (67), *Planet of the Apes* (68), *Patton—Blood and Guts* (69).

SCHARY, DORE (1905–   ). American writer-producer with newspaper and theatrical experience. AA best screenplay *Boys' Town* (38); produced for MGM 1942–45; Head of production RKO 1945–48; head of production MGM 1948–56; since independent. *Lonelyhearts* (59), *Sunrise at Campobello* (60), *Act One* (w, p, d) (63), etc.

SCHELL, MARIA (1926–   ). Austrian leading lady who has been in British and American films. *The Angel with the Trumpet* (49), *The Magic Box* (51), *So Little Time* (52), *The Heart of the Matter* (52), *Der Traumende Mund* (53), *The Last Bridge* (Austrian) (54), *Die Ratten* (55), *White Nights* (It.) (57), *Une Vie* (Fr.) (58), *The Brothers Karamazov* (58), *Cimarron* (61), *The Mark* (GB) (61), *99 Women* (69), etc.

SCHELL, MAXIMILIAN (1930–   ). Austrian leading man who has been in international films. *Kinder Mutter und Ein General* (58), *The Young Lions* (58), *Judgment at Nuremberg* (AA) (61), *Five-Finger Exercise* (62), *The Condemned of Altona* (63), *The Reluctant Saint* (63), *Topkapi* (64), *Return from the Ashes* (65), *The Deadly Affair* (66), *Beyond the Mountains* (66), *Counterpoint* (67), *The Castle* (68), *Krakatoa* (68), *First Love* (w, p, d only) (70), etc.

SCHENCK, AUBREY (1908–   ). American producer. *Shock* (46), *Repeat Performance* (48), *Beachhead* (53), *Up Periscope* (58), *Frankenstein 70* (59), *Robinson Crusoe on Mars* (64), *Don't Worry We'll Think of a Title* (66), etc.

SCHENCK, JOSEPH M. (1878–1961). Russian-born executive, in America from 1900, at first as pharmacist, then fairground showman and owner. By 1924 was chairman of United Artists and creator of its theatre chain. In 1933 he founded Twentieth Century Productions and by 1935 was head of Twentieth-Century Fox. In 1953 he created Magna Productions with Mike Todd. In 1950 he was voted a special Academy Award.

SCHENCK, NICHOLAS M. (1881–1969). Russian-born executive, brother of Joseph M. Schenck, with whom after arrival in America in 1900 he ran an amusement park. Later developed theatre chain which emerged as Loew's Consolidated Enterprises; became president of Loew's and thus financial controller of MGM.

SCHERTZINGER, VICTOR (1880–1941). American director, former concert violinist. Wrote the first film music score, for *Civilisation* (15). As director: *Forgotten Faces* (29), *Nothing but the Truth* (31), *Uptown New York* (32), *The Cocktail Hour* (33), *One Night of Love* (34), *Love Me Forever* (35), *The Music Goes Round* (36), *Something to Sing About* (37), *The Mikado* (GB) (39), *Road to Singapore* (40), *Rhythm on the River* (41), *Road to Zanzibar* (41), *Kiss the Boys Goodbye* (41), etc.

SCHIAFFINO, ROSANNA (1939–   ). Italian leading lady in international films. *Two Weeks in Another Town* (62), *The Victors* (63), *El Greco* (66), *Arrivederci Baby* (66), etc.

SCHILDKRAUT, JOSEPH (1895–1964). Austrian leading man and character actor, of theatrical family. On American stage from early 20s. Films include *Orphans of the Storm* (21), *Dust of Desire* (23), *The Road to Yesterday* (25), *King of Kings* (27), *Show Boat* (29), *Mississippi Gambler* (30), *Night Ride* (31), *Carnival* (GB) (32), *The Blue Danube* (GB) (32), *The Garden of Allah* (36), *The Life of Émile Zola* (as Dreyfus) (AA) (37), *Suez* (38), *Idiot's Delight* (38), *The Man in the Iron Mask* (39), *Flame of the Barbary Coast* (44), *The Cheaters* (45), *Monsieur Beaucaire* (46), *End of the Rainbow* (47), *Gallant Legion* (48), *The Diary of Anne Frank* (59), etc. Published autobiography 1959: *My Father and I.*

SCHILLING, GUS (1908–1957). Wry-faced American comic actor from musical comedy and burlesque. *Citizen Kane* (debut; as the waiter) (41), *A Thousand and One Nights* (44), *Lady from Shanghai* (47), *On Dangerous Ground* (52), *Glory* (56), etc.

†SCHLESINGER, JOHN (1926–   ). British director, former small-part actor and TV director. *Terminus* (60), *A Kind of Loving* (62), *Billy Liar* (63), *Darling* (65), *Far from the Madding Crowd* (67), *Midnight Cowboy* (US) (69).

SCHNEE, CHARLES (1916–1963). American screenwriter. *The Next Voice You Hear* (50), *The Furies* (50), *The Bad and the Beautiful* (AA) (52), *Torch Song* (produced only) (53), then for some years acted as MGM production executive. Last screenplay: *Two Weeks in Another Town.*

SCHNEER, CHARLES (1920–). American producer, mainly of trick films using 'Superdynamation'. *The Seventh Voyage of Sinbad* (58), *The Three Worlds of Gulliver* (59), *I Aim at the Stars* (61), *Mysterious Island* (62), *Jason and the Argonauts* (63), *The First Men in the Moon* (64), *You Must Be Joking* (65), *Half a Sixpence* (67), *The Executioner* (69), etc.

SCHNEIDER, ROMY (1938–) (Rosemarie Albach-Retty). Austrian leading lady in international films. *The Story of Vickie* (German) (58), *Forever My Love* (61), *Boccaccio 70* (62), *The Cardinal* (63), *The Trial* (63), *The Victors* (63), *Good Neighbour Sam* (64), *What's New Pussycat* (65), *10.30 p.m. Summer* (66), *Triple Cross* (66), *Don't You Cry* (70), etc.

SCHNITZLER, ARTHUR (1862–1931). Austrian playwright whose chief bequests to the cinema are *Liebelei* and *La Ronde*.

SCHOEDSACK, ERNEST B. (1893–). American director, former cameraman, who with Merian C. Cooper made *Grass* (26), *Chang* (27), *The Four Feathers* (29), *Rango* (31), *The Hounds of Zaroff* (32), *King Kong* (33), *Son of Kong* (34), *Long Lost Father* (34), *Outlaws of the Orient* (37), *Dr Cyclops* (39), *Mighty Joe Young* (49), etc.

schooldays have often been depicted in films with a thick sentimental veneer, as in *Goodbye Mr Chips*, *Good Morning, Miss Dove* and *Blossoms in the Dust*. But more usually the pupils have serious problems to worry about, as in *Young Woodley*, *The Guinea Pig*, *Friends for Life*, *Tea and Sympathy* and *Tom Brown's Schooldays*; while with at least equal frequency our sympathies are elicited on behalf of the staff: *The Housemaster*, *Bright Road*, *The Blackboard Jungle*, *Spare the Rod*, *Edward My Son*, *The Blue Angel*, *The Children's Hour*, *The Corn is Green*. *Term of Trial*, *To Sir With Love*, *Spinster*, *The Prime of Miss Jean Brodie*. More light-hearted treatment of the whole business is evident in *The Trouble with Angels* and *Margie*, and in some cases the treatment has undeniably been farcical: *Boys Will Be Boys*, *The Ghost of St Michael's*, *Good Morning Boys*, *A Yank at Eton*, *Vice Versa*, *Bottoms Up* and *The Happiest Days of Your Life*. The strangest schools on film are those depicted in *Zéro de Conduite* and its semi-remake *If* . . . while very special schools were seen in *Battement de Cœur* (for pickpockets), *School for Secrets* (for 'boffins'), *Old Bones of the River* (for African tiny tots), *The Goose Steps Out* (for young Nazis), *Orders to Kill*, *Carve Her Name with Pride* and *From Russia with Love* (for spies).

SCHUFFTAN, EUGENE (1894–). German cinematographer. *People on Sunday* (30), *L'Atlantide* (32), *Drôle de Drame* (36), *Quai des Brumes* (38), *It Happened Tomorrow* (44), *Ulysses* (54), *Eyes without a Face* (59), *Something Wild* (61), *The Hustler* (AA) (62), *Lilith* (64), etc. Invented the Schufftan process, a variation on the 'glass shot'

Schulberg, B. P.

(qv), by which mirror images are blended with real backgrounds.

SCHULBERG, B. P. (1892–1957). American executive, former publicist; general manager of Paramount (1926–1932), then independent producer.

SCHULBERG, BUDD (1914–). American novelist whose work has been adapted for the screen: *On the Waterfront* (AA) (54), *The Harder They Fall* (56), *A Face in the Crowd* (57), *Wind Across the Everglades* (59), etc. Son of B. P. Schulberg.

SCHUNZEL, REINHOLD (1886–1954). German actor and director who came to Hollywood in the 30s. *Rich Man, Poor Girl* (d) (38), *Balalaika* (d) (39), *The Great Awakening* (d) (41), *Hostages* (a) (43), *The Man in Half Moon Street* (a) (44), *The Woman in Brown* (a) (48), *Washington Story* (a) (52), etc.

SCHUSTER, HAROLD (1902–). American director, former editor, *Wings of the Morning* (37), *Dinner at the Ritz* (37), *Zanzibar* (40), *My Friend Flicka* (43), *The Tender Years* (47), *So Dear to My Heart* (49), *Kid Monk Baroni* (52), *Slade* (53), *Dragoon Wells Massacre* (57). *The Courage of Black Beauty* (58), etc. Much TV work.

SCHWARTZ, ARTHUR (1900–). American producer and composer, former lawyer. *Navy Blues* (c) (42), *Thank Your Lucky Stars* (c) (43), *Cover Girl* (p) (44), *The Band Wagon* (c) (53), *You're Never Too Young* (c) (55), others.

SCHWARZ, MAURICE (1891–1960). American actor famous in the Yiddish theatre; many of his successes, such as *Tevya the Milkman*, were filmed for limited circulation. Appeared in Hollywood's version of *Salome* (53).

scientists have been the subject of many films, though few real-life ones have led sufficiently dramatic lives to warrant filming. Warners led the way in the 30s with *The Story of Louis Pasteur* and *Dr Ehrlich's Magic Bullet*. In 1939 Mickey Rooney played *Young Tom Edison*, followed by Spencer Tracy as *Edison the Man*. Then in 1943, Greer Garson played *Madame Curie*. At this point the movie fan's thirst for scientific knowledge died out, and John Huston's *Freud* in 1962 did not revive it.

See also: *inventors*.

†SCOFIELD, PAUL (1922–). Distinguished British stage actor whose films have been infrequent. *That Lady* (55), *Carve Her Name with Pride* (58), *The Train* (64), *A Man for All Seasons* (AA, BFA) (66), *King Lear* (69).

score. The music composed for a film.

SCOTT, ADRIAN (1912–). American producer: *Farewell My Lovely (Murder My Sweet)* (44), *My Pal Wolf* (44), *Cornered* (46), *So Well*

Remembered (47), *Crossfire* (47), etc.; career affected by Un-American Activities investigation (48).

SCOTT, GEORGE C. (1926–   ). American stage actor, in occasional films: *Anatomy of a Murder* (59), *The Hustler* (62), *The List of Adrian Messenger* (63), *Dr Strangelove* (64), *The Bible* (66), *Not with My Wife You Don't* (66), *The Flim Flam Man* (67), *Patton* (69), etc. TV series: *East Side West Side* (63).

SCOTT, GORDON (1927–   ) (Gordon M. Werschkul). American leading man who after being fireman, cowboy and lifeguard was signed to play Tarzan in *Tarzan's Hidden Jungle* (55); made four further episodes, has lately been in Italy making muscleman epics: *Arm of Fire* (64), *The Tramplers* (66), etc.

SCOTT, GORDON L. T. (1920–   ). British producer, former production manager: *Look Back in Anger* (58), *Petticoat Pirates* (61), *The Pot Carriers* (63), *Crooks in Cloisters* (64), etc.

SCOTT, JANETTE (1938–   ). British leading lady, former child star. *No Place for Jennifer* (debut) (49), *No Highway* (50), *The Magic Box* (51), *As Long As They're Happy* (52), *Now and Forever* (55), *The Good Companions* (57), *The Devil's Disciple* (59), *The Old Dark House* (63), *The Beauty Jungle* (64), *Crack in the World* (65), etc.

SCOTT, LIZABETH (1922–   ) (Emma Matzo). American leading lady, formerly Tallulah Bankhead's stage understudy. *You Came Along* (45), *The Strange Love of Martha Ivers* (46), *Dead Reckoning* (46), *I Walk Alone* (47), *Desert Fury* (47), *Pitfall* (48), *The Racket* (51), *The Stolen Face* (GB) (52), *Scared Stiff* (53), *Bad For Each Other* (53), *The Weapon* (GB) (55), *Loving You* (56), etc. Recently on TV.

SCOTT, MARGARETTA (1912–   ). British stage (from 1929) and screen (from 1934) actress who usually plays upper-middle-class women. *Dirty Work* (34), *Things to Come* (36), *Quiet Wedding* (40), *Sabotage at Sea* (42), *Fanny by Gaslight* (43), *The Man from Morocco* (45), *Mrs Fitzherbert* (47), *Idol of Paris* (48), *Where's Charley* (52), *Town on Trial* (56), *The Last Man to Hang* (56), *A Woman Possessed* (58), *An Honourable Murder* (60), *Crescendo* (69), etc.

SCOTT, MARTHA (1914–   ). American actress with stage experience; film debut as heroine of *Our Town* (40). Later: *Cheers for Miss Bishop* (41), *One Foot in Heaven* (42), *In Old Oklahoma* (43), *So Well Remembered* (47), *The Desperate Hours* (55), *The Ten Commandments* (56), etc.

SCOTT, PETER GRAHAM (1923–   ). British director, from TV. *Panic in Madame Tussauds* (48), *Sing along with Me* (52), *The Headless Ghost*

(59), *Captain Clegg* (62), *The Pot Carriers* (62), *Bitter Harvest* (63), *Father Came Too* (64), *Mister Ten Per Cent* (67), etc.

SCOTT, RANDOLPH (1903–   ) (Randolph Crane). Rugged American outdoor star, in films from 1931 after stage experience. *Sky Bride* (31), *Island of Lost Souls* (32), *Supernatural* (32), *Home on the Range* (33), *Roberta* (34), *She* (35), *So Red the Rose* (35), *Follow the Fleet* (36), *Go West Young Man* (36), *Last of the Mohicans* (36), *High, Wide and Handsome* (37), *Rebecca of Sunnybrook Farm* (38), *The Texans* (38), *Jesse James* (39), *Virginia City* (40), *My Favourite Wife* (40), *When the Daltons Rode* (40). *Western Union* (41), *Belle Starr* (41), *Paris Calling* (41), *To the Shores of Tripoli* (42), *The Spoilers* (42), *Pittsburgh* (42), *Bombardier* (43), *Gung Ho* (43), *The Desperadoes* (43), *Belle of the Yukon* (44), *China Sky* (44), *Captain Kidd* (45), *Badman's Territory* (46), *Abilene Town* (47), *Christmas Eve* (47), *Fighting Man of the Plains* (49), *Sugarfoot* (51), *Santa Fe* (51), *Hangman's Knot* (53), *The Stranger Wore a Gun* (53), *The Bounty Hunter* (54), *A Lawless Street* (55), *Seven Men from Now* (56), *Decision at Sundown* (57), *Ride Lonesome* (58), *Guns in the Afternoon* (*Ride the High Country*) (62), many others.

SCOTT, ZACHARY (1914–1965). American leading man with considerable stage experience. *The Mask of Dimitrios* (film debut) (44), *The Southerner* (45), *Mildred Pierce* (46), *Stallion Road* (47), *The Unfaithful* (48), *Born To Be Bad* (51), *Let's Make It Legal* (53), *Appointment in Honduras* (53), *Bandido* (56), *The Young One* (60), *It's Only Money* (62), others.

SCOTTO, VINCENTE (1876–1952). French composer. *Jofroi* (34), *Pepe le Moko* (36), *La Fille du Puisatier* (40), *Domino* (43), *L'Ingénue Libertine* (50), etc.

SCOURBY, ALEXANDER (c. 1908–   ). American stage character actor whose occasional films include *Affair in Trinidad* (52), *The Big Heat* (53), *The Silver Chalice* (55), *Giant* (56), *Seven Thieves* (59), *The Big Fisherman* (59), *Confessions of a Counterspy* (*Man on a String*) (60).

screenplay: see *shooting script*.

SCROOGE. Dickens' *A Christmas Carol*, the tale of miser Scrooge haunted by his past, has been filmed countless times. Among the best-remembered are the Essanay version of 1908, the Edison version of 1910, the Seymour Hicks' versions of 1913 and 1935; the 1916 version with Rupert Julian, who also directed; the MGM 1938 version with Reginald Owen; and the 1951 version with Alastair Sim.

seances on the screen have often been shown to be fake, as in *Seance on a Wet Afternoon*, *Bunco Squad*, *Palmy Days*, *The Spiritualist* and *The Medum*. But just occasionally they do result in something being called up from over there: it happened in *Blithe Spirit*, *The Haunting*, *The Uninvited*, and *Night of the Demon*.

THE SEA HAWK. Rafael Sabatini's swashbuckling Elizabethan romance about a feuding family was screened with reasonable fidelity in 1924 with Milton Sills. The Errol Flynn pirate yarn of 1940 jettisoned almost everything but the title.

SEARLE, FRANCIS (c. 1905–   ). British director. *A Girl in a Million* (46), *Things Happen at Night* (48), *Cloudburst* (also wrote) (51), *Wheel of Fate* (also wrote) (53), many second features.

SEARLE, JACKIE (1920–   ). American boy actor of the 30s, usually in mean roles. Now plays Western villains. *Tom Sawyer* (31), *Skippy* (31), *Peck's Bad Boy* (35), *Little Lord Fauntleroy* (36), *That Certain Age* (38), *Little Tough Guys in Society* (39), *Hearts in Springtime* (41), *The Paleface* (49), many others; much on TV.

SEARS, FRED F. (1913–1957). American director of second features from 1945. *Ambush at Tomahawk Gap* (53), *The Werewolf* (55), *Rock Around the Clock* (56), *Cell 2455 Death Row* (56), *Don't Knock the Rock* (57), *Rumble on the Docks* (57), etc.

SEARS, HEATHER (1935–   ). British actress with repertory experience. *Dry Rot* (56), *The Story of Esther Costello* (*The Golden Virgin*) (57), *Room at the Top* (59), *Sons and Lovers* (60), *Phantom of the Opera* (62), *Saturday Night Out* (64), *Black Torment* (64), etc.

THE SEASHELL AND THE CLERGYMAN (France 1928). For many years this surrealist fantasy filled with sexual symbols was justly cited as the cinema's furthest excursion into the avant-garde. Its creator, Germaine Dulac, produced nothing of equal interest. The film is also notable for provoking a famous remark by the British Board of Film Censors in banning the picture: 'It is so obscure as to have no apparent meaning. If there is a meaning, it is doubtless objectionable.'

seaside resorts have provided lively settings for many British comedies: Douglas in *No Limit*, Brighton in *Bank Holiday*, Blackpool in *Sing As We Go*, and a variety of south coast resorts in *The Punch and Judy Man*, *French Dressing*, *All Over the Town*, *Barnacle Bill*. Sometimes the resort has provided a contrast to more serious goings-on, as in *The Entertainer*, *Brighton Rock*, *Room at the Top*, *The Dark Man*, *A Taste of Honey*, *I Was Happy Here*, *Family Doctor*, *The System*, *The Damned*. Hollywood usually comes a cropper when depicting British resorts, either comically as in *The Gay Divorce* or seriously as in *Separate Tables*; its own resorts have a monotonous look, whether in *Moon Over Miami* and *Fun in Acapulco*, nostalgically in *Some Like It Hot*, trendily in *Beach Party* and its many sequels, or morosely in *Tony Rome*. The French Riviera has never been notably well captured on film since Vigo's *A Propos de Nice*, but among the movies to have a go with the aid of back projection are *On the Riviera*, *That Riviera Touch* and *Moment to Moment*, while the French had a go for themselves in *St Tropez Blues* and others. A Mediterranean resort was the setting of the climax of *Suddenly Last Summer*; other European watering-places featured memorably in *Une Si Jolie Petite Plage*, *Sunday in August* and *The Lady with the Little Dog*. The most ingenious use of the seaside for purposes of film fantasy was certainly in *Oh What a Lovely War*.

SEASTROM (or **SJOSTROM**), **VICTOR** (1879–1960). Distinguished Swedish actor-director with stage experience. *Ingeborg Holm* (13), *Terje Vigen* (a, d) (16), *Jerusalem* (d) (18), *Ordet* (*The Word*) (a) (21), *The Phantom Carriage* (d) (20), *The Master of Man* (US) (d) (23), *He Who Gets Slapped* (US) (d) (24), *The Scarlet Letter* (US) (d) (26), *The Divine Woman* (US) (d) (28), *The Wind* (US) (d) (28), *Under the Red Robe* (GB) (d) (36), *Ordet* (remake) (a) (43), *To Mennesker* (d) (50), *Wild Strawberries* (a) (57), many others.

SEATON, GEORGE (1911–). American writer-director. Acted and produced on stage; joined MGM writing staff (33); later independent or working with producer William Perlberg. *A Day at the Races* (co-w) (37), *The Song of Bernadette* (w) (43), *Diamond Horseshoe* (w, d) (45), *Junior Miss* (w, d) (45), *The Shocking Miss Pilgrim* (w, d) (47), *Miracle on 34th Street* (w, d) (AA) (47), *The Big Lift* (w, d) (51), *For Heaven's Sake* (w, d) (51), *Anything Can Happen* (w, d) (53), *Little Boy Lost* (w, d) (53), *The Country Girl* (w, d) (AA) (54), *The Proud and Profane* (w, d) (56), *The Tin Star* (p) (57), *Teacher's Pet* (d) (58), *The Pleasure of His Company* (d) (61), *The Counterfeit Traitor* (w, d) (63), *Thirty-six Hours* (w, d) (64), *What's So Bad About Feeling Good?* (w, p, d) (68), *Airport* (w, d) (69), many others.

THE SEA WOLF. Jack London's stark psychological novel of an obsessed sea captain, Wolf Larsen, has been filmed seven times. In 1913 it starred Hobart Bosworth, in 1920 Noah Beery, in 1925 Ralph Ince, in 1930 Milton Sills, and in 1941 Edward G. Robinson. 1950 brought a disguised Western version, *Barricade*, with Raymond Massey, and in 1957 yet another straight version, under the title *Wolf Larsen*, was made with Barry Sullivan.

SEBERG, JEAN (1938–). American leading lady who won contest for role of Preminger's *Saint Joan* (57), after which her career faltered but has picked up in French films. *Bonjour Tristesse* (57), *The Mouse That Roared* (59), *Breathless* (*A Bout de Souffé*) (60), *Playtime* (62), *In the French Style* (63), *Lilith* (64), *Moment to Moment*

(65), *Estouffade a la Caraibe* (66), *The Road to Corinth* (68), *Pendulum* (69), *Paint Your Wagon* (69), *Airport* (69), etc.

SECOMBE, HARRY (1921–   ). Burly Welsh comedian and singer, who apart from a number of second-feature appearances in the early 50s has filmed only rarely: *Jet Storm* (56), *Davy* (57), *Oliver!* (68), *Song of Norway* (70).

second unit director. One who directs not the actors but the spectacular location sequences, stunt men, scenic backgrounds, etc., and is thus sometimes responsible for a film's most striking effects; e.g. Andrew Marton's chariot race sequence in *Ben Hur* (59).

SECONDS (US 1966). An interesting if unsuccessful attempt by John Frankenheimer to make a horror thriller for our times, with Rock Hudson as a middle-aged executive trapped by a sinister organization into paying for rejuvenation until they decide he will be more profitable as a corpse. Begins and ends in splendidly nasty form, but suffers from a flagging middle section. Original story by David Ely, cinematography by James Wong Howe.

SEDGWICK, EDWARD (1893–1953). American director of routine films: *Live Wires* (21), *The First Degree* (23), *Two Fisted Jones* (25), *Spring Fever* (27), *I'll Tell the World* (34), *Ma and Pa Kettle Back on the Farm* (50), many others.

SEGAL, ALEX (1915–   ). American director, from TV. *Ransom* (56), *All the Way Home* (63), *Joy in the Morning* (65), etc.

SEGAL, GEORGE (1935–   ). American leading man. *The New Interns* (64), *Invitation to a Gunfighter* (64), *Ship of Fools* (65), *King Rat* (65), *Lost Command* (66), *Who's Afraid of Virginia Woolf?* (66), *The Quiller Memorandum* (66), *The St Valentine's Day Massacre* (67), *Bye Bye Braverman* (68), *No Way to Treat a Lady* (68), *The Southern Star* (69), *The Bridge at Remagen* (69), etc.

SEGALL, HARRY (1897–   ). American writer who started the heavenly fantasies of the 40s with his play 'Halfway to Heaven'. *Fatal Lady* (36), *Here Comes Mr Jordan* (41), *Angel on My Shoulder* (46), *For Heaven's Sake* (50), *Monkey Business* (52), etc.

SEILER, LEWIS (1891–1964). American director. Many Tom Mix silents; then *Air Circus* (co-d) (28), second features through 30s, *Dust Be My Destiny* (39), *It All Came True* (40), *South of Suez* (41), *The Big Shot* (42), *Guadalcanal Diary* (43), *Molly and Me* (44), *If I'm Lucky* (46), *Whiplash* (48), *The Tanks Are Coming* (51), *The Winning Team* (52), *The System* (53), *Women's Prison* (55), *Battle Stations* (56), *The True Story of Lynn Stuart* (58), many others.

Seiter, William A.

SEITER, WILLIAM A. (1891–1964). American director, in Hollywood from 1918, then directing shorts. Later: *Boy Crazy* (22), *The Teaser* (25), *Good Morning Judge* (28), *The Love Racket* (30), *Girl Crazy* (32), *If I Had a Million* (part) (33), *Diplomaniacs* (33), *Professional Sweetheart* (33), *Fraternally Yours* (34), *Roberta* (34), *Dimples* (36), *His Affair* (37), *Room Service* (38), *It's a Date* (40), *Broadway* (42), *The Destroyer* (43), *The Affairs of Susan* (45), *I'll Be Yours* (47), *One Touch of Venus* (48), *Dear Brat* (51), *Make Haste to Live* (54), many others.

SEITZ, GEORGE B. (1888–1944). American director, known as the serial king. A writer-director from 1913, he worked on *The Perils of Pauline*, and directed *The Fatal Ring* (17) and all subsequent Pearl White serials. In the 20s, he acted in his own serials: *Velvet Fingers*, *The Sky Ranger*, etc. Turning to features, he directed nearly forty between 1927 and 1933, then moved to MGM and kept up an even more rapid output, including episodes of the Hardy Family series. *The Women in His Life* (35), *Andy Hardy Meets a Debutante* (39), *Kit Carson* (40), *Sky Murder* (40), *Andy Hardy's Private Secretary* (41), *China Caravan* (42), etc.

SEITZ, JOHN (1893–   ). American cinematographer, in Hollywood from 1916. *The Four Horsemen of the Apocalypse* (21), *The Prisoner of Zenda* (23), many distinguished silents; later *Huckleberry Finn* (39), *Sullivan's Travels* (41), *Hail the Conquering Hero* (44), *Double Indemnity* (44), *The Lost Weekend* (45), *Sunset Boulevard* (50), *The San Francisco Story* (52), *Hell on Frisco Bay* (55), *The Man in the Net* (58), *Guns of the Timberland* (60), etc.

SEKELY, STEVE (1899–   ) (Istvan Szekely). Hungarian director, in Hollywood from the mid-30s. *Women in Bondage* (44), *The Scar* (48), *Stronghold* (51), *The Blue Camellia* (54), *The Day of the Triffids* (62), etc.

SELANDER, LESLEY (c. 1903–   ). American director who has been making low-budget Westerns and other action pictures since 1936 and is still at it. *Cattle Pass* (37), *The Round-Up* (41), *The Vampire's Ghost* (46), *Belle Starr's Daughter* (48), *I Was an American Spy* (51), *Flight to Mars* (51), *The Highwayman* (52), *The Lone Ranger and the Lost City of Gold* (58), *Town Tamer* (65), *Fort Utah* (67), many others. Also hundreds of TV action films.

SELIG, WILLIAM N. (1864–1948). Pioneer American producer: *The Count of Monte Cristo* (08), *The Spoilers* (13), many serials, etc.

SELLARS, ELIZABETH (1923–   ). British leading actress on stage from 1941, latterly much on TV. Occasional films include *Floodtide* (debut) (48), *Madeleine* (50), *Cloudburst* (51), *The Gentle Gunman* (52), *The Barefoot Contessa* (54), *Three Cases of Murder* (55), *The*

Shiralee (57), *The Day They Robbed the Bank of England* (61), *The Chalk Garden* (64), *The Mummy's Shroud* (67).

†SELLERS, PETER (1925–   ). British comic actor who has recently become an international star. From variety stage and radio's 'Goon Show'. *Down Among the Z Men* (52), *Orders Are Orders* (54), *John and Julie* (55), *The Lady Killers* (55), *The Smallest Show on Earth* (57), *The Naked Truth* (58), *Tom Thumb* (58), *Up the Creek* (58), *Carlton-Browne of the F.O.* (58), *The Mouse That Roared* (59), *I'm All Right, Jack* (59), *The Battle of the Sexes* (60), *Two-Way Stretch* (60), *Never Let Go* (61), *The Millionairess* (61), *Mr Topaze* (also directed) (61), *Only Two Can Play* (62), *Lolita* (62), *Waltz of the Toreadors* (62), *The Dock Brief* (63), *The Wrong Arm of the Law* (63), *The Pink Panther* (63), *Dr Strangelove* (64), *The World of Henry Orient* (64), *A Shot in the Dark* (64), *What's New, Pussycat?* (65), *The Wrong Box* (66), *After the Fox* (66), *Casino Royale* (66), *The Bobo* (67), *Woman Times Seven* (67), *The Party* (68), *I Love You Alice B. Toklas* (68), *The Magic Christian* (69), *Hoffman* (70).

SELTEN, MORTON (1860–1940) (Morton Stubbs). British stage actor who played distinguished old gentlemen in some 30s films. *Service for Ladies* (32), *Ten Minute Alibi* (35), *The Ghost Goes West* (36), *Fire over England* (36), *A Yank at Oxford* (38), *The Divorce of Lady X* (38), *The Thief of Bagdad* (40), etc.

SELZNICK, DAVID O. (1902–1965). American independent producer, former writer. Worked for RKO from 1931, MGM from 1933; founded Selznick International Pictures in 1936. *A Star Is Born* (37), *The Prisoner of Zenda* (37), *Nothing Sacred* (37), *Tom Sawyer* (38), *Gone with the Wind* (39), *Rebecca* (40), *Since You Went Away* (43), *Spellbound* (45), *Duel in the Sun* (46), *The Third Man* (co-p) (49), *Indiscretion (Stazione Termini)* (51), *A Farewell to Arms* (57), *Tender Is the Night* (62), many others.

SEMON, LARRY (1890–1928). American silent slapstick comedian, popular in innumerable two-reelers of the 20s; also some features, *The Simple Life* (18), *The Wizard of Oz* (24), *The Sawmill* (25), *Spuds* (27), etc.

SENNETT, MACK (1880–1960) (Michael Sinnott). American 'king of comedy' who in the 20s produced countless slapstick shorts featuring the Keystone Kops, Chester Conklin, Louise Fazenda, Charlie Chaplin, Mack Swain, Billy West, Fred Mace, Heinie Conklin, Slim Summerville and others. By the time sound came, Sennett had exhausted all the possible tricks of his 'fun factory' and found the new methods not to his taste. His output waned almost to nothing, but he was given a special Academy Award in 1937: 'For his lasting contribution to the comedy technique of the screen . . . the Academy presents a Special Award to that master of fun, discoverer of stars, sympathetic, kindly, understanding genius—Mack Sennett'. A biography, *King of Comedy*, was published in 1955.

SENSO (Italy 1953). Luchino Visconti's grand stab at a historical romantic epic making psychological sense emerged as a rather lifeless melodrama but was distinguished by superb colour photography. In Britain and America a dubbed and shortened version was issued under the title *The Wanton Countess*. Alida Valli and Farley Granger starred.

serials demand a book to themselves. They began in the early years of the century and continued until the early fifties, their plethora of adventurous and melodramatic incident being usually divided into fifteen or twenty chapters of about twenty minutes each. They were the domain of mad doctors, space explorers, clutching hands, mysterious strangers, diabolical villains and dewy-eyed heroines. Each chapter ended with a 'cliffhanger' in which the hero or heroine was left in some deadly danger from which it was plain he could not escape; but at the beginning of the next chapter escape he did. A few favourite serials are *Fantomas*, *The Perils of Pauline*, *Batman*, *Flash Gordon's Trip to Mars* and *Captain Marvel*. Almost all of them were American. They were finally killed by the advent of TV and by the increasing length of the double-feature programme.

series of feature films used to be popular enough, and many are individually noted in this book; in recent years the series concept has been taken over by TV, and in any case low-budget movies featuring cut-to-pattern characters could no longer be made to pay their way in theatres. When one looks back over these old heroes, who flourished chiefly in the 30s and 40s, most of them turn out to be sleuths of one kind or another. They included *Sherlock Holmes*, *The Saint*, *The Lone Wolf*, *Father Brown*, *Nero Wolfe*, *Duncan McLain*, *The Crime Doctor*, *Sexton Blake*, *Mr Moto*, *Perry Mason*, *Bulldog Drummond*, *Nancy Drew*, *Mr Wong*, *Charlie Chan*, *Ellery Queen*, *Boston Blackie*, *The Falcon*, *Hildegarde Withers*, *Hercule Poirot*, *Dick Tracy*, *Torchy Blane*, *Michael Shayne*, *Philip Marlowe* and, more recently, *Inspector Clouseau* and *Tony Rome*. Nor should one forget crime anthologies like *Inner Sanctum* and *The Whistler*. The spy vogue, a recent happening, is naturally headed by *James Bond*: in his wake you may discern *Counterspy*, *Coplan*, *Flint*, *The Tiger*, *The Man from Uncle*, *Harry Palmer*, and *Superdragon*. Among the more muscular outdoor heroes may be counted *Hopalong Cassidy*, *The Three Mesquiteers*, *The Lone Ranger*, *Captain Blood*, *Zorro*, *Robin Hood*, *Tarzan*, *Jungle Jim*, *The Cisco Kid*, *The Man with No Name* and the Italian giants who go under such names as *Maciste*, *Goliath*, *Hercules* and *Ursus*. The longest surviving series villain is certainly *Fu Manchu*.

As for monsters, take your pick from *Frankenstein, Dracula, The Mummy, The Creature from the Black Lagoon, The Invisible Man, The Wolf Man, Dr X*; while if you prefer comedy freaks there are *Topper* and *Francis*. There have been a goodly number of domestic comedies and dramas, including *Squibs, The Jones Family, The Hardy Family, The Cohens and the Kellys, Blondie, Ma and Pa Kettle, Maisie, Henry Aldrich, Scattergood Baines, Lum and Abner, Jeeves, Gidget* and the *Four Daughters* saga. Other comedy series have ranged from the subtleties of *Don Camillo* to the prat-falls of *Old Mother Riley, Mexican Spitfire*, the *Doctor* series, and *Carry On*. Animals have had series to themselves, as for instance *Flicka, Lassie, Rusty* and *Flipper*. So have children of various ages : *Our Gang, Gasoline Alley, The Dead End Kids, The East Side Kids, The Bowery Boys*. The best-established musical series were *Broadway Melody* and *The Big Broadcast*. And three cheers for *Dr Kildare, Dr Christian, Dr Defoe, Dr Mabuse* and *Dr Goldfoot* . . . to say nothing of Professor *Quatermass*.

SERLING, ROD (1924–   ). American TV playwright who has contributed scores of scripts to such series as *Twilight Zone* (which he also introduced). Film writing includes *Patterns of Power* (56), *Saddle the Wind* (58), *Requiem for a Heavyweight (Blood Money)* (63), *Yellow Canary* (63), *Seven Days in May* (64), *Assault on a Queen* (66), *Planet of the Apes* (67).

SERNAS, JACQUES (1925–   ). Lithuanian-born leading man, in international films. *The Golden Salamander* (GB) (50), *Jump into Hell* (US) (55), *Helen of Troy* (US/Italy) (55), *Maddalena* (France) (56), *The Sign of the Gladiator* (Italy) (60), *Son of Spartacus* (Italy) (62), etc.

SERSEN, FRED (1890–1962). American special effects photographer, long with Fox, for whom he produced such spectacles as the fire in *In Old Chicago*, the storm in *The Rains Came*, and the canal-building in *Suez*.

SERVAIS, JEAN (1910–   ). French character actor with stage experience. *Criminel* (31), *La Valse Eternelle* (36), *La Danse de Mort* (47), *Une Si Jolie Petite Plage* (48), *Le Plaisir* (51), *Rififi* (55), *Les Jeux Dangereux* (58), *That Man from Rio* (64), *Lost Command* (66), etc.

SETON, BRUCE (1909–1969). British leading man, later character actor ; military background. *Blue Smoke* (34), *Sweeney Todd* (36), *Love from a Stranger* (38) ; war service ; *The Curse of the Wraydons* (46), *Bonnie Prince Charlie* (48), *Whisky Galore* (49), *John Paul Jones* (US) (59), etc. TV series: *Fabian of the Yard* (54).

SETTON, MAXWELL (1909–   ). British independent producer, former lawyer. *The Spider and the Fly* (50), *So Little Time* (52), *They Who Dare* (54), *Footsteps in the Fog* (55), *Town on Trial* (56), *I Was Monty's*

Double (58), etc. Recently held executive posts for Bryanston and Columbia.

SEVEN BRIDES FOR SEVEN BROTHERS (US 1954). A highly successful MGM musical which appeared at the end of the peak period spurred by Gene Kelly, and somehow failed to prolong it. Marred by obvious budget economies, it nevertheless brought tremendous gusto to its Western retelling of the story of the rape of the Sabine women. Produced by Jack Cummings, directed by Stanley Donen, with music by Gene de Paul, lyrics by Johnny Mercer, choreography by Michael Kidd; book by Albert Hackett, Frances Goodrich and Dorothy Kingsley. Howard Keel and Jane Powell led a talented cast.

SEVEN DAYS IN MAY (US 1964). A fine political melodrama directed by John Frankenheimer and written by Rod Serling from a novel by Fletcher Knebel and Charles W. Bailey II. About a militarist attempt to depose a weak president, it gives first-class opportunities to Fredric March as the president, Burt Lancaster as the ambitious general and Kirk Douglas as his bewildered aide; and apart from an unnecessary sex interest it moves with tremendous pace and attack.

SEVEN KEYS TO BALDPATE. The famous stage comedy-thriller by Earl Derr Biggers and George M. Cohan has been filmed five times; with Cohan himself in 1917, Douglas Maclean in 1926, Richard Dix in 1929, Gene Raymond in 1935, and Philip Terry in 1947.

SEVEN SAMURAI (Japan 1954). The film on which *The Magnificent Seven* (qv) was based; a spellbinding piece of oriental savagery which runs nearly three hours even in the abbreviated Western version but never allows the eye to wander. Director Akira Kurosawa and actor Toshiro Mifune share the credit. AA best foreign film 1955.

SEVENTH HEAVEN. Frank Borzage directed Janet Gaynor (AA) and Charles Farrell in the immensely popular 1927 version of this simple garret love story set in Paris before the 1914 war, from which the hero returns blinded. Henry King remade it in 1937, with Simone Simon and James Stewart. The story has its origins in a play by Austin Strong.

THE SEVENTH SEAL (Sweden 1957). Ingmar Bergman's most fascinating and infuriating film, an outpouring of medieval religious images of life and death, pain and joy. Its meaning probably can't be fully analysed, even by Bergman himself, but almost every scene is in some way memorable, and the film stands as a textbook of filmcraft. Photographed by Gunnar Fischer, with music by Eric

Nordgren. The cast includes Nils Poppe, Gunnar Bjornstrand, Max von Sydow, and Bengt Ekerot as Death.

THE SEVENTH VEIL (GB 1945). An incredibly successful piece of commercial film-making, one of the first post-war returns to the prewar novelette school; about a concert pianist undergoing psychiatric treatment because she can't decide which of three men to marry. Expertly concocted by producer Sidney Box, glossily directed by Compton Bennett. With Ann Todd, James Mason, Herbert Lom, Albert Lieven. When the film was televised in Britain over ten years later, cinemas all over the country suffered, and the event helped to toughen the attitude of the film trade to television.

SEWELL, VERNON (1903–   ). British director, former engineer, photographer, art director and editor. *The Silver Fleet* (43), *Latin Quarter* (46), *The Ghosts of Berkeley Square* (47), *Uneasy Terms* (48), *The Ghost Ship* (52), *Where There's a Will* (55), *Battle of the VI* (58), *House of Mystery* (61), *Strongroom* (62), *The Curse of the Crimson Altar* (68), etc.

sewers have figured in several thrillers, most notably *The Third Man* with its exciting final chase; its sewer complex was recently spoofed in *Carry On Spying*. In 1948 in *He Walked by Night* Richard Basehart played a criminal who invariably escaped through the sewers; and our old friend *The Phantom of the Opera* was similarly skilled. As recently as the British thriller *Invasion* a sewer detour was used; while the Frankenstein monster was saved from the burning windmill by falling through to the sewer, where he was found at the beginning of *Bride of Frankenstein*. In more serious films, sewers are of course featured in the many versions of *Les Misérables*, while the Polish resistance film *Kanal* takes place entirely—and nauseatingly—in the sewers of Warsaw.

sex. This was once called 'romance': the beginnings of corruption set in with de Mille's silent comedies such as *Why Change Your Wife?* and Lubitsch's classics *Forbidden Paradise* and *The Marriage Circle*. These gentlemen carried their sophistication into the early sound period, assisted by such stars as Valentino, Harlow, Dietrich, Clara Bow and Ginger Rogers; and there was considerable help from a film called *The Private Life of Henry VIII* and a lady named Mae West; but around 1934 the Hays Code and the Legion of Decency forced innocence upon Hollywood to such an extent that the smart hero and heroine of 1934's *It Happened One Night* just wouldn't dream of sharing a bedroom without a curtain between them. The later 30s, perforce, were the heyday of the boy next door and the *ingénue*: nice people all, impersonated by such stars as Gary Cooper, Dick Powell, Ray Milland, David Niven, Ruby Keeler, Janet Gaynor, Deanna Durbin and Irene Dunne. Meanwhile a strong rearguard action was being fought by actors like

William Powell, Myrna Loy, Melvyn Douglas, Ann Sheridan and Cary Grant, but usually the blue pencil had been wielded so heavily on their scripts that it was difficult to tell what was really being implied. The best way out was found in such comedies as *The Philadelphia Story*, which were basically earthy but gave every appearance of keeping it all in the mind. The war years produced a certain slackening of restrictions; for instance, the pin-up girl became not only permissible but desirable as a way of building up military morale. Preston Sturges brought sex out into the open in *The Palm Beach Story* and *The Miracle of Morgan's Creek*; Spencer Tracy and Katharine Hepburn started (in *Woman of the Year*) a series of films portraying the battle of the sexes in a recognizably human way. The 'love goddesses' became progressively more blatant in their appeal: Jane Russell, Marilyn Monroe, Jayne Mansfield. (But in the 50s it turned out that one of the earthiest of them, Sophia Loren, was also the best actress.) By now the production code had been broken down to the extent of permitting words like 'virgin' and 'mistress' (*The Moon Is Blue*), the recognition of adultery and prostitution as human facts (*Wives and Lovers*, *Kiss Me Stupid*), depiction of the lustfulness of males (*Tom Jones*, *Alfie*) and the presentation, albeit in a fantasy, of girls as 'pleasure units' (*Our Man Flint*). Indeed, after *Georgy Girl*, *Night Games* and *Who's Afraid of Virginia Woolf?*, it seems that public frankness can go very little further.

SEXTON BLAKE. The hawk-nosed detective, hero of several generations of boys, seems to be attributable to no single author. On screen he was portrayed in the 30s by George Curzon, in the 40s by David Farrar and in the 50s by Geoffrey Toone.

SEYLER, ATHENE (1889–). British comedy actress with long stage career dating from 1908. *The Perfect Lady* (film debut) (32), *The Citadel* (38), *Quiet Wedding* (40), *Dear Octopus* (43), *Nicholas Nickleby* (47), *Queen of Spades* (48), *Young Wives' Tale* (51), *Pickwick Papers* (53), *Yield to the Night* (56), *Campbell's Kingdom* (58), *The Inn of the Sixth Happiness* (58), *Make Mine Mink* (59), *Nurse on Wheels* (63), many others.

SEYMOUR, ANNE (1909–). American character actress. *All the King's Men* (49), *Man on Fire* (57), *Home from the Hill* (59), *The Subterraneans* (60), *Sunrise at Campobello* (60), *Mirage* (65), *Blindfold* (66), etc. TV series: *Empire*.

SEYMOUR, DAN (1915–). Burly American character actor, the scowling menace of countless films. *Casablanca* (42), *To Have and Have Not* (44), *Cloak and Dagger* (46), *Key Largo* (48), *Rancho Notorious* (52), *The Big Heat* (53), *Moonfleet* (55), *The Sad Sack* (57), *Watusi* (59), etc.

SEYRIG, DELPHINE (1932–   ). French leading actress. *Pull My Daisy* (58), *Last Year in Marienbad* (61), *Muriel* (63), *La Musica* (66), *Accident* (GB) (67), *Mr Freedom* (68), *Stolen Kisses* (68), etc.

SHADOW OF A DOUBT (US 1943). A very effective, and pleasingly understated, Hitchcock thriller about a small-town family visited by a romantic big-city uncle who turns out to be the Merry Widow Murderer. Hitch's technique has never been more supple, and Thornton Wilder's script is a great asset. Joseph Cotten and Teresa Wright give responsive performances. The film was remade, inadequately, in 1959 as a second feature called *Step Down to Terror*.

SHADOWS (US 1959). An improvised film shot on 16mm in New York by John Cassavetes with unknown actors. About young people in the big city, its chief interest was in its technique, which influenced the 'cinema vérité' school.

SHAKESPEARE, WILLIAM (1564–1616). British poet and dramatist whose plays have received plenty of attention from film-makers. *The Taming of the Shrew* was filmed in 1908 by D. W. Griffith; in 1929 with Douglas Fairbanks, Mary Pickford, and the immortal credit line 'additional dialogue by Sam Taylor'; in 1953, more or less, as *Kiss Me Kate*; and in 1966 with Elizabeth Taylor, Richard Burton, and script credits to three writers none of whom is Shakespeare. *As You Like It* was filmed in 1912 with Rose Coghlan and Maurice Costello; the only sound filming was in 1936 by Paul Czinner, with Elisabeth Bergner and Laurence Olivier. *A Midsummer Night's Dream* was tackled in major fashion by Warners in 1935, but the elaborate Max Reinhardt production failed to please at the box-office; in 1968 a 'realistic' version by Peter Hall was equally unsuccessful.

Of the tragedies, *Othello* has been frequently attempted, by Emil Jannings in 1922, Orson Welles in 1953, Sergei Bondartchuk in 1955 and Laurence Olivier in 1966; a 1961 British film called *All Night Long* was a modern up-dating of the plot, and Ronald Colman's Academy-Award winning performance in *A Double Life* (47) had him as an actor who starts playing the Moor in private life. *Hamlet* was played by Sir Johnston Forbes Robertson in 1913, Asta Nielsen in 1922, Olivier in 1948, and Innokenti Smoktunovsky in 1964. *Macbeth* is thought to be an unlucky play; but Sir Herbert Beerbohm Tree appeared in a version for Griffith in 1916; Orson Welles directed himself in the role in 1953, Paul Douglas in 1955 was an updated *Joe Macbeth*, and in 1960 Maurice Evans appeared in a version originally intended for TV but shown theatrically. *King Lear* has recently been filmed with Paul Scofield; there was a one-reel Vitagraph version in 1909 and Frederic Warde starred in a 1916 production. *Romeo and Juliet* was also made in 1916, starring Francis X. Bushman and Beverly Bayne; this superseded several one-reel versions. In 1936 MGM produced its Leslie Howard/ Norma Shearer version directed by George Cukor; in 1954 Renato Castellani directed an unsuccessful colour version with Laurence Harvey and Susan Shentall; in 1961 came the inevitable modernization in *West Side Story*: and 1968 brought another expensive production by Franco Zeffirelli. (There have also been several ballet versions.) There were early potted versions of *Julius Caesar* before the spectacular Italian production of 1914; the play was not filmed again until MGM's excellent 1953 version. The plot was used in a curious British second feature called *An Honourable Murder* (59), with the action moved to a modern executive suite; and another all-star version in colour followed in 1970.

Of the histories, most of *Henry IV* has been compressed by Orson Welles into his *Chimes at Midnight*. *Henry V* was splendidly dealt with by Olivier in 1944. *Richard III* existed in several primitive versions, and John Barrymore recited a speech from it in *Show of Shows* (28); but again it was left to Olivier to do it properly.

The oddest screen fate of a Shakespeare play was surely that of *The Tempest*, which in 1956 yielded its entire plot to that winning bit of science fiction *Forbidden Planet*.

SHAMROY, LEON (1901–   ). American cinematographer, in Hollywood from the 30s. *The Black Swan* (AA) (42), *Stormy Weather* (43), *Wilson* (AA) (44), *Leave Her to Heaven* (AA) (45), *Where Do We Go from Here?* (45), *Twelve O'clock High* (49), *The Robe* (53), *The Egyptian* (54), *The Best Things in Life Are Free* (56), *The King and I* (56), *South Pacific* (58), *Porgy and Bess* (59), *Cleopatra* (62), *The Cardinal* (63), *What a Way To Go* (64), *The Agony and the Ecstasy* (65), *The Glass Bottom Boat* (66), *Caprice* (also as actor) (67), *Planet of the Apes* (67), *Justine* (69), many others.

SHANE (US 1953). A serious, atmospheric Western about a pioneer family protected by a mysterious stranger; written by A. B. Guthrie Jnr from Jack Schaefer's novel. George Stevens directed it with great feeling and turned it into a classic. Photographed by Loyal Griggs (AA), music by Victor Young; with Alan Ladd, Jean Arthur, Van Heflin.

SHANE, MAXWELL (1905–   ). American writer-director, former publicist. *You Can't Beat Love* (co-w) (37), *One Body Too Many* (w) (43), *Fear in the Night* (w, d) (46) (remade as *Nightmare* in 1956), *City across the River* (w, d, p) (49), *The Naked Street* (w, d) (55), etc. Working in TV.

SHANGHAI EXPRESS (US 1932). This nostalgic melodrama, which even when new seemed to be spoofing itself, has over the years acquired the patina of a Hollywood classic. All about the intertwining of the lives of a Chinese war lord, a high class prostitute, and a stiff-upper-lip British officer on a train beset by rebels, it had suitable performances from Warner Oland, Marlene Dietrich and Clive Brook. Josef von Sternberg directed from a script by Harry Hervey; Lee Garmes (AA) was cinematographer. There was one direct remake, *Peking Express* (52), but many films borrowed the basic situations: *Half Way to Shanghai, Night Plane from Chungking, The House of Tao Ling,* even *The General Died at Dawn* and *The Lady Vanishes.*

SHANNON, HARRY (1890–1964). American character actor, often seen as sympathetic father or rustic; musical comedy experience. *Hands Up* (31), *Young Tom Edison* (40), *The Eve of St Mark* (44), *The Gunfighter* (50), *High Noon* (52), *Executive Suite* (54), *Come Next Spring* (56), *Hell's Crossroads* (57), many others.

SHAPIRO, STANLEY (1925–). American writer-producer associated with glossy comedies; long experience in radio and TV. *The Perfect Furlough* (w) (58), *Pillow Talk* (co-w) (AA) (59), *Operation Petticoat* (co-w) (59), *Come September* (co-w) (60), *That Touch of Mink* (co-w) (62), *Bedtime Story* (w, p) (64), *How to Save a Marriage* (p) (68), etc.

SHARAFF, IRENE (c. 1910–). American costume designer, long with Fox. Recent films include *An American in Paris* (AA) (51), *The King and I* (AA) (56), *West Side Story* (AA) (61), *Hello Dolly* (69).

SHARIF, OMAR (1933–) (Michael Shalhouz). Egyptian leading man now in international films. *Goha* (59), *Lawrence of Arabia* (62), *The Fall of the Roman Empire* (64), *Behold a Pale Horse* (64), *The Yellow Rolls-Royce* (64), *Genghis Khan* (65), *Dr Zhivago* (66), *The Night of the Generals* (66), *Marco the Magnificent* (66), *More Than a Miracle* (67), *Funny Girl* (68), *Mayerling* (68), *Mackenna's Gold* (68), *The Appointment* (69), *Che!* (69), *A Last Valley* (70), etc.

SHARP, DON (1922–). Australian-born director, in British film industry from 1952, at first as writer. *Ha'penny Breeze* (w) (52), *Robbery Under Arms* (w) (56), *The Professionals* (59), *Linda* (60), *Kiss of the Vampire* (62), *Devil Ship Pirates* (63), *Witchcraft* (64), *Those Magnificent Men in Their Flying Machines* (second unit) (65), *Rasputin the Mad Monk* (65), *The Face of Fu Manchu* (65), *Our Man in Marrakesh* (66), *The Million Eyes of Su Muru* (66), *Rocket to the Moon* (67), etc.

SHATNER, WILLIAM (1931–). American leading actor, seen mostly on TV as guest star and in series *Star Trek*. Films include *The Brothers Karamazov* (58), *The Explosive Generation* (61), *The Intruder* (*The Stranger*) (61), *The Outrage* (64).

SHAUGHNESSY, ALFRED (1916–). British producer. *Brandy for the Parson* (51), *Cat Girl* (57), *Heart of a Child* (57), *Just My Luck* (script only) (59), *The Impersonator* (script and direction only) (61), *Lunch Hour* (63), etc.

SHAUGHNESSY, MICKEY (1920–). Tough-looking American comic actor with stage experience. *The Last of the Comanches* (debut) (52), *From Here to Eternity* (53), *Conquest of Space* (55), *Jailhouse Rock* (57), *Don't Go Near the Water* (57), *North to Alaska* (60), *A Global Affair* (63), *A House is Not a Home* (64), *Never a Dull Moment* (68), etc.

SHAVELSON, MELVILLE (1917–). American screenwriter, in Hollywood from early 40s. *The Princess and the Pirate* (44), *Always Leave Them Laughing* (50), *Room for One More* (52), *The Seven Little Foys* (also directed) (56), *Beau James* (also directed) (57), *Houseboat* (also directed) (58), *The Five Pennies* (also directed) (59), *The Pigeon That Took Rome* (also produced and directed) (62), *A New Kind of Love* (also produced and directed) (63), *Cast a Giant Shadow* (also produced and directed) (66), many others, usually in collaboration with JACK ROSE (1911–).

SHAW, BERNARD (1856–1950). Distinguished Irish playwright who for many years refused to allow film versions of his works: he was reconciled to the idea by Gabriel Pascal. The following versions have been made: *How He Lied to Her Husband* (30), *Arms and the Man* (31), *Pygmalion* (38), *Major Barbara* (40), *Caesar and Cleopatra* (45), *Androcles and the Lion* (53), *Saint Joan* (57), *The Doctor's Dilemma* (58), *The Devil's Disciple* (59), *The Millionairess* (61), *My Fair Lady* (from *Pygmalion*) (64), etc.

SHAW, IRWIN (1912–). American novelist whose film scripts include *Talk of the Town* (42), *I Want You* (51), *Fire Down Below* (57), *The Young Lions* (from his own novel) (58), *Tip on a Dead Jockey* (58), *Two Weeks in Another Town* (novel only) (62), etc.

SHAW, ROBERT (1927–). British actor, mainly on stage from 1954. *The Dam Busters* (film debut) (55), *Sea Fury* (59), *The Valiant* (61), *Tomorrow at Ten* (62), *From Russia with Love* (63), *The Caretaker* (63), *The Luck of Ginger Coffey* (64), *The Battle of the Bulge* (65), *A Man for All Seasons* (as Henry VIII) (66), *Custer of the West* (67), *The Battle of Britain* (69), *The Royal Hunt of the Sun* (69), *Figures in a Landscape* (70), etc. Also novelist. TV series: *The Buccaneers* (56).

SHAW, SEBASTIAN (1905–). British leading man of the 30s, latterly character actor. On stage from 1913 (as child). *The Squeaker* (37), *The Spy in Black* (39), *East of Piccadilly* (41), *The Glass Mountain* (48), *It Happened Here* (64), *A Midsummer Night's Dream* (68), etc. Also on TV.

SHAW, SUSAN (1929–) (Patsy Sloots). British leading lady groomed by the Rank 'charm school'. *The Upturned Glass* (debut) (47),

Holiday Camp (47), *London Belongs to Me* (48), *The Woman in Question* (50), *The Intruder* (51), *The Good Die Young* (52), *Stock Car* (54), *The Switch* (63), etc.

SHAW, VICTORIA (1935–   ) (Jeanette Elphick). Australian leading lady in American films. *Cattle Station* (Aust.) (55), *The Eddy Duchin Story* (56), *Edge of Eternity* (59), *The Crimson Kimono* (60), *Alvarez Kelly* (66), etc.

SHAW, WINI (1910–   ). American singer of Hawaiian descent, used as voice of non-singing stars in many Warner musicals of the 30s. Actually appeared in *Three on a Honeymoon* (34), *Gold Diggers of 1935, In Caliente* (35), *Melody for Two* (37), etc.

SHAWLEE, JOAN (1929–   ) (formerly Joan Fulton). American character comedienne with night club and stage experience. *Men in Her Diary* (45), *Cuban Pete* (46), *I'll Be Yours* (47), *The Marrying Kind* (52), *Conquest of Space* (54), *A Star is Born* (54), *Some Like It Hot* (59), *The Apartment* (60), *Irma La Douce* (63), *The Wild Angels* (66), *The St Valentine's Day Massacre* (67), etc. TV series: *Aggie* (57).

SHAWN, DICK (c. 1929–   ) (Richard Schulefand). American comedian, in occasional films. *Wake Me When It's Over* (60), *It's a Mad Mad Mad Mad World* (63), *A Very Special Favour* (65), *What Did You Do in the War, Daddy?* (66), *Penelope* (66), *The Producers* (68), etc.

SHAYNE, ROBERT (c. 1910–   ) (Robert Shaen Dawe). American general purpose actor. *Keep 'Em Rolling* (34), *Shine On Harvest Moon* (44), *The Swordsman* (47), *The Neanderthal Man* (lead role) (53), *Spook Chasers* (58), *Valley of the Redwoods* (61), etc.

SHE. Seven silent versions are said to have been made of Rider Haggard's adventure phantasy about a lost tribe, an ageless queen and a flame of eternal life in darkest Africa. Only the last remains, made in London and Berlin by G. B. Samuelson, with Betty Blythe and Carlyle Blackwell. In 1934 in Hollywood, Merian Cooper and Ernest Schoedsack remade the story in a north pole setting, with Helen Gahagan and Randolph Scott. In 1965 came a lifeless Hammer version directed by Robert Day, with Ursula Andress and John Richardson; this was followed in 1968 by a sequel, *The Vengeance of She*, that was more than slightly potty.

SHE ONLY DANCED ONE SUMMER (Sweden 1951). This glum romantic tragedy came complete with nude bathing scene and dour puritan priests, amounting to almost a parody of itself. But it was commercial enough to cause a renewal of interest in European films. Arne Matsson directed: Ulla Jacobson and Folke Sundquist were the doomed lovers.

879

SHEAN, AL (1868–1949) (Alfred Schoenberg). German-born entertainer, long in American vaudeville; part of the famous 'Mr
Gallagher and Mr Shean' act. After his partner's death he played
character roles in Hollywood films: *Murder in the Air* (35), *San
Francisco* (36), *The Great Waltz* (38), *Ziegfeld Girl* (41), *Atlantic City*
(44), etc.

SHEARER, MOIRA (1926–   ) (Moira King). Scottish-born ballet
dancer who came to films for the leading role in *The Red Shoes* (48).
Later: *Tales of Hoffman* (52), *The Story of Three Loves* (53), *The Man
Who Loved Redheads* (55), *Peeping Tom* (59), *Black Tights* (60).
Retired.

SHEARER, NORMA (1900–   ). American star actress of the 20s and
30s, widow of Irving Thalberg, MGM executive producer. *The
Stealers* (debut) (20), *The Snob* (24), *He Who Gets Slapped* (24), *The
Tower of Lies* (25), *The Waning Sex* (26), *The Student Prince* (27),
The Actress (28), *The Trial of Mary Dugan* (first sound film) (29),
The Divorcee (AA) (29), *The Last of Mrs Cheyney* (29), *Hollywood
Desire* (29), *Their Own Desire* (30), *Let Us Be Gay* (30), *Strangers May
Kiss* (30), *Private Lives* (31), *A Free Soul* (31), *Strange Interlude* (31),
Smilin' Through (32), *Riptide* (34), *The Barretts of Wimpole Street* (34),
Romeo and Juliet (36), *Marie Antoinette* (38), *Idiot's Delight* (39), *The
Women* (39), *Escape* (40), *We Were Dancing* (42), *Her Cardboard
Lover* (42), etc. Retired. (†Sound films complete).

SHEEKMAN, ARTHUR (1892–   ). American comedy writer, often in
collaboration. *Monkey Business* (31), *Roman Scandals* (33), *Dimples*
(36), *Wonder Man* (45), *Welcome Stranger* (46), *Saigon* (47), *Young
Man with Ideas* (52), *Bundle of Joy* (56), *Ada* (61), etc.

SHEFFIELD, JOHNNY (1931–   ). American boy actor of the 30s,
especially in the *Tarzan* and later the *Bomba* series. Also appeared
in *Babes in Arms* (39), *Roughly Speaking* (45), etc.

THE SHEIK. Rudolph Valentino first appeared as the romantic Arab
in 1922, with Agnes Ayres as his willing co-star, in an adaptation
of E. Mayne Hull's novelette. It was one of his most successful roles,
and *Son of the Sheik* came out in 1926 with Vilma Banky partnering
him. His death prevented further episodes, but in 1937 Ramon
Novarro made fun of the idea in *The Sheik Steps Out*.

SHELDON, SIDNEY (1917–   ). American writer-director. *The Bachelor
and the Bobbysoxer* (w) (AA) (47), *Dream Wife* (co-w, d) (53), *You're
Never Too Young* (w) (55), *The Buster Keaton Story* (w, p, d) (57),
Jumbo (w) (62), etc.

SHELLEY, BARBARA (1933–   ). British leading lady who has
filmed in Italy; latterly associated with horror films. *Cat Girl* (57),

Blood of the Vampire (59), *Village of the Damned* (61), *Shadow of the Cat* (62), *Postman's Knock* (62), *The Gorgon* (64), *The Secret of Blood Island* (65), *Rasputin the Mad Monk* (65), *Dracula, Prince of Darkness* (65), etc.

SHELLEY, MARY WOLLSTONECRAFT (1797–1851). British writer, wife of the poet, who somewhat unexpectedly is remembered as the creator of *Frankenstein*, which she composed to pass the time during a wet summer.

SHELTON, JOY (1922–   ). British leading lady. *Millions Like Us* (43), *Waterloo Road* (45), *No Room at the Inn* (48), *A Case for PC 49* (51), *Impulse* (54), *No Kidding* (60), *HMS Defiant* (62), etc.

SHENSON, WALTER (c. 1921–   ). American producer, former publicist; based in Britain. *Korea Patrol* (53), *The Mouse That Roared* (59), *A Matter of Who* (61), *A Hard Day's Night* (64), *Help!* (65), *A Talent for Loving* (69), etc.

SHEPLEY, MICHAEL (1907–1961) (Michael Shepley-Smith). British stage actor who usually played amiable buffoons. *Black Coffee* (30), *Goodbye Mr Chips* (39), *Quiet Wedding* (40), *The Demi Paradise* (43), *Maytime in Mayfair* (49), *An Alligator Named Daisy* (56), *Don't Bother to Knock* (61), etc.

SHEPPERD, JOHN (1907–   ) (also known as SHEPPERD STRUDWICK). American leading man and latterly character actor, usually in gentle, understanding roles. Stage experience. *Congo Maisie* (debut) (40), *Remember the Day* (41), *The Loves of Edgar Allen Poe* (42), etc.; war service; *Enchantment* (47), *Joan of Arc* (48), *All the King's Men* (50), *A Place in the Sun* (51), *Autumn Leaves* (56), *The Sad Sack* (57), *The Unkillables* (67), etc.

SHER, JACK (1913–   ). American writer-director, former columnist. *My Favourite Spy* (w) (52), *Off Limits* (w) (53), *Four Girls in Town* (w, d) (56), *Kathy 'O* (w, d) (58), *The Wild and the Innocent* (w, d) (59), *The Three Worlds of Gulliver* (w, d) (60), *Paris Blues* (co-w) (61), *Critic's Choice* (w) (63), *Move Over Darling* (co-w) (63), etc.

SHERIDAN, ANN (1915–1967) (Clara Lou Sheridan). American leading lady of the 40s, known as the 'oomph' girl. Came to Hollywood 1933 by winning a beauty contest. *The Notorious Sophie Lang* (34), *The Glass Key* (35), *San Quentin* (38), *Angels with Dirty Faces* (38), *Dodge City* (39), *Castle on the Hudson* (40), *They Drive by Night* (40), *City for Conquest* (40), *Honeymoon for Three* (41), *The Man Who Came to Dinner* (42), *King's Row* (42), *Juke Girl* (42), *Edge of Darkness* (43), *Thank Your Lucky Stars* (43), *Shine On Harvest Moon* (44), *The Dough-girls* (44), *One More Tomorrow* (46), *Nora Prentiss* (47), *The Unfaithful* (47), *Good Sam* (48), *I Was a Male War Bride* (*You Can't Sleep Here*)

(49), *Woman on the Run* (50), *Just Across the Street* (52), *Come Next Spring* (55), *The Opposite Sex* (56), *Woman and the Hunter* (57), others. Emerged from retirement for a 1966 TV series, *Pistols and Petticoats*.

SHERIDAN, DINAH (1920–). British leading lady. *Irish and Proud of It* (36), *Full Speed Ahead* (39), *Salute John Citizen* (42), *For You Alone* (44), *Hills of Donegal* (47), *Calling Paul Temple* (48), *The Story of Shirley Yorke* (48), *Paul Temple's Triumph* (50), *Where No Vultures Fly* (51), *Genevieve* (53), etc. Retired to marry Rank executive John Davis (now divorced).

SHERIFF, PAUL (1903–) (Paul Shouvalov). Russian scenarist in Britain since mid-30s. *French Without Tears* (39), *Quiet Wedding* (40), *The Gentle Sex* (43), *The Way to the Stars* (45), *Vice Versa* (48), *Flesh and Blood* (51), *Gentlemen Marry Brunettes* (55), *Interpol* (57), *The Doctor's Dilemma* (58), *The Grass Is Greener* (60), etc.

SHERLOCK HOLMES. Conan Doyle's classic fictional detective, around whom a detailed legend has been created by ardent followers, has a long screen history. There were American one-reel films featuring him in 1903, 1905 and 1908. Also in 1908 there began a series of twelve Danish one-reelers starring Forrest Holger-Madsen. In 1910 there were two German films and in 1912 six French. A second French series began in 1913; also in this year an American two-reel version of *The Sign of Four* featured Harry Benham. British six-reelers were made of *A Study in Scarlet* (14) and *Valley of Fear* (16); also in 1916 the famous stage actor William Gillette put his impersonation of Holmes on film for Essanay. In 1917 came a German version of *The Hound of the Baskervilles*; then nothing till 1922, when John Barrymore played Holmes and Roland Young was Watson in Goldwyn's *Sherlock Holmes*, based on Gillette's stage play. In Britain in the same year Maurice Elvey directed a full-length version of *The Hound of the Baskervilles* and followed it with over 25 two-reelers starring Eille Norwood, remaining faithful to the original stories. In 1929 Carlyle Blackwell played Holmes in a German remake of *The Hound of the Baskervilles*; and in the same year Clive Brook played in a talkie, *The Return of Sherlock Holmes*, with H. Reeves-Smith as Watson. Arthur Wontner, a perfect Holmes, first played the role in *Sherlock Holmes' Final Hour* (GB) (31), later appearing in *The Sign of Four* (32), *The Missing Rembrandt* (33), *The Triumph of Sherlock Holmes* (35), and *Silver Blaze* (36) (Ian Fleming was Watson). Raymond Massey was Holmes in *The Speckled Band* (GB) (31), with Athole Stewart as Watson; in 1932 Robert Rendel was in *The Hound of the Baskervilles* (GB). Clive Brook again appeared in *Sherlock Holmes* (US) (32), with Reginald Owen as Watson; Owen then played Holmes in *A Study in Scarlet* (US) (33). The Germans made three more Holmes films in the mid-30s, including yet another remake of *The Hound*, which in 1939 was again tackled by Fox in Hollywood, this time with Basil Rathbone as the detective and Nigel Bruce as Watson. Its success led to a hurried remake of the Gillette play under the title *The Adventures of Sherlock Holmes* (39); two years later the same two actors began a series of twelve films in which the settings were modernized and most of the stories unrecognizable, although the acting and much of the writing were well in character. The titles were *Sherlock Holmes and the Voice of Terror* (41), *Sherlock Holmes and the Secret Weapon* (42), *Sherlock Holmes in Washington* (42), *Sherlock Holmes Faces Death* (43), *Spider Woman* (44), *The Scarlet Claw* (44), *Pearl of Death* (44), *House of Fear* (45), *Woman in Green* (45), *Pursuit to Algiers* (45), *Terror by Night* (46), *Dressed to Kill* (*Sherlock Holmes and the Secret Code*) (46). Then a long silence was broken by Peter Cushing and André Morell in the leads of a British remake of *The Hound of the Baskervilles* (59). In 1960 and 1961 Christopher Lee played Holmes in two German films which have not been exported; and in 1965 John Neville and Donald Houston appeared in an original story involving the famous pair with Jack the Ripper: *A Study in Terror*. Also in 1965 a BBC TV series featured Douglas Wilmer and Nigel Stock, with Peter Cushing later taking over as Holmes; the period atmosphere was carefully sought but the stories suffered from being padded out to the standard TV length. There was also a Franco-American TV series in 1954 with Ronald Howard and Howard Marion-Crawford; and in 1969 Billy Wilder made *The Private Life of Sherlock Holmes* with Robert Stephens.

SHERMAN, GEORGE (1908–   ). American director who graduated slowly from second feature Westerns. *Wild Horse Rodeo* (37), *Death Valley Outlaws* (41), *Outside the Law* (41), *Mantrap* (43), *Mystery Broadcast* (44), *The Lady and the Monster* (44), *The Bandit of Sherwood Forest* (46), *Last of the Redskins* (48), *Sword of the Desert* (49), *Panther's Moon* (50), *The Golden Horde* (51), *Against All Flags* (52), *War Arrow* (54), *Dawn at Socorro* (54), *Count Three and Pray* (55), *Comanche* (56), *Son of Robin Hood* (58), *The Enemy General* (60), *Panic Button* (64), *Smoky* (66), many others.

SHERMAN, LOWELL (1885–1934). American leading man with stage experience. *Way Down East* (20), *Monsieur Beaucaire* (24), *The Divine Woman* (27), *Mammy* (30), *The Greeks Had a Word for Them* (32), *False Faces* (32), *She Done Him Wrong* (directed only) (33), *Morning Glory* (33), *Broadway through a Keyhole* (33), etc.

SHERMAN, RICHARD and ROBERT (* —   ). American songwriters who have worked mainly on Disney films. *Mary Poppins* (AA) (64), *The Happiest Millionaire* (67), *The One and Only Genuine Family Band* (68), etc.

SHERMAN, VINCENT (1906–   ). American director, formerly stage actor. *The Return of Doctor X* (39), *All Through the Night* (41), *The*

Sherriff, R. C.

Hard Way (42), *Old Acquaintance* (43), *In Our Time* (44), *Mr Skeffing-ton* (45), *The Unfaithful* (47), *The New Adventures of Don Juan* (48), *The Hasty Heart* (49), *Lone Star* (51), *Affair in Trinidad* (52), *The Garment Jungle* (57), *Naked Earth* (57), *The Young Philadelphians* (59), *Ice Palace* (60), *The Second Time Around* (61), *Cervantes* (66), etc.

SHERRIFF, R. C. (1896–   ). Prolific British playwright and screen-writer. Plays filmed include *Journey's End* (30), *Badger's Green* (47), *Home at Seven* (52), etc. Scripts include *The Invisible Man* (33), *Goodbye Mr Chips* (39), *Lady Hamilton* (41), *Odd Man Out* (47), *Quartet* (48), *No Highway* (50), *The Dam Busters* (55), many others.

SHERWOOD, MADELEINE (1926–   ). American character actress. *Cat on a Hot Tin Roof* (58), *Hurry Sundown* (67), *Pendulum* (69), etc. TV series: *The Flying Nun* (67–68).

SHERWOOD, ROBERT (1896–1955). American dramatist. Plays filmed include *Reunion in Vienna* (32), *The Petrified Forest* (36), *Tovarich* (38), *Idiot's Delight* (39), *Abe Lincoln in Illinois* (39), etc. Other scripts: *Waterloo Bridge* (32), *The Adventures of Marco Polo* (38), *Rebecca* (40), *The Best Years of Our Lives* (45), *The Bishop's Wife* (48), *Jupiter's Darling (The Road to Rome)* (54).

SHIELDS, ARTHUR (1900–   ). Irish character actor, an Abbey player, long in Hollywood. *The Plough and the Stars* (37), *Drums along the Mohawk* (39), *The Long Voyage Home* (40), *The Keys of the Kingdom* (44), *The Corn Is Green* (45), *The River* (51), *The Quiet Man* (52), *The King and Four Queens* (56), *Night of the Quarter Moon* (59), *The Pigeon That Took Rome* (62), etc. Brother of Barry Fitzgerald.

SHIGETA, JAMES (1933–   ). Hawaiian leading man who usually plays Japanese in Hollywood films. *The Crimson Kimono* (60), *Cry for Happy* (60), *Bridge to the Sun* (61), *Flower Drum Song* (61), *Paradise Hawaiian Style* (66), *Nobody's Perfect* (68), etc.

SHINDO, KANETO (1912–   ). Japanese director. *Children of Hiroshima* (53), *The Wolf* (56), *The Island* (62), *Ningen* (63), *Onibaba* (64), *Kuroneko* (67), etc.

SHINE, BILL (1911–   ). Amiable British small part actor often seen as vacuous dandy. *The Scarlet Pimpernel* (34), *Farewell Again* (37), *Let George Do It* (40), *Perfect Strangers* (45), *Melba* (53), *Father Brown* (54), *Jack the Ripper* (58), many others.

SHINER, RONALD (1903–1966). British comedy actor, on stage from 1928, films from 1934, at first in bit parts, later as star. *King Arthur Was a Gentleman* (42), *The Way to the Stars* (45), *Worm's Eye View* (50), *Reluctant Heroes* (51), *Laughing Anne* (53), *Top of the Form* (54), *Up to His Neck* (55), *Keep It Clean* (56), *Dry Rot* (56), *Girls at Sea* (58), *Operation Bullshine* (59), *The Night We Got the Bird* (60), etc.

SHIP OF FOOLS (US 1965). A rather splendid 60s reversion to the star-studded 'Grand Hotel' type of film, with sociological overtones added. The period is 1933, the ship is full of Germans and Jews, and most of the ironies are naïvely and quaintly based on hind-sight; but the dramatic situations are well handled, Stanley Kramer's direction of the several stories is well controlled if rather stately, and there is a feast of good acting, notably from Simone Signoret, Oscar Werner, Vivien Leigh and Heinz Ruhmann.

ships, of the modern passenger kind, have provided a useful setting for many films, most recently in *Ship of Fools* (see above). Three notable versions of the Titanic disaster were *Atlantic* (30), *Titanic* (53) and *A Night to Remember* (58); while sinking ships also figured in *We're Not Dressing* (34), *Souls at Sea* (37), *History Is Made at Night* (37), *The Blue Lagoon* (48), *Our Girl Friday* (52), *The Admirable Crichton* (57) (and earlier versions), and *The Last Voyage* (60). A sinister time was had on board ship in *Journey into Fear*, *Across the Pacific*, *King Kong*, *My Favourite Blonde*, *The Ghost Ship*, *The Mystery of the Marie Celeste*, *The Sea Wolf*, *The Hairy Ape*, *Dangerous Crossing* and *Ghost Breakers*; laughter, however, was to the fore in *Monkey Business* (31), *The Lady Eve* (41), *Luxury Liner* (48), *Doctor at Sea* (55), *The Captain's Table* (58), *A Countess from Hong Kong* (66), and *A Night at the Opera* (35) with its famous cabin scene. The romance of a cruise was stressed in *Dodsworth* (36), *Now Voyager* (42), and the two versions of *Love Affair* (39) (the second being *An Affair to Remember* [56]); while in the 'Winter Cruise' section of *Encore* (51) it was almost forced on Kay Walsh. In *Assault on a Queen* (66), the leading characters plan to hi-jack the Queen Mary. The wierdest ship was the ship of the dead in *Outward Bound* (30), and its remake *Between Two Worlds* (44).

Mississippi riverboats have featured in *Mississippi*, *Rhythm on the River*, *Mississippi Gambler*, *The Secret Life of Walter Mitty*. *The Naughty Nineties*, *The Adventures of Mark Twain*, *Four for Texas*, *Frankie and Johnny*, and the several versions of *Showboat*; also in the TV series *Riverboat*.

Sailing ships of olden days are too numerous to detail.

SHIRLEY, ANNE (1918–   ) (Dawn Paris). American child star of the 20s (under the name Dawn O'Day) who later graduated to leading lady roles. *So Big* (32), *Anne of Green Gables* (35), *Stella Dallas* (37), *Vigil in the Night* (39), *Anne of Windy Willows* (40), *West Point Widow* (41), *All That Money Can Buy* (41), *Farewell My Lovely* (last to date) (44), etc.

SHOEMAKER, ANN (1895–   ). American character actress with stage experience. *A Dog of Flanders* (35), *Alice Adams* (35), *Stella Dallas* (37), *Babes in Arms* (39), *Conflict* (45), *A Woman's Secret* (49), *Sunrise at Campobello* (60), *The Fortune Cookie* (66), many others.

SHOLEM, LEE (c. 1900–   ). American director. *Tarzan's Magic Fountain* (48), *Redhead from Wyoming* (52), *Tobor the Great* (53), *Emergency Hospital* (56), *Pharaoh's Curse* (56), *Sierra Stranger* (57), etc.

SHONTEFF, LINDSAY (* –   ). British director, from TV. *The Curse of Simba* (63), *Devil Doll* (64), *Licensed to Kill* (65), *Run with the Wind* (66), etc.

THE SHOP AROUND THE CORNER (US 1940). Written by Samson Raphaelson from a play by Nikolaus Laszlo, produced and directed by Ernst Lubitsch, this was a charming piece of Hollywood schmaltz, though none of the cast really suggested Budapest shop assistants. James Stewart and Margaret Sullivan were the couple who disliked each other by day but fell in love through a Lonely Hearts Bureau; in support were Frank Morgan, Joseph Schildkraut, Felix Bressart. In 1949 Robert Z. Leonard remade it as a musical, *In the Good Old Summertime*, with Judy Garland and Van Johnson.

SHOPWORN ANGEL (US 1929). A well-remembered comedy-drama about a hard-boiled Broadway gold-digger (Nancy Carroll) who ultimately gave up her rich provider (Paul Lukas) for a poor doughboy on his way to war (Gary Cooper). This version was directed by Richard Wallace; H. C. Potter remade it in 1938, with Margaret Sullavan, Walter Pidgeon and James Stewart. In 1958 it turned up again as *That Kind of Woman*, with Sidney Lumet directing Sophia Loren, George Sanders and Tab Hunter.

SHORE, DINAH (1917–   ) (Frances Rose Shore). American singer, married to George Montgomery. In radio from 1938, occasional films from 1942. *Thank Your Lucky Stars* (43), *Up in Arms* (44), *Belle of the Yukon* (45), *Till the Clouds Roll By* (46), *Aaron Slick from Punkin Crick* (52), etc. Recently much on TV.

SHOSTAKOVITCH, DMITRI (1906–   ). Russian composer whose film music has included *The New Babylon* (28), *The Youth of Maxim* (35), *The Fall of Berlin* (47), *Hamlet* (64), *War and Peace* (64).

SHOTTER, WINIFRED (1904–   ). British leading lady of the 30s, chiefly remembered in the Aldwych farces beginning with *Rookery Nook* (30).

SHOWALTER, MAX (1917–   ) (formerly known as Casey Adams). American supporting actor often seen as reporter, newscaster or good guy friend. *Always Leave Them Laughing* (50), *With a Song in My Heart* (52), *Bus Stop* (56), *The Naked and the Dead* (58), *Elmer Gantry* (60), *Bon Voyage* (62), *Fate Is the Hunter* (64), etc.

SHOWBOAT. Jerome Kern and Oscar Hammerstein II's operetta from Edna Ferber's novel was filmed by Harry Pollard in 1929 with Laura la Plante and Joseph Schildkraut; by James Whale in 1936

with Irene Dunne, Allan Jones and Paul Robeson; and by George
Sidney in 1951 with Kathryn Grayson, Howard Keel and William
Warfield.

SHUMLIN, HERMAN (1898–   ). American stage producer who directed two films in the 40s: *Watch on the Rhine* (43), *Confidential Agent*
(45).

SHUTE, NEVIL (1899–1960). Australian best-selling novelist. Works
filmed include *The Pied Piper, Landfall, A Town Like Alice, On the
Beach.*

SIDNEY, GEORGE (1878–1945) (Sammy Greenfield). American
comedian, once popular in vaudeville. *Potash and Perlmutter* (23),
Millionaires (26), *Clancy's Kosher Wedding* (27), *The Cohens and Kellys
in Paris* (28), *Manhattan Melodrama* (34), *Good Old Soak* (37), others.

SIDNEY, GEORGE (1911–   ). American director, former musician
and MGM shorts director. *Free and Easy* (41), *Thousands Cheer* (43),
Bathing Beauty (44), *Anchors Aweigh* (45), *The Harvey Girls* (46),
Cass Timberlane (47), *The Three Musketeers* (48), *The Red Danube*
(49), *Annie Get Your Gun* (50), *Showboat* (51), *Scaramouche* (52),
Young Bess (53), *Kiss Me Kate* (53), *Jupiter's Darling* (54), *The Eddy
Duchin Story* (56), *Jeanne Eagels* (57), *Pal Joey* (57), *Who Was That
Lady?* (59), *Pepe* (60), *Bye Bye Birdie* (62), *Viva Las Vegas* (63), *The
Swinger* (66), *Half a Sixpence* (67), etc.

SIDNEY, SYLVIA (1910–   ). American leading lady of the 30s, on
stage from 15 years old. *Thru Different Eyes* (film debut) (29), *City
Streets* (31), *An American Tragedy* (31), *Street Scene* (32), *Merrily We
Go to Hell* (32), *Madame Butterfly* (33), *Thirty-Day Princess* (34),
Mary Burns, Fugitive (35), *The Trail of the Lonesome Pine* (36), *Fury*
(36), *Sabotage* (GB) (37), *Dead End* (37), *You Only Live Once* (37),
You and Me (38), *The Wagons Roll at Night* (41), *Blood on the Sun* (45),
Mr Ace (45), *The Searching Wind* (46), *A Stranger Walked In* (*Love
from a Stranger*) (47), *Les Misérables* (52), *Violent Saturday* (54),
Behind the High Wall (56), others. Recently on TV. Real name:
Sophia Kosow.

†SIEGEL, DON (1912–   ). American director, former editor; an
expert at crime thrillers, he has recently been attracting the atten-
tion of highbrow critics. *Hitler Lives* (short) (AA) (45), *Star in the
Night* (short) (AA) (45), *The Verdict* (46), *Night Unto Night* (48),
The Big Steal (49), *Duel at Silver Creek* (52), *No Time for Flowers* (52),
Count the Hours (54), *China Venture* (54), *Riot in Cell Block Eleven* (54),
Private Hell 36 (55), *An Annapolis Story* (55), *Invasion of the Body
Snatchers* (56), *Crime in the Streets* (57), *Spanish Affair* (57), *Baby Face
Nelson* (57), *The Line Up* (58), *The Gun Runners* (58), *The Hound Dog
Man* (59), *Edge of Eternity* (59), *Flaming Star* (60), *Hell Is for Heroes*

Siegel, Sol C.

(62), *The Killers* (64), *The Hanged Man* (64), *Madigan* (67), *Coogan's Bluff* (68), *Two Mules for Sister Sara* (69).

SIEGEL, SOL C. (1903–). American producer, in films from 1929. *Kiss and Tell* (44), *Blue Skies* (46), *House of Strangers* (49), *Fourteen Hours* (51), *Call Me Madam* (53), *High Society* (56), *Les Girls* (57), *Home from the Hill* (59), many others, mostly as staff producer of Paramount and MGM. Recently independent: *Walk Don't Run* (66), *Alvarez Kelly* (66), *No Way to Treat a Lady* (68).

SIEGFRIED (Germany 1924). This, with its sequel *Kriemhilde's Revenge*, is Fritz Lang's version of the Niebelungen saga, full of dragons and national heroes. Heavy-going Teutonic spectacle, but in its day a triumph of filmcraft.

SIGNORET, SIMONE (1921–) (Simone Kaminker). Distinguished French leading actress, married to Yves Montand. *Bolero* (42), *Les Démons à l'Aube* (45), *Macadam* (46), *Dédée d'Anvers* (47), *Manèges* (49), *Four Days' Leave* (49), *La Ronde* (50), *Casque d'Or* (BFA) (51), *Thérèse Raquin* (53), *Les Diaboliques* (54), *The Witches of Salem* (BFA) (56), *Room at the Top* (AA, BFA) (59), *Term of Trial* (62), *Ship of Fools* (65), *The Sleeping-Car Murder* (66), *Is Paris Burning?* (66), *The Deadly Affair* (66), *The Seagull* (68), *Le Rose et le Noir* (70), etc.

silent films began to grow unfashionable during 1927, though for eighteen months or so producers continued to put out so called 'silent versions' of their talkies: these versions were unspeakably bad, as the new talkies used very little camera movement and a great deal of dialogue which had to be given in sub-titles. By 1930 silents had all but disappeared, with exceptions such as Flaherty's *Tabu* (32), Chaplin's *City Lights* (31) and *Modern Times* (36), and an unsuccessful 1952 experiment called *The Thief*, which eschewed dialogue though it did have a music and effects track.

SILLIPHANT, STERLING (1918–). American writer-producer with much TV experience (*Naked City*, *Route 66*, etc.). Former advertising executive. *The Joe Louis Story* (w) (53), *Five Against the House* (w, co-p) (55), *Nightfall* (w) (56), *Damn Citizen* (w) (57), *The Slender Thread* (p) (66), *In the Heat of the Night* (w) (AA) (67), *Charly* (68), *A Walk in the Spring Rain* (69), etc.

SILLS, MILTON (1882–1930). Stalwart American leading man of the silent screen. *The Rack* (15), *The Claw* (17), *Eyes of Youth* (19), *The Weekend* (20), *Burning Sands* (22), *Adam's Rib* (23), *Madonna of the Streets* (24), *The Sea Hawk* (24), *Paradise* (26), *Valley of the Giants* (27), *His Captive Woman* (29), *The Sea Wolf* (30), many others.

SILVA, HENRY (1928–). Pale-eyed Puerto Rican actor, often seen as sadistic villain or assorted Latin types. *Viva Zapata* (52), *Crowded*

Paradise (56), *A Hatful of Rain* (57), *The Bravados* (58), *Green Mansions* (59), *Cinderfella* (60), *The Manchurian Candidate* (62), *Johnny Cool* (leading role) (63), *The Reward* (65), *The Plainsman* (66), *The Hills Ran Red* (It.) (66), *Never a Dull Moment* (68), etc.

SILVERA, FRANK (1914–   ). American general purpose actor with stage experience. *Viva Zapata* (52), *Killer's Kiss* (55), *Crowded Paradise* (56), *The Mountain Road* (60), *Mutiny on the Bounty* (62), *The Appaloosa* (66), *Che!* (69), etc.

SILVERHEELS, JAY (1920–   ). Red Indian actor, mainly in Western films. *The Prairie* (47), *Fury at Furnace Creek* (48), *Broken Arrow* (50), *War Arrow* (53), *The Lone Ranger* (55), others; then into TV's *Lone Ranger* series. 1965: *Indian Paint.*

SILVERS, PHIL (1912–   ). American vaudeville star comedian in occasional films from 1941. *Tom, Dick and Harry* (debut) (41), *You're in the Army Now* (42), *Roxie Hart* (42), *My Gal Sal* (42), *Coney Island* (43), *Cover Girl* (44), *A Thousand and One Nights* (45), *Where Do We Go from Here* (45), *Summer Stock* (*If You Feel Like Singing*) (50), *Lucky Me* (54), *Forty Pounds of Trouble* (63), *It's a Mad Mad Mad Mad World* (63), *A Funny Thing Happened on the Way to the Forum* (66), *Follow That Camel* (GB) (67), *Buona Sera, Mrs Campbell* (68), etc. Famous on TV as Sergeant Bilko.

SILVERSTEIN, ELIOT (c. 1925–   ). American director, from TV. *Belle Sommers* (62), *Cat Ballou* (65), *The Happening* (67), *A Man Called Horse* (69).

SIM, ALASTAIR (1900–   ). Scottish stage and screen character actor and comedian, formerly professor of elocution. *The Riverside Murder* (debut) (34), *The Private Secretary* (35), *Keep Your Seats Please* (36), *The Squeaker* (37), *Alf's Button Afloat* (38), *This Man Is News* (39), *Inspector Hornleigh* (39), *This Man in Paris* (40), *Cottage to Let* (41), *Let the People Sing* (42), *Waterloo Road* (44), *Green for Danger* (46), *Hue and Cry* (46), *Captain Boycott* (47), *London Belongs to Me* (48), *The Happiest Days of Your Life* (49), *Stage Fright* (50), *Laughter in Paradise* (51), *Scrooge* (51), *Folly To Be Wise* (52), *Innocents in Paris* (52), *An Inspector Calls* (54), *The Belles of St Trinians* (54), *Escapade* (55), *The Green Man* (57), *The Doctor's Dilemma* (58), *Left, Right and Centre* (59), *School for Scoundrels* (60), *The Millionairess* (61), etc.

SIM, SHEILA (1922–   ). British leading lady, married to Richard Attenborough. Stage experience before film debut in *A Canterbury Tale* (44). Later: *Great Day* (45), *Dancing with Crime* (47), *The Guinea Pig* (48), *Dear Mr Prohack* (49), *The Magic Box* (51), *The Night My Number Came Up* (55), etc. Retired.

SIMENON, GEORGES (1903–   ). French crime novelist, creator of Inspector Maigret. Works filmed include *Les Inconnus dans la Maison*

(43), *Panique* (46), *Temptation Harbour* (GB) (46), *La Marie du Port* (50), *The Man on the Eiffel Tower* (US) (50), *Le Fruit Defendu* (52), *The Brothers Rico* (US) (57), *Maigret Sets a Trap* (58) etc. BBC TV made a very successful *Maigret* series, also another series from his books called *Thirteen Against Fate.*

SIMMONS, ANTHONY (c. 1924–   ). British writer-director, known for short films: *Sunday by the Sea* (53), *Bow Bells* (54), *The Gentle Corsican* (56), etc. Features: *Your Money or Your Wife* (59), *Four in the Morning* (65).

SIMMONS, JEAN (1929–   ). British leading lady, married (1) Stewart Granger, (2) Richard Brooks. Started in films as teenage actress without even a test. *Give Us the Moon* (debut) (43), *The Way to the Stars* (45), *Great Expectations* (46), *Black Narcissus* (47), *Uncle Silas* (47), *Hamlet* (48), *The Blue Lagoon* (48), *Adam and Evelyn* (49), *Trio* (50), *So Long at the Fair* (50), *The Clouded Yellow* (51), to US: *Androcles and the Lion* (53), *Young Bess* (53), *The Actress* (53), *The Robe* (53), *The Egyptian* (54), *Désirée* (54), *Guys and Dolls* (56), *Hilda Crane* (56), *This Could Be the Night* (57), *The Big Country* (57), *Home Before Dark* (59), *Spartacus* (60), *The Grass Is Greener* (61), *All the Way Home* (63), *Life at the Top* (65), *Mister Buddwing* (66), *Divorce American Style* (67), *Rough Night in Jericho* (67), *The Happy Ending* (69), etc.

SIMMS, LARRY (1934–   ). American boy actor, notably in the *Blondie* series from 1938–48. (He was Baby Dumpling). Also: *The Last Gangster* (37), *Mr Smith Goes to Washington* (39), *Madame Bovary* (49), etc.

SIMON, MICHEL (1895–   ) (François Simon). Heavyweight French character actor, in films from the 20s after music hall experience. *Feu Mathias Pascal* (25), *The Passion of Joan of Arc* (28), *La Chienne* (31), *Boudu Sauve les Eaux* (32), *Lac aux Dames* (34), *L'Atalante* (34), *Jeunes Filles de Paris* (36), *Drôle de Drame* (37), *Les Disparus de Saint-Agil* (38), *Quai des Brumes* (38), *Fric Frac* (39), *La Fin du Jour* (39), *Circonstances Attenuantes* (39), *Vautrin* (43), *Un Ami Viendra Ce Soir* (45), *Panique* (46), *Fabiola* (48), *La Beauté du Diable* (49), *The Strange Desire of Monsieur Bard* (53), *Saadia* (53), *La Joyeuse Prison* (56), *It Happened in Broad Daylight* (58), *The Head* (59), *Austerlitz* (59), *Candide* (60), *The Devil and Ten Commandments* (62), *The Train* (64), *Two Hours to Kill* (65), *The Two of Us* (67), many others.

SIMON, NEIL (1927–   ). American comedy playwright whose Broadway success has been remarkable. Works filmed include *Come Blow Your Horn* (63), *Barefoot in the Park* (67), *The Odd Couple* (68), *Sweet Charity* (68).

SIMON, SIMONE (1914–   ). Pert French leading lady with brief stage experience. *Le Chanteur Inconnu* (debut) (31), *Lac aux Dames* (34); to US: *Girls' Dormitory* (36), *Seventh Heaven* (37), *Josette* (38), *La Bête Humaine* (39), *All That Money Can Buy* (41), *Cat People* (42), *Tahiti Honey* (43), *Temptation Harbour* (GB) (47), *Donna Senza Nome* (Italian) (49), *La Ronde* (50), *Olivia* (50), *Le Plaisir* (51), *Double Destin* (54), *The Extra Day* (GB) (56), etc.

SIMON, S. SYLVAN (1910–1951). American director with radio experience. *A Girl with Ideas* (37), *Four Girls in White* (39), *Whistling in the Dark* (41), *Rio Rita* (42), *Song of the Open Road* (44), *Son of Lassie* (45), *Her Husband's Affairs* (47), *The Lust for Gold* (49), *Born Yesterday* (producer only) (50), etc.

SIMPSON, ALAN (1929–   ). British TV and film comedy writer, with RAY GALTON (qv).

SIMPSON, RUSSELL (1878–1959). American character actor, in Hollywood from silent days. *Billy the Kid* (31), *Way Down East* (36), *Ramona* (37), *Dodge City* (39), *The Grapes of Wrath* (40), *Outside the Law* (41), *They Were Expendable* (45), *My Darling Clementine* (46), *The Beautiful Blonde from Bashful Bend* (49), *Seven Brides for Seven Brothers* (54), *Friendly Persuasion* (56), *The Horse Soldiers* (59), many others.

SIMS, JOAN (1930–   ). British stage, TV and film comedienne, often in cameo roles. *Colonel March Investigates* (53), *Meet Mr Lucifer* (54), *The Belles of St Trinians* (54), *Dry Rot* (56), *The Naked Truth* (58), *Carry On Regardless* (60), *Twice Round the Daffodils* (62), *Strictly for the Birds* (64), many others.

†SINATRA, FRANK (1915–   ). American leading actor and vocalist, former band singer. A teenage rave in the 40s, he later became respected as an actor and a powerful producer. *Las Vegas Nights* (41), *Ship Ahoy* (42), *Reveille with Beverly* (43), *Higher and Higher* (acting debut) (43), *Step Lively* (44), *Anchors Aweigh* (45), *Till the Clouds Roll By* (46), *It Happened in Brooklyn* (46), *The Kissing Bandit* (47), *Words and Music* (47), *The Miracle of the Bells* (48), *Take Me Out to the Ball Game (Everybody's Cheering)* (48), *On the Town* (49), *Double Dynamite* (50), *Meet Danny Wilson* (51), *From Here to Eternity* (AA) (53), *Suddenly* (54), *Young at Heart* (54), *The Tender Trap* (55), *Not as a Stranger* (55), *The Man with the Golden Arm* (56), *Johnny Concho* (56), *The Pride and the Passion* (56), *Guys and Dolls* (56), *High Society* (56), *Pal Joey* (57), *Some Came Running* (58), *A Hole in the Head* (59), *Can Can* (59), *Ocean's Eleven* (60), *The Devil at Four o'Clock* (61), *Sergeants Three* (62), *The Manchurian Candidate* (62), *Come Blow Your Horn* (63), *Robin and the Seven Hoods* (64), *None But the Brave* (also directed) (65), *Von Ryan's Express* (65), *Marriage on the Rocks* (65),

Cast a Giant Shadow (66), *Assault on a Queen* (66), *The Naked Runner* (GB) (67), *Tony Rome* (67), *The Detective* (68), *Lady in Cement* (68).

SINATRA, NANCY (1940–   ). American leading lady, daughter of Frank Sinatra. *For Those Who Think Young* (64), *The Last of the Secret Agents* (66), *Speedway* (68), etc.

SINCLAIR, HUGH (1903–62). British stage leading man, in occasional films. *A Girl Must Live* (39), *Alibi* (42), *They Were Sisters* (45), *Corridor of Mirrors* (48), *The Rocking Horse Winner* (50), *The Second Mrs Tanqueray* (52), etc.

SINDEN, DONALD (1923–   ). British leading man, on stage from mid-30s. *The Cruel Sea* (film debut) (53), *Doctor in the House* (54), *Simba* (55), *Eyewitness* (57), *Doctor at Large* (58), *Operation Bullshine* (59), *Twice Round the Daffodils* (62), *Decline and Fall* (68), etc. TV series: *Our Man at St Mark's*.

SINGER, ALEXANDER (1932–   ). American director. *A Cold Wind in August* (62), *Psyche 59* (64), *Love Has Many Faces* (65).

SINGER, CAMPBELL (1909–   ). British character actor, often seen as heavy father, commissionaire, sergeant-major or policeman. *Première* (37), *Take My Life* (47), *The Ringer* (52), *Simba* (55), *The Square Peg* (58), *The Pot Carriers* (62), many others. Also writes plays.

SING AS WE GO (GB 1934). You can almost smell the tripe and onions in this cheerful Gracie Fields vehicle scripted by J. B. Priestley. As things have happened, it also preserves the most authentic flavour on film of Britain's industrial north in the 30s.

THE SINGING FOOL (US 1928). Remembered because Al Jolson sang 'Sonny Boy' in it, this early talkie is otherwise a dismal tearjerker about a brash entertainer who comes to his senses when his little boy dies. Directed by Lloyd Bacon from a play by Leslie S. Barrows.

SINGIN' IN THE RAIN (US 1952). One of the most exhilarating and fast-moving comedy-musicals ever to come out of Hollywood, this enjoyably professional piece is also a gentle satire on the movie modes and manners of the 20s. Adolph Green and Betty Comden wrote the script, Arthur Freed and Nacio Herb Brown the words and music, Harold Rosson was cinematographer, and Gene Kelly and Stanley Donen directed. Kelly also starred, along with Donald O'Connor, Debbie Reynolds, Millard Mitchell and Jean Hagen.

SINGLETON, PENNY (1912–   ) (Dorothy McNulty). American leading lady, formerly in vaudeville, who from 1938 played the comic strip heroine 'Blondie' in two films a year for ten years. First film *After the Thin Man* (36); others negligible. Retired.

SIODMAK, CURT (1902–   ). German writer-director, in films from 1929, Hollywood from 1937. *People on Sunday* (co-w) (29), *The Tunnel* (co-w) (34), *Her Jungle Love* (co-w) (38), *Frankenstein Meets the Wolf Man* (w) (42), *Son of Dracula* (w) (43), *The Beast with Five Fingers* (w) (47), *Bride of the Gorilla* (w, d) (51), *The Magnetic Monster* (d) (51), *Love Slaves of the Amazon* (w, d) (57), *Ski Fever* (w, d) (66), etc.

SIODMAK, ROBERT (1900–   ). American director with early experience in Germany and France. *People on Sunday* (29), *The Weaker Sex* (32), *La Vie Parisienne* (35), *Pièges* (39), *West Point Widow* (41), *Son of Dracula* (43), *Phantom Lady* (44), *The Suspect* (44), *Christmas Holiday* (44), *The Spiral Staircase* (45), *The Strange Affair of Uncle Harry* (45), *The Killers* (46), *The Dark Mirror* (46), *Cry of the City* (48), *Criss Cross* (48), *The File on Thelma Jordon* (49), *The Great Sinner* (49), *Deported* (50), *The Whistle at Eaton Falls* (51), *The Crimson Pirate* (52), *Le Grand Jeu* (53), *Mein Vatel der Schauspieler* (56), *Katja* (59), *The Rough and the Smooth* (59), *Tunnel 28 (Escape from East Berlin)* (62), *Custer of the West* (67), others.

SIR ARNE'S TREASURE (Sweden 1919). A famous silent film directed by Mauritz Stiller from the novel by Selma Lagerlöf. It tells a 16th-century tale of three Scottish mercenaries in the Swedish army who rob a priest but are prevented from escaping by an icy winter which freezes up their ship; also of the girl Estelle who falls in love with one of them but is killed. The story was remade by Gustav Molander in 1954.

SIRK, DOUGLAS (1900–   ) (Detlef Sierck). Danish director, with stage experience; in America from early 40s. *Der Letzte Akkord* (36), *La Habanera* (37), *Summer Storm* (44), *Hitler's Madman* (44), *A Scandal in Paris* (46), *Personal Column (Lured)* (47), *Sleep My Love* (48), *The First Legion* (also produced) (51), *No Room for the Groom* (52), *Magnificent Obsession* (54), *All That Heaven Allows* (55), *Written on the Wind* (56), *Battle Hymn* (56), *The Tarnished Angels (Pylon)* (57), *A Time to Love and a Time to Die* (58), *Imitation of Life* (59), others.

SITTING BULL (c. 1834–1890). Sioux Indian chief, almost always on the warpath. The villain of countless westerns; J. Carrol Naish played him in a 1954 biopic.

SITTING PRETTY. This title was used for a 1933 comedy directed by Harry Joe Brown, with Jack Oakie and Jack Haley as two song-writers hitch-hiking their way to Hollywood. It is however chiefly associated with the 1947 comedy starring Clifton Webb as Lynn Belvedere, baby-sitter extraordinary. Webb appeared in two sequels, *Mr Belvedere Goes to College* (49) and *Mr Belvedere Rings the Bell* (51).

SJOBERG, ALF (1903–   ). Swedish director, former stage actor and director. *The Road to Heaven* (42), *Frenzy* (44), *Miss Julie* (51), *Barabbas* (53), *Karin Mansdotter* (54), *The Judge* (60), others.

SJOSTROM, VICTOR; see SEASTROM, VICTOR.

SJOMAN, VILGOT (1924–   ). Swedish director, chiefly famous (and notorious) for '*491*' (66), *I Am Curious: Blue* (67), and *I Am Curious: Yellow* (67).

SKELTON, RED (1910–   ) (Richard Skelton). American comedian of radio and TV; made numerous films in 40s, very few since. *Having Wonderful Time* (debut) (38), *Lady Be Good* (40), *Whistling in the Dark* (41), *Ship Ahoy* (42), *Whistling in Dixie* (42), *Du Barry Was a Lady* (43), *Whistling in Brooklyn* (43), *Bathing Beauty* (44), *The Show-off* (46), *Merton of the Movies* (47), *Three Little Words* (50), *The Clown* (53), *The Great Diamond Robbery* (54), *Public Pigeon Number One* (57), *Those Magnificent Men in Their Flying Machines* (65), etc.

SKINNER, CORNELIA OTIS (1901–   ). American stage actress, daughter of Otis Skinner the tragedian. Toyed with Hollywood in 1944, when she appeared in *The Uninvited* and *Kismet*, and her autobiographical book *Our Hearts Were Young and Gay* (co-written with Emily Kimbrough) was filmed with Gail Russell. 1967: *The Swimmer*.

SKINNER, OTIS (1858–1942). American stage actor who appeared in one film, *Kismet* (20). Charles Ruggles played him in *Our Hearts Were Young and Gay* (44).

SKIPWORTH, ALISON (1875–1952). Ample American character comedienne with stage experience. *Raffles* (30), *Night after Night* (32), *If I Had a Million* (33), *Alice in Wonderland* (33), *Becky Sharp* (35), *The Princess Comes Across* (36), *Wide Open Faces* (38), *Ladies in Distress* (39), etc.

SKIRBALL, JACK H. (1896–   ). American independent producer, former salesman. *Miracle on Main Street* (38), *Lady from Cheyenne* (41), *Saboteur* (42), *Shadow of a Doubt* (43), *It's in the Bag* (*The Fifth Chair*) (45), *Guest Wife* (46), *Payment on Demand* (51), etc.

SKOURAS, SPYROS (1893–   ). Greek-American executive, former hotelier. President of Twentieth-Century Fox 1943–62; instigator of CinemaScope.

slapstick. One of the earliest (1895) Lumière shorts, *L'Arroseur Arrosé*, was a knockabout farce, and in 1966 *A Funny Thing Happened on the Way to the Forum* was keeping the tradition going. Out of simple slapstick developed the great silent clowns, each with his own brand of pathos: Harold Lloyd, Charlie Chaplin, Buster Keaton, Fatty Arbuckle, Harry Langdon, Mabel Normand, Larry Semon, Laurel and Hardy. Pure destructive slapstick without humanity was superbly dispensed by Mack Sennett, especially in his Keystone Kops shorts. France had produced Max Linder; Britain lagged behind, but in the 20s Betty Balfour, Monty Banks and Lupino Lane kept the flag flying. Many of these names survived in some degree when sound came, but cross-talk was an added factor in the success of Wheeler and Wolsey, Charlie Chase, Edgar Kennedy, Leon Errol, Hugh Herbert, Joe E. Brown, W. C. Fields, Eddie Cantor, Abbott and Costello and above all the Marx Brothers. Similarly in Britain there was an influx of stage comics with firm music-hall traditions: George Formby, Will Hay, Max Miller, Gracie Fields, Leslie Fuller, the Crazy Gang, Arthur Askey, Gordon Harker, Sandy Powell, Frank Randle and Old Mother Riley. The 40s in Hollywood brought the more sophisticated slapstick of Danny Kaye, writer-director Preston Sturges, and the Bob Hope gag factory, with extreme simplicity keeping its end up via Olsen and Johnson and Jerry Lewis. In the 50s, TV finally brought a female clown, Lucille Ball, to the top; though competition was thin. France since the war has had Fernandel, Louis de Funes, Jacques Tati and Pierre Etaix; Britain Norman Wisdom and Morecambe and Wise; Italy Toto and Walter Chiari. In Hollywood romantic stars now take turns at donning the clown's hat, without making a career of it; and the fashion has recently been for epic comedies of violence and destruction, such as *It's a Mad Mad Mad Mad World*, *The Great Race*, and *Those Magnificent Men in Their Flying Machines*.

SLATE, JEREMY (1925–). American general purpose actor. *Wives and Lovers* (63), *I'll Take Sweden* (65), *The Sons of Katie Elder* (66), *The Devil's Brigade* (68), etc.

SLATER, JOHN (1916–). British cockney character actor and comedian of stage and TV, occasionally in films. *Love on the Dole* (debut) (40), *Went the Day Well* (42), *A Canterbury Tale* (44), *Passport to Pimlico* (48), *Johnny You're Wanted* (54), *Violent Playground* (58), *Three on a Spree* (61), *A Place to Go* (63), many others.

SLAUGHTER, TOD (1885–1956) (N. Carter Slaughter). Barnstorming British actor who toured the provinces with chop-licking revivals of outrageous old melodramas, all of which he filmed after a fashion: *Maria Marten* (35), *Sweeney Todd* (36), *The Face at the Window* (39), *The Curse of the Wraydons* (43), *The Greed of William Hart* (48), etc.

SLEZAK, WALTER (1902–   ). Austrian character actor, of theatrical family; in America since 1930. *Once Upon a Honeymoon* (English-speaking debut) (42), *Lifeboat* (44), *Step Lively* (44), *The Spanish Main* (45), *Cornered* (45), *Sinbad the Sailor* (47), *The Pirate* (48), *The Inspector General* (49), *Call Me Madam* (53), *White Witch Doctor* (54), *The Steel Cage* (54), *Come September* (61), *Emil and the Detectives* (64), *Wonderful Life* (GB) (64), *Twenty-four Hours to Kill* (65), *A Very Special Favour* (65), *Caper of the Golden Bulls* (67), *Dr Coppelius* (68), others. Published autobiography 1962: *What Time's the Next Swan?*

SLOANE, EVERETT (1909–1965). American character actor, on stage before joining Orson Welles for *Citizen Kane* (41). Later: *Journey into Fear* (42), *The Lady from Shanghai* (47), *The Men* (50), *Murder Inc.* (51), *The Big Knife* (55), *Lust for Life* (56), *Patterns of Power* (57), *Home from the Hill* (59), *The Patsy* (64), *The Disorderly Orderly* (65), many others, also TV appearances.

SLOANE, OLIVE (1896–1963). British character actress of stage and screen whose best role was in *Seven Days to Noon* (50). Countless other small roles since film debut in *Soldiers of the King* (33).

SLOCOMBE, DOUGLAS (1913–   ). British cinematographer, former journalist. *Dead of Night* (45), *The Captive Heart* (46), *Hue and Cry* (46), *The Loves of Joanna Godden* (47), *It Always Rains on Sunday* (47), *Saraband for Dead Lovers* (48), *Kind Hearts and Coronets* (49), *Cage of Gold* (50), *The Lavender Hill Mob* (51), *The Man in the White Suit* (52), *The Titfield Thunderbolt* (53), *Man in the Sky* (56), *The Smallest Show on Earth* (57), *Tread Softly Stranger* (58), *Circus of Horrors* (59), *The Young Ones* (61), *The L-shaped Room* (62), *Freud* (63), *The Servant* (63), *Guns at Batasi* (64), *A High Wind in Jamaica* (65), *The Blue Max* (66), *Promise Her Anything* (66), *The Vampire Killers* (67), *Fathom* (67), *Robbery* (67), *Boom* (68), *The Lion in Winter* (68), *The Italian Job* (69), *The Lonely Heart* (70), etc.

slow motion. An effect obtained by running the camera faster than usual. When the film passes through the projector at normal speed, each movement appears slower, as it occupies more frames of film. For scientific purposes (e.g. recording the growth of plants) cameras are so arranged that a single frame of film is exposed at regular intervals, thus giving an impression of accelerated growth.

SMALL, EDWARD (1891–   ). Veteran American independent producer, former actor and agent, in Hollywood from 1924. Films include *I Cover the Waterfront* (35), *The Man in the Iron Mask* (39), *The Corsican Brothers* (41), *Brewster's Millions* (45), *Down Three Dark Streets* (55), *Witness for the Prosecution* (57), *I'll Take Sweden* (65). *Forty Guns to Apache Pass* (66), many others; also TV series.

SMART, RALPH (1908–   ). British producer-director, latterly of TV series *The Invisible Man, Danger Man,* etc. Former editor and writer. Directed *Bush Christmas* (46), *A Boy, a Girl and a Bike* (48), *Bitter Springs* (50), *Never Take No for an Answer* (co-d) (51), *Curtain Up* (52), *Always a Bride* (54), etc.

SMEDLEY-ASTON, E. M. (1912–   ). British producer: *The Extra Day* (56), *Two-Way Stretch* (60), *Offbeat* (61), *The Wrong Arm of the Law* (63), etc.

†SMIGHT, JACK (1926–   ). American director, from TV. *I'd Rather Be Rich* (64), *The Third Day* (65), *Harper* (*The Moving Target*) (66), *Kaleidoscope* (66), *The Secret War of Harry Frigg* (67), *No Way to Treat a Lady* (68), *The Illustrated Man* (69).

SMILIN' THROUGH. The popular sentimental stage play by Jane Cowl and Jane Murfin, about a tragedy affecting the romances of two generations, was filmed in 1932 by Sidney Franklin, with Norma Shearer, Leslie Howard and Fredric March. In 1941 Frank Borzage remade it with Jeanette Macdonald, Brian Aherne and Gene Raymond.

SMITH, ALEXIS (1921–   ). American leading lady of the 40s who won an acting contest from Hollywood high school. *Dive Bomber* (debut) (41), *The Smiling Ghost* (41), *Gentleman Jim* (42), *The Constant Nymph* (42), *The Doughgirls* (44), *Conflict* (45), *Rhapsody in Blue* (45), *San Antonio* (45), *Night and Day* (46), *Of Human Bondage* (46), *Stallion Road* (47), *The Woman in White* (47), *The Decision of Christopher Blake* (48), *Any Number Can Play* (50), *Undercover Girl* (52), *Split Second* (53), *The Sleeping Tiger* (GB) (55), *The Eternal Sea* (56), *The Young Philadelphians* (*The City Jungle*) (59), etc. Married to Craig Stevens.

SMITH, BERNARD (c. 1905–   ). American producer, former publisher and story editor. *Elmer Gantry* (AA) (60), *How the West was Won* (62), *Seven Women* (65), *Alfred the Great* (69).

SMITH, SIR C. AUBREY (1863–1948). Distinguished British character actor, on stage from 1892, films from 1915. A splendidly authoritative figure in many Hollywood films of the 30s and 40s. *Builder of Bridges* (US) (15), *The Witching Hour* (16), *The Bachelor Father* (31), *Morning Glory* (32), *Queen Christina* (33), *House of Rothschild* (34), *The Tunnel* (GB) (35), *Clive of India* (35), *Lives of a Bengal Lancer* (35), *Romeo and Juliet* (36), *The Prisoner of Zenda* (37), *Sixty Glorious Years* (GB) (38), *The Four Feathers* (GB) (39), *Rebecca* (40), *Dr Jekyll and Mr Hyde* (41), *Madame Curie* (43), *The White Cliffs of Dover* (44), *Ten Little Niggers* (45), *An Ideal Husband* (GB) (47), many others.

SMITH, CHARLES (c. 1920–   ). American character actor who in the 40s played Dizzy in the *Henry Aldrich* series and other amiably doltish roles. *The Shop Around the Corner* (40), *Tom Brown's Schooldays* (40), *Three Little Girls in Blue* (45), *Two Weeks With Love* (50), *City of Bad Men* (53), many others.

SMITH, CONSTANCE (1929–   ). British leading lady. *Brighton Rock* (47), *Don't Say Die* (50), *The Thirteenth Letter* (US) (51), *Red Skies of Montana* (US) (52), *Treasure of the Golden Condor* (US) (53), *Tiger by the Tail* (55), etc.

SMITH, CYRIL (1892–1963). British character actor of stage and screen, often a henpecked husband but equally likely to be a grocer, dustman or policeman. On stage from 1900, films from 1908, and was in over 500 of the latter, including *School for Secrets* (46), *It's Hard To Be Good* (48), *Mother Riley Meets the Vampire* (52), *John and Julie* (54), *Sailor Beware* (his stage role) (56), etc.

SMITH, JOHN (1931–   ) (Robert Van Orden). Boyish American leading man with varied experience before film debut in *The High and the Mighty* (54). Later: *Ghost Town* (56), *The Bold and the Brave* (57), *The Magnificent Showman* (*Circus World*) (64), *Waco* (66), etc. TV series: *Cimarron City* (58), *Laramie* (59–62).

SMITH, KENT (1907–   ). American stage actor (from 1932) whose film debut was in *Cat People* (42). Later: *Hitler's Children* (42), *This Land Is Mine* (43), *The Spiral Staircase* (45), *Nora Prentiss* (47), *Magic Town* (47), *The Voice of the Turtle* (48), *The Damned Don't Cry* (50), *Paula* (52), *Comanche* (56), *Moon Pilot* (61), *Youngblood Hawke* (64), *The Trouble with Angels* (66), *Games* (67), *Death of a Gunfighter* (69), etc. TV series: *Peyton Place*; also frequent TV guest star.

†SMITH, MAGGIE (1934–   ). British leading actress with stage experience. *Nowhere To Go* (58), *The VIPs* (63), *Young Cassidy* (65), *Othello* (66), *The Honey Pot* (67), *Hot Millions* (68), *The Prime of Miss Jean Brodie* (69).

SMITH, PETE (1892–   ). American producer of punchy one-reel shorts on any and every subject from 1935 to the 50s, all narrated by 'a Smith named Pete'. Former publicist. Special Academy Award 1953 'for his witty and pungent observations on the American scene'.

SMITH, ROGER (1932–   ). American leading man. *The Young Rebels* (56), *Operation Mad Ball* (57), *Never Steal Anything Small* (59), *Auntie Mame* (59), *Rogues Gallery* (68), etc. TV series: 77 *Sunset Strip* (58–64), *Mr Roberts* (65).

SMITH, THORNE (1892–1934). American humorous novelist. Works filmed include *Topper*, *Turnabout*, *I Married a Witch*.

SMOKTUNOVSKY, INNOKENTI (1925–   ). Leading Russian stage actor, seen in a few films including *Nine Days of One Year* (60), *Hamlet* (64), *Tschaikovsky* (69).

THE SNAKE PIT (US 1948). Directed by Anatole Litvak from the novel by Mary Jane Ward, this deliberately unsensational study of mental illness did not entirely escape the problem of dramatizing a subject too serious for fiction. But Olivia de Havilland gave a fine performance and the film did much to assist Hollywood's new 'adult' post-war image. Photographed by Leo Tover, with music by Alfred Newman.

sneak preview. An unheralded tryout of a film at a public performance, usually in place of a second feature. Intended to gauge audience reaction, it is often followed by considerable re-editing before the official première.

snow, when needed for a movie scene, has been known to consist of a variety of ingredients including bleached cornflakes, soapflakes, chopped feathers, shredded asbestos, balsa chips, sawdust, and a wide range of plastic products.

SNOW WHITE AND THE SEVEN DWARFS (US 1937). The first full-length Disney cartoon has remained popular through the years, perhaps because it so admirably suits its creator's Grimm-like imagination. He has certainly never again presented so precisely differentiated a group of comedians as Bashful, Sleepy, Grumpy, Sneezy, Happy, Dopey and Doc.

soap opera, a term used disparagingly of TV domestic drama serials, originated because such offerings were invariably sponsored by the big soap companies who needed to attract the housewife.

social comedy. Silent romantic comedies were completely unrealistic, though they sometimes found it prudent to pretend satirical intent to cloak their lowbrow commercialism. Social comedy really came in as a substitute for sex comedy when the Hays office axe fell in 1934. Frank Capra took by far the best advantage of it, with his series of films showing an America filled to bursting point with good guys who only wanted a simple and comfortable home life in some small town where corruption never raised its ugly head. The best of these films were *Mr Deeds Goes to Town, You Can't Take It with You* and *Mr Smith Goes to Washington*; by the time *Meet John Doe* came along in 1941 war had soured the mood again. There was no British equivalent to Capra, unless one counts a few attempts by Priestley (*The Good Companions, Let the People Sing*) and such amusing depictions of the middle class as *Quiet Wedding* and *Dear Octopus*; but in the late 40s came the Ealing comedies, delightful and apparently realistic, but presenting a picture of England just as false as Capra's America. In both countries the 50s saw the development of an affluent society in which cynicism was fashionable and few reforms seemed worth urging except in bitterly serious fashion.

social conscience has long been a feature of Hollywood film production. Other countries have presented the odd feature pointing to flaws in their national make-up, but America has seemed particularly keen to wash its own dirty linen on screen, perhaps because this is rather easier than actually cleaning up the abuses.

The evolution of this attitude can be traced back as far as 1912 and Griffith's *The Musketeers of Pig Alley*, showing slum conditions; and, of course, Chaplin was a master at devising humour and pathos out of the unpleasant realities of poverty, a fact which endeared him to poor people all over the world. But it was not till the late 20s that the flood of socially conscious films began in earnest. Vidor's *The Crowd* investigated the drabness of everyday life for a city clerk. John Baxter's British *Dosshouse* was a lone entry on the lines of *The Lower Depths*. *City Streets* and *One-Third of a Nation* treated slum conditions; Vidor's *Our Daily Bread* concerned a young couple driven out of the city by poverty only to find farming just as precarious. *Little Caesar* and the gangster dramas which followed always assumed a crusading moral tone deploring the lives of vice and crime which they depicted; there was a somewhat more honest ring to *I Was a Fugitive from a Chain Gang*, which showed how circumstance can drive an honest man into anti-social behaviour. Capra sugared his pill with comedy: *American Madness* (the madness was money) and the popular comedies which followed all pitted common-man philosophy against urban sophistication and corruption.

In the mid-30s there were certainly many abuses worth fighting. *Black Legion* began Hollywood's campaign against the Ku Klux Klan, later followed up in *The Flaming Cross*, *Storm Warning* and *The Cardinal*. Lynch law, first tackled in *Fury*, was subsequently the subject of *They Won't Forget*, *The Ox Bow Incident* and *The Sound of Fury*. Juvenile delinquency was probed in *Dead End*, *Angels with Dirty Faces* and *They Made Me a Criminal*, but the 'Dead End Kids' were later played for comedy. Prison reform was advocated in *Each Dawn I Die*, *Castle on the Hudson*, and many other melodramas of questionable integrity. *The Good Earth* invited concern for the poor of other nations; *Mr Smith Goes to Washington* and *The Glass Key* were among many dramas showing that politicians are not incorruptible; *Love on the Dole* depicted the poverty of industrial Britain; *The Grapes of Wrath* and *Tobacco Road* pondered the plight of farming people deprived of a living by geographical chance and thoughtless government. In *Sullivan's Travels*, Preston Sturges came to the curious conclusion that the best thing you can do for the poor is make them laugh.

During World War II the nations were too busy removing the abuse of Nazidom to look inward, and indeed much poverty was alleviated by conscription and a fresh national awareness which, together with the increased need for industrial manpower, greatly improved the lot of the lower classes. But with victory came a whole crop of films, led by *The Best Years of Our Lives* and *Till the End of Time*, about the rehabilitation of war veterans. Concern about mental illness was shown in *The Snake Pit*, about paraplegia in *The Men*, and about labour relations in *The Whistle at Eaton Falls*. Alcoholism was treated in *The Lost Weekend* and *Smash-Up*, and the racial issues were thoroughly aired in *Lost Boundaries, Crossfire, Home of the Brave, No Way Out, Gentleman's Agreement* and *Pinky*. Pleas for nations to help and understand each other were made in such films as *The Well* and the French *Race for Life*.

With the development in the 50s of the affluent society, the number of reforms worth urging was drastically reduced. Teenage hoodlums figured largely in a score of films of which the best were *The Wild One* and *Rebel without a Cause*. Mentally handicapped children were sympathetically portrayed in *A Child Is Waiting*. In recent years, however, it is one world issue which has dominated the film-makers' social consciousness, that of the panic button; and this has manifested itself in films as diverse as *On the Beach, Dr Strangelove, Fail Safe* and *The Bedford Incident*.

SOFAER, ABRAHAM (1896–   ). Burmese actor, on British stage since 1921. Films include *Dreyfus* (debut) (31), *Rembrandt* (36), *A Matter of Life and Death* (46), *Judgment Deferred* (51), *Elephant Walk* (US) (54), *The Naked Jungle* (US) (54), *Bhowani Junction* (56), *King of Kings* (61), *Captain Sinbad* (US) (63), *Head* (68), *Che!* (69), etc.

soft focus. A diffused effect used in photographing ageing leading ladies who can't stand good definition; also frequently used for exotic shots in musical numbers, etc.

SOKOLOFF, VLADIMIR (1889–1962). Russian character actor, in Hollywood from 1936. *The Loves of Jeanne Ney* (27), *West Front 1918* (30), *L'Atalantide* (32), *Mayerling* (35), *The Life of Émile Zola* (37), *Spawn of the North* (38), *Juarez* (39), *Road to Morocco* (42), *For Whom the Bell Tolls* (43), *Cloak and Dagger* (46), *Back to Bataan* (46), *Istanbul* (56), *Confessions of a Counterspy* (60), many others.

SOLDATI, MARIO (1906–   ). Italian director, from 1939. *Scandal in the Roman Bath* (51), *The Wayward Wife* (53), *The Stranger's Hand* (54), *Woman of the River* (55), many others.

soldiers depicted at length in films include Alexander the Great (by Richard Burton), Hannibal (by Victor Mature), Ghenghis Khan (by Omar Sharif), Alexander Nevsky (by Cherkassov), Clive of India (by Ronald Colman), Napoleon (by Charles Boyer, Marlon Brando, Herbert Lom and others), Bonnie Prince Charlie (by David Niven), General Gordon (by Charlton Heston), Custer (by Errol Flynn and Robert Shaw), La Fayette (by Michel le Royer), Davy Crockett (by Fess Parker and others), Sergeant York (by Gary Cooper), Audie Murphy (by Audie Murphy), Rommel (by Erich von Stroheim and James Mason) and General Patton (by George C. Scott).

SOLON, EWEN (c. 1923–   ). New Zealand character actor in Britain, especially on TV in series *Maigret, The Revenue Men. The Sundowners* (59), *Jack the Ripper* (60), *The Hound of the Baskervilles* (60), *The Terror of the Tongs* (61), etc.

SOMLO, JOSEF (1885–   ). Hungarian producer with long experience at UFA; in Britain from 1933. *Dark Journey* (37), *The Mikado* (39), *Old Bill and Son* (40), *Uncle Silas* (47), *The Man Who Loved Redheads* (55), *Behind the Mask* (59), etc.

SOMMER, ELKE (1940–   ) (Elke Schletz). German leading lady, now in international films. *Don't Bother to Knock* (GB) (60), *The Victors* (GB) (63), *The Prize* (US) (63), *A Shot in the Dark* (US) (64), *The Art of Love* (US) (65), *Four Kinds of Love* (It.) (65), *The Money Trap* (US) (65), *The Oscar* (US) (66), *Boy, Did I Get a Wrong Number* (US) (66), *Deadlier than the Male* (GB) (66), *The Venetian Affair* (US) (66), *The Corrupt Ones* (*The Peking Medallion*) (US) (67), *The Wicked Dreams of Paula Schultz* (US) (68), etc.

SONDERGAARD, GALE (1899–   ). Tall, dark American actress, often in sinister roles. *Anthony Adverse* (AA) (36), *The Life of Émile Zola* (37), *The Cat and the Canary* (39), *The Bluebird* (40), *The Letter* (40), *The Mark of Zorro* (40), *The Strange Death of Adolf Hitler* (43), *Spider Woman* (43), *The Invisible Man's Revenge* (44), *Spider Woman Strikes Back* (46), *Anna and the King of Siam* (46), *Road to Rio* (47), *East Side West Side* (49), etc. Retired and did not film again till *Slaves* (69).

THE SONG OF BERNADETTE (US 1943). An enormous box-office success in the middle of World War II, this calculated piece of Hollywood religion turned Franz Werfel's book into sentimental hokum. The miracles of Lourdes have since been more movingly and convincingly treated; Henry King's direction was lethargic; and attempts at acting were smothered by syrupy music and phoney sets. Jennifer Jones' debut as Bernadette was highly successful, but Linda Darnell as the Virgin Mary took some swallowing. The film began a cycle of religious epics, including *Going My Way, The Bells of St Mary, The Miracle of the Bells*, etc. (See *religion*.)

SONG OF CEYLON (GB 1934). A documentary written, photographed and directed by Basil Wright for the Ceylon Tea Marketing Board, who must have been very surprised when they saw what they had got: a leisurely 40-minute poetic impression of the island without any direct propaganda. As an 'art house' picture it remains fascinating. Produced by John Grierson, with music by Walter Leigh.

SONS AND LOVERS (GB 1960). A decent and enjoyable film adaptation of D. H. Lawrence's autobiographical novel about growing up in the Nottinghamshire coalfields fifty years ago. Surprisingly produced by Jerry Wald, with Dean Stockwell making a reasonable attempt at the central part and more assured performances coming from Trevor Howard and Wendy Hiller, the film was perhaps most of all enjoyable for the background detail and for Freddie Francis' black-and-white photography. Jack Cardiff directed with care.

SONS OF THE LEGION (FRATERNALLY YOURS) (US 1933). The quintessential Laurel and Hardy comedy, in which the boys, henpecked as always, devise frantic schemes to get to a weekend convention—and then wish they hadn't. Sociologically, the movie pinpoints its period with total precision.

SORDI, ALBERTO (1919–). Italian leading man and comic actor, seen abroad in *I Vitelloni* (53), *The Sign of Venus* (55), *A Farewell to Arms* (67), *The Best of Enemies* (60), *Those Magnificent Men in Their Flying Machines* (65), *To Bed or Not To Bed* (65), etc.

SOREL, JEAN (1934–) (Jean de Rochbrune). French leading man. *The Four Days of Naples* (62), *A View from the Bridge* (62), *Vaghe Stella Dell'Orsa* (65), *Le Bambole* (66), *Belle de Jour* (67), etc.

SORRELL AND SON. H. B. Warner played Sorrell in both British versions of Warwick Deeping's family novel; in 1927 the son was Nils Asther and the director Herbert Brenon, while in 1933 Hugh Williams replaced Asther and Jack Raymond directed.

SOTHERN, ANN (1909–) (Harriette Lake). Pert American comedienne and leading lady with stage experience. *Let's Fall in Love* (debut) (34), *Kid Millions* (35), *Trade Winds* (38), *Hotel for Women* (39), *Maisie* (39), *Brother Orchid* (40), *Congo Maisie* (40), *Gold Rush Maisie* (41) (and seven others in this series before 1947), *Lady Be Good* (41), *Panama Hattie* (42), *Cry Havoc* (43), *Indian Summer* (47), *A Letter to Three Wives* (49), *Nancy Goes to Rio* (50), *Lady in a Cage* (63), *The Best Man* (64), *Sylvia* (65), *Chubasco* (67), etc. TV series: *Private Secretary* (52–54), *The Ann Sothern Show* (58–60).

The Sound of Music

THE SOUND OF MUSIC (AA) (US 1965). The huge commercial success of this sentimental Rodgers and Hammerstein musical with its simple story, happy ending and sumptuous Austrian locations seems to mark a genuine public desire for less sophisticated fare than the 60s have been giving; but producers are either unwilling or unable to satisfy it. It won Academy Awards for Robert Wise's direction, William Reynolds' editing, Jane Corcoran's sound recording, Irwin Kostal's scoring, and Ted McCord's photography.

SOUS LES TOITS DE PARIS (France 1930). This early sound film, a light romantic drama of the Paris garrets, has a well-remembered title and established the fame of writer-director René Clair, but it now seems rather heavier than his usual style, with his accustomed humour breaking through only occasionally. Albert Prejean and Pola Illery had the leading roles.

THE SOUTHERNER (US 1944). Jean Renoir's most successful American film, comparable to *The Grapes of Wrath* in its feeling for a poor Texas family scratching a living from cotton-growing. Zachary Scott and Betty Field are man and wife, with Beulah Bondi magnificent as the cantankerous granny and J. Carrol Naish as a suspicious neighbour. Photographed by Lucien Andriot, with music by Werner Janssen; from a novel, 'Hold Autumn in Your Hand', by George Sessions Perry.

SPAAK, CATHERINE (1945–). Belgian leading lady, daughter of Charles Spaak. *Le Trou* (60), *The Empty Canvas* (64), *Weekend at Dunkirk* (65), *Libertine* (68), etc.

SPAAK, CHARLES (1903–). Belgian screenwriter associated with many French films: *La Kermesse Heroïque* (35), *Les Bas-Fonds* (36), *La Grande Illusion* (37), *La Fin du Jour* (39), *Panique* (46), *Justice Est Faite* (co-w) (50), *Thérèse Raquin* (53), *Crime and Punishment* (56), *Charmants Garçons* (57), *The Vanishing Corporal* (61), *Cartouche* (62), etc.

space exploration on screen began in 1899 with Melies; in the 20s Fritz Lang made *The Woman in the Moon* and in the 30s there was *Buck Rogers in the Twenty-fifth Century*, but not until 1950 did the subject seem acceptable as anything but fantasy. In that year an adventure of the comic strip type, *Rocketship XM*, competed for box-office attention with George Pal's semi-documentary *Destination Moon*, and suddenly the floodgates were opened. During the next few years we were offered such titles as *Riders to the Stars*, *Fire Maidens from Outer Space*, *Satellite in the Sky*, *From the Earth to the Moon*, *Conquest of Space*, *Forbidden Planet*, *It! The Terror from Beyond Space*, *Robinson Crusoe on Mars*, *The First Men in the Moon* and *2001: A Space Odyssey*. Nor was the traffic all one way: Earth had many strange visitors from other planets, notably in

The Thing from Another World, The Day the Earth Stood Still, Devil Girl from Mars, Stranger from Venus, It Came from Outer Space, Invasion of the Body Snatchers (the best and subtlest of them all), *The War of the Worlds, The Quatermass Experiment, Quatermass II, Visit to a Small Planet* and *This Island Earth.*

SPARKS, NED (1883–1957). Hard-boiled, cigar-chewing Canadian comic actor often seen in Hollywood films of the 30s as grouchy reporter or agent. *The Big Noise* (27), *The Miracle Man* (30), *Forty-second Street* (33), *Two's Company* (GB) (37), *The Star Maker* (39), *For Beauty's Sake* (40), *Magic Town* (47), etc.

SPARKUHL, THEODORE (1894–). German photographer in Hollywood from the early 30s. *Carmen* (18), *Manon Lescaut* (26), *La Chienne* (31), *Too Much Harmony* (33), *Enter Madame* (35), *Beau Geste* (39), *The Glass Key* (42), *Star Spangled Rhythm* (43), *Blood on the Sun* (46), *Bachelor Girls* (47), many others. Retired.

SPARV, CAMILLA (1943–). Swedish-born leading lady in Hollywood films. *The Trouble with Angels* (66), *Murderers' Row* (66), *Dead Heat on a Merry-go-Round* (66), *Department K* (67), *Mackenna's Gold* (68), etc.

SPELLBOUND. There are two films of this title. In 1940 John Harlow made a low-budget British attempt to explore spiritualism, with Derek Farr as a distraught young man attempting to get in touch with his dead sweetheart. The years have been unkind to this naïve little movie, but it broke fresh ground at the time. In 1945 Alfred Hitchcock in Hollywood used the title for his glossy adaptation of Francis Beeding's *The House of Dr Edwardes*, with Ingrid Bergman and Gregory Peck, in loving close-up, discovering whether or not Peck, a psychiatrist, is in fact a murderous amnesiac. Full of tricks, but satisfying, the movie had a memorable dream sequence designed by Salvador Dali.

SPENSER, JEREMY (1937–). British leading man, former child actor, also on stage. *Portrait of Clare* (48), *Prelude to Fame* (50), *Appointment with Venus* (51), *Summer Madness* (55), *The Prince and the Showgirl* (57), *Wonderful Things* (58), *Ferry to Hong Kong* (58), *The Roman Spring of Mrs Stone* (61), *King and Country* (64), *He Who Rides a Tiger* (65), *Fahrenheit 451* (66), etc.

SPERLING, MILTON (1912–). American producer. *Cloak and Dagger* (46), *Three Secrets* (50), *Murder Inc.* (51), *Blowing Wild* (54), *The Court Martial of Billy Mitchell* (also co-wrote) (55), *The Bramble Bush* (also co-wrote) (59), *The Battle of the Bulge* (65), etc.

SPIEGEL, SAM (1901–). Polish-born producer, in Hollywood from 1941. *Tales of Manhattan* (42), *The Stranger* (45), *We Were Strangers* (48), *The African Queen* (51), *On the Waterfront* (54), *End as a Man*

(The Strange One) (57), *The Bridge on the River Kwai* (57), *Lawrence of Arabia* (62), *The Chase* (66), *The Night of the Generals* (66), *The Happening* (67), *The Swimmer* (68), etc. Was known for a time as S. P. EAGLE.

spies are currently enjoying enormous popularity as the heroes of over-sexed, gimmick-ridden melodramas. Real-life spies have been less frequently depicted, the world of James Bond being much livelier than those of Moyzich *(Five Fingers)*, Odette Churchill *(Odette V.C.)*, *Nurse Edith Cavell*, Violette Szabo *(Carve Her Name with Pride)*, *Mata Hari*, or the gangs in *The House on 92nd Street*, *13 Rue Madeleine*, and *Ring of Spies*.

Fictional spy films first became popular during and after World War I: they added a touch of glamour to an otherwise depressing subject, even though the hero often faced the firing squad in the last reel. Right up to 1939 romantic melodramas on this theme were being made: *I Was a Spy*, *The Man Who Knew Too Much*, *The Thirty-nine Steps*, *Lancer Spy*, *The Spy in Black*, *Dark Journey*, *British Agent*, *Secret Agent*, *The Lady Vanishes*, *Espionage Agent*, *Confessions of a Nazi Spy*. The last-named brought the subject roughly up to date, and with the renewed outbreak of hostilities new possibilities were hastily seized in *Foreign Correspondent*, *Night Train to Munich*, *Casablanca*, *The Conspirators*, *They Came to Blow Up America*, *Berlin Correspondent*, *Across the Pacific*, *Escape to Danger*, *Ministry of Fear*, *Confidential Agent*, *Sherlock Holmes and the Secret Weapon*, *Hotel Reserve*, and innumerable others. (It was fashionable during this period to reveal that the villains of comedy-thrillers and who-done-its were really enemy agents.) During the post-war years two fashions in film spying became evident: the downbeat melodrama showing spies as frightened men and women doing a dangerous job *(Notorious, Cloak and Dagger, Hotel Berlin, Orders To Kill)* and the 'now it can be told' semi-documentary revelation *(O.S.S., Diplomatic Courier, The Man Who Never Was, The Two-Headed Spy, The Counterfeit Traitor, Operation Crossbow)*. In the late 40s Nazis and Japs were replaced by reds, and we had a spate of melodramas under such titles as *I Married a Communist*, *I Was a Communist for the FBI*, *I Was an American Spy*, *Red Snow* and *The Red Danube*.

There had always been spy comedies. Every comedian made one or two: the Crazy Gang in *Gasbags*, Duggie Wakefield in *Spy for a Day*, Jack Benny in *To Be or Not To Be*, Bob Hope in *They Got Me Covered*, Radford and Wayne in *It's Not Cricket*, George Cole in *Top Secret*, right up to the 'Carry On' team in *Carry On Spying* and Morecambe and Wise in *The Intelligence Men*. There were also occasional burlesques like *All Through the Night* and sardonic comedies like *Our Man in Havana*. But it was not until the late 50s that the spy reasserted himself as a romantic image who could be taken lightly; and not until 1962 was the right box-office combination of sex and suspense found in *Dr No*. Since then we have been deluged with pale imitations of James Bond to such an extent that almost every leading man worth his salt has had a go. Cary Grant in *Charade*, David Niven in *Where the Spies Are*, Rod Taylor and Trevor Howard in *The Liquidator*, Dirk Bogarde in *Hot Enough for June*, Michael Caine in *The Ipcress File*, Paul Newman in *Torn Curtain*, James Coburn in *Our Man Flint*, Gregory Peck in *Arabesque*, Yul Brynner in *The Double Man*, Tom Adams in *Licensed To Kill*. There have also been elaborations such as the extreme sophistication of *The Manchurian Candidate*, the cold realism of *The Spy Who Came In from the Cold*, the op-art spoofing of *Modesty Blaise*, even the canine agent of *The Spy with a Cold Nose* and spies from outer space in *This Island Earth*. And the TV screens are filled with such tricky heroes as those in *The Man from UNCLE*, *Amos Burke Secret Agent*, *The Baron*, *I Spy* and *The Avengers*. It seems that spying is one of the film-makers' most durable themes.

SPILLANE, MICKEY (1918–   ) (Frank Morrison). Best-selling American crime novelist of the love-'em and kill-'em variety. Works filmed include *I The Jury* (53), *The Long Wait* (54), *Kiss Me Deadly* (55), and *The Girl Hunters* (64) (in which he played his own tough private eye Mike Hammer). Also appeared in *Ring of Fear* (54). Darren McGavin played Hammer in a 1960 TV series.

SPINETTI, VICTOR (c. 1933–   ). British comic actor with stage experience. *A Hard Day's Night* (64), *The Wild Affair* (64), *Help* (65), *The Taming of the Shrew* (66), *Heironymous Merkin* (69), etc.

THE SPIRAL STAIRCASE (US 1946). Basically a superior 'thunderstorm mystery', this admirably cinematic extension of a suspense novel by Ethel Lina White was notable for Robert Siodmak's direction, Nicholas Musuraca's photography, and the performance of Dorothy McGuire as a deaf-mute servant girl terrorized by a maniac in a lonely house.

THE SPOILERS. Rex Beach's action novel has been filmed five times, with interest centring on its climactic fight scene between the two male leads, who were as follows. 1914: William Farnum and Tom Santschi. 1922: Milton Sills and Noah Beery. 1930: William Boyd and Gary Cooper. 1942: John Wayne and Randolph Scott. 1956: Jeff Chandler and Rory Calhoun.

SPOLIANSKY, MISCHA (1898–   ). Russian composer, in Germany from 1930, Britain from 1934. *Don Juan* (34), *Sanders of the River* (35), *King Solomon's Mines* (37), *Jeannie* (42), *Don't Take It To Heart* (44), *Wanted for Murder* (46), *The Happiest Days of Your Life* (50), *Trouble in Store* (53), *Saint Joan* (57), *North-West Frontier* (59), many others.

sportsmen who have been the subject of biopics include Babe Ruth (William Bendix) in *The Babe Ruth Story*; Grover Cleveland Alexander (Ronald Reagan) in *The Winning Team*; Lou Gehrig (Gary Cooper) in *The Pride of the Yankees*; Monty Stratton (James Stewart) in *The Stratton Story*; Jim Piersall (Anthony Perkins) in *Fear Strikes Out*; Jim Corbett (Errol Flynn) in *Gentleman Jim*; John L. Sullivan (Greg McClure) in *The Great John L.*; Knute Rockne (Pat O'Brien) in *Knute Rockne All-American*; Jim Thorpe (Burt Lancaster) in *Jim Thorpe All-American* (*Man of Bronze*); Ben Hogan (Glenn Ford) in *Follow the Sun*; Annette Kellerman (Esther Williams) in *Million Dollar Mermaid*.

SPRING IN PARK LANE (GB 1947). An unexpectedly successful light comedy with music, this agreeable but witless affair about a footman who—of course—is really an earl in disguise was dated even when released, but coasted to fame on a blithe teaming of talents. Anna Neagle and Michael Wilding were a popular romantic team, Tom Walls and Nigel Patrick furnished light relief, and the palatial settings were lapped up by the British public after six years of total war. It was directed by Herbert Wilcox from a script by Nicholas Phipps. In the following year the same team attempted a sequel, *Maytime in Mayfair*, but this time the soufflé fell flat.

SPRINGSTEEN, R. G. (1904–). American director who has been making efficient low-budget Westerns since 1930, a pleasant exception being *Come Next Spring* (56), a rural drama. Otherwise: *Hellfire* (39), *Honeychile* (48), *The Enemy Within* (49), *The Toughest Man in Arizona* (53), *Track the Man Down* (53), *Cole Younger, Gunfighter* (58), *Battle Flame* (59), *Black Spurs* (64), *Taggart* (65), *Waco* (66), *Johnny Reno* (66), *Red Tomahawk* (66), many others.

THE SPY WHO CAME IN FROM THE COLD (GB 1965). A deliberately dour and chilling look at the spy game, made as a corrective to the James Bond cult. John le Carre's tale provided a splendid series of doublecrosses, and Richard Burton and Oskar Werner extracted plenty of feeling from skeletal parts, but Ossie Morris's photography was perhaps a little too grainy and harsh to be fair. Martin Ritt directed.

THE SQUAW MAN (US 1913). A Western generally considered as a milestone in Hollywood's history, being the first major film to be produced there. An enormous success, it starred Dustin Farnum (who later regretted his refusal to take a percentage of the profits instead of salary) and was directed by Cecil B. De Mille for Jesse L. Lasky. A remake starring Jack Holt was made in 1918, and a talkie version starring Warner Baxter appeared in 1931.

SQUIBS. The cockney flower-seller heroine of George Pearson's silent comedy put in her first successful appearance in 1921. Public acclaim produced three sequels: *Squibs Wins the Calcutta Sweep* (22), *Squibs MP* (23), *Squibs' Honeymoon* (23). Pearson then grew tired of the tomboyish character and cast Betty Balfour in other roles, but she reappeared in a not-too-successful talkie version in 1936, with Gordon Harker and Stanley Holloway.

SQUIRE, RONALD (1886–1958) (Ronald Squirl). Jovial British character actor of stage (since 1909) and screen (since 1934). *Don't Take It to Heart* (44), *While the Sun Shines* (46), *Woman Hater* (48), *The Rocking-Horse Winner* (50), *Encore* (52), *My Cousin Rachel* (US) (53), *The Million Pound Note* (54), *Now and Forever* (55), *Count Your Blessings* (58), etc.

STACK, ROBERT (1919–   ). Tall American leading man who after varied experience went to Hollywood and applied for screen test. *First Love* (debut) (39), *The Mortal Storm* (40), *First Love* (41), *To Be or Not To Be* (42), *Eagle Squadron* (42); war service; *A Date with Judy* (48), *Mr Music* (50), *The Bullfighter and the Lady* (51), *Bwana Devil* (53), *Sabre Jet* (54), *The High and the Mighty* (54), *Written on the Wind* (56), *The Tarnished Angels* (*Pylon*) (57), *The Last Voyage* (60), *The Caretakers* (*Borderlines*) (63), *Is Paris Burning?* (66), *The Corrupt Ones* (*The Peking Medallion*) (67), *Le Soleil des Voyous* (67), etc. TV series: *The Untouchables* (59–62), *The Name of the Game* (68–69).

STAFFORD, FREDERICK (1928–   ). Austrian leading man who after many he-man roles in European movies imitating James Bond was signed by Alfred Hitchcock to play the lead in *Topaz* (69).

STAGECOACH (US 1939). A classic Western which cleverly utilizes not only the usual ingredients but the never-failing trick of putting a miscellaneous group of people together in a dangerous situation. Directed by John Ford from Dudley Nichols' screenplay, with John Wayne, Claire Trevor, Thomas Mitchell, Donald Meek, etc. Remade in 1966 to little effect.

STAHL, JOHN M. (1886–1950). American director, former stage actor; in films from 1914. *Wives of Men* (18), *Husbands and Lovers* (23), *The Child Thou Gavest Me* (24), *The Naughty Duchess* (28), *Seed* (31), *Back Street* (32), *Imitation of Life* (34), *Magnificent Obsession* (35), *Parnell* (37), *Letter of Introduction* (38), *When Tomorrow Comes* (39), *Our Wife* (41), *Holy Matrimony* (43), *The Keys of the Kingdom* (44), *Leave Her to Heaven* (45), *The Foxes of Harrow* (47), many others.

STALLINGS, LAURENCE (1894–   ). American writer. *The Big Parade* (25), *What Price Glory* (co-w) (26), *So Red the Rose* (co-w) (35), *North-West Passage* (co-w) (39), *Jungle Book* (42), *Salome Where She*

Danced (45), *She Wore a Yellow Ribbon* (co-w) (49), *The Sun Shines Bright* (52), etc.

STAMP, TERENCE (1940–   ). British juvenile lead. *Billy Budd* (62), *Term of Trial* (62), *The Collector* (65), *Modesty Blaise* (66), *Far from the Madding Crowd* (67), *Poor Cow* (67), *Blue* (68), *Theorem* (It.) (68), *The Mind of Mr Soames* (69).

STAMP-TAYLOR, ENID (1904–1946). British character actress with stage experience. *Feather Your Nest* (37), *Action for Slander* (37), *The Lambeth Walk* (38), *Hatter's Castle* (41), *The Wicked Lady* (45), *Caravan* (46), etc.

STANDER, LIONEL (c. 1908–   ). Gravel-voiced American character actor, on stage and screen from the early 30s. *The Scoundrel* (34), *Mr Deeds Goes to Town* (36), *A Star Is Born* (37), *Guadalcanal Diary* (42), *The Spectre of the Rose* (46), *Unfaithfully Yours* (48), *St Benny the Dip* (51), *Cul de Sac* (GB) (66), *Promise Her Anything* (GB) (66), *A Dandy in Aspic* (68), etc.

STANDING, SIR GUY (1873–1937). British stage actor, father of Kay Hammond, in some Hollywood films: *The Eagle and the Hawk* (33), *Double Door* (34), *Lives of a Bengal Lancer* (35), *The Return of Sophie Lang* (36), *Lloyds of London* (37), etc.

STANDING, JOHN (1934–   ). British character actor, son of Kay Hammond. *King Rat* (65), *Walk Don't Run* (66), *The Psychopath* (66), etc.

STANLEY, KIM (1925–   ) (Patricia Reid). American stage actress; played leads in *The Goddess* (57), *Seance on a Wet Afternoon* (64).

STANWYCK, BARBARA (1907–   ) (Ruby Stevens). Durable American star actress, former night club dancer, signed for Hollywood after small stage roles. *The Locked Door* (debut) (29), *So Big* (31), *The Bitter Tea of General Yen* (32), *Gambling Lady* (34), *Annie Oakley* (35), *The Plough and the Stars* (37), *Stella Dallas* (37), *Union Pacific* (39), *Golden Boy* (39), *Remember the Night* (40), *Meet John Doe* (41), *The Lady Eve* (41), *Ball of Fire* (41), *The Great Man's Lady* (42), *The Gay Sisters* (42), *Striptease Lady* (*Lady of Burlesque*) (43), *Double Indemnity* (44), *Christmas in Connecticut* (*Indiscretion*) (45), *My Reputation* (46), *The Bride Wore Boots* (46), *The Strange Love of Martha Ivers* (46), *Cry Wolf* (47), *The Two Mrs Carrolls* (47), *The Other Love* (48), *Sorry, Wrong Number* (48), *The Furies* (50), *Clash by Night* (52), *Jeopardy* (53), *Blowing Wild* (54), *Executive Suite* (54), *The Violent Men* (56), *Crime of Passion* (57), *A Walk on the Wild Side* (62), *Roustabout* (64), *The Night Walker* (65), many others. TV series: *The Big Valley* (65–68).

STAPLETON, MAUREEN (1925–   ). American character actress. *Lonelyhearts* (59), *The Fugitive Kind* (60), *A View from the Bridge* (62), *Bye Bye Birdie* (62), *Airport* (69), etc.

STAPLEY, RICHARD: see WYLER, RICHARD.

STAR! (US 1968). A supremely professional if unconvincing account of the life of Gertrude Lawrence, done in the musical style of the 30s and 40s and all the better for it. Meticulously directed by Robert Wise on a mammoth budget, with skilled cinematography by Ernest Laszlo. Julie Andrews shows great stamina but her numbers somehow disappoint; Daniel Massey as Noel Coward steals the show.

star is a word coined by some forgotten publicist in the early years of the century who presumably touted his leading actors as twinkling heavenly lights. It came in the thirties to mean any actor who was billed above the title; but nowadays real stars are hard to find, and the word is generally applied only to those thought likely actually to draw patrons to the box office.

A STAR IS BORN. This 1937 screenplay by Dorothy Parker, Alan Campbell and Robert Carson has become a Hollywood legend and in some cases a reality: the marriage of two stars goes on the rocks because one of them is on the way up and the other on the way down. It was then tailored for Janet Gaynor and Fredric March with strong support from Adolphe Menjou and Lionel Stander as Hollywood types; William Wellman directed, Howard Greene was photographer, and Max Steiner wrote the music. In 1954 George Cukor directed Judy Garland and James Mason in the star roles, with Charles Bickford and Jack Carson; it was a long and lumpy film but with moments of magic including a couple of show-stopping musical numbers which seemed to distil the essence of Garland.

STARK, GRAHAM (1922–   ). British comedy actor of films and TV, mostly in cameo roles. *The Millionairess* (61), *Watch It, Sailor* (62), *A Shot in the Dark* (64), *Becket* (64), *Alfie* (66), *Finders Keepers* (66), etc.

STARK, RAY (c. 1914–   ). American producer and executive, recently head of Seven Arts. *The World of Suzie Wong* (60), *Lolita* (62), *Oh Dad, Poor Dad* (66), *This Property Is Condemned* (66), *Funny Girl* (67), etc.

STARRETT, CHARLES (1904–   ). American cowboy star of innumerable second features in the 30s and 40s. Made debut in *The Quarter Back* (26), playing himself (a professional footballer); other non-cowboy roles include *Fast and Loose* (30), *Sky Bride* (32), *Green Eyes* (34). Inactive since 1952.

STATE FAIR. This agreeable piece of rural Americana was first filmed in 1933 by Henry King, from a script by Sonya Levien and Paul Green. Will Rogers, Lew Ayres and Janet Gaynor were the stars. In 1945, with the benefit of added songs by Rodgers and Hammerstein, it was remade by Walter Lang with Charles Winninger, Dick Haymes and Jeanne Crain; and again, with a different score, in 1961 by Jose Ferrer, with Tom Ewell, Pat Boone and Ann-Margret.

STEEL, ANTHONY (1920–   ). Athletic British leading man with slight stage experience. *Saraband for Dead Lovers* (film debut) (48), *The Wooden Horse* (50), *Laughter in Paradise* (51), *The Malta Story* (52), *Albert RN* (53), *The Sea Shall Not Have Them* (55), *Storm over the Nile* (56), *The Black Tent* (56), *Checkpoint* (56), *A Question of Adultery* (57), *Harry Black* (58), *Honeymoon* (60), *The Switch* (63), *Hell is Empty* (66), *Anzio* (68), etc.

STEELE, BARBARA (1938–   ). British leading lady who has appeared mainly in Italian horror films. *Bachelor of Hearts* (58), *Sapphire* (59), *Black Sunday* (*The Devil's Mask*) (60), *The Pit and the Pendulum* (US) (61), *The Terror of Dr Hichcock* (62), *Eight and a Half* (63), *The Spectre* (64), *Sister of Satan* (*The Revenge of the Blood Beast*) (65), etc.

STEELE, BOB (1907–   ) (Robert Bradbury). American actor on stage from two years old. Since 1920 he played cowboy roles in over 400 second features, and was one of the 'Three Mesquiteers'.

STEELE, TOMMY (1936–   ) (Tommy Hicks). Energetic British cockney performer and pop singer who has made several films. *Kill Me Tomorrow* (55), *The Tommy Steele Story* (57), *The Duke Wore Jeans* (59), *Tommy the Toreador* (60), *It's All Happening* (62), *The Happiest Millionaire* (US) (67), *Half a Sixpence* (67), *Finian's Rainbow* (US) (68), *Where's Jack?* (69).

†STEIGER, ROD (1925–   ). Burly American leading character actor who became known on stage and TV after training at New York's Theatre Workshop. *Teresa* (51), *On the Waterfront* (54), *The Big Knife* (55), *Oklahoma* (55), *The Court Martial of Billy Mitchell* (*One Man Mutiny*) (55), *Jubal* (56), *The Harder They Fall* (56), *Back from Eternity* (57), *Run of the Arrow* (57), *Across the Bridge* (GB) (57), *Al Capone* (58), *Seven Thieves* (59), *The Mark* (61), *Hands Over the City* (It.) (63), *The Pawnbroker* (BFA) (65), *The Loved One* (65), *Doctor Zhivago* (66), *The Girl and the General* (66), *In the Heat of the Night* (AA, BFA) (67), *No Way to Treat a Lady* (68), *The Sergeant* (68), *The Illustrated Man* (69), *Three Into Two Won't Go* (69), *Waterloo* (as Napoleon) (70).

STEIN, PAUL (1891–1952). Austrian director who made films in America and Britain. *Ich Liebe Dich* (23), *My Official Wife* (US) (26), *Forbidden Woman* (US) (27), *Sin Takes a Holiday* (US) (30), *A*

Woman Commands (US) (31), *Lily Christine* (GB) (32), *The Outsider* (GB) (38), *The Saint Meets the Tiger* (GB) (41), *Talk about Jacqueline* (GB) (42), *Kiss the Bride Goodbye* (GB) (43), *Twilight Hour* (GB) (44), *The Lisbon Story* (GB) (46), *Counterblast* (GB) (48), *The Twenty Questions Murder Mystery* (GB) (49), etc.

STEINBECK, JOHN (1902–1968). American novelist; among films of his works are *Of Mice and Men* (40), *The Grapes of Wrath* (40), *Tortilla Flat* (42), *The Moon Is Down* (43), *The Red Pony* (49), *East of Eden* (54), *The Wayward Bus* (57), etc.

STEINER, MAX (1888–   ). Austrian composer, in America from 1924; became one of Hollywood's most reliable and prolific writers of film music. *Cimarron* (31), *A Bill of Divorcement* (32), *King Kong* (33), *The Lost Patrol* (34), *The Informer* (AA) (35), *She* (35), *The Charge of the Light Brigade* (36), *A Star Is Born* (37), *Gone with the Wind* (39), *The Letter* (40), *The Great Lie* (41), *Now Voyager* (AA) (42), *Casablanca* (42), *Since You Went Away* (AA) (44), *Rhapsody in Blue* (45), *The Big Sleep* (46), *The Treasure of the Sierra Madre* (47), *Johnny Belinda* (48), *The Fountainhead* (49), *The Glass Menagerie* (50), *Room for One More* (52), *The Charge at Feather River* (53), *The Caine Mutiny* (54), *Battle Cry* (55), *Come Next Spring* (56), *Band of Angels* (57), *The FBI Story* (59), *The Dark at the Top of the Stairs* (60), *Parrish* (61), *Youngblood Hawke* (64), scores of others.

STELLA DALLAS. This weepy novel of frustrated mother-love, written by Olive Higgins Prouty, was filmed by Henry King in 1925, with Belle Bennett and Ronald Colman, and by King Vidor in 1937, with Barbara Stanwyck and John Boles.

STEN, ANNA (1908–   ) (Anjuschka Stenski Sujakevitch). Russian leading actress imported to Hollywood by Goldwyn in 1933 in the hope of rivalling Garbo; but somehow she didn't click. Stayed, and still appears in occasional character roles. *Storm over Asia* (Russ.) (28), *Nana* (34), *We Live Again* (34), *The Wedding Night* (35), *A Woman Alone* (38), *So Ends Our Night* (41), *They Came to Blow Up America* (43), *She Who Dares* (44), *Let's Live a Little* (48), *Soldier of Fortune* (55), *The Nun and the Sergeant* (62), etc.

STEPANEK, KAREL (1899–   ). Czech character actor, in Britain from 1940. Usually plays Nazis or other villains. *They Met in the Dark* (43), *The Captive Heart* (46), *The Fallen Idol* (48), *State Secret* (50), *Cockleshell Heroes* (55), *Sink the Bismarck* (60), *Operation Crossbow* (65), *Before Winter Comes* (69), many others.

STEPHEN, SUSAN (1931–   ). British leading lady of the 50s. *His Excellency* (51), *The Red Beret (Paratrooper)* (53), *For Better For Worse* (54), *Golden Ivory* (54), *The Barretts of Wimpole Street* (57), *Carry On Nurse* (59), etc.

STEPHENS, ANN (1931–   ). British juvenile actress of the 40s. *In Which We Serve* (42), *Dear Octopus* (43), *The Upturned Glass* (47), *The Franchise Affair* (51), *Intent to Kill* (58), others.

STEPHENS, MARTIN (1949–   ). British juvenile player. *The Hellfire Club* (61), *Village of the Damned* (62), *The Innocents* (62), *Battle of the Villa Fiorita* (65), *The Witches* (66), etc.

STEPHENS, ROBERT (1931–   ). British stage actor, in occasional films. *Circle of Deception* (60), *Pirates of Tortuga* (US) (61), *A Taste of Honey* (61), *Cleopatra* (62), *The Small World of Sammy Lee* (63), *Morgan* (66), *Romeo and Juliet* (68), *The Prime of Miss Jean Brodie* (69), *The Private Life of Sherlock Holmes* (69), etc.

STEPHENSON, HENRY (1871–1956) (H. S. Garroway). British stage actor who came to Hollywood films in his sixties and remained to play scores of kindly old men. *Cynara* (debut) (32), *Little Women* (33), *Mutiny on the Bounty* (35), *Little Lord Fauntleroy* (36), *The Charge of the Light Brigade* (36), *Marie Walewska* (38), *The Young in Heart* (39), *The Adventures of Sherlock Holmes* (40), *This Above All* (42), *The Green Years* (46), *Oliver Twist* (48), *Challenge to Lassie* (49), etc.

STEPHENSON, JAMES (1888–1941). British-born stage actor, in Hollywood from 1938. *When Were You Born?* (debut) (38), *Boy Meets Girl* (38), *Confessions of a Nazi Spy* (38), *Beau Geste* (39), *Calling Philo Vance* (40), *The Sea Hawk* (40), *The Letter* (40), *International Squadron* (41), etc.

STERLING, FORD (1883–1939) (George F. Stitch). American comic actor, a leading Keystone Cop and slapstick heavy; also in *Drums of the Desert* (26), *Gentlemen Prefer Blondes* (28), *Kismet* (30), *Alice in Wonderland* (33), *The Black Sheep* (35), etc.

STERLING, JAN (1923–   ) (Jane Sterling Adriance). Blonde American leading lady with slight stage experience. *Johnny Belinda* (48), *Rhubarb* (51), *Ace in the Hole* (51), *Split Second* (52), *Pony Express* (53), *Alaska Seas* (54), *The High and the Mighty* (54), *Women's Prison* (55), *The Female on the Beach* (55), *1984* (56), *The Harder They Fall* (56), *Love in a Goldfish Bowl* (61), etc.

STERLING, ROBERT (1917–   ) (William Sterling Hart). American leading man of the 40s, mainly in second features. *Only Angels Have Wings* (39), *I'll Wait for You* (41), *The Secret Heart* (46), *Bunco Squad* (48), *Roughshod* (50), *Thunder in the Dust* (51), *Column South* (53), *Return to Peyton Place* (61), *Voyage to the Bottom of the Sea* (62), etc. TV series: *Topper* (53–55), *Ichabod and Me* (61).

STEVENS, CONNIE (1938–   ) (Concetta Ingolia). American leading lady with mixed Italian, English, Irish and Mohican blood.

Eighteen and Anxious (57), *Rock A Bye Baby* (58), *Parrish* (61), *Susan Slade* (61), *Two on a Guillotine* (64), *A Summer Tour* (65), *Never Too Late* (65), etc. TV series: *Hawaiian Eye* (59–62).

STEVENS, CRAIG (1918–   ) (Gail Shekles). American leading man, married to Alexis Smith. Stage experience; routine roles in Hollywood from *Affectionately Yours* (41). Later: *Since You Went Away* (43), *The Lady Takes a Sailor* (47), *The French Line* (54), *Abbott and Costello Meet Dr Jekyll and Mr Hyde* (55), *Gunn* (66), *The Limbo Line* (68), etc. Much on TV: series include *Peter Gunn* (58–60), *Man of the World* (62), *Mr Broadway* (64).

†STEVENS, GEORGE (1904–   ). American director, in Hollywood from 1923. In the late 30s and early 40s he made smooth and lively entertainments, but his infrequent later productions have tended towards elephantiasis. *The Cohens and Kellys In Trouble* (33), *Bachelor Bait* (34), *Kentucky Kernels* (34), *Laddie* (34), *The Nitwits* (34), *Alice Adams* (34), *Annie Oakley* (35), *Swing Time* (36), *A Damsel in Distress* (37), *Quality Street* (37), *Vivacious Lady* (38), *Gunga Din* (39), *Vigil in the Night* (40), *Penny Serenade* (40), *Woman of the Year* (41), *Talk of the Town* (42), *The More the Merrier* (43), *I Remember Mama* (47), *A Place in the Sun* (AA) (51), *Something to Life For* (52), *Shane* (53), *Giant* (AA) (56), *The Diary of Anne Frank* (59), *The Greatest Story Ever Told* (65), *The Only Game in Town* (69).

STEVENS, INGER (1935–   ) (Inger Stensland). Swedish leading lady, in America from childhood. Stage experience. *Man on Fire* (film debut) (57), *Cry Terror* (58), *The Buccaneer* (59), *The New Interns* (64), *A Guide for the Married Man* (67), *Firecreek* (67), *Madigan* (68), *Five Card Stud* (68), *Hang 'Em High* (68), *House of Cards* (68), etc. TV series: *The Farmer's Daughter* (63–65).

STEVENS, K. T. (1919–   ) (Gloria Wood). American leading lady of a few 40s films: daughter of director Sam Wood. *Kitty Foyle* (40), *The Great Man's Lady* (41), *Address Unknown* (44), *Vice Squad* (53), *Tumbleweed* (53), *Missile to the Moon* (58), etc.

STEVENS, LESLIE (1924–   ). American writer. *The Left-Handed Gun* (58), *Private Property* (also produced and directed) (59), *The Marriage-Go-Round* (from his play) (60), *Hero's Island* (also produced and directed) (62), etc. TV series as creator-producer-director: *Stony Burke*, *The Outer Limits*.

STEVENS, MARK (1916–   ). American leading man with varied early experience; usually in routine roles. *Objective Burma* (debut) (45), *From This Day Forward* (45), *The Dark Corner* (46), *I Wonder Who's Kissing Her Now* (47), *The Snake Pit* (48), *The Street With No Name* (48), *Sand* (49), *Mutiny* (53), *Cry Vengeance* (also p, d) (54),

Time Table (also p, d) (55), *September Storm* (60), *Fate Is the Hunter* (64), *Frozen Alive* (66), *Sunscorched* (66). Much on TV since 1955.

STEVENS, ONSLOW (1902–) (Onslow Ford Stevenson). American stage actor occasionally seen in film character roles. *Heroes of the West* (debut) (32), *Counsellor at Law* (33), *The Three Musketeers* (36), *When Tomorrow Comes* (39), *Mystery Sea Raider* (40), *House of Dracula* (45), *O.S.S.* (46), *Night Has a Thousand Eyes* (48), *The Creeper* (48), *State Penitentiary* (50), *Them* (54), *Tarawa Beachhead* (58), *All the Fine Young Cannibals* (60), *Geronimo's Revenge* (63), etc.

STEVENS, RISE (1913–). American opera singer, seen in a few films including *The Chocolate Soldier* (41), *Going My Way* (44), *Carnegie Hall* (47).

STEVENS, ROBERT (c. 1925–). American director, from TV. *The Big Caper* (57), *Never Love a Stranger* (58), *I Thank a Fool* (62), *In the Cool of the Day* (63), etc.

STEVENS, RONNIE (1925–). British comic actor with stage and TV experience. Film appearances (usually cameos) include *Made in Heaven* (52), *An Alligator Named Daisy* (55), *I Was Monty's Double* (58), *I'm All Right, Jack* (59), *Dentist in the Chair* (60), *San Ferry Ann* (65), *Some Girls Do* (68), etc.

STEVENS, STELLA (1938–). American leading lady. *Say One For Me* (debut) (58), *Lil Abner* (59), *Too Late Blues* (61), *The Courtship of Eddie's Father* (63), *The Nutty Professor* (63), *Synanon* (65), *The Secret of My Success* (65), *The Silencers* (66), *How to Save a Marriage* (67), *The Mad Room* (69), etc.

STEVENS, WARREN (c. 1928–). American general purpose actor, *The Frogmen* (51), *The Barefoot Contessa* (53), *Forbidden Planet* (56), *Hot Spell* (58), *No Name on the Bullet* (59), *Forty Pounds of Trouble* (62), *An American Dream* (66), *Madigan* (68), many others. TV series: *77th Bengal Lancers* (56), *The Richard Boone Show* (64).

STEVENSON, ROBERT (1905–). British director, in Hollywood from 1939; married to Anna Lee. *Tudor Rose* (36), *King Solomon's Mines* (37), *The Ware Case* (38), *Tom Brown's Schooldays* (39), *Back Street* (41), *Jane Eyre* (43), *Dishonoured Lady* (47), *To the Ends of the Earth* (48), *Walk Softly, Stranger* (50), *My Forbidden Past* (51), *The Las Vegas Story* (52), *Old Yeller* (57), *Johnny Tremain* (57), *The Absent-minded Professor* (60), *In Search of the Castaways* (61), *Mary Poppins* (64), *The Monkey's Uncle* (65), *That Darn Cat* (65), *Blackbeard's Ghost* (67), *The Love Bug* (69), etc.

STEVENSON, ROBERT LOUIS (1850–1894). British novelist and short story writer. Works filmed include *Dr Jekyll and Mr Hyde* (many versions),

Treasure Island (many versions), *The Body Snatcher*, *The Suicide Club*, *Kidnapped*, *The Master of Ballantrae*, *Ebb Tide*, *The Wrong Box*.

STEWART, ANITA (1895–1961) (Anna May Stewart). American silent screen leading lady. *A Million Bid* (13), *The Goddess* (15), *Mary Regan* (19), *Her Kingdom of Dreams* (20), *Never the Twain Shall Meet* (25), *Sisters of Eve* (28), many others.

STEWART, ATHOLE (1879–1940). British stage character actor. Films include *The Speckled Band* (31), *The Clairvoyant* (34), *Dusty Ermine* (37), *The Spy in Black* (39), *Tilly of Bloomsbury* (40).

STEWART, DONALD OGDEN (1894–   ). American playwright and screenwriter. Scripts include *Smilin' Through* (32), *The Barretts of Wimpole Street* (34), *The Prisoner of Zenda* (37), *The Philadelphia Story* (AA) (40), *Keeper of the Flame* (43), *Life with Father* (47), *Edward, My Son* (49), etc.

STEWART, ELAINE (1929–   ) (Elsy Steinberg). American leading lady of a few 50s films; former usherette. *Sailor Beware* (51), *The Bad and the Beautiful* (52), *Young Bess* (53), *Brigadoon* (54), *The Tattered Dress* (56), *The Adventures of Hajji Baba* (57), *The Rise and Fall of Legs Diamond* (60), *The Most Dangerous Man Alive* (61), etc.

STEWART, HUGH (1910–   ). British producer, former editor, *Trottie True* (49), *The Long Memory* (52), *Man of the Moment* (55) (and all subsequent Norman Wisdom comedies); *The Intelligence Men* (65), etc.

†STEWART, JAMES (1908–   ). American leading actor of inimitable slow drawl and gangly walk; has been portraying slow-speaking, honest heroes for thirty-five years. *Murder Man* (35), *Rose Marie* (36), *Next Time We Love* (36), *Wife versus Secretary* (36), *Small Town Girl* (36), *Speed* (36), *The Gorgeous Hussy* (36), *Born to Dance* (36), *After the Thin Man* (36), *Seventh Heaven* (37), *The Last Gangster* (37), *Navy Blue and Gold* (37), *Of Human Hearts* (38), *Vivacious Lady* (38), *Shopworn Angel* (38), *You Can't Take It with You* (38), *Made for Each Other* (38), *Ice Follies of 1939, It's a Wonderful World* (39), *Mr Smith Goes to Washington* (39), *Destry Rides Again* (39), *The Shop around the Corner* (39), *The Mortal Storm* (40), *No Time for Comedy* (40), *The Philadelphia Story* (40), *Come Live with Me* (40), *Pot o' Gold* (41), *Ziegfeld Girl* (41); war service; *It's a Wonderful Life* (46), *Magic Town* (47), *Call Northside 777* (47), *On Our Merry Way* (48), *Rope* (48), *You Gotta Stay Happy* (48), *The Stratton Story* (49), *Malaya* (49), *Winchester 73* (50), *Broken Arrow* (50), *The Jackpot* (50), *Harvey* (50), *No Highway* (GB) (51), *The Greatest Show on Earth* (51), *Bend of the River* (52), *Carbine Williams* (52), *The Naked Spur* (53), *Thunder Bay* (53), *The Glenn Miller Story* (53), *Rear Window* (54), *The Far Country*

(54), *Strategic Air Command* (55), *The Man from Laramie* (55), *The Man Who Knew Too Much* (56), *The Spirit of St Louis* (57), *Night Passage* (57), *Vertigo* (58), *Bell, Book and Candle* (58), *Anatomy of a Murder* (59), *The FBI Story* (59), *The Mountain Road* (60), *Two Rode Together* (61), *The Man Who Shot Liberty Vallance* (62), *Mr Hobbs Takes a Vacation* (62), *How the West Was Won* (62), *Take Her She's Mine* (63), *Cheyenne Autumn* (64), *Dear Brigitte* (65), *Shenandoah* (65), *The Flight of the Phoenix* (65), *The Rare Breed* (66), *Firecreek* (67), *Bandolero* (68), *The Cheyenne Social Club* (project) (70).

STEWART, PAUL (c. 1908–   ). American character actor, with stage experience; film debut with Orson Welles in *Citizen Kane* (41); thereafter frequently seen in sinister roles. *The Window* (48), *Twelve o'Clock High* (49), *The Bad and the Beautiful* (52), *Kiss Me Deadly* (55), many others; also director and star of several TV series including *Deadline, Playhouse 90*, etc.

STEWART, SOPHIE (1909–   ). British stage and radio actress, in occasional films. *Maria Marten* (35), *As You Like It* (36), *The Return of the Scarlet Pimpernel* (38), *Nurse Edith Cavell* (39), *The Lamp Still Burns* (43), *Uncle Silas* (47), *Yangtse Incident* (56), etc.

STILLER, MAURITZ (1883–1928). Swedish director who went to Hollywood in the 20s with Garbo, but died shortly after. *Vampyren* (12), *Sir Arne's Treasure* (19), *Erotikon* (20), *The Atonement of Gosta Berling* (24), *The Blizzard* (US) (26), *Hotel Imperial* (27), *Street of Sin* (28), etc.

STOCK, NIGEL (1919–   ). British character actor, former boy performer. *Lancashire Luck* (38), *Brighton Rock* (46), *Derby Day* (51), *The Dam Busters* (55), *Eye Witness* (57), *H.M.S. Defiant* (62), *The Lost Continent* (68), *The Lion in Winter* (68), many others. Much on TV: Dr Watson in *Sherlock Holmes* series.

stock shot. One not made at the time of filming but hired from a library. It can be either newsreel, specially shot material such as planes landing at an airport, views of a city, etc., or spectacular material lifted from older features. (e.g. *Storm over the Nile* [55] had a large proportion of action footage from the original *Four Feathers* [39], and the same shots have turned up in several other films including *Master of the World* [61] and *East of Sudan* [64]).

STOCKFIELD, BETTY (1905–1966). British stage actress, in occasional films. *City of Song* (30), *The Impassive Footman* (32), *The Beloved Vagabond* (36), *Derrière la Façade* (Fr.) (40), *Flying Fortress* (42), *Édouard et Caroline* (Fr.) (50), *The Lovers of Lisbon* (55), *True as a Turtle* (57), etc.

STOCKWELL, DEAN (1936–   ). American leading man, former boy performer. *Anchors Aweigh* (45), *The Green Years* (46), *Song of the Thin Man* (46), *Gentlemen's Agreement* (48), *The Boy with Green Hair* (49), *Kim* (51), *Compulsion* (59), *Sons and Lovers* (60), *Long Day's Journey into Night* (62), *Rapture* (65), *Psych-Out* (68), etc. Also on stage.

STOCKWELL, GUY (c. 1937–   ). American leading actor. *The War Lord* (65), *Blindfold* (65), *And Now Miguel* (66), *Beau Geste* (66), *The Plainsman* (66), *Tobruk* (66), *The King's Pirate* (67), *The Million Dollar Collar* (67), *In Enemy Country* (68), etc.

STOKER, BRAM (1847–1912). British novelist, the creator of *Dracula*. Was also Henry Irving's manager.

STOKOWSKI, LEOPOLD (1882–   ) (Leopold Stokes or Boleslowowicz). British-born orchestral conductor. Appeared in several films including *One Hundred Men and a Girl* (37), *Fantasia* (40).

STOLL, GEORGE (1905–   ). American musical director, with MGM from 1945. *Anchors Aweigh* (AA) (45), *Neptune's Daughter* (49), *I Love Melvin* (53), *The Student Prince* (54), *Hit the Deck* (55), *Meet Me in Las Vegas* (56), many others.

STOLOFF, MORRIS (1893–   ). American musical director, in Hollywood from 1936. Scored *Lost Horizon* (37), *You Can't Take It With You* (38), *Cover Girl* (AA) (44), *A Song to Remember* (45), *The Jolson Story* (AA) (46), *The 5000 Fingers of Dr T* (52), *Picnic* (55), many others.

STONE, ANDREW (1902–   ). American producer-director (latterly with his wife Virginia) who made it a rule since the mid-50s not to shoot in a studio, always on location. Formed Andrew Stone Productions 1943. *The Great Victor Herbert* (39), *Stormy Weather* (directed only) (42), *Hi Diddle Diddle* (43), *Sensations of 1945*, *Highway 301* (51), *The Steel Trap* (52), *The Night Holds Terror* (54), *Julie* (56), *Cry Terror* (58), *The Decks Ran Red* (59), *The Last Voyage* (60), *Ring of Fire* (61), *The Password Is Courage* (62), *Never Put It In Writing* (64), *The Secret of My Success* (65), *Song of Norway* (69), etc.

STONE, GEORGE E. (1903–1967) (George Stein). Polish-born character actor, who in Hollywood films played oppressed little men; formerly in vaudeville. Hundreds of films include *The Front Page* (30), *Little Caesar* (30), *Cimarron* (31), *Anthony Adverse* (36), *The Housekeeper's Daughter* (38), *His Girl Friday* (41), the *Boston Blackie* series, *Dancing in the Dark* (50), *The Robe* (53), *Guys and Dolls* (55), *The Man with the Golden Arm* (56), etc. Played the court usher in the *Perry Mason* TV series.

Stone, Harold J.

STONE, HAROLD J. (1911–   ). American character actor. *The Harder They Fall* (56), *Garment Center* (57), *Man Afraid* (57), *Spartacus* (60), *The Chapman Report* (62), *The Man with X Ray Eyes* (63), etc. Much on TV.

STONE, LEWIS (1879–1953). Distinguished American stage actor, a leading man of silent films and later a respected character actor. *Honour's Altar* (debut) (15), *The Prisoner of Zenda* (22), *Scaramouche* (23), *The Lost World* (24), *Madame X* (30), *The Mask of Fu Manchu* (32), *Mata Hari* (32), *Grand Hotel* (33), *Queen Christina* (33), *David Copperfield* (34), *Treasure Island* (35), *The Thirteenth Chair* (37), *You're Only Young Once* (37), *Judge Hardy's Children* (38), *Love Finds Andy Hardy* (38), *Out West with the Hardys* (39) (and ten further episodes of this series, ending in 1947), *Yellow Jack* (39), *The Bugle Sounds* (41), *Three Wise Fools* (46), *The World and His Wife* (*The State of the Union* (48), *Key to the City* (50), *Scaramouche* (52), *The Prisoner of Zenda* (52), *All the Brothers Were Valiant* (53), many others.

STONE, MILBURN (1904–   ). American character actor, in Hollywood from the mid-30s; has been in hundreds of low-budget action features, usually as villain or tough hero; more recently became famous as 'Doc' in the *Gunsmoke* TV series.

STONE, PETER (1930–   ). American screenwriter. *Charade* (63), *Father Goose* (AA) (64), *Mirage* (65), *Sweet Charity* (68), etc.

STOOGES, THE THREE. A trio of American comics specializing in a violent kind of slapstick. In two-reelers from 1930; latterly made a few features, e.g. *The Three Stooges Meet Hercules* (63), *The Outlaws is Coming* (64). The original participants were three seasoned ex-vaudevillians: LARRY FINE and MOE and CURLY HOWARD. When CURLY died in 1947, he was replaced by another brother, SHEMP HOWARD; he died in 1955 and was replaced by JOE DE RITA.

stop motion. The method by which much trick photography is effected: the film is exposed one frame at a time, allowing time for re-arrangement of models, etc., between shots, and thus giving the illusion in the completed film of motion by something normally inanimate. The monsters in *King Kong* (33) are the supreme example of this method.

STOPPA, PAOLO (1906–   ). Italian character actor, in films from 1932. More recently: *La Beauté du Diable* (49), *Miracle in Milan* (50), *The Seven Deadly Sins* (52), *Love Soldiers and Women* (55), *La Loi* (59), *The Leopard* (63), *Becket* (64), *After the Fox* (66), etc.

STORM, GALE (1922–   ) (Josephine Cottle). American leading lady of the 40s. *Tom Brown's Schooldays* (39), *Foreign Agent* (42), *Nearly*

Eighteen (43), *The Right to Live* (45), *Sunbonnet Sue* (46), *It Happened on Fifth Avenue* (47), *Abandoned* (49), *Underworld Story* (50), *The Texas Rangers* (51), etc. Later popular on TV with *The Gale Storm Show* (56–59).

STORM OVER ASIA (Russia 1929). Also known as *The Heir to Genghis Khan*, this beautifully-made propagandist melodrama concerned a Mongol fur trapper found in 1918 to be a descendant of Genghis Khan. Tried and half-executed for treason, he is reprieved to become a puppet monarch. Directed by V. I. Pudovkin.

storms of one kind or another have been brilliantly staged in *The Hurricane, The Wizard of Oz, When Tomorrow Comes, Reap the Wild Wind, Typhoon, Lord Jim, A High Wind in Jamaica, The Blue Lagoon, Portrait of Jennie, Noah's Ark* and *The Bible*, to name but a handful; they have also been essential situation-builders in such films as *Five Came Back, Hatter's Castle, Our Man Flint, The Card, Storm Fear* and *The Blue Lagoon*. A whole genre of films, known as the 'thunderstorm mystery', grew up in the 30s when every screen murder took place in a desolate mansion during a thunderstorm with no means of communication with the outside world; typical of these are *The Black Cat* (41), *The Cat and the Canary, The Ghost Breakers, Night Monster, Hold That Ghost, You'll Find Out* and *The Spiral Staircase*. Finally there is nothing like a good electrical storm for breathing life into a monster, as evidenced in a score of films from *Frankenstein* to *The Electric Man* and after.

THE STORY OF LOUIS PASTEUR (US 1936). The first of Warner Brothers' famous series of historical biographies: later films dealt with Zola, Reuter, Dr Ehrlich, Juarez, etc. In this case popularization managed to make scientific research remarkably exciting. Paul Muni (AA) was Pasteur; William Dieterle directed from a script by Sheridan Gibney and Pierre Collings, and Erich Wolfgang Korngold wrote the music. These films were very successful commercially; but when John Huston revived the form in 1962 with *Freud*, it was a box-office disaster.

STOSSEL, LUDWIG (1883–   ). Austrian character actor in Hollywood from the mid-30s. *Four Sons* (39), *Man Hunt* (41), *Woman of the Year* (41), *Hitler's Madman* (43), *Cloak and Dagger* (46), *A Song Is Born* (48), *Call Me Madam* (53), *Me and the Colonel* (58), *G.I. Blues* (60), many others.

STOUT, ARCHIE (1886–   ). American cinematographer in Hollywood from 1914. Later films include *Fort Apache* (48), *Hard Fast and Beautiful* (51), *The Quiet Man* (AA) (52), *The Sun Shines Bright* (53), *The High and the Mighty* (54).

STOWE, HARRIET BEECHER (1811–1896). American novelist, author of the much-filmed *Uncle Tom's Cabin* (qv).

STRADLING, HARRY (c. 1910–1970). British-born cinematographer, long in US. *La Kermesse Héroïque* (35), *Knight without Armour* (37), *Pygmalion* (38), *The Citadel* (38), *Jamaica Inn* (39), *Suspicion* (41), *The Picture of Dorian Gray* (AA) (44), *The Pirate* (48), *The Barkleys of Broadway* (49), *A Streetcar Named Desire* (51), *Valentino* (51), *Hans Christian Andersen* (52), *Helen of Troy* (55), *The Eddy Duchin Story* (56), *Guys and Dolls* (56), *The Pajama Game* (57), *A Face in the Crowd* (57), *The Dark at the Top of the Stairs* (60), *My Fair Lady* (AA) (64), *How to Murder Your Wife* (65), *Moment to Moment* (65), *Walk, Don't Run* (66), *Funny Girl* (68), *Support Your Local Sheriff* (68), *Hello Dolly* (69), many others.

STRADNER, ROSE (1913–1958). Austrian actress who made a few Hollywood films. *The Last Gangster* (38), *Blind Alley* (39), *The Keys of the Kingdom* (44), etc.

STRANGE, GLENN (1911–   ). Giant-size American character actor, in Hollywood from 1937, mainly in cowboy roles. Also played the monster in *House of Frankenstein* (35), *Abbott and Costello meet Frankenstein* (49), etc.

STRANGE INTERLUDE (US 1932). Eugene O'Neill's sombre romantic drama, with its sense of time and opportunity wasted, was a strange choice for MGM to film at the time, but Norma Shearer and Clark Gable provided powerful box-office lure, and the long monologues were overcome by billing the movie as 'the film in which you hear the characters THINK!' Robert Z. Leonard directed unobtrusively.

STRASBERG, SUSAN (1938–   ). American leading lady, daughter of Lee Strasberg, founder of the New York Actors Studio. Stage and TV experience. *Picnic* (film debut) (55), *Stage Struck* (57), *Taste of Fear* (59), *Kapo* (60), *Hemingway's Adventures of a Young Man* (62), *The High Bright Sun* (65), *Psych-Out* (68), *The Brotherhood* (68), etc.

STRAUSS, ROBERT (1913–   ). American comedy actor (occasionally in menacing roles); former salesman. *Sailor Beware* (52), *Stalag 17* (53), *The Seven Year Itch* (54), *Attack* (57), *The Last Time I Saw Archie* (61), *The Family Jewels* (65), etc.

STRAYER, FRANK (1891–1964). American director of second features. *Rough House Rosie* (27), *Enemy of Men* (30), *The Monster Walks* (32), *The Vampire Bat* (33), *The Ghost Walks* (35), *Blondie* (and many others in this series) (38), *The Daring Young Man* (42), *Messenger of Peace* (50), etc.

stretch-printing. The reason silent films look jerky is that they were shot at 16 frames a second whereas modern sound projectors operate at 24, making everything move half as fast again as normal. One means of overcoming this is stretch-printing in the lab: every second frame is printed twice. This still gives a curious effect, as for every two frames slower than normal sound speed we still get one frame faster.

STREISAND, BARBRA (1942–   ). American singer and entertainer. First films: *Funny Girl* (AA) (68), *Hello Dolly* (69), *On a Clear Day You Can See Forever* (69).

strikes: see *labour relations.*

STRITCH, ELAINE (1922–   ). American character actress and comedienne, mainly on stage. *The Scarlet Hour* (55), *A Farewell to Arms* (57), *The Perfect Furlough* (58), etc. TV series: *My Sister Eileen* (62).

STRICK, JOSEPH (1923–   ). American director. *The Savage Eye* (59), *The Balcony* (64), *Ulysses* (67), *Ring of Bright Water* (GB) (produced only) (69), *Tropic of Cancer* (69).

STRICKLYN, RAY (1930–   ). American 'second lead' with stage experience. *The Proud and the Profane* (56), *The Last Wagon* (57), *Ten North Frederick* (58), *Young Jesse James* (60), etc.; more recently on TV.

STROCK, HERBERT L. (1918–   ). American director, former publicist and editor. *The Magnetic Monster* (52), *Riders to the Stars* (54), *Battle Taxi* (55), *Teenage Frankenstein* (57), *How to Make a Monster* (58), *Rider on a Dead Horse* (62), *The Crawling Hand* (63), etc. Much TV work.

STRODE, WOODY or WOODROW (c. 1923–   ). Tall American Negro actor. *The Lion Hunters* (51), *The Ten Commandments* (56), *Sergeant Rutledge* (60), *Spartacus* (60), *Two Rode Together* (62), *The Man Who Shot Liberty Valance* (62), *Genghis Khan* (65), *The Professionals* (66), *Shalako* (68), *Che!* (69), etc.

STROMBERG, HUNT (1894–1968). American producer, long with MGM, who went independent in the 40s. *Breaking into Society* (as director) (24), *Fire Patrol* (as director) (26), *Torrent* (27), *Our Dancing Daughters* (28), *Red Dust* (32), *The Thin Man* (34), *The Great Ziegfeld* (AA) (36), *Maytime* (38), *Marie Antoinette* (38), *Idiot's Delight* (39), *The Women* (39), *Northwest Passage* (40), *Pride and Prejudice* (41), *Guest in the House* (44), *Lured* (47), *Too Late for Tears* (49), *Between Midnight and Dawn* (50), *Mask of the Avenger* (51), many others.

Stross, Raymond

STROSS, RAYMOND (1916–   ). British producer, in films from 1933; married to Anne Heywood. *As Long As They're Happy* (52), *An Alligator Named Daisy* (56), *The Flesh Is Weak* (56), *A Question of Adultery* (58), *A Terrible Beauty* (59), *The Very Edge* (62), *The Leather Boys* (63), *Ninety Degrees in the Shade* (65), *The Midas Run* (69), etc.

STRUDWICK, SHEPPERD; see SHEPPERD, JOHN.

STRUSS, KARL (c. 1890–   ). American cinematographer. *Ben Hur* (26), *Sunrise* (AA) (27), *Abraham Lincoln* (30), *The Sign of the Cross* (32), *Dr Jekyll and Mr Hyde* (32), *The Great Dictator* (40), *Bring on the Girls* (44), *Suspense* (46), *The Macomber Affair* (47), *Rocketship XM* (50), *Limelight* (52), *Tarzan and the She-Devil* (53), many others. Recently making TV commercials.

STUART, BINKIE (c. 1932–   ). British child actress of the 30s. *Moonlight Sonata* (37), *Little Dolly Daydream* (38), *My Irish Molly* (39), etc.

STUART, GLORIA (1909–   ) (Gloria Stuart Finch). American leading lady of the 30s. *The Old Dark House* (32), *The Invisible Man* (33), *Roman Scandals* (33), *Prisoner of Shark Island* (36), *Rebecca of Sunnybrook Farm* (38), *The Three Musketeers* (39), *She Wrote the Book* (last to date) (46), etc.

STUART, JOHN (1898–   ) (John Croall). British leading man of the 20s, character actor of the 40s and after. *Her Son* (debut) (20), *We Women* (25), *The Pleasure Garden* (26), *Blackmail* (29), *Elstree Calling* (30), *Atlantic* (30), *Number Seventeen* (31), *Taxi for Two* (32), *The Pointing Finger* (34), *Abdul the Damned* (35), *Old Mother Riley's Ghost* (41), *The Phantom Shot* (46), *Mine Own Executioner* (47), *The Magic Box* (51), *Quatermass II* (57), *Blood of the Vampire* (58), *Sink the Bismarck* (60), many others.

THE STUDENT PRINCE. The Sigmund Romberg/Dorothy Donnelly operetta about a Ruritarian prince who loves a barmaid was filmed by Lubitsch in 1927 with Ramon Novarro and Norma Shearer. There was no sound version until 1954, when Richard Thorpe directed Ann Blyth and Edmund Purdom (the latter using Mario Lanza's voice).

THE STUDENT OF PRAGUE. The old German legend, about a man who sold his reflection to the devil and bought it back only at the expense of his life, was filmed in 1913 by Paul Wegener, with Stellan Rye; in 1926 by Henrik Galeen, with Conrad Veidt; and in 1936 by Arthur Robison, with Anton Walbrook.

stunt men, who risk their lives doubling for the stars when the action gets too rough, have been featured in remarkably few movies: *Hollywood Stunt Men, Lucky Devils, The Lost Squadron, Sons of Adventure,*

Callaway Went Thataway and *Singing in the Rain*. *Hell's Angels* was
said to be the film on which most stunt men were killed; more
recently Paul Mantz lost his life while stunt-flying for *The Flight
of the Pheonix*, which was subsequently dedicated to him. Most
famous stunt man is probably Yakima Canutt, who later became
a famous second-unit director; Richard Talmadge, who doubled
for Douglas Fairbanks and also directed a few films himself; and
Cliff Lyons, who stood in for most of the western stars. Stunt men
who became famous in their own right include George O'Brien,
Jock Mahoney and Rod Cameron.

†STURGES, JOHN (1911–   ). American director of smooth if in-
creasingly pretentious action films, former editor and documen-
tarist. *The Man Who Dared* (46), *Shadowed* (46), *Alias Mr Twilight*
(47), *For the Love of Rusty* (47), *Keeper of the Bees* (48), *The Best Man
Wins* (48), *The Sign of the Ram* (48), *The Walking Hills* (49), *The
Capture* (49), *Mystery Street* (50), *The Magnificent Yankee* (50), *Right
Cross* (50), *Kind Lady* (51), *The People Against O'Hara* (51), *It's a
Big Country* (part) (51), *The Girl in White* (52), *Fast Company* (52),
Jeopardy (53), *Escape from Fort Bravo* (53), *Bad Day at Black Rock*
(54), *Underwater* (55), *The Scarlet Coat* (55), *Backlash* (56), *Gunfight
at the OK Corral* (57), *The Law and Jake Wade* (58), *The Old Man
and the Sea* (58), *Last Train from Gun Hill* (58), *Never So Few* (59),
The Magnificent Seven (60), *By Love Possessed* (61), *Sergeants Three*
(62), *A Girl Named Tamiko* (63), *The Great Escape* (63), *The Satan Bug*
(65), *The Hallelujah Trail* (65), *The Hour of the Gun* (67), *Ice Station
Zebra* (68), *Marooned* (69).

STURGES, PRESTON (1898–1959) (Edmond P. Biden). American writer-
director who through the early 40s was Hollywood's wonder boy;
after that something happened to his talent and he moved to
France, where he made one film with none of his old style. Early
life as businessman, inventor and playwright. Became staff writer
for Paramount and offered them a script for nothing on condition
that he should direct it himself. So: *The Great McGinty* (40),
Christmas in July (40), *Sullivan's Travels* (41), *The Lady Eve* (41),
The Palm Beach Story (42), *The Great Moment* (43), *The Miracle of
Morgan's Creek* (43), *Hail the Conquering Hero* (44), *Mad Wednesday*
(*The Sin of Harold Diddlebock*) (46), *Unfaithfully Yours* (48), *The
Beautiful Blonde from Bashful Bend* (49), *The Diary of Major Thompson*
(56), *Paris Holiday* (guest appearance only) (58). (†List as director
complete.)

STYNE, JULE (1905–   ) (Jules Styne). British-born composer, in
US from childhood. Former pianist and conductor. Film songs
include 'There Goes That Song Again', 'Give Me Five Minutes
More', 'It's Magic', 'Three Coins in the Fountain'. Shows filmed

include *Gentlemen Prefer Blondes, Bells Are Ringing, Gypsy, Funny Girl.*

submarines have been the setting for so many war action films that only a few can be noted. Pure entertainment was the object of *Submarine Patrol, Submarine Command, Torpedo Run, Destination Tokyo, Run Silent Run Deep, Crash Dive, The Deep Six* and *Ice Station Zebra.* Somewhat deeper thoughts were permitted in *Morning Departure, The Silent Enemy, Les Maudits,* and *We Dive at Dawn.* Submarines became objects of farce in *Jack Ahoy, Let's Face It,* and *Operation Petticoat.*

More unusual submarine vehicles appeared in *Voyage to the Bottom of the Sea, Around the World Under the Sea, Twenty Thousand Leagues Under the Sea, Thunderball, You Only Live Twice, Above Us the Waves* and *The Beast from 20,000 Fathoms.*

SUBOTSKY, MILTON (1921–   ). American independent producer and writer. *Rock Rock Rock* (56), *The Last Mile* (58), *City of the Dead* (GB) (60), *It's Trad Dad* (GB) (63), *Dr Terror's House of Horrors* (GB) (64), *Dr Who and the Daleks* (GB) (65), *The Skull* (GB) (66), *The Psychopath* (GB) (66), *Daleks Invasion Earth 2150 AD* (GB) (66), *Torture Garden* (67), etc.

SUCKSDORFF, ARNE (1917–   ). Swedish documentarist who has normally written and photographed his own films, which vary from six minutes to feature length. *The West Wind* (42), *Shadows on the Snow* (45), *Rhythm of a City* (47), *A Divided World* (48), *The Road* (48), *The Wind and the River* (51), *The Great Adventure* (53), *The Flute and the Arrow* (57), *The Boy in the Tree* (60), *My Home Is Copacabana* (65), etc.

suicide has been the central subject of two recent films, *Le Feu Follet* and *The Slender Thread,* in which the motives for it in two particular cases are examined. It has, of course, been part of countless other plots, including factual or legendary ones such as *Cleopatra, Romeo and Juliet* and *Scott of the Antarctic.* Innumerable melodramas have begun with apparent suicides which have been proved by the disbelieving hero to be murder; the latest of these is probably *The Third Secret.* In *An Inspector Calls* a girl's suicide caused guilt complexes in an entire family for different reasons. In *An American Dream* the hero virtually commits suicide by walking into a room full of gangsters out to kill him. In *Leave Her to Heaven* the leading character commits suicide in such a way that her husband will be blamed for her murder. Several Japanese films have been based on the suicide pilots or *Kamikaze,* and there has also been a graphic account of the principles of *Hara Kiri.* Suicide has often been the way out for villains in mystery pictures: drowning for Herbert Marshall in *Foreign Correspondent,* shooting for Leo G.

Carroll in *Spellbound*, poison for Rosamund John in *Green for Danger* and Barry Fitzgerald in *Ten Little Niggers*. And one could not begin to count the films in which characters have been narrowly saved from suicide, like Ray Milland in *The Lost Weekend*. Attempted suicide was even played for comedy by Laurel and Hardy in *The Flying Deuces*, and by Jack Lemmon in *Luv*, while in *It's a Wonderful Life* James Stewart was dissuaded from suicide by a friendly angel.

†SULLAVAN, MARGARET (1911–1960). American leading actress in light films of the 30s and 40s; she had a special whimsical quality which was unique. *Only Yesterday* (33), *Little Man What Now* (34), *So Red the Rose* (35), *The Good Fairy* (35), *Next Time We Love* (36), *The Moon's Our Home* (36), *Three Comrades* (38), *Shopworn Angel* (38), *The Shining Hour* (39), *The Shop around the Corner* (39), *The Mortal Storm* (40), *So Ends Our Night* (40), *Back Street* (41), *Appointment for Love* (41), *Cry Havoc* (43), *No Sad Songs for Me* (50).

SULLIVAN, BARRY (1912–   ). American leading man with stage experience. *Lady in the Dark* (43), *Two Years before the Mast* (44), *And Now Tomorrow* (44), *Three Guys Named Mike* (51), *The Bad and the Beautiful* (52), *Jeopardy* (54), *Queen Bee* (55), *Seven Ways from Sundown* (60), *The Light in the Piazza* (62), *Stagecoach to Hell* (64), *My Blood Runs Cold* (64), *Harlow* (electronovision version) (65), *An American Dream* (*See You in Hell, Darling*) (66), *Intimacy* (66), *Buckskin* (68), *Willie Boy* (69), etc. TV series: *Harbourmaster* (57), *The Road West* (66).

SULLIVAN, FRANCIS L. (1903–1956). Heavyweight British character actor, often seen as advocate. On stage from 1921, films from 1933. *The Missing Rembrandt* (debut) (33), *Chu Chin Chow* (33), *Great Expectations* (US) (35), *The Mystery of Edwin Drood* (US) (35), *Sabotage* (36), *Action for Slander* (37), *Dinner at the Ritz* (37), *Twenty-one Days* (38), *The Citadel* (38), *The Four Just Men* (39), *Pimpernel Smith* (41), *Fiddlers Three* (44), *Caesar and Cleopatra* (45), *Great Expectations* (46), *Oliver Twist* (48), *Night and the City* (51), *Plunder of the Sun* (US) (51), *The Prodigal* (US) (55), many others.

SULLIVAN'S TRAVELS (US 1941). Perhaps the most meaningful, eccentric and devastating of all Preston Sturges' comedies. About a film director who goes off in search of truth but finally discovers that all people want is to laugh, it is a remarkably sure-footed combination of farce, melodrama and sentiment, and its appeal seems to have increased over the years. Written and directed by Sturges, produced by Paul Jones, photographed by John F. Seitz; with memorable performances by Joel McCrea, Veronica Lake, and the familiar Sturges repertory of supporting players.

SUMMERFIELD, ELEANOR (1921–   ). British character comedienne, on stage from 1939. *London Belongs to Me* (film debut) (47), *Scrooge* (51), *It's Great To Be Young* (56), *Dentist in the Chair* (59), *On the Beat* (62), many others. TV series: *My Wife's Sister.*

SUMMERS, JEREMY (1931–   ). British director, from TV. *The Punch and Judy Man* (62), *Crooks in Cloisters* (64), *Ferry Cross the Mersey* (64), *House of a Thousand Dolls* (67), etc.

SUMMERS, WALTER (1896–   ). British director of the 20s and 30s. *Ypres* (25), *Mons* (26), *The Battle of the Coronel and Falkland Islands* (31), *Deeds Men Do* (32), *The Return of Bulldog Drummond* (33), *Mutiny on the Elsinore* (36), *Music Hath Charms* (co-d) (36), *At the Villa Rose* (38), *Dark Eyes of London* (38), *Traitor Spy* (40), etc.

SUMMERTIME (SUMMER MADNESS) (GB 1955). This adaptation of Arthur Laurents' play 'The Time of the Cuckoo' successfully balanced its slight emotional story against the exotic background of Venice. Katharine Hepburn gave a brilliant performance as the lonely spinster tourist attracted by a handsome but married Italian (Rossano Brazzi); David Lean's direction was subtle and witty, and Jack Hildyard's colour photography proved a major asset.

SUMMERVILLE, SLIM (1892–1946) (George J. Summerville). Lanky, mournful-looking American character comedian, former gagman and director for Mack Sennett. *All Quiet on the Western Front* (30), *The Front Page* (31), *Life Begins at Forty* (35), *The Road Back* (37), *Rebecca of Sunnybrook Farm* (38), *Jesse James* (39), *Tobacco Road* (41), *Miss Polly* (41), *Niagara Falls* (42), *The Hoodlum Saint* (46), many others.

SUNDBERG, CLINTON (1919–   ). American character actor, former teacher; usually plays flustered clerk or head waiter. *Undercurrent* (46), *Living in a Big Way* (47), *Annie Get Your Gun* (50), *Main Street to Broadway* (52), *The Caddy* (53), *The Birds and the Bees* (56), *The Wonderful World of the Brothers Grimm* (63), many others.

SUNRISE (US 1927). An interesting example of the German influence on Hollywood (written by Karl Mayer, directed by F. W. Murnau), this melodrama won a special Academy Award for 'artistic quality of production'. There were awards too for the camerawork (Charles Rosher, Karl Struss) and for Janet Gaynor as the young wife whose life is threatened by her temporarily unbalanced husband (George O'Brien). The story takes place during a journey, and the use of locations to this extent was rare for Hollywood at the time.

SUNSET BOULEVARD (US 1950). A harsh look at Hollywood directed by Billy Wilder from a script by himself, Charles Brackett and D. M. Marsham jnr. Gloria Swanson enjoys herself as the faded star who makes a tragic comeback, but she, Erich von Stroheim, Anna Q. Nilsson and Buster Keaton come so close to playing themselves it's macabre. William Holden plays the star's kept man who encourages her false hopes. Photographed by John F. Seitz with music by Franz Waxman.

SURTEES, ROBERT L. (1906–). Distinguished American cinematographer, in Hollywood from 1927. *Thirty Seconds over Tokyo* (44), *Our Vines Have Tender Grapes* (45), *The Unfinished Dance* (47), *Act of Violence* (48), *Intruder in the Dust* (49), *King Solomon's Mines* (AA) (50), *Quo Vadis* (51), *The Bad and the Beautiful* (AA) (52), *Escape from Fort Bravo* (53), *Trial* (55), *Oklahoma* (55), *The Swan* (56), *Raintree County* (57), *Merry Andrew* (58), *Ben Hur* (AA) (59), *Mutiny on the Bounty* (62), *The Hallelujah Trail* (65), *The Collector* (65), *The Satan Bug* (65), *Lost Command* (66), *Doctor Dolittle* (67), *The Graduate* (67), *Sweet Charity* (68), many others.

SUSCHITSKY, WOLFGANG (1912–). Austrian cinematographer in Britain. *No Resting Place* (51), *Cat and Mouse* (57), *The Small World of Sammy Lee* (63), *Ulysses* (67), etc. Also documentaries.

SUSPICION (US 1941). The film for which Joan Fontaine won an Academy Award was toned down from a novel by Frances Iles: the ending was changed as it was felt that no one would accept Cary Grant as a wife-murderer. Hitchcck directed rather coldly, and the production was only average.

SUSSKIND, DAVID (1920–). American TV and theatre personality and producer who has also produced a few films: *Edge of the City* (57), *A Raisin in the Sun* (61), *Requiem for a Heavyweight* (62), *All the Way Home* (63), etc.

SUTHERLAND, A. EDWARD (1895–). American director, in Hollywood from 1914. *Wild Wild Susan* (25), *Dance of Life* (29), *Palmy Days* (31), *Mississippi* (35), *The Flying Deuces* (39), *The Boys from Syracuse* (40), *Beyond Tomorrow* (41), *Invisible Woman* (41), *Nine Lives Are Not Enough* (42), *Dixie* (43), *Follow the Boys* (44), *Abie's Irish Rose* (46), *Having Wonderful Crime* (46), *Bermuda Affair* (56), many others. Moved into TV.

SUTTON, DUDLEY (1933–). British character actor. *The Leather Boys* (63), *Rotten to the Core* (65), *Crossplot* (69), etc.

SUTTON, GRADY (1908–). American character comedian usually seen as vacuous country cousin; in Hollywood from 1926. *The Story of Temple Drake* (32), *Alice Adams* (35), *Stage Door* (37), *Alexander's Ragtime Band* (38), *The Bank Dick* (41), *The Great Moment* (44), *My Wild Irish Rose* (48), *White Christmas* (54), *The Birds and the Bees* (56), *My Fair Lady* (64), *Paradise Hawaiian Style* (66), many others. TV series: *The Pruitts of Southampton*. (66).

SUTTON, JOHN (1908–1963). British actor with stage experience; in Hollywood from 1937, usually as second lead or smooth swashbuckling villain. *Bulldog Drummond Comes Back* (37), *The Adventures of Robin Hood* (38), *The Invisible Man Returns* (40), *A Yank in the RAF* (41), *Ten Gentlemen from West Point* (42), *Jane Eyre* (43), *Claudia and David* (46), *The Three Musketeers* (48), *The Golden Hawk* (52), *East of Sumatra* (54), *The Bat* (59), many others.

SVENGALI, the evil genius of George du Maurier's Victorian romance 'Trilby', has been seen at least five times on screen. In 1915 Wilton Lackaye and Clara Kimball Young appeared in a version under the title *Trilby*. There was a British one-reeler in 1922 in the 'Tense Moments with Great Authors' series, and in 1923 James Young directed a second Hollywood version with Arthur Edmund Carewe and Andrée Lafayette. In 1931, under the title *Svengali*, Archie Mayo directed a sound remake with John Barrymore as the hypnotist to Marian Marsh's heroine, and in 1954 Donald Wolfit and Hildegarde Neff appeared in a British version directed by Noel Langley.

SWAIN, MACK (1876–1935). American silent actor, a Mack Sennett heavy from 1914; most memorable in *The Gold Rush* (24). Last part, *Midnight Patrol* (32).

SWANSON, GLORIA (1898–   ). American leading lady of the silent screen who started as a Mack Sennett bathing beauty and is still making comebacks. *The Meal Ticket* (15), *Teddy at the Throttle* (17), *The Pullman Bride* (17), *Shifting Sands* (18), *Don't Change Your Husband* (18), *Male and Female* (19), *Why Change Your Wife?* (19), *The Affairs of Anatol* (21), *Prodigal Daughters* (23), *Madame Sans Gene* (25), *Untamed Lady* (26), *Sadie Thompson* (28), *Queen Kelly* (unfinished) (28), *Indiscreet* (31), *Perfect Understanding* (33), *Music in the Air* (34), *Father Takes a Wife* (41), *Sunset Boulevard* (50), *Three for Bedroom C* (52), *Nero's Mistress* (Italian) (56), many others. Also recent TV guest appearances.

SWANSON, MAUREEN (1932–   ). British leading lady who retired to marry after a brief career. *Moulin Rouge* (53), *A Town Like Alice* (56), *Robbery under Arms* (57), etc.; only recent film *The Clue of the Twisted Candle* (61).

SWARTHOUT, GLADYS (1904–   ). American opera singer who acted in a few films: *Rose of the Rancho* (35), *Give Us This Night* (36), *Champagne Waltz* (37), *Romance in the Dark* (38), *Ambush* (39), etc.

the Swedish Cinema was at the forefront of world production as early as 1910. Famous directors such as Victor Sjostrom and Mauritz Stiller were well known by 1912, and tended to make films of Swedish legends, which appealed by their very strangeness. *Sir Arne's Treasure* (19), *Thy Soul Shall Bear Witness* (20), *The Atonement of Gosta Berling* (24), are among the best-known titles of the Swedish silent period; but in the mid-20s all Sweden's best talent—including the newly-discovered Greta Garbo—moved towards Hollywood and the home industry was eclipsed until the late 40s saw the appearance of talents like Werner (*Midvinterblot*), Sucksdorff (*Rhythm of a City*) and Sjoberg (*Frenzy*). In the 50s the Swedish vein of romantic pessimism was developed to its ultimate in the semi-mystic but commercial films of Ingmar Bergman, who despite a recent temporary retirement remains the most significant name in the Scandinavian cinema.

SWEET, BLANCHE (1895–   ). American silent heroine. *The Lonedale Operator* (11), *Judith of Bethulia* (13), *The Secret Sin* (15), *The Deadliest Sex* (20), *Tess of the D'Urbervilles* (24), *Singed* (27), *The Silver Horde* (30), etc. Retired.

SWEET SMELL OF SUCCESS (US 1957). An odd, unexpected and harsh attack on Broadway columnists written in venom by Clifford Odets and Ernest Lehman, directed with tremendous polish by Alexander Mackendrick, fresh from Ealing. Not very likeable but highly cinematic, with photography by James Wong Howe, music by Elmer Bernstein, and arresting performances by Burt Lancaster and Tony Curtis.

SWENSON, INGA (1932–   ). American actress whose rare films include *Advise and Consent* (61), *The Miracle Worker* (62).

SWERLING, JO (1894–   ) (Joseph Swerling). Russian-American writer, long in Hollywood. *Dirigible* (31), *Platinum Blonde* (32), *Man's Castle* (35), *Made for Each Other* (38), *The Westerner* (40), *Blood and Sand* (42), *Lifeboat* (43), *Leave Her to Heaven* (46), *Thunder in the East* (52), many others. Recently inactive.

SWIFT, DAVID (1919–   ). American radio and TV writer-producer-director (TV series include *Mr Peepers, Grindl*). Recently turned to films: *Pollyanna* (60), *The Parent Trap* (61), *Love is a Ball (All This and Money Too)* (63), *The Interns* (63), *Under the Yum Yum Tree* (64), *Good Neighbour Sam* (64), *How to Succeed in Business without Really Trying* (w, p, d) (67), etc.

SWINBURNE, NORA (1902–   ). British actress on stage from 1914, screen occasionally from 1921. *Alibi* (30), *Potiphar's Wife* (31), *Fanny by Gaslight* (43), *Quartet* (48), *The River* (51), *The End of the Affair* (55), *Conspiracy of Hearts* (59), *Interlude* (68), many others; also TV appearances.

swinging London was a myth, a creation of *Time Magazine* which rebounded through the world's press and lasted for several silly seasons from 1965. It also helped British production finances by persuading American impresarios that London was where the action is, and its influence was felt in scores of trendy and increasingly boring films, including *Georgy Girl, Alfie, The Jokers, Kaleidoscope, Smashing Time, Help!, The Knack, Blow Up, Casino Royale, I'll Never Forget Whatshisname, To Sir With Love, Up the Junction, Bedazzled, Poor Cow, The Strange Affair, Salt and Pepper, Joanna* and *Otley.*

THE SWISS FAMILY ROBINSON. The classic children's novel by Johann Wyss was filmed in Hollywood in 1940 by Edward Ludwig, with Thomas Mitchell, Edna Best, Freddie Bartholemew and Terry Kilburn. In 1960 Ken Annakin remade it as a Walt Disney spectacular, with John Mills, Dorothy McGuire, James Macarthur and Tommy Kirk as the desert island castaways.

SWITZER, CARL ('ALFALFA') (1926–1959). American boy actor of the 30s, a graduate of 'Our Gang'; later in character roles. *General Spanky* (37), *The War Against Mrs Hadley* (42), *State of the Union* (48), *Track of the Cat* (54), *The Defiant Ones* (58), many others.

SYDNEY, BASIL (1894–1968). British actor of heavy roles, on stage from 1911. *Romance* (film debut) (20), *The Midshipmaid* (32), *The Tunnel* (35), *Rhodes of Africa* (36), *The Four Just Men* (39), *Ships with Wings* (41), *Went the Day Well* (42), *Caesar and Cleopatra* (45), *The Man Within* (47), *Hamlet* (48), *Treasure Island* (50), *Ivanhoe* (52), *Hell Below Zero* (54), *The Dam Busters* (55), *The Three Worlds of Gulliver* (60), many others; also on TV.

SYKES, ERIC (1924–   ). British TV scriptwriter turned comedian Has been in occasional films: *Invasion Quartet* (61), *Village of Daughters* (62), *Kill or Cure* (63), *Heavens Above* (63), *The Bargee* (63), *One-Way Pendulum* (64), *Those Magnificent Men in Their Flying Machines* (65), *Rotten to the Core* (65), *The Liquidator* (65), *The Spy with a Cold Nose* (67), *The Plank* (also directed) (67), *Shalako* (68), etc.

SYLVESTER. The celebrated cartoon cat with the lisping Bronx accent, always in pursuit of Tweetie Pie but never quite managing to win, has been appearing since the 40s in Warner shorts, voiced by the inimitable Mel Blanc. As he once said himself, 'There mutht be an eathier way for a puthy cat to get thome thuthtenanth . . .'

SYLVESTER, WILLIAM (1922–   ). American leading man, in British films since 1949. *Give Us This Day* (50), *The Yellow Balloon* (52), *Albert RN* (53), *High Tide at Noon* (57), *Gorgo* (59), *Offbeat* (60), *Ring of Spies* (63), *Devil Doll* (64), *Devils of Darkness* (65), *The Syndicate* (67), *The Hand of Night* (67), *2001, A Space Odyssey* (68), many others. Also on TV.

SYMS, SYLVIA (1934–). British leading lady with brief stage and TV experience. *My Teenage Daughter* (film debut) (56), *Ice Cold in Alex* (58), *Flame in the Streets* (60), *Victim* (61), *The Quare Fellow* (62), *The World Ten Times Over* (63), *East of Sudan* (64), *Operation Crossbow* (65), *The Big Job* (65), *Run Wild Run Free* (69), etc.

synchronisation. The arranging of sound and picture to match. Only rarely is this done by shooting them simultaneously; the normal process involves re-recording and much laboratory work to give the optimum results.

SZSABO, ISTVAN (1938–). Hungarian director. *Age of Illusion* (65), *Father* (66), etc.

T

TAFLER, SYDNEY (1916–   ). British character actor on stage from 1936. *The Little Ballerina* (film debut) (46), *Passport to Pimlico* (48), *Mystery Junction* (51), *Venetian Bird* (53), *The Sea Shall Not Have Them* (55), *Carve Her Name with Pride* (58), *Sink the Bismarck* (60), *The Bulldog Breed* (61), *The Seventh Dawn* (64), scores of others; also on TV.

take. A take is a single recording of a scene during the making of a film. Sometimes one take is enough; but directors have been known to shoot as many as fifty before they are satisfied with the results.

TALBOT, LYLE (1904–   ) (Lisle Henderson). American leading man and heavy of the 30s, still playing character roles. *Love Is a Racket* (32), *One Wild Night* (37), *Up In Arms* (43), *Sensations of 1945*, *Down among the Sheltering Palms* (53), *There's No Business Like Show Business* (54), *City of Fear* (58), innumerable others.

TALBOT, NITA (1930–   ). American leading lady and comedienne who seems set to follow in the wisecracking footsteps of Eve Arden. *That Funny Feeling* (65), *A Very Special Favour* (65), etc. TV series: *Hot Off the Wire* (60).

A TALE OF TWO CITIES. Apart from three very early one-reel versions, Dickens' novel of the French Revolution was filmed in 1917 with William Farnum, in 1926 (as *The Only Way*) with Martin Harvey, in 1935 with Ronald Colman and in 1958 with Dirk Bogarde.

TALES OF HOFFMAN (GB 1951). An ambitious if rather foolhardy attempt to combine opera and ballet in a popular form. Lacking a modern story, it did not have the box-office value of *The Red Shoes*, made three years earlier by the same team, Michael Powell and Emeric Pressburger. All very Teutonic, with heavy colour, music by Offenbach, décor by Hein Heckroth, choreography by Frederick Ashton, photography by Christopher Challis; and dancing and singing by the best talent money can buy.

TALES OF MANHATTAN (US 1942). Directed by Julien Duvivier, this string of anecdotes linked by the travels of one tail coat can be credited with starting or revivifying the short story compendium movie, later developed in such movies as *Flesh and Fantasy*, *Quartet*, *Full House*, *The Story of Three Loves*, *It's a Great Country* and many others. In itself it was unremarkable apart from Charles Laughton's splendid bit of pathos as a poor conductor; the Negro sequence was incredibly 'Uncle Tom'; and what might have been the best story, starring W. C. Fields, was removed before release because the film was too long.

talkies caused the biggest revolution the film industry has known, and provoked critical resentment difficult to understand until one sees a very early talkie and realizes what a raucous and unpleasant experience it must have been until Hollywood caught up with itself. The main steps of development were as follows. In 1923 Lee de Forest (qv) made primitive shorts. In 1926 Warners created Vitaphone, a disc process, and Fox pioneered sound on film with Movietone. Also in 1926 came *Don Juan*, the first film with synchronized music and effects. The first speaking and singing came in 1927 with Al Jolson in *The Jazz Singer*. In 1928 the first all-talking film, *The Singing Fool*, set the seal of popular success on the new medium.

TALMADGE, CONSTANCE (1898–   ). American silent heroine and comedienne, sister of Norma Talmadge. *Intolerance* (15), *Matrimaniac* (16), *The Honeymoon* (17), *Happiness à la Mode* (19), *Lessons in Love* (21), *Her Primitive Lover* (22), *The Goldfish* (24), *Her Sister from Paris* (25), *Venus* (last to date) (29), many others.

TALMADGE, NATALIE (1899–1969). American leading lady of a few silent comedies; retired to marry Buster Keaton. Younger sister of Norma and Constance Talmadge.

TALMADGE, NORMA (1897–1957). American silent heroine, sister of Constance Talmadge. *Battle Cry of Peace* (14), *Going Straight* (15), *Forbidden City* (18), *The Sign on the Door* (21), *Within the Law* (23), *Secrets* (24), *The Lady* (25), *Camille* (27), *The Dove* (28), *Dubarry Woman of Passion* (last film) (30), many others.

TALMADGE, RICHARD (1896–   ). American stunt man of the 20s, who doubled for Fairbanks, Lloyd, etc., and later became a star of action films such as *The Speed King, Laughting at Danger* and *Fighting Demon*. Later became a director of stunt sequences, and has recently worked on *How the West Was Won, What's New Pussycat? Hawaii* and *Casino Royale*. Real name: Ricardo Metzetti.

TALMAN, WILLIAM (1915–1968). American character actor usually seen as crook or cop: for seven years was well occupied in TV's *Perry Mason* series as the D.A. who never won a case. Films include *Red Hot and Blue* (49), *The Armoured Car Robbery* (50), *One Minute to Zero* (52), *The Hitch Hiker* (52), *City That Never Sleeps* (53), *This Man Is Armed* (56), *Two-Gun Lady* (59), *The Ballad of Josie* (67).

TAMBA, TETSURO (c. 1929–   ). Japanese actor who has appeared in occidental films: *Bridge to the Sun* (61), *The Seventh Dawn* (64), *You Only Live Twice* (67), *The Five Man Army* (70).

935

TAMBLYN, RUSS (1934–   ). Buoyant American dancer and tumbler, in small film roles from 1948. *Seven Brides for Seven Brothers* (54), *Hit the Deck* (55), *Don't Go Near the Water* (56), *Peyton Place* (57), *Tom Thumb* (58), *Cimarron* (61), *West Side Story* (61), *The Wonderful World of the Brothers Grimm* (63), *The Haunting* (63), *Son of a Gunfighter* (65), etc.

TAMIROFF, AKIM (1899–   ). Russian leading character actor, in America from 1923. *Sadie McKee* (34) (film debut), *Lives of a Bengal Lancer* (35), *Naughty Marietta* (35), *China Seas* (36), *The Story of Louis Pasteur* (36), *The General Died at Dawn* (36), *The Great Gambini* (37), *Spawn of the North* (38), *Union Pacific* (39), *Geronimo* (40), *The Way of All Flesh* (40), *The Great McGinty* (40), *The Corsican Brothers* (41), *For Whom the Bell Tolls* (43), *The Bridge of San Luis Rey* (44), *A Scandal in Paris* (46), *The Gangster* (47), *My Girl Tisa* (48), *Outpost in Morocco* (50), *You Know What Sailors Are* (GB) (53), *Confidential Report* (55), *The Black Sleep* (56), *Me and the Colonel* (57), *Topkapi* (64), *The Liquidator* (65), *Alphaville* (65), *Lieut. Robin Crusoe* (66), *After the Fox* (66), *Great Catherine* (68), scores of others.

TANDY, JESSICA (1909–   ). British-born actress wife of Hume Cronyn. *The Seventh Cross* (44), *Dragonwyck* (46), *The Green Years* (46), *Forever Amber* (48), *A Woman's Vengeance* (48), *Rommel, Desert Fox* (51), *The Light in the Forest* (58), *Hemingway's Adventures of a Young Man* (62), *The Birds* (63), etc.

TANI, YOKO (1932–   ). Japanese leading lady, in international films. *The Wind Cannot Read* (57), *The Quiet American* (58), *Savage Innocents* (59), *Piccadilly Third Stop* (60), *Marco Polo* (61), *Who's Been Sleeping in My Bed* (63), *Invasion* (66), etc.

TANNER, TONY (1932–   ). British light actor and revue artiste. *Strictly for the Birds* (64), *A Home of Your Own* (65), *The Pleasure Girls* (65), *Stop the World I Want to Get Off* (66), etc.

TARADASH, DANIEL (1913–   ). American screenwriter who has worked on *Golden Boy* (39), *Rancho Notorious* (48), *From Here to Eternity* (AA) (53), *Désirée* (54), *Storm Centre* (also directed) (55), *Picnic* (55), *Bell, Book and Candle* (58), *Morituri* (65), *Hawaii* (66), etc.

TARGET FOR TONIGHT (GB 1941). A feature-length documentary about an RAF bombing raid. Using no actors, it seemed at the time an amazing realistic achievement; but the slang and the understatement have dated it badly, and the aerial photography has since been surpassed. Produced by Ian Dalrymple, written and directed by Harry Watt, with music by Leighton Lucas.

TARKINGTON, BOOTH (1869–1946). American novelist. Films of his books include *Alice Adams*, *Penrod* (qv), *Monsieur Beaucaire* (qv), *The Magnificent Ambersons* (qv).

TARZAN. The brawny jungle hero, an English milord lost in Africa as a child and grown up with the apes, was a creation of novelist Edgar Rice Burroughs (1875–1950); the first Tarzan story was published in 1914. The films quickly followed. *Tarzan of the Apes* (18) starred Elmo Lincoln with Enid Markey as Jane; so did *Romance of Tarzan* (18). *The Return of Tarzan* (20) had Gene Polar and Karla Schramm. *Son of Tarzan* (20) was a serial with Kamuela C. Searle in the title role; Tarzan was P. Dempsey Tabler. Elmo Lincoln returned in another serial, *The Adventures of Tarzan* (21), with Louise Lorraine. *Tarzan and the Golden Lion* (27) starred James Pierce and Dorothy Dunbar. Another serial, *Tarzan the Mighty* (28), had Frank Merrill and no Jane; a runner-up, *Tarzan the Tiger* (30), had the same crew. In 1932 came Johnny Weissmuller in the first of MGM's long line of Tarzan pictures: *Tarzan the Ape Man*, with Maureen O'Sullivan as Jane. There followed *Tarzan and His Mate* (34), *Tarzan Escapes* (36), *Tarzan Finds a Son* (38), *Tarzan's Secret Treasure* (41), and *Tarzan's New York Adventure* (42). Meanwhile in 1935 an independent company had made a serial starring Herman Brix which was later released as two features, *Tarzan and the Green Goddess* and *New Adventures of Tarzan*; and in 1933 producer Sol Lesser had started his Tarzan series with *Tarzan the Fearless*, starring Buster Crabbe; he followed this up with *Tarzan's Revenge* (38) starring Glenn Morris. In 1943 Lesser took over Weissmuller (but not O'Sullivan or any other Jane) for *Tarzan Triumphs*, followed by *Tarzan's Desert Mystery* (44), *Tarzan and the Amazons* (reintroducing Jane in the shape of Brenda Joyce) (45), *Tarzan and the Leopard Woman* (45), *Tarzan and the Huntress* (47), and *Tarzan and the Mermaids* (48). Then Weissmuller was replaced by Lex Barker for *Tarzan's Magic Fountain* (48), *Tarzan and the Slave Girl* (49), *Tarzan's Peril* (50), *Tarzan's Savage Fury* (51), and *Tarzan and the She-Devil* (52). Gordon Scott next undertook the chore in *Tarzan's Hidden Jungle* (55), *Tarzan and the Lost Safari* (57), *Tarzan's Fight for Life* (58), *Tarzan's Greatest Adventure* (59) and *Tarzan the Magnificent* (60). MGM now remade *Tarzan the Ape Man* (60) starring Denny Miller; and, with Jock Mahoney, *Tarzan Goes to India* (62) and *Tarzan's Three Challenges* (64). The latest additions are *Tarzan and the Valley of Gold* (66), *Tarzan and the Great River* (67), and *Tarzan and the Jungle Boy* (68), all with Mike Henry. A TV series (66–67) starred Ron Ely.

TASHLIN, FRANK (1913–   ). American comedy writer-director, former cartoonist. *The Fuller Brush Man* (w) (48), *The Paleface* (w) (48), *The Good Humour Man* (w) (50), *Kill the Umpire* (w) (51), *Susan Slept Here* (d) (54), *Artists and Models* (w, d) (55), *The Girl Can't Help It* (w, p, d) (57), *Will Success Spoil Rock Hunter?* (w, p, d,) (57), *Rockabye Baby* (w, d) (58), *Say One for Me* (p, d) (59), *Cinderfella* (w, d) (60), *It's Only Money* (d) (63), *The Man from the*

Diners Club (d) (64), *The Alphabet Murders* (d) (65), *The Glass Bottom Boat* (d) (66), *Caprice* (d) (67), *The Private Navy of Sgt O'Farrell* (d) (68), etc.

TASHMAN, LILYAN (1899–1934). American silent screen sophisticate. *Experience* (21), *Manhandled* (24), *Don't Tell the Wife* (27), *New York Nights* (29), *Murder by the Clock* (31), *Scarlet Dawn* (32), *Frankie and Johnny* (33), etc.

A TASTE OF HONEY (GB 1961). A strange and influential little film produced and directed by Tony Richardson from a play by Shelagh Delaney, and lovingly photographed by Walter Lassally. Finding humour and compassion in the depressing background of industrial Lancashire, viewed through the eyes of a gawky adolescent schoolgirl, it paints vivid sketches of her tarty mum and the harmless homosexual who looks after her when a sailor leaves her pregnant. With the help of excellent performances from Rita Tushingham, Dora Bryan (BFA) and Murray Melvin, it succeeds in its determination to wring poetry out of squalor.

TATE, REGINALD (1896–1955). British character actor, mainly on stage. *Riverside Murder* (35), *Dark Journey* (37), *Next of Kin* (42), *The Life and Death of Colonel Blimp* (43), *Uncle Silas* (47), *Robin Hood* (52), *King's Rhapsody* (55), etc.

TATI, JACQUES (1908–   ) (Jacques Tatischeff). French pantomimist and actor who after years on the music halls and in small film roles began to write and direct his own quiet comedies which were really little more than strings of sight gags on a theme: *Jour de Fête* (47), *Monsieur Hulot's Holiday* (52), *Mon Oncle* (58), *Playtime* (68).

TAUBER, RICHARD (1892–1948). Austrian operatic singer, long in Britain where he made a number of artless musical comedy films: *Blossom Time* (32), *Land without Music* (35), *Pagliacci* (37), *The Lisbon Story* (45), etc.

TAUROG, NORMAN (1899–   ). American director, former child actor, in Hollywood from 1917. *Lucky Boy* (28), *Skippy* (AA) (31), *Huckleberry Finn* (33), *We're Not Dressing* (34), *Mrs Wiggs of the Cabbage Patch* (35), *Strike Me Pink* (36), *Mad about Music* (38), *The Adventures of Tom Sawyer* (38), *Boys' Town* (38), *Broadway Melody of 1940*, *Young Tom Edison* (40), *A Yank at Eton* (42), *Girl Crazy* (42),

The Hoodlum Saint (46), *The Bride Goes Wild* (48), *Please Believe Me* (50), *Room for One More* (52), *Living It Up* (54), *The Birds and the Bees* (56), *Bundle of Joy* (57), *Don't Give Up the Ship* (59), *Palm Springs Weekend* (63), *Tickle Me* (65), *Sergeant Deadhead* (65), *Speedway* (67), many others.

TAYLOR, DEEMS (1886–1966). American journalist and musician whose chief connection with films was to act as narrator for *Fantasia* (40) and to help write *A Pictorial History of the Movies*.

TAYLOR, DON (1920–   ). American light leading man, with stage experience. *Naked City* (48), *For the Love of Mary* (48), *Ambush* (49), *Father of the Bride* (50), *Submarine Command* (51), *The Blue Veil* (51), *Stalag 17* (53), *Men of Sherwood Forest* (54), *I'll Cry Tomorrow* (57), etc. Recently directing: *The Savage Guns* (62), *Ride the Wild Surf* (64), *Jack of Diamonds* (67), *The Five Man Army* (70), etc.; also TV films.

†TAYLOR, ELIZABETH (1932–   ). British-born leading lady with a well-publicized private life. Was evacuated to Hollywood during World War II and began as a child star. *Lassie Come Home* (43), *Jane Eyre* (43), *The White Cliffs of Dover* (44), *National Velvet* (44), *The Rich Full Life* (44), *Life with Father* (45), *Courage of Lassie* (45), *A Date with Judy* (48), *Julia Misbehaves* (48), *Little Women* (49), *Conspirator* (49), *The Big Hangover* (49), *Father of the Bride* (50), *Father's Little Dividend* (51), *A Place in the Sun* (51), *The Light Fantastic* (51), *Ivanhoe* (52), *The Girl Who Had Everything* (53), *Rhapsody* (54), *Elephant Walk* (54), *Beau Brummell* (54), *The Last Time I Saw Paris* (55), *Giant* (56), *Raintree County* (57), *Cat on a Hot Tin Roof* (58), *Suddenly Last Summer* (59), *Butterfield 8* (AA) (60), *Cleopatra* (62), *The VIPs* (63), *The Sandpiper* (65), *Who's Afraid of Virginia Woolf?* (AA) (66), *The Taming of the Shrew* (67), *Doctor Faustus* (67), *The Comedians* (67), *Reflections in a Golden Eye* (67), *Boom* (68), *Secret Ceremony* (68), *The Only Game in Town* (69). Currently married to Richard Burton; previously to Conrad Hilton, Michael Wilding, Michael Todd, Eddie Fisher.

TAYLOR, ESTELLE (1899–1958). American stage actress who made some silent films. *While New York Sleeps* (22), *The Ten Commandments* (23), *Don Juan* (26), *The Whip Woman* (27), *When East Is East* (28), etc.

TAYLOR, GILBERT (1914–   ). British cinematographer, in films since 1929. *The Guinea Pig* (48), *Seven Days to Noon* (50), *The Yellow Balloon* (52), *It's Great To Be Young* (55), *The Good Companions* (57), *Ice Cold in Alex* (58), *The Rebel* (60), *Dr Strangelove* (63), *Repulsion* (65), *The Bedford Incident* (65), *Before Winter Comes* (69), etc.

Taylor, Kent

TAYLOR, KENT (1907–) (Louis Weiss). Smart American leading man in routine low-budgeters since 1931 *Merrily We Go to Hell* (32), *Death Takes a Holiday* (34), *Bombers' Moon* (43), *Smooth as Silk* (46), *Ghost Town* (56), *Harbour Lights* (63), scores of others. TV series: *Boston Blackie* (51–52).

TAYLOR, LAURETTE (1884–1946) (Laurette Cooney). American stage leading lady who filmed her great success *Peg O My Heart* (22) and stayed in Hollywood for a few more silent films: *Happiness, One Night in Rome*, etc.

TAYLOR, ROBERT (1911–1969) (Spangler Arlington Brough). Durable American leading man signed by MGM while still at university. *Handy Andy* (debut) (34), *Magnificent Obsession* (35), *Broadway Melody of 1936, The Gorgeous Hussy* (36), *Personal Property* (37), *Camille* (37), *His Affair* (38), *A Yank at Oxford* (38), *The Crowd Roars* (38), *Three Comrades* (39), *Waterloo Bridge* (40), *Escape* (40), *Billy the Kid* (41), *When Ladies Meet* (41), *Johnny Eager* (41), *Her Cardboard Lover* (42), *Cargo of Innocents* (42), *Bataan* (42), *Song of Russia* (43), war service, *Undercurrent* (47), *High Wall* (48), *Conspirator* (50), *Ambush* (50), *Devil's Doorway* (50), *Quo Vadis* (51), *Ivanhoe* (52), *Knights of the Round Table* (54), *Many Rivers to Cross* (55), *The Adventures of Quentin Durward* (56), *The Power and the Prize* (56), *Tip on a Dead Jockey* (57), *Saddle the Wind* (57), *The Law and Jake Wade* (58), *The Hangman* (59), *The House of the Seven Hawks* (59), *The Killers of Kilimanjaro* (60), *Guns of Wyoming (Cattle King)* (62), *A House Is Not a Home* (64), *The Night Walker* (65), *Johnny Tiger* (66), *Return of the Gunfighter* (66), *Savage Pampas* (66), *The Glass Sphinx* (67), others. TV series: *The Detectives* (59–61).

TAYLOR, ROD (1929–). Australian-born, Hollywood-based leading man with stage experience. *Long John Silver* (55), *The Catered Affair* (56), *Giant* (56), *Raintree County* (57), *Separate Tables* (58), *The Time Machine* (60), *The Birds* (63), *The VIPs* (63), *Sunday in New York* (63), *Fate Is the Hunter* (64), *Thirty-six Hours* (64), *Young Cassidy* (65), *Do Not Disturb* (65), *The Liquidator* (65), *The Glass Bottom Boat* (66), *Hotel* (67), *Dark of the Sun* (67), *Chuka* (67), *Nobody Runs Forever* (68), *The Man Who Had Power Over Women* (70), etc. TV series: *Hong Kong* (60).

TAYLOR, SAM (1895–1958). American screenwriter of the 20s: *The Freshman, Exit Smiling*, etc. Remembered chiefly for the credit line to the 1928 version of *The Taming of the Shrew*: 'by William Shakespeare, with additional dialogue by Sam Taylor'.

TAYLOR-YOUNG, LEIGH (1944–). American leading lady. *I Love You Alice B. Toklas* (68), *The Adventurers* (69), *The Buttercup Chain* (69).

940

TAZIEFF, HAROUN (1914–). French explorer-photographer, best known for *Rendezvous du Diable* (*Volcano*) (58), *The Forbidden Volcano* (67).

teachers have been notably played by Robert Donat in *Goodbye Mr Chips*; Jennifer Jones in *Good Morning Miss Dove*; Bette Davis in *The Corn is Green*; Jack Hawkins in *Mandy*; Judy Garland in *A Child is Waiting*; Anne Bancroft in *The Miracle Worker*; Shirley Maclaine in *Spinster*; Glenn Ford in *The Blackboard Jungle*; Sidney Poitier in *To Sir With Love*; Sandy Dennis in *Up the Down Staircase*; Dorothy Dandridge in *Bright Road*; Max Bygraves in *Spare the Rod*; Otto Kruger in *The Housemaster*; Cecil Trouncer in *The Guinea Pig*; Maggie Smith in *The Prime of Miss Jean Brodie*; Joanne Woodward in *Rachel, Rachel*.

Comic teachers were to the fore in *Boys Will Be Boys* (Will Hay, the best of them all); the *St Trinian's* films; *Carry On Teacher*; *Old Mother Riley Headmistress*; *Bottoms Up* (Jimmy Edwards); *Fun at St Fanny's* (Fred Emney); and *Vice Versa* (James Robertson Justice).

See also: *schools*.

TEAL, RAY (1902–). American character actor who has probably played more sheriffs (good or bad) than he can count. In films from 1938 after stage experience. *The Cherokee Strip* (40), *A Wing and a Prayer* (44), *Captain Kidd* (45), *Joan of Arc* (48), *The Men* (50), *The Lion and the Horse* (53), *Montana Belle* (53), *Hangman's Knot* (54), *Ambush at Tomahawk Gap* (54), *Run for Cover* (55), *The Indian Fighter* (55), *Saddle the Wind* (57), *One-Eyed Jacks* (61), *Cattle King* (63), *Taggart* (64), many others.

TEARLE, CONWAY (1882–1938) (Frederick Levy). American leading actor of silent days; half-brother of Godfrey Tearle. *Stella Maris* (18), *The Virtuous Vamp* (20), *Woman of Bronze* (23), *Bella Donna* (25), *Gold Diggers of Broadway* (29), *Vanity Fair* (32), *Should Ladies Behave?* (34), *Klondike Annie* (36), *Romeo and Juliet* (36), etc.

TEARLE, SIR GODFREY (1884–1953). Distinguished British stage actor, on stage from 1893; occasional films from 1906, when he played Romeo in a one-reeler. *If Youth But Knew* (30), *The Thirty-nine Steps* (35), *One of Our Aircraft Is Missing* (42), *The Rake's Progress* (45), *Private Angelo* (48), *The Titfield Thunderbolt* (53), etc.

TEASDALE, VERREE (c. 1897–). American general purpose actress, mostly in comedy. *Syncopation* (29), *Fashions of 1934*, *The Milky Way* (36), *Topper Takes a Trip* (38), *Turnabout* (40), many others.

teaser: a poster, trailer, or other piece of publicity which whets the appetite for a forthcoming film without giving full details about it, sometimes not even the title. The term was also applied to early

the telephone

pornographic films 1900–05, e.g. *Lovers Interrupted, Making Love in a Hammock*, etc.

the telephone has been a very useful instrument to film scenarists. It brought sinister, menacing and threatening calls in *Sorry—Wrong Number, The Small World of Sammy Lee, Midnight Lace, I Saw What You Did, Experiment in Terror, Sudden Fear* and *Strangers on a Train. Chicago Calling* and *The Slender Thread* were among the films based entirely on someone trying to contact another character by telephone. *Bells Are Ringing, The Glenn Miller Story* and *Bye Bye Birdie* had musical numbers based on telephones. Shelly Berman, Jeanne de Casalis and Billy de Wolfe are among the revue artists famous for telephone sketches. Single phone calls were of high dramatic significance in *The Spiral Staircase, Little Caesar, Fail Safe, Dr Strangelove, Murder Inc, Dial M for Murder, Call Northside 777*, and *Phone Call from a Stranger*, while the phone had a special inference in several call girl pictures including *Butterfield 8. Our Man Flint, Indiscreet, Strange Bedfellows, Come Blow Your Horn* and *It's a Mad Mad Mad Mad World* are among the many films deriving comedy from the telephone . . . while the most chilling moment in many a thriller has been the discovery that the phone is disconnected. In *The President's Analyst* the telephone company turned out to be the supreme enemy of civilization.

telephoto lens. One which brings far-off objects apparently very close, but has the disadvantage of distorting and flattening perspective.

television, arch-enemy of the film-makers, was used during the 50s as an object of derision (*The Titfield Thunderbolt, Happy Anniversary, No Down Payment, Meet Mr Lucifer*), or totally ignored. Yet it had featured in films even before World War II: *Television Spy, Murder by Television, Raffles*, and a host of science fiction serials. More recently, television studios have provided a useful background for comedy (*You Must Be Joking, A Hard Day's Night*), for thrillers (*The Glass Web, Arabesque*) and for melodramas (*Seven Days in May, The Third Secret*). The only serious movie study of the effects of television is *A Face in the Crowd*; and the funniest scenes about television programmes are probably those in *The Apartment*.

television series based on motion picture originals almost outnumber the other kind. They include *The Thin Man, The Whistler, King's Row, Casablanca, My Friend Flicka, How to Marry a Millionaire, Margie, The Roaring Twenties, I Remember Mama, Blondie, Claudia, Jungle Jim, Hawkeye, The Invisible Man, Hudson's Bay, The Asphalt Jungle, Mr Smith Goes to Washington, Father of the Bride, Life with Father, National Velvet, Bus Stop, No Time for Sergeants, Going My Way, The Greatest Show on Earth, Les Girls, Peyton Place, The Naked City, Flipper, The Virginian, Hopalong Cassidy, The Munsters* (indirectly),

The Wackiest Ship in the Army, Mr Roberts, Gidget, Please Don't Eat the Daisies, Twelve O'clock High, Dr Kildare, The Farmer's Daughter, The Long Hot Summer, Tarzan, The Rounders, The Saint, Gideon's Way, The Man Who Never Was, Batman, Mr Deeds Goes to Town, The Courtship of Eddie's Father.

TELLEGEN, LOU (1884–1954). Dutch matinée idol who made many silent films in Hollywood: *Queen Elizabeth* (12), *The Explorer* (15), *The World and Its Women* (19), *Single Wives* (23), *The Redeeming Sin* (25), etc. Published autobiography 1931: *Women Have Been Kind*.

TEMPEST, DAME MARIE (1864–1942) (Marie Susan Etherington). British stage actress whose very rare films included *Moonlight Sonata* (37), *Yellow Sands* (38).

†TEMPLE, SHIRLEY (1928–   ). American child star of the 30s, performing in short films at three. Features: *The Red-Haired Alibi* (32), *To the Last Man* (33), *Out All Night* (33), *Carolina* (34), *Mandalay* (34), *Stand Up and Cheer* (34), *Now I'll Tell* (34), *Change of Heart* (34), *Little Miss Marker* (her first star vehicle) (34), *Baby Take a Bow* (34), *Now and Forever* (34), *Bright Eyes* (34), *The Little Colonel* (35), *Our Little Girl* (35), *Curly Top* (35), *The Littlest Rebel* (35), *Captain January* (36), *Poor Little Rich Girl* (36), *Dimples* (36), *Stowaway* (36), *Wee Willie Winkie* (37), *Heidi* (37), *Rebecca of Sunnybrook Farm* (38), *Little Miss Broadway* (38), *Just around the Corner* (38), *The Little Princess* (39), *Susannah of the Mounties* (39), *The Blue Bird* (40), *Young People* (40), *Kathleen* (41), *Miss Annie Rooney* (42), *Since You Went Away* (44), *I'll Be Seeing You* (44), *Kiss and Tell* (45), *Honeymoon* (47), *The Bachelor and the Bobbysoxer* (47), *That Hagen Girl* (47), *Fort Apache* (48), *Mr Belvedere Goes to College* (49), *Adventure in Baltimore* (49), *The Story of Seabiscuit* (49), *A Kiss for Corliss* (49). Later appeared on TV in *Shirley Temple Storybook*, and in the 60s went into local California politics. Won special Academy Award 1934 'in grateful recognition of her outstanding contribution to screen entertainment'.

THE TEN COMMANDMENTS. Cecil B. de Mille made two films under this title. The 1923 version spent only half its length on the biblical story, paralleling this with a modern tale about what happens when the moral laws are broken nowadays. It starred Richard Dix, Rod la Rocque and Estelle Taylor. The 1956 version spent four hours on the Bible story alone, and with less cinematic flair than the silent picture. Charlton Heston was Moses and Yul Brynner Pharaoh.

LA TERRA TREMA (Italy 1948). A famous dramatic film written and directed by Luchino Visconti and photographed by G. R. Aldo, about a family of poor Sicilian fishermen and their struggle against exploitation.

TERRISS, ELLALINE (1871–   ). British stage actress, widow of Sir Seymour Hicks; in a few films. *Blighty* (27), *Glamour* (31), *The Iron Duke* (35), *The Four Just Men* (39), etc.

TERRY, ALICE (1899–   ) (Alice Taafe). American leading lady of the silent screen. *Not My Sister* (16), *The Four Horsemen of the Apocalypse* (21), *The Prisoner of Zenda* (23), *Mare Nostrum* (27), *The Garden of Allah* (28), etc. Married Rex Ingram and retired.

TERRY, PAUL (1887–   ). American animator, the creator of 'Terry-toons' which have been filling Fox supporting programmes for over thirty years. Now retired.

TERRY, PHILIP (1909–   ). American leading man of the 40s, mainly in second features. *The Parson of Panamint* (41), *Pan-Americana* (45), *The Lost Weekend* (45), *Seven Keys to Baldpate* (47), etc.

TERRY-THOMAS (1911–   ) (Thomas Terry Hoar-Stevens). British comedian with inimitable gap-toothed manner; has recently become Hollywood's favourite idea of the English silly ass. Also on stage and TV. *Private's Progress* (56), *Blue Murder at St Trinians* (57), *The Naked Truth* (58), *Tom Thumb* (58), *Carleton Browne of the FO* (58), *I'm All Right, Jack* (59), *School for Scoundrels* (60), *His and Hers* (61), *A Matter of Who* (62), *Bachelor Flat* (62), *The Wonderful World of the Brothers Grimm* (63), *Kill or Cure* (63), *It's a Mad Mad Mad Mad World* (63), *The Mouse on the Moon* (63), *Those Magnificent Men in Their Flying Machines* (65), *How to Murder Your Wife* (65), *You Must Be Joking* (65), *Munster Go Home* (66), *Kiss the Girls and Make Them Die* (66), *Rocket to the Moon* (67), *The Perils of Pauline* (67), *Don't Look Now* (68), *Where Were You When the Lights Went Out?* (68), *2000 Years Later* (69), *Monte Carlo or Bust* (69), etc.

TERZIEFF, LAURENT (1935–   ). French leading man. *Les Tricheurs* (58), *Le Bois des Amants* (59), *La Notte Brava* (60), *Kapo* (60), *Thou Shalt Not Kill* (61), *The Seven Deadly Sins* (62), *Ballade Pour un Voyou* (64), *Le Triangle* (65), *Le Voyage au Pere* (66), *Two Weeks in September* (67), *The Milky Way* (68), etc.

TESTER, DESMOND (1919–   ). British boy actor of the 30s. *Midshipman Easy* (35), *Tudor Rose* (36), *Sabotage* (37), *The Drum* (38), *The Stars Look Down* (39), *The Turners of Prospect Road* (47), etc.

TETZEL, JOAN (1924–   ). American leading actress with stage experience, married to Oscar Homolka. *Duel in the Sun* (46), *The Paradine Case* (47), *The File on Thelma Jordon* (50), *Joy in the Morning* (65), etc.

TETZLAFF, TED (1903–   ). American director, formerly photographer. *World Première* (41), *Riff Raff* (46), *The Window* (48), *Johnny Allegro (Hounded)* (48), *The White Tower* (50), *The Treasure *of Lost Canyon* (52), *Time Bomb* (*Terror on a Train*) (53), *Son of Sinbad* (55), *The Young Land* (57), etc.

†TEWKSBURY, PETER (1924–   ). American director, from TV (*Father Knows Best*, *My Three Sons*, etc). *Sunday in New York* (64), *Emil and the Detectives* (65), *Doctor You've Got to be Kidding* (67), *Stay Away Joe* (68).

THACKERY, BUD (1903–   ). American cinematographer, especially for Republic, where he photographed innumerable westerns and serials. Moved into TV. Recently: *Coogan's Bluff* (68).

THALBERG, IRVING (1899–1936). American producer, MGM's boy wonder of the early 30s, responsible for the literary flavour of films like *The Barretts of Wimpole Street* (34), *Mutiny on the Bounty* (35), *Romeo and Juliet* (36); also for hiring the Marx Brothers. A biography by Bob Thomas, *Thalberg*, was published in 1969.

THANK YOUR LUCKY STARS (US 1943). A typical example of the all-star musicals mounted by the big Hollywood studios during World War II—and the best of them. The idea was to gather together all the stars on the payroll doing sketches or numbers joined by a thin story line and ending in a patriotic morale-boost for the boys overseas. In the same year MGM did *Thousands Cheer* and Paramount *Star-Spangled Rhythm*; this Warner job has better songs, a more amusing story, and the bright idea of making most of the stars do things one wouldn't expect from them. Eddie Cantor, Edward Everett Horton and S. Z. Sakall did the linking.

THATCHER, TORIN (1905–   ). Tough-looking British character actor, on stage from 1923; latterly on stage again after some years in Hollywood. *General John Regan* (film debut) (34), *Major Barbara* (40), *The Captive Heart* (45), *Great Expectations* (46), *The Crimson Pirate* (52), *The Robe* (53), *Love is a Many-Splendoured Thing* (55), *Witness for the Prosecution* (57), *The Canadians* (60), *Jack the Giant Killer* (62), *The Sandpiper* (65), *Hawaii* (66), *The King's Pirate* (67), many others.

THAXTER, PHYLLIS (1921–   ). American leading lady of the 40s, recently back in character roles. Stage experience. *Thirty Seconds Over Tokyo* (debut) (44), *Weekend at the Waldorf* (45), *Bewitched* (45), *Tenth Avenue Angel* (47), *Blood on the Moon* (48), *Come Fill the Cup* (51), *Springfield Rifle* (53), *Women's Prison* (54), *The World of Henry Orient* (64), etc.

theatres have provided an effective setting for many films apart from the countless putting-on-a-show musicals. Films concerned exclusively with matters theatrical include *The Royal Family of Broadway*, *Twentieth Century*, *The Great Profile*, *The Country Girl*,

Stage Door, Heller in Pink Tights, Take the Stage, To Be or Not to Be, Main Street to Broadway, Les Enfants du Paradis, Prince of Players, The Velvet Touch, All About Eve, Curtain Up and *Variety Jubilee*, while a theatre was also the principal setting for *Those Were the Days, The Lost People, The High Terrace, Four Hours to Kill, The Phantom of the Opera* and *The Climax*. Thrillers with climaxes in a theatre include *The Thirty-Nine Steps, Torn Curtain, Charlie Chan at the Opera, Cover Girl Killer, The Westerner, The Deadly Affair, No Way to Treat a Lady* and *King Kong*; comedies include *A Night at the Opera, A Haunting We Will Go, Knock On Wood, The Intelligence Men, Trouble in Paradise, The Secret of My Success, My Learned Friend* and *Meet Mr Lucifer*. Less frequent are uses of the theatre as a setting for romance, but it served this purpose in *All This and Heaven Too, The Lady with a Little Dog,* and *Letter from an Unknown Woman*.

THESE THREE (US 1936). This was a disguised version, directed by William Wyler, of Lillian Hellman's play 'The Children's Hour' about a lesbian relationship between two schoolmistresses and the scandal caused by a malicious girl. The affair had to be changed to a more normal one. In 1962 Wyler had another go, censorship being more relaxed, and filmed the original more or less intact, with Audrey Hepburn and Shirley Maclaine. (The title in Britain was changed to *The Loudest Whisper*.)

THESIGER, ERNEST (1879–1961). Witty, skeletal-looking British character actor, on stage from 1909. Made an enjoyable film debut in *The Old Dark House* (32) as Horace Femm, and later created eccentric characters in *The Bride of Frankenstein* (35), *Henry V* (44), *Caesar and Cleopatra* (45), *The Ghosts of Berkeley Square* (47), *The Man in the White Suit* (51), *Father Brown* (54), *The Roman Spring of Mrs Stone* (61), others.

THEY WON'T FORGET (US 1937). Among the first of Hollywood's anti-lynching melodramas, this was a stark and shattering affair to come from Warners in the escapist years. Convincingly set in the deep south, diligently directed by Mervyn le Roy, and not shirking a tragic ending, it was somewhat marred by the miscasting of Claude Rains as a southern senator. Notable for the debut of sweater girl Lana Turner as the murder victim.

THE THIEF OF BAGDAD. This Arabian Nights tale was superbly filmed with Douglas Fairbanks in 1924 (US); again in 1940 (GB/US) with Sabu and some remarkable trick photography, directed by Michael Powell, Tim Whelan and Ludwig Berger; and in 1961 (Italy) with Steve Reeves.

THIELE, WILLIAM (1890–   ). German director who after *Drei von Der Tankstelle* (30) went to Hollywood but found little work apart from several Tarzan pictures.

THE THIN MAN. In Dashiell Hammett's crime novel of the 20s, the thin man is the murderer's first victim. Oddly enough the tag stuck to William Powell (not all that thin) who played Nick Charles the detective, and he starred in five sequels: *After the Thin Man* (37), *Another Thin Man* (38), *Shadow of the Thin Man* (42), *The Thin Man Goes Home* (44), *Song of the Thin Man* (46). (There was also, later, a TV series with Peter Lawford and Phyllis Kirk.) Myrna Loy played Nora Charles in all the features, and it was said that her domestic scenes with Powell in the original film marked the first time a sophisticated, affectionate marriage had been realistically portrayed on the screen.

THE THING FROM ANOTHER WORLD (US 1952). Interesting as one of the first films to combine the old horror with the new science fiction, this was a competent job but disappointingly thin and tame considering its credits. Written by Charles Lederer and photographed by Russell Harlan, it was produced by Howard Hawks (and some say also directed by him despite the credit to Christian Nyby; there are also rumours that Orson Welles had a hand). The gripping early scenes about a USAF base at the north pole threatened by a temporarily frozen 'intellectual carrot' from a flying saucer weakened when the visitor thawed out and proved to be James Arness in a metallic suit.

THINGS TO COME (GB 1935). This film from H. G. Wells' prophetic tract, though naïve in some of its dialogue scenes, provided not only a tolerably accurate forecast of World War II and the atomic bomb but splendid imaginative spectacle and a musical theme by Sir Arthur Bliss which remains fresh and stirring. William Cameron Menzies directed, and among a cast which refused to be dwarfed were Raymond Massey and Ralph Richardson.

THIRARD, ARMAND (1899–   ). French cinematographer. *Remorques* (41), *Quai des Orfevres* (47), *Manon* (49), *The Wages of Fear* (53), *Act of Love* (54), *Les Diaboliques* (54), *And God Created Woman* (56), *The Truth* (60), etc.

THE THIRD MAN (GB 1949). A lucky combination of talents gave this romantic thriller set in war-torn Vienna an almost poetic quality and an excitement which have kept it vivid. The photogenic ruins provided a suitable background for all four star actors, Joseph Cotten, Valli, Trevor Howard and Orson Welles; Graham Greene wrote a bitter, well-timed script; Robert Krasker photographed lovingly; and Carol Reed directed every scene with the surest of touches except the last one, which was perhaps misjudged. And then there was that insistent zither music by Anton Karas. . . . BFA best British film.

947

THE THIRTY-NINE STEPS. Neither film version has borne much resemblance to John Buchan's lively spy yarn apart from the hero's initial predicament and the Scottish setting for the chase. Hitchcock, however (GB 1935), working from Charles Bennett's pacy script, scattered touches of macabre comedy and romantic banter which hit just the right note; Ralph Thomas (GB 1959) reworked the same ideas stolidly and without flair. And Kenneth More, Taina Elg and Barry Jones were somehow no match for Robert Donat, Madeleine Carroll and Godfrey Tearle.

THIS GUN FOR HIRE (US 1942). This was not only a moderately intelligent though considerably reshaped version of Graham Greene's *A Gun for Sale*: it was also notable for giving Alan Ladd his first starring role as the professional killer, a role which catapulted him into the front rank of box-office attractions. Frank Tuttle directed. The story was remade in 1956 as *Short Cut to Hell*, directed by James Cagney: Robert Ivers played the gunman, but both he and the movie passed without comment.

THIS MODERN AGE. A series of current affairs two-reelers sponsored in 1946 by Rank as the British answer to 'The March of Time'. Although decently produced by Sergei Nolbandov, the monthly issues were not a popular addition to already overlong programmes, and the attempt was given up in 1949.

THOMAS, DANNY (1914–   ) (Amos Jacobs). American night club comedian and star of his own seven-year TV series. Made a few films: *The Unfinished Dance* (47), *Big City* (48), *Call Me Mister* (51), *I'll See You in My Dreams* (52), *The Jazz Singer* (53).

THOMAS, GERALD (1920–   ). British director, former editor, in films from 1946. *Time Lock* (57), *Vicious Circle* (57), *The Duke Wore Jeans* (58), *Carry On Sergeant* (58) (and all the subsequent 'Carry Ons'), *Watch Your Stern* (60), *Twice Round the Daffodils* (62), *The Big Job* (65), *Don't Lose Your Head* (66), *Follow That Camel* (67), etc.

THOMAS, JAMESON (1892–1939). British actor who usually played 'the other man'. Went to Hollywood in the early 30s but did not command leading roles. *Blighty* (27), *A Daughter of Love* (28), *Piccadilly* (29), *High Treason* (30), *Hate Ship* (30), *Elstree Calling* (30), *The Phantom President* (32), *It Happened One Night* (34), *Lives of a Bengal Lancer* (35), *Mr Deeds Goes to Town* (36) *Death Goes North* (38), etc.

THOMAS, LOWELL (1892–   ). American broadcaster and lecturer who partly controls Cinerama and appeared as travelling commentator in some of its episodes: *Search for Paradise* (58), etc.

THOMAS, OLIVE (1888–1920). American 'Ziegfeld girl' who played a few comedy roles in films. *Beatrice Fairfax* (16), *Limousine Life* (18),

The Follies Girl (19), *The Glorious Lady* (19), *Footlights and Shadows* (20), etc.

THOMAS, RALPH (1915–). British director, former trailer maker, who with producer Betty Box has tackled some ambitious subjects in a rather stolid manner. *Helter Skelter* (48), *Traveller's Joy* (49), *Appointment with Venus* (51), *Venetian Bird* (53), *Doctor in the House* (54), *Above Us the Waves* (55), *The Iron Petticoat* (56), *Campbell's Kingdom* (57), *A Tale of Two Cities* (57), *The Wind Cannot Read* (58), *The Thirty-nine Steps* (59), *No Love for Johnnie* (61), *The Wild and the Willing* (62), *Hot Enough for June* (64), *The High Bright Sun* (65), *Deadlier Than the Male* (66), *Some Girls Do* (68), etc.

THOMAS, WILLIAM C.; see PINE, WILLIAM H.

THOMPSON, CARLOS (1916–). (Juan Carlos Mundanschaffter). Argentinian stage and screen matinée idol who has made some Hollywood films: *Fort Algiers* (53), *The Flame and the Flesh* (54), *Valley of the Kings* (54), *Magic Fire* (56), etc. TV series: *Sentimental Agent* (62).

THOMPSON, MARSHALL (1926–). American leading man who began by playing quiet juvenile roles. *Reckless Age* (44), *Gallant Bess* (45), *The Romance of Rosy Ridge* (46), *Homecoming* (48), *Words and Music* (48), *The Violent Hour* (50), *My Six Convicts* (52), *Battle Taxi* (55), *To Hell and Back* (55), *Clarence the Cross-Eyed Lion* (65), *Around the World Under the Sea* (66), many others. TV series: *Angel* (60), *Daktari* (66–68).

THORBURN, JUNE (1931–1967). British leading lady with repertory experience. *The Pickwick Papers* (film debut) (53), *The Cruel Sea* (53), *True as a Turtle* (56), *Tom Thumb* (58), *The Three Worlds of Gulliver* (59), *The Scarlet Blade* (63), etc.

THORNDIKE, ANDREW (1909–). East German director who with his wife Annelie made the strident anti-Nazi documentary series *The Archives Testify*; also *The German Story*, *The Russian Miracle*, etc.

THORNDIKE, DAME SYBIL (1882–). Distinguished British stage actress who has appeared in very occasional films. *Moth and Rust* (debut) (21), *Dawn* (29), *To What Red Hell* (30), *Hindle Wakes* (31), *Tudor Rose* (36), *Major Barbara* (40), *Nicholas Nickleby* (47), *Stage Fright* (50), *The Magic Box* (51), *Melba* (53), *Alive and Kicking* (58), *Shake Hands with the Devil* (59), *Hand in Hand* (61), etc.

THORPE, JERRY (c. 1930–). American director, from TV. *The Venetian Affair* (66), *The Day of the Evil Gun* (also produced) (68), etc.

THORPE, RICHARD (1896–) (Rollo Smolt Thorpe). American director, formerly in vaudeville. *The Feminine Touch* (28), *Forgotten*

Woman (32), *The Last of the Pagans* (35), *Night Must Fall* (38**)**, *Huckleberry Finn* (39), *Tarzan Finds a Son* (39), *Wyoming* (40), *Tarzan's New York Adventure* (42), *Above Suspicion* (43), *Her Highness and the Bellboy* (45), *Fiesta* (47), *The Sun Comes Up* (48), *East of the Rising Sun* (*Malaya*) (49), *The Great Caruso* (51), *The Prisoner of Zenda* (52), *Ivanhoe* (52), *The Student Prince* (54), *Knights of the Round Table* (54), *The Prodigal* (55), *The Adventures of Quentin Durward* (56), *Jailhouse Rock* (57), *The House of the Seven Hawks* (59), *The Tartars* (60), *Fun in Acapulco* (63), *The Golden Head* (65), *That Funny Feeling* (65), *The Truth About Spring* (65), *The Scorpio Letters* (67), *Pistolero* (67), etc.

THOSE MAGNIFICENT MEN IN THEIR FLYING MACHINES (GB 1965). This amiable romp about the first London-to-Paris air race was only moderately well written by Jack Davies and directed by Ken Annakin; but it serves as an example of a big budget and a lot of stars on a wide screen being acceptable in the mid-60s in place of real talent. The primitive airplanes were the real stars. In 1969 a follow-up by the same team, this time about vintage car racing, came off less well: it was known in Britain as *Monte Carlo or Bust* and in the States as *Those Daring Young Men in their Jaunty Jalopies*.

THREE COINS IN THE FOUNTAIN (US 1954). This highly commercial film taught Hollywood the travelogue possibilities of CinemaScope to freshen up a tired story, and encouraged the trek of producers from Hollywood to locations all over the world, thus changing the face of film-making. A simple trio of romantic stories, from John Secondari's novel, the action was deftly directed by Jean Negulesco, who ten years later attempted a disguised remake under the title *The Pleasure Seekers*. But by now there was no novelty left and the picture crept by almost unnoticed.

3-D. Three-dimensional film-making had been tried in 1935 by MGM, as a gimmick involving throwaway paper glasses with one red and one green eyepiece to match the double image on the screen. In 1953, Hollywood really got the idea that this device would save an ailing industry, and a number of cheap exploitation pictures were shot in 3-D before anyone got down to the practical problem of renting out and re-collecting the necessary polaroid spectacles, which threw cinema managers into fits. *Bwana Devil* was an awful picture; *Man in the Dark* and *Fort Ti* were a shade better, except that the action kept stopping for something to be hurled at the audience; *House of Wax*, a Warner horror remake of *The Mystery of the Wax Museum*, had better production values and seemed to catch on with the public. All the studios began to make 3-D films— *Kiss Me Kate*, *The Charge at Feather River*, *Sangaree*—but by the time these were ready, trade interest had shifted to Fox's new Cinema-Scope process, which although it gave no illusion of depth was at least a different shape and didn't need glasses. Nor did it entail such problems as running both projectors at once, with consequent intervals every twenty minutes; or long pauses when the film broke in order to mutilate the second copy in precisely the same way; or one machine running a little slower than the other, with gradual loss of synchronization. The remaining 3-D films were released 'flat', and the industry breathed a sigh of relief. So did the critics, who had wondered whether they would ever again see a film which did not involve frequent violent action. The Russians did claim at the time that they were inventing a 3-D process which would not require the use of glasses, but we are still waiting for that.

THE THREE MUSKETEERS. Apart from numerous European versions, Alexandre Dumas' classic swashbuckler has been a Hollywood favourite too. Edison made a version in 1911; so did Edward Laurillard in 1913, C. V. Heinkel in 1914, and Fred Niblo (the Douglas Fairbanks spectacular) in 1921. In the last-named production the musketeers were played by Eugene Pallette, Leon Barry and George Siegmann. Walter Abel was D'Artagnan in a 1936 version for RKO, with Paul Lukas, Moroni Olsen and Onslow Stevens: Rowland V. Lee directed. Don Ameche *sang* in a 1939 musical comedy version (sometimes known as *The Singing Musketeer*) with the Ritz Brothers, no less, as the trio. Directed by Allan Dwan, it was very, very funny. Gene Kelly made an acrobatic D'Artagnan for MGM in 1948, with Van Heflin, Gig Young and Robert Coote.

THREE SMART GIRLS (US 1937). A minor domestic comedy about three teenagers who save Dad from the clutches of a gold digger and restore him to the arms of Mum, this was notable as the first feature appearance, and a highly successful one, of Deanna Durbin. Henry Koster directed this and the 1939 sequel, *Three Smart Girls Grow Up.*

THULIN, INGRID (1929–   ). Swedish leading actress, often in Ingmar Bergman's films. *Wild Strawberries* (57), *So Close to Life* (58), *The Face* (59), *The Four Horsemen of the Apocalypse* (US) (62), *Winter Light* (62), *The Silence* (63), *Return from the Ashes* (US) (65), *The War Is Over* (Fr.) (66), *Night Games* (66), *Persona* (67), *The Damned* (69), etc.

THUNDER ROCK (GB 1942). Rather belated in its message, but still one of World War II's most thoughtful films, this intriguing fantasy was about an isolationist in a lighthouse spurred to get back into the world's affairs by the ghosts of passengers drowned near the rock a hundred years before. Memorably acted by Michael Redgrave, Barbara Mullen, Lilli Palmer, Frederick Valk and James Mason.

THURBER, JAMES (1894–1961). American humorist whose chief gifts to Hollywood were the original stories of *The Secret Life of Walter Mitty* and *The Male Animal*. TV series based on his cartoons: *My World and Welcome to It* (69).

THY SOUL SHALL BEAR WITNESS (Sweden 1920). A fantasy directed by Victor Sjostrom, who also played the leading role of a drunkard whose soul is taken in death's wagon to review the misery he has caused. Remade recently in Sweden, also in France in 1940 by Julien Duvivier, as *La Charrette Fantôme*, with Pierre Fresnay as the drunkard.

TIBBETT, LAWRENCE (1897–1960). American opera star who made some films in the 30s: *Rogue Song* (30), *New Moon* (30), *Cuban Love Song* (32), *Metropolitan* (36), *Under Your Spell* (37), etc.

TIERNEY, GENE (1920–). American leading lady, a New York socialite who turned to the stage and then Hollywood. *The Return of Frank James* (debut) (40), *Tobacco Road* (41), *Hudson's Bay* (41), *Belle Starr* (41), *Sundown* (41), *The Shanghai Gesture* (42), *Rings on Her Fingers* (42), *China Girl* (43), *Heaven Can Wait* (43), *Laura* (44), *A Bell for Adano* (45), *Leave Her to Heaven* (45), *Dragonwyck* (46), *The Razor's Edge* (46), *The Iron Curtain* (48), *Where the Sidewalk Ends* (50), *On the Riviera* (51), *Never Let Me Go* (53), *Personal Affair* (GB) (54), *The Egyptian* (54), *The Left Hand of God* (55), etc.; retired; came back in *Advise and Consent* (62), *Toys in the Attic* (63), *The Pleasure Seekers* (64).

TIERNEY, LAWRENCE (1919–). American 'tough-guy' actor brother of Scott Brady. *The Ghost Ship* (44), *Dillinger* (title role) (45), *Step by Step* (46), *San Quentin* (47), *Shakedown* (50), *The Hoodlum* (51), *A Child Is Waiting* (62), *Custer of the West* (67), etc.

TIFFIN, PAMELA (1943–). American leading lady, former child model. *Summer and Smoke* (60), *One Two Three* (61), *State Fair* (61), *The Hallelujah Trail* (65), etc.

TILBURY, ZEFFIE (1863–1945). American character actress. *Werewolf of London* (35), *The Last Days of Pompeii* (35), *Maid of Salem* (37), *Balalaika* (39), *Tobacco Road* (41), *She Couldn't Say No* (45), etc.

TILL, ERIC (1929–). British director, from TV. *Hot Millions* (68), *The Walking Stick* (69).

tilt. An upward or downward camera movement.

TINGWELL, CHARLES (c. 1924–). Australian actor, now in British TV and films; usually in self-effacing roles. Early films in Australia include *Always Another Dawn* (48) and *Bitter Springs* (50); more recently *Life in Emergency Ward Ten* (58), *Cone of Silence* (60),

Murder She Said (63), *The Secret of Blood Island* (65), *Dracula—Prince of Darkness* (65), etc.

TINLING, JAMES (1889–c. 1955). American second-feature director. *Silk Legs* (27), *Arizona* (30), *Broadway* (33), *Charlie Chan in Shanghai* (35), *Pepper* (36), *45 Fathers* (37), *Mr Moto's Gamble* (38), *Riders of the Purple Sage* (41), *Sundown Jim* (42), *The House of Tao Ling* (47).

tinting has plainly gone out of fashion now that virtually all films are in colour, but in black-and-white days the use of single colours could lead to interesting effects. In the 20s and earlier it was common practice to tint night scenes blue, sunlit scenes yellow, etc.; I saw one Russian film made in 1917 in which the only scene in black-and-white was that in which the hero hanged himself! When talkies came in these colour effects were forgotten, but towards the mid-30s when colour was threatening, a tint seemed better than nothing. Films released wholly in sepia included *The Ghost Goes West, Bad Man of Brimstone, The Firefly, Maytime, The Girl of the Golden West, Dodge City, The Oklahoma Kid, Of Mice and Men* and *The Rains Came*: while the 'real' scenes of *The Wizard of Oz* were also sepia, leaving full colour until we landed in Oz. *A Midsummer Night's Dream* was released with a blue rinse, as were the water ballet reels of *A Day at the Races*. Other colours have been used for short sequences. Green for *Portrait of Jennie* (the storm), *Luck of the Irish* (the leprechaun forest) and *Lost Continent* (to obscure the poor monster animation). Red for the *Hell's Angels* battle scenes and for the flash at the end of *Spellbound* when the villain turns a gun on himself. Even monochrome has its effectiveness, as shown in *A Matter of Life and Death* and *Bonjour Tristesse*.

TIOMKIN, DMITRI (1899–   ). Russian/American composer of innumerable film scores. *Alice in Wonderland* (33), *Lost Horizon* (37), *The Great Waltz* (38), *The Moon and Sixpence* (42), *Shadow of a Doubt* (43), *Duel in the Sun* (46), *Portrait of Jennie* (48), *The Men* (50), *High Noon* (AA) (52), *The High and the Mighty* (AA) (54), *Land of the Pharaohs* (55), *The Friendly Persuasion* (56), *Giant* (56), *Night Passage* (57), *Gunfight at the O.K. Corral* (57), *The Old Man and the Sea* (AA) (58), *The Unforgiven* (60), *The Alamo* (60), *The Guns of Navarone* (61), *55 Days at Peking* (62), *The Fall of the Roman Empire* (64), many others. 1968–69 produced US/Russian film *Tschaikovsky*. Published autobiography 1960: *Please Don't Hate Me*.

TISSE, EDOUARD (1897–1961). Franco-Russian cinematographer who worked closely with Eisenstein. *Strike* (24), *The Battleship Potemkin* (25), *The General Line* (*The Old and the New*) (27), *Que Viva Mexico* (32), *Aerograd* (36), *Alexander Nevsky* (39), *Ivan the Terrible* (42 and 46), *Glinka* (54), etc.

title changes. The reason for changing any title is to make it more attractive at the box office. Even a famous play or novel may not be the right bait for film fans; so *The Private Ear and the Public Eye* becomes *The Pad and How to Use It*, *Orpheus Descending* turns into *The Fugitive Kind*, and *The Clansman* is filmed as *The Birth of a Nation*. Even when a film has been well publicized during production, the title can be changed at the whim of the producer whenever he feels that what he has on his hands is by no means a one-hundred-per-cent copper-bottomed winner. The following, for instance, are all fairly recent:

Night of the Tiger	to *Ride Beyond Vengeance*
Joyhouse	to *The Love Cage*
Whatever Happened to Cousin Charlotte?	to *Hush, Hush, Sweet Charlotte*
Act of Mercy	to *Guns of Darkness*
The Great Train Robbery	to *The Big Job*
Passage of Love	to *I Was Happy Here*
Mother Superior	to *The Trouble with Angels*
The Richmond Story	to *Alvarez Kelly*
King of the Mountain	to *Bedtime Story*
Female of the Species	to *Deadlier than the Male*
Operation Paradise	to *Kiss the Girls and Make Them Die*
Une Nouvelle Aventure de Lemmy Caution	to *Alphaville*
All in Good Time	to *Wedlocked* and finally *The Family Way*
Eight Arms to Hold You	to *Help!*
The Centurions	to *Not For Honour and Glory* and then to *Lost Command*
The White Colt	to *Run Wild, Run Free*
Monte Carlo Or Bust (GB title)	to *Those Daring Young Men in Their Jaunty Jalopies* (US title)
Grigsby	to *The Last Grenade*
The Chairman (retained in US)	to *The Most Dangerous Man in the World*

Some very well-known films were rechristened at the very last moment. *Seven Brides for Seven Brothers* was made as *Sobbin' Women*, and *Three Coins in the Fountain* as *We Believe in Love*. *The Bad and the Beautiful* was almost released as *Tribute to a Bad Man*, a title which was later used for a different movie. And *I Love Louisa*, which has never in fact been used, was the working title for no fewer than three well-known movies: *Dancing in the Dark*, *The Band Wagon* and *What a Way to Go*.

Sometimes the new title seems weaker than the original, but decisions of this kind are far from easy, being usually taken at fraught moments. *Dr Goldfoot and the Sex Machine*, for instance, had to be changed because a real Dr Goldfoot protested; so it became *Dr G and the Bikini Machine*. For years British producers have been toying with a rustic love story called *Bats with Baby Faces*, but during production it was finally decided that people would take the film for a horror story, so it became, ill-advisedly, *Sky West and Crooked*; and after a fairly calamitous British release it was changed again for world markets into *Gypsy Girl*. A recent black comedy started production as *My Last Duchess*; this was felt to be too subtle to convey the theme of light-hearted wife murder, so the title became successively, in descending order of wit, *Arrivederci Baby*, *You Just Kill Me*, and *You're Dead Right*; but before release it reverted to *Arrivederci Baby* in most of the world and *See You Later Baby* for the apparently ignorant British. Then at the last minute it was shown to Londoners as *Drop Dead Darling*. Perhaps the most desperate last-minute change happened to *Morituri*, a title which had had world-wide publicity up to and including press shows. Suddenly the chill word came from New York: patrons were staying away from the movie like flies, ninety-nine per cent of them being unable to understand the title, and the few who could considering it less than entertaining to be reminded of their own mortality. So Fox changed the title, in one of the most drastic and expensive publicity actions of recent years; but so as to retain any goodwill they had accumulated for the old title, they incorporated it, with one of the clumsiest results ever perpetrated on the public:

The Saboteur, Code Name Morituri

Some other examples of re-thinking during production:

A modernization of *Volpone* began, unpromisingly, as *The Tale of a Fox*, brightened somewhat into *Anyone for Venice?*, and was released as *The Honey Pot*; but after poor business it was shown in the States as *It Comes Up Murder*. The film of Tennessee Williams' *The Milk Train Doesn't Stop Here Any More* was announced at first as *Boom*, then *Goforth*, then *Sunburst*, before *Boom* was finally revived and given the accolade. *A Suitable Case for Treatment*, a title utterly unappealing except to the handful of TV cognoscenti, was personalized into *Morgan*, the name of the leading character—with the old title in small print underneath, presumably for luck.

When AIP began to film H. P. Lovecraft's *The House at the End of the World*, and publicized it under this title, it seemed that we might for once get a fairly subtle horror film. Alas, the treatment was more fitted to the titles under which the film was released: in Britain *Monster of Terror*, in America *Die, Monster, Die*. Then there was a film announced in Britain as *Jules Verne's Rocket to the Moon*, and in the US at *P. T. Barnum's Rocket to the Moon*. Owing to poor business the American title was abandoned and became *Those Fantastic Flying Fools*; this too was unsuccessful and the distributor finally settled on *Blast-Off*.

title changes

When the Rank Organisation decided some years ago to film Rumer Godden's novel *An Episode of Sparrows*, about children who steal from church to feed starving animals, they made a most pleasing job of it. But John Davis as distributor had not much faith in John Davis as producer, and the film was released under the title *Innocent Sinners*, with a highly dubious publicity campaign which left no doubt that the sin involved was sexual. It is almost pleasing to record that the film failed at the box-office, whereas under its original title, with a tasteful campaign, it would certainly have had reasonable if limited success. Sam Spiegel and Columbia even took a full-page ad in 'Variety' to spoof their own indecision about titling a film which started out in mid-1966 as *The Innocent*. The ad, published in December, took the form of a comic-strip conversation between two executives, as follows:

September. Mr. A: 'Let's call it *The Innocent*.'
            Mr. B: 'Not bad. But I wanna call it *The Happening*.'
October.   Mr. A: 'Let's call it *Mr. Innocent*.'
            Mr. B: 'That's better. But I wanna call it *The Happening*.'
November.   Mr. A: 'Let's call it *It's What's Happening*.'
            Mr. B: 'Very interesting. But I still wanna call it *The Happening*.'
December.   Mr. A: 'Let's call it *The Happening*.'
            Mr. B: 'Great idea. Who thought of it?'

Sometimes a film is hauled back and retitled after its first release, as a last trump card when nothing else will save the situation. John Huston's enterprising but ill-fated *Freud* was touted as *The Secret Passion*, or in some cases, even more meaninglessly, as *Freud—The Secret Pasison*. (In no guise did it take money.) Billy Wilder's mordant. *Ace in the Hole* reached the sticks as *The Big Carnival* Danny Kaye's stolid-sounding *The Inspector General* was later corrected to *Happy Times* (the title of one of its songs). In America *Mr Topaze* became *I Like Money*, and *The Sea Wall* was shown as *This Angry Age* (a title justified by nothing in the movie). When William Dieterle's superb *All That Money Can Buy* failed to please the multitude, it was variously tried out as *The Devil and Daniel Webster* and *Daniel and the Devil*. A British drama called *The Tall Headlines* was about the effect on a family when its eldest son is hanged for murder. The title was commercially a non-starter, so the film was withdrawn and later revived under the utterly cheating tag *The Frightened Bride*. And a recent ragbag of sensations which failed as *Our Incredible World* quickly re-emerged as *The Mystery and the Pleasure*.

Novels keep their original titles fairly seldom, being designed to attract a much more specialized public than the film version must command. But there may be other reasons. One presumes that Launder and Gilliatt might have kept *That Uncertain Feeling* as the title of their adaptation from Kingsley Amis' book, had it not been for the constant reissues of an old Lubitsch film of the same name and for the more recent releases of similar-sounding films such as *That Certain Feeling* and *This Happy Feeling*. So they thought up a new joke and called it *Only Two Can Play*. A unique reason for not filming one novel under its original title was that the censor forbade it: so notorious in 1932 was William Faulkner's *Sanctuary* that it had to be filmed as *The Story of Temple Drake*. (Thirty years later it was remade under the original title.)

Very often a wily distributor with reissues to sell will alter the titles in the hope of persuading exhibitors that he is offering something new. A classic reissue bill of a few years back, presented as an all-action war show, consisted of two seriously-intentioned films with hardly a battle scene between them: *The Men*, which dealt with the hospital problems of paralysed veterans, became *Battle Stripe*, and *North Star*, Goldwyn's propaganda tribute to the Russian peasants in World War II, was carefully re-edited to avoid any suspicion of communist leanings and emerged as *Armoured Attack*. Another shining example of a publicist having an eye to the main chance dates from 1942, when President Roosevelt was asked to name the base from which U.S. planes had bombed Tokyo. The President, who knew his movies, smiled and said: 'Shangri-La'. Columbia Pictures promptly put out a film called *The Lost Horizon at Shangri-La*, an edited version of their five-year-old classic *Lost Horizon*.

One British purveyor of Continental 'X' attractions has hit upon the bright idea of reviving them under their original foreign titles if an English title was previously used—and sometimes vice versa. The advantage of this is that any patron complaining of having paid to see *Le Repos du Guerrier* and getting a second helping of *Warrior's Rest* has only his own ignorance to blame. (The distributors, incidentally, had hoped to issue this particular film under the title *Love on a Pillow*, but the censor wasn't having any.)

Retitling reissues is acknowledged in the trade to be a bit naughty, but Hollywood thinks remakes are fair game. Of course, the title of a really big film is still a strong drawing card when it is remade ten or twenty years later, so presumably *Cimarron* and *Stagecoach* and *The Four Horsemen of the Apocalypse* and *The Prisoner of Zenda* can go on being remade indefinitely under the same titles, but with a change of cast for each generation. It is different with medium-budget pictures which are likely to be forgotten within a year or two: if the plot has a clever twist, why waste it? Brush up the characters, vary the location, think of a fresh title and you have an original movie . . . more or less. Well-known though it is, the basic plot of *The Asphalt Jungle* has been re-used twice by Metro since the original came out in 1950; in *The Badlanders* it had a Western setting, and in *Cairo* an Eastern. *The More the Merrier*, a 1943 comedy, recently reappeared as *Walk, Don't Run*, with Cary Grant replacing Charles Coburn. The first picture to exploit the situation in which a group of assorted people are marooned among savages after a plane crash was (probably) *Five Came Back* in 1939; it was remade as *Back from Eternity* in 1955, and ten years later *Sands of the Kalahari* trod very similar ground except that the savages had become baboons; while *The Flight of the Phoenix* was pretty similar, too, despite its emphasis on re-building the plane. The version of *The Maltese Falcon* which everyone remembers was made in 1941 by John Huston, but Warners had also made talkies of the story in 1932 and 1936, the latter disguised as *Satan Met a Lady*; and Huston himself spoofed the plot in *Beat the Devil* (1954). Warners, in fact, are way ahead in this particular field. The plot of *Kid Galahad*, a successful boxing picture, was remade four years later as *The Wagons Roll at Night*, with the sport changed to lion-taming; *Tiger Shark* was recast and became *Manpower*; while a 1932 gangster movie called *The Mouthpiece* turned up in 1940 as *The Man Who Talked Too Much* and in 1955 as *Illegal*. Raymond Chandler's detective stories *Farewell My Lovely* and *The High Window* (American titles: *Murder My Sweet* and *The Brasher Doubloon*) were filmed straight in the mid-40s, but each had in fact appeared twice before on celluloid, disguised as adventures of The Falcon and Michael Shayne. Four famous films remade as Westerns were *The Sea Wolf*, *The Petrified Forest*, *Kiss of Death* and *House of Strangers*; they became *Barricade*, *Escape in the Desert*, *The Fiend Who Walked the West* and *Broken Lance*.

It seems fair enough for a famous film to get a new title when music is added: *Pygmalion* can change to *My Fair Lady*, *The Women* to *The Opposite Sex*, *Anna and the King of Siam* to *The King and I*. But was it quite proper to remake *Love Affair* and call it *An Affair To Remember*, *Vessel of Wrath* and call it *The Beachcomber*, *My Favourite Wife* and call it *Move Over Darling*? Here are a few others to ponder over:

Bachelor Mother (39)	to *Bundle of Joy* (56)
High Sierra (40)	to *I Died a Thousand Times* (55)
Outward Bound (30)	to *Between Two Worlds* (44)
Dark Victory (39)	to *Stolen Hours* (64)
To Have and Have Not (44)	to *The Breaking Point* (50) and *The Gun Runner* (56)
Resurrection (27 and 31)	to *We Live Again* (35)
The Front Page (30)	to *His Girl Friday* (40)
Morning Glory (32)	to *Stage Struck* (57)
Shanghai Express (32)	to *Peking Express* (51)
Lady for a Day (33)	to *A Pocketful of Miracles* (62)

It Happened One Night (34)	to *You Can't Run Away from It* (56)
Little Miss Marker (34)	to *Sorrowful Jones* (49)
The Mystery of the Wax Museum (32)	to *House of Wax* (52)
Rome Express (33)	to *Sleeping Car to Trieste* (48)
An American Tragedy (32)	to *A Place in the Sun* (52)
Oh Mr Porter (38)	to *Up the Creek* (58)
Waterloo Bridge (31 and 40)	to *Gaby* (55)
Red Dust (32)	to *Mogambo* (54)
The Animal Kingdom (32)	to *One More Tomorrow* (46)
The Street With No Name (48)	to *House of Bamboo* (55)
The Ghost Breakers (40)	to *Scared Stiff* (53)
The Millionaire (30)	to *That Way With Women* (47)
Ceiling Zero (35)	to *International Squadron* (39)
Ball of Fire (41)	to *A Song is Born* (48)
Libelled Lady (36)	to *Easy to Wed* (46)
Mother Carey's Chickens (40)	to *Summer Magic* (60)
The Major and the Minor (42)	to *You're Never Too Young* (55)
Nothing Sacred (37)	to *Living It Up* (53)
The Informer (35)	to *Up Tight* (68)

If the borrowing is admitted in the credits of the remake, it doesn't seem so much like cheating; but two fairly recent examples are inexcusable. One of Hitchcock's most celebrated thrillers, *Shadow of a Doubt*, was quietly remade by Universal as a second feature known in the US as *Step Down to Terror* and in Britain as *The Silent Stranger*; while anyone watching a Warner second called *Law versus Gangster* might recognize not only the storyline of *White Heat* (49) but most of the action sequences from the original, including long shots of Jimmy Cagney.

The most remade, and disguised, film, is probably the 1932 Cooper-Schoedsack thriller *The Most Dangerous Game*, released in Britain as *The Hounds of Zaroff*. It was remade in 1944 as *Johnny Allegro* (*Hounded* in Britain), and in 1946 as *A Game of Death*. In 1956 it was modernized as *Run for the Sun*; and it can't be long now before someone has another shot at it.

There are, of course, cases where a change of title is logical, to avoid having two films of the same name in release. *Gaslight*, Thorold Dickinson's highly-acclaimed Victorian thriller, was released in Britain in 1940. Metro subsequently bought up the negative and released their remake in 1943, as *Gaslight* in the US, but in Britain, to avoid confusion, as *The Murder in Thornton Square*. Later some copies of the original were released in the US under the inexplicable title *Angel Street*. Similarly, the British farce *Sailor Beware* was released in the US as *Panic in the Parlor* to avoid confusion with a Martin and Lewis comedy. Universal's 1964 version of *The Killers* was first intended to be known as *Johnny*

North, but the original title was adopted at the last minute; so when the 1947 version was released to TV, it had to be called *A Man Afraid*. And the Marilyn Monroe *Bus Stop* was shown on TV as *The Wrong Kind of Girl* because a TV series was thought to have worn out the welcome of the original title.

The case of *The Children's Hour* is complicated but instructive. When William Wyler first, in 1936, came to film this play about lesbians, the code compelled him to emasculate it, so rather than promise what he couldn't give he changed the title to *These Three*. In 1962 he remade it with full force and kept the original title; but in Britain, where the play was not widely known, *The Children's Hour* was felt not to accord with the film's 'X' certificate, and the picture was released as *The Loudest Whisper*.

The industry has long had its favourite title words, though most of them have no more justification in fact than superstitions. A producer is still encouraged by front office to call his film *The Big* this or *The Great* that, despite the fact that hundreds of others have done so before him and even these trusted crowd-pulling epithets are subject to the law of diminishing returns. During the 30s, *Murder* and *Death* were surprisingly well thought of, and later we had epidemics of *Naked, Man, Woman, Girl, Lady, Violent, High, Long, Night, Song, Teenage, Party, Thunder, Beach* and *Spy*. (The most evocative Christian name, it seems, is *Johnny*, which during the last twenty years or so has been the word preceding such diverse title epithets as *Allegro, Angel, Belinda, O'Clock, Cool, Concho, Dark, Frenchman, Guitar, Holiday, In the Clouds, One-Eye, Rocco, Stool Pigeon, Tremain*, and *Trouble*.)

During the last few years the industry has apparently found *Operation* to be a most useful ingredient of a title, almost a cure-all. You could tack it on to almost anything and come up with something appealing to the masses, as in *Operation Murder, Operation Bikini, Operation Eichmann, Operation Snatch, Operation Mad Ball, Operation Pacific, Operation Amsterdam, Operation Petticoat*. At the height of Sean Connery's sudden world-wide popularity, an old British Service comedy called *On the Fiddle*, in which he appeared as a gormless private, was dusted off for the American market as *Operation SNAFU* and did big business. (SNAFU is an American army term which can be bowdlerized as 'situation normal, all fowled up'.) And when Cary Grant's comedy *Father Goose* did less than was expected at the box-office, the posters were redesigned to make the title look like *Operation Father Goose*. So imagine the shock MGM had when its all-star spy thriller *Operation Crossbow* failed to reach the box-office heights, and market research insisted that the title was to blame. 'It sounds like Robin Hood' was the cry from the Mid-West. A change was obviously in order, and what did the picture end up as? *The Great Spy Mission*. You can't beat subtlety.

There are unfavourite words too. Wherever films are bought and sold it has long been whispered that there can be no hope of box-office success when the title contains the word *Miracle*. Instances cited include *The Miracle of Morgan's Creek*, *The Modern Miracle*, *The Miracle Worker*, *Miracle in Milan*, *The Miracle of Fatima*, *The Miracle of the Bells*, and *The Miracle* itself. It isn't surprising that such films are sometimes retitled, but the odd thing is that the alternatives are so unappealing. The delightful *Miracle on 34th Street*, for instance, went out dolefully to Britishers as *The Big Heart*, *A Miracle Can Happen* became *On Our Merry Way*, *Miracle of the White Stallions* changed to *Flight of the White Stallions* (but still did no business).

Another highly suspect word in Britain is *Experiment*, despite the success of Quatermass; indeed there seems little reason for this phobia, but *Experiment in Terror* was changed to *The Grip of Fear* on account of it, and it is true that little trade was drummed up by *Experiment Perilous*, *Experiment Alcatraz* or *Experiment in Evil*.

Titles are often used again to cover plots quite different from the original. Since 1942, for instance, there have been three films called *Nightmare*, none of them in any way connected; indeed, one was a remake of another film called *Fear in the Night*, while a second owed more than a little of its plot to *The Thirty-nine Steps*. When *Monkey Business* appeared in 1951, it was a Cary Grant comedy about rejuvenation, not a remake of the Marx Brothers extravaganza released in 1931; but the latter movie, then being revived, was withdrawn by arrangement between the two renters concerned so that it should not harm the business of the new arrival.

By far the majority of title switches are in fact sea changes. When the title has to be translated into another language, it can be affected by anything from local idioms to national characteristics, and the often weird results are beyond the comfortable scope of these notes. But simple transatlantic changes, in the same language, between Great Britain and the US, are a study in themselves, and can offer a surprising amount of insight into national psychology.

Taking the eastward direction first, it is accepted that Hollywood gained its early stranglehold on British audiences because the audiences liked what they saw and clamoured for more. Yet to this day there are many facets of the American way of life which British renters think their customers won't stomach. Obviously, the names of American politicians, sportsmen and less familiar entertainers will be the first to go, with such transitions as:

Tennessee Johnson	to *The Man on America's Conscience*
Darby's Rangers	to *The Young Invaders*
Jim Thorpe, All-American	to *Man of Bronze*
Captain John Smith and Pocahontas	to *Burning Arrows*

title changes

Abe Lincoln in Illinois	to *Spirit of the People*
The Great John L.	to *A Man Called Sullivan*
Chief Crazy Horse	to *Valley of Fury*
The Bob Mathias Story	to *The Flaming Torch*
The Helen Morgan Story	to *Both Ends of the Candle*

Even the devil has a different nickname in the US, so *Alias Nick Beal* had to become *The Contact Man* (and the film lost some of its point).

Of course there are hundreds of American phrases and allusions incomprehensible to British ears. Here are some of the changes occasioned by that particular difficulty:

Miss Grant Takes Richmond	to *Innocence Is Bliss*
Buck Privates	to *Rookies*
It's in the Bag (new in 1945)	to *The Fifth Chair*
Pot O' Gold	to *The Golden Hour*
The Petty Girl	to *Girl of the Year*
(in northern Britain, a petty is a lavatory)	
The Big Boodle	to *A Night in Havana*
The Catered Affair	to *Wedding Breakfast*
Sorority Girl	to *The Bad One*
Dead Ringer	to *Dead Image*
Dragstrip Riot	to *The Reckless Age*
The Fuller Brush Girl	to *The Affairs of Sally*
Hot Rod Gang	to *Fury Unleashed*
The Wheeler Dealers	to *Separate Beds*
Take Me Out to the Ball Game	to *Everybody's Cheering*
The Bachelor and the Bobby-soxer	to *Bachelor Knight*
The WAC from Walla Walla	to *Army Capers*
Never Wave at a WAC	to *The Private Wore Skirts*
Gobs and Gals	to *Cruising Casanovas*
Hallelujah I'm a Bum	to *Hallelujah I'm a Tramp*
(bum in Britain is a vulgarism for backside)	
Love Is a Ball	to *All This and Money Too*
Off Limits	to *Military Policemen*
(the British equivalent is 'out of bounds')	
Synanon	to *Get Off My Back*
Sob Sister	to *The Blonde Reporter*
Sons of the Desert	to *Fraternally Yours*
Angels in the Outfield	to *Angels and the Pirates*
Young Man with a Horn	to *Young Man of Music*
Lafayette Escadrille	to *Hell Bent for Glory*

Dancing Co-Ed	to	*Every Other Inch a Lady*
Never Give a Sucker an Even Break	to	*What a Man*
The Bank Dick	to	*The Bank Detective*
Mail Order Bride	to	*West of Montana*
Spinout	to	*California Holiday*
Scudda-Hoo Scudda-Hay	to	*Summer Lightning*
A Girl, A Guy and a Gob	to	*The Navy Steps Out*
The Flim Flam Man	to	*One Born Every Minute*
Sorority House	to	*That Girl from College*
Summer Stock	to	*If You Feel Like Singing*
Buckskin Frontier	to	*The Iron Road*
Eight on the Lam	to	*Eight on the Run*
Lady of Burlesque	to	*Striptease Lady*
I, Jane Doe	to	*Diary of a Bride*

In 1951 a film called *The Enforcer* (which has no British equivalent) was translated as *Murder Inc*. This caused some confusion when a second film called *Murder Inc* came along a few years later.

Even American place-names are thought by British renters to be off-putting—despite the success of films like *Arizona*, *Texas*, *Union Pacific*, *In Old Oklahoma*, and hundreds of others. Anyway, this is what happened in a few cases:

That Jane from Maine	to	*It Happened to Jane*
From Hell to Texas	to	*Manhunt*
The Doolins of Oklahoma	to	*The Great Manhunt*
Castle on the Hudson	to	*Years Without Days*
Indianapolis Speedway	to	*Devil on Wheels*
Christmas in Connecticut	to	*Indiscretion*
The Young Philadelphians	to	*The City Jungle*
Chicago Masquerade	to	*Little Egypt*
The Lady from Boston	to	*Pardon My French*
Washington Story	to	*Target for Scandal*
Little Big Horn	to	*The Fighting Seventh*
Kansas City Confidential	to	*The Secret Four*
Waco	to	*The Outlaw and the Lady*
The View from Pompey's Head	to	*Secret Interlude*
Saskatchewan	to	*O'Rourke of the Royal Mounted*
Broadway Bill	to	*Strictly Confidential*
Alleghany Uprising	to	*The First Rebel*
An Annapolis Story	to	*The Blue and the Gold*
The Whistle at Eaton Falls	to	*Richer Than the Earth*

Even folksy humour as evidenced by *Aaron Slick from Punkin Crick*, or by *Curtain Call at Cactus Crick*, is thought to be impermissible. These two films came through, respectively, as *Marshmallow Moon* and *Take the Stage*.

The British are also very dubious of propaganda, or anything that smacks of old-fashioned Yankee jingoism. It just has to be put down, as follows:

America, America	to *The Anatolian Smile* (the thought processes involved here are beyond guesswork)
Stars and Stripes Forever	to *Marching Along*
An American Guerilla in the Philippines	to *I Shall Return*
First Yank into Tokyo	to *Mask of Fury*
A Yank in Indo-China	to *Hidden Secret*
The Magnificent Yankee	to *The Man with Thirty Sons* (the joke couldn't be intentional, one supposes)
Mission Over Korea	to *Eyes of the Skies*
Captain Carey, USA	to *After Midnight*
An American Dream	to *See You in Hell, Darling*
All American	to *The Winning Way*

How Britishers ever let *Yankee Doodle Dandy* through, I just don't know. But quotations from American patriotic songs are obviously OK as the British won't know the context: the fact that such titles as *Halls of Montezuma, To the Shores of Tripoli* and *So Proudly We Hail* are meaningless to them is apparently of no importance.

Sometimes there are censorship reasons, obvious or not, why an American title just won't do in Britain. Take *BF's Daughter*, for instance; although the title of a John Marquand novel, it had to become *Polly Fulton* in Britain, where a BF is a bloody fool. The monarchy must be protected, so *The Royal Bed* became *The Queen's Husband* and *Royal Wedding* turned into *Wedding Bells*. *A Royal Scandal* was obviously unthinkable: it turned up as *Czarina*. Religion sets similar problems: *The Man Who Played God*, in case anyone got the same idea, became *The Silent Voice*. *Damn Yankees*, being both offensive and over-American, was changed to *What Lola Wants*, and quickly sank without trace.

Suggestions of sex must obviously be toned down for strait-laced Britishers:

Vice Squad	to *The Girl in Room 17*
Girls in the Night	to *Life After Dark*
Models Inc	to *That Kind of Girl*
I Was a Male War Bride	to *You Can't Sleep Here*
Professional Sweetheart	to *Imaginary Sweetheart*

Yet currently *Any Wednesday* is showing as *Bachelor Girl Apartment*.

Excess of any kind seems to scare British renters. When the gangster films of the early 30s were causing a press storm, the obvious solution was to tone down not the films but the titles. Who could object to *Public Enemy* when it became *Enemies of the*

Public? This devious change officially made the public, not the gangster, into the hero. *The Hatchet Man* became *The Mysterious Mr Wong*, *I am a Fugitive from a Chain Gang* lost its last four words, *Scarface* was subtitled *The Shame of a Nation*. Weirdest of all (it must have had a very adaptable plot-line), *Public Enemy's Wife* became *G-Man's Wife*.

Much later, *Confessions of an Opium Eater* became *Evils of Chinatown*, *Son of Slade* (a very violent Western) became *Texas Rose*, *The Bottom of the Bottle* became *Beyond the River*, *The Violent Men* became *Rough Company*, and *Scandal Sheet* became *The Dark Page*. Even *The Killer That Stalked New York*, in which the killer was smallpox, became *Frightened City*; and a moving little drama called *The Judge Steps Out* was shown as *Indian Summer* (a British judge 'stepping out' was apparently unthinkable).

At least on one occasion the British were less sensitive than their American cousins. Agatha Christie's murder puzzle *Ten Little Niggers* was filmed by René Clair in 1945—in America, where the title could not be used. The nursery rhyme was rewritten, and the picture became *Ten Little Indians*. This brought more protests from the minority groups, so it was released as *And Then There Were None*. But Britons staunchly saw it under the original title, despite the fact that the china figures were plainly Indians, and only Indians were mentioned in the dialogue. The recent remake settled firmly on Indians all round, which made it less puzzling.

When two versions of a film exist, and both are sold to TV, the earlier one is sometimes given a different title. Thus you may come across something called *Forbidden Alliance* which turns out to be the Laughton version of *The Barretts of Wimpole Street*; similarly *Flight Commander* is the 1930 *Dawn Patrol*, *Tops is the Limit* is the Bing Crosby *Anything Goes*, *The Wrong Kind of Girl* is *Bus Stop* (this to avoid confusion with a TV series), and *Oriental Dream* is the Ronald Colman *Kismet*.

British renters seem convinced that no audience can see a joke in a title. This often deprives we Britishers of a choice morsel of wit. Not, I grant you, in *Who Killed Doc Robbin?* (shown as *Sinister House*) or *Callaway Went Thataway* (shown as *The Star Said No*). But surely we might have kept *State of the Union* rather than *The World and His Wife*, *The Desk Set* instead of *His Other Woman*, *Advance to the Rear* instead of *Company of Cowards*, *Take a Letter Darling* and not *Green-Eyed Woman*? I might have gone to see something called *The Bar Sinister*, but not *It's a Dog's Life*. And how dull for *I Can Get It For You Wholesale* (now on TV as *Only the Best!*) to be shown as *This Is My Affair*—especially as the latter is the rejected American title of a Robert Taylor movie shown in Britain as *His Affair*. (Got that?)

Indeed, when all allowances have been made, some title changes must remain inexplicable. It isn't surprising that Universal, having filmed J. M. Barrie's *Alice Sit by the Fire*, should feel like changing the title. But why, for America, did they settle on *Darling How Could You*, and for Britain, *Rendezvous*? One agrees with the British distributor that *Requiem for a Heavyweight* won't break any box-office records. But then, nor will *Blood Money*. Why did the concise *Edge of the City* revert in Britain to the title of its original story, *A Man Is Ten Feet Tall*? And at a time when Alan Ladd and others were doing very nicely with one-word titles like *Saigon*, *Calcutta*, *China* and *Santiago*, why was *Malaya* shown in Britain as *East of the Rising Sun* (which is geographically inaccurate of Malaya anyway)?

Here are some other curious fates suffered by American titles at British hands:

Kiss the Blood Off My Hands	to *Blood on My Hands*
Abbott and Costello Meet Frankenstein	to *Abbott and Costello Meet the Ghosts*
Out of the Past	to *Build My Gallows High*
Walk East on Beacon	to *Crime of the Century*
I, Mobster	to *The Mobster*
Savage Wilderness	to *The Last Frontier*
The Fortune Hunter	to *The Outcast*
The Strange One	to *End as a Man*
Three Stripes in the Sun	to *The Gentle Sergeant*
Tank Commandos	to *Tank Commando* (did they shorten it?)
The Whistle at Eaton Falls	to *Richer than the Earth*
Million Dollar Mermaid	to *The One-Piece Bathing Suit*
Bend of the River	to *Where the River Bends*
Edge of Doom	to *Stronger Than Fear*
Count the Hours	to *Every Minute Counts*
Holiday	to *Free to Live* (also released as *Unconventional Linda*)
Conquest	to *Marie Walewska*
Southwest Passage	to *Camels West* (even the direction changed)
Saturday's Hero	to *Idols in the Dust*
Manfish	to *Calypso*
At Gunpoint	to *Gunpoint!*
Last of the Comanches	to *The Sabre and the Arrow*
Navy Wife	to *Mother, Sir*
The Big Land	to *Stampeded*
The Midnight Story	to *Appointment with a Shadow*
The Trap	to *The Baited Trap*
Top Secret Affair	to *Their Secret Affair*
The Poppy is also a Flower	to *Danger Grows Wild*
The Fortune Cookie	to *Meet Whiplash Willie*

Pillars of the Sky	to *The Tomahawk and the Cross*
South Sea Sinner	to *East of Java*
A Lovely Way to Die	to *A Lovely Way to Go*
Susan and God	to *The Gay Mrs Trexel*
Caper of the Golden Bulls	to *Carnival of Thieves*
The Mad Doctor	to *A Date With Destiny*
Underworld (1927)	to *Paying the Penalty*
The Corrupt Ones	to *The Peking Medallion*
The Whole Town's Talking	to *Passport to Fame*
Mr Winkle Goes to War	to *Arms and the Woman*
Claudelle Inglish	to *Young and Eager*
Will Success Spoil Rock Hunter?	to *Oh! For a Man*
Pride of the Marines	to *Forever in Love*
Three Stripes in the Sun	to *The Gentle Sergeant*
They Shall Have Music	to *Melody of Youth*
The True Story of Jesse James	to *The James Brothers*
Love from a Stranger	to *A Stranger Walked In*

In particular, since horror films always keep their market, which is based on an appetite for excess, why the following fairly recent attempts to tone down the bogeymen?

Frankenstein Versus the Space Monster	to *Duel of the Space Monsters*
Blood of Dracula	to *Blood Is My Heritage*
The Hideous Sun-Demon	to *Blood on His Lips*
The Night Monster	to *House of Mystery*
The Astounding She-Monster	to *Mysterious Invader*
Teenage Cavemen	to *Out of the Darkness*
Revenge of the Colossal Man	to *The Terror Strikes*
Attack of the Giant Leeches	to *Demons of the Swamp*
The Ape Man	to *Lock Your Doors*
The Corpse Vanishes	to *The Case of the Missing Brides*

It is rare for British renters deliberately to toughen up American titles. But it happened to *A Woman's Devotion* which became *War Shock*, to *Dino* (*Killer Dino*), and to *No Place To Land* (*Man Mad*). There were also two occasions when Hollywood chose British adventure themes but did them so badly that they had to be disguised: *Royal African Rifles* became *Storm Over Africa*, and *El Alamein* was released as *Desert Patrol*. The prize for falsification should probably go to the witch-hunting *I Married a Communist*, which RKO played in Britain as *The Woman on Pier 13*—a title 'justified' by an incident at the very end of the picture.

The westward traffic to America seems to keep relatively few British titles intact, the reasons for change being usually to substitute the concrete for the allusive and action for subtlety, in other words to suggest excitements of the kind not provided by the

967

picture. Consider the following examples in which sex has been made to rear its head:

Summer of the Seventeenth Doll	to	Season of Passion
A Tale of Five Cities	to	A Tale of Five Women
The Romantic Age	to	Naughty Arlette
The World Ten Times Over	to	Pussycat Alley
Catch Us If You Can	to	Having a Wild Weekend
Our Girl Friday	to	The Adventures of Sadie
London Town	to	My Heart Goes Crazy
The Forsyte Saga	to	That Forsyte Woman
Lady Hamilton	to	That Hamilton Woman
The Beauty Jungle	to	Contest Girl
The System	to	The Girl-Getters
Love Story	to	A Lady Surrenders
Trottie True	to	The Gay Lady
Portrait from Life	to	The Girl in the Painting
The Last Page	to	Manbait
Downhill	to	When Boys Leave Home
Sabotage	to	A Woman Alone
Young and Innocent	to	The Girl Was Young
Who Goes There?	to	The Passionate Sentry
My Teenage Daughter	to	Teenage Bad Girl
Waterfront	to	Waterfront Women
The Last Days of Dolwyn	to	Woman of Dolwyn
I See a Dark Stranger	to	The Adventuress
Ballad in Blue	to	Blues For Lovers
English Without Tears	to	Her Man Gilbey
Knave of Hearts	to	Lover Boy
Happy Ever After	to	Tonight's the Night
The Weak and the Wicked	to	Young and Willing
Yield to the Night	to	Blonde Sinner

A general toughening process is evident in the following changes:

The Informers (formerly The Snout)	to	Underworld Informers
HMS Defiant	to	Damn the Defiant
Vengeance	to	The Brain
The Woman in Question	to	Five Angles on Murder
Cosh Boy	to	The Slasher
Latin Quarter	to	Frenzy
The Seekers	to	Land of Fury
Time Bomb	to	Terror on a Train
There Is Another Sun	to	Wall of Death
The Smallest Show on Earth	to	Big Time Operators
Odd Man Out	to	Gang War
Busman's Honeymoon	to	Haunted Honeymoon

The Planter's Wife	to	*Outpost in Malaya*
Rough Shoot	to	*Shoot First*
St Martin's Lane	to	*Sidewalks of London*
Serious Charge	to	*A Touch of Hell*
Teheran	to	*The Plot to Kill Roosevelt*
White Cradle Inn	to	*High Fury*
The Late Edwina Black	to	*Obsessed*
Britannia Mews	to	*The Forbidden Street*

More particularly, observe from the following how unacceptable are quotations and allusions, which are invariably replaced by something unmistakably personal, full of the promise of action:

Dangerous Moonlight	to	*Suicide Squadron*
Singlehanded	to	*Soldier of the King*
Seagulls over Sorrento	to	*Crest of the Wave*
Life for Ruth	to	*Walk in the Shadow*
Derby Day	to	*Four Against Fate*
Ill Met by Moonlight	to	*Night Ambush*
A Terrible Beauty	to	*Night Fighters*
The Red Beret	to	*Paratrooper*
A Matter of Life and Death	to	*Stairway to Heaven*
The Full Treatment	to	*Stop Me Before I Kill*
Fortune Is a Woman	to	*She Played with Fire*
The Million Pound Note	to	*Man with a Million*
The White Unicorn	to	*Bad Sister*
A Town Like Alice	to	*The Rape of Malaya*
Seven Thunders	to	*The Beasts of Marseilles*
Cry the Beloved Country	to	*African Fury*
The Naked Truth	to	*Your Past Is Showing*
The Sound Barrier	to	*Breaking the Sound Barrier*
The High Bright Sun	to	*McGuire Go Home*
The Gift Horse	to	*Glory at Sea*
The Small Voice	to	*The Hideout*
Obsession	to	*The Hidden Room*
Where No Vultures Fly	to	*Ivory Hunter* (which is just what the hero wasn't)
The Way to the Stars	to	*Johnny in the Clouds*
Morning Departure	to	*Operation Disaster*
The Man Who Watched Trains Go By	to	*Paris Express*
Rich and Strange	to	*East of Shanghai*
The Small Back Room	to	*Hour of Glory*
The First of the Few	to	*Spitfire*
The Man Within	to	*The Smugglers*
Stranger in the House	to	*Cop-Out*
To Dorothy a Son	to	*Cash on Delivery*
Escapement	to	*The Electronic Monster*

The Quatermass Experiment	to	*The Creeping Unknown*
Quatermass II	to	*Enemy from Space*
Quatermass and the Pit	to	*Five Million Years to Earth*
Pimpernel Smith	to	*Mister V*
49th Parallel	to	*The Invaders*
The First of the Few	to	*Spitfire*
The Passionate Friends	to	*One Woman's Story*

It appears that America does not take to any title formed by a character's name: not, at least, if it's a British character:

Father Brown	to	*The Detective*
Captain Clegg	to	*Night Creatures*
Barnacle Bill	to	*All at Sea*
Albert RN	to	*Break to Freedom*

It seems too that when the British go in for horror they are a shade too reticent about it:

City of the Dead	to	*Horror Hotel*
The Quatermass Experiment	to	*The Creeping Unknown*
The Trollenberg Terror	to	*The Crawling Eye*
Night of the Demon	to	*Curse of the Demon*
Night of the Eagle	to	*Burn, Witch, Burn*
Fanatic	to	*Die, Die, My Darling*

Fashion has a lot to do with title changes. The spy vogue, for instance, produced the following amendments:

The Intelligence Men	to	*Spylarks*
Hot Enough for June	to	*Agent 8¾*
Licensed to Kill	to	*The Second Best Secret Agent in the Whole Wide World*

But then it seems spies were just as popular way back in 1939, when a Rex Harrison comedy called *Ten Days in Paris* turned up in the US as *Spy in the Pantry*.

Sometimes American distributors of British films have the excuse of unintelligibility for their title changes. It was reasonable enough that *The Chiltern Hundreds* (pretty unintelligible to most Britons, too) should become *The Amazing Mr Beecham*, and that *The Card* should be translated as *The Promoter*. Similarly *The Guinea Pig* means less to an American audience than *The Outsider*. *The Battle of the River Plate* is how we remember the famous naval action of 1939; but to an American audience *Pursuit of the Graf Spee* pinpoints it better as well as being more actionful. And *I Live in Grosvenor Square* just might perplex Mid-Westerners, who can immediately grasp *A Yank in London*.

There are some words which the American code will not, or would not, allow. *Fanny by Gaslight*, having possibilities of *double entendre*, must change to *Man of Evil*; *The Rake's Progress*, Hogarth or not, emerges as *Notorious Gentleman*, and *The Passionate Friends* as *One Woman's Story*. The celebrated stand of the Hays Office to the effect that the word 'behind' is impermissible unless immediately followed by a noun, does not alas appear to have affected any British titles. (Under this ruling, a certain well-known poem would have to begin: 'If winter comes, can Spring be far in back of?')

Ealing's group of Scottish comedies survived the Atlantic crossing quite pleasingly: *Whisky Galore* changed to *Tight Little Island*, *Rockets Galore* to *Mad Little Island*, and *The Maggie* to *High and Dry*. But it would be interesting to hear, in view of the honourable box-office history of Stevenson's schizophrenic doctor, why *The Two Faces of Dr Jekyll* was changed to *House of Fright*. Even less understandable is the change of the British *Give Us This Day*, taken from a story called *Christ in Concrete*. One can sympathize with the distributor's reluctance to use either of these alternatives, but what he finally hit on, *Salt to the Devil*, is equally unlikely to have sold any tickets. And why has *I Was Happy Here* become *Time Lost and Time Remembered*?

A curious thing happened when the sombre historical romance *Saraband for Dead Lovers* crossed the water. One might reasonably have expected something more punchy, less downbeat; instead it was simply shortened to *Saraband*. Oddlier and oddlier *Tomorrow We Live* was released in the States as *At Dawn We Die* . . .

Let me conclude with three personal favourites. Whoever rechristened the story of deaf little *Mandy* as *The Crash of Silence* surely deserves some kind of prize. The runner-up, perhaps, is the gentleman who discarded *The Woman with No Name* in favour of *Her Panelled Door*. And a special award for topicality. That mild theatrical comedy *The Amorous Prawn* would not normally have expected much American exposure. But its plot line made it possible to play it very profitably in the States, just after a certain well-reported British scandal, as *The Playgirl and the War Minister*.

TOBACCO ROAD (US 1941). Generally regarded as a minor film in the John Ford canon, this adaptation of Erskine Caldwell's savage picture of the southern 'poor whites' was successfully played for laughs and a few tears, and has grown more pleasing with the years. Among the apathetic, even stupid, but delightfully resilient characters, Charley Grapewin's performance as Jeeter stands out as something rare and wholly attractive; there is interesting work, too, by Marjorie Rambeau, Elizabeth Patterson, William Tracy and Slim Summerville.

TO BE OR NOT TO BE (US 1942). A bitter farce remarkable for the furore it caused on its release because it found humour in the Nazi occupation of Warsaw. Dealing with a troupe of actors who outwit the Nazis, it seems now not only inoffensive but funnier than it was at the time, with a string of running jokes put over as only Ernst

Lubitsch knew how. Carole Lombard, whose last film this was, and Jack Benny were perfect comedy leads, and the cast included Sig Ruman, Stanley Ridges, Lionel Atwill, Felix Bressart and Tom Dugan.

TOBIAS, GEORGE (1901–). American character actor with stage experience. *Saturday's Children* (debut) (40), *City for Conquest* (40), *Sergeant York* (41), *Yankee Doodle Dandy* (42), *This Is the Army* (43), *Thank Your Lucky Stars* (43), *Between Two Worlds* (44), *Objective Burma* (45), *Mildred Pierce* (46), *Sinbad the Sailor* (47), *Rawhide* (50), *The Glenn Miller Story* (53), *The Seven Little Foys* (55), *A New Kind of Love* (63), *The Glass Bottom Boat* (66), many others. TV series: *Hudson's Bay, Adventures in Paradise, Bewitched.*

TOBIN, DAN (c. 1909–). Lightweight American character actor. *Woman of the Year* (41), *Undercurrent* (46), *The Big Clock* (48), *The Velvet Touch* (49), *Dear Wife* (52), *Wedding Breakfast* (56), etc. TV series: *Perry Mason* (57–66).

TOBIN, GENEVIEVE (1904–). Vivacious American actress of French parentage. Mainly stage experience; made some films during 30s. *The Lady Surrenders* (debut) (31), *One Hour With You* (32), *Easy to Wed* (34), *The Petrified Forest* (36), *The Great Gambini* (37), *Dramatic School* (38), *Zaza* (39), etc.

TODD, ANN (1909–). British leading actress on stage from 1928. *Keeps of Youth* (film debut) (31), *The Return of Bulldog Drummond* (34), *The Squeaker* (37), *South Riding* (38), *Poison Pen* (39), *Ships with Wings* (41), *The Seventh Veil* (46), *The Paradine Case* (US) (48), *So Evil My Love* (48), *Madeleine* (49), *The Sound Barrier* (52), *The Green Scarf* (54), *Time without Pity* (57), *Taste of Fear* (58) *Son of Captain Blood* (Italian) (62), *Ninety Degrees in the Shade* (65), etc. Now directing travel films.

TODD, ANN (1932–) (A. T. Mayfield). American child star of the 30s and 40s. *Zaza* (39), *Blood and Sand* (41), *King's Row* (42), *The Jolson Story* (46), *Bomba and the Lion Hunters* (52), etc.

TODD, MIKE (1907–1958) (Avrom Goldenborgen). Dynamic American producer of Broadway spectacles. His one personally produced film was in similar vein: *Around the World in Eighty Days* (56). The wide-screen system *Todd-Ao* is named after him. A biography, *The Nine Lives of Mike Todd*, by Art Cohn, was published in 1959.

TODD, RICHARD (1919–). British leading man, in repertory from 1937 until spotted by a film talent scout. *For Them That Trespass* (debut) (48), *The Hasty Heart* (49), *Stage Fright* (50), *Lightning Strikes Twice* (US) (51), *Robin Hood* (52), *Venetian Bird* (53), *The Sword and the Rose* (54), *Rob Roy* (54), *A Man Called Peter* (55), *The Virgin Queen* (US) (55), *The Dam Busters* (55), *Yangtse Incident* (56), *Chase a*

Crooked Shadow (57), *Danger Within* (58), *The Long, The Short and the Tall* (59), *The Hellions* (60), *Never Let Go* (61), *The Longest Day* (62), *The Boys* (62), *The Very Edge* (63), *Operation Crossbow* (65), *The Battle of the Villa Fiorita* (65), *Coast of Skeletons* (65), etc.

TODD, THELMA (c. 1908–35). American wise-cracking heroine of the early 30s: *Monkey Business* (31), *Horse Feathers* (32), *Counsellor at Law* (33), *Maid in Hollywood* (34), etc.; also many two-reel comedies with Patsy Kelly. Died in mysterious circumstances.

TOGNAZZI, UGO (c. 1924–   ). Italian leading actor. *His Women* (*Il Mantenuto*) (also directed) (61), *The Fascist* (*Il Federale*) (62), *Queen Bee* (*Ape Regina* or *The Conjugal Bed*) (63), *The Magnificent Cuckold* (64), *An American Wife* (65), *A Question of Honour* (66), *Barbarella* (68), etc.

TO HAVE AND HAVE NOT. Ernest Hemingway's tough, soft-hearted adventure novel has been filmed three times; in 1944 by Howard Hawks, with Bogart, Bacall, and not much left of the plot; in 1951 by Michael Curtiz, as *The Breaking Point*, with John Garfield and Patricia Neal; and in 1958, as *The Gun Runners*, with Audie Murphy and Rossana Podesta.

TOKAR, NORMAN (1920–   ). American director, from radio; in films, has worked exclusively for Disney. *Big Red* (62), *Savage Sam* (63), *Sammy the Way Out Seal* (63), *A Tiger Walks* (64), *Those Calloways* (65), *Follow Me Boys* (65), *The Ugly Dachshund* (66), *The Happiest Millionaire* (67), *The Horse in the Grey Flannel Suit* (68), *Rascal* (69), etc.

TOKYO OLYMPIAD (Japan 1964). This documentary by Kon Ichikawa and a score of photographers is in its quiet way as remarkable as Leni Riefenstahl's film of the 1936 games. Here the athletes are seen not as gods but as men and women suffering the ultimate in physical stress; the probing cameras achieve many remarkable effects.

TOLABLE DAVID. This novel by Joseph Hergesheimer was first, and most successfully, filmed in 1921, with Richard Barthelmess as the gentle youth making good in the tough outdoor life; it was directed by Henry King from a scenario by Edmund Goulding. In 1931 John G. Blystone directed a disappointing sound remake with Richard Cromwell.

TOLAND, GREGG (1904–1948). Distinguished American cinematographer who worked mainly with Goldwyn from the late 20s. *The Unholy Garden* (31), *Roman Scandals* (33), *Tugboat Annie* (33), *Nana* (34), *We Live Again* (34), *Mad Love* (35), *Les Misérables* (35), *These Three* (36), *Dead End* (37), *The Goldwyn Follies* (38), *Escape to Happiness* (*Intermezzo*) (39), *Wuthering Heights* (AA) (39), *Raffles* (40), *The*

Grapes of Wrath (40), *The Long Voyage Home* (40), *The Westerner* (40), *Citizen Kane* (41), *The Little Foxes* (41); war service; *The Best Years of Our Lives* (46), *The Kid from Brooklyn* (47), *The Bishop's Wife* (48), *Enchantment* (48), many others.

TOLER, SIDNEY (1875–1947). American actor with stage experience. Played small parts in many films from 1928: *Madame X* (29), *Call of the Wild* (35), *Quality Street* (37), *Three Comrades* (38), etc.; then took over from Warner Oland as Charlie Chan and played the role 25 times.

TOM AND JERRY. Short cartoons featuring the mean-minded, accident-prone cat and his inventive and likeable little adversary have been in production at MGM, with a break in the 50s, since 1937, with Fred Quimby (qv) as executive producer until his death. They have been much criticized for their excessive violence, but their humour, coupled with the impossibility of the situations, has won the day. The Academy Award-winning titles are *The Milky Way* (40), *Yankee Doodle Mouse* (43), *Mouse Trouble* (44), *Quiet Please* (45), *Cat Concerto* (46), *The Little Orphan* (48), *The Two Mousketeers* (51), *Johann Mouse* (52).

TOMBES, ANDREW (c. 1891–   ). American supporting actor often seen as cop, undertaker, bartender or harassed official. *Moulin Rouge* (33), *Charlie Chan at the Olympics* (37), *Too Busy to Work* (39), *Phantom Lady* (44), *Can't Help Singing* (44), *Oh You Beautiful Doll* (49), *How To Be Very Very Popular* (55), many others.

TOM BROWN'S SCHOOLDAYS. The two major film versions of this famous Victorian story of life at Rugby School were: 1. US 1939, with Cedric Hardwicke as Dr Arnold and Jimmy Lydon as Tom, directed by Robert Stevenson. 2. GB 1951, with Robert Newton and John Howard Davies, directed by Gordon Parry.

TOMELTY, JOSEPH (1910–   ). Irish character actor, in British films since 1945. *Odd Man Out* (46), *The Sound Barrier* (52), *Meet Mr Lucifer* (54), *Simba* (55), *A Kid for Two Farthings* (56), *The Black Torment* (64), many others.

TOM JONES (GB 1963). Bawdy, rollicking, phenomenally popular adaptation of Fielding's eighteenth-century novel about the misfortunes of a foundling. Produced and directed by Tony Richardson, scripted by John Osborne, photographed by Walter Lassally, designed by Ralph Brinton, with a cast led by Albert Finney, Hugh Griffith and Edith Evans. For the most part vivid and hilarious, it runs out of breath before the end; and the colour process sometimes looks like an awful mistake while at other points perfectly capturing the texture of an old print. AA best film, best direction, best music (John Addison); BFA best film.

TOMLINSON, DAVID (1917–   ). Amiable British leading man and comedian, a latter-day Ralph Lynn. Brief professional experience before film debut in *Quiet Wedding* (40). After RAF service: *Journey Together* (45), *The Way to the Stars* (45), *Master of Bankdam* (47), *Miranda* (48), *Sleeping Car to Trieste* (48), *The Chiltern Hundreds* (49), *Hotel Sahara* (51), *Three Men in a Boat* (55), *Up the Creek* (58), *Follow That Horse* (60), *Tom Jones* (63), *Mary Poppins* (64), *The Truth about Spring* (65), *City in the Sea* (*War Gods of the Deep*) (65), *The Liquidator* (66), *The Love Bug* (69), many others.

TOM SAWYER. Mark Twain's boy hero has been played on film by Jack Pickford in 1917 (also in *Huck and Tom* [18]), Jackie Coogan in 1920, Tommy Kelly in 1938 (the Selznick production) and, also in 1938, by Billy Cook in *Tom Sawyer, Detective*.

TONE, FRANCHOT (1905–1968). American leading man of stage and screen. *The Wiser Sex* (film debut) (32), *Gabriel over the White House* (33), *Moulin Rouge* (34), *Mutiny on the Bounty* (35), *Suzy* (36), *Quality Street* (36), *They Gave Him a Gun* (37), *Three Comrades* (39), *The Trail of the Vigilantes* (40), *Nice Girl* (41), *The Wife Takes a Flyer* (42), *Five Graves to Cairo* (43), *His Butler's Sister* (43), *Phantom Lady* (44), *Dark Waters* (44), *That Night with You* (45), *Because of Him* (46), *Her Husband's Affairs* (47), *I Love Trouble* (48), *Every Girl Should Be Married* (48), *The Man on the Eiffel Tower* (50), then back to stage, *Advise and Consent* (62), *La Bonne Soupe* (64), *In Harm's Way* (65), *Nobody Runs Forever* (68), etc.

TONTI, ALDO (1910–   ). Italian cinematographer. *Ossessione* (44), *Europe 51* (50), *The Mill on the Po* (51), *War and Peace* (56), *Cabiria* (57), *Reflections in a Golden Eye* (67), etc.

TOOMEY, REGIS (1902–   ). American character actor, on screen since 1928, usually as cop or victim in routine crime dramas. *Framed* (29), *Murder by the Clock* (32), *G-Men* (35), *The Big Sleep* (46), *The Nebraskan* (53), *Guys and Dolls* (55), *Man's Favourite Sport* (63), *Peter Gunn* (67), scores of others. TV series: *Burke's Law*.

TOP HAT (US 1935). The most delightful and enduring of the Astaire-Rogers musicals of the 30s, with an agreeable wisp of plot and amusing if dated comedy dialogue handled by an expert team of supporting comics: Edward Everett Horton, Eric Blore, Helen Broderick and Erik Rhodes. Irving Berlin's score, one of his best, includes 'The Piccolino', 'Cheek to Cheek' and 'Isn't it a Lovely Day' as well as the title number; and Astaire and Rogers are at their peak. Script by Dwight Taylor and Alan Scott, photography by David Abel, direction by Mark Sandrich, production by Pandro S. Berman.

TOPOL (1935–   ) (Haym Topol). Israeli leading actor who gained fame with London stage run of *Fiddler on the Roof*. Films include *Cast a Giant Shadow* (65), *Sallah* (66), *Before Winter Comes* (69).

TOPPER (US 1937). Hal Roach produced this mixture of slapstick, sophistication and the supernatural, from Thorne Smith's novel, and started a new trend in Hollywood comedy. Roland Young was perfectly cast as the henpecked businessman beset by jovial ghosts in the forms of Cary Grant and Constance Bennett; only Norman Macleod's direction tended to lack the necessary lightness of touch. Young also appeared in two sequels, *Topper Takes a Trip* (39) and *Topper Returns* (41). In the 50s *Topper* was personified by Leo G. Carroll in a TV series.

TORCHY BLANE. A series of half a dozen second features, made in 1939–48, starring Glenda Farrell as a wisecracking girl reporter and Barton Maclane as the puzzled policeman who gets the comeback for her zany ideas. Most of the films were directed by William Beaudine.

TOREN, MARTA (1926–1957). Swedish leading lady signed by Hollywood scout while at dramatic school. *Casbah* (debut) (48), *Rogues Regiment* (49), *One-Way Street* (50), *Panthers Moon* (51), *Sirocco* (51), *The Man Who Watched the Trains Go By* (52), *Maddalena* (54), etc.

TORN, RIP (1931–   ) (Elmore Torn). American general purpose actor, mainly on stage and TV. Films include *Baby Doll* (56), *Time Limit* (57), *Cat on a Hot Tin Roof* (58), *King of Kings* (61), *Sweet Bird of Youth* (62), *The Cincinnati Kid* (65), *You're a Big Boy Now* (66), *Beach Red* (67), *The Rain People* (69) *Tropic of Cancer* (69).

TORRENCE, ERNEST (1878–   ). Scottish actor, in American silent films, usually as villain; former opera singer. *Tolable David* (21), *The Hunchback of Notre Dame* (23), *The Covered Wagon* (23), *Peter Pan* (24), *King of Kings* (27), *The Cossacks* (28), *The Bridge of San Luis Rey* (29), *The New Adventures of Get-Rich-Quick Wallingford* (31), *Cuban Love Song* (32), *Sherlock Holmes* (33), many others.

TORRE-NILSSON, LEOPOLDO (1924–   ). Argentinian director, usually of sharp-flavoured melodramas which he also writes. *The House of the Angel* (57), *The Fall* (59), *The Hand in the Trap* (60), *Summer Skin* (61), *Four Women for One Hero* (62), *The Roof Garden* (63), *The Eavesdropper* (65), *Martin Fierro* (68), etc.

TORRES, RAQUEL (1908–   ). Mexican leading lady whose chief Hollywood role was in *White Shadows of the South Seas* (26).

TORS, IVAN (1916–   ). Hungarian writer-producer-director, in Hollywood from 1941. *Song of Love* (w) (47), *The Forsyte Saga* (w) (49), *Storm over Tibet* (w, p) (52), *The Magnetic Monster* (w, p) (53),

Gog (w, p) (54), *Riders to the Stars* (p) (55), *Battle Taxi* (p) (56), *Flipper* (p) (60), *Rhino* (p, d) (63), *Zebra in the Kitchen* (65), *Around the World under the Sea* (65), etc.; TV series as producer include *The Man and the Challenge, Sea Hunt, Flipper.*

TOTHEROH, ROLLIE (1891–1967). American cinematographer who worked notably for Charles Chaplin: *The Pilgrim* (24), *City Lights* (31), *The Great Dictator* (40), *Monsieur Verdoux* (47), etc.

TOTO (1897–1967) (Antonio Furst de Curtis-Gagliardi). Italian comedian, from music hall and revue. *Fermo con le Mani* (36), *Toto Le Moko* (49), *Cops and Robbers* (53), *Gold of Naples* (54), *Racconti Romani* (55), *Persons Unknown* (58), *Toto of Arabia* (63), *The Commander* (67), many others.

TOTTER, AUDREY (c. 1918–   ). American leading lady of the 'hard-boiled' type, with stage and radio experience. *Main Street After Dark* (debut) (44), *Her Highness and the Bellboy* (45), *The Postman Always Rings Twice* (45), *The Lady in the Lake* (46), *Tenth Avenue Angel* (47), *The Unsuspected* (48), *The Contact Man* (*Alias Nick Beal*) (49), *The Set-Up* (49), *Tension* (51), *The Blue Veil* (52), *Assignment Paris* (53), *Women's Prison* (54), *A Bullet for Joey* (55), *The Carpetbaggers* (64), *Harlow* (electronovision version) (65), *Chubasco* (68), others. TV series: *Our Man Higgins* (62).

TOUMANOVA, TAMARA (1917–   ). Russian ballerina who has made occasional appearances in American films: *Days of Glory* (43), *Torn Curtain* (67), etc.

TOURNEUR, JACQUES (1904–   ). Franco-American director, son of Maurice Tourneur, with a special flair for the macabre. *Nick Carter, Master Detective* (39), *Cat People* (42), *I Walked with a Zombie* (43), *The Leopard Man* (43), *Days of Glory* (44), *Experiment Perilous* (44), *Build My Gallows High* (*Out of the Past*) (47), *Berlin Express* (48), *Stars in My Crown* (50), *The Flame and the Arrow* (51), *Appointment in Honduras* (53), *Wichita* (55), *Great Day in the Morning* (56), *Night of the Demon* (57), *Timbuktu* (59), *The Giant of Marathon* (61), *A Comedy of Terrors* (63), *City under the Sea* (*War Gods of the Deep*) (65), etc.

TOURNEUR, MAURICE (1876–1961) (Maurice Thomas). French director who made some American films. *Mother* (14), *Man of the Hour* (15), *Trilby* (15), *Poor Little Rich Girl* (17), *The Bluebird* (18), *The Last of the Mohicans* (20), *Treasure Island* (20), *The Christian* (GB) (23), *Aloma of the South Seas* (26), *Mysterious Island* (26), *L'Équipage* (27), *Maison de Danses* (31), *Koenigsmark* (35), *Volpone* (40), *The Devil's Hand* (42), *L'Impasse des Deux Anges* (48), etc.

TOVER, LEO (1902–   ). American cinematographer in Hollywood from 1918. More recently: *Dead Reckoning* (47), *The Snake Pit* (48),

The Heiress (49), *The Secret of Convict Lake* (51), *The President's Lady* (53), *Soldier of Fortune* (55), *The Sun Also Rises* (57), *Journey to the Centre of the Earth* (59), *Follow That Dream* (62), *Sunday in New York* (63), *Strange Bedfellows* (64), *A Very Special Favour* (65), many others.

TOWER OF LONDON (US 1939). A historical melodrama notable chiefly for treating the story of Richard III as a horror yarn: Basil Rathbone and Boris Karloff, who played Richard and his executioner, had just finished *Son of Frankenstein*. Rowland V. Lee directed. Vincent Price, who played Clarence, played Richard in an inferior 1962 remake by Roger Corman.

TOWERS, HARRY ALAN (1920–   ). British executive producer with varied experience in films and TV. Recently making popular crime and adventure films with international casts and finance. *Victim Five* (also wrote) (64), *Mozambique* (also wrote) (64), *The Face of Fu Manchu* (65), *Ten Little Indians* (65), *Our Man in Marrakesh* (*Bang, Bang, You're Dead*) (66), *The Brides of Fu Manchu* (66), *Rocket to the Moon* (67), etc.

TOYE, WENDY (1917–   ). British director, former dancer. Drew attention with two ingenious short films, *The Stranger Left No Card* (52) and *On the Twelfth Day* (55). Features: *Three Cases of Murder* (54), *All for Mary* (55), *True as a Turtle* (56), *We Joined the Navy* (62), *The King's Breakfast* (68), etc.

TRACK OF THE CAT (US 1954). An interesting but unsuccessful experiment by William Wellman to create a fresh filmic texture and atmosphere by shooting in colour but restricting his subjects to black and white—in this case snowy landscapes and forests—with the very occasional flash of colour. Unfortunately the story in this case, a kind of backwoods 'Cold Comfort Farm', was laborious and unappealing, and the cast led by Robert Mitchum looked understandably glum. William Clothier was the cinematographer.

tracking shot. One taken with a moving camera, usually forwards or backwards, and often on an actual track.

TRACY, ARTHUR (1903–   ). American singer who made his greatest success in England, especially with his rendering of 'Marta'. *The Big Broadcast* (32), *Limelight* (GB) (36), *The Street Singer* (GB) (37), *Follow Your Star* (GB) (38), etc.

TRACY, LEE (1898–1968). American leading actor of stage (from 1919) and screen (sporadically from 1929). Has inimitable nasal delivery. *Big Time* (debut) (29), *Liliom* (30), *Love Is a Racket* (32), *Doctor X* (32), *Blessed Event* (32), *Clear All Wires* (33), *Dinner at Eight* (33), *Bombshell* (33), *I'll Tell the World* (34), *The Lemon Drop Kid* (34), *Two-Fisted* (35), *Sutter's Gold* (36), *Criminal Lawyer* (37), *Spellbinder*

(39), *The Power of the Press* (43), *I'll Tell the World* (45), *High Tide* (47), *The Best Man* (64), etc. Also TV appearances.

†TRACY, SPENCER (1900–1967). Distinguished American actor with stage experience from 1922; exclusively on screen from 1930. His uneven features gained him gangster roles to begin with, then he made a corner in priests and friends of the hero; but his chief mature image was that of a tough, humorous fellow who was also a pillar of integrity. *Up the River* (30), *Quick Millions* (31), *Six-Cylinder Love* (31), *Goldie* (31), *She Wanted a Millionaire* (32), *Sky Devils* (32), *Disorderly Conduct* (32), *Young America* (32), *Society Girl* (32), *Painted Woman* (32), *Me and My Girl* (32), *Twenty Thousand Years in Sing Sing* (32), *Face in the Sky* (33), *The Power and the Glory* (33), *Shanghai Madness* (33), *The Mad Game* (33), *A Man's Castle* (33), *Looking for Trouble* (34), *The Show-Off* (34), *Bottoms Up* (34), *Now I'll Tell* (34), *Marie Galante* (34), *It's a Small World* (35), *Dante's Inferno* (35), *The Murder Man* (35), *Whipsaw* (35), *Riff Raff* (36), *Fury* (36), *San Francisco* (36), *Libelled Lady* (36), *Captains Courageous* (AA) (37), *They Gave Him a Gun* (37), *The Big City* (38), *Mannequin* (38), *Test Pilot* (38), *Boys' Town* (AA) (38), *Stanley and Livingstone* (39), *I Take This Woman* (39), *Northwest Passage* (40), *Edison the Man* (40), *Boom Town* (40), *Men of Boys' Town* (41), *Dr Jekyll and Mr Hyde* (41), *Woman of the Year* (42), *Tortilla Flat* (42), *Keeper of the Flame* (43), *A Guy Named Joe* (43), *The Seventh Cross* (44), *Thirty Seconds over Tokyo* (44), *Without Love* (45), *Sea of Grass* (46), *Cass Timberlane* (47), *State of the Union* (48), *Edward My Son* (GB) (49), *Adam's Rib* (49), *Malaya* (49), *Father of the Bride* (50), *Father's Little Dividend* (51), *Pat and Mike* (52), *Plymouth Adventure* (52), *The Actress* (53), *Broken Lance* (54), *Bad Day at Black Rock* (55), *The Mountain* (56), *The Desk Set* (56), *The Old Man and the Sea* (58), *The Last Hurrah* (58), *Inherit the Wind* (60), *The Devil at Four O'clock* (61), *Judgment at Nuremberg* (61), *It's a Mad Mad Mad Mad World* (63), *Guess Who's Coming to Dinner* (BFA) (67).

TRACY, WILLIAM (1917–1967). American actor who used to play sly or dumb young fellows. *Brother Rat* (38), *Strike Up the Band* (40), *Tobacco Road* (41), *About Face* (42), *Fall In* (44), *The Walls of Jericho* (49), *Mr Walkie Talkie* (54), *The Wings of Eagles* (56), etc.

TRADER HORN (US 1930). MGM's safari to darkest Africa to shoot scenes, with actors, for this picture was the first such expedition by a major Hollywood studio. The result, though directed by W. S. Van Dyke, showed that there was much to learn, and the film now seems very naïve. Co-star Edwina Booth caught a jungle fever from which she is said to have later died.

THE TRAIL OF THE LONESOME PINE. This backwoods melodrama was first filmed in 1916 with Charlotte Walker and Earle Foxe. In

1923 it was remade with Mary Miles Minter, Antonio Moreno and Ernest Torrance. In 1936 Henry Hathaway made a sound version with Sylvia Sidney, Henry Fonda and Fred Macmurray, and this version was significant as the first outdoor film in the newly-perfected three-colour Technicolor.

trains have above all served film-makers as a splendid background for suspense thrillers. Scores of sequences crowd to mind, all enhanced by the dramatic background of a speeding train: *The Lady Vanishes, North by Northwest, From Russia with Love, The Narrow Margin, The Tall Target, How the West Was Won, 3.10 to Yuma, Lady on a Train, Cat Ballou, Jesse James, Bad Day at Black Rock, Night of the Demon, Time Bomb, Rome Express, Sleeping Car to Trieste, Northwest Frontier, Man without a Star, The Thirty-nine Steps, Secret Agent, Ministry of Fear, Von Ryan's Express, Across the Bridge, Double Indemnity, Strangers on a Train, The Iron Horse, Union Pacific, Canadian Pacific, Next of Kin, Berlin Express, The Great Locomotive Chase, Terror by Night, Crack-Up, Rampage, The Train* . . . the list could be almost endless. More serious films using trains include *La Bête Humaine* (and its remake *Human Desire*), *Metropolitan* (and its remake *A Window in London*), *Brief Encounter, The Last Journey, Sullivan's Travels, Indiscretion of an American Wife, Anna Karenina, Terminus, Night Mail, The Manchurian Candidate,* and *Doctor Zhivago*; while spectacular crashes were featured in *The Greatest Show on Earth, Hatter's Castle, Seven Sinners, The Wrong Box, Lawrence of Arabia, Crack in the World, The Ghost Train,* and *King Kong*. The subway, elevated or underground railway was featured in *Practically Yours, On the Town, The Bachelor Party, Boys' Night Out, Union Station, The FBI Story, The Young Savages, Underground, Bulldog Jack, Daleks Invasion Earth 2150 A.D.,* and *The Liquidator*. The back platforms of American trains have become familiar, especially in political films like *Abe Lincoln in Illinois, Wilson* and *All the King's Men*; but also in *Hail the Conquering Hero, Double Indemnity, The Merry Monahans* and *Mr Deeds Goes to Town*. Comedy train sequences include the Marx Brothers chopping up moving carriages for fuel in *Go West,* the Ale and Quail Club in *The Palm Beach Story,* Buster Keaton's splendidly inventive *The General, The Great St Trinian's Train Robbery,* Laurel and Hardy going to sleep in the same bunk in *The Big Noise,* Hal Roach's *Broadway Limited,* John Barrymore in *Twentieth Century,* Peter Sellers in *Two-Way Stretch,* the Western sequence of *Around the World in Eighty Days,* the whole of *The Titfield Thunderbolt* and *Oh Mr Porter* . . . and many scenes of jaywalking on top of moving carriages, including *Professor Beware, The Merry Monahans* and *Fancy Pants*. Musical sequences with a train motif or setting are found in *A Hard Day's Night, Some Like It Hot, The Harvey Girls* ('The Atchison, Topeka and the Santa Fe'), *At the Circus* ('Lydia the Tattooed Lady'), *Sun Valley Serenade* ('Chattanooga Choo Choo'), *Dumbo*

('Casey Junior'), *The Jazz Singer* ('Toot Toot Tootsie, Goodbye'), *Easter Parade* ('When the Midnight Choo Choo Leaves for Alabam'), *Forty-second Street* ('Shuffle off to Buffalo'). TV series involving trains as a regular motif include *Casey Jones*, *The Wild Wild West*, *The Iron Horse*, and *Union Pacific*.

transvestism. There have been many films, mostly lightweight ones, making effective use of situations in which men dress up as women. *Charley's Aunt* has proved a perennial, and in silent days Julian Eltinge, a female impersonator, made several popular films. Well-known actors in female attire have included Lon Chaney in *The Unholy Three*, Lionel Barrymore in *The Devil Doll*, William Powell in *Love Crazy*, Cary Grant in *I Was a Male War Bride*, Alec Guinness in *Kind Hearts and Coronets*, Peter Sellers in *The Mouse That Roared*, William Bendix and Dennis O'Keefe in *Abroad With Two Yanks*, Jimmy Durante in *You're in the Army Now*, Lee J. Cobb in *In Like Flint*, Ray Walston in *Caprice*, Jerry Lewis in *Three On a Couch*, Stan Laurel in *That's My Wife* and *Jitterbugs*, Bing Crosby in *High Time*, Bob Hope in *Casanova's Big Night*, Tony Curtis and Jack Lemmon in *Some Like It Hot*, Tony Perkins in *Psycho*, Dick Shawn in *What Did You Do in the War, Daddy?*, Phil Silvers and Jack Gilford in *A Funny Thing Happened on the Way to the Forum*; and the device seems to have become a standard ingredient of recent spy stories including *Thunderball*, *Licensed to Kill*, *Where the Bullets Fly*, and *Gunn*.

Women disguised as men are rarer; but one can instance such notable examples as Katharine Hepburn in *Sylvia Scarlett*, Annabella in *Wings of the Morning*, Signe Hasso in *The House on 92nd Street*, Nita Talbot in *A Very Special Favour*, Marlene Dietrich in *Morocco*, Greta Garbo in *Queen Christina*, Mary Pickford in *Kiki*, Debbie Reynolds in *Goodbye Charlie*, Jessie Matthews in *Gangway*, and the ambiguous hero-heroine-villain of *Homicidal*.

TRAUBEL, HELEN (1903–   ). American soprano. Appeared in *Deep in My Heart* (54), *The Ladies' Man* (61), *Gunn* (67).

TRAUNER, ALEXANDER (1906–   ). French art director who has worked on international films. *Quai des Brumes* (38), *Le Jour Se Lève* (39), *Les Visiteurs du Soir* (42), *Les Enfants du Paradis* (44), *Les Portes de la Nuit* (45), *Manèges* (49), *Othello* (52), *Love in the After-noon* (56), *The Nun's Story* (58), *The Apartment* (60), *One Two Three* (61), *Irma La Douce* (63), *The Night of the Generals* (66), *A Flea in Her Ear* (68), many others.

TRAVERS, BEN (1886–   ). British playwright responsible for the Tom Walls/Ralph Lynn Aldwych farces which were all filmed in the early 30s: *Rookery Nook* (30), *A Cuckoo in the Nest* (33), *A Cup of Kindness* (33), *Turkey Time* (34), *Banana Ridge* (41), etc. Also wrote film scripts: *Fighting Stock* (36), *Just My Luck* (37), *Uncle Silas* (47), etc.

TRAVERS, BILL (1922–   ). Tall British leading man, married to Virginia McKenna; stage experience from 1947. *The Square Ring* (54), *Geordie* (55), *Bhowani Junction* (56), *The Barretts of Wimpole Street* (57), *The Smallest Show on Earth* (57), *The Seventh Sin* (US) (58), *The Bridal Path* (59), *Gorgo* (60), *Invasion Quartet* (61), *Two Living, One Dead* (Sw.) (62), *Born Free* (66), *Duel at Diablo* (US) (66), *A Midsummer Night's Dream* (68), *Ring of Bright Water* (69), etc.

TRAVERS, HENRY (1874–1965) (Travers Heagerty). British character actor, on stage from 1894, in America from 1901. Came to films in the 30s and usually played benign old gentlemen. *The Invisible Man* (33), *Reunion in Vienna* (33), *Seven Keys to Baldpate* (36), *On Borrowed Time* (38), *Dark Victory* (39), *Anne of Windy Willows* (40), *High Sierra* (41), *Mrs Miniver* (42), *The Moon Is Down* (43), *The Naughty Nineties* (45), *The Bells of St Mary* (46), *It's a Wonderful Life* (as an angel) (46), *The Yearling* (47), *The Girl from Jones Beach* (last appearance) (49), etc.

TRAVERS, LINDEN (1913–   ) (Florence Lindon-Travers). British leading lady of stage (from 1931), screen shortly after. *Double Alibi* (36), *The Lady Vanishes* (38), *The Terror* (39), *The Stars Look Down* (39), *The Ghost Train* (41), *The Missing Million* (42), *Beware of Pity* (46), *No Orchids for Miss Blandish* (48), *Quartet* (48), etc. Retired.

TRAVIS, RICHARD (1913–   ) (William Justice). American leading man of 40s and 50s second features. *The Man Who Came to Dinner* (41), *The Big Shot* (42), *Busses Roar* (43), *Jewels of Brandenberg* (44), *Alaska Patrol* (46), *Skyliner* (48), *Operation Haylift* (50), *Mask of the Dragon* (51), *Fingerprints Don't Lie* (51), *City of Shadows* (55), etc.; then into TV.

TREACHER, ARTHUR (1894–   ). Tall British character comedian, the perfect butler for 30 years. On stage from 20s, Hollywood from 1933. *David Copperfield* (34), *A Midsummer Night's Dream* (35), *The Little Princess* (39), *National Velvet* (44), *Delightfully Dangerous* (45), *The Countess of Monte Cristo* (48), *Love That Brute* (50), *Mary Poppins* (64), many others, including a series of 'Jeeves' films in the 30s.

TREASURE ISLAND. Robert L. Stevenson's adventure classic for boys was filmed three times by American companies. In 1920 Charles Ogle was Long John and Jim Hawkins was played by a girl— Shirley Mason. Maurice Tourneur directed. In 1935, in a splendid production for MGM, Victor Fleming directed Wallace Beery and Jackie Cooper; in 1950, in Britain for Disney, Byron Haskin directed Robert Newton, who was born to play Long John, and

Bobby Driscoll. Newton afterwards played the role in a feature, LONG JOHN SILVER (54), and 26 TV half-hours filmed in Australia.

THE TREASURE OF THE SIERRA MADRE (US 1948). Written and directed by John Huston from the novel by the mysterious B. Traven, this sombre but gripping saga of thieves falling out over gold, after an arduous search in bandit country, won Academy Awards for Huston on both counts and for his father Walter Huston who played the oldest of the rascals. Humphrey Bogart and Tim Holt were also involved, the photography was by Ted McCord and the music by Max Steiner. The film has not worn too well—it has a studio look—but at the time it was hailed as another stride forward by Hollywood towards productions of adult integrity.

treatment. The first expansion of a script idea into sequence form, giving some idea of how the story is to be told, i.e. with examples of dialogue, camera angles, etc.

TREE, DAVID (1915–   ). British comedy actor with stage experience. *Knight Without Armour* (37), *Pygmalion* (as Freddy Eynsford-Hill) (38), *Q Planes* (39), *French Without Tears* (39), *Major Barbara* (40). Then war service, in which he lost an arm; subsequently retired.

TREEN, MARY (c. 1912–   ). American comedy actress who usually plays nurses, office girls, or the heroine's plain friend. *Babbitt* (35), *Colleen* (36), *First Love* (40), *I Love a Soldier* (44), *From This Day Forward* (45), *Let's Live a Little* (48), *The Caddy* (53), *The Birds and the Bees* (56), *Rockabye Baby* (58), *Paradise Hawaiian Style* (56), many others.

TREVELYAN, JOHN (1904–   ). British executive, secretary of the British Board of Film Censors since 1958, responsible for a more liberal policy allowing such controversial films as *Saturday Night and Sunday Morning*, *Tom Jones*, *The Servant*, *The Silence*, *Repulsion* and *Who's Afraid of Virginia Woolf?*

TREVOR, AUSTIN (1897–   ) (A. Schilsky). British character actor with long stage experience. *At the Villa Rose* (30), *Alibi* (as Hercule Poirot) (31), *Lord Edgware Dies* (as Hercule Poirot) (34), *Dark Journey* (37), *Goodbye Mr Chips* (39), *Champagne Charlie* (44), *The Red Shoes* (48), *Father Brown* (54), *The Horrors of the Black Museum* (59), etc.

TREVOR, CLAIRE (1909–   ) (Claire Wemlinger). American character actress on stage from childhood. Made many routine films before gaining critical notice. *Life in the Raw* (debut) (33), *Hold That Girl* (34), *Dante's Inferno* (35), *Career Woman* (36), *Dead End* (37), *The Amazing Dr Clitterhouse* (38), *Stagecoach* (39), *I Stole a Million* (39), *Dark Command* (40), *Honky Tonk* (41), *Crossroads* (42), *Woman*

983

of the Town (43), *Farewell My Lovely* (*Murder My Sweet*) (44), *Johnny Angel* (45), *Crack Up* (46), *Bachelor Girls* (47), *Key Largo* (AA) (48), *The Lucky Stiff* (49), *Hard, Fast and Beautiful* (49), *Best of the Badmen* (50), *The Stranger Wore a Gun* (52), *The High and the Mighty* (54), *The Man without a Star* (55), *The Mountain* (56), *Marjorie Morningstar* (58), *Two Weeks in Another Town* (62), *How to Murder Your Wife* (65), *Capetown Affair* (67), etc.

THE TRIAL (France 1962). Orson Welles' attempt to put Kafka on the screen was mainly filmed in a French railway station and offered some opportunity for bravura direction and photography; but there were obvious technical inadequacies as well as an all-pervading portentousness, so that as a whole it didn't work except as a vehicle for the off-beat talents of Anthony Perkins as the victimized 'K' and Welles himself as a lawyer.

TRIESAULT, IVAN (1902–   ). Estonian character actor, former dancer, in Hollywood for many years, usually as frowning villainous henchman. *Mission to Moscow* (43), *The Hitler Gang* (44), *Notorious* (46), *To the Ends of the Earth* (48), *Five Fingers* (52), *Fraulein* (58), *The 300 Spartans* (62), *Barabbas* (62), *Von Ryan's Express* (65), *Batman* (66), many others.

TRINDER, TOMMY (1909–   ). British cockney music-hall comedian, in occasional films. *Laugh It Off* (40), *Sailors Three* (41), *The Foreman Went to France* (42), *Champagne Charlie* (44), *Fiddlers Three* (44), *Bitter Springs* (49), *You Lucky People* (54), *The Beauty Jungle* (64), etc.

TRINTIGNANT, JEAN-LOUIS (1930–   ). French leading man. *Race for Life* (55), *And God Created Woman* (56), *Austerlitz* (59), *Château en Suede* (63), *Mata Hari* (64), *Angelique* (64), *A Man and a Woman* (66), *Trans-Europe Express* (66), *Les Biches* (68), '*Z*' (68), *Ma Nuit Chez Maud* (69), *The American* (70).

TRIUMPH OF THE WILL (Germany 1934). A pictorial record of the sixth Nazi congress at Nuremberg, this controversial film still has a sensational impact and is probably the most powerful propaganda film ever made. Leni Riefenstahl's direction and editing, abetted by Sepp Allgeier's luminous photography, make the Nazis seem more like gods than men; and for this reason the film has been denied a commercial reissue in Britain. The early sequence showing Hitler's plane coming down from the clouds is perhaps the cleverest of all.

TRNKA, JIRI (1910–1969). Czech animator and puppeteer, many of whose short films have been shown abroad. *The Emperor's Nightingale* (49), *Song of the Prairie* (49), *The Good Soldier Schweik* (54), *Jan Hus* (56), *A Midsummer Night's Dream* (57), etc.

TRONSON, ROBERT (1924–   ). British director, from TV. *The Man at the Carlton Tower* (62), *The Traitors* (63), *On the Run* (63), *Ring of Spies* (64), etc.

TROTTI, LAMAR (1900–1952). Prolific American scriptwriter and producer. *Judge Priest* (co-w) (34), *Steamboat Round the Bend* (co-w) (35), *Ramona* (w) (36), *Slave Ship* (w) (37), *In Old Chicago* (w) (38), *Young Mr Lincoln* (w) (39), *Hudson's Bay* (w) (41), *The Ox Bow Incident* (w, p) (42), *Wilson* (w, p) (43), *The Razor's Edge* (w, p) (46), *Mother Wore Tights* (w, p) (47), *Yellow Sky* (w, p) (48), *Cheaper by the Dozen* (w, p) (50), *I'd Climb the Highest Mountain* (w, p) (51), *Stars and Stripes Forever* (w, p) (52), *With a Song in My Heart* (w, p) (52), many others.

TROUBLE IN PARADISE (US 1932). One feels that Ernst Lubitsch probably enjoyed making this more than any of his other American films: a roguish, pacy tale of cross and double cross among society jewel thieves, it is told with a lively visual wit and has such a gallery of attractive performances as to make it a sophisticated classic. Herbert Marshall, Miriam Hopkins, Kay Francis, C. Aubrey Smith, Charles Ruggles, Edward Everett Horton are all at their best. Written by Samson Raphaelson with sets designed by Hans Dreier.

THE TROUBLE WITH HARRY (US 1956). Alfred Hitchcock's favourite of his own films is a determinedly gay black comedy which lacks cinematic spontaneity, all its humour coming straight from Jack Trevor Story's original novel about a corpse on the heath which villagers keep burying and digging up again for their own reasons. The autumnal Vermont setting, delightful in itself, is a distraction to a movie which would have worked better in black and white. Mildred Natwick, Edmund Gwenn and Shirley Maclaine make the most of the macabre situations.

TROUGHTON, PATRICK (1920–   ). British character actor, mainly on TV. *Escape* (48), *Hamlet* (48), *Treasure Island* (50), *The Black Knight* (52), *Richard III* (56), *The Gorgon* (64), many others in small roles.

TROUNCER, CECIL (1898–1953). British stage character actor with splendidly resonant diction. Few film appearances include *Pygmalion* (38), *While the Sun Shines* (46), *London Belongs to Me* (48), *The Guinea Pig* (49), *The Lady with a Lamp* (51), *Pickwick Papers* (52), *The Weak and the Wicked* (54).

TROWBRIDGE, CHARLES (1882–1967). American character actor, former architect; usually played professors or kindly fathers. *I Take This Woman* (31), *The Thirteenth Chair* (36), *Confessions of a Nazi Spy* (39), *The Mummy's Hand* (40), *Mildred Pierce* (45), *The Wings of Eagles* (57), many others.

The True Glory

THE TRUE GLORY (GB 1945). This brilliantly-made, rather too literary documentary, composed of newsreel material from D-Day to the fall of Berlin, still has that brilliant surface polish which at the time of its release made it by far the best compilation film to have been seen. Directed by Carol Reed and Garson Kanin, with music by William Alwyn.

true-life adventures; see under THE LIVING DESERT.

TRUEX, ERNEST (1890–   ). American character actor of 'little man' roles, in films since the 20s. *Whistling in the Dark* (33), *The Adventures of Marco Polo* (38), *Christmas in July* (40), *His Girl Friday* (41), *Always Together* (48), *The Leather Saint* (56), *Twilight for the Gods* (58), *Fluffy* (65), many others; latterly much on TV.

†TRUFFAUT, FRANÇOIS (1932–   ). French 'new wave' director, former critic. *Les Mistons* (58), *Les Quatre Cents Coups* (59), *Shoot the Pianist* (60), *Jules and Jim* (61), *Love at Twenty* (part) (62), *Silken Skin* (64), *Fahrenheit 451* (66), *The Bride Wore Black* (67), *Stolen Kisses* (68), *Mississippi Mermaid* (69).

TRUMAN, MICHAEL (1916–   ). British director, former editor. *Touch and Go* (54), *Go to Blazes* (62), *The Girl in the Headlines* (63), etc.

TRUMAN, RALPH (1900–   ). British stage character actor who makes occasional film appearances. *Henry V* (44), *Beware of Pity* (46), *Oliver Twist* (48), *Quo Vadis* (51), *The Man Who Knew Too Much* (56), *El Cid* (61), many others.

TRUMBO, DALTON (1905–   ). American screenwriter, one of the 'Hollywood Ten' who were blacklisted by McCarthy. *The Remarkable Andrew* (42), *A Guy Named Joe* (43), *Our Vines Have Tender Grapes* (45), *Exodus* (60), *The Sandpiper* (65), *Hawaii* (66), *The Fixer* (68), many others.

TRYON, TOM (1926–   ). American leading man with stage and TV experience. *The Scarlet Hour* (debut) (55), *Three Violent People* (56), *I Married a Monster from Outer Space* (57), *Moon Pilot* (61), *Marines Let's Go* (61), *The Cardinal* (63), *In Harm's Way* (65), *The Glory Guys* (65), etc.

TSU, IRENE (1943–   ). Chinese glamour girl in Hollywood. *Caprice* (66), *The Green Berets* (67), etc.

TUCKER, FORREST (1919–   ). Rugged American leading man, mostly in routine action pictures from 1940. *The Westerner* (debut) (40), *Keeper of the Flame* (43), *The Yearling* (47), *Sands of Iwo Jima* (50), *The Wild Blue Yonder* (52), *Crosswinds* (53), *Trouble in the Glen* (GB) (54), *Break in the Circle* (GB) (56), *The Abominable Snowman* (GB) (57), *Auntie Mame* (58), *The Night They Raided Minsky's* (68), many others. Recently on stage. TV series: *Crunch and Des* (55), *F Troop* (65–67).

TUCKER, SOPHIE (c. 1885–1966) (Sophia Abuza). The 'red hot momma' of American vaudeville. Infrequent screen appearances include *Honky Tonk* (29), *Gay Love* (GB) (34), *Broadway Melody of 1938, Sensations of 1945.*

TUFTS, SONNY (1911–   ) (Bowen Charleston Tufts). Tall, good-humoured American 'second lead', in Hollywood from the early 40s. *So Proudly We Hail* (43), *I Love a Soldier* (44), *Here Come the Waves* (45), *The Virginian* (46), *Swell Guy* (47), *The Crooked Way* (49), *Easy Living* (49), *The Gift Horse* (GB) (52), *No Escape* (53), *Cat Women of the Moon* (53), *The Seven Year Itch* (55), *Come Next Spring* (56), *The Parson and the Outlaw* (57), *Town Tamer* (65).

TULLY, MONTGOMERY (1904–   ). British writer and director. *Murder in Reverse* (w, d) (45), *Spring Song* (w, d) (47), *Boys in Brown* (d) (49), *A Tale of Five Cities* (d) (51), *The Glass Cage* (d) (55), *The Hypnotist* (d) (57), *Escapement* (d) (58), *Clash by Night* (d) (63), *Who Killed the Cat* (d) (66), *Battle Beneath the Earth* (d) (68), many other second features and TV episodes.

TULLY, TOM (c. 1902–   ). American character actor with stage experience; usually in tough-looking but soft-hearted roles. *Destination Tokyo* (44), *Adventure* (45), *The Town Went Wild* (45), *June Bride* (48), *Where the Sidewalk Ends* (50), *The Caine Mutiny* (54), *Ten North Frederick* (57), *The Wackiest Ship in the Army* (61), *Coogan's Bluff* (68), etc. TV series *The Line-Up* (59).

TUNBERG, KARL (1908–   ). American screenwriter, in Hollywood from 1937. *My Lucky Star* (38), *Down Argentine Way* (40), *Orchestra Wives* (42), *Kitty* (45), *You Gotta Stay Happy* (47), *Scandal at Scourie* (53), *The Scarlet Coat* (55), *Ben Hur* (59), *Taras Bulba* (62), *Harlow* (electronovision version) (65), *Where Were You When the Lights Went Out?* (68), many others.

TURNER, FLORENCE (1888–1946). American actress who in 1907 became the first 'movie star' known by name; also as 'the Vitagraph Girl'. *A Dixie Mother* (10), *Francesca da Rimini* (12), *The Welsh Singer* (GB) (13), *My Old Dutch* (GB) (14), etc. Went back to Hollywood in roles of diminishing stature; retired in the mid-20s.

TURNER, JOHN (1932–   ). British leading man with stage experience, also known as TV's 'Knight Errant'. *Behemoth, the Sea Monster* (60), *Petticoat Pirates* (61), *Sammy Going South* (62), *The Black Torment* (64), etc.

TURNER, LANA (1920–   ) (Julia Turner). American leading lady of the 40s; began as the 'girl next door' type but became increasingly sophisticated. *They Won't Forget* (debut) (37) *The Adventures of Marco Polo* (38), *Calling Dr Kildare* (39), *Love Finds Andy Hardy* (39), *Choose Your Partner* (40), *Ziegfeld Girl* (41), *Dr Jekyll and Mr Hyde* (41), *Honky Tonk* (41), *Johnny Eager* (41), *Somewhere I'll Find You* (42), *Slightly Dangerous* (43), *Marriage Is a Private Affair* (44), *Keep Your Powder Dry* (44), *Weekend at the Waldorf* (45), *The Postman Always Rings Twice* (45), *Green Dolphin Street* (46), *Cass Timberlane* (47), *Homecoming* (48), *The Three Musketeers* (48), *A Life of Her Own* (50), *The Merry Widow* (52), *The Bad and the Beautiful* (52), *Latin Lovers* (53), *The Flame and the Flesh* (54), *Betrayed* (55), *The Prodigal* (55), *The Rains of Ranchipur* (55), *Diane* (56), *Another Time Another Place* (GB) (57), *Peyton Place* (57), *The Lady Takes a Flyer* (58), *Imitation of Life* (59), *Portrait in Black* (60), *By Love Possessed* (61), *Bachelor in Paradise* (62), *Who's Got the Action* (63), *Love Has Many Faces* (65), *Madame X* (66), *The Big Cube* (69), etc. TV series: *The Survivors* (69).

TURN OF THE TIDE (GB 1935). This small, well-intentioned little drama about family rivalry in a Yorkshire fishing village is said to have persuaded Lord Rank to enter the film industry because it showed that a fiction film could be a teaching instrument. Norman Walker directed: John Garrick and Geraldine Fitzgerald were the leading players.

TURPIN, BEN (1874–1940). Cross-eyed American silent comedian, mainly popular in short slapstick skits of the 20s. In films from 1915 after vaudeville experience. *Uncle Tom's Cabin* (19), *Small Town Idol* (21), *Show of Shows* (29), *The Love Parade* (30), scores of others.

TURPIN, DICK (1705–1739) was a seasoned criminal without too many obvious redeeming characteristics. Film-makers have seized on his ride to York and his affection for his horse as an excuse to view him through rose-tinted glasses. So he was played as a hero by Matheson Lang in 1922, Tom Mix in 1925, Victor McLaglen in 1933, Louis Hayward in 1951, and David Weston (for Walt Disney) in 1965.

TURPIN, GERRY (c. 1930–   ). British cinematographer. *The Queen's Guards* (61), *Seance on a Wet Afternoon* (64), *The Whisperers* (67), *Deadfall* (68), *Oh What a Lovely War* (69), *The Man Who Had Power Over Women* (70), etc.

TUSHINGHAM, RITA (1940–   ). British leading character actress with stage experience. *A Taste of Honey* (61), *The Leather Boys* (63), *A Place To Go* (63), *Girl with Green Eyes* (64), *The Knack* (65), *Dr Zhivago* (66), *The Trap* (66), *Smashing Time* (67), *Diamonds for Breakfast* (68), *The Guru* (69), *The Bed-Sitting Room* (69).

Twentieth-Century Fox Film Corporation

†TUTIN, DOROTHY (1930–   ). Leading British actress. Occasional films: *The Importance of Being Earnest* (52), *The Beggar's Opera* (53), *A Tale of Two Cities* (57), *Cromwell* (69).

TUTTLE, FRANK (1892–1963). American director of mainly routine films; in Hollywood from the 20s. *Kid Boots* (27), *Roman Scandals* (33), *The Glass Key* (35), *Waikiki Wedding* (37), *Lucky Jordan* (43), *Hostages* (43), *The Hour Before the Dawn* (43), *A Man Called Sullivan* (45), *Suspense* (46), *Swell Guy* (47), *The Magic Face* (51), *Gunman in the Streets* (51), *Hell on Frisco Bay* (55), *A Cry in the Night* (56), etc.

TWAIN, MARK (1835–1910) (Samuel Langhorne Clemens). Beloved American humorist and travel writer; was played by Fredric March in *The Adventures of Mark Twain* (44). Works filmed include *Tom Sawyer* (qv), *Huckleberry Finn* (qv), *A Connecticut Yankee* (qv), *The Prince and the Pauper* (qv), *The Celebrated Jumping Frog* (as *The Best Man Wins*), *The Million-Pound Banknote*.

TWELVE ANGRY MEN (US 1957). One of the most successful results (though not commercially) of the TV invasion of Hollywood: a meticulously detailed reconstruction of Reginald Rose's gripping jury-room TV play, directed by Sidney Lumet. Those present include Henry Fonda, E. G. Marshall, Jack Warden, George Voskovec, Ed Begley.

TWELVE O'CLOCK HIGH (US 1949). A belated, thoughtful tale of World War II which achieved freshness and realism by concentrating less on the action possibilities of the hazards undergone by American bomber pilots based in Britain than on the strains of command, with Gregory Peck giving a fine performance as the commanding officer who finally cracks up. Written by Sy Bartlett and Bernie Lay Jnr; photographed by Leon Shamroy; directed by Henry King. A successful TV series under the same title began in 1964.

TWELVETREES, HELEN (1908–1958) (Helen Jurgens). American leading lady of the 30s; films fairly unmemorable. *The Ghost Talks* (29), *The Painted Desert* (31), *Is My Face Red?* (32), *King for a Night* (33), *Times Square Lady* (35), *Hollywood Round Up* (37), etc.

Twentieth-Century Fox Film Corporation. An American production and distribution company formed in 1935 by a merger of Joseph Schenck's Twentieth Century Pictures with William Fox's Fox Film Corporation. Fox had started in nickelodeon days as a showman, then a distributor. Putting his profits into production, he started the careers of several useful stars including Theda Bara, and pioneered the Movietone sound-on-film process; but in the early 30s, after a series of bad deals, he lost power. The new company had Darryl F. Zanuck as production head from 1935 to 1956; he returned in 1962 as president after the resignation of Spyros Skouras, who had reigned from 1942. These two men are therefore largely responsible for the Fox image, which usually gave the impression of more careful budget-trimming and production-processing than did the films of the rest of the 'big five'. Fox's successful personality stars include Shirley Temple, Alice Faye, Don Ameche, Betty Grable and Marilyn Monroe; its best Westerns include *The Big Trail, Drums along the Mohawk, My Darling Clementine* and *The Gunfighter*; in drama it can claim *What Price Glory, Dante's Inferno, The Grapes of Wrath, How Green Was My Valley, The Ox-Bow Incident, The Song of Bernadette, Wilson, The Snake Pit*, and *Gentlemen's Agreement*. In 1953 Spyros Skouras successfully foisted the new screen shape, CinemaScope, on to world markets, but Fox have not used it with greater success than anyone else, their most elaborate 'spectaculars' being *The Robe, There's No Business Like Show Business, The King and I, South Pacific, The Diary of Anne Frank, The Longest Day, Cleopatra, Those Magnificent Men in Their Flying Machines, The Sound of Music*, and *Star!*. In 1969 the name of the company was officially changed to Twenty-first Century Fox.

TWENTY THOUSAND YEARS IN SING SING (US 1932). An early exposé of American prison life, from a book by Warden Lewis E. Lawes; its type quickly became too familiar. Spencer Tracy and Bette Davis starred. In 1940 the story was remade as *Castle on the Hudson* with John Garfield and Ann Sheridan.

TWIST, DEREK (1905–   ). British director, former editor and associate producer. *The End of the River* (47), *All over the Town* (48), *Green Grow the Rushes* (51), *Police Dog* (55), *Family Doctor* (57), etc.; also TV films.

2001: A SPACE ODYSSEY (GB 1968). This bird's-eye-view of the universe past and present, made by Stanley Kubrick from a novel by Arthur C. Clarke, worked like a huge confidence trick: the special effects (AA, BFA) were so spellbinding that comparatively few patrons complained of the obscure story line and general lack of human feeling. As prophecy it was certainly less optimistic than H. G. Wells' 1936 *Things To Come*.

TYLER, TOM (1903–1954) (William Burns). American cowboy star of innumerable second features in the 30s: *The Cowboy Cop* (26), *The Sorcerer* (29), *Riding the Lonesome Trail* (34), *Pinto Rustlers* (38), *Roamin' Wild* (39), etc. Also played small roles in such films as *Gone with the Wind* (39), *Stagecoach* (39), *The Mummy's Hand* (as the mummy) (40); and had the title role in *The Adventures of Captain Marvel* (serial) (41).

TZELNIKER, MEIER (1894–   ). British character actor well known in the Yiddish theatre. Occasional film roles include *Mr Emmanuel* (44), *It Always Rains on Sunday* (48), *Last Holiday* (50), *The Teckman Mystery* (54), *Make Me an Offer* (54), *A Night to Remember* (58), *Expresso Bongo* (60), *The Sorcerers* (67).

U

UGETSU MONOGATARI (Japan 1953). Rather oddly voted by an international critics' poll in 1958 as one of the ten best films ever made, this genuinely strange and beautiful drama would be unlikely to win such an accolade now. Laid in sixteenth-century Japan, it tells of a potter lured away from home into a castle of ghosts. Slight, charming, impeccably directed by Kenji Mizoguchi. Translated into English the title emerges as *Tales of a Pale and Mysterious Moon after the Rain*.

ULLMAN, DANIEL (1920–). American scriptwriter. *The Maze* (53), *Seven Angry Men* (54), *Wichita* (55), *Good Day for a Hanging* (59), *Face of a Fugitive* (59), *Mysterious Island* (61), etc.

ULMER, EDGAR G. (1900–). Austrian-born director long in Hollywood specializing in second features and exploitation subjects. In recent years, somewhat mysteriously revered by French critics. *The Black Cat* (34), *The Singing Blacksmith* (38), *Isle of Forgotten Sins* (43), *Bluebeard* (44), *The Wife of Monte Cristo* (46), *Ruthless* (48), *The Man from Planet X* (53), *The Naked Dawn* (55), *Daughter of Dr Jekyll* (57), *The Amazing Transparent Man* (60), *Beyond the Time Barrier* (61), *Atlantis, The Lost Kingdom* (*L'Atalantide*) (62), many others.

ULYSSES. The Homerian hero was played by Kirk Douglas in a 1954 Italian production by Dino de Laurentiis: it concentrated on spectacle and the monstrous Cyclops. Joseph Strick's 1967 film of the same title was a very different affair, being based on James Joyce's experimental novel about twenty-four hours in the life of an Irish Jew in Dublin. Although it could hardly do more than present excerpts from the original, it had much charm and imagination, though its faithful retention of Joyce's language caused it to be banned in many areas. Milo O'Shea and Barbara Jefford led the cast.

UMBERTO D (Italy 1952). Neo-realistic drama in the mould of *Bicycle Thieves* and also directed by Vittorio de Sica from a script by Cesare Zavattini; about a proud but lonely old man who, unable to raise his rent, contemplates suicide. Uses non-professional actors.

THE UMBRELLAS OF CHERBOURG (LES PARAPLUIES DE CHERBOURG) (France 1964). Naïve, charming, all-singing love story directed by Jacques Demy with music by Michel Legrand. The tale of star-

crossed lovers would be nothing without the musical treatment and
the delightful use of colour; as it is, the film has been considered a
masterpiece though it is unlikely to spark off a cycle of cinematic
light operas.

UMEKI, MIYOSHI (1929–   ). Japanese leading lady who won an
Academy Award for her performance in *Sayonara* (57). TV series;
The Courtship of Eddie's Father (69).

UNCLE TOM'S CABIN, an anti-slavery novel of excellent intentions and
unabashed sentimentality, was written in 1852 by American
novelist Harriet Beecher Stowe (1811–1896). It features the
dastardly white villain Simon Legree, the cheerful Negro Uncle
Tom, and poor Little Eva who is taken to heaven by an angel.
The main film versions include a 1903 one-reeler by Edwin S.
Porter, a Pathé three-reeler of 1910 and an American three-reeler
of 1913. In 1914 came a longer American version with Marie Eline
as Little Eva. 1918 brought a full-length version with Marguerite
Clark in the dual role of Topsy and Eva. Then in 1927 Harry
Pollard directed a full-blown silent spectacle which was frequently
revived with sound effects in later years: Virginia Grey was Eva.
The subject might have been thought too dated or too touchy for
sound treatment, but in 1965 a colour and widescreen European
co-production was directed by Geza von Radvanyi and featured
Herbert Lom as Simon Legree and Gertrud Mittermayer as
Eva.

uncredited appearances by well-known stars are usually intended as
gags to liven up a film which can do with an extra laugh. Thus the
brief cameos of Cary Grant and Jack Benny in *Without Reservations*;
Lana Turner in *Du Barry was a Lady*; Robert Taylor in *I Love
Melvin*; Bing Crosby in *My Favourite Blonde, The Princess and the
Pirate* and other Bob Hope films; Alan Ladd in *My Favourite Brunette*;
Peter Lorre in *Meet Me in Las Vegas*; Basil Rathbone and Nigel
Bruce in *Crazy House*; Myrna Loy in *The Senator was Indiscreet*; Peter
Sellers and David Niven in *Road to Hong Kong*; Vincent Price in
Beach Party; Boris Karloff in *Bikini Beach*; Groucho Marx in *Will
Success Spoil Rock Hunter?*; Elizabeth Taylor in *Scent of Mystery*;
Richard Burton in *What's New Pussycat?*; Jack Benny and Jerry
Lewis in *It's a Mad Mad Mad Mad World*; Robert Vaughn in
The Glass Bottom Boat; Bob Hope and others in *The Oscar*; Rock
Hudson in *Four Girls in Town*; Jack Benny and Jimmy Durante in
Beau James; Red Skelton in *Susan Slept Here*; Bing Crosby and Bob
Hope in *Scared Stiff*; Martin and Lewis and Jane Russell in *Road to
Bali*; Bogart and Bacall in *Two Guys from Milwaukee*; Gene Kelly in
Love is Better Than Ever; Clark Gable and Robert Taylor in *Callaway
Went Thataway*; Humphrey Bogart in *The Love Lottery*: Jack Benny
in *The Great Lover*; Ray Milland in *Miss Tatlock's Millions*; John

Wayne in *I Married a Woman*; and Margaret Rutherford in *The ABC Murders*.

Sometimes a sequel not featuring the star of the first story will have a brief reminiscence of him with no credit: this happened to Cary Grant in *Topper Takes a Trip* and to Simone Signoret in *Life At the Top*. Then there are deliberate in-jokes like Walter Huston playing bit parts in his son John's movies, Peter Finch playing a messenger in *The First Men in the Moon* because he happened to be there when the hired actor failed to turn up, Joseph Cotten playing a non-speaking part in *Touch of Evil* because he dropped in to watch the location shooting and Orson Welles sent a make-up man over for old times' sake, Helen Hayes playing a small role in *Third Man on the Mountain* because her son James Macarthur was in the cast. Occasionally when stars are replaced during production, long shots of them remain in the completed film: thus Vivien Leigh in *Elephant Walk* and George Brent in *Death of a Scoundrel*. The best gag was played by Al Jolson who, determined to get into *The Jolson Story* at all costs, played himself in the theatre runway long shots during 'California Here I Come'.

There remain a few mysteries. In *The Great Ziegfeld*, 'A Pretty Girl is Like a Melody' was sung by Stanley Morner, soon to become quite famous as Dennis Morgan. He was not credited. Nor were the following who had important roles to play and were well-known at the time: Constance Collier in *Anna Karenina*, Marlene Dietrich in *Touch of Evil*, Henry Daniell in *Mutiny on the Bounty*, Audrey Totter in *The Carpetbaggers*, Dorothy Malone and John Hubbard in *Fate is the Hunter*, Wilfrid Lawson in *Tread Softly Stranger*, Leo McKern in *The High Commissioner* (*Nobody Lives Forever*). And in *Those Magnificent Men in Their Flying Machines*, Cicely Courtneidge and Fred Emney had roughly equal dialogue in their one scene; yet he was credited and she was not. The reasons surely can't have anything to do with modesty.

See also: *directors' appearances*.

UNDER THE CLOCK (US 1944). Love and marriage in the course of forty-eight hours between a soldier and a girl who meet accidentally in a New York station. Slight, but charmingly played by Judy Garland and Robert Walker, subtly directed by Vincente Minnelli. US title: *The Clock*.

UNDER TWO FLAGS. Ouida's romantic melodrama of the Foreign Legion was filmed in 1916 by J. Gordon Edwards, with Theda Bara as 'Cigarette'; in 1922 by Tod Browning, with Priscilla Dean and Jack Kirkwood; and in 1936 by Frank Lloyd, with Claudette Colbert and Ronald Colman.

UNDERDOWN, EDWARD (1908–). British actor on stage from 1932; once a jockey. Often cast as dull Englishman. *The Warren Case* (33) (debut), *Wings of the Morning* (37), *They Were Not Divided* (50), *Beat the Devil* (54), *The Camp on Blood Island* (58), *The Day the Earth Caught Fire* (62), *Khartoum* (66), *The Hand of Night* (67), etc.

underground railways have been used remarkably little in films considering their dramatic possibilities. There were chases through the London system in *Underground* itself, *Bulldog Jack* and *Waterloo Road*; it was also used for a comedy scene in *Rotten to the Core*, a murder in *Man Hunt*, *Otley*, and *The Liquidator*, and a musical number in *Three Hats for Lisa*. The New York subway was the setting for musical numbers in *Dames* ('I Only Have Eyes for You') and *On the Town* ('Miss Turnstiles' ballet), and it also featured in a romantic comedy (*Practically Yours*) and was the scene of a brutal beating-up in *The Young Savages* and a nasty accidental death in *P.J.*; while the whole of *Dutchman* took place on it.

The New York elevated railway, on the other hand, was most dramatically used in *King Kong*, and provided effective backing in *The Lost Weekend*, *Union Station*, *The Bachelor Party* and *The FBI Story*.

undertakers, or morticians, have provided comedy relief in many a western, relying on frequent shootings to bring in business: perhaps this theme was first explored in *The Westerner* (39). The comedy elements of the profession were also presented by Vincent Price and Peter Lorre in *A Comedy of Terrors*, by Terry Thomas in *Strange Bedfellows*, and by almost the entire cast of *The Loved One*. Literature's most famous undertaker is perhaps Mr Sowerberry in *Oliver Twist*, played by Gibb McLaughlin in the 1948 version and by Leonard Rossiter in *Oliver!*.

underwater sequences of note were found in *Reap the Wild Wind*, *The Silent Enemy*, *The Beast from 20,000 Fathoms*, *The Golden Mistress*, *Twenty Thousand Leagues Under the Sea*, *Around the World Under the Sea*, *Voyage to the Bottom of the Sea*, *Thunderball*, and *Lady in Cement*.
See also: *submarines*.

UNDERWORLD (US 1927). Released in Britain as *Paying the Penalty*, this melodrama written by Ben Hecht and directed by Josef von Sternberg did much to trigger off the gangster cycle. George Bancroft played 'Bull Weed', the anti-hero; Evelyn Brent was 'Feathers McCoy', his moll, and Clive Brook 'Rolls Royce', his side-kick.

unemployment in Britain was the somewhat unpopular subject of *Doss House*, *Love on the Dole*, and *The Common Touch*; in Europe, *Joyless Street*, *Little Man What Now?* and *Berliner Ballade*. America has seemed almost to boast about its unemployed, who were featured in *The Crowd*, *Our Daily Bread*, *Grapes of Wrath*, *Hallelujah I'm a Bum*, *Sullivan's Travels*, *I Was a Fugitive from a Chain Gang*, *Down Went*

McGinty, One More Spring, Mr Deeds Goes to Town, Man's Castle, My Man Godfrey and *Tobacco Road*, among many others.

UNFAITHFULLY YOURS (US 1948). Vintage satirical comedy, and the last good one to be written and directed by Preston Sturges. Rex Harrison plays Sir Alfred de Carter (!), a jealous orchestral conductor who suspects his wife of infidelity and plots three revenges during a concert: murder during Rossini, renunciation during Wagner, suicide during Tschaikovsky.

THE UNINVITED (US 1943). Claimed as Hollywood's first attempt at a serious ghost story, this set-bound adventure now seems rather tame, with its phoney Devon village and cliff-top house in which a girl is driven to desperation by the spirit of her mother but saved by that of her father's mistress. But at least it broadened Hollywood's horizons, and Lewis Allen, directing his first film, led us deftly through the talky script. With Gail Russell, Ray Milland, Donald Crisp, Cornelia Otis Skinner; from a novel, 'Uneasy Freehold', by Dorothy Macardle.

United Artists Corporation was founded in 1919 by Mary Pickford, Douglas Fairbanks, Charlie Chaplin and D. W. Griffith, the object being to make and distribute their own and other people's quality product. Among the company's early successes were *His Majesty the American, Pollyanna* (the first film sold on a percentage basis), *Broken Blossoms, Way Down East,* and *A Woman of Paris.* In the mid-20s Joe Schenck was brought in to run the company, and he in turn gained Valentino, Goldwyn, Keaton and Swanson; but later all were bought out by various syndicates. Howard Hughes contributed *Hell's Angels* and *Scarface,* but in the 30s the UA product began to thin out, partly because the company was purely a distributor and financer of independent producers, without any studio of its own or any large roster of stars under contract. The hardest times, with only inferior product to sell, were between 1948 and 1953; but since then a new board of directors fought back to a powerful position through careful choice of product, and UA is now back at the top of the tree again with a recent history that includes *The Magnificent Seven, Tom Jones,* the James Bond pictures, and *The Battle of Britain.*

Universal Pictures was founded in 1912 by Carl Laemmle, an exhibitor turned producer. Universal City grew steadily, and included among its output many of the most famous titles of Von Stroheim, Valentino and Lon Chaney. In 1930 came *All Quiet on the Western Front,* and soon after *Dracula and Frankenstein,* the precursors of a long line of horror pictures. Laemmle lost power in the mid-30s and the studio settled down to be one of Hollywood's 'little two', producing mainly modest, low-budget co-features without too many intellectual pretensions. There were occasional notable pictures: *Destry Rides Again, Hellzapoppin, Flesh and Fantasy*. The stars under contract were durable: Boris Karloff, Lon Chaney jnr, Donald O'Connor, Abbott and Costello, Jeff Chandler, Audie Murphy. More ambition was noted in the 50s, when the era of the bread-and-butter picture was ended by TV. Decca Records gained a large measure of control, but in 1962 a merger gave the ultimate power to the Music Corporation of America, ex-agents and TV producers. The last few years have seen a steady resumption of prestige, with films like *Spartacus*, the Doris Day–Rock Hudson sex comedies, *Charade, The War Lord*, and Ross Hunter's soapily sentimental but glossy remakes of Hollywood's choicest weepies. The company, now a division of MCA Inc, is currently one of Hollywood's most powerful sources of box-office films, though its venture into 'enlightened' European production was fairly disastrous.

universities have scarcely been studied seriously by movie-makers· Of Britain's most venerable, Cambridge has served as a background for one light comedy, *Bachelor of Hearts*, and Oxford for another (*A Yank at Oxford*) which was subsequently parodied by Laurel and Hardy (*A Chump at Oxford*). Provincial universities score one comedy (*Lucky Jim*) and one drama (*The Wild and the Willing*). American campuses have usually featured in films of the *Hold That Co-Ed* type, the pleasantest to remember being *The Freshman* and *Horse Feathers*, with *How To Be Very Very Popular* a poor third.

UNSWORTH, GEOFFREY (* –   ). British cinematographer. Assistant on *A Yank at Oxford* (38), *Sixty Glorious Years* (38), *The Thief of Bagdad* (40), *A Matter of Life and Death* (45), etc.; worked solo on many films since, including *The Million Pound Note* (53), *Hell Drivers* (57), *A Night to Remember* (58), *Northwest Frontier* (59), *The 300 Spartans* (62), *Becket* (BFA) (64), *Genghis Khan* (65), *Half a Sixpence* (67), *2001: A Space Odyssey* (68), *The Bliss of Mrs Blossom* (68), *The Assassination Bureau* (68), *A Matter of Honour* (69), *Three Sisters* (70), etc.

UP IN ARMS (US 1944). Exuberant comedy-musical which introduced Danny Kaye as a big star, after years in slapstick two-reelers. Directed by Elliott Nugent, with songs by Harold Arlen.

URE, MARY (1933–   ). British leading actress of stage and (occasionally) screen. *Storm over the Nile* (debut) (55), *Windom's Way* (59), *Look Back in Anger* (59), *Sons and Lovers* (60), *The Mind Benders* (63), *The Luck of Ginger Coffey* (64), *Custer of the West* (67), *Where Eagles Dare* (68).

URECAL, MINERVA (1896–1966). American character actress. *Oh Doctor* (37), *Boys of the City* (40), *The Bridge of San Luis Rey* (44), *Who's*

Urquhart, Robert

Guilty (47), *The Lost Moment* (48), *Harem Girl* (52), *Miracle in the Rain* (56), *The Seven Faces of Dr Lao* (64), etc. TV series: *Tugboat Annie.*

URQUHART, ROBERT (1922–). Scottish character actor, in films since 1951 after stage experience. *You're Only Young Twice* (debut) (51), *Knights of the Round Table* (54), *You Can't Escape* (56), *The Curse of Frankenstein* (56), *Dunkirk* (58), *55 Days at Peking* (62), *Murder at the Gallop* (64), *Country Dance* (70), etc.

USTINOV, PETER (1921–). Multi-talented actor/director/playwright/screenwriter/raconteur. As actor: *The Goose Steps Out* (debut: as Will Hay schoolboy) (41), *The Way Ahead* (44), *Private Angelo* (49), *Quo Vadis* (51), *Beau Brummell* (54), *The Sundowners* (60), *Spartacus* (AA) (60), *Romanoff and Juliet* (61), *Billy Budd* (62), *Topkapi* (AA) (64), *John Goldfarb Please Come Home* (64), *Lady L* (65), etc. Wrote and directed *School for Secrets* (46), *Vice Versa* (48), *Private Angelo* (49), *Romanoff and Juliet* (61), *Billy Budd* (62), *Lady L* (65). 1967: acting in *Blackbeard's Ghost*, filming *Viva Max.*

UYS, JAMIE (1921–). South African writer-producer-director, chiefly known for *Rip Van Winkle* (60), *Dingaka* (66).

V

VADIM, ROGER (1928–   ) (Roger Vadim Plemiannikow). French writer-director. *Futures Vedettes* (w) (54), *And God Created Woman* (w, d) (56), *Heaven Fell That Night* (w, d) (57), *Les Liaisons Dangereuses* (w, d) (59), *Warrior's Rest* (w, d) (62), *Vice and Virtue* (w, d) (62), *La Ronde* (w, d) (64), *Nutty Naughty Château* (*Château en Suède*) (64), *The Game is Over* (w, d) (66), *Histoires Extraordinaires* (part) (68), *Barbarella* (68), etc.

THE VAGABOND KING : see IF I WERE KING.

VAGUE, VERA : see BARBARA JO ALLEN.

VALENTI, JACK (1921–   ). American executive, dynamic President of the Motion Picture Association of America.

VALENTINE, JOSEPH (1903–   ) (Giuseppe Valentino). Italian-American cinematographer, long in Hollywood. Films include *Possessed* (47), *Sleep My Love* (47), *Rope* (48), *Joan of Arc* (AA) (48).

†VALENTINO, RUDOLPH (1895–1926). Italian-American leading man, the great romantic idol of the 20s: his personality still shows. His sudden death caused several suicides and his funeral was a national event. *My Official Wife* (14), *Patria* (16), *Alimony* (18), *A Society Sensation* (18), *All Night* (18), *The Delicious Little Devil* (19), *A Rogue's Romance* (19), *The Homebreaker* (19), *Virtuous Sinners* (19), *The Big Little Person* (19), *Out of Luck* (19), *Eyes of Youth* (19), *The Married Virgin* (20), *An Adventuress* (20), *The Cheater* (20), *Passion's Playground* (20), *Once to Every Woman* (20), *Stolen Moments* (20), *The Wonderful Chance* (20), *The Four Horsemen of the Apocalypse* (the part that made him a super-star) (21), *Unchained Seas* (21), *Camille* (21), *The Conquering Power* (21), *The Sheik* (21), *Moran of the Lady Letty* (21), *Beyond the Rocks* (22), *The Young Rajah* (22), *Blood and Sand* (22), *Monsieur Beaucaire* (24), *A Sainted Devil* (24), *Cobra* (24), *The Eagle* (25), *Son of the Sheik* (25). Among the published biographies of him are his wife Natacha Rambova's *Rudy* (26), George S. Ullman's *The Real Valentino* (27), Alan Arnold's *Valentino* (52), and Robert Oberfirst's *Rudolph Valentino, The Man Behind the Myth* (62).

VALK, FREDERICK (1901–1956). Heavyweight Czech stage actor, in Britain from 1939. Films include *Gasbags* (40), *Thunder Rock* (42), *Dead of Night* (45), *Latin Quarter* (46), *An Outcast of the Islands* (51), *Top Secret* (52), *The Colditz Story* (53), *Zarak* (55).

Vallee, Rudy

VALLEE, RUDY (1901–   ). American character comedian, the former crooning idol of the late 20s. *The Vagabond* (29), *Sweet Music* (34), *Gold Diggers in Paris* (38), *Second Fiddle* (39), *Too Many Blondes* (41), *The Palm Beach Story* (42), *Happy Go Lucky* (43), *It's in the Bag* (45), *The Bachelor and the Bobbysoxer* (47), *The Beautiful Blonde from Bashful Bend* (49), *Ricochet Romance* (54), *Gentlemen Marry Brunettes* (55), *The Helen Morgan Story* (57), *How to Succeed in Business Without Really Trying* (his stage role) (67), *Live a Little, Love a Little* (68), etc. Recently on cabaret tours.

VALLI, ALIDA (1921–   ) (Alida Maria Altenburger). Italian leading actress, in films from the mid-30s. *I Due Sergenti* (36), *Manon Lescaut* (39), *Piccolo Mondo Antico* (41), *Eugénie Grandet* (46), *The Paradine Case* (US) (48), *The Miracle of the Bells* (48), *The Third Man* (49), *Walk Softly Stranger* (49), *The White Tower* (50), *The Lovers of Toledo* (52), *Senso* (53), *The Stranger's Hand* (53), *Heaven Fell That Night* (57), *The Sea Wall* (*This Angry Age*) (57), *Le Dialogue des Carmélites* (59), *Ophelia* (61), *Une Aussi Longue Absence* (61), etc.

VALLI, VIRGINIA (1898–1968) (Virginia McSweeney). American silent screen heroine who retired in 1932 to marry Charles Farrell. *Efficiency Edgar's Courtship* (17), *The Storm* (22), *A Lady of Quality* (23), *Paid to Love* (27), *Isle of Lost Ships* (32), etc.

VALLONE, RAF (1916–   ). Italian leading man, former journalist, *Bitter Rice* (48), *Vendetta* (49), *Il Cristo Proibito* (50), *Anna* (51), *Thérèse Raquin* (53), *The Beach* (53), *The Sign of Venus* (55), *El Cid* (61), *A View from the Bridge* (US) (61), *Phaedra* (62), *The Cardinal* (63), *Harlow* (65), *Beyond the Mountains* (66), *The Italian Job* (69), etc.

VANBRUGH, IRENE (1872–1949). Distinguished British stage actress whose rare film appearances included *The Gay Lord Quex* (27), *Moonlight Sonata* (37).

VAN CLEEF, LEE (1925–   ). American actor who after many years as a sneaky western villain found fame and fortune as strong silent hero/villain of Italian westerns. *High Noon* (52), *Shane* (53), *A Man Alone* (55), *Joe Dakota* (57), *Guns Girls and Gangsters* (58), *For a Few Dollars More* (65), *The Good The Bad and The Ugly* (66), *The Big Gundown* (66), etc.

VAN DINE, S. S. (1888–1939) (Willard Huntingdon Wright). American author who created the wealthy man-about-town detective Philo Vance, personified on screen by several actors. William Powell played him in *The Canary Murder Case* (29), *The Greene Murder Case* (29), *The Benson Murder Case* (30), and *The Kennel Murder Case* (33). Basil Rathbone had one attempt, *The Bishop Murder Case* (30). Warren William took over for *The Dragon Murder Case* (34) and

The Gracie Allen Murder Case (39). Meanwhile there were Paul Lukas in *The Casino Murder Case* (35), Edmund Lowe in *The Garden Murder Case* (36), and Grant Richards in *Night of Mystery* (37). 1940 brought James Stephenson in *Calling Philo Vance*; in 1947 there was William Wright in *Philo Vance Returns*; and Alan Curtis in 1948 appeared in two poor attempts, *Philo Vance's Gamble* and *Philo Vance's Secret Mission*.

VAN DOREN, MAMIE (1933–   ) (Joan Lucille Olander). American leading lady, the blonde bombshell of the second feature, in Hollywood from 1954. *Forbidden* (debut) (54), *Yankee Pasha* (54), *The Second Greatest Sex* (55), *Running Wild* (55), *The Girl in Black Stockings* (56), *Teacher's Pet* (58), *The Navy Versus the Night Monsters* (66), etc.

VAN DRUTEN, JOHN (1901–1957). British dramatist who latterly lived in America. Plays filmed include *Young Woodley, I am a Camera. Old Acquaintance, The Voice of the Turtle*.

VAN DYKE, DICK (1925–   ). American TV comedian rapidly establishing himself in movies. *Bye Bye Birdie* (63), *What a Way To Go* (64), *Mary Poppins* (64), *The Art of Love* (65), *Lt Robin Crusoe* (65), *Divorce American Style* (67), *Fitzwilly* (67), *Chitty Chitty Bang Bang* (68), *Billy Bright* (69), *Some Kind of Nut* (69), etc. TV series: *The Dick Van Dyke Show* (61–66).

VAN DYKE, W. S. (1889–1944). American director, with stage experience; former assistant to D. W. Griffith. *White Shadows of the South Seas* (26), *Trader Horn* (30), *Cuban Love Song* (32), *Eskimo* (33), *The Thin Man* (34), *The Painted Veil* (34), *Naughty Marietta* (35), *San Francisco* (36), *They Gave Him a Gun* (37), *Rosalie* (37), *Marie Antoinette* (38), *Sweethearts* (38), *It's a Wonderful World* (39), *Bitter Sweet* (40), *Rage in Heaven* (41), *I Married an Angel* (41), *Shadow of the Thin Man* (42), *Journey for Margaret* (42), then war service.

VANEL, CHARLES (1892–   ). French character actor, with stage experience. *Les Misérables* (33), *Le Grand Jeu* (34), *La Belle Equipe* (36), *Légion d'Honneur* (38), *Carrefour* (39), *La Ferme du Pendu* (45), *In Nomme della Legge* (49), *The Wages of Fear* (53), *Maddalena* (54), *Les Diaboliques (The Fiends)* (55), *Rafles sur la Ville* (57), *Le Dialogue des Carmélites* (59), *La Vérité* (60), *Un Homme de Trop* (67), many others.

VAN EYCK, PETER (1913–1969). Blond German actor, in America from mid-30s, later international. *The Moon Is Down* (42), *Five Graves to Cairo* (43), *Rommel, Desert Fox* (51), *The Wages of Fear* (53), *Retour de Manivelle* (57), *The Girl Rosemarie* (58), *The Snorkel* (58), *Foxhole in Cairo* (60), *Station Six Sahara* (63), *The Spy Who Came in from the Cold* (65), *Million Dollar Man* (67), *Shalako* (68), many others.

Van Eyssen, John

VAN EYSSEN, JOHN (c. 1923–). South African actor who appeared in a number of British films before turning agent. *Quatermass II* (56), *Dracula* (57), *I'm All Right Jack* (59), *The Criminal* (60), *Exodus* (60), etc. 1969: chief production executive in Britain for Columbia.

VAN FLEET, JO (1922–). American stage actress who has made several films. *East of Eden* (AA) (55), *The Rose Tattoo* (56), *I'll Cry Tomorrow* (57), *Gunfight at the OK Corral* (57), *The King and Four Queens* (57), *Wild River* (60), *Cool Hand Luke* (67), *I Love You Alice B. Toklas* (68), etc.

VAN HEUSEN, JIMMY (1919–). American songwriter, usually with lyrics by Johnny Burke. 'Swinging on a Star' (AA 1944), 'Sunday, Monday or Always', 'Sunshine Cake', many others; films include *Road to Rio* (47), *A Yankee in King Arthur's Court* (49), *Road to Bali* (53), *Little Boy Lost* (53), etc.

VAN PARYS, GEORGES (1902–). French composer. *Le Million* (31), *Jeunesse* (34), *Café de Paris* (38), *Le Silence Est d'Or* (46), *Fanfan La Tulipe* (51), *Adorables Créatures* (52), *Les Diaboliques (The Fiends)* (55), *French Cancan* (55), *Charmants Garçons* (57), many others.

VAN ROOTEN, LUIS (1906–). Mexican-born American character actor. *The Hitler Gang* (as Himmler) (44), *Two Years Before the Mast* (44), *To the Ends of the Earth* (48), *Champion* (49), *Detective Story* (51), *The Sea Chase* (55), etc.

VAN SLOAN, EDWARD (1882–1964). American character actor with stage experience; often seen as elderly professors. *Dracula* (30), *Frankenstein* (31), *The Mummy* (33), *Death Takes a Holiday* (34), *The Last Days of Pompeii* (35), *Dracula's Daughter* (36), *The Doctor Takes a Wife* (40), *The Mask of Dijon* (last film) (47), etc.

VAN UPP, VIRGINIA (c. 1913–). American executive producer, at Columbia in the late 40s. Former writer: *Young and Willing* (40), *The Crystal Ball* (42), *Cover Girl* (44), *The Impatient Years* (also produced) (44), *Together Again* (also produced) (45), etc.

VAN ZANDT, PHILIP (1904–1958). Dutch character actor, in Hollywood films. *Citizen Kane* (41), *House of Frankenstein* (45), *April Showers* (48), *Viva Zapata* (52), *Knock on Wood* (54), *The Pride and the Passion* (57), etc.

VARCONI, VICTOR (1896–) (Mihaly Varkonyi). Hungarian actor long in Hollywood. *The Volga Boatmen* (26), *King of Kings* (27), *The Doomed Battalion* (31), *Roberta* (34), *The Plainsman* (36), *Disputed Passage* (39), *Reap the Wild Wind* (42), *For Whom the Bell Tolls* (43), *Samson and Delilah* (50), etc.

VARDA, AGNES (1928–   ). French writer-director of the 'left bank' school. *La Pointe Courte* (56), *Cleo de 5 à 7* (62), *Le Bonheur* (65), *Les Créatures* (66), etc.

VARDEN, EVELYN (1895–1958). American stage character actress who made several films: *Pinky* (49), *Cheaper by the Dozen* (50), *Phone Call from a Stranger* (52), *The Student Prince* (54), *Night of the Hunter* (55), *The Bad Seed* (56), etc.

VARDEN, NORMA (c. 1898–   ). British character actress, usually as haughty aristocrat in comedies; went to Hollywood in the 40s. *A Night Like This* (32), *The Iron Duke* (35), *Foreign Affairs* (36), *Shipyard Sally* (39), *Random Harvest* (42), *The Green Years* (46), *Strangers on a Train* (51), *Gentlemen Prefer Blondes* (53), *Witness for the Prosecution* (58), *The Sound of Music* (65), *Doctor Dolittle* (67), many others.

variable area and *variable density*. Types of sound track. Variable area appears as a spiky symmetrical line (like a long folded ink blot). Variable density is the same width throughout but with horizontal bars of varying light and shade.

VARIETY (Germany 1925). Also known as VAUDEVILLE, this trapeze melodrama has a plot very similar to the later *Three Maxims* and *Trapeze*. Solemnly but stylishly directed by E. A. Dupont, with Emil Jannings, Warwick Ward and Lya de Putti.

VARLEY, BEATRICE (1896–   ). British character actress who has been playing worried little elderly ladies for thirty years. *Hatter's Castle* (41), *So Well Remembered* (47), *No Room at the Inn* (49), *Hindle Wakes* (53), *The Feminine Touch* (55), scores of others. Also stage and TV.

VARNEL, MARCEL (1894–1947). French-born director, in Hollywood from 1924; came to Britain 1935 and made some of the best comedies of Will Hay (*Oh Mr Porter* [38]), the Crazy Gang (*Alf's Button Afloat* [39]), George Formby (*Get Cracking* [43]), etc.; also *Hi Gang* (41), *The First Gentleman* (47), others. His son MAX VARNEL is now a TV director.

VARSI, DIANE (1938–   ). American leading lady who retired after a few films. *Peyton Place* (57), *Ten North Frederick* (57), *Compulsion* (59), *Wild in the Streets* (68), *Killers Three* (68), *Bloody Mama* (70), etc.

VAUGHAN, FRANKIE (1928–   ). British song and dance man of stage and TV. His several films include *Ramsbottom Rides Again* (55), *These Dangerous Years* (57), *Wonderful Things* (58), *The Lady Is a Square* (58), *Heart of a Man* (59), *Let's Make Love* (US) (61), *The Right Approach* (US) (62), *It's All Over Town* (64), etc. Real name: Frank Abelsohn.

Vaughan, Peter

VAUGHAN, PETER (1923–   ). British character actor of solid presence, *Sapphire* (59), *Village of the Damned* (60), *The Punch and Judy Man* (63), *Fanatic* (65), *The Naked Runner* (67), *Hammerhead* (68), *The Bofors Gun* (68), *Alfred the Great* (69), etc.

VAUGHN, ROBERT (1932–   ). American leading man of serious mien, with stage experience: chiefly familiar as TVs man from *U.N.C.L.E.* Films include *No Time to be Young* (58), *The Young Philadelphians* (59), *The Magnificent Seven* (60), *The Caretakers* (63), *The Venetian Affair* (66), *Bullitt* (68), *The Mind of Mr Soames* (GB) (69), *The Bridge at Remagen* (69).

VEDRES, NICOLE (1911–1965). French director, mainly of probing documentaries. *Paris 1900* (47), *La Vie Commence Demain* (50), *Au Frontières de l'Homme* (53), etc.

VEIDT, CONRAD (1893–1943). Distinguished German character actor who also filmed in Britain and Hollywood. *The Cabinet of Dr Caligari* (19), *Waxworks* (24), *Lucrezia Borgia* (25), *The Student of Prague* (26), *The Hands of Orlac* (26), *The Beloved Rogue* (US) (27), *The Man Who Laughs* (27), *Rasputin* (30), *Congress Dances* (31), *Rome Express* (GB) (32), *I Was a Spy* (GB) (33), *F.P.1* (33), *The Wandering Jew* (GB) (33), *Jew Suss* (GB) (34), *Bella Donna* (GB) (34), *The Passing of the Third Floor Back* (GB) (35), *King of the Damned* (GB) (35), *Under the Red Robe* (GB) (36), *Dark Journey* (GB) (37), *The Spy in Black* (GB) (39), *Contraband* (GB) (40), *The Thief of Bagdad* (GB) (40), *A Woman's Face* (US) (41), *Whistling in the Dark* (US) (41), *All through the Night* (US) (41), *The Men in Her Life* (*Ballerina*) (US) (42), *Nazi Agent* (US) (42), *Casablanca* (US) (42), *Above Suspicion* (US) (43), etc.

VEILLER, ANTHONY (1903–1965). American scriptwriter, in Hollywood from 1930. *Her Cardboard Lover* (42), *The Killers* (46), *Along the Great Divide* (51), *Moulin Rouge* (53), *Red Planet Mars* (also p) (53), *Safari* (56), *The List of Adrian Messenger* (63), many others.

VELEZ, LUPE (1909–1944). Mexican leading lady usually seen in temperamental roles. Started in Hal Roach two-reelers; then *Gaucho* (27), *Lady of the Pavements* (29), *Resurrection* (31), *The Half Naked Truth* (32), *Cuban Love Song* (32), *Strictly Dynamite* (34), *Mexican Spitfire* (39) (and several sequels) etc. Real name: Guadelupe Velez de Villalobos.

VENABLE, EVELYN (1913–   ). American leading lady of the 30s, usually in demure roles. *Cradle Song* (23), *Mrs Wiggs of the Cabbage Patch* (34), *Alice Adams* (35), *The Frontiersman* (38), *He Hired the Boss* (last to date) (43), etc. Married Hal Mohr.

VENESS, AMY (1876–1960). British character actress who latterly played cheerful old souls. *My Wife's Family* (31), *Hobson's Choice* (31), *Lorna Doone* (35), *Aren't Men Beasts?* (37), *Yellow Sands* (39),

The Man in Grey (43), *This Happy Breed* (44), *Here Come the Huggetts* (49), *Doctor in the House* (54), etc.

ventriloquists rarely stray from music hall to cinema, but Michael Redgrave played a demented one in *Dead of Night* and a similar theme was explored in the 1964 *Devil Doll*. A vent's dummy was used for comedy in *Knock on Wood*, for satire in *How I Won the War*, and for mystery in *The Dummy Talks*. The most movie-exposed performing ventriloquist is certainly Edgar Bergen, who with his dummy Charlie McCarthy and Mortimer Snerd appeared in a dozen or more films between 1937 and 1944.

VENTURA, LINO (1918–). Italian leading man, former boxer *Touchez Pas Au Grisbi* (53), *Marie Octobre* (57), *Crooks in Clover* (63), *Les Aventuriers* (67), others.

VERA-ELLEN (1927–) (Vera-Ellen Westmeyr Rohe). Diminutive, vivacious American leading lady of musicals; former band singer and dancer. *Wonder Man* (45), *Three Little Girls in Blue* (46), *Carnival in Costa Rica* (47), *Words and Music* (48), *On the Town* (49), *Three Little Words* (50), *Love Happy* (50), *Happy Go Lovely* (51), *Call Me Madam* (53), *White Christmas* (54), *Let's Be Happy* (56), etc. Retired.

VERDUGO, ELENA (1926–). Spanish-American leading lady. *Down Argentine Way* (40), *The Moon and Sixpence* (42), *House of Frankenstein* (45), *Song of Scheherazade* (47), *Cyrano de Bergerac* (50), *Thief of Damascus* (52), *How Sweet It Is* (68), etc. TV series: *Meet Millie* (52), *The New Phil Silvers Show* (63).

VERMILYEA, HAROLD (1889–1958). Russian-American character actor, former operatic singer. *O.S.S.* (46), *The Big Clock* (48), *Edge of Doom* (51), etc.

VERNE, JULES (1828–1905). French adventure novelist whose inventive science-fiction themes have latterly endeared him to Hollywood. Films of his works since 1954 include *Twenty Thousand Leagues Under the Sea*, *Around the World in 80 Days*, *From the Earth to the Moon*, *Journey to the Centre of the Earth*, *Five Weeks in a Balloon*, *Master of the World*, *The Children of Captain Grant* (*In Search of the Castaways*) and *Rocket to the Moon*.

VERNE, KAREN (1915–1968) (Ingabor Katrine Klinckerfuss). Norwegian leading lady who made a number of Hollywood films. *Ten Days in Paris* (GB) (39), *All Through the Night* (41), *King's Row* (42), *The Seventh Cross* (44), *A Bullet for Joey* (55), *Ship of Fools* (65), *Torn Curtain* (67), etc.

VERNEUIL, HENRI (1920–). French director, former journalist. *La Table aux Crevés* (50), *Forbidden Fruit* (52), *Public Enemy Number One* (53), *Paris Palace Hotel* (56), *The Cow and I* (59), *L'Affaire d'une Nuit* (*It Happened All Night*) (61), *The Big Snatch* (*Melodie en Sous-Sol*) (63), *Guns for San Sebastian* (68), many others.

VERNO, JERRY (1895–   ). British cockney character actor. *His Lordship* (32), *The Thirty-nine Steps* (35), *Farewell Again* (37), *Old Mother Riley in Paris* (38), *The Common Touch* (41), *The Red Shoes* (48), *The Belles of St Trinian's* (54), *After the Ball* (57), many others.

VERNON, ANNE (1925–   ) (Edith Vignaud). Vivacious French leading lady who has also filmed in Britain and Hollywood. *Le Mannequin Assassiné* (48), *Warning to Wantons* (GB) (48), *Shakedown* (US) (49), *Edward and Caroline* (50), *Rue de l'Estrapade* (52), *The Love Lottery* (GB) (54), *Time Bomb* (GB) (54), *Le Long des Trottoirs* (56), *Les Lavandières de Portugal* (57), *The Umbrellas of Cherbourg* (64), etc.

VERNON, RICHARD (c. 1907–   ). British character actor of stage and TV, usually in soft-spoken aristocratic roles. Films include *Accidental Death* (63), *A Hard Day's Night* (64), *Goldfinger* (64), *The Secret of My Success* (65), many others. TV series: *The Man in Room 17*.

VERSOIS, ODILE (1930–   ) (Militza de Poliakoff-Baidarov). French leading lady, sister of Marina Vlady. *Les Dernières Vacances* (46), *Into the Blue* (GB) (48), *Bel Amour* (51), *A Day to Remember* (GB) (53), *The Young Lovers* (*Chance Meeting*) (GB) (55), *To Paris with Love* (GB) (55), *Passport to Shame* (GB) (58), *Cartouche* (*Swords of Blood*) (62), *Benjamin* (68), etc.

VERTOV, DZIGA (1896–1954). Russian director and film theorist. Many documentaries; also *One-Sixth of the World* (27), *The Man with the Movie Camera* (28), *Three Songs of Lenin* (34), *In the Line of Fire* (41), etc.

VICAS, VICTOR (1918–   ). Franco-Russian director. *Double Destiny* (54), *Count Five and Die* (GB) (58), *Les Disparus* (60), etc.

VICKERS, MARTHA (1925–   ) (M. MacVicar). American leading lady of the 40s. *The Falcon in Mexico* (44), *The Big Sleep* (46), *Love and Learn* (47), *Ruthless* (48), *Bad Boy* (49), *Daughter of the West* (51), *The Burglar* (57), *Four Fast Guns* (60), etc.

VICTIM (GB 1962). This first British film to tackle homosexuality did so under cover of a detective story. Whether or not this invalidates it as social comment, it was an exciting film. Written by Janet Green, produced and directed by Michael Relph and Basil Dearden, photographed by Otto Heller; with Dirk Bogarde doing well in the difficult, ambiguous central role.

VICTOR, CHARLES (1896–1965). British character actor with long stage experience; in films from 1938, usually in cockney roles. *While the Sun Shines* (46), *The Calendar* (48), *The Ringer* (52), *Those People*

Next Door (53), *The Embezzler* (55), *Now and Forever* (57), scores of others.

VICTOR, HENRY (1898–1945). British character actor who went to Hollywood in the 30s and played villainous bit roles. *She* (25), *The Guns of Loos* (28), *The Fourth Commandment* (28), *The Mummy* (33), *Our Fighting Navy* (37), *Confessions of a Nazi Spy* (39), *Zanzibar* (40), *King of the Zombies* (41), etc.

THE VICTORS (GB 1963). By devising the anti-war film to end them all, writer-producer-director Carl Foreman pushed bits of this World War II compendium into absurdity: there simply wasn't a decent character around. But it does have moving and horrifying sequences, also some which impress as pure cinema. Photographed by Christopher Challis, with a generally effective American-international cast.

VIDAL, HENRI (1919–1959). Tough-looking French leading man, in films from 1940. *Les Maudits* (46), *Quai de Grenelle* (50), *Port du Désir* (54), *The Wicked Go to Hell* (55), *Porte des Lilas* (56), *Come Dance with Me* (59), etc.

VIDOR, CHARLES (1900–1959). Hungarian-American director, in Hollywood from 1932. *The Mask of Fu Manchu* (32), *Sensation Hunters* (34), *The Great Gambini* (37), *The Lady in Question* (40), *The Tuttles of Tahiti* (42), *The Desperadoes* (43), *Cover Girl* (44), *Together Again* (44), *A Song to Remember* (45), *Over 21* (45), *Gilda* (46), *The Guilt of Janet Ames* (48), *Hans Christian Andersen* (52), *Love Me or Leave Me* (55), *The Swan* (56), *The Joker Is Wild* (58), *A Farewell to Arms* (58), *Song without End* (unfinished) (59), many others.

VIDOR, FLORENCE (1895–). American leading lady of the silent screen. *Barbara Frietchie* (24), *The Grand Duchess and the Waiter* (26), *Are Parents People?* (26), *Lying Lips* (27), *The Patriot* (28), *Chinatown Nights* (29), etc. Married Jascha Heifetz, and retired.

VIDOR, KING (1894–). American director, former journalist, in Hollywood from 1915. *Peg o' My Heart* (23), *The Big Parade* (26), *The Crowd* (28), *Showpeople* (28), *Hallelujah* (29), *Not So Dumb* (30), *Billy the Kid* (30), *The Champ* (31), *Street Scene* (31), *Bird of Paradise* (32), *Cynara* (32), *The Stranger's Return* (33), *Our Daily Bread* (also wrote and produced) (33), *The Wedding Night* (34), *So Red the Rose* (35), *The Texas Rangers* (36), *Stella Dallas* (also p) (37), *The Citadel* (GB) (38), *Northwest Passage* (40), *Comrade X* (40), *H. M. Pulham Esquire* (41), *An American Romance* (also p) (44), *Duel in the Sun* (46), *On Our Merry Way* (co-d) (47), *The Fountainhead* (49), *Beyond the Forest* (49), *Lightning Strikes Twice* (51), *Japanese War Bride* (52), *Ruby Gentry* (52), *The Man without a Star* (54), *War and Peace* (56),

Solomon and Sheba (59), etc. Published autobiography 1953: *A Tree is a Tree.* (†Talkies complete.)

VIERNY, SACHA (1919–   ). French cinematographer. *Hiroshima Mon Amour* (58), *Last Year in Marienbad* (61), *Muriel* (63), *Do You Like Women?* (64), *Belle de Jour* (67), etc.

VIERTEL, BERTHOLD (1885–   ). Austrian director who moved to Britain and Hollywood from 1931. *The Wise Sex* (31), *The Man from Yesterday* (32), *Little Friend* (34), *The Passing of the Third Floor Back* (35), *Rhodes of Africa* (36), etc.

VIGO, JEAN (1905–1934) (Jean Almereyda). Influential French director on the strength of three semi-experimental, dream-like films: *A propos de Nice* (30), *Zéro de Conduite* (32), *L'Atalante* (34).

VILLARD, FRANK (1917–   ) (François Drouineau). French leading man, often in shifty roles. *Le Dernier Des Six* (41), *Gigi* (48), *Manèges* (*The Wanton*) (49), *L'Ingénue Libertine* (50), *Le Garçon Sauvage* (51), *Huis Clos* (54), *Crime Passionel* (55), *Mystères de Paris* (57), *Le Cave se Rebiffe* (61), *Mata Hari* (64), etc.

VILLIERS, JAMES (c. 1930–   ). British actor, usually in snooty or villainous roles. *The Entertainer* (60), *The Damned* (64), *King and Country* (64), *The Nanny* (65), *Half a Sixpence* (67), *Some Girls Do* (68), *Otley* (68), *A Nice Girl Like Me* (69), etc.

VINSON, HELEN (c. 1905–   ) (Helen Rulfs). Cool, aristocratic leading lady of Hollywood films of the 30s and 40s. *Jewel Robbery* (31), *I am a Fugitive from a Chain Gang* (32), *The Power and the Glory* (33), *The Tunnel* (GB) (35), *Vogues of 1938*, *In Name Only* (39), *Torrid Zone* (40), *Nothing But the Truth* (41), *They Are Guilty* (44), *The Lady and the Doctor* (last to date) (46), etc.

THE VIRGINIAN. Owen Wister's western novel was filmed in 1914 with Dustin Farnum, in 1930 with Gary Cooper, and in 1945 with Joel McCrea; in 1964 it turned up as a long-running TV series with James Drury. *Spawn of the North* (38) borrowed the basic plot, and in its turn was remade as *Alaska Seas* (54).

VIRIDIANA (Spain 1961). Luis Bunuel's startlingly allusive allegory of good and evil, with the latter winning in the end, is a ramshackle but absorbing film rounding up all the diverse moods of his earlier career: poetic, sacrilegious, melodramatic, enigmatic, hilarious and often moving.

VISCONTI, LUCHINO (1906–   ) (L. V. de Modrone). Italian writer-director, former art director. *Ossessione* (42), *La Terra Trema* (48), *Bellissima* (51), *Siamo Donne* (part) (52), *Senso* (53), *White Nights*

(57), *Rocco and His Brothers* (60), *Boccaccio 70* (62), *The Leopard* (64), *The Damned* (69), etc. Also stage producer.

LES VISITEURS DU SOIR (France 1942). A medieval fantasy written by Jacques Prevert and directed by Marcel Carne; remarkable in that, though made under the German occupation, it contrived to point an allegory of the resistance. (The devil turns the lovers to stone; but their hearts still beat no matter how hard he whips them.) As a film slow-moving, though full of elegant visuals, it has excellent performances from Jules Berry as the Devil and Arletty as his agent. Music by Maurice Thiriet, décor by Wakhevitch.

VistaVision. In 1953, when some companies were reluctant to follow Fox's lead and adopt CinemaScope, Paramount introduced Vista-Vision, a non-anamorphic process retaining the old frame ratio of 4 x 3. The chief innovation was that none of the essential action took place at the top or bottom of the picture, so that exhibitors with appropriate lens and aperture plates could choose their own screen ratio (from 4 x 3 to 2 x 1). At 2 x 1 on a big screen, VistaVision did not look very different from CinemaScope, especially as the loss of definition involved in magnifying the image was offset by printing the negative on 70mm stock and reducing this to 35mm during printing.

VITALE, MILLY (1938–). Italian leading lady. American films include *The Juggler* (53), *The Seven Little Foys* (55), *A Breath of Scandal* (60).

VITTI, MONICA (1933–) (Monica Luisa Ceciarelli). Italian leadin lady currently in international demand. *L'Avventura* (59), *La Notte* (60), *L'Eclisse* (62), *Dragées au Poivre* (63), *Nutty Naughty Château* (64), *The Red Desert* (64), *Modesty Blaise* (GB) (65), *The Chastity Belt* (67), etc.

VIVA MARIA (France 1965). A highly fashionable, and mostly very diverting, period extravaganza written and directed by Louis Malle, involving Brigitte Bardot and Jeanne Moreau in a Mexican revolution and a great many irrelevant visual gags. Melodrama and sex are nicely balanced by bouts of great cinematic fun . . . and everything is enhanced by Henri Decae's luxuriant colour photography.

VLADY, MARINA (1938–) (Marina de Poliakoff-Baidarov). French leading lady, sister of Odile Versois. *Orage d'Eté* (49), *Avant Le Déluge* (53), *The Wicked Go to Hell* (55), *Crime and Punishment* (56), *Toi le Venin* (59), *La Steppa* (61), *Climats* (62), *Enough Rope* (63), *Dragées au Poivre* (63), *Queen Bee* (64), *Chimes at Midnight* (66), etc.

VOGEL, PAUL C. (1899–). American cinematographer. *The Lady in the Lake* (46), *Black Hand* (49), *Battleground* (AA) (49), *Rose Marie*

(54), *High Society* (56), *The Wings of Eagles* (56), *The Time Machine* (60), *The Rounders* (64), etc.

VOGEL, VIRGIL (* –). American director, from TV. *The Mole People* (56), *Terror in the Midnight Sun* (58), *Son of Ali Baba* (64), etc.

VOGLER, KARL MICHAEL (1928–). German stage actor who has appeared in a few international films. *Those Magnificent Men in Their Flying Machines* (65), *The Blue Max* (67), *How I Won the War* (67), *Patton* (69), etc.

VOIGHT, JON (1939–). American leading actor who shot to fame in *Midnight Cowboy* (69). 1970: *The Revolutionary*.

volcanoes in the late 30s seemed all to belong to Paramount Studios' which used them as the climax of most of Dorothy Lamour's jungle pictures. They more recently turned up in *The Devil at Four o'clock*, and in *Journey to the Centre of the Earth* in which the way was down an extinct Icelandic crater and back on a fountain of lava up the inside of Etna. The famous eruption of Vesuvius was staged for the various versions of *The Last Days of Pompeii*, and *Krakatoa: East of Java* featured another historical disaster. A volcano was also the climax of Hal Roach's *Man and His Mate* and of its recent remake *One Million Years B.C.*; but the most spectacular pictures were obtained for the documentary compilation simply called *Volcano*.

VON HARBOU, THEA (1888–1954). German screenwriter, mainly associated with Fritz Lang's silent films. *Der Mude Tod* (21), *Dr Mabuse* (22), *Nibelungen Saga* (24), *Chronicles of the Grey House* (25), *Metropolis* (26), *The Spy* (28), *The Woman in the Moon* (29), *The Testament of Dr Mabuse* (32), *The Old and the Young King* (35), *Annélie* (41), *Fahrt Ins Gluck* (45), *The Affairs of Dr Holl* (51), others.

VON SEYFFERTITZ, GUSTAV (1863–1943). German actor who made some Hollywood films. *Old Wives for New* (18), *Sparrows* (26), *The Student Prince* (27), *The Bat Whispers* (31), *Shanghai Express* (32), *She* (35), *In Old Chicago* (38), *Nurse Edith Cavell* (39), etc. During World War I was known as G. Butler Clonblough.

†VON STERNBERG, JOSEPH (1894–1969) (Josef Stern). Austrian director, in US from early 20s. A great pictorial stylist and the creator of Marlene Dietrich's American image. *The Salvation Hunters* (25), *The Seagull* (unreleased) (26), *Underworld* (27), *The Last Command* (28), *The Dragnet* (28), *Docks of New York* (28), *The Case of Lena Smith* (29), *Thunderbolt* (29), *The Blue Angel* (in Germany) (30), *Morocco* (30), *Dishonoured* (31), *An American Tragedy* (31), *Shanghai Express* (32), *Blonde Venus* (32), *The Scarlet Empress* (34), *The Devil is a Woman* (35), *The King Steps Out* (36), *Crime and Punishment* (36),

I Claudius (unfinished) (37), *Sergeant Madden* (39), *The Shanghai Gesture* (41), *Jet Pilot* (50), *Macao* (51), *The Saga of Anatahan* (Jap.) (53). Wrote screenplays of most of his films. Published autobiography 1965: *Fun in a Chinese Laundry*. A critical study by Herman G. Weinberg was published in 1967.

VON STROHEIM, ERICH (1885–1957) (Hans Erich Maria Stroheim von Nordenwall). Austrian actor and director, mainly in Hollywood, where his extravagance in the 20s was notorious and harmed his later career. Former soldier. *Blind Husbands* (a, d) (19), *The Devil's Pass Key* (d) (19), *Foolish Wives* (a, d) (21), *Merry Go Round* (d) (22), *Greed* (d) (23), *The Merry Widow* (d) (25), *The Wedding March* (a, d) (27), *Queen Kelly* (w, d) (unfinished) (28), etc. Never directed again, but acted in *The Great Gabbo* (29), *As You Desire Me* (31), *Walking Down Broadway* (33), *The Crime of Dr Crespi* (35), *La Grande Illusion* (37), *Mademoiselle Docteur* (37), *L'Alibi* (38), *So Ends Our Night* (41), *Five Graves to Cairo* (43), *North Star* (44), *The Great Flamarion* (45), *La Danse de Mort* (47), *Sunset Boulevard* (50), *La Maison du Crime* (52), *Napoleon* (54), *L'Homme au Cents Visages* (56), others. A biography, *Hollywood Scapegoat*, by Peter Noble, was published in 1954.

VON SYDOW, MAX (1929–   ). Swedish actor, a member of Ingmar Bergman's company. *Miss Julie* (51), *The Seventh Seal* (56), *Wild Strawberries* (57), *So Close to Life* (58), *The Face* (59), *The Virgin Spring* (60), *Through a Glass Darkly* (61), *Winter Light* (62), *The Mistress* (62), *The Greatest Story Ever Told* (as Jesus) (US) (65), *The Reward* (US) (65), *Hawaii* (US) (66), *The Quiller Memorandum* (GB) (66), *Hour of the Wolf* (67), *The Shame* (68), *The Kremlin Letter* (US) (69).

VORHAUS, BERNARD (c. 1898–   ). German director, mostly in Britain and Hollywood. *Money for Speed* (GB) (33), *Broken Melody* (GB) (35), *Cotton Queen* (GB) (37), *Three Faces West* (US) (40), *Lady from Louisiana* (US) (41), *Bury Me Dead* (US) (47), *So Young So Bad* (US) (50), *The Lady from Boston* (US) (51), etc.

VOSKOVEC, GEORGE (1905–   ). Czech stage actor, long in US. Occasional films include *Twelve Angry Men* (57), *The Spy Who Came in from the Cold* (65), *Mister Buddwing* (66).

VYE, MURVYN (1913–   ). Burly American character actor who usually plays heavies. Stage experience. *Golden Earrings* (48), *A Connecticut Yankee at King Arthur's Court* (49), *Pick-Up* (51), *Road to Bali* (52), *Green Fire* (54), *Pearl of the South Pacific* (55), *Al Capone* (59), *Pay or Die* (60), etc. TV series; *The Bob Cummings Show*.

W

THE WAGES OF FEAR (France 1953). A long, solid shocker with serious undertones about four drivers with a cargo of nitro-glycerine. It showed that France could make a big commercial thriller as well as anybody, and very nearly forced acceptance of continental movies in British cinemas (it was given a full circuit release, sub-titles and all, but not enough others in a similar category came along to make foreign films a habit, and dubbing finally won the day). Written and directed by Henri-Georges Clouzot from a novel by Georges Arnaud; photographed by Armand Thirard with music by Georges Auric. With Yves Montand, Charles Vanel, Peter van Eyck. BFA (best film).

WAGGNER, GEORGE (1894–). American director, mainly of routine low-budgeters, in Hollywood from 1920. *The Wolf Man* (41), *The Climax* (also produced) (44), *Cobra Woman* (also produced) (45), *The Fighting Kentuckian* (49) (also wrote), *Operation Pacific* (also wrote) (51), *Bitter Creek* (54), *Destination 60,000* (also wrote) (57), *Pale Arrow* (58), many others.

WAGNER, FRITZ ARNO (1894–1958). German cinematographer: *Nosferatu* (23), *The Loves of Jeanne Ney* (27), *The Spy* (28), *Westfront 1918* (30), *Die Dreigroschenoper* (31), *Kameradschaft* (31), *Amphitryon* (35), *Ohm Kruger* (41), *Hotel Adlon* (55), many others.

WAGNER, ROBERT (1930–). American leading man spotted by talent scout while still at college. *Halls of Montezuma* (debut) (50), *With a Song in My Heart* (52), *Titanic* (53), *Prince Valiant* (54), *Broken Lance* (54), *White Feather* (55), *The Mountain* (56), *A Kiss Before Dying* (56), *The Hunters* (57), *Say One for Me* (58), *All the Fine Young Cannibals* (59), *The Longest Day* (62), *The Condemned of Altona* (63), *The Moving Target* (*Harper*) (66), *The Biggest Bundle of Them All* (66), *Don't Just Stand There* (68), *Winning* (69), etc. TV series: *It Takes a Thief* (67–68).

WAJDA, ANDRZEJ (1926–). Polish director. *A Generation* (54), *Kanal* (55), *Ashes and Diamonds* (58), *Innocent Sorcerers* (60), *The Siberian Lady Macbeth* (61), *Love at Twenty* (part only) (62), *Ashes* (64), etc.

WAKEFIELD, DUGGIE (1899–1951). British music-hall comedian, in character as a simpleton who always triumphed. Films include *Look Up and Laugh* (35), *Spy for a Day* (39), etc.

WAKEFIELD, HUGH (1888–   ). British character actor, on stage from childhood. Usually seen in monocled roles. *City of Song* (30), *The Sport of Kings* (31), *The Man Who Knew Too Much* (34), *The Crimson Circle* (36), *The Street Singer* (37), *Blithe Spirit* (45), *One Night with You* (48), *Love's a Luxury* (52), *The Million Pound Note* (54), etc.

WALBROOK, ANTON (1900–1968) (Adolf Wohlbruck). Distinguished German leading actor who came to Britain in the mid-30s. *Maskerade* (34), *The Student of Prague* (35), *Michael Strogoff* (US) (36), *Victoria the Great* (37), *The Rat* (37), *Sixty Glorious Years* (38), *Gaslight* (39), *Dangerous Moonlight* (40), *49th Parallel* (41), *The Life and Death of Colonel Blimp* (43), *The Man from Morocco* (44), *The Red Shoes* (48), *The Queen of Spades* (48), *La Ronde* (50), *Vienna Waltzes* (51), *Oh Rosalinda* (55), *Lola Montes* (55), *Saint Joan* (57), *I Accuse* (57), etc. Also on stage.

WALBURN, RAYMOND (1887–1969). American comedy actor with an inimitable bumbling pomposity; on stage from 1912, films from early 30s. *The Count of Monte Cristo* (34), *The Great Ziegfeld* (36), *Mr Deeds Goes to Town* (36), *Born to Dance* (37), *Professor Beware* (38), *Eternally Yours* (40), *Christmas in July* (41), *Dixie* (43), *Hail the Conquering Hero* (43), *The Man in the Trunk* (43), *The Cheaters* (45), *Henry the Rainmaker* (48), *State of the Union* (48), *Riding High* (49), *Father Takes the Air* (51), *Beautiful But Dangerous* (53), *The Spoilers* (55), etc.

WALD, JERRY (1911–1962). Live-wire American writer-producer, said to be the original of Budd Schulberg's novel 'What Makes Sammy Run?' Former journalist, in Hollywood from early 30s. *Stars over Broadway* (w) (35), *Hollywood Hotel* (w) (38), *George Washington Slept Here* (p) (42), *Mildred Pierce* (45), *Johnny Belinda* (p) (48), *The Glass Menagerie* (p) (50), *Clash by Night* (p) (52), *Queen Bee* (p) (55), *Peyton Place* (p) (57), *The Sound and the Fury* (p) (58), *Sons and Lovers* (p) (60), *The Stripper* (*Woman of Summer*) (p) (62), many others.

WALKER, CHARLOTTE (1878–1958). American leading lady with stage experience, in silent films. Mother of Sara Haden. *Kindling* (15), *Trail of the Lonesome Pine* (16), *Eve in Exile* (19), *Classmates* (24), *The Manicure Girl* (25), *Paris Bound* (29), *Scarlet Pages* (30), *Millie* (31), etc.

WALKER, CLINT (1927–   ). Giant-size American leading man, former cowboy star of TV's *Cheyenne*. No acting training. *Fort Dobbs* (57), *Yellowstone Kelly* (60), *Gold of the Seven Saints* (61), *Send Me No Flowers* (64), *Night of the Grizzly* (66), *The Dirty Dozen* (GB) (67), *Sam Whiskey* (68), *The Great Bank Robbery* (69), etc.

WALKER, HAL (1896–c. 1956). American director, mainly of routine films; stage experience. *Road to Utopia* (44), *Duffy's Tavern* (45), *My Friend Irma Goes West* (50), *At War with the Army* (51), *Road to Bali* (52), etc.

WALKER, HELEN (1921–1968). American leading lady of the 40s. *Lucky Jordan* (43), *Abroad with Two Yanks* (44), *Murder He Says* (45), *Cluny Brown* (46), *The Homestretch* (47), *Nightmare Alley* (47), *Impact* (49), *My True Story* (51), *Problem Girls* (52), *The Big Combo* (last role) (55), etc.

WALKER, JOSEPH (c. 1900–). American cinematographer. *It Happened One Night* (34), *Mr Deeds Goes to Town* (36), *Lost Horizon* (37), *Here Comes Mr Jordan* (41), *It's a Wonderful Life* (46), *The Jolson Story* (46), *Born Yesterday* (51), many others. Pioneer of zoom lens.

WALKER, NORMAN (1892–). British director. *Tommy Atkins* (27), *The Middle Watch* (31), *Turn of the Tide* (35), *The Man at the Gate* (40), *Hard Steel* (41), *They Knew Mr Knight* (45), etc.

WALKER, ROBERT (1919–1951). Modest-seeming American leading man of the 40s. *Bataan* (42), *Madame Curie* (43), *Thirty Seconds over Tokyo* (44), *Under the Clock* (45), *Till the Clouds Roll By* (46), *Song of Love* (47), *One Touch of Venus* (48), *Please Believe Me* (50), *Strangers on a Train* (51), *My Son John* (51), etc. His son ROBERT WALKER JNR (1941–) who looks remarkably like his father, has been seen in *The Hook* (63), *Ensign Pulver* (64), *The Ceremony* (64), *The Happening* (67), *The War Wagon* (67), etc.

WALKER, STUART (c. 1890–?1940). American director, former stage producer. *The Misleading Lady* (32), *White Woman* (33), *The Eagle and the Hawk* (33), *Great Expectations* (34), *The Mystery of Edwin Drood* (35), *Werewolf of London* (35), *Bulldog Drummond's Bride* (39), *Emergency Squad* (40), etc.

WALKER, SYD (1887–1945). British comic actor and monologuist. Films include *Over She Goes* (37), *Oh Boy* (38), *Hold My Hand* (39), *What Would You Do, Chums* (his catchphrase) (39), etc.

WALLACE, EDGAR (1875–1932). Prolific British crime story writer, Films of his books include *The Case of the Frightened Lady* (30 and 40), *The Calendar* (32 and 48), *The Crimson Circle* (30 and 37 and 61), *The Terror* (28 and 39), *Kate Plus Ten* (38), *Sanders of the River* (35). *The Squeaker* (37), *The Four Just Men* (39), *The Mind of Mr Reeder* (39) (and series), *The Ringer* (32 and 52), *King Kong* (32), and many episodes of a second feature series made at Merton Park in the 60s.

WALLACE, JEAN (1923–) (Jean Wallasek). American leading lady, married to Cornel Wilde. *You Can't Ration Love* (44), *Jigsaw*

(48), *The Good Humour Man* (50), *Song of India* (50), *Sudden Fear* (55), *The Big Combo* (55), *Maracaibo* (58), *Lancelot and Guinevere* (63), *Beach Red* (67), etc.

WALLACE, RICHARD (1894–1951). American director, former cutter for Mack Sennett. *MacFadden's Flats* (27), *Innocents of Paris* (30), *Seven Days' Leave* (31), *The Road to Reno* (32), *Shopworn Angel* (33), *The Little Minister* (35), *The Young in Heart* (39), *Captain Caution* (40), *The Navy Steps Out* (41), *She Knew All the Answers* (41), *Bride by Mistake* (44), *It's in the Bag* (*The Fifth Chair*) (45), *Sindbad the Sailor* (46), *Tycoon* (47), *Let's Live a Little* (48), *A Kiss for Corliss* (50), many others.

WALLACH, ELI (1915–). American stage actor (from 1940) who has latterly concentrated on films, often in villainous roles which he spices with 'the method'. *Baby Doll* (debut) (56), *The Line Up* (58), *Seven Thieves* (59), *The Magnificent Seven* (60), *The Misfits* (61), *Hemingway's Adventures of A Young Man* (62), *How the West Was Won* (62), *The Victors* (63), *The Moonspinners* (64), *Kisses For My President* (64), *Lord Jim* (65), *Genghis Khan* (65), *How to Steal a Million* (66), *The Good The Bad and The Ugly* (It.) (67), *The Tiger Makes Out* (67), *How to Save a Marriage* (68), *Mackenna's Gold* (68), *A Lovely Way to Die* (68).

WALLER, FATS (1904–1943). American Negro jazz pianist. Few film appearances include *Hooray for Love* (35), *King of Burlesque* (36), *Stormy Weather* (43).

WALLER, FRED (1886–1954). American research technician who invented Cinerama and saw it open successfully only two years before his death.

WALLIS, HAL B. (1898–). American producer, latterly independent, responsible for a long line of solidly commercial films. In films from 1922. *Little Caesar* (30), *The Story of Louis Pasteur* (36), *Jezebel* (38), *King's Row* (42), *Casablanca* (42), *The Strange Love of Martha Ivers* (46), *My Friend Irma* (49), *Gunfight at the OK Corral* (57), *G.I. Blues* (60), *Becket* (64), *Boeing-Boeing* (65), *The Sons of Katie Elder* (65), *Five Card Stud* (68), *True Grit* (69), *Anne of the Thousand Days* (69), scores of others (often as executive producer for major studios).

WALLS, TOM (1883–1949). British actor and director, on stage from 1905 after experience as policeman, busker, jockey, etc. Associated from mid-20s with the Aldwych farces, which he produced and later transferred to the screen, as well as playing amiable philanderers in them. Subsequently in character roles. *Rookery Nook* (31), *Turkey Time* (32), *A Cuckoo in the Nest* (34), *Fighting Stock* (35), *Pot Luck* (36), *Foreign Affairs* (37), *For Valour* (37), *Dishonour Bright* (37),

> *Second Best Bed* (38), *Strange Boarders* (38), *Halfway House* (43), *Johnny Frenchman* (45), *Master of Bankdam* (48), *The Interrupted Journey* (49), many others.

WALPOLE, HUGH (1884–1941). British novelist who has been oddly neglected by the cinema but did some scripting in 30s Hollywood and appeared as the vicar in *David Copperfield* (34).

WALSH, DERMOT (1924–   ). British leading man, usually in second features. *My Sister and I* (49), *The Frightened Man* (52), *The Floating Dutchman* (53), *The Night of the Full Moon* (56), *Woman of Mystery* (57), *Crash Drive* (59), *The Trunk* (61), *The Cool Mikado* (63), many others. TV series: *Richard the Lionheart*.

WALSH, KAY (1914–   ). British character actress, former leading lady. Trained in West End revue. *How's Chances* (debut) (34), *I See Ice* (38), *In Which We Serve* (42), *This Happy Breed* (44), *The October Man* (47), *Vice Versa* (48), *Oliver Twist* (48), *Encore* (50), *Stage Fright* (50), *Last Holiday* (51), *Cast a Dark Shadow* (55), *The Horse's Mouth* (59), *Tunes of Glory* (60), *Eighty Thousand Suspects* (63), *The Beauty Jungle* (64), *A Study in Terror* (65), *The Witches* (*The Devil's Own*) (66), *Connecting Rooms* (69), many others. Also on TV.

WALSH, RAOUL (1892–   ). Veteran American director of many commercial and several distinguished pictures. In films from 1912; former actor and assistant to D. W. Griffith. *Carmen* (15), *The Thief of Bagdad* (24), *What Price Glory* (26), *Sadie Thompson* (28), *In Old Arizona* (29), *The Big Trail* (30), *The Bowery* (33), *Every Night at Eight* (35), *Artists and Models* (38), *St Louis Blues* (39), *They Drive by Night* (40), *High Sierra* (41), *They Died with Their Boots On* (41), *Strawberry Blonde* (41), *Manpower* (41), *Desperate Journey* (42), *Gentleman Jim* (43), *Northern Pursuit* (44), *Uncertain Glory* (44), *The Horn Blows at Midnight* (45), *Objective Burma* (45), *San Antonio* (46), *The Man I Love* (46), *Pursued* (47), *Silver River* (48), *White Heat* (49), *Colorado Territory* (49), *Along the Great Divide* (49), *Captain Horatio Hornblower* (50), *Distant Drums* (51), *The World in His Arms* (52), *Glory Alley* (52), *Blackbeard the Pirate* (53), *A Lion is in the Streets* (54), *Saskatchewan* (54), *Battle Cry* (55), *The Tall Men* (55), *The Revolt of Mamie Stover* (57), *The King and Four Queens* (57), *Band of Angels* (57), *The Naked and the Dead* (58), *The Sheriff of Fractured Jaw* (GB) (58), *Esther and the King* (60), *Marines Let's Go* (61), *A Distant Trumpet* (64), many others.

WALSTON, RAY (1917–   ). American character comedian with stage experience. *Damn Yankees* (58), *South Pacific* (58), *Say One for Me* (59), *The Apartment* (61), *Tall Story* (62), *Wives and Lovers* (63), *Who's Minding the Store* (63), *Kiss Me Stupid* (65), *Caprice* (67), *Paint Your Wagon* (69), etc. TV series: *My Favourite Martian* (63–65).

WALTER, JESSICA (c. 1940–   ). American leading lady. *The Group* (66), *Grand Prix* (67), *Number One* (69).

WALTERS, CHARLES (1911–   ). American director specializing in musicals. Former stage dancer and director of musical sequences in films. *Presenting Lily Mars* (seq) (43), *Meet Me in St Louis* (seq) (44), *Good News* (47), *Easter Parade* (48), *If You Feel Like Singing (Summer Stock)* (50), *Easy to Love* (53), *Lili* (53), *The Glass Slipper* (55), *The Tender Trap* (55), *High Society* (56), *Don't Go Near the Water* (57), *Ask Any Girl* (59), *Please Don't Eat the Daisies* (60), *Jumbo* (62), *The Unsinkable Molly Brown* (64), *Walk, Don't Run* (66), etc.

WALTERS, THORLEY (1913–   ). British comedy actor on stage and screen from 1934. Film parts usually cameos, as incompetent officers, etc. *They Were Sisters* (45), *Private's Progress* (56), *Carleton Browne of the FO* (58), *Two-Way Stretch* (60), *Murder She Said* (62), *Ring of Spies* (64), *Joey Boy* (65), *Rotten to the Core* (65), *Dracula, Prince of Darkness* (65), *The Wrong Box* (66), *Frankenstein Must Be Destroyed* (69), etc.

WALTHALL, HENRY B. (1878–1936). American leading man of the silent screen, in films from 1909. *In Old Kentucky* (09), *A Convict's Sacrifice* (10), *The Birth of a Nation* (14), *The Raven* (15), *Ghosts* (15), *His Robe of Honour* (18), *Single Wives* (23), *The Scarlet Letter* (25), *The Barrier* (26), *Abraham Lincoln* (31), *Police Court* (32), *Laughing at Life* (33), *Viva Villa* (34), *China Clipper* (36), many others.

WALTON, SIR WILLIAM (1902–   ). British composer whose film scores include *Henry V* (44), *Hamlet* (48), *Richard III* (56).

W.A.M.P.A.S. (Western Association of Motion Picture Advertisers). A group of publicity executives who, from 1922 to 1931, gave annual certificates of merit to promising female starlets, known as 'Wampas baby stars'. Among those who succeeded were Bessie Love (nominated 1922), Laura la Plante (23), Clara Bow (24), Mary Astor (26), Joan Crawford (26), Dolores del Rio (26), Janet Gaynor (26), Lupe Velez (28), Jean Arthur (29), Loretta Young (29), Joan Blondell (31), Anita Louise (31).

WANAMAKER, SAM (1919–   ). American stage actor and director who has also appeared in films; now resident in Britain. *My Girl Tisa* (48), *Give Us This Day* (50), *Mr Denning Drives North* (51), *The Secret* (55), *The Criminal* (60), *Taras Bulba* (62), *The Man in the Middle* (64), *Those Magnificent Men in Their Flying Machines* (65), *The Spy Who Came in from the Cold* (65), *Warning Shot* (66), *The Day the Fish Came Out* (67), *File of the Golden Goose* (directed only) (69), *The Executioner* (directed only) (69, etc.

WANGER, WALTER (1894–1968) (W. Feuchtwanger). American independent producer who during a long career held at various times senior executive posts with major studios. Personal productions include *Queen Christina* (33), *The President Vanishes* (35), *Private Worlds* (35), *Mary Burns Fugitive* (35), *The Trail of the Lonesome Pine* (36), *You Only Live Once* (37), *History is Made at Night* (37), *52nd Street* (38), *Stand In* (38), *Blockade* (38), *Trade Winds* (38), *Algiers* (38), *Stagecoach* (39), *Foreign Correspondent* (40), *The Long Voyage Home* (40), war service, *Scarlet Street* (45), *The Lost Moment* (47), *Tap Roots* (48), *Joan of Arc* (48), *Riot in Cell Block Eleven* (64), *Invasion of the Body Snatchers* (55), *I Want to Live* (58), *Cleopatra* (62).

WAR AND PEACE. The main film versions of Tolstoy's epic novel were a Russian one of 1916; King Vidor's of 1955, with Henry Fonda and Audrey Hepburn, photographed by Aldo Tonti; and Sergei Bondartchuk's seven-hour colossus of 1967, photographed by Anatole Petrinsky.

war heroes who have become the subject of biopics include Eddie Rickenbacker (Fred MacMurray, *Captain Eddie*); Audie Murphy (himself, *To Hell and Back*); Guy Gabaldon (Jeffrey Hunter, *Hell to Eternity*); Sergeant York (Gary Cooper, *Sergeant York*); Douglas Bader (Kenneth More, *Reach for the Sky*); Guy Gibson (Richard Todd, *The Dam Busters*); Ernie Pyle (Burgess Meredith, *The Story of G.I. Joe*); John Hoskins (Sterling Hayden, *The Eternal Sea*).

THE WAR LORD (US 1965). An interesting Hollywood attempt to create a genuine medieval drama instead of the usual hokum, with Charlton Heston as an eleventh-century baron involved in outmoded ritual and suspected witchcraft. Written by John Collier and Millard Kaufman from a play by Leslie Stevens; photographed by Russell Metty; directed by Franklin Schaffner.

THE WAR OF THE WORLDS (US 1953). This George Pal version of the H. G. Wells fantasy about a Martian invasion was by no means as imaginative as it might have been, but was notable for introducing a streak of viciousness into scientific fiction: neither side showed much mercy, and the noise was deafening.

WARD, MICHAEL (1915–). British comic actor usually seen as nervous photographer or twee shopwalker. *An Ideal Husband* (47), *Sleeping Car to Trieste* (48), *Street Corner* (53), *Private's Progress* (55), *I'm All Right, Jack* (59), *Carry On Screaming* (66), etc.

WARD, POLLY (1908–) (Byno Poluski). British-born leading lady of several 30s comedies. *Shooting Stars* (28), *His Lordship* (32), *The Old Curiosity Shop* (34), *Feather Your Nest* (37), *Thank Evans* (38), *It's in the Air* (38), *Bulldog Drummond Sees It Through* (40), *Women Aren't Angels* (last to date) (42), etc.

WARDEN, JACK (1925–   ). Burly American character actor, also on stage and TV. *From Here to Eternity* (53), *Twelve Angry Men* (57), *A Man is Ten Feet Tall* (*Edge of the City*) (57), *The Bachelor Party* (57), *Escape from Zahrain* (62), *Mirage* (65), *Blindfold* (65), etc. TV series: *The Wackiest Ship in the Army*, (65).

WARHOL, ANDY (1926–   ). American 'underground' film-maker of the 60s: his works usually run for several hours and are totally boring except to the initiated. They include *Sleep* (63), *Blow Job* (64), *Harlot* (65), *The Chelsea Girls* (shown on two screens side by side, with different images) (66), and *F**k*, or *Blue Movie* (69).

Warner Brothers Pictures Inc. is a family affair started in 1923 by four American exhibitor brothers. After a very shaky start it soared to pre-eminence through their gamble on talking pictures in the shape of *The Jazz Singer* and *The Singing Fool*. Through the 30s and 40s the company kept its popularity through tough gangster films starring James Cagney, Edward G. Robinson and Humphrey Bogart, and musicals with Dick Powell and Ruby Keeler; and its prestige by exposés like *Confessions of a Nazi Spy* and *Mission to Moscow* and biographies of Zola, Pasteur, Ehrlich and Reuter. Other Warner stars included Bette Davis and Errol Flynn, both enormously popular with all classes. Warner films were not usually over-budgeted but contrived to look immaculate through solid production values and star performances. Since 1950 the company's product has been more variable, as deals have had to be done with independent producers, and there has been a patchy flirtation with TV; yet on the serious side directors like Kazan have been encouraged, popular taste is taken care of by spectaculars like *My Fair Lady* and *The Great Race*, and the company took a calculated risk (which paid off in spades) with *Who's Afraid of Virginia Woolf?* In the mid-60s came a merger with Seven Arts, and in 1969 Jack Warner, the surviving brother, retired.

WARNER, DAVID (1941–   ). Lanky British stage actor who has made film appearances: *Tom Jones* (as Blifil) (63), *Morgan* (66), *Work is a Four-Letter Word* (68), *A Midsummer Night's Dream* (68), *The Bofors Gun* (68), *The Fixer* (68), *The Seagull* (68), *The Ballad of Cable Hogue* (69).

WARNER, H. B. (1876–1958). Distinguished British actor, on stage from 1883; in Hollywood as film actor from *c.* 1917. *The Beggar of Cawnpore* (15), *The Man Who Turned White* (19), *One Hour Before Dawn* (20), *Zaza* (22), *King of Kings* (27), *Sorrell and Son* (27), *The Divine Lady* (28), *The Trial of Mary Dugan* (29), *Five Star Final* (31), *Mr Deeds Goes to Town* (36), *Lost Horizon* (37), *Victoria the Great* (37), *You Can't Take It With You* (38), *Bulldog Drummond Strikes Back* (39), *The Rains Came* (39), *All That Money Can Buy* (41), *Topper Returns* (41), *The Corsican Brothers* (41), *It's a Wonderful Life* (46), *Prince of*

Thieves (48), *Sunset Boulevard* (50), *Savage Drums* (51), *The Ten Commandments* (56), many others.

WARNER, JACK (1894–   ) (Jack Waters). Genial British character actor, former music-hall comedian; TV's 'Dixon of Dock Green'. *The Dummy Talks* (debut) (43), *The Captive Heart* (46), *Hue and Cry* (46), *It Always Rains on Sunday* (47), *Here Come the Huggetts* (48), *The Huggetts Abroad* (49), *The Blue Lamp* (50), *Valley of Eagles* (51), *Scrooge* (51), *The Quatermass Experiment* (55), *Home and Away* (56), *Carve Her Name With Pride* (58), *Jigsaw* (62), many others.

WARNER, JACK L. (1892–   ). American executive producer, surviving member of the four Warner Brothers who started up a small production company in the 20s and pioneered sound pictures with *The Jazz Singer* (27). The other brothers: Albert, Harry M., and Sam. Jack has published his autobiography (1965): 'My First Hundred Years in Hollywood'.

WARNING SHADOWS (German 1922). Directed by Arthur Robison, this structurally interesting but very Teutonic fantasy concerns a shadow-man who forces the inhabitants of an unhappy household to see themselves in a shadowy play. Full of weird effects largely achieved by expressionist use of light and shadow.

WARREN, CHARLES MARQUIS (1912–   ). American writer-director. *Little Big Horn* (51), *Hellgate* (52), *Arrowhead* (53), *Flight to Tangier* (54), *Seven Angry Men* (55), *The Black Whip* (56), etc. Moved into TV and became creator and executive producer of *Gunsmoke*, *Rawhide*, *The Virginian*, etc. Recent film: *Charro* (p, d) (69).

WARREN, C. DENIER (1889–   ). Chubby American character comedian, in British films; vaudeville experience. *Counsel's Opinion* (33), *Kentucky Minstrels* (34), *A Fire Has Been Arranged* (35), *Cotton Queen* (37), *Trouble Brewing* (39), *Kiss the Bride Goodbye* (44), *Old Mother Riley, Headmistress* (50), *Bluebeard's Ten Honeymoons* (60), etc.

WARREN, ROBERT PENN (1905–   ). American novelist. Works filmed include *All the King's Men* (49), *Band of Angels* (57).

WARRENDER, HAROLD (1903–1953). British stage and screen actor. *Friday the Thirteenth* (33), *Contraband* (40), *Sailors Three* (41), *Scott of the Antarctic* (49), *Pandora and the Flying Dutchman* (51), *Intimate Relations* (53), etc.

WARRICK, RUTH (c. 1915–   ). American leading lady of the 40s. Former radio singer. *Citizen Kane* (debut) (41), *The Corsican Brothers* (41), *Journey Into Fear* (42), *Forever and a Day* (43), *Mr Winkle Goes to War (Arms and the Woman)* (44), *Guest in the House* (44), *China Sky* (45), *Swell Guy* (47), *Arch of Triumph* (48), *Three Husbands* (50), *Killer with a Label* (50), *Let's Dance* (52), *Ride Beyond Vengeance* (65),

How to Steal the World (68), etc. TV series: *Father of the Bride* (61), *Peyton Place* (65).

WARWICK, JOHN (1905–   ) (John McIntosh Beattie). Australian leading man, later character actor, in British films. *Down on the Farm* (35), *Lucky Jade* (37), *The Face at the Window* (39), *Danny Boy* (40), *The Missing Million* (42), *Dancing with Crime* (47), *Street Corner* (53), *Up to His Neck* (54), *Just My Luck* (57), *Horrors of the Black Museum* (59); also many of the 'Scotland Yard' series as police inspector.

WARWICK, ROBERT (1878–1965) (Robert Taylor Bien). American character actor, adept at executives and heavy fathers. A star of such silent films as *A Modern Othello*, *The Mad Lover*, *Thou Art the Man*; later in *So Big* (32), *Night Life of the Gods* (35), *A Tale of Two Cities* (36), *The Life of Émile Zola* (37), *The Adventures of Robin Hood* (38), *Sullivan's Travels* (41), *The Palm Beach Story* (42), *I Married a Witch* (43), *Gentlemen's Agreement* (48), *Francis* (49), *Sugarfoot* (51), *Mississippi Gambler* (53), *Lady Godiva of Coventry* (55), *Night of the Quarter Moon* (59), many others.

WASHBOURNE, MONA (1903–   ). British stage character actress, whose occasional films include *Wide Boy* (48), *Child's Play* (53), *Doctor in the House* (54), *The Good Companions* (57), *Brides of Dracula* (60), *Billy Liar* (63), *Night Must Fall* (63), *One-Way Pendulum* (64), *My Fair Lady* (*US*) (64), *The Third Day* (US) (65), etc.

WASHINGTON, GEORGE (1732–1799). The first American president, the lad who could not tell a lie, has been impersonated in many films, including *Alexander Hamilton* (Alan Mowbray, who also had the role in *The Phantom President* and *Where Do We Go From Here?*); *America* (24) (Arthur Dewey); *The Howards of Virginia* (George Houston); *The Remarkable Andrew* (Montagu Love); *Unconquered* (Richard Gaines); *John Paul Jones* (John Crawford); *Lafayette* (Howard St John).

water, in inconvenient quantity, played a dramatic part in *Way Down East*; *Noah's Ark*; *The Rains Came* and its remake *The Rains of Ranchipur*; *The Bible*; *Floods of Fear*; *The Hurricane*; *Campbell's Kingdom*; *When Worlds Collide*; *Rain*; *Whistling in Dixie*; *Foreign Correspondent*; *Who Was That Lady?*; and no doubt a hundred others.
    See also: *rain*.

WATERLOO BRIDGE. Robert E. Sherwood's sentimental romance, about a ballet dancer who turns prostitute when her rich lover is reported killed at the war and commits suicide when he returns, was filmed in 1930 by James Whale, with Kent Douglass and Mae Clarke; in 1940 by Mervyn le Roy, with Robert Taylor and Vivien

Waterloo Road

Leigh; and in 1955 (as *Gaby*) by Curtis Bernhardt, with John Kerr, Leslie Caron and a happy ending.

WATERLOO ROAD (GB 1944). A small and now dated melodrama about a soldier who takes French leave to beat up his wife's seducer, this film can now be seen as the beginning of the British realist movement which eventually led to *Saturday Night and Sunday Morning*. Getting out of the studio into South London slums, it gave at the time a fresh and vivid sensation now impossible to recapture. Written and directed by Sidney Gilliat; photographed by Arthur Crabtree; with John Mills, Joy Shelton, Stewart Granger and Alastair Sim.

WATERS, ETHEL (1900–   ). Distinguished American Negro actress and singer. Films include *On With The Show* (29), *Tales of Manhattan* (42), *Cabin in the Sky* (43), *Pinky* (49), *Member of the Wedding* (52), *The Long Hot Summer* (58), etc. Published autobiography 1953: *His Eye is on the Sparrow*. TV series: *Beulah* (53).

WATERS, RUSSELL (1908–   ). British character actor usually in meek and mild parts. The 'hero' of many of Richard Massingham's short and light-hearted instructional films, he later appeared in *The Woman in the Hall* (47), *The Happiest Days of Your Life* (50), *Maggie* (54), *Left, Right and Centre* (59), many others.

WATKIN, PIERRE (c. 1894–1960). American character actor often seen as lawyer, doctor or kindly father. *Dangerous* (35), *Pride of the Yankees* (41), *Whistling in Dixie* (43), *Shanghai Chest* (46), *Knock On Any Door* (59), *The Dark Page* (51), *Johnny Dark* (54), many others.

WATKINS, PETER (1937–   ). British director from TV (*Culloden*, *The War Game*). First film: *Privilege* (67).

WATLING, JACK (1923–   ). Boyish British leading man who made film debut in *Sixty Glorious Years* (38). After war service: *Journey Together* (45), *The Courtneys of Curzon Street* (47), *Quartet* (48), *The Winslow Boy* (48), *Meet Mr Lucifer* (54), *The Sea Shall Not Have Them* (55), *The Admirable Crichton* (57), *A Night To Remember* (58), *Mary Had A Little* (61), many others; also on TV.

WATSON, BOBS (c. 1930–   ). American boy actor of the 30s and 40s; noted for his ability to weep at the drop of a hat. *In Old Chicago* (38), *Kentucky* (39), *On Borrowed Time* (39), *Dr Kildare's Crisis* (41), *Men of Boys Town* (41), *The Bold and the Brave* (56), *First to Fight* (67), etc. Recently on TV.

WATSON, LUCILE (1879–1962). Canadian character actress with stage experience; usually in imperious roles. *What Every Woman Knows* (34), *Sweethearts* (39), *Waterloo Bridge* (40), *Rage in Heaven* (41),

The Great Lie (41), *Watch on the Rhine* (43), *My Reputation* (44), *The Razor's Edge* (46), *Harriet Craig* (50), *My Forbidden Past* (last film) (51), etc.

WATSON, MINOR (1889–1965). American character actor who often played lawyers or kindly fathers. *Our Betters* (33), *Babbitt* (34), *When's Your Birthday* (37), *Boys' Town* (38), *Moon over Miami* (41), *The Big Shot* (42), *The Virginian* (46), *The File on Thelma Jordon* (49), *Mister 880* (50), *My Son John* (51), *Trapeze* (56), etc.

WATSON, ROBERT (1888–1965). American character actor who became famous for his resemblance to Hitler; played the lead in *The Hitler Gang* (43) and other films of this type. Otherwise played many small roles: *Moonlight and Melody* (33), *Mary of Scotland* (36), *The Devil with Hitler* (42), *Nazty Nuisance* (43), *The Big Clock* (48), *Red Hot and Blue* (49), *Singing in the Rain* (52), *The Story of Mankind* (57), etc.

WATSON, WYLIE (1889–1966) (John Wylie Robertson). British character actor, usually in 'little man' roles; formerly in music hall. *The Thirty-nine Steps* (35) (as 'Mr Memory'), *London Belongs to Me* (48), *Whisky Galore* (48), *The Sundowners* (60), many others. Retired to Australia.

WATT, HARRY (1906–   ). British director with varied early experience before joining GPO Film Unit as assistant in 1931. *Night Mail* (36), *North Sea* (38), *Squadron 992* (40), *Target For Tonight* (41), *Nine Men* (also wrote) (44), *Fiddlers Three* (44), *The Overlanders* (46), *Eureka Stockade* (48), *Where No Vultures Fly* (51), *West of Zanzibar* (53), *The Siege of Pinchgut* (59), etc.

WATTIS, RICHARD (1912–   ). Bespectacled British character comedian with stage experience. *The Happiest Days of Your Life* (49), *The Clouded Yellow* (51), *Hobson's Choice* (54), *I am a Camera* (55), *Simon and Laura* (55), *The Prince and the Showgirl* (58), *The VIPs* (63), *Moll Flanders* (65), *Up Jumped a Swagman* (65), *Wonderwall* (68), many others; also on TV.

WAXMAN, FRANZ (1906–1967) (Franz Wachsmann). German composer, in America from 1934. Among his many film scores are *Bride of Frankenstein* (35), *Sutter's Gold* (36), *Fury* (36), *Captains Courageous* (38), *The Young in Heart* (38), *Rebecca* (40), *The Philadelphia Story* (40), *Woman of the Year* (42), *Air Force* (42), *Mr Skeffington* (44), *Objective Burma* (45), *Humoresque* (46), *The Paradine Case* (48), *Alias Nick Beal* (49), *Sunset Boulevard* (AA) (50), *A Place in the Sun* (AA) (51), *My Cousin Rachel* (53), *Rear Window* (54), *Mister Roberts* (56), *Sayonara* (57), *The Nun's Story* (59), *Cimarron* (60), *Taras Bulba* (62), *Lost Command* (66), etc.

Waxman, Harry

WAXMAN, HARRY (1912–   ). British cinematographer. *Brighton Rock* (46), *They Were Not Divided* (48), *Valley of Eagles* (51), *The Baby and the Battleship* (56), *Innocent Sinners* (57), *The Secret Partner* (60), *The Roman Spring of Mrs Stone* (61), *The Day The Earth Caught Fire* (62), *Lancelot and Guinevere* (63), *Crooks in Cloisters* (64), *The Nanny* (65), *Khartoum* (2nd unit) (66), *The Family Way* (66), *The Trygon Factor* (67), *The Anniversary* (67), *Wonderwall* (68), *Twisted Nerve* (68), etc.

THE WAY AHEAD (GB 1944). World War II's best film tribute to the British Army, as seen through the eyes of a group of very unwilling conscripts. The film survives chiefly by virtue of the good comedy writing of its first half; the final baptism of fire is more routine. Directed by Carol Reed from a script by Eric Ambler and Peter Ustinov (originally intended as a short army propaganda film); photographed by Guy Green; music by Davis Rawnsley. With David Niven, Stanley Holloway, Raymond Huntley, Jimmy Hanley, William Hartnell, Peter Ustinov, etc.

WAY DOWN EAST (US 1920). D. W. Griffith's sentimental melodrama is remembered now for its brilliantly and hazardously filmed ice-floe sequence. Written by Griffith from a play by Lottie Blair Parker; photographed by Hendrik Sartov and Billy Bitzer. With Lillian Gish, Richard Barthelmess. Remade as a talkie in 1936 with Rochelle Hudson and Henry Fonda.

THE WAY TO THE STARS (GB 1945). A gentle, satisfying film about the RAF in World War II. Hardly a plane is seen, as the action takes place mainly in a small hotel near the airfield. Both writer Terence Rattigan and director Anthony Asquith are in their best and most typical forms, and a distinguished cast includes Michael Redgrave, John Mills, Rosamund John, Douglass Montgomery, Stanley Holloway, Renee Asherson and Joyce Carey.

WAYNE, DAVID (1916–   ) (Wayne McKeekan). Wiry American character actor, in films since late 40s, also stage star. *Portrait of Jennie* (48), *Adam's Rib* (49), *My Blue Heaven* (50), *Up Front* (51), *With a Song in my Heart* (52), *Wait till the Sun Shines Nellie* (52), *The I Don't Care Girl* (53), *Tonight We Sing* (53), *How to Marry a Millionaire* (53), *The Tender Trap* (55), *The Three Faces of Eve* (57), *The Last Angry Man* (59), *The Big Gamble* (60), etc. TV series: *Norby* (51).

WAYNE, JOHN (1907–   ) (Marion Michael Morrison). Tough, genial American leading man, former professional footballer, in films from 1930. *The Big Trail* (31), *The Big Stampede* (32), *Westward Ho* (35), *Born to the West* (38), *Wyoming Outlaw* (39), *Stagecoach* (39), *The Long Voyage Home* (40), *Seven Sinners* (40), *The Dark*

Command (40), *Lady From Louisiana* (41), *Reap the Wild Wind* (42), *The Spoilers* (42), *Flying Tigers* (43), *In Old Oklahoma* (44), *Dakota* (45), *They Were Expendable* (45), *Angel and the Badman* (47), *Fort Apache* (48), *Red River* (48), *Three Godfathers* (49), *She Wore a Yellow Ribbon* (49), *Rio Grande* (50), *Sands of Iwo Jima* (50), *Operation Pacific* (51), *The Quiet Man* (52), *Jet Pilot* (52), *Island in the Sky* (53), *Trouble Along the Way* (53), *Hondo* (54), *The High and the Mighty* (54), *The Conqueror* (55), *The Sea Chase* (55), *Blood Alley* (56), *The Searchers* (56), *The Wings of Eagles* (57), *Legend of the Lost* (57), *Rio Bravo* (58), *The Barbarian and the Geisha* (58), *The Horse Soldiers* (59), *North to Alaska* (59), *The Alamo* (also produced and directed) (60), *Hatari* (62), *The Man Who Shot Liberty Valance* (62), *How the West Was Won,* (62), *The Comancheros* (62), *The Longest Day* (62), *Donovan's Reef* (63), *McLintock* (63), *Circus World* (*The Magnificent Showman*) (64), *In Harm's Way* (65), *The Sons of Katie Elder* (65), *Cast a Giant Shadow* (66), *The War Wagon* (67), *The Green Berets* (68), *Hellfighters* (68), *The Undefeated* (69), *True Grit* (69), many others.

WAYNE, MICHAEL (1934–   ). American producer, son of John Wayne. Most notable film to date, *McLintock* (63).

WAYNE, NAUNTON (1901–   ). Mild-mannered British light comedy actor, on stage from 1920, films from 1931; became well known with Basil Radford in many films as Englishmen abroad. *The First Mrs Fraser* (debut) (31), *Going Gay* (33), *For Love of You* (34), *The Lady Vanishes* (38), *Night Train to Munich* (40), *Crooks' Tour* (41), *Next of Kin* (42), *Dead of Night* (45), *The Calendar* (47), *It's Not Cricket* (48), *Quartet* (48), *Passport to Pimlico* (48), *Obsession* (49), *Highly Dangerous* (50), *The Titfield Thunderbolt* (53), *You Know What Sailors Are* (53), *Nothing Barred* (61), others.

WAYNE, PATRICK (1939–   ). American actor, son of John Wayne. Seen in *The Searchers* (56), *The Alamo* (60), *The Comancheros* (62), *McLintock* (63).

WEAVER, DENNIS (1924–   ). American character actor. *The Raiders* (52), *War Arrow* (54), *Seven Angry Men* (55), *Touch of Evil* (58), *The Gallant Hours* (60), *Duel at Diablo* (66), etc. TV series: *Gunsmoke* (as Chester) (58–64), *Kentucky Jones* (65).

WEAVER, FRITZ (1926–   ). American stage actor. Films include *Fail Safe* (64), *The Maltese Bippy* (69), *A Walk in the Spring Rain* (70).

WEAVER, MARJORIE (1913–   ). American leading lady, mainly of second features. *China Clipper* (36), *Three Blind Mice* (38), *Young Mr Lincoln* (39), *Maryland* (40), *The Mad Martindales* (42), *We're Not Married* (52), others.

Webb, Clifton

WEBB, CLIFTON (1893–1966). (Webb Parmelee Hollenbeck). American leading character actor, former dancer and stage star. In films, became in middle age well-known in waspish roles. *Polly with a Past* (20), *New Toys* (24), *The Heart of a Siren* (25), then long absence; *Laura* (44), *The Dark Corner* (45), *The Razor's Edge* (46), *Sitting Pretty* (48), *Mr Belvedere Goes to College* (49), *Cheaper by the Dozen* (50), *For Heaven's Sake* (50), *Mr Belvedere Rings the Bell* (51), *Elopement* (52), *Dreamboat* (52), *Stars and Stripes Forever* (53), *Titanic* (53), *Mr Scoutmaster* (53), *Three Coins in the Fountain* (54), *Woman's World* (54), *The Man Who Never Was* (56), *Boy on a Dolphin* (57), *The Remarkable Mr Pennypacker* (58), *Holiday for Lovers* (59), *Satan Never Sleeps* (62), etc.

WEBB, JACK (1920–   ). American TV star and executive: starred and directed in *Dragnet* and other series; was briefly head of Warner TV. Occasional films include *The Men* (50), *You're in the Navy Now* (52), *Dragnet* (also produced and directed) (54), *Pete Kelly's Blues* (also produced and directed) (55), *The D.I.* (also produced and directed) (57), *The Last Time I Saw Archie* (also produced and directed) (62), others.

WEBB, JAMES R. (c. 1912–   ). American screenwriter. *The Charge at Feather River* (53), *Phantom of the Rue Morgue* (co-w) (54), *Trapeze* (56), *The Big Country* (co-w) (58), *Pork Chop Hill* (59), *How the West was Won* (AA) (63), *Guns for San Sebastian* (67), *Alfred the Great* (co-w) (69), many others.

WEBB, ROBERT D. (1903–   ). American director, former cameraman. *White Feather* (55), *On the Threshold of Space* (55), *The Proud Ones* (56), *Love Me Tender* (56), *The Way to the Gold* (57), *Seven Women from Hell* (61), *The Agony and the Ecstasy* (second unit) (65), *Capetown Affair* (67), etc.

WEBBER, ROBERT (1928–   ). American leading man with stage and TV experience. *Highway 301* (51), *Twelve Angry Men* (57), *The Stripper (Woman of Summer)* (63), *Hysteria* (GB) (64), *The Sandpiper* (65), *The Third Day* (65), *No Tears for a Killer* (It.) (65), *The Moving Target (Harper)* (66), *The Silencers* (67), *The Dirty Dozen* (67), etc.

WEBSTER, PAUL FRANCIS (c. 1910–   ). American lyricist. Various Shirley Temple songs in the 30s; later *Love is a Many Splendoured Thing* (AA) (54), *Friendly Persuasion* (56), *The Sandpiper* (AA) (65), etc.

weddings have formed a happy ending for innumerable films, and an unhappy start for others, but some are more memorable than the rest. Weddings on a lavish scale were seen in *Camelot, Royal Wedding, The Scarlet Empress, The Private Life of Henry VIII*. More domestic occasions were in *Quiet Wedding, The Member of the Wedding, The*

Catered Affair, Father of the Bride, June Bride, A Kind of Loving.
Weddings were interrupted in *The Philadelphia Story, The Bride
Wasn't Willing, I Married a Witch, The Runaround, You Gotta Stay
Happy, The Bride Went Wild, The Lion in Winter* and *I Love You
Alice B. Toklas.* Macabre weddings were found in *The Night Walker,
The Bride Wore Black, The Bride of Frankenstein, The Bride and the
Beast, Chamber of Horrors.* The wedding night was the centre of
interest in *The Man in Grey, The Wicked Lady, Wedding Night* and
My Little Chickadee. And the funniest wedding still remains that in
Our Wife, when cross-eyed justice of the peace Ben Turpin married
Mr Hardy to his best man Mr Laurel.

WEGENER, PAUL (1874–1948). Distinguished German actor-writer-
director. *The Student of Prague* (a) (13), *The Golem* (a, d) (14 and
20), *Vanina* (a) (22), *Svengali* (a, w, d) (27), *Lucrezia Borgia* (a)
(27), *Ein Mann Will Nach Deutschland* (d) (34), *Der Grosse König*
(a) (41), *Der Grosse Mandarin* (a) (48), many others.

WEIDLER, VIRGINIA (1927–1968). American child actress who usually
played a little horror. *Mrs Wiggs of the Cabbage Patch* (34), *Souls at
Sea* (37), *The Women* (39), *The Philadelphia Story* (40), *Born to Sing*
(42), *The Youngest Profession* (43), etc. Retired.

WEILL, KURT (1900–1950). German composer whose scores includ
Die Dreigroschenoper, One Touch of Venus and *Knickerbocker Holiday,*
all filmed.

WEINGARTEN, LAURENCE (c. 1893–   ). American producer, in films
from c. 1917. *Broadway Melody* (28), *A Day at the Races* (37), *Escape*
(40), *Adam's Rib* (49), *The Tender Trap* (54), *Cat on a Hot Tin Roof,*
(58), *The Unsinkable Molly Brown* (64), scores of others.

WEIS, DON (1922–   ). American director; came to Hollywood from
college as trainee. *Bannerline* (51), *I Love Melvin* (53), *A Slight Case
of Larceny* (53), *Ride the High Iron* (57), *Critics' Choice* (63), *Pajama
Party* (63), *Looking for Love* (64), *Billie* (65), *Pajama Party in a Haunted
House* (66), *The King's Pirate* (66), etc.; has also spent years in TV.

WEISBART, DAVID (1915–1967). American producer, former editor; in
Hollywood from 1935. *Mara Maru* (52), *Rebel Without a Cause* (55),
Love Me Tender (56), *Holiday for Lovers* (59), *Kid Galahad* (63),
Rio Conchos (64), *Goodbye Charlie* (65), *Valley of the Dolls* (67), many
others.

WEISSMULLER, JOHNNY (1904–   ). American leading man, former
Olympic athlete who from 1932 played Tarzan (qv) more often
than anyone else. In late 40s and early 50s appeared in 'Jungle
Jim' second features, also on TV. Only 'straight' role: *Swamp Fire*
(46). Guest appearance: *The Phynx* (69).

Welch, Joseph L.

WELCH, JOSEPH L. (1891–1960). Real-life American judge who became famous during the army-MacCarthy hearings in 1953 and was later persuaded to play the judge in *Anatomy of a Murder* (59).

WELCH, RAQUEL (1942–   ). Curvaceous American leading lady, former model. *Roustabout* (64), *A House Is Not a Home* (64), *A Swinging Summer* (65), *Fantastic Voyage* (66), *One Million Years BC* (66), *The Biggest Bundle of Them All* (66), *Bandolero!* (68), *Lady in Cement* (68), *100 Rifles* (69), *Tilda* (70), *Laurie Lee* (70), *Myra Breckinridge* (70), etc.

WELD, TUESDAY (1943–   ) (Susan Ker Weld). American juvenile lead, a model from childhood. *Rock Rock Rock* (56), *Rally Round the Flag Boys* (57), *The Five Pennies* (59), *Return to Peyton Place* (61), *Wild in the Country* (62), *Bachelor Flat* (63), *I'll Take Sweden* (65), *The Cincinnati Kid* (65), *Lord Love a Duck* (66), *Pretty Poison* (68), *An Exile* (70), etc. Also on TV, including *Dobie Gillis* series (59–62).

†WELLES, ORSON (1915–   ). American actor-producer-director with early radio and stage experience: one-time 'enfant terrible' of Hollywood whose unconventionality forced him to work in Europe, where, away from studio routine, his ambitious projects have not always brought results, and he seems to have spent his career trying to live up to the brilliance of his first film. As director/actor/writer: *Citizen Kane* (AA script with Herman J. Mankiewicz) (41), *The Magnificent Ambersons* (did not act) (42), *Journey into Fear* (direction completed by Norman Foster) (43), *The Stranger* (did not write) (46), *The Lady from Shanghai* (47), *Macbeth* (48), *Othello* (51), *Confidential Report* (55), *Touch of Evil* (58), *The Trial* (62), *Chimes at Midnight* (66), *The Immortal Story* (68).

As actor only, for other directors: *Jane Eyre* (43), *Follow the Boys* (44), *Tomorrow is Forever* (45), *Black Magic* (47), *Prince of Foxes* (49), *The Black Rose* (50), *Trent's Last Case* (53), *Si Versailles m'Etait Conte* (53), *Man Beast and Virtue* (53), *Napoleon* (54), *Three Cases of Murder* (55), *Trouble in the Glen* (55), *Moby Dick* (56), *Pay the Devil* (57), *The Long Hot Summer* (58), *Roots of Heaven* (58), *Compulsion* (58), *Ferry To Hong Kong* (58), *David and Goliath* (59), *Austerlitz* (60), *Crack in the Mirror* (60), *The Mongols* (60), *Lafayette* (61), *The Trial* (62), *The VIPs* (63), *Is Paris Burning* (66), *A Man for All Seasons* (66), *Sailor from Gibraltar* (66), *Oedipus the King* (67), *House of Cards* (68), *The Southern Star* (69), *The Battle of the Neretva* (70), *Waterloo* (70), *Catch 22* (70).

A biography by Peter Noble, *The Fabulous Orson Welles*, was published in 1956.

WELLMAN, WILLIAM (1896–   ). American director, former pilot, actor and Foreign Legionary; in Hollywood from 1921. *The Man Who Won* (23), *You Never Know Women* (26), *Wings* (27), *Beggars of*

Life (28), *Public Enemy* (31), *The Conquerors* (32), *Central Airport* (33), *Looking for Trouble* (34), *Small Town Girl* (35), *Call of the Wild* (35), *Robin Hood of Eldorado* (36), *Nothing Sacred* (37), *A Star is Born* (AA) (37), *Men with Wings* (also produced) (38), *Beau Geste* (39), *The Light that Failed* (39), *Pioneer Woman* (41), *The Great Man's Lady* (42), *The Ox Bow Incident* (42), *Roxie Hart* (42), *Buffalo Bill* (43), *The Story of G.I. Joe* (45), *Magic Town* (46), *Yellow Sky* (48), *The Iron Curtain* (48), *Battleground* (49), *The Next Voice You Hear* (50), *Westward the Women* (50), *Across the Wide Missouri* (51), *My Man and I* (52), *The High and the Mighty* (54), *Track of the Cat* (54), *Blood Alley* (55), *Darby's Rangers* (57), *Lafayette Escadrille (Hell Bent for Glory)* (58), others. Recently inactive.

WELLS, GEORGE (1909–). American writer, with MGM since 1944. *Take me Out to the Ball Game (Everybody's Cheering)* (48), *Three Little Words* (50), *Everything I Have Is Yours* (also produced) (52), *Jupiter's Darling* (produced only) (55), *Designing Woman* (AA) (57), *Ask Any Girl* (59), *The Honeymoon Machine* (62), *The Horizontal Lieutenant* (63), *Penelope* (66), *The Impossible Years* (68), etc.

WELLS, H. G. (1866–1946). Distinguished British author, several of whose novels have been filmed: *The Island of Dr Moreau (Island of Lost Souls)* (32), *The Invisible Man* (33), *The Man Who Could Work Miracles* (35), *Things To Come* (36), *Kipps* (41), *The History of Mr Polly* (49), *The War of the Worlds* (53), *The Time Machine* (60), etc.

WENDKOS, PAUL (1922–). American director. *The Burglar* (57), *Tarawa Beachhead* (58), *Gidget* (59), *Face of a Fugitive* (59), *Because They're Young* (60), *Angel Baby* (60), *Gidget Goes to Rome* (63), *52 Miles to Terror* (66), *Guns of the Magnificent Seven* (69), etc. Also directs TV series.

WERKER, ALFRED (1896–). American director, in Hollywood from 1917. *Little Lord Fauntleroy* (21), *Nobody's Children* (28), *Bachelor's Affairs* (32), *The House of Rothschild* (34), *Kidnapped* (38), *The Adventures of Sherlock Holmes* (39), *Moon Over Her Shoulder* (41), *The Mad Martindales* (42), *Whispering Ghosts* (42), *A Haunting We Will Go* (42), *Shock* (45), *Lost Boundaries* (46), *Repeat Performance* (47), *Pirates of Monterey* (48), *Sealed Cargo* (51), *Walk East on Beacon* (52), *Devil's Canyon* (53), *Canyon Crossroads* (55), *At Gunpoint* (58), many others.

†WERNER, OSKAR (1922–) (Josef Bschliessmayer). Austrian leading actor with international stage and screen credits. *Eroica* (49), *Decision Before Dawn* (51), *Lola Montes* (55), *Jules et Jim* (61), *Ship of Fools* (65), *The Spy Who Came in from the Cold* (65), *Fahrenheit 451* (66), *Interlude* (68), *The Shoes of the Fisherman* (68), etc.

WESSELY, PAULA (1908–). German leading actress. *Maskerade* (34), *Julika* (36), *Spiegel des Lebens* (38), *Die Kluge Marianne* (43), *Maria*

West, Adam

Theresia (51), *The Third Sex* (57), *Die Unvollkommene Ehe* (59), many others; also producer.

WEST, ADAM (c. 1938–   ). American light leading man. *The Young Philadelphians* (59), *Geronimo* (62), *Mara of the Wilderness* (65), *Batman* (66), *The Girl Who Knew Too Much* (68). TV series: *The Detectives, Batman*.

†WEST, MAE (1892–   ). American leading lady, the archetypal sex symbol, splendidly vulgar, overdressed, yet endearingly self-mocking. Wrote many of her own stage plays and film scripts, which bulge with double meanings. *Night After Night* (32), *She Done Him Wrong* (also wrote) (33), *I'm No Angel* (also wrote) (33), *Going to Town* (34), *Belle of the Nineties* (34), *Klondike Annie* (also wrote) (36), *Go West Young Man* (also wrote) (36), *Every Day's a Holiday* (37), *My Little Chickadee* (also co-wrote) (39), *The Heat's On* (43). Recently on TV in episodes of *Mr Ed* series. Published autobiography 1959: *Goodness Had Nothing To Do With It*. 1970: starring in *Myra Breckinridge*.

†WEST, ROLAND (1887– *   ). American director of the late silent period. *De Luxe Annie* (18), *The Silver Lining* (21), *Nobody* (22), *The Unknown Purple* (23), *The Monster* (25), *The Bat* (26), *The Dove* (27), *Alibi* (29), *The Bat Whispers* (31).

WEST SIDE STORY (AA) (US 1961). A film version by Robert Wise and Jerome Robbins (both AA) of the stage musical re-telling the Romeo and Juliet story in a New York slum setting. A downbeat book (Ernest Lehman) is lifted by good art direction (Boris Leven: AA) and Leonard Bernstein's music. Natalie Wood, Richard Beymer and Russ Tamblyn head the cast. George Chakiris wins the AA for supporting actor.

WESTCOTT, HELEN (1929–   ) (Myrthas Helen Hickman). American leading lady, former child actress. *A Midsummer Night's Dream* (35), *The New Adventures of Don Juan* (48), *The Gunfighter* (50), *With a Song in My Heart* (52), *The Charge at Feather River* (53), *Hot Blood* (55), *The Last Hurrah* (58), etc.

WESTERBY, ROBERT (1909–1968). British screenwriter, in films from 1947. *Broken Journey* (48), *The Spider and the Fly* (50), *They Who Dare* (54), *War and Peace* (co-w) (56), *Town on Trial* (56), *Cone of Silence* (60), *Greyfriars Bobby* (60), *The Three Lives of Thomasina* (64), etc.

Westerns have been with us almost as long as the cinema itself; and although Britain supplied *Carry On Cowboy* and a number of continental countries are now making passable horse operas of their own, it is natural enough that almost all Westerns should have come from America.

The Great Train Robbery was a Western, and two of the most popular stars of the early silent period, Broncho Billy Anderson and William S. Hart, played Western heroes, establishing the conventions and the legends still associated with the opening of America's west—Hollywood style. The attractions of Western stories included natural settings, cheapness of production, ready-made plots capable of infinite variation, and a general air of tough simplicity which was saleable the world over. Many of Hollywood's most memorable films of the teens and 20s were Westerns: *The Squaw Man, The Spoilers, The Vanishing American, The Covered Wagon, The Iron Horse, The Virginian, In Old Arizona, The Cisco Kid, Cimarron.* The Western adapted itself to sound with remarkable ease, and throughout the 30s provided many entertainments of truly epic stature: *Wells Fargo, Arizona, The Texas Rangers, Union Pacific, The Plainsman, Drums Along the Mohawk, Jesse James, The Westerner, Destry Rides Again, Stagecoach.* By now the major directorial talents in the field were established: they included John Ford, William Wyler, Howard Hawks, King Vidor, Victor Fleming, Michael Curtiz, Henry King, Frank Lloyd. And each year brought in the wake of the epics scores of cheap but entertaining second features, usually running in familiar series with such stars as Buck Jones, Tom Mix, Tim McCoy, John Wayne, Bob Steele, William Boyd ('Hopalong Cassidy'), Ken Maynard, Tom Tyler, Gene Autry, and the Three Mesquiteers. The singing cowboy familiarized by Autry led to the arrival of other practitioners in the 40s: Roy Rogers, Eddie Dean, Lee 'Lasses' White. The 40s also developed a tendency to base Westerns more firmly on history, telling such stories as *Brigham Young, Northwest Passage, My Darling Clementine, Santa Fe Trail, They Died with Their Boots On.* But by the end of the decade this genre had worn itself out except in the case of Ford, whose films became increasingly stylish and personal. Elsewhere Westerns deteriorated into routine action adventures starring actors a little past their best: Gary Cooper, Errol Flynn, Dennis Morgan, Alan Ladd. Howard Hawks' *Red River* was a useful move towards realism, and was followed in the early 50s by films like *The Gunfighter* and *Shane*, intent on proving how unpleasant a place the real West must have been. Side by side with realism came the 'message' Western, given its impetus by *Broken Arrow* (50), the first Western since silent days to sympathize with the Indians. It was followed by Western allegories like *High Noon* and *3.10 to Yuma*, in which the action elements were restricted or replaced by suspense in taut stories of good versus evil. In these ways the Western became a highly respectable form, attracting actors of the calibre of James Stewart, Marlon Brando, Glenn Ford, Henry Fonda, Burt Lancaster, Richard Widmark and Kirk Douglas, all of whom tended to play half-cynical heroes who preserved their sense of right by indulging in violent action in the last reel. The later 50s brought many spectacular Western productions including *Gunfight at the OK Corral*, *Last Train from Gun Hill*, *One-Eyed Jacks*, *Warlock* and *The Magnificent Seven*; but no new ground was broken. Second features continued to prosper in the capable hands of Randolph Scott, Joel McCrea and Audie Murphy.

The galloping success of TV made potted Westerns so familiar that even the biggest epics made for the cinema found it hard to attract a paying audience. Ford persevered with *The Man Who Shot Liberty Valance* and *Cheyenne Autumn*, both rehashes of earlier and better work; Cinerama made a patchy spectacle called *How the West Was Won*; novelty Westerns have tried violence, horror and sentimentality as gimmicks. However hard the times, one can't imagine Westerns ever dying out altogether.

WESTLEY, HELEN (1879–1942). American character actress of stage and screen; usually played crotchety but kind-hearted dowagers. *Moulin Rouge* (33), *Roberta* (34), *Splendour* (35), *Alexander's Ragtime Band* (38), *Lilian Russell* (40), *Lady with Red Hair* (41), *The Smiling Ghost* (42), etc.

WESTMAN, NYDIA (1907–). American character comedienne, usually in fluttery, nervous roles. *King of the Jungle* (33), *The Invisible Ray* (36), *The Cat and the Canary* (39), *When Tomorrow Comes* (40), *The Late George Apley* (47), *The Velvet Touch* (49), *The Ghost and Mr Chicken* (66), many others.

WESTON, DAVID (1938–). British actor of TV and films. *Doctor in Distress* (63), *Becket* (64), *The Legend of Young Dick Turpin* (65), etc.

WESTON, JACK (1926–). American roly-poly character actor, often an incompetent minor villain. *Mirage* (65), *Wait Until Dark* (67), *The Thomas Crown Affair* (68), *The April Fools* (69), many others. TV series: *The Hathaways* (61).

WEXLER, HASKELL (1926–). American cinematographer. *The Savage Eye* (59), *Angel Baby* (60), *The Hoodlum Priest* (61), *A Face in the Rain* (62), *America America* (63), *The Best Man* (64), *The Loved One* (co-ph) (65), *Who's Afraid of Virginia Woolf?* (66), *In the Heat of the Night* (AA) (67), *The Thomas Crown Affair* (68), etc.

†WHALE, JAMES (1889–1957). British stage director of somewhat mysterious personality; went to Hollywood 1930 to film his stage production of *Journey's End* and stayed to make other movies including four classics of the macabre. *Waterloo Bridge* (30), *Frankenstein* (31), *The Imprudent Maiden* (32), *The Old Dark House* (32), *The Kiss Before the Mirror* (33), *The Invisible Man* (33), *By Candlelight* (33), *One More River* (34), *Bride of Frankenstein* (35), *Remember Last Night* (35), *Showboat* (36), *The Road Back* (37), *The*

Great Garrick (37), *Sinners in Paradise* (37), *Wives under Suspicion* (38), *Port of Seven Seas* (38), *The Man in the Iron Mask* (39), *Green Hell* (40), *They Dare Not Love* (40). Retired 1940 apart from one unfinished film in 1952.

WHALEN, MICHAEL (c. 1907–   ) (Joseph Kenneth Shovlin). American leading man of the 30s. *Country Doctor* (36), *Time Out for Murder* (38), *Sign of the Wolf* (41), *Tahiti Honey* (43), *Gas House Kids in Hollywood* (48), *Mark of the Dragon* (51), *The Phantom from Ten Thousand Leagues* (56), many others, mainly second features.

WHEATLEY, ALAN (1907–   ). Suave British character actor best known as the Sheriff of Nottingham in TV's *Robin Hood*. In many films from 1937: latest include *Inn for Trouble* (60), *Shadow of the Cat* (61), *Tomorrow at Ten* (63), *A Jolly Bad Fellow* (64), etc.

WHEELER, BERT (1895–1968). American comedian who teamed as double act with ROBERT WOOLSEY (qv) in *Rio Rita* (29), *Half Shot at Sunrise* (30), *Cracked Nuts* (30), *Caught Plastered* (32), *Diplomaniacs* (33), *The Nitwits* (35), *The Rainmakers* (36), *Mummy's Boys* (37), *High Flyers* (38), etc. Appeared solo in *The Gay City* (41).

WHEELER, LYLE (1905–   ). American art director. *The Prisoner of Zenda* (37), *Tom Sawyer* (38), *Gone with the Wind* (AA) (39), *Rebecca* (40), *Laura* (44), *Anna and the King of Siam* (AA) (46), *Fourteen Hours* (51), *The Robe* (AA) (53), *Love Is a Many-Splendoured Thing* (55), *Daddy Longlegs* (55), *The Diary of Anne Frank* (AA) (59), *Journey to the Centre of the Earth* (59), *The Cardinal* (63), many others.

WHELAN, ARLEEN (c. 1916–   ). American leading lady of the 40s. *Kidnapped* (38), *Young Mr Lincoln* (39), *Charley's American Aunt* (42), *Ramrod* (47), *The Sun Shines Bright* (52), *The Badge of Marshal Brennan* (57), etc.

WHELAN, TIM (1893–1957). American director who often filmed in Britain. *Safety Last* (23), *It's a Boy* (GB) (33), *The Mill on the Floss* (GB) (36), *Farewell Again* (GB) (37), *The Divorce of Lady X* (GB) (37), *St Martin's Lane* (GB) (38), *Q Planes* (GB) (39), *Ten Days in Paris* (GB) (39), *The Thief of Bagdad* (GB) (co-d) (40), *A Date with Destiny* (40), *International Lady* (41), *Twin Beds* (42), *Nightmare* (42), *Seven Days' Leave* (42), *Higher and Higher* (42), *Step Lively* (44), *Badman's Territory* (46), *This Was a Woman* (GB) (47), *Texas Lady* (55), etc.

WHILEY, MANNING (1915–   ). British actor, usually in sinister roles. *Consider Your Verdict* (38), *The Trunk Crime* (39), *The Ghost of St Michael's* (41), *The Seventh Veil* (45), *Teheran* (47), *Little Big Shot* (last to date) (52), etc.

WHISKY GALORE (US: TIGHT LITTLE ISLAND) (GB 1948). One of the most successful of regional comedies, this lively romp from Ealing Studios was taken from Compton Mackenzie's novel about a boatload of whisky wrecked on a remote Scottish island. Brilliantly directed by Alexander Mackendrick and photographed by Gerald Gibbs, with a first-rate cast of character actors: Basil Radford, Duncan Macrae, Joan Greenwood, Jean Cadell, Wylie Watson, Gordon Jackson, etc.

THE WHISPERERS (GB 1967). The film that won a BFA for Edith Evans is in itself an often likeable but often unduly melodramatic little mood piece, chiefly commendable for daring to tackle the unfashionable and therefore uncommercial problems of old age. Bryan Forbes wrote and directed with considerable intelligence but failed to sort out various elementary confusions of character and verisimilitude.

THE WHISTLER. Based on a popular American radio show, this crime anthology ran as a film series from 1944 to 1950, with Richard Dix playing the hero of each. The only other connection was the whistled theme tune at the beginning. The first story was the old chestnut about the man who hires someone to kill him and then changes his mind. In the late 50s there was a TV series using the same title.

WHISTLING IN THE DARK. This crime comedy play by Lavinia Cross and Edward Carpenter was first filmed in 1933 by Elliott Nugent, with Ernest Truex as the little man who beats the crooks in the end. In 1940 it was revamped as a vehicle for Red Skelton, directed by S. Sylvan Simon, who also handled two sequels, *Whistling in Dixie* (42) and *Whistling in Brooklyn* (43).

WHITE, BARBARA (1924–). British leading lady of the 40s. *It Happened One Sunday* (44), *The Voice Within* (45), *Quiet Weekend* (46), *While the Sun Shines* (46), *Mine Own Executioner* (47), *This Was a Woman* (last to date) (48), etc.

WHITE, CAROL (1941–). British leading lady. *Linda* (58), *Slave Girls* (66), *Poor Cow* (67), *I'll Never Forget Whatshisname* (68), *Daddy's Gone A-Hunting* (69), *The Man Who Had Power Over Women* (70), etc.

WHITE CARGO. This much-caricatured play was based on a book by Vera Simonton called *Hell's Playground*: it dealt with the difficulties of acclimatization for Malayan rubber planters, and in particular with a shapely native distraction called Tondelayo. It was filmed in Britain by J. B. Williams in 1929, with Leslie Faber and Gypsy Rhouma, and in Hollywood in 1942 with Walter Pidgeon and Hedy Lamarr.

WHITE, CHRISSIE (1894–   ). British leading lady of the silent screen, especially popular when teamed with her husband HENRY EDWARDS (qv). Films include *Broken Threads, David Garrick, Barnaby Rudge, Sweet Lavender, Trelawny of the Wells, The City of Beautiful Nonsense, Possession*; latest appearance in *General John Regan* (34).

WHITE HEAT (US 1949). This bid to revive gangster movies ten years after the last gangster was jailed succeeded brilliantly as tough entertainment but its new violence left a nasty taste in the mouth. James Cagney is splendidly maniacal, Raoul Walsh's direction swift: the script by Ivan Goff and Ben Roberts is full of tension.

WHITE, JESSE (1918–   ) (Jesse Wiedenfeld). American comic character actor, usually seen as nervous cigar-chewing crook. Wide stage experience. *Harvey* (debut) (51), *Death of a Salesman* (52), *Not as a Stranger* (55), *Designing Woman* (57), *The Rise and Fall of Legs Diamond* (59), *It's Only Money* (62), *A House is Not a Home* (64), *Dear Brigitte* (65), *The Reluctant Astronaut* (67), many others.

WHITE, PEARL (1889–1938). American leading lady, 'queen of the silent serials'. On stage from six years old. At first a stunt woman, then in such serials as *The Perils of Pauline* (14) and *The Exploits of Elaine* (15), involving circus-like thrills. Later in features: *House of Hate* (18), *The White Moll* (20), *Know Your Men* (21), *A Virgin Paradise* (21), etc.; retired 1921. A pseudo-biography, *The Perils of Pauline*, was filmed with Betty Hutton in 1947.

WHITE SHADOWS IN THE SOUTH SEAS (US 1929). Robert Flaherty had a hand in scripting and photographing this South Seas melodrama, and also co-directed with W. S. Van Dyke. The story dealt with an alcoholic doctor who finds contentment with a native girl on a remote island.

WHITELAW, BILLIE (c. 1932–   ). British leading actress of stage and TV, also in occasional films: *Bobbikins* (59), *Hell is a City* (60), *No Love for Johnnie* (61), *Payroll* (61), *The Comedy Man* (63), *Charlie Bubbles* (BFA) (68), *Twisted Nerve* (68), *The Adding Machine* (69), etc.

WHITELEY, JON (1945–   ). British boy actor. *Hunted* (52), *The Kidnappers* (special AA) (53), *Moonfleet* (55), *The Weapon* (56), *The Spanish Gardener* (56), *Capetown Affair* (67), etc.

WHITMAN, STUART (1929–   ). American leading man, former boxer and stage and TV actor. *When Worlds Collide* (52), *Darby's Rangers* (57), *Ten North Frederick* (58), *The Decks Ran Red* (58), *The Story of Ruth* (60), *Murder Inc* (61), *The Mark* (62), *The Comancheros* (62), *Reprieve* (63), *Shock Treatment* (64), *Signpost to Murder* (64), *Rio Conchos* (64), *Those Magnificent Men in Their Flying Machines* (65),

Whitmore, James

Sands of the Kalahari (65), *An American Dream* (*See You in Hell, Darling*) (66), etc.

WHITMORE, JAMES (c. 1920–   ). American character actor with stage experience. *Undercover Man* (film debut) (49), *The Asphalt Jungle* (50), *Across the Wide Missouri* (51), *Kiss Me Kate* (53), *Them* (54), *Battle Cry* (55), *Oklahoma* (55), *The Eddie Duchin Story* (56), *Who Was That Lady?* (60), *Chuka* (67), *Planet of the Apes* (67), *Madigan* (68), *Guns of the Magnificent Seven* (69), etc. TV series: *The Law and Mr Jones* (60–61).

WHITNEY, PETER (1916–   ) (Peter King Engle). Portly American character player, in films from 1941. *Murder He Says* (as twins) (44), *Hotel Berlin* (45), *The Iron Curtain* (48), *The Big Heat* (53), *Great Day in the Morning* (56), *Sword of Ali Baba* (65), *Chubasco* (67), etc. TV series: *Beverly Hillbillies*.

WHITSUN-JONES, PAUL (1929–   ). Rotund British character actor, usually in comedy. *The Constant Husband* (55), *The Moonraker* (57), *Room at the Top* (59), *Tunes of Glory* (60), etc.

WHITTINGHAM, JACK (1910–   ). British screenwriter. *Q Planes* (39), *Kiss the Bride Goodbye* (44), *Twilight Hour* (45), *I Believe in You* (51), *Hunted* (52), *The Divided Heart* (54), *The Birthday Present* (also produced) (57), etc.

WHITTY, DAME MAY (1865–1948). Distinguished British character actress, on stage from 1881. Made film debut in her stage role in *Night Must Fall* (38), and was thereafter in demand to play strong-willed but kindly old ladies. *Marie Walewska* (38), *The Lady Vanishes* (38), *Raffles* (39), *A Bill of Divorcement* (40), *Suspicion* (41), *Mrs Miniver* (42), *Forever and a Day* (43), *The Constant Nymph* (43), *Lassie Come Home* (43), *Madame Curie* (43), *The White Cliffs of Dover* (44), *Devotion* (45), *My Name is Julia Ross* (46), *Green Dolphin Street* (47), *If Winter Comes* (47), *The Sign of the Ram* (48), etc.

WHORF, RICHARD (1906–1966). American actor with stage experience; films include *Midnight* (34), *Blues in the Night* (41), *Yankee Doodle Dandy* (42), *Keeper of the Flame* (43), *The Cross of Lorraine* (43), *Christmas Holiday* (44), etc. Became director: *Blonde Fever* (44), *Till the Clouds Roll By* (46), *It Happened in Brooklyn* (47), *Champagne for Caesar* (49), etc. Later moved to TV and directed innumerable episodes of such series as *Rawhide*, *Wagon Train* and *The Beverly Hillbillies*.

WHO'S AFRAID OF VIRGINIA WOOLF? (US 1966). This somewhat misguidedly opened-out film version of Edward Albee's electrifying domestic comedy-drama was rather dingily photographed by Haskell Wexler and sometimes dully directed by Mike Nichols, but its basic force and entertainment value could not be totally disguised, particularly in view of a brilliant performance by Richard Burton and excellent ones by Elizabeth Taylor, George Segal and Sandy Dennis. But its chief interest for historians will be that it further extended the bounds of what is permissible on public screens, its unbridled treatment of matters sexual being decorated by 'blue' jokes and expletives.

WHY WE FIGHT. A brilliant series of World War II documentaries using all the resources of the cinema, compiled by Frank Capra and the U.S. Signal Corps Film Unit from material shot by Allied cameramen and from pre-war newsreel material. Each lasted just over an hour, and was kept absorbingly entertaining as well as instructive by the use of music, diagrams and optical work. Titles were *Prelude to War, The Nazis Strike, Divide and Conquer, The Battle of Britain, The Battle of Russia, The Battle of China.*

WICKES, MARY (c. 1912–   ). American character comedienne. *The Man Who Came to Dinner* (as the nurse) (41), *Higher and Higher* (43), *June Bride* (48), *Young Man with Ideas* (52), *The Actress* (54), *Good Morning, Miss Dove* (56), *It Happened to Jane* (59), *The Trouble with Angels* (66), *Where Angels Go Trouble Follows* (68), many others.

WICKI, BERNHARD (1919–   ). Swiss actor (*Der Fallende Stern* [50], *The Last Bridge* [54], *Kinder Mutter und ein General* [54], *Jackboot Mutiny* [55], *The Face of the Cat* [57], *La Notte* [61], etc.) and director *The Bridge* (59), *The Miracle of Malachias* (61), *The Longest Day* (co-d) (62), *The Visit* (US) (63), *Morituri* (65), etc.

WIDDOES, KATHLEEN (1939–   ). American actress with stage experience. *The Group* (66), *Petulia* (68), *The Seagull* (68).

WIDERBERG, BO (1930–   ). Swedish writer-director. *Raven's End* (63), *Karlek* (63), *Thirty Times Your Money* (66), *Elvira Madigan* (67), etc.

WIDMARK, RICHARD (1915–   ) American leading man with stage and radio experience; at one time typed as cold-eyed killer, now in more sympathetic roles. *Kiss of Death* (debut) (48), *The Street with No Name* (48), *Yellow Sky* (48), *Down to the Sea in Ships* (49), *Night and the City* (50), *No Way Out* (50), *Panic in the Streets* (50), *Halls of Montezuma* (51), *Red Skies of Montana* (51), *Destination Gobi* (52), *Pickup on South Street* (53), *Hell and High Water* (54), *Garden of Evil* (54), *Broken Lance* (54), *The Cobweb* (55), *Backlash* (56), *The Last Wagon* (56), *Run for the Sun* (56), *Time Limit* (also co-produced) (57), *Saint Joan* (57), *The Law and Jake Wade* (58), *The Tunnel of Love* (58), *Warlock* (59), *The Baited Trap* (59), *The Alamo* (60), *Judgment at Nuremberg* (61), *How the West Was Won* (63), *Cheyenne Autumn* (64), *The Bedford Incident* (65), *Alvarez Kelly* (66), *The Way West* (67), *Madigan* (68), *Death of a Gunfighter* (69), etc.

WIENE, ROBERT (1881–1938). German director of expressionist films. *The Cabinet of Dr Caligari* (19), *Genuine* (20), *Raskolnikov* (23), *The Hands of Orlac* (24), etc.

WILBUR, CRANE (* –). American writer-director. *Canon City* (48), *The Story of Molly X* (49), *Outside the Wall* (49), *Inside the Walls of Folsom Prison* (50), *House of Wax* (script only) (53), *The Bat* (59), *Solomon and Sheba* (script only) (59), etc.

WILCOX, FRED M. (c. 1905–1964). American director, former publicist; films mainly routine. *Lassie Come Home* (43), *The Secret Garden* (49), *Shadow in the Sky* (51), *Code Two* (53), *Forbidden Planet* (56), *I Passed for White* (also wrote and produced) (60), etc.

WILCOX, HERBERT (1891–). British independent producer-director, in films from 1919 (as salesman); married to Anna Neagle. *The Wonderful Story* (20), *The Dawn of the World* (21), *Chu Chin Chow* (23), *Nell Gwyn* (24), *Dawn* (26), *Wolves* (28), *Rookery Nook* (30), *Good Night Vienna* (32), *Carnival* (32), *Bitter Sweet* (33), *Nell Gwyn* (34), *Sorrell and Son* (34), *Peg of Old Drury* (35), *Limelight* (36), *The Three Maxims* (36), *The Frog* (37), *Victoria the Great* (37), *Sixty Glorious Years* (38), *Our Fighting Navy* (38), *Nurse Edith Cavell* (US) (39), *Sunny* (US) (39), *No No Nanette* (US) (40), *Irene* (US) (40), *They Flew Alone* (42), *Yellow Canary* (43), *I Live in Grosvenor Square* (45), *Piccadilly Incident* (46), *The Courtneys of Curzon Street* (47), *Spring in Park Lane* (48), *Elizabeth of Ladymead* (49), *Maytime in Mayfair* (50), *Odette* (51), *The Lady with a Lamp* (52), *Trent's Last Case* (52), *Laughing Anne* (53), *Lilacs in the Spring* (54), *King's Rhapsody* (55), *Yangtse Incident* (56), *My Teenage Daughter* (56), *Those Dangerous Years* (57), *The Lady Is a Square* (58), *Heart of a Man* (59), etc.

WILCOXON, HENRY (1905–). British leading man with stage experience, in Hollywood from early 30s, latterly as executive for C. B. De Mille. *The Perfect Lady* (31), *The Flying Squad* (32), *Cleopatra* (34), *The Crusades* (35), *The Last of the Mohicans* (36), *Mrs Miniver* (42), *Samson and Delilah* (49), *Scaramouche* (52), *The Greatest Show on Earth* (53), *The Ten Commandments* (also co-produced) (56), *The Buccaneer* (also produced) (59), *The Private Navy of Sergeant O'Farrell* (69) etc.

WILD, JACK (1953–). British juvenile actor who played the Artful Dodger in *Oliver!* (68). TV series: *H. R. Pufnstuf* (69).

THE WILD ONE (US 1954). A Stanley Kramer production written by John Paxton and directed by Laslo Benedek, about a gang of motor-cycle hooligans who terrorize a small Western town. Photographed by Hal Mohr, with music by Leith Stevens, it starred Marlon Brando in a typical role, with Mary Murphy and Lee

Marvin. Banned by the British Board of Film Censors, it was shown at only one English cinema (then managed by the author of this book), with local watch committee approval.

WILD STRAWBERRIES (Sweden 1957). Ingmar Bergman's quietly showmanlike film about old age, superbly written (by himself), photographed (by Gunnar Fischer) and acted (by Victor Sjostrom). Its movement from past to present and back is particularly well achieved, and for once Bergman manages to make almost all his points explicit.

WILDE, CORNEL (1915–). American leading man with varied early experience including Broadway stage. In small film roles from 1940 but did not star till he played Chopin in *A Song to Remember* (45). Later: *A Thousand and One Nights* (45), *Leave Her to Heaven* (45), *The Bandit of Sherwood Forest* (46), *Centennial Summer* (46), *Forever Amber* (48), *It Had to Be You* (48), *Two Flags West* (50), *The Greatest Show on Earth* (53), *Passion* (54), *The Scarlet Coat* (55), *Hot Blood* (56), *Storm Fear* (also directed) (56), *Omar Khayyam* (57), *The Devil's Hairpin* (also produced and directed) (57), *Maracaibo* (also produced and directed) (58), *Lancelot and Guinevere* (also produced and directed) (63), *The Naked Prey* (65) (also produced and directed), *Beach Red* (also produced and directed) (67), many others.

WILDE, OSCAR (1856–1900). British playwright, poet and wit, the subject in 1960 of two film biographies: *Oscar Wilde* starring Robert Morley and *The Trials of Oscar Wilde* starring Peter Finch. The former was directed by Gregory Ratoff from a script by Jo Eisinger, and had Ralph Richardson as Carson, John Neville as Lord Alfred, and Edward Chapman as the Marquis of Queensbury. The latter, written and directed by Ken Hughes, had James Mason, John Fraser and Lionel Jeffries respectively in these roles. Films have been made of several of Wilde's works, including *The Importance of Being Earnest, An Ideal Husband, Lady Windermere's Fan, The Picture of Dorian Gray, Lord Arthur Savile's Crime* (in *Flesh and Fantasy*) and *The Canterville Ghost*.

†WILDER, BILLY (1906–). Austro-Hungarian writer-director, in Hollywood from 1934. A specialist for years in bitter comedy and drama torn from the world's headlines, he has lately specialized in rather heavy-going bawdy farce. Films as writer: *People on Sunday* (30), followed by 10 other German films; *Adorable* (French) (34), *Music in the Air* (co-w) (34), *Lottery Lover* (co-w) (35), *Bluebeard's Eighth Wife* (co-w) (38), *Midnight* (co-w) (39), *What a Life* (co-w) (39), *Ninotchka* (co-w) (39), *Arise My Love* (co-w) (40), *Ball Of Fire* (co-w) (41), *Hold Back The Dawn* (co-w) (41). Films as writer-director (script always in collaboration): *Mauvaise Graine* (French)

(33), *The Major and the Minor* (42), *Five Graves To Cairo* (43), *Double Indemnity* (44), *The Lost Weekend* (AA) (45), *The Emperor Waltz* (47), *A Foreign Affair* (48), *Sunset Boulevard* (50), *Ace in the Hole* (51), *Stalag 17* (53), *Sabrina* (54), *The Seven Year Itch* (55), *The Spirit of St. Louis* (57), *Love in the Afternoon* (57), *Witness For the Prosecution* (58), *Some Like It Hot* (59), *The Apartment* (AA) (60), *One Two Three* (61), *Irma La Douce* (63), *Kiss Me Stupid* (64), *The Fortune Cookie* (66), *The Private Life of Sherlock Holmes* (69). Also produced most of these.

WILDER, THORNTON (1897–   ) .American playwright and novelist. Works filmed include *Our Town*, *The Bridge of San Luis Rey* (several times), *The Matchmaker*; also wrote screenplay of Hitchcock's *Shadow of a Doubt*.

WILDER, W. LEE (1904–   ). Austrian-American producer, brother of Billy Wilder. Films mainly low-budget oddities: *The Great Flamarion* (44), *Phantom From Space* (53), *The Snow Creature* (54), *Bluebeard's Ten Honeymoons* (60), etc.

WILDING, MICHAEL (1912–   ). British leading man, recently turned agent. Former artist and stage actor. *Tilly of Bloomsbury* (debut) (40), *Sailors Three* (40), *Kipps* (41), *Cottage To Let* (41), *In Which We Serve* (42), *Dear Octopus* (43), *English Without Tears* (44), *Carnival* (46), *Piccadilly Incident* (46), *The Courtneys of Curzon Street* (47), *An Ideal Husband* (47), *Spring in Park Lane* (48), *Maytime in Mayfair* (50), *Under Capricorn* (50), *Stage Fright* (50), *Into the Blue* (51), *The Law and the Lady* (US) (52), *Derby Day* (52), *Trent's Last Case* (53), *The Egyptian* (54), *The Glass Slipper* (55), *Zarak* (56), *Danger Within* (57), *The World of Suzie Wong* (60), *The Naked Edge* (61), *The Best of Enemies* (61), *A Girl Named Tamiko* (63), *The Sweet Ride* (68), *Waterloo* (69), etc.

WILKE, ROBERT J. (c. 1913–   ). American character actor, usually in mean, shifty, or villainous roles. *San Francisco* (36), *Sheriff of Sundown* (44), *The Last Days of Boot Hill* (47), *Kill the Umpire* (50), *Twenty Thousand Leagues under the Sea* (54), *Night Passage* (57), *The Gun Hawk* (63), *The Hallelujah Trail* (65), *Tony Rome* (67), etc.

WILLIAM, WARREN (1896–1948) (Warren Krech). Suave American leading man with stage experience. *The Woman from Monte Carlo* (32), *The Mouthpiece* (33), *Lady for a Day* (33), *Imitation of Life* (34), *The Case of the Lucky Legs* (35), *Satan Met a Lady* (36), *The Firefly* (37), *The Lone Wolf's Spy Hunt* (39) (and others in this series), *Lillian Russell* (40), *The Wolf Man* (41), *Counter Espionage* (42), *One Dangerous Night* (43), *Fear* (46), *Bel Ami* (47), etc.

WILLIAMS, ADAM (c. 1927–   ). American 'second lead'. *Queen for a Day* (50), *Without Warning* (52), *Crashout* (55), *Garment Centre* (57),

Darby's Rangers (58), *North by Northwest* (59), *The Last Sunset* (61), *The Glory Guys* (67), etc.

WILLIAMS, BILL (1916–) (William Katt). American leading man, an innocent-type hero of the 40s. Former professional swimmer and singer. *Murder in the Blue Room* (debut) (44), *Those Endearing Young Charms* (45), *Till the End of Time* (46), *Deadline at Dawn* (47), *The Great Missouri Raid* (51), *The Outlaw's Daughter* (53), *Wiretapper* (56), *A Dog's Best Friend* (61), *Tickle Me* (65), etc. TV series: *Assignment Underwater* (61).

WILLIAMS, BRANSBY (1870–1964). Distinguished British stage actor who made an early talkie appearance in an experimental Lee de Forest Phonofilm. Later appeared in *The Gold Cure* (25), *Jungle Woman* (26), *Troublesome Wives* (28), *Song of the Road* (37), etc.

WILLIAMS, CARA (1925–) (Bernice Kamiat). American TV and radio comedienne. Occasional films include *Happy Land* (43), *Don Juan Quilligan* (45), *Sitting Pretty* (48), *The Girl Next Door* (53), *The Defiant Ones* (58), *The Man From the Diners Club* (63). TV series: *Pete and Gladys* (60–61), *The Cara Williams Show* (64).

WILLIAMS, ELMO (1913–). American editor and producer. Produced, edited and directed *The Cowboy* (54); worked as editor on several major productions; now head of 20th-Century Fox British productions.

WILLIAMS, EMLYN (1905–). Welsh actor and playwright, on stage from 1927. *The Case of the Frightened Lady* (film debut) (32), *Men of Tomorrow* (33), *Sally Bishop* (33), *Broken Blossoms* (36), *The Citadel* (38), *The Stars Look Down* (39), *Major Barbara* (40), *You Will Remember* (40), *Hatter's Castle* (41), *The Last Days of Dolwyn* (also wrote and directed) (48), *Three Husbands* (50), *Ivanhoe* (52), *The Deep Blue Sea* (56), *I Accuse* (57), *Beyond This Place* (59), *The L-Shaped Room* (62), *Eye of the Devil* (66), *The Walking Stick* (69), *David Copperfield* (69), others. Plays filmed include *Night Must Fall*, *The Corn is Green*.

WILLIAMS, ESTHER (1923–). Aquatic American leading lady, former swimming champion. *Andy Hardy's Double Life* (debut) (42), *A Guy Named Joe* (43), *Bathing Beauty* (44), *Thrill of a Romance* (45), *Easy to Wed* (45), *This Time for Keeps* (46), *Fiesta* (47), *On an Island with You* (48), *Take Me Out to the Ball Game* (*Everybody's Cheering*) (48), *Neptune's Daughter* (49), *Pagan Love Song* (50), *Duchess of Idaho* (51), *Texas Carnival* (52), *Shirts Ahoy* (52), *Million Dollar Mermaid* (52), *Dangerous When Wet* (53), *Easy to Love* (54), *Jupiter's Darling* (54), *The Unguarded Moment* (56), *The Big Show* (61), etc. Retired.

WILLIAMS, GRANT (1930–). American leading man who never quite made the bigtime. *Written on the Wind* (56), *The Incredible*

Shrinking Man (57), *The Monolith Monsters* (58), etc. TV series: *Hawaiian Eye* (59–63).

WILLIAMS, GUINN 'BIG BOY' (1900–62). American character actor, usually in amiably tough roles. In Hollywood 1919 as an extra. *Noah's Ark* (29), *Mr Wise Guy* (42), *The Desperadoes* (43), *Thirty Seconds Over Tokyo* (44), *Bad Men of Tombstone* (49), *Hangman's Knot* (53), *The Outlaw's Daughter* (55), *The Comancheros* (62), scores of others.

WILLIAMS, GUY (1924–   ). American leading man, the 'Zorro' of Walt Disney's TV series and films. Also in *The Prince and the Pauper* (62), *Captain Sinbad* (63), etc.

WILLIAMS, HARCOURT (1880–1957). Distinguished British stage actor whose film appearances, usually in weak roles, include *Henry V* (44), *Brighton Rock* (47), *Hamlet* (48), *Third Time Lucky* (48), *The Late Edwina Black* (51), *Roman Holiday* (53), *Around the World in Eighty Days* (56).

WILLIAMS, HUGH (1904–1969). British leading man and playwright, on stage from 1921. *Charley's Aunt* (film debut) (30), *In a Monastery Garden* (31), *Rome Express* (33), *Sorrell and Son* (34), *David Copperfield* (US) (34), *The Amateur Gentleman* (36), *Dark Eyes of London* (38), *Wuthering Heights* (US) (39), *A Girl in a Million* (46), *An Ideal Husband* (47), *Take My Life* (47), *The Blind Goddess* (48), *Elizabeth of Ladymead* (49), *The Gift Horse* (52), *The Fake* (53), *Twice Upon a Time* (53), *Khartoum* (66), etc. Recently on stage: his play *The Grass is Greener* was filmed in 1961.

WILLIAMS, JOHN (1903–   ). Suave British stage actor who has appeared in films, usually in polished comedy roles. *Emil and the Detectives* (35), *Next of Kin* (42), *A Woman's Vengeance* (48), *Dick Turpin's Ride* (51), *Dial M for Murder* (54), *Sabrina Fair* (54), *To Catch a Thief* (55), *The Solid Gold Cadillac* (56), *Witness for the Prosecution* (57), *Visit to a Small Planet* (60), *Last of the Secret Agents* (66), *The Secret War of Harry Frigg* (67), *A Flea in Her Ear* (68), etc.

WILLIAMS, KENNETH (1926–   ). British comic actor adept at 'small boy' characters and a variety of outrageous voices. Also on stage, radio and TV. *The Beggar's Opera* (52), *Carry on Sergeant* (58), (and all the other 'Carry Ons'), *Raising the Wind* (61), *Twice Round the Daffodils* (62), *Don't Lose Your Head* (67), *Follow That Camel* (68), etc.

WILLIAMS, RHYS (1897–1969). Welsh character actor, long in Hollywood; former technical adviser. *The Spiral Staircase* (45), *Scandal at Scourie* (53), *There's No Business Like Show Business* (54), *The Ken-*

tuckian (55), *The Fastest Gun Alive* (56), *The Sons of Katie Elder* (65), many others.

WILLIAMS, TENNESSEE (1914–   ). American playwright whose sleazy characters have proved popular screen fodder. Films of his plays include *The Glass Menagerie* (50), *A Streetcar Named Desire* (52), *The Rose Tattoo* (56), *Suddenly Last Summer* (59), *The Fugitive Kind* (60), *Summer and Smoke* (61), *The Night of the Iguana* (64), *Boom* (68), etc.

WILLIAMSON, LAMBERT (1907–   ). British composer. Film scores include *Edge of the World* (38), *End of the River* (48), *One Night With You* (48).

†WILLIAMSON, NICOL (1940–   ). British leading actor of stage and screen. *Inadmissible Evidence* (68), *The Bofors Gun* (68), *Laughter in the Dark* (69), *The Reckoning* (69), *Hamlet* (69).

WILLMAN, NOEL (1918–   ). British actor and stage director whose film roles have often been coldly villainous. *Pickwick Papers* (52), *The Net* (53), *Beau Brummell* (54), *Cone of Silence* (60), *The Girl on the Boat* (62), *Kiss of the Vampire* (63), *The Reptile* (65), *The Vengeance of She* (68), etc.

WILLS, CHILL (c. 1903–   ). Gravel-voiced American character actor, in films from 1938, mainly low-budget Westerns. Also the voice of the talking mule in the 'Francis' series. More recently: *High Lonesome* (50), *Bronco Buster* (52), *City That Never Sleeps* (53), *Timberjack* (55), *The Alamo* (61), *The Deadly Companions* (62), *The Cardinal* (63), etc. TV series: *Frontier Circus* (61), *The Rounders* (67).

WILMER, DOUGLAS (1920–   ). British character actor of stage, screen and TV. *Richard III* (56), *An Honourable Murder* (60), *El Cid* (61), *Cleopatra* (62), *The Fall of the Roman Empire* (64), *One Way Pendulum* (65), *Brides of Fu Manchu* (66), others. TV series: *Sherlock Holmes*.

WILSON, DOOLEY (c. 1904–   ). American Negro character actor, memorable as the pianist in *Casablanca* (42).

WILSON, HARRY LEON (1867–1939). American comedy novelist: chief works filmed are *Ruggles of Red Gap* and *Merton of the Movies*.

WILSON, MARIE (1916–   ) (Kathleen Elizabeth White). American leading lady often seen as 'dumb blonde'. *Satan Met a Lady* (36), *Fools for Scandal* (38), *Boy Meets Girl* (40), *Broadway* (42), *The Young Widow* (47), *Linda Be Good* (48), *My Friend Irma* (title role) (49), *A Girl in Every Port* (51), *Marry Me Again* (54), *Mr Hobbs Takes a Vacation* (62), etc.

WILSON, MICHAEL (1914–   ). American screenwriter whose career was interrupted by the McCarthy witch-hunt. *Five Fingers* (52),

Wilson, Richard

A Place in the Sun (AA) (52), *Friendly Persuasion* (uncredited) (56),
The Bridge on the River Kwai (uncredited) (57), *The Sandpiper* (65),
Planet of the Apes (67), *Che!* (69), etc.

WILSON, RICHARD (1915–). American producer and director,
former radio actor. *The Golden Blade* (p) (54), *Man with a Gun*
(p, d, w) (55), *Raw Wind in Eden* (d) (58), *Al Capone* (d) (59), *Pay
or Die* (p. d) (60), *Invitation to a Gunfighter* (p, d) (64), *Three in an
Attic* (p, d) (68), etc.

WILSON, WHIP (1915–1964). American cowboy actor who appeared in
a great number of second features in the 30s and 40s.

WIMPERIS, ARTHUR (1874–1953). British librettist and screenwriter,
usually in collaboration. *The Private Life of Henry VIII* (32), *Sanders
of the River* (35), *The Four Feathers* (39), *Mrs Miniver* (AA) (42),
Random Harvest (43), *The Red Danube* (48), *Calling Bulldog Drummond* (51), *Young Bess* (53), others.

WINCHELL, WALTER (1897–). American columnist and commentator with a keen eye for crime and show business. Appeared
in a few 30s movies such as *Love and Hisses* (37); wrote *Broadway
Thro a Keyhole* (33); narrated TV series *The Untouchables* (59–63).

WINDOM, WILLIAM (1923–). American leading man, usually in
minor film roles. *To Kill a Mockingbird* (62), *For Love or Money* (63),
One Man's Way (64), *The Americanisation of Emily* (64), *The Detective*
(68), etc. TV series: *The Farmer's Daughter* (63–66), *My World and
Welcome To It* (69).

WINDSOR, BARBARA (1937–). British cockney actress specializing
in dumb blondes. *Lost* (55), *Too Hot to Handle* (59), *Sparrows Can't
Sing* (64), *Carry on Spying* (64), *Crooks in Cloisters* (64), etc.

WINDSOR, MARIE (1923–) (Emily Marie Bertelson). American
leading lady with stage and radio experience; films mainly routine.
All American Co-Ed (41), *Song of the Thin Man* (47), *Force of Evil*
(48), *Outpost in Morocco* (49), *Dakota Lil* (50), *The Narrow Margin*
(51), *The Tall Texan* (53), *City That Never Sleeps* (53), *Abbott and
Costello Meet the Mummy* (55), *The Killing* (56), *The Unholy Wife*
(57), *Bedtime Story* (64), *Chamber of Horrors* (66), many others.

WINDUST, BRETAIGNE (1906–60). American director, from the New
York stage. *Winter Meeting* (47), *June Bride* (48), *Pretty Baby* (50),
The Enforcer (*Murder Inc*) (51), *Face to Face* (52), *The Pied Piper of
Hamelin* (59), etc.

WINGS (US 1928: AA). The last of the silent spectaculars and the first
film to win an Oscar. A field day of stunt flying with a World
War I background, directed by William Wellman, with Charles
Rogers, Clara Bow and Richard Arlen.

WINNER, MICHAEL (1936–   ). British director, in films from mid-50s. *Man with a Gun* (58), *Shoot to Kill* (60), *Some Like It Cool* (also wrote and produced) (61), *Haunted England* (w, d) (61), *Play it Cool* (d) (62), *The Cool Mikado* (w, d) (63), *West Eleven* (d) (63), *The System* (p, d) (64), *You Must Be Joking* (d) (65), *The Jokers* (d) (66), *I'll Never Forget Whatshishname* (67), *Hannibal Brooks* (69), *The Games* (69).

WINNINGER, CHARLES (1884–1968). Chubby American character actor, in films from 1916 as vaudeville appearances permitted. *Showboat* (as Captain Andy) (29), *Gambling Daughters* (31), *Night Nurse* (32), *Showboat* (35), *Three Smart Girls* (36), *Destry Rides Again* (39), *Coney Island* (43), *Broadway Rhythm* (44), *State Fair* (45), *Give My Regards to Broadway* (48), *The Sun Shines Bright* (53), *Raymie* (60), many others.

WINSLOW, GEORGE (1946–   ) (George Wenzlaff). American boy actor whose throaty voice earned him the nickname 'Foghorn'. *Room for One More* (52), *My Pal Gus* (52), *Mr Scoutmaster* (53), *Artists and Models* (55), *Wild Heritage* (58), etc.

WINTER, VINCENT (1947–   ). British child actor, in films since *The Kidnappers* (53) (special AA). Later: *The Dark Avenger* (*The Warriors*) (55), *Time Lock* (56), *Beyond This Place* (59), *Gorgo* (60), *Greyfriars Bobby* (61), *Almost Angels* (*Born to Sing*) (63), *The Three Lives of Thomasina* (64), etc.

WINTERS, JONATHAN (1925–   ). American comedian with TV and night-club experience. *It's a Mad Mad Mad Mad World* (63), *The Loved One* (65), *The Russians Are Coming, The Russians Are Coming* (66), *Penelope* (66), *Oh Dad Poor Dad* (67), etc.

WINTERS, ROLAND (1904–   ). Heavily-built American character actor with stage and radio experience, in Hollywood from 1946; played Charlie Chan in six Monogram features 1948–52. Other films include *13 Rue Madeleine* (46), *Inside Straight* (52), *So Big* (53), etc. Recently on TV.

WINTERS, SHELLEY (1922–   ) (Shirley Schrift). American leading character actress with vaudeville and stage experience, in Hollywood from 1943. *Nine Girls* (44), *Knickerbocker Holiday* (44), *1001 Nights* (45), *A Double Life* (48), *Cry of the City* (48), *Take One False Step* (49), *The Great Gatsby* (49), *Winchester 73* (50), *A Place in the Sun* (51), *My Man and I* (52), *Executive Suite* (54), *The Big Knife* (55), *The Night of the Hunter* (55), *I Am a Camera* (55), *I Died a Thousand Times* (56), *The Diary of Anne Frank* (AA) (59), *Lolita* (62), *Wives and Lovers* (63), *The Chapman Report* (63), *The Balcony* (64), *A Patch of Blue* (AA) (65), *Alfie* (GB) (66), *The Moving Target* (*Harper*) (66),

Enter Laughing (67), *The Scalp Hunters* (67), *Wild in the Streets* (68), *Buona Sera Mrs Campbell* (68), *The Mad Room* (69), *Bloody Mama* (70).

WINTLE, JULIAN (1913–   ). British producer, former editor, in films from 1934. Co-founder of Independent Artists 1958. *Hunted* (51), *High Tide at Noon* (57), *Tiger Bay* (59), *Very Important Person* (61), *This Sporting Life* (63), *And Father Came Too* (64), many others; also TV series *The Human Jungle*.

WINWOOD, ESTELLE (1883–   ) (Estelle Goodwin). British stage character actress who has played in several American films. *The House of Trent* (34), *Quality Street* (37), *The Glass Slipper* (55), *The Swan* (56), *Twenty-three Paces to Baker Street* (56), *Alive and Kicking* (GB) (58), *Darby O'Gill and the Little People* (59), *Dead Ringer* (64), *Camelot* (67), *Games* (67), *The Producers* (68), etc.

wipe. A wipe is an optical device used for quick changes of scene: a line appears at one edge or corner of the screen and 'wipes' across, bringing the new picture with it. Wipes can also be devised in complex patterns or as expanding images, etc.

WISBERG, AUBREY (c. 1905–   ). British-born writer-producer of Hollywood films, mainly second features. *So Dark the Night* (w) (41), *The Man from Planet X* (w, p) (51), *The Neanderthal Man* (w, p) (53), *Captain Kidd and the Slave Girl* (w, p) (54), *Son of Sinbad* (w) (55), many others.

WISDOM, NORMAN (1920–   ). British slapstick comedian, also on stage and TV. *Trouble in Store* (film debut) (53), *One Good Turn* (54), *Up in the World* (56), *Just My Luck* (58), *The Square Peg* (58), *Follow a Star* (59), *There Was a Crooked Man* (60), *The Bulldog Breed* (61), *On The Beat* (62), *A Stitch in Time* (63), *The Early Bird* (65), *Press for Time* (66), *The Night They Raided Minsky's* (US) (68), *What's Good for the Goose* (69), etc.

WISE, ERNIE: see ERIC MORECAMBE.

†WISE, ROBERT (1914–   ). American director, former editor (worked on *Citizen Kane, All That Money Can Buy, The Magnificent Ambersons*). In Hollywood from 1933. *Mademoiselle Fifi* (44), *Curse of the Cat People* (44), *The Body Snatcher* (45), *A Game of Death* (46), *Criminal Court* (46), *Born to Kill* (47), *Mystery in Mexico* (47), *Blood on the Moon* (48), *The Set-Up* (49), *Three Secrets* (50), *Two Flags West* (50), *The House on Telegraph Hill* (51), *The Day the Earth Stood Still* (51), *Captive City* (52), *Destination Gobi* (52), *Something for the Birds* (52), *Desert Rats* (52), *So Big* (53), *Executive Suite* (54), *Helen of Troy* (55), *Tribute to a Bad Man* (56), *Somebody Up There Likes Me* (56), *Until They Sail* (57), *This Could Be the Night* (57), *Run Silent Run Deep* (58), *I Want To Live* (58), *Odds Against Tomorrow* (59),

West Side Story (AA) (61), *Two for the Seesaw* (62), *The Haunting* (GB) (63), *The Sound of Music* (AA) (65), *The Sand Pebbles* (66), *Star!* (68), *The Andromeda Strain* (project) (70).

WISEMAN, JOSEPH (1919–   ). American stage actor who has made several film appearances. *Detective Story* (51), *Viva Zapata* (52), *The Prodigal* (55), *The Garment Jungle* (57), *The Unforgiven* (60), *Dr No* (title role) (62), *The Night They Raided Minsky's* (68), *Stiletto* (69), etc.

witchcraft has not been frequently tackled by film-makers, usually for censorship reasons, and *Witchcraft Through the Ages* (qv) remains the most comprehensive cinematic treatise on the subject. Dreyer's *Day of Wrath* took it seriously, as did *The Witches of Salem* and *Il Demonio* but all were chiefly concerned with the morals of witch-hunting. Witch doctors are familiar figures from African adventure films like *King Solomon's Mines* and *Men of Two Worlds*; more lightheartedly, witches featured in *The Wizard of Oz, I Married a Witch* and *Bell Book and Candle*, as well as in TV's *Bewitched* and all the films featuring Merlin. A nasty cannibalistic coven was seen in Gosta Werner's *Midvinterblot* and several recent thrillers (*Night of the Demon, City of the Dead, Night of the Eagle, Witchcraft, The Witches*) purported to believe in the effects of witchcraft.

See also: *the devil.*

WITCHCRAFT THROUGH THE AGES (HAXAN) (Sweden 1920). A unique and still horrifying film by Benjamin Christensen: a semi-documentary with fictional elements, reconstructing pagan ritual with such care as to make it a handbook of diabolism.

WITHERS, GOOGIE (1917–   ). British leading lady of stage and screen, married to John McCallum with whom she retired some years ago to Australia. *Trouble Brewing* (39), *One of Our Aircraft is Missing* (42), *The Loves of Joanna Godden* (46), *Pink String and Sealing Wax* (46), *It Always Rains on Sunday* (47), *Hamlet* (48), *Miranda* (48), *Traveller's Joy* (50), *White Corridors* (51), *Derby Day* (52), *Devil on Horseback* (54), *Port of Escape* (55), etc.

WITHERS, GRANT (1904–1959). American general purpose actor in films since the 20s. *Tiger Rose* (29), *Sinner's Holiday* (30), *Red-Haired Alibi* (32), *Society Fever* (35), *Men of Steel* (37), *Mr Wong, Detective* (39), *Mexican Spitfire Out West* (41), *The Apache Trail* (43), *My Darling Clementine* (46), *Tripoli* (50), *Run for Cover* (55), *The White Squaw* (58), many others.

WITHERS, JANE (1926–   ). American child star of the 30s, more mischievous and less pretty than Shirley Temple. *Bright Eyes* (34), *Ginger* (35), *The Farmer Takes a Wife* (35), etc. Continued in 40s as character actress: *The Mad Martindales* (42), *North Star* (43), *Faces in the Fog* (44), *Affairs of Geraldine* (46), *Giant* (56), *The Right Approach* (62), *Captain Newman* (63), etc.

WITHERSPOON, CORA (1890–1957). American character comedienne often seen as shrewish wife; on stage from 1910, films from 1931. *Madame X* (38), *The Bank Dick* (41), *This Love of Ours* (45), *The Mating Season* (50), *The First Time* (52), etc.

WITNESS FOR THE PROSECUTION (US 1957). A remarkably enjoyable film version by Billy Wilder (who also wrote the screenplay with Harry Kurnitz) of Agatha Christie's twisty courtroom who-done-it. Chiefly notable for Charles Laughton's picture-stealing performance as the wily defence counsel, it also boasts a cunning portrayal by Marlene Dietrich.

WITNEY, WILLIAM (c. 1910–   ). American director, mainly of routine Westerns for Republic. *Roll On Texas Moon* (46), *Night Time in Nevada* (49), *The Fortune Hunter* (52), *City of Shadows* (54), *Stranger at My Door* (56), *The Bonnie Parker Story* (58), *Paratroop Command* (59), *Master of the World* (61), *Girls on the Beach* (65), *Arizona Raiders* (66), *Forty Guns to Apache Pass* (67), many others.

THE WIZARD OF OZ (US 1939). Despite décor which now seems vulgar, this well-loved film survives as Hollywood's best retelling of a fairy story, mainly because of the delightful score by Harold Arlen and E. Y. Harburg, and because Judy Garland, though actually too old for Dorothy, successfully portrayed the essential innocence and wonder which make such stories live. An excellent supporting cast included Ray Bolger as the Scarecrow, Jack Haley as the Tin Man, Bert Lahr as the Cowardly Lion, Margaret Hamilton as the Wicked Witch and Frank Morgan as the Wizard. Mervyn le Roy produced, Victor Fleming directed, Harold Rosson was cameraman; the Technicolor which added so much at the time now seems garish. There had been two silent versions of Frank Baum's book, in 1910 and 1924.

THE WOLF MAN. The werewolf or lycanthrope, a man who turns into a ravaging beast at full moon, is a fairly ancient Central European mythological figure. Hollywood did not develop the idea until *Werewolf of London* (34), a one-shot in which Henry Hull, a victim of his own well-intentioned research, was firmly despatched before the end. Not until 1941 was the possibility of a series character envisaged. *The Wolf Man* had a splendid cast: Claude Rains, Warren William, Patric Knowles, Bela Lugosi, Maria Ouspenskaya, and Lon Chaney jnr as Lawrence Talbot, heir to a stately English home but unlucky enough to be bitten by a werewolf and thus condemned to monstrous immortality until despatched by a silver bullet. In this film he was battered to apparent death by Claude Rains, but arose from the family crypt for *Frankenstein Meets the Wolf Man* (43), which ended with him and the Frankenstein monster being swept away in a flood. In *House of Frankenstein* he was discovered in a block of ice and promptly thawed out, only to be shot with the requisite silver bullet by a gypsy girl. The producers, however, played so unfair as to revive him for *House of Dracula* (46), in which he lived to be the only movie monster with a happy ending: brain surgery cured him and he even got the girl. Years later, however, in *Abbott and Costello Meet Frankenstein* (49), it seemed that his affliction was again tormenting him; this time we last saw him falling into a rocky and turbulent sea. Mr Chaney had by now done with the character apart from a cod appearance in an episode of TV's *Route 66*; But Hammer Films revived the basic plot in *Curse of the Werewolf* (61), with Oliver Reed as the mangy hero. To date this has provoked no sequels. One should also mention *I Was a Teenage Werewolf* (57), and *Werewolf in a Girls' Dormitory* (with its theme song 'The Ghoul in School') (61), but the less said about these the better.

WOLFE, IAN (1896–   ). American character actor who usually plays worried, grasping or officious roles. *The Barretts of Wimpole Street* (33), *Clive of India* (35), *Hudson's Bay* (40), *The Moon Is Down* (43), *The Invisible Man's Revenge* (44), *The Great Caruso* (50), *Gaby* (56), *The Lost World* (60), *Games* (67), many others.

WOLFF, LOTHAR (1909–   ). German producer-director, former editor; with 'The March of Time' for many years, and still associated with Louis de Rochemont. *Lost Boundaries* (p) (45), *Martin Luther* (co-w, p) (53), *Windjammer* (p) (57), *Question Seven* (p, d) (61), *Fortress of Peace* (p) (63), etc.

WOLFIT, SIR DONALD (1902–1968). Distinguished British stage actor long engaged in bringing Shakespeare to the provinces. In films briefly in 1934 (*Death at Broadcasting House, Drake of England*); not again until 1952, since when he has given several ripe characterizations. *The Ringer* (52), *Pickwick Papers* (53), *Svengali* (54), *Guilty* (56), *I Accuse* (57), *Blood of the Vampire* (58), *Room at the Top* (59), *The House of Seven Hawks* (59), *The Mark* (61), *Lawrence of Arabia* (62), *Dr Crippen* (63), *Becket* (64), *Ninety Degrees in the Shade* (65), *Life at the Top* (65), *Decline and Fall* (68), etc. TV series: *Ghost Squad*. Published autobiography 1955: *First Interval*.

WOLHEIM, LOUIS (1880–1931). German-born character actor, often of semi-brutish roles, with American stage experience; in Hollywood from 1919. *Dr Jekyll and Mr Hyde* (20), *Little Old New York* (22), *America* (24), *Two Arabian Knights* (27), *The Racket* (28), *Tempest* (28), *Frozen Justice* (29), *All Quiet on the Western Front* (31), *Sin Ship* (also directed) (31), etc.

Wolper, David

WOLPER, DAVID (1928–   ). American documentarist who has now turned feature film producer with *If It's Tuesday This Must Be Belgium* (69), *The Bridge at Remagen* (69), etc.

A WOMAN OF PARIS (US 1923). Charlie Chaplin wrote and directed but did not appear in this society melodrama, with Edna Purviance as the distraught heroine and Adolphe Menjou as a smooth philanderer. Chaplin has kept it under cover for forty years but it is said to contain moments of still-effective cinema.

WOMAN OF THE DUNES (SUNA NO ONNA) (Japan 1964). A strange erotic fable about an entomologist on a remote beach who is trapped into living with a nubile woman in a deep sandpit. Overlong, but an exciting piece of pure cinema, written by Kobo Abe, directed by Hiroshi Teshigahara, with Eiji Okada and Kyoko Kishida.

WOMAN TO WOMAN. This tearjerking play by Michael Morton, about a doomed love affair between a British officer and a French dancer, was first filmed by Graham Cutts in 1923, and achieved some renown as one of the better examples of British silent cinema. Clive Brook and Betty Compson had the leads, and Miss Compson appeared with Georges Barraud in the talkie remake of 1929, directed by Victor Saville. In 1946 Maclean Rogers directed an updated version with Douglass Montgomery and Joyce Howard.

THE WOMEN. Clare Booth Luce's venomous comedy was filmed twice by MGM; in 1939 with an all-woman cast headed by Norma Shearer, Rosalind Russell, Paulette Goddard and Joan Crawford. In 1956 it became a semi-musical called *The Opposite Sex*, with June Allyson and Ann Sheridan.

WONG, ANNA MAY (1902–60) (Wong Liu Tsong). Chinese-American actress popular in the 30s. *Red Lantern* (19), *The Thief of Bagdad* (24), *Piccadilly* (GB) (29), *On the Spot* (30), *Shanghai Express* (32), *Chu Chin Chow* (GB) (33), *Java Head* (GB) (34), *Limehouse Blues* (36), *Bombs Over Burma* (42), *Impact* (49), etc.; reappeared after long absence in *Portrait in Black* (60).

WONTNER, ARTHUR (1875–1960). Gaunt British character actor with a long stage career dating from 1897. His occasional films range from *The Bigamist* (15) to *Genevieve* (53), but he will be best remembered as Sherlock Holmes (qv) in several British films of the 30s.

WOOD, CHARLES (c. 1931–   ). British playwright with a penchant for military matters. Wrote the scripts for *Help* (65), *The Knack* (65), *How I Won the War* (67), *The Charge of the Light Brigade* (67).

WOOD, NATALIE (1938–   ) (Natasha Gurdin). Former American child actress, now a leading feminine star. *Happy Land* (43), *Tomorrow is Forever* (45), *The Bride Wore Boots* (46), *No Sad Songs for Me* (50),

The Blue Veil (52), *Rebel Without a Cause* (55), *A Cry in the Night* (56), *The Searchers* (56), *Marjorie Morningstar* (58), *Kings Go Forth* (59), *Cash McCall* (60), *Splendour in the Grass* (61), *West Side Story* (61), *Gypsy* (62), *Love with the Proper Stranger* (64), *Sex and the Single Girl* (64), *The Great Race* (65), *Inside Daisy Clover* (66), *This Property Is Condemned* (66), *Penelope* (66), *Bob and Carol and Ted and Alice* (69), etc.

WOOD, PEGGY (1892–). American character actress, former opera singer. *Handy Andy* (34), *The Housekeeper's Daughter* (39), *The Story of Ruth* (60), *The Sound of Music* (65), etc. TV series: *Mama* (49–56).

WOOD, SAM (1883–1949). American director, in business before becoming assistant to C. B. De Mille c. 1915; directing from 1920. *The Beloved Villain* (20), *Under the Lash* (22), *Bluebeard's Eighth Wife* (23), *One Minute to Play* (26), *The Latest from Paris* (28), *Within the Law* (30), *Stamboul Quest* (32), *The Late Christopher Bean* (33), *Get-Rich-Quick Wallingford* (34), *A Night at the Opera* (35), *The Unguarded Hour* (36), *A Day at the Races* (37), *Madame X* (37), *Lord Jeff* (38), *Goodbye Mr Chips* (39), *Raffles* (39), *Our Town* (40), *Kitty Foyle* (40), *The Devil and Miss Jones* (41), *The Pride of the Yankees* (42), *Kings Row* (42), *Saratoga Trunk* (43) (released 46), *For Whom the Bell Tolls* (also produced) (43), *Casanova Brown* (44), *Guest Wife* (45), *Heartbeat* (46), *Ivy* (47), *Command Decision* (48), *Ambush* (49), etc.

WOODS, ARTHUR B. (c. 1904–1943). British director. *On Secret Service* (34), *Radio Parade* (35), *Drake of England* (35), *The Dark Stairway* (37), *The Return of Carol Deane* (38), *They Drive by Night* (38), *The Nursemaid Who Disappeared* (39), *Busman's Honeymoon* (40), etc. Killed on war service.

WOODS, AUBREY (1928–). British character actor. *Nicholas Nickleby* (47), *Queen of Spades* (48), *Father Brown* (54), *School for Scoundrels* (59), *Spare the Rod* (61), *Just Like a Woman* (66), etc.

WOODBRIDGE, GEORGE (1907–). Portly British character actor, often seen as tavernkeeper or jovial policeman. *Tower of Terror* (42), *Green for Danger* (46), *Bonnie Prince Charlie* (48), *The Story of Gilbert and Sullivan* (53), *The Constant Husband* (55), *Dracula* (58), *Two-Way Stretch* (60), *Dracula Prince of Darkness* (65), many others. TV series: *Stryker of the Yard*.

WOODBURY, JOAN (1915–). American leading lady of 40s second features. *Without Children* (35), *Forty Naughty Girls* (38), *The Mystery of the White Room* (39), *The Desperadoes* (43), *Flame of the West* (46), *Here Comes Trouble* (49), *The Ten Commandments* (56), many others.

WOODS, DONALD (c. 1904–   ). American leading man of the 40s who usually didn't get the girl. *Anna Karenina* (35), *Forgotten Girls* (40), *Love, Honour and Oh Baby* (41), *I Was a Prisoner on Devil's Island* (41), *Wonder Man* (45), *Barbary Pirate* (49), *Undercover Agent* (54), *Thirteen Ghosts* (60), *Kissing Cousins* (64), *Moment to Moment* (65), many others.

WOODWARD, EDWARD (1930–   ). British stage actor who achieved popularity on TV as *Callan* (66–69). Films include *Where There's a Will* (54), *Becket* (64), *The File of the Golden Goose* (69).

WOODWARD, JOANNE (1930–   ). American leading actress, married to Paul Newman, with stage and TV experience. *Count Three and Pray* (debut) (55), *A Kiss Before Dying* (56), *The Three Faces of Eve* (AA) (57), *The Sound and the Fury* (58), *No Down Payment* (58), *Rally Round the Flag Boys* (58), *From the Terrace* (59), *The Fugitive Kind* (60), *Paris Blues* (61), *Woman of Summer* (*The Stripper*) (62), *A New Kind of Love* (64), *Signpost to Murder* (64), *Big Hand for a Little Lady* (66), *A Fine Madness* (66), *Rachel, Rachel* (68), *Winning* (69), *Hall of Mirrors* (69), etc.

WOOLAND, NORMAN (1910–   ). British actor, former radio announcer. *Hamlet* (film debut) (48), *Escape* (49), *Romeo and Juliet* (53), *The Master Plan* (55), *Richard III* (56), *Guilty* (56), *The Rough and the Smooth* (59), *The Fall of the Roman Empire* (64), *Saul and David* (65), *The Projected Man* (66), etc.

WOOLCOTT, ALEXANDER (1887–1943). Waspish American columnist and critic, the original inspiration for Kaufman and Hart's *The Man Who Came To Dinner*. Sole film appearance in *The Scoundrel* (35).

WOOLF, JAMES (1919–1966). British producer. With brother JOHN WOOLF (1913–   ) founded Romulus Films 1949 and made *Pandora and the Flying Dutchman* (51), *The African Queen* (52), *Three Men in a Boat* (56), *Room at the Top* (59), etc. Alone, James produced *The L-shaped Room* (62), *The Pumpkin Eater* (64), *Life at the Top* (65), *King Rat* (65). After his death, John produced *Oliver!* (AA) (68). Both are sons of leading producer-distributor C. M. Woolf, who died in 1942.

WOOLFE, H. BRUCE (1880–1965). British producer, best known for his war reconstructions of the 20s (*Armageddon, Ypres, The Battle of the Somme*, etc.) and for the *Secrets of Nature* series begun in 1919. Head of British Instructional Films from 1926; later in charge of production for children.

WOOLLEY, MONTY (1888–1963) (Edgar Montillion Woolley). American character actor and personality, former Yale professor who came to Broadway stage in 1936 and later repeated his hilarious role in the film of *The Man Who Came to Dinner* (41). Later: *The Pied Piper* (42), *The Light of Heart* (43), *Holy Matrimony* (43), *Irish Eyes Are Smiling* (44), *Since You Went Away* (44), *Molly and Me* (45), *Night and Day* (46), *The Bishop's Wife* (48), *Miss Tatlock's Millions* (50), *As Young as You Feel* (52), *Kismet* (55), etc.

WOOLSEY, ROBERT (1889–1938). American comedian; see BERT WHEELER.

WORKER, ADRIAN (1916–). British producer and managing director of Shepperton Studios.

WORLD OF PLENTY (GB 1943). A feature-length survey of the global food problem, notable as the first documentary to get a full circuit release in Britain. Directed by Paul Rotha from a script by himself and Eric Knight, it showed advanced use of newsreel material, specially-staged scenes, and Adprint diagrams, and confidently adapted the technique invented by 'The March of Time'.

WORLOCK, FREDERICK (1886–). British character actor with long stage career; in Hollywood since the 30s. *Miracles for Sale* (39), *The Sea Hawk* (40), *Rage in Heaven* (41), *The Black Swan* (43), *Sherlock Holmes Faces Death* (44), *Terror by Night* (46), *Joan of Arc* (48), *Spinout* (66), etc.

WORTH, BRIAN (1914–). British light leading man. *The Lion Has Wings* (39), *One Night with You* (48), *Hindle Wakes* (52), *An Inspector Calls* (54), *Ill Met by Moonlight* (57), *Peeping Tom* (60), etc.

WORTH, IRENE (1916–). American leading actress, in recent years mainly on British stage. Rare film appearance in *Orders to Kill* (BFA) (58).

WOUK, HERMAN (1915–). American best-selling novelist. Works filmed include *The Caine Mutiny* (54), *Marjorie Morningstar* (58), *Youngblood Hawke* (64).

WRAY, FAY (1907–). American leading lady of the 30s, a great screamer. *Gasoline Love* (23), *The Wedding March* (26), *The Unholy Garden* (31), *Dirigible* (31), *The Hounds of Zaroff* (32), *King Kong* (33), *The Affairs of Cellini* (34), etc. Later came back as character actress: *Treasure of the Golden Condor* (53), *Hell on Frisco Bay* (55), etc. TV series: *Pride of the Family* (53).

WREDE, CASPAR (1929–). Finnish director, in British TV. Films include *The Barber of Stamford Hill* (62), *Private Potter* (64).

Wright, Basil

WRIGHT, BASIL (1907–   ). British producer-director. In films from 1929: worked with John Grierson in creation of 'documentary'. *Windmill in Barbados* (d) (30), *Song of Ceylon* (p, d) (34), *Night Mail* (co-d) (36), *Waters of Time* (p, d) (51), *World Without End* (d) (53), *The Immortal Land* (p, d) (58), *A Place for Gold* (p, d) (61), etc.

WRIGHT, TERESA (1918–   ). American leading actress with stage experience. *The Little Foxes* (film debut) (41), *Mrs Miniver* (AA) (42), *The Pride of the Yankees* (42), *Shadow of a Doubt* (43), *Casanova Brown* (44), *The Best Years of Our Lives* (46), *Pursued* (47), *Enchantment* (48), *The Men* (50), *Something to Live For* (52), *The Actress* (53), *Track of the Cat* (54), *The Search for Bridey Murphy* (56), *Escapade in Japan* (57), *The Happy Ending* (69), etc.

WRIGHT, TONY (1925–   ). British light leading man, with stage experience. *The Flanagan Boy* (film debut) (51), *Jumping for Joy* (54), *Jacqueline* (56), *Seven Thunders* (57), *Faces in the Dark* (60), *Journey to Nowhere* (62), etc. TV series: *Compact*.

writers honoured by film biographies include Sean O'Casey in *Young Cassidy* (with Rod Taylor), *Hans Christian Andersen* (with Danny Kaye), *The Wonderful World of the Brothers Grimm* (with Karl Boehm and Laurence Harvey), Ernie Pyle in *The Story of G.I. Joe*, also known as *War Correspondent* (with Burgess Meredith), Byron in *The Bad Lord Byron* (with Dennis Price), Robert Browning in *The Barretts of Wimpole Street* (with Fredric March and later Bill Travers), Zola in *The Life of Émile Zola* (with Paul Muni), *Jack London* (with Michael O'Shea), the Brontë sisters in *Devotion* (with Olivia de Havilland, Ida Lupino and Nancy Coleman; also with Arthur Kennedy as Branwell Bronte and Sidney Greenstreet as Thackeray), *Oscar Wilde* (qv) in two films, *Omar Khayyam* (with Cornel Wilde), F. Scott Fitzgerald in *Beloved Infidel* (with Gregory Peck) and *The Adventures of Mark Twain* (with Fredric March).

WUTHERING HEIGHTS (US 1939). A good example of the superior prewar Hollywood film. Emily Brontë's brooding novel of the Yorkshire moors was shortened in incident, shot in America, scripted by Charles Macarthur and Ben Hecht, directed by William Wyler; yet it emerged truer to its original in mood than any of the earlier British silent attempts. Laurence Olivier as Heathcliff dominated the film; Merle Oberon, David Niven and Geraldine Fitzgerald gave sound performances; Gregg Toland's photography was first-rate. A subsequent Mexican version of the story by Luis Bunuel, *Abismos de Pasion* (50), has not been widely seen. There were also several British silent versions, and a 1970 remake is promised.

WYATT, JANE (1912–   ). Pleasing American leading lady of the 30s and 40s, with stage experience. *The Luckiest Girl in the World*

(36), *Lost Horizon* (37), *Kisses for Breakfast* (41), *The Kansan* (42), *The Iron Road* (43), *None But the Lonely Heart* (44), *Boomerang* (47), *Gentleman's Agreement* (47), *Bad Boy* (49), *Task Force* (49), *Our Very Own* (50), *The Man Who Cheated Himself* (51), *Never Too Late* (65), many others. Spent several years in TV series *Father Knows Best*.

WYCHERLY, MARGARET (1881–1956). British-born character actress with American stage experience. *The Thirteenth Chair* (29), *Sergeant York* (41), *Keeper of the Flame* (43), *The Yearling* (46), *White Heat* (49), *Man with a Cloak* (51), *That Man from Tangier* (53), others.

WYLER, WILLIAM (1902–   ). Distinguished German-American director, former film publicist, in Hollywood from 1920. Director from 1925, starting with low-budget silent westerns. †Talkies: *Anybody Here Seen Kelly?* (29), *The Shakedown* (29), *Love Trap* (29), *Hell's Heroes* (30), *The Storm* (30), *A House Divided* (31), *Tom Brown of Culver* (32), *Her First Mate* (33), *Counsellor at Law* (33), *Glamour* (34), *The Good Fairy* (35), *The Gay Deception* (35), *These Three* (36), *Come and Get It* (co-d) (36), *Dodsworth* (36). *Dead End* (37), *Jezebel* (38), *Wuthering Heights* (39), *The Letter* (40), *The Westerner* (40), *The Little Foxes* (41), *Mrs Miniver* (AA) (42); war service; *The Memphis Belle* (documentary) (44), *The Fighting Lady* (documentary) (44), *The Best Years of Our Lives* (AA) (46), *The Heiress* (49), *Detective Story* (51), *Carrie* (52), *Roman Holiday* (53), *The Desperate Hours* (55), *The Friendly Persuasion* (56), *The Big Country* (58), *Ben Hur* (59), *The Loudest Whisper* (*The Children's Hour*) (62), *The Collector* (65), *How to Steal a Million* (66), *Funny Girl* (68), *Lord Byron Jones* (70).

WYMAN, JANE (1914–   ) (Sarah Jane Fulks). American leading lady of the 40s, at first in dumb blonde roles, later as serious actress. In Hollywood from mid-30s. *My Man Godfrey* (36), *Brother Rat* (38), *Flight Angels* (40), *Bad Men of Missouri* (41), *The Body Disappears* (41), *You're in the Army Now* (41), *My Favourite Spy* (42), *Princess O'Rourke* (43), *Crime By Night* (44), *The Doughgirls* (44), *Make Your Own Bed* (44), *The Lost Weekend* (45), *Night and Day* (46), *Magic Town* (46), *The Yearling* (47), *Johnny Belinda* (AA) (48), *Three Guys Named Mike* (49), *Here Comes the Groom* (51), *The Blue Veil* (52), *Just For You* (53), *So Big* (53), *Magnificent Obsession* (54), *All That Heaven Allows* (55), *Miracle in the Rain* (56), *Pollyanna* (60), *Bon Voyage* (63), *How To Commit Marriage* (69), etc.

WYMARK, PATRICK (1926–   ) (Patrick Cheeseman). British TV actor, in occasional films. The voice of Churchill in *The Finest Hours* (64), *A King's Story* (65); also in *The Criminal* (60), *Repulsion* (65), *The Secret of Blood Island* (65), *The Psychopath* (66), *Where Eagles Dare* (68). *Cromwell* (69), etc. TV series: *The Plane Makers*, *The Power Game*.

Wymore, Patrice

WYMORE, PATRICE (1926–   ). American leading lady. *Tea for Two* (50), *Rocky Mountain* (50), *The Big Trees* (52), *She's Working Her Way Through College* (52), *She's Back on Broadway* (53), *Chamber of Horrors* (66), etc.

WYNN, ED (1886–1966) (Isaiah Edwin Leopold). American vaudeville, radio and TV comic who after initial film failure in *Rubber Heels* (27) returned to Hollywood in the 50s as a character actor of fey old gentlemen. *The Great Man* (56), *Marjorie Morningstar* (58), *The Diary of Anne Frank* (59), *The Absent-minded Professor* (60), *Mary Poppins* (64), *Dear Brigitte* (64), *The Greatest Story Ever Told* (65), etc.

WYNN, KEENAN (1916–   ). American character actor, son of Ed Wynn. In Hollywood from early 40s after stage experience. *See Here Private Hargrove* (44), *Under the Clock* (45), *Weekend at the Waldorf* (45), *The Hucksters* (47), *Annie Get Your Gun* (50), *Kiss Me Kate* (53), *The Glass Slipper* (55), *The Great Man* (57), *A Hole in the Head* (59), *The Absent-minded Professor* (61), *Dr Strangelove* (64), *The Americanization of Emily* (65), *The Great Race* (65), *The War Wagon* (67), *Mackenna's Gold* (68), *Smith* (69), *Once Upon a Time in the West* (69), many others.

WYNTER, DANA (c. 1930–   ) (Dagmar Wynter). British leading lady, in films from 1951. *White Corridors* (51), *Colonel March Investigates* (53), *Invasion of the Body Snatchers* (US) (56), *Something of Value* (57), *Shake Hands with the Devil* (59), *Sink the Bismarck* (60), *The List of Adrian Messenger* (63), *If He Hollers Let Him Go* (68), *Airport* (69), etc. TV series: *The Man Who Never Was* (66).

WYNYARD, DIANA (1906–1964) (Dorothy Isobel Cox). Distinguished British stage actress. On stage from 1925; made her film debut in Hollywood: *Rasputin and the Empress* (32). Later: *Cavalcade* (33), *Reunion in Vienna* (33), *Over the River* (34), *Freedom Radio* (39), *Gaslight* (39), *Kipps* (41), *The Prime Minister* (41), *An Ideal Husband* (47), *The Feminine Touch* (53), etc.

Y

A YANK AT OXFORD (GB 1938). The first major production of MGM-British under Michael Balcon, a significant precedent and a happy blending of talent from both countries. It was a simple enough romantic comedy-drama, but packed with appeal. Robert Taylor was the stranger to English academic routine, Lionel Barrymore his father, Vivien Leigh and Maureen O'Sullivan his girl friends. Jack Conway directed. Imitations included *A Chump at Oxford* (40), with Laurel and Hardy, and *A Yank at Eton* (42) with Mickey Rooney.

YANKEE DOODLE DANDY (US 1942). Biopic about George M. Cohan, famous American playwright/entertainer; held together by the immense zest of James Cagney (AA), with Walter Huston and Joan Leslie in tow. Tuneful songs helped; so did the skilled direction of Michael Curtiz.

YARBROUGH, JEAN (1900–). American director of second features, former prop man. *Devil Bat* (41), *Lure of the Islands* (42), *Good Morning, Judge* (43), *In Society* (44), *The Naughty Nineties* (45), *The Brute Man* (46), *Curse of the Allenbys* (47), *The Creeper* (48), *Abbott and Costello Lost in Alaska* (52), *Jack and the Beanstalk* (52), *Women of Pitcairn Island* (57), *Saintly Sinners* (61), *Hillbillies in a Haunted House* (67), many others.

YATES, HERBERT (1880–1966). American executive, ex-president of Republic Pictures, where his word was law in the 40s and many of his productions starred his wife, Vera Hruba Ralston.

†YATES, PETER (1929–). British director. *Summer Holiday* (62), *One-way Pendulum* (64), *Robbery* (67), *Bullitt* (US) (68), *John and Mary* (US) (69), etc.

YORDAN, PHILIP (c. 1913–). Prolific American writer-producer. Screenplay credits include *Syncopation* (42), *Dillinger* (45), *House of Strangers* (49) (and a Western remake of the same story, *Broken Lance* (AA) [54]), *Detective Story* (51), *Johnny Guitar* (54), *El Cid* (61), *Fifty-five Days at Peking* (62), *The Fall of the Roman Empire* (64), many others. Also wrote and produced *The Harder They Fall* (56), *Men in War* (57), *God's Little Acre* (58), *Day of the Outlaw* (59), *Studs Lonigan* (60), *The Day of the Triffids* (62), *The Thin Red Line* (64), *The Battle of the Bulge* (65), etc.

YORK, DICK (1928–   ). American actor whose films include *My Sister Eileen* (55), *Operation Mad Ball* (57), *They Came to Cordura* (58), *Inherit the Wind* (60), etc. Recent TV series: *Going My Way*, *Bewitched*.

YORK, MICHAEL (1942–   ). British leading man with stage experience. *The Taming of the Shrew* (67), *Accident* (67), *Smashing Time* (67), *Romeo and Juliet* (68), *The Strange Affair* (68), *The Guru* (69), *Alfred the Great* (69), *Justine* (69), etc.

YORK, SUSANNAH (1942–   ). British leading lady of stage and screen, presently in great demand. *Tunes of Glory* (debut) (60), *There Was a Crooked Man* (60), *The Greengage Summer* (61), *Freud* (62), *Tom Jones* (63), *The Seventh Dawn* (64), *Scene Nun Take One* (64), *Sands of the Kalahari* (65), *Kaleidoscope* (66), *A Man for All Seasons* (66), *Mr Sebastian* (67), *The Killing of Sister George* (68), *Lock Up Your Daughters* (69), *They Shoot Horses Don't They* (69), *Country Dance* (70), etc.

YORKIN, BUD (1926–   ) (Alan Yorkin). American director, from TV. *Come Blow Your Horn* (63), *Never Too Late* (65), *Divorce American Style* (67), *Inspector Clouseau* (68), etc.

YOU CAN'T TAKE IT WITH YOU (US 1938: AA best picture). Vintage crazy comedy from the stage play by George S. Kaufman and Moss Hart about a family of New Yorkers who do exactly what they want to in life and even convert a stuffy tycoon whose son falls for their daughter. Directed by Frank Capra (AA); played with all the stops out by Lionel Barrymore, Jean Arthur, James Stewart, Spring Byington, Edward Arnold, Mischa Auer, Ann Miller, Samuel S. Hinds, Donald Meek, H. B. Warner and Halliwell Hobbes.

YOUNG, ALAN (1919–   ) (Angus Young). British-born comic actor, in Canada since childhood. *Margie* (debut) (46), *Mr Belvedere Goes to College* (49), *Androcles and the Lion* (53), *Tom Thumb* (58), *The Time Machine* (59), etc. TV series: *Mister Ed*.

YOUNG, ARTHUR (1898–1959). Portly British stage actor; film appearances usually in self-important roles. *No Limit* (35), *Victoria the Great* (37), *My Brother Jonathan* (48), *The Lady with a Lamp* (51), *An Inspector Calls* (54), *The Gelignite Gang* (56), etc.

YOUNG, CARLETON (c. 1908–   ). American character actor, from radio; father of Tony Young. *The Glory Brigade* (53), *The Court Martial of Billy Mitchell* (55), *The Horse Soldiers* (59), *Sergeant Rutledge* (60), many others.

YOUNG, CLARA KIMBALL (1890–1960). Popular American heroine of the silent screen. *Cardinal Wolsey* (debut) (12), *Beau Brummell* (13),

Goodness Gracious (16), *Eyes of Youth* (19), *Cheating Cheaters* (19), *Forbidden Woman* (20), *My Official Wife* (26), etc. Later played small roles: *Souls for Sables* (33), *The Frontiersman* (39), *Mr Celebrity* (42), etc.

YOUNG, COLLIER (1908–). American writer-producer: *The Hitch-Hiker* (53), *The Bigamist* (54), *Mad at the World* (55), *Huk* (56), etc. Recently working in TV.

YOUNG, FREDERICK (1902–). Distinguished British cinematographer. *Bitter Sweet* (33), *Nell Gwyn* (34), *When Knights Were Bold* (36), *Victoria the Great* (37), *Sixty Glorious Years* (38), *Goodbye Mr Chips* (39), *The Young Mr Pitt* (41), *49th Parallel* (41), etc.; war service; *Bedelia* (46), *So Well Remembered* (47), *Edward My Son* (49), *Treasure Island* (50), *Ivanhoe* (52), *Lust for Life* (56), *Invitation to the Dance* (56), *Bhowani Junction* (56), *Island in the Sun* (56), *Lawrence of Arabia* (AA) (62), *The Seventh Dawn* (64), *Lord Jim* (65), *Rotten to the Core* (65), *Doctor Zhivago* (AA) (65), *The Deadly Affair* (67), *You Only Live Twice* (67), etc.

YOUNG, GIG (1913–) (Byron Barr: also known as Bryant Fleming). American light comedy leading man with a pleasantly bemused air. *Misbehaving Husbands* (40), *They Died With Their Boots On* (41), *Dive Bomber* (41), *The Gay Sisters* (in which he played a character called Gig Young and thereafter used the name) (41), *Old Acquaintance* (43), *Air Force* (43), etc.; war service; *Escape Me Never* (46), *The Woman in White* (47), *Wake of the Red Witch* (48), *The Three Musketeers* (49), *Come Fill the Cup* (51), *City That Never Sleeps* (54), *Young at Heart* (55), *Ask Any Girl* (59), *That Touch of Mink* (62), *For Love or Money* (63), *Strange Bedfellows* (65), *The Shuttered Room* (67), etc. TV series: *The Rogues* (64).

YOUNG, HAROLD (1897–). American director who made distinguished British films for Korda but was little heard from on his return to Hollywood. *Catherine the Great* (34), *The Scarlet Pimpernel* (35), *52nd Street* (38), *Code of the Streets* (39), *Juke Box Jenny* (42), *The Frozen Ghost* (43), *I'll Remember April* (44), etc.

YOUNG, LORETTA (1913–) (Gretchen Young). American leading lady whose career in films began when she accidentally, at 15, answered a studio call meant for her elder sister, Polly Ann Young. *Laugh Clown Laugh* (debut) (28), *Loose Ankles* (29), *The Squall* (30), *Kismet* (30), *I Like Your Nerve* (31), *The Devil to Pay* (31), *Platinum Blonde* (32), *The Hatchet Man* (32), *Big Business Girl* (32), *Life Begins* (32), *Zoo in Budapest* (33), *The House of Rothschild* (34), *Midnight Mary* (35), *Man's Castle* (35), *The Crusaders* (35), *Clive of India* (35), *Call of the Wild* (35), *Shanghai* (36), *Ramona* (36), *Ladies in Love* (37), *Wife, Doctor and Nurse* (37), *Second Honeymoon* (38), *Four Men and a Prayer* (38), *Suez* (38), *Kentucky* (38), *Three Blind Mice* (38), *The Story of Alexander Graham Bell* (39), *The Doctor Takes a Wife* (39), *He Stayed for Breakfast* (40), *Lady from Cheyenne* (41), *Ballerina (The Men in Her Life)* (41), *A Night to Remember* (42), *China* (43), *Ladies Courageous* (44), *And Now Tomorrow* (44), *The Stranger* (45), *Along Came Jones* (46), *The Perfect Marriage* (46), *The Farmer's Daughter* (AA) (47), *The Bishop's Wife* (48), *Come to the Stable* (49), *Cause for Alarm* (51), *Half Angel* (51), *Paula* (52), *Because of You* (52), *It Happens Every Thursday* (53), others. More recently appeared for several years (53–60) in her own TV show of anthology dramas. Published autobiography 1962: *The Things I Had To Learn.*

YOUNG MR LINCOLN (US 1939). Biopic directed by John Ford, picturing Abraham Lincoln before he became a political figure. Written by Lamar Trotti, with a first-class performance by Henry Fonda and an all-pervading genuine feeling for American pioneer life.

THE YOUNG ONES (GB 1961). Derivative but zestful British musical determined to sell teenage music not only to other kids but to adults. Cliff Richard and his gang proved so endearing that two agreeable but overlong sequels were made: *Summer Holiday* (63), *Wonderful Life* (64). Sidney Furie's direction was undisciplined but full of bright ideas.

YOUNG, OTIS (1932–   ). American Negro actor. TV series: *The Outcasts* (68).

YOUNG, ROBERT (1907–   ). American leading man invariably cast in amiable, dependable roles. A former clerk, with stage experience. *The Lullaby* (debut) (31), *Strange Interlude* (31), *The Kid from Spain* (32), *Hell Below* (32), *Tugboat Annie* (33), *Lazy River* (34), *The House of Rothschild* (34), *Spitfire* (34), *Whom the Gods Destroy* (35), *West Point of the Air* (35), *It's Love Again* (GB) (36), *Secret Agent* (GB) (36), *Stowaway* (36), *The Emperor's Candlesticks* (37), *I Met Him in Paris* (37), *The Bride Wore Red* (37), *Josette* (38), *Frou Frou* (38), *Three Comrades* (39), *Rich Man, Poor Girl* (39), *Honolulu* (39), *Miracles for Sale* (39), *Maisie* (39), *Northwest Passage* (40), *The Mortal Storm* (40), *Florian* (40), *Western Union* (41), *The Trial of Mary Dugan* (41), *Lady Be Good* (41), *H. M. Pulham Esquire* (41), *Cairo* (42), *Journey for Margaret* (42), *Sweet Rosie O'Grady* (43), *Claudia* (43), *The Canterville Ghost* (44), *The Enchanted Cottage* (44), *Those Endearing Young Charms* (45), *Lady Luck* (46), *Claudia and David* (46), *The Searching Wind* (46), *They Won't Believe Me* (47), *Crossfire* (47), *Sitting Pretty* (48), *The Forsyte Saga* (49), *Pride for Sale* (50), *Ellen (The Second Woman)* (51), *Goodbye My Fancy* (51), *The Half-Breed* (52), *The Secret of the Incas* (54), others. Latterly played in TV series *Father Knows Best* (54–60), *Marcus Welby M.D.* (69).

YOUNG, ROLAND (1887–1953). British character actor with stage experience; made a screen career in Hollywood and is affectionately remembered for a gallery of whimsical or ineffectual types. *Sherlock Holmes* (debut) (22), *Moriarty* (22), then nothing till talkies came in; *The Unholy Night* (29), *Madame Satan* (30), *New Moon* (30), *One Hour With You* (32), *Wedding Rehearsal* (GB) (32), *The Guardsman* (32), *His Double Life* (33), *David Copperfield* (as Uriah Heep) (34), *Ruggles of Red Gap* (34), *One Rainy Afternoon* (36), *The Man Who Could Work Miracles* (GB) (36), *Call It a Day* (37), *King Solomon's Mines* (GB) (37), *Topper* (title role) (37), *Ali Baba Goes to Town* (38), *Sailing Along* (GB) (38), *The Young in Heart* (39), *Topper Takes a Trip* (39), *No No Nanette* (40), *The Philadelphia Story* (40), *Flame of New Orleans* (41), *The Lady Has Plans* (42), *They All Kissed the Bride* (42), *Tales of Manhattan* (42), *Forever and a Day* (43), *Standing Room Only* (44), *Ten Little Niggers* (*And Then There Were None*) (45), *Bond Street* (GB) (47), *The Great Lover* (49), *Let's Dance* (50), *St Benny the Dip* (51), *That Man from Tangier* (53), others.

YOUNG, STEPHEN (1939–   ) (Stephen Levy). Canadian leading man, former extra. TV series: *Seaway* (64), *Judd For The Defense* (66–68).

YOUNG, TERENCE (1915–   ). British screenwriter (*On the Night of the Fire* [39], *Dangerous Moonlight* [40], etc.) who became a successful director: *Corridor of Mirrors* (48), *They Were Not Divided* (50), *The Tall Headlines* (52), *The Red Beret* (53), *That Lady* (55), *Zarak* (56), *Too Hot to Handle* (60), *Doctor No* (62), *From Russia With Love* (63), *The Amorous Adventures of Moll Flanders* (65), *Thunderball* (65), *Danger Grows Wild* (*The Poppy is Also a Flower*) (66), *Triple Cross* (66), *Wait Until Dark* (67), *Mayerling* (68), *The Christmas Tree* (69), etc.

YOUNG, TONY (c. 1932–   ). American leading man, from TV series *Gunslinger*. Films include *He Rides Tall* (63), *Taggart* (64).

YOUNG, VICTOR (1900–1956). American composer with over 300 film scores to his credit, including *For Whom the Bell Tolls* (43), *Shane* (53), *The Greatest Show on Earth* (53), *Three Coins in the Fountain* (54), *Around the World in Eighty Days* (56).

YOUNGSON, ROBERT (1917–   ). American producer specializing in compilation films. Started as writer/director of short films, including *World of Kids* (AA) (50), *This Mechanical Age* (AA) (51). Later released omnibus editions of silent comedy snippets: *The Golden Age of Comedy* (58), *When Comedy Was King* (59), *Days of Thrills and Laughter* (60), *Thirty Years of Fun* (62), etc.

YOU'RE A BIG BOY NOW (US 1966). A frantic freewheeling comedy about a bashful boy's awakening to sex, written and directed by

Yung, Sen

Francis Ford Coppola like a string of New Yorker cartoons kaleido-scopically presented. With Peter Kastner.

YUNG, SEN (also known as VICTOR SEN YUNG) (1915–   ). Chinese-American character actor familiar 1938–48 as Charlie Chan's number one son. Also in *The Letter* (40), *Across the Pacific* (42), *The Left Hand of God* (55), *Flower Drum Song* (61), *A Flea in Her Ear* (68), etc. TV series: *Bonanza*.

YURKA, BLANCHE (1893–   ). American character actress. *Queen of the Mob* (40), *City for Conquest* (41), *The Bridge of San Luis Rey* (44), *The Flame* (48), *The Furies* (50), *Sons of the Musketeers* (51), *Thunder in the Sun* (58), others.

Z

ZAMPA, LUIGI (1905–   ). Italian director, formerly scriptwriter. Films, all on neo-realist lines, include *To Live in Peace* (46), *City On Trial* (52), *The Woman of Rome* (54).

ZAMPI, MARIO (1903–63). Italian director, long in Britain, mainly involved in semi-crazy comedies which he usually wrote and produced. *The Fatal Night* (48), *Laughter in Paradise* (50), *Top Secret* (52), *Happy Ever After* (54), *The Naked Truth* (56), *Too Many Crooks* (58), *Five Golden Hours* (61), etc.

ZANUCK, DARRYL F. (1902–   ). American production executive. Started career in 20s, writing stories for Rin Tin Tin. Production chief for Warners 1931. Co-founder 20th-Century Productions (33); merged with Fox (35). Vice-president in charge of production for 20th Century-Fox (35–52), then independent; returned in 62 as Executive President. Many distinguished films include *Clive of India* (35), *Lloyds of London* (37), *In Old Chicago* (38), *Drums Along the Mohawk* (40), *The Grapes of Wrath* (40), *How Green Was My Valley* (42), *Wilson* (45), *Gentlemen's Agreement* (48), *All About Eve* (50), *Twelve o'Clock High* (51), *Viva Zapata* (52), *Island in the Sun* (57), *Roots of Heaven* (58), *The Longest Day* (also directed scenes) (62). Under the name Mark Canfield wrote the screenplay of *Crack in the Mirror* (60).

ZANUCK, RICHARD (1934–   ). American producer who started career as assistant to his father. Solo ventures: *Compulsion* (59), *Sanctuary* (61), *The Chapman Report* (62), etc. Now vice-president in charge of production for 20th Century-Fox.

ZAVATTINI, CESARE (1902–   ). Italian scriptwriter and film theorist. *Shoeshine* (46), *Bicycle Thieves* (48), *Miracle in Milan* (51), *First Communion* (51), *Umberto D* (52), *Gold of Naples* (55), *The Roof* (56), *Two Women* (61), *Marriage Italian Style* (64), etc.

ZAZIE DANS LE METRO (France 1960). Breakneck comedy, an up-to-date French *Hellzapoppin*, about a demoniac ten-year-old girl on the loose in Paris. A non-stop stream of cinematic trickery directed with great glee by Louis Malle.

ZEFFIRELLI, FRANCO (1922–   ). Italian stage director whose first films are *The Taming of the Shrew* (66), *Romeo and Juliet* (68).

1063

Zeman, Karel

ZEMAN, KAREL (1910–   ). Czech producer-director of trick and fantasy films, of which the best known internationally are *Journey To Primeval Times* (55), and *Baron Munchausen* (61).

ZERO DE CONDUITE (France 1933). A nightmarish fantasy of schoolboy life, directed in surrealist vein by Jean Vigo. Music by Maurice Jaubert, photography by Boris Kaufmann.

ZETTERLING, MAI (1925–   ). Swedish leading lady, first noticed abroad in *Frenzy* (44). English-speaking debut: *Frieda* (47). Later: *The Bad Lord Byron* (48), *Quartet* (48), *Knock on Wood* (54), *A Prize of Gold* (55), *Seven Waves Away* (56), *Only Two Can Play* (61), *The Main Attraction* (62), *The Bay of St Michel* (63), etc. Recently turned to direction with *The War Game* (62), *Loving Couples* (64), *Night Games* (66), BBC travelogues, *Doctor Glas* (68), etc.

ZIEGFELD FOLLIES (US 1944; released 1946). Spectacular, plotless musical revue 'inspired' by the great showman Florenz Ziegfeld (glimpsed in Heaven in the person of William Powell). Several MGM performers are seen at or near their best: Fred Astaire in two numbers with Lucile Bremer and a comedy dance routine with Gene Kelly, Judy Garland burlesquing a star's press interview, Lena Horne singing 'Love', etc. Mostly directed by Vincente Minnelli.

ZIMBALIST, EFREM JNR (1923–   ). American leading man with stage experience; usually plays characters who inspire confidence. *House of Strangers* (50), *Band of Angels* (57), *Too Much Too Soon* (58), *By Love Possessed* (61), *A Fever in the Blood* (61), *The Chapman Report* (62), *The Reward* (65), *Wait Until Dark* (67), etc. Perhaps best known as the older private eye in TV series *77 Sunset Strip* (58–63), *The F.B.I.* (65–69).

ZIMBALIST, SAM (1904–1958). American producer. *The Crowd Roars* (38), *Boom Town* (40), *King Solomon's Mines* (50), *Quo Vadis* (51), *Mogambo* (53), *Beau Brummell* (54), *Ben Hur* (59) (died during production).

†ZINNEMANN, FRED (1907–   ). Austrian-born director, with varied experience before coming to Hollywood in 1929. Was an extra (in 'All Quiet'), script clerk, and director of shorts (*That Mothers Might Live* (AA) [38], several episodes of 'Crime Does Not Pay', etc.). Features: *Kid Glove Killer* (42), *Eyes in the Night* (42), *The Seventh Cross* (44), *Little Mister Jim* (46), *My Brother Talks to Horses* (47), *The Search* (48), *Act of Violence* (49), *The Men* (50), *Teresa* (51), *High Noon* (52), *The Member of the Wedding* (53), *From Here to Eternity* (AA) (53), *Oklahoma* (55), *A Hatful of Rain* (57), *The Nun's Story* (58), *The Sundowners* (60), *Behold a Pale Horse* (64), *A Man for All Seasons* (67).

ZOLA, EMILE (1840–1902). Prolific French novelist of the seamy side. Works filmed include *Nana*, *Gervaise*, *La Bete Humaine* and *Therese Raquin*. A 1937 biopic, *The Life of Emile Zola*, starred Paul Muni and centred on Zola's participation in the Dreyfus case.

zombies originate from Haitian legend, and are generally held to be dead people brought back to life by voodoo. In movies they invariably shamble along with sightless eyes, looking pretty awful but doing no real damage. They were most convincingly displayed in Victor Halperin's 1932 *White Zombie*; other examples of the species turned up in *Revolt of the Zombies*, *The Zombies of Mora Tau*, *I Walked With a Zombie*, *King of the Zombies*, *The Ghost Breakers* (and its remake *Scared Stiff*), and *Dr Terror's House of Horrors*. The species also gave its name to a strong rum punch, and one treasures the memory of a movie in which the Ritz Brothers walked up to a bar and ordered three zombies. 'I can see that', said the barman, 'but what'll you have to drink?'

zoom. A lens of variable length, normally used for swiftly magnifying a distant object or moving rapidly away from a close one.

ZORBA THE GREEK (Greece 1965). A zestful, uncontrolled, open-air film, written and directed by Michael Cacoyannis from a novel by Nikos Kazantzakis, about a huge peasant who persuades a timid Englishman to share his joy in life even when surrounded by disaster. Marred by over-indulgent writing and an unnecessary sub-plot about a widow who is stoned to death by Cretan peasants, the film remains a pleasure to watch by virtue of Walter Lassally's photography, Mikos Theodorakis' music, and the performances of Anthony Quinn, Alan Bates, and (in moderation) Lila Kedrova.

ZORINA, VERA (1917–   ) (Eva Brigitta Hartwig). German-born ballet dancer and actress whose American films include *The Goldwyn Follies* (39), *On Your Toes* (39), *I Was An Adventuress* (40), *Louisiana Purchase* (41), *Star Spangled Rhythm* (43), *Follow the Boys* (44). Now retired.

ZORRO (Don Diego de Vega). The black-garbed Robin Hood of Spanish California originated as the hero of a 1919 strip cartoon by Johnston McCulley. (Zorro, incidentally, is Spanish for fox.) Films featuring the devil-may-care righter of wrongs include *The Mark of Zorro* (20) with Douglas Fairbanks, and its 1925 sequel *Don Q, Son of Zorro*; *The Bold Caballero* (37) with Robert Livingston; *Zorro Rides Again* (37), a serial with John Carroll; *Zorro's Fighting Legion* (39), a serial with Reed Hadley; Mamoulian's splendid remake of *The Mark of Zorro* (40), with Tyrone Power; *The Ghost of Zorro* (49), a serial with Clayton Moore; *The Sign of Zorro* (60) with Guy Williams; and *Zorro and the Three Musketeers* (62) with Gordon Scott.

Zucco, George

ZUCCO, GEORGE (1886–1960). Sepulchral-toned British stage actor, long in Hollywood and typecast in horror films in which he admirably exuded upper-bracket malignancy. *Dreyfus* (debut) (31), *The Good Companions* (32), *The Man Who Could Work Miracles* (35), *Marie Antoinette* (38), *The Cat and the Canary* (39), *The Hunchback of Notre Dame* (40), *Arise My Love* (40), *The Mummy's Hand* (40), *The Adventures of Sherlock Holmes* (as Moriarty) (40), *Sherlock Holmes in Washington* (42), *The Black Swan* (42), *Dead Men Walk* (43), *The Black Raven* (43), *The Mad Ghoul* (43), *House of Frankenstein* (45), *Fog Island* (45), *Dr Renault's Secret* (46), *The Pirate* (47), *Joan of Arc* (48), *Madame Bovary* (49), *Let's Dance* (50), *David and Bathsheba* (51), *The First Legion* (51), many others.

ZUGSMITH, ALBERT (1910–   ). American producer-director with a taste for exploitation subjects. Produced: *Written on the Wind* (57), *The Tattered Dress* (57), *The Incredible Shrinking Man* (58), *Touch of Evil* (58), etc. Directed: *High School Confidential* (60), *Teacher was a Sexpot* (60), *The Private Life of Adam and Eve* (61), *Confessions of an Opium Eater* (*Evils of Chinatown*) (63), *Fanny Hill* (produced only) (64), *Movie Star American Style* (or *LSD I Hate You*) (66), *The Incredible Sex Revolution* (project) (67), etc.

ZUKOR, ADOLPH (1873–   ). Hungarian-born film pioneer. Emigrated to America, became film salesman, nickelodeon owner, and independent producer (in 1913, by persuading New York stage stars James O'Neill, James K. Hackett and Minnie Maddern Fiske to appear in productions of, respectively, *The Count of Monte Cristo*, *The Prisoner of Zenda* and *Tess of the D'Urbervilles*). This was the start of 'Famous Players', which in 1916 merged with Jesse Lasky's production interests and later became Paramount Pictures. He has remained board chairman of the latter since 1935. His autobiography, 'The Public Is Never Wrong', was published in 1945. Special Academy Award 1948 'for his services to the industry over a period of forty years'.

ALPHABETICAL LIST OF THEMES EXPLORED

UNDER THESE HEADINGS in the main text will be found notes on the main use of these subjects in films past and present, with examples.

abortion
actor-directors
actors
advertising
air balloons
airplanes
alcoholics
amnesia
ancient Egypt
angels
animals
anti-semitism
Arabian Nights
army comedies
automobiles
babies
bad language
ballet
baseball
bathtubs
Berlin
the Bible
big business
bigamists
birds
black comedy
blindness
boffins
boobs
boxing
the British Empire
brothels
bullfights
burlesque

buses
butlers
case histories
the chase
child stars
Christ
Christmas
churches
circuses
clairvoyance
coal mines
the cold war
colour
colour sequences
comedy teams
comic strips
communism
compilation films
composers
concentration camps
concerts
confidence tricksters
courtesans
courtroom scenes
crazy comedy
criminals
custard pies
deaf mutes
death
dentists
department stores
desert islands
deserts
the devil

Devil's Island
directors'
   appearances
disguise
doctors
documentary
dreams
drug addiction
drunk scenes
duels
elephants
the end of the world
Enoch Arden
entertainers
epidemics
episodic films
excerpts
explorers
falling
families
fantasy
fire
firing squads
flashbacks
fog
the Foreign Legion
forest fires
funerals
fun fairs
gambling
gangsters
governesses
helicopters
hillbillies

Hollywood on film
homosexuality
horror
hotels
houses
hypnosis
impresarios
India
in-jokes
insanity
insects
inventors
Ireland
jewel thieves
Jews
kidnapping
kings and queens
labour relations
leprechauns
lesbianism
letters
light comedies
lifts (elevators)
London
lynch law
Mau Mau
mirrors
monks
monster animals
mother love
motor cycles
motor racing
multiple roles
musicals
musical remakes
mystery
narrators
naval comedy
Negroes
New York
nuns

nurses
nymphomaniacs
offices
old age
opera singers
orchestral conductors
painters
Paris
parties
pirates
police
politics
pre-credits sequences
priests
prison
prisoners of war
private eyes
prophecy
prostitutes
psychology
railway stations
rain
rape
Red Indians
reincarnation
religion
reporters
robberies
romantic teams
Rome
sailors
satire
schooldays
scientists
seances
seaside resorts
servants
serials
series
sewers
sex

ships
slapstick
social comedy
social conscience
space exploration
spies
sportsmen
storms
strikes
stunt men
submarines
suicide
swinging London
teachers
telephones
television
television series
theatres
3-D
tinting
title changes
trains
transvestism
uncredited
   appearances
underground
   railways
undertakers
   (morticians)
underwater scenes
unemployment
universities
ventriloquists
volcanoes
war heroes
weddings
westerns
witchcraft
writers
zombies

ALPHABETICAL LIST OF FICTIONAL SCREEN CHARACTERS

THE FOLLOWING are noted in the main text:

Ali Baba
Arsène Lupin
Arthur
Betty Boop
Blondie
Boston Blackie
The Bowery Boys
Bugs Bunny
Bulldog Drummond
Charlie Chan
The Cohens and the Kellys
The Cisco Kid
The Crime Doctor
Dead End (Kids)
Dracula
Ellery Queen
The Falcon
Flash Gordon
Frankenstein
Fu Manchu
Godzilla
Gold Diggers
The Hardy Family
Hopalong Cassidy
The Invisible Man
James Bond
Joe Palooka
The Jones Family

Jungle Jim
The Kettles
Dr Kildare
The Lone Wolf
Matt Helm
Mexican Spitfire
Mr Magoo
Mr Moto
The Mummy
Nancy Drew
Old Mother Riley
Our Gang
Penrod
Philo Vance
Popeye
Robin Hood
Robinson Crusoe
The Saint
Scattergood Baines
Sexton Blake
Sherlock Holmes
Squibs
Tarzan
The Thin Man
Tom and Jerry
Tom Sawyer
Torchy Blane

KEY TO DEDICATION

SO MANY PEOPLE have written to say that they are driving themselves mad tracking down the references in the dedication (which also appeared in the second edition) that I now take pity on them and offer the following 'solutions'. All the names belong to characters who have pleased me in one movie or another, and the list represents a great many happy memories.

To those who are still playing the game—*don't read on!*

C. K. DEXTER HAVEN The divorced but still hopeful husband, played by Cary Grant, in the most witty, warm and polished of sophisticated comedies, *The Philadelphia Story*.

JAMES BLANDINGS Cary Grant again, in a charming post-war domestic comedy, *Mr Blandings Builds his Dream House*, about the average middle-class fellow who is foiled in all his attempts to achieve the simple life.

ELWOOD P. DOWD James Stewart as the gentle dipsomaniac in *Harvey*, taking with him everywhere an invisible but lovable six-foot white rabbit.

FLOYD THURSBY The man much heard of but never seen in *The Maltese Falcon*, that most nonchalant of thrillers, in which he is reported dead in the second reel. But one wonders . . .

WALTER PARKS THATCHER The splendidly disgruntled guardian in *Citizen Kane*, played by George Coulouris with a relish equalled by all concerned in this supremely fast-moving and entertaining classic.

WOLF J. FLYWHEEL Who else but Groucho Marx? This is his *Big Store* persona.

CARL DENHAM Robert Armstrong, the intrepid film producer in *King Kong*. It says much for Armstrong's full-blooded ham performance that he is not overshadowed by the monsters.

SHERIDAN WHITESIDE The epitome of invective and abuse, Monty Woolley in *The Man Who Came to Dinner*. A great lip-curling comedy performance, even though he was robbed of his stage opening line, 'I may vomit'.

SAUL FEMM The little arsonist played by Brember Wills in *The Old Dark House*, one of a rich gallery of grotesques.

JOSEPH TURA 'That great, great, Polish actor' . . . Jack Benny in *To Be or Not to Be*, the best part he ever had; the film was a grey farce full of Lubitsch delight.

LONGFELLOW DEEDS He who came to town, in the person of Gary Cooper, and proved to the satisfaction of Frank Capra and Robert Riskin that country ways are smarter and saner than city ones.

LAURA JESSON Celia Johnson in *Brief Encounter*, a highly sensitive and moving performance in a little film that is still a masterpiece for those prepared to get under its skin and into its period.

AHMED BEN HASSAN Rudolph Valentino in *The Sheik* and *Son of the Sheik*, a bravura performance which preserves its simple magic through the decades and overcomes even the handicap of washy 16-mm prints.

RUDOLPH RASSENDYLL The hero of *The Prisoner of Zenda*, most perfectly portrayed by Ronald Colman in the 1937 version, an impeccable Boys' Own Paper adventure story.

LAWRENCE TALBOT It's the wolf man, played always by Lon Chaney Jnr, who may not have been 'the screen's master character actor' as billed, but was certainly eager to please.

JAKIE RABINOWITZ Al Jolson in the pioneer talkie, *The Jazz Singer*. For the record, his first words in the movie are not 'Listen to this, Ma', but 'You ain't heard nothing yet' in the second reel.

EDYTHE VAN HOPPER The marvellously repulsive Florence Bates, in her first film role as the rich dowager in *Rebecca*, getting every last cent's worth out of Monte Carlo.

WALDO LYDECKER Another performance that was talked about, by Clifton Webb as the acidulous columnist of *Laura*, who typed in his bath and had a bad word for everybody.

PHILIP MARLOWE Raymond Chandler's cynical but honest private eye. Although various gentlemen made a good job of him, the palm must go to Humphrey Bogart in *The Big Sleep*.

THEO KRETSCHMAR-SCHULDORFF Anton Walbrook as the gentle German in *The Life and Death of Colonel Blimp*, an expensive British movie which contrived to present its public with an enemy hero in the middle of a world war.

MAX CORKLE A tribute to James Gleason, one of those great Hollywood character comedians who absolutely never let us down. This was one of his prize performances, in *Here Comes Mr Jordan*.

DR LUDOVIC PRAETORIUS That ingratiating grotesque, Ernest Thesiger, in a role he made his own, that of the evil genius in *The Bride of Frankenstein*. Can anyone forget the casual way he offers the monster a cigar when they meet head-on in the cavernous tomb?

LOLA FROHLICH Marlene Dietrich in *The Blue Angel*; enough said.

EMILY KOCKENLOCKER A Preston Sturges movie must get a look in, and here is Diana Lynn with a typical Sturges surname as the sassy still centre of his wildest movie *The Miracle of Morgan's Creek*.

MR LAUREL AND MR HARDY Who could omit from such an affectionate list those dear simple bowler-hatted souls whose genius, as is often the way with artists, was not realized until they were on the point of leaving us? After forty years, the majority of their two-reelers still present undiluted joy, and there seems no reason why they should not continue to do so for succeeding generations.